See inside for an illustration of  THE CRIMINAL JUSTICE SYSTEM

# THE CRIMINAL JUSTICE SYSTEM

## ENTRY INTO THE SYSTEM

**CRIME**

**Reported and observed crime**

**Investigation**

**Arrest**

**Charges filed**

**Initial appearance**

Released without prosecution

Released without prosecution

Unsolved crime or no arrest

Charges dropped or dismissed

## PROSECUTION AND PRETRIAL SERVICES

Charges dropped or dismissed

**Bail or detention hearing**

**Grand jury**

Refusal to indict

Charge dismissed

**Felonies**

Gather information

Gather information

**Preliminary hearing**

**Arraignment**

**Misdemeanors**

## ADJUDICATION

Reduction of charge

**Plea bargain**

**Trial**

Acquitted

Found guilty

Guilty plea

**Appeal**

Appeal rejected

Appeal filed

New trial granted

**Preliminary hearing**

**Arraignment**

Charge dismissed

**Plea bargain**

**Trial**

Acquitted

Found guilty

Guilty plea

# INTRODUCTION TO
# *Criminal Justice*

**THIRTEENTH EDITION**

# INTRODUCTION TO
# *Criminal Justice*

## LARRY J. SIEGEL
University of Massachusetts, Lowell

## JOHN L. WORRALL
University of Texas at Dallas

**WADSWORTH**
CENGAGE Learning™

Australia • Brazil • Japan • Korea • Mexico • Singapore • Spain • United Kingdom • United States

## WADSWORTH
### CENGAGE Learning™

*Introduction to Criminal Justice*,
**Thirteenth Edition**
**Larry J. Siegel and John L. Worrall**

Senior Publisher: Linda Schreiber-Ganster

Senior Acquisitions Editor:
Carolyn Henderson Meier

Senior Developmental Editor: Shelley Murphy

Senior Assistant Editor: Erin Abney

Editorial Assistant: Virginette Acacio

Media Editor: Ting Jian Yap

Senior Marketing Manager: Michelle Williams

Marketing Assistant: Sean Foy

Marketing Communications Manager:
Heather Baxley

Senior Content Project Manager: Christy Frame

Creative Director: Rob Hugel

Senior Art Director: Maria Epes

Senior Print Buyer: Rebecca Cross

Rights Acquisitions Account Manager:
Dean Dauphinais

Production Service: Aaron Downey,
Matrix Productions Inc.

Photo Editor: Kim Adams Fox

Text Designer: Diane Beasley

Copy Editor: Connie Day

Cover Designer: Riezebos Holzbaur Design
Group

Cover Image: Urban nightlife: Brian Weed/
Shutterstock. Two police officers:
Konstantin Sutyagin/Shutterstock.

Compositor: PreMediaGlobal

For product information and technology assistance, contact us at
**Cengage Learning Customer & Sales Support, 1-800-354-9706**

For permission to use material from this text or product,
submit all requests online at **cengage.com/permissions**
Further permissions questions can be emailed to
**permissionrequest@cengage.com**

Library of Congress Control Number: 2010941230

ISBN-13: 978-0-495-91338-2

ISBN-10: 0-495-91338-3

**Wadsworth**
20 Davis Drive
Belmont, CA 94002
USA

Cengage Learning is a leading provider of customized learning solutions with office locations around the globe, including Singapore, the United Kingdom, Australia, Mexico, Brazil, and Japan. Locate your local office at:
**www.cengage.com/global**

Cengage Learning products are represented in Canada by Nelson Education, Ltd.

To learn more about Wadsworth, visit **www.cengage.com/wadsworth**

Purchase any of our products at your local college store or at our preferred online store **www.cengagebrain.com**

Printed in the United States of America
1 2 3 4 5 6 7 14 13 12 11 10

This book is dedicated to my children, Eric, Andrew, Julie,
and Rachel, and to my grandchildren, Jack, Kayla, and Brooke.
It is also dedicated to Jason Macy (thanks for marrying Rachel)
and Therese J. Libby (thanks for marrying me).
L. J. S.

This book is dedicated to my wife, Sabrina.
Thank you for your continued love and support.
J. L. W.

# ABOUT THE AUTHORS

**LARRY J. SIEGEL** was born in the Bronx in 1947. While living on Jerome Avenue and attending City College of New York in the 1960s, he was swept up in the social and political currents of the time. He became intrigued with the influence contemporary culture had on individual behavior: Did people shape society or did society shape people? He applied his interest in social forces and human behavior to the study of crime and justice. After graduating CCNY, he attended the newly opened program in criminal justice at the State University of New York at Albany, earning both his M.A. and Ph.D. degrees there. After completing his graduate work, Dr. Siegel began his teaching career at Northeastern University, where he was a faculty member for nine years. After leaving Northeastern, he held teaching positions at the University of Nebraska–Omaha and Saint Anselm College in New Hampshire. He

is currently a professor at the University of Massachusetts, Lowell. Dr. Siegel has written extensively in the area of crime and justice, including books on juvenile law, delinquency, criminology, criminal justice, and criminal procedure. He is a court-certified expert on police conduct and has testified in numerous legal cases. The father of four and grandfather of three, Larry Siegel and his wife, Terry, now reside in Bedford, New Hampshire, with their two dogs, Watson and Cody.

**JOHN L. WORRALL** is Professor of Criminology and Program Head at the University of Texas at Dallas. A Seattle native, he received a B.A., double majoring in psychology and law and justice, from Central Washington University in 1994. Both his M.A. (criminal justice) and Ph.D. (political science) were received from Washington State University, where he graduated in 1999. From 1999–2006, he was a member of the criminal justice faculty at California State University, San Bernardino. He joined UTD in Fall 2006.

Dr. Worrall has published articles and book chapters on a wide range of topics ranging from legal issues in policing to crime measurement. He is the author of *Crime Control in America: What Works?* (2nd ed., Allyn & Bacon, 2008) and *Criminal Procedure: From First Contact to Appeal* (3rd ed., Prentice Hall, 2010); coauthor of *Police Administration* (3rd ed., Cengage, 2012), *Policing Today* (Prentice Hall, 2010), and *Criminal Evidence: An Introduction* (Oxford University Press, 2005); and co-editor of *The Changing Role of the American Prosecutor* (SUNY, 2009). He is also editor of the journal *Police Quarterly*.

# BRIEF CONTENTS

# CONTENTS

**CHAPTER 6**

# The Police: Organization, Role, and Function    202

**CHAPTER 7**

# Issues in Policing    240

**CHAPTER 8**

# Police and the Rule of Law    284

## PART THREE

## COURTS AND ADJUDICATION  325

### CHAPTER 9

### The Courts and the Judiciary  326

### CHAPTER 10

### The Prosecution and the Defense  358

### CHAPTER 11

### Pretrial and Trial Procedures  390

### CHAPTER 15
## Prison Life: Living in and Leaving Prison    548

## PART FIVE

## CONTEMPORARY CHALLENGES IN CRIMINAL JUSTICE    603

### CHAPTER 16
## Juvenile Justice    604

### CHAPTER 17
## Crime and Justice in the New Millennium    640

**CHAPTER 18**

## Terrorism, Homeland Security, and the Future of Criminal Justice    676

# BOXED FEATURES

## ANALYZING CRIMINAL JUSTICE ISSUES

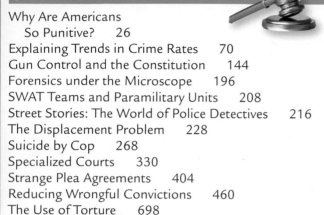

## IMAGES OF JUSTICE

## EVIDENCE-BASED JUSTICE

## CRIMINAL JUSTICE AND TECHNOLOGY

## RACE, GENDER, AND CULTURE IN CRIMINAL JUSTICE

## CAREERS IN CRIMINAL JUSTICE

**A**t about 1:30 in the afternoon on November 5, 2009, at Fort Hood, Texas, U.S. Army Major Nidal Malik Hasan, a psychiatrist, entered the Soldier Readiness Center, where Army personnel receive routine medical treatment, took a seat at an empty table, and prayed silently. Then he stood up, took out an FN Five-seven automatic pistol, shouted *"Allahu Akbar!"* and opened fire. Hasan got off more than 100 rounds, killing 13 people and wounding 30 others. As he left the building in pursuit of more victims, base civilian police Sergeant Kimberly Munley arrived on the scene, engaged in a fire-fight with Hasan, and was shot three times. Civilian police officer Sergeant Mark Todd then arrived at the scene, fired at Hasan, hit him with a number of shots, knocking him over, and placed him in handcuffs.

Hasan, an American-born Muslim of Palestinian descent, has been charged with 13 counts of premeditated murder and 32 counts of attempted murder under the Uniform Code of Military Justice; he may face additional charges at court-martial. In the aftermath of the shooting, internal Army reports indicated that officers within the Army were aware of Hasan's drift toward radical Islam and that he was in communication with radical leader Anwar al-Awlaki. The FBI, informed of Hasan's contacts in 2008, did not consider him a threat.

The Fort Hood massacre case illustrates both the complexity and the significance of crime in America. Hasan was not only an Army officer but also a medical doctor—hardly the expected profile of a terrorist mass murderer. And what should be done with a killer such as Hasan? He appeared to be suffering from mental illness. Should his state of mind prevent his being convicted of a horrendous crime that he obviously committed? The case shows that agents of the justice system must be prepared to deal with new and deadly forms of criminality, ranging from international terrorism to transnational criminal cartels.

Each year the criminal justice system routinely processes millions of cases involving theft, violence, drug trafficking, and other crimes, and these are rarely reviewed on TV or in the newspapers. Some involve petty thefts from the neighborhood grocery store. Others involve complex international drug-smuggling schemes that net the conspirators millions of dollars. Agents of the justice system must contend with criminal activity ranging from neighborhood teens out on a shoplifting spree to international drug cartels that use sophisticated technology to launder money in overseas capitals.

The justice system has become an enterprise that costs taxpayers more than $100 billion each year. It employs millions of people in law enforcement, courts, and correctional agencies. *Introduction to Criminal Justice* was written to help students interested in justice better understand this enormous and complex system and to aid their journey in introductory-level criminal justice courses. The text analyzes and describes the agencies of justice and the variety of procedures they use to apprehend, adjudicate, and treat criminal offenders. It covers what most experts believe are the critical issues in criminal justice and analyzes their impact on the justice system. Our primary goals in writing this, the thirteenth edition, remain as they have been for the previous twelve editions:

- To provide students with in-depth knowledge about criminal justice agencies
- To be as thorough and up-to-date as possible
- To be objective and unbiased
- To challenge students to think critically about justice

Every attempt has been made to present the material in an interesting, balanced, and objective manner, making sure that no single political or theoretical position dominates the text. Instead, we present the many diverse views that shape the contemporary criminal justice system and characterize its interdisciplinary nature. Diversity of opinion is what the study of criminal justice is all about and is the central focus of the text. We have tried to provide a text that is scholarly and informative, comprehensive yet interesting, and well organized and objective while at the same time thought-provoking.

## ORGANIZATION OF THE TEXT

Part One gives the student a basic introduction to crime, law, and justice—from as far back as the American Revolution to a decade into the new millennium. The first chapter briefly describes the history of criminal justice, the agencies of justice, and the formal justice process, and it introduces students to the concept of the informal justice system, which involves discretion, deal making, and plea bargains. The chapter also describes the major perspectives on justice. Chapter 2 addresses such questions as: How is crime measured? Where and when does it occur? Who commits crime? Who are its victims? What social factors influence the crime rate? And what patterns can be found in the incidence of crime? Chapter 3 covers theories about the cause of crime and the factors that contribute to victimization. Chapter 4 provides a discussion of the criminal law and its relationship to criminal justice.

Part Two provides an overview of the law enforcement field. Four chapters cover the history and development of law enforcement; the role, organization, and function of police in modern society; issues in policing; and police and the rule of law.

Part Three is devoted to the adjudication process, from pretrial indictment to the sentencing of criminal offenders. Three chapters focus on organization of the court system, an analysis of the prosecution and defense functions, pretrial procedures, and the criminal trial. The topics included range from court structure to the processing of felony cases, indigent defense systems, attorney competence, legal ethics, pretrial services, and bail reform. Part Three concludes with a chapter on punishment and sentencing.

The three chapters in Part Four focus on the correctional system, including probation, intermediate sanctions, and restorative justice. The traditional correctional system of jails, prisons, community-based corrections, and parole are also discussed at length. Such issues as technocorrections and the problem of prisoner reentry are explored.

Part Five covers special topics in criminal justice. Chapter 16 contains information on preventive detention of youths, waiving youths to the adult court, and such recent changes as prohibition of the death penalty for children. This part also features two new chapters devoted to two key challenges that the criminal justice system faces in the new millennium. Chapter 17 examines corporate enterprise crime, cyber crime, and transnational organized crime, and Chapter 18 addresses terrorism and homeland security and speculates about the future of criminal justice.

## WHAT'S NEW IN THIS EDITION

Because the study of criminal justice is a dynamic field of scientific inquiry and the concepts and processes of justice are constantly evolving, the thirteenth edition of *Introduction to Criminal Justice* has been thoroughly revised. We have tried hard to make the text more concise, "student-friendly," and accessible. Great care has been taken to address both the structure and the process of justice. We have attempted to ensure that each chapter is comprehensive, self-contained, and effectively organized.

To make the book more relevant and to reflect problems now facing the justice system, we have added two new chapters that address such cutting-edge issues as transnational gangs, cyber crime, terrorism, corporate enterprise crime, and homeland security. To make room for these new chapters—and to provide a better balance among the three components of the criminal justice system (police, courts, and corrections)—we have condensed the material on courts and adjudication by merging into a single chapter the two chapters that formerly covered pretrial procedures and the criminal trial.

*Introduction to Criminal Justice* now devotes even more attention to analyzing what works—and what does not work—to prevent and control crime. *Evidence-Based Justice* features, new to this edition, summarize research on some of the most popular and controversial crime-control initiatives. We have also updated all chapters with the latest research, discussing the pros and cons, and the successes and failures, of numerous efforts that the justice system has undertaken to make society safer.

The thirteenth edition also includes two new features designed to help readers understand the crucial but challenging area of case law. First, for the most important and influential cases, such as *Miranda v. Arizona*, we have included a feature (*The Evolution of . . .*) that explains how the principles on which the original holding was based have evolved over time, through subsequent decisions. We list in chronological order the cases, the years in which they were decided, and their holdings. Second, we have added summaries of *Significant Cases* at the end of certain chapters. For example, Chapter 12, Punishment and Sentencing, ends with a table listing key cases, the year in which each was decided, the underlying issue, and the decision. Taken together, these new features not only help readers identify the essential decisions in the cases upon which much of the criminal justice system is built, but also trace how those holdings have been clarified and refined over time.

## Chapter-by-Chapter Changes

**Chapter 1, Crime and Criminal Justice,** begins with a vignette on the FBI's "Operation Rotten Tomato," an investigation into the selling of tomato products that fell short of basic quality standards set by the Food and Drug Administration. We have added more material on the history of crime in the United States, including the outlaw Jesse James, who made his living robbing banks and trains, and Marshall Wyatt Earp, who helped put men like James behind bars. We introduce a new section that embodies a major concept in the book: evidence-based justice, which involves basing policy decisions on the scientific collection of data to determine what programs work and what they cost. A new *Analyzing Criminal Justice Issues* feature in Chapter 1 asks, "Why Are Americans So Punitive?" And a new *Evidence-Based Justice* feature inquires, "Does Monitoring Sex Offenders Really Work?"

**Chapter 2**, **The Nature and Extent of Crime,** begins with the story of Dr. Amy Bishop, a Harvard-trained neurobiologist, who shot to death three of her colleagues and severely wounded three others after she was denied tenure. We also cover the case of Bernard Kerik, former commissioner of the New York City Police, who was sentenced to four years in prison for accepting gratuities while in office. All crime and victim data has been updated. There is new information on international crime trends. One new *Evidence-Based Justice* feature asks, "Is the Crime Rate Really Declining?" and another explores the equally controversial issue of the relationship between immigration and crime.

**Chapter 3, Understanding Crime and Victimization,** begins with an update on a controversial story that rocked American politics, the investigation into the Emperors Club, a call girl ring frequented by New York's hard-charging governor, Eliot Spitzer. An *Evidence-Based Justice* feature reviews the use of closed-circuit TV surveillance cameras in areas that are at risk for crime. A new section reviews the work of prominent psychologist John Bowlby, who finds that attachments formed soon after birth, when infants bond with their mothers, strongly influence behavior later in life. There is also a new section on state (organized) crime, which targets the role of the political structure in shaping crime.

**Chapter 4, Criminal Law: Substance and Procedure,** updates legal changes in gay marriage law and discusses New Hampshire General Court HB 43, which made New Hampshire the fifth state to legalize same-sex marriage. An *Analyzing Criminal Justice Issues* feature on gun control and the Constitution covers *District of Columbia v. Heller*, in which the Court ruled that the Second Amendment protects an individual's right to own weapons for self-defense. There is a new section on the concept of criminal harm, which holds that for an act to be considered a crime, the actor's willingness to cause harm must be proved. There is also a section on stand-your-ground laws, which allow the use of deadly force when a person reasonably believes it necessary to prevent the commission of a "forcible felony," including carjacking, robbery, and assault. New sections on changing legal doctrines discuss rape, technology, environmental crimes, and medical marijuana laws.

**Chapter 5, The Police: History and Contemporary Structure,** opens with a new vignette featuring collaboration between police and civilians at the U.S.–Mexico border. A new *Analyzing Criminal Justice Issues* feature explores some of the problems in the forensic sciences, including the growing DNA-testing backlog. A revised and expanded section on the emergence of professionalism in law enforcement features the work of the Wickersham Commission. A new *Ethical Challenges* assignment pertaining to the FBI's Combined DNA Index System (CODIS) is also included. Finally, a revised section on communications spotlights the movement in law enforcement agencies toward "plain language" dispatch.

**Chapter 6, The Police: Organization, Role, and Function,** begins with a discussion of the recession's effect on police hiring. A new *Evidence-Based Justice* feature summarizes the research on policing and its effect on crime. A new *Criminal Justice and Technology* feature examines the use of in-car cameras. The coverage of community policing was extensively revised to make room for a new section on intelligence-led policing, including discussion of fusion centers and the gathering and sharing of tactical and strategic information. Finally, there is a new *Analyzing Criminal Justice Issues* feature on displacement and diffusion in the context of problem-oriented policing.

**Chapter 7, Issues in Policing,** begins with a chapter-opening discussion of policing and U.S.–Mexico border violence. The chapter was also carefully edited for length. A new *Criminal Justice and Technology* feature on the taser is included, as is a new *Evidence-Based Justice* feature on the effectiveness of tasers. A new section on the National Law Enforcement Officers Memorial is included toward the end of the chapter. The *Careers in Criminal Justice* feature has been revised to discuss differences in qualifications and training for federal prosecutors compared to those of local prosecutors.

**Chapter 8, Police and the Rule of Law,** begins with a discussion of the Supreme Court's recent decision in *Arizona v. Gant*. Two new features on Supreme Court cases have also been added. They summarize the development of case law decided in the wake of *Carroll v. United States* (automobile searches) and *Miranda v. Arizona* (confessions and interrogations). Chapter content has been updated to include the most recent U.S. Supreme Court cases pertaining to policing, through the 2009–2010 term. The automobile search section has also been extensively revised and expanded. Finally, the chapter summary is now accompanied by a *Significant Cases* table—specifically, a summary of key cases related to policing.

**Chapter 9, The Courts and the Judiciary,** begins with a discussion of the Supreme Court's controversial decision in *District Attorney's Office v. Osborne*, an Alaska case dealing with DNA testing. A new *Evidence-Based Justice* feature discusses the latest research on the effectiveness of drug courts. The latest data on judicial salaries, court caseloads, and other aspects of judicial administration in America is also included.

**Chapter 10, The Prosecution and the Defense,** begins with a discussion of the use of federal forfeiture laws by prosecutors in child sexual abuse cases. A new *Evidence-Based Justice* feature addresses recent research on no-drop prosecution policies. The restructured Defending the Accused section (which was formerly called The Right to Counsel) now focuses strictly on mechanisms of defense representation, reserving the legal material and court cases for the next chapter.

**Chapter 11, Pretrial and Trial Procedures,** is a new chapter. It combines former Chapters 12 (Pretrial Procedures) and 13 (The Criminal Trial) into a single, more concise chapter. The opening vignette features the Supreme Court's recent decision in *Montejo v. Louisiana*, a case dealing with the intersection of *Miranda* and the Sixth Amendment right to counsel. The chapter includes two new case features, "The Evolution of *Gideon v. Wainwright*" and "The Evolution of *Batson v. Kentucky*." It concludes with a *Significant Cases* summary of key Supreme Court cases pertaining to the pretrial and trial stages of the criminal process.

**Chapter 12, Punishment and Sentencing,** opens with a vignette featuring the case of William Johnson, a man who has been on Florida's death row for 32 years. An *Evidence-Based Justice* feature on three-strikes laws has also been added. It summarizes the research on whether such laws have a deterrent effect. The section on capital punishment includes a new feature, "The Evolution of *Furman v. Georgia*," which traces important death penalty cases decided over the past several decades. A *Significant Cases* table summarizes key sentencing cases decided by the Supreme Court.

**Chapter 13, Community Sentences: Probation, Intermediate Sanctions, and Restorative Justice,** has undergone a number of changes. It begins with the high-profile media case of pop singer Rihanna, beaten and bruised after an altercation with her rapper boyfriend Chris Brown. Brown was later sentenced to probation. There is a new section on probation conditions in the Internet Age, which we cover because probation orders now regulate Internet use, including entry into chatrooms, adult entertainment websites, purchasing drugs via the Internet, and so on. A *Criminal Justice and Technology* feature discusses how probationers are being monitored with the aid of technological innovations. An *Evidence-Based Justice* feature called "Prison versus Probation" reviews evidence that treating offenders in the community may be more effective than institutional programs. There are new sections on *HotSpot probation*, organizing probation caseloads around *area (rather than client) needs*, specialized probation, and the use of swift and sure punishment to discourage violations of probation. We also cover the House of Healing (HOH), a community-living residential program located in Erie, Pennsylvania, that at any one time cares for a maximum of eight female offenders and their children. Another *Evidence-Based Justice* feature examines the Brooklyn-based Drug Treatment Alternative-to-Prison (DTAP) Program. The section on restorative justice has been expanded, and a new *Race, Gender, and Culture in Criminal Justice* feature reviews restorative justice in Australia and New Zealand, including one innovative effort that is based in part on native Maori practices.

**Chapter 14, Corrections: History, Institutions, and Populations,** has a new opening vignette that discusses Arizona's Maricopa County (Phoenix) Sheriff Joe Arpaio's effort to promote himself as "America's Toughest Sheriff" and his Tent City, which is considered the nation's toughest jail. The data on prison and jail populations has been revised and updated. There is more material on jail populations and new-generation jails. A new *Criminal Justice and Technology* feature addresses efforts to increase prison security and reduce escapes.

**Chapter 15, Prison Life: Living in and Leaving Prison,** has an update to the opening vignette on Kathy Boudin, a woman who served 20 years in prison for her role in the 1981 robbery of a Brinks truck by a terrorist cell. It reveals how her life changed behind bars and talks about her subsequent release into the community. There is a new section on sexual coercion, long considered routine in penal institutions. There is new information on problems encountered in female institutions. New sections cover anger management and efforts to control violent criminal behavior both in the institution and upon the offender's release into the community. Another new section looks at faith-based programs and reviews research showing that inmates who are involved in religious programs and education do better after their release than those in comparison groups. The problems of reentry are reviewed in some detail. A new section on "making good" explores what helps inmates turn their lives around. What helps some go straight when so many others fail? There are new *Evidence-Based Justice* features on cognitive-behavioral therapy and on the Boston Reentry Initiative (BRI). A *Criminal Justice and Technology* feature looks at the use of technology to improve prison life and security.

**Chapter 16, Juvenile Justice,** begins with the story of 16-year-old John Odgren, who committed a senseless, cold-blooded murder in Lincoln-Sudbury Regional High School, in suburban Massachusetts, a case that raises the issue of mental illness and delinquency. There is a *Race, Gender, and Culture in Criminal Justice* feature on minority overrepresentation in juvenile justice. We cover the important 2009 case of *Safford Unified School District v. Redding,* which drew national headlines when it limited the scope of school drug searches. An *Evidence-Based Justice* feature asks, "Is Waiver Effective?" and reviews the debate surrounding transfers of juvenile offenders to adult or criminal court. We cover *Graham v. Florida,* the case in which the Supreme Court prohibited imposing a sentence of life without parole on a juvenile offender who did not commit homicide.

**Chapter 17, Crime and Justice in the New Millennium,** is a totally new chapter that addresses the effect of the technological revolution on crime and justice. The chapter reviews three independent yet interrelated emerging criminal activities that are presenting challenges to the criminal justice system: corporate enterprise crime, cyber crime, and transnational organized crime. Among the topics we covered are globalization and justice, fraud on Wall Street, the subprime mortgage scandal, enforcement of laws against corporate crime, the extent and costs of cyber crime and the enforcement of laws against it, transnational organized crime (including Russian organized crime and Mexican drug cartels), transnational sex trafficking, and controlling transnational crime.

**Chapter 18, Terrorism, Homeland Security, and the Future of Criminal Justice,** is a new chapter that expands on the previous edition's Chapter 5 and adds a section on the future of criminal justice to conclude the book. The section on the criminal justice response to terrorism now features data and details on terrorism prosecutions and convictions in federal court. It also includes a new *Images of Justice* feature on both al-Hurra, the Arabic-language satellite television network for the Middle East funded by the United States, and as-Sahab, al Qaeda's media arm. A new section on the Supreme Court and terrorism summarizes key cases decided in the wake of 9/11. And as we have noted, the concluding section discusses several trends and developments that are likely to affect the criminal justice system in the coming decades.

## SPECIAL FEATURES

We have created a comprehensive, proven learning system designed to help students get the most out of their first course in criminal justice. In addition to the many changes already mentioned, we have included a wealth of new photographs to appeal to visual learners and make material more relevant and meaningful. Carefully updated tables and completely redrawn figures highlight key chapter concepts. Marginal definitions of key terms; concise, bulleted end-of-chapter summaries that align with chapter learning objectives; and a comprehensive end-of-book glossary all help students master the material. Internet research links appearing in the text's margins enable students to explore topics productively via the Web.

## Boxed Features

We have included a number of thematic boxes to introduce students to some of the field's most crucial programs, policies, and issues and to provide them with an opportunity to analyze the material in greater depth.

- **Careers in Criminal Justice**  We have updated this popular addition to the previous edition with the latest career paths in criminal justice. These features contain detailed information on salaries, educational requirements, and future prospects.

- **Images of Justice**  These features examine how the criminal justice system is portrayed in films and TV shows and also how the media influence crime and justice. For example, in Chapter 11, an *Images of Justice* box discusses the so-called "*CSI* effect" and looks at the academic research that has sought to determine whether it really exists.

- **Race, Gender, and Culture in Criminal Justice**  These features are aimed at helping students better understand the problems of women and minorities in the justice system and how justice works for them. To highlight the differences in criminal justice in other cultures, some of these features offer a comparative perspective. For example, cultural differences are highlighted in a *Race, Gender, and Culture in Criminal Justice* feature in Chapter 8 that discusses interrogation law in three other countries. And Chapter 7 contains one that goes into detail on the subject of racial profiling.

- **Criminal Justice and Technology**  This feature focuses on some of the latest efforts to fight crime using contemporary technological methods. For example, Chapter 9's *Criminal Justice and Technology* feature introduces the use of virtual reality in the courtroom.

- **Analyzing Criminal Justice Issues**  This feature helps students learn to think critically about current justice issues and practices. For example, an *Analyzing Criminal Justice Issues* feature in Chapter 12 discusses efforts to reduce wrongful convictions.

- **(NEW) Evidence-Based Justice**  This new feature summarizes scientific evidence related to the effectiveness of various criminal justice strategies and programs. For example, an *Evidence-Based Justice* feature in Chapter 6 examines the research on the crime prevention effects of police work.

- **(NEW) The Evolution of . . .**  This new feature summarizes the evolution of key Supreme Court decisions. For example, Chapter 8 contains two new features, "*The Evolution of Carroll v. United States*," the key vehicle search case, and "The Evolution of *Miranda v. Arizona*," which of course deals with confessions and interrogations. The feature summarizes nearly every subsequent Supreme Court case that builds on, expands, or restricts the original holding.

## Other Important Chapter Features

We have included numerous learning tools in every chapter to enhance student mastery of the material. A few of the most valuable study aids we provide are described below.

- **Ethical Challenges in Criminal Justice: A Writing Assignment**  Each chapter includes a writing assignment that challenges students to solve an ethical dilemma they may someday confront while working within the justice system. All the book's ethical dilemmas have been either heavily revised or rewritten in response to reviewer feedback and to ensure that each one is concretely related to the content of the chapter where it appears. The dilemma in Chapter 18, for example, focuses on what should be done with detained terror suspects whom the United States deems not to be a threat but whose home countries don't want them back.

- **Perspectives on Justice** Running throughout the book are brief boxes titled Perspectives on Justice. These are designed to clarify competing viewpoints on what criminal justice is all about and what it should emphasize. For example, some people believe that the primary mission of the justice system is punishing criminals, whereas others focus more on treatment and rehabilitation. The Perspectives boxes indicate how each competing view has influenced the way the system of justice operates and identify programs and policies to which the different views are linked.

- **Web Links** These are designed to guide students to websites that provide them with additional information when they want to conduct further research on the topics covered in the text.

- **Concept Summaries** Throughout the chapters, these tables or lists summarize important concepts found in the chapter so that students can compare and contrast ideas, views, cases, findings, and so on. For example, a Concept Summary in Chapter 3 reviews the major premises and the research focus of various theories of the causes of crime.

- **(NEW) Significant Cases** Several chapters contain reference to multiple Supreme Court decisions. At the end of each of these chapters is a new *Significant Cases* feature. For example, Chapter 12 provides a table summarizing significant cases in punishment and sentencing. Such tables list the name of each case, the year it was decided, the key issue at stake, and the Supreme Court's decision. It was not possible to summarize every significant case, but we believe readers will benefit from the comprehensiveness of the selections we have included.

## ANCILLARY MATERIALS

Cengage Learning provides a number of supplements to help instructors use *Introduction to Criminal Justice* in their courses and to aid students in preparing for exams. Supplements are available to qualified adopters. Please consult your local sales representative for details.

To access additional course materials, including CourseMate, please visit www.cengagebrain.com. At the CengageBrain.com home page, search for the ISBN of your title (from the back cover of your book) using the search box at the top of the page. This will take you to the product page where these resources can be found.

### For the Instructor

*INSTRUCTOR'S EDITION* Designed just for instructors, the *Instructor's Edition* includes a visual walk-through that illustrates the key pedagogical features of the text as well as the media and supplements that accompany it. Use this handy tool to learn about the many options this text offers to keep your class engaging and informative.

*INSTRUCTOR'S RESOURCE MANUAL WITH TEST BANK* An improved and completely updated *Instructor's Resource Manual with Test Bank* has been developed by Lisa Anne Zilney at Montclair State University. The manual includes learning objectives, detailed chapter outlines, key terms, suggested readings, questions for review and discussion, and Internet assignments. Each chapter's test bank contains questions in multiple-choice, true–false, fill-in-the-blank, and essay formats, with a full answer key. The test bank is keyed to the learning objectives that appear at the beginning of each chapter in the textbook and includes the page numbers in the main text where the answers can be found. Finally, each question in the test bank has been carefully reviewed by experienced criminal justice instructors for quality, accuracy, and content coverage. Our "Instructor Approved" seal, which appears on the front cover, is our assurance that you are working with an assessment and grading resource of the highest caliber.

*POWERLECTURE WITH EXAMVIEW* This one-stop digital library and presentation tool includes preassembled Microsoft® PowerPoint® lecture slides linked to the learning objectives for each chapter. Also included are an electronic copy of the *Instructor's Resource Manual with Test Bank*, the *Student Study Guide*, ExamView computerized testing, and more. Based on the learning objectives outlined at the beginning of each chapter, the enhanced **PowerLecture** enables you to bring together text-specific lecture outlines and art from this text, along with new video clips, animations, and learning modules from the Web or your own materials—culminating in a powerful, personalized, media-enhanced presentation. The **PowerLecture** DVD also integrates **ExamView**®, a computerized test bank available for use on PC and Macintosh computers to customize tests of up to 250 items that can be delivered in print or online. With ExamView you can create, deliver, and customize tests and study guides (both print and online) in minutes. You can easily edit and import your own questions and graphics, change test layouts, and reorganize questions. And using ExamView's complete word-processing capabilities, you can enter an unlimited number of new questions and/or edit existing questions.

*LESSON PLANS* Prepared by Samantha Carlo at Miami Dade College, these instructor-created lesson plans bring accessible, masterful suggestions to every lesson. Each lesson plan includes a sample syllabus, learning objectives, lecture notes, discussion topics, in-class activities, tips for classroom presentation of chapter material, a detailed lecture outline, and assignments. Lesson plans are available on the PowerLecture resource and the instructor website.

*WEBTUTOR™ ON BLACKBOARD® AND WEBCT®* Jump-start your course with customizable, rich, text-specific content within your Course Management System. Whether you want to web-enable your class or to put an entire course online, WebTutor delivers. WebTutor offers a wide array of resources, including media assets, a test bank, practice quizzes linked to chapter learning objectives, and additional study aids. Visit www.cengage.com/webtutor to learn more.

*THE WADSWORTH CRIMINAL JUSTICE VIDEO LIBRARY* So many exciting new videos—so many great ways to enrich your lectures and spark discussion of the material in this text! Your Cengage Learning representative will be happy to provide details on our video policy by adoption size. The library includes the following selections and many others.

- *ABC® Videos.* ABC videos feature short, high-interest clips from current news events, as well as historical raw footage going back 40 years. Perfect for discussion starters or to enrich your lectures and spark interest in the material in the text, these brief videos provide students with a new lens through which to view the past and present, one that will greatly enhance their knowledge and understanding of significant events and open up new dimensions in learning. Clips are drawn from such programs as *World News Tonight, Good Morning America, This Week, PrimeTime Live, 20/20,* and *Nightline,* as well as numerous ABC News specials and material from the Associated Press Television News and British Movietone News collections.

- *Cengage Learning's "Introduction to Criminal Justice Video Series"* features videos supplied by the BBC Motion Gallery. These timely, engaging clips from CBS and BBC news programs—everything from nightly news broadcasts and specials to *CBS News Special Report* programs, *CBS Sunday Morning, 60 Minutes*, and more—are perfect classroom discussion starters.

- *Films for the Humanities.* Choose from nearly 200 videos on a variety of topics, such as elder abuse, supermax prisons, suicide and the police officer, the making of an FBI agent, and domestic violence.

## Criminal Justice Media Library

Cengage Learning's Criminal Justice Media Library includes nearly 300 media resources on the topics you cover in your courses. Available to stream from any Web-enabled computer, the Criminal Justice Media Library includes such valuable resources as Career Profile Videos featuring interviews with criminal justice professionals from a range of roles and locations, simulations that enable students to step into various roles and practice their decision-making skills, video clips on current topics from ABC® and other sources, animations that illustrate key concepts, interactive learning modules that help students check their knowledge of important topics, and Reality Check exercises that compare expectations and preconceived notions against the real-life thoughts and experiences of criminal justice professionals. The Criminal Justice Media Library can be uploaded and used within many popular Learning Management Systems. And you can customize it with your own course material. You can also purchase an institutional site license. Please contact your Cengage Learning representative for ordering and pricing information.

## For the Student

*CENGAGENOW™* CengageNOW is an easy-to-use online resource that helps students study effectively, without wasting time, to get the grade they want—NOW. By using CengageNOW Personalized Study (a diagnostic study tool containing valuable text-specific resources), students focus only on what they don't know and thus learn more in less time, an approach that often leads to a better grade. If the textbook does not include an access code card, students can go to www.ichapters.com to purchase CengageNOW.

*STUDY GUIDE* An extensive student guide has been developed and updated for this edition by Todd Scott at Schoolcraft Community College. Because different students learn in different ways, the guide includes a variety of pedagogical aids to help them, as well as integrated art and figures from the main text. Each chapter is outlined and summarized, major terms and figures are defined, and self-tests are provided with the answers keyed to each chapter's learning objectives.

*COURSEMATE* Cengage Learning's Criminal Justice CourseMate brings course concepts to life with interactive learning, study, and exam preparation tools that support the printed textbook. CourseMate includes an integrated ebook, quizzes keyed to chapter learning objectives, flashcards, videos, and more, and it introduces EngagementTracker, a first-of-its-kind tool that monitors student engagement in the course. The accompanying instructor website offers access to password-protected resources such as an electronic version of the *Instructor's Manual* and PowerPoint® slides.

*CLeBOOK* Cengage Learning's Criminal Justice ebooks enable students to access our textbooks in an easy-to-use online format. Highlight, take notes, bookmark, search your text, and (for most texts) link directly into multimedia. In short, CLeBooks combine the best features of paper books and ebooks in one package.

## Careers in Criminal Justice Website

*Available bundled with this text at no additional charge.* Featuring plenty of self-exploration and profiling activities, the interactive Careers in Criminal Justice Website helps students investigate and focus on the criminal justice career choices that are right for them. Includes interest assessment, video testimonials from career professionals, résumé and interview tips, and links for reference.

*CURRENT PERSPECTIVES: READINGS FROM INFOTRAC® COLLEGE EDITION* These readers, which are designed to give students a closer look at special topics in criminal justice, include free access to InfoTrac College Edition. The timely articles are selected by experts in each topic from within InfoTrac College Edition. They are available free when bundled with the text, and they include the following titles:

- Cyber Crime
- Victimology
- Juvenile Justice
- Racial Profiling
- White-Collar Crime
- Terrorism and Homeland Security
- Public Policy and Criminal Justice
- Technology and Criminal Justice
- Ethics in Criminal Justice
- Forensics and Criminal Investigation
- Corrections
- Law and Courts
- Policy in Criminal Justice

## ACKNOWLEDGMENTS

Many people helped make this book possible. Our marvelous acquisitions editor, Carolyn Henderson Meier, is always at our side and is an unofficial coauthor. A lot of credit for getting this book out must go to our wonderful, fantastic, patient, competent, (and did we mention fabulous?) development editor, Shelley Murphy. Special thanks to our incredible production manager Christy Frame, our fantastic production editor Aaron Downey, the obsessive-compulsive copyeditor Connie Day, the indefatigable photo editor Kim Adams Fox, and our incredible marketing manager, the astonishing Michelle Williams, all of whom do great and magnificent jobs.

To the reviewers for the twelfth and thirteenth editions, whose names are listed below, as well as to the reviewers for all previous editions, our enthusiastic and continuing thanks.

### Thirteenth Edition Reviewers

Sonya Brown, Tarrant County College
Ellen Smith Chupik, Moraine Valley Community College
James A. Curry, Baylor University
Wendelin Hume, University of North Dakota
Fred O. Jones, Simpson College
Douglas L. Kuck, University of South Carolina-Aiken
Douglas R. Larkins, Arkansas State University
Holly Ventura Miller, University of Texas at San Antonio
Kathleen Nicolaides, University of North Carolina-Charlotte
Terry L. Pippin, College of Southern Nevada
Robert Werling, California State University, Stanislaus

## Twelfth Edition Reviewers

George Ackerman, Keiser University
Steven M Christiansen, Joliet Junior College
William J. Hull, Corinthian Colleges, Inc
Terry Miller, Valencia Community College
Dan Moeser, East Tennessee State University
Robert W. Peetz, Midland College
O. Elmer Polk, Kennesaw State University
Michael J. Witkowski, University of Detroit Mercy

## Reviewers of All Previous Editions

Nola Allen
Allen Anderson
Jerry Armor
Thomas R. Arnold
William Ashlen
Kelly Asmussen
David Barger
Roger Barnes
Joe Becraft
Charles Beene
Eugene Bouley Jr.
Cathy C. Brown
Michael P. Brown
Steve Brown
Joseph Bruce
George S. Burbridge
Nicholas Carimi Jr.
Kathy Lynn Cook
Steven G. Cox
Robert Culbertson
Robert Doyle
Steven A. Egger
Michael T. Eskey
David Falcone
Gerhard Falk
Irwin Flack
Lorie Fridell
Patrick Gartin
Steven Gilham
Kathryn Golden
Peter Grimes
Ed Groskopf
Earl Hamb
John P. Harlan
Donald Harrelson
George Hernandez
William Hobbs
Dennis Hoffman
Robert G. Huckabee
Barton Ingraham
Michael Israel
Dorothy K. Kagehiro

John Klofas
James M. Knight Sr.
Nella Lee
Matthew Leone
Robert Lockwood
Otwin Marenin
Thomas McAninch
Patrick McConnell
Richard McCorkle
John Mezhir
Tom Mieczowski
Al Mirrane
Frank Morn
Anthony T. Muratore
Michael Neustrom
Deborah Newman
Linda O'Daniel
Robert Page
William Prince
Edward Qualey
Helen S. Ridley
Ronald Robinson
Rudy SanFillipo
John Sargent
William Selke
E. H. Shelby
Gayle Shuman
Zoann Snyder-Joy
Ronald Sopenoff
Henry Starkel
Rebecca Stevens
Karen Terry
Mark Tezak
Howard Timm
Donald Torres
Robert C. Wadman
S. N. Wailes
Laurin A. Wollan Jr.
Kevin Wright

*Larry J. Siegel*
*John L. Worrall*

# INTRODUCTION TO
# *Criminal Justice*

# THE NATURE OF CRIME, LAW, AND CRIMINAL JUSTICE

THE STUDY OF CRIMINAL JUSTICE should begin with a basic understanding of crime, law, and justice. There are differing views on what are the proper goals of this vast system. Some view the system as a treatment dispensing institution designed to rehabilitate criminal offenders; others view it as an agency of social control that protects decent citizens from criminal predators. Some people who work in the system, like Daisy Mongeau, an Investigator with the New Hampshire Public Defender's Office in Concord, are more concerned with providing people accused of crime with fair and equitable treatment before the law. She finds that a lot of her friends just can't understand why she works so hard to defend people who are guilty—even those who have confessed to the crime. "They don't seem to understand," she says, "that everyone is entitled to a criminal defense even if they actually committed the crime!"

When asked what is her greatest reward she says, "Getting the prosecutor to drop the case because of what a witness told me during an investigation." She finds that "clients are thrilled that someone actually believed them and helped them win the case. These are people not used to being given a helping hand."

The modern criminal justice system has evolved since ancient times. Some elements such as courts and punishment have been with us for thousands of years. Others, like police and corrections, are newer concepts, some developing in the United States in the nineteenth century. For example, probation and community treatment is a relatively new concept begun in 1841; today probation officers supervise 4 million clients. One of them, Samantha J. O'Hara, is a U.S. Probation Officer for the U.S. District Court in the Southern District of Iowa, headquartered in Des Moines. O'Hara thoroughly enjoys her job. "I like learning of people's stories and how they became involved in their offenses. The contact with a variety of people, including offenders, their families, assistant U.S. Attorneys, defense counsel, case agents, and the federal judges makes for an extremely diverse mix. It is personally rewarding to me," she adds, "to see that the final product is helpful to the U.S. District court judges, later the Federal Bureau of Prisons, and eventually to my colleagues in the U.S. Probation Officer supervision units across the country." ■

PART ONE OF THIS TEXT covers the basic issues and concepts of crime, law, and justice. Chapter 1 covers the justice process and the organizations that are entrusted with conducting its operations: the police, courts, and corrections; it provides overview of the justice system and sets out its most important agencies, processes, and concepts. Chapter 2 looks at the nature and extent of crime, and Chapter 3 tries to answer the question, why do people commit crime? Chapter 4 covers the criminal law, analyzing both its substantive and procedural components.

"[People] don't seem to understand that everyone is entitled to a criminal defense even if they actually committed the crime! Getting the prosecutor to drop the case because of what a witness told me during an investigation [is my greatest reward]. Clients are thrilled that someone actually believed them and helped them win the case. These are people not used to being given a helping hand."

"I like learning of people's stories and how they became involved in their offenses. The contact with a variety of people, including offenders, their families, assistant U.S. Attorneys, defense counsel, case agents, and the federal judges makes for an extremely diverse mix. It is personally rewarding to me, to see that the final product is helpful to the U.S. District court judges, later the Federal Bureau of Prisons, and eventually to my colleagues in the U.S. Probation Officer supervision units across the country."

# CHAPTER 1

# Crime and Criminal Justice

## CHAPTER OBJECTIVES

1. Be able to define the concept of criminal justice.
2. Be aware of the long history of crime in America.
3. Discuss the formation of the criminal justice system.
4. Name the three basic component agencies of criminal justice.
5. Comprehend the size and scope of the contemporary justice system.
6. Trace the formal criminal justice process.
7. Know what is meant by the term "criminal justice assembly line."
8. Discuss the "wedding cake" model of justice.
9. Be familiar with the various perspectives on criminal justice.
10. Understand the ethical issues that arise in criminal justice.

**T**he FBI labeled it "Operation Rotten Tomato"—and for good reason! On February 18, 2010, Frederick Salyer of Pebble Beach, California, owner and CEO of the SK Foods corporation (supplier of a range of tomato products), was arrested by federal agents and charged by the U.S. Attorney's office with violations of the Racketeer Influenced and Corrupt Organizations Act (RICO). The indictment alleged that Salyer had engaged in a variety of corrupt practices, including bribery and food misbranding and adulteration, wire fraud, and obstruction of justice.[1] It seems that over a period of 10 years, Salyer and his associates at SK had bribed the purchasing managers of some of its largest customers, such as Kraft Foods and Frito-Lay, to ensure that they purchased products from SK at elevated, above-market prices. But that was not all. The government also alleged that SK Foods used false documents to conceal its willingness to sell tomato products that fell short of basic quality standards set by the Food and Drug Administration. Unbeknownst to them, consumers were eating tomato sauce with mold levels so high that they violated federal standards. And because SK products were mislabeled, consumers who thought they were getting "organic" tomato paste were actually buying out-of-date conventional tomato products, paying a higher price for inferior goods. SK Foods declared bankruptcy in May 2009, and its assets were purchased by Singapore-based Olam International. A number of employees of SK and its customers pled guilty to charges of taking and/or receiving bribes; if convicted, Sayler faces 20 years in prison. ∎

**criminal justice system**
The system of law enforcement, adjudication, and correction that is directly involved in the apprehension, prosecution, and control of those charged with criminal offenses.

The public relies on the agencies of the **criminal justice system** for protection from elaborate schemes such as Salyer's intricate tomato scam. This loosely organized collection of agencies is responsible for protecting the public, maintaining order, enforcing the law, identifying transgressors, bringing the guilty to justice, and treating criminal behavior. The public depends on this vast system, which employs more than 2 million people and costs taxpayers more than $200 billion per year, to protect them from criminals and to bring justice to their lives. The criminal justice system is now expanding and taking on new duties, including protecting the country from terrorists and cyber criminals, groups that were almost unknown a decade ago. Member agencies must cooperate to investigate complex criminal conspiracies. (Operation Rotten Tomato, for example, was a joint effort of the FBI, the Internal Revenue Service, the Food and Drug Administration, and the Department of Justice Antitrust Division.) The contemporary justice system is constantly evolving to meet these new challenges.

This text serves as an introduction to the study of criminal justice. This chapter covers some basic issues and concepts, beginning with a discussion of the concept and study of criminal justice. The major processes of the criminal justice system are then examined to provide an overview of how the system functions. Because no single view exists of the underlying goals that help shape criminal justice, the varying perspectives on what criminal justice really is—or should be—are set out in some detail.

## IS CRIME A RECENT DEVELOPMENT?

Older people often say, "Crime is getting worse every day" and "I can remember when it was safe to walk the streets at night," but their memories may be colored by wishful thinking. Crime and violence have existed in the United States for more than 200 hundred years. In fact, the crime rate may have been much higher in the nineteenth and early twentieth centuries than it is today.

Crime and violence have been common since the nation was first formed.[2] Guerilla activity was frequent before, during, and after the Revolutionary War. Bands supporting the British (Tories) and the American revolutionaries engaged in savage attacks on each other, using hit-and-run tactics, burning, and looting.

The struggle over slavery during the mid-nineteenth century generated decades of conflict, crime, and violence, including a civil war. Slave patrols were made up of small groups of white men who enforced discipline upon slaves. Their duties included searching slave quarters for weapons that might be used in insurrections and breaking up clandestine slave meetings. They hunted down fugitive slaves and inflicted on the escapees brutal punishments, which could include both maiming and killing them, practices that horrified even some plantation owners.[3]

After the war, night riders and Ku Klux Klan members were active in the South, using vigilante methods to maintain the status quo and terrorize former slaves. The violence also spilled over into bloody local conflicts in the hill country of southern Appalachia. Factional hatred, magnified by the lack of formal law enforcement and by grinding poverty, gave rise to violent attacks and family feuding.

### Crime in the Old West

After the Civil War, many former Union and Confederate soldiers headed west with the dream of finding gold or starting a cattle ranch. Some even resorted to murder, theft, and robbery. The notorious John Wesley Hardin (who is alleged to have killed 30 men) studied law in prison and became a practicing attorney before his death. Henry McCarty, better known as the infamous "Billy the Kid," participated in range wars and may have killed more than 20 people before being gunned down in 1881 by Sheriff Pat Garrett; Billy had just turned 22. Others formed outlaw bands that terrorized the western territories. There is no more storied bad man in the history of the America than the outlaw Jesse James, who made his living robbing banks and trains. A folk hero, James remained an active outlaw until April 3, 1882, when he was shot in the back by Bob Ford, a fellow gang member, who did the deed in order to claim a $5,000 reward. Folk tales aside, James was in fact more of an impulsive killer than a latter-day Robin Hood: In September 1864, during the Civil War, Jesse, riding with the guerilla band led by Bloody Bill Anderson, held up a train in the town of Centralia, Missouri, and helped to kill 22 unarmed Union soldiers on board.[4] The James gang was not the only band of outlaws that plied its trade in the Old West. Train robbery was popularized by the Reno brothers in Indiana and perfected by Kid Curry (Harvey Alexander Logan), Butch Cassidy (Robert Leroy Parker), and the Sundance Kid (Harry Alonzo Longabaugh). Legend has it that Butch and Sundance fled from Wyoming to Bolivia to hide out and rob banks and were killed by soldiers in a 1908 shootout. But there are some who believe they sneaked back into the United States and lived quiet lives until their deaths in the 1930s!

Facing these outlaws were an equally colorful group of lawmen who developed reputations that have persisted for more than a century. Of these, none is more famous than Wyatt Earp. In 1876 he became chief deputy marshal of Dodge City, Kansas, a lawless frontier town, and he later moved on to Deadwood, in the Dakota Territory. In 1879 Earp and his brothers Morgan and Virgil journeyed to Tombstone, Arizona, where he eventually was appointed acting deputy U.S. marshal for the Arizona Territory. The Earps, along with their gunslinging dentist friend, Doc Holliday, participated in the famous O.K. Corral gunfight in 1881, during which they killed several members of a rustler gang known as the Cowboys.

## Crime in the Cities

The Old West was not the only area where gang activity flourished. In East Coast cities, gangs bearing colorful names such as the Hudson Dusters and the Shirttails battled rivals for control of the streets. In New York City, many gangs, including the Plug Uglies, the Swamp Angels, the Daybreak Boys, and the Bowery Boys, competed for dominance in the Five Point section of the lower East Side. Gang battles were extremely brutal, and men were killed with knives, hatchets, cleavers, and anything else that could puncture or slice flesh. One gang leader, William Poole, who was born in 1821, followed in his father's footsteps, opening a New York City butcher shop. In the 1850s his local street gang became the enforcers for the anti-immigrant Know-Nothing or Native American Party. In 1854 Poole, who was also known as "Bill the Butcher," severely beat John Morrissey, an Irish gang leader. Morrissey and his boys swore vengeance and fatally shot Poole on February 25, 1855, at Stanwix Hall in New York. As legend has it, Poole's dying words were "Good-bye, boys: I die a true American!"[5] Poole's story was told in the 2002 film *Gangs of New York*.

The Civil War also produced widespread business crime. The great robber barons bribed government officials and plotted to corner markets and obtain concessions for railroads, favorable land deals, and mining and mineral rights on government land. The administration of President Ulysses S. Grant was tainted by numerous corruption scandals.

From 1900 to 1935, the nation experienced a sustained increase in criminal activity. This period was dominated by Depression-era outlaws who later became mythic figures. Charles "Pretty Boy" Floyd was a folk hero among the sharecroppers of eastern Oklahoma, and the whole nation eagerly followed the exploits of its premier bank robber, John Dillinger, until he killed in front of a Chicago movie house. The infamous "Ma" Barker and her sons Lloyd, Herman, Fred, and Arthur are believed responsible for killing more than 10 people, and Bonnie Parker and Clyde Barrow killed more than 13 before they were slain in a shootout with federal agents.

The crime problem, then, is not a recent phenomenon; it has been evolving along with the nation itself. Crime has provided a mechanism for the frustrated to vent their anger, for business leaders to maintain their position of wealth and power, and for those outside the economic mainstream to take a shortcut to the American dream. To protect itself from this ongoing assault, the public has supported the development of a wide array of government agencies whose stated purpose is to control and prevent crime; to identify, apprehend, and bring to trial those who violate the law; and to devise effective methods of criminal correction. These agencies make up the criminal justice system.

## CREATING CRIMINAL JUSTICE

The debate over the proper course for effective crime control can be traced back to the publication in 1764 of Cesare Beccaria's famous treatise *On Crime and Punishments*. Beccaria, an Italian social philosopher, made a persuasive argument against the use of torture and capital punishment, common practices in the eighteenth century. He argued that only the minimum amount of punishment was needed to control crime if criminals could be convinced that their violations of law were certain to be discovered and punished.[6] Beccaria's work provides a blueprint for criminal justice: Potential law violators would most certainly be deterred if agencies of government could swiftly detect, try, and punish anyone foolish enough to violate the criminal law.

It was not until 1829, however, that the first police agency, the London Metropolitan Police, was created both to keep the peace and to identify and apprehend criminal suspects. A huge success in England, police agencies began to appear in the United States during the mid-nineteenth century. Another nineteenth-century innovation, the penitentiary (or prison) was considered a liberal reform that replaced physical punishments.

Although significant and far reaching, these changes were isolated developments. As criminal justice developed over the next century, these fledgling agencies of justice rarely worked together in a systematic fashion. It was not until 1919—when the Chicago Crime Commission, a professional association funded by private contributions, was created—that the work of the criminal justice system began to be recognized.[7] The Chicago Crime Commission acted as a citizens' advocate group and kept track of the activities of local justice agencies. The commission still carries out its work today and is active in administering anticrime programs.[8]

In 1931 President Herbert Hoover appointed the National Commission of Law Observance and Enforcement, which is commonly known as the Wickersham Commission. This national study group made a detailed analysis of the U.S. justice system and helped usher in the era of treatment and rehabilitation. Its final report found that thousands of rules and regulations govern the system, making it difficult for justice personnel to navigate the system's legal and administrative complexity. Some of the problems the commission encountered are still with us today: controlling illegal substances, the risk of compromising individual liberties, limiting the costs of justice, and recognizing cultural differences within society.[9]

The modern era of criminal justice can be traced to a series of research projects, begun in the 1950s, under the sponsorship of the American Bar Foundation (ABF).[10] Originally designed to provide in-depth analysis of the organization, administration, and operation of criminal justice agencies, the ABF project discovered that the justice system contained many procedures that had been kept hidden from the public view. The research focus then shifted to an examination of these previously obscure processes—investigation, arrest, prosecution, and plea negotiations. Justice professionals had a great deal of latitude in decision making, and how this discretion was used became a prime focus of the research effort. For the first time, the term "criminal justice system" began to be used, reflecting a view that justice agencies could be connected in an intricate, yet often unobserved, network of decision-making processes.

## Federal Involvement

In 1967 the President's Commission on Law Enforcement and Administration of Justice (the Crime Commission), which had been created by President Lyndon B. Johnson, published its final report, *The Challenge of Crime in a Free Society*.[11] This group of practitioners, educators, and attorneys had been charged with creating a comprehensive view of the criminal justice process and recommending reforms. Concomitantly, Congress passed the Safe Streets and Crime Control Act of 1968, providing for the expenditure of federal funds for state and local crime control efforts.[12] This act helped launch a massive campaign to restructure the justice system. It funded the National Institute of Law Enforcement and Criminal Justice, which encouraged research and development in criminal justice. Renamed the National Institute of Justice in 1979, it has remained a major source of funding for the implementation and evaluation of innovative experimental and demonstration projects in the criminal justice system.[13]

The Safe Streets Act provided funding for the **Law Enforcement Assistance Administration (LEAA)**, which, throughout its 14-year history, granted hundreds of millions of dollars in federal aid to local and state justice agencies. On April 15, 1982, the program came to an end when Congress ceased funding it. Although the LEAA attracted its share of criticism, it supported many worthwhile programs, including the development of a vast number of criminal justice departments in colleges and universities and the use of technology in the criminal justice system.

**Law Enforcement Assistance Administration (LEAA)** Federal agency that provided technical assistance and hundreds of millions of dollars in aid to state and local justice agencies between 1969 and 1982.

## Evidence-Based Justice: A Scientific Evolution

With continued funding from federal agencies such as the National Institute of Justice, the Office of Juvenile Justice and Delinquency Prevention, and the Bureau of Justice Statistics—as well as from private foundations such as the Pew and Annie E. Casey foundations—the study of criminal justice has embraced careful research analysis to support public policy initiatives. Whereas programs, policies, and procedures may have been shaped by political goals in the past, a mature justice system now relies more on the scientific collection of data to determine whether programs work and what policies should be adopted. According to this "What Works" movement,[14] empirical evidence, carefully gathered using careful scientific methods, must be collected and analyzed in order to determine whether criminal justice programs work and whether they actually reduce crime rates and offender recidivism. Programs must now undergo rigorous review to ensure that they achieve their stated goals and have a real and measurable effect on behavior.

**Evidence-based justice** efforts have a few unifying principles:[15]

**evidence-based justice** Determining whether criminal justice programs actually reduce crime rates and offender recidivism through the use of the scientific method.

1. *Target audience.* Programs must be reaching the right audience. A drug treatment program that is used with groups of college students caught smoking pot may look successful, but can it work with hard-core substance abusers? It is important for programs to work with high-risk offenders who have the greatest probability of recidivating. Targeting low-risk offenders may make programs look good, but it really proves little because the client group might not have repeated their criminal offenses even if left untreated.

2. *Randomized experiments.* Whenever possible, random experiments are conducted. Two groups of drug users are randomly selected, the first group is placed in the special treatment program, and the other is treated in a traditional fashion, such as being put in prison. If the recidivism rates of the experimental group are superior, we have strong evidence that the novel treatment method really works. Although it is sometimes difficult to select

subjects randomly, other methods (such as matching subjects on key characteristics such as age, race, gender, and prior record) can be substituted.

3. *Intervening factors.* Evidence-based programming must consider intervening factors that enhance or impede program success. A community-based crime prevention program that is used in a high-income neighborhood may be met with general approval and prove effective in reducing local problems, such as kids drinking at night in the local park. But will the program work in a high-crime area where well-armed gangs frighten residents? Conversely, a program that is deemed a failure with a group of at-risk kids living in an inner-city neighborhood, may work quite well with at-risk youngsters living in a rural environment.

4. *Measurement of success.* Evidence-based programs must develop realistic measures of success. For example, a treatment may seem to work, but careful analysis might reveal that the effect quickly wears off; long-term measures of program effectiveness are needed. Program retention must also be considered: A program for teens may seem to work because those who complete the program are less likely to commit crime in the future. But before success is declared and the program is adopted on a national level, research must closely evaluate such issues as the dropout rate: Are potential failures removed before the program is completed in order to ensure overall success (and continued funding)? And what about selectivity? Is the program open to everyone, including repeat offenders, or is it limited to people who are considered to have the greatest potential for success?

5. *Cost-effectiveness.* Programs may work, but the cost may be too high. In an era of tight budgets, program effectiveness must be balanced with cost. It is not enough for a program to be effective; it must also prove to be efficient.

These are but a few of the issues being considered today under the umbrella of evidence-based justice. Some well-known programs and policies that are both popular and have high visibility, such as the school-based Drug Abuse and Resistance Education (DARE) program, have been questioned because scientific evidence shows that the best intentions do not necessarily result in the best practice.[16] In addition, scientific research is now being used to dispute commonly held beliefs that may be misleading and erroneous. Throughout the text, we will highlight programs that have passed careful, evidence-based evaluations *and* some that have failed to stand up to such scrutiny.

## THE CONTEMPORARY CRIMINAL JUSTICE SYSTEM

The contemporary criminal justice system is society's instrument of social control. Some behaviors are considered so dangerous that they must be either strictly controlled or outlawed outright; some people are so destructive that they must be monitored or even confined. The agencies of justice seek to prevent or reduce outlawed behavior by apprehending, adjudicating, and sanctioning lawbreakers. Society maintains other forms of informal **social control**, such as parental and school discipline, but these are designed to deal with moral—not legal—misbehavior. Only the criminal justice system has the power to control crime and punish outlawed behavior through the arm of the criminal law.

The contemporary criminal justice system can be divided into three main components: law enforcement agencies, which investigate crimes and apprehend suspects (see the accompanying Careers in Criminal Justice feature); the court system, which charges, indicts, tries, and sentences offenders; and the correctional system, which incapacitates convicted offenders and attempts to aid in their treatment and rehabilitation (see Figure 1.1).

**social control**
A society's ability to control individual behavior in order to serve the best interests and welfare of the society as a whole.

**FIGURE 1.1**
Components of the Criminal Justice System

**Police**

Police departments are those public agencies created to maintain order, enforce the criminal law, provide emergency services, keep traffic on streets and highways moving freely, and develop a sense of community safety. Police officers work actively with the community to prevent criminal behavior; they help divert members of special needs populations, such as juveniles, alcoholics, and drug addicts, from the criminal justice system; they participate in specialized units such as a drug prevention task force or antirape unit; they cooperate with public prosecutors to initiate investigations into organized crime and drug trafficking; they resolve neighborhood and family conflicts; and they provide emergency services, such as preserving civil order during strikes and political demonstrations.

**Courts**

The criminal courthouse is the scene of the trial process. Here the criminal responsibility of defendants accused of violating the law is determined. Ideally, the court is expected to convict and sentence those found guilty of crimes while ensuring that the innocent are freed without any consequence or burden. The court system is formally required to seek the truth, to obtain justice for the individual brought before its tribunals, and to maintain the integrity of the government's rule of law. The main actors in the court process are the judge, whose responsibilities include overseeing the legality of the trial process, and the prosecutor and the defense attorney, who are the opponents in what is known as the adversary system. These two parties oppose each other in a hotly disputed contest—the criminal trial—in accordance with rules of law and procedure.

**Corrections**

In the broadest sense, correctional agencies include community supervision or probation, various types of incarceration (including jails, houses of correction, and state prisons), and parole programs for both juvenile and adult offenders. These programs range from the lowest security, such as probation in the community with minimum supervision, to the highest security, such as 23-hour lockdown in an ultra-maximum-security prison. Corrections ordinarily represent the postadjudicatory care given to offenders when a sentence is imposed by the court and the offender is placed in the hands of the correctional agency.

Criminal justice agencies are political entities whose structure and function are lodged within the legislative, judicial, and executive branches of the government:

■ *Legislative*. Under our current justice system, the legislature defines the law by determining what conduct is prohibited and establishes criminal penalties for those who violate the law. The legislative branch of government helps shape justice policy by creating appropriations for criminal justice agencies and acting as a forum for the public expression of views on criminal justice issues.

■ *Judicial*. The judiciary interprets existing laws and determines whether they meet constitutional requirements. It also oversees criminal justice practices and has the power to determine whether existing operations fall within the bounds of the state constitution and, ultimately, the U.S. Constitution. The courts have the right to overturn or ban policies that conflict with constitutional rights.

■ *Executive*. The executive branch of government is responsible for the day-to-day operation of justice agencies. It does not make or interpret the laws but is trusted with their enforcement. In this capacity, it must create and oversee the agencies of justice, determine their budget, and guide their direction and objectives. Laws cannot be enforced unless the executive supplies crime control agencies with sufficient funding to support their efforts.

## CAREERS IN CRIMINAL JUSTICE

# Police Officer

### Duties and Characteristics of the Job

Police officers are responsible for enforcing the written laws and ordinances of their jurisdiction. Police officers patrol within their jurisdiction and respond to calls wherever police attention is needed. Duties can be routine, such as writing a speeding ticket, or more involved, such as responding to a domestic disturbance or investigating a robbery. Their nonpatrol duties include testifying in court and writing reports of their

© AP Photo/Elaine Thompson

*On November 30, 2009, in the Leschi neighborhood of Seattle, sheriff's deputies look over a rifle they removed from the home of Maurice Clemmons, a career criminal, who was a suspect in the slaying of four Lakewood, Washington, police officers. After evading police for two days following the shooting, Clemmons was shot and killed by a police officer in Seattle. Police work can be dangerous, and even though shootouts are uncommon, a police officer must be prepared for the use of violence as part of the job.*

law enforcement actions. Some officers will choose or be chosen to work in specialized units such as the well-known special weapons and tactics (SWAT) teams or canine (K9) corps.

Police officers patrol jurisdictions of various sizes and have varying duties based on the nature of their jurisdiction. For example, sheriffs and their deputies enforce the laws within a county. State police primarily patrol state highways and respond to calls for backup from police units across their state. Institutions such as colleges and universities often have their own police forces as well, which enforce laws and rules in this specific area.

Police work can be an intense and stressful job; it sometimes entails encounters with hostile and potentially violent people. Police are asked to put their lives on the line to preserve order and safety. Their actions are watched closely and reflect upon their entire department. Because the places that police protect must be watched at all times, police work shifts may fall on weekends and holidays. Quite often it is the younger police officers who take these less desirable shifts. Additionally, police officers often have to work overtime; 45-hour workweeks are common.

### Job Outlook

Government spending ultimately determines how many officers a department has. Overall opportunities in local police departments will be excellent for individuals who meet the stringent psychological, personal, and physical qualifications. Many openings are created by the need to replace workers who retire and those who leave local agencies for federal jobs or for employment in private-sector security.

## Scope of the System

Because of its varied and complex mission, the contemporary criminal justice system in the United States is monumental in size. It now costs federal, state, and local governments more than $200 billion per year for civil and criminal justice— up more than 300 percent since 1982 (Figure 1.2).

As Figure 1.3 shows, the greatest increase in spending has been for correctional services. Over the past decade, state jurisdictions have conducted a massive correctional building campaign, adding tens of thousands of prison cells. It costs about $70,000 to build a prison cell, and about $22,000 per year is needed to keep an inmate in prison. Juvenile institutions cost about $30,000 per year per resident.

Per capita expenditure across the three government types and criminal justice functions is now more than $720 each year for every American! One reason why

Most police officers are employed at the local level, so this is where a majority of the jobs are found. There are generally more opportunities for employment in larger departments, such as those that serve large urban or suburban areas. Not surprisingly, most opportunities exist in areas with comparatively high crime rates or low salaries.

## Salary

The most recent data available indicates that police and sheriffs' patrol officers have annual wages of more than $51,000. The lowest-paid 10 percent earned about $30,000, and the highest-paid 10 percent earned about $80,000. Median annual wages were about $46,000 in federal government, $57,000 in state government, and $51,000 in local government. Officers, of course, made more:

| Position | Minimum salary | Maximum salary |
| --- | --- | --- |
| Police chief | $90,570 | $113,930 |
| Deputy chief | 74,834 | 96,209 |
| Police captain | 72,761 | 91,178 |
| Police lieutenant | 65,688 | 79,268 |
| Police sergeant | 58,739 | 70,349 |
| Police corporal | 49,421 | 61,173 |

## Opportunities

Police work is often appealing to many because of the good benefits and retirement policies. These factors may contribute to the fact that for the better-paying positions, such as state police, there may be more applicants than available positions. This competition means that those with qualifications such as a college education will have a better chance of being hired. After several years, those with the proper education who build a reputation for good work can rise in the ranks of their department or be assigned to other desirable positions, such as detective or investigator.

## Qualifications

To be a police officer, you must be in good shape mentally and physically, as well as meet certain education requirements and pass written tests. New police officers undergo thorough, rigorous training and testing—normally by spending 12 to 14 weeks at a local police academy—before they go out on the streets. During training, new officers learn diverse skills that will be necessary for their job, such as knowledge of laws and individual rights, self-defense, and first aid. Applicants can also expect to be asked to pass lie detector and drug tests.

Because of the enormous responsibility associated with being a police officer, certain personal qualities are considered indispensable for future officers. These include responsibility, good communication skills, good judgment, and the ability to make quick decisions.

## Education and Training

In most cases, one needs a high school diploma to be a police officer, but more and more jurisdictions are requiring at least some college education. Some college credits may be enough for an applicant to obtain a position on the police force, but more education, generally in the form of a bachelor's degree in a relevant field (especially criminal justice) is necessary for being promoted and moving up in rank.

Sources: "Police and Detectives," *Occupational Outlook Handbook*, 2010–2011 edition (Bureau of Labor Statistics, U.S. Department of Labor), retrieved March 16, 2010, from www.bls.gov/oco/ocos160.htm.

the justice system is so expensive to run is that it employs more than 2.4 million people in thousands of independent law enforcement, court-related, and correctional agencies. The nation now has almost 18,000 law enforcement agencies, including more than 12,000 local police departments, 3,000 county sheriffs' offices, and 49 state police departments (every state has one except Hawaii). In addition, there are 2,000 other specialized law enforcement agencies ranging from transit police in large cities to county constables.

These police and law enforcement agencies now employ more than a million people; more than 700,000 are sworn personnel with general arrest powers, and the rest are civilian employees. Of these, about 600,000 are in local agencies, 330,000 work in county sheriffs' offices, and the rest (90,000) work for state police.[17] There are nearly 17,000 courts; more than 8,000 prosecutorial agencies employ around 80,000 people; and about 1,200 correctional institutions (such as

**FIGURE 1.2**

Direct Expenditure by Level of Government

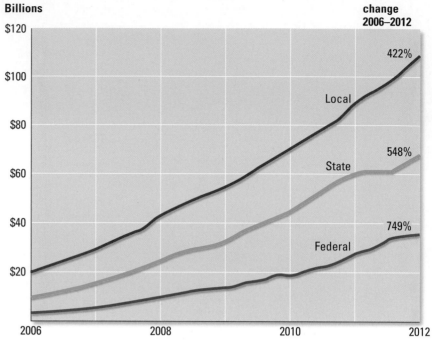

Source: Bureau of Justice Statistics, *Justice Expenditure and Employment Extracts*, http://bjs.ojp.usdoj.gov/content/glance/exptyp.cfm.

**FIGURE 1.3**

Direct Expenditure by Criminal Justice Function

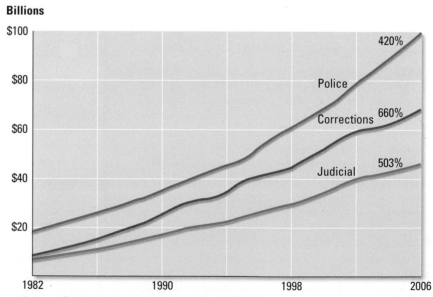

Source: Bureau of Justice Statistics, *Justice Expenditure and Employment Extracts*, http://bjs.ojp.usdoj.gov/content/glance/exptyp.cfm.

jails, prisons, and detention centers) employ around half a million people. There are also thousands of community corrections agencies, including more than 3,500 probation and parole departments (see Exhibit 1.1).

The system is massive because it must process, treat, and care for millions of people. Although the crime rate has declined substantially in the past decade,

## Elements of the Correctional System

**Probation**—Court-ordered community supervision of convicted offenders by a probation agency. Offenders on probation are required to obey specific rules of conduct while in the community.

**Prison**—A state or federal correctional facility that houses convicted criminals sentenced to a period of confinement that is typically more than one year.

**Jail**—A county correctional facility that holds people pending trial, awaiting sentencing, serving a sentence that is usually less than one year, or awaiting transfer to other facilities after conviction.

**Parole**—Community supervision after a period of incarceration.

### FIGURE 1.4
**Adult Correctional Populations**

Adult correctional populations, 1980–2008

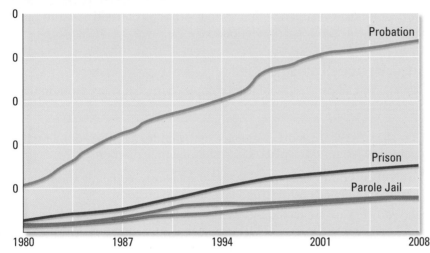

Source: Bureau of Justice Statistics, *Correctional Surveys,* http://bjs.ojp.usdoj.gov/content/glance/corr2.cfm.

**CourseMate** For more information about **data on the criminal justice system**, visit the Criminal Justice CourseMate at CengageBrain.com, then access the "Web Links" for this chapter.

more than 14 million people are still being arrested each year, including more than 2 million for serious felony offenses.[18] In addition, the juvenile courts handle about 1.5 million juveniles. Today, state and federal courts convict a total of over 1 million adults on felony charges.[19] It is not surprising, considering these numbers, that today more than 7 million people are under some form of correctional supervision, including 2 million men and women in the nation's jails and prisons and an additional 5 million adult men and women being supervised in the community while on probation or parole (see Figure 1.4). How can this trend be explained? The answer is that people are more likely to be convicted than in the past and, if sent to prison or jail, to serve more of their sentence (Table 1.1). The cost of corrections is now about $68 billion per year, a cost of about $30,000 per inmate, reinforcing the old saying that "It costs more to put a person in the state pen than to send a student to Penn State."

### TABLE 1.1

**Number and Rate of Persons Sentenced in State Courts for Committing a Felony**

| Year | Estimated Number | Rate per 100,000 Residents Age 18 or Older |
|---|---|---|
| 1990 | 829,340 | 447 |
| 1994 | 872,220 | 448 |
| 1998 | 927,720 | 454 |
| 2002 | 1,051,000 | 489 |
| 2006 | 1,132,290 | 503 |

Source: Matthew R. Durose, Donald Farole, and Sean P. Rosenmerkel, *Felony Sentences in State Courts, 2006* (Washington, D.C.: Bureau of Justice Statistics, 2009), http://bjs.ojp.usdoj.gov/index.cfm?ty=pbdetail&iid=2152.

## THE FORMAL CRIMINAL JUSTICE PROCESS

Another way of understanding criminal justice is to view it as a process that takes an offender through a series of decision points beginning with arrest and concluding with reentry into society. During this process, key decision makers resolve whether to maintain the offender in the system or to discharge the suspect without further action. This decision making is often a matter of individual discretion, based on a variety of factors and perceptions. Legal factors, including the seriousness of the charges, available evidence, and the suspect's prior record, are usually considered legitimate influences on decision making. Troubling is the fact that the suspect's race, gender, class, and age may also influence decision outcomes. Critics believe that such extralegal factors determine the direction a case will take, whereas supporters argue that the system is relatively fair and unbiased.[20]

In reality, few cases are actually processed through the entire formal justice system. Most are handled informally and with dispatch. The system of justice has been roundly criticized for its "backroom deals" and bargain justice. It is true that most criminal suspects are treated informally, but more important is the fact that every defendant charged with a serious crime is entitled to a full range of legal rights and constitutional protections.

## Formal Procedures

The formal criminal process includes a complex series of steps, from initial contact to postrelease.

*INITIAL CONTACT* In most instances, an offender's initial contact with the criminal justice system takes place as a result of a police action:

■ Patrol officers observe a person acting suspiciously, conclude the suspect is under the influence of drugs, and take her into custody.

■ Police officers are contacted by a victim who reports a robbery; they respond by going to the scene of the crime and apprehending a suspect.

■ An informer tells police about some ongoing criminal activity in order to receive favorable treatment.

■ Responding to a request by the mayor or other political figure, the local department may initiate an investigation into an ongoing criminal enterprise such as gambling, prostitution, or drug trafficking.

■ A person walks into the police station and confesses to committing a crime—for example, he killed his wife after an altercation.

Initial contact can also be initiated by citizens when no crime is involved—for example, when a parent files a petition in juvenile court alleging that his child is beyond control and needs to be placed in a state detention facility.

*INVESTIGATION* The purpose of the criminal investigation is to gather enough evidence to identify a suspect and support a legal arrest. An investigation can take just a few minutes, as when a police officer sees a crime in progress and apprehends the suspect quickly. Or it can take many years and involve hundreds of law enforcement agents. Dennis Rader, the notorious BTK (Bind, Torture, Kill) serial killer, began his murderous streak in 1974 and was finally apprehended in 2005 after an investigation that lasted more than 20 years.[21]

During the investigatory stage, police officers gather information in an effort to identify the perpetrator of a crime, understand the perpetrator's methods and motives, and determine whether the crime was an individual event or one of many similar crimes committed by a single individual. Gathering information means engaging in such activities as interviewing victims and witnesses at the crime scene, canvassing the neighborhood to locate additional witnesses, securing the crime scene, and then conducting a thorough search for physical evidence, such as weapons, fluids, and fingerprints.

Experienced officers recognize that all material gathered during a criminal investigation must be carefully collected, recorded, classified, processed, and stored. Because they may have to testify at trial under strict rules of evidence, they know that even early in the investigatory process, all evidence must be marked for identification and protectively packaged. If the police fail to follow proper procedures, the "chain of evidence" may be broken, tainting the evidence and making it inadmissible in court. Similarly, police must follow proper procedures while interviewing and/or searching suspects, being careful to uphold the constitutionally guaranteed right to privacy. If police overstep the boundaries set by the law to protect the rights of the accused, relevant information may later be excluded from trial.

*ARREST*  An arrest is considered legal when all of the following conditions exist:

- The police officer believes there is sufficient evidence, referred to as "probable cause," that a crime is being or has been committed and that the suspect is the person who committed it.

- The officer deprives the individual of freedom.

- The suspect believes that he is now in the custody of the police and has lost his liberty. The police officer is not required to use the word "arrest" or any similar term to initiate an arrest, nor does the officer have to handcuff or restrain the suspect or bring him to the police station.

Under most circumstances, to make an arrest in a misdemeanor, the officer must have witnessed the crime personally, a principle known as the **in-presence requirement**. However, some jurisdictions have waived the in-presence requirement in specific classes of crimes, such as domestic violence offenses, enabling police officers to take formal action after the crime has been committed even if they were not present when it occurred. Arrests can also be made when a magistrate, presented with sufficient evidence by police and prosecutors, issues a warrant authorizing the arrest of the suspect.

**in-presence requirement**
The principle that in order to make an arrest in a misdemeanor, the arresting officer must have personally witnessed the crime being committed.

*CUSTODY*  After an arrest and while the suspect is being detained, the police may wish to search for evidence, conduct an interrogation, or even encourage a confession. Witnesses may be brought to view the suspect in a lineup or in a one-on-one confrontation. Because these procedures are so crucial and can have a great impact at trial, the U.S. Supreme Court has granted suspects in police custody protection from the unconstitutional abuse of police power, such as illegal searches and intimidating interrogations. If a suspect who is under arrest is to be questioned about her involvement in or knowledge of a crime, the police must advise her of her right to remain silent and inform her that she is under no obligation to answer questions. Furthermore, recognizing that the police can take advantage of or exploit the suspect's psychological distress, the Court has ordered interrogating officers to advise the suspect that she is entitled to have a lawyer present and that the state will provide one at no charge if she cannot afford legal services. This so-called *Miranda* **warning** must be given if the police intend to use the answers against the person in a criminal case. If the arrested person chooses to remain silent, the questioning must stop. (*Miranda* will be discussed further in Chapter 8.)

*Miranda* **warning**
*Miranda v. Arizona* established that suspects under arrest must be advised that they have no obligation to answer questions and that they are entitled to have a lawyer present during questioning, if necessary, at no expense to themselves.

*CHARGING*  If the arresting officers or their superiors believe that sufficient evidence exists to charge a person with a crime, the case will be turned over to the prosecutor's office. The prosecutor's decision whether to charge the suspect with a specific criminal act involves many factors, including evidence sufficiency, crime seriousness, case pressure, and political issues, as well as personal factors such as a prosecutor's own specific interests and biases.

Charging is a critical decision in the justice process. Depending on the prosecutor's interpretation of the case, the suspect could be charged with a felony or a misdemeanor, and the subsequent differences between the charges can be vast. It is also possible that after conducting a preliminary investigation of its legal merits, prosecutors may decide to take no further action in a case; this is referred to as a **nolle prosequi**.

*PRELIMINARY HEARING/GRAND JURY* Created in England in the twelfth century, the grand jury's original purpose was to act as a buffer between the king (and his prosecutors) and the common citizen. The practice was instituted in the colonies, and later the U.S. Constitution mandated that before a trial can take place, the government must first show probable cause to believe that the accused committed the crime for which he is being charged. In about half the states and in the federal system, this determination is made by a grand jury in a closed hearing. In its most classic form, the **grand jury** consists of 12 to 23 persons, who convene in private session to evaluate accusations against the accused and determine whether the evidence warrants further legal action. If the prosecution can present sufficient evidence, the grand jury will issue a **true bill of indictment**, which specifies the exact charges on which the accused must stand trial.

In some instances, and especially in the federal system, prosecutors have used the grand jury as an investigative instrument directed against ongoing criminal conspiracies, including racketeering and political corruption. In this capacity, the grand jury has wide, sweeping, and almost unrestricted power to subpoena witnesses, solicit their testimony, and hand down indictments. Because the power to use the grand jury in this way is virtually in complete control of the prosecutor, and thus its proper application depends on his or her good faith, critics have warned of abuse and potential "witch hunts."[22]

In most states (and ironically in England, where the practice began), the grand jury system has been either replaced or supplemented by the preliminary hearing. In a preliminary hearing, the prosecution files a charging document (usually called an "information") before a lower trial court, which then conducts an open hearing on the merits of the case. During this procedure, which is often referred to as a "probable cause hearing," the defendant and the defendant's attorney may appear and dispute the prosecutor's charges. The suspect will be called to stand trial if the presiding magistrate or judge accepts the prosecutor's evidence as factual and sufficient.

Both the grand jury and the preliminary hearing are designed to protect citizens from malicious or false prosecutions that can damage their reputations and cause them both financial distress and psychological anguish.

*ARRAIGNMENT* Before the trial begins, the defendant will be arraigned, or brought before the court that will hear the case. At this time, formal charges are read; the defendant is informed of his constitutional rights (the right to be represented by legal counsel and to have the state provide one if he is indigent); an initial plea (not guilty or guilty) is entered in the case; a trial date is set; and bail issues are considered.

**nolle prosequi**
The term used when a prosecutor decides to drop a case after a complaint has been formally made. Reasons for a nolle prosequi include evidence insufficiency, reluctance of witnesses to testify, police error, and office policy.

**grand jury**
A type of jury responsible for investigating alleged crimes, examining evidence, and issuing indictments.

**true bill of indictment**
A written statement charging a defendant with the commission of a crime, drawn up by a prosecuting attorney and considered by a grand jury. If the grand jury finds sufficient evidence to support the indictment, it will issue a true bill of indictment.

© AP Images/Marcio Jose Sanchez

*Some jurisdictions maintain the grand jury system for indictments, whereas others now use preliminary hearings. The federal justice system still employs the grand jury. Former San Francisco Giants baseball player Barry Bonds arrives at the federal courthouse in San Francisco, California, on June 6, 2008. Bonds pleaded not guilty to 15 felony charges of lying to a federal grand jury about his use of performance-enhancing drugs.*

*BAIL/DETENTION* Bail is a money bond levied to ensure the return of a criminal defendant for trial, allowing the defendant to remain in the community prior to trial. Defendants who do not show up for trial forfeit their bail. Those people who cannot afford to put up bail or who cannot borrow sufficient funds for it will remain in state custody prior to trial. In most instances, this means an extended stay in a county jail or house of correction. If they are stable members of the community and have committed nonviolent crimes, defendants may be released on their own recognizance (promise to the court), without bail.

*PLEA BARGAINING* After an arraignment, if not before, the defense and prosecution discuss a possible guilty plea in exchange for reducing or dropping some of the charges or agreeing to a request for a more lenient sentence or some other consideration, such as placement in a treatment facility rather than a maximum-security prison. It is generally accepted that almost 90 percent of all cases end in a plea bargain, rather than a criminal trial.

*TRIAL/ADJUDICATION* If an agreement cannot be reached or if the prosecution does not wish to arrange a negotiated settlement of the case, a criminal trial will be held before a judge (bench trial) or jury, who will decide whether the prosecution's evidence against the defendant is sufficient beyond a reasonable doubt to prove guilt. If a jury cannot reach a decision—that is, if it is deadlocked—the case is left unresolved, leaving the prosecution to decide whether it should be retried at a later date.

*SENTENCING/DISPOSITION* If after a criminal trial the accused has been found guilty as charged, he will be returned to court for sentencing. Possible dispositions may include a fine, probation, some form of community-based corrections, a period of incarceration in a penal institution, and, in rare instances, the death penalty.

*APPEAL/POSTCONVICTION REMEDIES* After conviction, the defense can ask the trial judge to set aside the jury's verdict because the jury has made a mistake of law, such as misinterpreting the judge's instructions or convicting on a charge that was not supported by the evidence. Failing that, the defendant may file an appeal if, after conviction, she believes that her constitutional rights were violated by errors in the trial process. Appellate courts review such issues as whether evidence was used properly, whether the judge conducted the trial in an approved fashion, whether jury selection was properly done, and whether the attorneys in the case acted appropriately. If the court finds that the appeal has merit, it can rule that the defendant be given a new trial or, in some instances, order her outright release.

*CORRECTIONAL TREATMENT* After sentencing, the offender is placed within the jurisdiction of state or federal correctional authorities. The offender may serve a probationary term, be placed in a community correctional facility, serve a term in a county jail, or be housed in a prison. During this stage of the criminal justice process, the offender may be asked to participate in rehabilitation programs designed to help her make a successful readjustment to society.

*RELEASE* Upon completion of the sentence and period of correction, the offender will be free to return to society. Most inmates do not serve the full term of their sentence but are freed through an early-release mechanism, such as parole or pardon, or by earning time off for good behavior. Offenders sentenced to community supervision simply finish their term and resume their lives in the community.

*POSTRELEASE* After termination of their correctional treatment, offenders may be asked to spend some time in a community correctional center, which acts as a bridge between a secure treatment facility and absolute freedom. Offenders may find that their conviction has cost them some personal privileges, such as the right to hold certain kinds of employment. These may be returned by court order once the offenders have proved their trustworthiness and willingness to abide by society's rules.

## The Criminal Justice Assembly Line

To justice expert Herbert Packer, the image that comes to mind from the criminal justice process is an assembly-line conveyor belt down which moves an endless stream of cases, never stopping, carrying them to workers who stand at fixed stations and who perform, on each case as it comes by, the same small but essential operation that brings it one step closer to being a finished product—or, to exchange the metaphor for the reality, a closed file.[23] Criminal justice is seen as a screening process in which each successive stage (prearrest investigation, arrest, postarrest investigation, preparation for trial or entry of plea, conviction, disposition) involves a series of routinized operations whose success is gauged primarily by their ability to pass the case along to a successful conclusion.[24]

According to this view, each of the stages is a decision point through which cases flow. At the investigatory stage, police must decide whether to pursue the case or to terminate involvement because insufficient evidence exists to identify a suspect, because the case is considered trivial, or because the victim decides not to press charges. At the bail stage, a decision must be made whether to set bail so high that the defendant remains in custody, to set a moderate bail, or to release the defendant on her own recognizance. Each of these decisions can have a critical effect on the defendant, the justice system, and society. If an error is made, an innocent person may suffer or, conversely, a dangerous individual may be released to continue to prey upon the community.

In practice, many suspects are released before trial because of a procedural error, evidence problems, or other reasons that result in a case dismissal by the prosecutor (nolle prosequi). Although most cases that go to trial wind up in a conviction, others are dismissed by the presiding judge because of a witness's or complainant's failure to appear or because of procedural irregularities. Thus the justice process can be viewed as a funnel that holds many cases at its mouth and relatively few at its stem end.

Theoretically, nearly every part of the process requires that individual cases be disposed of as quickly as possible. However, the criminal justice process is slowed by congestion, inadequate facilities, limited resources, inefficiency, and the nature of governmental bureaucracy. When defendants are not processed smoothly, often because of the large caseloads and inadequate facilities that exist in many urban jurisdictions, the procedure breaks down, and the ultimate goal of a fair and efficient justice system cannot be achieved.

Figure 1.5 illustrates the approximate number of offenders removed from the criminal justice system at each stage of the process. As the figure shows, most people who commit crime escape detection, and of those who do not, relatively few are bound over for trial, convicted, and eventually sentenced to prison. However, more than a million people are convicted on felony charges each year—about 30 percent of all people arrested on felony charges. Researchers Matthew Durose, Donald Farole, and Sean Rosenmerkel found that about 69 percent of people convicted on felony charges are sentenced to a period of incarceration, either in state prison (41%) and or in a local jail (28%). Of the remainder, an estimated 27 percent received a probation sentence with no jail or prison time. Four percent of felons were not sentenced to any incarceration or probation but received a sentence that included fines, restitution, treatment, community service, or some other penalty (for example, house arrest or periodic drug testing).[25] The average prison sentence was about 5 years; most imprisoned felons are able to get out early via parole, early release for good behavior, or both. Concept Summary 1.1 shows the interrelationship of the component agencies of the criminal justice system and the criminal justice process.

**FIGURE 1.5**
The Criminal Justice Funnel

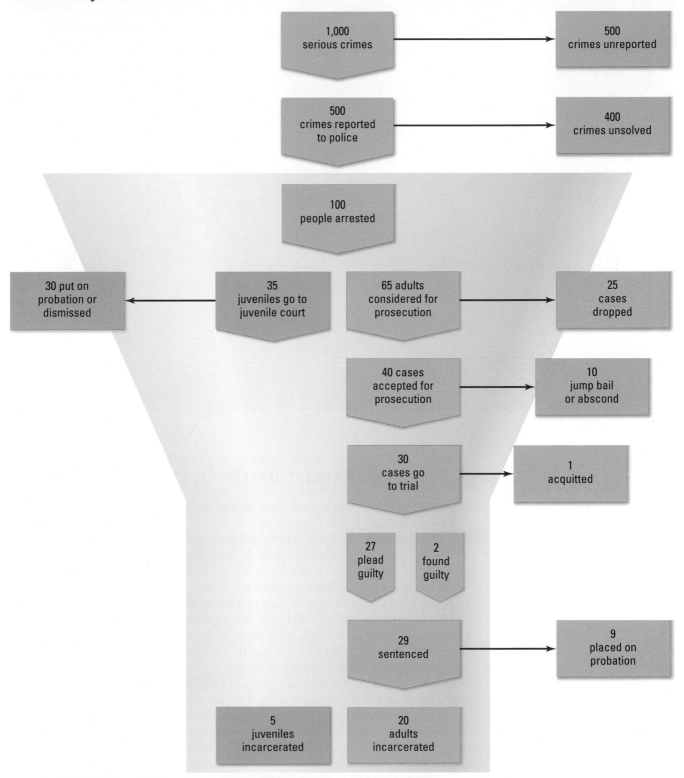

Sources: Thomas H. Cohen and Tracey Kyckelhahn, *Felony Defendants in Large Urban Counties, 2006* (Washington, D.C.: Bureau of Justice Statistics, 2010; Matthew Durose, Donald Farole, and Sean Rosenmerkel, *Felony Sentences in State Courts, 2006* (Washington, D.C.: Bureau of Justice Statistics, 2009).

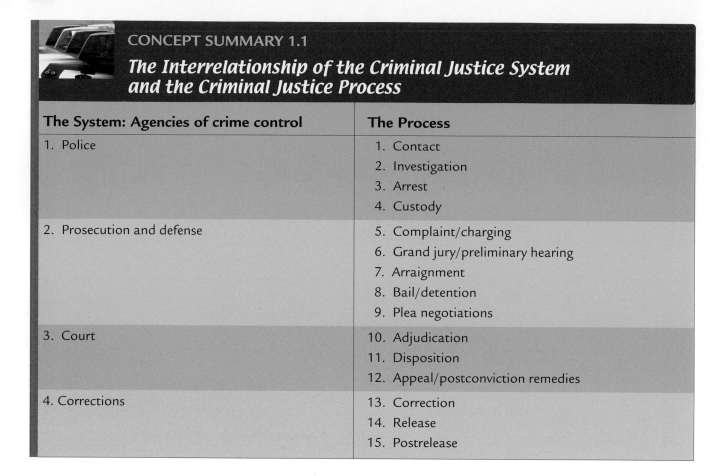

CONCEPT SUMMARY 1.1

*The Interrelationship of the Criminal Justice System and the Criminal Justice Process*

| The System: Agencies of crime control | The Process |
|---|---|
| 1. Police | 1. Contact |
| | 2. Investigation |
| | 3. Arrest |
| | 4. Custody |
| 2. Prosecution and defense | 5. Complaint/charging |
| | 6. Grand jury/preliminary hearing |
| | 7. Arraignment |
| | 8. Bail/detention |
| | 9. Plea negotiations |
| 3. Court | 10. Adjudication |
| | 11. Disposition |
| | 12. Appeal/postconviction remedies |
| 4. Corrections | 13. Correction |
| | 14. Release |
| | 15. Postrelease |

# THE INFORMAL CRIMINAL JUSTICE SYSTEM

The traditional model of the criminal justice system depicts the legal process as a series of decision points through which cases flow. Each stage of the system is defined by time-honored administrative procedures and controlled by the rule of law. The public's perception of the system, fueled by the media, is that it is composed of daredevil, crime-fighting police officers who never ask for overtime or sick leave, crusading district attorneys who stop at nothing to send the mob boss up the river, wily defense attorneys who neither ask clients for up-front cash nor cut short office visits to play golf, no-nonsense judges who are never inept political appointees, and tough wardens who rule the yard with an iron hand. Yet it would be overly simplistic to assume that the system works this way for every case. Although a few cases illustrate all the rights and procedures that make up the traditional, formal model, many are settled in an informal pattern of cooperation between the major actors in the justice process. For example, police may be willing to make a deal with a suspect to gain his cooperation, and the prosecutor may bargain with the defense attorney to get a plea of guilty as charged in return for a promise of leniency. Law enforcement agents and court officers are allowed tremendous discretion in their decisions whether to make an arrest, to bring formal charges, to handle a case informally, to substitute charges, and so on. Crowded courts operate in a spirit of getting the matter settled quickly and cleanly, instead of engaging in long, drawn-out criminal proceedings with an uncertain outcome.

The recognition of the informal justice process has spurred development of two concepts—the courtroom work group and the wedding cake model—that help us better understand how U.S. justice really operates.

# The Courtroom Work Group

Whereas the traditional model regards the justice process as an adversary proceeding in which the prosecution and defense are combatants, the majority of criminal cases are cooperative ventures in which all parties get together to work out a deal.

This **courtroom work group**, which is made up of the prosecutor, defense attorney, judge, and other court personnel, functions to streamline the process of justice through the extensive use of plea bargaining and other trial alternatives. Instead of looking to provide a spirited defense or prosecution, these legal agents (who have often attended the same schools, know one another, and have worked together for many years) try to work out a case to their own professional advantage. Their goal is to remove "unnecessary" delays and avoid formal trials at all costs. Because most defendants who have gotten this far in the system are assumed to be guilty, the goal is to process cases efficiently rather than to seek justice.

Political scientist David Neubauer has identified five essential ingredients of the courtroom work group:

> **courtroom work group**
> A term used to imply that all parties in the justice process work together in a cooperative effort to settle cases efficiently rather than to engage in a true adversarial procedure.

1.  *Shared decision making.* The legal process provides the trial judge with formal authority over the outcome of court proceedings. However, the judge's reliance on other members for information about the case results in a shared decision-making process. Shared decision making allows the judge to remain the informal leader of the work group and also serves to diffuse blame for mistakes.

2.  *Shared norms.* Each member of the work group agrees to behave in a predictable manner. The most important shared norm is shielding the work group from nonmembers; the greatest uncertainty comes from outsider contributors (such as witnesses and jurors) that work group members cannot control. There are standards of professional conduct (e.g., be firm in your decisions) and policy (e.g., all members agree on the seriousness of certain cases).

3.  *Socialization.* Newcomers are taught the informal expectations of the work group as part of their orientation. Senior members who possess great formal authority, such as judges, may be oriented to work group methods by those with less authority, such as deputy clerks. The socialization process shapes the overall behavior of the group by limiting the use of judicial authority and by communicating the group's informal work rules.

4.  *Reward and sanction.* To be meaningful, group rules must be enforced. Group members who abide by the norms are rewarded; those who do not are sanctioned. Conformity to group norms is secured by both extending rewards and leveling sanctions.

5.  *Goal modification.* Although all members share the goal of "doing justice," that goal is often cloudy because of the difficulty in defining justice and in measuring whether it has been achieved. As a result, members pursue organizational objectives, such as disposing of cases efficiently rather than worrying about effectiveness.[26]

In most criminal cases, cooperation, not conflict, between prosecution and defense appears to be the norm. The adversarial process comes into play in only a few widely publicized criminal cases involving rape or murder. Consequently, more than 80 percent of all felony cases and over 90 percent of misdemeanors are settled without trial.

What has developed is a system in which criminal court experiences can be viewed as a training ground for young defense attorneys looking for seasoning and practice. It provides a means for newly established lawyers to receive government compensation for cases they take to get their practice going and as an arena in which established firms can place their new associates for experience before they assign them to paying clients. Similarly, successful prosecutors often look forward to a political career or a highly paid partnership in a private firm. To further their career aspirations, prosecutors must develop and maintain a winning track record in criminal cases. Although the courtroom work group limits the constitutional rights of defendants, it may be essential for keeping the overburdened justice system afloat. Moreover, it is not clear that the informal justice system is inherently unfair to both the victim and the offender. Rather, evidence shows that the defendants who benefit the most from informal court procedures commit the least serious crimes, whereas most chronic offenders gain relatively little.[27]

## The "Wedding Cake" Model of Justice

Samuel Walker, a justice historian and scholar, has come up with a dramatic way of describing the informal justice process. He compares it with a four-layer cake, as depicted in Figure 1.6.[28]

*LEVEL 1* The first layer of Walker's model is made up of the celebrated cases involving the wealthy and famous, such as media figure O. J. Simpson, style guru Martha Stewart, and NBA all-star Gilbert Arenas (who in 2010 was sentenced to 30 days in a halfway house for bringing guns into the Washington Wizards locker room. The first level may also contain people who are not so famous or powerful but victimize someone who is—John Hinckley Jr., who shot President Ronald Reagan, might fall into this category, as would Mark David Chapman, who murdered Beatle John Lennon in 1980. Other cases fall into the first layer because they are widely reported in the media and become the subject of a TV investigation. Theodore Kaczynski may have been a recluse living in the Montana wilderness, but his crimes attracted national attention when, over a 17-year

**FIGURE 1.6**
The Criminal Justice Wedding Cake

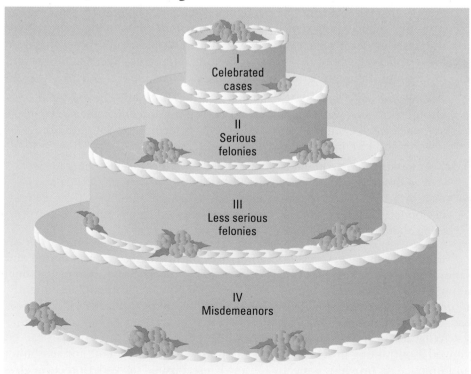

Source: Based on Samuel Walker's *Sense and Nonsense about Crime* (Monterey, Calif.: Brooks/Cole, 1983).

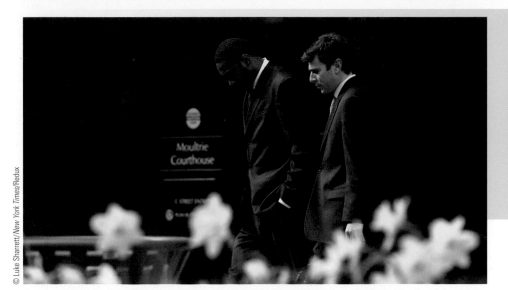

Washington Wizards guard Gilbert Arenas, left, leaves District of Columbia Superior Court in Washington after his sentencing on March 26, 2010. Arenas was ordered to spend 30 days in a halfway house for his conviction on gun charges stemming from a locker-room confrontation with a teammate. Arenas, one of the nation's most celebrated athletes, would be classified in the top layer of the criminal justice "wedding cake." Might less wealthy and less famous people, who would occupy the lower layers, not fare as well?

© Luke Sharrett/*New York Times*/Redux

period, he mailed or hand-delivered a series of increasingly sophisticated bombs that killed 3 Americans and injured 24 more. Along the way, he became known as the Unabomber.

Cases in the first layer of the criminal justice "wedding cake" usually receive the full array of criminal justice procedures, including competent defense attorneys, expert witnesses, jury trials, and elaborate appeals. The media typically focus on Level I cases, and the TV-watching public gets the impression that most criminals are sober, intelligent people, and most victims are members of the upper classes—a patently false impression.

*LEVEL II* In the second layer are the serious felonies—rapes, robberies, and burglaries—that have become all too familiar in U.S. society. These are serious crimes committed by experienced offenders. Burglaries are included if the amount stolen is high and the techniques that were used indicate the suspect is a pro. Violent crimes, such as rape and assault, are vicious incidents against an innocent victim and may involve a weapon and extreme violence. Robberies involve large amounts of money and suspects who brandish handguns or other weapons and are considered career criminals. Police, prosecutors, and judges all agree that these cases demand the full attention of the justice system. Offenders in such Level II cases receive a full jury trial and, if convicted, can look forward to a prison sentence.

*LEVEL III* Although they can also be felonies, crimes that fall in the third layer of the wedding cake are less serious offenses committed by young or first-time offenders or involving people who knew each other or were otherwise related: An inebriated teenager committed a burglary and netted $50; the rape victim had gone on a few dates with her assailant before he attacked her; the robbery involved members of rival gangs and no weapons; the assault was the result of a personal dispute, and there is some question who hit whom first. Agents of the criminal justice system relegate these cases to the third level because they see them as less important and less deserving of attention. Level III crimes may be dealt with by an outright dismissal, a plea bargain, reduction in charges, or (most typically) a probationary sentence or intermediate sanction, such as victim restitution.

*LEVEL IV* The fourth layer of the cake is made up of the millions of misdemeanors, such as disorderly conduct, shoplifting, public drunkenness, and minor assault. The lower criminal courts handle these cases in assembly-line fashion. Few defendants insist on exercising their constitutional rights, because the delay would cost them valuable time and money. Because the typical penalty is a small fine, everyone wants to get the case over with.[29]

The wedding cake model of informal justice is an intriguing alternative to the traditional criminal justice flowchart. Criminal justice officials handle individual cases differently, yet there is a high degree of consistency in the way particular types or classes of cases are dealt with in every legal jurisdiction. For example, police and prosecutors in Los Angeles and Boston handle the murder of a prominent citizen in similar fashion. They also deal similarly with the death of an unemployed street person killed in a brawl. Yet in both jurisdictions, the two cases, both involving a murder, will be handled very differently: The bigwig's killer will receive a full-blown jury trial (with details on the 6 o'clock news), whereas the drifter's killer will get a quick plea bargain. The model is useful because it shows that all too often, public opinion about criminal justice is formed on the basis of what happened in an atypical case.

## ▋ PERSPECTIVES ON JUSTICE

Since the 1960s, when the field of criminal justice began to be the subject of both serious academic study and attempts at unified policy formation, significant debate has continued over the meaning of the term "criminal justice" and how the problem of crime control should be approached. After decades of research and policy analysis, criminal justice is still far from a unified field. Practitioners, academics, and commentators alike have expressed irreconcilable differences concerning its goals, purpose, and direction. Some conservatives believe the solution to the crime problem is to increase the number of police, apprehend more criminals, and give them long sentences in maximum-security prisons. In contrast, liberals call for increased spending on social services and community organization. Others worry about giving the government too much power to regulate and control behavior and to interfere with individual liberty and freedom.

Given the multitude of problems facing the justice system, this lack of consensus is particularly vexing. The agencies of justice must try to eradicate such diverse social problems as substance abuse, gang violence, pornography, cyber crime, and terrorism, all the while respecting individual liberties and civil rights. The agencies of the justice system also need adequate resources to carry out their complex tasks effectively, but this hope often seems to be wishful thinking. Experts are still searching for the right combination of policies and actions that will significantly reduce crime and increase public safety, while upholding individual freedom and social justice.

Considering the complexity of criminal justice, it is not surprising that no single view, perspective, or philosophy dominates the field. What are the dominant views of the criminal justice system today? What is the role of the justice system, and how should it approach its tasks?

### The Crime Control Perspective

More than 20 years ago, political scientist James Q. Wilson made the persuasive argument that most criminals are not poor unfortunates who commit crime to survive but greedy people who choose theft or drug dealing for quick and easy profits.[30] Criminals, he argued, lack inhibition against misconduct, value the excitement and thrill of breaking the law, have a low stake in conformity, and are willing to take greater chances than the average person. If they could be convinced that their actions will bring severe punishment, only the irrational would be willing to engage in crime. Restraining offenders and preventing their future misdeeds, Wilson argued, is a much more practical goal of the criminal justice system than trying to eradicate the root causes of crime: poverty, poor schools, racism, and family breakup.

Wicked people exist. Nothing avails except to set them apart from innocent people. And many people, neither wicked nor innocent, but watchful, dissembling, and calculating of their chances, ponder our reaction to wickedness as a clue to what they might profitably do.[31]

Wilson's views helped define the **crime control perspective** on criminal justice. According to this view, the proper role of the justice system is to prevent crime through the judicious use of criminal sanctions. People want protection from dangerous criminals and expect the government to do what is necessary—punish criminals—to make them feel secure; crime control is part of the democratic process.[32] Because the public is outraged by such crimes as mass school shootings such as the one at Columbine High School in Colorado, it demands an efficient justice system that hands out tough sanctions to those who violate the law.[33]

According to crime control philosophy, if the justice system operated in an effective manner, most potential criminals would be deterred from crime, and the few who broke the law would be apprehended, tried, and punished so that they would never again risk committing crime. Crime rates trend upward, the argument goes, when criminals do not sufficiently fear apprehension and punishment. If the efficiency of the system could be increased and the criminal law could be toughened, crime rates would decline. Effective law enforcement, strict mandatory punishment, and expanding the use of prison are the keys to reduce crime rates. Although crime control may be expensive, reducing the appeal of criminal activity is well worth the price.

*EFFECTIVENESS AND EFFICIENCY* According to the crime control perspective, the focus of justice should be on the victim of crime, not on the criminal, so that innocent people can be protected from the ravages of crime. This objective can be achieved through more effective police protection, tough sentences (including liberal use of the death penalty), and the construction of prisons designed to safely incapacitate hardened criminals. If the system could be made more efficient, few would be tempted to break the law, and its effectiveness would improve.

Crime control advocates do not want legal technicalities to help the guilty go free and tie the hands of justice. They lobby for the abolition of legal restrictions that limit a police officer's ability to search for evidence and interrogate suspects. Police departments would be more effective crime fighters, they argue, if administrators employed a proactive, aggressive law enforcement style without having to worry about charges that their forceful tactics violated the right of criminal defendants.[34] The police may sometimes be forced to use tactics that abridge civil liberties for the sake of effectiveness, such as profiling people at an airport on the basis of their race or ethnic origin in an effort to identify and apprehend suspected terrorists. Civil libertarians are wary of racial profiling, but crime control advocates argue that we are in the midst of a national emergency and that the ends justify the means.

*ABOLISHING LEGAL ROADBLOCKS* One impediment to effective crime control is the legal roadblocks set up by the courts to protect the due process rights of criminal defendants. Several hundred thousand criminals go free every year in cases dropped because courts find that police have violated the suspects' *Miranda rights*.[35] Crime control advocates lobby for abolition of the exclusionary rule, which requires that illegally seized evidence be barred from criminal proceedings. Their voices have been heard: A more conservative Supreme Court has given police greater latitude to search for and seize evidence and has eased restrictions on how police operate. However, research shows that even in this permissive environment, police routinely violate suspects' rights when searching for evidence, and the majority of these incidents are never reviewed by the courts because the search was not followed up by arrest or citation.[36]

**crime control perspective**
A model of criminal justice that emphasizes the control of dangerous offenders and the protection of society through harsh punishment as a deterrent to crime.

## ANALYZING CRIMINAL JUSTICE ISSUES

# Why Are Americans So Punitive?

Why is the general public in the United States more punitive and more willing to get tough on crime than people in other nations? According to criminal justice scholars James Unnever and Francis Cullen, criminal justice policies in the United States have been harsh and punitive for nearly 40 years, resulting in a prison population of more than 2 million. Rather than believing that crime can be controlled through social programs and criminals rehabilitated through individualized treatment interventions, Americans have embraced the "crime control" model's emphasis on the harsh punishment of offenders as a means of protecting innocent individuals from being victimized. Conservative ideas on public policy, they note, have shifted the United States from a center-left to a center-right position. Three prominent theories have emerged to explain why the American public seems willing to support the idea of "getting tough on crime": the escalating crime–distrust model, the moral decline model, and the racial animus model.

### The Escalating Crime–Distrust Model

The escalating crime–distrust model rests on the public's perception that crime is increasing and that rising crime rates will disrupt their way of life. People view crime as a menace because they have lost faith in the ability of government, and especially of the courts, to protect them from the injurious effects of crime. Whereas fifty years ago, the public was willing to attack the "root causes of crime," such as poverty and unemployment, today this approach is seen as foolhardy. Offenders are not community members to be saved but threats to public safety; criminals no longer deserve a second chance but are outsiders who should be imprisoned. In contemporary American society, concern for the offender has largely been replaced by concern for the victim. The court system is widely viewed as a misguided liberal entity that puts the rights of criminals ahead of concern for victims, thereby contributing to the volume of crime. Thus fear of crime, concern about crime, and prior victimization significantly increase punitive attitudes.

### The Moral Decline Model

According to the moral decline model, people who feel uncertain about the world, where we are going, and the social climate are most likely to be punitive. This view rests on the concept of a world that is in "moral decay." People who feel that the conventional social bonds that hold society together are dissolving look for punitive public policies to take their place. The family is in decline, they believe. Schools are failing, America is being threatened by overseas adversaries and is in danger of losing its supremacy, and moral values are being undermined by forces ranging from Internet pornography to the glorification of morally questionable rock stars. In this climate, where basic values are under attack, softer approaches to crime, such as probation and community treatment, simply will not work. The justice system must get tough with this growing moral threat.

### The Racial Animus Model

The racial animus model focuses on the racial beliefs and values that have shaped crime control policies. Sadly, a long history of racism on the part of members of the justice system resulted in horrific

Crime control advocates also question the criminal justice system's ability to rehabilitate offenders. Most treatment programs are ineffective because the justice system is simply not equipped to treat people who have a long history of antisocial behavior. Even when agents of the system attempt to prevent crime by working with young people, the results are unsatisfactory. From both a moral and a practical standpoint, the role of criminal justice should be the control of antisocial people. If not to the justice system, then to whom can the average citizen turn for protection from society's criminal elements?

In recent years, the crime control model has emerged as the dominant vision of justice. Its proponents have helped shaped public attitudes toward crime and its control. As a result, the American public seems quite punitive toward criminals (see the nearby Analyzing Criminal Justice Issues feature[37]), and about two-thirds approve availability of the death penalty.

miscarriages of justice. Just as attacks and lynchings were common 80 years ago, some more recent incidents show that the criminal justice system is not yet entirely immune to racism:

- In 1955, Emmitt Till was beaten and lynched in Mississippi, allegedly for whistling at a white woman. Two men were tried for the crime but were acquitted.
- In 1964, three civil rights workers (Michael Schwerner, Andrew Goodman, and James Chaney) were abducted and killed in Philadelphia, Mississippi. In 2005, Edgar Killen, by then 80 years old, was convicted of manslaughter in the case and given a 60-year prison sentence.
- In 1998, James Byrd Jr. was abducted, tied to the back of a truck, and dragged to his death in Jasper, Texas. Two of the murderers, who were associated with a white supremacist prison gang, were sentenced to death; the third received life in prison.

Although racism's influence on the justice system has surely declined, there is evidence that perceptions of race still shape the contours of how Americans think about crime and its control. White America has developed a mental image of the typical offender as a young, inner-city black male who offends with little remorse. People who subscribe to this view will oppose even policies that are in their own best interests because they may benefit groups that they hold in disregard. In sum, the racial animus model contends that racial and ethnic intolerance is integral to any understanding of why Americans endorse get-tough policies.

## Testing the Models

When Unnever and Cullen tested the validity of the foregoing models by using data from a national public opinion survey, they found that punitive sentiments can emerge from all three views but that the racial animus model seemed to be most powerful determinant of punitiveness. People view crime and justice through a racial lens. The American public's endorsement of mass imprisonment and the death penalty rests on the belief that the targets of these harsh crime control efforts are African American young men, a group already feared and loathed by the white majority. The fact that a disliked subgroup is also associated with crime legitimizes the public's feelings and prejudices. These feelings are supported by political pundits who constantly dwell on the failings of the court system and the "coddling of criminals," Unnever and Cullen conclude that

> when politicians justify their support for getting tough on criminals by citing public-opinion polls, they are either explicitly or implicitly basing their policy decisions on racialized punitive attitudes. In short, the data show that when it comes to public opinion about crime and its control, race and racism matter.

## Critical Thinking

Do you agree with this analysis? Are punitive crime control measures a function of racial animus, or are people genuinely scared of crime and just want the agencies of the justice system to take drastic action. Have the media stirred the pot by providing a racially biased vision of who commits crime, sells drugs, and joins gangs?

Source: James Unnever and Francis Cullen, "The Social Sources of Americans' Punitiveness: A Test of Three Competing Models," *Criminology* 48 (2010): 99–129.

## The Rehabilitation Perspective

If the crime control perspective views the justice system in terms of protecting the public and controlling criminal elements, then the **rehabilitation perspective** sees the justice system as a means of caring for and treating people who cannot manage themselves. Advocates of this perspective view crime as an expression of frustration and anger created by social inequality. Crime can be controlled by giving people the means to improve their lifestyle through conventional endeavors.

The rehabilitation concept assumes that people are at the mercy of social, economic, and interpersonal conditions and interactions. Criminals themselves are the victims of racism, poverty, strain, blocked opportunities, alienation, family disruption, and other social problems. They live in socially disorganized neighborhoods that are incapable of providing proper education, health care, or civil services. Society must help them compensate for their social problems.

**rehabilitation perspective**
A perspective on criminal justice that sees crime as an expression of frustration and anger created by social inequality that can be controlled by giving people the means to improve their lifestyles through conventional endeavors.

*ALTERNATIVES TO CRIME*  Rehabilitation advocates believe that government programs can help reduce crime on both a societal (macro) and an individual (micro) level. On the macro, or societal, level, research shows that as the number of legitimate opportunities to succeed declines, people are more likely to turn to criminal behaviors, such as drug dealing, to survive. Increasing economic opportunities through job training, family counseling, educational services, and crisis intervention is a more effective crime reducer than prisons and jails. As legitimate opportunities increase, violence rates decline.[38]

On the micro, or individual, level, rehabilitation programs can help at-risk youths avoid entry into criminal careers by providing them with legitimate alternatives to crime and with counseling to help them grasp opportunities. Drug offenders, a population known to be resistant to change, have shown marked improvement given the proper course of treatment.[39]

Even if preventive measures have not worked, incarcerating offenders without proper treatment is not the right course of action. Given the proper therapy, incarcerated offenders can significantly lower their rates of recidivism.[40] Within correctional settings, programs that develop interpersonal skills, induce a prosocial change in attitudes, and improve thinking patterns have been shown to significantly reduce recidivism rates.[41]

Society has a choice: Pay now, by funding treatment and educational programs, or pay later, when troubled youths enter costly correctional facilities over and over again. This view is certainly not lost on the public. Although the public may want to get tough on crime, many people are willing to make exceptions—for example, by advocating leniency for younger offenders.[42]

## The Due Process Perspective

**due process perspective**
A perspective on criminal justice that emphasizes individual rights and constitutional safeguards against arbitrary or unfair judicial or administrative proceedings.

Advocates of the **due process perspective** argue that the greatest concern of the justice system should be treating all those accused of crime fairly.[43] This means providing impartial hearings, competent legal counsel, equitable treatment, and reasonable sanctions. The use of discretion within the justice system should be strictly monitored to ensure that no one suffers from racial, religious,

Due process advocates fear that the justice process is often imprecise and that life-threatening mistakes are routinely made by police, prosecutors, and judges. Consequently, we must be ever vigilant to guard against violations of constitutional rights. Here Polk County public defender Robert Young hugs James Bain, right, during a hearing at the Polk County Courthouse Thursday, on December 17, 2009, in Bartow, Florida. Bain was released after spending 35 years in prison for a 1974 rape conviction. New DNA evidence proved that he could not have committed the crime.

or ethnic discrimination. The system must be attuned to the civil rights afforded every citizen by the U.S. Constitution. Therefore, it is vexing to due process advocates when the Supreme Court extends the scope of law enforcement's reach, enabling police agencies to monitor and control citizens at the expense of their right to privacy.

Although many views exist of what the true goals of justice should be, the system undoubtedly must be expected to operate in a fair and unbiased manner. Those who advocate the due process orientation point out that the justice system remains an adversary process that pits the forces of an all-powerful state against those of a solitary individual accused of committing a crime. If concern for justice and fairness did not exist, the defendant who lacked resources could easily be overwhelmed.

Miscarriages of justice are common. Numerous criminal convictions have been overturned because newly developed DNA evidence later showed that the accused could not have committed the crimes. Many of those who were falsely convicted spent years in prison before their release.[44] Evidence also shows that many innocent people have been executed for crimes they did not commit. From 1976 to 1999, 566 people were executed. During that same period, 82 convicts awaiting execution were exonerated—a ratio of one freed for every seven put to death.[45] Because such mistakes can happen, even the most apparently guilty offender deserves all the protection the justice system can offer. Having a competent attorney who mounts a spirited defense may mean the difference between life and death. When Talia Roitberg Harmon and William Lofquist studied the cases of people who had been falsely convicted of murder, they found that those who employed private counsel were much more likely to be exonerated than those who could not afford a private attorney.[46] Is it fair that a life-or-death outcome may rest on the ability to afford private counsel?

Those who question the due process perspective claim that the legal privileges that are afforded to criminal suspects have gone too far and that the effort to protect individual rights now interferes with public safety. Is it fair, they argue, for evidence to be suppressed when it is obtained in violation of the constitutional right to be free from illegal search and seizure, even if it means that a guilty person goes free? Yet, many people who appear guilty may actually be victims of slipshod justice. Recent (2008) research sponsored by the Pew Foundation found that a majority of death penalty convictions that have been overturned were due to "serious, reversible error," including egregiously incompetent defense counsel, suppression of exculpatory evidence, false confessions, racial manipulation of the jury, questionable "snitch" and accomplice testimony, and faulty jury instructions.[47] Certainly, the danger of convicting an innocent person still remains a frightening possibility.

## The Nonintervention Perspective

Supporters of the **nonintervention perspective** believe that justice agencies should limit their involvement with criminal defendants. Regardless of whether intervention is designed to punish people or to treat them, the ultimate effect of any involvement is harmful. Whatever their goals or design, programs that bring people in contact with a social control agency—such as the police, a mental health department, the correctional system, or a criminal court—will have long-term negative effects. Once involved with such an agency, criminal defendants may be watched, people might consider them dangerous and untrustworthy, and they can develop a lasting record that has negative connotations. Bearing an official label disrupts their personal and family life and harms parent–child relationships. Eventually, they may even come to believe what their official record suggests; they may view themselves as bad, evil, outcasts, troublemakers, or crazy. Thus, official intervention promotes, rather than reduces, the tendency to engage in antisocial activities.[48]

Noninterventionists are concerned about the effect of the stigma that convicted criminals bear when they are branded "rapist" or "child abuser."

**nonintervention perspective**
A perspective on criminal justice that favors the least intrusive treatment possible: decarceration, diversion, and decriminalization.

On October 28, 2009, a group of sign-waving supporters demonstrate for Measure 2F, a reform to legalize private possession of up to an ounce of marijuana by adults 21 and older in the town of Breckenridge, Colorado. Supporters urged people to pass 2F, which would legalize possession of smoking paraphernalia and of up to 1 ounce of marijuana. Pot possession would still be a state crime, but rather than making an arrest, town police officers would have to take users to the county sheriff's department to be cited. The measure passed overwhelmingly in the November election. Do you believe that pot should be legalized?

As horrifying as these crimes are, such labels imply chronic criminality, and they will stick with the perpetrators forever. Noninterventionists point out that this may not be in the best interests of society. Once labeled, people may find it difficult to be accepted back into society, even after they have completed their sentence. It is not surprising, considering these effects of stigma and labeling, that recidivism rates are so high. When people are given less stigmatizing forms of punishment, such as probation, they are less likely to become repeat offenders.[49]

Fearing the harmful effects of stigma and labels, noninterventionists have tried to place limitations on the government's ability to control people's lives. They have called for the **decriminalization** (reduction of penalties) and legalization of nonserious victimless crimes, such as the possession of small amounts of marijuana, public drunkenness, and vagrancy.

Noninterventionists demand the removal of nonviolent offenders from the nation's correctional system, a policy referred to as **deinstitutionalization**. First offenders who commit minor crimes should instead be placed in informal, community-based treatment programs, a process referred to as pretrial diversion.

Sometimes the passage of new criminal laws can stigmatize offenders beyond the scope of their offense, a phenomenon referred to as widening the net of justice. For example, a person who purchases pornography on the Internet may be labeled a dangerous sex offender, or someone caught for a second time with marijuana may be considered a habitual drug abuser. Noninterventionists have fought implementation of community notification–type laws that require convicted sex offenders to register with state law enforcement officials and that allow officials to publicly disclose when a registrant moves into a community. Their efforts have resulted in rulings stating that these laws can be damaging to the reputation and future of offenders who have not been given an opportunity to defend themselves from the charge that they are chronic criminal sex offenders.[50] As a group, noninterventionist initiatives have been implemented to help people avoid the stigma associated with contact with the criminal justice system.

## The Equal Justice Perspective

The **equal justice perspective** asserts that all people should receive the same treatment under the law. Efforts to distinguish between criminal offenders and create a system of individualized treatment create a sense of unfairness that

**decriminalization**
Reducing the penalty for a criminal act without legalizing it.

**deinstitutionalization**
The policy of removing from secure confinement as many first offenders of minor, nonviolent crimes as possible and treating them in the community.

**equal justice perspective**
A perspective on criminal justice based on the idea that all people should receive the same treatment under the law and should be evaluated on the basis of their current behavior, not on what they have done in the past.

undermines the goals of the system. Frustration arises when two people commit the same crime but receive different sentences or punishments. The resulting anger and sense of unfairness will increase the likelihood of recidivism.

To remedy this situation, the criminal justice system must reduce discretion and unequal treatment. Each criminal act must be treated independently and punished proportionately. Punishment must not be based either on past events for which people have already paid their debt to society or on what they may do in the future. The treatment of criminal offenders must be based solely on present behavior. Punishment must be equitably administered and based on the principle of "just deserts."

The equal justice perspective has had considerable influence in molding the nation's sentencing policy. An ongoing effort has been made to reduce discretion and guarantee that every offender convicted of a particular crime receives equal and precisely computed punishment. This change has been particularly welcome, given the charges of racial discrimination that have beset the sentencing process. A number of initiatives have been designed to achieve this result, including mandatory sentences, which require that all people convicted of a crime receive the same prison sentence. Truth-in-sentencing laws require offenders to serve a substantial portion of their prison sentence behind bars, thus limiting their eligibility for early release on parole.[51]

## The Restorative Justice Perspective

According to the **restorative justice perspective**, the true purpose of the criminal justice system is to promote a peaceful and just society; the justice system should aim for peacemaking, not punishment.[52] The restorative justice perspective draws its inspiration from religious and philosophical teachings ranging from Quakerism to Zen. Advocates of restorative justice view the efforts of the state to punish and control as "crime encouraging" rather than "crime discouraging." The violent punishing acts of the state, they claim, are not unlike the violent acts of individuals.[53] Therefore, mutual aid, not coercive punishment, is the key to a harmonious society. Without the capacity to restore damaged social relations, society's response to crime has been almost exclusively punitive.

According to restorative justice, resolution of the conflict between criminal and victim should take place in the community in which that conflict originated,

**restorative justice perspective**
A perspective on criminal justice that sees the main goal of the criminal justice system as making a systematic response to wrongdoing that emphasizes healing victims, offenders, and communities wounded by crime. It stresses peacemaking, not punishment.

Inmate James Burton Jr. waters the "Restorative Justice Gardens" at the Southeast Correctional Center in Charleston, Missouri, on September 5, 2007. Inmates have produced tens of thousands of pounds of fresh vegetables from a six-acre garden at the state prison complex, all of it donated to the Bootheel Food Bank in Sikeston, Missouri, which serves some of the poorest counties in the state. Should society attempt to restore law violators to the community, or should violators merely be punished for their misdeeds?

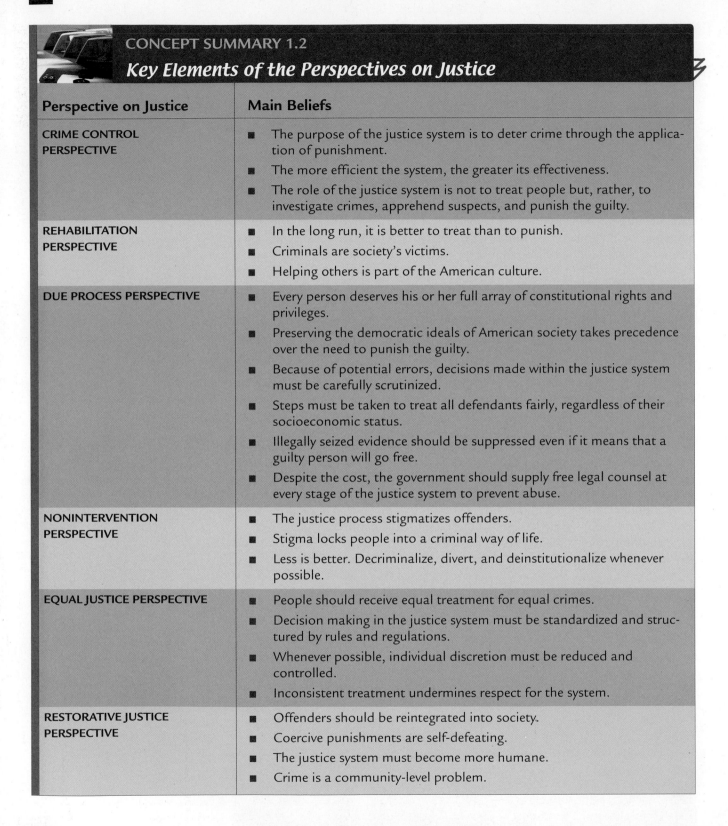

CONCEPT SUMMARY 1.2
## Key Elements of the Perspectives on Justice

| Perspective on Justice | Main Beliefs |
|---|---|
| **CRIME CONTROL PERSPECTIVE** | ■ The purpose of the justice system is to deter crime through the application of punishment.<br>■ The more efficient the system, the greater its effectiveness.<br>■ The role of the justice system is not to treat people but, rather, to investigate crimes, apprehend suspects, and punish the guilty. |
| **REHABILITATION PERSPECTIVE** | ■ In the long run, it is better to treat than to punish.<br>■ Criminals are society's victims.<br>■ Helping others is part of the American culture. |
| **DUE PROCESS PERSPECTIVE** | ■ Every person deserves his or her full array of constitutional rights and privileges.<br>■ Preserving the democratic ideals of American society takes precedence over the need to punish the guilty.<br>■ Because of potential errors, decisions made within the justice system must be carefully scrutinized.<br>■ Steps must be taken to treat all defendants fairly, regardless of their socioeconomic status.<br>■ Illegally seized evidence should be suppressed even if it means that a guilty person will go free.<br>■ Despite the cost, the government should supply free legal counsel at every stage of the justice system to prevent abuse. |
| **NONINTERVENTION PERSPECTIVE** | ■ The justice process stigmatizes offenders.<br>■ Stigma locks people into a criminal way of life.<br>■ Less is better. Decriminalize, divert, and deinstitutionalize whenever possible. |
| **EQUAL JUSTICE PERSPECTIVE** | ■ People should receive equal treatment for equal crimes.<br>■ Decision making in the justice system must be standardized and structured by rules and regulations.<br>■ Whenever possible, individual discretion must be reduced and controlled.<br>■ Inconsistent treatment undermines respect for the system. |
| **RESTORATIVE JUSTICE PERSPECTIVE** | ■ Offenders should be reintegrated into society.<br>■ Coercive punishments are self-defeating.<br>■ The justice system must become more humane.<br>■ Crime is a community-level problem. |

not in some far-off prison. The victim should be given a chance to voice his story, and the offender can directly communicate her need for social reintegration and treatment. The goal is to enable the offender to appreciate the damage she has caused, to make amends, and to be reintegrated into society.

Restorative justice programs are now being geared to these principles. Mediation and conflict-resolution programs are now common in efforts to resolve harmful human interactions ranging from domestic violence to hate crimes.[54] Police officers, as elements of community policing programs, are beginning to use mediation techniques to settle disputes instead of resorting to formal arrest.[55] Financial and community service restitution programs as an alternative to imprisonment have been in operation for more than two decades.

## Perspectives in Perspective

The variety of tactics being used to combat crime today aptly illustrates the impact of the various perspectives on the operations of the criminal justice system. Advocates of each view have attempted to promote their vision of what justice is all about and how it should be applied. During the past decade, the crime control and equal justice models have dominated. Laws have been toughened and the rights of the accused curtailed, the prison population has grown, and the death penalty has been employed against convicted murderers. Because the crime rate has been dropping, these policies seem to be effective. They may be questioned if crime rates once again begin to rise. At the same time, efforts to rehabilitate offenders, to provide them with elements of due process, and to administer the least intrusive treatment have not been abandoned. Police, courts, and correctional agencies supply a wide range of treatment and rehabilitation programs to offenders in all stages of the criminal justice system. Whenever possible, those accused of a crime are treated informally in nonrestrictive, community-based programs, and the effects of stigma are guarded against.

Although the legal rights of offenders are being closely scrutinized by the courts, the basic constitutional rights of the accused remain inviolate. Guardians of the process have made sure that defendants are afforded the maximum protection possible under the law. For example, criminal defendants have been awarded the right to *competent* legal counsel at trial; merely having a lawyer to defend them is not considered sufficient legal protection.

In sum, understanding the justice system today requires analyzing a variety of occupational roles, institutional processes, legal rules, and administrative doctrines. Each predominant view of criminal justice offers a vantage point for understanding and interpreting these complex issues. No single view is *the* right or correct one. Each individual must choose the perspective that best fits his or her ideas and judgment—or they can all be discarded and the individual's own view substituted. The various perspectives on justice and their key elements are set out in Concept Summary 1.2.

## ETHICS IN CRIMINAL JUSTICE

Both the general public and criminal justice professionals are concerned with the application of ethics.[56] Both would like every police officer on the street, every district attorney in court, and every correctional administrator in prison to be able to discern what is right, proper, and moral; to be committed to ethical standards; and to apply equal and fair justice. These demands are difficult to meet, however, because justice system personnel are often forced to work in an environment in which moral ambiguity is the norm. Should a police officer be forced to arrest, a prosecutor to charge, and a correctional official to punish a woman who for many years was the victim of domestic abuse and in desperation retaliated against her abusive spouse? Who is the victim here, and who is the aggressor? And what about the parent who attacks the man who has sexually abused her young child? Should she be prosecuted as a felon? And what happens if the parent mistakenly attacks and injures the wrong person? Can a clear line be drawn between righteous retribution and vigilante justice? As students of justice, we are concerned with identifying the behavioral standards that should govern everyone involved in the administration of justice. And if these standards can be identified, can we find ways to disseminate them to police departments, courts, and correctional agencies around the nation?

## EVIDENCE-BASED JUSTICE

# *Does Monitoring Sex Offenders Really Work?*

Keeping tabs on sex offenders remains a controversial issue. Do Internet-based sex offender registration lists violate the privacy of offenders who have served their time? After all, there is no arsonist, drug dealer, or murderer list, even though these offenders may present a danger to society. Should people who have served their time be left alone? Or are neighbors entitled to know when a former sex offender moves into the community?

There is no question that sex offender registration lists are legal. The Supreme Court, in *Connecticut Dept. of Public Safety v. Doe* (2003), upheld the legality of sex offender registration when it ruled that persons convicted of sexual offenses may be required to register with a state's Department of Public Safety and may then be listed on a sex offender registry that contains registrants' names, addresses, photographs, and descriptions and can be accessed on the Internet. In a 9–0 opinion upholding the plan, the Court reasoned that, because these defendants had been convicted of a sex offense, disclosing their names on the registry without a hearing did not violate their right to due process.

Thus sex offender registration laws have been ruled constitutional, are pervasive (they are used in all 50 states), appeal to politicians who may be swayed by media crusades against child molesters (such as "To Catch a Predator" on *Dateline NBC*), and appease the public's desire to "do something" about child predators. But do they actually work? Does registration deter offenders from committing further sex offenses and reduce the incidence of predatory acts against children?

To answer this question, criminologists Kristen Zgoba and Karen Bachar recently conducted an in-depth study of the effectiveness of the New Jersey registration law and found that, although it was maintained at great cost to the state, the system did not produce effective results. On the one hand, sex offense rates in New Jersey were in steep decline before the system was installed, and the rate of decline actually slowed down after 1995 when the law took effect. The study showed that the greatest rate of decline in sex offending occurred prior to the passage and implementation of Megan's Law. Zgoba and Bachar also found that the passage and implementation of Megan's Law did not reduce the number of rearrests for sex offenses, nor did it have any demonstrable effect on the time between when sex offenders were released from prison and the time they were rearrested for any new offense, such as a drug offense, theft, or another sex offense.

Zgoba and Bachar's results can be used to rethink legal changes such as sex offender registration. Rather than deterring them from committing crime, such laws may merely cause sex offenders to be more cautious, while giving parents a false sense of security. For example, sex offenders may target victims in other states or in communities where they do not live and parents are less cautious.

Sources: *Connecticut Dept. of Public Safety v. Doe*, 538 U.S. 1 (2003); Kristen Zgoba and Karen Bachar, "Sex Offender Registration and Notification: Research Finds Limited Effects in New Jersey," National Institute of Justice, April 2009, www.ncjrs.gov/pdffiles1/nij/225402.pdf.

Ethics in criminal justice is an especially important topic today, considering the power granted to those who work in, operate, and control the justice system. We rely on the justice system to exert power over people's lives and to be society's instrument of social control, so we give the system and its agents the authority to deny people their personal liberty on a routine basis. A police officer's ability to arrest and use force, a judge's power to sentence, and a correctional administrator's authority to punish an inmate give them considerable personal power, which must be governed by ethical considerations. Without ethical decision making, individual civil rights may suffer, and personal liberties guaranteed by the U.S. Constitution may be trampled upon. The need for an ethical criminal justice system is further enhanced by cyber-age advances in record keeping and data recording. Agents of the criminal justice system now have immediate access to our most personal information, ranging from arrest record to medical history. Issues of privacy and confidentiality, which can have enormous economic, social, and political consequences, are now more critical than ever.

Take, for instance, the Megan's Law movement, which began in New Jersey in 1994, after 7-year-old Megan Kanka was murdered by a paroled child molester who had moved in across the street. The form of Megan's Laws differs from state to state, but most require law enforcement officials to maintain a registry of convicted sex offenders living in the area and make this registry available to the public. Although monitoring convicted sex offenders may seem like an effective crime deterrent, the American Civil Liberties Union has fought the effort around the nation because they consider such laws overreaching and dangerous. In one case, the local chapter of the ACLU strongly objected to a legislative effort introduced in Louisiana that required registered sex offenders to (a) inform colleges and universities where they were either employed or enrolled of their status, so that (b) the institution could inform all students and staff that there are sex offenders working and studying at the institution.[57] The monitoring of sex offenders has also been challenged on the grounds that it simply does not work, an issue discussed in the accompanying Evidence-Based Justice feature.

Ethical issues transcend all elements of the justice system. Yet specific issues shape the ethical standards in each branch.

## Ethics and Law Enforcement

Ethical behavior is particularly important in law enforcement because police officers have the authority to deprive people of their liberty. And in carrying out their daily activities, they also have the right to use physical and even deadly force.

Depriving people of liberty and using force are not the only police behaviors that require ethical consideration. Police officers have considerable discretion in choosing whom to investigate, how far the investigation should go, and how much effort is required—does an investigation merit undercover work, listening devices, surveillance? While carrying out their duties, police officers must be responsive to the public's demand for protection and at the same time remain sensitive to the rights and liberties of those they must deter from committing crime and/or control. In this capacity, they serve as the interface between the power of the state and the citizens it governs. This duality creates many ethical dilemmas. Consider the following:

■ Should law enforcement agents target groups who they suspect are heavily involved in crime and violence, or does this practice lead to racial/ethnic profiling? Is it unethical for a security agent to pay closer attention to a young Arab male getting on an airline flight than she pays to a clean-cut American soldier from upstate New York? Why suspect a blue-eyed, blonde soldier of being a terrorist when the 9/11 terrorists were of Arab descent? But don't forget that Tim McVeigh, who grew up in rural Pendleton, New York, and spent more than three years in the Army, went on to become the Oklahoma City Bomber. How can police officers balance their need to protect public security with the ethical requirement that they protect citizens' legal rights?

■ Should police officers tell the truth even if it means that a guilty person will go free? Let's say that a police officer stops a car for a traffic violation and searches it illegally. In so doing, he finds a weapon that was used in a particularly heinous shooting in which three children were killed. Would it

*As part of his probation, Leroy Schad must have signs on his car and home stating that he is a sex offender. He's allowed to leave his Hudson, Kansas, home only for counseling, for doctors' appointments, and to register as a sex offender at the sheriff's office. Schad, 72, was convicted in March 2007 of aggravated indecent solicitation of a child. Is it ethical to punish people through labeling and humiliation, and does ethics apply even to those who prey upon children? The American Civil Liberties Union, an opponent of registration, has said, "Sex offender registration becomes a lifelong invasion of a person's privacy,...ability to resume a normal life, and...ability to assimilate with mainstream society. Sex offender registration causes hysteria and suspicion without solving the problem. Instead, it is counterproductive, pushing the sex offender into a different neighborhood, or even worse, underground." Do you agree?*

**EXHIBIT 1.2**

## The Dilemma of Red Light Cameras

Police in Dallas, Texas, installed "red light cameras" that take snapshots of busy intersections, capturing the license plates of cars that are running the light, under the assumption that this use of technology would simultaneously save lives and generate millions of dollars in extra fines. But things did not work out as planned, and in March 2008, one-quarter of the cameras were removed. The decision was based not on their ineffectiveness but on the fact that they worked all too well! The data showed that drivers pay attention to cameras at intersections—resulting in fewer violations and consequently shrinking revenue from fines. Even though the cameras reduced injuries, they reduced revenue so much that the cameras could not even pay for themselves. Red light violations went down by as much as 29 percent from month to month. A good thing—but not necessarily, if you rely on traffic fines to make up a healthy chunk of your budget. Accordingly, after losing millions in fines, the city turned off about a quarter of the least profitable cameras, saying it couldn't justify the cost of running them.

Is it ethical to remove or reduce a crime/safety device that is effective but does not generate profits? Should financial concerns ever play a role in the justice system?

Source: Alex Johnson, "Do Red Light Cameras Work Too Well? Some Cities Rethink Devices as Drivers Pay Heed, Reducing Fine Revenue," March 21, 2008, msnbc.com, www.msnbc.msn.com/id/23710970.

be ethical for the officer to lie on the witness stand and say he noticed the gun on the car seat in plain sight (and hence subject to legal and proper seizure)? Or should he tell the truth and risk having the charges against the suspect dismissed, leaving the offender free to kill again?

■ Should police officers be loyal to their peers even when they know that these officers have violated the law? A new officer soon becomes aware that his partner is taking gratuities from local gangsters in return for looking the other way and allowing their prostitution and bookmaking operations to flourish. Should the rookie file a complaint and turn in his partner? Will she be labeled a "rat" and lose the respect of her fellow officers? After all, gambling and prostitution are not violent crimes and do not really hurt anyone. Or do they?

■ Is it ethical for police agencies to profit financially from their law enforcement activities? Police departments have instituted a number of money-making schemes ranging from selling ads on the back of police cars to ticket-writing campaigns. In some instances, individual officers can benefit. For example, when contractors are required to have paid police officer details present at job sites, officers are paid two or three times the standard wage. Profiting from police services is controversial, and it can also have unexpected consequences, as Exhibit 1.2 shows.

How can law enforcement officers be aided in making ethical decisions? Various national organizations have produced model codes of conduct that can serve as behavioral guides. One well-known document created by the International Association of Chiefs of Police says,[58]

> As a Law Enforcement Officer my fundamental duty is to serve mankind; to safeguard lives and property; to protect the innocent against deception, the weak against oppression or intimidation, and the peaceful against violence or disorder; and to respect the Constitutional Rights of all men to liberty, equality and justice. . . .

## Ethics and the Court Process

Ethical concerns do not stop with an arrest. As an officer of the court and the "people's attorney," the prosecutor must seek justice for all parties in a criminal matter and should not merely be targeting a conviction. To be fair, prosecutors must share evidence with the defense, not use scare tactics or intimidation, and represent the public interest. It would be inexcusable and illegal for prosecutors to suppress critical evidence, a practice that might mean the guilty walk free and the innocent are convicted.

Prosecutorial ethics may be tested when the dual role of a prosecutor causes her to experience role conflict. On the one hand, she represents the people and has an obligation to present evidence, uphold the law, and obtain convictions as vigorously as possible. In the adversary system, it is the prosecutor who takes the side of the victims and on whom they depend for justice.

However, as a fair and impartial officer of the court, the prosecutor must oversee the investigation of crime and make sure that all aspects of the investigation meet constitutional standards. If during the investigation it appears that the police have violated the constitutional rights of suspects—for example, by extracting an illegal confession or conducting an illegal search—the prosecutor has an ethical obligation to take whatever action is necessary and appropriate to remedy legal or technical errors, even if that means rejecting a case in which the defendant's rights have been violated. Moreover, the canon of legal ethics in most states forbids the prosecutor from pursuing charges when there is no probable cause and mandates that all evidence that might mitigate guilt or reduce the punishment be turned over to the defense.

**THE DEFENSE ATTORNEY** As an officer of the court, along with the judge, prosecutors, and other trial participants, the defense attorney seeks to uncover the basic facts and elements of the criminal act. In this dual capacity of being both an advocate for defendants and an officer of the court, this attorney often experiences conflicting obligations to his client and his profession. Suppose a client confides that she is planning to commit a crime. What are the defense attorney's ethical responsibilities in this case? Obviously, the lawyer would have to counsel the client to obey the law; if the lawyer assisted the client in engaging in illegal behavior, he would be subject to charges of unprofessional conduct and even to criminal liability.

## Ethics and Corrections

Ethical issues do not cease to arise when a defendant has been convicted. The ethical issues surrounding punishment are too vast to discuss here, but they include the following:

■ Is it fair and ethical to execute a criminal? Can capital punishment ever be considered a moral choice?

■ Should people be given different punishments for the same criminal law violation? Is it fair and just when some convicted murderers and rapists receive probation for their crimes, while others are sentenced to prison for the same offense?

■ Is it fair to grant leniency to criminals who agree to testify against their co-conspirators and therefore allow them to benefit from their perfidy, while others not given the opportunity to "squeal" are forced to bear the full brunt of the law?

■ Should some criminal inmates be granted early release because they can persuade the parole board that they have been rehabilitated, while others, who are not so glib, convincing or well spoken, are forced to serve their entire sentence behind bars?

■ Should technology be used to monitor offenders in the community? Would it be ethical to track a probationer's movements with a GPS unit attached to an ankle bracelet she is required to wear at all times? Should her Internet use and computer downloads be monitored? Should profit be an issue in correctional administration? There has been a trend to privatize aspects of corrections, ranging from outsourcing food and health services to running the prisons themselves. Is it ethical to turn the care and custody of incarcerated people over to corporations that may give profit higher priority than treatment?

Ethical standards are also challenged by the discretion afforded to correctional workers and administrators. Discretion is involved when a correctional officer decides to report an inmate for disorderly conduct, which might jeopardize his or her parole. And although the Supreme Court has issued many rulings related to prisoners' rights, implementing these mandates is left to others, who may or may not carry them out in an orderly way.

Correctional officers have significant coercive power over offenders. They are under a legal and professional obligation not to use unnecessary force or to take advantage of inmates' powerlessness. One example of abuse is an officer beating an inmate; another is a staff member coercing sex from an inmate. These abuses of power can occur because of the powerlessness of the offender relative to the correctional professional. One national survey uncovered evidence that this breach of ethics is significant: Correctional inmates reported 8,210 allegations of sexual violence. About 42 percent of the reported allegations of sexual violence involved staff-on-inmate sexual misconduct, and 11 percent involved staff sexual harassment of inmates. In other words, staff members were involved in more cases of sexual violence and harassment in correctional facilities than were inmates![59]

Ethical considerations pervade all elements of the justice system. Making ethical decisions is an increasingly important task in a society that is becoming more diverse, pluralistic, and complex every day.

## Ethical Challenges in Criminal Justice: A Writing Assignment

Some people believe drugs should be legalized and controlled so that they could not fall into the hands of adolescents. Drug sales would be controlled in the same manner as the sale of alcohol and cigarettes. Write an essay addressing this issue from each of the perspectives of justice discussed in the chapter. In other words, how would a crime control, a rehabilitation, a due process, a nonintervention, an equal justice, and a restorative justice advocate react to the suggestion that drugs be legalized? You should refer to the sections that describe the core values of all of these perspectives before you submit your answer. You might want to include a comment on the position each perspective might take on the legalization of drug use.

## SUMMARY

**1. Be able to define the concept of criminal justice.**

- The criminal justice system consists of the agencies that dispense justice and the process by which justice is carried out.

**2. Be aware of the long history of crime in America.**

- America has experienced crime throughout most of its history.

- In the Old West, justice was administered by legendary lawmen such as Wyatt Earp.

**3. Discuss the formation of the criminal justice system.**

- There was little in the way of a formal criminal justice system until the nineteenth century when the first police agencies were created.

- The term "criminal justice system" became prominent in the United States around 1967, when the President's Commission on Law Enforcement and the Administration of Justice began a nationwide study of the nation's crime problem.

■ Criminal justice is a field that applies knowledge gleaned from various disciplines in an attempt to understand what causes people to commit crimes and how to deal with the crime problem.

**4. Name the three basic component agencies of criminal justice.**

■ Criminal justice consists of the study of crime and of the agencies concerned with its prevention and control.

■ On an ideal level, the criminal justice system functions as a cooperative effort among the primary agencies—police, courts, and corrections.

**5. Comprehend the size and scope of the contemporary justice system.**

■ The contemporary criminal justice system in the United States is monumental in size.

■ It now costs federal, state, and local governments more than $200 billion per year to maintain a criminal justice system that now employs more than 2 million people.

■ The system now processes, treats, and cares for millions of people. More than 14 million people are still being arrested each year; and there are more than 7 million people in the correctional system.

**6. Trace the formal criminal justice process.**

■ The process consists of the actual steps the offender takes from the initial investigation through trial, sentencing, and appeal.

■ The justice process comprises 15 stages, each of which is a decision point through which cases flow.

■ Each of these decisions can have a critical effect on the defendant, the justice system, and society.

**7. Know what is meant by the term "criminal justice assembly line."**

■ Herbert Packer described the criminal justice process as an assembly-line conveyor belt down which moves an endless stream of cases

■ The system acts as a "funnel": Most people who commit crime escape detection, and of those who do not, relatively few are bound over for trial, and even fewer are convicted and eventually sentenced to prison.

■ The justice funnel holds many cases at its mouth and relatively few at its stem end.

**8. Discuss the "wedding cake" model of justice.**

■ In many instances, the criminal justice system works informally to expedite the disposal of cases.

■ Criminal acts that are very serious or notorious may receive the full complement of criminal justice processes, from arrest to trial. However, less serious cases are often settled when a bargain is reached between the prosecution and the defense.

**9. Be familiar with the various perspectives on criminal justice.**

■ The role of criminal justice can be interpreted in many ways.

■ People who study the field or work in its agencies bring their own ideas and feelings to bear when they try to decide on the right course of action to take or recommend. Therefore, there are a number of different perspectives on criminal justice today.

■ Perspectives range from the most conservative—crime control—to the most liberal—restorative justice.

**10. Understand the ethical issues that arise in criminal justice.**

■ The justice system must deal with many ethical issues.

■ The challenge is to determine what is fair and just and to balance that with the need to protect the public.

## KEY TERMS

criminal justice system, 4
Law Enforcement Assistance Administration (LEAA), 7
evidence-based justice, 7
social control, 8
in-presence requirement, 15
*Miranda* warning, 15

nolle prosequi, 16
grand jury, 16
true bill of indictment, 16
courtroom work group, 21
crime control perspective, 25
rehabilitation perspective, 27
due process perspective, 28

nonintervention perspective, 29
decriminalization, 30
deinstitutionalization, 30
equal justice perspective, 30
restorative justice perspective, 31

## CRITICAL THINKING QUESTIONS

1. Can a single standard of ethics be applied to all criminal justice agencies? Or is the world too complex to legislate morality and ethics?

2. Describe the differences between the formal and informal justice systems. Is it fair to treat some offenders informally?

3. What are the layers of the criminal justice "wedding cake"? Give an example of a crime for each layer.

4. What are the basic elements of each perspective on justice? Which perspective best represents your own point of view?

5. How would each perspective on criminal justice view the use of the death penalty as a sanction for first-degree murder?

## NOTES

1. Federal Bureau of Investigation, "Operation Rotten Tomato: Fraud in the Food Industry," February 18, 2010, www.fbi.gov/page2/feb10/tomato_021810.html.

2. This section leans heavily on Ted Robert Gurr, "Historical Trends in Violent Crime: A Critical Review of the Evidence," in *Crime and Justice: An Annual Review of Research*, vol. 3, ed. Michael Tonry and Norval Morris (Chicago: University of Chicago Press, 1981); Richard Maxwell Brown, "Historical Patterns of American Violence," in *Violence in America: Historical and Comparative Perspectives*, ed. Hugh Davis Graham and Ted Robert Gurr (Beverly Hills, Calif.: Sage, 1979).

3. Sally Hadden, *Slave Patrols: Law and Violence in Virginia and the Carolinas* (Cambridge, Mass.: Harvard University Press, 2001).

4. T. J. Stiles, *Jesse James, Last Rebel of the Civil War* (New York: Vintage, 2003); Ted Yeatman, *Frank & Jesse James: The Story Behind the Legend* (Nashville, Tenn: Cumberland House, 2003).

5. Herbert Asbury, *Gangs of New York* (New York: Basic Books, 2001). Reprint Edition.

6. Cesare Beccaria, *On Crimes and Punishments* (1764; reprint, Indianapolis: Bobbs-Merrill, 1963).

7. Samuel Walker, *Popular Justice* (New York: Oxford University Press, 1980).

8. Visit the commission's website, www.chicagocrimecommission.org/about.html (accessed May 2, 2010).

9. Lexis/Nexis, "Records of the Wickersham Commission on Law Observance and Enforcement," www.lexisnexis.com/academic/2upa/Allh/WickershamComm.asp.

10. For an insightful analysis of this effort, see Samuel Walker, "Origins of the Contemporary Criminal Justice Paradigm: The American Bar Foundation Survey, 1953–1969," *Justice Quarterly* 9 (1992): 47–76.

11. President's Commission on Law Enforcement and the Administration of Justice, *The Challenge of Crime in a Free Society* (Washington, D.C.: U.S. Government Printing Office, 1967).

12. See Public Law 90–351, Title I—Omnibus Crime Control Safe Streets Act of 1968, 90th Congress, June 19, 1968.

13. For a review, see Kevin Wright, "Twenty-Two Years of Federal Investment in Criminal Justice Research: The National Institute of Justice, 1968–1989," *Journal of Criminal Justice* 22 (1994): 27–40.

14. Lawrence Sherman, Denise Gottfredson, Doris MacKenzie, John Eck, Peter Reuter, and Shawn Bushway, Preventing Crime: *What Works, What Doesn't, What's Promising* (Washington, D.C.: U.S. Department of Justice, Office of Justice Programs, 1997).

15. See, generally, Brandon Welsh and David Farrington, *Preventing Crime: What Works for Children, Offenders, Victims and Places* (London: Springer-Verlag, 2006).

16. Dennis Rosenbaum and Gordon Hanson, "Assessing the Effects of School-Based Drug Education: A Six-Year Multilevel Analysis of Project D.A.R.E.," *Journal of Research in Crime and Delinquency* 35 (1998): 381–412.

17. Brian A. Reaves, *Census of State and Local Law Enforcement Agencies, 2004* (Washington, D.C.: Bureau of Justice Statistics, 2007).

18. Federal Bureau of Investigation, *Crime in the United States, 2005* (Washington, D.C.: U.S. Government Printing Office, 2006), Table 29.

19. Matthew R. DuRose and Patrick A. Langan, *Felony Sentences in State Courts, 2002* (Washington, D.C.: Bureau of Justice Statistics, 2004).

20. For an analysis of this issue, see William Wilbanks, *The Myth of a Racist Criminal Justice System* (Monterey, Calif.: Brooks/Cole, 1987); Stephen Klein, Joan Petersilia, and Susan Turner, "Race and Imprisonment Decisions in California," *Science* 247 (1990): 812–816; Alfred Blumstein, "On the Racial Disproportionality of the United States Prison Population," *Journal of Criminal Law and Criminology* 73 (1982): 1259–1281; Darnell Hawkins, "Race, Crime Type, and Imprisonment," *Justice Quarterly* 3 (1986): 251–269.

21. Court TV Crime Library, Marilyn Bardsley, Rachael Bell, and David Lohr, "BTK—Birth of a Serial Killer," www.crimelibrary.com/serial_killers/unsolved/btk/index_1.html (accessed March 25, 2007).

22. American Bar Association Grand Jury System, www.abanet.org/media/faqjury.html (accessed April 25, 2008).

23. Herbert L. Packer, *The Limits of the Criminal Sanction* (Stanford, Calif.: Stanford University Press, 1975), 21.

24. Ibid.

25. Matthew Durose, Donald Farole, and Sean Rosenmerkel, *Felony Sentences in State Courts, 2006* (Washington, D.C.: Bureau of Justice Statistics, 2009), http://bjs.ojp.usdoj.gov/content/pub/pdf/fssc06st.pdf

26. David W. Neubauer, *America's Courts and the Criminal Justice System* (Pacific Grove, Calif.: Brooks/Cole, 1996), pp. 72–75.

27. Douglas Smith, "The Plea Bargaining Controversy," *Journal of Criminal Law and Criminology* 77 (1986): 949–967.

28. Samuel Walker, *Sense and Nonsense about Crime* (Belmont, Calif.: Wadsworth, 1985).

29. Malcolm Feeley, *The Process Is the Punishment* (New York: Russell Sage, 1979).

30. James Q. Wilson, *Thinking about Crime* (New York: Vintage, 1983).

31. Ibid., p. 128.

32. Vanessa Barker, "The Politics of Punishing," *Punishment & Society* 8 (2006): 5–32.

33. John DiIulio, *No Escape: The Future of American Corrections* (New York: Basic Books, 1991).

34. Richard Timothy Coupe and Laurence Blake, "The Effects of Patrol Workloads and Response Strength on Arrests at Burglary Emergencies," *Journal of Criminal Justice* 33 (2005): 239–255.

35. Paul Cassell, "How Many Criminals Has Miranda Set Free?" *Wall Street Journal*, March 1, 1995, p. A15.

36. Jon Gould and Stephen Mastrofski, "Suspect Searches: Assessing Police Behavior under the U.S. Constitution," *Criminology & Public Policy* 3 (2004): 315–362.

37. *Sourcebook of Criminal Justice Statistics, 2009* (Albany, New York: Hindelang Criminal Justice Research Center University at Albany), www.albany.edu/sourcebook/pdf/t2522009.pdf.

38. Karen Parker and Patricia McCall, "Structural Conditions and Racial Homicide Patterns: A Look at the Multiple Disadvantages in Urban Areas," *Criminology* 37 (1999): 447–448.

39. Denise Gottfredson, "Participation in Drug Treatment Court and Time to Rearrest," *Justice Quarterly* 21 (2004): 637–658.

40. John Hepburn, "Recidivism among Drug Offenders Following Exposure to Treatment," *Criminal Justice Policy Review* 16 (2005): 237–259.

41. Francis Cullen, John Paul Wright, and Mitchell Chamlin, "Social Support and Social Reform: A Progressive Crime Control Agenda," *Crime and Delinquency* 45 (1999): 188–207.

42. Jane Sprott, "Are Members of the Public Tough on Crime? The Dimensions of Public 'Punitiveness,'" *Journal of Criminal Justice* 27 (1999): 467–474.

43. Packer, *The Limits of the Criminal Sanction*, p. 175.

44. "DNA Testing Has Exonerated 28 Prison Inmates, Study Finds," *Criminal Justice Newsletter*, June 17, 1996, p. 2.

45. Caitlin Lovinger, "Death Row's Living Alumni," *New York Times*, August 22, 1999, p. 1.

46. Talia Roitberg Harmon and William S. Lofquist, "Too Late for Luck: A Comparison of Post-Furman Exonerations and Executions of the Innocent," *Crime and Delinquency* 51 (2005): 498–520.

47. Pew Foundation, "Death Penalty," www.pewcenteronthestates.org/topic_category.aspx?category=510 (accessed February 28, 2008).

48. Eric Stewart, Ronald Simons, Rand Conger, and Laura Scaramella, "Beyond the Interactional Relationship between Delinquency and Parenting Practices: The Contribution of Legal Sanctions," *Journal of Research in Crime and Delinquency* 39 (2002): 36–60.

49. Cassia Spohn and David Holleran, "The Effect of Imprisonment on Recidivism Rates of Felony Offenders: A Focus on Drug Offenders," *Criminology* 40 (2002): 329–359.

50. *Doe v. Pryor M.D.* Ala, Civ. No. 99-T-730-N, J. Thompson, August 16, 1999.

51. This section is based on Paula M. Ditton and Doris James Wilson, *Truth in Sentencing in State Prisons* (Washington, D.C.: Bureau of Justice Statistics, 1999).

52. Herbert Bianchi, *Justice as Sanctuary* (Bloomington: Indiana University Press, 1994); Nils Christie, "Conflicts as Property," *British Journal of Criminology* 17 (1977): 1–15; L. Hulsman, "Critical Criminology and the Concept of Crime," *Contemporary Crises* 10 (1986): 63–80.

53. Larry Tifft, Foreword, in Dennis Sullivan, *The Mask of Love* (Port Washington, N.Y.: Kennikat Press, 1980), p. 6.

54. Robert Coates, Mark Umbreit, and Betty Vos, "Responding to Hate Crimes through Restorative Justice Dialogue," *Contemporary Justice Review* 9 (2006): 7–21; Kathleen Daly and Julie Stubbs, "Feminist Engagement with Restorative Justice," *Theoretical Criminology* 10 (2006): 9–28.

55. Christopher Cooper, "Patrol Police Officer Conflict Resolution Processes," *Journal of Criminal Justice* 25 (1997): 87–101.

56. This section leans heavily on Jocelyn M. Pollock, *Ethics in Crime and Justice, Dilemmas and Decisions*, 4th ed. (Belmont, Calif.: Wadsworth, 2004).

57. ACLU of Louisiana, "Uncompassionate Sex Offender Registration Impedes Individual's Efforts to Gain Education, Earn Honest Pay," April 8, 2003, www.laaclu.org/News/2003/April%208%20Sex%20Offender%20Reg.html.

58. International Association of Chiefs of Police, "Law Enforcement Code of Ethics," www.theiacp.org/documents/index.cfm?fuseaction=document&document_id=95 (accessed March 25, 2010).

59. Allen Beck and Timothy Hughes, *Prison Rape Elimination Act of 2003, Sexual Violence Reported by Correctional Authorities, 2004* (Washington, D.C.: Bureau of Justice Statistics, 2005).

# CHAPTER 2

# The Nature and Extent of Crime

## CHAPTER OBJECTIVES

1. Be able to discuss how crime is defined.
2. Define and discuss some of the different types of crime.
3. Be familiar with the methods used to measure crime.
4. Discuss the development of the NIBRS program.
5. Be able to discuss the strengths and weaknesses of various measures of crime.
6. Recognize the trends in the crime rate.
7. Comment on the factors that influence crime rates.
8. Be familiar with trends in crime in other cultures.
9. Know the various crime patterns.
10. Understand the concept of the criminal career.

© AP Photo/Huntsville Police Dept.

**B**ack in 2006 Dr. Amy Bishop, a Harvard-trained neurobiologist, along with her husband Jim Anderson, invented a portable cell growth incubator designed to replace the old practice of growing cells in a petri dish. Their highly sophisticated endeavor held much promise, and they were able to raise more than $1 million in start-up money to organize a biotech business. Four years later, however, this highly educated woman was in the news for an entirely different reason. While attending a faculty meeting at the University of Alabama's Huntsville campus, Bishop shot three of her colleagues to death and severely wounded three others. The alleged reason: Despite her achievements Bishop was denied tenure—that is, a lifetime academic appointment. The case soon took on other bizarre twists. According to Massachusetts law enforcement authorities, in 1986, when she was 19 years old, Bishop had killed her own brother Seth with a shotgun blast. Although there were suspicions of foul play at the time, the incident was ruled an accident, and Bishop was not charged; the case has since been reopened. Then it turned out she was also a suspect in another violent incident: A package containing two bombs had been sent to the Newton home of Dr. Paul Rosenberg, a professor and doctor at Boston's Children's Hospital, soon after he had criticized her doctoral research.[1] So it may be that Dr. Amy Bishop will be heading to prison at about the same time the device she created will be heading to market. ∎

Stories about such violent acts help convince most Americans that we live in a violent society. Bishop was not a gang kid from the inner city, but a highly educated woman with a Ph.D. from one of the most prestigious schools in the world. If a person with such impeccable credentials can become a mass killer, who can be truly safe? When people read headlines about a violent crime spree, they begin to fear crime and take steps to protect themselves, perhaps avoiding public places and staying at home in the evening.[2] When asked whether they fear walking in their neighborhood at night, 34 percent of all American citizens today say "yes"—the same percentage who gave this answer to the same question in 1965, more than 45 years ago![3] About one-quarter say they have bought a gun for self-protection, and 12 percent claim they carry guns for defense.[4]

Are Americans justified in their fear of crime? Should they barricade themselves behind armed guards? Are crime rates actually rising, or are they falling? And where do most crimes occur, and who commits them? To answer these and similar questions, crime experts have devised elaborate methods of crime data collection and analysis. Without accurate data on the nature and extent of crime, it would not be possible to formulate theories that explain the onset of antisocial behaviors or to devise criminal justice policies that facilitate their control or elimination. Accurate data collection is also critical for assessing the nature and extent of crime, tracking changes in the crime rate, and measuring the individual and social factors that may influence criminality. In fact, even though the violent acts of the Amy Bishops of this world give people the impression that females are becoming as deadly as males, the official data indicates that about 90 percent of all people arrested for murder are men.[5]

In this chapter, we first define what is meant by the term "crime" and the various ways crime is viewed. We then review some major categories of criminal activity in America and around the world before we turn to the measurement of crime, how crime data is collected, and what this information tells us about crime patterns and trends. We also examine the concept of criminal careers and discover what available crime data can tell us about the onset, continuation, and termination of criminality.

## HOW IS CRIME DEFINED?

The justice system focuses on crime and its control. While for most of us the concept of "crime" seems rather simple—a violation of criminal law—the question remains: Why are some acts considered a violation of the law when other, seemingly more serious, acts are legal and noncriminal? There are actually three views of how and why some behaviors become illegal and are considered crimes while others remain noncriminal.

### Consensus View

On February 18, 2010, Bernard Kerik, a former commissioner of the New York City Police, was sentenced to four years in prison for accepting gratuities while in office. At his hearing, U.S. Attorney Preet Bharara said, "It is a very sad day when the former commissioner of the greatest police department in the world is sentenced to prison for base criminal conduct." He added, "Today's sentencing of Bernard Kerik is one of the most powerful recent reminders that no one in this country is above the law."[6]

According to what is known as the **consensus view of crime**, behaviors that become crimes are those that (a) are essentially harmful to a majority of citizens in the society and therefore (b) have been controlled or prohibited by the existing criminal law. There is general agreement about which behaviors society needs to control by law and which should be beyond state regulation.

The criminal law, then, is a set of rules, codified by state authorities, that expresses the norms, goals, and values of *the vast majority of society*; it represents

**consensus view of crime**
The view that the great majority of citizens agree that certain behaviors must be outlawed or controlled, and that criminal law is designed to protect citizens from social harm.

*On February 18, 2010, Bernard Kerik makes a brief public statement upon leaving federal court in White Plains, New York. Kerik, a former New York police commissioner who rose to national prominence, was sentenced to four years in prison after pleading guilty to eight felony charges, including tax fraud and lying to White House officials. According to the consensus view of crime, the law applies equally to all people, regardless of their wealth, fame, or "importance."*

the *consensus* of public opinion about right and wrong. In a democratic society no one is above the law, even the New York City Police commissioner; the law applies evenly to everyone.

The consensus view rests on the assumption that criminal law has a social control function—restraining those whose behavior would otherwise endanger the social framework by taking advantage of others' weakness for their own personal gain. Criminal law works to control behaviors that are inherently destructive and dangerous in order to maintain the existing social fabric and ensure the peaceful functioning of society.

## Conflict View

The **conflict view of crime** holds that the ongoing class struggle between the rich and poor, the haves and have-nots, controls the content of criminal law and thereby shapes the definition of crime. According to this view, criminal law is created and enforced by the ruling class as a mechanism for controlling dissatisfied have-not members of society. The law is the instrument that enables the wealthy to maintain their position of power and control the behavior of those who oppose their ideas and values or who might rebel against the unequal distribution of wealth.[7] Laws defining property crimes, such as larceny and burglary, are created to protect the wealth of the affluent: People who steal from the wealthy are severely punished; the wealthy who manipulate the economic system for their personal gain are "above the law." Drug laws are developed to ensure that workers will be productive and sober. Laws defining violent crimes are created to keep the angry and frustrated lower classes under control. People who violate these laws are subject to severe punishments. In contrast, perpetrators of business and white-collar crimes receive relatively lenient punishments, considering the extent of the harm and damage they cause.

## Interactionist View

Falling between the consensus and conflict visions, the **interactionist view of crime** suggests that criminal law is structured to reflect the preferences and opinions of people who hold social power in a particular legal jurisdiction and use their influence to shape the legal process. These **moral entrepreneurs** wage campaigns (*moral crusades*) to control behaviors they view as immoral and wrong

**conflict view of crime**
The view that criminal law is created and enforced by those who hold political and economic power and is a tool used by the ruling class to control dissatisfied have-not members of society.

**interactionist view of crime**
The view that criminal law reflects the preferences and opinions of people who hold social power in the society and use their influence to impose their own values and moral code on the rest of the population.

**moral entrepreneurs**
People who wage campaigns to control behaviors they view as immoral or wrong.

## CONCEPT SUMMARY 2.1
### Definition of Crime

| Consensus View | Conflict View | Interactionist View |
|---|---|---|
| The will of the majority shapes the law and defines crimes. | The law is a tool of the ruling class. | Social crusaders and moral entrepreneurs define crime. |
| Agreement exists on right and wrong. | Crime is a politically defined concept. | The definition of crime is subjective, reflecting contemporary values and morals. |
| Laws apply to all citizens equally. | "Real crimes" are not outlawed. The law is used to control the underclass. | Criminal labels are life-transforming events. |

(e.g., abortion) or, conversely, to legalize behaviors they consider harmless social eccentricities (e.g., carrying a handgun for self-protection; smoking pot). Because drug use offends their moral sense, it is currently illegal to purchase marijuana and hashish, while liquor and cigarettes are sold openly, even though far more people die of alcoholism and smoking than from drug abuse each year.[8] Even the definition of serious violent offenses, such as rape and murder, depends on the prevailing moral values of those who shape the content of the criminal law. For example, Florida has implemented a "stand your ground law" that legalizes the killing of an unarmed thief or intruder who is found in the owner's parked car; in other states, shooting an unarmed person merely because she or he was sitting in one's car might be considered murder. Fifty years ago a man could not be prosecuted for raping his wife; today, every state criminalizes marital rape. In sum, the definition of crime better reflects prevailing moral values than any objective standard of right and wrong.

The basics of these three views are set out in Concept Summary 2.1.

Although these views of crime differ, they generally agree (1) that criminal law defines crime, (2) that the definition of crime is constantly changing and evolving, (3) that social forces mold the definition of crimes, and (4) that criminal law has a social control function. Therefore, as used here, the term **crime** is defined as follows:

> *Crime is a violation of social rules of conduct, interpreted and expressed by a written criminal code, created by people holding social and political power. Its content may be influenced by prevailing public sentiments, historically developed moral beliefs, and the need to protect public safety. Individuals who violate these rules may be subject to sanctions administered by state authority, which include social stigma and loss of status, freedom, and on occasion, their lives.*

**crime**
A violation of social rules of conduct, interpreted and expressed by a written criminal code, created by people holding social and political power. Its content may be influenced by prevailing public sentiments, historically developed moral beliefs, and the need to protect public safety.

## WHAT ARE THE DIFFERENT CATEGORIES OF CRIME?

Millions of criminal acts occur each year, and their diversity and variety are staggering. Crimes range in seriousness from shoplifting to serial murder. Some crimes are violent and destructive; others are motivated by economic gain; and a third group, public order crimes, are made up of acts (such as prostitution and drug use) that threaten or violate the moral standards of society, or at least the segment of society that has the power to shape and control the law.

# Violent Crimes

Americans are bombarded with television news stories and newspaper articles featuring grisly accounts of violent gangs, serial murder, child abuse, and rape. Although rates of violent crime have declined significantly over the past decade, most Americans still worry about becoming a victim of crime. Some criminal acts are **expressive violence**, acts that vent rage, anger, or frustration, and some are **instrumental violence**, acts designed to improve the financial or social position of the criminal—for example, through an armed robbery or murder for hire. What are the forms of violence that most people fear?

*GANG VIOLENCE* After remaining dormant for many years, organized youth gangs today terrorize neighborhoods in urban communities around the United States. From Boston to Los Angeles, gangs have become actively involved in drug distribution, extortion, and violence.

Whereas youth gangs once relied on group loyalty and emotional involvement with neighborhood turf to encourage membership, modern gangs seem more motivated by the quest for drug profits and street power. It is common for drug cliques to form within gangs and for established drug dealers to make use of gang members, also called "gang bangers," for protection and distribution services. As a consequence, gang-related killings have become so commonplace that the term "gang homicide" is now recognized as a separate and unique category of criminal behavior.[9]

At one time, gang activity occurred only in the nation's largest cities, especially Philadelphia, New York, Detroit, Los Angeles, and Chicago. These cities still have large gang populations, but today smaller and medium-size cities—such as Cleveland and Columbus, Ohio, and Milwaukee, Wisconsin—also have been the locus of gang activity. One reason why gang populations are swelling is that established urban gang members migrate to other regions to set up local branches.

The National Youth Gang Survey (NYGS) measures gang activity around the United States.[10] Its most recent effort finds that a significant majority of urban areas report the presence of gangs and that gangs exist in all social strata, from rural counties to metropolitan areas.[11] More than one-third of cities and towns with populations of at least 2,500 now experience gang problems. This translates to an estimated 3,550 jurisdictions nationwide. Not surprisingly, the numbers of gangs and gang members are on the rise: In the United States, there are now more than 27,000 gangs containing almost 800,000 gang members.

*MULTIPLE MURDER* On Monday, April 16, 2007, 23-year-old Seung-Hui Cho methodically took the lives of 32 people—27 students and 5 professors—at Virginia Tech, before taking his own life.[12] In the aftermath of the tragedy, Cho was described as a loner unable to make social connections.[13] Ten months later, on February 14, 2008, Steven Kazmierczak entered Cole Hall at Northern Illinois University, armed with a shotgun and three handguns. Standing on the stage he methodically began shooting into the crowded classroom, killing 5 and wounding 16 others before taking his own life.[14] These tragedies highlight the threat of mass killings by seemingly deranged gunmen.

There are three different types of multiple killers:

- **Mass murderers** kill many victims in a single violent outburst.
- **Spree killers** spread their murderous outburst over a few days or weeks.
- **Serial killers** kill over a long period of time but typically assume a "normal" identity between murders.

Mass murderers, such as Seung-Hui Cho, serial killers, such as Jeffrey Dahmer of Milwaukee, and spree killers, such as John Allen Muhammed (the D.C. sniper), have become familiar to the American public.[15] The threat of the unknown, random, and deranged assailant has become a part of modern reality.

**expressive violence**
Violent behavior motivated by rage, anger, or frustration.

**instrumental violence**
Violent behavior that results from criminal activity designed to improve the financial status of the culprit, such as shooting someone during a bank robbery.

**mass murderer**
Type of multiple killer who kills many victims in a single violent outburst.

**spree killer**
Type of multiple killer who spreads the murderous outburst over a few days or weeks.

**serial killer**
Type of multiple killer who kills over a long period of time but typically assumes a "normal" identity between murders.

There is no single explanation for serial, spree, or mass murder. Such widely disparate factors as mental illness, sexual frustration, neurological damage, child abuse and neglect, smothering maternal relationships, and childhood anxiety have been suggested as possible causes. However, most experts view multiple murderers as sociopaths who from early childhood demonstrated bizarre behavior (such as torturing animals), enjoy killing, are impervious to their victims' suffering, and bask in the media limelight when caught.[16]

*INTIMATE VIOLENCE*  Although violent attacks by strangers produce the most fear and create the most graphic headlines, Americans face greater physical danger from people with whom they are in close and intimate contact: spouses, other relatives, and dating partners.

One area of intimate violence that has received a great deal of media attention is child abuse, which is any physical or emotional trauma to a child for which no reasonable explanation, such as an accident or ordinary disciplinary practices, can be found. Child abuse can result from physical beatings administered by hands, feet, weapons, belts, or sticks, or from burning.

The Department of Health and Human Services has been monitoring the extent of child maltreatment through its annual survey of child protective services (CPS). An estimated 3 million cases, involving the alleged maltreatment of approximately 6 million children, are now referred to CPS agencies each year. These cases involve a variety of maltreatment problems ranging from neglect to sexual abuse. In the most recent findings, approximately 25 percent of the reported cases (approximately 800,000) were substantiated after investigation.[17] Most maltreated kids are the victims of neglect; about 11 percent of confirmed cases, or almost 90,000 youths, suffer physical abuse each year. About 8 percent of the cases involve sexual abuse—including prostitution, use in pornography, and molestation by adults—but the actual number may be much higher. More than 50,000 kids are thrown out of their home each year by a parent or guardian and may be forced into abusive relationships as survival mechanisms.[18] An estimated 1,600 children die each year because of abuse, a rate of slightly more than 2 deaths per 100,000 children. Although these figures seem staggering, the incidents and rate of abuse have actually been in decline. Fifteen years ago, more than 1 million children were identified as victims of abuse or neglect, and nationwide, and the rate of victimization of children was approximately 15 per 1,000 children, compared to 11 per 1,000 today.

Regardless of how it is defined, the effects of abuse can be devastating. Children who have experienced some form of maltreatment have a devalued sense of self, mistrust others, tend to assume others are hostile in situations where the intentions of others are ambiguous, tend to generate antagonistic solutions to social problems, and exhibit suspicion of close relationships.[19]

**hate crimes (bias crimes)**
Criminal acts directed toward a particular person or members of a group because they share a discernible racial, ethnic, religious, or gender characteristic.

*HATE CRIMES*  Violent acts directed toward a particular person or toward the members of a group merely because the targets share a discernible racial, ethnic, religious, or gender characteristic are known as **hate crimes**, or **bias crimes**.[20] Hate crimes can include the desecration of a house of worship or cemetery, harassment of a minority-group family that has moved into a previously all-white neighborhood, or a racially motivated murder.

Hate crimes usually involve convenient, vulnerable targets who are incapable of fighting back. For example, there have been numerous reported incidents of teenagers attacking vagrants and the homeless in an effort to rid their town or neighborhood of people they consider undesirable.[21] Another group targeted for hate crimes is gay men and women: Gay bashing has become common in U.S. cities.

Currently, the FBI annually records 7,800 hate crime incidents—motivated by bias against a race, religion, disability, ethnicity, or sexual orientation—that involve almost 10,000 victims and 7,000 offenders. About two-thirds of the victims are individuals, and the majority of such crimes involve racial attacks against African Americans. One-third of hate crimes are directed toward institutions or organizations (for example, someone vandalizes a mosque or paints racist graffiti on a building that contains the offices of a civil rights group).[22] As incomprehensible as it seems, the FBI records about 80 hate crimes a year directed against the physically handicapped or mentally ill.

## Public Order Crimes

Societies have long banned or limited behaviors that are believed to run contrary to social norms, customs, and values. These behaviors are commonly referred to as **public order crimes**, or victimless crimes, although the latter term can be misleading. Public order crimes involve acts that interfere with how society operates and functions. They are criminalized because those who shape the law believe that they conflict with social norms, prevailing moral rules, and current public opinion. They are considered a threat to society because they disrupt the "public order" and the ability of people to work and function efficiently. Included within this category are sex- related crimes such as prostitution and trafficking in pornography and the trafficking and sale of illegal substances.

**public order crimes**
Behaviors that are illegal because they run counter to existing moral standards. Obscenity and prostitution are considered public order crimes.

*PROSTITUTION* A crime that typically involves engaging in sexual acts for money or compensation, prostitution is for good reason often referred to as "the world's oldest profession"; it was a common practice in ancient Greece and Babylon. Today fewer than 80,000 prostitution arrests are being made annually, with the gender ratio being about 2:1 female to male. The number of prostitution arrests has been trending downward for some time; about 100,000 arrests were made in 1995. It is possible that (1) fewer people are seeking the services of prostitutes, (2) police are reluctant to make arrests in prostitution cases, or (3) more sophisticated prostitutes using the Internet or other forms of technology to "make dates" are better able to avoid detection by police. Advertising on Internet sites, known as *ehooking,* may be responsible for a hidden and hard-to-measure resurgence in sex for hire, especially in times of economic turmoil.[23]

*SUBSTANCE ABUSE* Even though the United States has been waging a "war on drugs" for some time, millions of Americans still abuse substances on a routine basis. How widespread is the problem? A number of national surveys attempt to chart trends in drug abuse in the general population. *Monitoring the Future,* an annual national survey of drug abuse among high school students, indicates that drug use has declined from a high point in the 1970s, when more than half of all high school seniors routinely used illegal substances. Drug use has been rather stable for the past ten years.[24] Although this trend is promising, more than one-third of all high school seniors still report using an illicit substance during the past 12 months, as do 27 percent of 10th graders and more than 14 percent of 8th graders.[25] In a similar vein, the National Household Survey on Drug Abuse and Health, sponsored by the federal government, finds that about 20 million Americans aged 12 or older are current (past month) illicit drug users and/or had used an illicit drug during the prior month. This means that about 8.0 percent of the population aged 12 years or older uses illicit drugs such as marijuana/hashish, cocaine (including crack), heroin, hallucinogens, or inhalants, or uses prescription-type psychotherapeutics nonmedically.[26] Clearly, even though drug usage appears to have stabilized, it is still a significant social problem.

Substance abuse is of much concern to criminal justice policymakers because there is unquestionably a link between substance abuse and criminal activities. Alcohol abuse, for example, is suspected of being involved in half of all U.S. murders, suicides, and accidental deaths.[27] Strong links also exist between alcohol consumption and certain types of homicide, especially those that occur during robberies and other criminal offenses.[28]

*Alcohol, legal and easily obtained, is related to half of all U.S. murders, suicides, and accidental deaths. Alcohol-related deaths number 100,000 a year—far more than deaths related to all illegal drugs combined. Should pot be legalized and alcohol banned? Before you answer, remember they tried to do that once before.*

Although the association between substance abuse and crime is powerful, the true relationship between them is still uncertain, because many users have had a history of criminal activity before the onset of their substance abuse. Here are some of the possible relationships:

■ Chronic criminal offenders begin to abuse drugs and alcohol after they have engaged in crime—that is, crime causes drug abuse.

■ Substance abusers turn to a life of crime to support their habits—that is, drug abuse causes crime.

■ Drug use and crime co-occur in individuals—that is, both crime and drug abuse are caused by some other common factor, such as risk taking, for example (risk takers use drugs and also commit crime).[29]

■ Drug users suffer social and personal problems—such as heavy drinking and mental instability— that are linked to crime.[30]

## Economic Crimes

Millions of property- and theft-related crimes occur each year. Most are the work of amateur or occasional criminals whose decision to steal is spontaneous and whose acts are unskilled, unplanned, and haphazard. Many thefts, ranging in seriousness from shoplifting to burglary, are committed by school-age youths who are unlikely to enter into a criminal career.

Added to the pool of amateur thieves are the millions of adults whose behavior may occasionally violate the criminal law—shoplifters, pilferers, tax cheats—but whose primary income derives from conventional means and whose self-identity is noncriminal. Most of these property crimes occur when an immediate opportunity, or *situational inducement*, to commit crime arises.[31]

Professional thieves, in contrast, derive a significant portion of their income from crime. Professionals do not delude themselves that their acts are impulsive, one-time efforts. They also do not employ elaborate rationalizations to excuse the harmfulness of their action (e.g., "Shoplifting doesn't really hurt anyone"). Professionals pursue their craft with vigor, attempting to learn from older, experienced criminals the techniques that will garner them the most money with the least risk. Their numbers are relatively few, but professionals engage in crimes that produce greater losses to society and perhaps cause more significant social harm. Typical forms include pickpocketing, burglary, shoplifting, forgery and counterfeiting, extortion, and swindling.[32]

*WHITE-COLLAR CRIME*  Some criminal activities involve people and institutions whose acknowledged purpose is profit through illegal business transactions. Included within the category of **white-collar crime** are such acts as income tax evasion, credit card fraud, and bank fraud. White-collar criminals also use their positions of trust in business or government to commit crimes. Their activities might include soliciting bribes or kickbacks, as well as embezzlement. Some white-collar criminals set up businesses for the sole purpose of victimizing the general public. They engage in land swindles, securities theft, medical fraud, and so on. And, in addition to acting as individuals, some white-collar criminals enter into conspiracies designed to improve the market share or profitability of corporations. This type of white-collar crime, which includes antitrust violations, price fixing, and false advertising, is known as **corporate crime**.

Estimating the extent of white-collar crime and its influence on victims is difficult because victimologists often ignore those who suffer the consequences of such crime. Some experts place its total monetary value in the hundreds of billions of dollars. Beyond their monetary cost, white-collar crimes often damage property and kill people. Violations of safety standards, pollution of the environment, and industrial accidents due to negligence can be classified as corporate violence. White-collar crime also destroys confidence, saps the integrity of commercial life, and has the potential to cause devastating destruction.

*ORGANIZED CRIME*  Organized crime involves the criminal activity of people and organizations whose acknowledged purpose is economic gain through illegal enterprise.[33] These criminal cartels provide outlawed goods and services demanded by the general public: prostitution, narcotics, gambling, loan sharking, pornography, and untaxed liquor and cigarettes. In addition, organized criminals infiltrate legitimate organizations, such as unions, to drain off their funds and profits for illegal purposes.

Federal and state agencies have been dedicated to wiping out organized crime, and some well-publicized arrests have resulted in the imprisonment of important leaders. The membership of the traditional Italian and Irish crime families has dropped an estimated 50 percent over a 20-year period.

**white-collar crime**
White-collar crimes involve the violation of rules that control business enterprise. They include employee pilferage, bribery, commodities law violations, mail fraud, computer fraud, environmental law violations, embezzlement, Internet scams, extortion, forgery, insurance fraud, price fixing, and environmental pollution.

**corporate crime**
Crime committed by a corporation, or by individuals who control the corporation or other business entity, for such purposes as illegally increasing market share, avoiding taxes, or thwarting competition.

© AP Photo/Moises Castillo, Fi e

*Organized crime has become a transnational phenomenon. Here, on March 7, 2009, police lead suspected gunmen Domingo Choj, right, and Hector Rolando Toj, back, at an air force base in Guatemala City. Nine gunmen were arrested after hours of fighting in western Guatemala. One of the men is a Mexican national and is suspected of being a recruiter for the Zetas, a group of Gulf cartel hit men. Mexican crime syndicates are spreading their tentacles as never before, using their trademark brutality to take over in places such as Guatemala and even Colombia, long the heart of Latin America's drug world. They now operate in at least 47 countries.*

## CAREERS IN CRIMINAL JUSTICE

# Statistician

### Duties and Characteristics of the Job

Statisticians use numerical data to examine, understand, and predict various phenomena. In the criminal justice system, they use their skills to study crime rates and trends and to create more accurate methods of crime measurement. Usually, statisticians focus on demographic information to analyze people's behaviors and trends within a society. A statistician's job includes designing surveys, deciding which methods should be used to analyze the data collected, and making predictions based on patterns within the data. Once this analysis is complete, statisticians will present the data, often in the form of written reports or scholarly articles. Although the concepts and mathematical calculations they perform may be abstract, the knowledge they produce is often used to describe events in the real world and to impel action on the part of those who read the findings of the researcher.

Statisticians generally work normal hours in a comfortable office setting. However, certain projects may require longer hours and travel to sites where data is being collected. Statisticians may earn a master's or doctorate degree, but their education is never fully complete, because they need to keep up to date on the latest findings in their field and to know the newest methods of analysis. Statisticians must also attend conferences to learn the latest developments in their field and the findings of other statisticians. They can work for a variety of employers, including private companies involved in security, and for private research institutes such as the Rand Corporation, although most work for the government or at colleges and universities. Like other academics, statisticians conduct research, publish, and teach. Note that the skills a statistician has are useful beyond their pure mathematical purposes and can be adapted for work in various fields, such as criminology and criminal justice.

### Job Outlook

Steady growth is predicted in the number of opportunities for employment as a statistician in the near future. However, faster growth is expected in jobs that

---

New groups—including Russian and eastern European, Hispanic, and African American gangs—have filled the vacuum created by federal prosecutors. Thousands of Russian immigrants are believed to be involved in criminal activity, primarily in Russian enclaves in New York City. Besides extortion from fellow eastern European immigrants, Russian organized crime groups have engaged in narcotics trafficking, fencing stolen property, money laundering, and other traditional organized crime schemes.[34]

Beyond these criminal activities, the criminal justice system is now confronted by emerging forms of illegal behavior—transnational crimes, billion dollar business enterprise crimes, international sex trafficking, terrorism, and cyber crime. Because of their importance, these crimes will be discussed in greater detail in Chapters 17 and 18.

## HOW MUCH CRIME IS THERE? HOW DO WE MEASURE IT?

Understanding how much crime takes place every year, what are the trends and patterns in crime, and who commits criminal behavior is essential in planning effective crime control policies. Without such knowledge, it would be impossible to know whether policies were effective and whether they were worth the cost. Take the case of the death penalty. Many people advocate its use to deter people from committing murder, but it would be impossible to know whether capital punishment is indeed an effective deterrent without a means of calculating murder rates and trends. Capital punishment might be justified if murder rates most often do not present themselves under the title "statistician" but, rather, under different titles in various fields requiring the skills of a statistician. Criminologists and psychologists who conduct research are two examples of those who need the strong analytical skills and statistical knowledge possessed by statisticians.

Statisticians are increasingly being employed in the private sector as market analysts who look at purchasing trends, but statisticians are still employed primarily by state, local, and federal agencies and by colleges and universities.

### Salary

Median annual wage-and-salary wages of statisticians were $72,610 in May 2008. The middle 50 percent earned between $52,730 and $95,170. The lowest-earning 10 percent earned less than $39,740, and the highest-earning 10 percent earned more than $117,190. The average annual salary for statisticians employed by the federal government was $92,322 in March 2009, and mathematical statisticians averaged $107,015.

### Opportunities

Opportunities will be best for those whose training is not based purely on statistics but is combined with another disciplinary focus, such as sociology or criminology.

### Qualifications

Statisticians' primary requirements for employment are educational. A bachelor's degree in statistics or mathematics sets a solid base for more education, either in further study of math or in another area of interest. Employment in this field requires an interest in and skill with numbers and analytical thinking. Statisticians must not only collect and interpret potentially complex data; they must also be able to explain their findings and predictions to nonstatisticians. Finally, multiple computer programs can be used to collect and examine data, and it will be beneficial for future statisticians to be familiar with the software most commonly used in their field of interest.

### Education and Training

A bachelor's degree in the appropriate field can gain a statistician entry into that field, but in order to advance, statisticians need further education in the form of a master's or doctorate.

Sources: "Statisticians," *Occupational Outlook Handbook*, 2010–2011 edition (Washington, D.C.: Bureau of Labor Statistics, U.S. Department of Labor), retrieved June 19, 2010, from www.bls.gov/oco/ocos045.htm.

---

fell dramatically soon after the death penalty was imposed. If, however, imposition of the death penalty had little if any effect on murder rates, justifications for its use would be damaged. Because obtaining accurate crime data is so essential, there are many career opportunities for statisticians in the criminal justice system (see the accompanying Careers in Criminal Justice feature).

## SOURCES OF CRIME DATA

The primary sources of crime data routinely used to measure the nature and extent of crime are surveys and official records collected, compiled, and analyzed by government agencies such as the federal government's Bureau of Justice Statistics and the Federal Bureau of Investigation (FBI). Criminal justice data analysts use these techniques to measure the nature and extent of criminal behavior and the personality, attitudes, and background of criminal offenders. What are these sources of crime data, how are they collected, and how valid are their findings?

**CourseMate** For more information about the **Bureau of Justice Statistics**, visit the Criminal Justice CourseMate at CengageBrain.com, then access the "Web Links" for this chapter.

### The Uniform Crime Report (UCR)

The Federal Bureau of Investigation collects the most important crime record data from local law enforcement agencies and publishes it yearly in the bureau's **Uniform Crime Report (UCR)**. The UCR includes crimes reported to local law enforcement departments and the number of arrests made by police agencies.[35] The FBI receives and compiles records from more than 17,000 police departments serving a majority of the U.S. population. Its major unit of analysis

**Uniform Crime Report (UCR)**
The official crime data collected by the FBI from local police departments.

### EXHIBIT 2.1

## Part I Crime Offenses

**CRIMINAL HOMICIDE**

*Murder and Nonnegligent Manslaughter* The willful (non-negligent) killing of one human being by another. Deaths caused by negligence, attempts to kill, assaults to kill, suicides, accidental deaths, and justifiable homicides are excluded. Justifiable homicides are limited to (1) the killing of a felon by a law enforcement officer in the line of duty and (2) the killing of a felon, during the commission of a felony, by a private citizen.

*Manslaughter by Negligence* The killing of another person through gross negligence. Traffic fatalities are excluded. Manslaughter by negligence is a Part I crime.

**FORCIBLE RAPE**

The carnal knowledge of a female forcibly and against her will. Included are rapes by force and attempts or assaults to rape. Statutory offenses (no force used but victim under age of consent) are excluded.

**ROBBERY**

Taking or attempting to take anything of value from the care, custody, or control of a person or persons by force or threat of force or violence and/or by putting the victim in fear.

**AGGRAVATED ASSAULT**

An unlawful attack by one person upon another for the purpose of inflicting severe or aggravated bodily injury. This type of assault is usually accompanied by the use of a weapon or by means likely to produce death or great bodily harm. Simple assaults are excluded.

**BURGLARY/BREAKING OR ENTERING**

Unlawful entry into a structure to commit a felony or a theft. Attempted forcible entry is included.

**LARCENY/THEFT (EXCEPT MOTOR VEHICLE THEFT)**

The unlawful taking, carrying, leading, or riding away of property from the possession or constructive possession of another. Examples are thefts of bicycles or automobile accessories, shoplifting, pocket picking, and the stealing of any property or article that is not taken by force and violence or by fraud. Attempted larcenies are included. Embezzlement, con games, forgery, worthless checks, and so on are excluded.

**MOTOR VEHICLE THEFT**

The theft or attempted theft of a motor vehicle. A motor vehicle is self-propelled and runs on the surface and not on rails. Specifically excluded from this category are motorboats, construction equipment, airplanes, and farming equipment.

**ARSON**

Any willful or malicious burning or attempt to burn, with or without intent to defraud, a dwelling house, public building, motor vehicle, or aircraft, personal property of another, or the like.

---

**Part I crimes**
Those crimes used by the FBI to gauge fluctuations in the overall volume and rate of crime. The offenses included were the violent crimes of murder and nonnegligent manslaughter, forcible rape, robbery, and aggravated assault and the property crimes of burglary, larceny, motor vehicle theft, and arson.

**Part II crimes**
All other crimes reported to the FBI; these are less serious crimes and misdemeanors, excluding traffic violations.

involves **Part I crimes**: murder and nonnegligent manslaughter, forcible rape, robbery, aggravated assault, burglary, larceny, arson, and motor vehicle theft. Exhibit 2.1 defines these crimes.

The FBI tallies and annually publishes the number of reported offenses by city, county, standard metropolitan statistical area, and geographical divisions of the United States. In addition to these statistics, the UCR shows the number and characteristics (age, race, and gender) of individuals who have been arrested for these and all other crimes, except traffic violations; these other crimes are referred to as **Part II crimes**.

*COMPILING THE UNIFORM CRIME REPORT* The methods used to compile the UCR are quite complex. Each month, law enforcement agencies report the number of Part I crimes known to them. This data is collected from records of all crime complaints that victims, officers who discovered the infractions, or other sources reported to these agencies.

Whenever criminal complaints are revealed through investigation to be unfounded or false, they are eliminated from the actual count. However, the number of actual offenses known is reported to the FBI whether or not anyone is arrested for the crime, the stolen property is recovered, or prosecution ensues.

The UCR uses three methods to express crime data. First, the number of crimes reported to the police and arrests made are expressed as raw figures (e.g., "An estimated 16,000 persons were murdered nationwide in 2009"). Second, crime rates per 100,000 people are computed. That is, when the UCR indicates that the murder rate was 5.6 in 2009, it means that almost 6 people in every 100,000 were murdered between January 1 and December 31, 2009. This is the equation used:

$$\frac{\text{Number of Reported Crimes}}{\text{Total U.S. Population}} \times 100{,}000 = \text{Rate per } 100{,}000$$

Third, the FBI computes changes in the rate of crime over time. This might be expressed as "The number of murders decreased 4 percent between 2008 and 2009."

***CLEARANCE RATES*** In addition, each month law enforcement agencies report how many crimes were **cleared**. Crimes are cleared in two ways: (1) when at least one person is arrested, charged, and turned over to the court for prosecution; or (2) by exceptional means, when some element beyond police control precludes the physical arrest of an offender (e.g., the offender leaves the country). Data on the number of clearances involving the arrest of only juvenile offenders, data on the value of property stolen and recovered in connection with Part I offenses, and detailed information pertaining to criminal homicide are also reported.

> **cleared**
> An offense is cleared by arrest or solved when at least one person is arrested or charged with the commission of the offense and is turned over to the court for prosecution.

Traditionally, slightly more than 20 percent of all reported Part I crimes are cleared by arrest each year. Not surprisingly, as Figure 2.1 shows, more serious crimes such as murder and rape are cleared at much higher rates than less serious property crimes such as larceny/theft. Factors contribute to this difference in clearance rate:

■ The media give more attention to serious violent crimes, and as a result, local and state police departments are more likely to devote time and spend more resources in their investigations.

■ There is more likely to be a prior association between victims of violent/serious crimes and their attackers, a fact that aids police investigations.

■ Even if they did not know one another beforehand, violent crime victims and offenders interact, which facilitates identification.

■ Serious violent crimes often produce physical evidence (blood, body fluids, fingerprints) that can be used to identify suspects.

**FIGURE 2.1**
Percentage of Crimes Cleared by Arrest

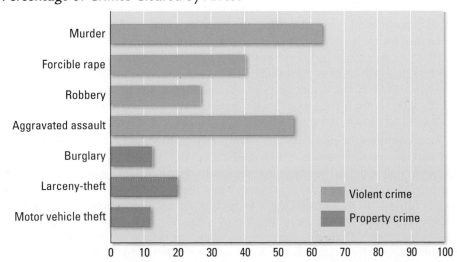

Source: FBI, Uniform Crime Reports, 2009, www.fbi.gov/ucr/cius2009/offenses/clearances/index.html.

## EVIDENCE-BASED JUSTICE

# *Is the Crime Rate Really Declining?*

The FBI's Uniform Crime Report (UCR) program, long considered the definitive source of official crime data and trends, tells us that crime rates have been in steep decline for the past decade. Some find it perplexing that property rates have trended downward despite a flagging economy and high unemployment. Now a recent study of more than a hundred retired New York Police Department captains and higher-ranking officers has cast doubt on the accuracy of this data. According to a survey conducted by crime experts John Eterno and Eli Silverman, these former police commanders were under intense pressure to reduce crime. In order to placate hard-charging commissioners such as William Bratton, some local commanders manipulated crime statistics in order to suggest that their efforts at crime control were working. How did they cheat? One method was to check eBay and other websites to find prices for items that had been reported stolen that were actually lower than the value provided by the crime

victim. They would then use the lower values to reduce felony grand larcenies, crimes that are in the UCR, to misdemeanor petit larcenies, which go unrecorded. Some commanders reported sending officers to crime scenes to persuade victims not to file complaints or altering crime details so they did not have to be reported to the FBI. For example, an attempted burglary must be reported, but not an illegal trespass. Although it is possible that the New York police administrators were under more pressure to reduce crime than their counterparts around the country, the fact that members of the largest police department in the United States may have fudged UCR data suggests that the decade-long decline in crime may have been influenced by police reporting practices.

John Eterno and Eli B. Silverman, "The NYPD's Compstat: Compare Statistics or Compose Statistics?" *International Journal of Police Science & Management* 12 (2010): in press. See also John Eterno and Eli B. Silverman, *Unveiling Compstat: The Global Policing Revolution's Naked Truths* (London: CRC Press/Taylor and Francis Group, London, 2011).

**VALIDITY OF THE UNIFORM CRIME REPORT** Despite continued reliance on the UCR, its accuracy has been suspect. The three main areas of concern are reporting practices, law enforcement practices, and methodological problems.

- *Reporting practices.* Many victims do not report these incidents to police; therefore, these crimes do not become part of the UCR. The reasons for not reporting vary. Some victims do not trust the police or have confidence in their ability to solve crimes. Others do not have property insurance and therefore believe reporting theft is useless. In other cases, victims fear reprisals from an offender's friends or family or, in the case of family violence, from their spouse or boyfriend or girlfriend.[36] According to surveys of crime victims, less than 40 percent of all criminal incidents are reported to the police. Some of these victims justify nonreporting by stating that the incident was "a private matter," that "nothing could be done," or that the victimization was "not important enough."[37] Changes in reporting can shape the crime trends reported in the UCR. When Eric Baumer and Janet Lauritsen examined data from 1973 to 2005, their findings showed that shifts in victim reporting can account for about half of the total yearly change in the official UCR crime rate.[38]

- *Law enforcement practices.* The way police departments record and report criminal and delinquent activity also affects the validity of UCR statistics. Some police departments define crimes loosely—reporting a trespass as a burglary or an assault on a woman as an attempted rape—whereas others pay strict attention to FBI guidelines. These reporting practices may help explain interjurisdictional differences in crime.[39] Arson is seriously underreported because many fire departments do not report to the FBI and because those that do file such reports define many fires that may well have been set by arsonists as "accidental" or "spontaneous."[40]

Some local police departments make systematic errors in UCR reporting. They may count an arrest only after a formal booking procedure, even though the UCR requires arrests to be counted if the suspect is released without a formal charge. One survey of arrests found an error rate of about 10 percent in every Part I offense category.[41] More serious allegations claim that in some cases, police officials may deliberately alter reported crimes to improve their department's public image. Police administrators' interested in lowering the crime rate may falsify crime reports by classifying a burglary as a nonreportable trespass.[42] See the accompanying Evidence-Based Justice feature for more on this issue.

Ironically, boosting police efficiency and professionalism may actually help increase crime rates: As people develop confidence in the police, they may be more motivated to report crime.[43] Higher crime rates may occur as departments adopt more sophisticated computer technology and hire better-educated, better-trained employees.[44]

■ *Methodological issues.* Several methodological issues contribute to skepticism about the UCR's validity:

  ■ No federal crimes are reported.

  ■ Reports are voluntary and vary in accuracy and completeness.

  ■ Not all police departments submit reports.

  ■ The FBI uses estimates in its total crime projections.

  ■ If an offender commits multiple crimes, only the most serious is recorded. Thus, when a narcotics addict rapes, robs, and murders a victim, only the murder is recorded. Consequently, many lesser crimes go unreported.

  ■ Each act is listed as a single offense for some crimes but not for others. When a man robs six people in a bar, the offense is listed as one robbery; but if he had assaulted or murdered them, his acts would have been listed as six assaults or six murders.

  ■ Incomplete acts are lumped together with completed ones.

  ■ Important differences exist between the FBI's definition of certain crimes and those used in a number of states.[45]

In addition to these issues, the complex scoring procedure used in the UCR program means that many serious crimes are not counted. If, during an armed bank robbery, the robber strikes a teller with the butt of a handgun, runs from the bank, and steals an automobile at the curb, he has technically committed robbery, aggravated assault, and motor vehicle theft, which are three Part I offenses. However, the UCR records only the most serious crime, the robbery.[46]

## National Incident-Based Reporting System (NIBRS)

Clearly there must be a more reliable source for crime statistics than the UCR as it stands today. Beginning in 1982, a five-year redesign effort was undertaken to provide more comprehensive and detailed crime statistics. The effort resulted in the **National Incident-Based Reporting System (NIBRS)**, a program that collects data on each reported crime incident. Instead of allowing local police agencies simply to indicate the kinds of crimes that individual citizens report to the police and to submit summary statements of resulting arrests, the new program requires them to provide at least a brief account of each incident and arrest, including the incident, victim, and offender information.

Under NIBRS, law enforcement authorities provide the FBI with information on each criminal incident that occurs in their jurisdiction and involves any of 46 specific offenses, including the 8 Part I crimes; arrest information on the

**National Incident-Based Reporting System (NIBRS)**
A form of crime data collection created by the FBI requiring local police agencies to provide at least a brief account of each incident and arrest within 22 crime patterns, including the incident, victim, and offender information.

46 offenses as well as 11 lesser offenses is also provided in the NIBRS. These expanded crime categories include numerous additional crimes, such as blackmail, embezzlement, drug offenses, and bribery. This allows a national database on the nature of crime, victims, and criminals to be developed. Other collected information includes statistics gathered by federal law enforcement agencies, as well as data on hate, or bias, crimes. When fully implemented, NIBRS will provide

**CourseMate** For more information about **NIBRS**, visit the Criminal Justice CourseMate at CengageBrain.com, then access the "Web Links" for this chapter.

- Expansion of the number of offense categories included
- Details on individual crime incidents (offenses, offenders, victims, property, and arrests)
- Links between arrests and crime clearances
- Inclusion of all offenses that occur in an incident, rather than only the most serious offense
- The ability to distinguish between attempted and completed crimes
- Links between offense, offender, victim, property, and arrestee variables, which permit examination of interrelationships.[47]

Thus far, more than 20 states have implemented their NIBRS programs, and 12 others are in the process of finalizing their data collections. When this program is fully implemented and adopted across the nation, it should bring about greater uniformity in cross-jurisdictional reporting and improve the accuracy of official crime data. Whether it can capture cases missing from the UCR remains to be seen.[48]

## National Crime Victimization Survey (NCVS)

Because more than half of all victims do not report their experiences to the police, the UCR cannot measure all the annual criminal activity. To address the nonreporting issue, the federal government's Bureau of Justice Statistics sponsors the **National Crime Victimization Survey (NCVS)**, a comprehensive, nationwide survey of victimization in the United States. Begun in 1973, the NCVS provides a detailed picture of crime incidents, victims, and trends.[49]

**National Crime Victimization Survey (NCVS)**
The nation's primary source of information on criminal victimization. Each year, data from a national sample measure the frequency, characteristics, and consequences of criminal victimization by such crimes as rape, sexual assault, robbery, assault, theft, household burglary, and motor vehicle theft.

How is the NCVS conducted? At the present time, once a year, U.S. Census Bureau personnel interview household members in a nationally representative sample. In the most recent survey, about 42,000 households and 78,000 individuals aged 12 or older were contacted.[50] Households stay in the sample for three years. New households are rotated into the sample on an ongoing basis. The NCVS collects information on crimes suffered by individuals and households, whether or not those crimes were reported to law enforcement. It estimates the proportion of each crime type reported to law enforcement, and it summarizes the reasons that victims give for reporting or not reporting. In 1993, the survey was redesigned to provide detailed information on the frequency and nature of rape, sexual assault, personal robbery, aggravated and simple assault, household burglary, theft, and motor vehicle theft. In 2006, the techniques used were once again changed so that results are now comparable to those in previous years (see below for more on the changes).[51]

The survey provides information about victims (age, sex, race, ethnicity, marital status, income, and educational level), offenders (sex, race, approximate age, and victim–offender relationship), and the crimes (time and place of occurrence, use of weapons, nature of injury, and economic consequences). Questions also cover the experiences of victims with the criminal justice system, self-protective measures used by victims, and possible substance abuse by offenders. Supplements are added periodically to the survey to obtain detailed information on topics such as school crime.

*NCVS: ADVANTAGES AND PROBLEMS* The greatest advantage of the NCVS over official data sources such as the UCR is that it can provide estimates of the total amount of annual crimes, not only those that are reported to police. Nonreporting is a significant issue: Only about half of all violent victimizations and about one-third of all property crimes are reported to the police. As a result, the NCVS data provide a more nearly complete picture of the nation's crime problem. Also, because some crimes are significantly underreported, the NCVS is an indispensable measure of their occurrence. Take the crime of rape and sexual assault, of which only about 40 percent of incidents are reported to police. The Uniform Crime Report records about 90,000 rapes or attempted rapes occurred, compared to the 200,000 uncovered by the NCVS. In addition, the NCVS helps us understand why crimes are not reported to police and whether the type and nature of the criminal event influences whether the police will ever know it occurred. Again with the crime of rape, research shows that victims are much more likely to report rape if it is accompanied by another crime, such as robbery, than they are if the rape is a stand-alone event. Official data alone cannot provide that type of information.[52]

Although its utility and importance are unquestioned, the NCVS may also suffer from some methodological problems. As a result, its findings must be interpreted with caution. Among the potential problems:

- Overreporting due to victims' misinterpretation of events. A lost wallet may be reported as stolen, or an open door may be viewed as a burglary attempt.

- Underreporting due to the embarrassment of reporting crime to interviewers, fear of getting in trouble, or simply forgetting an incident.

- Inability to record the personal criminal activity of those victims interviewed, such as drug use or gambling; murder is also not included, for obvious reasons.

- Sampling errors, which may produce a group of respondents who do not represent the nation as a whole.

- Inadequate question format that invalidates responses. Some groups, such as adolescents, may be particularly susceptible to reporting error because of faulty question format.[53]

*THE FUTURE OF THE NCVS*  For the past 30 years, the NCVS has served, along with the UCR, as one of the two major measures of crime and victimization in the United States. It now faces some important challenges. A recent analysis conducted by the National Research Council found that its effectiveness has been undermined by budget limitations.[54]

In order to keep going in spite of tight resources, the survey's sample size and methods of data collection have been altered. Although the current sample size is still valid for its purpose, victimization is a relatively rare event, and when they are contacted, many respondents do not have incidents to report. Consequently, the NCVS now has to combine multiple years of data in order to comment on change over time, which is less desirable than an annual measure of year-to-year change.

Reflecting these issues, significant changes were made in 2006 to the way the NCVS data is collected. The methodological changes included a new sampling method, a change in the method of handling first-time interviews with households, and a change in the method of interviewing. Some selected areas were dropped from the sample, while others were added. Finally, computer-assisted personal interviewing (CAPI) replaced paper and pencil interviewing (PAPI). Although the limitations of the NCVS cannot be overlooked, no available substitute provides national information on crime and victimization, along with extensive details on victims and the social context of the criminal event.

## Self-Report Surveys

Whereas the NCVS is designed to measure victimization directly and criminal activity indirectly, participants in **self-report surveys** are asked to describe, in detail, their recent and lifetime participation in criminal activity. Self-reports are generally given anonymously in groups, so that the people being surveyed are

**self-report survey**
A research approach that questions large groups of subjects, such as high school students, about their own participation in delinquent or criminal acts.

assured that their responses will remain private and confidential. Secrecy and anonymity are essential to maintaining the honesty and validity of responses. Self-report survey questions might ask:

- How many times in the past year have you taken something worth more than $50?
- How many times in the past year did you hurt someone so badly that they needed medical care?
- How many times in the past year did you vandalize or damage school property?
- How many times in the past year did you use marijuana?

Most self-report studies have focused on juvenile delinquency and youth crime, but they can also be used to examine the offense histories of select groups such as prison inmates, drug users, and even police officers.[55]

In addition to crime-related items, most self-report surveys contain questions about attitudes, values, and behaviors. There may be questions about a participant's substance abuse history and his or her family relations, such as "Did your parents ever strike you with a stick or a belt?" Criminologists can then use statistical analysis of the responses to determine whether people who report being abused as children are also more likely to use drugs as adults. When psychologist Christiane Brems and her associates used this approach to collect data from 274 women and 556 men receiving drug detoxification services, they found that 20 percent of men and more than 50 percent of women reported childhood physical or sexual abuse. Individuals who report an abuse history also reported earlier age of onset of drinking, more problems associated with the use of alcohol/drugs, more severe psychopathology, and more lifetime arrests.[56]

**MONITORING THE FUTURE**  One of the most important sources of self-report data is the *Monitoring the Future* (MTF) study, which researchers at the University of Michigan Institute for Social Research (ISR) have been conducting annually since 1978. This national survey typically involves more than 2,500 high school seniors.[57] The MTF is considered the national standard for measuring substance abuse trends among American teens.

The MTF data indicates that the number of people who break the law is far greater than the number projected by official statistics. Almost everyone questioned is found to have violated a law at some time, including truancy, alcohol abuse, false ID use, shoplifting or larceny under $50, fighting, marijuana use, and damage to the property of others. Furthermore, self-reports dispute the notion that criminals and delinquents specialize in one type of crime or another; rather, offenders seem to engage in a mixed bag of crime and deviance.[58]

**VALIDITY OF SELF-REPORTS**  Critics of self-report studies frequently suggest that it is unreasonable to expect people to candidly admit illegal acts. This is especially true of those with official records, who may be engaging in the most criminality. At the same time, some people may exaggerate their criminal acts, forget some of them, or be confused about what is being asked. Some surveys contain an overabundance of trivial offenses, such as shoplifting small items or using false identification to obtain alcohol, often lumped together with serious crimes to form a total crime index. Consequently, comparisons between groups can be highly misleading.

The "missing cases" phenomenon is also a concern. Even if 90 percent of a school population voluntarily participate in a self-report study, researchers can never be sure whether the few who refuse to participate or are absent that day constitute a significant portion of the school's population of persistent high-rate offenders. Research indicates that offenders with the most extensive prior criminality are also the most likely "to be poor historians of their own crime commission rates."[59] And the most serious chronic offenders in the teenage population are the least likely to be willing to cooperate with criminologists administering self-report tests.[60]

**CONCEPT SUMMARY 2.2**
*Data Collection Methods*

### Uniform Crime Report (UCR)

■ Data is collected from records compiled by police departments across the nation, which include crimes reported to police, and arrests.

■ Strengths of the UCR are that it measures homicides and arrests and that it is a consistent, national sample.

■ Weaknesses of the UCR are that it omits crimes not reported to police, omits most drug usage, and contains reporting errors.

### National Crime Victimization Survey (NCVS)

■ Data is collected from a large national survey.

■ Strengths of the NCVS are that it includes crimes not reported to the police, uses careful sampling techniques, and is a yearly survey.

■ Weaknesses of the NCVS are that it relies on victims' memory and honesty and that it omits substance abuse.

### Self-Report Surveys

■ Data is collected from local surveys.

■ Strengths of self-report surveys are that they include nonreported crimes and substance abuse and that offenders' personal information is included.

■ Weaknesses of self-report surveys are that they rely on the honesty of offenders and that they omit offenders who refuse to or are unable to participate and who may be the most deviant.

Institutionalized youths, who are not generally represented in the self-report surveys, are not only more delinquent than the general youth population, but are also considerably more misbehaving than the most delinquent youths identified in the typical self-report survey.[61] Consequently, self-reports may measure only nonserious, occasional delinquents, while ignoring hard-core chronic offenders.

There is also evidence that reporting accuracy differs among racial, ethnic, and gender groups. It is possible that some groups are more worried about image than others and less willing to report crime, deviance, and/or victimization for fear that it would make them or their group look bad.[62]

To address these criticisms, various techniques have been used to verify self-report data.[63] The "known group" method compares youths who are known to be offenders with those who are not to see whether the former report more delinquency. Research shows that when kids are asked whether they have ever been arrested or sent to court, their responses accurately reflect their true-life experiences.[64]

Although these studies are supportive, self-report data must be interpreted with some caution. Asking subjects about their past behavior may capture more serious crimes but miss minor criminal acts. For example, people remember armed robberies and rapes better than minor assaults and altercations.[65] In addition, some classes of offenders, such as substance abusers, may have a tough time accounting for their prior misbehavior.[66]

## Evaluating Sources of Crime Data

The UCR, the NCVS, and self-reports are the standard sources of data used by criminologists to track trends and patterns in the crime rate. Each has its own strengths and weaknesses. The UCR contains information on the number and characteristics of people arrested—information that the other data sources lack. Some recent research indicates that for serious crimes, such as drug trafficking, arrest data can provide a meaningful measure of the level of criminal activity in a particular neighborhood environment, which other data sources cannot provide. It is also the source of information on particular crimes such as murder, which the other data sources cannot provide.[67] It remains the standard unit of analysis

### EXHIBIT 2.2

## Alternative Crime Measures

### COHORT RESEARCH DATA

Collecting cohort data involves observing over time a group of people who share certain characteristics. Researchers might select all girls born in Boston in 1970 and then follow their behavior patterns for 20 years. The research data might include their school experiences, arrests, and hospitalizations, along with information about their family life (marriages, divorces, and parental relations, for example). Data may also be collected directly from the subjects during interviews and meetings with family members. If the cohort is carefully drawn, it may be possible to accumulate a complex array of data that can be used to determine which life experiences are associated with criminal careers. Another approach is to take a contemporary cohort, such as men in prison in New York in 2009, and then look back into their past and collect data from educational, family, police, and hospital records—a format known as a retrospective cohort study. If criminologists wanted to identify childhood and adolescent risk factors for criminality, they might acquire the inmates' prior police and court records, school records, and so on.

### EXPERIMENTAL DATA

Sometimes criminologists conduct controlled experiments to collect data on the cause of crime. To conduct experimental research, criminologists manipulate, or intervene in, the lives of their subjects to see the outcome or the effect of the intervention. True experiments usually have three elements: (1) random selection of subjects, (2) a control or comparison group, and (3) an experimental condition. For example, to determine whether viewing violent media content is a cause of aggression, a criminologist might randomly select one group of subjects and have them watch an extremely violent and gory film (such as *Evil Dead 2* or *Texas Chainsaw Massacre*) and then compare their behavior to that of a second randomly selected group who watch something mellow (such as a *Shrek* film or *WALL-E*). The behavior of both groups would be monitored; if the subjects who had watched the violent film were significantly more aggressive than those who had watched the nonviolent film, an association between media content and behavior would be supported. The fact that both groups were randomly selected would prevent some preexisting condition from invalidating the results of the experiment.

### OBSERVATIONAL AND INTERVIEW RESEARCH

Sometimes criminologists focus their research on relatively few subjects, interviewing them in depth or observing them as they go about their activities. This research often results in the kind of in-depth data that large-scale surveys do not yield. In one such effort, Claire Sterk-Elifson focused on the lives of middle-class female drug abusers. The 34 interviews she conducted provide insight into a group whose behavior might not be captured in a large-scale survey. Sterk-Elifson found that these women were introduced to cocaine at first "just for fun": "I do drugs," one 34-year-old lawyer told her, "because

upon which most criminological research is based. However, UCR data omits many criminal incidents that victims choose not to report to police, and it is subject to the reporting caprices of individual police departments.

The NCVS includes unreported crime and important information on the personal characteristics of victims. However, the data consists of estimates made from relatively limited samples of the total U.S. population, so that even narrow fluctuations in the rates of some crimes can have a major impact on findings. It also relies on personal recollections, which may be inaccurate. The NCVS also does not include data on important crime patterns, including patterns in murder and drug abuse, that are critical issues for crime analysis.

Self-report surveys can provide information on the personal characteristics of offenders—such as their attitudes, values, beliefs, and psychological profiles—that is unavailable from any other source. Yet at their core, self-reports rely on the honesty of criminal offenders and drug abusers, a population not generally known for accuracy and integrity.

Although their tallies of crimes are certainly not in sync, the crime patterns and trends recorded by the three methods are often quite similar (see Concept Summary 2.2 on page 61).[68] All of the sources of crime data agree about the personal characteristics of serious criminals (such as age and gender) and about

I like the feeling. I would never let drugs take over my life." Unfortunately, many of these subjects succumbed to the power of drugs and suffered both emotional and financial stress.

### META-ANALYSIS AND SYSTEMATIC REVIEW

Meta-analysis involves gathering data from a number of previous studies. Compatible information and data are extracted and pooled together. When analyzed, the grouped data from several different studies provide a more powerful and valid indicator of relationships than the results of a single study. A systematic review is another widely accepted means of evaluating the effectiveness of public policy interventions. It involves collecting the findings from previously conducted scientific studies that address a particular problem, appraising and synthesizing the evidence, and using the collective evidence to address a particular scientific question.

### DATA MINING

A relatively new criminological technique, data mining employs multiple advanced computational methods, including artificial intelligence (the use of computers to perform logical functions), to analyze large data sets that usually involve one or more data sources. The goal is to identify significant and recognizable patterns, trends, and relationships that are not easily detected through traditional analytical techniques. Data mining might be employed to help a police department determine whether burglaries in its jurisdiction exhibit a particular pattern. To determine whether such a pattern exists, a criminologist

might apply data-mining techniques with a variety of sources, including calls for service data, crime or incident reports, witness statements, suspect interviews, tip information, telephone toll analysis, and Internet activity. The data mining might uncover a strong relationship between the time of day and the place of occurrence. The police could use the findings to plan an effective burglary elimination strategy.

### CRIME MAPPING

Crime mapping is a research technique that employs computerized crime maps and other graphical representations of crime data patterns. The simplest maps display crime locations or concentrations and can be used, for example, to help law enforcement agencies increase the effectiveness of their patrol efforts. More complex maps can be used to chart trends in criminal activity. For example, criminologists might be able to determine whether certain neighborhoods in a city have significantly higher crime rates than others—whether they are so-called hot spots of crime.

Sources: David Farrington, Lloyd Ohlin, and James Q. Wilson, *Understanding and Controlling Crime* (New York: Springer-Verlag, 1986), pp. 11–18; Claire Sterk-Elifson, "Just for Fun? Cocaine Use among Middle-Class Women," *Journal of Drug Issues* 26 (1996): 63–76; William F. Whyte, *Street Corner Society* (Chicago: University of Chicago Press, 1955) 38; Herman Schwendinger and Julia Schwendinger, *Adolescent Subcultures and Delinquency* (New York: Praeger, 1985); David Farrington and Brandon Welsh, "Improved Street Lighting and Crime Prevention," *Justice Quarterly* 19 (2002): 313–343; Colleen McCue, Emily Stone, and Teresa Gooch, "Data Mining and Value-Added Analysis," *FBI Law Enforcement Bulletin* 72 (2003): 1–6; Jerry Ratcliffe, "Aoristic Signatures and the Spatio-Temporal Analysis of High Volume Crime Patterns," *Journal of Quantitative Criminology* 18 (2002): 23–43.

where and when crime occurs (such as urban areas, nighttime, and summer months). In addition, the problems inherent in each source are consistent over time. Therefore, even if the data sources do not provide an exact, precise, and valid count of crime at any given time, they are reliable indicators of changes and fluctuations in yearly crime rates.

In addition to the primary sources of crime data—UCR, NCVS, and self-report surveys—a number of other methods are routinely used to acquire data. These are discussed in Exhibit 2.2.

## CRIME TRENDS

Crime is not new to the last century.[69] Studies have indicated that a gradual increase in the crime rate, especially in violent crime, occurred from 1830 to 1860. Following the Civil War, this rate increased significantly for about 15 years. Then, from 1880 up to the time of World War I, with the possible exception of the years immediately preceding and following the war, the number of reported crimes decreased. After a period of readjustment, the crime rate steadily declined until the Depression (about 1930), when another crime wave was recorded.

## RACE, GENDER, AND CULTURE IN CRIMINAL JUSTICE

# Crime in Other Cultures

Although the United States once led the Western world in overall crime, there has been a marked decline in U.S. crime rates, which are now below those of other industrial nations, including England and Wales, Denmark, and Finland.

Making international comparisons is often difficult because the legal definitions of crime vary from country to country. There are also differences in the way crime is measured. For example, in the United States, crime may be measured by counting criminal acts reported to the police or by using victim surveys, whereas in many European countries, the number of cases solved by the police is used as the measure of crime. Despite these problems, valid comparisons can still be made about crime across different countries using a number of reliable data sources. For example, the United Nations Survey of Crime Trends and Operations of Criminal Justice Systems (UNCJS) is one of the best-known source of information on cross-national data. There is also the United Nations International Study on the Regulation of Firearms. INTERPOL, an international police agency, collects data from police agencies in 179 countries. The World Health Organization (WHO) has conducted surveys on global violence. The *European Sourcebook of Crime and Criminal Justice Statistics* provides data from police agencies in 36 European nations. Finally, the International Crime Victims Survey (ICVS), which is conducted in 60 countries and managed by the Ministry of Justice of the Netherlands, the Home Office of the United Kingdom, and the United Nations Interregional Crime and Justice Research Institute, has become a reliable source of cross-cultural crime and victimization trends.

What do these data sources tell us about crime in other cultures? The ICVS is perhaps the best source today on determining crime and victimizations rates and trends. According to the most recent ICVS, an estimated 16 percent of the population in the nations included in the most recent survey had been victims of at least one of ten common crimes (such as burglary, robbery, theft, and assault) in the course of the last year. The countries with the highest scores are Ireland, England and Wales, New Zealand, and Iceland. Lowest overall victimization rates are found in Spain, Japan, Hungary, and Portugal. Just as in the United States, there has been a distinct downward trend in the level of crime and victimization during

the past decade. Also similarly, some cities have much higher crime rates than others. The cities in developed countries with the lowest victimization rates are Hong Kong, Lisbon, Budapest, Athens, and Madrid; highest victimization rates are found in London and Tallinn, Estonia. Although victimization rates are still high, most of the countries show a distinct downward trend in the level of victimization since 1995. The drops are most pronounced in property crimes such as vehicle-related crimes (bicycle theft, thefts from cars, and joyriding) and burglary. In most countries, crime rates are back at the level of the late 1980s. One reason is that people around the world are taking precautions to prevent crime. Improved security may well have been one of the main forces behind the universal drop in crimes such as joyriding and household burglary.

What do the cross-national data tell us about individual crimes?

### Homicide

Many nations, especially those experiencing social or economic upheaval, have murder rates much higher than the United States. Colombia has about 63 homicides per 100,000 people, and South Africa has 51, compared to fewer than 6 in the United States. During the past decade, there were more homicides in Brazil than in the United States, Canada, Italy, Japan, Australia, Portugal, Britain, Austria, and Germany *taken together*. Why are murder rates so high in Brazil? Law enforcement officials link the upsurge in violence to drug trafficking, gang feuds, vigilantism, and disputes over trivial matters, in which young, unmarried, uneducated males are involved.

### Rape

Violence against women is related to economic hardship and the social status of women. Rates are high in poor nations in which women are oppressed. Where women are more emancipated, the rates of violence against women are lower.

For many women, sexual violence starts in childhood and adolescence and may occur in the home, school, and community. Studies conducted in a wide variety of nations ranging from Cameroon to New Zealand found high rates of reported forced sexual initiation. In some nations, as many as 46 percent of adolescent women and 20 percent of adolescent men

*Rio de Janeiro State Police (PMERJ) carry a body down a stairway in a slum where a shootout took place an hour earlier. Because crime is an international phenomenon, there is an ongoing effort to collect accurate cross-national crime data.*

report sexual coercion at the hands of family members, teachers, boyfriends, or strangers.

Sexual violence has significant health consequences, including suicide, stress, mental illnesses, unwanted pregnancies, sexually transmitted diseases, HIV/AIDS, self-inflicted injuries, and (in the case of child sexual abuse) adoption of high-risk behaviors such as multiple sexual partners and drug use.

## Robbery

Countries with more reported robberies than the United States include England and Wales, Portugal, and Spain. Countries with fewer reported robberies include Germany, Italy, and France, as well as Middle Eastern and Asian nations.

## Burglary

The United States has lower burglary rates than Australia, Denmark, Finland, England and Wales, and Canada. It has higher reported burglary rates than Spain, Korea, and Saudi Arabia.

## Vehicle Theft

Australia, England and Wales, Denmark, Norway, Canada, France, and Italy now have higher rates of vehicle theft than the United States.

## Child Abuse

A World Health Organization report found that child physical and sexual abuse takes a significant toll around the world. In a single year, about 57,000 children under 15 years of age are murdered. The homicide rates for children aged 0 to 4 years were over twice as high as rates among children aged 5 to 14 years. Many more children are subjected to nonfatal abuse and neglect; 8 percent of male and 25 percent of female children up to age 18 experience sexual abuse of some kind.

## Gun Crimes

There has also been a common assumption that the United States is the most heavily armed nation on earth, but there is new evidence that people around the world are arming themselves in record numbers. Residents in the 15 countries of the European Union have an estimated 84 million firearms. Of these, 67 million (80 percent) are in civilian hands. With a total population of 375 million people, this amounts to 17 guns for every 100 people.

## Critical Thinking

1. Although risk factors at all levels of social and personal life contribute to youth violence, young people in all nations who experience change in societal-level factors—such as economic inequalities; rapid social change; and the availability of firearms, alcohol, and drugs—seem the most likely to get involved in violence. Can anything be done to help alleviate these social problems?

2. The United States is notorious for employing much tougher penal measures than European nations. Do you believe that our tougher measures would work abroad and should be adopted there as well? Is there a downside to putting lots of people in prison?

Sources: Jan van Dijk, John van Kesteren, and Paul Smit, "Criminal Victimisation in International Perspective: Key Findings from the 2004–2005 ICVS and EU ICS, 2008," http://rechten.uvt.nl/icvs/pdffiles/ICVS2004_05.pdf; Virendra Kumar and Sarita Kanth, "Bride Burning," *Lancet* 364 (2004): 18–19; Etienne Krug, Linda Dahlberg, James Mercy, Anthony Zwi, and Rafael Lozano, *World Report on Violence and Health* (Geneva: World Health Organization, 2002); Graeme Newman, *Global Report on Crime and Justice* (New York: Oxford University Press, 1999).

As measured by the UCR, crime rates increased gradually following the 1930s until the 1960s, when the growth rate became much greater. The homicide rate, which had actually declined from the 1930s to the 1960s, also began a sharp increase that continued for almost 30 years.

By 1991 police recorded about 14.6 million crimes. Since then, with a few exceptions, the number of crimes has been in decline. About 10.6 million crimes were reported in 2009—a drop of 4 million reported crimes since the 1991 peak, despite a boost of about 50 million in the general population. Are the crime trends and patterns experienced in the United States unique or do they occur in other cultures as well? This issue is explored in the accompanying Race, Gender, and Culture in Criminal Justice feature.

## Trends in Violent Crime and Property Crime

Especially welcome has been a significant drop in UCR violent crimes—murder, rape, robbery, and assault. About 1.3 million violent crimes are now being reported to the police each year, a rate of around 460 per 100,000 Americans. Of course, people are still disturbed by media reports of violent incidents, but in reality there are 500,000 fewer violent crimes being reported today than in 1991, when almost 2 million incidents occurred, a violence rate of 758 per 100,000. This means that the violence rate has dropped almost 40 percent from its peak.

The property crime rate—including burglary, larceny, motor vehicle theft, and arson—has also been in decline, dropping more than 10 percent during the past decade. At its peak, in 1991, about 13 million property crimes were reported, a rate of almost 5,000 per 100,000 citizens. Currently, a little more than 9 million property crimes are reported annually to police, a rate of about 3,300 per 100,000 population. Property crimes remain a serious national problem, and losses totaling an estimated $15 billion now result from property crimes each year.

## Trends in Victimization

According to the latest NCVS survey, U.S. residents aged 12 or older experienced about 23 million violent and property victimizations. About 16 million households now experience one or more property crimes or had a member aged 12 or older who experienced one or more violent crimes.[70]

Like the UCR data, NCVS data shows that criminal victimizations have declined significantly during the past 30 years. In 1973 an estimated 44 million victimizations were recorded, compared to 23 million today. Figure 2.2 presents the recent trends in violent crime, and Figure 2.3 tracks property victimizations. As these figures show, the NCVS supports the downward trend in the crime rate; both property crimes and violent crimes have declined more than 30 percent in the past decade.

## Trends in Self-Reporting

Self-report results appear to be more stable than the UCR. When the results of recent self-report surveys are compared with various studies conducted over a 20-year period, a uniform pattern emerges: The use of drugs and alcohol increased markedly in the 1970s, leveled off in the 1980s, and then began to increase in the mid-1990s until 1997, when the use of most drugs began to decline. Theft, violence, and damage-related crimes seem more stable. Although a self-reported crime wave has not occurred, neither has there been any visible reduction in self-reported criminality. Table 2.1 contains data from the most recent *Monitoring the Future* survey. A surprising number of these "typical" teenagers reported involvement in serious criminal behavior. About 11 percent reported hurting someone badly enough that the victim needed medical care (5 percent said they did it more than once); about 27 percent reported stealing something worth less than $50, and another 10 percent stole something worth more than $50; 25 percent reported shoplifting; 11 percent damaged school property.

**FIGURE 2.2**
**Trends in Violent Crime**

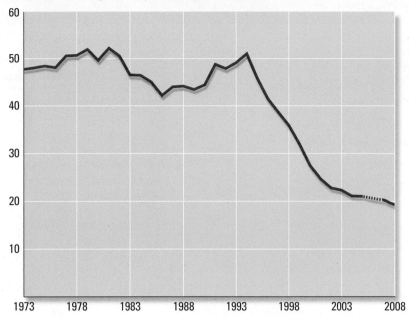

Victimization rate per 1,000 persons age 12 and over

Note: The violent crimes included are rape, robbery, aggravated and simple assault, and homicide.
Source: Bureau of Justice Statistics, http://bjs.ojp.usdoj.gov/content/glance/viort.cfm.

**FIGURE 2.3**
**Trends in Property Crimes**

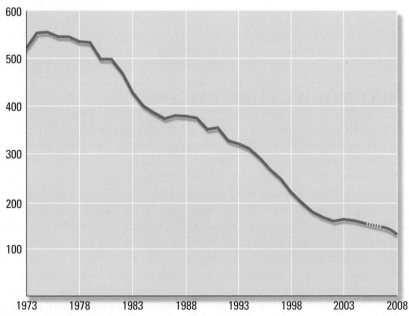

Victimization rate per 1,000 households

Note: Property crimes include burglary, theft, and motor vehicle theft.
Source: Bureau of Justice Statistics, http://bjs.ojp.usdoj.gov/content/glance/house2.cfm.

If the MTF data is accurate, the crime problem is much greater than UCR and NCVS data would lead us to believe. There are approximately 21 million youths between the ages of 15 and 19, and 3 percent of the students in this age group say they have used a weapon to steal one or more times in the past year.[71] At this rate, high school students must have committed a minimum of 630,000

### TABLE 2.1

**Monitoring the Future Survey of Criminal Activity of High School Seniors**

| Crime | Percent Engaging in Offenses | |
| --- | --- | --- |
|  | Committed at Least Once | Committed More than Once |
| Set fire on purpose | 1 | 2 |
| Damaged school property | 5 | 7 |
| Damaged work property | 3 | 3 |
| Auto theft | 2 | 3 |
| Auto part theft | 2 | 2 |
| Break and enter | 12 | 13 |
| Theft, less than $50 | 12 | 17 |
| Theft, more than $50 | 4 | 5 |
| Shoplift | 12 | 16 |
| Gang or group fight | 9 | 7 |
| Hurt someone badly enough to require medical care | 7 | 6 |
| Used force or a weapon to steal | 1 | 2 |
| Hit teacher or supervisor | 1 | 2 |
| Participated in serious fight | 7 | 6 |

Source: *Monitoring the Future, 2009* (Ann Arbor, Mich.: Institute for Social Research, 2010).

armed robberies during the past 12 months; in comparison, the UCR tallied about 440,000 armed robberies for *all* age groups

## WHAT THE FUTURE HOLDS

Speculating about the future of crime trends is risky because current conditions can change rapidly, but some criminologists have tried to predict future patterns. There are approximately 50 million school-age children in the United States, and many are under age 10; this is a greater number than we have had for decades. Many come from stable homes, but some lack stable families and adequate supervision. These children will soon enter their prime crime years, and as a result, crime rates may increase in the future.[72] However, whereas kids increase crime rates, seniors depress them. Even if teens commit more crime in the future, their contribution may be offset by the aging of the population, which will produce a large number of senior citizens and elderly, a group with a relatively low crime rate.[73]

Although population trends are important, the economy, technological change, and social factors may shape the direction of the crime rate.[74] The narcissistic youth culture that stresses materialism is being replaced by more moralistic cultural values.[75] Positive social values have a "contagion effect"; that is, the values held by the baby boomers will influence the behavior of all citizens, even crime-prone teens. The result may be moderation in the potential growth of the crime rate. Such prognostication is reassuring, but there is, of course, no telling what changes are in store that may influence crime rates either up or down. Technological developments such as e-commerce on the Internet have created new classes of crime. Although crime rates have trended downward, it is too early to predict that this trend will continue into the foreseeable future. The nearby Analyzing Criminal Justice Issues feature reviews the factors that influence crime rates and trends.

## CRIME PATTERNS

Criminologists look for stable crime rate patterns to gain insight into the nature of crime. The cause of crime may be better understood by examining the rate. If, for example, criminal statistics consistently show that crime rates are higher in poor neighborhoods in large urban areas, then the cause of crime may be related to poverty and neighborhood decline. If, in contrast, crime rates are spread evenly across society, and rates are equal in poor and affluent neighborhoods, this would suggest that crime has little economic basis. Instead, crime might be linked to socialization, personality, intelligence, or some other trait unrelated to class position or income. In this section we examine crime traits and patterns.

### The Ecology of Crime

Patterns in the crime rate seem to be linked to temporal and ecological factors. Some of the most important of these are discussed here.

*DAY, SEASON, AND CLIMATE* Most reported crimes occur during the warm summer months of July and August. During the summer, teenagers, who usually have the highest crime levels, are out of school and have greater opportunity to commit crime. People spend more time outdoors during warm weather, making themselves easier targets. Similarly, homes are left vacant more often during the summer, making them more vulnerable to property crimes. Two exceptions to this trend are murders and robberies, which occur frequently in December and January (although rates are also high during the summer).

Crime rates may be higher on the first day of the month than at any other time. Government welfare and Social Security checks arrive at this time, and with them come increases in such activities as breaking into mailboxes and accosting recipients on the streets. Also, people may have more disposable income at this time, and the availability of extra money may be related to behaviors associated with crime, such as drinking, partying, gambling, and so on.[76]

Another reason for seasonal differences in the crime rate is that weather effects (such as temperature swings) may have an impact on violent crime. The association between temperature and crime is thought to resemble an inverted U-shaped curve: Crime rates increase with rising temperatures and then begin to decline at some point (85 degrees) when it may be too hot for any physical exertion.[77] One way to protect yourself from violent crime: Turn off your air conditioner.[78]

*REGIONAL DIFFERENCES* Large urban areas have by far the highest rates of violence, and rural areas have the lowest per capita crime rates. Exceptions to this trend are low-population resort areas with large transient or seasonal populations—such as Atlantic City, New Jersey. Typically, the western and southern states have had consistently higher crime rates than the Midwest and Northeast (Figure 2.4, page 72). This pattern has convinced some criminologists that regional cultural values influence crime rates; others believe that regional differences can be explained by economic differences.

One argument for higher crime rates in the West and South is related to the influx of immigrants into these areas. This issue is explored in the Evidence-Based Justice feature on page 74.

## ANALYZING CRIMINAL JUSTICE ISSUES

# Explaining Trends in Crime Rates

Crime experts consider the explanation of crime trends one of their most important goals. Yet it is difficult to point to a single explanation for crime rate change. Let's look at a few of the most important social, ecological, and policy factors that are considered to be influences on the direction taken by crime rates.

## Age Structure of the Population

The age composition of the population has a significant influence on crime trends: Teenagers have extremely high crime rates, whereas seniors rarely commit crime. The greater the proportion of teens in the population, the higher the crime rate and the greater the number of persistent offenders. When the "baby boomers" hit their teens in the mid-1960s, the crime rate skyrocketed. Because the number of senior citizens is expanding and the population is aging, crime rates may remain relatively low for some time.

## Immigration

Immigration has become one of the most controversial issues in American society, and some people believe that immigrants should be prevented from entering the country because they have a disruptive effect on society. Research suggests the opposite, however, and some scholars, such as Harvard sociologist Robert Sampson, find that immigrants as a whole engage in criminal activities less than the general population. When Ramiro Martinez and his colleagues examined the association between drug crimes and immigration in Miami, Florida, and San Diego, California, they also found that immigration is *negatively* associated with homicides and with drug-related homicides specifically. This research indicates that as the number of immigrants in the population increases, the crime rate may actually decline; in other words, immigration has a suppressor effect on crime.

## Economy/Jobs

Although it seems logical that high unemployment should increase crime rates and that a good economy should reduce criminal activity, especially theft-related crimes, there is actually significant debate over the association between the economy and crime rates.

■ It is possible that a *poor economy actually helps lower crime rates* because unemployed parents are at home to supervise children and guard the family's possessions. Because there is less to spend, a poor economy reduces the number of valuables worth stealing. And it is unlikely that law-abiding, middle-

aged workers will suddenly turn to a life of crime if they are laid off during an economic downturn.

■ It is also possible that over the long haul, a *strong economy helps lower crime rates*, whereas long periods of sustained economic weakness and unemployment may eventually lead to increased rates: Crime skyrocketed in the 1930s during the Great Depression.

One reason for this confusion is that short-term economic swings have different impacts on different segments of the population. When manufacturing moved overseas during the latter half of the twentieth century, it had a much greater impact on young minority men living in cities hit hardest by deindustrialization than on highly educated suburban dwellers who could get jobs in service and technology industries.

## Abortion

There is evidence that the recent drop in the crime rate can be attributed to the availability of legalized abortion. In 1973, *Roe v. Wade* legalized abortion nationwide, and the drop in crime rate began approximately 18 years later, in 1991. Crime rates began to decline when the first groups of potential offenders affected by the abortion decision began reaching the peak age of criminal activity. It is possible that the link between crime rates and abortion is the result of two mechanisms: (1) selective abortion on the part of women most likely to have children who would eventually engage in criminal activity, and (2) improved child rearing caused by better maternal, familial, and/or fetal care because women are having fewer children.

## Gun Availability

As the number of guns in the population increases, so do violent crime rates. There is evidence that more guns than ever before are finding their way into the hands of young people. Surveys of high school students indicate that up to 10 percent carry guns at least some of the time. As the number of gun-toting students increases, so does the seriousness of violent crime, as happens when a schoolyard fight turns into murder.

## Gang Membership

According to government sources, there are now 800,000 gang members in the United States. Criminal gangs commit as much as 80 percent of the crime in many communities, including armed robbery, assault, auto theft, drug trafficking, extortion, fraud, home invasions, identity theft, murder, and weapons trafficking. Gang members are far more likely to possess guns than those not affiliated with gangs; criminal activity increases when kids join gangs. Drug-dealing gangs are heavily armed, a condition that persuades non–gang-affiliated kids to arm themselves for self-protection. The result is an arms race that generates an increasing spiral of violence.

## Drug Use

As drug use increases, crime rates increase. The surge in the violent crime rate between 1985 and 1993 has been tied directly to the crack cocaine epidemic that swept the nation's largest cities. Well-armed drug gangs did not hesitate to use violence to control territory, intimidate rivals, and increase market share. When crack use declined in urban areas after 1993, so did crime rates. A sudden increase in drug use may be a harbinger of future increases in the crime rate, especially if guns are easily obtained and the economy is weak.

## Media

The jury is still out, but some experts believe that violent media can influence the direction of crime rates. As the availability of media with a violent theme skyrocketed in the 1980s with the introduction of home video players, cable TV, and computer and video games, teen violence rates increased as well.

## Medical Technology

Some crime experts believe that the presence and quality of health care can have a significant impact on murder rates. The big breakthrough occurred in the 1970s, when technology that was developed to treat injured soldiers in Vietnam was applied to trauma care in the nation's hospitals. Ever since then, fluctuations in the murder rate have been linked to the level and availability of emergency medical services.

## Aggressive Law Enforcement

Reductions in crime rates may be attributed to adding large numbers of police officers and using them in aggressive police practices that target "quality of life" crimes, such as panhandling, graffiti, petty drug dealing, and loitering. By showing that even the smallest infractions will be dealt with seriously, aggressive police departments may be able to discourage potential criminals from committing more serious crimes. Cities that encourage aggressive, focused police work may be able to lower homicide rates in the area.

## Incarceration

It is also possible that tough laws imposing lengthy prison terms on drug dealers and repeat offenders can affect crime rates. The fear of punishment may inhibit some would-be criminals, and placing a significant number of potentially high-rate offenders behind bars seems to help lower crime rates. As the nation's prison population has expanded, the crime rate has fallen.

## Prisoner Reentry

Even though putting people in prison may have a short-term positive effect on crime rates, in the long run, increasing punishments may backfire. The recidivism rate of paroled inmates is quite high, and about two-thirds of those released from state custody will eventually return to prison. Inmates reentering society may have a significant effect on local crime rates, and most reoffend shortly after being released.

## Cultural Change

In contemporary society, cultural change (such as increases in the number of single-parent families, high school dropout rates, racial conflict, and teen pregnancies) can affect crime rates.

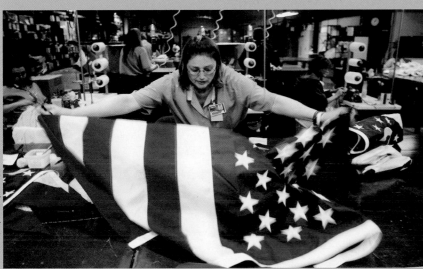

On January 12, 2010, an Ohio Reformatory for Women prisoner works on an American flag at the institution in Marysville, Ohio. Budget cuts are trimming the Ohio Penal Industries program, which officials say equips inmates with valuable job skills and helps reduce recidivism. Crime rates may increase if programs designed to teach job skills to returning former inmates are cut back or ended.

© AP Photo/*Dayton Daily News*, Jim Noelker

*continued*

# Explaining Trends in Crime Rates (continued)

## Criminal Opportunity

As criminal opportunities increase, so do crime rates. The decline in the burglary rate over the past decade may be explained in part by the abundance, and subsequent decline in price, of commonly stolen merchandise such as smart phones and iPads. If the risk of getting caught outweighs the value of the goods, why bother? Improving home and commercial security devices may also discourage would-be burglars, convincing them to turn to other forms of crime, such as theft from motor vehicles. On the other hand, new targets may increase crime rates: Subway crime increased in New York when thieves began targeting people carrying iPods and expensive cell phones.

Each of these factors may contribute to shifts in crime rate trends. They also have theoretical implications for social policy. For example, if crime is influenced by economic and justice-related factors, then criminals must be rational decision makers who will choose to commit crime if the need arises and the threat of punishment is limited. Effective crime control efforts might then be linked to convincing prospective offenders that crime does not pay and offering them alternative avenues to economic gain, such as job training and vocational education.

## Critical Thinking

While crime rates have been declining in the United States, they have been increasing in Europe. Is it possible that factors that correlate with crime rate changes in the United States have little utility in predicting changes in other cultures? What other factors may increase or reduce crime rates?

Sources: Amy Anderson and Lorine Hughes, "Exposure to Situations Conducive to Delinquent Behavior: The Effects of Time Use, Income, and Transportation," *Journal of Research in Crime and Delinquency* 46 (2009): 5–34; The National Gang Intelligence Center, National Gang Threat Assessment, 2009, www.atf.gov/pub/gang_related/2009_nat_gang_threat_assessment.pdf; Scott Decker, Charles Katz, and Vincent Webb, "Understanding the Black Box of Gang Organization: Implications for Involvement in Violent Crime, Drug Sales, and Violent Victimization, *Crime and Delinquency* 54 (2008): 153–172; Robert Sampson and Lydia Bean, "Cultural Mechanisms and Killing Fields: A Revised Theory of Community-Level Racial Inequality," in *The Many Colors of Crime: Inequalities of Race, Ethnicity, and Crime in America,* ed. Ruth D. Peterson, Lauren Krivo, and John Hagan (New York: New York University Press, 2006), pp. 8–36 ; Ramiro Martinez Jr. and Matthew Amie Nielsen, "Local Context and Determinants of Drug Violence in Miami and San Diego: Does Ethnicity and Immigration Matter?" *International Migration Review* 38 (2004): 131–157; Martin Killias, "The Opening and Closing of Breaches: A Theory on Crime Waves, Law Creation and Crime Prevention," *European Journal of Criminology* 3 (2006): 11–31; Matthew Miller, David Hemenway, and Deborah Azrael, "State-Level Homicide Victimization Rates in the U.S. in Relation to Survey Measures of Household Firearm Ownership, 2001–2003," *Social Science & Medicine* 64 (2007): 656–664; Alfred Blumstein, "The Crime Drop in America: An Exploration of Some Recent Crime Trends," *Journal of Scandinavian Studies in Criminology & Crime Prevention* 7 (2006): 17–35; Thomas Arvanites and Robert Defina, "Business Cycles and Street Crime," *Criminology* 44 (2006): 139–164; Fahui Wang, "Job Access and Homicide Patterns in Chicago: An Analysis at Multiple Geographic Levels Based on Scale-Space Theory," *Journal of Quantitative Criminology* 21 (2005): 195–217; John J. Donohue and Steven D. Levitt, "The Impact of Legalized Abortion on Crime," *The Quarterly Journal of Economics* 116 (2001): 379–420.

## FIGURE 2.4
**Crime in the United States by Region, Geographic Division, and State**

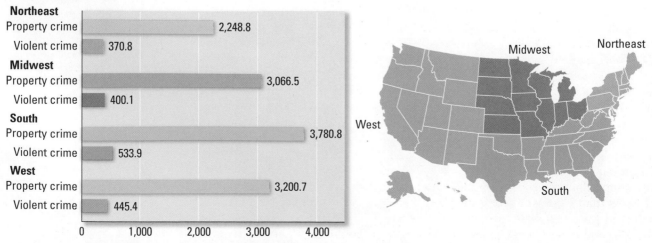

Source: FBI, *Crime in the United States, 2008,* www.fbi.gov/ucr/cius2008/offenses/standard_links/regional_estimates.html.

## Social Class, Socioeconomic Conditions, and Crime

It makes sense that crime is inherently a lower-class phenomenon. After all, people at the lowest rungs of the social structure have the greatest incentive to commit crimes, and those people who are undergoing financial difficulties are the ones most likely to become their targets.[79] It seems logical that people who are unable to obtain desired goods and services through conventional means may consequently resort to theft and other illegal activities—such as selling narcotics—to obtain them. These activities are referred to as **instrumental crimes**. Those living in poverty are also believed to engage in disproportionate amounts of **expressive crimes**, such as rape and assault, as a result of their rage, frustration, and anger against society. Alcohol and drug abuse, common in impoverished areas, help fuel violent episodes.[80]

Official statistics indicate that crime rates in inner-city, high-poverty areas are generally higher than those in suburban or wealthier areas.[81] Surveys of known criminals consistently show that prisoners were members of the lower class and unemployed or underemployed in the years before their incarceration. Income inequality, poverty, and resource deprivation are all associated with the most serious violent crimes, including homicide and assault.[82] Members of the lower class are more likely to suffer psychological abnormality, including high rates of anxiety and conduct disorders, conditions that may promote criminality.[83] Community-level indicators of poverty and disorder—deteriorated neighborhoods, lack of informal social control, income inequality, presence of youth gangs, and resource deprivation—are all associated with the most serious violent crimes, including homicide and assault.[84]

Contemporary research also shows that the association between poverty and crime may be a community-level rather than an individual-level phenomenon. That is, even though a particular individual who is poor may not commit crime, groups of people living in communities that lack economic and social opportunities are influenced by their neighborhood disadvantage.[85] These community conditions also produce high levels of frustration: Residents believe they are relatively more deprived than residents in more affluent areas and may then turn to criminal behavior to relieve their frustration.[86] Family life is disrupted, and law-violating youth groups thrive in a climate that undermines adult supervision.[87] Conversely, when the poor are provided with economic opportunities via welfare and public assistance, crime rates drop.[88]

**instrumental crimes**
Criminal acts intended to improve the financial or social position of the criminal.

**expressive crimes**
Criminal acts that serve to vent rage, anger, or frustration.

### PERSPECTIVES ON JUSTICE

#### Rehabilitation

Rehabilitation advocates believe that social class is correlated with crime and that programs emphasizing jobs, counseling, and opportunity—instead of punishment—are the key to reducing crime rates.

## Age and Crime

There is general agreement that age is inversely related to criminality.[89] Regardless of economic status, marital status, race, sex, and so on, younger people commit crime more often than their older peers. Official statistics tell us that young people are arrested at a rate disproportionate to their numbers in the population; victim surveys generate similar findings for crimes in which assailant age can be determined. Whereas youths under 18 make up about 6 percent of the total U.S. population, they account for about 25 percent of serious crime arrests and 17 percent of arrests for all crimes. As a general rule, the peak age for property crime is believed to be 16, and for violence, 18. In contrast, adults 45 and over, who make up about one-third of the population, account for only 7 percent of arrests for serious crime. The elderly are particularly resistant to the temptations of crime; they make up more than 14 percent of the population and less than 1 percent of arrests. Elderly males 65 and over are predominantly arrested for alcohol-related matters (such as public drunkenness and drunk driving) and elderly females for larceny (such as shoplifting). The elderly crime rate has remained stable for the past 20 years.[90]

## EVIDENCE-BASED JUSTICE

# Immigration and Crime

Some critics call for tough new laws limiting immigration and/or strictly enforcing immigration laws because they believe that immigrants are prone to crime and represent a social threat. How true are their perceptions? Not very true, according to the report "Crime, Corrections, and California: What Does Immigration Have to Do with It?" released by the Public Policy Institute of California. According to the data, immigrants are far less likely than the average U.S. native to commit crime. Significantly lower rates of incarceration and institutionalization among foreign-born adults suggest that long-standing fears that immigration is a threat to public safety are unjustified. Among the key findings:

■ People born outside the United States make up about 35 percent of California's adult population but represent about 17 percent of the state prison population.

■ U.S.-born adult men are incarcerated in state prisons at rates up to 3.3 times higher than foreign-born men.

■ Among men ages 18 to 40—the age group most likely to commit crime—those born in the United States are 10 times more likely than immigrants to be in county jail or state prison.

■ Noncitizen men from Mexico aged 18 to 40—a group disproportionately likely to have entered the United States illegally—are more than 8 times *less* likely than U.S.-born men in the same age group to be in a correctional setting (0.48% vs. 4.2%).

These findings are striking because immigrants in California are more likely than the U.S.-born to be young and male and to have low levels of education—all characteristics associated with higher rates of crime and incarceration. Yet the report shows that institutionalization rates of young male immigrants with less than a high school diploma are extremely low, particularly when compared with U.S.-born men with low levels of education.

The low rates of criminal involvement by immigrants may be due in part to current U.S. immigration policy, which screens immigrants for criminal history and assigns extra penalties to noncitizens who commit crimes.

Here we can see how data collection and analysis can be used to dispel a widespread, albeit erroneous, assumption about human behavior.

Source: Kristin F. Butcher and Anne Morrison Piehl, "Crime, Corrections, and California: What Does Immigration Have to Do with It?" Public Policy Institute of California, 2008, www.ppic.org/main/publication.asp?i=776.

Research shows that on average, kids who are persistent offenders begin committing crime in their childhood, rapidly increase their offending activities in late adolescence, and then begin a slowdown in adulthood. Early starters tend to commit more crime and are more likely to continue to be involved in criminality over a longer period of time.[91]

Why are kids more involved in crime than adults? One view relies on the special status of youth in contemporary society. Adolescents are impatient, and because their future is uncertain, they are unwilling or unable to delay gratification. Deviance in adolescence is fueled by the need for money and sex and is reinforced by close relationships with peers who defy conventional morality. At the same time, teenagers are becoming independent from parents and other adults who enforce conventional standards of morality and behavior. They have a new sense of energy and strength and are involved with peers who are similarly vigorous and frustrated.

In adulthood, people become better able to delay gratification and forgo the immediate gains that law violations bring. They also start wanting to take responsibility for their behavior and to adhere to conventional mores, such as establishing long-term relationships and starting a family. Getting married, raising a family, and creating long-term family ties provide the stability that helps people desist from crime.[92]

Another view ties the association between age and crime to biological traits. Young people are simply stronger and more vigorous than adults and better equipped to deal with the rigors of crime. Young men also possess more abundant levels of testosterone, the principal male steroid hormone that has been linked to aggression and violence. Hormone levels decline during the life cycle, which may explain why violence rates diminish over time.[93]

Aging out of crime, then, may be a function of the natural history of the human life cycle rather than due to a change in social circumstances.[94]

## Gender and Crime

Male crime rates are much higher than those of females. Victims report that their assailant was male in more than 80 percent of all violent personal crimes. The most recent Uniform Crime Report arrest statistics indicate that males account for more than 80 percent of all arrests for serious violent crimes and almost 70 percent of the arrests for serious property crimes. Murder arrests are 8 males to 1 female. Even though gender differences in the crime rate have persisted over time, there seems little question that females are now involved in more crime than ever before and that there are more similarities than differences between male and female offenders.[95] UCR arrest data shows that over the past decade, while male arrest rates have declined by 9 percent, female arrest rates have increased by 9 percent. Most notable have been increased female arrests for serious crimes such as robbery (up 10 percent) and burglary (up 15 percent). Thus, during a period of slowing overall growth in crime rates, women have increased their participation in crime. How can these differences be explained?

## Explaining Gender Differences in the Crime Rate

Early criminologists pointed to emotional, physical, and psychological differences between males and females to explain the differences in crime rates: Men are physically and emotionally stronger and better equipped to commit crimes. Another early view of female crime focused on the supposed dynamics of sexual relationships. Female criminals were viewed as either sexually controlling or sexually naive, either manipulating men for profit or being manipulated by them. The female's criminality was often masked because criminal justice authorities were reluctant to take action against a woman.[96]

Although these early writings are no longer taken seriously, some experts still believe that gender-based traits are a key determinant of crime rate differences. Among the suspected differences are physical strength and hormonal influences. According to this view, male sex hormones (androgens) account for more aggressive male behavior, and gender-related hormonal differences explain the gender gap in the crime rate.[97]

***SOCIALIZATION AND DEVELOPMENT*** Another view is that, unlike boys, a majority of young girls are socialized to avoid being violent and aggressive and are supervised more closely by parents. It comes as no surprise when research shows that most girls develop moral values that strongly discourage antisocial behavior.[98] The few female criminals are troubled individuals, alienated at home, who pursue crime as a means of compensating for their disrupted personal lives.[99] The streets are a second home to girls whose emotional adjustment was hampered by a strained home life marked by such conditions as absent fathers and overly competitive mothers.

Delinquent girls sent to adult prisons had troubled lives that set them on a criminal career path.[100] In contrast, girls who are able to turn their lives around, who become mothers themselves and

*Robyn Ramsey, 25, is arrested after a police chase in Lancaster, California. Ramsey, detained in a car theft case, stole a sheriff's sport utility vehicle and led deputies on a two-hour pursuit through the Antelope Valley before being captured. Bonnie Ramsey, Robyn's mother, said her daughter had been addicted to methamphetamine but was trying to recover. Some experts say hormonal differences explain the gender gap in the crime rate, but when either males or females take drugs, their decision-making skills are impaired, and more crime ensues.*

© Associated Press/AP Photo/Antelope Valley Press/Kelly Lacefield take on the responsibility of child care, are able to forgo a life filled with delinquency and substance abuse.[101]

Some experts explain these differences in socialization by pointing to gender-based differences in human development that help shape behavior choices. Girls are believed to have cognitive traits that shield them from criminal behaviors.

**COGNITIVE DIFFERENCES**  Psychologists note significant cognitive differences between boys and girls that may affect their antisocial behaviors. Girls have been found to be superior to boys in verbal ability, while boys test higher in visual-spatial performance. Girls acquire language faster, learning to speak earlier and with better pronunciation. Girls are far less likely to have reading problems than boys, whereas boys do much better on standardized math tests. (This difference is attributed by some experts to boys receiving more attention from math teachers.) In most cases these cognitive differences are small, are narrowing, and are usually attributed to cultural expectations. Their superior verbal skills may enable girls to talk rather than fight. When faced with conflict, women might be more likely to try negotiating rather than either responding passively or resisting physically, especially when they perceive an increased threat of harm or death.[102]

**FEMINIST VIEWS**  In the 1970s, feminists focused attention on the social and economic role of women in society and its relationship to female crime rates.[103] **Liberal feminist theory** suggested that the traditionally lower crime rate for women could be explained by their second-class economic and social position. It was believed that as women's social roles changed and their lifestyles became more like those of males, the crime rates for the genders would converge.

Crime experts, responding to this research, began to refer to the "new female criminal." The rapid increase in the female crime rate during the 1960s and 1970s, especially in what had traditionally been male-oriented crimes (such as burglary and larceny), supported the feminist view. In addition, self-report studies seem to indicate that the pattern of female criminality, if not its frequency, is similar to that of male criminality and that the factors predisposing male criminals to crime have an equal impact on female criminals.[104] Crime experts began to assess the association among economic issues, gender roles, and criminality.

**IS CONVERGENCE LIKELY?**  In sum, gender differences in the crime rate have been explained by such statements as these:

- Males are stronger and better able to commit violent crime.
- Hormonal differences make males more aggressive.
- Girls are socialized to be less aggressive than boys.[105]
- Girls have better verbal skills and use them to diffuse conflict.
- Boys are granted greater personal freedom; girls are subject to greater parental control.

Will the gender differences in the crime rate eventually dissolve? Some crime experts find that gender-based crime rate differences remain significant and argue that the emancipation of women has had relatively little influence on female crime rates.[106] They dispute the idea that increases in the female arrest rate reflect economic or social change brought about by the women's movement. For one thing, many female criminals come from the socioeconomic class least affected by the women's movement. Their crimes seem more a function of economic inequality than of women's rights. For another, the offense patterns of women are still quite different from those of men, who commit a disproportionate share of serious crimes, such as robbery, burglary, murder, and assault.[107] According to Darrell Steffensmeier and his associates, recent trends may be explained more by changes in police activity than in criminal activity: Police today may be more willing to arrest girls for crimes.[108] Police may be abandoning

**liberal feminist theory**
An ideology holding that women suffer oppression, discrimination, and disadvantage as a result of their sex and calling for gender equality in pay, opportunity, child care, and education.

their traditional deference toward women in an effort to be "gender neutral." In addition, new laws such as dual arrest laws in domestic cases, which mandate that both parties be taken into custody, result in more women suffering arrest in domestic incidents.[109] Whether male and female crime rates will eventually converge remains to be seen.

## Race and Crime

Official crime data indicates that minority group members are involved in a disproportionate share of criminal activity. African Americans make up about 12 percent of the general population, yet they account for about 38 percent of arrests for Part I violent crime and for 30 percent of property crime arrests. They also are responsible for a disproportionate number of Part II arrests (except for alcohol-related arrests, which involve primarily white offenders).

It is possible that this data reflects true racial differences in the crime rate, but it is also likely that bias in the justice process plays a part. We can evaluate this issue by comparing racial differences in self-report data with those found in official delinquency records. Charges of racial discrimination in the justice process would be substantiated if whites and blacks self-reported equal numbers of crimes but minorities were arrested and prosecuted far more often. Self-report studies such as the MTF survey, for example, generally show similarity in offending differences between African American and European American youths for most crimes, but for some serious offenses, such as stealing more than $50 (13% vs. 7%) and using a weapon to steal (7% vs. 2%), African American youths do in fact admit more offending than white youths (a finding that is reflective of the UCR arrest data.[110] How can the disproportionate number of African American youngsters arrested for serious crimes be explained?

*SYSTEM BIAS* Some critics charge that race-based differences in the crime rate can be explained by unequal treatment by the justice system. According to what is known as the **"racial threat hypothesis,"** as the percentage of minorities in the population increases, so does the amount of social control that police direct at minority group members.[111] Police are more likely to aggressively patrol minority neighborhoods; to suspect, search, and arrest minority group members; and to make arrests for minor infractions among members of these groups, thus helping to raise the minority crime rate.[112] For example, as Malcolm Holmes and his colleagues found, in southwestern border communities, police maintain order and reinforce the physical and social isolation of the barrio. As the numbers of poor Hispanics increase, affluent Anglos may mobilize politically to demand greater levels of police protection.[113] When politicians use veiled hints of racial threat in their political campaigns, the result is efforts to control and punish minority citizens.[114]

The "racial threat" effect does not end with the police, nor does system bias. As the percentage of minorities in a state jurisdiction increases, so does the use of draconian sentencing practices. As they are processed through the system, minority group members, especially those who are indigent or unemployed, continue to receive disparate treatment. Black and Latino adults are less likely than whites to be offered the opportunity to post bail in violent crime cases and consequently are more likely to be kept in detention pending trial.[115] They also receive longer prison sentences than whites who commit similar crimes and have similar criminal histories. Take, for instance, the use of habitual offender statutes that provide very long sentences for a second or third conviction ("three strikes and you're out"). A recent study by Matthew Crow and Kathrine Johnson looked at the use of habitual sentencing practices in Florida and concluded that race and ethnicity still matter: Minority drug and violent offenders are viewed as particular threats to dominant, mainstream values and are more likely to be charged as habitual offenders than are European Americans.[116] Nor is this solely a state court problem. After reviewing sentences in the federal court system,

**racial threat hypothesis**
The view that young minority males are subject to greater police control—for example, formal arrest—when their numbers increase within the population.

Jill Doerner and Stephen Demuth found that particularly harsh punishments are focused disproportionately on the youngest Hispanic and black male defendants: Young Hispanic male defendants have the highest odds of incarceration, and young black male defendants receive the longest sentences.[117] Yet when African Americans are victims of crime, their predicaments draw less public concern and media attention than are afforded white victims.[118] Murderers of whites (and females) are much more likely to be punished with death than those whose victims are black males, a fact not lost on the minority population.[119]

*CULTURAL BIAS*  Another explanation of racial differences in the crime rate rests on the effects of the legacy of racial discrimination on personality and behavior.[120] The fact that U.S. culture influences African American crime rates is underscored by the fact that black violence rates are much lower in other nations—both those that are predominantly white, such as Canada, and those that are predominantly black, such as Nigeria.[121]

Some criminologists view black crime as a function of socialization in a society where the black family was torn apart and black culture destroyed in such a way that recovery has proved impossible. Early experiences, beginning with slavery, have left a wound that has been deepened by racism and lack of opportunity.[122] Children of the slave society were thrust into a system of forced dependency and ambivalence and antagonism toward one's self and one's group.

In an important work, *All God's Children: The Bosket Family and the American Tradition of Violence*, crime reporter Fox Butterfield chronicles the history of the Boskets, a black family, through five generations.[123] He focuses on Willie Bosket, who is charming, captivating, and brilliant. He is also one of the worst criminals in the New York State penal system. By the time he was in his teens, he had committed more than 200 armed robberies and 25 stabbings. Butterfield shows how the early struggles in the South, with its violent slave culture, led directly to Willie Bosket's rage and violence on the streets of New York City. Beginning in South Carolina in the 1700s, the Southern slave society was a place where white notions of honor demanded immediate retaliation for the smallest slight. According to Butterfield, contemporary black violence is a tradition inherited from white Southern violence. The need for respect has turned into a cultural mandate that can provoke retaliation at the slightest hint of insult.

*STRUCTURAL BIAS*  A third view is that racial differences in the crime rate are a function of disparity in the social and economic structure of society. William Julius Wilson, one of the nation's most prominent sociologists, provided a description of the plight of the lowest levels of the underclass, which he labeled the truly disadvantaged, most often minority group members who dwell in urban inner cities, occupy the bottom rung of the social ladder, and are the victims of discrimination. Because the truly disadvantaged rarely come into contact with the actual source of their oppression, they direct their anger and aggression at those with whom they are in close contact, such as neighbors, businesspeople,

U.S. President Barack Obama serves lunch to the homeless and disadvantaged at So Others Might Eat, a soup kitchen in northwest Washington, on Martin Luther King Day, January 18, 2010. There is a link between social structure and crime, so efforts to reduce the effects of poverty may result in a reduced crime rate.

© Luke Sharrett/New York Times/Redux

and landlords. Plagued by underemployment or unemployment, they begin to lose self-confidence, a feeling exacerbated by the plight of kin and friendship groups who also experience extreme economic marginality. Self-doubt is a neighborhood norm that threatens to overwhelm those forced to live in areas of concentrated poverty. Wilson argued that for the first time in the twentieth century, most adults in inner-city ghetto neighborhoods were not working during a typical week. He found that inner-city life was only marginally affected by the surge in the nation's economy brought about by new industrial growth connected with technological development. Poverty in these inner-city areas is pervasive and unchanging—if anything, it is steadily worsening as residents are further shut out of the economic mainstream.

Wilson focuses on the plight of the African American community, which had enjoyed periods of relative prosperity in the 1950s and 1960s. He suggests that as difficult as life was for African Americans in the 1940s and 1950s, they at least had a reasonable hope of steady work. Now, because of the globalization of the economy, those opportunities have evaporated. In the past, growth in the manufacturing sector fueled upward mobility and lay the foundation for today's African American middle class. Those opportunities no longer exist, because manufacturing plants have been moved to inaccessible rural and overseas locations where the cost of doing business is lower. With manufacturing opportunities all but obsolete in the United States, service and retail establishments that depended on blue-collar spending have similarly disappeared, leaving behind an economy based on welfare and government supports. In less than 20 years, formerly active African American neighborhoods have become crime-infested inner-city ghettos.

In his most recent work, *More than Just Race: Being Black and Poor in the Inner City*, Wilson tries to explain the persistence of poverty in black neighborhoods: He finds that both culture and structure play a role in crime. For example, a law and order political philosophy and fear of racial conflict have led to high incarceration rates among African American males. Black women can get jobs in services industries, but employers are less likely to hire black men, especially those with a criminal record. As a result, there has been a decline in the ability of black men to be providers, further undermining the stability of the African American family. Here we can see how structure and culture intertwine to produce stress in the African American community.[124]

*IS CONVERGENCE POSSIBLE?* Considering these overwhelming social problems, is it possible that racial crime rates will soon converge? One argument is that if economic conditions improve in the minority community, then differences in crime rates will eventually disappear.[125] A trend toward residential integration, under way since 1980, may also help reduce crime rate differentials.[126] Convergence in crime rates will occur if economic and social obstacles can be removed.

In sum, the weight of the evidence shows that although there is little difference in the self-reported crime rates of racial groups, Hispanics and African Americans are more likely to be arrested for serious violent crimes. The causes of minority crime have been linked to poverty, racism, hopelessness, lack of opportunity, and urban problems experienced by all too many minority group citizens.

## Chronic Offending and Crime

Crime data shows that most offenders commit a single criminal act and, upon arrest, discontinue their antisocial activity. Others commit a few less serious crimes. A small group of criminal offenders, however, account for a majority of all criminal offenses. These persistent offenders are referred to as **career criminals** or **chronic offenders**. The concept of the chronic or career offender is most closely associated with the research efforts of Marvin Wolfgang, Robert Figlio, and Thorsten Sellin.[127] In their landmark 1972 study *Delinquency in a Birth Cohort*, they used official records to follow the criminal careers of a

**career criminals**
Persistent repeat offenders who organize their lifestyle around criminality.

**chronic offenders**
As defined by Marvin Wolfgang, Robert Figlio, and Thorsten Sellin, delinquents arrested five or more times before the age of 18, who commit a disproportionate amount of all criminal offenses.

**FIGURE 2.5**
**Distribution of Offenses in the Philadelphia Cohort**

Source: Marvin Wolfgang, Robert Figlio, and Thorsten Sellin, *Delinquency in a Birth Cohort* (Chicago: University of Chicago Press, 1972).

*Career criminals are responsible for a significant portion of the total crime rate. Here, George Hyatte appears in a courtroom for an extradition hearing in Columbus, Ohio. George and his wife, Jennifer Hyatte, were arrested at the America's Best Value Inn in Columbus after a cab driver tipped off authorities that he had driven them there. Hyatte, a career-criminal inmate serving a 41-year sentence for robbery and related charges, killed a guard in the course of a daring escape attempt—a crime that might bring him the death penalty.*

cohort of 9,945 boys born in Philadelphia in 1945 from the time of their birth until they reached 18 years of age in 1963. Official police records were used to identify delinquents. About one-third of the boys (3,475) had some police contact. The remaining two-thirds (6,470) had none. Each delinquent was given a seriousness weight score for every delinquent act.[128] The weighting of delinquent acts enabled the researchers to differentiate between a simple assault requiring no medical attention for the victim and serious battery in which the victim needed hospitalization. The best-known discovery of Wolfgang and his associates was that of the so-called chronic offender. The cohort data indicated that 54 percent (1,862) of the sample's delinquent youths were repeat offenders, whereas the remaining 46 percent (1,613) were one-time offenders. The repeaters could be further categorized as nonchronic recidivists and chronic recidivists. The former consisted of 1,235 youths who had been arrested more than once but fewer than five times and who made up 35.6 percent of all delinquents. The latter were a group of 627 boys arrested five times or more, who accounted for 18 percent of the delinquents and 6 percent of the total sample of 9,945. (See Figure 2.5.)

The chronic offenders (known today as "the chronic 6 percent") were involved in the most dramatic amounts of delinquent behavior. They were responsible for 5,305 offenses, or 51.9 percent of all the offenses committed by the cohort. Even more striking was the involvement of chronic offenders in serious criminal acts. Of the entire sample, the chronic 6 percent committed 71 percent of the homicides, 73 percent of the rapes, 82 percent of the robberies, and 69 percent of the aggravated assaults.

Wolfgang and his associates found that arrests and court experience did little to deter the chronic offender. In fact, punishment was inversely related to chronic offending: The more stringent the sanction that chronic offenders received, the more likely they would be to engage in repeated criminal behavior.

In a second cohort study, Wolfgang and his associates selected a new, larger birth cohort, born in Philadelphia in 1958, which contained both male and female subjects.[129] Although the proportion of delinquent youths was about the same as that in the 1945 cohort, they again found a similar pattern of chronic offending. Chronic female delinquency was relatively rare—only 1 percent of the females in the survey were chronic offenders. Wolfgang's pioneering effort to identify the chronic career offender has been replicated by a number of other researchers in a variety of locations in the United States.[130] The chronic offender has also been found abroad.[131]

*WHAT CAUSES CHRONICITY?*  As might be expected, kids who have been exposed to a variety of personal and social problems at an early age—a concept referred to as **early onset**—are the most at risk to repeat offending. One important study of delinquent offenders in Orange County, California, conducted by Michael Schumacher and Gwen Kurz, found several factors that characterized the chronic offender, including problems in the home and at school.[132] Other research studies have found that involvement in criminal activity (getting arrested before age 15), relatively low intellectual development, and parental drug involvement were key predictive factors for chronicity.[133] Offenders who accumulate large debts, use drugs, and resort to violence are more likely to persist in crime.[134] In contrast, those who spend time in a juvenile facility and later in an adult prison are more likely to desist.[135]

**early onset**
The principle or fact that kids who have been exposed to a variety of personal and social problems at an early age are the most at risk to repeat offending.

**three-strikes laws**
Sentencing codes that require that an offender receive a life sentence after conviction for a third felony. Some states allow parole after a lengthy prison stay—for example, 25 years.

*POLICY IMPLICATIONS*  The chronic offender has become a central focus of crime control policy. Apprehension and punishment seem to have little effect on the offending behavior of chronic offenders, and most repeat their criminal acts after their release from a correctional facility.[136] Because chronic offenders rarely learn from their mistakes, sentencing policies designed to incapacitate chronic offenders for long periods of time, without hope of probation or parole, have been established. Incapacitation rather than rehabilitation is the goal. Among the policies spurred by the chronic offender concept are mandatory sentences for violent or drug-related crimes; **three-strikes laws**, which require people convicted of a third felony offense to serve a mandatory life sentence; and **truth-in-sentencing laws**, which require that convicted felons spend a significant portion of their sentence behind bars. Whether such policies can reduce crime rates or are merely get-tough measures designed to placate conservative voters remains to be seen.

## PERSPECTIVES ON JUSTICE

### Crime Control

The discovery of the chronic offender was a key element in the development of sentences that provide extended terms for repeat offenders. It stands to reason that if only a few hard-core offenders commit most crimes, locking them up for life can have a dramatic effect on the crime rate. This is a cornerstone of the crime control model.

**truth-in-sentencing laws**
Laws requiring convicted felons to spend a significant portion of their sentence behind bars.

## Ethical Challenges in Criminal Justice: A Writing Assignment

Critics complain that kids watch too much violent TV and that media violence is a cause of juvenile crime. How would you address their claims? Write an essay on the factors that influence crime rates. You may want to refer to the Analyzing Criminal Justice Issues feature titled "Explaining Trends in Crime Rates" before you answer. In your essay, you might want to provide alternative explanations for the factors associated with juvenile crime.

# SUMMARY

## 1. Be able to discuss how crime is defined.

- There are three views on how behaviors become crimes: the consensus, conflict, and interactionist views.

- The consensus view holds that criminal behavior is defined by laws that reflect the values and morals of a majority of citizens. The conflict view states that criminal behavior is defined in such a way that economically powerful groups can retain their control over society. The interactionist view portrays criminal behavior as a relativistic, constantly changing concept that reflects society's current moral values.

## 2. Define and discuss some of the different types of crime.

- Violent crimes involve acts ranging from mass murder to child abuse.

- Public order crimes involve acts that interfere with how society operates and functions. Such crimes as prostitution and drug trafficking are criminalized because those who shape the law believe that they conflict with social norms, prevailing moral rules, and current public opinion.

- Millions of property- and theft-related crimes occur each year, ranging from simple theft, such as larceny, to complex white-collar frauds and schemes.

## 3. Be familiar with the methods used to measure crime.

- One of the most important sources is the Uniform Crime Report (UCR) compiled by the FBI. This national survey compiles criminal acts reported to local police. The acts called Part I crimes are murder, rape, burglary, robbery, assault, larceny-theft, and motor vehicle theft.

- The federal government also sponsors the National Crime Victimization Survey (NCVS), which asks people about their experiences with crime.

- A third form of information is self-report surveys, which ask offenders themselves to tell about their criminal behaviors.

## 4. Discuss the development of the NIBRS program.

- The National Incident-Based Reporting System (NIBRS) is a program that collects data on each reported crime incident.

- This program requires local police agencies to provide at least a brief account of each incident and arrest, including the incident, victim, and offender information.

- Thus far, more than 20 states have implemented their NIBRS programs, and 12 others are in the process of finalizing their data collection.

## 5. Be able to discuss the strengths and weaknesses of various measures of crime.

- The validity of the UCR has been suspect because many people fail to report crime to police as a consequence of fear, apathy, or lack of respect for law enforcement.

- Many crime victims do not report criminal incidents to the police because they believe that nothing can be done or that they should not expose themselves to further risk.

- Self-reports depend on the accuracy of respondents, many of whom are drug users or delinquent.

## 6. Recognize the trends in the crime rate.

- Crime rates were high in the 1930s, declined afterward, and then began a rapid increase in the 1960s.

- Crime rates have been in a downward trend for about a decade.

- The violent crime rate has been in decline but shows signs of a recent uptrend.

## 7. Comment on the factors that influence crime rates.

- Changes in the crime rate have been attributed to social factors, including the age structure of society. Increases in the crime rate have been tied to drug epidemics.

- The effect of the economy on crime rates is less certain.

- Criminal justice policy seems to influence crime rates.

## 8. Be familiar with trends in crime in other cultures.

- Crime rates were traditionally higher in the United States than abroad.

- In recent years, crime rates have been climbing overseas while declining in the United States.

- Crime rates may be spiraling upward in nations undergoing rapid changes in their social and economic makeup.

## 9. Know the various crime patterns.

- Crime occurs more often in large cities during the summer and at night. Some geographical areas (the South and West) have higher crime rates than others (the Midwest and New England).

■ Arrest data indicate that males, minorities, the poor, and the young have relatively high rates of criminality.

■ Victims of crime tend to be poor, young, male, and members of a minority group.

**10. Understand the concept of the criminal career.**

■ One of the most important findings in the crime statistics is the existence of the chronic offender.

■ Repeat, career criminals are responsible for a significant amount of all law violations.

■ Career criminals begin their careers early in life and, instead of aging out of crime, persist in their criminal behavior into adulthood.

## KEY TERMS

consensus view of crime, 44
conflict view of crime, 45
interactionist view of crime, 45
moral entrepreneurs, 45
crime, 46
expressive violence, 47
instrumental violence, 47
mass murderer, 47
spree killer, 47
serial killer, 47
hate crimes (bias crimes), 48

public order crimes, 49
white-collar crime, 51
corporate crime, 51
Uniform Crime Report (UCR), 53
Part I crimes, 54
Part II crimes, 54
cleared, 55
National Incident-Based Reporting System (NIBRS), 57
National Crime Victimization Survey (NCVS), 58

self-report survey, 59
instrumental crimes, 73
expressive crimes, 73
liberal feminist theory, 76
racial threat hypothesis, 77
career criminals, 79
chronic offenders, 79
early onset, 81
three-strikes law, 81
truth-in-sentencing laws, 81

## CRITICAL THINKING QUESTIONS

1. Would you answer honestly if a national crime survey asked you about your criminal behavior, including drinking and drug use? If not, why not? If you answered no, do you question the accuracy of self-report surveys?

2. How would you explain gender differences in the crime rate? Do you think males are more violent than females? Why?

3. Assuming that males are more violent than females, does this mean that crime has a biological rather than a social basis (because males and females share a similar environment)?

4. The UCR states that crime rates are higher in large cities than in small towns. What does that say about

the effects of TV, films, and music on teenagers' behavior?

5. What social and environmental factors do you believe influence the crime rate? For example, do you think a national emergency such as the September 11, 2001, terrorist attacks would increase or decrease crime rates or have relatively little effect or influence?

6. If the characteristics of chronic offenders could be determined, should people with those traits be monitored from birth?

## NOTES

1. Shelley Murphy, Donovan Slack, and Meghan Irons, "Ala. Suspect Was Questioned in Bomb Case, Officials Thought Woman May Have Had Motive to Target Newton Doctor in 1993, *Boston Globe*, February 15, 2010, www.boston.com/news/local/massachusetts/articles/2010/02/15/more_questions_on_professor_held_in_ala/.

2. Mirka Smolej and Janne Kivivuori, "The Relation between Crime News and Fear of Violence," *Journal of Scandinavian Studies in Criminology & Crime Prevention* 7 (2006): 211–227.

3. The Gallup Organization, Inc., *The Gallup Poll,* www.gallup.com/poll/1603/Crime.aspx (accessed December 16, 2009).

4. Data provided by the *Sourcebook of Criminal Justice Statistics*, Hindelang Criminal Justice Research Center, University at Albany, 2010, www.albany.edu/sourcebook/pdf/t2402007.pdf.

5. Federal Bureau of Investigation, *Crime in the United States, 2009* (Washington, D.C.: U.S. Government Printing Office, 2010), www.fbi.gov/ucr/cius2009/index.html. Herein cited in notes as FBI, *Uniform Crime Report* and referred to in text as Uniform Crime Report or UCR. When possible, data has been updated with 2009 preliminary results.

6. Basil Katz, "Former NY Police Commissioner Sentenced to Prison," Reuters, February 18, 2010, www.reuters.com/article/idUSTRE61H5EU20100218.

7. For a general discussion of Marxist thought on criminal law, see Michael Lynch, Raymond Michalowski, and W. Byron Groves, *The New Primer in Radical Criminology: Critical Perspectives on Crime, Power, and Identity*, 3rd ed. (Monsey, N.Y.: Criminal Justice Press, 2000).

8. The National Council on Alcoholism and Drug Dependence, www.ncadd.org (accessed May 18, 2005).

9. Gary Bailey and N. Prabha Unnithan, "Gang Homicides in California: A Discriminant Analysis," *Journal of Criminal Justice* 22 (1994): 267–275.

10. Arlen Egley Jr., and Christina O'Donnell, *Highlights of the 2007 National Youth Gang Survey* (Washington, D.C.: U.S. Department of Justice, Office of Juvenile Justice and Delinquency Prevention, 2009).

11. National Youth Gang Center, *National Youth Gang Survey Analysis*, www.nationalgangcenter.gov/Survey-Analysis (accessed December 23, 2009).

12. Ian Urbina and Manny Fernardez, "Memorial Services Held in U.S. and around World," *New York Times*, April 21, 2007.

13. Raymond Hernandez, "A Friend, a 'Good Listener,' and a Victim in a Day of Tragedy," *New York Times*, April 17, 2007.

14. Abbie Boudreau and Scott Zamost, "Girlfriend: Shooter Was Taking Cocktail of 3 Drugs," CNN. February 20, 2008 (accessed February 25, 2008) www.cnn.com/2008/CRIME/02/20/shooter. girlfriend/.

15. James Alan Fox and Jack Levin, "Multiple Homicide: Patterns of Serial and Mass Murder," in *Crime and Justice: An Annual Edition*, vol. 23, ed. Michael Tonry (Chicago: University of Chicago Press, 1998), pp. 407–455.

16. Ibid.

17. Data in this section comes from U.S. Department of Health and Human Services, Administration for Children and Families, *Child Maltreatment, 2007*, www.acf.hhs.gov/programs/cb/pubs/cm07/cm07.pdf (accessed December 22, 2009).

18. Richard Estes and Neil Alan Weiner, *The Commercial Sexual Exploitation of Children in the U.S., Canada and Mexico* (Philadelphia: University of Pennsylvania, 2001).

19. Joseph Price and Kathy Glad, "Hostile Attributional Tendencies in Maltreated Children," *Journal of Abnormal Child Psychology* 31 (2003): 329–344.

20. James Garofalo, "Bias and Non-Bias Crimes in New York City: Preliminary Findings." Paper presented at the annual meeting of the American Society of Criminology, Baltimore, November 1990.

21. "Boy Gets 18 Years in Fatal Park Beating of Transient," *Los Angeles Times*, December 24, 1987, p. 9B.

22. FBI, *Hate Crime Statistics, 2008*, www.fbi.gov/ucr/hc2008/incidents.html (accessed February 3, 2010).

23. Scott Shuger, "Hookers.com: How e-Commerce Is Transforming the Oldest Profession," *Slate Magazine*, www.slate.com/id/73797/ (accessed April 15, 2009).

24. The annual survey is conducted by Lloyd Johnston, Jerald Bachman, Patrick O'Malley, and John Schulenberg of the Institute of Social Research, University of Michigan, Ann Arbor, www.monitoringthefuture.org/pubs/monographs/overview2008.pdf

25. Monitoring the Future, "2008 Data from In-School Surveys of 8th-, 10th-, and 12th-Grade Students," www.monitoringthefuture.org/data/08data.html#2008data-drugs.

26. Department of Health and Human Services, "Results from the 2007 National Survey on Drug Use and Health: National Findings," www.oas.samhsa.gov/nsduh/2k7nsduh/2k7Results.cfm#TOC (accessed April 20, 2009).

27. Ruth Engs and David Hanson, "Boozing and Brawling on Campus: A National Study of Violent Problems Associated with Drinking over the Past Decade," *Journal of Criminal Justice* 22 (1994): 171–180.

28. Robert Nash Parker, "Bringing 'Booze' Back In: The Relationship between Alcohol and Homicide," *Journal of Research in Crime and Delinquency* 32 (1993): 3–38.

29. Evelyn Wei, Rolf Loeber, and Helene White, "Teasing Apart the Developmental Associations between Alcohol and Marijuana Use and Violence," *Journal of Contemporary Criminal Justice* 20 (2004): 166–183.

30. Susan Martin, Christopher Maxwell, Helene White, and Yan Zhang, "Trends in Alcohol Use, Cocaine Use, and Crime," *Journal of Drug Issues* 34 (2004): 333–360.

31. John Hepburn, "Occasional Criminals," in *Major Forms of Crime*, ed. Robert Meier (Beverly Hills: Sage, 1984), pp. 73–94.

32. James Inciardi, "Professional Crime," in *Major Forms of Crime*, ed. Robert Meier (Beverly Hills: Sage, 1984), p. 223.

33. See, generally, Jay Albanese, *Organized Crime in America*, 2d ed. (Cincinnati, Ohio: Anderson, 1989), p. 68.

34. James O. Finckenauer and Yuri A. Voronin, *The Threat of Russian Organized Crime* (Washington, D.C.: National Institute of Justice, 2001).

35. FBI, *Crime in the United States, 2008*.

36. Richard Felson, Steven Messner, Anthony Hoskin, and Glenn Deane, "Reasons for Reporting and Not Reporting Domestic Violence to the Police," *Criminology* 40 (2002): 617–648.

37. Shannan Catalano, *Criminal Victimization 2003* (Washington, D.C.: Bureau of Justice Statistics, 2004). Herein cited as NCVS, 2003.

38. Eric Baumer and Janet Lauritsen, "Reporting Crime to the Police, 1973–2005: A Multivariate Analysis of Long-term Trends in the National Crime Survey (NCS) and National Crime Victimization Survey (NCVS), *Criminology* 48 (2010): forthcoming.

39. Duncan Chappell, Gilbert Geis, Stephen Schafer, and Larry Siegel, "Forcible Rape: A Comparative Study of Offenses Known to the Police in Boston and Los Angeles," in *Studies in the Sociology of Sex*, ed. James Henslin (New York: Appleton Century Crofts, 1971), pp. 169–193.

40. Patrick Jackson, "Assessing the Validity of Official Data on Arson," *Criminology* 26 (1988): 181–195.

41. Lawrence Sherman and Barry Glick, "The Quality of Arrest Statistics," *Police Foundation Reports* 2 (1984): 1–8.

42. David Seidman and Michael Couzens, "Getting the Crime Rate Down: Political Pressure and Crime Reporting," *Law and Society Review* 8 (1974): 457.

43. Robert Davis and Bruce Taylor, "A Proactive Response to Family Violence: The Results of a Randomized Experiment," *Criminology* 35 (1997): 307–333.

44. Robert O'Brien, "Police Productivity and Crime Rates: 1973–1992," *Criminology* 34 (1996): 183–207.

45. Leonard Savitz, "Official Statistics," in *Contemporary Criminology*, ed. Leonard Savitz and Norman Johnston (New York: Wiley, 1982), pp. 3–15.

46. FBI, *UCR Handbook* (Washington, D.C.: U.S. Government Printing Office, 1998), p. 33.

47. Bureau of Justice Statistics, "About Incident-Based Statistics and the National Incident-Based Reporting System (NIBRS)," www.ojp.usdoj.gov/bjs/ibrs.htm (accessed April 1, 2008).

48. Lynn Addington, "The Effect of NIBRS Reporting on Item Missing Data in Murder Cases," *Homicide Studies* 8 (2004): 193–213.

49. Bureau of Justice Statistics, "The Nation's Two Crime Measures," www.ojp.usdoj.gov/bjs/pub/html/ntcm.htm.

50. Michael Rand, *Criminal Victimization, 2008* (Washington, D.C.: Bureau of Justice Statistics, 2009), www.ojp.usdoj.gov/bjs/pub/pdf/cv08.pdf.

51. Michael Rand and Shannan Catalano, *Criminal Victimization, 2006* (Washington, D.C.: Bureau of Justice Statistics, 2007), www.ojp.usdoj.gov/bjs/pub/pdf/cv06.pdf.

52. Lynn A. Addington and Callie Marie Rennison, "Rape Co-occurrence: Do Additional Crimes Affect Victim Reporting and Police Clearance of Rape?" *Journal of Quantitative Criminology* 24 (2008): 205–226.

53. L. Edward Wells and Joseph Rankin, "Juvenile Victimization: Convergent Validation of Alternative Measurements," *Journal of Research in Crime and Delinquency* 32 (1995): 287–307.

54. Robert M. Groves and Daniel L. Cork, "Surveying Victims: Options for Conducting the National Crime Victimization Survey"

(Washington, D.C.: National Research Council, 2008), www.nap.edu/catalog/12090.html.

55. Saul Kassin, Richard Leo, Christian Meissner, Kimberly Richman, Lori Colwell, Amy-May Leach, and Dana La Fon, "Police Interviewing and Interrogation: A Self-Report Survey of Police Practices and Beliefs," *Law and Human Behavior* 31 (2007): 381–400.

56. Christiane Brems, Mark Johnson, David Neal, and Melinda Freemon, "Childhood Abuse History and Substance Use among Men and Women Receiving Detoxification Services," *American Journal of Drug & Alcohol Abuse* 30 (2004): 799–821.

57. Lloyd Johnston, Patrick O'Malley, and Jerald Bachman, *Monitoring the Future, 2009* (Ann Arbor, Mich.: Institute for Social Research, 2009).

58. D. Wayne Osgood, Lloyd Johnston, Patrick O'Malley, and Jerald Bachman, "The Generality of Deviance in Late Adolescence and Early Adulthood," *American Sociological Review* 53 (1988): 81–93.

59. Leonore Simon, "Validity and Reliability of Violent Juveniles: A Comparison of Juvenile Self-Reports with Adult Self-Reports Incarcerated in Adult Prisons." Paper presented at the annual meeting of the American Society of Criminology, Boston, November 1995, p. 26.

60. Stephen Cernkovich, Peggy Giordano, and Meredith Pugh, "Chronic Offenders: The Missing Cases in Self-Report Delinquency Research," *Journal of Criminal Law and Criminology* 76 (1985): 705–732.

61. Terence Thornberry, Beth Bjerregaard, and William Miles, "The Consequences of Respondent Attrition in Panel Studies: A Simulation Based on the Rochester Youth Development Study," *Journal of Quantitative Criminology* 9 (1993): 127–158.

62. Julia Yun Soo Kim, Michael Fendrich, and Joseph S. Wislar, "The Validity of Juvenile Arrestees' Drug Use Reporting: A Gender Comparison," *Journal of Research in Crime and Delinquency* 37 (2000): 419–432; Donald Tomaskovic-Devey, Cynthia Pfaff Wright, Ronald Czaja, and Kirk Miller, "Self-Reports of Police Speeding Stops by Race: Results from the North Carolina Reverse Record Check Survey," *Journal of Quantitative Criminology* 22 (2006): 279–297.

63. See Spencer Rathus and Larry Siegel, "Crime and Personality Revisited: Effects of MMPI Sets on Self-Report Studies," *Criminology* 18 (1980): 245–251; John Clark and Larry Tifft, "Polygraph and Interview Validation of Self-Reported Deviant Behavior," *American Sociological Review* 31 (1966): 516–523.

64. Mallie Paschall, Miriam Ornstein, and Robert Flewelling, "African-American Male Adolescents' Involvement in the Criminal Justice System: The Criterion Validity of Self-Report Measures in Prospective Study," *Journal of Research in Crime and Delinquency* 38 (2001): 174–187.

65. Jennifer Roberts, Edward Mulvey, Julie Horney, John Lewis, and Michael Arter, "A Test of Two Methods of Recall for Violent Events," *Journal of Quantitative Criminology* 21 (2005): 175–193.

66. Lila Kazemian and David Farrington, "Comparing the Validity of Prospective, Retrospective, and Official Onset for Different Offending Categories," *Journal of Quantitative Criminology* 21 (2005): 127–147.

67. Barbara Warner and Brandi Wilson Coomer, "Neighborhood Drug Arrest Rates: Are They a Meaningful Indicator of Drug Activity? A Research Note," *Journal of Research in Crime and Delinquency* 40 (2003): 123–139.

68. Alfred Blumstein, Jacqueline Cohen, and Richard Rosenfeld, "Trend and Deviation in Crime Rates: A Comparison of UCR and NCVS Data for Burglary and Robbery," *Criminology* 29 (1991): 237–248. See also Michael Hindelang, Travis Hirschi, and Joseph Weis, *Measuring Delinquency* (Beverly Hills: Sage, 1981).

69. Clarence Schrag, *Crime and Justice: American Style* (Washington, D.C.: U.S. Government Printing Office, 1971), p. 17.

70. Rand, *Criminal Victimization, 2008.*

71. United States Census Bureau, Data Set: 2005–2007 American Community Survey 3-Year Estimates, http://factfinder.census.gov/servlet/STTable?_bm=y&-geo_id=01000US&-qr_name=ACS_2007_3YR_G00_S0101&-ds_name=ACS_2007_3YR_G00_.

72. James A. Fox, *Trends in Juvenile Violence: A Report to the United States Attorney General on Current and Future Rates of Juvenile Offending* (Boston: Northeastern University, 1996).

73. Steven Levitt, "The Limited Role of Changing Age Structure in Explaining Aggregate Crime Rates," *Criminology* 37 (1999): 581–599.

74. Darrell Steffensmeier and Miles Harer, "Making Sense of Recent U.S. Crime Trends, 1980 to 1996/1998: Age Composition Effects and Other Explanations," *Journal of Research in Crime and Delinquency* 36 (1999): 235–274.

75. Ibid., p. 265.

76. Ellen Cohn, "The Effect of Weather and Temporal Variations on Calls for Police Service," *American Journal of Police* 15 (1996): 23–43.

77. R. A. Baron, "Aggression as a Function of Ambient Temperature and Prior Anger Arousal," *Journal of Personality and Social Psychology* 21 (1972): 183–189.

78. James Rotton and Ellen Cohn, "Outdoor Temperature, Climate Control, and Criminal Assault," *Environment & Behavior* 36 (2004): 276–306.

79. Felipe Estrada and Anders Nilsson, "Segregation and Victimization: Neighbourhood Resources, Individual Risk Factors and Exposure to Property Crime," *European Journal of Criminology* 5 (2008): 193–216.

80. Parker, "Bringing 'Booze' Back In."

81. Victoria Brewer and M. Dwayne Smith, "Gender Inequality and Rates of Female Homicide Victimization across U.S. Cities," *Journal of Research in Crime and Delinquency* 32 (1995): 175–190.

82. Chin-Chi Hsieh and M. D. Pugh, "Poverty, Income Inequality, and Violent Crime: A Meta-Analysis of Recent Aggregate Data Studies," *Criminal Justice Review* 18 (1993): 182–199.

83. Richard Miech, Avshalom Caspi, Terrie Moffitt, Bradley Entner Wright, and Phil Silva, "Low Socioeconomic Status and Mental Disorders: A Longitudinal Study of Selection and Causation during Young Adulthood," *American Journal of Sociology* 104 (1999): 1096–1131; Marvin Krohn, Alan Lizotte, and Cynthia Perez, "The Interrelationship between Substance Use and Precocious Transitions to Adult Sexuality," *Journal of Health and Social Behavior* 38 (1997): 87–103, at 88; Richard Jessor, "Risk Behavior in Adolescence: A Psychosocial Framework for Understanding and Action," in *Adolescents at Risk: Medical and Social Perspectives*, ed. D. E. Rogers and E. Ginzburg (Boulder, Colo.: Westview, 1992).

84. Robert J. Sampson, "Disparity and Diversity in the Contemporary City: Social (Dis)order Revisited," *British Journal of Sociology* 60 (2009): 1–31.

85. Ramiro Martinez, Jacob Stowell, and Jeffrey Cancino, "A Tale of Two Border Cities: Community Context, Ethnicity, and Homicide," *Social Science Quarterly* 89 (2008): 1–16.

86. Robert Agnew, "A General Strain Theory of Community Differences in Crime Rates," *Journal of Research in Crime and Delinquency* 36 (1999): 123–155.

87. Bonita Veysey and Steven Messner, "Further Testing of Social Disorganization Theory: An Elaboration of Sampson and Groves's Community Structure and Crime," *Journal of Research in Crime and Delinquency* 36 (1999): 156–174.

88. Lance Hannon and James DeFronzo, "Welfare and Property Crime," *Justice Quarterly* 15 (1998): 273–288.

89. Travis Hirschi and Michael Gottfredson, "Age and the Explanation of Crime," *American Journal of Sociology* 89 (1983): 552–584, at 581.

90. For a comprehensive review of crime and the elderly, see Kyle Kercher, "Causes and Correlates of Crime Committed by the Elderly," in *Critical Issues in Aging Policy*, ed. E. Borgatta and

R. Montgomery (Beverly Hills: Sage, 1987), pp. 254–306; Darrell Steffensmeier, "The Invention of the 'New' Senior Citizen Criminal," *Research on Aging* 9 (1987): 281–311.

91.  Misaki Natsuaki, Xiaojia Ge, and Ernst Wenk, "Continuity and Changes in the Developmental Trajectories of Criminal Careers: Examining the Roles of Timing of First Arrest and High School Graduation," *Journal of Youth & Adolescence* 37 (2008): 431–444.

92.  Ryan King, Michael Massoglia, and Ross MacMillan, "The Context of Marriage and Crime: Gender, the Propensity to Marry, and Offending in Early Adulthood," *Criminology* 45 (2007): 33–65.

93.  Walter Gove, "The Effect of Age and Gender on Deviant Behavior: A Biopsychosocial Perspective," in *Gender and the Life Course*, ed. A. S. Rossi (New York: Aldine, 1985), pp. 115–144.

94.  James Q. Wilson and Richard Herrnstein, *Crime and Human Nature* (New York: Simon & Schuster, 1985), pp. 126–147.

95.  Paul Tracy, Kimberly Kempf-Leonard, and Stephanie Abramoske-James, "Gender Differences in Delinquency and Juvenile Justice Processing: Evidence from National Data, Crime and Delinquency 55 (2009): 171–215

96.  Otto Pollack, *The Criminality of Women* (Philadelphia: University of Pennsylvania, 1950).

97.  Alan Booth and D. Wayne Osgood, "The Influence of Testosterone on Deviance in Adulthood: Assessing and Explaining the Relationship," *Criminology* 31 (1993): 93–118.

98.  Daniel Mears, Matthew Ploeger, and Mark Warr, "Explaining the Gender Gap in Delinquency: Peer Influence and Moral Evaluations of Behavior," *Journal of Research in Crime and Delinquency* 35 (1998): 251–266.

99.  Gisela Konopka, *The Adolescent Girl in Conflict* (Englewood Cliffs, N.J.: Prentice-Hall, 1966); Clyde Vedder and Dora Somerville, *The Delinquent Girl* (Springfield, Ill.: Charles C. Thomas, 1970).

100.  Emily Gaarder and Joanne Belknap, "Tenuous Borders: Girls Transferred to Adult Court," *Criminology* 40 (2002): 481–517.

101.  Derek Kraeger, Ross Matsueda, and Elena Erosheva, "Motherhood and Criminal Desistance in Advantaged Neighborhoods," *Criminology* 48 (2010): 221–258.

102.  Debra Kaysen, Miranda Morris, Shireen Rizvi, and Patricia Resick, "Peritraumatic Responses and Their Relationship to Perceptions of Threat in Female Crime Victims," *Violence Against Women* 11 (2005): 1515–1535.

103.  Freda Adler, *Sisters in Crime* (New York: McGraw-Hill, 1975); Rita James Simon, *The Contemporary Woman and Crime* (Washington, D.C.: Government Printing Office, 1975).

104.  David Rowe, Alexander Vazsonyi, and Daniel Flannery, "Sex Differences in Crime: Do Mean and Within-Sex Variation Have Similar Causes?" *Journal of Research in Crime and Delinquency* 32 (1995): 84–100; Michael Hindelang, "Age, Sex, and the Versatility of Delinquency Involvements," *Social Forces* 14 (1971): 525–534; Martin Gold, *Delinquent Behavior in an American City* (Belmont, Calif.: Brooks/Cole, 1970); Gary Jensen and Raymond Eve, "Sex Differences in Delinquency: An Examination of Popular Sociological Explanations," *Criminology* 13 (1976): 427–448.

105.  Mears, Ploeger, and Warr, "Explaining the Gender Gap in Delinquency."

106.  Darrell Steffensmeier and Renee Hoffman Steffensmeier, "Trends in Female Delinquency," *Criminology* 18 (1980): 62–85. See also Darrell Steffensmeier and Renee Hoffman Steffensmeier, "Crime and the Contemporary Woman: An Analysis of Changing Levels of Female Property Crime, 1960–1975," *Social Forces* 57 (1978): 566–584; Joseph Weis, "Liberation and Crime: The Invention of the New Female Criminal," *Crime and Social Justice* 1 (1976): 17–27; Carol Smart, "The New Female Offender: Reality or Myth?" *British Journal of Criminology* 19 (1979): 50–59; Steven Box and Chris Hale, "Liberation/Emancipation, Economic Marginalization or Less Chivalry," *Criminology* 22 (1984): 473–478.

107.  Meda Chesney-Lind, "Female Offenders: Paternalism Reexamined," in *Women, the Courts and Equality*, ed. Laura Crites and Winifred Hepperle (Newbury Park, Calif.: Sage, 1987), pp. 114–139, at 115.

108.  Darrell Steffensmeier, Jennifer Schwartz, Hua Zhong, and Jeff Ackerman, "An Assessment of Recent Trends in Girls' Violence Using Diverse Longitudinal Sources: Is the Gender Gap Closing?" *Criminology* 43 (2005): 355–406.

109.  Susan Miller, Carol Gregory, and Leeann Iovanni, "One Size Fits All? A Gender-Neutral Approach to a Gender-Specific Problem: Contrasting Batterer Treatment Programs for Male and Female Offenders," *Criminal Justice Policy Review* 16 (2005): 336–359.

110.  Johnston, O'Malley, and Bachman, *Monitoring the Future*, pp. 102–104.

111.  Hurbert Blalock Jr., *Toward a Theory of Minority-Group Relations* (New York: Capricorn Books, 1967).

112.  Robin Shepard Engel and Jennifer Calnon, "Examining the Influence of Drivers' Characteristics during Traffic Stops with Police: Results from a National Survey," *Justice Quarterly* 21 (2004): 49–90.

113.  Malcolm Holmes, Brad Smith, Adrienne Freng, and Ed Muñoz, "Minority Threat, Crime Control, and Police Resource Allocation in the Southwestern United States," *Crime and Delinquency* 54 (2008): 128–152.

114.  Bradley Keen and David Jacobs, "Racial Threat, Partisan Politics, and Racial Disparities in Prison Admissions," *Criminology* 47 (2009): 209–238.

115.  Michael Leiber and Kristan Fox, "Race and the Impact of Detention on Juvenile Justice Decision Making," *Crime and Delinquency* 51 (2005): 470–497; Traci Schlesinger, "Racial and Ethnic Disparity in Pretrial Criminal Processing," *Justice Quarterly* 22 (2005): 170–192.

116.  Matthew Crow and Kathrine Johnson, "Race, Ethnicity, and Habitual-Offender Sentencing: A Multilevel Analysis of Individual and Contextual Threat," *Criminal Justice Policy Review* 19 (2008): 63–83.

117.  Jill Doerner and Stephen Demuth, "The Independent and Joint Effects of Race/Ethnicity, Gender, and Age on Sentencing Outcomes in U.S. Federal Courts," *Justice Quarterly* 27 (2010): 1–27.

118.  Alexander Weiss and Steven Chermak, "The News Value of African-American Victims: An Examination of the Media's Presentation of Homicide," *Journal of Crime and Justice* 21 (1998): 71–84.

119.  Jefferson Holcomb, Marian Williams, and Stephen Demuth, "White Female Victims and Death Penalty Disparity Research," *Justice Quarterly* 21 (2004): 877–902.

120.  Barry Sample and Michael Philip, "Perspectives on Race and Crime in Research and Planning," in *The Criminal Justice System and Blacks*, ed. Georges-Abeyie, pp. 21–36.

121.  Ruth Peterson, Lauren Krivo, and Mark Harris, "Disadvantage and Neighborhood Violent Crime: Do Local Institutions Matter?" *Journal of Research in Crime and Delinquency* 37 (2000): 31–63

122.  James Comer, "Black Violence and Public Policy," in *American Violence and Public Policy*, ed. Lynn Curtis (New Haven, Conn.: Yale University Press, 1985), pp. 63–86

123.  Fox Butterfield, *All God's Children: The Bosket Family and the American Tradition of Violence* (New York: Avon, 1996).

124.  William Julius Wilson, More than Just Race: Being Black and Poor in the Inner City (New York: Norton, 2009); William Julius Wilson and Richard Taub, *There Goes the Neighborhood: Racial, Ethnic, and Class Tensions in Four Chicago Neighborhoods and Their Meaning for America* (New York: Knopf, 2006); William Julius Wilson, *The Truly Disadvantaged* (Chicago: University of Chicago Press, 1987); *When Work Disappears: The World of the*

*Urban Poor* (New York: Knopf, 1996); *The Bridge over the Racial Divide: Rising Inequality and Coalition Politics*, Wildavsky Forum Series, 2 (Berkeley: University of California Press, 1999).

125. Roy Austin, "Progress toward Racial Equality and Reduction of Black Criminal Violence," *Journal of Criminal Justice* 15 (1987): 437–459.

126. Reynolds Farley and William Frey, "Changes in the Segregation of Whites from Blacks during the 1980s: Small Steps toward a More Integrated Society," *American Sociological Review* 59 (1994): 23–45.

127. Marvin Wolfgang, Robert Figlio, and Thorsten Sellin, *Delinquency in a Birth Cohort* (Chicago: University of Chicago Press, 1972).

128. See Thorsten Sellin and Marvin Wolfgang, *The Measurement of Delinquency* (New York: Wiley, 1964), p. 120.

129. Paul Tracy and Robert Figlio, "Chronic Recidivism in the 1958 Birth Cohort." Paper presented at the American Society of Criminology meeting, Toronto, October 1982; Marvin Wolfgang, "Delinquency in Two Birth Cohorts," in *Perspective Studies of Crime and Delinquency*, ed. Katherine Teilmann Van Dusen and Sarnoff Mednick (Boston: Kluwer-Nijhoff, 1983), pp. 7–17. The following sections rely heavily on these sources.

130. Lyle Shannon, *Criminal Career Opportunity* (New York: Human Sciences Press, 1988).

131. D. J. West and David P. Farrington, *The Delinquent Way of Life* (London: Hienemann, 1977).

132. Michael Schumacher and Gwen Kurz, *The 8% Solution: Preventing Serious Repeat Juvenile Crime* (Thousand Oaks, Calif.: Sage, 1999).

133. Peter Jones, Philip Harris, James Fader, and Lori Grubstein, "Identifying Chronic Juvenile Offenders," *Justice Quarterly* 18 (2001): 478–507.

134. Lila Kazemian and Marc LeBlanc, "Differential Cost Avoidance and Successful Criminal Careers," *Crime and Delinquency* 53 (2007): 38–63.

135. Rudy Haapanen, Lee Britton, and Tim Croisdale, "Persistent Criminality and Career Length," *Crime and Delinquency* 53 (2007): 133–155.

136. Michael Ezell and Amy D'Unger, "Offense Specialization among Serious Youthful Offenders: A Longitudinal Analysis of a California Youth Authority Sample" (Durham, N.C.: Duke University, 1998, unpublished report).

# CHAPTER 3

# Understanding Crime and Victimization

## CHAPTER OUTLINE

*Careers in Criminal Justice: Criminologist*

- **THE CAUSE OF CRIME**

- **CHOICE THEORY**
Rational Criminals
Rational Crimes
Situational Crime Prevention
General Deterrence
Specific Deterrence/Incarceration

- **SOCIOBIOLOGICAL THEORIES**
Biochemical Factors
Neurological Factors
Genetic Factors

- **PSYCHOLOGICAL THEORIES**
Psychodynamic Theory
Behavioral Theory
Cognitive Theory
Personality and Crime
*Images of Justice: The Media and Violence*
IQ and Crime

- **SOCIOLOGICAL THEORIES**
Social Structure Theory
The Disorganized Neighborhood
Social Process Theories

- **CRITICAL CRIMINOLOGY**
State (Organized) Crime
Support for Critical Theory

- **DEVELOPMENTAL THEORIES**
Criminal Careers
Latent Trait Theory
Life Course Theory

- **THEORIES OF VICTIMIZATION**
Victim Precipitation
Lifestyle Theory
Routine Activities Theory

## CHAPTER OBJECTIVES

1. Understand why, to some, crime seems rational.
2. Know the strategies used to reduce crime by rational criminals.
3. Identify the various biological traits linked to crime.
4. Know the various psychological views of the cause of crime.
5. Identify the personality traits linked to crime.
6. Compare and contrast the various social structure theories of crime.
7. Distinguish among the three types of social process theories.
8. Know what is meant by critical criminology.
9. Understand the basics of developmental theory.
10. Identify the various theories of victimization.

© Timothy A. Clary/AFP/Getty Images

**T**he Emperors Club VIP provided its "members" with the companionship of young, beautiful women for "total relaxation massage, entertainment purposes, modeling or private dancing." It introduced "fashion models, pageant winners and exquisite students, graduates, and women of successful careers (finance, art, media, etc.) to gentlemen of exceptional standards," charging somewhere between $3,000 an hour and $31,000 per day for their services. This high-priced prostitution ring might never have been exposed had it not been for a federal investigation of one of its clients, New York's hard-charging governor, Eliot Spitzer, who at one time was considered a future presidential candidate. Known in the club as Client #9, Spitzer had paid $80,000 for the services of the Club's young sex workers, including aspiring 23-year-old singer Ashley Dupre (born Ashley Youmans in 1985). When a federal investigation uncovered his involvement with the Emperors Club, the scandal rocked the nation, and on March 17, 2008, Spitzer was forced to resign in disgrace.[1] Spitzer was not the only one affected by the investigation. Kristin Davis (AKA the Manhattan Madam), who ran the club, received a 3-month-jail sentence and after her release considered running for governor. A number of her associates pled guilty to conspiracy charges stemming from their participation in the Emperors Club and received a 1-year probationary sentence.[2] One of them, Temeka Rachelle Lewis, 32, of Brooklyn, New York, stands out. Lewis is a graduate of the prestigious University of Virginia with a bachelor's degree in English language and literature. She was an honor student all her life and grew up in what has been described as "a good church-going family," who were reportedly in shock over the revelations.[3] As for Ashley Dupre, she made thousands of dollars when her recording "What We Want" was played more than 3 million times on the Internet after the scandal erupted. The New York Post hired her to write a weekly advice column dealing with sex and relationships, she appeared in the May 2010 issue of Playboy, and she has been in talks to develop a reality TV show. ∎

## CAREERS IN CRIMINAL JUSTICE

# Criminologist

### Duties and Characteristics of the Job

Criminologists are academics who analyze patterns in criminal activity and attempt to determine the causes of, future trends in, and potential solutions to crime in society. Criminologists are concerned with questions such as how to effectively deter crime, who will commit crime and why, and how to predict and prevent criminal behavior. Like statisticians, criminologists often design and carry out research projects to collect and analyze data with the intention of answering some aspect of these larger questions. Their ideas are written up into reports or articles for various agencies and publications and are used for academic, law enforcement, and policy purposes.

Criminologists often work with law enforcement at the local, state, or federal level. In these positions, they might do research on problems specific to the district they are working with, or they might examine case files and attend crime scenes to help determine whether a suspect's profile is accurate. Other criminologists seek positions at universities and colleges, where they conduct research, write books and articles, and teach courses about crime and criminal justice. In general, criminologists work normal 40-hour weeks in office settings.

### Job Outlook

The demand for criminologists is expected to reflect the general demand for sociologists, which at present is expected to grow slowly at the government and law enforcement levels. There is much greater demand for criminologists working in the university setting, however. Those with more education can expect better job opportunities and higher salaries.

### Salary

Criminologists' median annual earnings are $70,000. However, salaries will vary widely, depending on the employer. A doctorate-level criminologist working at a college or university can expect pay comparable to that of other faculty. Starting pay for an assistant professor ranges from $45,000 to $70,000. A full professor has an average annual salary of about $100,000. Pay will vary with the institution and the individual's level of advancement.

## THE CAUSE OF CRIME

How can we explain the behavior of Kristin Davis, Ashley Dupre, Temeka Lewis, or Eliot Spitzer? Certainly their illegal behavior was not the product of a disturbed childhood or extreme poverty. What could possess successful, attractive people to engage in a risky criminal conspiracy? Was it an impulsive personality or some other form of psychological abnormality? Or perhaps a matter of rational choice: They may have reasoned that no one was really being hurt by their actions, so where was the harm?

Despite years of study and research, crime experts are still not certain why people commit crime or why some people become crime victims. One of the enduring goals of **criminology**—the scientific study of the nature, extent, cause, and control of criminal behavior—is to develop an understanding of the nature and cause of crime and victimization. Without knowing why crime occurs, it would be difficult to create effective crime reduction programs. No one could be sure whether efforts were being aimed at the proper audience or, if they were, whether the prevention efforts were the ones most likely to cause positive change. A crime prevention program based on providing jobs for unemployed teenagers will be effective only if crime is, in fact, linked to unemployment. Similarly, a plan to reduce prison riots by reducing the sugar intake of inmates is feasible only if research shows a link between diet and violence. Criminologists study these crime patterns in part to help agents of the criminal justice system plan and construct programs to reduce crime. If you are interested in becoming a criminologist, you may want to read the accompanying Careers in Criminal Justice feature.

**criminology**
The scientific study of the nature, extent, cause, and control of criminal behavior.

## Opportunities

Those entering the field of criminology should be aware that they will face competition from other qualified candidates for a limited number of jobs, especially at the more financially rewarding positions with the federal government. However, the predicted increase in retirement in the near future will probably open up new positions. There is more opportunity in the university setting for criminologists than for psychologists or sociologists.

Many individuals who get a degree in criminology or work as criminologists can use their education and experience and successfully launch careers in related jobs, such as police officer, federal agent, or psychologist.

## Qualifications

Because of the academic nature of criminology, the primary requirement for a career in this field is proper academic training. Educational requirements usually include courses on human behavior and the criminal justice system, and they should involve developing skills in statistics and writing. Training should also include familiarity with computer programs used for statistical analysis, such as SAS or SPSS. Because criminology requires collecting and examining data, conducting research, and presenting these ideas to others, personal qualities such as intellectual curiosity and strong communicative and analytical skills are important. Those who want to be involved in law enforcement in a hands-on manner or do not like math and writing reports may not be interested in this career.

Certain states require potential criminologists to pass a written test in order to become licensed before they can work. Additionally, those working with law enforcement agencies will have to pass background and security checks.

## Education and Training

Although some criminologists enter the field with a bachelor's degree, a majority pursue postgraduate education. Typically, this means a master's degree in criminology and/or criminal justice. Other social science degrees can be acceptable. This is generally enough for those desiring work at law enforcement agencies. However, some positions—for example, teaching at the university level—will require a doctorate in one of the previously mentioned fields.

Sources: "Social Scientists, Other," *Occupational Outlook Handbook*, 2010–2011 edition (Washington, D.C.: Bureau of Labor Statistics, U.S. Department of Labor), retrieved May 19, 2010, www.bls .gov/oes/current/oes193041.htm; Comprehensive Career Profile List: Criminologist, http://careers.stateuniversity.com/pages/714/ Criminologist.html, retrieved May 19, 2010.

In the following sections, the most important theories of crime causation are discussed in some detail. We then look at the concept of victimization and discuss theories that attempt to explain why some people are likely to be victimized while others tend not to be victimized by crime.

## CHOICE THEORY

One prominent view of criminality argues that most people adopt the conventional American goals and values of striving for success, material attainment, and hard work.[4] People who commit crime also want the best things in life, scrambling around to obtain their "piece of the pie."[5] However, because achieving success is not always easy, some people decide to cut corners. They use illegal means to get what they want. If they commit crime, it is because they have chosen an illegal path to obtain the goals that might otherwise have been out of reach.

Having decided to take a criminal path to success, they choose to commit crime after weighing the potential benefits and consequences of their criminal act. People will commit a crime if they believe that doing so will yield immediate benefits without the threat of long-term risks. Risk evaluations may cover a wide range of topics: What's the chance of getting caught? How difficult will it be to commit the crime? Is the profit worth the effort? Should I risk committing crime in my own neighborhood where I know the territory, or is it worth traveling to a strange place in order to increase my profits?[6]

People who decide to get involved in crime weigh the chances of arrest (based on their past experiences), plus the subjective psychic rewards of crime, including the excitement and social status it brings and perceived opportunities for easy

*Of all the characters in the Eliot Spitzer scandal, Ashley Dupre probably made out the best, writing an advice column and selling her music on the Web. Even so, it's difficult to understand why an attractive and intelligent young woman would become a call girl, albeit a high-paid one. Neither is it easy to understand the behavior of Spitzer, New York's hard-charging governor. Often, as here, criminologists must try to explain the seemingly inexplicable.*

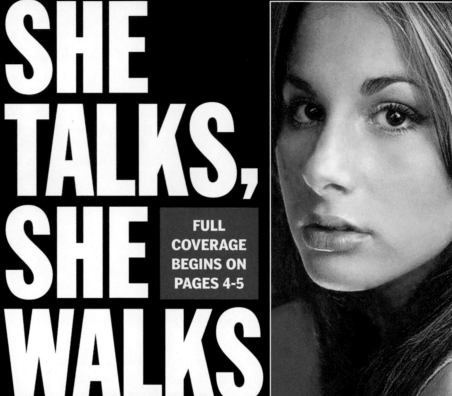

Weather: Cloudy, chance of rain, 52/40     SPORTS ★ FINAL     Saturday, March 15, 2008

# DAILY◉NEWS

50¢     **2.5 MILLION READERS EVERY DAY**     NYDailyNews.com

**WIN TICKETS** TO **YANKEES** VS. **BOSTON** AT HISTORIC YANKEE STADIUM     **ENTER TODAY! SEE PAGE 14**

# SHE TALKS, SHE WALKS

**FULL COVERAGE BEGINS ON PAGES 4-5**

## Spitzer hooker is granted immunity as feds focus on Eliot's campaign cash

gains. If the rewards are great, the perceived risk small, and the excitement high, the likelihood of their committing additional crimes increases.[7] Successful shoplifters say they will do it again in the future; past experience has taught them the rewards of illegal behavior.[8]

Drug trafficking fits this pattern. Before concluding a drug sale, experienced traffickers mentally balance the chances of making a large profit against the probability of being apprehended and punished for drug dealing. They know that most drug deals are not detected and that the potential for enormous, untaxed profits is great. They evaluate their lifestyle and determine how much cash they need to maintain their standard of living, which is usually extravagant. They may have borrowed to finance the drug deal, and their creditors are not usually reasonable if loans cannot be repaid promptly. They also realize that they could be the target of a sting operation by undercover agents and that if caught, they will get a long mandatory sentence in a forbidding federal penitentiary. If the greedy culprits conclude that the potential for profits is great enough, their need for cash urgent, and the chances of apprehension minimal, they will carry out the deal. If, however, they believe that the transaction will bring them only a small profit and entails a large risk of apprehension and punishment, they may forgo the deal. According to this view, crime is a matter of rational choice, involving a calculated decision made after a motivated offender weighs the potential costs and benefits of illegal activity. To deter the commission of crime, punishment must be sufficiently strict, sure, and swift to outweigh any benefits of law violation. A 30-year prison sentence should deter potential bank robbers, regardless of the amount of money in the bank's vault. However, no matter how severely the law punishes a criminal act, it will have negligible **deterrent effect** if potential law violators believe that they have little chance of being caught or that the wheels of justice are slow and inefficient.

**deterrent effect**
The assumed ability of the threat of criminal sanctions to discourage crime before it occurs.

## Rational Criminals

Whether to commit a specific crime is a personal decision based on the evaluation of available information. When deciding to commit crime, potential offenders weigh their chances of getting caught and punished and then balance them with the perceived benefits of crime. Benefits include not only monetary gains but also psychological rewards, such as excitement and increased social status among their peers.[9] Criminals are likely to desist from crime if they believe that their future illegal earnings will be relatively low and that attractive and legal opportunities to generate income are available.[10] In contrast, criminals may be motivated when they know people who have made big scores and are successful at crime. Although the prevailing wisdom is that "crime does not pay," a small but significant subset of criminals earn close to $50,000 a year from crime, and their success may help motivate other would-be offenders.[11] In this sense, rational choice is a function of a person's perception of conventional alternatives and opportunities.

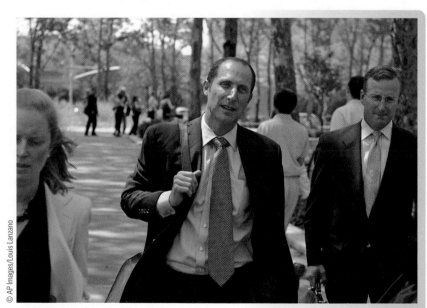

© AP Images/Louis Lanzano

The rational criminal may also decide to forgo or desist from illegal behaviors. Experienced criminals may begin to fear apprehension and punishment—a target appears too well protected, the police in the area are very active, local judges have vowed to crack down on crime—it just does not feel safe enough to break the law.[12]

*The fact that some criminals "choose" crime is clear in cases involving high-level corporate and white-collar crimes. Matthew Tannin (center), former hedge fund manager for the investment firm Bear Stearns, enters a Brooklyn federal court for a hearing on July 18, 2008. He was charged with securities fraud in the wake of the collapse of the subprime mortgage market, which foreshadowed Bear Stearns's own downfall. Whereas some violent crimes may seem impulsive and unplanned, is it possible to say that perpetrating a complex securities fraud scheme did not involve rational choice?*

## Rational Crimes

That crime is rational can be observed in a wide variety of criminal events. White-collar and organized crime figures engage in elaborate and well-planned conspiracies, ranging from international drug deals to the looting of savings and loan institutions.

But even predatory street criminals exhibit stealth and planning in their criminal acts. Burglars may try to determine which homes are easy targets by reading newspaper stories about weddings or social events that mean the attendees' homes will be unguarded. They choose houses that are easily accessible, are screened from public view, and offer good escape routes—for example, at the end of a cul-de-sac abutting a wooded area. They target high-value homes that do not have burglar alarms or other security devices.[13] Burglars seem to prefer working between 9 A.M. and 11 A.M. and in mid-afternoon, when parents are either working or dropping off or picking up children at school.

## EVIDENCE-BASED JUSTICE

# CCTV

Police departments in England and the United States, especially in Chicago and New York City, have installed thousands of closed-circuit TV (CCTV) surveillance cameras in areas that are at risk for crime. The idea is to have video surveillance of streets that are experiencing high crime rates. For example, in July 2003, the Chicago Police Department positioned remote-controlled and viewable cameras called Police Observation Devices—commonly referred to as PODs—to view and record crime in high-risk areas. Each POD was equipped with flashing blue lights on top to ensure that its highly visible presence would inform the public that the area was under police surveillance

Do these measures really work? After an a careful review of 41 studies conducted around the world, Brandon Welsh and David Farrington found that CCTV interventions (a) have a small but desirable effect on reducing area crime, (b) are most effective in reducing crime in parking lots, (c) are most effective in reducing vehicle crimes, and (d) are more effective in reducing crime in England, where there is a high level of public support for the use of CCTV cameras in public settings to prevent crime, than in the United States, where people are wary of the "Big Brother is watching you" implications of monitoring via surveillance technology. Thus, although American police agencies may be willing to spend millions on CCTV systems, these may be less effective than expected in reducing street crime.

One element of situational crime prevention is to make it difficult to commit crimes, thereby discouraging would-be criminals. This crime prevention principle is applied around the world. Here a private security guard watches closed-circuit cameras to keep tabs on students and visitors at the Rikkyo Elementary School in Tokyo. At this school, small, gray plastic tags tucked inside students' backpacks beam a message to the computer, and the computer records the time students enter or leave. Rikkyo officials hope this radio frequency identification technology will serve as an early-warning system for children who are missing or abducted.

Source: Brandon Welsh and David Farrington, *Making Public Places Safer: Surveillance and Crime Prevention* (New York: Oxford University Press, 2008).

Burglars appear to monitor car and pedestrian traffic and to avoid selecting targets on heavily traveled streets.[14]

Even violent criminals exhibit elements of rationality. Research shows that armed robbers choose targets close to their homes or in areas that they routinely travel. Familiarity with the area gives them knowledge of escape routes; this is referred to as their awareness space.[15] Robbers also report being wary of people who are watching the community for signs of trouble. Robbery levels are relatively low in neighborhoods where residents keep a watchful eye on their neighbors' property.[16] Robbers avoid freestanding buildings, where they can more easily be surrounded by police. Others select targets that are known to do a primarily cash business, such as bars, supermarkets, and restaurants.[17] If crime is a rational choice, how can it be prevented or controlled?

## Situational Crime Prevention

Some advocates of rational choice theory argue that crime prevention can be achieved by reducing the opportunities people have to commit particular crimes, a technique known as *situational crime prevention*. This technique was first popularized in the United States in the early 1970s by Oscar Newman, who coined the term *defensible space*. The idea is that crime can be prevented or displaced through the use of residential architectural designs that reduce criminal opportunity, such as well-lit housing projects that maximize surveillance.[18]

Contemporary choice theorists maintain that situational crime prevention can be achieved by creating a strategy or overall plan to reduce specific crimes and then developing specific tactics to achieve those goals. Ronald Clarke has set out the main types of crime prevention tactics in use today:[19]

- *Increase the effort needed to commit the crime.* Increasing the effort needed to commit crimes involves using target-hardening techniques and access control: placing steering locks on cars, putting unbreakable glass on storefronts, locking gates and fencing yards, having owners' photos on credit cards, controlling the sale of spray paint (to reduce graffiti), and installing caller ID (a device that displays the telephone number of the party placing the call, which can reduce the number of obscene or crank calls).

- *Increase the risks of committing the crime.* It is also possible to increase the risks of committing a crime by improving surveillance lighting, creating neighborhood watch programs, controlling building entrances and exits, putting in burglar alarms and security systems, and increasing the number and effectiveness of private security officers and police patrols. Research shows that crime rates are reduced when police officers use aggressive crime reduction techniques and promote community safety by increasing lighting and cleaning up vacant lots.[20] The accompanying Evidence-Based Justice feature examines a crime prevention method that has become popular in a number of communities.

- *Reduce the rewards for committing the crime.* Reward reduction strategies include making car radios removable so they can be taken into the home at night, marking property so that it is more difficult to sell when stolen, and having gender-neutral phone lists to discourage obscene phone calls.

- *Induce shame or guilt.* Inducing guilt or shame might include such techniques as embarrassing offenders (e.g., publishing "John lists" in the newspaper to punish those arrested for soliciting prostitutes) and improving compliance by providing trash bins whose easy access might shame chronic litterers into using them. When caller ID was installed in New Jersey, the number of obscene phone calls reported to police declined significantly because of the threat of exposure.[21]

- *Reduce provocation.* Some crimes are the result of extreme provocation—for example, road rage. It might be possible to reduce provocation by creating programs that reduce conflict. An early closing time for local bars and pubs might limit assaults that result from late-night drinking. Posting guards outside schools at closing time might prevent childish taunts from escalating into full-blown brawls.

- *Remove excuses.* Crime may be reduced by making it difficult for people to excuse their criminal behavior by saying things like "I didn't know that was illegal" or "I had no choice." To achieve this goal, municipalities have set up roadside displays that electronically flash a car's speed as it passes, eliminating the driver's excuse that she did not know how fast she was going when stopped by police. Litter boxes, brightly displayed, can eliminate the claim that "I just didn't know where to throw my trash."

## General Deterrence

If crime is a matter of choice, it follows that it can be controlled by convincing criminals that breaking the law is a bad or dangerous choice to make. If people believe that they are certain to be apprehended by the police, quickly tried, and severely

**general deterrence**
A crime control policy that depends on the fear of criminal
penalties.

penalized, they are more likely to dismiss any thought of breaking the law.[22] In other words, people will not choose crime if they fear legal punishment. The harsher the punishment, the more certain its application, and the speedier the judgment, the more effective it will be. This principle is referred to as **general deterrence**. If the justice system could be made more effective, those who care little for the rights of others would be deterred by fear of the law's sanctioning power.[23]

Research shows that some people who report that they fear punishment will be deterred from committing certain crimes.[24] The prevailing wisdom is that the certainty of being punished is a greater deterrent to crime than its severity. In other words, people are more likely to be deterred from crime if they believe that they will get caught. If police can be more proactive, cracking down on crime, potential criminals will become wary and may choose not to commit crimes such as robbery.[25] What happens to them after apprehension seems to have a lesser impact.[26]

Although certainty of punishment has some influence on crime, little hard evidence is yet available that fear of the law alone can be a general deterrent to crime.[27] Even the harshest punishment, the death penalty, appears to have very little effect on the murder rate.[28] The certainty of being punished may influence a few offenders, such as those who might not have become criminals anyway, but it has little effect on others, especially those who are involved with criminal peers or live in a crimogenic environment.[29] A recent (2009) meta-analysis of the existing literature shows that the most significant deterrent effects can be achieved in minor crimes and offenses, whereas more serious crimes such as homicide are harder to discourage.[30] Because criminals may more readily be deterred from committing some crimes—for example, tax noncompliance, speeding, and illegal parking—future research should be directed at identifying and targeting these preventable offenses.[31]

What factors inhibit the sanctioning power of the criminal law? One is the lack of efficiency of the justice system. About 20 percent of serious reported crimes result in an arrest. Relatively few criminals are eventually tried, convicted, and sentenced to prison. Chronic offenders and career criminals may believe that the risk of apprehension and imprisonment is limited and conclude that the certainty of punishment—a key element in deterrence—is minimal. Even if they do fear punishment, their anxiety may be neutralized by the belief that a crime gives them a significant chance for large profit. Active burglars report that the fear of capture and punishment is usually neutralized by the hope of making a big score; greed overcomes fear.[32]

The concept of general deterrence assumes a rational criminal—that is, an offender who carefully weighs and balances the pains and benefits of the criminal act. However, a majority of arrested criminals are under the influence of drugs or alcohol at the time of their arrest. Therefore, many offenders may be incapable of having the rational thought patterns upon which the concept of general deterrence rests. Relatively high rates of substance abuse, including alcohol and illegal drugs, may render even the harshest criminal penalties for violent crimes ineffective deterrents.[33]

In sum, the theory of rational choice views criminals as calculating individuals who can be deterred from crime by the threat of punishment. Yet research has so far failed to turn up clear and convincing evidence that the threat of punishment or its implementation can deter would-be criminals.

## Specific Deterrence/Incarceration

Even if the threat of punishment cannot deter would-be criminals, actual punishment at the hands of the justice system should be sufficient to convince arrested offenders never to repeat their criminal acts. If punishment were severe enough, a convicted criminal would never dare repeat his or her offense. What rational person would? This view is called **specific deterrence**. Prior to the twentieth century, specific deterrence was a motive for the extreme tortures and physical punishments commonly inflicted on convicted criminals. By breaking the convicts physically, legal authorities hoped to control their spirit and behavior.[34] The more enlightened society in America today no longer uses such cruel and

**specific deterrence**
Punishment severe enough to
convince convicted offenders
never to repeat their criminal
activity.

unusual punishments on its citizens. Instead, we rely on incarcerating criminals as the primary mode of punishment; more than 500 out of every 100,000 adults is now behind bars.[35]

The theory of specific deterrence relies on the belief that experience will shape criminal choices. Those who have been caught and sent to prison soon learn that crime just does not pay; being punished today will make people wary of committing crime in the future. Convinced that the pains of punishment outweigh the benefits of crime, they may be more willing to desist from a criminal career.[36]

Yet there seem to be problems with this approach: Many offenders who are arrested soon repeat their criminal acts.[37] A majority of inmates repeat their criminal acts soon after returning to society, and most inmates have served time previously. Even those people imprisoned in super-maximum-security prisons, receiving the harshest treatment possible (solitary confinement 23 hours a day), are as likely to repeat their crimes upon release as those serving time in traditional institutions.[38]

Why have these draconian punishments failed as a specific deterrent?

- Specific deterrence assumes a rational criminal, someone who learns from experience. Many offenders have impulsive personalities that interfere with their ability to learn from experience.

- Being convicted and punished may expose people to more experienced offenders who encourage them to commit more crime and teach them criminal techniques.

- A majority of criminal offenders have lifestyles marked by heavy substance abuse, lack of formal education, and disturbed home lives, which inhibit conventional behavior. Punishment does little to help an already troubled person readjust to society.

- Punishment can produce a short-term specific deterrent effect, but because it also produces rage and anger, it fails to produce longer-term behavior change. People who are harshly treated may want to prove that they cannot be broken by the system.[39]

- The stigma of having been in prison labels people and helps lock offenders into a criminal career instead of convincing them to avoid one.

- Criminals who are punished may also believe that the likelihood of getting caught twice for the same type of crime is remote: "Lightning never strikes twice in the same spot," they may reason; no one is that unlucky.[40]

- Experiencing the harshest punishments may cause severe psychological problems, while reducing the opportunities for interaction with law-abiding people.[41]

- An incapacitation strategy is terribly expensive. The prison system costs billions of dollars each year. Even if incarceration could reduce the crime rate, the costs would be enormous.

- Most inmates come from a few impoverished communities. When they are released, they disrupt their neighborhoods, undermine social institutions, and create community disorganization. Rather than act as a crime suppressant, incarceration may have the long-term effect of accelerating crime rates.[42]

- If money can be made from criminal activity, there will always be someone to take the place of the incarcerated offender. New criminals will be recruited and trained, offsetting any benefit that can be attributed to incarceration.

- Most criminal offenses are committed by teens and very young adult offenders who are unlikely to be sent to prison for a single felony conviction. Aging criminals are already past the age when they are likely to commit crime. As a result, a strict incarceration policy may keep people in prison beyond the time when they cease being a threat to society, while a new cohort of high-risk adolescents is on the street.[43]

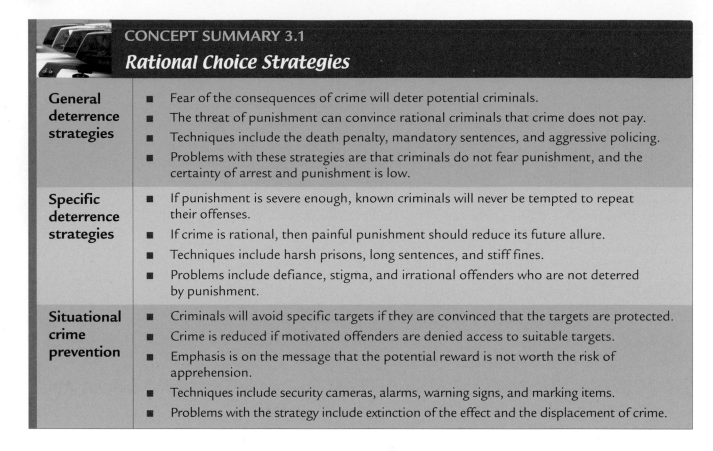

**CONCEPT SUMMARY 3.1**
*Rational Choice Strategies*

| | |
|---|---|
| **General deterrence strategies** | ■ Fear of the consequences of crime will deter potential criminals. <br> ■ The threat of punishment can convince rational criminals that crime does not pay. <br> ■ Techniques include the death penalty, mandatory sentences, and aggressive policing. <br> ■ Problems with these strategies are that criminals do not fear punishment, and the certainty of arrest and punishment is low. |
| **Specific deterrence strategies** | ■ If punishment is severe enough, known criminals will never be tempted to repeat their offenses. <br> ■ If crime is rational, then painful punishment should reduce its future allure. <br> ■ Techniques include harsh prisons, long sentences, and stiff fines. <br> ■ Problems include defiance, stigma, and irrational offenders who are not deterred by punishment. |
| **Situational crime prevention** | ■ Criminals will avoid specific targets if they are convinced that the targets are protected. <br> ■ Crime is reduced if motivated offenders are denied access to suitable targets. <br> ■ Emphasis is on the message that the potential reward is not worth the risk of apprehension. <br> ■ Techniques include security cameras, alarms, warning signs, and marking items. <br> ■ Problems with the strategy include extinction of the effect and the displacement of crime. |

Thus there is some question whether punishing criminals brings the desired effect. There is evidence that using harsh punishments, such as incarceration, brings about crime rate relief.[44] Not all experts are skeptics; some believe that punishing people can reduce crime rates.[45] After all, the crime rate has in fact dropped dramatically during the past decade, while the prison population has grown. Although it is difficult to measure precisely, there is at least some evidence that crime rates and incarceration rates are related.[46] Economist Steven Levitt, author of the widely read book *Freakonomics*, concludes that each person put behind bars results in a decrease of 15 serious crimes per year.[47] He argues that the social benefits associated with crime reduction equal or exceed the social and financial costs of incarceration.[48] So the debate over the effectiveness of punishing people to lower crime rates continues to rage.

The basic components of these strategies are set out in Concept Summary 3.1.

## SOCIOBIOLOGICAL THEORIES

As the nineteenth century came to a close, some criminologists began to suggest that crime was caused not so much by human choice but by inherited and uncontrollable biological and psychological traits: intelligence, body build, personality, biomedical makeup. The newly developed scientific method was applied to the study of social relations, including criminal behavior.

The origin of scientific criminology is usually traced to the research of Cesare Lombroso (1836–1909). Lombroso, an Italian army physician fascinated by human anatomy, became interested in finding out what motivated criminals to commit crimes. He physically examined hundreds of prison inmates and other criminals to discover any similarities among them. On the basis of his research, Lombroso proposed that criminals manifest *atavistic anomalies*: primitive, animal-like physical qualities such as an asymmetric face or excessive jaw, eye defects, large eyes, a receding forehead, prominent cheekbones, long arms, a twisted nose, and swollen lips.[49] Lombroso's views were discredited in the twentieth century, and biological explanations of crime were abandoned.

There has been a recent resurgence of interest in the biology of crime. Contemporary biological theory assumes that variation in human physical traits can explain behavior. Instead of being born equal and influenced by social and environmental conditions, each person possesses a unique biochemical, neurological, and genetic makeup. People may develop physical or mental traits at birth, or soon thereafter, that affect their social functioning over the life course and influence their behavior choices. So behavior has both biological and sociological elements, hence the term "sociobiological, or biosocial, theories." It is possible, then, that while biochemical makeup influences behavior, social factors (such as nurturing parents and supportive environments) can mitigate its effects.[50] Biological and environmental factors have an interactive effect. Biosocial theory can be divided into four subareas, the biochemical, neurological, evolutionary, and genetic effects on behavior.

## Biochemical Factors

Biocriminologists sometimes focus on the influence of biochemical factors on criminal behavior. It is believed that ingestion of or exposure to toxic substances or harmful chemicals, and poor diet in utero, at birth, and beyond, may affect people throughout their life course. Such factors can either trigger, or make people susceptible to, hostile or aggressive responses. Thus people who are exposed to toxic biochemical substances may be more likely than others to take hostile action when exposed to stressful events. What are suspected biochemical influences on behavior?

*ENVIRONMENTAL CONTAMINANTS* Exposure to environmental contaminants such as the now-banned PCBs (polychlorinated biphenyls), a chemical that was once used in insulation materials, as well as to lead, mercury, and other metals, has been shown to influence brain functioning and intelligence levels.[51] Exposure to these contaminants may lead to cognitive and learning dysfunctions, factors associated with antisocial behaviors.[52] Psychologist Bernard Rimland, for one, argues that childhood behavior problems stem from environmental contaminants. In his 2008 book *Dyslogic Syndrome*, Rimland disputes the notion that bad or ineffective parenting is to blame for troubled or disobedient children:

> . . . most "bad" children . . . suffer from toxic physical environments [and] . . . research clearly shows that the culprits primarily responsible for the dyslogical behavior of millions of America's children are not their parents, but rather the poor-quality food substitutes they eat, the pollutants in the air they breathe, the chemically contaminated water they drink, and other less well-known physical insults that cause malfunctioning brains and bodies. . . . They struggle at school, they struggle through life, and in their wake they leave a trail of misery—of disrupted and saddened lives. But it's not truly their fault, and it's rarely their parents' fault.[53]

*FOOD PRODUCTS AND DIET* Some research efforts have linked antisocial behavior to vitamin and mineral deficiencies, food additives, and improper diet. Ingestion of common food additives such as calcium propionate, used to preserve bread, has been linked to problem behaviors.[54] Research shows that excessive amounts of harmful substances such as food dyes and artificial colors and flavors seem to provoke hostile, impulsive, and otherwise antisocial behaviors.[55]

***HYPOGLYCEMIA*** Another area of biological research focuses on hypoglycemia, a condition that occurs when blood glucose (sugar) falls below the levels necessary for normal and efficient brain functioning. Symptoms of hypoglycemia include irritability, anxiety, depression, crying spells, headaches, and confusion. Research shows that persistent abnormality in the way the brain metabolizes glucose is linked to substance abuse.[56]

***HORMONES*** One area of concern has been testosterone, the most abundant male hormone (androgen), which controls secondary sex characteristics such as facial hair and voice timbre. Excessive levels of testosterone have been linked to violence and aggression.[57] Children who have low levels of the stress hormone cortisol tend to be more violent and antisocial than those with normal levels.[58] A growing body of evidence suggests that hormonal changes are also related to mood and behavior and that adolescents experience more intense mood swings, anxiety, and restlessness than their elders; this may contribute to the high violence rates found among teenage males.[59]

In sum, biochemical studies suggest that criminal offenders have abnormal levels of certain organic or inorganic substances that influence their behavior and in some way make them prone to antisocial behavior.

## Neurological Factors

Another area of interest to biosocial theorists is the relationship of brain activity to behavior. Neurological deficits have been linked to a full range of criminal activity, including serial murder.[60] There is a suspected link between brain dysfunction and conduct disorder (CD), which is considered a precursor to long-term chronic offending. Children with CD lie, steal, bully other children, get into fights frequently, and break schools' and parents' rules; many are callous and lack empathy and/or guilt.[61] Studies conducted in the United States and other nations have indicated that the relationship between impairment in executive brain functions (such as abstract reasoning, problem-solving skills, and motor behavior skills) and aggressive behavior is significant.[62] Children who suffer from measurable neurological deficits at birth are believed also to suffer, throughout their life course, from a number of antisocial traits ranging from habitual lying to antisocial violence.[63] Aggressive adolescents—most commonly boys—often misinterpret their surroundings, feel threatened, and act inappropriately aggressive. They tend to strike back when being teased, blame others when getting into a fight, and overreact to accidents.[64]

Some suspect that the cause of abnormal neurological function is impairment in **neurotransmitters**, which are chemical compounds that influence or activate brain functions. Neurotransmitters studied in relation to aggression include dopamine, serotonin, monoamine oxidase, and gamma aminobutyric acid. Evidence exists that abnormal levels of these chemicals are associated with aggression.[65] Studies of habitually violent criminals show that low serotonin levels are linked with poor impulse control, hyperactivity, increased irritability, and sensation seeking.[66]

***ADHD*** People with an abnormal cerebral structure, referred to as minimal brain dysfunction, may experience periods of explosive rage. Brain dysfunction is sometimes manifested as attention-deficit/hyperactivity disorder (ADHD), another suspected cause of antisocial

**neurotransmitters**
Chemical substances that carry impulses from one nerve cell to another. Neurotransmitters are found in the space (synapse) that separates the transmitting neuron's terminal (axon) from the receiving neuron's terminal (dendrite).

*This scan compares a normal brain (left) and the brain of an individual with ADHD (right). The areas of orange and white demonstrate a higher rate of metabolism; the areas of blue and green represent an abnormally low metabolic rate. Why is ADHD so prevalent in the United States today? Some experts believe our immigrant forebears were risk-takers who impulsively left their homelands for a life in the new world. They may have brought with them a genetic predisposition to ADHD.*

© Dr. Alan Zametkin/Clinical Brain Imaging, courtesy of Office of Scientific Information, NIMH

## CONCEPT SUMMARY 3.2
### *Biosocial Views of Crime Causation*

| View | Major Premise | Strengths | Research Focus |
|---|---|---|---|
| **Biochemical** | Crime, especially violence, is a function of diet, vitamin intake, hormonal imbalance, or food allergies. | Explains irrational violence; it shows how the environment interacts with personal traits to influence behavior. | Diet, hormones, enzymes, environmental contaminants, and lead intake. |
| **Neurological** | Criminals and delinquents often suffer brain impairment. Attention-deficit/hyperactivity disorder and other brain dysfunctions are related to antisocial behavior. | Explains irrational violence; it shows how brain activity influences behavior. | ADHD, learning disabilities, brain injuries, and brain chemistry. |
| **Genetic** | Criminal traits and predispositions are inherited. | Explains why a small percentage of youths in high-crime areas become chronic offenders. | Twin behavior, sibling behavior, and parent–child similarities. |

behavior. Several studies have shown that children with attention problems experience increased levels of antisocial behavior and aggression during childhood, adolescence, and adulthood.[67] Boys and girls who suffer from ADHD are impaired both academically and socially, factors that are related to long-term antisocial behaviors.[68]

The condition may cause poor school performance, bullying, stubbornness, and a lack of response to discipline. Although the origin of ADHD is still unknown, suspected causes include neurological damage, prenatal stress, and even food additives and chemical allergies. Research shows that youths with ADHD who grow up in a dysfunctional family are the most vulnerable to chronic delinquency that continues into their adulthood.[69]

## Genetic Factors

Although the earliest biological studies of crime tried and failed to discover a genetic basis for criminality, modern biosocial theorists are still concerned with the role of heredity in producing crime-prone people. The relationship may be either direct or indirect. A direct association might include possessing particular genes highly correlated with crime.[70] An indirect association occurs when genetic makeup is associated with a personality trait or physical trait that is linked to antisocial behavior. Personality conditions linked to aggression (such as psychopathy, impulsivity, and neuroticism) and psychopathology (such as schizophrenia) have been found to be heritable.[71]

If inherited traits are related to criminality, twins should be more similar in their antisocial activities than other sibling pairs. However, because most twins are brought up together, determining whether behavioral similarities are a function of environmental influences or genetics is difficult. To overcome this problem, biosocial theorists usually compare identical, or monozygotic (MZ), twins with fraternal, or dizygotic (DZ), twins of the same sex. MZ twins are genetically identical, so their behavior would be expected to be more similar than that of DZ twins. Preliminary studies have shown that this is true.[72] Some evidence exists that genetic makeup is a better predictor of criminality than either social or environmental variables.[73]

The various biosocial views of criminal behavior are summarized in Concept Summary 3.2.

## PSYCHOLOGICAL THEORIES

The view that criminals may be suffering from psychological abnormality or stress has also had a long history.

### Psychodynamic Theory

Psychodynamic theory, the creation of Viennese physician Sigmund Freud (1856–1939), still holds a prominent position in psychological thought.[74] According to the psychodynamic view, some people encounter problems during their early development that cause an imbalance in their personality. Some have mood disorders and are extremely anxious, fearful, and impulsive. Patients with psychosis are people whose primitive impulses have broken through and actually control their personality; they may hear voices telling them what to do, or see visions. One type of psychosis is schizophrenia, a condition marked by incoherent thought processes, a lack of insight, hallucinations, and feelings of persecution.

*CRIME AND MENTAL ILLNESS* Psychodynamic theorists believe that law violators have suffered damage to their personalities early in their development and that this damage renders them powerless to control their impulses. They may suffer delusions and feel persecuted, worthless, and alienated.[75] As a result, they seek immediate gratification of their needs without considering right and wrong or the needs of others. Mental illness dogs offenders across the life course: Delinquent adolescents have higher rates of clinical mental disorders than adolescents in the general population.[76] As adult criminals, people who have been arrested for multiple crimes are more likely to suffer from a psychiatric disorder, particularly a psychotic disorder, than nonchronic offenders.[77] Even if apprehended, the mentally ill are much more likely to experience repeated incarcerations if they continue to suffer from major psychiatric disorders (such as depressive disorder, bipolar disorder, schizophrenia, and nonschizophrenic psychotic disorders).[78] In sum, there is a body of research showing that people who suffer from severe mental illness and distress seem to be more antisocial than members of the general population and that punishment may do little to reduce their criminal offending.[79]

Despite this evidence, some doubt remains about whether the mentally ill commit more crime than the mentally sound. It is also possible that the link is caused by the treatment of the mentally ill: The police may be more likely to arrest the mentally ill, giving the illusion that the latter are crime-prone.[80] However, even though some mental health problems increase the risk of arrest, others elicit out more cautious or compassionate police responses that may result in treatment rather than arrest.[81] Further research is needed to clarify this important relationship.

### Behavioral Theory

A second branch of psychological theory views behavior as learned through interactions with others. Behavior that is rewarded becomes habitual; behavior that is punished becomes extinguished. One sub-branch of behavioral theory of particular relevance to criminology is **social learning theory**. According to social learning theorists, people act aggressively because, as children, they modeled their behavior after the violent acts of adults.[82] Later in life, antisocial behavioral patterns are reinforced by peers and other acquaintances.[83]

Social learning theorists conclude that the antisocial behavior of potentially violent people can be triggered by a number of different influences: verbal taunts and threats; the experience of direct pain; and perceptions of relative social disability, such as poverty and racial discrimination. Those who have learned

**social learning theory** The view that human behavior is learned through observation of human social interactions, either directly from those in close proximity or indirectly from the media.

violence and have seen it rewarded are more likely than others to react violently when subjected to these stimuli.

One area of particular interest to social learning theorists is whether the entertainment media can influence violence. This topic is discussed in the accompanying Images of Justice feature.

## Cognitive Theory

Cognitive psychologists are concerned with the way people perceive and mentally represent the world in which they live. Some researchers focus on how people process and store information, viewing the operation of human intellect as similar to the way computers analyze available information; the emphasis is on information processing. Aggressive people may base their behavior on faulty information. They perceive other people as more aggressive than they really are. Consequently, they are more likely to be vigilant, on edge, or suspicious. When they attack victims, they may believe they are defending themselves, when they are simply misreading the situation.[84] The college student who rapes his date may have a cognitive problem, rendering him incapable of distinguishing among behavioral cues. He misidentifies rejection as a come-on or as "playing hard to get."

Another area of cognitive psychology is moral development theory. According to this theory, people go through a series of stages beginning early in childhood and continuing through their adult years.[85] Each stage is marked by a different view of right and wrong. For example, a child may do what is right simply to avoid punishment and censure. Later in life, the same person will develop a sensitivity to others' needs and do what is right to avoid hurting others. Upon reaching a higher level of maturity, the same person may behave in accordance with his or her perception of universal principles of justice, equality, and fairness.

According to developmental psychologists, criminals may lack the ability to make moral judgments. Criminals report that their outlooks are characterized by self-interest and impaired moral development. They are unlikely to consider the rights of others, and they are not concerned with maintaining the rules of society.[86]

## Personality and Crime

Some psychologists view criminal behavior as a function of a disturbed personality structure. Personality can be defined as the reasonably stable patterns of behavior, including thoughts and emotions, that distinguish one person from another.[87]

The terms "antisocial," "psychopath," and "sociopath" are commonly used to describe people who have an **antisocial personality** (although the APA considers "psychopath" and "sociopath" outdated, these terms are still commonly used). *The Diagnostic and Statistical Manual of Mental Disorders* of the American Psychiatric Association (APA) defines the antisocial personality as a pervasive pattern of disregard for, and violation of, the rights of others that begins in childhood or early adolescence and continues into adulthood. Those suffering from this disease usually exhibit at least three of the following behaviors:

**antisocial personality**
A personality characterized by a lack of warmth and feeling, inappropriate behavioral responses, and an inability to learn from experience (also called sociopath or psychopath).

- Failure to conform to social norms with respect to lawful behaviors, as indicated by repeatedly performing acts that are grounds for arrest.
- Deceitfulness, as indicated by repeatedly lying, using aliases, or conning others for personal profit or pleasure.
- Impulsivity or failure to plan ahead.
- Irritability and aggressiveness, as indicated by repeated physical fights or assaults.
- Reckless disregard for the safety of self or others.
- Consistent irresponsibility, as indicated by repeated failure to sustain consistent work behavior or to honor financial obligations
- Lack of remorse, as indicated by being indifferent to or rationalizing having hurt, mistreated, or stolen from another[88]

## IMAGES OF JUSTICE

# The Media and Violence

Do the media influence behavior? Does broadcast violence cause aggressive behavior in viewers? This has become a hot topic because of the persistent theme of violence on television and in films. Critics have called for drastic measures, ranging from banning TV violence to putting warning labels on heavy-metal albums out of fear that listening to hard-rock lyrics produces delinquency.

If there is in fact a TV–violence link, the problem is indeed alarming. Systematic viewing of TV begins at 2.5 years of age and continues at a high level during the preschool and early school years. Marketing research indicates that adolescents aged 11 to 14 view violent horror movies at a higher rate than any other age group. Children this age use older peers and siblings and apathetic parents to gain access to R-rated films.

A number of researchers have found that viewing media violence *contributes* to aggression. For example, developmental psychologist John Murray carefully reviewed existing research on the effect of TV violence on children and concluded that viewing media violence is related to both short- and long-term increases in aggressive attitudes, values, and behaviors. There is also evidence that kids who watch TV are more likely to persist in aggressive behavior as adults. A recent study conducted by researchers at Columbia University found that kids who watch more than an hour of TV each day show an increase in assaults, fights, robberies, and other acts of aggression later in life and into adulthood. One reason is that excessive TV viewing may create changes in personality and

cognition that produce long-term behavioral changes. Dimitri Christakis and his associates found that for every hour of television watched daily between the ages of 1 and 3, the risk of developing attention problems increased by 9 percent over the life course; attention problems have been linked to antisocial behaviors.

There are several explanations for the effects of television and film violence on behavior:

- Media violence can provide aggressive "scripts" that children store in memory. Repeated exposure to these scripts can increase their retention and lead to changes in attitudes.
- Media violence increases the arousal levels of viewers and makes them more prone to act aggressively. Studies measuring the galvanic skin response of subjects—a physical indication of arousal based on the amount of electricity conducted across the palm of the hand—show that viewing violent media led to increased arousal levels in young children.
- Media violence promotes such negative attitudes as suspiciousness and the expectation that the viewer will become involved in violence. Frequent viewing of aggression and violence makes them seem common and socially acceptable behavior.
- Media violence allows aggressive youths to justify their behavior. It is possible that, instead of causing violence, media helps violent youths rationalize their behavior as a socially acceptable and common activity.

Those suffering from this personality disorder are believed to be dangerous, aggressive, antisocial individuals who act in a callous manner. They neither learn from their mistakes nor are deterred by punishments.[89] Although they may appear charming and have at least average intelligence, people with antisocial personality disorder lack emotional depth, are incapable of caring for others, and maintain an abnormally low level of anxiety. Forensic psychologist James Blair and his colleagues found that approximately 15 to 25 percent of U.S. prison inmates meet diagnostic criteria for psychopathy. Once they are released, former inmates who suffer from psychopathy are three times more likely than other prisoners to reoffend within a year of release, and four times more likely to reoffend violently.[90]

What causes an antisocial personality to develop? There are three independent views:

- *Socialization.* Some experts link it to improper socialization, having a psychopathic parent, parental rejection, lack of love during childhood, and inconsistent discipline.[91]

■ Media violence may disinhibit aggressive behavior, which is normally controlled by other learning processes. **Disinhibition** takes place when adults are viewed as being rewarded for violence and when violence is seen as socially acceptable. This contradicts previous learning experiences in which violent behavior was viewed as wrong.

## Is There a Media–Violence Link?

This research is quite persuasive, but not all biosocial theorists accept that watching TV and movies or playing violent video games eventually leads to episodes of interpersonal violence. The mere fact that kids who are exposed to violent media also engage in violent behaviors is not proof of a causal connection. It is also possible that kids who are already violent seek out violent media to enforce or justify their preexisting behaviors: What would we expect violent gang boys to watch on TV? *Hannah Montana* and *SpongeBob*? There is little evidence that areas that experience the highest levels of violent TV viewing also have rates of violent crime that are above the norm. Millions of children watch violence every night but do not become violent criminals. If violent TV shows did, indeed, cause interpersonal violence, then there should be few ecological and regional patterns in the crime rate, but there are many. To put it another way, how can regional differences in the violence rate be explained, considering the fact that people all across the nation watch the same TV shows and films? Nor can the violence–media link explain recent crime trends. Despite a rampant increase in violent TV shows, films, and video games, the violence rate among teens has been in significant decline.

One reason for the ongoing debate may be that media violence may affect one subset of the population but have relatively little effect on others. Media violence may influence people who are predisposed to aggressive or antisocial behavior. Thus, if the impact of media on behavior is not in fact universal, it may have the greatest effect on those who are the most socially and psychologically vulnerable.

## Critical Thinking

1. Should the government control the content of TV shows and limit the amount of weekly violence? How could the national news be shown if violence were omitted? What about boxing matches and hockey games?

2. How can we explain the fact that millions of kids watch violent TV shows and remain nonviolent? If there is a TV–violence link, how can we explain the fact that violence rates may have been higher in the Old West than they are today? Do you think kids in violent gangs stay home and watch TV shows?

Sources: George Comstock, "A Sociological Perspective on Television Violence and Aggression," *American Behavioral Scientist* 51 (2008): 1184–1211; John Murray, "Media Violence: The Effects Are Both Real and Strong," *American Behavioral Scientist* 51 (2008): 1212–1230; Tom Grimes and Lori Bergen, "The Epistemological Argument against a Causal Relationship between Media Violence and Sociopathic Behavior among Psychologically Well Viewers," *American Behavioral Scientist* 51 (2008): 1137–1154; Dimitri Christakis, Frederick Zimmerman, David DiGiuseppe, and Carolyn McCarty, "Early Television Exposure and Subsequent Attentional Problems in Children," *Pediatrics* 113 (2004): 708–713; Craig Anderson and Brad J. Bushman, "The Effects of Media Violence on Society," *Science* 295 (2002): 2377–2379; Brad Bushman and Craig Anderson, "Media Violence and the American Public," *American Psychologist* 56 (2001): 477–489.

■ *Arousal level*. Psychopaths may suffer from a low level of arousal as measured by the activity of their autonomic nervous system.[92] They may be thrill seekers who engage in high-risk antisocial activities to raise their general neurological arousal level.

■ *Brain dysfunction*. The antisocial personality traits can be linked to brain dysfunction or damage.[93] Research shows that psychopaths may have brain-related physical anomalies that cause them to process emotional input differently than do nonpsychopaths.[94]

**disinhibition**
Unconstrained behavior resulting from a loss of inhibition via some external influence, such as drugs or alcohol, or from a brain injury.

**ATTACHMENT AND CRIME** For some people, psychological problems make them unable to form attachments with others. According to prominent psychologist John Bowlby, attachments are formed soon after birth, when infants bond with their mothers. They will become frantic, crying and clinging, to prevent separation or to reestablish contact with a missing parent.[95] Bowlby's most important finding was that to grow up mentally healthy, "the infant and young child should experience a warm, intimate, and continuous relationship with his mother

*Although some research shows that people who act aggressively in social settings have lower IQ scores than their peers, other findings suggest that the association between intelligence and crime is insignificant. Should mentally challenged offenders be punished in the same manner as those who are not intellectually impaired? Here, Daryl Atkins walks into the York-Poquoson courtroom in York, Virginia. Atkins's 2002 case led the U.S. Supreme Court to bar execution of the mentally retarded as cruel and unusual—and hence unconstitutional. Ironically, upon rehearing the case in July 2005, a jury in Virginia decided that Atkins was intelligent enough to be executed and that the stimulation of the trial process had raised his IQ above 70, rendering him competent to be put to death under Virginia law. In January 2008, his sentence was commuted to life in prison as a consequence of prosecutorial misconduct in the original case.*

(or permanent mother substitute) in which both find satisfaction and enjoyment."[96] According to this view, failing to develop proper attachment may cause people to fall prey to a number of psychological disorders. Psychologists believe that children with attachment problems may be impulsive and have difficulty concentrating and, consequently, experience difficulty in school. Having detachment problems has been linked to a variety of antisocial behaviors, including sexual assault and child abuse.[97] It has been suggested that boys disproportionately experience disrupted attachment and that these disruptions are causally related to disproportionate rates of male offending.[98]

## IQ and Crime

One of the most enduring controversies in the psychology of crime is the relationship between intelligence, as measured by standardized intelligence quotient (IQ) tests, and violent or criminal behavior. Numerous studies link low IQ to violent and aggressive behavior and crime.[99] Some research examines samples of people to determine whether those with low IQ are also more aggressive in social settings. Evidence shows that people who act aggressively in social settings also have lower IQ scores than their peers.[100] Some studies have found a direct IQ–delinquency link among samples of adolescent boys.[101]

Although this evidence is persuasive, many experts dispute that an IQ–crime relationship exists. They offer the following reasons:

■ IQ tests are biased and reflect middle-class values. As a result, socially disadvantaged people do poorly on IQ tests, and members of that group are also the ones most likely to commit crime.

■ The measurement of intelligence is often varied and haphazard, and results may depend on the particular method used.[102]

■ People with low IQs are stigmatized and negatively labeled by middle-class decision makers such as police officers, teachers, and guidance counselors. It is stigma and labeling—not a low IQ—that causes criminal behavior. Because of their favorable treatment higher-IQ offenders avoid the stigma of criminal punishment, which helps reduce their chances of recidivism.

■ Having a low IQ may influence some criminal patterns, such as arson and sex crimes, but not others, further clouding the waters.[103]

## SOCIOLOGICAL THEORIES

Official, self-report, and victim data all indicate social patterns in the crime rate.[104] Some regions are more crime-prone than others. Distinct differences are found in crime rates across states, cities, and neighborhoods. If crime rates are higher in Los Angeles, California, than in Woodstock, Vermont, it is probably not because Californians are more likely to suffer personality defects or eat more sugar than Vermonters. Crime rates are higher in large urban areas that house concentrations of the poor than they are in sparsely populated rural areas in which residents are relatively affluent. Prisons are filled with the poor and hopeless, not the rich and famous. Because crime patterns have a social orientation, sociological explanations of crime are common in criminology.

Sociological criminology is usually traced to the pioneering work of sociologist Émile Durkheim (1858–1917), who viewed crime as a social phenomenon.[105] In formulating his theory of anomie, Durkheim held that crime is an essential part of society and a function of its internal conflict. As he used the term, **anomie** means the absence or weakness of rules and social norms in any person or group; without these rules or norms, an individual may lose the ability to distinguish between right and wrong.

As the field of sociological criminology emerged in the twentieth century, greater emphasis was placed on environmental conditions, whereas the relationship between crime and physical or mental traits (or both) was neglected. Equating the cause of criminal behavior with social factors, such as poverty and unemployment, was instrumental in the development of treatment-oriented crime prevention techniques. If criminals are made and not born—if they are forged in the crucible of societal action—then it logically follows that crime can be eradicated by eliminating the social elements responsible for crime. The focus of crime prevention shifted from punishing criminals to treatment and rehabilitation.

> **anomie**
> The absence or weakness of rules, norms, or guidelines on what is socially or morally acceptable.

## Social Structure Theory

At their core, **social structure** theories equate poverty and income inequality both in the United States and abroad with high crime rates.[106] This association is especially powerful in the United States, because we live in a stratified society. Social strata are created by the unequal distribution of wealth, power, and prestige. Social classes are segments of the population whose members share relatively similar attitudes, values, and norms and have an identifiable lifestyle. In U.S. society, it is common to identify people as members of the upper, middle, or lower socioeconomic class, with a broad range of economic variations existing within each group. The upper-upper class is made up of a small number of exceptionally well-to-do families who maintain enormous financial and social resources. There are now more than 43 million Americans living in poverty, which is defined, for a family of four, as earnings of about $21,000 per year. Such families have scant, if any, resources and suffer socially and economically as a result. The top 20 percent of households earn more than $90,000 per year, and the bottom 20 percent average about $19,000; in contrast to the average American, the "super-rich"—the top one-tenth of 1 percent (0.1%)—average about $1.6 million in income each year.[107] This concentration of wealth is not unique to the United States; it is a worldwide phenomenon. According to the most recent World Wealth Report, there are about 10 million high-net-worth individuals in the world today (people with more than $1 million in assets, excluding their primary residence); they have a net worth of more than $40 trillion.[108]

About 20 million high school dropouts face dead-end jobs, unemployment, and social failure. Because of their meager economic resources, lower-class citizens are often forced to live in slum areas plagued by substandard housing, inadequate health care, poor educational opportunities, underemployment, and despair. They live in areas with deteriorated housing and abandoned buildings, which are magnets for crime, drug dealing, and prostitution.[109] Violence and crime have been found to spread in these areas in a pattern similar to an epidemic of a contagious disease.[110] When lower-class youths are exposed to a continual stream of violence, they are more likely to engage in violent acts themselves.[111] Living in poor areas magnifies the effect of personal, social, and economic problems. Kids whose families are poor *and* who reside in a poverty-stricken area are more likely to engage in antisocial behavior than kids from poor families growing up in more affluent areas. The combination of having a poor family and living in a disorganized area may be devastating.[112]

> **social structure**
> The stratifications, classes, institutions, and groups that characterize a society.

*RACIAL DISPARITY* The problems of lower-class culture are particularly acute for racial and ethnic minorities. The burdens of underclass life are often felt most acutely by minority group members. Whereas many urban European Americans use their economic, social, and political advantages to live in sheltered gated communities patrolled by security guards and police, most minorities do not have access to similar protections and privileges.[113]

Almost 25 percent of African Americans and 22 percent of Latino Americans still live in poverty, compared to less than 10 percent of whites. According to the U.S. Census Bureau, the median family income of Latinos and African Americans is two-thirds that of whites.[114]

These economic and social disparities continually haunt members of the minority underclass and their children. Even if they value education and other middle-class norms, their desperate life circumstances (including high unemployment and nontraditional family structures) may prevent them from developing the skills, habits, and aspirations that lead first to educational success and later to success in the workplace; these deficits have been linked to crime and drug abuse.[115]

If they do commit crime, minority youths are more likely to be officially processed to the juvenile court than Caucasian youths. This makes it more likely that they will develop an official record at an early age, an outcome that may increase the odds of their being incarcerated as adults.[116] According to a recent report by the Pew Foundation, whereas 1 in 30 of all men between the ages of 20 and 34 in the United States is behind bars, for black males in that age group the figure is 1 in 9; and 1 in 100 black women in their mid- to late 30s is incarcerated, compared to 1 in 355 European American women.[117]

The crushing burden of urban poverty brings on the development of a **culture of poverty**.[118] This subculture is marked by apathy, cynicism, helplessness, and distrust. The culture is passed from one generation to the next, creating a permanent underclass referred to as the "truly disadvantaged."[119]

Considering the social disability suffered by the lower class, it is not surprising that some people turn to crime as a means of support and survival. According to the social structure approach, a significant majority of people who commit violent crimes and serious theft offenses live in the lower-class culture, and a majority of all serious crimes occur in inner-city areas. The social forces operating in lower-class, inner-city areas produce high crime rates. What are these forces, and how do they produce crime?

**culture of poverty**
The view that people in the lower class of society form a separate culture with its own values and norms that are in conflict with those of conventional society.

## The Disorganized Neighborhood

The effects of income inequality, poverty, racism, and despair are viewed by many crime experts as a key cause of youth crime and drug abuse. Kids who grow up poor and live in households that lack economic resources are much more likely to get involved in serious crime than their wealthier peers.[120] According to this view, crime is a natural outcome of life in neighborhoods characterized by physical deterioration and by conflicting values and social systems. Disorganized neighborhoods are undergoing the disintegration of their existing culture and services, the diffusion of cultural standards, and successive changes from purely residential to a mixture of commercial, industrial, transient, and residential populations. In these areas, the major sources of informal social control—family, school, neighborhood, and civil services—are broken and ineffective.

Impoverished urban areas are believed to be crime-prone for a number of reasons:

■  Long-term, unremitting poverty undermines a community and its residents. Crime rates are sensitive to the destructive social forces operating in lower-class urban neighborhoods.

- Residents develop a sense of hopelessness and mistrust of conventional society. Residents of such areas are frustrated by their inability to become part of the "American Dream."

- Kids growing up in these disadvantaged areas are at risk for criminality because they hear from adults that there is little chance of success in the conventional world.

- Poverty undermines the basic stabilizing forces of the community—family, school, peers, and neighbors—rendering them weakened, attenuated, and ineffective.

- The ability of the community to control its inhabitants—to assert informal social control—is damaged and frayed.

- The community has become socially disorganized, leaving its residents free to succumb to the lure of antisocial behaviors. Without social controls, kids are free to join gangs, violate the law, and engage in uncivil and destructive behaviors.

- Residents are constantly exposed to disruption, violence, and incivility—factors that increase the likelihood that they themselves will become involved in delinquency.[121]

- Because the poor and affluent often live in close proximity within large urban areas, actual or perceived income inequality creates a sense of relative deprivation that encourages people to commit crime.[122]

It is not surprising, considering these social problems, that disorganized neighborhoods also experience rapid population turnover.[123] Changes in racial and economic composition seem to destabilize neighborhoods and elevate their crime rates.[124] In contrast, stable neighborhoods, even those with a high rate of poverty, experience relatively low crime rates and have the strength to restrict substance abuse and criminal activity.[125] As areas decline, residents flee to safer, more stable localities. Those who can move to more affluent neighborhoods find that their lifestyles and life chances improve immediately and continue to do so over their life span.[126] As the more affluent residents flee, leaving behind a neighborhood with nonexistent employment opportunities, inferior housing patterns, and unequal access to health care, poverty becomes concentrated in these areas.[127] Urban areas marked by concentrated poverty become isolated and insulated from the social mainstream and more prone to criminal activity, violence, and homicide.[128]

Those who cannot leave because they cannot afford to live in more affluent communities face an increased risk of victimization. Because of racial differences in economic well-being, those "left behind" are all too often minority citizens.[129] Whites may feel threatened as the number of minorities in the population increases, generating competition for jobs and political power.[130] As racial prejudice increases, the call for "law and order" aimed at controlling the minority population grows louder.[131]

In contrast to areas plagued by poverty, cohesive communities with high levels of social control and social integration, where people know one another and develop interpersonal ties, may also develop **collective efficacy**: mutual trust, a willingness to intervene in the supervision of children, and the maintenance of public order.[132] It is the cohesion among neighborhood residents, combined with shared expectations for informal social control of public space, that promotes collective efficacy.[133] Residents in these areas are able to enjoy a better life because the fruits of cohesiveness can be better education, health care, and housing opportunities.[134]

The crime-producing influences of economic disadvantages are felt by all residents.[135] However, minority group members living in these areas suffer the

**collective efficacy**
A condition of mutual trust and cooperation that develops in neighborhoods that have a high level of formal and informal social control.

added disadvantages of race-based income inequality and institutional racism.[136] The fact that significant numbers of African Americans are forced to live under these conditions can help explain the distinct racial patterns in the official crime statistics.

Unfortunately, the problems found in disorganized areas are stubborn and difficult to overcome. Even when an attempt is made to revitalize a neighborhood—for example, by creating institutional support programs such as community centers and better schools—the effort may be undermined by the chronic lack of economic and social resources.[137]

*DEVIANT VALUES AND CULTURES*  Living in deteriorated inner-city neighborhoods, forced to endure substandard housing and schools, and cut off from conventional society, slum dwellers are faced with a constant assault on their self-image and sense of worth. Although the media bombard them with images glorifying a materialistic lifestyle, they cannot purchase fine clothes, a luxury automobile, or their own home. Residents may become resentful and angry when they realize that they are falling further and further behind the social mainstream.[138] Residents who live in these high-crime areas, where drug abuse is common, also suffer. Because they believe that their neighbors lack ties to conventional cultural values, their own social ties in the neighborhood become weak and attenuated. This may further reduce already weakened levels of informal social control.[139]

How is it possible for them to adjust and satisfy their needs? One method of adjusting is to create an independent value system. Whereas middle-class values favor education, hard work, sexual abstinence, honesty, and sobriety, lower-class values in slum areas applaud goals that are realistically obtainable in a disorganized society: being cool, promiscuous, intemperate, and fearless. Thus, lower-class **focal concerns** include scorning authority, living for today, seeking excitement, and scoffing at formal education.[140]

Some people living in disorganized areas band together to form an independent lower-class subculture—a small reference group that provides members with a unique set of values, beliefs, and traditions distinct from those of conventional society. Within this subculture, lower-class youths can achieve success unobtainable within the larger culture, while also gaining a sense of identity and achievement. Members of the criminal subculture adopt a set of norms and principles in direct opposition to middle-class society. They engage in short-run hedonism, living for today by taking drugs, drinking, and engaging in unsafe sex. They resist efforts by family members and other authority figures to control their behavior and instead join autonomous peer groups and gangs.[141] Members may be prone to violence, for example, because the routine activities of their subculture require them to frequent locations, such as bars and dance clubs, where aggressive behavior is the norm and where they are exposed to other violence-prone people.[142] Cultural values might include excluding police officers from social conflicts and handling problems personally. When Charis Kubrin and Ronald Weitzer examined the ecological and socioeconomic correlates of homicide in St. Louis, they found that a certain type of homicide (what they call "cultural retaliatory homicide") is more common in some neighborhoods than in others.[143] Residents in these communities often solve problems informally, without calling the police, even if it means having to kill someone in retaliation for a perceived or actual slight or provocation. The neighborhood culture codes support this type of problem solving, even if it leads to violence and death. In sum, in lower-class areas, social, cultural, and economic forces interact to produce a violent environment.

**focal concerns**
Central values and goals that, some sociological theorists believe, differ by social class.

## PERSPECTIVES ON JUSTICE

### Rehabilitation

Social structure theory is linked to the rehabilitation perspective on justice. If poverty and strain cause crime, then efforts to improve economic opportunity can help reduce crime rates. Jobs and social welfare programs are part of the government's effort to give members of the lower class opportunities to succeed legitimately. Reducing crime rates by revitalizing a community's social and economic health is extremely difficult because the problems of decayed, transitional neighborhoods are overwhelming. Rehabilitation efforts are dwarfed by the social problems ingrained in these areas.

*STRAIN* In lower-class neighborhoods, **strain**, or status frustration, occurs because legitimate avenues for success are all but closed. Frustrated and angry, with no acceptable means of achieving success, people may use deviant methods, such as theft or violence, to obtain their goals. Because they feel relatively deprived, the poor channel their anger and frustration into antisocial behaviors.[144]

The concept of strain can be traced to the pioneering work of famed sociologist Robert Merton, who recognized that members of the lower class experience anomie, or normlessness, when the means they have for achieving culturally defined goals, mainly wealth and financial success, are insufficient.[145] As a result, people begin to seek alternative solutions to meet their need for success: They may steal, sell drugs, or extort money. Merton referred to this method of adaptation as *innovation*—the use of innovative but illegal means to achieve success in the absence of legitimate means. Other youths, faced with the same dilemma, might reject conventional goals and choose to live as drug users, alcoholics, and wanderers; Merton referred to this as *retreatism*. Still others might join revolutionary political groups and work to change the system to one of their liking; Merton referred to this as *rebellion*.

Criminologist Robert Agnew has expanded anomie theory by recognizing other sources of strain in addition to failure to meet goals. These include both negative experiences, such as child abuse, and the loss of positive supports, such as the end of a stable romantic relationship (see Figure 3.1).[146] Some people, especially those with an explosive temperament, those with low tolerance for adversity, those with poor problem-solving skills, and those who are overly sensitive or emotional, are less likely to cope well with strain.[147] As their perceptions of strain increase, so does their involvement in antisocial behaviors.[148] In contrast, those people who can call on others for help and support from family, friends, and social institutions are better able to cope with strain.[149]

## Social Process Theories

Not all social theorists agree that the root cause of crime can be found solely within the culture of poverty.[150] After all, self-report studies indicate that many middle- and upper-class youths take drugs and commit serious criminal acts. As adults, they commit white-collar and corporate crimes. Conversely, the majority of people living in the poorest areas hold conventional values and forgo criminal activity. Simply living in a violent neighborhood does not produce violent

**strain**
The emotional turmoil and conflict caused when people believe that they cannot achieve their desires and goals through legitimate means.

**FIGURE 3.1**
**Agnew's Sources of Strain and Their Consequences**

© AP Images/Garfield County Sheriff

*Is crime learned? These booking photos show Patricia Marion Gray, 53, and her son Nathan Gray, 32, who were arrested near Rifle, Colorado, after a meeting with an undercover agent for a purported deal involving weapons, marijuana, and money. Did Nathan learn his criminal ways from his mom? Or can there be another explanation for their co-offending?*

people. Research shows that family, peer, and individual characteristics play a large role in predicting violence.[151] These patterns indicate that forces must be operating in all strata of society to affect individual involvement in criminal activity.

If crime is spread throughout the social structure, then it follows that the factors that cause crime should be found within all social and economic groups. People commit crimes as a result of the experiences they have while they are being socialized by the various organizations, institutions, and processes of society. People are most strongly impelled toward criminal behavior by poor family relationships, destructive peer-group relations, educational failure, and labeling by agents of the justice system. Although lower-class citizens have the added burdens of poverty, strain, and blocked opportunities, middle- or upper-class citizens also may turn to crime if their socialization is poor or destructive.

Social process theorists point to research efforts linking family problems to crime as evidence that socialization, not social structure, is the key to understanding the onset of criminality:

- Marital distress and conflict are significantly related to harsh and hostile negative parenting styles. Adolescents who live in this type of environment develop poor emotional well-being, a tendency to externalize problems, and antisocial behavior.[152] Kids who report having troubled home lives also exhibit lower levels of self-esteem and are more prone to antisocial behaviors.[153]

- Adolescents who do not receive affection from their parents during childhood are more likely to use illicit drugs and be more aggressive as they mature.[154]

- Kids who experience family breakup and shifting family structures may be at risk for crime. For example, youths who reside with a single biological parent who cohabits with a nonbiological partner have been found to exhibit an unusually high rate of antisocial behavior.[155]

- The effects of family dysfunction are felt well beyond childhood. Kids who experience high levels of family conflict grow up to have stressful adult lives, punctuated by periods of depression.[156] Children whose parents are harsh, angry, and irritable grow up to behave in the same way toward their own children, creating risk problems for their own offspring.[157] Thus the seeds of adult dysfunction are planted early in childhood.

In contrast, effective parenting may neutralize crime-producing forces in the environment:

- Parents who are supportive and who effectively control their children in a noncoercive fashion are more likely to raise children who refrain from delinquency; this is called **parental efficacy**.[158]

- Delinquency is reduced when parents provide the type of structure that integrates children into families, while giving them the ability to assert their individuality and regulate their own behavior.[159]

**parental efficacy**
Parenting that is supportive, effective, and noncoercive.

Educational experience has also been found to have a significant impact on behavioral choices. Schools contribute to fostering criminality when they set problem youths apart by creating a track system that labels some as college-bound and others as academic underachievers. Studies show that chronic delinquents do poorly in school, lack educational motivation, and are frequently held back.[160] Research indicates that high school dropouts are more likely to become involved in crime than those who complete their education, especially if dropping out follows a history of school-related behavioral problems.[161] School climate may be the culprit: Many students are also subject to violence and intimidation on school grounds; school crime surveys suggest that about 1.5 million violent incidents occur in public elementary and secondary schools each year.[162] Bullying is a sad but common occurrence in the U.S. educational system; more than 15 percent of U.S. schoolchildren say they have been bullied by other students during the current school term.[163]

Associating with peers also exerts tremendous influence on behavior, attitudes, and beliefs.[164] Popular kids who hang out with their friends without parental supervision are at risk for delinquent behaviors mainly because they have more opportunity to get into trouble.[165] Conversely, their less popular peers, who routinely suffer peer rejection, are more likely to display aggressive behavior and to disrupt group activities through bickering, bullying, or other antisocial behavior.[166] Deviant peers may then sustain or amplify antisocial behavior trends—for example, riding around, staying out late, and partying—and amplify delinquent careers.[167] Because delinquent friends tend to be "sticky" (once acquired, they are not easily lost), peer influence may continue through the life span.[168] Delinquent friends may help kids neutralize the fear of punishment: The fear of punishment is diminished among kids who hang with delinquent friends, and loyalty to delinquent peers may outweigh the fear of punishment.[169] Having prosocial friends who are committed to conventional success may help shield youths from crime-producing inducements in their environment.[170]

In sum, significant evidence exists that the direction and quality of interpersonal interactions and relationships influence behavior throughout the life span. However, disagreement arises over the direction this influence takes:

- *Social learning theory* suggests that people learn the techniques and attitudes of crime from close relationships with criminal peers. Crime is a learned behavior.

- *Social control theory* maintains that everyone has the potential to become a criminal but that most people are controlled by their bonds to society. Crime occurs when the forces that bind people to society are weakened or broken.

- *Social reaction (labeling) theory* says that people become criminals when significant members of society label them as such and they accept those labels as a personal identity.

*SOCIAL LEARNING THEORY*  Those who advocate learning theories hold that people enter into a life of crime when, as adolescents, they are taught the attitudes, values, and behaviors that support a criminal career. They may learn the techniques of crime from a variety of intimates, including parents and family members.[171]

The best-known example of the learning perspective is Edwin Sutherland's **differential association theory**.[172] Sutherland, considered by many to be the preeminent American criminologist, believed that the attitudes and behaviors that cause crime are learned in close and intimate relationships with significant others. People learn to commit crime in the same way they learn any other behavior. Children learn to ride a bike by observing more experienced riders, practicing riding techniques, and hearing how much fun it is to ride. In the same fashion, some kids may meet and associate with criminal "mentors" who teach them how to be successful criminals and gain the greatest benefits from their criminal activities.[173] The more deviant an adolescent's social network and network of affiliations, including parents, peers and romantic partners, the more likely that adolescent is to engage in antisocial

**differential association theory**
The view that criminal acts are related to a person's exposure to antisocial attitudes and values.

behavior. It's likely that deviant affiliations provide attitudes ("definitions") toward delinquency.[174]

Adolescents who are exposed to an excess of definitions in support of deviant behavior will eventually view those behaviors as attractive, appropriate, and suitable, and then engage in a life of crime.[175] In other words, if one of your friends whom you look up to drinks and smokes, it is a lot easier for you to engage in those behaviors yourself and to believe they are appropriate.[176]

The closer the source of these definitions, the more powerful the effect. Romantic partners, for example, have a significant influence on each other's behavior; partners may "learn" from each other.[177] As a result, crime appears to be intergenerational. Youths whose parents are deviant and criminal are more likely to become criminal themselves; children learn crime from their parents.[178] The more kids are involved with criminal parents, the more likely they are to commit crime. This finding supports the hypothesis that children learn criminal attitudes from exposure to deviant parents, rather than crime being inherited (because time of exposure, not merely having criminal parents, is what predicts crime).[179]

***SOCIAL CONTROL THEORY*** When they were in high school, most students knew a few people who seemed detached and alienated from almost everything and everyone. They did not care about school, they had poor relationships at home, and although they may have belonged to a tough crowd, their relationships with their peers were superficial and often violent. Very often these same people got into trouble at school, had run-ins with the police, and were involved in drugs and antisocial behaviors.

> **social control theory**
> The view that most people do not violate the law because of their social bonds to family, peer group, school, and other institutions. If these bonds are weakened or absent, individuals are much more likely to commit crime.

These observations form the nucleus of **social control theory**. This approach to understanding crime holds that all people may have the inclination to violate the law but that most such impulses are held in check by their relationships with conventional institutions and individuals, such as family, school, and peer group. For some people, when these relationships are strained or broken, they become free to engage in deviant acts that otherwise would be avoided. Crime occurs when the influence of official and informal sources of social control is weakened or absent.

The most influential advocate of control theory is sociologist Travis Hirschi, who suggests that people's social bonds are formed from a number of different elements (see Figure 3.2). According to Hirschi, people whose bond to society is secure are unlikely to engage in criminal misconduct because they have a strong stake in society. Those who find their social bond weakened are much more likely to succumb to the temptations of criminal activity. After all, crime does have rewards, such as excitement, action, material goods, and pleasures. Hirschi does not give a definitive explanation of what causes a person's social bond to weaken, but there are probably two main sources: disrupted home life and poor school ability (leading to subsequent school failure and dislike of school). Hirschi's social bond theory is widely accepted, and there is a significant body of work that supports its key concepts. Both males and females who are detached from their parents and uninvolved in conventional activities are the ones most at risk for gang involvement and antisocial behavior.[180] Youths who are detached from the educational experience are at risk of turning to criminality; those who are committed to school are less likely to engage in delinquent acts.[181] Lack of attachment is a more powerful predictor of delinquency and youth crime than actual school failure and/or educational underachievement.[182]

However, not all research supports Hirschi. The most significant concern is Hirschi's contention that delinquents are detached loners whose bond to friends has been broken. It is commonly believed that delinquents are not "lone wolves" whose only personal relationships are exploitive; rather, their friendship patterns seem quite close to those of conventional youths.[183] Many join gangs and engage in group activities: They play sports, go to parties, and hang out with their peers.

**FIGURE 3.2**
**Elements of the Social Bond**

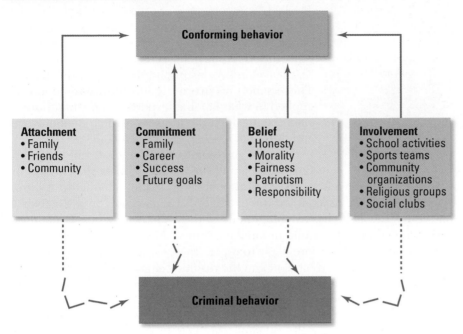

Some types of offenders, such as drug abusers, report having closer and more intimate relations with their peers than nonabusers.[184]

Hirschi would counter that what appears to be a close friendship is really a relationship of convenience and that "birds of a feather flock together" only when it suits their criminal activities. Though co-offending is common, research shows that most juvenile offenses are committed by individuals acting alone and that group offending, when it does occur, is incidental rather than the norm.[185] Associating with kids who support deviant acts may neutralize the positive influences of other elements of the social bond. For example, Hirschi assumes that kids who are involved in school activities are less likely to engage in antisocial behavior—that is, involvement reduces crime. Yet when kids join a sports team, they often get involved with others whose carefree behaviors may encourage criminality.[186] Participating on high school sports teams may help lower the incidence of some serious antisocial behaviors, such as robbery and burglary, as predicted by Hirschi, but it also produces higher levels of status offense–type behaviors, such as drinking. Although these issues remain, Hirschi's version of social control theory is an enduring vision of the social processes that produce criminality.

*SOCIAL REACTION THEORY* According to **social reaction (labeling) theory**, officially designating people as "troublemakers," and thus stigmatizing them with a permanent deviant label, leads them to criminality. People who commit undetected antisocial acts are called "secret deviants" or "primary deviants." Their illegal act has little influence or impact on their lifestyle or behavior. However, if another person commits the same act and his or her behavior is discovered by social control agents, the labeling process may be triggered. That person may be given a deviant label, such as "mentally ill" or "criminal." The deviant label transforms him or her into an outsider, shunned by the rest of society. In time, the stigmatized person may come to believe that the deviant label is valid and assume it as a personal identity. For example, the student placed in special education classes begins to view himself as "stupid" or "backward," the mental

**social reaction (labeling) theory**
The view that society produces criminals by stigmatizing certain individuals as deviants, a label that they come to accept as a personal identity.

## PERSPECTIVES ON JUSTICE

### *Noninterventionism*

Labeling theory principles support the noninterventionist view that an offender's contacts with the criminal justice system should be limited. Among the most prominent policy initiatives based on labeling theory are efforts to divert first offenders from the normal justice process and shepherd them into treatment programs, to order offenders to pay victim restitution instead of entering them into the justice process, and to deinstitutionalize nonviolent offenders (that is, remove them from the prison system).

**critical criminology**
The view that crime results because the rich and powerful impose their own moral standards and economic interests on the rest of society.

**FIGURE 3.3**
The Labeling Process

**Initial criminal act**
People commit crimes for a number of reasons.

**Detection by the justice system**
Arrest is influenced by racial, economic, and power relations.

**Decision to label**
Some are labeled "official" criminals by police and court authorities.

**Creation of a new identity**
Those labeled are known as troublemakers, criminals, and so on, and they are shunned by conventional society.

**Acceptance of labels**
Labeled people begin to see themselves as outsiders. Secondary deviance. Self-labeling.

**Deviance amplificaton**
Stigmatized offenders are locked into criminal careers.

patient accepts society's view of her as "crazy," and the convicted criminal considers himself "dangerous" or "wicked."

Accompanying the deviant label are a variety of degrading social and physical restraints—handcuffs, trials, incarceration, bars, cells, and a criminal record—that leave an everlasting impression on the accused. These sanctions are designed to humiliate and are applied in what labeling experts call *degradation ceremonies*, in which the target is made to feel unworthy and despised.

Labels and sanctions work to define the whole person, meaning that a label evokes stereotypes that are used to forecast other aspects of the labeled person's character. A person labeled "mentally ill" is assumed to be dangerous, evil, cruel, or untrustworthy, even though he or she has exhibited none of these characteristics. Even among people who commit the same or similar crimes, those who are more harshly labeled or punished are more likely to repeat their criminal offenses than those who are spared harmful treatment and the resulting stigma.[187]

Faced with such condemnation, negatively labeled people may begin to adopt their new degraded identity. They may find no alternative but to seek others who are similarly stigmatized and form a deviant subculture. They are likely to make deviant friends and join gangs, associations that escalate their involvement in criminal activities.[188] Instead of deterring crime, labeling begins a deviance amplification process. If apprehended and subjected to even more severe negative labels, the offender may be transformed into a real deviant—one who view himself or herself as in direct opposition to conventional society. The deviant label may become a more comfortable and personally acceptable social status than any other. The individual whose original crime may have been relatively harmless is transformed by social action into a career deviant, a process referred to as *secondary deviance*. The entire labeling process is illustrated in Figure 3.3.

Labeling theorists also believe that the labeling process includes racial, gender, and economic discrimination. For example, judges may sympathize with white defendants and help them avoid criminal labels, especially if they seem to come from "good families," whereas minority youths are not afforded that luxury.[189] This may help explain racial and economic differences in the crime rate.

## CRITICAL CRIMINOLOGY

**Critical criminology** views the economic and political forces operating in society as the fundamental cause of criminality. The criminal law and criminal justice system are seen as vehicles for controlling the poor. The criminal justice system helps the powerful and rich impose their own morality and standards of good behavior on the entire society, while protecting their property and physical safety from the have-nots, even though the cost may be the legal rights of the lower class. Those in power control the content and direction of the law and the legal system. Crimes are defined in a way that meets the needs of the ruling classes. Thus, a poor person's theft of property worth five dollars can be punished much more severely than the misappropriation of millions by a large corporation. Those in the middle class are drawn into this pattern of control because they are led to believe that they, too, have a stake in maintaining the status quo and should support the views of the upper class; they are taught to fear the lower class.[190]

Critical criminologists often take a broad view of deviant behavior, and they most vigorously oppose racism, sexism, and genocide, rather than focusing on burglary, robbery, and rape.[191] They trace the history of criminal sanctions to show how those sanctions have been related to the needs of the wealthy. They attempt to show how police, courts, and correctional agencies have served as tools of the powerful members of society. Because of social and economic inequality, members of the lower class are forced to commit larceny and burglary, take part in robberies, and sell drugs as a means of social and economic survival. In some instances, the disenfranchised engage in rape, assault, and senseless homicides as a means of expressing their rage, frustration, and anger.

## State (Organized) Crime

Critical theorists argue that mainstream criminologists often focus on the crimes of the poor and powerless, while ignoring the illegal acts of the rich and powerful.[192] They have identified **state (organized) crime**—acts defined by law as criminal and committed by state officials, both elected and appointed, in pursuit of their jobs as government representatives. These antisocial behaviors arise from efforts either to maintain governmental power or to uphold the unfair advantages acquired by those who support the government.

State (organized) crimes are manifested in a number of ways. Some individuals abuse their state authority or fail to exercise it when working with people and organizations in the private sector. These *state–corporate* crimes may occur when a state institutions such as an environmental agency fails to enforce laws, resulting in the pollution of public waterways.[193] In industrial society, some government officials, secretly on the payroll of large private corporations, do everything they can to protect the property rights of the wealthy, while opposing the real interests of the poor. They might even go to war to support the capitalist classes who covet the labor and natural resources of other nations.

State crimes may also involve violation of citizen trust through crimes such as soliciting bribes (usually money or some other economic benefit, such as a gift or service). Politicians, judges, police, and government regulators engage in corruption that damages public trust in the government. And unfortunately, when corruption is uncovered and the perpetrator brought to justice, it is difficult to determine whether a real criminal has been caught or a political opponent framed and punished.

To carry out state crimes, government agents may engage in a variety of illegal behaviors, ranging from listening in on telephone conversations to intercepting emails without proper approval in order to stifle dissent and monitor political opponents. In some rogue states, governments agencies routinely deny citizens basic civil rights, holding them without trial and using "disappearances" and summary executions to rid themselves of political dissidents. Others may go as far as torturing opponents or employing death squads to eliminate any threat to their dominance.[194]

**state (organized) crime**
Criminal acts committed by state officials in pursuit of their jobs as government representatives.

© AP Photo/Fernando Sturla, Telam/File

*State-organized crimes are crimes inflicted by those in power upon their political opponents. Here, on July 2, 2010, Argentina's former dictator Jorge Rafael Videla is escorted by prison guards into a courthouse for a hearing in Buenos Aires. He faces charges for crimes he committed during Argentina's 1976–1983 military dictatorship. Now 84 years old, he is being tried for the murders of 31 political prisoners who were pulled from their jail cells shortly after his 1976 military coup and, according to the official story, shot while trying to escape.*

## Support for Critical Theory

A considerable body of research supports critical criminology. Criminologists routinely have found evidence that measures of social inequality, such as income level, deteriorated living conditions, and relative economic deprivation, are highly associated with crime rates, especially the felony murders that typically accompany robberies and burglaries.[195] The conclusion is that as people become economically marginalized, they will turn to violent crime for survival, producing an inevitable upswing in the number of street crimes and a corresponding spike in the murder rate.

Another area of critical research involves examining the criminal justice system to see whether it operates as an instrument of class oppression or as a fair, evenhanded social control agency. Research has found that jurisdictions with significant levels of economic disparity are also the most likely to have large numbers of people killed by police officers. Police may act more forcefully in areas where class conflict creates the perception that extreme forms of social control are needed to maintain order.[196] There is also evidence of racial discrimination. Police typically devote more resources to areas and neighborhoods that have large minority populations where there is fear that minorities are becoming more numerous and presenting a threat to the white majority.[197] Analysis of national population trends and imprisonment rates shows that as the percentage of minority group members increases in a population, the imprisonment rate does likewise.[198]

## DEVELOPMENTAL THEORIES

**developmental theories**
A view of crime holding that as people travel through the life course, their experiences along the way influence their behavior patterns. Behavior changes at each stage of the human experience.

**Developmental theories** seek to identify, describe, and understand the developmental factors that explain the onset and continuation of a criminal career. As a group, they do not ask the relatively simple question: Why do people commit crime? Instead, they focus on more complex issues: Why do some offenders persist in criminal careers, whereas others desist from or alter their criminal activity as they mature? Why do some people continually escalate their criminal involvement, whereas others turn their lives around? Do all criminals exhibit similar offending patterns, or are there different types of offenders and different paths to offending? Developmental theorists want to know not only why people enter a criminal way of life but also whether, once they do, they are able to alter the trajectory of their criminal involvement.

### Criminal Careers

Rather than ask why people commit crime, developmental theories focus on the development and maintenance of criminal careers. Criminals start their journey at different times. Some are "precocious"—their criminal careers begin early and persist into adulthood—whereas others stay out of trouble in their early adolescence and do not violate the law until late in their teenage years.[199]

**early onset**
The beginning of antisocial behavior during early adolescence, after which criminal behavior is more likely to persist throughout the life span.

One important aspect of criminal career development is **early onset**: People who are antisocial during adolescence are the ones most likely to remain criminals throughout their life span.[200] The earlier the onset of criminality, the more frequent, varied, and sustained the criminal career.[201] Early rule breaking increases the probability of future rule breaking because it weakens inhibitions to crime and strengthens criminal motivation. In other words, once kids get a taste of antisocial behavior, they like it and want to continue down a deviant path.[202]

Early-onset criminals seem to get involved in such behaviors as truancy, cruelty to animals, lying, and theft; they also appear to be more violent than their less precocious peers.[203] In contrast, late starters are more likely to be involved in nonviolent crimes such as theft.[204] What causes some kids to begin offending at an early age? Among the suspected root causes are poor parental discipline and monitoring, inadequate emotional support, distant peer relationships, and psychological issues and problems.[205]

Why is early onset so important? Early delinquent behavior creates a downward spiral in a young person's life.[206] Thereafter, tension may begin to develop with parents and other family members, emotional bonds to conventional peers become weakened and frayed, and opportunities to pursue conventional activities such as sports dry up and wither away. Replacing them are closer attachment to more deviant peers and involvement in a delinquent way of life.[207] Early starters are also the ones most likely to have troubled, disorganized lives. Not only are they more likely to commit crime as adults, but they are more likely to be "life failures"—experiencing high unemployment, living in substandard housing, and unable to maintain a stable romantic relationship.[208]

Developmental theories seem to fall into two distinct groups: latent trait theory and life course theory.

## Latent Trait Theory

**Latent trait theories** hold that human development is controlled by a master trait present at birth or soon after. Some criminologists believe that this master trait remains stable and unchanging throughout a person's lifetime, whereas others suggest that it can be later altered or influenced by experience. In either event, as people travel through their life course this trait is always there, influencing decisions and directing their behavior. Because this master trait is enduring, the ebb and flow of criminal behavior are directed by the impact of external forces such as criminal opportunity and the reactions of others.[209] Suspected latent traits include defective intelligence, impulsive personality, and lack of attachment.[210]

**latent trait theories**
The view that human behavior is controlled by a master trait, present at birth or soon after, that influences and directs behavior.

*GENERAL THEORY OF CRIME* The best-known latent trait theory is Michael Gottfredson and Travis Hirschi's General Theory of Crime.[211] In the general theory, Gottfredson and Hirschi argue that individual differences in the tendency to commit criminal acts can be found in a person's level of self-control. People with limited self-control tend to be impulsive, insensitive, physical (rather than mental), risk-taking, shortsighted, and nonverbal. They have a here-and-now orientation and refuse to work for distant goals. They lack diligence, tenacity, and persistence in a course of action. People lacking self-control tend to be adventuresome, active, physical, and self-centered. As they mature, they have unstable marriages, jobs, and friendships.

Criminal acts are attractive to such individuals because they provide easy and immediate gratification—or, as Gottfredson and Hirschi put it, "money without work, sex without courtship, revenge without court delays." Given the opportunity to commit crime, they will readily violate the law. Under the same set of circumstances, nonimpulsive people will refrain from antisocial behavior.

Criminal activity diminishes when the opportunity to commit crime is limited. People age out of crime because the opportunity to commit crimes diminishes with age. Teenagers simply have more opportunity to commit crimes than the elderly, regardless of their intelligence. Here the general theory integrates the concepts of latent traits and criminal opportunity: Possessing a particular trait, plus having the opportunity to commit crime, results in the choice to commit crime.[212] Numerous tests have demonstrated that people who lack self-control are more likely to commit crime and that this association is independent of other factors, such as where they live and their social relationships.[213]

*WHAT CAUSES IMPULSIVITY AND LOW SELF-ESTEEM?* Some social scientists believe that self-control may have a biological basis, stemming from such factors as neuropsychological deficits, birth complications, and low birth weight, all of which have been linked to low-self control.[214] When Kevin Beaver and his associates examined impulsive personality and self-control in twin pairs, they discovered evidence that these traits may be inherited rather than developed. That might explain the stability of these latent traits over the life course.[215] Others investigators, such as Chris Gibson and his associates, have found evidence that suggests the root cause of poor self-control is inadequate child-rearing practices.[216] How you are raised seems more important, they find, than where you were raised. Gottfredson and Hirschi would agree. They believe that parents who refuse or are unable to monitor a child's behavior, to recognize deviant behavior when it occurs, and to punish that behavior will produce children who lack self-control. Children who are not attached to their parents, who are poorly supervised, and whose parents are criminal or deviant themselves are the most likely to develop poor self-control.

The effect of poor parenting in producing children with low self-control may be intergenerational: Parents who themselves manifest low-self control are the ones most likely to use damaging and inappropriate supervision and punishment mechanisms, such as corporal punishment and inappropriate discipline modes that have been linked to lack of self-control in adolescents. These impulsive kids grow up to become poor parents who use improper discipline—and hence produce another generation of impulsive kids.[217]

## Life Course Theory

**life course theories**
The view that criminality is a dynamic process influenced by people's perceptions and experiences throughout their lives, which may change their behavior for the better or the worse.

In contrast to this view, **life course theories** view criminality as a dynamic process, influenced by a multitude of individual characteristics, traits, and social experiences. As people travel through the life course, they are constantly bombarded by changing perceptions and experiences. As a result, their behavior may change direction, sometimes for the better and sometimes for the worse (see Figure 3.4).

**FIGURE 3.4**
Life Course Theory

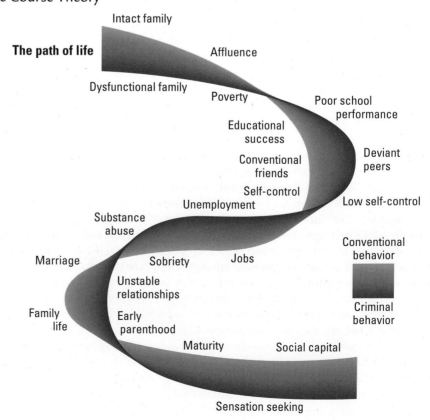

There are also differences in the types of crimes people commit. *Specialists* limit their criminal activities to a cluster of crime such as theft offenses, including burglary and shoplifting.[218] On the other hand, *generalists* engage in a wide variety of criminal activity ranging from drug abuse and burglary to rape, depending on the opportunity to commit crime and the likelihood of success.[219]

Life course theorists dispute the existence of an unchanging master trait that controls human development. Instead, they suggest that as people mature, the factors that influence their behavior also undergo change. At first, family relations may be most influential; in later adolescence, school and peer relations predominate; in adulthood, marital relations may be the most critical influence. Some antisocial youths who are in trouble throughout their adolescence may be able to find stable work and maintain intact marriages as adults. These life events help them desist from crime. In contrast, those who develop arrest records, get involved with the wrong crowd, and can find only menial jobs are at risk for criminal careers. Social forces that are critical at one stage of life may have little meaning or influence at another.

Life course theorists believe that crime is one among a group of antisocial behaviors that cluster together and typically involve family dysfunction, sexual and physical abuse, substance abuse, smoking, precocious sexuality and early pregnancy, educational underachievement, suicide attempts, sensation seeking, and unemployment.[220] According to this view, crime is a type of social problem rather than the product of other social problems.[221] People who suffer from one of these conditions typically exhibit many symptoms of the rest.[222] They find themselves with a range of personal dilemmas, from drug abuse to being accident-prone, to requiring more health care and hospitalization, to becoming teenage parents, to having mental health problems.[223] Problem behaviors have a cumulative effect: The more risk factors a person suffers in childhood, the greater the likelihood that these will carry over into adulthood.[224] The psychic scars of childhood are hard to erase.[225]

**AGE-GRADED THEORY** Two of the leading life course theorists, criminologists Robert Sampson and John Laub, have formulated what they call *age-graded theory*.[226] According to Sampson and Laub, "turning points" in a criminal career are life events that enable people to "knife off" from a criminal career path into one of conventional and legitimate activities. As they mature, people who have had significant problems with the law are able to desist from crime if they can become attached to a spouse who supports and sustains them. They may encounter employers who are willing to give them a chance despite their record. People who cannot sustain secure marital relations or are failures in the labor market are less likely to desist from crime. Getting arrested can help sustain a criminal career because it reduces the chances of marriage, employment, and job stability, factors that are directly related to crime.

According to Sampson and Laub, these life events help people build **social capital**—positive relations with individuals and institutions that are life-sustaining. Building social capital, which includes acquiring personal connections and relationships, is critical if a person hopes to reach his or her life's objectives.[227] For example, a successful marriage creates social capital when it improves a person's stature, creates feelings of self-worth, and encourages people to give him a chance.[228] Getting a good job inhibits crime by creating a stake in conformity—why commit crimes when you are doing well at your job? The relationship is reciprocal: People who are chosen as employees return the favor by doing the best job possible; those chosen as spouses blossom into devoted partners. Building social capital and strong social bonds reduces the likelihood of long-term deviance. Research shows that even people who have long histories of criminal activity and have been convicted of serious offenses reduce the frequency of their offending if they get married and fall into a domestic lifestyle.[229]

**social capital**
Positive relations with individuals and institutions that foster self-worth and inhibit crime.

## CONCEPT SUMMARY 3.3
### Concepts and Theories of Criminology: A Review

| Theory | Major Premise |
| --- | --- |
| CHOICE | People commit crime when they perceive that the benefits of law violation outweigh the threat and pain of punishment. |
| BIOCHEMICAL | Crime, especially violence, is a function of diet, vitamin intake, hormonal imbalance, or food allergies. |
| NEUROLOGICAL | Criminals and delinquents often suffer brain impairment. Attention-deficit/hyperactivity disorder and minimum brain dysfunction are related to antisocial behavior. |
| GENETIC | Delinquent traits and predispositions are inherited. The criminality of parents can predict the delinquency of children. |
| PSYCHODYNAMIC | The development of personality early in childhood influences behavior for the rest of a person's life. Criminals have weak egos and damaged personalities. They lack attachment to others. |
| SOCIAL STRUCTURE | The conflicts and problems of urban social life and communities control the crime rate. Crime is a product of transitional neighborhoods that manifest social disorganization and value conflict. |
| STRAIN | People who adopt the goals of society but lack the means to attain them seek alternatives, such as crime. Personal-level strain produces crime. |
| SOCIAL LEARNING | People learn to commit crime from exposure to antisocial behaviors. Criminal behavior depends on the person's experiences with rewards for conventional behaviors and punishments for deviant ones. Being rewarded for deviance leads to crime. |
| SOCIAL CONTROL | A person's bond to society prevents him or her from violating social rules. If the bond weakens, the person is free to commit crime. |
| SELF-CONTROL | People choose to commit crime when they lack self-control. People lacking self-control will seize criminal opportunities. |
| CRITICAL | People commit crime when the law, controlled by the rich and powerful, defines their behavior as illegal. The immoral actions of the powerful go unpunished. |
| DEVELOPMENTAL | Early in life, people begin relationships that determine their behavior through their life course. Life transitions control the probability of offending. |

People who are married often have schedules where they work 9-to-5 jobs, come home for dinner, take care of children if they have them, watch television, go to bed, and repeat the cycle over and over again. People who are not married have free rein to do what they want, especially if they are not employed. Getting married helps these people stay away from crime. If they do not make that commitment, they can continue their lifestyles, which are erratic.[230]

The major views of crime causation are summarized in Concept Summary 3.3.

## THEORIES OF VICTIMIZATION

For many years, criminological theory focused on the actions of the criminal offender. The role of the victim was virtually ignored. Then a number of scholars found that the victim is not a passive target in crime but someone whose behavior can influence his or her own fate. Hans Von Hentig portrayed the crime victim as someone who "shapes and molds the criminal."[231] The criminal may be a predator, but the victim may help the criminal by becoming a willing prey. Stephen Schafer extended this approach by focusing on the victim's responsibility in the "genesis of crime."[232] Schafer accused some victims of provoking or encouraging criminal behavior, a concept now referred to as **victim precipitation**. These early works helped focus attention on the role of the victim in the crime problem and led to the development of theories that try to explain why someone becomes a crime victim.

**victim precipitation**
The role of the victim in provoking or encouraging criminal behavior.

## Victim Precipitation

The concept of victim precipitation was popularized by Marvin Wolfgang's 1958 study of criminal homicide. Wolfgang found that crime victims were often intimately involved in their demise and that as many as 25 percent of all homicides could be classified as victim-precipitated.[233]

There are two types of victim precipitation. *Active precipitation* occurs when victims act provocatively, use threats or fighting words, or even attack first.[234] For example, some experts have suggested that female rape victims contribute to their attacks by their manner of dress or by pursuing a relationship with the rapist.[235] Although this finding has been disputed, courts have continued to return not-guilty verdicts in rape cases if a victim's actions can in any way be construed as consenting to sexual intimacy.[236] A number of research efforts have found that both male and female victims score high on impulsivity scales, indicating that they have an impulsive personality that might render them abrasive and obnoxious—and thus might incite victimization.[237]

*Passive precipitation* occurs when the victim exhibits some personal characteristic that unintentionally either threatens or encourages the attacker. The crime may occur because of personal conflict. For example, a woman may become the target of intimate violence when she increases her job status and her success provokes jealousy in a spouse or partner.[238] Passive precipitation may also occur when the victim belongs to a group whose mere presence threatens the attacker's reputation, status, or economic well-being. For example, hate crime violence may be precipitated by immigrants arriving in the community and competing for jobs and housing.[239] Gender may play a role in the decision-making process: Criminals may select female victims because they perceive them to be easier, less threatening targets.[240]

## Lifestyle Theory

Some criminologists believe that people may become crime victims because their lifestyle increases their exposure to criminal offenders. Victimization risk is increased by such behaviors as associating with violent young men, going out in public places late at night, and living in an urban area. Research confirms that young women who engage in substance abuse and come into contact with men who are also substance abusers increase the likelihood that they will be sexual assault victims.[241]

Although we often think of criminals as victimizing others, people who engage in crime and gang activity actually have very high rates of victimization themselves.[242] Carrying a weapon is another surefire way to become a crime victim. Males who carry weapons are approximately three times more likely to be victimized than those who go unarmed.[243] Kids who carry weapons to school are much more likely to become crime victims than those who avoid weapons. Carrying a weapon may embolden youths and encourage them to become involved in risk-taking behavior.[244]

One way for young males to avoid victimization: Limit their male friends and hang out with girls! The greater the number of girls in their peer group, the lower their chances of victimization.[245] Those who have a history of engaging in serious delinquency, getting involved in gangs, carrying guns, and selling drugs have an increased chance of being shot and killed.[246]

Having a risky lifestyle increases victimization risk across the life course. College students who spend several nights each week partying and who take recreational drugs are much more likely to suffer violent crime than those who avoid such risky behavior.[247] As adults, those who commit crimes increase their chances of becoming the victims of homicide.[248]

Lifestyle theory suggests that a person can reduce her or his chances of victimization by reducing risk-taking behavior: by staying home at night, moving to a rural area, staying out of public places, earning more money, and getting married. Yet knowing the pitfalls, why do some people forgo safety and engage in a high-risk lifestyle? One reason may be that victims share personality traits commonly found in law violators—namely, impulsivity and low self-control. Perhaps their impetuous and reckless nature leads them to seek risky situations that put them in greater danger than they might have imagined.[249]

## Routine Activities Theory

**routine activities theory**
The view that crime is a product of three everyday factors: motivated offenders, suitable targets, and a lack of capable guardians.

**Routine activities theory** holds that the incidence of criminal activity and victimization is related to the nature of normal, everyday patterns of human behavior. According to this view, predatory crime rates can be explained by three factors (see Figure 3.5): the supply of *motivated offenders* (such as large numbers of unemployed teenagers), *suitable targets* (goods that have value and can be easily transported, such as an iPod), and the absence of *capable guardians* (protections such as police and security forces or home security devices).[250]

The presence of these components increases the likelihood that a predatory crime will take place. For example, increasing the number of motivated offenders and placing them in close proximity to valuable goods will increase property victimizations. Even after-school programs, designed to reduce criminal

**FIGURE 3.5**
Routine Activities Theory

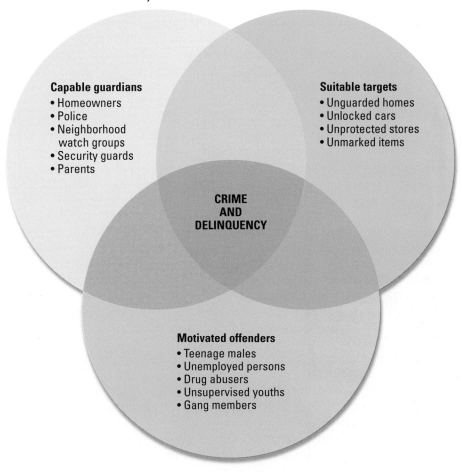

**Capable guardians**
• Homeowners
• Police
• Neighborhood watch groups
• Security guards
• Parents

**Suitable targets**
• Unguarded homes
• Unlocked cars
• Unprotected stores
• Unmarked items

**CRIME AND DELINQUENCY**

**Motivated offenders**
• Teenage males
• Unemployed persons
• Drug abusers
• Unsupervised youths
• Gang members

activity, may produce higher crime rates because they lump together motivated offenders—teenage boys—with vulnerable victims—teenage boys.[251]

Similarly, the presence of valuable targets increases the likelihood of crime and victimization. As average family income increases because of an increase in the number of working mothers, and consequently the average family is able to afford more luxury goods such as laptop computers and iPhones, a comparable increase in the crime rate might be expected. Why? Because the number of suitable targets has expanded while the number of capable guardians left to protect the home has been reduced.[252] The absence of suitable targets as been shown to reduce the chances of victimization: Crime rates go down during times of high unemployment because there is less to steal and more people are at home to guard their possessions.

Guardianship has also been found to be related to victimization. As people begin to buy more goods and services on the Internet, their chances of being victimized by fraudulent sellers and dealers increase; distance buying reduces the oversight of capable guardians.[253] Community crime rates have been found to decline as people begin to employ security devices, guard their homes, create neighborhood-level surveillance programs, and use other "target-hardening" methods.[254] Similarly, if victims fight back, their resistance can deter motivated offenders: The effort needed to rob or attack an aggressive victim who is willing to defend his or her property may simply make the crime less attractive.[255]

The routine activities approach is an important means of understanding crime and victimization patterns and predicting victim risk.

## Ethical Challenges in Criminal Justice: A Writing Assignment

There is an old saying that "people are a product of their environment." If that is so, it would explain why there is so much crime in areas afflicted by poverty. Write an essay addressing the association between poverty and crime. Refer to the sections on social structure theory to gain insight on the factors present in lower-class areas that may influence community crime rates. If you want to consider alternative viewpoints, you may want to address noncommunity factors. In that case, refer to the sections on social process, trait, and rational choice theories.

## SUMMARY

**1. Understand why, to some, crime seems rational.**

- People choose to commit crime after weighing the potential benefits and consequences of their criminal act.

- People will commit a crime if they believe doing so will provide immediate benefits without much threat of long-term risks.

- If the rewards are great, the perceived risk small, and the excitement high, the likelihood of committing additional crimes increases.

**2. Know the strategies used to reduce crime by rational criminals.**

- If crime is a matter of choice, then it can be controlled by convincing criminals that breaking the law is a bad or dangerous choice to make.

- General deterrence is designed to make potential criminals fear the consequences of crime.

- Specific deterrence strategies punish known criminals so severely that they will never be tempted to repeat their offenses.

- Situational crime prevention strategies are designed to convince would-be criminals to avoid specific targets. Techniques include security cameras, alarms, warning signs, and marking items.

**3. Identify the various biological traits linked to crime.**

- Biosocial theory focuses on the influence of biochemical factors on criminal behavior.

- Biochemical studies suggest that criminal offenders have abnormal levels of organic or inorganic substances that influence their behavior and in some way make them prone to antisocial behavior.

- The presence of brain abnormality causes irrational and destructive behaviors.

- Modern biocriminologists are concerned with the role of heredity in producing crime-prone people.

4. **Know the various psychological views of the cause of crime.**

- According to the psychodynamic view, some people encounter problems during their early development that cause an imbalance in their personality.

- Behavior theory holds that human behavior is learned through interactions with others. Behavior that is rewarded becomes habitual; behavior that is punished becomes extinguished.

- Cognitive psychologists are concerned with the way people perceive and mentally represent the world in which they live.

5. **Identify the personality traits linked to crime.**

- Psychologists have explored the link between personality and crime.

- The terms "antisocial," "psychopath," and "sociopath" are commonly used to describe people who have an antisocial personality—a pervasive pattern of disregard for, and violation of, the rights of others that begins in childhood or early adolescence and continues into adulthood.

- Attachment theory focuses on the ability to form attachments—emotional bonds to other people—as a key to psychodynamic development.

- One of the most enduring controversies in the psychology of crime is the relationship between intelligence and crime.

6. **Compare and contrast the various social structure theories of crime.**

- Social structure theories suggest that people's places in the socioeconomic structure influence their chances of becoming a criminal.

- Social disorganization theory suggests that the urban poor violate the law because they live in areas in which social control has broken down.

- Strain theories view crime as resulting from the anger people experience over their inability to achieve legitimate social and economic success.

- Cultural deviance theories hold that a unique value system develops in lower-class areas. Lower-class values approve of behaviors

such as being tough, never showing fear, and defying authority.

7. **Distinguish among the three types of social process theories.**

- Social learning theory suggests that people learn the techniques and attitudes of crime from close relationships with criminal peers. Crime is a learned behavior.

- Social control theory maintains that everyone has the potential to become a criminal but that most people are controlled by their bonds to society. Crime occurs when the forces that bind people to society are weakened or broken.

- Social reaction (labeling) theory holds that people become criminals when significant members of society label them as such and they accept those labels as a personal identity.

8. **Know what is meant by critical criminology.**

- Critical theorists suggest that crime in any society is caused by class conflict. Laws are created by those in power to protect their rights and interests.

- One of the theory's most important premises is that the justice system is biased and designed to protect the wealthy.

- Critical criminology tries to explain how the workings of the capitalist system produce inequality and crime.

9. **Understand the basics of developmental theory.**

- Life course theories argue that events that take place over the life course influence criminal choices.

- The cause of crime constantly changes as people mature. At first, the nuclear family influences behavior; during adolescence, the peer group dominates; in adulthood, marriage and career are critical.

- Latent trait theory suggests that a master trait guides people over the life course.

10. **Identify the various theories of victimization.**

- Victim precipitation theory looks at the victim's role in the criminal incident.

- Lifestyle theories suggest that victims put themselves in danger by engaging in high-risk activities, such as going out late at night, living in a high-crime area, and associating with high-risk peers.

- The routine activities theory maintains that a pool of motivated offenders exists and that these offenders will take advantage of suitable, unguarded targets.

## KEY TERMS

criminology, 90
deterrent, 93
general deterrence, 96
specific deterrence, 96
neurotransmitters, 100
social learning theory, 102
antisocial personality, 103
disinhibition, 105
anomie, 107
social structure, 107

culture of poverty, 108
collective efficacy, 109
focal concerns, 110
strain, 111
parental efficacy, 112
differential association theory, 113
social control theory, 114
social reaction (labeling)
    theory, 115
critical criminology, 116

state (organized) crime, 117
developmental theories, 118
early onset, 118
latent trait theories, 119
life course theories, 120
social capital, 121
victim precipitation, 123
routine activities theory, 124

## CRITICAL THINKING QUESTIONS

1. What factors that are present in a disorganized urban area produce high crime rates?

2. If research could show that the tendency to commit crime is inherited, what should be done with the young children of violence-prone criminals?

3. How can psychological and biological theories be used to explain crime patterns and trends?

4. Are all criminals impulsive? How could impulsivity be used to explain white-collar and/or organized crime?

5. If crime is a routine activity, what steps should you take to avoid becoming a crime victim?

## NOTES

1. "Emperor's Club: All about Eliot Spitzer's Alleged Prostitution Ring," *Huffington Post*, March 10, 2008, www.huffingtonpost.com/2008/03/10/emperors-club-all-about-_n_90768.html.

2. United States Attorney for the Southern District, Press Release, "Booker for Prostitution Ring Pleads Guilty to Federal Prostitution Conspiracy and Money Laundering Offenses," May 14, 2008, http://newyork.fbi.gov/dojpressrel/pressrel08/prostitutionring051408.pdf (accessed May 16, 2008).

3. Rich Schapiro and Adam Nichols, "Hooker Booker's Family Can't Understand Her Fall into Life of Sleaze," *New York Daily News*, March 13, 2008, www.nydailynews.com/news/2008/03/13/2008-03-13_hooker_bookers_family_cant_understand_he.html (accessed July 17, 2008).

4. Christopher Uggen and Melissa Thompson, "The Socioeconomic Determinants of Ill-Gotten Gains: Within-Person Changes in Drug Use and Illegal Earnings," *American Journal of Sociology* 109 (2003): 146–187.

5. Philippe Bourgois, *In Search of Respect: Selling Crack in El Barrio* (Cambridge: Cambridge University Press, 1995), p. 326.

6. Carlo Morselli and Marie-noële Royer, "Criminal Mobility and Criminal Achievement," *Journal of Research in Crime and Delinquency* 45 (2008): 4–21.

7. Ross Matsueda, Derek Kreager, and David Huizinga, "Deterring Delinquents: A Rational Choice Model of Theft and Violence," *American Sociological Review* 71 (2006): 95–122.

8. Jeffrey Bouffard, "Predicting Differences in the Perceived Relevance of Crime's Costs and Benefits in a Test of Rational Choice Theory," *International Journal of Offender Therapy and Comparative Criminology* 51 (2007): 461–485.

9. Matsueda, Kreager, and Huizinga, "Deterring Delinquents."

10. Liliana Pezzin, "Earnings Prospects, Matching Effects, and the Decision to Terminate a Criminal Career," *Journal of Quantitative Criminology* 11 (1995): 29–50.

11. Pierre Tremblay and Carlo Morselli, "Patterns in Criminal Achievement: Wilson and Abrahamse Revisited," *Criminology* 38 (2000): 633–660.

12. Gordon Knowles, "Deception, Detection, and Evasion: A Trade Craft Analysis of Honolulu, Hawaii's Street Crack Cocaine Traffickers," *Journal of Criminal Justice* 27 (1999): 443–455.

13. Andrew Buck, Simon Hakim, and George Rengert, "Burglar Alarms and the Choice Behavior of Burglars: A Suburban Phenomenon," *Journal of Criminal Justice* 21 (1993): 497–507; Julia MacDonald and Robert Gifford, "Territorial Cues and Defensible Space Theory: The Burglar's Point of View," *Journal of Environmental Psychology* 9 (1989): 193–205; Paul Cromwell, James Olson, and D'Aunn Wester Avary, *Breaking and Entering: An Ethnographic Analysis of Burglary* (Newbury Park, Calif.: Sage, 1991), pp. 48–51.

14. Matthew Robinson, "Lifestyles, Routine Activities, and Residential Burglary Victimization," *Journal of Criminal Justice* 22 (1999): 27–52.

15. William Smith, Sharon Glave Frazee, and Elizabeth Davison, "Furthering the Integration of Routine Activity and Social Disorganization Theories: Small Units of Analysis and the Study of Street Robbery as a Diffusion Process," *Criminology* 38 (2000): 489–521.

16. Paul Bellair, "Informal Surveillance and Street Crime: A Complex Relationship," *Criminology* 38 (2000): 137–167.

17. John Gibbs and Peggy Shelly, "Life in the Fast Lane: A Retrospective View by Commercial Thieves," *Journal of Research in Crime and Delinquency* 19 (1982): 229–230.

18. Oscar Newman, *Defensible Space: Crime Prevention through Urban Design* (New York: Macmillan, 1972).

19. Ronald Clarke, *Situational Crime Prevention* (Albany, N.Y.: Harrow and Heston, 1992).

20. Anthony Braga, David Weisburd, Elin Waring, Lorraine Green Mazerolle, William Spelman, and Francis Gajewski, "Problem-Oriented Policing in Violent Crime Places: A Randomized Controlled Experiment," *Criminology* 37 (1999): 541–580.

21. Ronald Clarke, "Deterring Obscene Phone Callers: The New Jersey Experience," in *Situational Crime Prevention*, ed. Ronald Clarke (Albany, N.Y.: Harrow and Heston, 1992), pp. 124–132.

22. James Q. Wilson, *Thinking about Crime* (New York: Basic Books, 1975); Ernest Van den Haag, *Punishing Criminals* (New York: Basic Books, 1975).

23. Herbert Packer, *The Limits of the Criminal Sanction* (Stanford, Calif.: Stanford University Press, 1968).

24. Steven Klepper and Daniel Nagin, "Tax Compliance and Perceptions of the Risks of Detection and Criminal Prosecution," *Law and Society Review* 23 (1989): 209–240.

25. Charis Kubrin, Steven Messner, Glenn Deane, Kelly McGeever, and Thomas D. Stucky, "Proactive Policing and Robbery Rates across U.S. Cities," *Criminology* 48 (2010), 57–97.

26. Daniel Nagin and Greg Pogarsky, "An Experimental Investigation of Deterrence: Cheating, Self-Serving Bias, and Impulsivity," *Criminology* 41 (2003): 167–195.

27. Raymond Paternoster, "Decisions to Participate in and Desist from Four Types of Common Delinquency: Deterrence and the Rational Choice Perspective," *Law and Society Review* 23 (1989): 7–29.

28. Kenneth Land, Raymond Teske Jr., and Hui Zheng, "The Short-Term Effects of Executions on Homicides: Deterrence, Displacement, or Both?" *Criminology* 47 (2009): 1009–1043.

29. Shelley Keith Matthews and Robert Agnew, "Extending Deterrence Theory," *Journal of Research in Crime and Delinquency* 45 (2008): 91–118.

30. Dieter Dolling, Horst Entorf, Dieter Hermann, and Thomas Rupp, "Deterrence Effective? Results of a Meta-Analysis of Punishment," *European Journal on Criminal Policy & Research* 15 (2009): 201–224.

31. Michael Tonry, "Learning from the Limitations of Deterrence Research," *Crime & Justice: A Review of Research* 37 (2008): 279–311.

32. Alex Piquero and George Rengert, "Studying Deterrence with Active Residential Burglars," *Justice Quarterly* 16 (1999): 451–462.

33. Robert Nash Parker, "Bringing 'Booze' Back In: The Relationship between Alcohol and Homicide," *Journal of Research in Crime and Delinquency* 32 (1993): 3–38.

34. Michel Foucault, *Discipline and Punishment* (New York: Random House, 1978).

35. Pew Charitable Trust, *One in 100: Behind Bars in America 2008* (Washington, D.C.: Pew Charitable Trusts, 2008), www .pewcenteronthestates.org/uploadedFiles/One%20in%20100.pdf.

36. Rudy Haapanen, Lee Britton, and Tim Croisdale, "Persistent Criminality and Career Length," *Crime and Delinquency* 53 (2007): 133–155.

37. Andrew Klein and Terri Tobin, "A Longitudinal Study of Arrested Batterers, 1995–2005: Career Criminals," *Violence against Women* 14 (2008): 136–157.

38. Daniel Mears and William Bales, "Supermax Incarceration and Recidivism," *Criminology* 47 (2009): 1131–1166); David Lovell, L. Clark Johnson, and Kevin Cain, "Recidivism of Supermax Prisoners in Washington State," *Crime and Delinquency* 53 (2007): 633–656.

39. Andrew Klein and Terri Tobin, "A Longitudinal Study of Arrested Batterers, 1995–2005: Career Criminals," *Violence against Women* 14 (2008): 136–157.

40. Greg Pogarsky and Alex R. Piquero, "Can Punishment Encourage Offending? Investigating the 'Resetting' Effect," *Journal of Research in Crime and Delinquency* 40 (2003): 92–117.

41. Bruce Arrigo and Jennifer Bullock, "The Psychological Effects of Solitary Confinement on Prisoners in Supermax Units: Reviewing What We Know and Recommending What Should Change," *International Journal of Offender Therapy and Comparative Criminology* 52 (2008): 622–640.

42. James Lynch and William Sabol, "Prisoner Reentry in Perspective," Urban Institute: www.urban.org/publications/410213.html (accessed March 15, 2007).

43. Jose Canela-Cacho, Alfred Blumstein, and Jacqueline Cohen, "Relationship between the Offending Frequency of Imprisoned and Free Offenders," *Criminology* 35 (1997): 133–171.

44. Christina Stahlkopf, Mike Males, and Daniel Macallair, "Testing Incapacitation Theory: Youth Crime and Incarceration in California," *Crime & Delinquency* 56 (2010): 253–268.

45. Reuel Shinnar and Shlomo Shinnar, "The Effects of the Criminal Justice System on the Control of Crime: A Quantitative Approach," *Law and Society Review* 9 (1975): 581–611.

46. William Spelman, "Specifying the Relationship between Crime and Prisons," *Journal of Quantitative Criminology* 24 (2008): 149–178.

47. Steven D. Levitt and Stephen J. Dubner, *Freakonomics: A Rogue Economist Explores the Hidden Side of Everything* (New York: William Morrow, 2006).

48. Steven Levitt, "Why Do Increased Arrest Rates Appear to Reduce Crime: Deterrence, Incapacitation, or Measurement Error?" *Economic Inquiry* 36 (1998): 353–372; see also Thomas Marvell and Carlisle Moody, "The Impact of Prison Growth on Homicide," *Homicide Studies* 1 (1997): 205–233.

49. Cesare Lombroso, *Crime: Its Causes and Remedies* (Montclair, N.J.: Patterson Smith, 1968).

50. Kevin Beaver, John Paul Wright, and Matt DeLisi, "Delinquent Peer Group Formation: Evidence of a Gene × Environment Correlation," *Journal of Genetic Psychology* 169 (2008): 227–244.

51. D. K. L. Cheuk and Virginia Wong, "Attention Deficit Hyperactivity Disorder and Blood Mercury Level: A Case-Control Study in Chinese Children," *Neuropediatrics* 37 (2006): 234–240; Jens Walkowiak, Jörg-A Wiener, Annemarie Fastabend, Birger Heinzow, Ursula Krämer, Eberhard Schmidt, Hans-J Steingürber, Sabine Wundram, and Gerhard Winneke, "Environmental Exposure to Polychlorinated Biphenyls and Quality of the Home Environment: Effects on Psychodevelopment in Early Childhood," *Lancet* 358 (2001): 92–93; Herbert Needleman, Christine McFarland, Roberta Ness, Stephen Fienberg, and Michael Tobin, "Bone Lead Levels in Adjudicated Delinquents: A Case Control Study," *Neurotoxicology and Teratology* 24 (2002): 711–717.

52. G. B. Ramirez, O. Pagulayan, H. Akagi, A. Francisco Rivera, L. V. Lee, A. Berroya, M. C. Vince Cruz, and D. Casintahan, "Tagum Study II: Follow-Up Study at Two Years of Age after Prenatal Exposure to Mercury," *Pediatrics* 111 (2003): 289–295.

53. Bernard Rimland, *Dyslogic Syndrome: Why Today's Children are "Hyper," Attention Disordered, Learning Disabled, Depressed, Aggressive, Defiant, or Violent—And What We Can Do about It* (London: Jessica Kingsley Publishers, 2008).

54. S. Dengate and A. Ruben, "Controlled Trial of Cumulative Behavioural Effects of a Common Bread Preservative," *Journal of Pediatrics and Child Health* 38 (2002): 373–376.

55. Karen Lau, W. Graham McLean, Dominic P. Williams, and C. Vyvyan Howard, "Synergistic Interactions between Commonly Used Food Additives in a Developmental Neurotoxicity Test," *Toxicological Science* 90 (2006): 178–187.

56. Diana Fishbein, "Neuropsychological Function, Drug Abuse, and Violence: A Conceptual Framework," *Criminal Justice and Behavior* 27 (2000): 139–159.

57. Alan Booth and D. Wayne Osgood, "The Influence of Testosterone on Deviance in Adulthood," *Criminology* 31 (2006): 93–117.

58. Keith McBurnett et al., "Aggressive Symptoms and Salivary Cortisol in Clinic-Referred Boys with Conduct Disorder," *Annals of the New York Academy of Sciences* 794 (1996): 169–177.

59. Christy Miller Buchanan, Jacquelynne Eccles, and Jill Becker, "Are Adolescents the Victims of Raging Hormones? Evidence for Activational Effects of Hormones on Moods and Behavior at Adolescence," *Psychological Bulletin* 111 (1992): 62–107.

60. J. Arturo Silva, Gregory B. Leong, and Michelle M. Ferrari, "A Neuropsychiatric Developmental Model of Serial Homicidal Behavior," *Behavioral Sciences and the Law* 22 (2004): 787–799.

61. Alice Jones, Kristin Laurens, Catherine Herba, Gareth Barker, and Essi Viding, "Amygdala Hypoactivity to Fearful Faces in Boys with Conduct Problems and Callous-Unemotional Traits," *American Journal of Psychiatry* 166 (2009): 95–102.

62. Jean Seguin, Robert Pihl, Philip Harden, Richard Tremblay, and Bernard Boulerice, "Cognitive and Neuropsychological Characteristics of Physically Aggressive Boys," *Journal of Abnormal*

*Psychology* 104 (1995): 614–624; Deborah Denno, "Gender, Crime and the Criminal Law Defenses," *Journal of Criminal Law and Criminology* 85 (1994): 80–180.

63. Yaling Yang, Adrian Raine, Todd Lencz, Susan Bihrle, Lori LaCasse, and Patrick Colletti, "Prefrontal White Matter in Pathological Liars," *British Journal of Psychiatry* 187 (2005): 320–325.

64. Society for Neuroscience News Release, "Studies Identify Brain Areas and Chemicals Involved in Aggression; May Speed Development of Better Treatment," 11/05/07, www .sfn.org/index .cfm?p;agename=news_110507d; Society for Neuroscience News Release, "New Research Sheds Light on Brain Differences in Adolescents, Understanding Their Impulsive Risk-Taking Behavior," November 6, 2007, www.sfn.org/index .cfm?pagename=news_110607b.

65. Susan Young, Andrew Smolen, Robin Corley, Kenneth Krauter, John DeFries, Thomas Crowley, and John Hewitt, "Dopamine Transporter Polymorphism Associated with Externalizing Behavior Problems in Children," *American Journal of Medical Genetics* 114 (2002): 144–149.

66. Matti Virkkunen, David Goldman, and Markku Linnoila, "Serotonin in Alcoholic Violent Offenders," in *The Ciba Foundation Symposium: Genetics of Criminal and Antisocial Behavior* (Chichester, England: Wiley, 1995).

67. Rolf Loeber and Dale Hay, "Key Issues in the Development of Aggression and Violence from Childhood to Early Adulthood," *Annual Review of Psychology* 48 (1997): 371–410.

68. D. R. Blachman and S. P. Hinshaw, "Patterns of Friendship among Girls with and without Attention-Deficit/Hyperactivity Disorder," *Journal of Abnormal Child Psychology* 30 (2002): 625–640.

69. Terrie Moffitt and Phil Silva, "Self-Reported Delinquency, Neuropsychological Deficit, and History of Attention Deficit Disorder," *Journal of Abnormal Child Psychology* 16 (1988): 553–569.

70. Brian Boutwell and Kevin Beaver, "A Biosocial Explanation of Delinquency Abstention," *Criminal Behaviour & Mental Health* 18 (2008): 59–74.

71. Gregory Carey and David DiLalla, "Personality and Psychopathology: Genetic Perspectives," *Journal of Abnormal Psychology* 103 (1994): 32–43.

72. See S. A. Mednick and Karl O. Christiansen, eds., *Biosocial Bases of Criminal Behavior* (New York: Gardner, 1977).

73. David Rowe and D. Wayne Osgood, "Heredity and Sociological Theories of Delinquency: A Reconsideration," *American Sociological Review* 49 (1984): 526–540.

74. For an analysis of Sigmund Freud, see Spencer Rathus, *Psychology* (New York: Holt, Rinehart, and Winston, 1990), pp. 412–420.

75. August Aichorn, *Wayward Youth* (New York: Viking, 1965).

76. Robert Vermeiren, "Psychopathology and Delinquency in Adolescents: A Descriptive and Developmental Perspective," *Clinical Psychology Review* 23 (2003): 277–318.

77. David Vinkers, Edwin de Beurs, and Marko Barendregt, "Psychiatric Disorders and Repeat Offending," *American Journal of Psychiatry* 166 (2009): 489.

78. Jacques Baillargeon, Ingrid Binswanger, Joseph Penn, Brie Williams, and Owen Murray, "Psychiatric Disorders and Repeat Incarcerations: The Revolving Prison Door," *American Journal of Psychiatry* 166 (2009): 103–109.

79. John Monahan, *Mental Illness and Violent Crime* (Washington, D.C.: National Institute of Justice, 1996).

80. Courtenay Sellers, Christopher Sullivan, Bonita Veysey, and Jon Shane, "Responding to Persons with Mental Illnesses: Police Perspectives on Specialized and Traditional Practices," *Behavioral Sciences and the Law* 23 (2005): 647–657.

81. Paul Hirschfield, Tina Maschi, Helene Raskin White, Leah Goldman Traub, and Rolf Loeber, "Mental Health and Juvenile Arrests: Criminality, Criminalization, or Compassion?" *Criminology* 44 (2006): 593–630.

82. This discussion is based on three works by Albert Bandura: *Aggression: A Social Learning Analysis* (Englewood Cliffs, N.J.: Prentice-Hall, 1973); *Social Learning Theory* (Englewood Cliffs, N.J.: Prentice-Hall, 1977); and "The Social Learning Perspective: Mechanisms of Aggression," in *The Psychology of Crime and Criminal Justice*, ed. H. Toch (New York: Holt, Rinehart, and Winston, 1979), pp. 198–226.

83. Mark Warr and Mark Stafford, "The Influence of Delinquent Peers: What They Think or What They Do?" *Criminology* 29 (1991): 851–866.

84. J. E. Lockman, "Self and Peer Perception and Attributional Biases of Aggressive and Nonaggressive Boys in Dyadic Interactions," *Journal of Consulting and Clinical Psychology* 55 (1987): 404–410.

85. Jean Piaget, *The Moral Judgement of the Child* (London: Kegan Paul, 1932).

86. Lawrence Kohlberg et al., *The Just Community Approach in Corrections: A Manual* (Niantic, Conn.: Connecticut Department of Corrections, 1973).

87. Walter Mischel, *Introduction to Personality*, 4th ed. (New York: Holt, Rinehart, and Winston, 1986), p. 1.

88. American Psychiatric Association, *Diagnostic and Statistical Manual of Mental Disorders*, 4th ed. (Washington, D.C.: American Psychiatric Association, 1994).

89. Albert Rabin, "The Antisocial Personality: Psychopathy and Sociopathy," in *The Psychology of Crime and Criminal Justice*, ed. H. Toch (New York: Holt, Rinehart, and Winston, 1979), pp. 236–251.

90. James Blair, Derek Mitchell, and Karina Blair, *The Psychopath: Emotion and the Brain* (New York: Blackwell Publishing, 2005).

91. David Lykken, "Psychopathy, Sociopathy, and Crime," *Society* 34 (1996): 30–38.

92. Christopher J. Patrick, "Emotion and Psychopathy: Startling New Insights," *Psychophysiology* 31 (1994): 319–330.

93. Adrian Raine, Todd Lencz, Susan Bihrle, Lori LaCasse, and Patrick Colletti, "Reduced Prefrontal Gray Matter Volume and Reduced Autonomic Activity in Antisocial Personality Disorder," *Archives of General Psychiatry* 57 (2000): 119–127.

94. Kent Kiehl, Andra Smith, Robert Hare, Adrianna Mendrek, Bruce Forster, Johann Brink, and Peter F. Liddle, "Limbic Abnormalities in Affective Processing by Criminal Psychopaths as Revealed by Functional Magnetic Resonance Imaging," *Biological Psychiatry* 5 (2001): 677–684.

95. John Bowlby, "Maternal Care and Mental Health," World Health Organization Monographs Series No. 2 (Geneva: World Health Organization, 1951), p. 53.

96. Ibid., p. 13.

97. Eric Wood and Shelley Riggs, "Predictors of Child Molestation: Adult Attachment, Cognitive Distortions, and Empathy," *Journal of Interpersonal Violence* 23 (2008): 259–275.

98. Karen L. Hayslett-McCall and Thomas J. Bernard, "Attachment, Masculinity, and Self-Control: A Theory of Male Crime Rates," *Theoretical Criminology* 6 (2002): 5–33.

99. Deborah Denno, "Sociological and Human Developmental Explanations of Crime: Conflict or Consensus?" *Criminology* 23 (1985): 711–741; Christine Ward and Richard McFall, "Further Validation of the Problem Inventory for Adolescent Girls: Comparing Caucasian and Black Delinquents and Nondelinquents," *Journal of Consulting and Clinical Psychology* 54 (1986): 732–733; L. Hubble and M. Groff, "Magnitude and Direction of WISC-R Verbal Performance IQ Discrepancies among Adjudicated Male Delinquents," *Journal of Youth and Adolescence* 10 (1981): 179–183.

100. Peter R. Giancola and Amos Zeichner, "Intellectual Ability and Aggressive Behavior in Nonclinical-Nonforensic Males," *Journal of Psychopathology and Behavioral Assessment* 16 (1994): 20–32.

101. Donald Lynam, Terrie Moffitt, and Magda Stouthamer-Loeber, "Explaining the Relation between IQ and Delinquency: Class, Race, Test Motivation, School Failure, or Self-Control?" *Journal of Abnormal Psychology* 102 (1993): 187–196; Alex Piquero, "Frequency, Specialization, and Violence in Offending Careers," *Journal of Research in Crime and Delinquency* 37 (2000): 392–418.

102. Murray Simpson, M. K. Simpson, and J. Hogg, "Patterns of Offending among People with Intellectual Disability: A Systematic Review, Part I: Methodology and Prevalence Data," *Journal of Intellectual Disability Research* 45 (2001): 384–396.

103. Ibid.

104. Terance Miethe and Robert Meier, *Crime and Its Social Context: Toward an Integrated Theory of Offenders, Victims, and Situations* (Albany, N.Y.: State University of New York Press, 1994).

105. Émile Durkheim, *The Division of Labor in Society* (New York: Free Press, 1964); Émile Durkheim, *Rules of the Sociological Method,* trans. S. A. Solvay and J. H. Mueller, ed. G. Catlin (New York: Free Press, 1966).

106. William Alex Pridemore, "A Methodological Addition to the Cross-National Empirical Literature on Social Structure and Homicide: A First Test of the Poverty-Homicide Thesis," *Criminology* 46 (2008): 133–154; John Hipp, "Income Inequality, Race, and Place: Does the Distribution of Race and Class within Neighborhoods Affect Crime Rates?" *Criminology* 45 (2007): 665–697.

107. U.S. Census Bureau Data, United States Census, www.census.gov/prod/2008pubs/p60-235.pdf (accessed May 15, 2009).

108. *Merrill Lynch,* "World Wealth Report, 2008, www.us.capgemini.com/DownloadLibrary/files/Capgemini_FS_WWR08.pdf.

109. William Spelman, "Abandoned Buildings: Magnets for Crime," *Journal of Criminal Justice* 21 (1993): 481–495.

110. Jeffrey Fagan and Garth Davies, "The Natural History of Neighborhood Violence," *Journal of Contemporary Criminal Justice* 20 (2004): 127–147.

111. Justin Patchin, Beth Huebner, John McCluskey, Sean Varano, and Timothy Bynum, "Exposure to Community Violence and Childhood Delinquency," *Crime and Delinquency* 2006 (52): 307–332.

112. Carter Hay, Edward Fortson, Dusten Hollist, Irshad Altheimer, and Lonnie Schaible, "Compounded Risk: The Implications for Delinquency of Coming from a Poor Family That Lives in a Poor Community," *Journal of Youth and Adolescence* 36 (2007): 593–605.

113. Maria Velez, Lauren Krivo, and Ruth Peterson, "Structural Inequality and Homicide: An Assessment of the Black–White Gap in Killings," *Criminology* 41 (2003): 645–672.

114. U.S. Department of Census Data, "Poverty Highlights," www.census.gov/hhes/www/poverty/poverty07/pov07hi.html.

115. James Ainsworth-Darnell and Douglas Downey, "Assessing the Oppositional Culture Explanation for Racial/Ethnic Differences in School Performances," *American Sociological Review* 63 (1998): 536–553.

116. Michael Leiber and Joseph Johnson, "Being Young and Black: What Are Their Effects on Juvenile Justice Decision Making?" *Crime & Delinquency* 54 (2008): 560–581.

117. Pew Foundation, "One in 100: Behind Bars in America 2008," www.pewcenteronthestates.org/uploadedFiles/8015PCTS_Prison08_FINAL_2-1-1_FORWEB.pdf.

118. Oscar Lewis, "The Culture of Poverty," *Scientific American* 215 (1966): 19–25.

119. William Julius Wilson, *The Truly Disadvantaged* (Chicago: University of Chicago Press, 1987).

120. David Bjerk, "Measuring the Relationship between Youth Criminal Participation and Household Economic Resources," *Journal of Quantitative Criminology* 23 (2007): 23–39.

121. Hilary Byrnes, Chen Meng-Jinn, Brenda Miller, and Eugene Maguin, "The Relative Importance of Mothers' and Youths' Neighborhood Perceptions for Youth Alcohol Use and Delinquency," *Journal of Youth and Adolescence* 36 (2007): 649–659.

122. Paul Eberts and Kent P. Sehwirian, "Metropolitan Crime Rates and Relative Deprivation," *Criminology* 5 (1968): 43–52.

123. E. Britt Patterson, "Poverty, Income Inequality, and Community Crime Rates," *Criminology* 29 (1991): 755–776.

124. Karen Parker, Brian Stults, and Stephen Rice, "Racial Threat, Concentrated Disadvantage and Social Control: Considering the Macro-Level Sources of Variation in Arrests," *Criminology* 43 (2005): 1111–1134.

125. Bridget Freisthler, Elizabeth Lascala, Paul Gruenewald, and Andrew Treno, "An Examination of Drug Activity: Effects of Neighborhood Social Organization on the Development of Drug Distribution Systems," *Substance Use & Misuse* 40 (2005): 671–686.

126. Micere Keels, Greg Duncan, Stefanie Deluca, Ruby Mendenhall, and James Rosenbaum, "Fifteen Years Later: Can Residential Mobility Programs Provide a Long-Term Escape from Neighborhood Segregation, Crime, and Poverty?" *Demography* 42 (2005): 51–72.

127. Gregory Squires and Charis Kubrin, "Privileged Places: Race, Uneven Development and the Geography of Opportunity in Urban America," *Urban Studies* 42 (2005): 47–68; Matthew Lee, Michael Maume, and Graham Ousey, "Social Isolation and Lethal Violence across the Metro/Nonmetro Divide: The Effects of Socioeconomic Disadvantage and Poverty Concentration on Homicide," *Rural Sociology* 68 (2003): 107–131.

128. Lee, Maume, and Ousey, "Social Isolation and Lethal Violence across the Metro/Nonmetro Divide"; Charis E. Kubrin, "Structural Covariates of Homicide Rates: Does Type of Homicide Matter?" *Journal of Research in Crime and Delinquency* 40 (2003): 139–170; Darrell Steffensmeier and Dana Haynie, "Gender, Structural Disadvantage, and Urban Crime: Do Macrosocial Variables Also Explain Female Offending Rates?" *Criminology* 38 (2000): 403–438.

129. Allen Liska and Paul Bellair, "Violent-Crime Rates and Racial Composition: Convergence over Time," *American Journal of Sociology* 101 (1995): 578–610.

130. Patricia McCall and Karen Parker, "A Dynamic Model of Racial Competition, Racial Inequality, and Interracial Violence," *Sociological Inquiry* 75 (2005): 273–294.

131. Steven Barkan and Steven Cohn, "Why Whites Favor Spending More Money to Fight Crime: The Role of Racial Prejudice," *Social Problems* 52 (2005): 300–314.

132. Jeffrey Michael Cancino, "The Utility of Social Capital and Collective Efficacy: Social Control Policy in Nonmetropolitan Settings," *Criminal Justice Policy Review* 16 (2005): 287–318; Chris Gibson, Jihong Zhao, Nicholas Lovrich, and Michael Gaffney, "Social Integration, Individual Perceptions of Collective Efficacy, and Fear of Crime in Three Cities," *Justice Quarterly* 19 (2002): 537–564; Felton Earls, *Linking Community Factors and Individual Development* (Washington, D.C.: National Institute of Justice, 1998).

133. Robert J. Sampson and Stephen W. Raudenbush, *Disorder in Urban Neighborhoods: Does It Lead to Crime?* (Washington, D.C.: National Institute of Justice, 2001).

134. Andrea Altschuler, Carol Somkin, and Nancy Adler, "Local Services and Amenities, Neighborhood Social Capital, and Health," *Social Science and Medicine* 59 (2004): 1219–1230.

135. Steffensmeier and Haynie, "Gender, Structural Disadvantage, and Urban Crime."

136. Karen Parker and Matthew Pruitt, "Poverty, Poverty Concentration, and Homicide," *Social Science Quarterly* 81 (2000): 555–582.

137. Ruth Peterson, Lauren Krivo, and Mark Harris, "Disadvantage and Neighborhood Violent Crime: Do Local Institutions Matter?" *Journal of Research in Crime and Delinquency* 37 (2000): 31–63.

138. Beverly Stiles, Xiaoru Liu, and Howard Kaplan, "Relative Deprivation and Deviant Adaptations: The Mediating Effects of Negative Self-Feelings," *Journal of Research in Crime and Delinquency* 37 (2000): 64–90.

139. Barbara Warner, "The Role of Attenuated Culture in Social Disorganization Theory," *Criminology* 41 (2003): 73–97.

140. Walter Miller, "Lower Class Culture as a Generating Milieu of Gang Delinquency," *Journal of Social Issues* 14 (1958): 5–19; see also Thorsten Sellin, *Culture Conflict and Crime,* Bulletin no. 41 (New York: Social Science Research Council, 1938).

141. Richard Cloward and Lloyd Ohlin, *Delinquency and Opportunity* (Glencoe, Ill.: Free Press, 1960).

142. Leslie Kennedy and Stephen Baron, "Routine Activities and a Subculture of Violence: A Study of Violence on the Street," *Journal of Research in Crime and Delinquency* 30 (1993): 88–112.

143. Charis Kubrin and Ronald Weitzer, "Retaliatory Homicide: Concentrated Disadvantage and Neighborhood Culture," *Social Problems* 50 (2003): 157–181.

144. Hipp, "Income Inequality, Race, and Place."

145. Robert Merton, "Social Structure and Anomie," *American Sociological Review* 3 (1938): 672–682.

146. Robert Agnew, "Foundation for a General Strain Theory of Crime and Delinquency," *Criminology* 30 (1992): 47–87; Robert Agnew, "Stability and Change in Crime over the Life Course: A Strain Theory Explanation," in *Advances in Criminological Theory,* vol. 7, *Developmental Theories of Crime and Delinquency,* ed. Terence Thornberry (New Brunswick, N.J.: Transaction, 1994).

147. Robert Agnew, Timothy Brezina, John Paul Wright, and Francis T. Cullen, "Strain, Personality Traits, and Delinquency: Extending General Strain Theory," *Criminology* 40 (2002): 43–71.

148. Lee Ann Slocum, Sally Simpson, and Douglas Smith, "Strained Lives and Crime: Examining Intra-Individual Variation in Strain and Offending in a Sample of Incarcerated Women," *Criminology* 43 (2005): 1067–1110.

149. Wan-Ning Bao, Ain Haas, and Yijun Pi, "Life Strain, Coping, and Delinquency in the People's Republic of China," *International Journal of Offender Therapy & Comparative Criminology* 51 (2007): 9–24.

150. Charles Tittle, Wayne Villemez, and Douglas Smith, "The Myth of Social Class and Criminality: An Empirical Assessment of the Evidence," *American Sociological Review* 43 (1978): 643–656.

151. Eric Stewart, Ronald Simons, and Rand Conger, "Assessing Neighborhood and Social Psychological Influences on Childhood Violence in an African American Sample," *Criminology* 40 (2002): 801–830.

152. Ming Cui and Rand D. Conger "Parenting Behavior as Mediator and Moderator of the Association between Marital Problems and Adolescent Maladjustment," *Journal of Research on Adolescence* 18 (2008): 261–284.

153. Robert Vermeiren, Jef Bogaerts, Vladislav Ruchkin, Dirk Deboutte, and Mary Schwab-Stone, "Subtypes of Self-Esteem and Self-Concept in Adolescent Violent and Property Offenders," *Journal of Child Psychology and Psychiatry* 45 (2004): 405–411.

154. Tiffany Field, "Violence and Touch Deprivation in Adolescents," *Adolescence* 37 (2002): 735–749.

155. Robert Apel and Catherine Kaukinen, "On the Relationship between Family Structure and Antisocial Behavior: Parental Cohabitation and Blended Households," *Criminology* 46 (2008): 35–70.

156. Todd Herrenkohl, Rick Kosterman, David Hawkins, and Alex Mason, "Effects of Growth in Family Conflict in Adolescence on Adult Depressive Symptoms: Mediating and Moderating Effects of Stress and School Bonding, *Journal of Adolescent Health* 44 (2009): 146–152.

157. Rand Conger, Institute for Social and Behavioral Research, Iowa State University, www.isbr.iastate.edu/staff/Personals/rdconger/ (accessed May 15, 2009).

158. John Paul Wright and Francis Cullen, "Parental Efficacy and Delinquent Behavior: Do Control and Support Matter?" *Criminology* 39 (2001): 677–706.

159. Carter Hay, "Parenting, Self-Control, and Delinquency: A Test of Self-Control Theory," *Criminology* 39 (2001): 707–736.

160. Lyle Shannon, *Assessing the Relationship of Adult Criminal Careers to Juvenile Careers: A Summary* (Washington, D.C.: U.S. Government Printing Office, 1982); Donald J. West and David P. Farrington, *The Delinquent Way of Life* (London: Heineman, 1977); Marvin Wolfgang, Robert Figlio, and Thorsten Sellin, *Delinquency in a Birth Cohort* (Chicago: University of Chicago Press, 1972).

161. Gary Sweeten, Shawn D. Bushway, and Raymond Paternoster, "Does Dropping Out of School Mean Dropping into Delinquency?" *Criminology* 47 (2009): 47–91.

162. Jill DeVoe, Katharin Peter, Sally Ruddy, Amanda Miller, Mike Planty, Thomas Snyder, and Michael Rand, *Indicators of School Crime and Safety, 2003* (Washington, D.C.: U.S. Department of Education and Bureau of Justice Statistics, 2004).

163. Catherine Dulmus, Matthew Theriot, Karen Sowers, and James Blackburn, "Student Reports of Peer Bullying Victimization in a Rural School," *Stress, Trauma & Crisis* 7 (2004): 1–15; Tonja Nansel, Mary Overpeck, and Ramani Pilla, "Bullying Behaviors among U.S. Youth: Prevalence and Association with Psychosocial Adjustment," *Journal of the American Medical Association* 285 (2001): 2094–3100.

164. Scott Menard, "Demographic and Theoretical Variables in the Age-Period Cohort Analysis of Illegal Behavior," *Journal of Research in Crime and Delinquency* 29 (1992): 178–199.

165. Amy Anderson and Lorine Hughes, "Exposure to Situations Conducive to Delinquent Behavior: The Effects of Time Use, Income, and Transportation," *Journal of Research in Crime and Delinquency* 46 (2009): 5–34.

166. Delbert Elliott, David Huizinga, and Suzanne Ageton, *Explaining Delinquency and Drug Use* (Beverly Hills, Calif.: Sage, 1985); Helene Raskin White, Robert Padina, and Randy La-Grange, "Longitudinal Predictors of Serious Substance Use and Delinquency," *Criminology* 6 (1987): 715–740.

167. Sylive Mrug, Betsy Hoza, and William Bukowski, "Choosing or Being Chosen by Aggressive-Disruptive Peers: Do They Contribute to Children's Externalizing and Internalizing Problems?" *Journal of Abnormal Child Psychology* 32 (2004): 53–66; Terence Thornberry and Marvin Krohn, "Peers, Drug Use and Delinquency," in *Handbook of Antisocial Behavior*, ed. David Stoff, James Breiling, and Jack Maser (New York: Wiley, 1997), pp. 218–233.

168. Mark Warr, "Age, Peers, and Delinquency," *Criminology* 31 (1993): 17–40.

169. Shelley Keith Matthews and Robert Agnew, "Extending Deterrence Theory: Do Delinquent Peers Condition the Relationship between Perceptions of Getting Caught and Offending?" *Journal of Research in Crime and Delinquency* 45 (2008): 91–118.

170. John Paul Wright and Francis Cullen, "Employment, Peers, and Life-Course Transitions," *Justice Quarterly* 21 (2004): 183–205.

171. Denise Kandel and Mark Davies, "Friendship Networks, Intimacy, and Illicit Drug Use in Young Adulthood: A Comparison of Two Competing Theories," *Criminology* 29 (1991): 441–467.

172. Edwin Sutherland and Donald Cressey, *Criminology* (Philadelphia: J. B. Lippincott, 1970), pp. 71–91.

173. Carlo Morselli, Pierre Tremblay, and Bill McCarthy, "Mentors and Criminal Achievement," *Criminology* 44 (2006): 17–43.

174. Robert Lonardo, Peggy Giordano, Monica Longmore, and Wendy Manning, "Parents, Friends, and Romantic Partners: Enmeshment in Deviant Networks and Adolescent Delinquency Involvement," *Journal of Youth and Adolescence* 38 (2009): 367–383.

175. Andy Hochstetler, Heith Copes, and Matt DeLisi, "Differential Association in Group and Solo Offending," *Journal of Criminal Justice* 30 (2002): 559–566.

176. Wesley Younts, "Status, Endorsement and the Legitimacy of Deviance," *Social Forces* 87 (2008): 561–590.

177. Dana Haynie, Peggy Giordano, Wendy Manning, and Monica Longmore, "Adolescent Romantic Relationships and Delinquency Involvement," *Criminology* 43 (2005): 177–210.

178. Terence Thornberry, Adrienne Freeman-Gallant, Alan Lizotte, Marvin Krohn, and Carolyn Smith, "Linked Lives: The Intergenerational Transmission of Antisocial Behavior," *Journal of Abnormal Child Psychology* 31 (2003): 171–184.

179. Terence P. Thornberry, "The Apple Doesn't Fall Far from the Tree (or Does It?): Intergenerational Patterns of Antisocial Behavior—The American Society of Criminology 2008 Sutherland Address," *Criminology* 47 (2009): 297–325; Terence Thornberry, Adrienne Freeman-Gallant, Alan Lizotte, Marvin Krohn, and Carolyn Smith, "Linked Lives: The Intergenerational Transmission of Antisocial Behavior," *Journal of Abnormal Child Psychology* 31 (2003): 171–184.

180. Kerryn Bell, "Gender and Gangs: A Quantitative Comparison," *Crime & Delinquency* 55 (2009): 363–387.

181. Allison Ann Payne, "A Multilevel Analysis of the Relationships among Communal School Organization, Student Bonding, and Delinquency," *Journal of Research in Crime and Delinquency* 45 (2008): 429-455.

182. Norman White and Rolf Loeber, "Bullying and Special Education as Predictors of Serious Delinquency," *Journal of Research in Crime and Delinquency* 45 (2008): 380–397.

183. Peggy Giordano, Stephen Cernkovich, and M. D. Pugh, "Friendships and Delinquency," *American Journal of Sociology* 91 (1986): 1170–1202.

184. Denise Kandel and Mark Davies, "Friendship Networks, Intimacy, and Illicit Drug Use in Young Adulthood: A Comparison of Two Competing Theories," *Criminology* 29 (1991): 441–467.

185. Lisa Stolzenberg and Stewart D'Alessio, "Co-Offending and the Age–Crime Curve," *Journal of Research in Crime and Delinquency* 45 (2008): 65–86.

186. Kathleen Miller, Merrill Melnick, Grace Barnes, Don Sabo, and Michael Farrell, "Athletic Involvement and Adolescent Delinquency," *Journal of Youth and Adolescence* 36 (2007): 711–723.

187. Ted Chiricos, Kelle Barrick, William Bales, and Stephanie Bontrager, "The Labeling of Convicted Felons and Its Consequences for Recidivism," *Criminology* 45 (2007): 547–581.

188. Jón Gunnar Bernburg, Marvin Krohn, and Craig Rivera, "Official Labeling, Criminal Embeddedness, and Subsequent Delinquency: A Longitudinal Test of Labeling Theory," *Journal of Research in Crime and Delinquency* 43 (2006): 67–88.

189. Christina DeJong and Kenneth Jackson, "Putting Race into Context: Race, Juvenile Justice Processing, and Urbanization," *Justice Quarterly* 15 (1998): 487–504.

190. W. Byron Groves and Robert Sampson, "Critical Theory and Criminology," *Social Problems* 33 (1986): 58–80.

191. Andrew Woolford, "Making Genocide Unthinkable: Three Guidelines for a Critical Criminology of Genocide," *Critical Criminology* 14 (2006): 87–106.

192. Jeffrey Ian Ross, *The Dynamics of Political Crime* (Beverly Hills, Calif.: Sage, 2003).

193. Ibid.

194. Jessica Wolfendale, "Training Torturers: A Critique of the "Ticking Bomb" Argument" *Social Theory & Practice* 31 (2006): 269–287; Vittorio Bufacchi and Jean Maria Arrigo, "Torture, Terrorism and the State: A Refutation of the Ticking-Bomb Argument," *Journal of Applied Philosophy* 23 (2006): 355–373.

195. Travis Pratt and Christopher Lowenkamp, "Conflict Theory, Economic Conditions, and Homicide: A Time-Series Analysis," *Homicide Studies* 6 (2002): 61–84.

196. David Jacobs and David Britt, "Inequality and Police Use of Deadly Force: An Empirical Assessment of a Conflict Hypothesis," *Social Problems* 26 (1979): 403–412.

197. Malcolm Holmes, Brad Smith, Adrienne Freng, and Ed Munoz, "Minority Threat, Crime Control, and Police Resource Allocation in the Southwestern United States," *Crime and Delinquency* 54 (2008): 128–153.

198. Thomas Arvanites, "Increasing Imprisonment: A Function of Crime or Socioeconomic Factors?" *American Journal of Criminal Justice* 17 (1992): 19–38.

199. Ick-Joong Chung, Karl G. Hill, J. David Hawkins, Lewayne Gilchrist, and Daniel Nagin, "Childhood Predictors of Offense Trajectories," *Journal of Research in Crime and Delinquency* 39 (2002): 60–91; Amy D'Unger, Kenneth Land, Patricia McCall, and Daniel Nagin, "How Many Latent Classes of Delinquent/Criminal Careers? Results from Mixed Poisson Regression Analyses," *American Journal of Sociology* 103 (1998): 1593–1630.

200. Lila Kazemian, David Farrington, and Marc Le Blanc, "Can We Make Accurate Long-term Predictions about Patterns of De-escalation in Offending Behavior?" *Journal of Youth and Adolescence* 38 (2009): 384–400.

201. David Nurco, Timothy Kinlock, and Mitchell Balter, "The Severity of Preaddiction Criminal Behavior among Urban, Male Narcotic Addicts and Two Nonaddicted Control Groups," *Journal of Research in Crime and Delinquency* 30 (1993): 293–316.

202. Sarah Bacon, Raymond Paternoster, and Robert Brame, "Understanding the Relationship between Onset Age and Subsequent Offending during Adolescence," *Journal of Youth and Adolescence* 38, (2009): 301–311.

203. W. Alex Mason, Rick Kosterman, J. David Hawkins, Todd Herrenkohi, Liliana Lengua, and Elizabeth McCauley, "Predicting Depression, Social Phobia, and Violence in Early Adulthood from Childhood Behavior Problems," *Journal of the American Academy of Child and Adolescent Psychiatry* 43 (2004): 307–315; Rolf Loeber and David Farrington, "Young Children Who Commit Crime: Epidemiology, Developmental Origins, Risk Factors, Early Interventions, and Policy Implications," *Development and Psychopathology* 12 (2000): 737–762; Patrick Lussier, Jean Proulx, and Marc LeBlanc, "Criminal Propensity, Deviant Sexual Interests and Criminal Activity of Sexual Aggressors against Women: A Comparison of Explanatory Models," *Criminology* 43 (2005): 249–281.

204. Dawn Jeglum Bartusch, Donald Lynam, Terrie Moffitt, and Phil Silva, "Is Age Important? Testing a General Versus a Developmental Theory of Antisocial Behavior," *Criminology* 35 (1997): 13–48.

205. Mary Campa, Catherine Bradshaw, John Eckenrode, and David Zielinski, "Patterns of Problem Behavior in Relation to Thriving and Precocious Behavior in Late Adolescence," *Journal of Youth and Adolescence* 37 (2008): 627–640.

206. W. Alex Mason, Rick Kosterman, J. David Hawkins, Todd Herrenkohi, Liliana Lengua, and Elizabeth McCauley, "Predicting Depression, Social Phobia, and Violence in Early Adulthood from Childhood Behavior Problems," *Journal of the American Academy of Child & Adolescent Psychiatry* 43 (2004): 307–315; Ronald Prinz and Suzanne Kerns, "Early Substance Use by Juvenile Offenders," *Child Psychiatry and Human Development* 33 (2003): 263–268.

207. Bacon, Paternoster, and Brame, "Understanding the Relationship Between Onset Age and Subsequent Offending During Adolescence."

208. Alex Piquero, David Farrington, Daniel Nagin, and Terrie Moffitt, "Trajectories of Offending and Their Relation to Life Failure in Late Middle Age: Findings from the Cambridge Study in Delinquent Development," *Journal of Research in Crime and Delinquency*, first published on January 7, 2010, http://jrc .sagepub.com.libproxy.uml.edu/cgi/rapidpdf/0022427809357713v1.

209. David Rowe, D. Wayne Osgood, and W. Alan Nicewander, "A Latent Trait Approach to Unifying Criminal Careers," *Criminology* 28 (1990): 237–270.

210. David Rowe and Daniel Flannery, "An Examination of Environmental and Trait Influences on Adolescent Delinquency," *Journal of Research in Crime and Delinquency* 31 (1994): 374–389.

211. Michael Gottfredson and Travis Hirschi, *A General Theory of Crime* (Stanford, Calif.: Stanford University Press, 1990).

212. Christian Seipel and Stefanie Eifler, "Opportunities, Rational Choice, and Self-Control: On the Interaction of Person and Situation in a General Theory of Crime," *Crime & Delinquency* 56 (2010): 167–197.

213. Michael Welch, Charles R. Tittle, Jennifer Yonkoski, Nicole Meidinger, and Harold G. Grasmick, "Social Integration, Self-Control, and Conformity," *Journal of Quantitative Criminology* 24 (2008): 73–92, www.springerlink.com.libproxy.uml.edu/content/ k04q0n5u78xm806p/fulltext.html; Gregory Morris, Peter Wood, and Gregory Dunaway, "Self-Control, Native Traditionalism, and Native American Substance Use: Testing the Cultural Invariance of a General Theory of Crime," *Crime and Delinquency* 52 (2006): 572–598; Alexander Vazsonyi, Janice Clifford Wittekind, Lara Belliston, and Timothy Van Loh, "Extending the General Theory of Crime to 'The East': Low Self-Control in Japanese Late Adolescents," *Journal of Quantitative Criminology* 20 (2004): 189–216.

214. Marie Ratchford and Kevin Beaver, "Neuropsychological Deficits, Low Self-Control, and Delinquent Involvement: Toward a Biosocial Explanation of Delinquency," *Criminal Justice and Behavior* 36 (2009): 147–162.

215. Kevin M. Beaver, J. Eagle Shutt, Brian Boutwell, Marie Ratchford, Kathleen Roberts, and J. C. Barnes, "Genetic and Environmental Influences on Levels of Self-Control and Delinquent Peer Affiliation: Results from a Longitudinal Sample of Adolescent Twins," *Criminal Justice and Behavior* 36 (2009): 41–60.

216. Chris Gibson, Christopher Sullivan, Shayne Jones, and Alex Piquero, "Does It Take a Village? Assessing Neighborhood

Influences on Children's Self-Control," *Journal of Research in Crime and Delinquency* 47 (2010): 31–62.

217. Stacey Nofziger, "The 'Cause' of Low Self-Control: The Influence of Maternal Self-Control," *Journal of Research in Crime and Delinquency* 45 (2008): 191–224.

218. Jacqueline Schneider, "The Link between Shoplifting and Burglary: The Booster Burglar," *British Journal of Criminology* 45 (2005): 395–401.

219. Glenn Deane, Richard Felson, and David Armstrong, "An Examination of Offense Specialization Using Marginal Logit Models," *Criminology* 43 (2005): 955–988; Christopher Sullivan, Jean Marie McGloin, Travis Pratt, and Alex Piquero, "Rethinking the 'Norm' of Offender Generality: Investigating Specialization in the Short-Term," *Criminology* 44 (2006): 199–233.

220. Helene Raskin White, Peter Tice, Rolf Loeber, and Magda Stouthamer-Loeber, "Illegal Acts Committed by Adolescents under the Influence of Alcohol and Drugs," *Journal of Research in Crime and Delinquency* 39 (2002): 131–153; Xavier Coll, Fergus Law, Aurelio Tobias, Keith Hawton, and Josep Tomas, "Abuse and Deliberate Self-Poisoning in Women: A Matched Case-Control Study," *Child Abuse and Neglect* 25 (2001): 1291–1293.

221. David Fergusson, L. John Horwood, and Elizabeth Ridder, "Show Me the Child at Seven II: Childhood Intelligence and Later Outcomes in Adolescence and Young Adulthood," *Journal of Child Psychology & Psychiatry & Allied Disciplines* 46 (2005): 850–859.

222. Richard Miech, Avshalom Caspi, Terrie Moffitt, Bradley Entner Wright, and Phil Silva, "Low Socioeconomic Status and Mental Disorders: A Longitudinal Study of Selection and Causation during Young Adulthood," *American Journal of Sociology* 104 (1999): 1096–1131; Marvin Krohn, Alan Lizotte, and Cynthia Perez, "The Interrelationship between Substance Use and Precocious Transitions to Adult Sexuality," *Journal of Health and Social Behavior* 38 (1997): 87–103.

223. Rolf Loeber, David Farrington, Magda Stouthamer-Loeber, Terrie Moffitt, Avshalom Caspi, and Don Lynam, "Male Mental Health Problems, Psychopathy, and Personality Traits: Key Findings from the First 14 Years of the Pittsburgh Youth Study," *Clinical Child and Family Psychology Review* 4 (2002): 273–297.

224. Rolf Loeber, Dustin Pardini, D. Lynn Homish, Evelyn Wei, Anne Crawford, David Farrington, Magda Stouthamer-Loeber, Judith Creemers, Steven Koehler, and Richard Rosenfeld, "The Prediction of Violence and Homicide in Young Men," *Journal of Consulting and Clinical Psychology* 73 (2005): 1074–1088.

225. David Gadd and Stephen Farrall, "Criminal Careers, Desistance and Subjectivity: Interpreting Men's Narratives of Change," *Theoretical Criminology* 8 (2004): 123–156.

226. Robert Sampson and John Laub, *Crime in the Making: Pathways and Turning Points through Life* (Cambridge, Mass.: Harvard University Press, 1993).

227. Nan Lin, *Social Capital: A Theory of Social Structure and Action* (Cambridge: Cambridge University Press, 2002).

228. Doris Layton MacKenzie and Spencer De Li, "The Impact of Formal and Informal Social Controls on the Criminal Activities of Probationers," *Journal of Research in Crime and Delinquency* 39 (2002): 243–278.

229. Alex Piquero, John MacDonald, and Karen Parker, "Race, Local Life Circumstances, and Criminal Activity over the Life Course," *Social Science Quarterly* 83 (2002): 654–671.

230. Personal communication with Alex Piquero, September 24, 2002.

231. Hans Von Hentig, *The Criminal and His Victim: Studies in the Sociobiology of Crime* (New Haven, Conn.: Yale University Press, 1948), p. 384.

232. Stephen Schafer, *The Victim and His Criminal* (New York: Random House, 1968), p. 152.

233. Marvin Wolfgang, *Patterns of Criminal Homicide* (Philadelphia: University of Pennsylvania Press, 1958).

234. Ibid.

235. Menachem Amir, *Patterns in Forcible Rape* (Chicago: University of Chicago Press, 1971).

236. Susan Estrich, *Real Rape* (Cambridge, Mass.: Harvard University Press, 1987).

237. Pamela Wilcox, Marie Skubak Tillyer, and Bonnie S. Fisher, "Gendered Opportunity? School-Based Adolescent Victimization," *Journal of Research in Crime and Delinquency* 46 (2009): 245–269.

238. Edem Avakame, "Females' Labor Force Participation and Intimate Femicide: An Empirical Assessment of the Backlash Hypothesis," *Violence and Victims* 14 (1999): 277–283.

239. Rosemary Gartner and Bill McCarthy, "The Social Distribution of Femicide in Urban Canada, 1921–1988," *Law and Society Review* 25 (1991): 287–311.

240. Wilcox, Tillyer, and Fisher, "Gendered Opportunity?

241. Elizabeth Reed, Hortensia Amaro, Atsushi Matsumoto, and Debra Kaysen, "The Relation between Interpersonal Violence and Substance Use among a Sample of University Students: Examination of the Role of Victim and Perpetrator Substance Use," *Addictive Behaviors* 34 (2009): 316–318.

242. Rolf Loeber, Mary DeLamatre, George Tita, Jacqueline Cohen, Magda Stouthamer-Loeber, and David Farrington, "Gun Injury and Mortality: The Delinquent Backgrounds of Juvenile Offenders," *Violence and Victims* 14 (1999): 339–351.

243. Rolf Loeber, Larry Kalb, and David Huizinga, *Juvenile Delinquency and Serious Injury Victimization* (Washington, D.C.: Office of Juvenile Justice and Delinquency Prevention, 2001).

244. Pamela Wilcox, David May, and Staci Roberts, "Student Weapon Possession and the 'Fear and Victimization Hypothesis': Unraveling the Temporal Order," *Justice Quarterly* 23 (2006): 502–529.

245. Dana Haynie and Alex Piquero, "Pubertal Development and Physical Victimization in Adolescence," *Journal of Research in Crime and Delinquency* 43 (2006): 3–35.

246. Loeber, DeLamatre, Tita, Cohen, Stouthamer-Loeber, and Farrington, "Gun Injury and Mortality."

247. Bonnie Fisher, John Sloan, Francis Cullen, and Chunmeng Lu, "Crime in the Ivory Tower: The Level and Sources of Student Victimization," *Criminology* 36 (1998): 671–710.

248. Adam Dobrin, "The Risk of Offending on Homicide Victimization: A Case Control Study," *Journal of Research in Crime and Delinquency* 38 (2001): 154–173.

249. Christopher Schreck, Eric Stewart, and Bonnie Fisher, "Self-Control, Victimization, and Their Influence on Risky Lifestyles: A Longitudinal Analysis Using Panel Data," *Journal of Quantitative Criminology* 22 (2006): 319–340.

250. Lawrence Cohen and Marcus Felson, "Social Change and Crime Rate Trends: A Routine Activities Approach," *American Sociological Review* 44 (1979): 588–608; Lawrence Cohen, Marcus Felson, and Kenneth Land, "Property Crime Rates in the United States: A Macrodynamic Analysis, 1947–1977, with Ex-Ante Forecasts for the Mid-1980s," *American Journal of Sociology* 86 (1980): 90–118; for a review, see James LeBeau and Thomas Castellano, "The Routine Activities Approach: An Inventory and Critique" (Carbondale: Center for the Studies of Crime, Delinquency, and Corrections, Southern Illinois University, 1987).

251. Denise Gottfredson and David Soulé, "The Timing of Property Crime, Violent Crime, and Substance Use among Juveniles," *Journal of Research in Crime and Delinquency* 42 (2005): 110–120.

252. Cohen, Felson, and Land, "Property Crime Rates in the United States."

253. Kristy Holtfreter, Michael Reisig, and Travis Pratt, "Low Self-Control, Routine Activities, and Fraud Victimization," *Criminology* 46 (2008): 189–220.

254. Pamela Wilcox, Tamara Madensen, and Marie Skubak Tillyer, "Guardianship in Context: Implications for Burglary Victimization Risk and Prevention," *Criminology* 45 (2007): 771–803.

255. Rob Guerette and Shannon Santana, "Explaining Victim Self-Protective Behavior Effects on Crime Incident Outcomes: A Test of Opportunity Theory," *Crime & Delinquency* 56 (2010): 198–226.

# CHAPTER 4

# Criminal Law: Substance and Procedure

## CHAPTER OBJECTIVES

1. Know the similarities and differences between substantive and procedural criminal law and between civil law and public law.
2. Understand the concept of substantive criminal law and be familiar with its history.
3. Discuss the sources of the criminal law.
4. Be familiar with the elements of a crime.
5. Define the term "strict liability."
6. Describe how crimes are classified.
7. Be able to discuss excuse and justification defenses for crime.
8. Discuss the concept of criminal procedure.
9. Know which amendments to the Constitution are the most important to the justice system.
10. List the elements of due process of law.

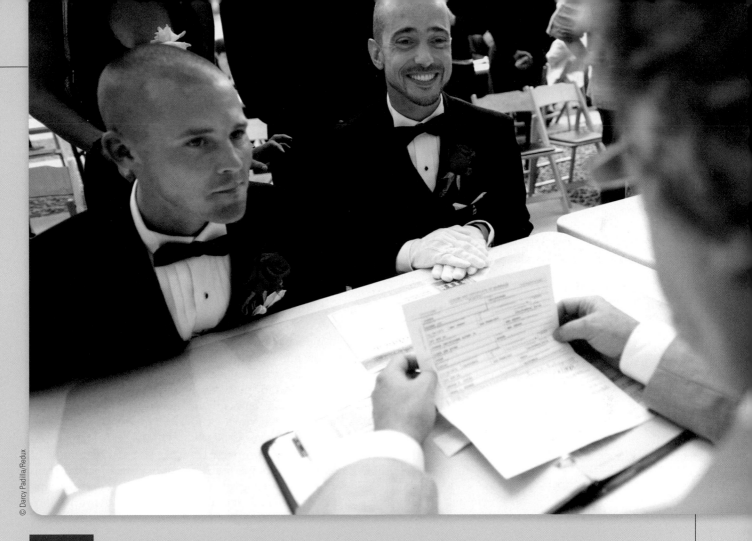

© Darcy Padilla/Redux

**O**n May 15, 2008, in a decision that made headlines across the nation, the California Supreme Court overturned a voter-approved ban on gay marriage, a decision that would allow gay couples to marry in the nation's largest state. In a 4–3 vote, the court found that under the California constitution, domestic partnerships are not a good enough substitute for marriage. The court's ruling, which made California the second state (the first was Massachusetts) to recognize gay marriage, was based on its interpretation of the state constitution. The court held in part that

> . . . in contrast to earlier times, our state now recognizes that an individual's capacity to establish a loving and long-term committed relationship with another person and responsibly to care for and raise children does not depend upon the individual's sexual orientation, and, more generally, that an individual's sexual orientation—like a person's race or gender—does not constitute a legitimate basis upon which to deny or withhold legal rights.[1]

In the aftermath of this ruling, a coalition of religious and social conservative groups placed a measure on the 2008 state ballot that amended the state constitution to prohibit gay marriage. On November 4, 2008, the measure passed with a 52 percent plurality.[2] Ironically, while liberal California banned gay marriages, same-sex couples will be able to marry in conservative New Hampshire beginning January 1, 2010, under New Hampshire General Court HB 436. The law's enactment made New Hamphsire the fifth state to legalize same-sex marriage, joining Massachusetts, Connecticut, Vermont, and Iowa. In California, a new law (SB 54) requires the state to recognize same-sex marriages performed in other states during the period when such marriages were legal in California.[3] ∎

EXHIBIT 4.1

## Three Categories of Torts

1. *Intentional torts* are injuries that the person knew or should have known would occur through his or her actions—for example, a person attacks and injures another (assault and battery) after a dispute.

2. *Negligent torts* are injuries caused because a person's actions were unreasonably unsafe or careless—for example, a traffic accident is caused by a reckless driver.

3. *Strict liability torts* are injuries that occur because a particular action caused damage prohibited by statute—for example, a victim is injured because a manufacturer made a defective product.

---

Here we see how a court ruling can instantly change the lives of thousands of people. These events illustrate that the law is a flexible document, changing to meet evolving social standards of morality and ethics. A hundred years ago "gay marriage" would have been inconceivable, but today it is a reality because of judicial interpretation of the law and the prevailing social climate. And because opponents of gay marriage were successful in amending the California constitution, a right and privilege enjoyed by citizens of that state suddenly disappeared. Conversely, in New Hampshire, a state known for its conservative "live free or die" philosophy (and state motto), gay marriage is now a right.

In modern U.S. society, the law governs nearly all phases of human enterprise, including commerce, family life, property transfer, and the regulation of interpersonal conflict. It contains elements that control personal relationships between individuals and public relationships between individuals and the government. The former is known as *civil law*, and the latter is called **criminal law**. The law, then, can generally be divided into four broad categories:

- *Substantive criminal law.* The branch of the law that defines crimes and their punishment is known as **substantive criminal law**. It involves such issues as the mental and physical elements of crime, crime categories, and criminal defenses.

- *Procedural criminal law.* Those laws that set out the basic rules of practice in the criminal justice system are **procedural criminal laws**. Some elements of the law of criminal procedure are the rules of evidence, the law of arrest, the law of search and seizure, and questions of appeal, jury selection, and the right to counsel.

- *Civil law.* The set of rules governing relations between private parties, including both individuals and organizations (such as business enterprises and corporations), is known as **civil law**. The civil law is used to resolve, control, and shape such personal interactions as contracts, wills and trusts, property ownership, and commerce. The element of civil law that is most relevant to criminal justice is **torts**, the law of personal injuries (see Exhibit 4.1 and Concept Summary 4.1).

- *Public law.* The branch of law that deals with the government and its relationships with individuals or other governments. **Public law** governs the administration and regulation of city, county, state, and federal government agencies.

The four elements of the law can be interrelated: A crime victim may also sue the perpetrator for damages in a civil court; some crime victims may forgo criminal action and choose to file a tort claim alone. It is also possible to seek civil damages from a perpetrator, even if he is found not guilty of crime (as in the case of the families of Nicole Brown and Ron Goldman, who successfully sued O. J. Simpson for damages), because the evidentiary standard in a tort action is less than that which evidence must meet for a criminal conviction.

---

**criminal law**
The body of rules that define crimes, set out their punishments, and mandate the procedures for carrying out the criminal justice process.

**substantive criminal law**
A body of specific rules that declare what conduct is criminal and prescribe the punishment to be imposed for such conduct.

**procedural criminal laws**
The methods that must be followed in obtaining warrants, investigating offenses, effecting lawful arrests, conducting trials, introducing evidence, sentencing convicted offenders, and reviewing cases by appellate courts.

**civil law**
All law that is not criminal, including tort, contract, personal property, maritime, and commercial law.

**torts**
The law of personal injuries.

**public law**
The branch of law that deals with the state or government agencies and controls their administrative relationships with individuals, corporations, or other branches of government.

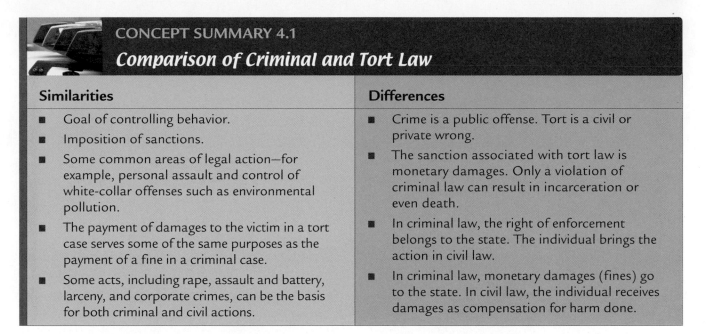

**CONCEPT SUMMARY 4.1**

*Comparison of Criminal and Tort Law*

| Similarities | Differences |
|---|---|
| ■ Goal of controlling behavior. | ■ Crime is a public offense. Tort is a civil or private wrong. |
| ■ Imposition of sanctions. | ■ The sanction associated with tort law is monetary damages. Only a violation of criminal law can result in incarceration or even death. |
| ■ Some common areas of legal action—for example, personal assault and control of white-collar offenses such as environmental pollution. | ■ In criminal law, the right of enforcement belongs to the state. The individual brings the action in civil law. |
| ■ The payment of damages to the victim in a tort case serves some of the same purposes as the payment of a fine in a criminal case. | ■ In criminal law, monetary damages (fines) go to the state. In civil law, the individual receives damages as compensation for harm done. |
| ■ Some acts, including rape, assault and battery, larceny, and corporate crimes, can be the basis for both criminal and civil actions. | |

(That is, in civil court defendants may be found guilty by a preponderance of the evidence, whereas in criminal court they must be found guilty beyond a reasonable doubt.)

In some instances, the government has the option of either pursuing a legal matter through the criminal process or filing a tort action, or both. White-collar crimes, for example, often involve both criminal and civil penalties.

If you are interested in becoming an attorney, read the accompanying Careers in Criminal Justice feature.

## THE DEVELOPMENT OF CRIMINAL LAW

The criminal law is a living document that is constantly evolving to keep pace with society and its needs. The substantive criminal law defines crime and punishment in U.S. society. Each state government and the federal government has its own criminal code, developed over many generations and incorporating moral beliefs, social values, and political, economic, and other societal concerns. The goals of the substantive criminal law are set out in Exhibit 4.2 on page 140.

The rules designed to implement the substantive law are known as procedural law. In contrast to the substantive law, the procedural law is concerned with the criminal process—the legal steps through which an offender passes—commencing with the initial criminal investigation and concluding with the release of the offender. Some elements of the law of criminal procedure (such as the rules of evidence, the right to notice of charges, questions of appeal, and the right to counsel) affect the substantive law. Many of the rights that have been extended to offenders over the past two decades lie within procedural law.

Because the law defines crime, punishment, and procedure, which are the basic concerns of the criminal justice system, it is essential for students to know something of the nature, purpose, and content of the substantive and procedural criminal law.

### The History of Criminal Law

The roots of the criminal codes used in the United States can be traced back to such early legal charters as the Babylonian Code of Hammurabi (2000 BCE) and the Mosaic Code of the Israelites (1200 BCE). Another early code, the Roman

# CAREERS IN CRIMINAL JUSTICE

## Attorney

### Duties and Characteristics of the Job

Attorneys use their experience and extensive knowledge of the law and the legal system to defend the rights of their clients. They can fulfill this role by representing the best interests of their clients in a legal setting by defending them during a trial or settling their grievances in or out of court. However, lawyers also act as legal advisors and engage in such activities as drawing up and/or interpreting legal documents and contracts. They frequently act as advisors by informing their clients about changes in existing laws. Attorneys often choose a field of specialization, such as tax law or intellectual property rights.

Attorneys typically work in firms—organizations of lawyers who pool their resources on legal cases. Some attorneys gain experience within existing firms and then leave to start their own practice. Some work for the federal, state, or local government, and others take advantage of increasing opportunities for employment within businesses.

Attorneys generally work in offices and courtrooms, though at times they may have to travel to meet clients at their homes or even in prison. They often work long hours; especially if a case goes to trial, a 60-plus-hour workweek is not uncommon for an attorney.

### Job Outlook

Job opportunities are expected to grow at an average rate for the next several years. Competition for education and professional positions will be considerable, especially at prestigious institutions and law firms. A good academic record from a prestigious law school, as well as work experience, mobility, and additional education in a field of specialty, will be especially helpful. Jobs will be most plentiful in urban areas, where there tend to be more law firms, big businesses, and government offices.

### Salary

Median annual earnings of all wage-and-salaried lawyers were recently $110,590. The middle half of those in this occupation earned between $74,980 and $163,320. Partners in large national firms in Chicago or New York may have an annual salary in the millions. An attorney's salary depends on type of employer, experience, region, and type of law being practiced. For example, lawyers employed by the federal government tend to make more than state-employed lawyers. Extremely successful sole practitioners can win millions in tort actions.

---

Twelve Tables (451 BCE) was formulated by a special commission of ten noble Roman men in response to pressure from the lower classes, who complained that the existing, unwritten legal code gave arbitrary and unlimited power to the wealthy classes. The original code was written on bronze plaques, which have been lost, but records of sections, which were memorized by every Roman male, survive. The remaining laws deal with debt, family relations, property, and other daily matters.

Although the early formal legal codes were lost during the Dark Ages, German and Anglo-Saxon societies developed legal systems featuring monetary compensation, called wergild (*wer* means "worth" and refers to what the person, and therefore the crime, was worth), for criminal violations. Guilt was determined by two methods: *compurgation*, which involved having the accused person swear an oath of innocence while being backed up by a group of 12 to 25 oath helpers, who would attest to his or her character; and *claims of innocence and ordeal*, which were based on the principle that divine forces would not allow an innocent person to be harmed.

Determining guilt by ordeal involved such measures as having the accused place his or her hand in boiling water or hold a hot iron. If the wound healed, the person was found innocent; if the wound did not heal, the accused was deemed guilty. Trial by combat allowed the accused to challenge his accuser to a duel,

## Opportunities

Gaining entrance into law school can be challenging; there are many talented applicants applying for a limited number of spots. The competition for jobs with prestigious firms is fierce because there are more graduating lawyers than there are job openings. Making the law review at one's law school, publishing law review articles while in school, and obtaining prestigious internships can be helpful in securing coveted jobs.

Training and practice as a lawyer can be a personally and financially rewarding career in itself. However, many lawyers use their education and experience as a means of launching other careers. It is not uncommon for lawyers to have successful careers as business administrators, politicians, law professors, or judges.

## Qualifications

The primary qualification for a career as an attorney is a legal education. A bachelor's degree in a program that gives one strong analytical and writing skills is recommended for preparation for law school.

Becoming a successful lawyer can be challenging and requires personality traits such as discipline, commitment, and the ability to work hard. Additionally, those who like an intellectual challenge and communicate well are more likely to enjoy being an attorney and to be successful.

## Education and Training

The primary requirements for a career as an attorney begin with proper educational training. Potential attorneys must have a bachelor's degree in order to gain entrance into an American Bar Association–accredited law school, which will prepare them for legal practice. After graduating from law school, attorneys must become certified before they can practice. Certification is obtained by passing a state bar exam. Completing these requirements can be challenging. Gaining admission to a law school requires not only hard work and discipline but also good grades and a desirable score on the Law School Admissions Test (LSAT).

Even after attorneys obtain a position, their education is not complete. Attorneys must stay informed of the latest developments in law and often attend conferences, and many states have continuing legal education (CLE) requirements that must be met.

For certain positions, such as law school professor and specialties such as patent law, further experience and education are be needed.

Source: "Lawyers," *Occupational Outlook Handbook*, 2010–2011 edition (Bureau of Labor Statistics, U.S. Department of Labor); retrieved May 19, 2010, from www.bls.gov/oco/ocos053.htm.

with the outcome determining the legitimacy of the accusation. Punishments included public flogging, branding, beheading, and burning.

## The Common Law

After the Norman Conquest of England in 1066, royal judges began to travel throughout the land, holding court in each county several times a year. When court was in session, the royal administrator, or judge, would summon a number of citizens who would, on their oath, tell of the crimes and serious breaches of the peace that had occurred since the judge's last visit. The royal judge would then decide what to do in each case, using local custom and rules of conduct as his guide—a system known as **stare decisis** (Latin for "to stand by decided cases"). Courts were bound to follow the law established in previous cases unless a higher authority, such as the king or the pope, overruled the law.

The present English system of law came into existence during the reign of Henry II (1154–1189), when royal judges began to publish their decisions in local cases. Judges began to use these written decisions as a basis for their decision making, and eventually a fixed body of legal rules and principles was produced. If the new rules were successfully applied in a number of different cases, they would become precedents, which would then be commonly applied in all similar cases—hence the term "common law." Crimes such as murder, burglary, arson, and rape are common-

**stare decisis**
To stand by decided cases: the legal principle by which the decision or holding in an earlier case becomes the standard by which subsequent similar cases are judged.

**EXHIBIT 4.2**

## Goals of the Substantive Criminal Law

■ *Enforce social control.* The substantive criminal law is the main instrument of control at the disposal of an existing government. The criminal law can be used by those who hold political power to eliminate behaviors they believe pose a threat to society or challenge the government's authority. The law prevents actions that challenge the legitimacy of the government, such as planning its overthrow, collaborating with its enemies, committing terrorist acts, or engaging in espionage.

■ *Distribute retribution.* By punishing people who infringe on the rights, property, and freedom of others, the law shifts the burden of revenge from the individual to the state. Although the thought of state-sponsored retribution may be offensive to some, it is greatly preferable to a system in which injured parties or their friends and relatives would seek to redress their injuries through personal vengeance or revenge.

■ *Express public opinion and morality.* Criminal law reflects public opinions and moral values. Some crimes, such as murder and forcible rape, are almost universally prohibited, but others, such as substance abuse, prostitution, and gambling, reflect contemporary moral values and may undergo change according to social conditions and attitudes. The criminal law is used to codify changing social values and educate the public about what is expected of them and their behavior.

■ *Deter criminal behavior.* Criminal law is designed through its application of punishment to control, restrain, and deter illegal acts before they actually occur. During the Middle Ages, public executions drove this point home; today, long prison sentences and an occasional execution are designed to achieve the same result.

■ *Punish wrongdoing.* If the deterrent power of criminal law fails to prevent crime, the law gives the state the ability to sanction or punish offenders. Those who violate criminal law are subject to physical coercion and punishment.

■ *Maintain social order.* All legal systems are designed to support and maintain the boundaries of the social system they serve. The free enterprise system is supported and sustained by criminal laws that protect property transfer and control market operations.

■ *Provide restoration.* Victims deserve restitution or compensation for their pain and loss. The criminal law can be used to restore to victims what they have lost. Because we believe in equity and justice, it is only fair that the guilty help repair the harm they have caused others by their crimes. Punishments such as fines, forfeiture, and restitution are connected to this legal goal.

**mala in se**
In common law, offenses that are by their own nature evil, immoral, and wrong; such offenses include murder, theft, and arson.

law crimes whose elements were initially defined by judges. They are referred to as **mala in se**, inherently evil and depraved. When the situation required it, the English Parliament enacted legislation to supplement the judge-made common law. These crimes were referred to as statutory or mala prohibitum crimes, which reflected existing social conditions. English common law evolved constantly to fit specific incidents that the judges encountered. For example, in the *Carriers* case (1473), an English court ruled that a merchant who had been hired to transport merchandise was guilty of larceny (theft) if he kept the goods for his own purposes.[4] Before the *Carriers* case, it was not considered a crime under the common law when people kept something that was voluntarily placed in their possession, even if the rightful owner had given them only temporary custody of the merchandise. Breaking with legal tradition, the court acknowledged that the commercial system could not be maintained unless the laws of theft were expanded. The definition of larceny was altered to meet the needs of a growing free enterprise economic system. The definition of theft was changed to include the taking of goods not only by force or stealth, but also by embezzlement and fraud.

Before the American Revolution, the colonies, then under British rule, were subject to the common law. After the colonies won their independence, state legislatures standardized common-law crimes such as murder, burglary, arson, and rape by putting them into statutory form in criminal codes. As in England, whenever common law proved inadequate to deal with changing social and moral

**EXHIBIT 4.3**

## *Louisiana: Feticide in the First Degree*

First degree feticide is:

The killing of an unborn child when the offender has a specific intent to kill or to inflict great bodily harm.

The offense of feticide shall not include acts that cause the death of an unborn child if those acts were committed during any abortion to which the pregnant woman or her legal guardian has consented or which was performed in an emergency.

The killing of an unborn child when the offender is engaged in the perpetration or attempted perpetration of aggravated rape, forcible rape, aggravated arson, aggravated burglary, aggravated kidnapping, second degree kidnapping, assault by drive-by shooting, aggravated escape, armed robbery, first degree robbery, second degree robbery, cruelty to juveniles, second degree cruelty to juveniles, terrorism, or simple robbery, even though he has no intent to kill or inflict great bodily harm.

Source: Louisiana First Degree Feticide Law, La. Rev. Stat. Ann. §§14:32.5–14.32.8, read with §§14:2(1), (7), (11) (2006).

issues, the states and Congress supplemented it with legislative statutes. Similarly, statutes prohibiting such offenses as the sale and possession of narcotics or the pirating of DVDs have been passed to control human behavior unknown at the time the common law was formulated. Today, criminal behavior is defined primarily by statute. With few exceptions, crimes are removed, added, or modified by the legislature of a particular jurisdiction.

## SOURCES OF THE CRIMINAL LAW

The contemporary U.S. legal system is codified by the state legislatures and the U.S. Congress. Each jurisdiction precisely defines "crime" in its legal code and sets out the appropriate punishments. However, like its English common-law roots, U.S. criminal law is not static and is constantly evolving. A state statute based on common law may define first-degree murder as the "unlawful killing, with malice and premeditation, of one human being by another." Over time, state court decisions might help explain the meaning of the term "malice" or clarify whether "*human being*" refers only to someone "born and alive" or can also refer to an unborn fetus. More than half the states have expanded their legal codes to include *feticide law*, which declares the killing of an unborn fetus to be murder (see Exhibit 4.3 for Louisiana's statute).

The content of the law may also be influenced by judicial decision making. A criminal statute may be no longer enforceable when an appellate judge rules that it is vague, deals with an act no longer of interest to the public, or is an unfair exercise of state control over an individual. Conversely, a judicial ruling may expand the scope of an existing criminal law, thereby allowing control over behaviors that heretofore were beyond its reach. In a famous 1990 case, 2 Live Crew (made up of Luther Campbell, Christopher Wong-Won, Mark Ross, and DJ Mr. Mixx), a prominent rap group, found its sales restricted in Florida as police began arresting children under 18 for purchasing the band's sexually explicit CD *As Nasty as They Want to Be*. The hit single "Me So Horny" was banned from local radio stations. Prosecutors tried but failed to get a conviction after group members were arrested at a concert. If members of the Crew had in fact been found guilty and the conviction had been upheld by the state's highest appellate court, obscenity laws would have been expanded to cover people singing (or rapping) objectionable music lyrics.

### Constitutional Limits

Regardless of its source, all criminal law in the United States must conform to the rules and dictates of the U.S. Constitution.[5] Any criminal law that even appears to conflict with the various provisions and articles of the Constitution must reflect a compelling need to protect public safety or morals.[6]

**ex post facto law**
A law that makes an act criminal after it was committed or retroactively increases the penalty for a crime; such laws are forbidden by the U.S. Constitution.

Criminal laws have been interpreted as violating constitutional principles if they are too vague or too broad to give clear meaning of their intent. A law forbidding adults to engage in "immoral behavior" could not be enforced because it does not use clear and precise language or adequately explain which conduct is forbidden.[7] The Constitution also prohibits laws that make a person's status a crime. Becoming or being a heroin addict is not a crime, although laws can forbid the sale, possession, and manufacture of heroin. The Constitution limits laws that are overly cruel and/or capricious. Whereas the use of the death penalty may be constitutionally approved, capital punishment would be forbidden if it were used for lesser crimes such as rape or employed in a random, haphazard fashion.[8] Cruel ways of executing criminals that cause excessive pain are likewise forbidden. One method used to avoid "cruelty" is lethal injection. In the 2008 case *Baze and Bowling v. Rees*, the Court upheld the use of lethal injection unless there is a "substantial risk of serious harm" and suffering before death—for example, if it can be shown that the drugs will not work effectively.[9]

The Constitution also forbids *bills of attainder*: legislative acts that inflict punishment without a judicial trial. This device, used by the English kings to punish rebels and seize their property, was particularly troublesome to American colonials when it was used to seize the property of people considered disloyal to the Crown; hence, attainder is forbidden in the Constitution. Nor does the Constitution permit the government to pass any **ex post facto law,** defined as the following:

- A law that makes an action, done before the passing of the law, and which was innocent when done, criminal; and punishes such action.

- A law that makes a crime more serious after the fact than it was when first committed.

- A law that inflicts a greater punishment than was available when the crime was committed.

- A law that makes convicting the offender easier than it was at the time the offender committed the crime.[10]

Sometimes there is great debate over what the Constitution actually means, and no issue has inspired more debate than the Second Amendment's instruction: "A well regulated militia, being necessary to the security of a free state, the right of the people to keep and bear arms, shall not be infringed." As a result, the policy and practice of gun control has been a topic of significant national debate. This issue is discussed in the nearby Analyzing Criminal Justice Issues feature.

## CLASSIFYING CRIMES

The decision of how a crime should be classified rests with the individual jurisdiction. Each state has developed its own body of criminal law and consequently determines its own penalties for the various crimes. Thus the criminal law of a given state defines and grades offenses, sets levels of punishment, and classifies crimes into categories. Over the years, crimes have been generally grouped into (1) felonies, misdemeanors, and violations, and (2) other statutory classifications, such as juvenile delinquency, sex offender categories, and multiple- or first-offender classifications. In general terms, felonies are considered serious crimes, misdemeanors are seen as less serious crimes, and violations may be noncriminal offenses such as traffic offenses and public drunkenness. Some states consider violations to be civil matters, whereas others classify them as crimes.

EXHIBIT 4.4

## *Alabama Definition of Burglary in the First Degree*

Section 13A-7-5, burglary in the first degree

A person commits the crime of burglary in the first degree if he knowingly and unlawfully enters or remains unlawfully in a dwelling with intent to commit a crime therein, and if, in effecting entry or while in dwelling or in immediate flight there from, he or another participant in the crime: (1) is armed with explosives or a deadly weapon, or (2) causes physical injury to any person who is not a participant in the crime, or (3) uses or threatens the immediate use of a dangerous instrument. Burglary in the first degree is a Class A felony.

Source: Alabama Criminal Code, Acts 1977, No. 607, p. 812, and §§ 2610; Acts 1979, No. 79-471, p. 862, and §§ 1.

## Felonies and Misdemeanors

The most common classification in the United States is the division between felonies and misdemeanors.[11] This distinction is based primarily on the degree of seriousness of the crime. Distinguishing between a felony and a misdemeanor is sometimes difficult. *Black's Law Dictionary* defines the two terms as follows:

> *A felony is a crime of a graver or more atrocious nature than those designated as misdemeanors. Generally it is an offense punishable by death or imprisonment in a penitentiary. A misdemeanor is lower than a felony and is generally punishable by fine or imprisonment otherwise than in a penitentiary.*[12]

Each jurisdiction in the United States determines by statute what types of conduct constitute felonies or misdemeanors. The most common definition of a *felony* is a crime punishable in the statute by death or by imprisonment in a state or federal prison. Another way of determining what category an offense falls into is by providing, in the statute, that a felony is any crime punishable by imprisonment for more than one year. In the former method, the place of imprisonment is critical; in the latter, the length of the prison sentence distinguishes a felony from a misdemeanor.

In the United States today, felonies include serious crimes against the person, such as criminal homicide, robbery, and rape, as well as such crimes against property as burglary and larceny. Misdemeanors include petit (or petty) larceny, assault and battery, and the unlawful possession of marijuana. The least serious, or petty, offenses, which often involve criminal traffic violations, are called infractions or violations. The felony/misdemeanor classification has a direct effect on the offender charged with the crime. A person convicted of a felony may be barred from certain fields of employment or some professions, such as law and medicine. A felony offender's status as an alien in the United States might also be affected, or the offender might be denied the right to hold public office, vote, or serve on a jury.[13] These and other civil liabilities exist only when a person is convicted of a felony offense, not of a misdemeanor.

## The Legal Definition of a Crime

Nearly all common-law crime contains both mental and physical elements. Consider the common-law crime of burglary in the first degree. Alabama's is defined as shown in Exhibit 4.4.

Note that in order to commit the crime of armed burglary in Alabama (and elsewhere), offenders must do the following things:

■ Willfully enter a dwelling

■ Be armed or arm themselves after entering the house, or commit an assault on a person who is lawfully in the house

■ Knowingly and intentionally commit the crime

## ANALYZING CRIMINAL JUSTICE ISSUES

# Gun Control and the Constitution

To millions of Americans, the massacre of more than 30 people at Virginia Tech on April 16, 2007, was a graphic reminder of the association between guns and crime. How could a mentally unbalanced person such as Seung-Hui Cho be allowed to purchase a deadly automatic weapon? Under Virginia's gun laws, Cho was legally entitled to purchase a Glock 19 9mm semiautomatic from a gun dealer and leave with it on the same day. He was a disturbed loner, but the commonwealth had no waiting period to buy a gun, and his status as a permanent resident alien made no difference. If he had taken the time to apply for a permit to carry a concealed weapon, he would have received it without a fuss, because Virginia law enforcement authorities were required to issue a permit to anyone who requested one if the applicant did not fit into a narrow range of disqualifying categories, one of which was having a criminal record, which he did not.

Could Cho's rampage have been avoided if the sale of handguns had been eliminated or strictly controlled? In the aftermath of these violent incidents, state and local jurisdictions, in addition to the federal government, have instituted laws restricting sales and possession of guns; some also regulate dealers who sell guns. This angers those gun enthusiasts who view gun control efforts as a threat to personal liberty and who call for severe punishment of criminals rather than control of handguns. They argue that the Second Amendment to the U.S. Constitution protects the right to bear arms. Does it?

### Supreme Court Review

Seventy years ago, in *United States v. Miller*, 307 U.S. 174 (1939), the Supreme Court ruled that the Second Amendment must be interpreted as intending to guarantee the states' rights to maintain and train a militia, not a personal right to bear arms. Miller had wanted to avoid registering a "sawed-off shotgun" that he possessed for personal use. The Court ruled, "In the absence of any evidence tending to show that possession or use of a shotgun having a barrel of less than 18 inches in length at this time has some reasonable relationship to the preservation or efficiency of a well-regulated militia, we cannot say that the Second Amendment guarantees the right to keep and bear such an instrument." Because Miller's shotgun was not for a militia-type purpose, it was not protected by the Second Amendment. The purpose of the Second Amendment is to support the national defense. Therefore, the only purpose for which owning and carrying a gun is protected under the Second Amendment is as part of "a well-regulated militia," acting on behalf of the national government.

The *Miller* decision still left open a number of issues, such as the regulation of handguns and whether municipalities can ban possession of all guns outright. In the 2008 decision *District of Columbia v. Heller*, the Court ruled that the Second Amendment protects an individual's right to own weapons for self-defense—not merely a right related to membership in a "well-regulated militia"—and therefore a municipal government is prohibited from banning gun ownership.

*People march down Capitol Avenue in Springfield, Illinois, on March 10, 2010, to show support for gun ownership rights during Illinois Gun Owner Lobby Day. They gathered at the state capital to urge legislators to reject bills that would restrict gun ownership and approve proposals that would allow people to carry concealed firearms. The Supreme Court has interpreted the Second Amendment to the U.S. Constitution to mean that state and local governments cannot ban handgun ownership but may impose some restrictions on who may buy guns and when they may be used.*

Nonetheless, the Court allowed the registration and regulation of handguns. Because *Heller* applied only to the District of Columbia, which is under federal control, the Court took up the case of *McDonald v. Chicago*. On June 28, 2010, the Supreme Court ruled that the individual's Second Amendment right to bear arms must be recognized by the states, though it left open the door to regulation, such as limiting the right of ex-felons or mental patients to own guns.

## Regulating Gun Ownership

Even though citizens have the right to own arms, there are still a number of laws regulating handgun purchase, sale, and ownership. The Federal Gun Control Act of 1968, which is still in effect, prohibits the direct mail order of firearms (except antique firearms) by consumers and mandates that anyone who wants to buy a gun from a source other than a private individual must do so through a federally licensed firearms dealer. It requires that all dealers be licensed, fill out forms detailing each trade, and avoid selling to people prohibited from owning guns, such as minors, ex-felons, and drug users. Dealers must record the source and properties of all guns they sell and must carefully account for their purchase. Gun buyers must provide identification and must sign waivers attesting to their ability to possess guns. The act also bans unlicensed individuals from acquiring handguns outside their state of residence, although long guns (rifles and shotguns) may (under federal law) be acquired from federally licensed firearms dealers located in other states, provided this is allowed by both the state of purchase and the state of residence.

The Brady Handgun Violence Prevention Act of 1993, amending the Gun Control Act of 1968, imposed a waiting period of five days before a licensed importer, manufacturer, or dealer may sell, deliver, or transfer a handgun to an unlicensed individual. Beginning November 30, 1998, the Brady Law changed and substituted an instant check, based on the FBI's National Instant Criminal Background Check System (NICS), on whether a prospective buyer is prohibited from purchasing a weapon. Gun purchases by any of the following are prohibited: people convicted of or under indictment for felony charges, fugitives, the mentally ill, those with dishonorable military discharges, those who have renounced U.S. citizenship, illegal aliens, illegal drug users, and those who have been convicted of domestic violence misdemeanors or are under domestic violence restraining orders.

In addition to the federal controls, a number of states have instituted laws restricting access to firearms by individuals who are subject to a restraining order or who have been convicted of a domestic violence misdemeanor; they also may allow law enforcement officers to confiscate firearms at a domestic violence scene.

Another approach is to severely punish people caught with unregistered handguns. The most famous attempt to regulate handguns using this method is the Massachusetts Bartley-Fox Law, which provides a mandatory one-year prison term for possessing a handgun (outside the home) without a permit.

Even if severely restricted, the government's ability to control guns is problematic. If legitimate gun stores were strictly regulated, private citizens could still sell, barter, or trade handguns. Unregulated gun fairs and auctions are common throughout the United States; many gun deals are made at gun shows with few questions asked. People obtain firearms illegally through a multitude of unauthorized sources, including unlicensed dealers, corrupt licensed dealers, and "straw" purchasers (people who buy guns for those who cannot purchase them legally).

If the sale of handguns were restricted, they would become more valuable, and illegal importation of guns might increase, as it has for other controlled substances such as narcotics. Regulating dealers is difficult, and tighter controls on them would only encourage private sales and bartering. Relatively few guns are stolen in burglaries, but many are sold to licensed gun dealers who circumvent the law by ignoring state registration requirements or making unrecorded or misrecorded sales to individuals and unlicensed dealers. Even a few corrupt dealers can supply tens of thousands of illegal handguns. Thus, despite legal controls, keeping guns out of the hands of criminals is not an easy task.

## Critical Thinking

1. Should the sale and possession of handguns be closely controlled and restricted?

2. Which of the gun control methods discussed do you feel would be most effective in deterring crime?

Sources: *District of Columbia v. Heller* (07-290) 2008; E. R. Vigdor and J. A. Mercy, "Do Laws Restricting Access to Firearms by Domestic Violence Offenders Prevent Intimate Partner Homicide?" *Evaluation Review* 30 (2006): 313–346; Gary Kleck and Jongyeon Tark, "Resisting Crime: The Effects of Victim Action on the Outcomes of Crimes," *Criminology* 42 (2005): 861–909; Robert Martin and Richard Legault, "Systematic Measurement Error with State-Level Crime Data: Evidence from the 'More Guns, Less Crime' Debate," *Journal of Research in Crime and Delinquency* 42 (2005): 187–210; Tomislav Kovandzic, Thomas Marvell, and Lynne Vieraitis, "The Impact of 'Shall-Issue' Concealed Handgun Laws on Violent Crime Rates: Evidence from Panel Data for Large Urban Cities," *Homicide Studies* 9 (2005): 292–323; Brady Handgun Violence Prevention Act, Pub. L. No. 103-159, 107 Stat. 1536 (Nov. 30, 1993), codified at 18 U.S.C. § 921 et seq.

To fulfill the legal definition, all elements of the crime must be proved, including these:

- The accused engaged in the guilty act (**actus reus**).
- The accused had the intent to commit the act (**mens rea**).
- Both the actus reus and the mens rea were concurrently present.
- The defendant's actions were the proximate cause of the injury resulting.
- Actual harm was caused. Thoughts of committing an act do not alone constitute a crime.

Each of these elements is discussed in greater detail next.

*ACTUS REUS*   The actus reus is an aggressive act, such as taking someone's money, burning a building, or shooting someone. The action must be voluntary for an act to be considered illegal. An accident or involuntary act would not be considered criminal. For example, if a person has a seizure while walking down the street, and as a result strikes another person in the face, he cannot be held criminally liable for assault. But if he knew beforehand that he could have a seizure and unreasonably put himself in a position where he was likely to harm others—for instance, by driving a car—he would be criminally liable for his behavior.

In addition, the failure or omission to act can be considered a crime on some occasions:

- *Failure to perform a legally required duty that is based on relationship or status.* These relationships include parent and child and husband and wife. If a husband finds his wife unconscious because she took an overdose of sleeping pills, he is obligated to seek medical aid. If he fails to do so and she dies, he can be held responsible for her death. Parents are required to look after the welfare of their children; failure to provide adequate care can be a criminal offense.
- *Imposition by statute.* Some states have passed laws that require a person who observes an automobile accident to stop and help the other parties involved.
- *A contractual relationship.* These relationships include lifeguard and swimmer, doctor and patient, and babysitter or au pair and child. Because lifeguards have been hired to ensure the safety of swimmers, they have a legal duty to come to the aid of drowning persons. If a lifeguard knows a swimmer is in danger and does nothing about it and the swimmer drowns, the lifeguard is legally responsible for the swimmer's death.

The duty to act is a legal and not a moral duty. The obligation arises from the relationship between the parties or from explicit legal requirements. For example, a private citizen who sees a person drowning is under no legal obligation to save that person. Although it may be considered morally reprehensible, the private citizen could walk away and let the swimmer drown without facing legal sanctions.

*MENS REA*   Under common law, for an act to constitute a crime, the actor must have criminal intent, or mens rea. To intend to commit a crime, the person must have clear knowledge of the consequences of his actions and must desire those consequences/outcomes to occur. A person who enters a store with a gun and shouts at the clerk to open the cash register is signaling his intent to commit a robbery. Criminal intent is implied if the results of an action, though originally unintended, are certain to occur. When Mohammed Atta and his terrorist band crashed airplanes into the World Trade Center on September 11, 2001, they did not intend to kill any particular person in the buildings. Yet the law would hold that anyone would be substantially certain that people in the building would be killed in the blast; therefore, the terrorists had the criminal intent to commit the crime of first-degree murder.

Mens rea is legally present when a person's reckless and/or negligent act produces social harm. Recklessness occurs when a person is or should be aware that his planned behavior is potentially harmful but goes ahead anyway, knowing his

EXHIBIT 4.5

## *New York State Law: § 270.10, Creating a Hazard*

A person is guilty of creating a hazard when:

1. Having discarded in any place where it might attract children, a container which has a compartment of more than one and one-half cubic feet capacity and a door or lid which locks or fastens automatically when closed and which cannot easily be opened from the inside, he fails to remove the door, lid, locking or fastening device; or

2. Being the owner or otherwise having possession of property upon which an abandoned well or cesspool is located, he fails to cover the same with suitable protective construction.

Creating a hazard is a class B misdemeanor.

Source: New York State Consolidated Laws, Article 270, Other Offenses Relating to Public Safety, Section 270.10, Creating a Hazard (2002).

actions may expose someone to risk or suffering. Even though he may not desire to hurt the eventual victim, his act is considered intentional because he was willing to gamble with the safety of others rather than taking precautions to avoid injury. It would be considered reckless for a disgruntled student to set a fire in a dormitory supply closet to protest new restrictions on visitation rights. If some of her classmates were killed in the blaze, she might be charged with manslaughter even though she did not intend to cause injury. Her actions would be considered reckless because she went ahead with her plan despite the fact that she surely knew that a fire could spread and cause harm.

In contrast, **criminal negligence**, another form of mens rea, occurs when a person's careless and inattentive actions cause harm. If a student who stayed up for three days studying for a test and then drove home fell asleep at the wheel, thereby causing a fatal accident, his behavior might be considered negligent because driving while in a drowsy state creates a condition that a reasonable person can assume will lead to injury. Negligence differs from recklessness, and is considered less serious, because the person did not knowingly gamble with another's safety but simply failed to foresee possible dangers.

**criminal negligence**
Liability that can occur when a person's careless and inattentive actions cause harm.

**STRICT LIABILITY** Certain statutory offenses exist in which mens rea is not essential. These offenses fall within a category known as a **public safety** or **strict liability crime**. A person can be held responsible for such a violation independent of the existence of intent to commit the offense. Strict liability criminal statutes generally include narcotics control laws, traffic laws, health and safety regulations, sanitation laws, and other regulatory statutes. A driver could not defend herself against a speeding ticket by claiming that she was unaware of how fast she was going and did not intend to speed, and a bartender could not claim that a juvenile to whom he sold liquor without checking an ID looked older than 21. No state of mind is generally required where a strict liability statute is violated.[14] Consider the New York State law § 270.10, about creating a hazard, which is set out in Exhibit 4.5.[15] Intent to commit is not required for a person to be found guilty on charges of creating a hazardous condition.

**public safety or strict liability crime**
A criminal violation—usually one that endangers the public welfare—that is defined by the act itself, irrespective of intent.

**THE CONCURRENCE OF MENS REA AND ACTUS REUS** The third element needed to prove that a crime was committed is the immediate relationship to or concurrence of the act with the criminal intent or result. The law requires that the offender's conduct be the proximate cause of any injury resulting from the criminal act. If, for example, a man chases a victim into the street intending to assault him, and the victim is struck and killed by a car, the accused could be convicted of murder if the court felt that his actions made him responsible for the victim's death. In other words, the victim would not have run into the street on his own accord and therefore would not have been killed. If, however, a victim dies from a completely unrelated illness after being assaulted, the court must determine whether the death was a probable consequence of the defendant's illegal conduct or would have resulted even if the assault had not occurred.

## EXHIBIT 4.6

# Common-Law Crimes

| Crime | Description | Example |
|---|---|---|
| **Crimes against the Person** | | |
| *First-Degree Murder* | Unlawful killing of another human being with malice aforethought and with premeditation and deliberation. | A woman buys poison and pours it into a cup of coffee her husband is drinking, intending to kill him for the insurance benefits. |
| *Voluntary Manslaughter* | Intentional killing committed under extenuating circumstances that mitigate the killing, such as killing in the heat of passion after being provoked. | A husband coming home early from work finds his wife in bed with another man. The husband goes into a rage and shoots and kills both lovers with a gun he keeps by his bedside. |
| *Battery* | Unlawful touching of another with intent to cause injury. | A man seeing a stranger sitting in his favorite seat in a cafeteria goes up to that person and pushes him out of the seat. |
| *Assault* | Intentional placing of another in fear of receiving an immediate battery. | A student aims an unloaded gun at her professor and threatens to shoot. He believes the gun is loaded. |
| *Rape* | Unlawful sexual intercourse with a female without her consent. | After a party, a man offers to drive a young female acquaintance home. He takes her to a wooded area and, despite her protests, forces her to have sexual relations with him. |
| *Robbery* | Wrongful taking and carrying away of personal property from a person by violence or intimidation. | A man armed with a loaded gun approaches another man on a deserted street and demands his wallet. |
| **Inchoate (Incomplete) Offenses** | | |
| *Attempt* | An intentional act for the purpose of committing a crime that is more than mere preparation or planning of the crime. The crime is not completed, however. | A person places a bomb in the intended victim's car so that it will detonate when the ignition key is used. The bomb is discovered before the car is started. Attempted murder has been committed. |

**CRIMINAL HARM** Thought alone is not a crime. For an act to be considered a crime, the actor's willingness to cause harm must be proved. It is the nature of the harm that ultimately determines what crime the person committed. If someone trips another with the intent of making that person fall down and be embarrassed in public, he has committed the crime of battery. If by some chance the victim dies from the fall, the harm that was caused elevates the crime to manslaughter even if that was not the intended result. In the crime of robbery, the actus reus is taking the property from the person or presence of another. In order to satisfy the harm requirement, the robber must acquire the victim's possessions, an act referred to as *asportation*. The legal definition of robbery is satisfied when possession of the property is transferred, even for a brief moment, to the robber. If a robber removes a victim's wallet from his pocket and immediately tosses it over a fence when he spies a police officer approaching, the robbery is complete because even the slightest change in possession of the property is sufficient to cause harm. Nor is the value of

EXHIBIT 4.6

## Common-Law Crimes (continued)

| Crime | Description | Example |
|-------|-------------|---------|
| Conspiracy | Voluntary agreement between two or more persons to achieve an unlawful object or to achieve a lawful object using means forbidden by law. | A doctor conspires with a con man to fake accidents and then bring the false "victims" to his office so he can collect medical fees from an insurance company. |
| Solicitation | With the intent that another person engage in conduct constituting a felony, a person solicits, requests, commands, or otherwise attempts to cause that person to engage in such conduct. | A terrorist approaches a person he believes is sympathetic to his cause and asks him to join in a plot to blow up a government building. |
| **Crimes against Property** | | |
| Burglary | Breaking and entering of a structure owned by another with the intent to commit a felony therein. | Intending to steal some jewelry and silver, a young man breaks a window and enters another's house at 10 P.M. |
| Arson | Intentional burning of a building, home, or other property of another. | A worker, angry that her boss did not give her a raise, goes to her boss's house and sets it on fire. |
| Larceny | Taking and carrying away the personal property of another with the intent to keep and possess the property. | While shopping, a woman sees a diamond ring displayed at the jewelry counter. When no one is looking, the woman takes the ring, places it in her pocket, and walks out of the store without paying. |

Source: Developed by Therese J. Libby, J.D.

the property important: Actual value is irrelevant so long as the property had some value to the victim. Exhibit 4.6 sets out common-law criminal offenses.

## CRIMINAL DEFENSES

In 1884 two British sailors, desperate after being shipwrecked for days, made the decision to kill and eat a suffering cabin boy. Four days later, they were rescued by a passing ship and returned to England. In the case of *Regina v. Dudley and Stephens*, English authorities, wanting to end the practice of shipwreck cannibalism, tried the two men for murder and convicted them. Clemency was considered, and a reluctant Queen Victoria commuted the death sentences to six months behind bars.[16] Were the seamen justified in killing a shipmate to save their lives? If they had not done so, they probably would have died. Can there ever be a good reason to take a life? Can the killing of another ever be justified? Before you answer, remember that people can kill in self-defense, to prevent lethal crimes, or in times of war. The passengers aboard United Airlines Flight 93 are considered heroes for attacking the hijackers on September 11, 2001. Certainly no rational person would condemn their acts, even though they may have resulted in the death of others. Often, the quality of the act is not most important; the way society defines and reacts to it determines whether a crime has been committed.

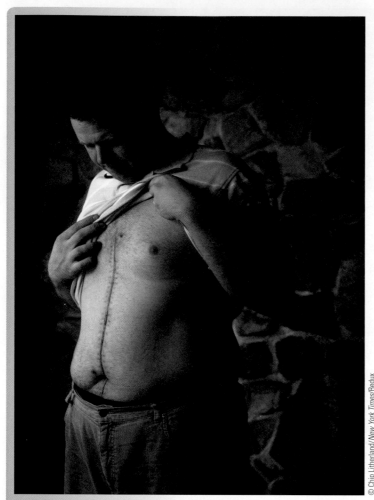

Jason Rosenbloom shows his scars from gunshot wounds sustained while he was in his home in Clearwater, Florida, on August 3, 2006. Rosenbloom was unarmed when he was shot twice by a neighbor during an argument over how many garbage bags Rosenbloom was allowed to put out on the curb. In the last year, 15 states have enacted laws that expand the right of self-defense, allowing crime victims to use deadly force in situations where violent acts might formerly have made them liable to prosecution for murder. Supporters call these provisions "stand your ground" laws. Opponents call them "shoot first" laws. The first of the new laws took effect in Florida, where guns may be used in self-defense. What would have happened if Jason had been carrying a gun and had used it for self-defense?

**excuse defense**
A defense in which a person states that his or her mental state was so impaired that he or she lacked the capacity to form sufficient intent to be held criminally responsible.

When people defend themselves against criminal charges, they must refute one or more of the elements of the crime of which they have been accused. Defendants may deny the actus reus by arguing that they were falsely accused and the real culprit has yet to be identified. Defendants may also claim that although they did engage in the criminal act they are accused of, they lacked the mens rea, or mental intent, needed to be found guilty of the crime. If a person whose mental state is impaired commits a criminal act, the person may seek to be excused of his or her criminal actions by claiming that he or she lacked the capacity to form sufficient intent to be held criminally responsible. Insanity, intoxication, ignorance, age, and entrapment are among the types of **excuse defenses**.

Another type of defense is **justification**. Here, the individual usually admits committing the criminal act but maintains that the act was justified under the circumstances and that he or she, therefore, should not be held criminally liable. Among the justification defenses are consent, necessity, duress, and self-defense. Persons standing trial for criminal offenses may defend themselves by claiming either that their actions were justified under the circumstances or that their behavior should be excused by their lack of mens rea. If either the physical or the mental elements of a crime cannot be proved, then the defendant cannot be convicted.

## Ignorance or Mistake

Ignorance or mistake can be an excuse if it negates an element of a crime. As a general rule, however, ignorance of the law is no excuse. Some courts have had to accept this excuse in cases in which the government failed to make enactment of a new law public. It is also a viable justification when the offender relies on an official statement of the law that is later deemed incorrect. Barring that, even immigrants and other new arrivals to the United States are required to be aware of the content of the law. For example, Chris Ahamefule Iheduru, a Nigerian immigrant, was convicted of sexual assault on the grounds that he had intimate relations with his 14-year-old stepdaughter after signing a contract with the girl to bear him a son (she gave birth to a daughter).[17] At trial, Iheduru testified that it is not illegal in his native country to have sex with a juvenile and that he did not know it was against the law in the United States. However, his ignorance of U.S. law did not shield him from conviction.

## Insanity

Insanity is a defense to criminal prosecution in which the defendant's state of mind negates his or her criminal responsibility. A successful insanity defense results in a verdict of "not guilty by reason of insanity." Insanity, in this case, is a legal category. As used in U.S. courts, it does not mean that everyone who suffers from a form of mental illness can be excused from legal responsibility. Many people who are depressed, suffer mood disorders, or have a psychopathic personality can be found legally sane. Instead, *insanity* means that the defendant's state of mind at the time the crime was committed made it impossible for her to have the necessary mens rea to satisfy the legal definition of a crime. Thus, a person can be undergoing treatment for a psychological disorder but still be judged legally

© Chip Litherland/New York Times/Redux

**EXHIBIT 4.7**

## Various Insanity Defense Standards

### THE *M'NAGHTEN* RULE

The *M'Naghten* rule, first formulated in England in 1843, defines a person as insane if at the time she committed the act she stands accused of, she was laboring under such a defect of reason, arising from a disease of the mind, that she could not tell or know the nature and quality of the act or, if she did know it, that she did not know what she was doing was wrong. In other words, she could not tell "right from wrong." The *M'Naghten* rule is used in the majority of the states.

### THE IRRESISTIBLE IMPULSE

The irresistible impulse test was formulated in Ohio in 1834. It is used quite often in conjunction with *M'Naghten* and defines a person as insane if he should or did know that his actions were illegal, but, because of a mental impairment, he couldn't control his behavior. His act was a result of an uncontrollable or irresistible impulse. A person who commits a crime during a "fit of passion" would be considered insane under this test. The most famous use of this defense occurred in 1994, when Lorena Bobbitt successfully defended herself against charges that she cut off the penis of her husband, John, after suffering abuse at his hands.

### THE *DURHAM* RULE

The *Durham* rule or "product test" was set forth by the United States Court of Appeals for the District of Columbia Circuit in 1954 and states that ". . . an accused is not criminally responsible if her unlawful act was the product of mental disease or defect." It was used for some time in the state of New Hampshire.

### THE INSANITY DEFENSE REFORM ACT (U.S.)

The Insanity Defense Reform Act, Title 18, U.S. Code, Section 17, was enacted by Congress in 1984 and states that a person accused of a crime can be judged not guilty by reason of insanity if "the defendant, as a result of a severe mental disease or defect, was unable to appreciate the nature and quality or the wrongfulness of her acts."

### THE SUBSTANTIAL CAPACITY TEST

The substantial capacity test was defined by the American Law Institute in its Model Penal Code. This argues that insanity should be defined as a lack of substantial capacity to control one's behavior. Substantial capacity is defined as "the mental capacity needed to understand the wrongfulness of [an] act, or to conform . . . behavior to the . . . law." This rule combines elements of the *M'Naghten* rule with the concept of "irresistible impulse."

sane if it can be proved that, at the time she committed the crime, she had the capacity to understand the wrongfulness of her actions.

If a defendant uses the insanity plea, it is usually left to psychiatric testimony to prove that this defendant understood the wrongfulness of her or his actions and was therefore legally sane or, conversely, was mentally incapable of forming intent. The jury must then weigh the evidence in light of the test for sanity currently used in the jurisdiction. These tests vary throughout the United States. The standards most commonly used are listed in Exhibit 4.7.

## Intoxication

As a general rule, intoxication, which may include drunkenness or being under the influence of drugs, is not considered a defense. However, a defendant who becomes involuntarily intoxicated under duress or by mistake may be excused for crimes committed. Involuntary intoxication may also lessen the degree of the crime. For example, a judgment may be decreased from first- to second-degree murder because the defendant uses intoxication to prove the lack of the critical element of mens rea, or mental intent. Thus, the effect of intoxication on criminal liability depends on whether the defendant uses alcohol or drugs voluntarily. For example, a defendant who enters a bar for a few drinks, becomes intoxicated, and strikes someone can be convicted of assault and battery. If, however, the defendant ordered a nonalcoholic drink that was subsequently spiked by someone else, the defendant may have a legitimate legal defense.

**justification**
A defense for a criminal act claiming that the criminal act was reasonable or necessary under the circumstances.

Because of the frequency of crime-related offenses involving drugs and alcohol, the impact of intoxication on criminal liability is a persistent issue in the criminal justice system. The connection among drug use, alcoholism, and violent street crime has been well documented. Although those in law enforcement and the judiciary tend to emphasize the use of the penal process in dealing with problems of chronic alcoholism and drug use, others in corrections and crime prevention favor approaches that depend more on behavioral theories and the social sciences. For example, in the case of *Robinson v. California*, the U.S. Supreme Court struck down a California statute making addiction to narcotics a crime, on the ground that it violated the defendant's rights under the Eighth and Fourteenth Amendments to the Constitution.[18] However, the landmark decision in *Powell v. Texas* placed severe limitations on the behavioral science approach in *Robinson* when it rejected the defense of chronic alcoholism of a defendant charged with the crime of public drunkenness.[19]

## Age

The law holds that a child is not criminally responsible for actions committed at an age that precludes a full realization of the gravity of certain types of behavior. Under common law, there is generally a conclusive presumption of incapacity for a child under age 7, a reliable presumption for a child between the ages of 7 and 14, and no presumption for a child over the age of 14. This generally means that a child under age 7 who commits a crime will not be held criminally responsible for these actions and that a child between the ages of 7 and 14 may be held responsible. These common-law rules have been changed by statute in most jurisdictions. Today, the maximum age of criminal responsibility for children ranges from 14 to 17 or 18, whereas the minimum age may be set by statute at age 7 or under age 14.[20] In addition, every jurisdiction has established a juvenile court system to deal with juvenile offenders and children in need of court and societal supervision. Thus, the mandate of the juvenile justice system is to provide for the care and protection of children under a given age, established by state statute. In certain situations, a juvenile court may transfer a more serious chronic youthful offender to the adult criminal court.

## Entrapment

Under the rule of law, a defendant may be excused from criminal liability if he can convince the jury that law enforcement agents used traps, decoys, and deception to induce criminal action. Law enforcement officers can legitimately set traps for criminals by getting information about crimes from informers, undercover agents, and codefendants. Police officers are allowed to use ordinary opportunities for defendants to commit crime and to create these opportunities without excessive inducement. However, when the police instigate the crime, implant criminal ideas, and coerce individuals into bringing about crime, defendants can claim to have been entrapped.

Entrapment then must be viewed within the context of the defendant's predisposition to commit a crime. A defendant with a criminal record would have a tougher time using this defense successfully than one who had never been in trouble. However, in one of the most important entrapment cases, *Jacobson v. United States* (1992), the Supreme Court ruled that a defendant with a past history of child pornography had been entrapped by the government into purchasing more. Keith Jacobson had ordered *Bare Boys* magazines depicting nude children. When his name came up in their *Bare Boys* files, government agents sent him mailings for more than two and a half years in an effort to get him to purchase more kiddie porn. Such purchases are a violation of the Child Protection Act of 1984. Jacobson was arrested after he gave in to the inducements and ordered a magazine showing young boys engaged in sexual activities. A search of his house revealed no materials other than those sent by the government (and the original *Bare Boys* magazines). On appeal, the Court held that Jacobson was entrapped because the state could not prove a predisposition to break the law, and the purchase of the sexually charged magazines was the result of government coaxing.[21]

# Justification Defenses

Criminal defenses may be based on the concept of justification. In these instances, defendants normally acknowledge that they committed the act but claim that they cannot be prosecuted because they were justified in doing so. Major types of criminal defenses involving justification are consent, self-defense, duress, and necessity.

*CONSENT* As a general rule, the victim's consent to a crime does not automatically excuse the defendant who commits the action. The type of crime involved generally determines the validity of consent as an appropriate legal defense. Such crimes as common-law rape and larceny require lack of consent on the part of the victim. In other words, a rape does not occur if the victim consents to sexual relations. In the same way, a larceny cannot occur if the owner voluntarily consents to the taking of property. Consequently, in such crimes, consent is an essential element of the crime, and it is a valid defense where it can be proved or shown that it existed at the time the crime was committed. But in other crimes, such as sexual relations with a minor child, consent cannot be a defense because the state presumes that young people are not capable of providing adequate or mature consent. Nor can consent be used to justify the crime of incest or bigamy.

One controversial area of consent is the crime of assisted suicide; it is still against the law to help someone commit suicide, even if the person consented to the procedure. The issue became prominent because of the involvement of Michigan doctor Jack Kevorkian in numerous physician-assisted suicides. Kevorkian was convicted in 1999 on charges of second-degree murder after the death of Thomas Youk, a man he helped commit suicide. It is today illegal for a doctor to write or fill a prescription for medications sufficient for a patient to commit suicide, or personally give medications sufficient to cause death, in every state except Oregon, which passed a "death with dignity act" in 1994. A number of other nations, including Belgium, Switzerland, and the Netherlands, allow at least some forms of assisted suicide.[22]

*SELF-DEFENSE* A criminal defendant can claim to be not guilty because he or she acted in self-defense. To establish self-defense, the defendant must prove he acted with a reasonable belief that he was in imminent danger of death or harm and had no reasonable means of escape from the assailant.

As a general legal rule, a person defending herself may use only such force as is reasonably necessary to prevent personal harm. A person who is assaulted by another with no weapon is ordinarily not justified in hitting the assailant with a baseball bat. A person verbally threatened by another is not justified in striking the other party with his fists. If a woman hits a larger man, the man would not generally be justified in striking the woman and causing her physical harm. In other words, for the self-defense privilege to be legally exercised, the danger to the defendant must be immediate. And even in cases where the victim was the one who initiated the fray and pummeled his opponent first, an imbalance in weaponry (such as gun versus fist) would mitigate a finding of self-defense.[23]

In some instances, a woman (or man) may kill his or her mate after years of abuse; this defense is known as *battered-wife syndrome* (or, in cases involving child abuse, *battered-child syndrome*). Although a history of battering can be used to mitigate the seriousness of the crime, a finding of not guilty most often requires the presence of imminent danger and the inability of the accused to escape from the assailant.

*STAND YOUR GROUND* Most self-defense statutes require a duty to retreat before reacting to a threat with physical violence. An exception is one's own home. According to the "castle exception" (from the old saying "A man's home

## EXHIBIT 4.8

# Provisions of Florida's Stand-Your-Ground Law

Section (1) A person is presumed to have held a reasonable fear of imminent peril of death or great bodily harm to himself or herself or another when using defensive force that is intended or likely to cause death or great bodily harm to another if:

(a) The person against whom the defensive force was used was in the process of unlawfully and forcefully entering, or had unlawfully and forcibly entered, a dwelling, residence, or occupied vehicle, or if that person had removed or was attempting to remove another against that person's will from the dwelling, residence, or occupied vehicle; and

(b) The person who uses defensive force knew or had reason to believe that an unlawful and forcible entry or unlawful and forcible act was occurring or had occurred.

. . . Section (3) A person who is not engaged in an unlawful activity and who is attacked in any other place where he or she has a right to be has no duty to retreat and has the right to stand his or her ground and meet force with force, including deadly force if he or she reasonably believes it is necessary to do so to prevent death or great bodily harm to himself or herself or another or to prevent the commission of a forcible felony.

Section (4) A person who unlawfully and by force enters or attempts to enter a person's dwelling, residence, or occupied vehicle is presumed to be doing so with the intent to commit an unlawful act involving force or violence.

Source: Florida Statutes, Home Protection; Use of Deadly Force; Presumption of Fear of Death or Great Bodily Harm, www.leg.state.fl.us/statutes/index.cfm?App_mode=Display_Statute&Search_String=&URL=Ch0776/SEC013.HTM&Title5->2005->Ch0776->Section%20013#0776.013.

is his castle"), a person is not obligated to retreat within his or her residence before fighting back. Some states, most notably Florida, now have "stand-your-ground" laws, which allow people to use force in a wide variety of circumstances and eliminate or curtail the need to retreat.

Florida's law, which was enacted on October 1, 2005, allows the use of deadly force when a person reasonably believes it necessary to prevent the commission of a "forcible felony," including carjacking, robbery, and assault (see Exhibit 4.8).

The traditional "castle doctrine" allowed people to use deadly force only when they reasonably believed that their lives were in danger. The new law allows average citizens to use deadly force when they reasonably believe that their homes or vehicles have been illegally invaded. The Florida law authorizes the use of defensive force by anyone "who is not engaged in an unlawful activity and who is attacked in any other place where he or she has a right to be." Furthermore, under the law, such a person has no duty to retreat and can stand his or her ground and meet force with force. The statute also grants civil and criminal immunity to anyone found to have had such a reasonable belief.[24]

**DURESS**   A duress (also called compulsion or coercion) defense may be used when the defendant claims he was forced to commit a crime as the only means of preventing death or serious harm to himself or others. For example, a bank employee might be excused from taking bank funds if she can prove that her family was being threatened and that consequently she was acting under duress. But widespread general agreement exists that duress is no defense for an intentional killing.

A famous, albeit unsuccessful, duress defense was mounted by Patty Hearst, the young daughter of wealthy newspaper owners, who on February 4, 1974, was kidnapped by the Symbionese Liberation Army (SLA), a heavily armed radical group. While in captivity, she began to sympathize with her kidnappers and actually joined them in a series of bank robberies. After the group was captured, Hearst's lawyers argued that her participation in the crimes was caused by the duress of her ordeal. Hearst testified that she feared for her life if she did not cooperate. Her performance on the stand did not convince jurors because she refused to answer many questions posed by the prosecution; she was convicted and sentenced to seven years in prison. (President Jimmy Carter commuted her sentence on February 1, 1979, and ordered her release.)

*NECESSITY* The defense of necessity is used when a crime was committed under extreme circumstances and could not be avoided. Unlike the duress defense, which involves threats made by another person, people act out of necessity according to their own judgment. Typically, to prove necessity, the burden is on the defendant to show that he acted to prevent imminent harm and that there were no legal alternatives to violating the law. Using these criteria, a successful necessity defense could be launched if a woman in labor, fearing that she was about to give birth, stole a car in order to get to the hospital for an emergency delivery. It might also be considered necessity if a hunter shot an animal of an endangered species that was about to attack his child. However, defendants must prove that their actions were "the lesser of two evils." Unlike the case of the pregnant woman above, a defendant could not claim necessity for stealing a car because he was late for a soccer game.

## In the Line of Duty

Police officers, firefighters, and other first responders can use their occupation in defense of an alleged law violation committed while in the line of duty. For example, a police officer who shoots a suspect he or she believes is drawing a weapon cannot be charged with murder, even if it turns out that the suspect was unarmed. However, there are a number of exceptions to this rule. First, the action must be contained within the scope of their duties. A police officer who uses physical force while buying marijuana from a dealer would be just as criminally liable as any citizen. Second, protection from criminal liability would be limited in cases of gross negligence or malicious intent. For example, police officers could be charged with criminal assault if they used a weapon to batter a suspect they were interrogating. Police officers who drove at excessive speeds while not on emergency calls have been charged with manslaughter for causing the death of motorists.[25]

Immunity enjoyed by government agents can also sometimes spill over to private citizens who come to the aid of police or other civil servants. For example, a third party who sees a police officer grappling with a suspect and comes to the officer's aid cannot be prosecuted for assault if it later turns out that the suspect was innocent of crime. Many states have passed "Good Samaritan" laws that provide immunity from both civil and criminal actions to private citizens who, in good faith, cause injury while attempting to help someone in distress, including both private citizens and government officials.

## Changing Defenses

Criminal defenses are undergoing rapid change. As society becomes more aware of existing social problems that may contribute to crime, it has become commonplace for defense counsels to defend their clients by raising a variety of new defenses based on preexisting conditions or syndromes with which their clients were afflicted. Examples include "battered-woman syndrome," "Vietnam syndrome," "child sexual abuse syndrome," "Holocaust survivor syndrome," and "adopted-child syndrome." In using these defenses, attorneys are asking judges either to recognize a new excuse for crime or to fit these conditions into preexisting defenses. For example, a person who used lethal violence in self-defense may argue that the trauma of serving in the Vietnam War caused him to overreact to provocation. Or a victim of child abuse may use her experiences to mitigate her culpability in a crime, asking a jury to consider her background when making a death penalty decision. In some instances, exotic criminal defenses have been gender-specific. Attorneys have argued that their female clients' behavior was a result of their premenstrual syndrome (PMS) and that male clients were aggressive because of an imbalance in their testosterone levels. These defenses have achieved relatively little success in the United States.[26]

Although criminal law reform may be guided by good intentions, it is sometimes difficult to put the changes into operation. Law reform may necessitate creating new enforcement agencies or severely tax existing ones. As a result, the system becomes strained, and cases are backlogged.

## REFORMING THE CRIMINAL LAW

In recent years, many states and the federal government have been examining their substantive criminal law. Because the law, in part, reflects public opinion and morality regarding various forms of behavior, what was considered criminal 40 years ago may not be considered so today. In some cases, states have reassessed their laws and reduced the penalties on some common practices such as public intoxication; this reduction of penalties is referred to as *decriminalization*. Such crimes, which in the past might have resulted in a prison sentence, may now be punished with a fine. In other instances, what was once considered a criminal act may be declared noncriminal or legalized. Sexual activity between consenting same-sex adults was punished as a serious felony under sodomy statutes in a number of states until the U.S. Supreme Court ruled such statutes illegal in 2003.

States may take action to decriminalize or even legalize some crimes because the general public simply ignores the laws, and law enforcement agents are reluctant to press charges even when they apprehend violators. Legal scholar Margaret Raymond calls these **penumbral crimes**—criminal acts defined by a high level of noncompliance with the stated legal standard, an absence of stigma associated with violation of the stated standard, and a low level of law enforcement or public sanction.[27] Because otherwise law-abiding people routinely violate these laws, the laws may be targets for penalty reduction and eventual legalization. For example, given that the 55-mile-per-hour speed limit has been so widely ignored, states have increased limits to 65 and even 70 miles per hour.

What are some of the new laws that are being created and some of the old ones that have been eliminated?

**penumbral crimes**
Criminal acts defined by a high level of noncompliance with the stated legal standard, an absence of stigma associated with violation of the stated standard, and a low level of law enforcement or public sanction.

**stalking**
The willful, malicious, and repeated following, harassing, or contacting of another person. Such behavior becomes a criminal act when it causes the victim to feel fear for his or her safety or the safety of others.

**obitiatry**
Helping people take their own lives: assisted suicide.

### Stalking Laws

More than 25 states have enacted **stalking** statutes, which prohibit and punish acts described typically as "the willful, malicious and repeated following and harassing of another person."[28] Stalking laws were originally formulated to protect women terrorized by former husbands and boyfriends, although celebrities are often plagued by stalkers as well. In celebrity cases, these laws often apply to stalkers who are strangers or casual acquaintances of their victims.

### Prohibiting Assisted Suicide

Some laws are created when public opinion turns against a previously legal practice. Physician-assisted suicide became the subject of a national debate when Dr. Jack Kevorkian began practicing what he calls **obitiatry**, helping people take their own lives.[29] In an attempt to stop Kevorkian, Michigan passed a statutory ban on assisted suicide, reflecting what lawmakers believed to be prevailing public opinion.[30] Convicted and imprisoned, Kevorkian was released on June 1, 2007, and now gives lectures on college campuses; 44 states, including Michigan, now disallow assisted suicide either by statute or by common law.[31]

### Registering Sex Offenders

Some legal changes have been prompted by public outrage over a particularly heinous crime. One of the most well known is Megan's Law, named after 7-year-old Megan Kanka of Hamilton Township, New Jersey, who was killed in 1994. Charged with the crime was a convicted sex offender, who, unbeknownst to the Kankas, lived across the street. On May 17, 1996, President Bill Clinton signed Megan's Law, which contained two components:

1. *Sex offender registration.* A revision of the 1994 Jacob Wetterling Act, which had required the states to register individuals convicted of sex crimes against children, also established a community notification system.

EXHIBIT 4.9

## Environmental Protection Laws

- Federal Insecticide, Fungicide and Rodenticide Act (FIFRA), 7 USC §§ 136–136y

- Energy Supply and Environmental Coordination Act, 15 USC §§ 791–798

- Toxic Substances Control Act (TSCA), 15 USC §§ 2601–2692

- Federal Water Pollution Control Act (also known as the Clean Water Act), 33 USC §§ 1251–1387

- Safe Drinking Water Act, 42 USC §§ 300f–300j–26

- Noise Control Act, 42 USC §§ 4901–4918, 42 USC § 4910 (criminal provision)

- Solid Waste Disposal Act (including, in Subchapter III, the Resource Conservation and Recovery Act [RCRA]), 42 USC §§ 6901–6992k

- Clean Air Act, 42 USC §§ 7401–7671

- Federal Hazardous Material Transportation Statute, 49 USC §§ 5101–5127

Source: U.S. Department of Justice, www.usdoj.gov/usao/eousa/foia_reading_room/usam/title5/11menv.htm.

2. *Community notification.* States were compelled to make private and personal information on registered sex offenders available to the public.

Variations of Megan's Law have been adopted by most state jurisdictions. Although civil libertarians have expressed concern that notification laws may interfere with an offender's postrelease privacy rights, recent research indicates that registered offenders find value in Megan's Law because it helps deter future abuse. And when DNA collection is included in the law, it helps reduce false accusations and convictions.[32]

## Clarifying Rape

Sometimes laws are changed to clarify the definition of crime and to quell public debate over the boundaries of the law. When does bad behavior cross the line into criminality, and when does it remain merely bad behavior? An example of the former can be found in changes to the law of rape. In seven states, including California, it is now considered rape if (a) the woman consents to sex, (b) the sex act begins, (c) she changes her mind during the act and tells her partner to stop, and (d) he refuses and continues. Before the legal change, such a circumstance was not considered rape but merely aggressive sex.[33]

## Controlling Technology

Changing technology and the ever-increasing role of technology in people's daily lives will require modifications of the criminal law. Such technologies as automatic teller machines and cellular phones have already spawned a new generation of criminal acts involving theft of access numbers and software piracy. For example, a modification to Virginia's Computer Crimes Act that took effect in 2005 makes *phishing*—sending out bulk email messages designed to trick consumers into revealing bank account passwords, Social Security numbers, and other personal information—a felony. Those convicted of selling the data or using the data to commit another crime, such as identity theft, now face twice as much prison time as before.

## Protecting the Environment

In response to the concerns of environmentalists, the federal government has passed numerous acts designed to protect the nation's well-being. Some of the most important are listed in Exhibit 4.9.

The Environmental Protection Agency has successfully prosecuted significant violations of these and other new laws, including data fraud cases (such as private laboratories submitting false environmental data to state and federal environmental agencies); indiscriminate hazardous waste dumping that resulted in serious injuries and death; industrywide ocean dumping by cruise ships; oil spills that caused

BP Mobile Incident Commander Keith Seilhan talks with oil cleanup workers in Gulf Shores, Alabama, on July 2, 2010. Seilhan is informing the workers that they have BP's permission to speak to members of the media if they wish. The Deepwater Horizon incident was a harrowing reminder that environmental laws are needed to protect the biosystem both from those who pollute on purpose and from those who are negligent in their handling of dangerous chemicals.

© AP Photo/Dave Martin

significant damage to waterways, wetlands, and beaches; and illegal handling of hazardous substances such as pesticides and asbestos that exposed children, the poor, and other especially vulnerable groups to potentially serious illness.[34]

## Legalizing Marijuana

A number of states are now exploring the legalization of marijuana for medical purposes. For example, New Jersey Senate Bill 119, signed into law on January 18, 2010, is typical of changes in the law. The bill protects "patients who use marijuana to alleviate suffering from debilitating medical conditions, as well as their physicians, primary caregivers, and those who are authorized to produce marijuana for medical purposes" from "arrest, prosecution, property forfeiture, and criminal and other penalties." It also provides for the creation of alternative treatment centers, "at least two each in the northern, central, and southern regions of the state. The first two centers issued a permit in each region shall be nonprofit entities, and centers subsequently issued permits may be nonprofit or for-profit entities." The bill allows marijuana to be prescribed for a variety of illnesses ranging from severe chronic pain, nausea, and vomiting to terminal illnesses such as cancer. Physicians determine how much marijuana a patient needs and give written instructions to be presented to an alternative treatment center. The maximum amount for a 30-day period is 2 ounces.[35] According to the Drug Policy Alliance, Alaska, California, Colorado, Hawaii, Maine, Michigan, Montana, Nevada, New Mexico, Oregon, Rhode Island, Vermont, and Washington have created laws that effectively remove state-level criminal penalties for growing and/or possessing medical marijuana. Another ten states, as well as the District of Columbia, have symbolic medical marijuana laws (laws that support medical marijuana but do not provide patients with legal protection under state law).[36]

Providing medical marijuana has strong public support, but the federal government still criminalizes any use of marijuana, and federal agents can arrest users even if they have prescriptions from doctors in states where medical marijuana is legal. The Supreme Court ruled in 2005 in *Gonzales v. Raich* that the federal government can prosecute medical marijuana patients, even in states with compassionate-use laws.[37] The Court ruled that under the Commerce Clause of the United States Constitution, which allows the United States Congress "To regulate Commerce … among the several States," Congress may ban the use of cannabis even where states approve its use for medicinal purposes. The reasoning: Because of high demand, marijuana grown for medical reasons would find its way into the hands of ordinary drug users. So although the law may change on a local or state level, federal rules take precedence.

## Responding to Terrorism

The criminal law also underwent extensive change in both substance and procedure in the aftermath of the September 11, 2001, terrorist attacks. These changes will be discussed further in Chapter 18.

## THE LAW OF CRIMINAL PROCEDURE

Whereas substantive criminal law primarily defines crimes, the law of criminal procedure consists of the rules and procedures that govern the processing of criminal suspects and the conduct of criminal trials. The right to remain silent, the right to an attorney, and the right to a speedy and fair trial are all critical elements of criminal procedure. The main source of the procedural law is the ten amendments added to the U.S. Constitution on December 15, 1791, which are collectively known as the Bill of Rights. These amendments were added to the Constitution to quell fears among some of the founding fathers (such as George Mason) that, as drafted, the Constitution did not offer protections from the tyrannical exercise of power by an all-powerful central government.[38] The British violation of the colonists' civil rights before and during the Revolution was still fresh in their minds when they demanded a "bill of rights" that would spell out the rights and privileges of individual citizens. On September 25, 1789, the First Congress of the United States therefore proposed, to the state legislatures, 12 amendments to the Constitution that answered the arguments most frequently advanced against it. The first two proposed amendments, which concerned the number of constituents for each representative and the compensation of members of Congress, were not ratified. Articles 3 to 12, however, were ratified by three-fourths of the state legislatures, and they constitute the Bill of Rights.[39]

## Judicial Interpretation

The purpose of these amendments was to prevent the government from usurping the personal freedoms of citizens. The U.S. Supreme Court's interpretation of these amendments has served as the basis for the creation of legal rights of the accused. When the Supreme Court justices are conservative, as they are now, they are less likely to create new rights and privileges and more likely to restrict civil liberties. Take what is known as the **exclusionary rule**: According to judicial doctrine, evidence seized by police in violation of the rights and privileges presented by the Constitution cannot be used in a court of law; it is as if the incriminating evidence did not exist. Thus, if police make an illegal arrest and find illegal substances hidden on the suspect's body, the contraband cannot be presented as evidence at a trial. Although that much is clear, it is up to judicial interpretation to define a citizen's constitutional rights and privileges and then determine when they are violated. There are countless cases defining what the police can and cannot do and when their actions trigger the exclusionary rule. Take for instance the 2009 case of *Herring v. U.S.*[40] Bennie Dean Herring had been searched after the police were informed that there was an outstanding warrant against him on a felony charge. The search turned up methamphetamine and a pistol. Soon after, it was discovered that the warrant had actually been withdrawn five months earlier and had been left in the computer system by mistake. Should the evidence be discarded because the police made an error? Or should the evidence be allowed at trial because the police acted in good faith based on a mistaken belief that there was a warrant out for Herring? After all, the warrant *was* in the computer, so relying on it was an honest mistake. But if that mistake were excused, what would stop police from putting tainted warrants in their computer, leaving them there, and claiming they made many "honest mistakes"? The majority of the Supreme Court settled this conundrum when it ruled that "When police mistakes leading to an unlawful search are

**exclusionary rule**
The principle that illegally obtained evidence cannot be used in a court of law.

the result of isolated negligence attenuated from the search, rather than systemic error or reckless disregard of constitutional requirements, the exclusionary rule does not apply." The court ruled that the errors in the *Herring* case did not amount to deliberate police misconduct that should trigger the exclusionary rule, and the conviction of Bennie Herrings was allowed to stand. We will revisit the exclusionary rule and its control over police conduct in Chapter 7.

Of primary concern in the law of criminal procedure are the Fourth, Fifth, Sixth, and Eighth Amendments, which limit and control the manner in which the federal government operates the justice system. In addition, the due process clause of the Fourteenth Amendment has been interpreted as imposing limits on government action at the state and local levels.

■  The Fourth Amendment bars illegal "searches and seizures," a right especially important for the criminal justice system because it means that police officers cannot indiscriminately use their authority to investigate a possible crime or arrest a suspect. Stopping, questioning, or searching an individual without legal justification represents a serious violation of the Fourth Amendment right to personal privacy.

■  The Fifth Amendment limits the admissibility of confessions that have been obtained unfairly. In 1966, in the landmark case of *Miranda v. Arizona*, the Supreme Court held that a person accused of a crime has the right to refuse to answer questions when placed in police custody.[41] The Fifth Amendment also guarantees defendants the right to a grand jury hearing and the right not to be tried twice for the same crime—that is, they are protected from double jeopardy. Its due process clause guarantees defendants the right to fundamental fairness and the expectation of fair trials, fair hearings, and similar procedural safeguards.

■  The Sixth Amendment guarantees the defendant the right to a speedy and public trial by an impartial jury, the right to be informed of the nature of the charges, and the right to confront any prosecution witnesses. It also contains the right of a defendant to be represented by an attorney, a privilege that has been extended to numerous stages of the criminal justice process, including pretrial custody, identification and lineup procedures, preliminary hearing, submission of a guilty plea, trial, sentencing, and postconviction appeal.

■  According to the Eighth Amendment, "Excessive bail shall not be required, nor excessive fines imposed, nor cruel and unusual punishments inflicted." Bail is a money bond put up by the accused to attain freedom between arrest and trial. Bail is meant to ensure a trial appearance, because the bail money is forfeited if the defendant misses the trial date. The Eighth Amendment does not guarantee a constitutional right to bail but instead prohibits the use of excessive bail, which is typically defined as an amount far greater than that imposed on similar defendants who are accused of committing similar crimes. The Eighth Amendment also forbids the use of cruel and unusual punishment. This prohibition protects both the accused and convicted offenders from actions regarded as unacceptable by a civilized society, including corporal punishment and torture.

■  The Fourteenth Amendment is the vehicle used to ensure that the protections enumerated in the Bill of Rights are applied by the states. It affirms that no state shall "deprive any person of life, liberty, or property, without due process of law." In essence, the same general constitutional restrictions previously applicable to the federal government can be imposed on the states.

## Due Process of Law

The concept of due process, found in both the Fifth and Fourteenth Amendments, has been used to evaluate the constitutionality of legal statutes and to set standards and guidelines for fair procedures in the criminal justice system. In seeking to define the meaning of the term, most legal experts conclude that it refers to the essential elements of fairness under law.[42] This definition basically refers to the legal system's need for rules and regulations that protect individual rights.

Due process can be divided into two distinct categories: substantive and procedural. *Substantive due process* refers to the citizen's right to be protected from criminal laws that may be biased, discriminatory, or otherwise unfair. These laws may be vague or may apply unfairly to one group over another. For example, in an important 2003 case, *Lawrence et al. v. Texas*, the U.S. Supreme Court declared that laws banning sodomy were unconstitutional in that they violated the due process rights of citizens because of their sexual orientation. A neighbor in 1998 had reported a "weapons disturbance" at the home of John G. Lawrence, and when police arrived they found Lawrence and another man, Tyron Garner, having sex. The two were held overnight in jail and later fined $200 each for violating the state's homosexual conduct law. In its decision, the Court said the following:

> Although the laws involved . . . here . . . do not do more than prohibit a particular sexual act, their penalties and purposes have more far-reaching consequences, touching upon the most private human conduct, sexual behavior, and in the most private of places, the home. They seek to control a personal relationship that, whether or not entitled to formal recognition in the law, is within the liberty of persons to choose without being punished as criminals. The liberty protected by the Constitution allows homosexual persons the right to choose to enter upon relationships in the confines of their homes and their own private lives and still retain their dignity as free persons.[43]

As a result of the decision, laws banning same-sex relations are now unconstitutional and unenforceable, a decision that paved the way for the legalization of gay marriage.

In contrast, *procedural due process* seeks to ensure that no person will be deprived of life, liberty, or property without proper and legal criminal process. Basically, procedural due process is intended to guarantee that fundamental fairness exists in each individual case. Specific due process procedures include the following:

- Prompt notice of charges
- A formal hearing
- The right to counsel or some other representation
- The opportunity to respond to charges
- The opportunity to confront and cross-examine witnesses and accusers
- The privilege to be free from self-incrimination
- The opportunity to present one's own witnesses
- A decision made on the basis of substantial evidence and facts produced at the hearing
- A written statement of the reasons for the decision
- An appellate review procedure

These concepts, which protect basic freedoms, are not unique to the United States.

## The Meaning of Due Process

Exactly what constitutes due process in a specific case depends on the facts of the case, the federal and state constitutional and statutory provisions, previous court decisions, and the ideas and principles that

© AP Images/Gloria Ferniz

*The right to due process of law extends to all people who come before the court, including immigrants and foreign nationals. Here Samuel Komba Kambo is interviewed at an Immigration and Customs Enforcement contract facility in San Antonio, Texas, where he was being detained by U.S. Immigration authorities. Kambo, a legal immigrant, spent nearly a year in jail while fighting deportation as the government tried to revoke his visa. He was released from custody in October 2007 after a U.S. district judge ruled that U.S. Immigration and Customs Enforcement had violated his due process rights. Kambo is a retired captain in the Republic of Sierra Leone Armed Forces and was involved in a coup to oust President Joseph Saidu Momoh and the All People's Congress (APC) government in 1992.*

### PERSPECTIVES ON JUSTICE

#### Due Process

*Lawrence et al. v. Texas* is a milestone in the ongoing effort to grant due process rights to all Americans. According to the due process perspective, no one should be denied the protection of the law simply because of his or her personal status—race, religion, ethnicity, or sexual orientation.

society considers important at a given time and in a given place.[44] Justice Felix Frankfurter emphasized this point in *Rochin v. California* (1952):

> Due process of law requires an evaluation based on a disinterested inquiry pursued in the spirit of science on a balanced order of facts, exactly and clearly stated, on the detached consideration of conflicting claims[,] . . . on a judgment not ad hoc and episodic but duly mindful of reconciling the needs both of continuity and of change in a progressive society.[45]

The interpretations of due process of law are not fixed but rather reflect what society deems fair and just at a particular time and place. The degree of loss suffered by the individual (victim or offender) balanced against the state's interests also determines which and how many due process requirements are ordinarily applied. When the Supreme Court justices are conservative, as they have been in the first decade of the twenty-first century, they are less likely to create new rights and privileges under the guise of due process. For example, the Court's decision in the case of *Sattazahn v. Pennsylvania* (2003) helped define the concept of double jeopardy. Sattazahn had been sentenced to death under a Pennsylvania law that requires that the sentencing jury must unanimously find that the case warranted capital punishment. If the jury cannot unanimously agree on the sentence, the court must enter a life sentence. After he was convicted of murder, Sattazahn's jury became deadlocked on the sentence; the trial judge discharged them and entered a life sentence. Later, Sattazahn appealed the conviction and received a new trial. At the second trial, the prosecutor again sought the death penalty and Sattazahn was again convicted, but this time the jury imposed a death sentence. Sattazahn appealed once again on the grounds that the imposition of the death sentence after he was originally awarded a life sentence was a violation of double jeopardy. However, the Supreme Court disagreed, finding that jeopardy was not compromised in this case. When a defendant is convicted of murder and sentenced to life imprisonment and succeeds in having the conviction set aside on appeal, jeopardy has not terminated, so a life sentence imposed in connection with the initial conviction raises no double-jeopardy bar to a death sentence on retrial. The Court also concluded that double-jeopardy protections were not triggered in this case because the jury deadlocked at the first sentencing and made no findings with respect to the alleged aggravating circumstance; the result could not be called an "acquittal" within the context of double jeopardy.[46] Sattazahn had gambled by appealing his conviction and lost.

This complicated case aptly illustrates how judicial interpretation controls the meaning of "double jeopardy" and how due process demands that the individual's rights be balanced against the state's interests.

## Ethical Challenges in Criminal Justice: A Writing Assignment

A young woman has been arrested for killing her abusive husband. According to her story, she came home from work to find her husband in the kitchen drunk and rambling. When she tried to reason with him, he slapped her repeatedly. Feeling that her life was in danger, she ran out of the room and into her first-floor bedroom, where she kept a handgun. After loading the gun, she ran back to the kitchen, where she saw him holding a large knife. She then shot him in the chest, killing him instantly. Her attorney intends to claim that she was a battered wife and her actions amounted to self-defense. Take the role of a prosecutor and decide whether you would charge the woman with homicide. What would you need to know before making your decision? Be sure to review the sections on legal definitions of a crime and on criminal defenses before writing your essay.

# SUMMARY

**1. Know the similarities and differences between substantive and procedural criminal law and between civil law and public law.**

- Substantive law defines crimes and their punishment.
- Procedural law sets out the basic rules of practice in the criminal justice system.
- Civil law governs relations between private parties.
- Public law regulates the activities of governmental agencies.

**2. Understand the concept of substantive criminal law and be familiar with its history.**

- The substantive criminal law defines crimes and their punishments.
- The underlying goal of the substantive criminal law is to enforce social control, distribute retribution, express public opinion and morality, deter criminal behavior, punish wrongdoing, maintain social order, and provide restoration.

**3. Discuss the sources of the criminal law.**

- The roots of the criminal codes used in the United States can be traced back to such early legal charters as the Babylonian Code of Hammurabi (2000 BCE), the Mosaic Code of the Israelites (1200 BCE), and the Roman Twelve Tables (451 BCE).
- After the Norman Conquest of Britain, royal judges decided what to do in each case, using local custom and rules of conduct as their guide in a system known as stare decisis (Latin for "to stand by decided cases").
- Eventually this system evolved into a common law of the country that incorporated local custom and practice into a national code.
- The contemporary American legal system was codified by state and federal legislatures.

**4. Be familiar with the elements of a crime.**

- Nearly all common-law crime contains both mental and physical elements.
- For an act to constitute a crime, it must be a voluntary and deliberate illegal act, or actus reus, such as taking someone's money, burning a building, or shooting someone.
- For an act to constitute a crime, it must be done with deliberate purpose or criminal intent, or mens rea.
- For an action to constitute a crime, the law requires that a connection be made between the mens rea and actus reus, thereby showing

that the offender's conduct was the proximate cause of the injury resulting.

**5. Define the term "strict liability."**

- Certain statutory offenses exist in which mens rea is not essential. These offenses fall in a category known as public safety or strict liability crimes.
- Traffic crimes, public safety, and business crimes are typically strict liability crimes.

**6. Describe how crimes are classified.**

- Felonies are considered serious crimes. Felonies include crimes against the person, such as criminal homicide, robbery, and rape, as well as such crimes against property as burglary and larceny.
- Misdemeanors are seen as less serious crimes. They include petit (or petty) larceny, assault and battery, and the unlawful possession of marijuana.
- Violations include public nuisance offenses such as traffic violations and public drunkenness.

**7. Be able to discuss excuse and justification defenses for crime.**

- Defendants may claim that even though they did engage in the criminal act they are accused of, they should be excused because they lacked mens rea; "I did not know what I was doing."
- Another type of defense is justification, such as self-defense, which involves maintaining that the act was justified under the circumstances; "Given the circumstances, anyone would have done what I did."

**8. Discuss the concept of criminal procedure.**

- The law of criminal procedure consists of the rules and procedures that govern the pretrial processing of criminal suspects and the conduct of criminal trials.
- The main source of the procedural law is the body of the Constitution and the first ten amendments added to the U.S. Constitution on December 15, 1791. These are collectively known as the Bill of Rights.

**9. Know which amendments to the Constitution are the most important to the justice system.**

- Of primary concern are the Fourth, Fifth, Sixth, and Eighth Amendments, which limit and control the manner in which the federal government operates the justice system.
- The Fourteenth Amendment applies these rights to the state and local governments.

## 10. List the elements of due process of law.

- The concept of due process is found in both the Fifth and Fourteenth Amendments.

- Due process has been used to evaluate the constitutionality of legal statutes and to set standards and guidelines for fair procedures in the criminal justice system.

- Due process can be divided into two distinct categories: substantive and procedural. Substantive due process refers to the citizen's right to be protected from criminal laws that may be biased, discriminatory, or otherwise unfair.

## KEY TERMS

criminal law, 136
substantive criminal law, 136
procedural criminal laws, 136
civil law, 136
torts, 136
public law, 136
stare decisis, 139

mala in se, 140
ex post facto laws, 142
actus reus, 146
mens rea, 146
criminal negligence, 147
public safety or strict liability
   crime, 147

excuse defenses, 150
justification, 151
penumbral crimes, 156
stalking, 156
obitiatry, 156
exclusionary rule, 159

## CRITICAL THINKING QUESTIONS

1. What are the specific aims and purposes of the criminal law? To what extent does the criminal law control behavior?

2. How would you cast your vote on an amendment legalizing recreational drugs? Why?

3. What is a criminal act? What is a criminal state of mind? When are individuals criminally liable for their actions?

4. Discuss the various kinds of crime classifications. To what extent or degree are they distinguishable?

5. Numerous states are revising their penal codes. Which major categories of substantive crimes—for example, laws banning prostitution—do you think should be revised?

6. Entrapment is a defense used when the defendant was lured into committing the crime. To what extent should law enforcement personnel induce the commission of an offense?

## NOTES

1. Supreme Court of California, *In Re Marriage Cases*, S147999, May 15, 2008, www.courtinfo.ca.gov/opinions/documents/S147999.PDF (accessed July 17, 2010).
2. Lisa Leff, "Calif. Overturns Gay Marriage Ban," *Time*, May 15, 2008, www.time.com/time/printout/0,8816,1806634,00.html (accessed July 17, 2008); "Bob Egelko and John Wildermuth," "Prop 8 Foes Concede Defeat, Vow to Fight On," SFGate, November 6, 2008, www.sfgate.com/cgi-bin/article.cgi?f=/c/a/2008/11/06/BA1313VJQH.DTL.
3. Marriage Recognition and Family Protection Act, 2010, http://www.eqca.org/site/pp.asp?c=kuLRJ9MRKrH&b=5305359,
4. *Carriers* Case, 13 Edward IV 9.pL.5 (1473).
5. See John Weaver, *Warren—The Man, the Court, the Era* (Boston: Little, Brown, 1967); see also "We the People," *Time*, July 6, 1987, p. 6.
6. *Kansas v. Hendricks*, 117 S.Ct. 2072 (1997); *Chicago v. Morales*, 119 S.Ct. 246 (1999).
7. *City of Chicago v. Morales et al.*, 527 U.S. 41 (1999).
8. Daniel Suleiman, "The Capital Punishment Exception: A Case for Constitutionalizing the Substantive Criminal Law," *Columbia Law Review* 104 (2004): 426–458.
9. *Baze and Bowling v. Rees*, 553 U.S. 35 (2008).
10. *Calder v. Bull*, 3 U.S. 386 (1798).
11. See American Law Institute, Model Penal Code, Sec. 104.
12. Henry Black, *Black's Law Dictionary*, rev. 5th ed. (St. Paul, Minn.: West, 1979), pp. 744, 1150.
13. Sheldon Krantz, *Law of Corrections and Prisoners' Rights, Cases, and Materials*, 3d ed. (St. Paul, Minn.: West, 1986), p. 702; Barbara Knight and Stephen Early Jr., *Prisoners' Rights in America* (Chicago: Nelson-Hall, 1986), Chapter 1; see also Fred Cohen, "The Law of Prisoners' Rights—An Overview," *Criminal Law Bulletin* 24 (1988): 321–349.
14. See *United States v. Balint*, 258 U.S. 250 (1922); see also *Morissette v. United States*, 342 U.S. 246 (1952).
15. New York State Consolidated Laws, Article 270, Other Offenses Relating to Public Safety, Section 270.10, Creating a Hazard (2002).
16. *Regina v. Dudley and Stephens*, 14 Q.B.D. 273 (1884).
17. Associated Press, "Nigerian Used Stepdaughter, 14, for a Son, Jury Finds," *Boston Globe*, October 8, 1998, p. 9.
18. *Robinson v. California*, 370 U.S. 660 (1962).
19. *Powell v. Texas*, 392 U.S. 514 (1968).
20. Samuel M. Davis, *Rights of Juveniles: The Juvenile Justice System* (New York: Boardman, 1974; updated 1993), Chapter 2; Larry Siegel and Joseph Senna, *Juvenile Delinquency: Theory, Practice, and Law* (St. Paul, Minn.: West, 1996).
21. *Jacobson v. United States*, 503 U.S. 540 (1992).
22. ERGO (Euthanasia Research & Guidance Organization), www.finalexit.org (accessed July 17, 2008).

23. "Criminal Law—Mutual Combat Mitigation—Appellate Court of Illinois Holds That Disproportionate Reaction to Provocation Negates Mutual Combat Mitigation—*People v. Thompson*, 821 N.E. 2d 664 (Ill. App. Ct. 2004)," *Harvard Law Review* 118 (2005): 2437–2444.

24. Patrik Jonsson, "Is Self-Defense Law Vigilante Justice? Some Say Proposed Laws Can Help Deter Gun Violence. Others Worry about Deadly Confrontations," *Christian Science Monitor*, February 24, 2006.

25. AOL News, Cop in Fatal Crash Was Driving 94 MPH, November 18, 2009, www.aolnews.com/story/milford-connecticut-police-officer-jason/773587.

26. Deborah W. Denno, "Gender, Crime, and the Criminal Law Defenses," *Journal of Criminal Law and Criminology* 85 (Summer 1994): 80–180.

27. Margaret Raymond, "Penumbral Crimes," *American Criminal Law Review* 39 (2002): 1395–1440.

28. National Institute of Justice, *Project to Develop a Model Anti-Stalking Statute* (Washington, D.C.: National Institute of Justice, 1994).

29. Marvin Zalman, John Strate, Denis Hunter, and James Sellars, "Michigan Assisted Suicide Three Ring Circus: The Intersection of Law and Politics," *Ohio Northern Law Review* 23 (1997): 863–903.

30. 1992 P.A. 270, as amended by 1993 P.A. 3, M.C. L. ss. 752.1021 to 752.1027.

31. Michigan Code of Criminal Procedure, "Assisting a Suicide," Section 750.329a.

32. Sarah Welchans, "Megan's Law: Evaluations of Sexual Offender Registries," *Criminal Justice Policy Review* 16 (2005): 123–140.

33. Matthew Lyon, "No Means No? Withdrawal of Consent during Intercourse and the Continuing Evolution of the Definition of Rape," *Journal of Criminal Law and Criminology* 95 (2004): 277–314.

34. Environmental Protection Agency, Criminal Enforcement Division, www.epa.gov/compliance/criminal/index.html (accessed July 17, 2010).

35. State of New Jersey 213th Legislature, Senate Bill 119, http://medicalmarijuana.procon.org/sourcefiles/NJS119.PDF.

36. Drug Policy Alliance Network, "Medical Marijuana," http://www.drugpolicy.org/marijuana/medical/ (accessed April 1, 2010).

37. *Gonzales v. Raich*, 545 U.S. 1 (2005).

38. National Archives, www.archives.gov/national-archives-experience/charters/bill_of_rights.html (accessed July 17, 2008).

39. Ibid.

40. *Herring v. United States*, no. 07-513 (2008).

41. *Miranda v. Arizona*, 384 U.S. 436 (1966).

42. James MacGregor Burns and Steward Burns, *The Pursuit of Rights in America* (New York: Knopf, 1991).

43. *Lawrence et al. v. Texas*, 539 U.S. 558 (2003).

44. *Rochin v. California*, 342 U.S. 165 (1952).

45. *Ibid.*, at 172.

46. *Sattazahn v. Pennsylvania*, 537 U.S. 101 (2003).

# THE POLICE AND LAW ENFORCEMENT

THE POLICE ARE THE GATEKEEPERS of the criminal justice process. They initiate contact with law violators and decide whether to formally arrest them and start their journey through the criminal justice system, settle the issue in an informal way (such as by issuing a warning), or simply take no action at all. The strategic position of police officers, their visibility and contact with the public, and their use of weapons and arrest power have kept them in the forefront of public thought about law enforcement.

Policing is not easy, and it is not always glamorous work, but many who choose this important career wouldn't have it any other way. Steve Bishopp, a sergeant with the Dallas Police Department, finds his job particularly rewarding: "I've come across some truly violent, vicious people that should never be out in society. I have worked many bloody and violent murders and sexual assaults, and putting those people in jail (particularly after assisting the prosecution in getting a conviction) gives me a huge sense of accomplishment and pride." Steve also enjoys being a role model for his four kids. These positives tend to outweigh the difficulties that can go along with constantly being in the spotlight and interacting with a public that doesn't always understand the nuances of the job.

Large cities such as Dallas are the exception; most officers work in smaller agencies with relatively few officers. But even though smaller towns may not see as much "action" as big cities, many of the same rules apply. For example, Larry Napolitano, a patrolman in Shrewsbury, Massachusetts, a town of 34,000 people, believes police officers must guard against complacency. They must always remain vigilant and prepared during any encounter; otherwise, they may not be ready for the danger that could arise. "When you stop a motor vehicle, you really have no knowledge of who that person is, what kind of day they had, or what they are capable of. You obviously stopped them for a reason, whether it be motor vehicle-related or for another reason, but you really don't know what lies ahead. If you get complacent and treat every stop the same way, it could get you seriously hurt or killed." ∎

*THE FOLLOWING FOUR CHAPTERS serve as an introduction to and overview of policing and law enforcement in contemporary society. Chapter 5 discusses the history of law enforcement and the various contemporary agencies. Chapter 6 covers the organization, role, and function of police agencies. Chapter 7 considers the most pressing issues facing police agencies. And Chapter 8 is devoted to police and the rule of law.*

*"When you stop a motor vehicle, you really have no knowledge of who that person is, what kind of day they had, or what they are capable of. You obviously stopped them for a reason, whether it be motor vehicle–related or for another reason, but you really don't know what lies ahead. If you get complacent and treat every stop the same way, it could get you seriously hurt or killed."*

*"I've come across some truly violent, vicious people that should never be out in society. I have worked many bloody and violent murders and sexual assaults, and putting those people in jail (particularly after assisting the prosecution in getting a conviction) gives me a huge sense of accomplishment and pride."*

# CHAPTER 5

# The Police: History and Contemporary Structure

## CHAPTER OBJECTIVES

1. Recount the early development of the police in England.
2. Recount the development of the police in colonial America.
3. Discuss twentieth-century police reforms and the emergence of professionalism.
4. Identify the main events in policing between 1960 and the present.
5. Identify the various levels of law enforcement.
6. Identify the most prominent federal law enforcement agencies.
7. Discuss the differences among local, county, state, and federal law enforcement agencies.
8. Be familiar with private policing, including the reasons for it and the controversies associated with it.
9. Identify various technologies currently used in law enforcement.

**T**he immigrant population in the United States stands at almost 40 million.[1] According to recent estimates, roughly one in three of these immigrants has entered the country illegally.[2] The vast majority have crossed into the United States from Mexico, leading to a variety of responses to secure the nation's southern border. Immigration and Customs Enforcement (ICE) has hired more agents, as has the Border Patrol. National Guard troops have even been stationed at the border, especially following the high-profile shooting death of an Arizona rancher.[3] Civilian patrol organizations have even come on board. Examples include the Minuteman Project and the Minuteman Civil Defense Corps,[4] both of which have lobbied for improved border security and asked volunteers to patrol the borders where Border Patrol agents cannot always be.

As law enforcement officials and civilians get more involved in patrolling the border, they are partnering in new and unprecedented ways. For example, the Texas Border Sheriff's Coalition has recently joined forces with BlueServo[SM] Inc. to launch a "virtual community watch" initiative. Interested persons can log on to a website, view live footage of select locations along the Texas–Mexico border, and report suspected illegal crossings to authorities.[5] As one local sheriff explained, "By putting more eyes on the Texas–Mexico border, law enforcement can better protect our state from powerful and ruthless Mexican crime cartels and violent transnational gangs."[6] ■

Although public–private partnerships are important, there is some concern that too much civilian involvement could become problematic. Critics of Minutemen-like organizations claim they are composed of modern-day vigilantes. Others worry that even those who patrol the border from behind their computer screens may be inclined to take the law into their own hands. Despite such concerns, there is continued interest in civilian patrol at the U.S.–Mexico border. This is most interesting, because even though much early law enforcement in this country relied on people serving in a volunteer capacity, the typical police officer we think of today is a paid government official, employed by a city, county, or state or by the federal government.

When we talk about civilian patrols at the border, it is also important to think about the vast private security apparatus in the United States. The number of private police in America, including most notably security guards, now exceeds the number of government police by about 3 to 1.[7] This means there are approximately three private police or security personnel for every sworn officer, and the number appears to be growing.

This chapter, the first of four on policing and law enforcement, covers the history of the police, the various organizations that perform police functions, and how technology is now being used to improve police operations. The evolution of policing has been dramatic and somewhat cyclical, as this chapter's opening suggests. Many years ago, during tribal times, the people appointed villagers to protect them from outside marauders who wanted to destroy their lives. Then the government assumed responsibility for policing, and law enforcement became a public function. Today, however, private security professionals and civilian volunteers are performing many of the same functions as government police. Does this represent a return to early policing?

# THE HISTORY OF POLICE

The origin of U.S. police agencies, like that of criminal law, can be traced to early English society.[8] England had no regular police force before the Norman Conquest. Every person living in the villages scattered throughout the countryside was responsible for aiding neighbors and protecting the settlement from thieves and marauders. This was known as the pledge system. People were grouped in collectives of ten families, called **tythings** (or **tithings**) and were entrusted with policing their own minor problems, such as dealing with disturbances, fire, wild animals, and other threats. The leader was called the tythingman. When trouble occurred, he was expected to make a **hue and cry** to assemble his helpers and warn the village. Ten tythings were grouped into a **hundred**, whose affairs were supervised by a hundredman appointed by the local nobleman. The hundredman (later to be called the parish **constable**) might be considered the first real police officer, and he dealt with more serious breaches of the law.[9]

Shires, which resembled the counties of today, were controlled by the **shire reeve**, who was appointed by the Crown or local landowner to supervise the territory and ensure that order would be kept. The shire reeve, a forerunner of today's sheriff (note the relatedness of the two terms), soon began to pursue and apprehend law violators as part of his duties.

In the thirteenth century, the **watch system** was created to help protect property in England's larger cities and towns. Watchmen patrolled at night and helped protect the community from robberies, fires, and disturbances. They reported to the area constable, who became the primary metropolitan law enforcement agent. In larger cities, such as London, the watchmen were organized within church parishes and were usually members of the parish they protected.

**tything (tithing)**
In medieval England, a collective group of ten families that pledged to help one another and provide mutual aid.

**hue and cry**
In medieval England, a call for mutual aid against trouble or danger.

**hundred**
In medieval England, a group of 100 families (ten tythings) responsible for maintaining order and trying minor offenses.

**constable**
In early English towns, an appointed peacekeeper who organized citizens for protection and supervised the night watch.

**shire reeve**
In early England, the chief law enforcement official in a county; forerunner of today's sheriff.

**watch system**
In medieval England, groups of men who organized in church parishes to guard at night against disturbances and breaches of the peace under the direction of the local constable.

In 1326 the office of **justice of the peace** was created to assist the shire reeve in controlling the county. Eventually, these justices took on judicial functions in addition to their primary role as peacekeeper. The local constable became the operational assistant to the justice of the peace, supervising the night watchmen, investigating offenses, serving summonses, executing warrants, and securing prisoners. This system helped delineate the relationship between police and the judiciary, which has persisted for more than 600 years.

**justice of the peace**
Official appointed to act as the judicial officer in a county.

## Private Police and Thief Takers

As the eighteenth century began, rising crime rates in the cities encouraged a new form of private, monied police, who were able to profit both legally and criminally from the lack of formal police departments. These private police agents, referred to as *thief takers*, were universally corrupt, taking profits not only from catching and informing on criminals but also from theft, receiving stolen property, intimidation, perjury, and blackmail. They often relieved their prisoners of money and stolen goods and made more income by accepting hush money, giving perjured evidence, swearing false oaths, and operating extortion rackets. Petty debtors were especially easy targets for those who combined thief taking with the keeping of alehouses and taverns. While prisoners were incarcerated, their health and safety were entirely at the whim of the keepers, or thief takers, who were free to charge virtually whatever they wanted for board and other necessities. Court bailiffs who also acted as thief takers were the most passionately detested legal profiteers. They seized debtors and held them in small lockups, where they forced their victims to pay exorbitant prices for food and lodging.

The thief takers' use of violence was notorious. They went armed and were prepared to maim or kill in order to gain their objectives. Before he was hanged in 1725, Jack Wild, the most notorious thief taker, "had two fractures in his skull and his bald head was covered with silver plates. He had seventeen wounds in various parts of his body from swords, daggers, and gunshots, [and] ... his throat had been cut in the course of his duties."[10]

Henry Fielding, famed author of the novel *Tom Jones*, along with Saunders Welch and Sir John Fielding (Henry's brother), sought to clean up the thief-taking system. Appointed a city magistrate in 1748, Fielding operated his own group of monied police out of Bow Street in London, directing and deploying them throughout the city and its environs, deciding which cases to investigate and what streets to protect. His agents were carefully instructed on their legitimate powers and duties. Fielding's Bow Street Runners were a marked improvement over the earlier monied police because they actually had an administrative structure that improved record keeping and investigative procedures.

Although an improvement, Fielding's forces were not adequate, and by the nineteenth century, state police officers were needed. Ironically, almost 200 years later, private policing is now considered essential. Private police forces are a rapidly growing entity, and in many instances local police forces work closely with private security firms and similar entities. In some gated communities and special tax assessment districts, property owners pay a special levy, in addition to their tax dollars, to hire additional private police, who may work in partnership with local law enforcement to investigate criminal activities.[11]

## The London Metropolitan Police

In 1829 Sir Robert Peel, England's home secretary, guided through Parliament an "Act for Improving the Police in and near the Metropolis." The legislation came to be known as the **Metropolitan Police Act.** Peel was also among the first influential figures in policing history to call for more than just a crime

**Metropolitan Police Act**
Sir Robert Peel's legislation that established the first organized police force in London.

## EXHIBIT 5.1

## Sir Robert Peel's Nine Principles of Policing

1. The basic mission for which the police exist is to prevent crime and disorder.

2. The ability of the police to perform their duties is dependent upon public approval of police actions.

3. Police must secure the willing co-operation of the public in voluntary observance of the law to be able to secure and maintain the respect of the public.

4. The degree of co-operation of the public that can be secured diminishes proportionately to the necessity of the use of physical force.

5. Police seek and preserve public favour not by catering to public opinion but by constantly demonstrating absolute impartial service to the law.

6. Police use physical force to the extent necessary to secure observance of the law or to restore order only when the exercise of persuasion, advice and warning is found to be insufficient.

7. Police, at all times, should maintain a relationship with the public that gives reality to the historic tradition that the police are the public and the public are the police; the police being only members of the public who are paid to give full-time attention to duties which are incumbent on every citizen in the interests of community welfare and existence.

8. Police should always direct their action strictly towards their functions and never appear to usurp the powers of the judiciary.

9. The test of police efficiency is the absence of crime and disorder, not the visible evidence of police action in dealing with it.

Source: Sir Robert Peel, www.nwpolice.org/peel.html (accessed April 6, 2010).

© Popperfoto/Getty Images

*Sir Robert Peel (1788–1850) was home secretary from 1822 to 1830 and prime minister of Great Britain twice in the 1830s and 1840s. He was also responsible for forming the Metropolitan Police, the first organized police force in London.*

fighter role for officers. He identified nine principles that he felt should characterize police forces.[12] These appear in Exhibit 5.1.

Peel's Metropolitan Police Act established the first organized police force in London. Composed of more than 1,000 men, the London police force was structured along military lines. Its members would be known from then on as *bobbies*, after their creator. They wore a distinctive uniform and were led by two magistrates, who were later given the title of commissioner. However, the ultimate responsibility for the police fell to the home secretary and, consequently, Parliament.

The early bobbies suffered many problems. Not only were many of them corrupt, but they were unsuccessful at stopping crime and were unduly influenced by the wealthy. Owners of houses of ill repute who in the past had guaranteed their undisturbed operation by bribing watchmen now turned their attention to the bobbies. Metropolitan Police administrators fought constantly to terminate cowardly, corrupt, and alcoholic officers, dismissing in the beginning about one-third of the bobbies each year.

Despite its recognized shortcomings, the London experiment proved a vast improvement over what had come before. It was considered so successful that the Metropolitan Police soon began providing law enforcement assistance to outlying areas that requested it. Another act of Parliament allowed justices of the peace to establish local police forces, and by 1856 every borough and county in England was required to form its own police force.

## Law Enforcement in Colonial America

Law enforcement in colonial America paralleled the British model. In the colonies, the county **sheriff** became the most important law enforcement agent. In addition to keeping the peace and fighting crime, sheriffs collected taxes, supervised elections, and handled a great deal of other legal business.

The colonial sheriff did not patrol or seek out crime. Instead, he reacted to citizens' complaints and investigated crimes that had occurred. His salary, which was related to his effectiveness, was paid on a fee system. Sheriffs received a fixed amount for every arrest made. Unfortunately, their tax-collecting chores were more lucrative than fighting crime, so law enforcement was not one of their primary concerns.

In the cities, law enforcement was the province of the town marshal, who was aided, often unwillingly, by a variety of constables, night watchmen, police justices, and city council members. However, local governments had little power of administration, and enforcement of the criminal law was largely an individual or community responsibility. After the American Revolution, larger cities relied on elected or appointed officials to serve warrants and recover stolen property, sometimes in cooperation with the thieves themselves. Night watchmen, referred to as *leatherheads* because of the leather helmets they wore, patrolled the streets calling the hour, while equipped with a rattle to summon help and a nightstick to ward off lawbreakers. Watchmen were not widely respected. Rowdy young men enjoyed tipping over watch houses with a leatherhead inside, and a favorite saying in New York was "While the city sleeps the watchmen do too."[13]

In rural areas in the South, "slave patrols" charged with recapturing escaped slaves were an early, if loathsome, form of law enforcement.[14] In the western territories, individual initiative was encouraged by the practice of offering rewards for the capture of felons. If trouble arose, the town vigilance committee might form a posse to chase offenders. These **vigilantes** were called on to use force or intimidation to eradicate such social problems as theft of livestock. For example, the San Francisco Vigilance Committee actively pursued criminals in the mid-nineteenth century.

As cities grew, it became exceedingly difficult for local leaders to organize ad hoc citizen vigilante groups. Moreover, the early nineteenth century was an era of widespread urban unrest and mob violence. Local leaders began to realize that a more structured police function was needed to control demonstrators and keep the peace.

## Early Police Agencies

The modern police department was born out of the urban mob violence that wracked the nation's cities in the nineteenth century. Boston created the first formal U.S. police department in 1838. New York formed its police department in 1844, Philadelphia in 1854. The new police departments replaced the night watch system and relegated constables and sheriffs to serving court orders and running jails.

At first, the urban police departments inherited the functions of the institutions they replaced. For example, Boston police were charged with maintaining public health until 1853, and in New York, the police were responsible for street sweeping until 1881. Politics dominated the departments and determined the recruitment of new officers and the promotion of supervisors. An individual with the right connections could be hired despite a lack of qualifications. Early police agencies were corrupt, brutal, and inefficient.[15]

In the late nineteenth century, police work was highly desirable because it paid more than most other blue-collar jobs. By 1880, the average factory worker earned $450 per year, while a metropolitan police officer made double that amount. For immigrant groups, having enough political clout to be appointed to

**CourseMate** For more information about **Sir Robert Peel's life**, visit the Criminal Justice CourseMate at CengageBrain.com, then access the "Web Links" for this chapter.

**sheriff**
The chief law enforcement officer in a county.

**vigilantes**
In the Old West, members of a vigilance committee or posse called upon to capture cattle thieves or other felons.

the police department was an important step up the social ladder.[16] However, job security was uncertain because it depended on the local political machine staying in power.

Police work itself was primitive. Few of even the simplest technological innovations common today, such as call boxes and centralized record keeping, were in place. Most officers patrolled on foot, without backup or the ability to call for help. Officers were commonly taunted by local toughs and responded with force and brutality. The long-standing conflict between police and the public was born in the difficulty that untrained, unprofessional officers had in patrolling the streets of nineteenth-century U.S. cities and in breaking up and controlling labor disputes. Police were not crime fighters as they are known today. Their major role was maintaining order, and their power was almost unchecked. The average officer had little training, no education in the law, and a minimum of supervision, yet the police became virtual judges of law and fact, with the ability to exercise unlimited discretion.[17]

At mid-nineteenth century, the detective bureau was set up as part of the Boston police. Until then, thief taking had been the province of amateur bounty hunters who hired themselves out to victims for a price. When professional police departments replaced bounty hunters, the close working relationships that developed between police detectives and their underworld informants produced many scandals and, consequently, high turnover in personnel.

Police during the nineteenth century were regarded as incompetent and corrupt, and they were disliked by the people they served. The police role was only minimally directed at law enforcement. Its primary function was serving as the enforcement arm of the reigning political power, protecting private property, and keeping control of the ever-rising numbers of foreign immigrants.

Police agencies evolved slowly in the second half of the nineteenth century. Uniforms were introduced in 1853 in New York. The first technological breakthroughs in police operations came in the area of communications. The linking of precincts to central headquarters by telegraph began in the 1850s. In 1867 the first telegraph police boxes were installed. An officer could turn a key in a box, and his location and number would automatically register at headquarters. Additional technological advances were made in transportation. The Detroit Police Department outfitted some of its patrol officers with bicycles in 1897. By 1913, the motorcycle was being used by departments in the eastern part of the nation. The first police car appeared in Akron, Ohio, in 1910, and the police wagon became popular in Cincinnati in 1912.[18] Nonpolice functions, such as care of the streets, began to be abandoned after the Civil War.

Big-city police were still disrespected by the public, unsuccessful in their role as crime stoppers, and uninvolved in progressive activities. The control of police departments by local politicians impeded effective law enforcement and fostered an atmosphere of graft and corruption.

## Twentieth-Century Reform

In an effort to reduce police corruption, civic leaders in a number of jurisdictions created police administrative boards to lessen local officials' control over the police. These boards were responsible for appointing police administrators and controlling police affairs. In many instances, these measures failed because the private citizens appointed to the review boards lacked expertise in the intricacies of police work.

Another reform movement was the takeover of some big-city police agencies by state legislators. Although police budgets were financed through local taxes, control of police was usurped by rural politicians in the state capitals. New York City temporarily lost authority over its police force in 1857. It was not until the first decades of the twentieth century that cities regained control of their police forces.

© AP Images/Boston Public Library

*Great precaution is taken to guard police headquarters in Pemberton Square during the Boston police strike of 1919. Here the cavalrymen of the state guard ride horses previously used by the mounted policemen who went on strike. The Boston police strike ended police unionism for decades and solidified power in the hands of reactionary, autocratic police administrators. In the aftermath of the strike, various local, state, and federal crime commissions began to investigate the extent of crime and the ability of the justice system to deal with it and made recommendations to improve police effectiveness.*

The Boston police strike of 1919 heightened interest in police reform. The strike came about basically because police officers were dissatisfied with their status in society. Other professions were unionizing and increasing their standards of living, but police salaries lagged behind. The Boston police officers' organization, the Boston Social Club, voted to become a union affiliated with the American Federation of Labor. The police officers struck on September 9, 1919. Rioting and looting broke out, resulting in Governor Calvin Coolidge's mobilization of the state militia to take over the city. Public support turned against the police, and the strike was broken. Eventually, all the striking officers were fired and replaced by new recruits. The Boston police strike ended police unionism for decades and solidified power in the hands of reactionary, autocratic police administrators. In the aftermath of the strike, various local, state, and federal crime commissions began to investigate the extent of crime and the ability of the justice system to deal with it and made recommendations to improve police effectiveness.[19] However, with the onset of the Great Depression, justice reform became a less important issue than economic revival, and for many years, little changed in policing.

## The Emergence of Professionalism

Around the turn of the twentieth century, a number of nationally recognized leaders called for measures to help improve and professionalize the police. In 1893 the International Association of Chiefs of Police (IACP), a professional society, was formed. Under the direction of its first president (District of Columbia chief of police Richard Sylvester), the IACP became the leading voice for police reform during the first two decades of the twentieth century. The IACP called for creating a civil service police force and for removing political influence and control. It also advocated centralized organizational structure and record keeping to curb the power of politically aligned precinct captains. Still another professional reform the IACP fostered was the creation of specialized units, such as delinquency control squads.

In 1929, President Herbert Hoover created the National Commission on Law Observance and Enforcement, otherwise known as the **Wickersham Commission** (for George W. Wickersham, its chairman), to study the U.S. criminal justice system and make recommendations for improvement. In 1931, it issued the so-called *Wickersham Commission Report*. Two volumes of the report

**CourseMate** For more information about **police labor relations**, visit the Criminal Justice CourseMate at CengageBrain.com, then access the "Web Links" for this chapter.

**Wickersham Commission**
Formally known as the National Commission on Law Observance and Enforcement, a commission created in 1929 by President Herbert Hoover to study the U.S. criminal justice system, including the police.

dealt specifically with police. Volume 2, called *Lawlessness in Law Enforcement*, portrayed the police in an unfavorable light, calling them inept, inefficient, racist, brutal, and even criminal. Volume 14, *The Police*, was authored mostly by August Vollmer, one of the most famous police reformers of the time. In it, he discussed methods that could be used to professionalize the police, several of which he had already used in his own law enforcement career.

While serving as police chief of Berkeley, California, Vollmer instituted university training for young officers. He also helped develop the School of Criminology at the University of California at Berkeley, which became the model for justice-related programs around the United States. Vollmer's protégés included O. W. Wilson, who pioneered the use of advanced training for officers when he took over and reformed the Wichita (Kansas) Police Department in 1928. Wilson was also instrumental in applying modern management and administrative techniques to policing. His text *Police Administration* became the single most influential work on the subject.[20]

## MODERN POLICING FROM THE 1960S TO THE 1990S

The modern era of policing can be traced from the 1960s to the 1990s. Several major events occurred during this important period of police history.

### Policing in the 1960s

Turmoil and crisis were the hallmarks of policing during the 1960s. Throughout this decade, the U.S. Supreme Court handed down a number of decisions designed to control police operations and procedures. Police officers were now required to obey strict legal guidelines when questioning suspects, conducting searches, and wiretapping. As the civil rights of suspects were significantly expanded, police complained that they were being "handcuffed by the courts."

Also during this time, civil unrest produced a growing tension between police and the public. African Americans, who were battling for increased rights and freedoms in the civil rights movement, found themselves confronting police lines. When riots broke out in New York, Detroit, Los Angeles, and other cities between 1964 and 1968, the spark that ignited conflict often involved the police. When students across the nation began marching in anti–Vietnam War demonstrations, local police departments were called on to keep order. Police forces were ill equipped and poorly trained to deal with these social problems. Not surprisingly, the 1960s were marked by a number of bloody confrontations between the police and the public.

Compounding these problems was a rapidly growing crime rate. The number of violent and property crimes increased dramatically. Drug addiction and abuse, common in all social classes, grew to be national concerns. Urban police departments could not control the crime rate, and police officers resented the demands placed on them by dissatisfied citizens.

### Policing in the 1970s

The 1970s witnessed many structural changes in police agencies themselves. The end of the Vietnam War significantly reduced tensions between students and police. However, the relationship between police and minorities was still rocky. Local fears and distrust, combined with conservative federal policies, encouraged police departments to control what was perceived as an emerging minority group "threat."[21]

Increased federal government support for criminal justice greatly influenced police operations.[22] During the decade, the Law Enforcement Assistance Administration (LEAA) devoted a significant portion of its funds to police agencies.

Although a number of police departments used this money to purchase little-used hardware, such as anti-riot gear, most of it went to supporting innovative research on police work and advanced training of police officers. Perhaps most significant, LEAA's Law Enforcement Education Program helped thousands of officers further their college education. Hundreds of criminal justice programs were developed on college campuses around the country, providing a pool of highly educated police recruits. LEAA funds were also used to import into law enforcement technology originally developed in other fields. Technological innovations involving computers transformed the way police kept records, investigated crimes, and communicated with one another. State training academies improved the way police learned to deal with such issues as job stress, community conflict, and interpersonal relations.

The 1960s were a time of social ferment. Here Chicago policemen with nightsticks in hand confront a demonstrator on the ground in Grant Park, Chicago, on August 26, 1968. The police force converged at Grant Park when protesters opposing the Vietnam War climbed on the statue of Civil War general John Logan. Conflicts such as this between police and the public inspired the creation of university-based criminal justice programs.

More women and minorities were recruited into police work. Affirmative action programs gradually helped alter the ethnic, racial, and gender composition of U.S. policing.

## Policing in the 1980s

As the 1980s began, the police role seemed to be changing significantly. A number of experts acknowledged that the police were not simply crime fighters and called for police to develop a greater awareness of community issues, which resulted in the emergence of the community policing concept.[23]

Police unions, which began to grow in the late 1960s, continued to have a great impact on departmental administration in the 1980s. Unions fought for and won increased salaries and benefits for their members. In many instances, unions eroded the power of the police chief to make unquestioned policy and personnel decisions. During the decade, chiefs of police commonly consulted with union leaders before making major decisions about departmental operations.

Although police operations improved markedly during this time, police departments were also beset by problems that impeded their effectiveness. State and local budgets were cut back during the Reagan administration, and federal support for innovative police programs was severely curtailed with the demise of the LEAA.

Police–community relations continued to be a major problem. Riots and incidents of urban conflict occurred in some of the nation's largest cities.[24] They triggered continuing concern about what the police role should be, especially in inner-city neighborhoods.

## Policing in the 1990s

The 1990s began on a sour note and ended with an air of optimism. The incident that helped change the face of U.S. policing occurred on March 3, 1991, when two African American men, Rodney King and Bryant Allen, were driving in Los Angeles. They refused to stop when signaled by a police car, instead increasing their speed. King, who was driving, was apparently drunk or on drugs. When police finally stopped the car, they delivered 56 baton blows and 6 kicks to King in a period of two minutes, producing 11 skull fractures, brain damage, and kidney damage. They did not realize that their actions were being videotaped by an observer, who later gave the tape to the media. The officers involved were tried in a suburban court and acquitted by an all-white jury. The acquittal set off six days of rioting in South Central Los Angeles, and the California National Guard was called in to restore order. In total, 54 people were killed, 2,383 were known to have been injured, and 13,212 people were arrested.[25] The police officers involved in the beatings were later tried and convicted in federal court.

The King case prompted an era of reform. Several police experts decreed that the nation's police forces should be evaluated not on their crime-fighting ability but on their courteousness, behavior, and helpfulness. Interest renewed in reviving an earlier style of police work featuring foot patrols and increased citizen contact. Police departments began to embrace new forms of policing that stressed cooperation with the community and problem solving; this is referred to as the **community policing** model. Ironically, urban police departments began to shift their focus to working closely with community members at a time when technological improvements made it easier to fight crime from a distance.

An ongoing effort was made to bring diversity to police departments, and African Americans began to be hired as chiefs of police, particularly in Los Angeles. As a result of the reform efforts, the intellectual caliber of the police rose dramatically, and they became smarter, better informed, and more sophisticated than ever before. Management skills became more sophisticated, and senior police managers began to implement sophisticated information technology systems. As a result, policing became intellectually more demanding, requiring specialized knowledge about technology, forensic analysis, and crime. Although a few notorious cases of police corruption and violence made headlines, by and large the police began to treat the public more fairly and more equitably than ever before.[26]

**community policing**
A law enforcement program that seeks to integrate officers into the local community to reduce crime and achieve good community relations. It typically involves personalized service and decentralized policing, citizen empowerment, and an effort to reduce community fear of crime, disorder, and decay.

## POLICING AND LAW ENFORCEMENT TODAY

Policing and law enforcement today are organized into four broad categories: federal, state, county, and local policing agencies (and many subcategories within).

The federal government has a number of law enforcement agencies designed to protect the rights and privileges of U.S. citizens. No single agency has unlimited jurisdiction. Each has been created to enforce specific laws and cope with particular situations. Federal police agencies have no particular rank order or hierarchy of command or responsibility, and each reports to a specific department or bureau.

### The U.S. Justice Department

The U.S. Department of Justice is the legal arm of the federal government. Headed by the attorney general, it is empowered to enforce all federal laws, represent the United States when it is party to court action, and conduct independent investigations through its law enforcement services.

The Department of Justice maintains several separate divisions that are responsible for enforcing federal laws and protecting U.S. citizens. The Civil Rights Division proceeds legally against violations of federal civil rights laws that protect citizens from discrimination on the basis of their race, creed, ethnic background, age, or sex. Areas of greatest concern include discrimination in education, housing, and employment, including affirmative action cases. The Tax Division brings legal actions against tax violators. The Criminal Division prosecutes violations of the Federal Criminal Code. Its responsibility includes enforcing statutes related to bank robbery (because bank deposits are federally insured), kidnapping, mail fraud, interstate transportation of stolen vehicles, drug trafficking, and other offenses.

*THE FEDERAL BUREAU OF INVESTIGATION* The Justice Department first became involved in law enforcement when the attorney general hired investigators to enforce the Mann Act (forbidding the transportation of women between states for immoral purposes). These investigators were formalized in 1908 into a distinct branch of the government, the Bureau of Investigation. The agency was later reorganized into the **Federal Bureau of Investigation (FBI)**, which was under the direction of J. Edgar Hoover from 1924 until his death in 1972.

Today's FBI is not a police agency but an investigative agency with jurisdiction over all law enforcement matters in which the United States is or may be an interested party. However, its jurisdiction is limited to federal laws, including all federal statutes not specifically assigned to other agencies. Areas covered by these laws include espionage, sabotage, treason, civil rights violations, murder and assault of federal officers, mail fraud, robbery and burglary of federally insured banks, kidnapping, and interstate transportation of stolen vehicles and property. The FBI headquarters in Washington, D.C., oversees more than 50 field offices, approximately 400 satellite offices known as resident agencies, 4 specialized field installations, and more than 60 foreign liaison posts. The foreign liaison offices, each of which is headed by a legal attaché or legal liaison officer, work abroad with U.S. and local authorities on criminal matters within FBI jurisdiction. In all, the FBI has approximately 33,000 employees, including some 13,500 special agents and 20,000 support personnel, who perform professional, administrative, technical, clerical, craft, trade, or maintenance operations.[27]

The FBI offers a number of important services to local law enforcement agencies. Its identification division, established in 1924, collects and maintains a vast fingerprint file. Its sophisticated crime laboratory, established in 1932, aids local police in testing and identifying such evidence as hairs, fibers, blood, tire tracks, and drugs. The Uniform Crime Report (UCR) is another service of the FBI. The UCR is an annual compilation of crimes reported to local police agencies, arrests, police killed or wounded in action, and other information. Finally, the FBI's National Crime Information Center is a computerized network linked to local police departments that provides ready information on stolen vehicles, wanted persons, stolen guns, and so on.

The FBI mission has been evolving to keep pace with world events (see Exhibit 5.2). With the end of the cold war and the reduction of East–West tension, the FBI's mission to investigate European-based spy rings has diminished. In some offices, agents have been reassigned to antiterror, antigang, and drug control efforts.[28]

> **Federal Bureau of Investigation (FBI)**
> The arm of the Justice Department that investigates violations of federal law, gathers crime statistics, runs a comprehensive crime laboratory, and helps train local law enforcement officers.

*BUREAU OF ALCOHOL, TOBACCO, FIREARMS AND EXPLOSIVES (ATF)* Formerly known as the Bureau of Alcohol, Tobacco, and Firearms, ATF helps control sales of untaxed liquor and cigarettes and, through the Gun Control Act of 1968 and the Organized Crime Control Act of 1970, has jurisdiction over the illegal sale, importation, and criminal misuse of firearms and explosives. On January 24, 2003, ATF's law enforcement functions were transferred from the Treasury Department to the Department of Justice (DOJ), and ATF became the Bureau of Alcohol, Tobacco, Firearms and Explosives. ATF's strategic plan is currently being revised to reflect the agency's new name and mission and function within the DOJ.

*U.S. MARSHALS* The Marshals Service is the nation's oldest federal law enforcement agency. Among its duties are the following:[29]

- *Judicial security.* Protection of federal judicial officials, which includes judges, attorneys, and jurors. The Marshals Service also oversees every aspect of courthouse construction, from design through completion, to ensure the safety of federal judges, court personnel, and the public.

- *Fugitive investigations.* Working with law enforcement authorities at federal, state, local, and international levels, the Marshals Service apprehends thousands of dangerous felons each year. The Marshals Service is the primary agency responsible for tracking and extraditing fugitives who are apprehended in foreign countries and are wanted for prosecution in the United States.

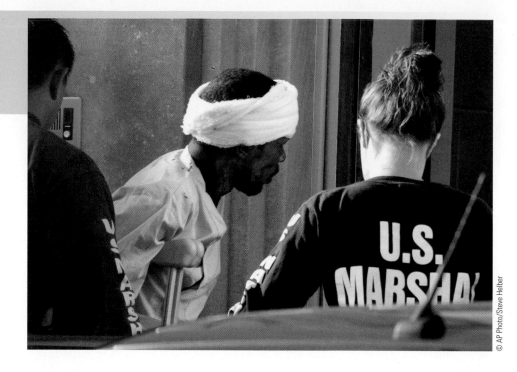

*An injured suspected pirate from Somalia is escorted into federal court by U.S. marshals in Norfolk, Virginia, on April 23, 2010. He is one of 11 suspects standing trial in connection with alleged attacks on U.S. naval vessels off the coast of Africa.*

© AP Photo/Steve Helber

■ *Witness security.* The Marshals Service Witness Security Program ensures the safety of witnesses who risk their lives testifying for the government in cases involving organized crime and other significant criminal activity. Since 1970, the Marshals Service has protected, relocated, and given new identities to more than 8,000 witnesses.

■ *Prisoner services.* The Marshals Service houses more than 55,000 federal unsentenced prisoners each day in federal, state, and local jails.

■ *Justice Prisoner and Alien Transportation System (JPATS).* In 1995, the air fleets of the Marshals Service and the Immigration and Naturalization Service merged to form a more efficient and effective system for transporting prisoners and criminal aliens.

■ *Asset Forfeiture Program.* The Marshals Service is responsible for managing and disposing of seized and forfeited properties acquired by criminals through illegal activities.

---

### EXHIBIT 5.2

## Reformulated FBI Priorities

1. Protect the United States from terrorist attack.

2. Protect the United States against foreign intelligence operations and espionage.

3. Protect the United States against cyber-based attacks and high-technology crimes.

4. Combat public corruption at all levels.

5. Protect civil rights.

6. Combat transnational and national criminal organizations and enterprises.

7. Combat major white-collar crime.

8. Combat significant violent crime.

9. Support federal, state, local, and international partners.

10. Upgrade technology to successfully perform the FBI's mission.

Source: FBI, www.fbi.gov/priorities/priorities.htm (accessed April 4, 2010).

# The Department of Homeland Security (DHS)

The Department of Homeland Security has a number of independent branches and bureaus.[30] Of them, three are well-known law enforcement agencies: Customs and Border Protection, Immigration and Customs Enforcement, and the U.S. Secret Service.

*CUSTOMS AND BORDER PROTECTION (CBP)*  This agency is responsible for preventing terrorists, human and drug smugglers, undocumented immigrants, and agricultural pests from entering the United States, while improving the flow of legitimate trade and travel.

Customs and Border Protection employs nearly 58,000 personnel, among them approximately 20,000 Border Patrol agents and CBP Air and Marine agents who patrol the country's borders and points of entry. CBP also partners with other countries through its Container Security Initiative and the Customs-Trade Partnership against Terrorism program. The goal of each is to help ensure that goods destined for the United States are screened before they are shipped. Finally, CBP facilitates trade by

- Protecting U.S. businesses from theft of intellectual property and unfair trade practices
- Collecting import duties, taxes, and fees
- Enforcing trade laws related to admissibility
- Regulating trade practices to collect the appropriate revenue
- Maintaining export controls
- Protecting U.S. agricultural resources via inspection activities at the ports of entry[31]

*IMMIGRATION AND CUSTOMS ENFORCEMENT (ICE)*  As the largest investigative arm of the Department of Homeland Security, ICE is responsible for identifying and addressing vulnerabilities in the nation's border and for enhancing economic, transportation, and infrastructure security. It has four main components.

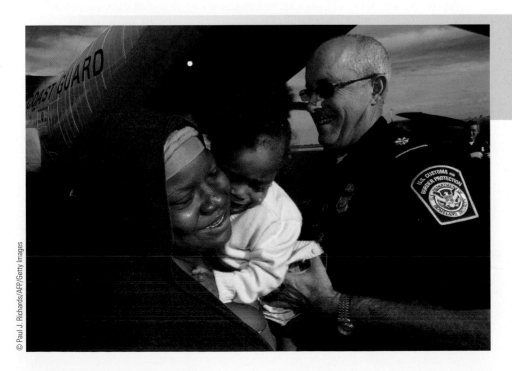

A U.S. Customs and Border Protection officer reunites a mother and child who were separated after being evacuated from Port-au-Prince, Haiti, after the January 12, 2010, magnitude 7.0 earthquake that killed an estimated 200,000 people.

- The *Office of Investigations* investigates a wide range of domestic and international activities arising from the movement of people and goods that violate immigration and customs laws and threaten national security.

- The *Office of Detention and Removal Operations* is responsible for public safety and national security by ensuring the departure from the United States of all removable aliens through the fair enforcement of the nation's immigration laws.

- The *Office of Intelligence* is responsible for the collection, analysis, and dissemination of strategic and tactical intelligence data for use by ICE and DHS.

- The *Office of International Affairs (OIA)* conducts and coordinates international investigations involving transnational criminal organizations responsible for the illegal movement of people, goods, and technology into and out of the United States.[32]

**THE SECRET SERVICE**   The U.S. Secret Service has two significant missions. The first is to protect the president and vice president, their families, heads of state, and other high-level officials. Part of this function involves investigating threats against protected officials and protecting the White House, the vice president's residence, and other buildings within Washington, D.C.

The second mission is to investigate counterfeiting and other financial crimes, including financial institution fraud, identity theft, computer fraud, and computer-based attacks on our nation's financial, banking, and telecommunications infrastructure. Criminal investigations cover a wide range of conduct:

> counterfeiting of U.S. currency (to include coins); counterfeiting of foreign currency (occurring domestically); identity crimes such as access device fraud, identity theft, false identification fraud, bank fraud and check fraud; telemarketing fraud; telecommunications fraud (cellular and hard wire); computer fraud; fraud targeting automated payment systems and teller machines; direct deposit fraud; investigations of forgery, uttering, alterations, false impersonations or false claims involving U.S. Treasury Checks, U.S. Saving Bonds, U.S. Treasury Notes, Bonds and Bills; electronic funds transfer (EFT) including Treasury disbursements and fraud within the Treasury payment systems; Federal Deposit Insurance Corporation investigations; Farm Credit Administration violations; and fictitious or fraudulent commercial instruments and foreign securities.[33]

## State Law Enforcement Agencies

Unlike municipal police departments, state police were legislatively created to deal with the growing incidence of crime in nonurban areas, a consequence of the increase in population mobility and the advent of personalized mass transportation in the form of the automobile. County sheriffs—elected officials with occasionally corrupt or questionable motives—had proved to be ineffective in dealing with the wide-ranging criminal activities that developed during the latter half of the nineteenth century. In addition, most local police agencies were unable to protect the public against highly mobile lawbreakers who randomly struck at cities and towns throughout a state. In response to citizens' demands for effective and efficient law enforcement, state governors began to develop plans for police agencies that would be responsible to the state, instead of being tied to local politics and possible corruption.

The Texas Rangers, created in 1835, was one of the first state police agencies formed. This agency still operates today (see Exhibit 5.3), but at the time it was mainly a military outfit that patrolled the Mexican border. It was followed by the Massachusetts State constables in 1865 and the Arizona Rangers in 1901. Pennsylvania formed the first truly modern state police in 1905.[34]

**EXHIBIT 5.3**

## Texas Rangers' Job Duties

According to the Texas Department of Justice, Texas Rangers' job duties are as follows:

■ The activities of the Texas Ranger Division consist primarily of making criminal and special investigations; apprehending wanted felons; suppressing major disturbances; the protection of life and property; and rendering assistance to local law enforcement officials in suppressing crime and violence;

■ The Texas Ranger Division will, through investigation and close personal contact with all federal, state, county, and city law enforcement agencies, be responsible for the gathering and dissemination of criminal intelligence pertaining to all facets of organized crime. The Texas Ranger Division joins with all other enforcement agencies in the suppression of the same;

■ Under orders of the Director, suppress all criminal activity in any given area, when it is apparent that the local officials are unwilling or unable to maintain law and order;

■ Upon the request or order of a judge of a court of record, serve as officers of the court and assist in the maintenance of decorum, the protection of life, and the preservation of property during any judicial proceeding;

■ When called upon, provide protection for elected officials at public functions and at any other time or place when directed to do so by a superior officer;

■ Establish direct personal contact and maintain close liaison with all agencies, or branches thereof, concerned with the investigation and suppression of criminal activities. These contacts are not to be limited to the state but shall be nationwide. Every effort will be exerted to maintain a full and free flow of information on active offenders and offenses between all interested agencies;

■ Participate in educational training programs and provide specialized instruction to local, state, and federal law enforcement representatives;

■ With the approval of the Director, conduct investigations of any alleged misconduct on the part of other Department personnel;

■ Be the primary Department investigator when a Department member is killed or suffers serious bodily injury, attributable to an intentional act;

■ Provide forensic hypnotists for use as an investigative tool in gathering additional information;

■ Provide forensic artwork for use as an investigative or procedural tool in major criminal cases;

■ Assist the Governor's Protective Detail in providing security for the Texas Governor during his official travel throughout the state, as well as other dignitaries.

Source: The Texas Ranger Job Duties, www.txdps.state.tx.us/director_staff/texas_rangers/jobduties.htm (accessed April 4, 2010).

Today, about 23 state police agencies have the same general police powers as municipal police and are territorially limited in their exercise of law enforcement regulations only by the state's boundaries. The remaining state police agencies are primarily responsible for highway patrol and traffic law enforcement. Some state police, such as those in California, direct most of their attention to the enforcement of traffic laws. Most state police organizations are restricted by legislation from becoming involved in the enforcement of certain areas of the law. For example, in some jurisdictions, state police are prohibited from becoming involved in strikes or other labor disputes, unless violence erupts.

The nation's 80,000 state police employees (55,000 officers and 25,000 civilians) are not only involved in law enforcement and highway safety but also carry out a variety of functions, which include maintaining a training academy and providing emergency medical services. State police crime laboratories aid local departments in investigating crime scenes and analyzing evidence. State police also provide special services and technical expertise in such areas as bomb site analysis and homicide investigation. Other state police departments, such as California's, are involved in highly sophisticated traffic and highway safety programs that include using helicopters for patrol and rescue, testing safety devices for cars, and conducting postmortem examinations to determine the causes of fatal accidents.

## County Law Enforcement Agencies

The county sheriff's role has evolved from that of the early English shire reeve, whose primary duty was to assist the royal judges in trying prisoners and enforcing sentences. From the time of the westward expansion in the United States until municipal departments were developed, the sheriff was often the sole legal authority over vast territories.

Today, more than 3,000 sheriff's offices operate nationwide, employing more than 330,000 full-time staff, including about 175,000 sworn personnel.[35] Nearly all sheriff's offices provide basic law enforcement services such as routine patrol (97%), responding to citizen calls for service (95%), and investigating crimes (92%).[36] Typically, a sheriff's department's law enforcement functions are restricted to unincorporated areas within a county, unless a city or town police department requests its help.

The duties of a county sheriff's department vary according to the size and degree of development of the county. The standard tasks of a typical sheriff's department are serving civil process (summons and court orders), providing court security, operating the county jail, and investigating crimes. Less commonly, sheriff's departments may serve as coroners, tax collectors, overseers of highways and bridges, custodians of the county treasury, and providers of fire, animal control, and emergency medical services. In years past, sheriff's offices also conducted executions.

Some sheriff's departments are exclusively oriented toward law enforcement; some carry out only court-related duties; some are involved solely in correctional and judicial matters and not in law enforcement. However, a majority are full-service programs that carry out judicial, correctional, and law enforcement activities. As a rule, agencies that serve large population areas (more than one million people) are devoted to maintaining county correctional facilities, whereas those in smaller population areas focus on law enforcement.

In the past, sheriffs' salaries were nearly always based on the fees they received for the performance of official acts. They received fees for every summons, warrant, subpoena, writ, or other process they served. They were also compensated for summoning juries or locking prisoners in cells. Today, sheriffs are salaried to avoid conflict of interest.

## Metropolitan Law Enforcement Agencies

Local police make up the majority of the nation's authorized law enforcement personnel. Metropolitan police departments range in size from the New York City Police Department, with almost 40,000 full-time officers and 10,000 civilian employees, to rural police departments, which may have only a single part-time officer. Today, local police departments have more than 450,000 sworn personnel.[37] In addition to sworn personnel, many police agencies hire civilian employees who bring special skills to the department. In this computer age, departments often employ information resource managers, who are charged with improving data processing, integrating the department's computer information database with others in the state, operating computer-based fingerprint identification systems and other high-tech investigative devices, and linking with national computer systems such as the FBI's national crime information system, which holds the records of millions of criminal offenders. To carry out these tasks, local departments employ an additional 130,000 civilians, bringing the entire number to more than 580,000 people.

Most individual metropolitan police departments perform a standard set of functions and tasks and provide similar services to the community. These include

- Traffic enforcement
- Narcotics and vice control
- Accident investigation
- Radio communications
- Patrol and peacekeeping

- Crime prevention
- Property and violent crime investigation
- Fingerprint processing
- Death investigation
- Search and rescue

The police role is expanding, so procedures must be developed to aid special-needs populations, including AIDS-infected suspects, the homeless, and victims of domestic and child abuse. For a summary of the key enforcement-related differences among federal, state, county, and metropolitan law enforcement agencies, see Concept Summary 5.1. Also see the accompanying Images of Justice feature for a discussion about how the media portray law enforcement agencies.

These are only a few examples of the multiplicity of roles and duties assumed today in some of the larger urban police agencies around the nation. Smaller agencies can have trouble carrying out these tasks effectively. The hundreds of small police agencies in each state often provide duplicate services. Police experts often debate whether unifying smaller police agencies into superagencies would improve services. Smaller municipal agencies can provide important specialized services that might have to be relinquished if they were combined and incorporated into larger departments. Another approach has been to maintain smaller departments but to link them via computerized information-sharing and resource-management networks.[38]

*POLICING IN SMALL CITIES*  Most TV police shows feature the work of big-city police officers, but an overwhelming number of departments have fewer than 50 officers and serve a population of less than 25,000. About 70 law enforcement agencies employ 1,000 or more full-time sworn personnel, including 48 local police departments with 1,000 or more officers. These agencies account for about one-third of all local police officers. In contrast, nearly 800 departments employ just one officer.[39]

## CONCEPT SUMMARY 5.1

### Differences among Federal, State, County, and Metropolitan Law Enforcement

| Agency | Jurisdiction | Crimes Most Often Targeted |
|---|---|---|
| Federal agencies (FBI, Secret Service) | Entire United States | Violations of federal law |
| State patrol | State | Traffic violations on highways |
| State police | State | Violations of state law |
| County sheriff | County, mostly unincorporated areas thereof | Violations of state laws and county ordinances |
| Metropolitan police | City limits | Violations of state laws and city ordinances |

## IMAGES OF JUSTICE

# 22 Seasons and Going Strong: Effects of COPS and Reality TV

*COPS*, the Fox television documentary that follows police officers around as they go about their jobs, recently entered its 22nd season. It is one of the longest-running television programs in America and is the second longest-running program on Fox. The show has followed officers in 140 cities throughout the United States and several foreign countries. *COPS* has been partly responsible for a series of related "reality-based" programs featuring not just police officers but also prosecutors, criminal investigators, bounty hunters, prison guards, crime scene investigators, and paramedics. Even parody programs such as *Reno 911* owe at least part of their success to *COPS*.

*COPS* and shows like it help make up the reality television genre. Unlike many reality programs that feature unscripted activities of everyone from musicians and dancers to survivalists and dating couples, *COPS* features police officers doing real work. But just how realistic is *COPS*? The consensus among researchers who have tried to answer this question is that there are few redeeming virtues (aside, perhaps, for television ratings) associated with programs such as *COPS*. As Ray Surette argued in his book *Media, Crime, and Criminal Justice*,

> . . . contrary to their image of reality, these programs are clearly structured along entertainment lines. They

commonly employ the oldest entertainment crime story structure known: *'crime→chase→capture.'* . . . They mix reconstructions, actors, and interviews and employ camera angles, music, lighting, and sets to enhance their dramatic and entertainment elements.

### Portrayal of Criminals

It is well known that criminals featured on the evening news tend to fit a certain demographic. Usually they are portrayed as poor minorities. They are also portrayed as unusually violent. In one study of *America's Most Wanted*, for example, researchers found that criminals were depicted as either violent or resistant in three out of four encounters, far in excess of what happens in the real world. There also appears to be an underrepresentation of white-collar crime in reality-based programming.

### Portrayal of the Police

Reality-based policing and crime programs also have a tendency to portray arrest rates that far exceed official arrest statistics. For example, Mary Beth Oliver found that "among crimes in the FBI Crime Index, reality-based police programs portrayed a significantly greater proportion of crimes as cleared ... than the proportion reported by the FBI." She also found that approximately half of all police officers on reality-based police programs used threats of verbal

---

While our attention is drawn to big-city police, it is important to think about policing in small towns. The officers who work in these locations rarely face the same problems as their big-city counterparts. Crime rates are lower, citizens know each other better, and the types of problems tend to differ from those of big cities. Researchers have found, in fact, that rural policing relies heavily on informal mechanisms, rather than arrest, for dealing with unwanted behaviors.[40] They have also found that officers engage citizens more informally and personably in such towns.[41] These findings are important because if the typical police officer works in a small town, then he affords some insight into what police work is really like. It is not necessarily about big busts, high-profile crimes, and rampant lawlessness.

## PERSPECTIVES ON JUSTICE

### Nonintervention

Small-town departments certainly take crime seriously, but some of them opt for an informal approach. Officers may refrain from making arrests if counseling an offender and talking to him or her would be more effective. This approach can help protect certain individuals from the harmful effects of a criminal stigma and help reinforce the bonds of community found in smaller cities.

aggression or actual physical aggression, whereas only about 20 percent of criminal suspects were found to be aggressive during the same encounters.

## Portrayal of Crime

Like the mainstream media, *COPS* and other reality-based policing and crime programs have a tendency to report only the most serious crimes. It is difficult to fault the programs or their parent networks for doing this, because viewers seem to want it. There is a certain appeal to witnessing a fleeing felon tackled in the middle of the street, compared with depiction of the same individual using the drug he or she has stolen.

## Fear of Crime

Oliver and Armstrong found that reality-based programming is linked to higher estimates of crime prevalence, particularly crimes committed by African Americans. In their words, "reality-based programs appear to embody many characteristics that point to the likelihood of several harmful influences: these shows portray a world that is much more crime infested than is actually the case, they cast people of color in the role of the villain, and they are perceived as realistic by many of their viewers."

## An Insatiable Thirst?

A recent *San Francisco Chronicle* article drew this conclusion after looking back on 20 years of *COPS*:

> *COPS* has succeeded spectacularly because it takes us on a titillating ride through trash-heap America.

In those blighted, benighted streets, the poor, emotionally maimed, drug-addicted and merely addled, are pulled over, spreadeagled, cuffed, bullied, then made to jump through the hoops of criminal-law enforcement for our viewing pleasure. . . . So culturally hungry have we become for the kick of televised police chases, dramatic arrests and victim-ventilating psychodrama, that even the miscreants themselves seem untroubled at signing the releases allowing their generally imbecilic actions and law-enforcement reactions to be broadcast on national television.

## Critical Thinking

1. Does reality television do justice to the men and women who make their living in the criminal justice system?

2. The police are already heavily scrutinized in the media, so does reality programming help or hurt?

Sources: Ray Surette, *Media, Crime, and Criminal Justice: Images, Realities, and Policies*, 3rd ed. (Belmont, Calif.: Wadsworth, 2007); Gray Cavender and Lisa Bond-Maupin, "Fear and Loathing on Reality Television: An Analysis of *America's Most Wanted* and *Unsolved Mysteries*," *Sociological Inquiry* 63 (1993): 305–317; Mary Beth Oliver and G. Blake Armstrong, "The Color of Crime: Perceptions of Caucasians' and African-Americans' Involvement in Crime," in *Entertaining Crime: Television Reality Programs*, ed. M. Fishman and G. Cavender (New York: Aldine De Gruyter, 1998), pp. 19–35; Mary Beth Oliver, "Portrayals of Crime, Race, and Aggression in 'Reality-Based' Police Shows: A Content Analysis," *Journal of Broadcasting and Electronic Media* 38 (1994): 179–192; John L. Worrall, "Constitutional Issues in Reality-Based Police Television Programming: Media Ride-Alongs," *American Journal of Criminal Justice* 25 (2001): 41–64; Richard Rapaport, "Dying and Living in 'COPS' America," *San Francisco Chronicle*, January 7, 2007.

## PRIVATE POLICING

Supplementing local police forces is a burgeoning private security industry. Private security service, or **private policing,** has become a multi-billion-dollar industry with 10,000 firms and more than 2 million employees.[42] Even some federal police services have been privatized to cut expenses.

Some private security firms have become billion-dollar companies. The Wackenhut Corporation is the U.S.-based division of Group 4 Securicor, the world's second-largest provider of security services. Among its clients are a number of Fortune 500 companies. It has several subsidiaries that work for the federal government. Wackenhut Services Incorporated (WSI) is a primary contractor to NASA and the U.S. Army. Wackenhut also provides security and emergency response services to local governments—helping them guard their public transport systems, among other services. Wackenhut helps

**private policing**
Crime prevention, detection, and the apprehension of criminals carried out by private organizations or individuals for commercial purposes.

# CAREERS IN CRIMINAL JUSTICE

## Security Professional

### Duties and Characteristics of the Job

There are two broad classes of security professionals: proprietary security personnel, who are directly employed by organizations that desire asset protection, and security services professionals, who provide security products and services for various organizations. The security services industry sells equipment (such as closed-circuit television and security systems), installs and maintains equipment, provides uniformed security guards, conducts investigations, performs risk assessments, protects high-value shipments, and so on.

The security professional who typically comes to mind is the retail security guard, or, more formally, a person employed in "retail loss prevention." To many people, the idea of working in retail security for a career is unappealing, because entry-level store security guards are not paid particularly well. What many people do not realize, however, is that a wide range of administrative, technical, supervisory, and managerial opportunities exist within the security field.

### Job Outlook

The security industry in the United States is extensive. By some estimates, it is a $100-billion-a-year business that continues to grow on an annual basis. According to ASIS International, the largest organization for security professionals, "Security is one of the fastest-growing professional careers worldwide." Opportunities exist at all levels within the security industry, and all businesses, no matter what their size, need qualified personnel to address their security concerns, prevent theft, deter workplace violence, and otherwise protect themselves to ensure normal business operations.

### Salary

Entry-level positions in retail loss prevention are among the lowest-paying security jobs, but the pay prospects improve as one ascends to a management position. Moving into other industries, such as banking and financial services, entry-level and

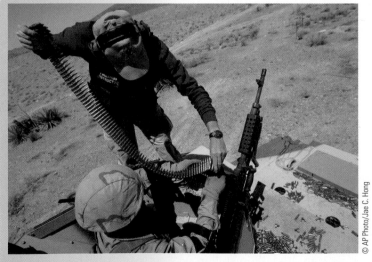

*Homeland insecurity. Firearms instructor Mark Herrin, top, helps private security officer Daril Rivera reload a machine gun during paramilitary training at a test site in Mercury, Nevada. Both are employed by Wackenhut, Inc., a private corporation that acts as a security contractor to the Department of Energy. Should private security officials be tasked with protecting America's sensitive nuclear sites?*

© AP Photo/Jae C. Hong

the U.S. government protect nuclear reactors, guards the Trans-Alaska Pipeline System, and maintains security in closed government facilities. It maintains a Custom Protection Officer Division, made up of highly trained uniformed security officers assigned to critical or complex facilities in such places as government buildings, banks, and other special situations. (The accompanying Careers in Criminal Justice feature discusses a career in the private security area.)

## Reasons for Private Policing

Why is private policing so popular? There are three answers to this question.

■ A preference for nongovernmental provision of important services, particularly crime control. Many people feel the private sector can do a more effective job than traditional government-led policing.

■ The growth of mass private property, particularly large shopping malls and other properties that attract large numbers of consumers and have little other police protection.

■ A belief that government police are not capable of providing the level of service and presence that the public desires.[43]

mid-level management positions command a salary ranging from $35,000 to $100,000, depending on several factors. Government/industry security professionals are also fairly well compensated. Entry-level management positions carry a salary range of $55,000 to $75,000 and beyond, depending on several factors.

## Opportunities

There are more opportunities for careers as a security professional than most people can fathom. Such careers are available in almost every area of human endeavor, including banking and financial services, commercial real estate, cultural properties (such as museums), educational institutions, gaming/wagering facilities, health care facilities, information systems, lodging and hospitality, manufacturing, transportation, utility and nuclear facilities, and agricultural operations.

## Qualifications

In most states, security professionals need to be licensed in order to work. This generally requires that applicants be 18 years of age or older, pass a background check, and complete relevant training.

Security professionals may also be expected to pass routine drug tests. Qualifications may be stricter, depending on the level of risk and responsibility associated with the position.

## Education and Training

For many security professions, a high school diploma is sufficient to secure an entry-level position. Some jobs require an associate or baccalaureate degree in criminal justice or a related discipline, sometimes combined with a certain amount of real-world experience. Some colleges and universities also offer dedicated security education degrees. ASIS offers three certifications for security professionals: Certified Protection Professional (CPP), the Professional Certified Investigator (PCI), and Physical Security Professional (PSP). These certifications require that certain knowledge and skills be demonstrated, but they also help differentiate applicants from one another, and they improve an applicant's professional credibility and earnings potential.

Source: ASIS International, *Career Opportunities in Security* (Alexandria, Va.: ASIS International, 2005), retrieved April 6, 2010, from www.asisonline.org/careercenter/careers2005.pdf.

## Criticisms of Private Policing

Private policing is controversial for a number of reasons. First, there is some concern that privatization puts the profit motive ahead of more lofty goals such as protection of public safety. Another concern is that private police could eventually replace government, or public, police. Fortunately, this looks unlikely. As one expert observed, "Private policing poses no risk of supplanting public law enforcement entirely, at least not in our lifetime, and it is far from clear to what extent the growing numbers of private security employees are actually performing functions previously carried out by public officers."[44]

There will also be more legal scrutiny as the private security business blossoms. A number of questions remain to be answered. One important issue is whether security guards are subject to the same search and seizure standards as police officers. The U.S. Supreme Court has repeatedly stated that purely private search activities do not violate the Fourth Amendment's prohibitions. Might security guards be subject to Fourth Amendment requirements if they are performing services that are traditionally reserved for the police, such as guarding communities?

## TECHNOLOGY AND LAW ENFORCEMENT

Budget realities demand that police leaders make the most effective use of their forces, and technology seems to be one method of increasing productivity at a relatively low cost. The introduction of technology has already been explosive. In 1964, only one city (St. Louis) had a police computer system; by 1968, 10 states

## CRIMINAL JUSTICE AND TECHNOLOGY

# Gunshot Locators

Faced with a surge in the number of shootings, Gary, Indiana, installed the ShotSpotter Gunshot Location System (GLS). The device uses a network of weatherproof acoustic sensors that locate and record gunshots. Most gunshots emit sound waves for a distance of up to two miles. The GLS sensors determine the direction from which the sound came. When several sensors are used in conjunction with one another, they can triangulate and determine the exact location where the gunshots were fired. Using this technology, the Gary Police Department seized 27 semiautomatic handguns in a single night. It happened over New Year's because the department knew, from previous experience, that many guns were fired into the air near midnight.

## Technology

ShotSpotter, the leading manufacturer of Gunshot Location Systems, bases its product on the same technology that geologists use to pinpoint an earthquake's epicenter. In fact, the original concept was conceived by a U.S. Geological Survey seismologist.

With at least three sensors, the system ties into a geographic information system (GIS) and maps the gunshot's location with a dot on a city map. Gunshots show up as red dots; different colors are used for other loud noises. The map then shows a dispatcher the gunshot's location, and this information is used to send the nearest officer to the scene.

An added feature of GLS technology is that it can be integrated with surveillance cameras so that both gunshots *and* shooters can be detected. ShotSpotter also markets the Rapid Deployment System, a portable version of its gunshot detector that can be used by SWAT teams and other first responders.

A few other companies have developed similar gunshot detection technologies. These include the SECURES Gunshot Detection and Localization System and the Safety Dynamics SENTRI. The Safety Dynamics product is especially adept at distinguishing gunshots from other noises in loud areas. Chicago used SENTRI in its "Operation Disruption," a crackdown on gun violence in a city that has a total ban on handguns.

---

and 50 cities had state-level criminal justice information systems. Today, almost every city of more than 50,000 people has some sort of computer-support services.[45] Local police departments, even in the smallest jurisdictions, now rely on computers in the field to link patrol officers with law enforcement databases, and this capability has grown considerably during the past decade.

Police officers now trained to prevent burglaries may someday have to learn to create high-tech forensic labs that can identify suspects involved in the theft of genetically engineered cultures from biomedical labs.[46] Criminal investigation will be enhanced by the application of sophisticated electronic gadgetry: computers, cell phones, and digital communication devices. Where else has technology affected law enforcement?

## Identifying Criminals

Police are becoming more sophisticated in their use of computer software to identify and convict criminals. One of the most important computer-aided tasks is the identification of criminal suspects. Computers now link neighboring agencies so they can share information on cases, suspects, and warrants. On a broader jurisdictional level, the FBI implemented the National Crime Information Center in 1967. This system provides rapid collection and retrieval of data about persons wanted for crimes anywhere in the 50 states.

Some police departments are using computerized imaging systems to replace mug books. Photos or sketches are stored in computer memory and are easily retrieved for viewing. Several software companies have developed identification programs that help witnesses create a composite picture of the perpetrator. A vast library of photographed or sketched facial features can be stored in computer files and accessed on a terminal screen. Witnesses can scan

CourseMate For more information about **police technology**, visit the Criminal Justice CourseMate at CengageBrain.com, then access the "Web Links" for this chapter.

CourseMate For more information about the **National Crime Information Center**, visit the Criminal Justice CourseMate at CengageBrain.com, then access the "Web Links" for this chapter.

## Advantages

The obvious advantage of gunshot location technology is rapid response by police. With real-time information on gunshot locations, police officers can be rapidly dispatched to the scene and given a realistic opportunity to apprehend the shooter. A related advantage is an improved ability to provide medical treatment for gunshot victims. In one unfortunate example, 35-year-old landscaper Jose Villatory was fatally shot as he was mowing a yard outside a Washington, D.C., apartment complex. Neighbors reported hearing the shot, but they did not call police because gunshots were so common in the area. Perhaps ShotSpotter or a similar device could have saved his life. Gunshot location systems have also given police a better chance of locating forensic evidence at crime scenes. This occurred in a Washington, D.C.–area sniper case, where a man was shooting people from a freeway overpass. He was turned in by someone, but a gunshot locator the FBI had installed helped agents locate spent shell casings.

## Limitations

While gunshot locators clearly help authorities identify the whereabouts of shooters, it is unclear whether the technology deters criminals. Gunshot locators have been credited for significant reductions in gunfire in several cities, but whether the devices themselves are responsible cannot be known for sure. Another concern is that despite built-in mechanisms to prevent false positives, the devices sometimes alert authorities to a gunshot when in fact none occurred. Finally, gunshot locators are prohibitively expensive for many cities. The cost to cover one square mile is approximately $150,000, followed by an additional $100,000 to $120,000 for every other square mile covered. If cameras are added to the technology, the cost can reach millions of dollars to cover a relatively small area within a single city.

## Critical Thinking

1. Can gunshot locators help the police catch criminals? Are they worth the cost?

2. Can gunshot locators deter criminals? If not, what needs to be done to deter gun crime?

Sources: Bill Siuru, "Gunshot Location Systems," *Law and Order* 55 (2007): 10, 12, 15–17; Lorraine G. Mazerolle, James Frank, Dennis Rogan, and Cory Watkins, *Field Evaluation of the ShotSpotter Gunshot Location System: Final Report on the Redwood City Trial* (Washington, D.C.: National Institute of Justice, 2000); Fernicia Patrik and Tod W. Burke, "Gunshot Sensor Technology: Can You Hear Me Now?" *Police and Security News* 23 (2007): 1–3.

---

thousands of noses, eyes, and lips until they find those that match the suspect's. Eyeglasses, mustaches, and beards can be added; skin tones can be altered. When the composite is created, an attached camera prints a hard copy for distribution.

In an effort to identify crime patterns and link them to suspects, some departments have begun to use computer software to analyze behavior patterns, a process called **data mining**.[47] By discovering patterns in crimes such as burglary, especially those involving multiple offenders, computer programs can be programmed to recognize a particular way of working a crime and thereby identify suspects most likely to fit the profile.

**data mining**
The use of sophisticated computer software to conduct analysis of behavior patterns in an effort to identify crime patterns and link them to suspects.

## Locating Criminals

Many technologies have also been developed for the purpose of locating criminals. Given that there are relatively few police compared to the number of citizens, officers cannot be everywhere at the same time. Nor can they readily identify or locate certain criminals who do not wish to be found. Several technological advances assist them in this regard.

The accompanying Criminal Justice and Technology feature describes the recent advent of gun detector technology. Cities can purchase devices that literally "listen" for gunfire so that officers can quickly be directed to the place where guns were recently fired. Companies have also developed gun detectors that officers can use to determine who is carrying an illegally concealed weapon. Millivision, one of the leaders in this area, has developed a portable gun detection device that officers can use from a distance. It does not reveal any anatomical information, only the outline of a gun.[48] Police departments even use closed-circuit television cameras to monitor certain urban areas from a distance.[49]

Another company has developed a device that can "listen" for a person hidden in the trunk of a vehicle. This is useful in the traffic stop context, when police officers are vulnerable to attack. The so-called Enclosed Space Detection System (ESDS) has been developed for police to ascertain whether one or more persons is hidden in a vehicle:

> The device works by detecting the motion of the vehicle caused by the shock wave produced by a beating heart. The shock wave couples to the surrounding vehicle, causing it to vibrate on its suspension. The motion sensors used with ESDS are the same type of sensors used to detect the low-frequency seismic movement of the earth. It is the highly specialized analysis software developed at Oak Ridge that enables the ESDS to detect the minute vibrations that are the telltale sign of an intruder hiding in a vehicle.[50]

More popular are so-called **thermal imagers**. These devices, which can be mounted on aircraft or handheld, use infrared technology to detect heat signals. Also known as "night vision," thermal imaging helps law enforcement officials detect everything from marijuana-growing operations to suspects hiding from officers in foot pursuits.

**CourseMate** For more information about **thermal imagers**, visit the Criminal Justice CourseMate at CengageBrain.com, then access the "Web Links" for this chapter.

**thermal imager**
A device that detects radiation in the infrared range of the electromagnetic spectrum and is used in law enforcement to detect variations in temperature (warm images stand out against cool backgrounds).

## Crime Scene Investigation

Using advanced technology to analyze crime scenes has caught the public interest now that *CSI*-type programs are routine TV fare. But in truth, CSI technology is now undergoing considerable change as cyber capabilities are being added to the investigator's bag of tricks.[51]

Traditionally, to investigate and evaluate a crime scene, detectives relied on photographic evidence and two-dimensional drawings. However, it can be difficult to visualize the positional relationships of evidence with two-dimensional tools. Now, through a combination of laser and computer technology, high-definition surveying (HDS) creates a virtual crime scene that enables investigators to maneuver every piece of evidence.

High-definition surveying gives law enforcement a complete picture of a crime scene. HDS reflects a laser light off objects in the crime scene and back to a digital sensor, creating three-dimensional spatial coordinates that are calculated and stored using algebraic equations. An HDS device projects light in the form of a laser in a 360-degree horizontal circumference, measuring millions of points and creating a "point cloud." The data points are bounced back to the receiver, collected, converted, and used to create a virtual image of any location. A personal computer can now take the data file and project that site onto any screen.

Not only does HDS technology allow the crime scene to be preserved exactly, but the perspective can also be manipulated to provide additional clues. For instance, if the crime scene is the front room of an apartment, the three-dimensional image allows the investigator to move around and examine different points of view. Or, if a victim was found seated, an investigator can see—and show a jury—what the victim might have seen just before the crime occurred. If witnesses outside said that they looked in a living room window, an investigator can zoom around and view what the witnesses could (or could not) have seen through that window.

HDS technology can also limit crime scene contamination. Investigators may inadvertently touch an object at a crime scene, leaving their fingerprints, or they may move evidence or take it from the scene, perhaps by picking up fibers on their shoes. Evidence is compromised if moved or disturbed from its resting place, which may contaminate the scene and undermine the case. HDS technology is a "stand-off" device, enabling investigators to approach the scene in stages by scanning from the outer perimeter and moving inward, reducing the chances of contamination. The investigative and prosecutorial value of virtual crime scenes is evident. If an HDS device is used at the scene, detectives, prosecutors, and juries can return to a crime scene in its preserved state. Showing a jury exactly what a witness could or could not have seen can be very valuable.

# Crime Mapping

It is now recognized that there are geographic "hot spots" where a majority of predatory crimes are concentrated.[52] Computer mapping programs that can translate addresses into map coordinates enable departments to identify problem areas for particular crimes, such as drug dealing. Computer maps allow police to identify the location, time of day, and linkage among criminal events and to concentrate their forces accordingly. Figure 5.1 illustrates a typical crime map that is now being used in Providence, Rhode Island.

Crime maps offer police administrators graphic representations of where crimes are occurring in their jurisdiction. Computerized crime mapping gives the police the power to analyze and correlate a wide array of data to create immediate, detailed visuals of crime patterns. The simplest maps display crime locations or concentrations and can be used to help direct patrols to the places they are most needed. More complex maps can be used to chart trends in criminal activity, and some have even proved valuable in solving individual criminal cases. For example, a serial rapist may be caught by observing and understanding the patterns of his crime so that detectives can predict where he will strike next and stake out the area with police decoys.

## FIGURE 5.1
### Violent Crime in Providence, Rhode Island

Note: Downtown is excluded from analysis due to small residential population.

Crime mapping makes use of new computer technology. Instead of antiquated pin maps, computerized crime mapping helps the police detect crime patterns and the pathologies of related problems. It enables them to work with multiple layers of information and scenarios, and thus to identify emerging hot spots of criminal activity far more successfully and target resources accordingly.

A number of the nation's largest departments are now using mapping techniques. The New York City Police Department's CompStat process relies on computerized crime mapping to identify crime hot spots.[53] The Chicago Police Department has developed the popular CLEARMAP Crime Incident web application. By visiting the department's web page, anyone can search a database of reported crime within the city and map incident locations.[54] The system received a prestigious Harvard Innovations in American Government award in 2007.

Some mapping efforts cross jurisdictional boundaries.[55] Examples of this approach have included the Regional Crime Analysis System in the greater Baltimore–Washington area and the multijurisdictional efforts of the Greater Atlanta PACT Data Center. The Charlotte–Mecklenburg Police Department (North Carolina) has used data collected by other city and county agencies in its crime-mapping efforts. By coordinating the departments of tax assessor, public works, planning, and sanitation, police department analysts have made links between disorder and crime that have been instrumental in supporting the department's community policing philosophy.

Crime maps alone may not be a panacea. Many officers are uncertain how to read such maps and assess their data. To maximize the potential of this new technique, police agencies need to invest in training and infrastructure before crime mapping can have an impact on their effectiveness.

*ALTERNATIVE MAPPING INITIATIVES* Mapping may soon serve other purposes than resource allocation. Law enforcement officials in the state of Washington have developed a new Internet-based mapping system that will provide critical information about public infrastructures to help them handle terrorist or emergency situations. The initiative, known as the Critical Incident Planning and Mapping System,[56] provides access to tactical response plans, satellite imagery, photos, floor plans, and the locations of hazardous chemicals.[57]

In West Virginia, local and state government entities are working with private firms to develop an emergency 911 system that can pinpoint the location of callers if they are unable to speak English, if they are unconscious, or even if they hang up. The West Virginia Statewide Addressing and Mapping Board is using geospatial information technology to produce maps that show a caller's exact location by a given number and street name. The project is designed to reduce emergency response times and improve disaster recovery planning, floodplain mapping, security, evacuation routing, counterterrorism efforts, crime analysis, and more.[58]

Mapping technology has recently been combined with GPS (global positioning system), a network of orbiting satellites that transmit signals to a portable device that tracks the precise whereabouts of a person or thing. Officers in one gruesome case found various parts of a man's badly decomposed body in Lake Powell, in Utah's Bryce Canyon National Park. They used a digital camera equipped with GPS technology to snap pictures of the exact locations where body parts and related evidence were found. The officers were then able to view all the photo locations on a map, which helped them determine that the body broke apart over time as the result of wave action, not because of foul play.[59] GPS technology is also used for a wide range of other applications, such as keeping track of the exact locations of officers' patrol cars.[60]

## Biometrics

**biometrics**
Automated methods of recognizing a person on the basis of a physiological or behavioral characteristic.

**Biometrics** is defined as automated methods of recognizing a person on the basis of a physiological or behavioral characteristic.[61] Some biometric measures, such as fingerprint identification, have been used for years by law enforcement to identify criminals. However, recent improvements in computer technology have expanded the different types of measures that can be used for identification. Biometrics is now used to identify individuals on the basis of voice, retina, facial features, and handwriting identification, just to name a few.

The field of biometrics can be used by all levels of government, including the military and law enforcement, and it is also helpful in private businesses. Financial institutions, retail shopping, and health and social fields can all use biometrics as a way to limit access to financial information or to secure Internet sites.

Unlike current personal identification methods, such as the personal identification numbers (PINs) used for bank machines and Internet transactions, biometric authenticators are unique to the user and thus cannot be stolen and used without that individual's knowledge.

The process of recording biometric data occurs in four steps. First, the raw biometric data is captured or recorded by a video camera or a fingerprint-reading device. Second, the distinguishing characteristics of the raw data are used to create a biometric template. Third, the template is changed into a mathematical representation of the biometric sample and stored in a database. Finally, a verification process will occur when an individual attempts to gain access to a restricted site. The individual will have to present his or her fingerprint or retina to be read and then matched to the biometric sample on record. Once verification is made, the individual is granted access to restricted areas. Currently, a number of programs are in effect. Immigration and Customs Enforcement has been using hand geometry systems at major U.S. airports to check frequent international travelers. Casinos around the country have started to implement facial recognition software into their buildings so that security is notified when a known cheater enters their premises.

> **CourseMate** For more information about **automated fingerprint systems**, visit the Criminal Justice CourseMate at CengageBrain.com, then access the "Web Links" for this chapter.

## Automated Fingerprint Identification Systems

The use of computerized automated fingerprint identification systems (AFIS) is growing in the United States. Using mathematical models, AFIS can classify fingerprints and identify up to 250 characteristics (minutiae) of the print. These automated systems use high-speed silicon chips to plot each point of minutiae and count the number of ridge lines between that point and its four nearest neighbors; this substantially improves their speed and accuracy over earlier systems.

Some police departments report that computerized fingerprint systems are enabling them to make over 100 identifications per month from fingerprints taken at crime scenes. AFIS files have been regionalized. The Western Identification Network (WIN), for example, consists of eight central site members (Alaska, Idaho, Montana, Nevada, Oregon, Utah, Wyoming, and the Portland Police Bureau), two interface members (California and Washington), multiple local members, and six federal members (the Drug Enforcement Administration, Federal Bureau of Investigation, Immigration and Naturalization Service, Internal Revenue Service, Postal Inspection Service, and Secret Service).[62] When it began, the system had a centralized automated database of 900,000 fingerprint records; today, with the addition of new jurisdictions (Alaska, California, and Washington), the system's number of searchable fingerprint records has increased to more than 14 million. Technology is constantly improving the effectiveness and reliability of the AFIS system, making it easier to use and more efficient in identifying suspects.[63]

## DNA Testing

**DNA profiling,** a procedure that gained national attention during the O. J. Simpson trial, makes it possible to identify suspects on the basis of the genetic material found in hair, blood, and other bodily tissues and fluids. When DNA is used as evidence in a rape trial, DNA segments are taken from the victim, from the suspect, and from blood and semen found on the victim. A DNA match indicates a four-billion-to-one likelihood that the suspect is the offender.

Every U.S. state and nearly every industrialized country now maintain DNA databases of convicted offenders.[64] These databases allow comparison of crime

**DNA profiling**
The identification of criminal suspects by matching DNA samples taken from their person with specimens found at the crime scene.

## ANALYZING CRIMINAL JUSTICE ISSUES

# Forensics under the Microscope

The *Chicago Tribune*'s recent "Forensics under the Microscope" series suggests that all is not well in the world of forensic sciences. Such concerns were echoed in a more recent National Academy of Sciences (NAS) report entitled *Strengthening Forensic Science in the United States: A Path Forward*. The authors of the report highlighted a series of problems with the forensic sciences, many of which are not well known to people on the outside—and particularly not to those who owe their knowledge of forensics and investigations to fictional television programs. Here are some of those problems:

■ **Case Backlog** The NAS called attention to another report in which it was learned that federal, state, and local laboratories reported a backlog of nearly 500,000 requests for forensic analysis. This backlog has been made even more serious by requests for quick test results. Labs are having trouble keeping up.

■ **DNA Demands** The ascendancy of DNA evidence and the opportunities to use it during investigations have further burdened crime labs. And even though the NAS, along with other experts and commissions, has heralded the advent of DNA testing as valuable tool for criminal investigation, there is only so much it can do. According to the NAS report, "DNA evidence comprises only about 10 percent of case work and is not always relevant to a particular case. Even if DNA evidence is available, it will assist in solving a crime only if it supports an evidential hypothesis that makes guilt or innocence more likely. For example, the fact that DNA evidence of a victim's husband is found in the house in which the couple lived and where the murder took place proves nothing. The fact that the husband's DNA is found under the fingernails of the victim who put up a struggle may have very different significance" (pp. 1-5 and 1-6).

■ **Questionable Evidence** The fact that DNA evidence is regarded as a gold standard in criminal investigations has begun to cast doubt on convictions secured through other, more traditional types of evidence. According to the report, "The fact is that many forensic tests—such as those used to infer the source of toolmarks or bite marks—have never been exposed to stringent scientific scrutiny. . . . Even fingerprint analysis has been called into question" (p. 1-6).

---

**CourseMate** For more information about the U.S. government's **DNA initiative**, visit the Criminal Justice CourseMate at CengageBrain.com, then access the "Web Links" for this chapter.

scene DNA to samples taken at other crime scenes and from known offenders. The United States has more than 3 million samples of offenders/arrestees in its state and federal DNA databases. The United States is not alone in gathering this material. Great Britain requires that almost any violation of law result in the collection of DNA samples from the violator.[65]

Two methods of DNA matching are used. The most popular technique, known as *RFLP* (restriction fragment length polymorphism), uses radioactive material to produce a DNA image on an x-ray film. The second method, *PCR* (polymerase chain reaction), amplifies DNA samples through molecular photocopying.[66]

DNA evidence is now used in criminal trials in more than 20 states.[67] Its use has also been upheld on appeal.[68] The use of DNA evidence in criminal trials received a boost in 1997, when the FBI announced that the evidence has become so precise that experts no longer have to supply a statistical estimate of accuracy while testifying at trial ("The odds are a billion to one that this is the culprit"); they can now state in court that there exists "a reasonable degree of scientific certainty" that the evidence came from a single suspect.[69]

Leading the way in the development of the most advanced forensic techniques is the Forensic Science Research and Training Center operated by the FBI in Washington, D.C., and Quantico, Virginia. The lab provides information and services to hundreds of crime labs throughout the United States. The National Institute of Justice is also sponsoring research to identify a wider variety of DNA segments for testing and is involved in developing a PCR-based

■ **Errors** The NAS also called attention to several disturbing examples of errors and fraud in the forensic sciences. In one case, a state-mandated examination of the West Virginia State Police laboratory revealed that the convictions of more than 100 people were in doubt. Another scandal involving the Houston Crime Laboratory came to light in 2003. An investigation revealed "routine failure to run essential scientific controls, failure to take adequate measures to prevent contamination of samples, failure to adequately document work performed and results obtained, and routine failure to follow correct procedures for computing statistical frequencies" (p. 1-8).

■ **Incompatible Fingerprint Identification Systems** Law enforcement agencies around the country have developed and put in place automated fingerprint identification systems in an effort to solve crimes. The problem, according to the NAS, is inadequate integration of these systems.

■ **Lack of Preparation for Mass Disasters** According to the NAS, "Threats to food and transportation, concerns about nuclear and cyber security, and the need to develop rapid responses to chemical, nuclear, radiological, and biological threats underlie the need to ensure that there is a sufficient supply of adequately trained forensic specialists . . . [but]

public crime laboratories are insufficiently prepared to handle mass disasters" (p. 1-13).

■ **The *CSI* Effect** The so-called *CSI* effect, named for the popular television program, is concerned with the real-world implications of Hollywood's fictional spin on the forensic sciences and criminal investigations. The NAS found that some prosecutors believe they must make their in-court presentations as visually appealing as possible in an effort to please jurors who think they understand forensic work from having watched their favorite television programs. Attempts to satisfy such unrealistic expectations may compromise the pursuit of justice.

### Critical Thinking

1. To what extent has the recent attention paid to wrongful convictions fueled calls for improvement, such as those in the NAS report?

2. What improvements *have* been made in recent years?

Sources: *Chicago Tribune*, "Forensics under the microscope," www.chicagotribune.com/news/watchdog/chi-forensics-specialpackage, 0,7787855.special (accessed April 6, 2010); National Academy of Sciences, National Research Council, *Strengthening Forensic Science in the United States: A Path Forward* (Washington, D.C.: The National Academies Press), www.nap.edu/catalog.php?record_id=12589 (accessed April 6, 2010).

DNA-profiling examination using fluorescent detection that will reduce the time required for DNA profiling.

The FBI is now operating the Combined DNA Index System (CODIS), which has assisted in nearly 50,000 investigations. CODIS is a computerized database that allows DNA obtained at a crime scene to be searched electronically to find matches among samples taken from convicted offenders and from other crime scenes. Early on, the system linked evidence taken from crime scenes in Jacksonville, Florida, to evidence obtained in Washington, D.C., thereby tying nine crimes to a single offender.[70] When Timothy Spence was executed in Virginia on April 27, 1994, he was the first person convicted and executed almost entirely on the basis of DNA evidence.[71] More recently, CODIS has been expanded to include a wealth of information, including profiles of individuals convicted of crimes—and even of arrestees, if state law permits.[72] Critics of this information-gathering cite concerns that some arrestees are innocent and that data retained from innocent persons could be improperly used in violation of privacy and civil liberties.[73]

DNA evidence—and the forensic sciences in general—are not without some problems. A recent study reported that although there is widespread knowledge about the utility of forensic evidence, it is not being adequately used by law enforcement agencies.[74] The authors found a significant number of unsolved homicides and rapes wherein forensic evidence had not been submitted to laboratories for analysis. In a related vein, see the nearby Analyzing Criminal Justice Issues feature for some discussion of an important report recently released by the National Academy of Sciences.

**CourseMate** For more information about **the science of DNA testing**, visit the Criminal Justice CourseMate at CengageBrain.com, then access the "Web Links" for this chapter.

## Communications

Computer technology is now commonplace in policing. Officers routinely and effectively use mobile computer systems and other information technology (IT) devices to gather information from, and transmit information about criminal incidents to, local, state, and national criminal information systems.[75]

Many larger departments have equipped officers with portable computers, which significantly reduce the time needed to write and duplicate reports. Police can now use terminals to draw accident diagrams, communicate with city traffic engineers, and merge their incident reports into other databases. Agencies are increasingly availing themselves of wireless technologies to perform their jobs with greater flexibility and productivity.[76]

Historically, police departments developed their own systems of codes for communicating information between dispatch and officers on the streets. Nowadays, in response to presidential and Homeland Security directives, departments are starting to change this protocol in favor of "plain language" dispatch and radio communication systems. The purpose is to facilitate communication with outside agencies and avoid becoming bogged down in codes and vernacular unique to a specific police department.

**CourseMate** For more information about **the latest (and future) police technologies**, visit the Criminal Justice CourseMate at CengageBrain.com, then access the "Web Links" for this chapter.

## Ethical Challenges in Criminal Justice: A Writing Assignment

The FBI's Combined DNA Index System (CODIS) helps law enforcement develop investigative leads in cases where biological evidence is secured from a crime scene. Biological samples are matched against DNA profiles of people in the database, including convicted criminals and arrestees. State and local law enforcement officials have access to the system and may be able to link several similar crimes to a single perpetrator.

Write an essay on the ethics of using this system. In doing so, answer these questions: Should every arrestee have a DNA sample taken? Does CODIS amount to an undesirable invasion of individual privacy, or does it represent a positive advance in police investigations that generates benefits for society? What other technological advances in law enforcement raise ethical questions? Why do they raise ethical questions? Refer to this chapter's "Technology and Law Enforcement" section for some guidance.

## SUMMARY

**1. Recount the early development of the police in England.**

■ Early in English history, law enforcement was a personal matter.

■ Under the pledge system, people were grouped into tythings and hundreds. The leader of a tything was called the tythingman. The leader of a hundred was called the hundredman and later came to be called the constable. This rudimentary beginning was the seed of today's police departments.

■ Shires, which resembled today's counties, were controlled by the shire reeve, the forerunner of the sheriff.

■ Under the thirteenth-century watch system, watchmen patrolled at night and helped protect communities from robberies, fires, and disturbances.

■ Early in the eighteenth century, paid private police called thief takers patrolled the streets.

■ The Metropolitan Police Act established the first organized police force in London.

**2. Recount the development of the police in colonial America.**

■ Law enforcement in colonial America resembled the British model.

■ The county sheriff became the most important law enforcement official.

■ Urban police departments were born out of urban mob violence.

■ Boston created America's first urban police department in 1838.

## 3. Discuss twentieth-century police reforms and the emergence of professionalism.

■ In the early years of the twentieth century, various reforms were undertaken with the intent of limiting local officials' control over the police.

■ The Boston police strike of 1919 fueled interest in police reform.

■ Nationally recognized leaders called for professionalization of the police. The International Association of Chiefs of Police, a key professional society, was formed.

## 4. Identify the main events in policing between 1960 and the present.

■ Police professionalism was interpreted to mean tough, rule-oriented police work featuring advanced technology and hardware. However, the view that these measures would quickly reduce crime proved incorrect.

■ During the 1970s, federal support for local law enforcement benefited police departments considerably. Criminal justice programs began to be formed in colleges and universities throughout the United States.

■ Between 1960 and the 1990s, police were beset by many problems, including questions about their treatment of minorities and why they were not more effective. This paved the way for a radical change in policing and the development of community policing.

## 5. Identify the various levels of law enforcement.

■ There are four main levels of law enforcement in the United States: federal, state, county, and local.

■ Most law enforcement is performed at the local level.

■ The typical local police department employs fewer than 50 officers.

## 6. Identify the most prominent federal law enforcement agencies.

■ The most prominent federal law enforcement agencies within the Justice Department are the Federal Bureau of Investigation (FBI), the Bureau of Alcohol, Tobacco, Firearms and Explosives (ATF), and the U.S. Marshals Service.

■ The most prominent federal law enforcement agencies within the Department of Homeland Security are Customs and Border Protection (CBP), Immigration and Customs Enforcement (ICE), and the Secret Service.

## 7. Discuss the differences among local, county, state, and federal law enforcement agencies.

■ Federal law enforcement agencies primarily enforce federal law.

■ State law enforcement agencies come in two main varieties. State police generally enforce state law and have broad police power. State patrols and highway patrols focus mainly on traffic enforcement on state highways and interstates.

■ County law enforcement officials enforce state laws and county ordinances. Most of their enforcement work occurs in unincorporated areas. Some sheriff's departments are oriented mainly toward law enforcement. Some also take on correctional responsibilities, such as running county jails.

■ City and metropolitan police are the most common law enforcement officials. They have broad authority to enforce state and local laws.

## 8. Be familiar with private policing, including the reasons for it and the controversies associated with it.

■ Private police outnumber public police (those employed by the federal, state, or local government) by roughly three to one.

■ Private police have emerged in response to (a) the desire for nongovernment provision of police services, (b) growth in mass private property, such as shopping malls, and (c) a belief that the private sector can do a better job than the public sector (government) in preventing and controlling crime.

■ Private policing is controversial because of concerns that (a) the profit motive will take precedence over crime control, (b) private police may replace public police, and (c) there are few constitutional constraints on private police.

## 9. Identify various technologies currently used in law enforcement.

■ Today, most police departments rely on advanced computer-based technology to identify suspects and collate evidence.

■ Various technologies, such as gun detectors, have been developed to aid the police in locating the whereabouts of criminals.

■ Many law enforcement agencies use mapping software to identify geographic "hot spots" of crime and to track their progress in crime control and prevention.

■ Automated fingerprint systems and computerized identification systems have become widespread. Some believe that technology may make police overly intrusive and interfere with civil liberties.

■ DNA testing, combined with DNA databases, helps law enforcement officials identify criminals.

■ Communications technologies continue to advance. Computers and wireless technology are used by the vast majority of police departments.

## KEY TERMS

tything (tithing), 170
hue and cry, 170
hundred, 170
constable, 170
shire reeve, 170
watch system, 170
justice of the peace, 171

Metropolitan Police Act, 171
sheriff, 173
vigilantes, 173
Wickersham Commission, 175
community policing, 178
Federal Bureau of Investigation
 (FBI), 179

private policing, 187
data mining, 191
thermal imager, 192
biometrics, 194
DNA profiling, 195

## CRITICAL THINKING QUESTIONS

1. List the problems faced by today's police departments that were also present during the early days of policing.

2. There is concern that history may be repeating itself in policing, as reliance on civilian volunteers and privatization increases. Is this cause for concern?

3. Distinguish among the duties of the state police, sheriff's departments, and local police departments.

4. What is the Department of Homeland Security? What are its component law enforcement agencies?

5. Private police outnumber public (government) police by about 3 to 1. Is this beneficial or harmful?

6. What are some of the technological advances that should help the police solve more crimes? What are the hazards of embracing these advances?

## NOTES

1. Steven Camorota, *Immigrants in the United States, 2007: A Profile of America's Foreign Born Population* (Washington, D.C.: Center for Immigration Studies, 2007).
2. Ibid.
3. Sue Major Holmes, "NM Governor Orders National Guard to Border," *Associated Press*, March 31, 2010, http://tinyurl.com/yd3ca4c (accessed April 4, 2010).
4. Minuteman Project, www.minutemanproject.com (accessed April 6, 2010).
5. Texas Border Watch Test Site, www.texasborderwatch.com (accessed April 4, 2010).
6. Ibid.
7. Elizabeth Joh, "The Paradox of Private Policing," *Journal of Criminal Law and Criminology* 95 (2004): 49–131.
8. This section relies heavily on such sources as Malcolm Sparrow, Mark Moore, and David Kennedy, *Beyond 911: A New Era for Policing* (New York: Basic Books, 1990); Daniel Devlin, *Police Procedure, Administration, and Organization* (London: Butterworth, 1966); Robert Fogelson, *Big-City Police* (Cambridge, Mass.: Harvard University Press, 1977); Roger Lane, *Policing the City, Boston 1822–1885* (Cambridge, Mass.: Harvard University Press, 1967); J. J. Tobias, *Crime and Industrial Society in the Nineteenth Century* (New York: Schocken, 1967); Samuel Walker, *A Critical History of Police Reform: The Emergence of Professionalism* (Lexington, Mass.: Lexington Books, 1977); Samuel Walker, *Popular Justice* (New York: Oxford University Press, 1980); John McMullan, "The New Improved Monied Police: Reform Crime Control and Commodification of Policing in London," *British Journal of Criminology* 36 (1996): 85–108.
9. Devlin, *Police Procedure, Administration, and Organization*, p. 3.
10. McMullan, "The New Improved Monied Police," p. 92; Joh, "The Paradox of Private Policing."

11. Edward J. Blekely and Mary G. Snyder, *Fortress America: Gated Communities in the United States* (Washington, D.C.: Brookings Institution Press, 1997).
12. Not everyone agrees there are only nine principles. There are also several variations on the nine principles. Those we have reprinted appear in several sources, but see Susan A. Lentz and Robert H. Chaires, "The Invention of Peels' Principles: A Study of Policing 'Textbook' History," *Journal of Criminal Justice* 35 (2007): 69–79.
13. Wilbur Miller, "The Good, the Bad, and the Ugly: Policing America," *History Today* 50 (2000): 29–32.
14. Phillip Reichel, "Southern Slave Patrols as a Transitional Type," *American Journal of Police* 7 (1988): 51–78.
15. Walker, *Popular Justice*, p. 61.
16. Ibid., p. 8.
17. Dennis Rousey, "Cops and Guns: Police Use of Deadly Force in Nineteenth-Century New Orleans," *American Journal of Legal History* 28 (1984): 41–66.
18. Law Enforcement Assistance Administration, *Two Hundred Years of American Criminal Justice* (Washington, D.C.: Government Printing Office, 1976).
19. National Commission on Law Observance and Enforcement, *Report on the Police* (Washington, D.C.: Government Printing Office, 1931), pp. 5–7.
20. Orlando W. Wilson, *Police Administration*, 4th ed. (New York: McGraw-Hill, 1977).
21. Pamela Irving Jackson, *Minority Group Threat, Crime, and Policing* (New York: Praeger, 1989).
22. For an overview of early federal support for local law enforcement, see John L. Worrall, "The Effects of Local Law Enforcement Block Grants on Serious Crime," *Criminology and Public Policy* 7 (2008): 325–350.
23. James Q. Wilson and George Kelling, "Broken Windows," *Atlantic Monthly* (March 1982): pp. 29–38.

24. Frank Tippett, "It Looks Just Like a War Zone," *Time* (May 27, 1985): 16–22; "San Francisco, New York Police Troubled by Series of Scandals," *Criminal Justice Newsletter* 16 (1985): 2–4; Karen Polk, "New York Police: Caught in the Middle and Losing Faith," *Boston Globe*, December 28, 1988, p. 3.

25. *Los Angeles Times, Understanding the Riots: Los Angeles before and after the Rodney King Case* (Los Angeles: *Times*, 1992).

26. David H. Bayley, "Policing in America," *Society* 36 (December 1998): 16–20.

27. Federal Bureau of Investigation, www.fbi.gov/quickfacts.htm (accessed April 6, 2010).

28. Kathleen Grubb, "Cold War to Gang War," *Boston Globe*, January 22, 1992, p. 1.

29. United States Marshals, www.usmarshals.gov/duties/factsheets/general-1209.pdf (accessed April 6, 2010).

30. Department of Homeland Security, www.dhs.gov/xabout/structure (accessed April 6, 2010).

31. Customs and Border Protection, www.cbp.gov/xp/cgov/about/mission/cbp_is.xml (accessed April 6, 2010).

32. Immigration and Customs Enforcement, www.ice.gov/about/index.htm (accessed April 6, 2010).

33. U.S. Secret Service, www.secretservice.gov/criminal.shtml (accessed April 6, 2010).

34. Bruce Smith, *Police Systems in the United States* (New York: Harper and Row, 1960).

35. Brian Reaves, *Census of State and Local Law Enforcement Agencies, 2004* (Washington, D.C.: Bureau of Justice Statistics, 2007).

36. Matthew Hickman and Brian Reaves, *Local Police Departments 2003* (Washington, D.C.: Bureau of Justice Statistics, 2006).

37. Reaves, *Local Police Departments, 2004*.

38. See, for example, Robert Keppel and Joseph Weis, *Improving the Investigation of Violent Crime: The Homicide Investigation and Tracking System* (Washington, D.C.: National Institute of Justice, 1993).

39. Reaves, *Local Police Departments, 2004*.

40. Brian K. Payne, Bruce L. Berg, and Ivan Y. Sun, "Policing in Small Town America: Dogs, Drunks, Disorder, and Dysfunction," *Journal of Criminal Justice* 33 (2005): 31–41.

41. John Liederbach and James Frank, "Policing the Big Beat: An Observational Study of County Level Patrol and Comparisons to Local Small Town and Rural Officers," *Journal of Crime and Justice* 29 (2006): 21–44.

42. William C. Cunningham and John J. Strauchs, "Security Industry Trends: 1993 and Beyond," *Security Management* 36 (1992): 27–30, 32, 34–36.

43. David A. Sklansky, "The Private Police," *UCLA Law Review* 46 (1999): 1165–1287.

44. Ibid., p. 1168.

45. Lois Pliant, "Information Management," *Police Chief* 61 (1994): 31–35.

46. Larry Coutorie, "The Future of High-Technology Crime: A Parallel Delphi Study," *Journal of Criminal Justice* 23 (1995): 13–27.

47. Rebecca Kanable, "Dig into Data Mining," *Law Enforcement Technology* 34 (2007): 62, 64–68, 70.

48. Millivision, www.millivision.com/technology.html (accessed April 6, 2010).

49. Rebecca Kanable, "Setting up Surveillance Downtown," *Law Enforcement Technology* (February 2008), www.officer.com/print/Law-Enforcement-Technology/Setting-up-surveillance-downtown/1$40869 (accessed April 6, 2010).

50. Oak Ridge National Laboratory, www.ornl.gov/sci/engineering_science_technology/sms/Hardy%20Fact%20Sheets/National%20Security%20-%20Human%20Presence.pdf (accessed April 6, 2010).

51. Raymond E. Foster, "Crime Scene Investigation," *Government Technology* (March 2005), www.govtech.com/gt/articles/93225 (accessed April 6, 2010).

52. This section is based on Derek Paulsen, "To Map or Not to Map: Assessing the Impact of Crime Maps on Police Officer Perceptions of Crime," *International Journal of Police Science & Management* 6 (2004): 234–246; William W. Bratton and Peter Knobler, *Turnaround: How America's Top Cop Reversed the Crime Epidemic* (New York: Random House, 1998), p. 289; Jeremy Travis, "Computerized Crime Mapping," *NIJ News*, January 1999.

53. James J. Willis, Stephen D. Mastrofski, and David Weisburd, "Making Sense of COMPSTAT: A Theory-Based Analysis of Organizational Change in Three Police Departments," *Law and Society Review* 41 (2007): 147–188.

54. Chicago Police Department, http://gis.chicagopolice.org/ (accessed April 6, 2010).

55. Nancy G. La Vigne and Julie Wartell, *Mapping across Boundaries: Regional Crime Analysis* (Washington, D.C.: Police Executive Research Forum, 2001).

56. Washington Association of Sheriffs and Police Chiefs, www.waspc.org/index.php?c=Critical%20Incident%20Planning%20and%20Mapping%20System (accessed April 6, 2010).

57. Dibya Sarker, "Washington State Develops Mapping System," *Federal Computer Week*, www.preparedresponse.com/media/news/news17.html (accessed April 6, 2010).

58. West Virginia Statewide Addressing and Mapping Board, www.addressingwv.org/flash.asp (accessed April 6, 2010).

59. Kevin Corbley, "GPS Photo Mapping in Law Enforcement," *Law Enforcement Technology* 35 (2008): 96, 98–101.

60. Geoffrey Gluckman, "Eye in the Sky: GPS Has Changed the Way Law Enforcement Does Fleet Management," *Law Enforcement Technology* 33 (2006): 68, 70–75.

61. "Introduction to Biometrics," www.biometrics.org (accessed April 6, 2010); Fernando L. Podio, "Biometrics—Technologies for Highly Secure Personal Authentication," *ITL Bulletin* (National Institute of Standards and Technology).

62. Western Identification Network, www.winid.org/winid/default.asp (accessed April 6, 2010).

63. Weipeng Zhang, Yan Yuan Tang, and Xinge You, "Fingerprint Enhancement Using Wavelet Transform Combined with Gabor Filter," *International Journal of Pattern Recognition & Artificial Intelligence* 18 (2004): 1391–1406.

64. Frederick Bieber, Charles Brenner, and David Lazer, "Finding Criminals through DNA of Their Relatives," *Science* 312 (2006): 1315–1316.

65. Ibid.

66. Ronald Reinstein, *Postconviction DNA Testing: Recommendations for Handling Requests* (Philadelphia: Diane, 1999).

67. "California Attorney General Endorses DNA Fingerprinting," *Criminal Justice Newsletter* 1 (1989): 1.

68. *State v. Ford*, 301 S.C. 485 (1990).

69. "Under New Policy, FBI Examiners Testify to Absolute DNA Matches," *Criminal Justice Newsletter* 28 (1997): 1–2.

70. "FBI's DNA Profile Clearinghouse Announces First 'Cold Hit,'" *Criminal Justice Newsletter* 16 (1999): 5.

71. "South Side Strangler's Execution Cited as DNA Evidence Landmark," *Criminal Justice Newsletter* 2 (1994): 3.

72. Federal Bureau of Investigation, "CODIS: Combined DNA Index System," www.fbi.gov/hq/lab/pdf/codisbrochure2.pdf (accessed April 6, 2010).

73. Karen Norrgard, "Forensics, DNA Fingerprinting, and CODIS," *Nature Education* 1(2008):1. Available at: www.nature.com/scitable/topicpage/Forensics-DNA-Fingerprinting-and-CODIS-736 (accessed April 6, 2010).

74. Kevin J. Strom and Matthew J. Hickman, "Unanalyzed Evidence in Law-Enforcement Agencies: A National Examination of Forensic Processing in Police Departments," *Criminology and Public Policy* 9(2010): 381–404.

75. Ralph Ioimo and Jay Aronson, "Police Field Mobile Computing: Applying the Theory of Task–Technology Fit," *Police Quarterly* 7 (2004): 403–428; "Facial AFIS Launched by Identix," *Biometric Technology Today* 11 (2003): 4.

76. Ed Lee, "Best Practices in Mobile Data Communications," *Law Enforcement Technology* 35 (2008): 40, 42–45.

# CHAPTER 6

# The Police: Organization, Role, and Function

## CHAPTER OBJECTIVES

1. Understand the organization of police departments.
2. Recognize the problems associated with the time-in-rank system.
3. Distinguish between the patrol function and the investigation function.
4. Describe the purposes of patrol.
5. Discuss various efforts to improve patrol.
6. Discuss key issues associated with the investigative function.
7. Understand the concept of community policing.
8. List several challenges associated with community policing.
9. Discuss the concept of problem-oriented policing.
10. Define intelligence-led policing and explain ways in which it occurs.
11. Explain the various police support functions.
12. Identify some of the cost-saving measures that may be employed to improve police productivity.

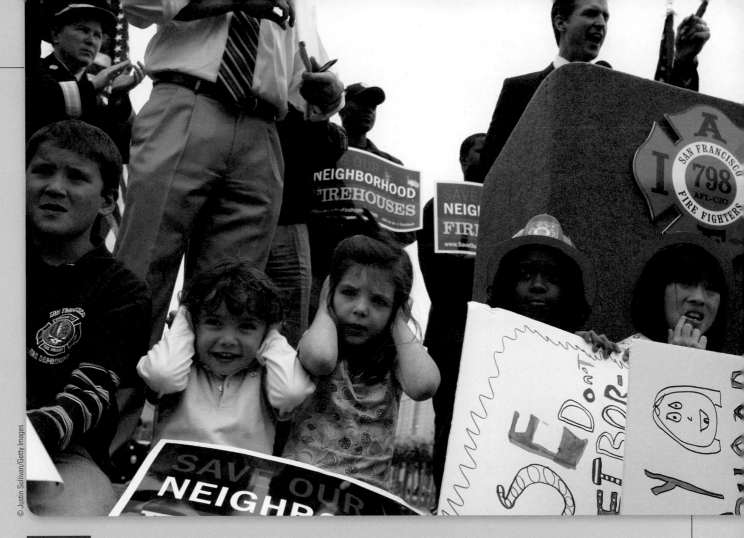

**C**ities all across the country are being forced to cope with budget cuts. Services are being curtailed, employees are being furloughed, and capital improvements are being delayed—if not canceled altogether. Throughout history, police department spending has rarely landed on the chopping block, but in light of the recession gripping America, no public agency is immune. No one likes to cut spending for crime prevention, but in some locales it has become necessary.

Police departments across the country are adopting a range of creative—and controversial—strategies to respond to mandates that they limit spending. Some of them, such as Temecula, California's, have placed limits on overtime, putting caps on the amount of extra work officers can put in.[1] Other cities, including Philadelphia, have left hundreds of positions unfilled.[2] Still others are offering senior officers early retirement. In one extreme case, the city of Toledo, Ohio, made cost-saving alterations to police and fire contracts without union input.[3] Citing falling tax revenues, officials said that economic conditions amounted to an "exigent circumstance" that gave them no choice.

A few agencies have been fortunate enough to buck the trend. Some, including the Dallas Police Department, continue to hire year in and year out. But the Dallas experience is not the norm. Spending limits and budget cuts seem to prevail more than growth and expansion. This trend raises interesting questions for public safety. Do cuts in hiring affect crime? Do other restrictions limit police effectiveness? Will we see an increase in crime because of criminal justice spending cuts? Only time will tell. It is possible to get some answers to these questions now, however. In this chapter, we look at what is known about police effectiveness in general. We also look at recent innovations in law enforcement that show promise for crime reduction, several of which do not require police force expansion and excessive spending. ∎

Most municipal police departments in the United States are independent agencies within the executive branch of government. On occasion, police agencies in two independent jurisdictions may cooperate and participate in mutually beneficial enterprises, such as sharing information on known criminals, or they may work with joint task forces of state, county, and federal agencies to investigate ongoing criminal cases. Aside from such cooperative efforts, police departments tend to be functionally independent organizations with unique sets of rules, policies, procedures, norms, and budgets. In other words, no two are exactly alike.

# THE POLICE ORGANIZATION

Although many police agencies are today in the process of rethinking their organization and goals, the majority are still organized in a hierarchical manner, as illustrated in Figure 6.1. Within this organizational model, each element of the department normally has its own chain of command and rank system. New York City ranks include the following, from lowest to highest:

- Police officer
- Detective specialist
- Detective investigator
- Sergeant (symbol of rank: 3 chevrons)
- Lieutenant (symbol of rank: 1 gold bar)
- Captain (symbol of rank: 2 gold bars)
- Deputy inspector (symbol of rank: gold oak leaf)
- Inspector (symbol of rank: gold eagle)
- Deputy chief (symbol of rank: 1 gold star)
- Assistant chief (symbol of rank: 2 gold stars)
- Bureau chief (symbol of rank: 3 gold stars)
- Chief of department (symbol of rank: 4 gold stars)
- Deputy commissioner (symbol of rank: 3 gold stars)
- First deputy commissioner (symbol of rank: 4 gold stars)
- Police commissioner (symbol of rank: 5 gold stars)

In a large municipal department, there may be a number of independent units headed by a bureau chief who serves as the senior administrator, a captain who oversees regional or precinct units and acts as liaison with other police agencies, a lieutenant who manages daily activities, and sergeants and patrol officers who carry out fieldwork. Smaller departments may have a captain or lieutenant as a unit head. At the head of the organization is the police chief, who sets policy and has general administrative control over all the department's various operating branches.

Problems regarding a police department's organizational structure are not uncommon, nor are they unique to policing agencies, as anyone who has ever dealt with any governmental bureaucracy is aware. Most often they are attributable to personnel changes (due to retirements, promotions, transfers, or resignations) or simply to a periodic internal reorganization. As a result, citizens may sometimes have difficulty determining who is responsible for a particular police function or operational policy, or two divisions may unknowingly compete with each other over jurisdiction on a particular case. The large number of operating divisions and the lack of any clear relationship among them almost guarantee that the decision-making practices of one branch will be unknown to another. These are common management problems that are not insurmountable, and they are typically resolved over time.

In promoting personnel, most departments also follow a system called the **time-in-rank system**. This means that before moving up the administrative ladder, an officer must spend a certain amount of time in the next lowest rank. Thus a

**CourseMate** For more information about the **New York City Police Department**, visit the Criminal Justice CourseMate at CengageBrain.com, then access the "Web Links" for this chapter.

**time-in-rank system**
The promotion system in which a police officer can advance in rank only after spending a prescribed amount of time in the preceding rank.

**FIGURE 6.1**
Organization of a Traditional Metropolitan Police Department

| Civilian advisory board | Chief of police / Assistant chief | Planning and research / Crime mapping / Program evaluation |

| Personnel / Affirmative action officer / Recruitment and promotion | Internal affairs / Trial board |

**Equipment**
- Repairs
- Station, grounds
- Uniforms
- Squad cars
- Computers

**Chief clerk**
- Payroll
- Property
- Supplies
- Purchasing
- Printing
- Statistics
- Budget and finance

**Special services**
- Ambulance
- Records, communications
- Morgue
- Radio
- Psychologist
- Computer programmer
- Court liaison
- Lockup

**Training**
- Academy
- In-service training
- Pistol range
- Physical fitness
- Stress-control program

**Vice**
- Gambling
- Liquor
- Prostitution
- Obscenity

**Detectives**
- Bunko (checks, fraud)
- Homicide
- Robbery
- Sex
- Fugitives
- Autos
- Narcotics

**Patrol**
- 1st district
- 2nd district
- 3rd district
- 4th district
- Foot patrol
- Canine corps
- SWAT (Special Weapons and Tactics)

**Community police unit**
- Neighborhood newsletter
- Ministations Station 1 Station 2 Station 3
- Community coordinating council liaison

**Traffic**
- Control
- Accidents
- Public vehicles
- Violator's school

**Prevention**
- Community relations
- Athletic league
- Project DARE
- Officer Friendly

**Juveniles**
- Detectives
- Juvenile court prosecutor
- School liaison
- Gang control unit

sergeant cannot become a captain without serving an appropriate amount of time as a lieutenant. In New York City, for example, promotions from police officer to sergeant, from sergeant to lieutenant, and from lieutenant to captain all occur via a civil service formula that involves such criteria as performance on a civil service written examination, length of service, citations awarded, and optional physical fitness test (for extra points). Promotion beyond the rank of captain is discretionary. Unlike the private sector, where people can be hired away from another company and given an immediate promotion and boost in pay, the time-in-rank system prohibits departments from allowing officers to skip ranks and sometimes prevents them from hiring an officer from another department and awarding her a higher rank. Although this system is designed to promote fairness and stability in police agencies and to limit favoritism, it may restrict administrative flexibility.

**CourseMate** For more information about **Copsonline**, visit the Criminal Justice CourseMate at CengageBrain.com, then access the "Web Links" for this chapter.

## THE POLICE ROLE

In countless books, movies, and TV shows, the public has been presented with a view of policing that romanticizes police officers as fearless crime fighters who think little of their own safety as they engage in daily shootouts with Uzi-toting drug runners, psychopathic serial killers, and organized crime hit men. Occasionally, but not often, fictional patrol officers and detectives seem aware of

*The role of the police involves activities ranging from emergency medical care to traffic control, but law enforcement and crime control are critical (and often misunderstood) elements of policing. Here a bank robbery suspect is being subdued. The suspect was able to make it only across the street from the bank before being apprehended.*

departmental rules, legal decisions, citizens' groups, civil suits, or physical danger. They are rarely faced with the economic necessity of moonlighting as security guards, taking on extra details, caring about an annual pay raise, or griping when someone less deserving gets a choice assignment for political reasons.

How close to real life is this portrayal of a selfless crime fighter? Not very, according to most research efforts. Police officers are asked to deal with hundreds of incidents each year, and crime fighting is only a small part of the daily routine. Studies of police work indicate that a significant portion of an officer's time is spent handling minor disturbances, service calls, and administrative duties. Police work, then, involves much more than catching criminals. Figure 6.2 shows the results of a national survey of police behavior.[4] This survey found that about 20 percent of Americans aged 16 and older (about 44 million people) have contacts with the police each year. The single largest number of these involve some form of motor vehicle or traffic-related issues. About 5 million annual contacts involve citizens asking for assistance—responding to a complaint about music being too loud during a party, warning kids not to shoot fireworks, and so on. This survey indicates that the police role is both varied and complex.

These results are not surprising when we consider the Uniform Crime Report (UCR) arrest data. Each year, about 700,000 local, county, and state police officers make about 14 million arrests, or about 20 each.[5] Of these, about 2 million are for serious crimes (Index I), or about 3 per officer. Given an even distribution of arrests, it is evident that the average police officer makes fewer than 2 arrests per month and fewer than 1 felony arrest every four months.

These figures should be interpreted with caution because not all police officers are engaged in activities that allow them to make arrests, such as patrol or detective

**FIGURE 6.2**
Police Encounters with Citizens Each Year

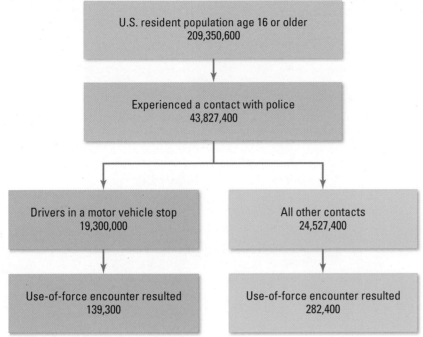

Source: Matthew Durose, Erica Schmitt, and Patrick Langan, *Contacts between the Police and the Public: Findings from the 2002 National Survey* (Washington, D.C., Bureau of Justice Statistics, 2005).

work, and many work in rural and suburban departments in areas with very low crime rates. About one-third of all sworn officers in the nation's largest police departments are in such units as communications, antiterrorism, administration, and personnel. Even if the number of arrests per officer were adjusted by one-third, it would still amount to about four serious crime arrests per officer per year, and these figures include such crimes as shoplifting and other minor larcenies. So although police handle thousands of calls each year, relatively few result in an arrest for a serious crime such as a robbery or burglary; in suburban and rural areas, years may go by before a police officer makes a felony arrest.

The evidence, then, shows that unlike TV and film portrayals, the police role involves many non-crime-related activities. Although the media depict police officers busting criminals and engaging in high-speed chases, the true police role is much more complex. Police officers function in a variety of roles, ranging from dispensers of emergency medical care to keepers of the peace on school grounds. Although officers in large urban departments may be called on to handle more felony cases than those in small towns, they too will probably find that most of their daily activities are not related to crime. What are some of the most important functions of police?

## THE PATROL FUNCTION

Regardless of style of policing, uniformed patrol officers are the backbone of the police department, usually accounting for about two-thirds of a department's personnel.[6] Patrol officers are the most highly visible members of the entire criminal justice system. They are charged with supervising specific areas of their jurisdiction, called **beats,** whether in a patrol car, or by motorcycle, horse, helicopter, or boat, or even on foot in some departments. Each beat, or patrol area, is covered 24 hours a day by different shifts. The major purpose of patrol is to

**beats**
Designated police patrol areas.

- Deter crime by maintaining a visible police presence
- Maintain public order (peacekeeping) within the patrol area
- Enable the police department to respond quickly to law violations or other emergencies

## ANALYZING CRIMINAL JUSTICE ISSUES

# SWAT Teams and Paramilitary Units

Most large police departments operate or participate as members in a SWAT (Special Weapons and Tactics), tactical, or police paramilitary unit (PPU). These units consist of highly trained officers who provide assistance or take over during a variety of incidents, including

- Terrorist incidents
- High-risk warrant situations
- Barricaded suspects
- Hostage situations
- Civil disturbances
- Heavily armed criminals

Devices and technologies commonly employed by PPUs include

- Military equipment and technology
- Submachine guns
- Tactical semiautomatic shotguns, M16 rifles, sniper rifles, and automatic shotguns referred to as "street sweepers"

- Less lethal technologies, including percussion grenades
- Tools for "dynamic entries," such as battering rams and hydraulic door spreaders
- Night vision tools
- Armored and/or military personnel carriers
- Body armor, Kevlar helmets
- Distinct—often black—uniforms

### History and Growth

Police paramilitary units emerged on the law enforcement scene in the 1960s in response to legitimate problems. Patrol officers were simply not equipped to address civil disobedience, dramatic protests, and other high-risk situations without proper training, protection, and armament. The realities of crime today have prompted more and more agencies to seek their own police paramilitary units.

Peter Kraska and Victor Kappeler, two PPU experts, found that in 1982 about 60 percent of agencies they surveyed reported participating in a PPU.

© AP Images/The Winchester Star/Scott Mason

*A key police support function is training, not just in the academy but throughout an officer's career. It is essential that officers remain sharp and continue to hone their skills. Here members of the Winchester, Virginia, Police Department SWAT team and military police officers from the nearby Quantico Marine Corps Base shield themselves as they detonate a blast at an abandoned house as part of a training exercise.*

- Identify and apprehend law violators
- Aid individuals and care for those who cannot help themselves
- Facilitate the movement of traffic and people
- Create a feeling of security in the community[7]

Patrol officers' responsibilities are immense. They may suddenly be faced with an angry mob, an armed felon, or a suicidal teenager and be forced to make split-second decisions on what action to take. At the same time, they must be sensitive to the needs of citizens who are often of diverse racial and ethnic back-

By the mid-1990s that number had reached nearly 90 percent. Kraska and Kappeler focused on large cities, but many small cities have joined with neighboring cities to participate in regional PPUs. Today, nearly every law enforcement agency that needs a PPU has access to one, even in rural areas.

## Overkill?

As criminals have become more sophisticated and prepared, a certain amount of growth in PPUs has been expected. Critics, however, have argued that PPUs are being used for much more than crisis situations. Kraska and Kappeler's research revealed that some agencies used their units to do ordinary patrol work. They reported on one patrol officer's experiences partnering with SWAT:

> We're into saturation patrols in hot spots. We do a lot of our work with the SWAT unit because we have bigger guns. We send out two, two-to-four man cars, we look for minor violations and do jump-outs, either on people on the street or automobiles. After we jump out, the second car provides periphery cover with an *ostentatious display of weaponry*. We're sending a clear message: If the shootings don't stop, we'll shoot someone. (p. 10)

Radley Balko, a researcher at the conservative Cato Institute, has recently authored a report calling the rise of paramilitary units and their use "overkill." He argues that the approximately 40,000 annual PPU raids are subjecting nonviolent drug offenders, bystanders, and innocent civilians to "the terror of having their homes invaded while they're sleeping, usually by teams of heavily armed paramilitary units dressed not as police officers but as soldiers" (p. 1).

## Walking a Fine Line?

Police paramilitary units perform an important function, but another source of concern is that their organization and appearance make them almost indistinguishable from the military. Moreover, Kraska and Kappeler found that many law enforcement PPUs actively train with military personnel. Some PPU members have military backgrounds. Thus the potential exists for some uncomfortable overlap between what the military should do and what the police should do.

The Posse Comitatus Act, passed in 1878, prohibits federal military personnel from engaging in local law enforcement activities. The National Guard can be used for law enforcement in some situations, but this is usually at the request of states, not the federal government. Yet according to Balko, there have been some interesting developments in recent years that have caused the lines between law enforcement and the military to become very thin. For example, in 1988 Congress ordered the National Guard to assist in state-level efforts to eradicate marijuana. Through various funding programs and partnerships, the federal government has also supplied local law enforcement agencies with many of the same technologies that the military possesses. What's wrong with this? Again, according to Balko,

> With all of this funding and free or discounted equipment and training from the federal government, police departments across the country needed something to do with it. So they formed SWAT teams—thousands of them. SWAT teams have since multiplied and spread across the country at a furious clip. (p. 8)

## Critical Thinking

1. Have the growth and use of PPUs become excessive?

2. Should the military be involved in domestic law enforcement? Why or why not?

Sources: Peter B. Kraska and Victor E. Kappeler, "Militarizing American Police: The Rise and Normalization of Paramilitary Units," *Social Problems* 44 (1997): 1–18; Radley Balko, *Overkill: The Rise of Paramilitary Police Raids in America* (Washington, D.C.: Cato Institute, 2006); Derek Lutterbeck, "Between Police and Military: The New Security Agenda and the Rise of Gendarmeries," *Cooperation and Conflict* 39 (2004): 45–68.

grounds. When police are present and visible, a sense of security is created in a neighborhood, and residents' opinions of the police improve.[8]

## Patrol Activities

Most experts agree that the bulk of patrol effort is devoted to what has been described as **order maintenance**, or **peacekeeping**: maintaining order and civility within the officer's assigned jurisdiction.[9] Order-maintenance policing generally targets behavior that falls somewhere between criminal and noncriminal. The patrol officer's discretion often determines whether a noisy neighborhood

**order maintenance (peacekeeping)**
Maintaining order and authority without the need for formal arrest ("handling the situation")—keeping things under control by means of threats, persuasion, and understanding.

## EVIDENCE-BASED JUSTICE

# The Police Presence and Deterrence

For many years, preventive police patrol was considered one of the greatest deterrents to criminal behavior. The visible presence of patrol cars on the street and the rapid deployment of police officers to the scene of the crime were viewed as particularly effective law enforcement techniques. However, research efforts have questioned the basic assumptions of patrol. The most widely heralded attempt at measuring patrol effectiveness was undertaken during the early 1970s in Kansas City, Missouri, under sponsorship of the Police Foundation, a private institute that studies police behavior. To evaluate the effectiveness of patrol, the researchers divided 15 police districts into three groups: One group retained normal patrol, the second (proactive) set of districts were supplied with two to three times the normal amount of patrol forces, and the third (reactive) group had their preventive patrols eliminated, with police officers responding only when summoned by citizens to the scene of a particular crime. Data from the Kansas City study indicated that these variations in patrol techniques had little effect on the crime patterns in the 15 districts. The presence or absence of patrol did not seem to affect residential or business burglaries, motor vehicle thefts, larcenies involving auto accessories, robberies, vandalism, or other criminal behavior. Moreover, variations in patrol techniques appeared to have little influence on citizens' attitudes toward police, their satisfaction with police, or their fear of future criminal behavior.

The Kansas City experiment gave the impression that there is little the police can do to reduce crime, but it is important to note that there were limitations associated with the research design. For example, officers sometimes entered reactive beats in order to respond promptly to calls for service. There are several other reasons why we shouldn't put too much faith in the Kansas City experiment:

■ Dozens of studies are almost evenly divided on whether patrol and crime go hand in hand. Almost as many researchers have found less crime in areas with a higher police presence as have found less crime in areas with a lower police presence.

■ Some studies from other countries have shown that when the police go on strike (they are usually prohibited by law from doing so in the United States), crime rates surge. This suggests that patrol certainly does *something* to reduce crime.

■ Recent federal funding for the hiring of additional police officers has been linked to significant reductions in crime rates in cities across the country.

■ When the Department of Homeland Security increases the terror threat alert level, more police are put on patrol. Researchers have found that these surges in the police presence have led to less crime.

■ Increasing the size of the local police force may have other benefits for the overall effectiveness of the justice system. Adding police and bolstering resources can increase prosecution and conviction rates. Inadequate resources make it difficult to gather sufficient evidence to ensure a conviction, and prosecutors are likely to drop these cases. Adding police resources helps increase prosecutorial effectiveness.

Sources: George Kelling, Tony Pate, Duane Dieckman, and Charles Brown, *The Kansas City Preventive Patrol Experiment: A Summary Report* (Washington, D.C.: Police Foundation, 1974); Richard C. Larson, "What Happened to Patrol Operations in Kansas City? A Review of the Kansas City Preventive Patrol Experiment," *Journal of Criminal Justice* 3 (1975): 267–297; Thomas B. Marvell and Carlisle E. Moody, "Specification Problems, Police Levels, and Crime Rates," *Criminology* 24 (1996): 609–646; Tuija Makinen and Hannu Takala, "The 1976 Police Strike in Finland," *Scandinavian Studies in Criminology* 7 (1980): 87–106; William N. Evans and Emily Owens, "COPS and Crime," *Journal of Public Economics* 91 (2007): 181–201; Government Accountability Office, *Community Policing Grants: COPS Grants Were a Modest Contributor to Declines in Crime in the 1990s* (Washington, D.C.: Government Accountability Office, 2005); Jonathan Klick and Alexander Tabarrok, "Using Terror Alert Levels to Estimate the Effect of Police on Crime," *Journal of Law and Economics* 48 (2005): 267–279; Joan Petersilia, Allan Abrahamse, and James Q. Wilson, "A Summary of RAND's Research on Police Performance, Community Characteristics, and Case Attrition," *Journal of Police Science and Administration* 17 (1990): 219–229.

dispute involves the crime of disturbing the peace or whether it can be controlled with street-corner diplomacy and the combatants sent on their way. Similarly, teenagers milling around in the shopping center parking lot can be brought in and turned over to the juvenile authorities or handled in a less formal and often more efficient manner.

Police encounter many troubling incidents that need some sort of fixing.[10] Enforcing the law might be one tool a patrol officer uses; threats, coercion, sympathy, understanding, and apathy might be others. SWAT teams often handle the most difficult situations (see the nearby Analyzing Criminal Justice Issues feature), but most important is keeping things under control so that no complaints arise. The real police role, then, may be that of a community problem solver.

Police officers practice a policy of selective enforcement, concentrating on some crimes but handling the majority in an informal manner. A police officer is supposed to know when to take action and when not to, whom to arrest and whom to deal with by issuing a warning or taking some other informal action. If a mistake is made, the officer can come under fire from his peers and superiors, as well as from the general public. Consequently, the patrol officer's job is extremely demanding and often unrewarding and unappreciated. The attitudes of police officers toward the public, not surprisingly, are sometimes characterized as being ambivalent and cynical.[11]

## Improving Patrol

In response to the aforementioned issues, police departments have initiated a number of programs and policies to try to improve patrol effectiveness. Some have proved more effective than others. Some are also more controversial than others.

*AGGRESSIVE PATROL*  The Kansas City study greatly influenced the way police experts viewed the effectiveness of patrol. Its lukewarm findings set the stage for community- and problem-oriented policing models, which stress social service over crime deterrence. However, it may be too soon to dismiss police patrol as a crime-fighting technique. Although the mere presence of police may not be sufficient to deter crime, the manner in which they approach their task may make a difference.

Police departments that use **proactive policing**, or an aggressive law enforcement style, may also help reduce crime rates. Jurisdictions that encourage patrol officers to stop motor vehicles to issue citations and to aggressively arrest and detain suspicious persons also experience lower crime rates than jurisdictions that do not follow such proactive policies.[12] Aggressive traffic enforcement can also have the added benefit of reducing more serious crimes.[13]

*TARGETING OF SPECIFIC CRIMES*  Evidence shows that targeting specific crimes can be successful.[14] One aggressive patrol program, known as the Kansas City Gun Experiment, was directed at restricting the carrying of guns in high-risk places at high-risk times. Working with academics from the University of Maryland, the Kansas City Police Department focused extra patrol attention on a hot-spot high-crime area identified by computer analysis of all gun crimes. Over a 29-week period, the gun patrol officers made thousands of car and pedestrian checks and traffic stops, and they made more than 600 arrests. Using frisks and searches, they found 29 guns, and an additional 47 weapons were seized by other officers in the experimental area. There were 169 gun crimes in the target beat in the 29 weeks before the gun patrol but only 86 while the experiment was under way, a decrease of 49 percent. Drive-by shootings dropped significantly, as did homicides, without any displacement to other areas in the city. The weapons seized could have been taken from high-rate

**proactive policing**
An aggressive law enforcement style in which patrol officers take the initiative against crime instead of waiting for criminal acts to occur. For example, they stop motor vehicles to issue citations and aggressively arrest and detain suspicious persons.

### PERSPECTIVES ON JUSTICE

#### Crime Control

The results of proactive policing are encouraging to crime control enthusiasts, but the downside of aggressive tactics must be considered before a general policy of vigorous police work can be adopted. Proactive police strategies may cause resentment in areas where minority citizens believe they are being unfairly targeted by police. Aggressive police tactics such as stopping, frisking, and rousting teenagers who congregate on street corners may be the seeds from which racial conflict grows. Overly aggressive police may also be the ones who are continually involved in incidents of unnecessary brutality. Due process advocates are troubled by these side effects and demand review boards to oversee police activities. Despite such reservations, many large police jurisdictions have adopted a crime control philosophy by having patrol officers become more aggressive and concentrate on investigating and deterring crimes.

offenders who were among the most likely perpetrators of gun-related crimes. Their lost opportunity to commit violent crimes may have resulted in an overall rate decrease. The gun sweeps also could have caused some of the most violent criminals to be taken off the streets. And, as word of the patrol got out, there may have been a general deterrent effect: People contemplating violent crime may have been convinced that the risk of apprehension was unacceptably high.[15]

**BROKEN WINDOWS POLICING**   The order maintenance function has become all the more important in light of George Kelling and James Q. Wilson's popular **broken windows model** of policing.[16] Their highly influential article made three key points:

> **broken windows model**
> The role of the police as maintainers of community order and safety.

1. *Neighborhood disorder creates fear.* Urban areas filled with street people, youth gangs, prostitutes, and the mentally disturbed are the ones most likely to maintain a high degree of crime.

2. *Neighborhoods give out crime-promoting signals.* A neighborhood filled with deteriorated housing, unrepaired broken windows, and disorderly behavior gives out crime-promoting signals. Honest citizens live in fear in these areas, and predatory criminals are attracted to them.

3. *Police need to aggressively target low-level "quality of life" crimes.* If they are to successfully reduce fear and prevent more serious crime from coming into neighborhoods, they must first address the minor problems that invite more serious ones.[17]

Broken windows policing is controversial because some people perceive it as harassment.[18] Why focus on low-level petty crimes when there are more serious problems? Others feel that broken windows policing is remarkably effective. Researchers have claimed it was responsible for the drastic reductions in crime that took place in New York City during the 1990s.[19] Other researchers have put broken windows policing to the test and found that, indeed, it can be an effective approach.[20] The downturn in the New York City violent crime rate during the 1990s has been attributed to aggressive police work aimed at lifestyle crimes: vandalism, panhandling, and graffiti.[21]

**INCREASE IN ARRESTS**   Can more formal police action, such as an arrest, reduce crime? Research studies show that contact with the police may cause some offenders to forgo repeat criminal behavior and deter future criminality.[22] For example, an arrest for drunk driving has been shown to reduce the likelihood of further driving while intoxicated, because arrestees are afraid that they will be rearrested if they drink and drive.[23] The effect of arrest may be immediate: As the number of arrests increases, reported crimes decrease substantially the following day.[24] News of increased and aggressive police activity could be rapidly diffused through the population and have an immediate impact that translates into lower crime rates. Some cities have adopted a zero-tolerance approach, making arrests for even nuisance crimes—for example, panhandling—to deter repeat offenders and give citizens the impression that crime will not be tolerated. This meshes with the broken windows approach just discussed.

**RAPID RESPONSE**   It is widely assumed that criminals can be caught if the police can simply get to the scene of a crime quickly. As one researcher put it,

> . . . the shorter the police travel time from assignment to arrival at a crime scene, the more likely it is that police can arrest offenders before they flee. This claim is then extended to rapid response producing three crime prevention effects. One is a reduction in harm from crimes interrupted in progress by police intervention. Another, more general benefit of rapid response time is a greater deterrent effect . . . The third hypothesized prevention effect comes from the incapacitation through imprisonment of offenders . . .[25]

## CONCEPT SUMMARY 6.1
### Improving Patrol

| Strategy | Tactic | Goal |
| --- | --- | --- |
| Aggressive patrol | Enforce law vigorously | Give message that crime will not be tolerated |
| Targeting of specific crimes | Crack down on persistent problems such as gun possession | Stop or seriously interrupt one type of crime |
| Broken windows policing | Target low-level offenses and incivilities | Prevent serious crime |
| Increase in arrests | Arrest even minor offenders; zero-tolerance approach | Convince people that crime does not pay |
| Rapid response | Respond to 911 calls quickly | Increase odds of catching lawbreakers |
| Procedural justice | Treat citizens with dignity and respect | Increase chances of citizens helping police fight crime, such as by calling officers |
| Use of technology | Employ latest communication and mapping technologies | Identify criminals and target crimes efficiently |

But does the research support this view? Does rapid response really increase the chances of police catching lawbreakers? Unfortunately, the jury is still out, but some researchers have found that a quick response can be beneficial.[26]

**PROCEDURAL JUSTICE** Patrol can be made more effective when police pay attention to how they treat citizens. For example, researchers have found that when officers treat citizens with dignity and respect, the citizens are more likely to be satisfied with the experience, to accept police decisions,[27] and even to participate in crime prevention programs.[28] Research also indicates that precinct-level efforts to ensure that officers are respectful of citizens can help lower the number of complaints and improve community relations.[29] In other words, the police must pay attention to **procedural justice**, a concern with making decisions that are arrived at through procedures viewed as fair.[30] If people view procedures as unfair, they will be less likely to support police in their crime-fighting efforts.[31]

**procedural justice**
A concern with making decisions that are arrived at through procedures viewed as fair.

© AP Images/Denis Poroy

Enforcement of our nation's antidrug laws is a top law enforcement priority. Here San Diego County deputy district attorney Damon Mosler points to the guns and drugs seized during a May 6, 2008, drug bust. Seventy-five San Diego State University students and 21 nonstudents were arrested after an undercover investigation of a college drug ring. Do you think arrests like this will deter other college students from committing similar crimes?

**USE OF TECHNOLOGY** Police departments have also relied on technology to help guide patrol efforts. The best-known program, CompStat, was begun in New York City as a means of directing police efforts in a more productive fashion.[32] William Bratton, who had been appointed New York City police chief, wanted to revitalize the department and break through its antiquated bureaucratic structures. He installed CompStat, a computerized system that gave local precinct commanders up-to-date information about where and when crime was occurring in their jurisdictions. Part of the CompStat program, twice-weekly "crime-control strategy meetings," brought precinct commanders together with the department's

## CRIMINAL JUSTICE AND TECHNOLOGY

# In-Car Cameras

During the 1990s, lawsuits alleging racial bias in police traffic stops began to be filed. This, coupled with some questionable shootings and other police–suspect encounters, prompted many agencies to install cameras in their patrol cars. Between 2000 and 2004, the Office of Community-Oriented Policing Services in the U.S. Justice Department awarded over $20 million in grants to local police departments so they could purchase and install in-car camera systems. Before the funding program, 11 percent of state police and highway patrol vehicles were equipped with cameras. A few years later, nearly 75 percent of these agencies were able to equip their police cars with cameras.

### Reasons for In-Car Cameras

In-car cameras offer several advantages. The International Association of Chiefs of Police (IACP) studied in-car camera programs in 20 states and came up with several reasons why this technology is desirable:

■ *Officer safety*. Perhaps the single most beneficial feature of an in-car camera is the positive effect it can have on officer safety. Having a recording of, say, traffic stops enables the officers to view it and critique their actions after the fact.

■ *Professionalism and performance*. Officers report altering their behavior to some extent when in front of the camera. The IACP found that many officers reported performing to the best of their ability, knowing their actions were being recorded. Other officers argue that a camera's recordings are useful for preparing courtroom testimony; there is less need to rely on memory, which bolsters an officer's credibility when he or she is testifying.

■ *Defense against complaints*. A recording of a police–citizen contact helps protect the officer and the department for which he or she works from meritless complaints or lawsuits. The IACP study revealed that roughly half of citizen complaints are withdrawn once complainants are made aware that a camera recorded the alleged incident.

■ *Leadership benefits*. Police administrators regard in-car cameras as desirable because they aid in investigations of misconduct and promote accountability of officers working in the field. Years of research on public perceptions of police have revealed that professionalism and courtesy promote citizen satisfaction and support. Cameras help further this.

■ *Training*. Just as individual officers may review the recordings from their in-car cameras, so can

top administrators, who asked them to report on crime problems in their precincts and tell what they were doing to turn things around. Those involved in the strategy sessions had both detailed data and electronic pin maps that showed how crime clustered geographically in the precinct and how patrol officers were being deployed. The CompStat program required local commanders to demonstrate their intimate knowledge of crime trends and to develop strategies to address them effectively. When the assembled police administrators presented their ideas, the local commander was required to demonstrate, in follow-up sessions, how he had incorporated the new strategies in the local patrol plan. CompStat proved extremely successful and made a major contribution to the dramatic decline in New York City's crime rate during the past decade. CompStat-like programs have since been implemented in several other jurisdictions around the country.[33] Concept Summary 6.1 summarizes efforts to improve patrol effectiveness.

Untold numbers of other technological innovations have assisted the police in their crime control and prevention efforts. Some have helped them detect and apprehend criminals more quickly. Others have been developed in response to community concerns, making departments more accessible to the communities they serve. Still others have been put in police cars to protect officers from allegations of impropriety. One such technology, the in-car camera, is featured in the accompanying Criminal Justice and Technology feature.

training personnel use the recordings to arm trainees with the knowledge they need and stories of "what not to do."

## Criticisms of In-Car Cameras

In-car cameras are not supported by all concerned. To this day, some agencies have yet to install cameras because of resistance on the part of line officers and their collective bargaining units. In Montgomery, Alabama, officials agreed to install in-car cameras in the city's police cruisers years ago, mainly in response to one officer's shooting of an unarmed suspect, but union officials say the cameras threaten officer privacy. Critics make these points about in-car cameras:

■ *Distraction from the job.* If cameras encourage officers to be on their best behavior, then some of them may obsess over the camera so much that their actions amount to performing for the camera rather than focusing on the task at hand. A small number of officers in the IACP study reported that the cameras distracted them from violators. Sometimes the officers would even worry more about positioning the camera for optimal viewing than about guarding their own safety.

■ *Too much reliance on the camera.* Some officers also reported relying more on recordings of their stops than on their own memory. This could be detrimental from a court testimony standpoint (see above), and some officers reported that their note-taking skills suffered as a consequence of heavy reliance on technology.

■ *Too much information.* There is a concern that the cameras reveal too much information. Union challenges, such as those in Montgomery, Alabama, underscore the controversy associated with requiring that officers always be on their toes because a camera is recording their every move. Is this desirable? Many agencies compromise by setting the cameras to turn on only when the vehicle's flashing lights and/or siren are turned on.

■ *Stress and job performance.* The IACP study found that some officers reported increased stress levels associated with the cameras. A small percentage reported reduced job satisfaction. Some officers even reported making fewer traffic stops because of the presence of a camera.

## Critical Thinking

1. What do you feel is the most important reason for in-car cameras? Is it a good reason?

2. Do in-car cameras make the police more effective or less effective? Why?

Sources: Ernesto Londono, "Police Car Camera Plan Stalls in Union Dispute," *Washington Post*, March 22, 2008, B01; International Association of Chiefs of Police, *The Impact of Video Evidence on Modern Policing: Research and Best Practices from the IACP Study on In-Car Cameras* (Alexandria, Va.: International Association of Chiefs of Police, 2002); Lonnie J. Westphal, "The In-Car Camera: Value and Impact," *Police Chief* 71 (2004): 59–60, 62, 65.

# THE INVESTIGATION FUNCTION

Since the first independent detective bureau was established by the London Metropolitan Police in 1841, criminal investigators have been romantic figures vividly portrayed in novels, movies, and TV shows. Think of Detective Alex Cross in James Patterson's widely read books (such as *Kiss the Girls* and *Along Came a Spider*), Eddie Murphy's portrayal of Axel Foley in *Beverly Hills Cop* and Clint Eastwood's role as Dirty Harry, and television shows such as *CSI: Crime Scene Investigation* and *Law & Order*.[34] The fictional police detective is usually depicted as a loner who is willing to break departmental rules, perhaps even violate the law, to capture the suspect. The average fictional detective views departmental policies and U.S. Supreme Court decisions as unfortunate roadblocks to police efficiency. Civil rights are either ignored or actively scorned.[35]

Although every police department probably has a few aggressive detectives who may take matters into their own hands at the expense of citizens' rights, modern criminal investigators are likely to be experienced civil servants, trained in investigatory techniques, knowledgeable about legal rules of evidence and procedure, and at least somewhat cautious about the legal and administrative consequences of their actions.[36] See the nearby Analyzing Criminal Justice Issues feature for more on the real world of detective work.

## ANALYZING CRIMINAL JUSTICE ISSUES

# Street Stories: The World of Police Detectives

In his book *Street Stories*, sociologist Robert Jackall narrates the stories and insights he gathered while interviewing and hanging with New York City detectives. Jackall formed close associations with veteran detectives and observed them in action as they controlled a crime scene, canvassed for witnesses, interviewed suspects, gathered evidence, and honed their interrogation techniques.

He found that detectives get great satisfaction from solving crimes and putting criminals behind bars. But they also see themselves as caught in a bureaucratic and moral dilemma: They are outsiders because they must play the game of the streets and work amid the mayhem caused by the city's most dangerous criminals and then bring the case to the organized and controlled processing unit that is the criminal court. Detectives believe that court rules victimize them and all too often neutralize their hard work. They get to know the suspect and her entire recorded criminal history. Talking with the suspect

for hours on end, they form ironclad beliefs based on their assessment of the suspect's character and record. Because the reliability of these assessments may be questionable, even the best detectives are sometimes dead wrong. Partly to guard against such errors of judgment, the law deliberately ignores individuals' criminal histories and allows no consideration at trial of the police detectives' assessment of the suspect's moral character. Of course, these rules conflict with the detectives' views of the case and of the culpability of the suspect.

Detectives also find themselves regularly competing for cases with other agencies such as the FBI and with other detective branches. They resent the federal agencies for their large budgets, their agents' lack of understanding of how the city works, and especially the federal agents' unwillingness to share information about criminal groups. Some detective squads regularly hide important information from other units, even within their own departments, so that these units won't steal the case or get credit for its

---

Investigative services can be organized in a variety of ways. In New York City, each borough or district has its own detective division that supervises investigators assigned to neighborhood police precincts (stations). Local squad detectives work closely with patrol officers to provide an immediate investigative response to crimes and incidents. New York City also maintains specialized borough squads—homicide, robbery, and special victims—to aid local squads and help identify suspects whose crimes may have occurred in multiple locations. There are also specialty squads that help in areas such as forensics. Other departments maintain special divisions with prime responsibility for addressing specific types of crimes. Some jurisdictions maintain **vice squads**, which are usually staffed by plainclothes officers or detectives specializing in victimless crimes, such as prostitution or gambling. Vice squad officers may set themselves up as customers for illicit activities to make arrests. For example, male undercover detectives may frequent public men's rooms and make advances toward other men. Those who respond are arrested for homosexual soliciting. In other instances, female police officers may pose as prostitutes. These covert police activities have often been criticized as violating the personal rights of citizens, and their appropriateness and fairness have been questioned.

**vice squads**
Police units assigned to enforce morality-based laws, such as those addressing prostitution, gambling, and pornography.

## How Do Detectives Detect?

Detectives investigate the causes of crime and attempt to identify the individuals or groups responsible for committing particular offenses. They may enter a case after patrol officers have made the initial contact, such as when a patrol car interrupts a crime in progress and the offenders flee before they can be apprehended. Detectives can investigate a case entirely on their own, sometimes solution. Borough-wide homicide squads steal good cases from precinct detectives, and bosses regularly appropriate credit for their subordinates' work on the streets.

Detectives have the privilege of seeing the underside of life, even the lives of the rich and famous. As Jackall puts it,

> Detectives' work regularly takes them behind respectable public faces, where they glimpse messy, sometimes tumultuous, sometimes sad, sometimes ironic, sometimes tragic, sometimes comic, sometimes despairing, sometimes vice-filled private lives. (p. 343)

They watch as a man walks into the squad room clad only in his underwear, claiming that he and a friend were just having a quiet conversation in his parked car when a robber reached through the window and snatched their clothes. They come across otherwise respectable professionals addicted to narcotics. In one case, while investigating the murder of a man dressed in women's clothes, they uncovered a genteel "butterfly society" of established professional men who cross-dress for Friday evening cocktails. These journeys behind public façades stir prurient interests in some detectives but arouse profound class resentments in most. Police officers come overwhelmingly from the working class. They are the sons and daughters of police officers and firefighters, and they are appalled at the antics of the rich and their ability to get away with crimes for which the poor would be sent to prison.

Because detectives are agents of the state, symbols of authority, and ultimate insiders with privileged access to hidden social arenas and forbidden knowledge, they become objects of fear, anger, and resentment. This dual role, Jackall concludes, shapes the meanings of detectives' work, their images of the world, and their self-images.

## Critical Thinking

1. Should detectives use deception and coercion to gather evidence, or do these practices reduce their credibility in the eyes of the community?

2. Should detectives be selected, trained, and promoted in the same way as patrol officers, or should investigations be carried out by a totally independent agency that focuses on the scientific gathering of evidence?

Source: Robert Jackall, *Street Stories: The World of Police Detectives* (Cambridge, Mass.: Harvard University Press, 2005).

---

by following up on leads provided by informants. Sometimes detectives go undercover in order to investigate crime: A lone agent can infiltrate a criminal group or organization to gather information on future criminal activity. Undercover officers can also pose as victims to capture predatory criminals who have been conducting street robberies and muggings.[37]

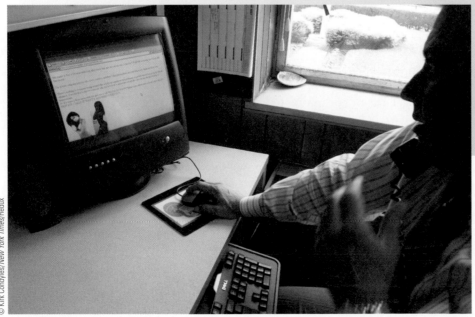

A detective monitors Craigslist's now defunct "Erotic Services" category. The company decided to close its doors on erotic services following a long legal battle, prompted in part by lawsuits claiming that the ads served to facilitate prostitution. Law enforcement officials across the country continue to monitor the website closely, sometimes placing decoy ads to catch would-be customers.

© Kirk Condyles/New York Times/Redux

EXHIBIT 6.1

## Investigative Functions

| Specific Focus | General Coverage | Informative Data Gathering |
| --- | --- | --- |
| Specific witnesses | Neighborhood canvas | Cell phone records |
| Specific evidence | Friends, family, and associates | Computer hard drives |
| Specific events | Coworkers | Other records |
| Specific facts | Victim/suspect time lines | Private papers |

*Source:* John B. Edwards, "Homicide Investigative Strategies," *FBI Law Enforcement Bulletin* 74 (2005): 11–21.

In his recent study of investigation techniques, Martin Innes found that police detectives rely heavily on interviews and forensic evidence to reconstruct or manufacture a narrative of the crime, creating in a sense the "story" that sets out how, where, and why the incident took place.[38] To create their story, contemporary detectives typically use a three-pronged approach:[39]

■ *Specific focus.* Detectives interview witnesses, gather evidence, record events, and collect facts that are available at the immediate crime scene.

■ *General coverage.* This process involves detectives who (a) canvass the neighborhood and make observations; (b) conduct interviews with friends, families, and associates; (c) contact coworkers or employers for information regarding victims and suspects; and (d) construct victim/suspect time lines to outline their whereabouts before the incident.

■ *Informative data gathering.* Detectives use modern technology to collect records of cell phones and pagers, computer hard drives (palm pilots, laptops, notebooks, desktops, and servers), diaries, notes, and documents. Information includes data used by persons of interest in the investigation that tells about their lives, interactions with others, and geographical connections (see Exhibit 6.1).

Detectives may successfully identify a criminal suspect if these methods pan out. But that is only the beginning of building an airtight case. Next, the detectives attempt to gain as much information as possible from their suspect, perhaps even getting him to confess.

## Sting Operations

**sting operation**
Organized groups of detectives who deceive criminals into openly committing illegal acts or conspiring to engage in criminal activity.

Another approach to detective work, commonly referred to as a **sting operation**, involves organized groups of detectives who deceive criminals into openly committing illegal acts or conspiring to engage in criminal activity.[40] Numerous sting operations have been aimed at capturing various types of criminals, ranging from professional thieves to sex offenders. To catch professional thieves, undercover detectives often pose as fences, set up ongoing fencing operations, and encourage thieves interested in selling stolen merchandise. Transactions are videotaped to provide prosecutors with strong cases. A similar approach is sometimes used to catch sex offenders.

Sting operations have drawbacks. By its very nature, a sting involves deceit by police agents that often borders on entrapment.[41] Covert police activities have been criticized as violating the personal rights of citizens while forcing officers into demeaning roles, such as having female officers act like prostitutes. (Ironically, 2005 research by Mary Dodge and her associates found that rather than considering it demeaning, female officers find their sting work as make-believe prostitutes exciting and consider it a stepping-stone toward promotion.[42])

At-large parolees lie on the floor as they are arrested in a sting operation at the auditorium at the California State Building in Oakland, California, on May 15, 2010. California corrections officials dangled an attractive offer before hundreds of the fugitives: Come in, get a $200 reward, and qualify for an amnesty program.

© AP Photo/John Storey

Sting operations may encourage criminals to commit new crimes because they have a new source for fencing stolen goods. Innocent people may hurt their reputations by buying merchandise from a sting operation when they had no idea that the items had been stolen. By putting the government in the fencing business, such operations blur the line between law enforcement and criminal activity.

## Undercover Work

Sometimes detectives go undercover to investigate crime.[43] Undercover work can take a number of forms. A lone agent can infiltrate a criminal group or organization to gather information on future criminal activity. Or a Drug Enforcement Administration agent may go undercover to gather intelligence on drug smugglers. Undercover officers can also pose as victims to capture predatory criminals who have been conducting street robberies and muggings.

Undercover work is considered a necessary element of police work, although it can prove dangerous for the agent. Police officers may be forced to engage in illegal or immoral behavior to maintain their cover. They also face significant physical danger in playing the role of a criminal and dealing with mobsters, terrorists, and drug dealers. In far too many cases, undercover officers are mistaken for real criminals and injured by other law enforcement officers or private citizens trying to stop a crime. Arrest situations involving undercover officers may also provoke violence when suspects do not realize they are in the presence of police and therefore violently resist arrest.

Undercover officers may also experience psychological problems. Being away from home, keeping late hours, and always worrying that their identity will be uncovered can create enormous stress. Officers have experienced post-undercover strain, resulting in trouble at work and, in many instances, ruined marriages and botched prosecutions. Hanging around with criminals for a long time, making friends with them, and earning their trust can also have a damaging psychological impact.

## Evaluating Investigations

Serious criticism has been leveled at the nation's detective forces for getting bogged down in paperwork and being relatively inefficient in clearing cases. One famous study of 153 detective bureaus found that a great deal of a detective's time was spent in nonproductive work and that investigative expertise did little to solve cases. Half of all detectives could be replaced without negatively influencing crime clearance rates.[44]

Although some question remains about the effectiveness of investigations, police detectives do make a valuable contribution to police work because their skilled interrogation and case-processing techniques are essential to eventual criminal conviction.[45] Nonetheless, in a majority of cases that are solved, the perpetrator is identified at the scene of the crime by patrol officers. Research by the Police Executive Research Forum shows that if a crime is reported while in progress, the police have about a 33 percent chance of making an arrest; the arrest probability declines to about 10 percent if the crime is reported 1 minute later, and to 5 percent if more than 15 minutes elapse. As the time between the crime and the arrest grows, the chances of a conviction are also reduced, probably because the ability to recover evidence is lost. To put it another way, the longer the gap between completion of the crime and the placing of the investigation into the hands of detectives, the lower the odds that the perpetrator will be identified and arrested.[46]

## Improving Investigations

A number of efforts have been made to revamp and improve investigation procedures. One practice has been to give patrol officers greater responsibility for conducting preliminary investigations at the scene of the crime. In addition, specialized units, such as homicide or burglary squads, now operate over larger areas and can bring specific expertise to bear. Technological advances in DNA and fingerprint identification have also boosted investigation effectiveness.

One reason for investigation ineffectiveness is that detectives often lack sufficient resources to carry out a lengthy ongoing probe of any but the most serious cases. Research shows the following:[47]

- *Unsolved cases*. Almost 50 percent of burglary cases are screened out by supervisors before assignment to a detective for a follow-up investigation. Of those assigned, 75 percent are dropped after the first day of the follow-up investigation. Although robbery cases are more likely to be assigned to detectives, 75 percent of them are also dropped after one day of investigation.

- *Length of investigation*. The vast majority of cases are investigated for no more than 4 hours stretching over 3 days. An average of 11 days elapses between the initial report of a crime and the suspension of the investigation.

- *Sources of information*. Early in an investigation, the focus is on the victim; as the investigation is pursued, emphasis shifts to the suspect. The most critical information for determining case outcome is the name and description of the suspect and related crime information. Victims are most often the source of information. Unfortunately, witnesses, informants, and members of the police department are consulted far less often. However, when these sources are tapped, they are likely to produce useful information.

- *Effectiveness*. Preliminary investigations by patrol officers are critical. In situations in which the suspect's identity is not known immediately after the crime is committed, detectives make an arrest in less than 10 percent of all cases.

Given these findings, detective work may be improved if greater emphasis is placed on collecting physical evidence at the scene of the crime, identifying witnesses, checking departmental records, and using informants. The probability of successfully settling a case is improved if patrol officers gather evidence at the scene of a crime and effectively communicate it to detectives working the case. Also recommended is the use of targeted investigations that direct attention at a few individuals, such as career criminals, who are known to have engaged in the behavior under investigation.

As the private security industry grows, a great many investigators are being employed by private detective agencies or security companies. Sound like an interesting career? Read the Careers in Criminal Justice feature in this chapter.

## Using Technology

Police departments are now employing advanced technology in all facets of their operations, from assigning patrol routes to gathering evidence. Similarly, investigators are starting to use advanced technology to streamline and enhance the investigation process. Gathering evidence at a crime scene and linking clues to a list of suspects can be a tedious job for many investigators. Yet linkage is critical if suspects are to be quickly apprehended before they are able to leave the jurisdiction, intimidate witnesses, or cover up any clues they may have left behind.

One innovative use of technology enables investigators to compare evidence found at the crime scene with material collected from similar crimes by other police agencies. Police agencies are using a program called Coplink to help with this time-consuming task. Coplink integrates information from different jurisdictions into a single database that detectives can access when working investigations.[48] The Coplink program allows investigators to search the entire database of past criminal records and compile a list of possible suspects even when only partial data is available, such as first or last name, partial license plate numbers, vehicle type, vehicle color, location of crime, or weapon used. The Coplink program enables police to access data from other police agencies in minutes, a process that otherwise could take days or weeks. The Coplink system allows for easy information sharing between law enforcement agencies, a task that has been problematic in the past. It is one of the new breed of computer-aided investigation techniques that are beginning to have a significant impact on capture ratios in the nation's police departments.

**CourseMate** For more information about **Coplink**, visit the Criminal Justice CourseMate at CengageBrain.com, then access the "Web Links" for this chapter.

## COMMUNITY POLICING

For generations, police agencies have been trying to gain the cooperation and respect of the communities they serve. At first, efforts at improving the relationships between police departments and the public involved programs with the general title of police–community relations (PCR). Developed at the station house and departmental levels, these initial PCR programs were designed to make citizens more aware of police activities, alert them to methods of self-protection, and improve general attitudes toward policing.

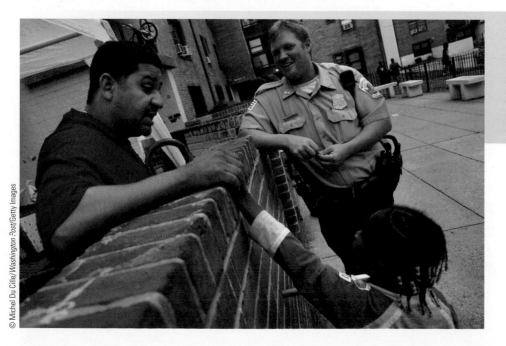

One method of implementing community policing is to improve the bonds between officers and the residents who live in the neighborhoods they serve. Here police officer Patrick Ecelberger, one of several District of Columbia officers assigned to a walking beat, chats with two neighborhood residents.

© Michel Du Cille/Washington Post/Getty Images

## CAREERS IN CRIMINAL JUSTICE

# *Private Detectives and Investigators*

### Duties and Characteristics of the Job

Private detectives' and investigators' work comes in a variety of forms, but they primarily collect information for a client. Most often this will involve interviewing individuals, conducting surveillance, and conducting searches for information. Private investigators often specialize in a certain type of case, such as corporate, financial, or legal investigation. Loss-prevention agents, commonly known as store detectives, prevent the loss, theft, or destruction of store merchandise at the hands of shoplifters, employees, and delivery persons. The kinds of cases that private investigators take on include locating missing persons, investigating computer-based crimes, uncovering fraud, and conducting background checks. Because their work often involves legal issues, private detectives and investigators may be asked to prepare materials for a trial by producing evidence or writing reports, aiding attorneys, or testifying in court.

Private detectives and investigators often have to work irregular hours, including nights and weekends, when conducting surveillance, interviews, or other forms of research. Investigators who own their own detective agency are exceptions to this tendency because they can send other investigators to do this work. Likewise, work settings can vary from safe places such as offices and homes to more dangerous settings.

### Job Outlook

The outlook is good for those seeking a career in this field. The best opportunities are for those seeking entry-level positions at detective agencies or as part-time store detectives. Larger discount and retail chains offer the most opportunities for those who seek store detective positions.

### Salary

Private detectives and investigators in full-time positions earn a median annual salary of $41,760. For investigators paid on a case-by-case basis, pay will depend on the number and pay rate of cases they choose to take or are assigned. Earnings vary greatly, depending on factors such as geographical region and employer.

### Opportunities

Job opportunities within the field are expected to grow in the coming years for numerous reasons, including the need to replace those who retire or change careers and an increase in litigation. Candidates entering the field should expect healthy competition from other applicants with degrees and relevant law enforcement experience. Opportunities for advancement may be limited, so after several years of experience, many private detectives and investigators start their own agencies.

### Qualifications

In many states, a private investigator needs a license in order to work. The strictness of the licensing requirements varies by state. Personality and work characteristics that will serve a potential applicant well when applying for positions include determination, responsibility, assertiveness, good communications skills, and the ability to handle confrontations. If a detective or investigator wants to specialize in a certain field, such as corporate investigating, relevant education and personal experience in that field may be necessary. In general, detectives and investigators are not armed; however, certain jobs may require that applicants be licensed and trained to be carry arms.

### Education and Training

Although there is no explicit educational minimum for this type of work, many applicants in this field have undergraduate degrees in a related field such as criminal justice or have some previous law enforcement or military experience. Education gives those who do not have such experience an advantage. Knowledge of how to conduct searches and surveillance techniques is also helpful.

Sources: "Private Detectives and Investigators," *Occupational Outlook Handbook*, 2010–2011 edition (Bureau of Labor Statistics, U.S. Department of Labor), retrieved April 9, 2010, from www.bls.gov/oco/ocos157.htm; *Occupational Employment and Wages, May 2008* (Bureau of Labor Statistics, U.S. Department of Labor), retrieved April 9, 2010, from www.bls.gov/oes/current/oes339021.htm.

---

**EXHIBIT 6.2**

# Three Key Components of Community-Oriented Policing

**COMMUNITY PARTNERSHIPS**

Collaborative partnerships between the law enforcement agency and the individuals and organizations they serve to develop solutions to problems and increase trust in police.

- Other government agencies
- Community members/groups
- Nonprofits/service providers
- Private businesses
- Media

**ORGANIZATIONAL TRANSFORMATION**

The alignment of organizational management, structure, personnel, and information systems to support community partnerships and proactive problem solving.

*Agency Management*

- Climate and culture
- Leadership
- Labor relations
- Decision making
- Strategic planning
- Policies
- Organizational evaluations
- Transparency
- Organizational structure

*Geographical assignment of officers*

- Despecialization
- Resources and finances

*Personnel*

- Recruitment, hiring, and selection
- Personnel supervision/evaluations
- Training

*Information Systems (Technology)*

- Communication/access to data
- Quality and accuracy of data

**PROBLEM SOLVING**

The process of engaging in the proactive and systematic examination of identified problems to develop and rigorously evaluate effective responses.

- Scanning: Identifying and prioritizing problems
- Analysis: Researching what is known about the problem
- Response: Developing solutions to bring about lasting reductions in the number and extent of problems
- Assessment: Evaluating the success of the responses
- Using the crime triangle to focus on immediate conditions (victim/offender/location)

Source: Office of Community Oriented Policing Services, www.cops.usdoj.gov/Default.asp?Item=36 (accessed April 6, 2010).

---

Although PCR efforts showed a willingness of police agencies to cooperate with the public, some experts believed that law enforcement agencies needed to undergo a significant transformation to create meaningful partnerships with the public. In their view, community relations and crime control effectiveness cannot be the province of a few specialized units housed within a traditional police department. Instead, the core police role must be altered if community involvement is to be won and maintained. To accomplish this goal, police departments should return to an earlier style of policing, in which officers on the beat had intimate contact with the people they served. Modern police departments generally rely on motorized patrol to cover wide areas, to maintain a visible police presence, and to ensure rapid response time. Although effective and economical, the patrol car removes officers from the mainstream of the community, alienating people who might otherwise be potential sources of information and help to the police.

In response to the limitations of earlier approaches to policing, **community-oriented policing (COP)** programs have been implemented in large cities, suburban areas, and rural communities.[49] Also described as simply "community policing," such programs promote interaction between officers and citizens and give officers the time to meet with local residents to talk about crime in the neighborhood and to use personal initiative to solve problems. Although not all

**CourseMate** For more information about **community policing**, visit the Criminal Justice CourseMate at CengageBrain.com, then access the "Web Links" for this chapter.

**community-oriented policing**
Programs designed to bring police and public closer together and create a more cooperative environment between them.

programs work (police–community newsletters and cleanup campaigns do not seem to do much good), the overall impression has been that patrol officers can reduce the level of fear in the community. Some studies have also showed that community policing programs reduce crime.[50] Exhibit 6.2 elaborates on the elements of community-oriented policing.

## Implementing Community Policing

The community policing concept was originally implemented through a number of innovative demonstration projects.[51] Among the most publicized were experiments in **foot patrol**, which took officers out of cars and had them walking beats in the neighborhood. Foot patrol efforts were aimed at forming a bond with community residents by acquainting them with the individual officers who patrolled their neighborhood, letting them know that police were caring and available. The first foot patrol experiments were conducted in cities in Michigan and New Jersey. An evaluation of foot patrol indicated that although it did not bring down the crime rate, residents in areas where foot patrol was added perceived greater safety and were less afraid of crime.[52]

Since the advent of these programs, the federal government has encouraged the growth of community policing by providing millions of dollars to hire and train officers.[53] The U.S. Justice Department's Office of Community Oriented Policing Services is the go-to source for community policing funding.[54] Hundreds of communities have adopted innovative forms of decentralized, neighborhood-based community policing models. Recent surveys indicate that a significant increase is evident in community policing activities in recent years and that certain core programs such as crime prevention activities have become embedded in the police role.[55]

## The Challenges of Community Policing

The core concepts of police work are changing as administrators recognize the limitations and realities of police work in modern society. If they are to be successful, community policing strategies must be able to react effectively to some significant administrative problems:

- *Defining community*. Police administrators must be able to define the concept of community as an ecological area characterized by common norms, shared values, and interpersonal bonds.[56] After all, the main focus of community policing is to activate the community norms that make neighborhoods more crime resistant. If, in contrast, community policing projects cross the boundaries of many different neighborhoods, any hope of learning and accessing community norms, strengths, and standards will be lost.[57]

- *Defining roles*. Police administrators must also establish the exact role of community police agents. How should they integrate their activities with those of regular patrol forces? For example, should foot patrols have primary responsibility for policing in an area, or should they coordinate their activities with officers assigned to patrol cars?

- *Changing supervisor attitudes*. Some supervisors are wary of community policing because it supports a decentralized command structure. This would mean fewer supervisors and, consequently, less chance for promotion and a potential loss of authority.[58] Those supervisors who learn to actively embrace community policing concepts are the ones best able to encourage patrol officers to engage in self-initiated activities, including community policing and problem solving.[59]

- *Reorienting police values*. Research shows that police officers who have a traditional crime control orientation are less satisfied with community policing efforts than those who are public service oriented.[60] In some instances, officers holding traditional values may go as far as looking down on their own comrades assigned to community policing, who as a result feel "stigmatized" and penalized by lack of agency support.[61]

- *Revising training.* Community policing requires that police departments alter their training requirements, especially during field training.[62] Future officers must develop community-organizing and problem-solving skills, along with traditional police skills. Their training must prepare them to succeed less on their ability to make arrests or issue citations and more on their ability to solve problems, prevent crime effectively, and deal with neighborhood diversity and cultural values.[63]

- *Reorienting recruitment.* To make community policing successful, mid-level managers who are receptive to and can implement community-change strategies must be recruited and trained.[64] The selection of new recruits must be guided by a desire to find individuals with attitudes that support community policing. They must be open to the fact that community policing will help them gain knowledge of the community, give them opportunities to gain skill and experience, and help them engage in proactive problem solving.[65]

- *Reaching out to every community.* Because each neighborhood has its own particular needs, community policing must become flexible and adaptive. In neighborhoods undergoing change in racial composition, special initiatives to reduce tensions may be required.[66] Some neighborhoods are cohesive and highly organized, and residents work together to solve problems. In other neighborhoods, it takes more work for community policing to succeed.

## Overcoming Obstacles

Although there are formidable obstacles to overcome, growing evidence suggests that community- and problem-oriented policing can work and fit well with traditional forms of policing.[67] Many police experts and administrators have embraced these concepts as revolutionary revisions of the basic police role. Community policing efforts have been credited with helping reduce crime rates in large cities such as New York and Boston. The most professional and highly motivated officers are the ones most likely to support community policing efforts.[68]

These results are encouraging, but there is no clear-cut evidence that community policing is highly successful at reducing crime or changing the traditional values and attitudes of police officers involved in the programs.[69] Some research does show that the arrest rate actually increases after COP programs have been implemented.[70] However, crime rate reductions in cities that have used COP may be the result of an overall downturn in the nation's crime rate, rather than a result of community policing efforts.

Despite these professional obstacles, community policing has become a common part of municipal police departments. The concept is also being exported around the world, with varying degrees of success; some nations do not seem to have the stability necessary to support community policing.[71] Where it is used, citizens seem to like community policing initiatives, and those who volunteer and get involved in community crime prevention programs report higher confidence in the police force and its ability to create a secure environment.[72] They also tend to be more likely to report crime.[73]

**CourseMate** For more information about **training, advice, and discussion on community policing**, visit the Criminal Justice CourseMate at CengageBrain.com, then access the "Web Links" for this chapter.

## PROBLEM-ORIENTED POLICING (POP)

Closely associated with, yet independent from, the community policing concept are **problem-oriented policing (POP)** strategies. Traditional police models focus on responding to calls for help in the least possible time, dealing with the situation, and getting on the street again as soon as possible.[74] In contrast, the core of problem-oriented policing is a proactive orientation.

Problem-oriented policing strategies require police agencies to identify particular long-term community problems—street-level drug dealers, prostitution rings, gang hangouts—and to develop strategies to eliminate them.[75] Like community policing, being problem solvers requires that police departments rely

**problem-oriented policing (POP)**
A style of police management that stresses proactive problem solving instead of reactive crime fighting.

on local residents and private resources. This means that police managers must learn how to develop community resources, design efficient and cost-effective solutions to problems, and become advocates as well as agents of reform.[76] A significant portion of police departments are using special units to confront specific social problems. For example, departments may employ special units devoted to youth issues ranging from child abuse to gangs.

Problem-oriented policing models are supported by the fact that a great deal of urban crime is concentrated in a few hot spots.[77] A large number of all police calls in metropolitan areas typically radiate from a relatively few locations: bars, malls, the bus depot, hotels, and certain apartment buildings.[78] By implication, concentrating police resources on these **hot spots of crime** could appreciably reduce crime.[79]

## Criminal Acts, Criminal Places

Problem-oriented strategies are being developed that focus on specific criminal problem areas, specific criminal acts, or both. They have proved so popular and effective[80] that an organization has emerged whose mission is to share information between police agencies concerning best practices. The Center for Problem-Oriented Policing makes available an extensive collection of problem-specific guides that police officers around the country can access, read, and apply to situations in their respective jurisdictions.[81] Examples of problem-solving efforts include combating auto theft and violence.

*COMBATING AUTO THEFT* Because of problem-oriented approaches (combined with advanced technology), car thieves in many jurisdictions are no longer able to steal cars with as much ease as before. To reduce the high number of car thefts occurring each year, some police departments have invested in bait cars, which are parked in high-theft areas and are equipped with technology that alerts law enforcement personnel when someone has stolen a vehicle. A signal goes off when either a door is opened or the engine starts. Then, equipped with global positioning satellite (GPS) technology, police officers can watch the movement of the car. Some cars are also equipped with microscopic videos and audio recorders, which enable officers to see and hear the suspect(s) within the car, and with remote engine and door locks, which can trap the thief inside. The technology has been used in conjunction with an advertising campaign to warn potential car thieves about the program. The system has been instituted in several cities, with impressive results. Motor vehicle theft dropped over 40 percent in Minneapolis over a three-year period in which bait cars were used and dropped 30 percent in Vancouver within six months of the time the program was begun. In addition to cutting down on auto theft, the system (which costs roughly $3,500 per car) tends to reduce the danger of high-speed pursuits because police officers can put obstacles on the road to stop the car.[82]

*REDUCING VIOLENCE* A number of efforts have been made to reduce violence by using problem-oriented community policing techniques. Police in Richmond, California, successfully applied such techniques, including citizen involvement, to help reduce murder rates.[83] Problem-oriented techniques have also been directed at combating gang-related violence. For example, the Tucson (Arizona) Police Department has created a **gang tactical detail** unit, which is aimed at proactively attacking neighborhood gang problems by targeting known offenders who have shown a propensity toward gang violence or criminal activity. Members of the tactical unit work directly with neighborhood community groups to identify specific gang problems within individual neighborhoods. Once the problem is identified, the unit helps devise a working solution that combines community involvement, intergovernmental assistance, and law enforcement intervention. The officers of the gang tactical detail attend meetings with community groups to identify gang-related

**hot spots of crime**
The relatively few locations—bars, malls, the bus depot, hotels, and certain apartment buildings—from which a significant portion of police calls typically originate in metropolitan areas.

**CourseMate** For more information about the **Center for Problem-Oriented Policing**, visit the Criminal Justice CourseMate at CengageBrain.com, then access the "Web Links" for this chapter.

**gang tactical detail**
A police unit created to combat neighborhood gang problems by targeting known offenders who have shown a propensity toward gang violence or criminal activity.

problems. They assist with gang-awareness presentations for schools and civic groups.[84]

Another well-known program, Operation Ceasefire, is a problem-oriented policing intervention aimed at reducing youth homicide and youth firearms violence in Boston. Evaluations of the program found that Ceasefire produced significant reductions in youth homicide victimization and gun assault incidents in Boston—reductions that were not experienced in other communities in New England or elsewhere in the nation.[85] The Jersey City, New Jersey, police recently applied a variety of aggressive crime-reducing techniques in some of the city's gang-ridden areas. Evaluations of the program show that crime rates were reduced when police officers used aggressive problem solving (e.g., drug enforcement) and community improvement techniques (e.g., increased lighting and cleaned vacant lots) in high-crime areas.[86] Recent research on efforts to reduce gun violence suggest that a strategy of "pulling levers" can be quite effective. This approach focuses on communicating penalties to criminals and using every get-tough strategy available when laws are violated.[87]

Although programs such as these seem successful, the effectiveness of any street-level problem-solving efforts must be interpreted with caution.[88] Criminals could merely be dispersing to other, safer areas of the city and planning to return shortly after the program has been declared a success and the additional police forces have been pulled from the area.[89] Nonetheless, evidence shows that simply saturating an area with police may not deter crime but that focusing efforts at a particular problem may have a crime-reducing effect.

Gauging the effectiveness of problem-oriented policing is difficult. On the one hand, it may have a deterrent effect: Hot-spots policing increases the community perception that police arrest many criminals and that most violators get caught. On the other hand, there is the possibility of **displacement**: Criminals move from an area targeted for increased police presence to another that is less well protected.[90] When the police leave, the criminals return to business as usual. The displacement issue is discussed further in the nearby Analyzing Criminal Justice Issues feature.

**displacement**
An effect that occurs when criminals move from an area targeted for increased police presence to another that is less well protected.

## INTELLIGENCE-LED POLICING

Since 9/11, policing has experienced a fundamental philosophical change. It has combined a homeland security focus with the many advances made in the realms of community- and problem-oriented policing.[91] An outgrowth of this combination is **intelligence-led policing (ILP)**: "the collection and analysis of information to produce an intelligence end product designed to inform police decision making at both the tactical and strategic levels."[92] More simply, ILP is intended to further shift the emphasis in police work away from reactive responses and individual case investigations. It instead emphasizes information sharing, collaboration, and strategic solutions to crime problems at various levels. It relies heavily on

- Confidential informants
- Offender interviews
- Careful analysis of crime reports and calls for service
- Suspect surveillance
- Community sources of information[93]

The British have a long history of sophisticated intelligence gathering and analysis. All 43 British constabularies, as well as the London Metropolitan Police, have had intelligence units for some time, to deal with problems ranging from drugs to organized crime.[94] The UK's National Drugs Intelligence Unit, created in the 1980s, gathers intelligence to aid in the enforcement of laws against

**intelligence-led policing (ILP)**
The collection and analysis of information to generate an "intelligence end product" designed to inform police decision making at both the tactical and the strategic level.

## ANALYZING CRIMINAL JUSTICE ISSUES

# The Displacement Problem

One of the most common criticisms of problem-oriented policing is that it simply pushes crime into surrounding areas. In other words, the criminal element follows the path of least resistance. This can be both a blessing and curse. On the one hand, a city mayor who is responsible to those in the city he or she serves may not care if a successful intervention pushed crime into a neighboring city; the people in the neighboring city don't elect the mayor! On the other hand, when crime moves elsewhere, it doesn't go away. This means that some problem-oriented strategies help one community (or neighborhood) but hurt the next.

Unfortunately, few efforts to investigate the effectiveness of problem-oriented policing consider the issue of displacement. Few take a hard look at whether crime went up in surrounding areas—or at other aspects of displacement. Researchers have identified five types of displacement:

■ Temporal: offenders change the times at which they offend

■ Spatial: offenders offend in different locations

■ Target: offenders choose different targets

■ Tactical: offenders use different methods to accomplish their objectives

■ Offense: offenders switch to different crime types

Note that four of these varieties of displacement do not require that offenders move to a different area. This complicates matters, because it means the police need to be cognizant of more than just spatial displacement. They have to look for unanticipated consequences. If, for example, a city sees a surge in car thefts from mall parking lots, the police may launch an initiative to aggressively patrol the areas to catch and deter criminals. Their work is not done, however, if they succeed. They also need to ensure that offenders didn't opt for different targets, such as residences—or cars parked in private driveways. This is difficult to do.

What factors influence whether displacement will occur? A recent study by the Center for Problem-Oriented Policing identifies three factors:

■ Offender motivation: What drives offenders to break the law is likely to influence displacement.

Drug-addicted offenders, for example, may substitute one type of theft for another in order to generate cash to sustain their habits.

■ Offender familiarity: A large body of literature confirms that offenders, like people in general, don't like to step out of their comfort zone. More often than not, if displacement is going to occur, it will occur close to the same location and offenders will opt for familiar targets and tactics.

■ Crime opportunity: When there are opportunities to offend, motivated offenders will do so. A community-wide initiative that puts all residents on high alert may do wonders to "harden" targets and make it difficult for offenders simply to move up the street to the next suitable target. Alternatively, if one specific location is targeted, but others are not, then those other areas may become attractive for motivated offenders.

Many problem-oriented policing initiatives do not result in displacement. In fact, some produce positive spillover effects, a phenomenon known as "diffusion." Diffusion involves the reduction of crime (or similar benefits) in areas other than the one initially targeted. Many studies have shown evidence of diffusion, so it is important for evaluators to be aware that there can be additional benefits associated with problem-oriented policing programs. But they can be just as difficult to detect as displacement.

## Critical Thinking

1.  Why may displacement not occur?

2.  What are the ideal boundaries for detecting displacement?

3.  How exactly could displacement be measured?

Sources: Rob T. Guerette, *Analyzing Crime Displacement and Diffusion* (Washington, D.C.: Office of Community-Oriented Policing Services, Center for Problem-Oriented Policing, 2009); Robert Barr and Ken Pease, "Crime Placement, Displacement and Deflection," in *Crime and Justice: A Review of Research*, Vol. 12, ed. Michael Tonry and N. Morris (Chicago: University of Chicago Press, 1990); Rob T. Guerette and Kate J. Bowers, "Assessing the Extent of Crime Displacement and Diffusion of Benefits: A Review of Situational Crime Prevention Evaluations," *Criminology* 47 (2009): 7–18.

drug trafficking. In 1992, the National Criminal Intelligence Service (NCIS) was formed, mainly to deal with the problem of organized crime. One of its responsibilities is to work with the chemical industry in the UK to identify and disrupt the production of synthetic drugs.[95]

In contrast, American law enforcement agencies have, until recently, had little intelligence-gathering capacity. If it occurred at all, intelligence gathering was mostly reserved for large police agencies. According to David Carter, one of the leading experts on ILP, "Early law enforcement initiatives typically had no analysis and essentially consisted of dossiers kept on individuals who were suspicious or were deemed to be threats of some sort, often based on intuitive, rather than empirical, threat criteria."[96] Current ILP initiatives attempt to compensate for this shortcoming.

Intelligence-led policing bears a great deal of similarity to problem-oriented policing. The two are somewhat different, however. Problem-oriented policing puts problem identification and solution in the hands of individual street-level officers. In contrast, ILP emphasizes a top-down managerial approach by which administrators set priorities for crime prevention and enforcement and then pass these priorities down through the agency.[97] ILP is also similar to community policing in that it relies on residents as part of the intelligence-gathering process. But it is different, too, because whereas community policing emphasizes the desires of the community, intelligence-led policing relies on problem identification through careful analysis of the criminal environment as a whole. Intelligence-led policing has even been likened to CompStat, which is discussed earlier in this chapter. See Table 6.1 for a summary of the differences and commonalities between CompStat and intelligence-led policing.

### TABLE 6.1

#### Comparison of CompStat and Intelligence-Led Policing

| CompStat | Commonalities | Intelligence-Led Policing |
|---|---|---|
| Single jurisdiction | Both have a goal of prevention | Multiple jurisdictions |
| Incident-driven | Both require:<br>■ Organizational flexibility<br>■ Consistent information input<br>■ A significant analytic component | Threat-driven |
| Street crime and burglary | | Criminal enterprises and terrorism |
| Crime mapping | | Commodity flow; trafficking and transiting logistics |
| Time-sensitive (24-hour feedback and response) | | Strategic |
| Disrupt crime series (e.g., burglary ring) | | Disrupt enterprises |
| Drives operations:<br>■ Patrol<br>■ Tactical unit<br>■ Investigators | | Drives operations:<br>■ Joint terrorism task forces<br>■ Organized crime investigations<br>■ Task forces |
| Analysis of offender MO (modus operandi) | | Analysis of enterprise MO (modus operandi) |

Source: Office of Community-Oriented Policing Services, *Intelligence-Led Policing: The Integration of Community Policing and Law Enforcement Intelligence, Part 4* (Washington, D.C.: COPS Office, n.d.), p. 43. Available at www.cops.usdoj.gov/pdf/e09042536_Chapter_04.pdf (accessed April 9, 2010).

To gain a more concrete grasp the concept of intelligence-led policing, consider these examples:

■ A county sheriff's office identifies narcotics control as its top priority and develops strategies accordingly. The office targets known offenders and groups, shuts down open-air drug markets and crackhouses, and participates in school-based drug awareness programs to help prevent drug use.

■ A statewide agency identifies vehicle insurance fraud as a top area for enforcement. The agency targets those involved in staged accidents, identifies communities in which insurance fraud is prevalent, [exposes] ongoing fraudulent activity, and mounts a public education campaign.

■ A police agency in a small city makes safe streets a priority. The agency focuses on directed enforcement in identified hot spots. It also targets career criminals whose apprehension will significantly reduce the number of crimes being committed. Preventive measures include enhanced patrols, improved street lighting, and crime watch programs.[98]

## Intelligence and the Intelligence Process

Because intelligence-led policing emphasizes policing based on intelligence, it is only fitting that we devote more attention to the concept of intelligence. Basically, there are two types of intelligence. **Tactical intelligence** "includes gaining or developing information related to threats of terrorism or crime and using this information to apprehend offenders, harden targets, and use strategies that will eliminate or mitigate the threat."[99] It consists of information that can be used immediately. An example of tactical intelligence is knowing that a wanted fugitive is at a particular location. This is information that can be used immediately for the purpose of making an arrest. **Strategic intelligence** provides information to decision makers about the changing nature of certain problems and threats for the purpose of "developing response strategies and reallocating resources."[100] It is more general and is used to direct operations. An example of strategic intelligence is awareness that a particular gang traffics in a particular type of drug. With this information, pressure can be brought to bear on the gang as a whole, even though law enforcement officials may not have the tactical intelligence necessary to make an arrest.

Intelligence gathering follows a six-step process (see Figure 6.3). The first step, planning and direction, involves deciding what it is that officials want to know and what data to collect to that end. The next step, collection, consists of gathering the data that will be used for making decisions. Step three, processing and collation, involves evaluating the reliability and validity of the data collected. Officials need to sift through the data and decide what information will be useful. Fourth comes analysis. This includes crime analysis (such as detecting patterns of certain types of crimes) and investigative analysis (such as examining bank records). The fifth step, dissemination, involves getting the information to the decision makers who need it. Finally, reevaluation entails getting feedback on the products generated by the intelligence function. Note that the process is cyclical and continues on indefinitely. Figure 6.3 emphasizes that intelligence is fluid and constantly subject to change.

**tactical intelligence**
Gaining or developing information related to threats of terrorism or crime and using this information to apprehend offenders, harden targets, and use strategies that will eliminate or mitigate the threat.

**strategic intelligence**
Information about the changing nature of certain problems and threats for the purpose of developing response strategies and reallocating resources.

**FIGURE 6.3**
The Intelligence Process

Source: Office of Justice Programs, *National Criminal Intelligence Sharing Plan* (Washington, D.C.: U.S. Department of Justice, 2003), p. 6.

# FUSION CENTERS

In the spring of 2002, law enforcement executives from around the country met at a Criminal Intelligence Sharing Summit. Summit participants called for the development of a national intelligence plan, one that could be used to prevent future terrorist attacks like the ones that occurred on 9/11. After this meeting, the Global Justice Information Sharing Initiative and the Intelligence Working Group were formed. These groups eventually developed the **National Criminal Intelligence Sharing Plan (NCISP)**.[101] The report outlined a number of "action steps" that could be taken to improve intelligence gathering and sharing among law enforcement agencies across the country. The NCISP sought to communicate

- A model intelligence-sharing plan
- A mechanism to promote intelligence-led policing
- A blueprint for law enforcement administrators to follow when enhancing or building an intelligence system
- A model for intelligence process principles and policies
- A plan that respects and protects individuals' privacy and civil rights
- A technology architecture to provide secure, seamless sharing of information among systems
- A national model for intelligence training
- An outreach plan to promote timely and credible intelligence sharing
- A plan that leverages existing systems and networks, yet allows flexibility for technology and process enhancements

As part of this process, many states and large cities have formed **fusion centers**. What is a fusion center? According to the National Fusion Center Guidelines, it is "an effective and efficient mechanism to exchange information and intelligence, maximize resources, streamline operations, and improve the ability to fight crime and terrorism by analyzing data from a variety of sources."[102] Often located in police departments, these centers are set up for the purpose of sharing information and intelligence within specific jurisdictions and across levels of government. Fusion centers often emphasize terrorism prevention and crime fighting with extensive use of technology. They frequently resemble a department's technological "nerve center" and are usually housed in a central location where information is collected and then shared with decision makers. There are four main goals for fusion centers:

- Provide support for a range of law enforcement activities, including anti-crime operations and terrorism prevention.
- Provide help for major incident operations and support for units charged with interdiction and criminal investigations
- Provide the means for community input, often through "tip lines."
- Provide assistance to law enforcement executives so they can make informed decisions about departmental priorities.[103]

Fusion centers are intended to provide a mechanism through which government agencies, law enforcement, and the private sector can work together for the common purpose of protecting the homeland and preserving public safety. They are based on a model of collaboration. Collaboration between agencies and across levels of government has been lacking throughout history, but the events of 9/11 affirmed a need for change. The concept of fusion centers will continue to catch on, and more will probably be developed as law enforcement becomes increasingly aware of the benefits they can yield.

**National Criminal Intelligence Sharing Plan (NCISP)**
A formal intelligence-sharing initiative that identifies the security and intelligence-sharing needs recognized in the wake of the 9/11 terrorist attacks.

**fusion center**
A mechanism to exchange information and intelligence, maximize resources, streamline operations, and improve the ability to fight crime and terrorism by analyzing data from a variety of sources.

# POLICE SUPPORT FUNCTIONS

As the model of a typical police department indicates (see Figure 6.1 near the beginning of the chapter), not all members of a department engage in what the general public regards as real police work—patrol, detection, and traffic control. Even in departments that are embracing community and problem-oriented policing, a great deal of police resources are devoted to support and administrative functions.

Many police departments maintain their own personnel service, which carries out such functions as recruiting new police officers, creating exams to determine the most qualified applicants, and handling promotions and transfers. Innovative selection techniques are constantly being developed and tested. For example, the Behavioral-Personnel Assessment Device (B-PAD) requires police applicants to view videotaped scenarios and respond as though they were officers handling the situation. Reviews indicate that this procedure may be a reliable and unbiased method of choosing new recruits.[104]

Larger police departments often maintain an internal affairs branch, which is charged with policing the police. The **internal affairs** division processes citizen complaints of police corruption, investigates allegations of unnecessary use of force by police officers, and even probes allegations of police participation in criminal activity, such as burglaries or narcotics violations. In addition, the internal affairs division may assist police managers when disciplinary action is brought against individual officers. Internal affairs is a controversial function because investigators are feared and distrusted by fellow police officers. Nonetheless, rigorous self-scrutiny is the only way that police departments can earn citizens' respect. Some type of citizen oversight of police practices and civilian review boards with the power to listen to complaints and conduct investigations have become commonplace in police departments.

Most police departments are responsible for the administration and control of their own budgets. This task includes administering payroll, purchasing equipment and services, planning budgets for future expenditures, and auditing departmental financial records.

Police departments maintain separate units charged with recording and disseminating information on wanted offenders, stolen merchandise, traffic violators, and so on. Modern data-management systems enable police to use their records in a highly sophisticated way. For example, officers in a patrol car who spot a suspicious-looking vehicle can instantly receive a computerized rundown on whether it has been stolen. And when property is recovered during an arrest, police using this sort of system can determine who reported the loss of the merchandise and arrange for its return.

Another important function of police communication is the effective and efficient dispatching of patrol cars. Again, modern computer technologies have been used to make the most of available resources.[105]

In many departments, training is continuous throughout an officer's career. Training usually begins at a police academy, which may be run exclusively for larger departments or be part of a regional training center that services smaller and varied governmental units. More than 90 percent of all police departments require preservice training, including nearly all departments in larger cities (population over 100,000). The average officer receives more than 600 hours of preservice training, including 400 hours in the classroom and the rest in field training. Police in large cities receive more than 1,000 hours of instruction divided almost evenly between classroom and field instruction.[106] Among the topics usually covered are law and civil rights, firearms handling, emergency medical care, and restraint techniques.[107]

After assuming their police duties, new recruits are assigned to field-training officers who "break them in" on the job. However, training does not stop here.

**internal affairs**
The police unit that investigates allegations of police misconduct.

On-the-job training is a continuous process in the modern police department and covers such areas as weapons skills, first aid, crowd control, and community relations. Some departments use roll-call training, in which superior officers or outside experts address police officers at the beginning of the workday. Other departments allow police officers time off to attend annual training sessions to sharpen their skills and learn new policing techniques.

Police departments provide emergency aid to the ill, counsel youngsters, speak to school and community agencies on safety and drug abuse, and provide countless other services designed to improve citizen–police interactions.

Larger police departments maintain specialized units that help citizens protect themselves from criminal activity. For example, they advise citizens on effective home security techniques or conduct Project ID campaigns—engraving valuables with an identifying number so that they can be returned if recovered after a burglary. Police also work in schools, some by patrolling them and others by teaching youths how to avoid drug use.[108]

Police agencies maintain (or have access to) forensic laboratories that enable them to identify substances to be used as evidence and to classify fingerprints.

Planning and research functions include designing programs to increase police efficiency and strategies to test program effectiveness. Police planners monitor recent technological developments and institute programs to adapt them to police services. Many small agencies do not have the luxury of extensive support divisions. The larger the agency, the more likely there will be several distinct support divisions and functions.

# IMPROVING POLICE PRODUCTIVITY

Police administrators have sought to increase the productivity of their line, support, and administrative staff. As used today, the term **police productivity** refers to the amount of order, maintenance, crime control, and other law enforcement activities provided by individual police officers and concomitantly by police departments as a whole. By improving police productivity, a department can keep the peace, deter crime, apprehend criminals, and provide useful public services without necessarily increasing its costs. This goal is accomplished by having each police officer operate with greater efficiency, thus using fewer resources to achieve greater effectiveness.

Police departments are experimenting with cost-saving reforms that maximize effectiveness while saving taxpayer dollars. David Hirschel and Charles Dean describe how a program to summon offenders to court via a field citation is considerably cheaper than a formal arrest. Factoring in the cost of rearresting offenders who fail to appear in court, a citation program would save about $72 per case. Considering the millions of arrests made each year, the adoption of a citation policy could produce considerable savings, not to mention the positive effects on the overcrowded jail system.[109] Other cost-saving productivity measures include consolidation, informal arrangements, sharing, pooling, contracting, police service districts, using civilian employees, multiple tasking, special assignment programs, and differential police responses.[110]

■ *Consolidation.* One way to increase police efficiency is to consolidate police services.[111] This means combining small departments (usually with fewer than ten employees) in adjoining areas into a superagency that serves the previously fragmented jurisdictions. Consolidation has the benefit of creating departments large enough to use expanded services (such as crime labs, training centers, communications centers, and emergency units) that are not cost-effective in smaller departments. This procedure is controversial because it demands that existing lines of political and administrative authority be drastically changed.

**police productivity**
The amount of order maintenance, crime control, and other law enforcement activities provided by individual police officers and concomitantly by police departments as a whole.

■ *Informal arrangements.* Unwritten cooperative agreements may be made between localities to perform collectively a task that would be mutually beneficial (such as monitoring neighboring radio frequencies so that needed backup can be provided).

■ *Sharing.* The provision or receiving of services that aid in the execution of a law enforcement function can be shared (such as the sharing of a communications system by several local agencies). Some agencies form mutual-aid pacts so that they can share infrequently used emergency services such as emergency response teams.[112] Some states have gone as far as setting up centralized data services that connect most local police agencies into a statewide information net.[113] Information sharing is becoming increasingly popular.

■ *Pooling.* Some police agencies combine the resources of two or more agencies to perform a specified function under a predetermined, often formalized arrangement with direct involvement by all parties. One example is the use of a city–county law enforcement building or training academy; another is the establishment of a crime task force.

■ *Contracting.* Another productivity measure is a limited and voluntary approach in which one government enters into a formal binding agreement to provide all or certain specified law enforcement services (such as communications or patrol service) to another government for an established fee. Many communities that contract for full law enforcement service do so at the time they incorporate to avoid the costs of establishing their own police capability. This often occurs in small cities located within a county that has a large established law enforcement agency. It is often cost-prohibitive for a small city to have its own full-service police agency, so contracting with a sheriff's department, for example, can be helpful.

■ *Service districts.* Some jurisdictions have set aside areas, usually within an individual county, where a special level of service is provided and financed through a special tax or assessment. In California, residents of an unincorporated portion of a county may petition to form such a district to provide more intensive patrol coverage than is available through existing systems. Such service may be provided by a sheriff, another police department, or a private person or agency.

■ *Civilian employees.* One common cost-saving method is to use civilians in administrative support or even in some line activities. Civilians' duties have included operating communications gear; performing clerical work, planning, and doing research; and staffing traffic control (meter monitors). Using civilian employees can be a real savings to taxpayers, because civilian salaries are considerably lower than those of regular police officers. In addition, trained, experienced officers are then able to spend more time on direct crime control and enforcement activities.

■ *Multiple tasking.* Some police officers are trained to carry out other functions of municipal government. For example, in a number of smaller departments, the roles of firefighters and police officers have been merged into a job called a public safety officer. The idea is to increase the number of people trained in both areas in order to be able to put more police at the scene of a crime, or more firefighters at a blaze, than was possible when the two tasks were separated. The system provides greater coverage at far less cost.

■ *Special assignments.* Some departments train officers for special assignments that are required only occasionally, such as radar operation, crowd control, and security.

■ *Differential police responses.* These strategies maximize resources by differentiating among police requests for services in terms of the form that the police response takes. Some calls will result in the dispatching of a sworn officer, others in the dispatching of a less highly trained civilian. Calls considered low in priority are handled by asking citizens to walk in or to mail in their requests.[114]

In sum, police departments are now implementing a variety of administrative models designed to stretch resources while still providing effective police services.

## Ethical Challenges in Criminal Justice: A Writing Assignment

You are chief of the Middle City Police Department. Your city has seen a surge in violent crime in a popular downtown tourist area. Having learned of the value of "broken windows" policing, you have ordered the officers patrolling the area to be on the lookout for low-level offenses in hopes that cleaning up the streets will send a message that serious crime won't be tolerated. Two weeks later, you begin to hear complaints from some residents that patrol officers are harassing them. They argue that officers target even the most minor infractions, making it very unpleasant for people who frequent the area. Now the mayor is pressuring you to adopt a different strategy. You are aware of broken windows success stories in surrounding cities, and you are also aware of the research on its effectiveness, but you are increasingly being called upon to defend your actions.

Write an essay on the ethics of broken windows policing. In doing so, answer these questions: Should minor offenses be prioritized over more serious crimes? What are the possible drawbacks of this approach? What points would you raise to defend broken windows policing? If you opt to abandon the broken windows strategy, what other approaches might you take to make policing in your city more effective? What ethical dilemmas, if any, do those strategies pose? For help and further insights into these issues, refer to the "Improving Patrol" section earlier in this chapter.

## SUMMARY

1. **Understand the organization of police departments.**

   ■ Today's police departments operate in a military-like fashion.

   ■ Policy generally emanates from the top of the hierarchy.

2. **Recognize the problems associated with the time-in-rank system.**

   ■ The time-in-rank system requires that before moving up the administrative ladder, an officer must spend a certain amount of time in the next lowest rank.

   ■ The time-in-rank system prohibits departments from allowing officers to skip ranks and sometimes prevents them from hiring an officer from another department and awarding her a higher rank.

3. **Distinguish between the patrol function and the investigation function.**

   ■ Patrol officers are the most highly visible components of the entire criminal justice system.

Patrol officers are charged with supervising specific areas of their jurisdiction, called beats.

   ■ Investigative work is less visible. Detectives often wear plain clothes. Investigators work closely with patrol officers to provide an immediate investigative response to crimes and incidents.

4. **Describe the purposes of patrol.**

   ■ The purposes of patrol include deterring crime by maintaining a visible police presence, maintaining public order (peacekeeping) within the patrol area, enabling the police department to respond quickly to law violations or other emergencies, identifying and apprehending law violators, aiding individuals and caring for those who cannot help themselves, facilitating the movement of traffic and people, and creating a feeling of security in the community.

5. **Discuss various efforts to improve patrol.**

   ■ Police departments have taken several steps to improve patrol, including aggressive patrol, proactive policing, targeting specific crimes, adopting a broken windows policing strategy, prioritizing certain types of arrests, responding to 911 calls quickly, paying attention to procedural justice, and using technology.

■ Some efforts to improve patrol have proved more effective than others. For example, it may be more effective to target specific types of crimes than to be concerned solely with rapid response.

### 6. Discuss key issues associated with the investigative function.

■ Contemporary detectives typically use a three-pronged approach. This consists of specific, general, and informative (data collection) elements.

■ Sting operations occur when organized groups of detectives deceive criminals into openly committing illegal acts or conspiring to engage in criminal activity.

■ Detectives frequently work undercover. Undercover work is considered a necessary element of police work, although it can be dangerous for the agent.

### 7. Understand the concept of community policing.

■ Community policing consists of a return to an earlier style of policing, in which officers on the beat had intimate contact with the people they served.

■ Community policing gives officers the time to meet with local residents to talk about crime in the neighborhood and to use personal initiative to solve problems.

### 8. List several challenges associated with community policing.

■ Implementing community policing can be challenging because of difficulties in defining community, choosing appropriate roles for officers, changing supervisor attitudes, reorienting police values, revising training, and recruiting different types of officers.

■ One of the most significant obstacles associated with community policing is reaching out to citizens.

### 9. Discuss the concept of problem-oriented policing.

■ Problem-oriented policing strategies require police agencies to identify particular long-term community problems and to develop strategies to eliminate them.

■ Concentrating police resources on so-called hot spots of crime could appreciably reduce crime.

### 10. Explain intelligence-led policing (ILP) and its relationship to community- and problem-oriented policing.

■ ILP consists of the collection and analysis of information to produce an "intelligence end product" designed to inform police decision making at both the tactical and strategic levels.

■ ILP emphasizes problem solving, but from the top down. It relies on community input, but priorities are set at the department level, not identified by residents.

### 11. Explain the various police support functions.

■ Other organizations or divisions that support patrol, investigations, and traffic include personnel, internal affairs, administration, records, dispatch, training, planning, and research.

■ The larger the police department, the more extensive its support divisions.

### 12. Identify some of the cost-saving measures that may be employed to improve police productivity.

■ Police departments have sought to improve their productivity by consolidating, adopting informal arrangements, sharing, pooling, contracting, assigning service districts, hiring civilians, multiple tasking, using special assignments, and trying differential response.

## KEY TERMS

time-in-rank system, 204
beats, 207
order maintenance (peacekeeping), 209
proactive policing, 211
broken windows model, 212
procedural justice, 213
vice squads, 216
sting operation, 218

community-oriented policing (COP), 223
foot patrol, 224
problem-oriented policing (POP), 225
hot spots of crime, 226
gang tactical detail, 226
displacement, 227
intelligence-led policing (ILP), 227

tactical intelligence, 230
strategic intelligence, 230
National Criminal Intelligence Sharing Plan (NCISP), 231
fusion center, 231
internal affairs, 232
police productivity, 233

## CRITICAL THINKING QUESTIONS

1. Should the primary police role be law enforcement or community service? Explain.

2. Should a police chief be permitted to promote an officer with special skills to a supervisory position, or should all officers be forced to spend time in rank? Why or why not?

3. Do the advantages of proactive policing outweigh the disadvantages? Explain.

4. Can the police and the community ever form a partnership to fight crime? Why or why not? Does the community policing model remind you of early forms of policing? Explain.

5. What is the relationship among community policing, problem-oriented policing, and intelligence-led policing? Are they similar or fundamentally different?

## NOTES

1. Jeff Horseman, "Temecula to Plug Budget Gap with Overtime Limits," *The Press-Enterprise*, February 23, 2010 (A4).

2. Carrie Johnson, "Double Blow for Police: Less Cash, More Crime," *Washington Post*, February 28, 2009. Available at www.washingtonpost.com/wp-dyn/content/article/2009/02/07/AR2009020701157.html (accessed April 8, 2010).

3. Caitlin Devitt, "Toledo Passes FY 2010 Budget That Unilaterally Amends Police Contract," *The Regions*, April 1, 2010 (Vol. 371, p. 24).

4. Matthew Durose, Erica Schmitt, and Patrick Langan, *Contacts between Police and the Public: Findings from the 2002 National Survey* (Washington, D.C.: Bureau of Justice Statistics, 2005).

5. FBI, "Uniform Crime Reports," www.fbi.gov/ucr/cius2007/arrests/index.html (accessed April 6, 2010).

6. Brian Reaves and Pheny Smith, *Law Enforcement Management and Administrative Statistics, 1993: Data for Individual State and Local Agencies with 100 or More Officers* (Washington, D.C.: Bureau of Justice Statistics, 1995).

7. American Bar Association, *Standards Relating to Urban Police Function* (New York: Institute of Judicial Administration, 1974), Standard 2.2.

8. James Hawdon and John Ryan, "Police–Resident Interactions and Satisfaction with Police: An Empirical Test of Community Policing Assertions," *Criminal Justice Policy Review* 14 (2003): 55–74.

9. Albert J. Reiss, *The Police and the Public* (New Haven, Conn.: Yale University Press, 1971), p. 19.

10. James Q. Wilson, *Varieties of Police Behavior: The Management of Law and Order in Eight Communities* (Cambridge, Mass.: Harvard University Press, 1968).

11. See Harlan Hahn, "A Profile of Urban Police," in *The Ambivalent Force*, ed. A. Niederhoffer and A. Blumberg (Hinsdale, Ill.: Dryden, 1976), p. 59.

12. James Q. Wilson and Barbara Boland, "The Effect of Police on Crime," *Law and Society Review* 12 (1978): 367–384.

13. Alexander Weiss and Sally Freels, "The Effects of Aggressive Policing: The Dayton Traffic Enforcement Experiment," *American Journal of Police* 15 (1996): 45–64.

14. Jennifer B. Robinson, "Measuring the Impact of a Targeted Law Enforcement Initiative on Drug Sales," *Journal of Criminal Justice* 36 (2008): 90–101.

15. Lawrence Sherman, James Shaw, and Dennis Rogan, *The Kansas City Gun Experiment* (Washington, D.C.: National Institute of Justice, 1994).

16. George Kelling and James Q. Wilson, "Broken Windows: The Police and Neighborhood Safety," *Atlantic Monthly* 249 (March 1982): 29–38.

17. Ibid.

18. Robert Panzarella, "Bratton Reinvents Harassment Model of Policing," *Law Enforcement News* 24 (1998): 14–15.

19. Eli Silverman, *NYPD Battles Crime: Innovative Strategies in Policing* (Boston: Northeastern University Press, 1999).

20. Barbara Brown, Douglas D. Perkins, and Graham Brown, "Crime, New Housing, and Housing Incivilities in a First-Ring Suburb: Multilevel Relationships across Time," *Housing Policy Debate* 15 (2004): 301–345.

21. Richard Rosenfeld, Robert Fornango, and Andres F. Rengifo, "The Impact of Order-Maintenance Policing on New York City Homicide and Robbery Rates: 1988–2001," *Criminology* 45 (2007): 355–384; Steven F. Messner, Sandro Galea, Kenneth J. Tardiff, and Melissa Tracy, "Policing, Drugs, and the Homicide Decline in New York City in the 1990s," *Criminology* 45 (2007): 385–414.

22. Mitchell Chamlin, "Crime and Arrests: An Autoregressive Integrated Moving Average (ARIMA) Approach," *Journal of Quantitative Criminology* 4 (1988): 247–255.

23. Perry Shapiro and Harold Votey, "Deterrence and Subjective Probabilities of Arrest: Modeling Individual Decisions to Drink and Drive in Sweden," *Law and Society Review* 18 (1984): 111–149.

24. Stewart D'Alessio and Lisa Stolzenberg, "Crime, Arrests, and Pretrial Jail Incarceration: An Examination of the Deterrence Thesis," *Criminology* 36 (1998): 735–761.

25. Lawrence W. Sherman, "Policing for Crime Prevention," in *Preventing Crime: What Works, What Doesn't, What's Promising*, ed. Lawrence W. Sherman, Denise C. Gottfredson, Doris L. MacKenzie, John Eck, Peter Reuter, and Shawn W. Bushway (Washington, D.C.: National Institute of Justice, 1998), Chapter 8.

26. John L. Worrall, *Crime Control in America: What Works?*, 2nd ed. (Boston: Allyn and Bacon, 2008), pp. 53–54.

27. Tom Tyler and Jeffrey Fagan, "Legitimacy and Cooperation: Why Do People Help the Police Fight Crime in Their Communities?" *Public Law and Legal Theory Working Paper Group* (Paper Number 06-99) (New York: Columbia Law School).

28. Mike D. Reisig, "Procedural Justice and Community Policing: What Shapes Residents' Willingness to Participate in Crime Prevention Programs?" *Policing: A Journal of Policy and Practice* 1 (2007): 359–369.

29. Robert Davis, Pedro Mateu-Gelabert, and Joel Miller, "Can Effective Policing Also Be Respectful? Two Examples in the South Bronx," *Police Quarterly* 8 (2005): 229–247.

30. Tom Tyler, "Procedural Justice, Legitimacy, and the Effective Rule of Law," in *Crime and Justice: A Review of Research*, ed. M. H. Tonry (Chicago: University of Chicago Press, 2003), pp. 283–357.

31. Jacinta M. Gau and Rod K. Brunson, "Procedural Justice and Order Maintenance Policing: A Study of Inner-City Young Men's Perceptions of Police Legitimacy," *Justice Quarterly* 27 (2010): 255–279; Patrick J. Carr, Laura Napolitano, and Jessica Keating, "We Never Call the Cops and Here Is Why: A Qualitative Examination of Legal Cynicism in Three Philadelphia Neighborhoods," *Criminology* 45 (2007): 445–480.

32. William Bratton, *Turnaround: How America's Top Cop Reversed the Crime Epidemic* (New York: Random House, 1998).

33. James J. Willis, Stephen D. Mastrofski, and David Weisburd, "CompStat and Bureaucracy: A Case Study of Challenges and Opportunities for Change," *Justice Quarterly* 21 (2004): 463–496.

34. See Belton Cobb, *The First Detectives* (London: Faber and Faber, 1957).

35. See, for example, James Q. Wilson, "Movie Cops—Romantic vs. Real," *New York Magazine* (August 19, 1968): 38–41.

36. For a view of the modern detective, see William Sanders, *Detective Work: A Study of Criminal Investigations* (New York: Free Press, 1977).

37. Mark Pogrebin and Eric Poole, "Vice Isn't Nice: A Look at the Effects of Working Undercover," *Journal of Criminal Justice* 21 (1993): 385–396; Gary Marx, *Undercover: Police Surveillance in America* (Berkeley: University of California Press, 1988).

38. Martin Innes, *Investigating Murder: Detective Work and the Police Response to Criminal Homicide* (Clarendon Studies in Criminology) (London: Oxford University Press, 2003).

39. John B. Edwards, "Homicide Investigative Strategies," *FBI Law Enforcement Bulletin* 74 (2005): 11–21.

40. Graeme R. Newman, *Sting Operations* (Washington, D.C.: Center for Problem-Oriented Policing, 2007).

41. Robert Langworthy, "Do Stings Control Crime? An Evaluation of a Police Fencing Operation," *Justice Quarterly* 6 (1989): 27–45.

42. Mary Dodge, Donna Starr-Gimeno, and Thomas Williams, "Puttin' on the Sting: Women Police Officers' Perspectives on Reverse Prostitution Assignments," *Policing: An International Journal of Police Strategies and Management* 7 (2005): 71–85.

43. Pogrebin and Poole, "Vice Isn't Nice"; Marx, *Undercover.*

44. Peter Greenwood and Joan Petersilia, *The Criminal Investigation Process: Summary and Policy Implications*, ed. Peter Greenwood et al. (Santa Monica, Calif.: RAND Corporation, 1975).

45. Mark Willman and John Snortum, "Detective Work: The Criminal Investigation Process in a Medium-Size Police Department," *Criminal Justice Review* 9 (1984): 33–39.

46. Police Executive Research Forum, *Calling the Police: Citizen Reporting of Serious Crime* (Washington, D.C.: Police Executive Research Forum, 1981).

47. John Eck, *Solving Crimes: The Investigation of Burglary and Robbery* (Washington, D.C.: Police Executive Research Forum, 1984).

48. A. Fischer, "Coplink Nabs Criminals Faster," *Arizona Daily Star*, January 7, 2001, p. 1; Alexandra Robbins, "A. I. Cop on the Beat," *PC Magazine*, 22 (2002); M. Sink, "An Electronic Cop That Plays Hunches," *New York Times*, November 2, 2002, p. B1; also see www.coplink.com (accessed April 6, 2010).

49. Albert Cardarelli, Jack McDevitt, and Katrina Baum, "The Rhetoric and Reality of Community Policing in Small and Medium-Sized Cities and Towns," *Policing* 21 (1998): 397–415.

50. Nadine M. Connell, Kristen Miggans, and Jean Marie McGloin, "Can a Community Policing Initiative Reduce Serious Crime?" *Police Quarterly* 11 (2008): 127–150.

51. For a general review, see Robert Trojanowicz and Bonnie Bucqueroux, *Community Policing: A Contemporary Perspective* (Cincinnati, Ohio: Anderson, 1990).

52. Police Foundation, *The Newark Foot Patrol Experiment* (Washington, D.C.: Police Foundation, 1981).

53. John Worrall and Jihong Zhao, "The Role of the COPS Office in Community Policing," *Policing* 26 (2003): 64–87.

54. Office of Community-Oriented Policing Services, www.cops.usdoj.gov/ (accessed April 6, 2010).

55. Jihong Zhao, Nicholas Lovrich, and Quint Thurman, "The Status of Community Policing in American Cities," *Policing* 22 (1999): 74–92.

56. Jack R. Greene, "The Effects of Community Policing on American Law Enforcement: A Look at the Evidence." Paper presented at the International Congress on Criminology, Hamburg, Germany, September 1988, p. 19.

57. Roger Dunham and Geoffrey Alpert, "Neighborhood Differences in Attitudes toward Policing: Evidence for a Mixed-Strategy Model of Policing in a Multi-Ethnic Setting," *Journal of Criminal Law and Criminology* 79 (1988): 504–522.

58. Scott Lewis, Helen Rosenberg, and Robert Sigler, "Acceptance of Community Policing among Police Officers and Police Administrators," *Policing* 22 (1999): 567–588.

59. Robin Shepard Engel, *How Police Supervisory Styles Influence Patrol Officer Behavior* (Washington, D.C.: National Institute of Justice, 2003).

60. Amy Halsted, Max Bromley, and John Cochran, "The Effects of Work Orientations on Job Satisfaction among Sheriffs' Deputies Practicing Community-Oriented Policing," *Policing* 23 (2000): 82–104

61. Venessa Garcia, "Constructing the 'Other' within Police Culture: An Analysis of a Deviant Unit within the Police Organization," *Police Practice and Research* 6 (2005): 65–80.

62. Allison T. Chappell, "Community Policing: Is Field Training the Missing Link?" *Policing* 30 (2007): 498–517.

63. Michael Palmiotto, Michael Birzer, and N. Prabha Unnithan, "Training in Community Policing: A Suggested Curriculum," *Policing* 23 (2000): 8–21.

64. Lisa Riechers and Roy Roberg, "Community Policing: A Critical Review of Underlying Assumptions," *Journal of Police Science and Administration* 17 (1990): 112–113.

65. John Riley, "Community-Policing: Utilizing the Knowledge of Organizational Personnel," *Policing* 22 (1999): 618–633.

66. Donald Green, Dara Strolovitch, and Janelle Wong, "Defended Neighborhoods: Integration and Racially Motivated Crime," *American Journal of Sociology* 104 (1998): 372–403.

67. David Kessler, "Integrating Calls for Service with Community- and Problem-Oriented Policing: A Case Study," *Crime and Delinquency* 39 (1993): 485–508.

68. L. Thomas Winfree, Gregory Bartku, and George Seibel, "Support for Community Policing versus Traditional Policing among Nonmetropolitan Police Officers: A Survey of Four New Mexico Police Departments," *American Journal of Police* 15 (1996): 23–47.

69. Jihong Zhao, Ni He, and Nicholas Lovrich, "Value Change among Police Officers at a Time of Organizational Reform: A Follow-Up Study of Rokeach Values," *Policing* 22 (1999): 152–170.

70. Jihong Zhao, Matthew Scheider, and Quint Thurman, "A National Evaluation of the Effect of COPs Grants on Police Productivity (Arrests) 1995–1999," *Police Quarterly* 6 (2003): 387–410.

71. Mike Brogden, "'Horses for Courses' and 'Thin Blue Lines': Community Policing in Transitional Society," *Police Quarterly* 8 (2005): 64–99.

72. Ling Ren, Liqun Cao, Nicholas Lovrich, and Michael Gaffney, "Linking Confidence in the Police with the Performance of the Police: Community Policing Can Make a Difference," *Journal of Criminal Justice* 33 (2005): 55–66.

73. Stephen M. Schnebly, "The Influence of Community-Oriented Policing on Crime-Reporting Behavior," *Justice Quarterly* 25 (2008): 223–251.

74. Walter Baranyk, "Making a Difference in a Public Housing Project," *Police Chief* 61 (1994): 31–35.

75. Herman Goldstein, "Improving Policing: A Problem-Oriented Approach," *Crime and Delinquency* 25 (1979): 236–258.

76. Jerome Skolnick and David Bayley, *Community Policing: Issues and Practices Around the World* (Washington, D.C.: National Institute of Justice, 1988), p. 12.

77. Lawrence Sherman, Patrick Gartin, and Michael Buerger, "Hot Spots of Predatory Crime: Routine Activities and the Criminology of Place," *Criminology* 27 (1989): 27–55.

78. Ibid., p. 45.

79. Dennis Roncek and Pamela Maier, "Bars, Blocks, and Crimes Revisited: Linking the Theory of Routine Activities to the Empiricism of 'Hot Spots,'" *Criminology* 29 (1991): 725–753.

80. David Weisburd, Cody W. Telep, Joshua C. Hinkle, and John E. Eck, "Is Problem-Oriented Policing Effective in Reducing Crime and Disorder? Findings from a Campbell Systematic Review," *Criminology and Public Policy* 9 (2010): 139–172.

81. Center for Problem-Oriented Policing, www.popcenter.org (accessed April 6, 2010).

82. C. Jewett, "Police Use Bait Cars to Reduce Theft," *Knight Ridder/ Tribune Business News*, March 3, 2003, p. 1.

83. Michael White, James Fyfe, Suzanne Campbell, and John Goldkamp, "The Police Role in Preventing Homicide: Considering the Impact of Problem-Oriented Policing on the Prevalence of Murder," *Journal of Research in Crime and Delinquency* 40 (2003): 194–226.

84. Tucson Police Department, "Gang Tactical Detail," http:// tpdinternet.tucsonaz.gov/Organization/divisions/sid.html (accessed May 16, 2008).

85. Anthony Braga, David Kennedy, Elin Waring, and Anne Morrison Piehl, "Problem-Oriented Policing, Deterrence, and Youth Violence: An Evaluation of Boston's Operation Ceasefire," *Journal of Research in Crime and Delinquency* 38 (2001): 195–225.

86. Anthony Braga, David Weisburd, Elin Waring, Lorraine Green Mazerolle, William Spelman, and Francis Gajewski, "Problem-Oriented Policing in Violent Crime Places: A Randomized Controlled Experiment," *Criminology* 37 (1999): 541–580.

87. Anthony A. Braga, Glenn L. Pierce, Jack McDevitt, Brenda J. Bond, and Shea Cronin, "The Strategic Prevention of Gun Violence among Gang-Involved Offenders," *Justice Quarterly* 25 (2008): 132–162.

88. Bureau of Justice Assistance, *Problem-Oriented Drug Enforcement: A Community-Based Approach for Effective Policing* (Washington, D.C.: National Institute of Justice, 1993).

89. Ibid., pp. 64–65.

90. Brian A. Lawton, Ralph B. Taylor, and Anthony J. Luongo, "Police Officers on Drug Corners in Philadelphia, Drug Crime, and Violent Crime: Intended, Diffusion, and Displacement Impacts," *Justice Quarterly* 22 (2005): 427–451.

91. David L. Carter and Jeremy G. Carter, "Intelligence-Led Policing: Conceptual and Functional Considerations for Public Police," *Criminal Justice Policy Review* 20 (2009): 310–325, p. 310.

92. Global Intelligence Working Group, *National Criminal Intelligence Sharing Plan* (Washington, DC: Office of Justice Programs, 2003), p. 6.

93. Jerry Ratcliffe, *What Is Intelligence-Led Policing?* Available at www.jratcliffe.net/research/ilp.htm (accessed April 9, 2010).

94. Carter and Carter, p. 310.

95. National Criminal Intelligence Service, http://drugs.homeoffice.gov.uk/organisation-search/UK-and-National/ncise42d.html?version=1 (accessed April 9, 2010).

96. Carter and Carter, p. 312.

97. Ratcliffe.

98. Marilyn B. Peterson, "Toward a Model for Intelligence-Led Policing in the United States." In *Turnkey Intelligence: Unlocking Your Agency's Intelligence Capability* (Lawrenceville, NJ: International Association of Law Enforcement Intelligence Analysts, Law Enforcement Intelligence Unit, and National White Collar Crime Center, 2002), p. 5.

99. David L. Carter, *Law Enforcement Intelligence: A Guide for State, Local, and Tribal Law Enforcement Agencies* (Washington, D.C.: U.S. Department of Justice, 2004), p. 8.

100. Ibid.

101. *National Criminal Intelligence Sharing Plan.* Available at www.it.ojp.gov/documents/NCISP_Plan.pdf (accessed April 9, 2010).

102. *Fusion Center Guidelines: Developing and Sharing Information and Intelligence in a New Era.* Available at www.it.ojp.gov/documents/fusion_center_guidelines.pdf (accessed April 9, 2010).

103. Charles R. Swanson, Leonard Territo, and Robert W. Taylor, *Police Administration: Structures, Processes, and Behavior*, 7th ed. (Upper Saddle River, N.J.: Prentice Hall, 2008), pp. 77–78.

104. William Boerner and Terry Nowell, "The Reliability of the Behavioral Personnel Assessment Device (B-PAD) in Selecting Police Recruits," *Policing* 22 (1999): 343–352.

105. See, for example, Richard Larson, *Urban Police Patrol Analysis* (Cambridge, Mass.: MIT Press, 1972).

106. Brian Reaves, *State and Local Police Departments, 1990* (Washington, D.C.: Bureau of Justice Statistics, 1992), p. 6.

107. Philip Ash, Karen Slora, and Cynthia Britton, "Police Agency Officer Selection Practices," *Journal of Police Science and Administration* 17 (1990): 258–269.

108. Dennis Rosenbaum, Robert Flewelling, Susan Bailey, Chris Ringwalt, and Deanna Wilkinson, "Cops in the Classroom: A Longitudinal Evaluation of Drug Abuse Resistance Education (DARE)," *Journal of Research in Crime and Delinquency* 31 (1994): 3–31.

109. J. David Hirschel and Charles Dean, "The Relative Cost-Effectiveness of Citation and Arrest," *Journal of Criminal Justice* 23 (1995): 1–12.

110. Adapted from Terry Koepsell and Charles Gerard, *Small Police Agency Consolidation: Suggested Approaches* (Washington, D.C.: Government Printing Office, 1979).

111. International Association of Chiefs of Police, *Consolidating Police Services: An IACP Planning Approach* (Alexandria, Va.: International Association of Chiefs of Police, 2003).

112. Mike D'Alessandro and Charles Hoffman, "Mutual Aid Pacts," *Law and Order* 43 (1995): 90–93.

113. Leonard Sipes Jr., "Maryland's High-Tech Approach to Crime Fighting," *Police Chief* 61 (1994): 18–20.

114. Robert Worden, "Toward Equity and Efficiency in Law Enforcement: Differential Police Response," *American Journal of Police* 12 (1993): 1–24.

# CHAPTER 7

# Issues in Policing

## CHAPTER OBJECTIVES

1. Know the benefits likely to accrue from higher education for police.
2. Discuss some of the issues associated with minority police officers.
3. Describe how the role of women in local police agencies has evolved over time.
4. Explain the concept of a police culture.
5. Know the reasons why experts believe police have a unique personality.
6. Recognize the different types of police officer styles.
7. Understand the factors that influence police discretion.
8. Know the consequences of stress and fatigue.
9. Distinguish between brutality and corruption.
10. Know the difference between deadly and nondeadly force.
11. Know the leading types of less-lethal weapons.

**I**n Juarez, Mexico, right across the border from El Paso, Texas, more than 2,600 people were killed in 2009 as rival drug cartels fought among themselves and with Mexican government officials in an effort to protect lucrative drug trafficking routes. Unfortunately, there is evidence that some of the crime and violence once concentrated across the border has spread into the United States. In early 2010, prompted in part by the killing in Mexico of two U.S. citizens affiliated with the American consulate, Texas Senators Kay Bailey Hutchison and John Cornyn wrote to President Obama, asking for additional federal support at the border, arguing that "The spillover violence in Texas is real and it is escalating. Our border patrol agents and local law enforcement are more regularly engaged with gunmen associated with drug cartels, but our resources and personnel are limited."[1] At about the same time, Texas Governor Rick Perry activated a plan that increased surveillance of border activity with additional ground, air, and maritime patrols.[2] Local police agencies in Texas have also sought federal funding for improved enforcement in towns near the border.[3]

Conventional crimes keep America's law enforcement agencies busy, but the added burden of coping with spillover violence at the U.S.–Mexico border makes an already difficult job even tougher. Local police, along with federal officials, have to walk a fine line as they seek to improve conditions in the region. On the one hand, there is a need to enforce America's antidrug laws and block the supply of illicit substances. On the other hand, U.S. trade with Mexico exceeds $1 billion each day by some estimates, so any efforts to further curb border violence should be measured against a need to preserve legitimate trade; officials must be mindful of the possible public relations fallout that could result from aggressive enforcement.[4] ■

The police have always been put in a difficult spot when it comes to enforcing the law and, at the same time, maintaining a favorable public image. Many people feel the police should control and prevent crime, even if doing so requires a no-nonsense, heavy-handed approach. Yet the police do not work in a vacuum. There can be unanticipated consequences associated with their actions, especially if they adopt a "get tough" stance. The situation along the U.S.–Mexico border illustrates that there is a never-ending balancing act at work.

Fortunately, a great deal of progress has been made in improving the public's opinion of the police. Most citizens today seem to approve of their local law enforcement agents. About 55 percent say they have a "great deal of confidence" in the police.[5] Although this is encouraging, approval is often divided along racial lines.[6] It may not be surprising that minority citizens report having less confidence in the police compared with Caucasians and are less likely to report crime to police agencies.[7] To combat these perceptions, police departments have gone to great lengths to improve relationships with minorities, and these efforts have begun to pay off. Surveys show improvement in the African American community's view of the local police: Minority groups value police services, welcome the presence of both white and African American police officers, and are generally supportive of the local police.[8]

The general public is not the only group concerned about police attitudes and behavior. Police administrators and other law enforcement experts have focused their attention on issues that may influence the effectiveness and efficiency of police performance in the field. Some of their concerns are outgrowths of the development of policing as a profession: Does an independent police culture exist, and what are its characteristics? Do police officers develop a unique working personality, and if so, does it influence their job performance? Are there police officer styles that make some police officers too aggressive and others inert and passive? Is policing too stressful an occupation?

Important questions are also being raised about the problems that police departments face while interacting with the society they are entrusted with supervising: Are police officers too forceful and brutal, and do they discriminate in their use of deadly force? When officers need to use force, what options are available? Should they use their guns or consider alternatives such as Tasers or less-lethal weapons? If so, under what circumstances? Are police officers corrupt, and how can police deviance be controlled? There is evidence that police officers are all too often involved in marital disputes and even incidents of domestic violence, which may be linked to anxiety and strain.[9] Stress and burnout become part of the job.[10] This chapter focuses on these and other problems facing police officers in contemporary society. We begin with a discussion of the makeup of the police and the police profession.

## WHO ARE THE POLICE?

The composition of the nation's police forces is changing. Traditionally, police agencies were composed of white males with a high school education who viewed policing as a secure position that brought them the respect of family and friends and a step up the social ladder. It was not uncommon to see police families in which one member of each new generation would enter the force. This picture has been changing and will continue to change. As criminal justice programs turn out thousands of graduates every year, an increasing number of police officers have at least some college education. In addition, affirmative action programs have helped slowly change the racial and gender composition of police departments to reflect community makeup.

### Police and Education

In recent years, many police experts have argued that police recruits should have a college education. This development is not unexpected, considering that higher education for police officers has been recommended by national commissions since 1931.[11]

Although most law enforcement agencies still do not require recruits to have an advanced degree, the number requiring some higher education in the hiring and promotion process is growing. Today, nearly all (98%) local police departments have an education requirement for new officer recruits:

- About 18 percent of departments have some type of college requirement.

- About 9 percent require a two-year degree.

- About one-third of all officers work in departments that have some type of college requirement, more than three times as high a proportion as in 1990.[12]

- When asked, most departments express a preference for criminal justice majors, usually because of their enhanced knowledge of the entire criminal justice system and issues in policing.[13]

Another promising trend is that, although they do not require college credits for promotion, most police departments recognize that college education is an important element in promotion decisions. The United States is not alone in this regard; police departments around the world are now encouraging recruits and in-service officers to earn college credits.[14]

What are the benefits of higher education for police officers? Better communication with the public, especially minority and ethnic groups, is believed to be one benefit. Educated officers write better and more clearly and are more likely to be promoted. Police administrators believe that education enables officers to perform more effectively, generate fewer citizen complaints, show more initiative in performing police tasks, and generally behave more professionally.[15] In addition, educated officers are less likely to have disciplinary problems, are viewed as better decision makers,[16] and are less inclined to use force.[17] Research indicates that educated officers are more likely to rate themselves higher on most performance indicators, indicating that higher education is associated with greater self-confidence and assurance.[18]

Although education has its benefits, little conclusive evidence has been found that educated officers are more effective crime fighters.[19] The diversity of the police role, the need for split-second decision making, and the often boring and mundane tasks that police are required to do are all considered reasons why formal education may not improve performance on the street.[20] Nonetheless, because police administrators value educated officers, and citizens find them to be exceptional in the use of good judgment and problem solving, the trend toward a better-educated police force is likely to continue.[21]

## Minorities in Policing

For the past two decades, U.S. police departments have made a concerted effort to attract minority police officers, and there have been some impressive gains. As might be expected, cities with large minority populations have a higher proportion of minority officers in their police departments.[22]

The reasons for this effort are varied. Ideally, police departments recruit minority citizens to field a more balanced force that truly represents the communities they serve. African Americans generally have less confidence in the police than whites and are skeptical of their ability to protect citizens from harm.[23] African Americans also seem more likely to have been victimized when well-publicized incidents of police misconduct occur.[24] Therefore, it comes as no surprise that public opinion polls and research surveys show that African American citizens report having less confidence in the police than either Hispanics or Caucasians.[25] African American juveniles seem particularly suspicious of police, even when they deny having had negative encounters with them.[26] A heterogeneous police force can be instrumental in gaining the confidence of the minority community by helping dispel the view that police departments are generally bigoted or biased organizations. Furthermore, minority police officers possess special qualities that can serve to improve police performance. Spanish-speaking officers can help with investigations in Hispanic neighborhoods, and Asian American officers are essential for undercover or surveillance work with Asian gangs and drug importers.

**THE AFRICAN AMERICAN EXPERIENCE**   The earliest known date when an African American was hired as a police officer was 1861 in Washington, D.C.; Chicago hired its first African American officer in 1872.[27] At first, African American officers suffered a great deal of discrimination. Their work assignments were restricted, as were their chances for promotion. They were often assigned solely to the patrol of African American neighborhoods, and in some cities they were required to call a white officer to make an arrest. White officers held highly prejudicial attitudes, and as late as the 1950s some refused to ride with African Americans in patrol cars.[28]

The experience of African American police officers has not been an easy one. In his classic book *Black in Blue*, written almost 40 years ago, Nicholas Alex pointed out that African American officers of the time suffered from what he called **double marginality**.[29] On the one hand, African American officers had to deal with the expectation that they would give members of their own race a break. On the other hand, they often experienced overt racism from their police colleagues. Alex found that African American officers' adaptation to these pressures ranged from denying that African American suspects should be treated differently from whites to treating African American offenders more harshly than white offenders (to prove their lack of bias). Alex offered several reasons why some African American officers were tougher on African American offenders: They desired acceptance from their white colleagues, they were particularly sensitive to any disrespect shown them by African American teenagers, and they viewed themselves as protectors of the African American community. Ironically, minority citizens may be more likely to accuse a minority officer of misconduct than a white officer—a circumstance that underscores the difficult position of the minority officer in contemporary society.[30]

**double marginality**
According to Nicholas Alex, the social burden that African American police officers carry by being both minority group members and law enforcement officers.

**MINORITY REPRESENTATION TODAY**   Figure 7.1 illustrates the increasing diversity in America's police departments. Almost 25 percent of local police officers are African American, Hispanic, or other minority races.

**FIGURE 7.1**
Minority Representation on Local Police Departments

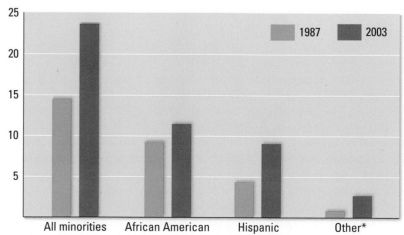

Percent of full-time sworn personnel

* Includes Asians, Pacific Islanders, American Indians, and Alaska Natives.
Source: Matthew Hickman and Brian Reaves, *Local Police Departments, 2003* (Washington D.C.: Bureau of Justice Statistics, 2006), p. iii.

The increased representation of minorities in police department ranks has fueled a number of changes. Minority police officers now seem more aggressive, more self-assured, and less willing to accept any discriminatory practices by the police department.[31] Researchers have found that they are more willing than white officers to use their authority to take official action. For example, the higher the percentage of black officers on the force, the higher the arrest rate for crimes such as assault.[32] Nor do black officers hesitate to use their arrest powers on African American suspects. Using observational data on police–citizen encounters in Cincinnati, Robert Brown and James Frank found that although white officers were more likely to arrest suspects than black officers were, black suspects were more likely to be arrested when the decision maker was a black officer.[33]

Yet as their numbers increase, minority officers appear to be experiencing some of the same problems and issues encountered by white officers.[34] They report feeling similar rates of job-related stress and strain, stemming from the same types of stressors, such as family conflict.[35] Minority officers do report more stress when they consider themselves "tokens," marginalized within the department.[36] They may also deal with stress in a somewhat different fashion: They are more likely to seek aid from fellow minority officers, whereas white officers are more likely to try to express their feelings to others, form social bonds, and try to get others to like them more.[37]

When affirmative action was first instituted, white police officers viewed it as a threat to their job security.[38] As more minorities have joined U.S. police forces, their situation seems to have changed. Caucasian officers are more likely to appreciate the contribution of minority officers. When Charles Katz examined the formation of a police gang unit in a midwestern city, he found that commanders chose minority officers so the unit could be representative of the community they served.[39] As one Hispanic officer told Katz, "When you talk to Hispanics, you have to know and be familiar with their culture. . . . [For example, you] always talk to the man of the house, never presenting your position to the kid or to the mother."[40] These benefits are not lost on citizens either, and research shows that the general public cares little about the racial or ethnic makeup of the police officers in their neighborhood and more about their effectiveness.[41]

Despite the many advances minority police officers have made, clear differences exist between white and, in particular, black police officers. A recent study by Peter Moskos, a professor at the John Jay College of New York, revealed that there are "two shades of blue."[42] That is, "[b]lack and white police officers have different attitudes towards the role of police in society, police department politics, and the minority community." Detailed findings from his research, which was based on several months of participant observation (he once worked as an officer in the city he studied) and interviewing, appear in Exhibit 7.1.

## Women in Policing

In 1910 in Los Angeles, Alice Stebbins Wells became the first woman to hold the title of police officer and to have arrest powers.[43] As Figure 7.2 shows, about 16 percent of all sworn officers in larger cities (over 250,000) are women; in all, about 11 percent of sworn officers are female.[44]

The road to success in police work has not been easy for women. For more than half a century, female officers endured separate criteria for selection, were given menial tasks, and were denied the opportunity for advancement.[45] Some relief was gained with the passage of the 1964 Civil Rights Act and its subsequent amendments. Courts have consistently supported the addition of women to police forces by striking down entrance requirements that eliminated almost all female candidates but that could not be proved to predict job performance (such as height and upper-body strength).[46] Women do not perform as well as men on strength tests and are much more likely to fail the entrance physical than

## EXHIBIT 7.1

## Summary of White and Black Police Attitudes

| Attitudes Shared | |
|---|---|
| **Subject** | **(No significant racial differences)** |
| The ghetto | Violent, bad, dirty |
| Departmental discipline | Department will sacrifice an officer for political reasons |
| Social ideology | Conservative |
| Victims who know their assailants | Deserve what they get |
| Lower-class whites | Fat, wife-beating, inbred, no teeth, cop-fighting, redneck drunks |
| Lower-class blacks | Baby-making, welfare-dependent, drug-using, cop-hating drunks |

| Attitudes Not Shared | | |
|---|---|---|
| **Subject** | **(Significant racial differences)** | |
| | **Black Police** | **White Police** |
| Residents of the ghetto | Good and bad people live in ghetto | All bad |
| Departmental discipline | Biased against blacks because an "old-boys' network" protects whites | Biased against whites because department is politically afraid to punish blacks |
| Hiring process | Process is tougher for blacks | Standards are lowered for blacks |
| Black police identity | Cop identity more important than race identity | Many are black before blue |
| White police identity | Too many racist redneck crackers | More "professional" |
| Self-identity as police | Strong, but just a job | Strong |
| Political ideology | Independent, conservative, or liberal | Independent or conservative |
| Role of police | Peacekeepers | Crime fighters |
| The city | Bad, but problems are everywhere | Bad, where trouble comes from |

Source: Peter C. Moskos, "Two Shades of Blue: Black and White in the Blue Brotherhood," *Law Enforcement Executive Forum* 8 (2008): 57–86.

male recruits. Critics contend that many of these tests do not reflect the actual tasks that police do on the job.[47] Nonetheless, the role of women in police work is still restricted by social and administrative barriers that have been difficult to remove.

Studies of policewomen indicate that they are still struggling for acceptance, believe that they do not receive equal credit for their job performance, and report that it is common for them to be sexually harassed by their coworkers.[48] One reason may be that many male police officers tend to view policing as an overtly masculine profession not appropriate for women. For example, officers in the Los Angeles Police Department make an important distinction between two models of officers—"hard chargers" and "station queens." The former display such characteristics as courage and aggressiveness; they are willing to place themselves in danger and handle the most hazardous calls.[49] The latter like to work in the station house doing paperwork or other administrative tasks. The term "queen" is designed as a pejorative to indicate that these officers are overly feminine.[50]

*District of Columbia Police Chief Cathy L. Lanier converses with another police officer while on patrol in Washington, D.C. Lanier rose to her position from humble beginnings: She was a high school dropout after ninth grade and an unwed mother at the age of 15. Despite a rough start, she later earned advanced academic degrees from Johns Hopkins University and the Naval Postgraduate School in Monterey, California, where she completed a master's in security studies. Lanier also attended the John F. Kennedy School of Government at Harvard University and is a graduate of the FBI Academy and the University of the District of Columbia. She has been on the force for 18 years.*

Female police officers may also be targeted for more disciplinary actions by administrators and, if cited, are more likely to receive harsher punishments than male officers.[51] Considering the sometimes hostile reception they get from male colleagues and supervisors, it is not surprising that female officers report significantly higher levels of job-related stress than male officers.[52] Women have also faced considerable obstacles to promotion within the ranks, although recently this issue has become rather clouded and complex. For example, Carol Archbold and Dorothy Schulz found that female officers were frequently encouraged by their male supervisors to seek promotion, but this dissuaded many of the women from seeking promotion for fear that they would be promoted because of their status as a woman rather than their competencies.[53]

**JOB PERFORMANCE**  Research indicates that female officers are highly successful police officers.[54] In an important study of recruits in the Metropolitan

**FIGURE 7.2**
Percentage of Women in Local Police Departments

**Percent of full-time sworn personnel**

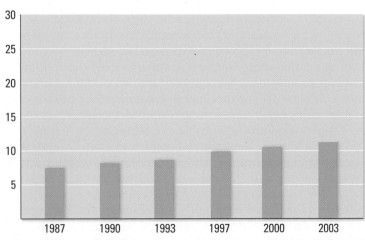

Source: Matthew Hickman and Brian Reaves, *Local Police Departments, 2003* (Washington D.C.: Bureau of Justice Statistics, 2006), p. iii.

Police Department of Washington, D.C., policewomen were found to display extremely satisfactory work performances.[55] Compared with male officers, women were found to respond to similar types of calls, and the arrests they made were as likely to result in conviction. Women were more likely than their male colleagues to receive support from the community and were less likely to be charged with improper conduct. On the other hand, there is evidence that female officers are more likely to be assaulted during domestic violence incidents.[56]

*GENDER CONFLICTS* Despite the overwhelming evidence supporting their performance, policewomen have not always been fully accepted by their male peers or the general public.[57] Surveys of male officers show that only one-third accept a woman on patrol and that more than half do not think women can handle the physical requirements of the job as well as men.[58] This form of bias is not unique to the United States. Research shows that policewomen working in northern England report being excluded from full membership in the force, based on gender inequality. Although policewomen in England are enthusiastic about crime-related work, their aspirations are frequently frustrated in favor of male officers.[59]

Female officers are frequently caught in the classic catch-22 dilemma: If they are physically weak, male partners view them as a risk in street confrontations; if they are more powerful and aggressive than their male partners, they are regarded as an affront to a male officer's manhood. Ironically, to adapt to this paternalistic culture, they may develop values and attitudes that support traditional concepts of police work instead of the new community policing models, which are viewed as taking a more humanistic, people-oriented approach.[60] The catch-22 dilemma can also lead to stress and burnout, but recent studies suggest that female officers may have achieved a measure of equality with their male colleagues when it comes to reporting these conditions.[61]

*MINORITY FEMALE OFFICERS* African American women, who account for less than 5 percent of police officers, occupy a unique status. In a study of African American policewomen serving in five large municipal departments, Susan Martin found that they perceive significantly more racial discrimination than both other female officers and African American male officers.[62] However, white policewomen were significantly more likely to perceive sexual discrimination than African American policewomen were.

Martin found that African American policewomen often incur the hostility of both white women and African American men, who feel that these officers they will take their place. On patrol, African American policewomen are treated differently by male officers than white policewomen are. Neither group of women is viewed as equals. White policewomen are protected and coddled, whereas African American policewomen are viewed as passive, lazy, and unequal. In the station house, male officers show little respect for African American women, who face "widespread racial stereotypes as well as outright racial harassment."[63] African American women also report having difficult relationships with African American male officers. Their relationships are strained by tensions and dilemmas "associated with sexuality and competition for desirable assignments and promotions."[64] Surprisingly, little unity is found among the female officers. As Martin concludes, "Despite changes in the past two decades, the idealized image of the representative of the forces of 'law and order' and protector who maintains 'the thin blue line' between 'them' and 'us' remains white and male."[65]

Despite these problems, the future of women in policing grows continually brighter.[66] Female officers want to remain in policing because it pays a good salary, offers job security, and is a challenging and exciting occupation.[67] These factors should continue to bring women to policing for years to come.

**CourseMate** For more information about conducting **research on law enforcement**, visit the Criminal Justice CourseMate at CengageBrain.com, then access the "Web Links" for this chapter.

# THE POLICE PROFESSION

All professions have unique characteristics that distinguish them from other occupations and institutions. Policing is no exception. Police experts have long sought to understand the unique nature of the police experience and to determine how the challenges of police work shape the profession and its employees.

## Police Culture

Police experts have found that the experience of becoming a police officer and the nature of the job itself cause most officers to band together in a police subculture characterized by cynicism, clannishness, secrecy, and insulation from others in society—the so-called **blue curtain**. Police officers tend to socialize together and believe that their occupation cuts them off from relationships with civilians. Officers perceive their working environment to be laden with danger or the risk of danger, and they become preoccupied with the danger and violence that surround them, always anticipating both.[68] Perceptions of danger have a unifying effect on officers and work to separate them from the chief source of danger—the public—and help create the boundaries of a police subculture. Joining the police subculture means always having to stick up for fellow officers against outsiders; maintaining a tough, macho exterior personality; and distrusting the motives and behavior of outsiders.[69] Six core beliefs are viewed as being at the heart of the police culture:

**blue curtain**
The secretive, insulated police culture that isolates officers from the rest of society.

- *Police are the only real crime fighters.* The public wants the police officer to fight crime; other agencies, both public and private, only play at crime fighting.

- *No one else understands the real nature of police work.* Lawyers, academics, politicians, and the public in general have little concept of what it means to be a police officer.

- *Loyalty to colleagues counts above everything else.* Police officers have to stick together because everyone is out to get the police and make the job more difficult.

- *The war against crime cannot be won without bending the rules.* Courts have awarded criminal defendants too many civil rights.

- *Members of the public are basically unsupportive and unreasonably demanding.* People are quick to criticize police unless they need police help themselves.

- *Patrol work is the pits.* Detective work is glamorous and exciting.[70]

The forces that support a police culture are generally believed to develop out of on-the-job experiences. Most officers originally join the police force because they want to help people, fight crime, and have an interesting, exciting, prestigious career with a high degree of job security.[71] Recruits often find that the social reality of police work does not mesh with their original career goals. They are unprepared for the emotional turmoil and conflict that accompany police work today.

Membership in the police culture helps recruits adjust to the rigors of police work and provides the emotional support needed for survival.[72] The culture encourages decisiveness in the face of uncertainty and the ability to make split-second judgments that may later be subject to extreme criticism. The police subculture also encourages its members to draw a sharp distinction between good and evil. Officers, more than mere enforcers of the law, are warriors in the age-old battle between right and wrong.[73] Also, criminals are referred to as "terrorists" and "predators," terms that convey the view that they are evil individuals ready to prey upon the poor and vulnerable. Because the predators represent a real danger, the police culture demands that its members be both competent and concerned with the safety of their peers and partners.

In sum, the police culture has developed in response to the insulated, dangerous lifestyle of police officers. Policing is a hazardous occupation, and the availability of the unquestioned support and loyalty of their peers is not something officers could readily do without.[74] Nonetheless, some experts fear that the police culture will divide officers from the people they serve and create an "us against the world" mentality.[75]

## Police Personality

**cynicism**
The belief that most people's actions are motivated solely by personal needs and selfishness.

Along with an independent police culture, some experts believe that police officers develop a unique set of personality traits that distinguish them from the average citizen.[76] To some commentators, the typical police personality can be described as dogmatic, authoritarian, and suspicious.[77] **Cynicism** has been found at all levels of policing, including chiefs of police, and throughout all stages of a police career.[78] Maintenance of these negative values and attitudes is believed to cause police officers to be secretive and isolated from the rest of society, producing the blue curtain.[79]

The police officer's working personality is shaped by constant exposure to danger and the need to use force and authority to reduce and control threatening situations.[80] Police feel suspicious of the public they serve and defensive about the actions of their fellow officers. There are two opposing viewpoints on the cause of this phenomenon. One position holds that police departments attract recruits who are by nature cynical, authoritarian, and secretive.[81] Other experts maintain that socialization and experience on the police force itself cause these character traits to develop.

Since the first research measuring police personality was published, numerous efforts have been made to determine whether the typical police recruit possesses a unique personality that sets her apart from the average citizen. The results have been mixed.[82] Although some research concludes that police values are different from those of the general adult population, other efforts reach an opposing conclusion. Some have found that police officers are more psychologically healthy than the general population, less depressed and anxious, and more social and assertive.[83] Still other research on police personality has found that police officers highly value such personality traits as warmth, flexibility, and emotion. These traits are far removed from rigidity and cynicism.[84] Thus no one position dominates on the issue of how the police personality develops—or even whether one exists.

In his classic study of police personality, *Behind the Shield* (1967), Arthur Neiderhoffer examined the assumption that most police officers develop into cynics as a function of their daily duties.[85] Among his most important findings were that police cynicism increased with length of service and that military-like police academy training caused new recruits to quickly become cynical about themselves.[86]

## Police Style

Policing encompasses a multitude of diverse tasks, including peacekeeping, criminal investigation, traffic control, and providing emergency medical service. Part of the socialization of a police officer is developing a working attitude, or style, through which he approaches policing. For example, some police officers may view their job as a well-paid civil service position that stresses careful compliance with written departmental rules and procedures. Other officers may see themselves as part of the "thin blue line" that protects the public from wrongdoers. They will use any means to get the culprit, even if it involves such cheating as planting evidence on an obviously guilty person who so far has escaped arrest. Should the police bend the rules to protect the public? This has been referred to as the "Dirty Harry problem," after the popular Clint Eastwood film character who routinely (and successfully) violated all known standards of police work.[87]

**police styles**
The working personalities adopted by police officers that can range from being a social worker in blue to being a hard-charging crime fighter.

Several studies have attempted to define and classify **police styles** into behavioral clusters. These classifications, called typologies, attempt to categorize law enforcement agents by groups, each of which has a unique approach to police

---

**EXHIBIT 7.2**

## The Four Basic Styles of Policing

### The Crime Fighter

To crime fighters, the most important aspect of police work is investigating serious crimes and apprehending criminals. Their focus is on the victim, and they view effective police work as the only force that can keep society's "dangerous classes" in check. They are the "thin blue line" protecting society from murderers and rapists. They consider property crimes less significant, and they believe that misdemeanors, traffic control, and social service functions would be better handled by other agencies of government. The ability to investigate criminal behavior that poses a serious threat to life and safety, combined with the power to arrest criminals, separates a police department from other municipal agencies. The crime fighters see diluting these functions with minor social service and nonenforcement duties as harmful to police efforts to create a secure society.

### The Social Agent

Social agents believe that police should be involved in a wide range of activities without regard for their connection to law enforcement. Instead of viewing themselves as criminal catchers, the social agents consider themselves community problem solvers. They are troubleshooters who patch the holes that appear where the social fabric wears thin. They are happy to work with special-needs populations, such as the homeless, school kids, and those who require emergency services. Social agents fit well within a community policing unit.

### The Law Enforcer

According to this view, duty is clearly set out in law, and law enforcers stress playing it "by the book."

Because the police are specifically charged with apprehending all types of lawbreakers, they see themselves as generalized law enforcement agents. Although law enforcers may prefer working on serious crimes—which are more intriguing and rewarding in terms of achievement, prestige, and status—they see the police role as one of enforcing all statutes and ordinances. They perceive themselves as neither community social workers nor vengeance-seeking vigilantes. Simply put, they are professional law enforcement officers who perform the functions of detecting violations, identifying culprits, and taking the lawbreakers before a court. Law enforcers are devoted to the profession of police work and are the officers most likely to aspire to command rank.

### The Watchman

The watchman style is characterized by an emphasis on the maintenance of public order as the police goal, not on law enforcement or general service. Watchmen ignore many infractions and requests for service unless they believe that the social or political order is jeopardized. They expect juveniles to misbehave and believe such mischief is best ignored or treated informally. Motorists will often be left alone if their driving does not endanger or annoy others. Vice and gambling are problems only when the currently accepted standards of public order are violated. Like the watchmen of old, these officers take action only if and when a problem arises. Watchmen are the most passive officers, more concerned with retirement benefits than crime rates.

Sources: William Muir, *Police: Streetcorner Politicians* (Chicago: University of Chicago Press, 1977); James Q. Wilson, *Varieties of Police Behavior* (Cambridge, Mass.: Harvard University Press, 1968).

---

work. The purpose of such classifications is to demonstrate that the police are not a cohesive, homogeneous group, as many believe, but individuals with differing approaches to their work.[88] The approach that police take to their task and their attitude toward the police role, as well as toward their peers and superior officers, have been shown to affect their work.[89]

An examination of the literature suggests that four styles of police work seem to fit the current behavior patterns of most police agents: the crime fighter, the social agent, the law enforcer, and the watchman. These four styles are described in Exhibit 7.2.

*CURRENT VIEWS ON POLICE CULTURE, PERSONALITY, AND STYLES*
Although some experts have found that a unique police personality and culture do exist, others have challenged that assumption.[90] No clear-cut agreement has been reached on the matter. In either event, changes in contemporary police

## CAREERS IN CRIMINAL JUSTICE

# FBI Agent

### Duties and Characteristics of the Job

Federal Bureau of Investigation special agents work for the federal government. Their primary duty is to conduct investigations of federal crimes and threats to national security. Their primary areas of investigation include white-collar crime, drug trafficking, and espionage. They may also lend aid,

Waldomar Mariscal, the son of Vicky Pelaez and Juan Lazaro, arrives at their home in Yonkers, New York, on June 29, 2010. Pelaez and Lazaro were among 11 arrested by the FBI on June 28 in connection with an alleged Russian spy ring.

services, and training to other law enforcement organizations. The actual law enforcement role of an agent is limited; apprehension and arrest are often delegated to local authorities.

Working as a federal agent is challenging. Federal agents may be required to travel to conduct investigations and can be away for long periods of time. Special agents often work overtime; a 45-hour workweek is the average for an agent. Finally, some find it troubling that they have to maintain secrecy about their work, even with their family.

### Job Outlook

Factors such as the high pay, good benefits, generous retirement policy (full retirement at age 55), and the prestige associated with the position make this career highly desirable and thus very competitive. However, the early retirement policy ensures that there will always be job openings. Recruitment is ongoing, and the FBI is always accepting applications.

### Salary

New special agents are paid as GS-10 and earn a base salary of $43,441. Salary also depends on where the agent is located, and it increases with overtime pay.

agencies will soon have a significant impact on police culture and personality, if they have not done so already. Police departments have become diverse, attracting women and minorities in growing numbers. Police are becoming more educated and technologically sophisticated. The vision of a monolithic department whose employees share similar and uniform values, culture, and personality traits seems somewhat naive in the presence of such diversity.

Furthermore, today's police officer is unlikely to be able to choose to embrace a particular style of policing while excluding others. Although some police officers may emphasize one area of law enforcement over another, their daily activities are likely to require them to engage in a wide variety of duties. A contemporary police officer can seldom choose to concentrate on crime fighting and ignore his other duties. Police departments are seeking public support through community police models and are reorienting the police role toward community outreach.[91]

## POLICE DISCRETION

**discretion**
The use of personal decision making and choice in carrying out operations in the criminal justice system.

A critical aspect of a police officer's professional responsibility is the personal discretion each officer has in carrying out his daily activities. **Discretion** can involve the selective enforcement of the law, as when a vice-squad plainclothes officer decides not to take action against a tavern that is serving drinks after hours. Patrol officers use discretion when they decide to arrest one suspect for disorderly conduct but escort another home. Because police have the ability

After these adjustments, a first-year agent can expect to earn between $61,000 and $69,900. Agents promoted to supervisory positions earn higher pay, as do those who work in a geographical area where pay is higher in general.

## Opportunities

The FBI does not put forth specific recommendations for what skills or specialties it is seeking. However, strong analytical and research skills are always desirable, and law, accounting, and engineering degrees are also sought after for their usefulness in federal investigations.

## Qualifications

Being a federal agent can be a demanding job, and the qualifications to become one are just as demanding. There are seven steps in the process of being hired as an agent. In order to even apply to be an agent, one must be a U.S. citizen, be at least 23 but younger than 37, hold a valid driver's license, and have earned a bachelor's degree. A potential federal agent must first qualify in one of five categories representing the different entry programs: accounting/finance, computer science/information technology, language, law, and diversified (a miscellaneous-type category). Once a candidate qualifies for one of these larger categories, he will need certain skills and/or experience that the agency currently desires within that category, and the skills desired can change over time. Candidates

must be willing to travel wherever their assignments take them and also be willing to move, because an agent can be asked to relocate at any time.

Certain personality characteristics and skills are important for potential special agents. Because a special agent's job is primarily investigative, strong research and analytical skills are very important.

## Education and Training

As a general rule, potential agents do not move directly from schooling into a federal position. Some entry programs require previous work experience before one can even apply. A bachelor's degree is the minimum education requirement; however, graduate study makes an application more likely to be accepted. Depending on the category of entry program, the degree should be in certain relevant fields. If accepted, the applicant spends several weeks at a training program in Quantico, Virginia, learning investigative procedures and other necessary skills. After completion of training, new special agents are paired with more experienced ones to observe how the knowledge they gained is to be applied in real-life settings.

Sources: "Police and Detectives," *Occupational Outlook Handbook*, 2010–2011 edition (Bureau of Labor Statistics, U.S. Department of Labor), www.bls.gov/oco/ocos160.htm (April 12, 2010); "Careers" (Federal Bureau of Investigation), www.fbijobs.gov/11.asp (retrieved April 12, 2010); "Princeton Review Career Profiles: FBI Agent," www.princetonreview.com/cte/profiles/dayInLife.asp?careerID=64 (retrieved April 12, 2010).

to deprive people of their liberty, arrest them, take them away in handcuffs, and even use deadly force to subdue them, their use of discretion is a vital concern.

The majority of police officers use a high degree of personal discretion in carrying out daily tasks, sometimes referred to in criminal justice as **low-visibility decision making**.[92] This terminology suggests that, unlike members of almost every other criminal justice agency, police are neither regulated in their daily procedures by administrative scrutiny nor subject to judicial review (except when their behavior clearly violates an offender's constitutional rights). As a result, the exercise of discretion by police may sometimes deteriorate into discrimination, violence, and other abusive practices. Nonetheless, the public recognizes the right of police to exercise their discretion, even if it means using force to control an unruly suspect while treating a more respectful one with deference and respect.[93]

**low-visibility decision making**
Decision making by police officers that is not subject to administrative review—for example, a decision not to arrest someone or not to stop a speeding vehicle.

## Factors Influencing Discretion

A number of factors influence police discretion.[94] Some are to be expected; others are more controversial.

*CRIME FACTORS* Police discretion is related to the severity of the offense. There is relatively little, if any, discretion used for the most serious crimes such as murder and aggravated assault.[95] Far more personal discretion is available when

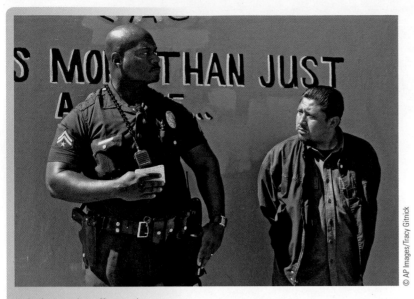

*Whether a police officer makes an arrest may depend on how the individual officer views offense severity. Here officer Deon Joseph waits for a squad car to transport Marco Rodriguez to a detox center in the Skid Row area of downtown Los Angeles, rather than to jail.*

police confront a suspect in a minor case involving a simple assault or trespass. Related to offense seriousness is the issue of who brings it to the attention of police. If, for example, a police officer stumbles upon an altercation or break-in, the discretionary response may be different from a situation in which the officer is summoned by police radio.[96]

***VICTIM FACTORS***  The relationship between the parties involved influences decision making and discretion. An altercation between two friends or relatives may be handled differently than an assault on a stranger. A case in point is policing domestic violence cases. Research indicates that police are reluctant to even respond to these kinds of cases because they are a constant source of frustration and futility.[97] Police sometimes intentionally delay responding to domestic disputes, hoping that by the time they get there the problem will be settled.[98] Victims, they believe, often fail to get help or change their abusive situation.[99]

***ENVIRONMENTAL FACTORS***  The degree of discretion that an officer will exercise is at least partially defined by the living and working environment.[100] An officer who lives in the community she serves probably shares a large part of the community's beliefs and values and is likely to be sensitive to and respect the wishes of neighbors, friends, and relatives. However, conflict may arise when the police officer commutes to an assigned area of jurisdiction, as is often the case in inner-city precincts. The officer who holds personal values that are at odds with those of the community can exercise discretion in ways that conflict with the community's values and result in ineffective law enforcement.[101]

According to the **overload hypothesis**, community crime rates may shape officer discretion. As local crime rates increase, police resources become strained to the breaking point; officers are forced to give less time and attention to each new case. The amount of attention they can devote to less serious crimes decreases, and they begin to treat petty offenders more leniently than officers in less crime-ridden neighborhoods might have done.[102]

**overload hypothesis**
The theory that police workload influences discretion so that as workload increases, less time and attention can be devoted to new cases, especially petty crimes.

***DEPARTMENTAL FACTORS***  The policies, practices, and customs of the local police department are another influence on discretion. These conditions vary from department to department and strongly depend on the judgment of the chief and others in the organizational hierarchy.[103] Efforts by the administration to limit or shape the behavior of the officer on patrol may prompt it to issue directives aimed at influencing police conduct. For example, in an effort to crack down on a particular crime—such as adolescent drug abuse—the department can create a strict arrest and referral policy for those engaging in that crime.

A patrol officer's supervisor can influence discretion. The ratio of supervisory personnel to subordinates may also influence discretion. Departments with a high ratio of sergeants to patrol officers may experience fewer officer-initiated actions than ones in which fewer eyes are observing the action in the streets. Supervisory style may also affect how police use discretion. Robin Shepard Engel found that patrol officers supervised by sergeants who are take-charge types and

## CONCEPT SUMMARY 7.1
### Factors that Influence Police Discretion

| Category | Elements |
|---|---|
| Crime factors | Offense severity, officer's perceptions of offense severity, and reasons for the call |
| Victim factors | Victim–offender relationship |
| Environmental factors | Community culture and values |
| Departmental factors | Policies and orders, supervisory style and control |
| Peer factors | Friendships, norms, subculture |
| Suspect behavior and characteristics | Suspect demeanor; suspect resistance; suspect race, gender, and age |
| Officer characteristics | Officer's education, experience, gender, and career aspirations |

like to participate in high levels of activity in the field themselves spend significantly more time per shift engaging in self-initiated and community policing or problem-solving activities than in administrative activities. In contrast, officers with supervisors whose style involves spending time mentoring and coaching subordinates are more likely to devote significantly more attention to engaging in administrative tasks.[104]

**PEER FACTORS** Police discretion is subject to peer pressure.[105] Police officers suffer a degree of social isolation because the job involves strange working conditions and hours, including being on 24-hour call, and their authority and responsibility to enforce the law may cause embarrassment during social encounters. At the same time, officers must handle irregular and emotionally demanding encounters involving the most personal and private aspects of people's lives. As a result, police officers turn to their peers for both on-the-job advice and off-the-job companionship, essentially forming a subculture that provides a source of status, prestige, and reward.

The peer group affects how police officers exercise discretion on two distinct levels. First, in an obvious, direct manner, other police officers dictate acceptable responses to street-level problems by displaying or withholding approval in office discussions. Second, the officer who takes the job seriously and desires the respect and friendship of others will take their advice, abide by their norms, and seek out the most experienced and most influential patrol officers on the force and follow their behavioral models.

**SUSPECT BEHAVIOR AND CHARACTERISTICS** Researchers have also found that suspect behavior and characteristics weigh heavily in the use of discretionary powers.[106] Suspect **demeanor** (the attitude and appearance of the offender) is one of the most important influences. If an offender is surly, talks back, or otherwise challenges the officer's authority, formal action is more likely to be taken.[107] According to this view, a negative demeanor will result in formal police action.[108] Suspects who behave in a civil manner, accept responsibility for their offense, and admit their guilt are less likely to be sanctioned than those who display a less courteous demeanor.[109]

**demeanor**
The way a person outwardly manifests his or her personality.

# RACE, GENDER, AND CULTURE IN CRIMINAL JUSTICE

## Racial Profiling

The term "racial profiling" has been coined to describe the racial influence over police discretion. A number of empirical studies have found that state and local police officers routinely stop and/or search African American motorists at a rate far greater than their representation in the driving pool:

■ Brian Withrow looked at police practices in Wichita, Kansas, and found that African American citizens are stopped at disproportionately higher rates than non–African American citizens and that African American and Hispanic citizens are more likely to be searched and arrested than non–African American and non-Hispanic citizens. Another of his studies, this one from San Jose, California, revealed that Hispanics made up 31 percent of the city's population but accounted for 43 percent of the people stopped.

■ Researchers at Northeastern University in Boston used four statistical tests to analyze 1.6 million traffic citations issued between April 1, 2001, and June 30, 2003, in towns across Massachusetts and found the following: ticketing resident minorities disproportionately more than whites, ticketing all minorities disproportionately more than whites, searching minorities more often than whites, and issuing warnings to whites more often than to minorities. According to the study, 15 police departments failed all four tests, 42 failed three tests, 87 failed two tests, and 105 failed one.

■ Richard Lundman's analysis of citizen encounters with police indicates (a) that minority citizens are more likely to be stopped than whites but (b) that searches of minority-driven vehicles are no more likely to yield drugs or contraband than searches of vehicles driven by whites.

■ Michael Smith and Geoffrey Alpert found that once blacks and Hispanics are stopped, they are more likely than whites to be searched and arrested. Similar findings were reported by the New Jersey attorney general's office, which found that nearly 80 percent of people searched during traffic stops were black or Hispanic.

### Does Race Matter?

Some experts question whether profiling and racial discrimination are as widespread as currently feared.

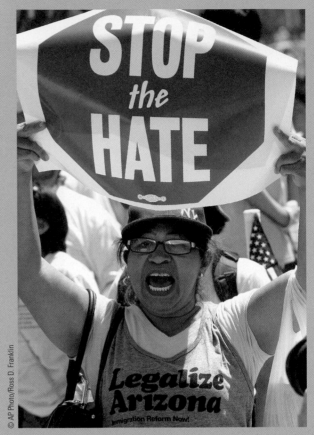

© AP Photo/Ross D. Franklin

*Amaria Lopez, of Phoenix, protests at the Arizona Capitol on Sunday, April, 25, 2010. Activists called on President Barack Obama to fight a tough new Arizona law targeting illegal immigrants, and they promised to march in the streets and invite arrest by refusing to comply if the measure goes into effect. The law, which continues to undergo legal challenges as of this writing, requires Arizona police officers to question people about their immigration status if there is reasonable suspicion that they are in the United States illegally. Opponents maintain that this law would undoubtedly lead to racial profiling.*

One approach has been to measure the attitudes that minority citizens hold toward police. When Ronald Weitzer surveyed residents in three Washington, D.C., neighborhoods, he found that African Americans value racially integrated police services and welcome the presence of both white and African American police officers, a finding that would seem improbable if most white officers were racially biased. The African American community is generally supportive of the local police, especially when officers respond quickly to calls for service. It is unlikely that African Americans would appreciate rapid responses from racist police.

Another approach is to directly measure whether police treat minority and majority citizens differently—

that is, use racial profiling in making decisions. Some studies show little evidence that police use racial profiling:

- David Eitle, Lisa Stolzenberg, and Stewart J. D'Alessio found that whites are more likely to be arrested for assaults than African Americans.

- Matt DeLisi and Bob Regoli found that whites are nine times more likely to experience DWI arrests than African Americans, a finding that would be unlikely if racial profiling were routine.

- Jon Gould and Stephen Mastrofski studied illegal police searches and found that race has little influence on police conduct. Although police may routinely conduct illegal searches, the suspect's race does not influence their tactics.

- Joseph Schafer, David Carter, and Andra Katz-Bannister found that although race plays some role in traffic stops, age and gender actually have a greater influence on police decision making.

- James Lange, Mark Johnson, and Robert Voas surveyed drivers on the New Jersey Turnpike and found that the proportion of speeding drivers who were identified as African American coincided with the proportion of African American drivers stopped by police. Their findings suggest that police are less likely to engage in racial profiling today and that efforts to control profiling have been successful.

- Geoffrey Alpert, Roger Dunham, and Michael Smith investigated racial profiling by the Miami-Dade Police Department and found that there was no pattern of discriminatory activity toward minority citizens during traffic stops, but there was some evidence of unequal treatment after the stop.

- Some studies show that searches of white suspects yield more contraband than black suspects, but this may be due to what Geoffrey Alpert has called the "carrying rate differential"—the likelihood that blacks rarely carry contraband for fear of getting caught. One young black male made this observation in his study: "We expect to be stopped and we know we're going to be searched—we're not stupid enough to carry."

## Can Racial Profiling Be Justified?

Whereas most experts condemn any form of racial profiling, two Harvard scholars, Mathias Risse and Richard Zeckhauser, have argued that profiling may have utility as a crime control tactic. First, they suggest that there is a significant correlation between membership in certain racial groups and the propensity

to commit certain crimes. This explains why profiling takes place. Second, they suggest that given such a propensity, stopping, searching, or investigating members of such groups differentially will help curb crime. That is, racial profiling has utility because it can eliminate more crime than other law enforcement practices for equivalent expenditures of resources and disruption. If these assumptions are true, then racial profiling is morally justified in a broad range of cases, including many cases that tend to be controversial. Some people consider profiling abusive, but Risse and Zeckhauser believe that police abuse is a separate issue and should not be considered an aspect of profiling.

A key element of Risse and Zeckhauser's position is that racial profiling is not as harmful as crime and therefore is not too high a price to pay in order to achieve reductions in crime rates. Most stops are not abusive, and police try to act as civilly as possible under the circumstances. But as legal scholars Samuel Gross and Katherine Barnes point out, the assumption that a stop-and-search is intrinsically a minor inconvenience is questionable. Its effect can be corrosive:

> As the level of the police officer's interest increases, the cost to the innocent citizen escalates rapidly. It's one thing to get a speeding ticket and an annoying lecture . . . it's quite another to be told to step out of the car and to be questioned. . . . The questions may seem intrusive and out of line, but you can hardly refuse to answer an armed cop. At some point you realize you are not just another law-abiding citizen who's being checked out . . . like everyone else. You've been targeted. The trooper is not going through a routine so he can let you go . . . he wants to find drugs on you. . . . Those of us who have not been through this sort of experience probably underestimate its impact. To be treated as a criminal is a basic insult to a person's self-image and his position in society. It cannot easily be shrugged off. . . .

In other words, although some may argue that profiling can reduce some forms of criminal behavior, such as drug trafficking, the social costs it brings are too high a price to pay for modest crime reductions.

Most researchers have looked at traffic stops and resulting searches in their efforts to determine whether racial profiling is a problem. Recently, economists have called for a different approach: focusing only on successful searches. A successful search is one that turns up evidence of contraband. Nicole Persico and Petra Todd have argued that an unbiased officer will focus his or her efforts on people who, if searched, is mostly likely to possess contraband. In contrast, a biased officer will take pleasure from

# Racial Profiling (continued)

searching people because they are minorities. This is known as the "outcome test," and it calls for looking past who is stopped and focusing on what the end result of a stop is. In other words, just because one group may be stopped more than another does not necessarily mean profiling is occurring. It could just be good police work! Robin Engel has been critical of this argument, claiming that it makes too many assumptions about how policing is really done.

## Critical Thinking

1. What, if anything, can be done to reduce racial bias on the part of police? Would adding minority officers help? Would it be a form of racism to assign minority officers to minority neighborhoods?

2. Would research showing that police are more likely to make arrests in interracial incidents than in intraracial incidents constitute evidence of racism?

3. Police spot three men of Middle Eastern descent carrying a large, heavy box into a crowded building. Should they stop and question them and demand to look into the carton? Is this racial profiling?

Sources: Brian Withrow, "Race-Based Policing: A Descriptive Analysis of the Wichita Stop Study," *Police Practice and Research* 5 (2004): 223–240; Brian Withrow, "A Comparative Analysis of Commonly Used Benchmarks in Racial Profiling: A Research Note," *Justice Research and Policy* 6 (2004): 71–92; Amy Farrell, Jack McDevitt, Lisa Bailey, Carsten Andresen, and Erica Pierce, "Massachusetts Racial and Gender Profiling Final Report" (Boston: Northeastern University, 2004), www.racialprofilinganalysis.neu.edu/IRJsite_docs/finalreport.pdf (accessed April 12, 2010); Richard Lundman, "Driver Race, Ethnicity, and Gender and Citizen Reports of Vehicle Searches by Police and Vehicle Search Hits," *Journal of Criminal Law and Criminology* 94 (2004): 309–350; Michael Smith and Geoffrey Alpert, "Explaining Police Bias: A Theory of Social Conditioning and Illusory Correlation," *Criminal Justice and Behavior* 34 (2007): 1262–1283; *Interim Report of the State Police Review Team Regarding Allegations of Racial Profiling* (Trenton, N.J.: Office of the Attorney General, 1999); Ronald Weitzer, "White, Black, or Blue Cops? Race and Citizen Assessments of Police Officers," *Journal of Criminal Justice* 28 (2000): 313–324; David Eitle, Lisa Stolzenberg, and Stewart J. D'Alessio, "Police Organizational Factors, the Racial Composition of the Police, and the Probability of Arrest," *Justice Quarterly* 22 (2005): 30–57; Matt DeLisi and Robert Regoli, "Race, Conventional Crime, and Criminal Justice: The Declining Importance of Skin Color," *Journal of Criminal Justice* 27 (1999): 549–557; Jon Gould and Stephen Mastrofski, "Suspect Searches: Assessing Police Behavior Under the U.S. Constitution," *Criminology and Public Policy* 3 (2004): 315–362; Joseph Schafer, David Carter, and Andra Katz-Bannister, "Studying Traffic Stop Encounters," *Journal of Criminal Justice* 32 (2004): 159–170; James Lange, Mark Johnson, and Robert Voas, "Testing the Racial Profiling Hypothesis for Seemingly Disparate Traffic Stops on the New Jersey Turnpike," *Justice Quarterly* 22 (2005): 193–223; Geoffrey P. Alpert, Roger G. Dunham, and Michael R. Smith, "Investigating Racial Profiling by the Miami-Dade Police Department: A Multimethod Approach," *Criminology and Public Policy* 6 (2007): 25–56; Geoffrey P. Alpert, "Eliminate Race as the Only Reason for Police-Citizen Encounters," *Criminology and Public Policy* 6 (2007): 671–678; Mathias Risse and Richard Zeckhauser, "Racial Profiling," *Philosophy and Public Affairs* 32 (2004): 131–170; Samuel Gross and Katherine Barnes, "Road Work: Racial Profiling and Drug Interdiction on the Highway," *Michigan Law Review* 101 (2003): 651–754, at 745–746; Nicola Persico and Petra E. Todd, "The Hit Rates Test for Racial Bias in Motor-Vehicle Searches," *Justice Quarterly* 25 (2008): 37–53; Robin S. Engel, "A Critique of the 'Outcome Test' in Racial Profiling Research," *Justice Quarterly* 25 (2008): 1–36.

What if a suspect acts out physically or resists? Suspects who physically resist are much more likely to receive some form of physical coercion in return, but those who offer verbal disrespect are not likely to be physically coerced.[110] Therefore, police officers' response to a suspect's challenge to their authority is dependent on the way the challenge is delivered. Verbal challenges are met with verbal responses, and physical with physical.[111]

It is not particularly surprising that suspects' attitudes and behavior influence police officers' decisions. But what about the way a suspect *looks*? Should gender, age, or race matter? Ideally, the answer is no, but reality tells a different story. We look at the controversial issue of racial profiling in the accompanying Race, Gender, and Culture in Criminal Justice feature starting on page 256, but one finding is fairly clear: Race matters. It either influences officers' behavior directly or affects the level of suspicion officers display toward minority versus white suspects.[112] Gender is also important. One study found that women are less likely to be arrested than men.[113] And as for age, researchers have found that young people tend to be arrested more often or dealt with more harshly than their older counterparts.[114]

***OFFICER CHARACTERISTICS*** The characteristics of police officers themselves are also important predictors of discretionary decision making. It is possible that officer education and experience are important, but researchers have yet to reach any consensus on this.[115] As for gender, researchers have found that female officers are less likely to use force than male officers.[116] Because female officers seem to have the ability to avoid violent encounters with citizens and to deescalate potentially violent arrest situations, they are typically the target of fewer citizen complaints.[117] Finally, there is some evidence that police officers' career aspirations affect their decision making. One study found that those officers who desired promotion tended to make the most arrests.[118]

Police discretion is one of the most often debated issues in criminal justice (see Concept Summary 7.1 on page 255). On its face, the unequal enforcement of the law smacks of unfairness and violates the Constitution's doctrines of due process and equal protection. Yet if some discretion were not exercised, police would be forced to function as robots merely following the book. Administrators have sought to control discretion so that its exercise may be both beneficial to citizens and nondiscriminatory.[119]

## PROBLEMS OF POLICING

Law enforcement is not an easy job. The role ambiguity, social isolation, and threat of danger present in working the streets are the police officer's constant companions. What effects do these strains have on police? The most significant problems are job stress, fatigue, violence and brutality, and corruption.

### Job Stress

The complexity of their role, the need to exercise prudent discretion, the threat of using violence and having violence used against them, and isolation from the rest of society all take a toll on law enforcement officers. Police officer stress leads to negative attitudes, burnout, loss of enthusiasm and commitment (cynicism), increased apathy, substance abuse problems, divorce, health problems, and many other social, personal, and job-related problematic behaviors.[120] Evidence suggests that police officers are often involved in marital disputes and even incidents of domestic violence, which may be linked to stress.[121] Stress may not be constant, but at some time during their career (usually the middle years), most officers will feel its effects.[122]

***CAUSES OF STRESS*** A number of factors have been associated with job stress. Some are related to the difficulties that police officers have in maintaining social and family relationships, considering their schedule and workload.[123] Police suffer stress in their personal lives when they bring the job home or when their work hours are shifted, causing family disruptions.[124] Those who perceive themselves as alienated from family and friends at home are more likely to feel stress on the job.[125]

Some stressors are job related. The pressure of being on duty 24 hours per day leads to stress and emotional detachment from both work and public needs. Policing is a dangerous profession, and officers are at risk of many forms of job-related injury. Every year, several officers are killed. On the other hand, law enforcement officers contemplating retirement also report high stress levels. So although the job may be dangerous, many officers are reluctant to leave it.[126]

Stress has been related to internal conflict with administrative policies that deny officers support and a meaningful role in decision making.[127] Stress may result when officers are forced to adapt to a department's new methods of policing, such as community-oriented policing, and they are skeptical about the change in policy.[128] Other stressors include poor training, substandard equipment, inadequate pay, lack of opportunity, job dissatisfaction, role conflict, exposure to brutality, and fears about competence, success, and safety.[129] Some officers may feel stress because they believe that the court system favors the rights of the criminal and handcuffs the police; others might be sensitive to a perceived lack of support from governmental officials and the general public.[130] Still others believe that their superiors care little about their welfare.[131]

Police psychologists have divided these stressors into four distinct categories:

■ External stressors, such as verbal abuse from the public, justice system inefficiency, and liberal court decisions that favor the criminal. What are perceived to be antipolice judicial decisions may alienate police and reduce their perceptions of their own competence.[132]

■ Organizational stressors, such as low pay, excessive paperwork, arbitrary rules, and limited opportunity for advancement.

■ Duty stressors, such as rotating shifts, work overload, boredom, fear, and danger.

■ Individual stressors, such as discrimination, marital difficulties, and personality problems.[133]

The effects of stress can be shocking. Police work has been related to both physical and psychological ailments. Police have a significantly high rate of premature death caused by such conditions as heart disease and diabetes. They also experience a disproportionate number of divorces and other marital problems. Research indicates that police officers in some departments, but not all, have higher suicide rates than the general public. (Recent research shows that New York City police have suicide rates equal to or lower than the general public, and some researchers have found a lower than average police suicide rate in other areas of the country.[134]) Alcohol and drug abuse have been linked to stress, as well.[135] Police who feel stress may not be open to adopting new ideas and programs such as community policing.[136]

***COMBATTING STRESS*** The more support police officers get in the workplace, the lower their feelings of stress and anxiety.[137] Consequently, departments have attempted to fight job-related stress by training officers to cope with its effects. Today, stress training includes diet information, biofeedback, relaxation and meditation, and exercise. Many departments include stress management as part of an overall wellness program that is also designed to promote physical and mental health, fitness, and good nutrition.[138] Some programs have included family members: They may be better able to help the officer cope if they have more knowledge about the difficulties of police work. Research also shows that because police perceive many benefits from their job and enjoy the quality of life it provides, stress-reduction programs might help officers focus on the positive aspects of police work.[139]

Stress is a critically important aspect of police work. Further research is needed to create valid methods of identifying police officers who are under considerable stress and to devise effective stress-reduction programs.[140]

# Fatigue

Nearly everyone has been tired at work from time to time. While on-the-job sleepiness is inconsequential for many workers, it can lead to disaster for others. No one wants airline pilots to fall asleep, and the prospect of a truck driver sleeping behind the wheel is equally disturbing. What about a police officer? A police officer who is overly tired may be at higher risk of acting inappropriately or being injured on the job.

The problem of "tired cops"[141] has largely been overlooked, but it should not be.[142] Police officers often work lengthy shifts with unpredictable hours. The *Boston Globe* investigated one agency and found that 16 officers worked more than 80 hours in a week.[143] One even worked 130 hours! While it is difficult to fault anyone for seeking overtime pay, too much work can lead to disaster. Here are some examples:

- A Michigan police officer working nearly 24 hours straight crashes his cruiser while chasing a fleeing motorist. He is critically injured.

- In California, a sheriff's deputy working alone drifts off a deserted highway and is killed instantly when his patrol car crashes into a tree.

- An officer in Florida, who has had trouble staying awake, runs a red light in her patrol car and crashes into a van driven by a deputy sheriff, injuring him severely.

- A police officer driving home from working in Ohio nods off at the wheel, begins swerving in and out of traffic, and runs off the road, striking and killing a man jogging down the sidewalk.[144]

*CONTROLLING POLICE FATIGUE* What can be done to control police fatigue? One option is for administrators to pay special attention to scheduling so that officers do not work too much overtime. Another is for administrators to adopt policies that place limitations on second jobs. Many officers moonlight as security guards, which may affect their on-the-job performance. A recent government report offered several other recommendations for limiting fatigue. Administrators should:

- Review the policies, procedures, and practices that affect shift scheduling and rotation, overtime, moonlighting, the number of consecutive hours allowed, and the way in which the department deals with overly tired employees.

- Assess how much of a voice officers are given in work-hour and shift-scheduling decisions. The number of hours that officers work and the time of day they are assigned to work affect their personal, social, family, and professional lives. Excluding officers from decisions affecting this arena increases stress, which in turn reduces their ability to deal with fatigue and tends to diminish their job performance and ability to deal with stress.

- Assess the level of fatigue that officers experience, the quality of their sleep, and how tired they are while on the job, as well as their attitudes toward fatigue and work-hour issues.

- Review recruit and in-service training programs to determine whether officers are receiving adequate information about the importance of good sleep habits, the hazards associated with fatigue and shift work, and strategies for managing them. Are officers taught to view fatigue as a safety issue? Are they trained to recognize drowsiness as a factor in vehicle crashes?[145]

## Violence and Brutality

Police officers are empowered to use force and violence in pursuit of their daily tasks. Some scholars argue that the use of violent measures is the core of the police role.[146] Even so, since their creation, U.S. police departments have wrestled with the charge that they are brutal, physically violent organizations. Early police officers resorted to violence and intimidation to gain the respect that was not freely given by citizens. In the 1920s, the Wickersham Commission detailed numerous instances of **police brutality**, including the use of the "third degree" to extract confessions.

**police brutality**
Actions such as using abusive language, making threats, using force or coercion unnecessarily, prodding with nightsticks, and stopping and searching people to harass them.

*Andrew Meyer, a journalism major at the University of Florida, is tased by a police officer during a 2007 Constitution Day forum after being disruptive during a question-and-answer session with Senator and former presidential candidate John Kerry. Meyer was heard shouting, "Don't tase me, bro, don't tase me!"—a phrase that went down as one of* Time *magazine's "Top 10 T-shirt worthy slogans" of the year.*

© AP Images/Independent Florida Alligator/Andrew Stanfill

Today, police brutality continues to be a concern, especially when police use excessive violence against members of the minority community. The nation looked on in disgust when a videotape was aired on network newscasts showing members of the Los Angeles Police Department beating, kicking, and using electric stun guns on Rodney King. Other incidents reported in both national and local media over the years also illustrate the persistent problems that police departments have in regulating violent contacts with citizens.

**WHO ARE THE PROBLEM COPS?**  Evidence shows that only a small proportion of officers are continually involved in problem behavior.[147] What kind of police officer gets involved in problem behavior? Aggressive cops may be ones who overreact to the stress of police work while at the same time feeling socially isolated. They believe that the true sources of their frustration—such as corrupt politicians or liberal judges—are shielded from their anger, so they take their frustrations out on readily available targets: vulnerable people in their immediate environment.[148]

Some officers are chronic offenders. Research conducted in a southeastern city by Kim Michelle Lersch and Tom Mieczkowski found that a few officers (7%) were chronic offenders who accounted for a significant portion of all citizen complaints (33 percent). Those officers receiving the bulk of the complaints tended to be younger and less experienced, and they had been accused of harassment or violence after a proactive encounter that they had initiated. Although repeat offenders were more likely to be accused of misconduct by minority citizens, there was little evidence that attacks were racially motivated.[149]

Efforts to deal with these problem cops are now being undertaken in police departments around the nation. A number of departments have instituted early-warning systems to change the behavior of individual officers who have been identified as having performance problems. The basic intervention strategy involves a combination of deterrence and education. According to the deterrence strategy, officers who are subject to intervention will presumably change their behavior in response to a perceived threat of punishment. Early-warning systems operate on the assumption that training, as part of the intervention, can help officers improve their performance. Evaluations show that early-warning systems appear to have a dramatic effect on reducing citizen complaints and other indicators of problematic police performance among those officers subject to intervention.[150]

*DEALING WITH PROBLEM COPS* Detailed rules of engagement that limit the use of force are common in major cities. However, the creation of departmental rules limiting behavior is often haphazard and is usually a reaction to a crisis situation (for example, a citizen is seriously injured) instead of part of a systematic effort to improve police–citizen interactions.[151] Some departments have developed administrative policies that stress limiting the use of force and containing armed offenders until specially trained backup teams are sent to take charge of the situation. Administrative policies have been found to be an effective control on deadly force, and their influence can be enhanced if the chief of police gives them the proper support.[152]

The most significant factors in controlling police brutality may be the threat of civil judgments against individual officers who use excessive force, police chiefs who ignore or condone violent behavior, and the cities and towns in which they are employed. Civilians routinely file civil actions against police departments when they believe that officers have violated their civil rights. Police may be sued when a victim believes that excessive force was used during his or her arrest or custody. Civilians may collect damages if they can show that the force used was unreasonable, considering all the circumstances known to the officer at the time he or she acted. Excessive-force suits commonly occur when police use a weapon, such as a gun or baton, to subdue an unarmed person who is protesting his or her treatment. The U.S. Supreme Court in 1978 (*Monell v. Department of Social Services*) ruled that local agencies could be held liable under the federal Civil Rights Act (42 U.S.C. 1983) for actions of their employees if such actions were part of an official custom or practice.[153]

The few "bad apples" who ruin it for the rest of the police force can have harmful effects on a department's public image. In response, many urban police departments have implemented neighborhood and community policing models to improve relations with the public. Improved trust in police may lead to a perception that brutality is not a problem.[154]

## Corruption

Police departments have almost always wrestled with the problem of controlling illegal and unprofessional behavior by their officers. **Corruption** pervaded the U.S. police when the early departments were first formed. In the nineteenth century, police officers systematically ignored violations of laws related to drinking, gambling, and prostitution in return for regular payoffs. Some entered into relationships with professional criminals, especially pickpockets. Illegal behavior was tolerated in return for goods or information. Police officers helped politicians gain office by allowing electoral fraud to flourish. Some senior officers sold promotions to higher ranks within the police department.[155]

Since the early nineteenth century, scandals involving police abuse of power have occurred in many urban cities, and elaborate methods have been devised to control or eliminate the problem. Although most police officers are not corrupt, the few who are dishonest bring discredit to the entire profession. And corruption is often hard to combat because the police code of silence demands that officers never turn in their peers, even if they engage in corrupt or illegal practices.[156] Fortunately, however, recent studies reveal that corruption is quite rare and that career-ending misconduct is the exception.[157]

*VARIETIES OF CORRUPTION* Police corruption can include a number of activities. In a general sense, it involves misuse of authority by police officers in a manner designed to produce personal gain for themselves or others.[158] However, debate continues over whether a desire for personal gain is an essential part of

**corruption**
Exercising legitimate discretion for improper reasons or using illegal means to achieve approved goals.

corruption. Some experts argue that the unnecessary use of force, unreasonable searches, and an immoral personal life also constitute police misconduct and should be considered as serious as corruption devoted to economic gain.

Scholars have attempted to create typologies categorizing the forms that the abuse of police powers can take. For example, the **Knapp Commission**, a public body set up to investigate the New York City police in the 1970s, classified abusers into two groups: **meat eaters** and **grass eaters**.[159] Meat eaters aggressively misuse police power for personal gain by demanding bribes, threatening legal action, or cooperating with criminals. Across the country, police officers have been accused, indicted, and convicted of shaking down club owners and other businesspeople.[160] In contrast, grass eaters accept payoffs when their everyday duties place them in a position to be solicited by the public. For example, police officers have been investigated for taking bribes to look the other way while neighborhood bookmakers ply their trade.[161] The Knapp Commission concluded that the vast majority of police officers on the take are grass eaters, although the few meat eaters who are caught capture all the headlines. In 1993, another police scandal prompted the formation of the **Mollen Commission**, which found that some New York cops were actively involved in violence and drug dealing.

Other police experts have attempted to create models to better understand police corruption. Several types of corruption have been identified:[162]

- *Internal corruption.* This corruption takes place among police officers themselves, involving both the bending of departmental rules and the outright performance of illegal acts. For example, Chicago police officers conspired to sell relatively new police cars to other officers at cut-rate prices, forcing the department to purchase new cars unnecessarily. A major scandal hit the Boston Police Department when a captain was indicted in an exam-tampering-and-selling scheme. Numerous officers bought promotion exams from the captain, and others had him lower the scores of rivals who were competing for the same job.[163]

- *Selective enforcement or nonenforcement.* This form occurs when police officers abuse or exploit their discretion. If an officer frees a drug dealer in return for valuable information, that is considered a legitimate use of discretion; if the officer does so for money, that is an abuse of police power.

- *Active criminality.* This is participation by police in serious criminal behavior. Police may use their positions of trust and power to commit the very crimes they are entrusted with controlling. The case of New York police detectives Louis Eppolito and Stephen Caracappa is perhaps the most shocking example of police criminality in recent history. Eppolito and Caracappa sold police files on key witnesses to the mob and were convicted on charges linking them to 11 mob hits.[164]

- *Bribery and extortion.* This includes practices in which law enforcement roles are exploited specifically to raise money. Bribery is initiated by the citizen; extortion is initiated by the officer. Bribery or extortion can be a one-shot transaction, as when a traffic violator offers a police officer $500 to forget about issuing a summons. Or the relationship can be an ongoing one, in which the officer solicits (or is offered) regular payoffs to ignore criminal activities, such as gambling or narcotics dealing. This is known as "being on the pad." Sometimes police officers accept routine bribes and engage in petty extortion without considering themselves corrupt. They consider these payments as unofficial fringe benefits of police work. For example, *mooching* involves receiving free gifts of coffee, cigarettes, meals, and so on in exchange for possible future acts of favoritism. *Chiseling* occurs when officers demand admission to entertainment events or price discounts. And *shopping* involves taking small items, such as cigarettes, from a store whose door was accidentally left unlocked after business hours.[165]

**Knapp Commission**
A public body that conducted an investigation into police corruption in New York City in the early 1970s and uncovered a widespread network of payoffs and bribes.

**meat eater**
A term used to describe a police officer who actively solicits bribes and vigorously engages in corrupt practices.

**grass eater**
A term used to describe a police officer who accepts payoffs when everyday duties place him or her in a position to be solicited by the public.

**Mollen Commission**
An investigative unit set up to inquire into police corruption in New York City in the 1990s.

*THE CAUSES OF CORRUPTION* No single explanation satisfactorily accounts for the various forms that the abuse of power takes:

CourseMate For more information about **police attitudes toward abuse of authority**, visit the Criminal Justice CourseMate at CengageBrain.com, then access the "Web Links" for this chapter.

- *Police personality.* One view puts the blame on the type of person who becomes a police officer. This position holds that policing tends to attract lower-class individuals who do not have the financial means to maintain a coveted middle-class lifestyle. As they develop the cynical, authoritarian police personality, accepting graft seems an all-too-easy method of achieving financial security.

- *Institutions and practices.* A second view is that the wide discretion that police enjoy, coupled with the low visibility they maintain with the public and their own supervisors, makes them likely candidates for corruption. In addition, the code of secrecy maintained by the police subculture helps insulate corrupt officers from the law. Similarly, police managers, most of whom have risen through the ranks, are reluctant to investigate corruption or punish wrongdoers. Thus, corruption may also be viewed as a function of police institutions and practices.[166]

- *Moral ambivalence.* A third position holds that corruption is a function of society's ambivalence toward many forms of vice-related criminal behavior that police officers are sworn to control. Unenforceable laws governing moral standards promote corruption because they create large groups with an interest in undermining law enforcement. These include consumers—people who gamble, wish to drink after the legal closing hour, or patronize a prostitute—who do not want to be deprived of their chosen form of recreation. Even though the consumers may not actively corrupt police officers, their existence creates a climate that tolerates active corruption by others.[167] Because vice cannot be controlled and the public apparently wants it to continue, the officer may have little resistance to inducements for monetary gain offered by law violators.

- *Environmental conditions.* A fourth position is that corruption may be linked to specific environmental and social conditions that enhance the likelihood that police officers may become involved in misconduct. For example, in some areas a rapid increase in the minority residential population may be viewed as a threat to dominant group interests. Police in these areas may become overly aggressive and routinely use coercive strategies. The conflict produced by these outcomes may lead to antagonism between the police and the minority public, and to eventual police misconduct of all types. One recent study, in which social/ecological conditions in New York City police precincts and divisions were associated with patterns of police misconduct from 1975 to 1996, found that misconduct cases involving bribery, extortion, excessive force, and other abuses of police authority were linked to trends in neighborhood structural disadvantage, increasing population mobility, and increases in the Latino population.[168]

- *Corrupt departments.* It has also been suggested that police corruption is generated at the departmental level and that conditions within the department produce and nurture deviance.[169] In some departments, corrupt officers band together and form what is called a "rotten pocket."[170] Rotten pockets help institutionalize corruption because their members expect newcomers to conform to their illegal practices and to a code of secrecy.

- *Officer characteristics.* A study of police misconduct in the New York City Police Department revealed that factors such as officer race, prior criminal history, and problems in prior jobs were associated with on-the-job misconduct. The authors argued that "[b]y screening out those with prior arrests and prior employment problems, departments can significantly reduce the likelihood of hiring future 'bad cops.'"[171]

*CONTROLLING CORRUPTION* How can police misconduct be controlled? One approach is to strengthen the internal administrative review process within police departments. A strong and well-supported internal affairs division has been linked to lowered corruption rates.[172] However, asking police to police themselves is not a simple task. Officers are often reluctant to discipline their peers. One review of disciplinary files of New York City police officers found that many miscreants escaped punishment when their cases were summarily dismissed by the police department without anyone ever interviewing victims or witnesses or making any other efforts to examine the evidence.[173] One reason may be the blue curtain mentality that inhibits police from taking action against their fellow officers. Surveys indicate that police officers are more reluctant than ordinary citizens to report unethical behavior on the part of their colleagues.[174] Engaging in illegal brutality or bending the rules of procedure falls under the code of silence.[175]

Another approach, instituted by then New York Commissioner Patrick Murphy in the wake of the Knapp Commission, is the **accountability system**. This holds that supervisors at each level are directly accountable for the illegal behaviors of the officers under them. Consequently, a commander can be demoted or forced to resign if one of her command officers is found guilty of corruption.[176] However, close scrutiny by a department can lower officer morale and create the suspicion that the officers' own supervisors distrust them.

Police departments have also organized outside review boards or special prosecutors to investigate reported incidents of corruption. However, outside investigators and special prosecutors are often limited by their lack of intimate knowledge of day-to-day operations. As a result, they depend on the testimony of a few officers who are willing to cooperate, either to save themselves from prosecution or because they have a compelling moral commitment. Outside evaluators also face the problem of the blue curtain, which is quickly closed when police officers feel that their department is under scrutiny.

A more realistic solution to corruption, albeit a difficult one, might be to change the social context of policing. Police operations must be made more visible, and the public must be given freer access to police operations. All too often, the public finds out about police problems only when a scandal hits the newspaper. Another option is that some of the vice-related crimes the police now deal with might be decriminalized or referred to other agencies. Although decriminalization of vice cannot in itself end the problem, it could lower the pressure placed on individual police officers and help eliminate their moral dilemmas.

**accountability system**
A system that makes police supervisors responsible for the behavior of the officers in their command.

## USE OF FORCE

Despite some highly publicized incidents that get a lot of media attention, data show that the use of force is not a very common event.[177] A national survey on police contacts with civilians sponsored by the federal government found that in a single year, of the 45 million people who had one or more police contacts, about 1.5 percent (664,500 persons) reported that an officer used or threatened to use force.[178] African Americans (3.5%) and Hispanics (2.5%) were more likely than whites (1.1%) to experience police threat or use of force during the contact; young people (ages 16 to 29) were almost three times more likely to experience force than people over 29. When force was applied, however, it was most likely to be pushing or grabbing. In 19 percent of the 664,500 force incidents, a police officer pointed a gun at the individual, and 14 percent resulted in injury to the citizen. And although 24 percent of the combatants cursed at, insulted, or verbally threatened the officer(s) during the incident, three-quarters claimed that the force was excessive, and more than 80 percent believed the officer acted improperly. So 45 million people were contacted by police, but only 90,000 or so were injured. Is that far too many or relatively few?

These data indicate that police use of force may not be as common as previously believed, but it still remains a central part of the police role. Although getting an accurate figure is difficult, at least 6,600 civilians have been killed by the police since 1976, and the true number is probably much higher.[179] Considering these numbers, police use of force is an important topic for study.

## Race and Force

The routine use of force may be diminishing, but there is still debate over whether police are more likely to get rough with minority suspects. The national survey on police contacts with civilians found that African Americans and Hispanics were more likely than whites to experience police threat or use of force as a consequence of police contact. Cities with large African American populations also experience the highest amount of lethal violence by police.[180]

Considering this evidence, it is not surprising that surveys of minority group members show they are more likely to disapprove of the police view of force than majority group members.[181] Minority citizens are much more likely to claim that police "hassle them" by stopping them or watching them closely when they have done nothing wrong.[182]

Race may be a factor that determines the outcome of police–citizen encounters, but it is certainly not the only one. Joel Garner's study of police encounters with citizens, using a wide variety of samples taken in different locales, found that race actually played an insignificant role in the decision to use force.[183] The suspect's behavior is a much more powerful determinant of police response than age or race. William Terrill studied 3,544 police–suspect encounters and found that situational factors often influence the extent to which force is applied. Use of force seems to escalate when a police officer gives a suspect a second chance (such as "Dump the beer out of your car, and I'll let you go"), but the suspect hesitates or defies the order.[184] People who resist police orders or actually grapple with officers are much more likely to be the target of force than those who are respectful, passive, and noncombative.

The general public seems to understand the situational use of force: Even people who condemn police violence—such as racial minorities—are more supportive of its use if the officer is in danger or a suspect is confrontational.[185] So the evidence suggests that whether African American or white, suspect behavior may be a more important determinant of force than race or ethnicity.

## Deadly Force

**Deadly force** is force that is likely to cause death or significant bodily harm. The FBI defines it as "the intentional use of a firearm or other instrument resulting in a high probability of death."[186] The justification for the use of deadly force can be traced to English common law, in which almost every criminal offense was a felony and bore the death penalty. The use of deadly force in the course of arresting a felon was considered expedient, saving the state the burden of trial (the "fleeing felon" rule).[187]

Although the media depict hero cops in a constant stream of deadly shootouts in which scores of bad guys are killed, the number of people killed by the police each year is somewhere between 300 and 500.[188] Although these data are encouraging, some researchers believe that the actual number of police shootings is far greater and may be hidden or masked by a number of factors. For example, coroners may be intentionally or accidentally underreporting police homicides by almost half.[189]

**deadly force**
The intentional use of a firearm or other instrument, resulting in a high probability of death.

*FACTORS RELATED TO POLICE SHOOTINGS* Is police use of deadly force a random occurrence, or are there social, legal, and environmental factors associated with its use? The following seven patterns have been related to police shootings.

- *Local and national violence levels.* The higher the levels of violence in a community, the more likely police in the area will use deadly force.[190]

# ANALYZING CRIMINAL JUSTICE ISSUES

## Suicide by Cop

As strange as it sounds, some individuals shot by the police actually *want* to be shot. The problem of "suicide by cop" occurs when an individual who is intent on ending his or her life engages in behavior that makes it likely that police will use deadly force.

An example is the case of John T. Garczynski Jr., a Florida Power and Light Company employee, separated from his wife and despondent over the breakup of his marriage and their financial situation. One night after their breakup, Garczynski met his wife at a bowling alley and gave her a packet containing a suicide note, an obituary, and a eulogy that he wanted read at his funeral. After Garczynski left the bowling alley and his wife discovered what was in the package, she called the police, who were then able to track down Garczynski with the help of his cellular phone company. When officers confronted him, he pointed a gun at them, so the officers fired. Garczynski died in a hail of 26 bullets.

Cases like Garczynski's can be difficult for police officers. As Rebecca Stincelli, author of the book *Suicide by Cop: Victims from Both Sides of the Badge*, has noted, "In the past, people have used rope, a gun, gas, [or] jumped off a building. A police officer is just another method ... They say it's nothing personal, [but] they are wrong. It's very personal." The FBI has raised a similar point, noting that "Suicide-by-cop incidents are painful and damaging experiences for the surviving families, the communities, and all law enforcement professionals."

How common is suicide by cop? One study of fatal shootings by Los Angeles police officers found that more than 10 percent could be classified as suicide by cop! Researchers have since placed such killings into three categories. The first is a "direct confrontation," where the suicidal party initiates a confrontation with police for the purpose of dying. The second is a "disturbed intervention," in which a suicidal subject takes advantage of the police presence to further his or her suicide attempt. The third is a "criminal intervention," where a criminal suspect would rather die than be apprehended.

### Critical Thinking

1.  What can police officers do to avoid potential suicide-by-cop situations? If they are forced into one, what options are available?

2.  To what extent can police officers infer, in a potential suicide-by-cop situation, that a person is intent on dying? Are other options available?

Sources: Stephanie Slater, "Suicidal Man Killed by Police Fusillade," *Palm Beach Post*, March 11, 2005, p. 1A; Rebecca Stincelli, *Suicide by Cop: Victims from Both Sides of the Badge* (Folsom, Calif.: Interviews and Interrogations Institute, 2004); Vivian Lord, *Suicide by Cop: Inducing Officers to Shoot* (Flushing, N.Y.: Looseleaf Law Publications, 2004); Anthony J. Pinizzotto, Edward F. Davis, and Charles E. Miller III, "Suicide by Cop: Defining a Devastating Dilemma," *FBI Law Enforcement Bulletin* 74 (2005): 15; "Ten Percent of Police Shootings Found to Be 'Suicide by Cop,'" *Criminal Justice Newsletter*, September 1, 1998, pp. 1–2; Robert J. Homant and Daniel B. Kennedy, "Suicide by Police: A Proposed Typology of Law Enforcement Officer–Assisted Suicide," *Policing: An International Journal of Police Strategies and Management* 23 (2000): 339–355.

---

A number of studies have found that fatal police shootings were closely related to reported national violent crime rates and criminal homicide rates. Police officers kill civilians at a higher rate in years when the general level of violence in the nation is higher. The perception of danger may contribute to the use of violent means for self-protection.[191]

■ *Exposure to violence.* Police officers may be exposed to violence when they are forced to confront the emotionally disturbed. Some distraught people attack police as a form of suicide.[192] This tragic event has become so common that the term "suicide by cop" has been coined to denote victim-precipitated killings by police. For example, during an 11-year period (1988 to 1998) more than 10 percent of the shootings by police officers in Los Angeles involved suicidal people intentionally provoking police (see the accompanying Analyzing Criminal Justice Issues feature for more details on suicide by cop).[193]

■ *Workload.* A relationship exists among police violence and the number of police on the street, the number of calls for service, the number and nature of police dispatches, the number of arrests made in a given jurisdiction, and police exposure to stressful situations.

■ *Firearms availability.* Cities that experience a large number of crimes committed with firearms are also likely to have high police violence rates. A strong association has been found between police use of force and gun density (the proportion of suicides and murders committed with a gun).[194]

■ *Social conflict.* The threat hypothesis. According to the threat hypothesis, more police are killed in cities with a large underclass.[195] The greatest number of police shootings occur in areas that have significant disparities in economic opportunity and high levels of income inequality.[196] Economic disadvantage within the minority community, coupled with political alienation, leads to a climate in which police–citizen conflict is sharpened. Politically excluded groups may turn to violence to gain ends that those not excluded can acquire with conventional tactics. One conflict-reduction approach is to add minority police officers. However, recent research by Brad Smith shows that the mere addition of minority officers to a department is not sufficient to reduce levels of police violence.[197] The presence of an African American mayor has also been linked with reductions in the likelihood of police–citizen violence.[198] Such a mayor may help reduce feelings of powerlessness in the minority community, which in turn reduces anger against the state, of which the police are the most visible officials.

■ *Administrative policies.* The philosophy, policies, and practices of individual police chiefs and departments significantly influence the police use of deadly force.[199] Departments that stress restrictions on the use of force generally have lower shooting rates than those that favor tough law enforcement and encourage officers to shoot when necessary. Poorly written or ambivalent policies encourage shootings because they allow the officer at the scene to decide when deadly force is warranted, often under conditions of high stress and tension.

■ *Race.* No other issue is as important to the study of the police use of deadly force as racial discrimination. A number of critics have claimed that police are more likely to shoot and kill minority offenders than they are whites. In a famous statement, sociologist Paul Takagi charged that police have "one trigger finger for whites and another for African-Americans."[200] Takagi's complaint was supported by a number of research studies that showed that a disproportionate number of police killings involved minority citizens— almost 80 percent in some of the cities surveyed.[201]

Do these findings alone indicate that police discriminate in the use of deadly force? Some pioneering research by James Fyfe helps provide an answer to this question. In his study of New York City shootings over a five-year period, Fyfe found that police officers were most likely to shoot suspects who were armed and with whom they became involved in violent confrontations. Once such factors as being armed with a weapon, being involved in a violent crime, and attacking an officer were considered, the racial differences in the police use of force ceased to be significant. Fyfe found that African American officers were almost twice as likely as white officers to have shot citizens. He attributed this finding to the fact that African American officers work and live in high-crime, high-violence areas where shootings are more common and that African American officers hold proportionately more line positions and fewer administrative posts than white officers, which would place them more often on the street and less often behind a desk.[202]

**CONTROLLING DEADLY FORCE** Because police use of deadly force is such a serious problem, ongoing

## PERSPECTIVES ON JUSTICE

### Due Process

The *Tennessee v. Garner* decision helps preserve important civil rights, particularly the U.S. Constitution's prohibition against unreasonable searches and seizures. Shooting an unarmed fleeing felon is now considered a violation of the felon's constitutional rights. Most police departments also have policies that restrict officers' use of force.

efforts have been made to control it. One of the most difficult problems that undermined its control was the continued use of the fleeing-felon rule in a number of states. However, in 1985 the U.S. Supreme Court outlawed the indiscriminate use of deadly force with its decision in the case of *Tennessee v. Garner*. In this case, the Court ruled that the use of deadly force against apparently unarmed and nondangerous fleeing felons is an illegal seizure of their person under the Fourth Amendment. Deadly force may not be used unless it is necessary to prevent escape and the officer has probable cause to believe that the suspect poses a significant threat of death or serious injury to the officer or others. The majority opinion stated that when the suspect poses no immediate threat to the officer and no threat to others, the harm resulting from failing to apprehend the suspect does not justify the use of deadly force to do so: "A police officer may not seize an unarmed, nondangerous suspect by shooting him dead."[203]

Individual state jurisdictions still control police shooting policy. Some states have adopted statutory policies that restrict the police use of violence. Others have upgraded training in the use of force. The Federal Law Enforcement Training Center (FLETC) has developed the FLETC use-of-force model, illustrated in Figure 7.3, to teach officers the proper method to escalate force in response to the threat they face. As the figure shows, resistance ranges from compliant and cooperative to assaultive with the threat of serious bodily harm or death. Officers are taught via lecture, demonstration, computer-based instruction, and training scenarios to assess a suspect's behavior and apply an appropriate and corresponding amount of force.[204]

Another method of controlling police shootings is through internal review and policy making by police administrative review boards and other top-level officials.[205] Since 1972, the New York City Police Department has conducted an internal investigation any time an officer's weapon is discharged (with the exception of training situations). The process works as follows:

■ NYPD policy requires an officer to provide immediate notification to his or her supervisor of any firearm discharge.

**FIGURE 7.3**
The Federal Law Enforcement Training Center's Use-of-Force Model

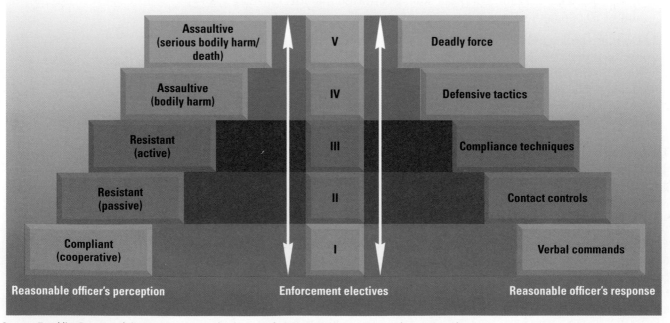

Source: Franklin Graves and Gregory Connor, Federal Law Enforcement Training Center, Glynco, Georgia.

- The department dispatches a "firearm-discharge investigative team" (also called a "shooting team") to the scene. The team investigates the scene, gives the shooting officer a breath-alcohol test, and prepares a detailed incident report pursuant to the department's *Firearm Discharges Investigation Manual.*

- If the incident involved shooting of a person, the commissioner is briefed the next day.

- The district attorney is notified of the shooting.

- The shooting team's final report is due 90 days after the incident, at which point it is examined by the patrol borough's Firearms Discharge Review Board (FDRB), the patrol borough commander, the department's FDRB, and ultimately the department chief. Accidental discharges and other shootings not of people do not receive full review.[206]

The review board approach is controversial because it can mean that the department recommends that one of its own officers be turned over for criminal prosecution.

There is evidence that police officers involved in shootings often suffer from "perceptual distortions."[207] That is, they sometimes perceive reality as different than it is. In the heat of the moment, they may lose track of time, hear things that didn't occur, and even see things that were not there. Knowing that these distortions can occur is important, because it suggests some latitude be given to officers who discharge their weapons; their actions should not always be judged with the benefit of 20-20 hindsight but rather with an understanding of what was going through their heads at the time. Realizing this, according to experts, "...may help concerned members of the public to appreciate the realities of what officers experience when they face decisions about whether to fire their weapons and to make more informed judgments about whether a given officer acted reasonably when he or she fired his or her weapon."[208]

## Nondeadly Force

**Nondeadly force** is force that is unlikely to cause death or significant bodily harm. Nondeadly force can range from the use of handcuffs and suspect compliance techniques to rubber bullets and stun guns. Officers resort to nondeadly force in a number of circumstances. They may begin with verbal commands and then escalate the force used when confronted with a resistant suspect. Researchers have found that the crime in question is strongly linked to the type of nondeadly force used and that officers are also influenced by past experience, the presence of other officers, and the presence and behavior of bystanders.[209] And even though nondeadly force is used more often than deadly force, it is still relatively rare—and at the lower end of the severity scale (e.g., grabbed by officer instead of hit). Researchers have estimated that police use or threaten to use nondeadly force in only 1.7 percent of all contacts and 20 percent of all arrests.[210]

Although nondeadly force is unlikely to cause death, it sometimes does. For example, medical examiners have attributed some Taser deaths (we discuss Tasers in more detail shortly) to a condition known as excited delirium, a supposed overdose of adrenaline that can occur in heated confrontations with the police. Not everyone agrees that **excited delirium** is an actual medical condition, but it has been listed as the cause of death in some situations, particularly when the suspect was found to be under the influence of stimulants.[211]

*CONTROLLING NONDEADLY FORCE* In *Graham v. Connor*, the Supreme Court created a reasonableness standard for the use of nondeadly force. The Court held that force is excessive when, considering all the circumstances known to the officer at the time he acted, the force used was unreasonable.[212] For example, an officer is approached in a threatening manner by someone wielding a knife. The assailant fails to stop when warned and is killed by the officer. The

**nondeadly force**
Force that is unlikely to cause death or significant bodily harm.

**excited delirium**
An overdose of adrenaline that can occur in heated confrontations with the police.

## CRIMINAL JUSTICE AND TECHNOLOGY

# *Tasers*

The Taser (an acronym for **T**homas **A**. **S**wift's **E**lectric **R**ifle) is named after the 1911 Victor Appleton novel *Tom Swift and His Electric Rifle* It fires electrified darts at uncooperative individuals who, when hit, can experience up to 50,000 volts of electricity. The company that makes the Taser, Taser International, manufactures a wide array of products, one of the most popular being the X26. The X26 uses a replaceable cartridge full of nitrogen to deploy two small probes. The probes can travel approximately 20 feet and can pierce through two inches of clothing, attack the individual's central nervous system, and cause muscle contractions and temporary paralysis.

One of Taser International's latest products is the Taser XREP, a self-contained, wireless device that can be deployed from a modified pump-action shotgun. Because it is wireless, it can be delivered to suspects at upwards of 100 feet away, posing minimal risk to the officer using it. The nose of the projectile contains four sharp probes. These attach to the body of the suspect and deploy a shock for 20 seconds. Most recently, Taser has released a product that can be used to incapacitate multiple suspects at once, something

officer would not be held liable if it turns out that the shooting victim was deaf and could not hear the officer's command and if the officer at the time of the incident had no way of knowing about the person's disability.

*LESS-LETHAL WEAPONS*  In the last few years, about 1,000 local police forces have started using some sort of less-lethal weapons designed to subdue suspects. The term "less-lethal" is the preferred description because even though these weapons fall into the nondeadly force category, some have been linked to deaths. Despite this, experts have heralded less-lethal weapons as helpful additions to the law enforcement arsenal.[213]

Among the most widely used nonlethal weapons are so-called **impact munitions**, including rubber bullets. At short distances, officers use pepper spray and Tasers, which deliver electric shocks from long wire tentacles, producing intense muscle spasms. Other technologies include guns that shoot giant nets, guns that squirt sticky glue, and lights that can temporarily blind a suspect.[214] All such technologies can reduce the risk of injury and death to both police officers and suspects during difficult encounters.[215]

Impact munitions include foam rubber bullets, wooden dowels, bean bags, and other projectiles that are usually fired from 12-gauge shotguns or 37/40-millimeter gas grenade launchers.[216] An example of one such device is Combined Tactical Systems' (CTS) 12-gauge launching cap. It can fire a large rubber projectile from a distance of 75 to 100 meters. Beanbags can also be fired from these types of devices. "Area rounds" are 12-gauge shotgun shells full of rubber pellets that deliver strong blows to people without penetrating the skin. Sponge point grenades, fired from grenade launchers, also help police subdue unruly individuals. Even rubber pellet–filled hand grenades have been used, as have flash grenades and flash-bang stun hand grenades.[217] Impact munitions are often used as an alternative to deadly force, but it is possible for their use to result in loss of life. When some of these devices are fired from distances of less than 30 feet, serious injury and death can result. A National Institute of Justice study of 373 impact munitions incidents revealed that eight individuals died as a result of injuries sustained from impact munitions.[218] At least one suspect died as a result of being hit in the neck with a beanbag round. The rest died as a result of having broken ribs pierce their heart or lungs.

**impact munitions**
Less-lethal weapons that are used to stun or otherwise incapacitate uncooperative suspects so they can be subdued. Examples include rubber bullets and bean bag projectiles.

the X26, its predecessors, and even the XREP cannot accomplish.

Well over 8,000 law enforcement agencies around the country use these and other Taser products—in addition to other less-lethal technologies. The Taser enjoys popularity, in part because it offers police officers an alternative to deadly force in certain situations. Tasers are not without controversy, however. Some organizations are opposed to their use, and they have been linked to some deaths, but for the most part, the evidence is supportive of Tasers (see the Evidence-Based Justice box in this chapter), so it is likely that they will continue to increase in popularity and be used by more and more law enforcement agencies.

## Critical Thinking

1. What advantages does the Taser offer over other less-lethal weapons?

2. Since Tasers are considered less-lethal weapons, will officers be more inclined to resort to their use? Why or why not?

Sources: Michael D. White, "The Taser as a Less Lethal Force Alternative: Findings on Use and Effectiveness in a Large Metropolitan Police Agency," *Police Quarterly* 10 (2007): 170–191; Taser International, www.taser.com/pages/default.aspx (accessed April 13, 2010); Taser International, *Advanced Taser M26 Field Report Analysis* (Scottsdale, AZ: Taser International, 2002).

---

A conducted energy device (CED) administers a nonlethal shock to an uncooperative suspect. The most well-known CED is the popular **Taser**, manufactured by Taser International.[219] It is described in the accompanying Criminal Justice and Technology feature. See also the Evidence-Based Justice feature on Taser effectiveness.

One of the most popular less-lethal weapons being used by law enforcement personnel is oleoresin capsicum, also known as pepper spray. This product, which is made from peppers, is so strong that when suspects are sprayed, their eyes automatically shut and they experience shortness of breath. Pepper spray is used in a variety of scenarios, from subduing an agitated individual to subduing groups that are uncooperative and causing problems.

Some law enforcement agencies have adopted more high-powered pepper spray models, including the PepperBall System, which is a semiautomatic high-pressure launcher that fires projectiles that contain the strongest form of oleoresin capsicum and burst on impact. The launcher is accurate up to 30 feet and can saturate an area up to 100 feet across, which allows police officers to safely stand back while incapacitating suspects.

Pepper spray is appropriately considered a less-lethal weapon because some people have died as a result of its use.[220] Researchers at the University of Texas Southwestern Medical Center identified 63 cases of death where pepper spray was thought to be the culprit. On closer examination, they found that only two of the deaths were linked to pepper spray, and those suspects were asthmatics whose conditions were aggravated by the use of pepper spray.[221]

**Taser**
A nonlethal conducted energy device that administers a shock to an uncooperative suspect by way of an electrified dart.

## Police as Victims

Police use of force continues to be an important issue, but control measures seem to be working. Fewer people are being killed by police, and fewer officers are being killed in the line of duty than ever before—about 50 each year. The number rose dramatically in 2001 because 23 officers were killed in the September 11 terrorist attacks, along with 343 firefighters. Before the 2001 spike, the number of officers slain in the line of duty had been trending downward for

### PERSPECTIVES ON JUSTICE

#### Crime Control and Due Process

Many aspects of police work require balancing crime control and due process perspectives of justice. Less-lethal weapons help the police control crime through their ability to help subdue unruly suspects, but such weapons also limit the chances that a suspect will be unnecessarily killed.

## EVIDENCE-BASED JUSTICE

# Are Tasers Effective?

As Tasers have found their way into mainstream law enforcement use, researchers have been drawn to the question of whether they present an effective alternative to conventional use-of-force measures. This research has yielded a wide range of conclusions, ranging from very supportive to very critical. Staunch advocates of Tasers include the manufacturer and much of the law enforcement community. Critics include most notably Amnesty International, the human rights organization. It has been especially critical of Taser death. Most research findings fall somewhere between these extremes.

For example, research has shown that Tasers are more effective at incapacitating suspects than pepper spray. Dozens of studies have concluded that Tasers pose minimal risk of death or serious injury, but much of the research has been conducted in laboratory settings on animals and healthy human volunteers. In response to this limitation, Michael White and Justin Ready compared news reports of fatal and nonfatal Taser incidents. They found that suspect drug use, mental illness, and continued resistance were associated with Taser deaths, but they concluded that more research is necessary if we are ever to know for sure. In the meantime, they suggest the development of model policy guidelines for Taser use, because the hope is that policy guidance for police can minimize any unfortunate consequences associated with Taser use. Indeed, the Police Executive Research Forum has come up with several recommendations for the proper use of Tasers and related CEDs:

■ CEDs should be used only against persons who are actively resisting or exhibiting active aggression, or to prevent individuals from harming themselves or others. CEDs should not be used against a passive suspect.

■ No more than one officer at a time should activate a CED against a person.

■ When activating a CED, law enforcement officers should use it for one standard cycle and stop to evaluate the situation (a standard cycle is five seconds). If subsequent cycles are necessary, agency policy should restrict the number and duration of those cycles to the minimum activations necessary to place the subject in custody.

■ Training protocols should emphasize that multiple activations and continuous cycling of a CED appear to increase the risk of death or serious injury and should be avoided where practical.

■ Training should include recognizing the limitations of CED activation and being prepared to transition to other force options as needed.

Sources: Taser International, www.taser.com/research/statistics/Pages/default.aspx (accessed April 13, 2010); Amnesty International, Amnesty International's Continued Concerns about Taser Use (Amnesty International, 2006), web.amnesty.org/library/index/engamr510302006 (accessed April 13, 2010); Taser International, *Advanced Taser M26 Field Report Analysis* (Scottsdale, AZ: Taser International, 2002); Robert J. Kaminski, "Research on Conducted Energy Devices: Findings, Methods, and Possible Alternatives," *Criminology and Public Policy* 8 (2009): 903–913; Michael D. White and Justin Ready, "Examining Fatal and Nonfatal Incidents Involving the Taser," *Criminology and Public Policy* 8 (2009): 865–891; James M. Cronin and Joshua A. Ederheimer, Conducted Energy Devices: Development of Standards for Consistency and Guidance (Washington, D.C.: Police Executive Research Forum, 2006), p. 23, www.policeforum.org/upload/CED-Guidelines_414547688_2152007092436.pdf (accessed April 12, 2010).

the previous decade.[222] In 2008, the last year for which data was available as of this writing, 41 law enforcement officers were feloniously killed. What were the circumstances surrounding their deaths? Of the 41 officers slain, 6 were killed in ambush situations, 9 were killed in arrest situations, and 8 were killed while handling traffic stops or during vehicle pursuits. The remaining 18 were killed responding to disturbance calls; investigating suspicious persons/circumstances; and during tactical operations, investigative activities, and prisoner transport.[223] Many more officers are assaulted than killed. Figure 7.4, which includes all officers killed between 1999 and 2008, makes this clear. Roughly 1,000 officers are assaulted for every officer who is killed.

One long-cherished myth is that police officers who answer domestic violence calls are at risk for violent victimization. The scenario goes that, when they are confronted, one of the two battling parties turns on the outsider who dares

**CourseMate** For more information about **concerns of police survivors**, visit the Criminal Justice CourseMate at CengageBrain.com, then access the "Web Links" for this chapter.

**FIGURE 7.4**
Law Enforcement Officers Feloniously Killed or Assaulted

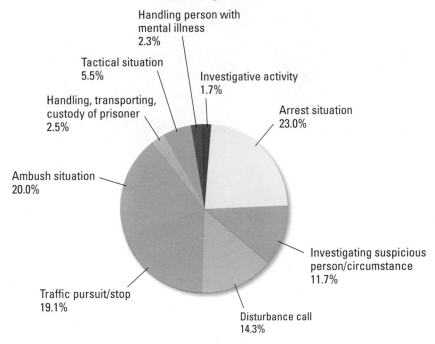

Percent of 530 officers feloniously killed

Handling person with mental illness 2.3%
Tactical situation 5.5%
Investigative activity 1.7%
Handling, transporting, custody of prisoner 2.5%
Arrest situation 23.0%
Ambush situation 20.0%
Traffic pursuit/stop 19.1%
Investigating suspicious person/circumstance 11.7%
Disturbance call 14.3%

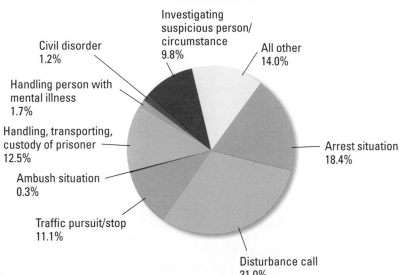

Percent of 586,915 officers assaulted

Investigating suspicious person/circumstance 9.8%
Civil disorder 1.2%
All other 14.0%
Handling person with mental illness 1.7%
Handling, transporting, custody of prisoner 12.5%
Arrest situation 18.4%
Ambush situation 0.3%
Traffic pursuit/stop 11.1%
Disturbance call 31.0%

Source: Federal Bureau of Investigation, *Law Enforcement Officers Killed and Assaulted, 2008* (Washington, D.C.: Federal Bureau of Investigation, 2006), http://www.fbi.gov/about-us/cjis/ucr/leoka/2008 (accessed October 8, 2010, Figure 4.).

interfere in a private matter. However, research conducted in Charlotte, North Carolina, indicates that domestic violence calls may be no more dangerous than many other routine police interactions.[224] So although police officers should be on their guard when investigating a call for assistance from an abused spouse, the risk of violence against them may be no greater than when they answer a call for a burglary or car theft.

*Every year, dozens of police officers are killed on the job, and thousands more are injured. Here Fredericksburg, Virginia, police officers Bill Hyer and Heather Marshall listen to their chief talk to the media and other officers on June 7, 2008, about the shooting death of their colleague, officer Todd Bahr. Bahr was responding to a domestic dispute when he was shot. The suspect died minutes later after exchanging gunfire with other officers.*

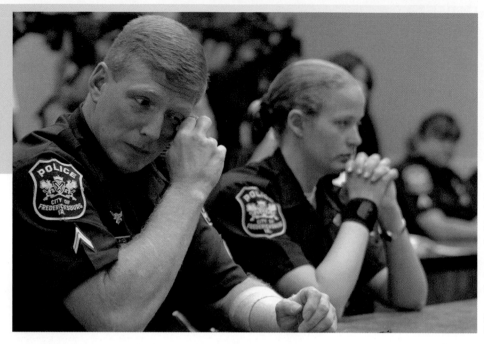

© AP Images/*The Free Lance-Star*/Robert A. Martin

**National Law Enforcement Officers Memorial**
The nation's monument to police officers who have died in the line of duty.

*MEMORIALIZING LOST OFFICERS* The **National Law Enforcement Officers Memorial** is the nation's monument to police officers who have died in the line of duty. Located in Washington, D.C., the monument consists of two curving marble walls that display the names of over 18,600 men and women who lost their lives while serving on duty as police officers. Only those who have died in the line of duty can have their names displayed on the wall. To die in the line of duty means that

> a law enforcement officer has died as a direct and proximate result of a personal injury sustained in the line of duty. This includes victim law enforcement officers who, while in an off-duty capacity, act in response to a law violation. It also includes victim law enforcement officers who, while in an off-duty capacity, are en route to or from a specific emergency or responding to a particular request for assistance; or the officer is, as required or authorized by law or condition of employment, driving his or her employer's vehicle to or from work; or when the officer is, as required by law or condition of employment, driving his or her own personal vehicle at work and is killed while en route to or from work.[225]

## Ethical Challenges in Criminal Justice: A Writing Assignment

The town has a strict policy prohibiting police officers from accepting or soliciting bribes or gratuities, so Councilman Bessey files a complaint against Officer Jones with the city's Civilian Review Board, claiming that Jones accepted a free lunch from a local restaurant. A hearing on the matter is scheduled, and if he is found liable, Jones faces three possible penalties: suspension, suspension and loss of rank, or dismissal.

Write an essay on the ethics of accepting gratuities. In doing so, answer these questions: Should police officers be permitted to accept gratuities, in this case free lunches? Why or why not? What penalty, if any, should Jones receive? Officer Jones had to know about the town's policy, but he nevertheless violated it. Why? What explanations can be offered for his behavior? What steps can police administrators take to control behaviors such as this? Consult this chapter's "Corruption" section for guidance as you write.

# SUMMARY

1. **Know the benefits likely to accrue from higher education for police.**

   - It is believed that a well-educated officer can communicate better with the public.
   - Police administrators believe well-educated officers perform more effectively.
   - Research shows that educated officers are less likely to have disciplinary problems.

2. **Discuss some of the issues associated with minority police officers.**

   - A heterogeneous police force can be instrumental in gaining the confidence of the minority community.
   - In some larger departments, the percentage of minorities on police forces now reflects their representation in the general population.

3. **Describe how the role of women in local police agencies has evolved over time.**

   - Today, about 16 percent of all sworn officers in larger cities (population over 250,000) are women. African American women account for less than 5 percent of police officers.
   - Women still lag behind white males in supervisory positions.
   - Women working in the male-dominated police profession often experience stress and anxiety.

4. **Explain the concept of a police culture.**

   - There is an independent and unique police culture, which insulates police officers from the rest of society. This culture has distinct rules and loyalties.
   - Police culture is characterized by cynicism, clannishness, secrecy, and insulation from others in society. Together, these elements of police culture have been called the "blue curtain."
   - Police culture is largely developed from on-the-job experiences.

5. **Know the reasons why experts believe police have a unique personality.**

   - Experts believe the police personality is shaped by constant exposure to danger and the need to use force and authority to defuse and control threatening situations.
   - Some experts believe that policing attracts recruits who are by nature cynical, authoritarian, and secretive. Others maintain that socialization and experience on the police force itself cause these character traits to develop.

6. **Recognize the different types of police officer styles.**

   - Police officers may develop a unique working style. Four distinct police styles have been identified: the crime fighter, the social agent, the law enforcer, and the watchman.
   - Some experts have challenged the argument that there are distinct officer styles.

7. **Understand the factors that influence police discretion.**

   - Discretion is the use of personal decision making and choice in carrying out operations in the criminal justice system.
   - A number of factors influence police discretion: the crime in question, victim factors, environmental factors, departmental factors, peer factors, suspect behavior and characteristics, and officer characteristics.

8. **Know the consequences of stress and fatigue.**

   - Stress leads to negative attitudes, burnout, loss of enthusiasm and commitment (cynicism), increased apathy, substance abuse problems, divorce, health problems, and many other social, personal, and job-related problematic behaviors
   - A police officer who is fatigued may be at higher risk of acting inappropriately or being injured on the job.

9. **Distinguish between brutality and corruption.**

   - Brutality refers to actions such as using abusive language, making threats, using force or coercion unnecessarily, prodding with nightsticks, and stopping and searching people to harass them.
   - Corruption consists of exercising legitimate discretion for improper reasons or using illegal means to achieve approved goals.

10. **Know the difference between deadly and nondeadly force.**

    - Deadly force is force that is likely to cause death or significant bodily harm.
    - Nondeadly force is force that is *unlikely* to cause death or significant bodily harm.

11. **Know the leading types of less-lethal weapons.**

    - The term "less-lethal" comes from the fact that such weapons are less lethal than guns, but it is still possible for death to result in exceptional cases.
    - Popular less-lethal weapons include impact munitions, conducted energy devices (such as Tasers), and pepper spray.

## KEY TERMS

double marginality, 244
blue curtain, 249
cynicism, 250
police styles, 250
discretion, 252
low-visibility decision making, 253
overload hypothesis, 254
demeanor, 255

police brutality, 161
corruption, 263
Knapp Commission, 264
meat eater, 264
grass eater, 264
Mollen Commission, 264
accountability system, 266
deadly force, 267

nondeadly force, 271
excited delirium, 271
impact munitions, 272
Taser, 273
National Law Enforcement
   Officers Memorial, 276

## CRITICAL THINKING QUESTIONS

1. Should male and female officers have exactly the same duties in a police department? If not, why not?

2. Do you think that working the street will eventually lead an officer to develop a cynical personality and distrust for civilians? Explain.

3. How can education help police officers?

4. Should a police officer who accepts a free meal from a restaurant owner be dismissed from the force? Why or why not?

5. A police officer orders an unarmed person running away from a burglary to stop. The suspect keeps running and is shot and killed by the officer. Has the officer committed a crime? Explain.

6. Would you like to live in a society that abolished police discretion and followed a full-enforcement policy? Why or why not?

## NOTES

1. State News Service, "Texas Senators Hutchison, Cornyn Request Action from President Obama on Escalating Violence in Mexico," March 17, 2010.
2. Associated Press, "Gov. Activates Spillover Violence Response Plan," March 16, 2010.
3. David Burge, "Law Agencies Seek Grant for Border Crime," *El Paso Times*, March 23, 2010. Available at www.elpasotimes.com/news/ci_14736032 (accessed April 13, 2010).
4. Gary Martin, "Customs Chief: Violence Not Crossing Border," *San Antonio Express-News*, April 8, 2010, p. 10A.
5. *Sourcebook of Criminal Justice Statistics*, online version, http://albany.edu/sourcebook/pdf/t2122007.pdf (accessed August 21, 2008).
6. Elaine B. Sharp and Paul E. Johnson, "Accounting for Variation in Distrust of Local Police," *Justice Quarterly* 26 (2009): 157–182.
7. Robert Sigler and Ida Johnson, "Reporting Violent Acts to the Police: A Difference by Race," *Policing* 25 (2002): 274–293.
8. Thomas Priest and Deborah Brown Carter, "Evaluations of Police Performance in an African American Sample," *Journal of Criminal Justice* 27 (1999): 457–465; Ronald Weitzer, "White, Black, or Blue Cops? Race and Citizen Assessments of Police Officers," *Journal of Criminal Justice* 28 (2000): 313–324.
9. Karen Kruger and Nicholas Valltos, "Dealing with Domestic Violence in Law Enforcement Relationships," *FBI Law Enforcement Bulletin* 71 (2002): 1–7.
10. Robert Loo, "A Typology of Burnout Types among Police Managers," *Policing* 27 (2004): 156–165.
11. See Larry Hoover, *Police Educational Characteristics and Curricula* (Washington, D.C.: U.S. Government Printing Office, 1975).
12. Matthew Hickman and Brian Reaves, *Local Police Departments, 2003* (Washington, D.C.: Bureau of Justice Statistics, 2006).
13. Brian Reaves and Matthew J. Hickman, *Police Departments in Large Cities, 1990–2000* (Washington, D.C.: Bureau of Justice Statistics, 2002).
14. Maggy Lee and Maurice Punch, "Policing by Degrees: Police Officers' Experience of University Education," *Policing and Society* 14 (2004): 233–249.
15. Bruce Berg, "Who Should Teach Police? A Typology and Assessment of Police Academy Instructors," *American Journal of Police* 9 (1990): 79–100.
16. David Carter and Allen Sapp, *The State of Police Education: Critical Findings* (Washington, D.C.: Police Executive Research Forum, 1988), p. 6.
17. Jason Rydberg and William Terrill, "The Effect of Higher Education on Police Behavior," *Police Quarterly* 13 (2010): 92–120.
18. John Krimmel, "The Performance of College-Educated Police: A Study of Self-Rated Police Performance Measures," *American Journal of Police* 15 (1996): 85–95.
19. Robert Worden, "A Badge and a Baccalaureate: Policies, Hypotheses, and Further Evidence," *Justice Quarterly* 7 (1990): 565–592.
20. See Lawrence Sherman and Warren Bennis, "Higher Education for Police Officers: The Central Issues," *Police Chief* 44 (1977): 32.
21. Worden, "A Badge and a Baccalaureate," 587–589.
22. Jihong Zhao and Nicholas Lovrich, "Determinants of Minority Employment in American Municipal Police Agencies: The Representation of African American Officers," *Journal of Criminal Justice* 26 (1998): 267–278.
23. David Murphy and John Worrall, "Residency Requirements and Public Perceptions of the Police in Large Municipalities," *Policing* 22 (1999): 327–342.

24. Steven Tuch and Ronald Weitzer, "The Polls: Trends, Racial Differences in Attitudes toward the Police," *Public Opinion Quarterly* 61 (1997): 662; Sutham Cheurprakobkit, "Police–Citizen Contact and Police Performance: Attitudinal Differences between Hispanics and Non-Hispanics," *Journal of Criminal Justice* 28 (2000): 325–336; Maguire and Pastore, eds., *Sourcebook of Criminal Justice Statistics*.

25. Cheurprakobkit, "Police–Citizen Contact and Police Performance"; Maguire and Pastore, eds., *Sourcebook of Criminal Justice Statistics*.

26. Yolander G. Hurst, James Frank, and Sandra Lee Browning, "The Attitudes of Juveniles toward the Police: A Comparison of African-American and White Youth," *Policing* 23 (2000): 37–53.

27. Jack Kuykendall and David Burns, "The African-American Police Officer: An Historical Perspective," *Journal of Contemporary Criminal Justice* 1 (1980): 4–13.

28. Ibid.

29. Nicholas Alex, *Black in Blue: A Study of the Negro Policeman* (New York: Appleton-Century-Crofts, 1969).

30. Kim Michelle Lersch, "Predicting Citizen Race in Allegations of Misconduct against the Police," *Journal of Criminal Justice* 26 (1998): 87–99.

31. Nicholas Alex, *New York Cops Talk Back* (New York: Wiley, 1976).

32. David Eitle, Lisa Stolzenberg, and Stewart J. D'Alessio, "Police Organizational Factors, the Racial Composition of the Police, and the Probability of Arrest," *Justice Quarterly* 22 (2005): 30–57.

33. Robert Brown and James Frank, "Race and Officer Decision Making: Examining Differences in Arrest Outcomes between Black and White Officers," *Justice Quarterly* 23 (2006): 96–126.

34. Stephen Leinen, *African-American Police, White Society* (New York: New York University Press, 1984).

35. Ni He, Jihong Zhao, and Ling Ren, "Do Race and Gender Matter in Police Stress? A Preliminary Assessment of the Interactive Effects," *Journal of Criminal Justice* 33 (2005): 535–547; Merry Morash, Robin Haarr, and Dae-Hoon Kwak, "Multilevel Influences on Police Stress," *Journal of Contemporary Criminal Justice* 22 (2006): 26–43.

36. Joseph L. Gustafson, "Tokenism in Policing: An Empirical Test of Kanter's Hypothesis," *Journal of Criminal Justice* 36 (2008): 1–10.

37. Robin Haarr and Merry Morash, "Gender, Race, and Strategies of Coping with Occupational Stress in Policing," *Justice Quarterly* 16 (1999): 303–336.

38. James Jacobs and Jay Cohen, "The Impact of Racial Integration on the Police," *Journal of Police Science and Administration* 6 (1978): 182.

39. Charles Katz, "The Establishment of a Police Gang Unit: An Examination of Organizational and Environmental Factors," *Criminology* 39 (2001): 37–73.

40. Ibid., p. 61.

41. Weitzer, "White, Black, or Blue Cops?"

42. Peter C. Moskos, "Two Shades of Blue: Black and White in the Blue Brotherhood," *Law Enforcement Executive Forum* 8 (2008): 57–86.

43. For a review of the history of women in policing, see Dorothy Moses Schulz, "From Policewoman to Police Officer: An Unfinished Revolution," *Police Studies* 16 (1993): 90–99; Cathryn House, "The Changing Role of Women in Law Enforcement," *Police Chief* 60 (1993): 139–144.

44. Reaves and Hickman, *Police Departments in Large Cities*.

45. Susan Martin, "Female Officers on the Move? A Status Report on Women in Policing," in *Critical Issues in Policing*, ed. Roger Dunham and Geoffery Alpert (Grove Park, Ill.: Waveland, 1988), pp. 312–331.

46. *Le Bouef v. Ramsey*, 26 FEP Cases 884 (September 16, 1980).

47. Michael Birzer and Delores Craig, "Gender Differences in Police Physical Ability Test Performance," *American Journal of Police* 15 (1996): 93–106.

48. James Daum and Cindy Johns, "Police Work from a Woman's Perspective," *Police Chief* 61 (1994): 46–49.

49. Steve Herbert, "'Hard Charger' or 'Station Queen'? Policing and the Masculinist State," *Gender, Place and Culture: A Journal of Feminist Geography* 8 (2001): 55–72.

50. Ibid., p. 58.

51. Matthew Hickman, Alex Piquero, and Jack Greene, "Discretion and Gender Disproportionality in Police Disciplinary Systems," *Policing* 23 (2000): 105–116.

52. Robin Haarr and Merry Morash, "Gender, Race, and Strategies of Coping with Occupational Stress in Policing, *Justice Quarterly* 16 (1999): 303–336."

53. Carol A. Archbold and Dorothy M. Schulz, "The Lingering Effects of Tokenism on Female Police Officers' Promotion Aspirations," *Police Quarterly* 11 (2008): 50–73.

54. Merry Morash and Jack Greene, "Evaluating Women on Patrol: A Critique of Contemporary Wisdom," *Evaluation Review* 10 (1986): 230–255.

55. Peter Bloch and Deborah Anderson, *Policewomen on Patrol: Final Report* (Washington, D.C.: Police Foundation, 1974).

56. Cara E. Rabe-Hemp and Amie M. Schuck, "Violence against Police Officers: Are Female Officers at Greater Risk?" *Police Quarterly* 10 (2007): 411–428.

57. Daum and Johns, "Police Work from a Woman's Perspective."

58. Mary Brown, "The Plight of Female Police: A Survey of NW Patrolmen," *Police Chief* 61 (1994): 50–53.

59. Simon Holdaway and Sharon K. Parker, "Policing Women Police: Uniform Patrol, Promotion, and Representation in the CID," *British Journal of Criminology* 38 (1998): 40–48.

60. Michael Birzer and Robert Nolan, "Learning Strategies of Selected Urban Police Related to Community Policing," *Policing* 25 (2002): 242–255.

61. William P. McCarty, Jihong "Solomon" Zhao, and Brett E. Garland, "Occupational Stress and Burnout between Male and Female Police Officers: Are There Any Gender Differences?" *Policing* 30 (2007): 672–691.

62. Susan Martin, "Outsider within the Station House: The Impact of Race and Gender on African-American Woman Police," *Social Problems* 41 (1994): 383–400, at 387.

63. Ibid., p. 392.

64. Ibid., p. 394.

65. Ibid., p. 397.

66. Ibid.

67. Eric Poole and Mark Pogrebin, "Factors Affecting the Decision to Remain in Policing: A Study of Women Officers," *Journal of Police Science and Administration* 16 (1988): 49–55.

68. Eugene Paoline, "Taking Stock: Toward a Richer Understanding of Police Culture," *Journal of Criminal Justice* 31 (2003): 199–214.

69. See, for example, Richard Harris, *The Police Academy: An Inside View* (New York: Wiley, 1973); John Van Maanen, "Observations on the Making of a Policeman," in *Order Under Law*, ed. R. Culbertson and M. Tezak (Prospect Heights, Ill.: Waveland, 1981), pp. 111–126; Jonathan Rubenstein, *City Police* (New York: Ballantine, 1973); John Broderick, *Police in a Time of Change* (Morristown, N.J.: General Learning Press, 1977).

70. Malcolm Sparrow, Mark Moore, and David Kennedy, *Beyond 911: A New Era for Policing* (New York: Basic Books, 1990), p. 51.

71. M. Steven Meagher and Nancy Yentes, "Choosing a Career in Policing: A Comparison of Male and Female Perceptions," *Journal of Police Science and Administration* 16 (1986): 320–327.

72. Michael K. Brown, *Working the Street* (New York: Russell Sage, 1981), p. 82.

73. Anthony Bouza, *The Police Mystique: An Insider's Look at Cops, Crime, and the Criminal Justice System* (New York: Plenum Press, 1990), p. 17.

74. Egon Bittner, *The Functions of Police in Modern Society* (Cambridge, Mass.: Oelgeschlager, Gunn, and Hain, 1980), p. 63.

75. Venessa Garcia, "Constructing the 'Other' within Police Culture: An Analysis of a Deviant Unit within the Police Organization," *Police Practice and Research* 6 (2005): 65–80.

76. Wallace Graves, "Police Cynicism: Causes and Cures," *FBI Law Enforcement Bulletin* 65 (1996): 16–21.

77. Richard Lundman, *Police and Policing* (New York: Holt, Rinehart, and Winston, 1980). See also Jerome Skolnick, *Justice without Trial* (New York: Wiley, 1966).

78. Micael Bjork, "Fighting Cynicism," *Police Quarterly* 11 (2008): 88–101.

79. William Westly, *Violence and the Police: A Sociological Study of Law, Custom, and Morality* (Cambridge, Mass.: MIT Press, 1970).

80. Skolnick, *Justice without Trial*, pp. 42–68.

81. Milton Rokeach, Martin Miller, and John Snyder, "The Value Gap between Police and Policed," *Journal of Social Issues* 27 (1971): 155–171.

82. Bruce Carpenter and Susan Raza, "Personality Characteristics of Police Applicants: Comparisons across Subgroups and with Other Populations," *Journal of Police Science and Administration* 15 (1987): 10–17.

83. Larry Tifft, "The 'Cop Personality' Reconsidered," *Journal of Police Science and Administration* 2 (1974): 268; David Bayley and Harold Mendelsohn, *Minorities and the Police* (New York: Free Press, 1969); Robert Balch, "The Police Personality: Fact or Fiction?" *Journal of Criminal Law, Criminology, and Police Science* 63 (1972): 117.

84. Lowell Storms, Nolan Penn, and James Tenzell, "Policemen's Perception of Real and Ideal Policemen," *Journal of Police Science and Administration* 17 (1990): 40–43.

85. Arthur Niederhoffer, *Behind the Shield: The Police in Urban Society* (Garden City, N.Y.: Doubleday, 1967).

86. Ibid., pp. 216–220.

87. Carl Klockars, "The Dirty Harry Problem," *Annals* 452 (1980): 33–47.

88. Jack Kuykendall and Roy Roberg, "Police Manager's Perceptions of Employee Types: A Conceptual Model," *Journal of Criminal Justice* 16 (1988): 131–135.

89. Stephen Matrofski, R. Richard Ritti, and Jeffrey Snipes, "Expectancy Theory and Police Productivity in DUI Enforcement," *Law and Society Review* 28 (1994): 113–138.

90. John P. Crank, *Understanding Police Culture* (Cincinnati, Ohio: Anderson, 1998).

91. Paoline, "Taking Stock."

92. Skolnick, *Justice without Trial*.

93. Carroll Seron, Joseph Pereira, and Jean Kovath, "Judging Police Misconduct: 'Street-Level' versus Professional Policing," *Law and Society Review* 38 (2004): 665–710.

94. William Terrill and Eugene A. Paoline III, "Nonarrest Decision Making in Police–Citizen Encounters," *Police Quarterly* 10 (2007): 308–331.

95. Kenneth Litwin, "A Multilevel Multivariate Analysis of Factors Affecting Homicide Clearances," *Journal of Research in Crime and Delinquency* 41 (2004): 327–351.

96. Lawrence W. Sherman, "Causes of Police Behavior: The Current State of Quantitative Research," in *The Ambivalent Force*, 3rd ed., ed. A. S. Blumberg and E. Niederhoffer (New York: Holt, Rinehart, and Wilson, 1985), pp. 183–195, at p. 187.

97. Helen Eigenberg, Kathryn Scarborough, and Victor Kappeler, "Contributory Factors Affecting Arrest in Domestic and Nondomestic Assaults," *American Journal of Police* 15 (1996): 27–51.

98. Leonore Simon, "A Therapeutic Jurisprudence Approach to the Legal Processing of Domestic Violence Cases," *Psychology, Public Policy, and Law* 1 (1995): 43–79.

99. Peter Sinden and B. Joyce Stephens, "Police Perceptions of Domestic Violence: The Nexus of Victim, Perpetrator, Event, Self and Law," *Policing* 22 (1999): 313–326.

100. Gregory Howard Williams, *The Law and Politics of Police Discretion* (Westport, Conn.: Greenwood, 1984).

101. Douglas Smith and Jody Klein, "Police Control of Interpersonal Disputes," *Social Problems* 31 (1984): 468–481.

102. David Klinger, "Negotiating Order in Patrol Work: An Ecological Theory of Police Response to Deviance," *Criminology* 35 (1997): 277–306.

103. Allison Chappell, John Macdonald, and Patrick Manz, "The Organizational Determinants of Police Arrest Decisions," *Crime and Delinquency* 52 (2006): 287–306.

104. Robin Shepard Engel, "Patrol Officer Supervision in the Community Policing Era," *Journal of Criminal Justice* 30 (2002): 51–64.

105. Westly, *Violence and the Police*.

106. John McCluskey, William Terrill, and Eugene Paoline III, "Peer Group Aggressiveness and the Use of Coercion in Police–Suspect Encounters," *Police Practice and Research* 6 (2005): 19–37.

107. Nathan Goldman, *The Differential Selection of Juvenile Offenders for Court Appearance* (New York: National Council on Crime and Delinquency, 1963).

108. Schafer, "Negotiating Order in the Policing of Youth Drinking"; Richard Lundman, "Demeanor or Crime? The Midwest City Police–Citizen Encounters Study," *Criminology* 32 (1994): 631–653; Robert Worden and Robin Shepard, "On the Meaning, Measurement, and Estimated Effects of Suspects' Demeanor toward the Police." Paper presented at the annual meeting of the American Society of Criminology, Miami, November 1994.

109. Joseph Schafer and Stephen Mastrofski, "Police Leniency in Traffic Enforcement Encounters: Exploratory Findings from Observations and Interviews," *Journal of Criminal Justice* 33 (2005): 225–238.

110. William Terrill and Stephen Mastrofski, "Situational and Officer-Based Determinants of Police Coercion," *Justice Quarterly* 19 (2002): 215–248.

111. William Terrill, *Police Coercion: Application of the Force Continuum* (New York: LFB Scholarly Publishing, 2001).

112. Geoffrey P. Alpert, John M. Macdonald, and Roger G. Dunham, "Police Suspicion and Discretionary Decision Making During Citizen Stops," *Criminology* 43 (2005): 407–434.

113. Christy A. Visher, "Gender, Police Arrest Decisions, and Notions of Chivalry," *Criminology* 21 (1983): 5–28.

114. Kenneth J. Novak, James Frank, Brad W. Smith, Robin Engel, and Shepard Engel, "Revisiting the Decision to Arrest: Comparing Beat and Community Officers," *Crime and Delinquency* 48 (2002): 70–98.

115. Roy Roberg, Kenneth Novak, and Gary Cordner, *Police and Society*, 3rd ed. (Los Angeles: Roxbury, 2005), p. 292.

116. Joel Garner, Christopher Maxwell, and Cederick Heraux, "Characteristics Associated with the Prevalence and Severity of Force Used by the Police," *Justice Quarterly* 19 (2002): 705–747.

117. Steven Brandl, Meghan Stroshine, and James Frank, "Who Are the Complaint-Prone Officers? An Examination of the Relationship between Police Officers' Attributes, Arrest Activity, Assignment, and Citizens' Complaints about Excessive Force," *Journal of Criminal Justice* 29 (2001): 521–529.

118. William F. Walsh, "Police Officer Arrest Rates," *Justice Quarterly* 3 (1986): 271–290.

119. Brown, *Working the Street*, p. 290.

120. Judith A. Waters and William Ussery, "Police Stress: History, Contributing Factors, Symptoms, and Interventions," *Policing* 30 (2007): 169–188.

121. Karen Kruger and Nicholas Valltos, "Dealing with Domestic Violence in Law Enforcement Relationships," *FBI Law Enforcement Bulletin* 71 (2002): 1–7.

122. Yates and Pillai, "Frustration and Strain among Fort Worth Police Officers."

123. Ni He, Jihong Zhao, and Carol Archbold, "Gender and Police Stress: The Convergent and Divergent Impact of Work Environment, Work–Family Conflict, and Stress Coping Mechanisms of Female and Male Police Officers," *Policing* 25 (2002): 687–709.

124. Francis Cullen, Terrence Lemming, Bruce Link, and John Wozniak, "The Impact of Social Supports on Police Stress," *Criminology* 23 (1985): 503–522.

125. Morash, Haarr, and Kwak, "Multilevel Influences on Police Stress."

126. Deborah Wilkins Newman and LeeAnne Rucker-Reed, "Police Stress, State-Trait Anxiety, and Stressors among U.S. Marshals," *Journal of Criminal Justice* 32 (2004): 631–641.

127. Jihong Zhao, Ni He, and Nicholas Lovrich, "Predicting Five Dimensions of Police Officer Stress: Looking More Deeply into Organizational Settings for Sources of Police Stress," *Police Quarterly* 5 (2002): 43–63.

128. Lawrence Travis III and Craig Winston, "Dissension in the Ranks: Officer Resistance to Community Policing and Support for the Organization," *Journal of Crime and Justice* 21 (1998): 139–155.

129. R. E. Farmer, "Clinical and Managerial Implications of Stress Research on the Police," *Journal of Police Science and Administration* 17 (1990): 205–218; Nancy Norvell, Dale Belles, and Holly Hills, "Perceived Stress Levels and Physical Symptoms in Supervisory Law Enforcement Personnel," *Journal of Police Science and Administration* 16 (1988): 75–79.

130. Donald Yates and Vijayan Pillai, "Attitudes toward Community Policing: A Causal Analysis," *Social Science Journal* 33 (1996): 193–209.

131. Harvey McMurray, "Attitudes of Assaulted Police Officers and Their Policy Implications," *Journal of Police Science and Administration* 17 (1990): 44–48.

132. Robert Ankony and Thomas Kelly, "The Impact of Perceived Alienation of Police Officers' Sense of Mastery and Subsequent Motivation for Proactive Enforcement," *Policing* 22 (1999): 120–132.

133. John Blackmore, "Police Stress," in *Policing Society*, ed. Clinton Terry (New York: Wiley, 1985), p. 395.

134. Stephen Curran, "Separating Fact from Fiction about Police Stress," *Behavioral Health Management* 23 (2003): 38–40; Peter Marzuk, Matthew Nock, Andrew Leon, Laura Portera, and Kenneth Tardiff, "Suicide among New York City Police Officers, 1977–1996," *American Journal of Psychiatry* 159 (2002): 2069–2072; Rose Lee Josephson and Martin Reiser, "Officer Suicide in the Los Angeles Police Department: A Twelve-Year Follow-Up," *Journal of Police Science and Administration* 17 (1990): 227–230.

135. Vicki Lindsay, "Police Officers and Their Alcohol Consumption," *Police Quarterly* 11 (2008): 74–87.

136. Yates and Pillai, "Attitudes toward Community Policing," 205–206.

137. Ibid.

138. Rosanna Church and Naomi Robertson, "How State Police Agencies Are Addressing the Issue of Wellness," *Policing* 22 (1999): 304–312; Farmer, "Clinical and Managerial Implications of Stress Research on the Police," p. 215.

139. Peter Hart, Alexander Wearing, and Bruce Headey, "Assessing Police Work Experiences: Development of the Police Daily Hassles and Uplifts Scales," *Journal of Criminal Justice* 21 (1993): 553–573.

140. Vivian Lord, Denis Gray, and Samuel Pond, "The Police Stress Inventory: Does It Measure Stress?" *Journal of Criminal Justice* 19 (1991): 139–149.

141. Bryan Vila and Dennis J. Kenney, "Tired Cops: The Prevalence and Potential Consequences of Police Fatigue," *NIJ Journal* 248 (2002): 16–21.

142. Luenda E. Charles, Cecil M. Burchfiel, Desta Fekedulegn, Bryan Vila, Tara A. Hartley, James Slaven, Anna Mnatsakanova, and John M. Violanti, "Shift Work and Sleep: The Buffalo Police Health Study," *Policing* 30 (2007): 215–227.

143. Vila and Kenney, "Tired Cops: The Prevalence and Potential Consequences of Police Fatigue," p. 18.

144. Ibid., p. 17.

145. Ibid., pp. 19–20.

146. Bittner, *The Functions of Police in Modern Society*, p. 46.

147. Frank Hughes and Lisa B. Andre, "Problem Officer Variables and Early-Warning Systems," *The Police Chief* 74 (2007): 164, 166, 168, 172.

148. Sean Griffin and Thomas Bernard, "Angry Aggression among Police Officers," *Police Quarterly* 6 (2003): 3–21.

149. Kim Michelle Lersch and Tom Mieczkowski, "Who Are the Problem-Prone Officers? An Analysis of Citizen Complaints," *American Journal of Police* 15 (1996): 23–42.

150. Samuel Walker, Geoffrey P. Alpert, and Dennis J. Kenney, *Early Warning Systems: Responding to the Problem Police Officer, Research in Brief* (Washington, D.C.: National Institute of Justice, 2001).

151. Samuel Walker, "The Rule Revolution: Reflections on the Transformation of American Criminal Justice, 1950–1988," *Working Papers, Series 3* (Madison: University of Wisconsin Law School, Institute for Legal Studies, December 1988).

152. Michael D. White, "Controlling Police Decisions to Use Deadly Force: Reexamining the Importance of Administrative Policy," *Crime and Delinquency* 47 (2001): 131.

153. Victor Kappeler, Stephen Kappeler, and Rolando Del Carmen, "A Content Analysis of Police Civil Liability Cases: Decisions of the Federal District Courts, 1978–1990," *Journal of Criminal Justice* 21 (1993): 325–337.

154. See, for example, Ronald Weitzer, "Citizen Perceptions of Police Misconduct: Race and Neighborhood Context," *Justice Quarterly* 16 (1999): 819–846.

155. Samuel Walker, *Popular Justice* (New York: Oxford University Press, 1980), p. 64.

156. Louise Westmarland, "Police Ethics and Integrity: Breaking the Blue Code of Silence," *Policing and Society* 15 (2005): 145–165.

157. Robert J. Kane and Michael D. White, "A Study of Career-Ending Misconduct among New York City Police Officers," *Criminology and Public Policy* 8 (2009): 737–769.

158. Herman Goldstein, *Police Corruption* (Washington, D.C.: Police Foundation, 1975), p. 3.

159. Knapp Commission, *Report on Police Corruption* (New York: Braziller, 1973), pp. 1–34.

160. Elizabeth Neuffer, "Seven Additional Detectives Linked to Extortion Scheme," *Boston Globe*, October 25, 1988, p. 60.

161. Kevin Cullen, "U.S. Probe Eyes Bookie Protection," *Boston Globe*, October 25, 1988, p. 1.

162. Michael Johnston, *Political Corruption and Public Policy in America* (Monterey, Calif.: Brooks/Cole, 1982), p. 75.

163. William Doherty, "Ex-Sergeant Says He Aided Bid to Sell Exam," *Boston Globe*, February 26, 1987, p. 61.

164. Alan Feuer and William K. Rashbaum, "Blood Ties: 2 Officers' Long Path to Mob Murder Indictments, March 12, 2005, *New York Times*; Lisa Stein, "Cops Gone Wild," *U.S. News and World Report*, March 21, 2005, p. 14.

165. Ellwyn Stoddard, "Blue Coat Crime," in *Thinking about Police*, ed. Carl Klockars (New York: McGraw-Hill, 1983), pp. 338–349.

166. Lawrence Sherman, *Police Corruption: A Sociological Perspective* (Garden City, N.Y.: Doubleday, 1974), pp. 40–41.

167. Samuel Walker, *Police in Society* (New York: McGraw-Hill, 1983), p. 181.

168. Robert Kane, "The Social Ecology of Police Misconduct," *Criminology* 40 (2002): 867–897.

169. Sherman, *Police Corruption*.

170. Robert Daley, *Prince of the City* (New York: Houghton Mifflin, 1978).

171. Kane and White, "A Study of Career-Ending Misconduct," p. 763.

172. Sherman, *Police Corruption*, p. 194.

173. Kevin Flynn, "Police Dept. Routinely Drops Cases of Officer Misconduct, Report Says," *New York Times*, September 15, 1999, p. 1.

174. Gary R. Rothwell and J. Norman Baldwin, "Whistle-Blowing and the Code of Silence in Police Agencies," *Crime and Delinquency* 53 (2007): 605–632.

175. Louise Westmarland, "Police Ethics and Integrity."

176. Barbara Gelb, *Tarnished Brass: The Decade after Serpico* (New York: Putnam, 1983); Candace McCoy, "Lawsuits against Police: What Impact Do They Have?" *Criminal Law Bulletin* 20 (1984): 49–56.

177. For a general review, see Tom McEwen, *National Data Collection on Police Use of Force* (Washington, D.C.: National Institute of Justice, 1996).

178. Matthew Durose, Erica Schmitt, and Patrick Langan, *Contacts between Police and the Public: Findings from the 2002 National Survey* (Washington, D.C.: Bureau of Justice Statistics, 2005).

179. Colin Loftin, David McDowall, Brian Wiersema, and Adam Dobrin, "Underreporting of Justifiable Homicides Committed by Police Officers in the United States, 1976–1998," *American Journal of Public Health* 93 (2003): 1117–1121; for trend data, see http://bjs.ojp.usdoj.gov/dataonline/Search/Homicide/Homicide.cfm (accessed April 12, 2010).

180. Brad Smith, "The Impact of Police Officer Diversity on Police-Caused Homicides," *Policy Studies Journal* 31 (2003): 147–162.

181. Brian Thompson and James Daniel Lee, "Who Cares If Police Become Violent? Explaining Approval of Police Use of Force Using a National Sample," *Sociological Inquiry* 74 (2004): 381–410.

182. Sandra Lee Browning, Francis Cullen, Liqun Cao, Renee Kopache, and Thomas Stevenson, "Race and Getting Hassled by the Police: A Research Note," *Police Studies* 17 (1994): 1–11.

183. Joel Garner, Christopher Maxwell, and Cederick Heraux, "Characteristics Associated with the Prevalence and Severity of Force Used by the Police," *Justice Quarterly* 19 (2002): 705–747.

184. William Terrill, "Police Use of Force: A Transactional Approach," *Justice Quarterly* 22 (2005): 107–138.

185. Thompson and Lee, "Who Cares If Police Become Violent?"

186. Sam W. Lathrop, "Reviewing Use of Force: A Systematic Approach," *FBI Law Enforcement Bulletin* 69 (2000): 16–20.

187. Ibid.

188. Bureau of Justice Statistics, *Homicide Trends in the U.S.: Justifiable Homicides*, http://bjs.ojp.usdoj.gov/content/homicide/justify.cfm (accessed April 12, 2010).

189. Lawrence W. Sherman and Robert H. Langworthy, "Measuring Homicide by Police Officers," *Journal of Criminal Law and Criminology* 70 (1979): 546–560.

190. Brad Smith, "The Impact of Police Officer Diversity on Police-Caused Violence," *Policy Studies Journal* 31 (2003): 147–163.

191. John MacDonald, Geoffrey Alpert, and Abraham Tennenbaum, "Justifiable Homicide by Police and Criminal Homicide: A Research Note," *Journal of Crime and Justice* 22 (1999): 153–164.

192. Richard Parent and Simon Verdun-Jones, "Victim-Precipitated Homicide: Police Use of Deadly Force in British Columbia," *Policing* 21 (1998): 432–449.

193. "10% of Police Shootings Found to Be 'Suicide by Cop,'" *Criminal Justice Newsletter* 29 (1998): 1.

194. Sherman and Langworthy, "Measuring Homicide by Police Officers."

195. Brad Smith, "Structural and Organizational Predictors of Homicide by Police," *Policing* 27 (2004): 539–557.

196. Jonathan Sorenson, James Marquart, and Deon Brock, "Factors Related to Killings of Felons by Police Officers: A Test of the Community Violence and Conflict Hypotheses," *Justice Quarterly* 10 (1993): 417–440; David Jacobs and David Britt, "Inequality and Police Use of Deadly Force: An Empirical Assessment of a Conflict Hypothesis," *Social Problems* 26 (1979): 403–412.

197. Smith, "The Impact of Police Officer Diversity on Police-Caused Violence."

198. David Jacobs and Jason Carmichael, "Subordination and Violence against State Control Agents: Testing Political Explanations for Lethal Assaults against the Police," *Social Forces* 80 (2002): 1223–1252.

199. James Fyfe, "Police Use of Deadly Force: Research and Reform," *Justice Quarterly* 5 (1988): 165–205.

200. Paul Takagi, "A Garrison State in a 'Democratic' Society," *Crime and Social Justice* 5 (1974): 34–43.

201. Mark Blumberg, "Race and Police Shootings: An Analysis in Two Cities," in *Contemporary Issues in Law Enforcement*, ed. James Fyfe (Beverly Hills, Calif.: Sage, 1981), pp. 152–166.

202. James Fyfe, "Shots Fired," Ph.D. dissertation, State University of New York, Albany, 1978.

203. *Tennessee v. Garner*, 471 U.S. 1 (1985).

204. Franklin Graves and Gregory Connor, "The FLETC Use-of-Force Model," *Police Chief* 59 (1992): 56–58.

205. Gregory B. Morrison, "Deadly Force Programs among Larger U.S. Police Departments," *Police Quarterly* 9 (2006): 331–360.

206. Bernard D. Rostker, Lawrence M. Hanser, William M. Hix, Carl Jensen, Andrew R. Morral, Greg Ridgeway, and Terry. L. Schell, *Evaluation of the New York City Police Department Firearm Training and Firearm-Discharge Review Process* (Santa Monica, Calif.: RAND Corporation, 2008), pp. 41–46.

207. David A. Klinger and Rod. K. Brunson, "Police Officers' Perceptual Distortions during Lethal Force Situations: Informing the Reasonableness Standard," *Criminology and Public Policy* 8 (2009): 117–140.

208. Ibid., pp. 136–137.

209. Brian A. Lawton, "Levels of Nonlethal Force: An Examination of Individual, Situational, and Contextual Factors," *Journal of Research in Crime and Delinquency* 44 (2007): 163–184.

210. Matthew J. Hickman, Alex R. Piquero, and Joel H. Garner, "Toward a National Estimate of Police Use of Nonlethal Force," *Criminology and Public Policy* 7 (2008): 563–604.

211. Theresa G. DiMaio and Vincent J. M. DiMaio, *Excited Delirium Syndrome: Cause of Death and Prevention* (Boca Raton, Fla.: CRC Press, 2005).

212. *Graham v. Connor*, 490 U.S. 386 (1989).

213. Gary M. Vilke and Theodore C. Chan, "Less Lethal Technology: Medical Issues," *Policing* 30 (2007): 341–357.

214. Warren Cohen, "When Lethal Force Won't Do," *U.S. News and World Report*, June 23, 1997, p. 12.

215. Michael R. Smith, Robert J. Kaminski, Jeffrey Rojek, Geoffrey P. Alpert, and Jason Mathis, "The Impact of Conducted Energy Devices and Other Types of Force and Resistance on Officer and Suspect Injuries," *Policing* 30 (2007): 423–446.

216. David Klinger, "Impact Munitions: A Discussion of Key Information," *Policing* 30 (2007): 385–397.

217. National Institute of Justice, *Department of Defense Nonlethal Weapons and Equipment Review: A Research Guide for Civil Law Enforcement and Corrections* (Washington, D.C.: National Institute of Justice, 2004).

218. National Institute of Justice, *Impact Munitions Use: Types, Targets, Effects* (Washington, D.C.: National Institute of Justice, 2004), p. 3.

219. Michael D. White and Justin Ready, "The TASER as a Less Lethal Force Alternative," *Police Quarterly* 10 (2007): 170–191.

220. For some research in this area, see R. J. Kaminski, S. M. Edwards, and J. W. Johnson, "Assessing the Incapacitative Effects of Pepper Spray during Resistive Encounters with Police," *Policing: An International Journal of Police Strategies and Management* 22 (1999): 7–29; R. J. Kaminski, S. M. Edwards, and J. W. Johnson,

"The Deterrent Effects of Oleoresin Capsicum on Assaults against Police: Testing the Velcro-Effect Hypothesis," *Police Quarterly* 1 (1998): 1–20.

221. National Institute of Justice, *The Effectiveness and Safety of Pepper Spray, Research for Practice* (Washington, D.C.: National Institute of Justice, 2003), www.ncjrs.gov/pdffiles1/nij/195739.pdf (accessed April 12, 2010).

222. Federal Bureau of Investigation, "Law Enforcement Officers Killed and Assaulted, 2000," press release, November 26, 2001.

223. Federal Bureau of Investigation, "Law Enforcement Officers Killed and Assaulted, 2004," www.fbi.gov/ucr/killed/2008/data/table_23.html (accessed April 12, 2010).

224. J. David Hirschel, Charles Dean, and Richard Lumb, "The Relative Contribution of Domestic Violence to Assault and Injury of Police Officers," *Justice Quarterly* 11 (1994): 99–118.

225. National Law Enforcement Officers Memorial Fund, www.nleomf.org/memorial/names/ (accessed April 12, 2010).

# CHAPTER 8

# Police and the Rule of Law

## CHAPTER OBJECTIVES

1. Understand how the Fourth Amendment controls law enforcement officials.
2. Define search and arrest.
3. Distinguish between search warrants and arrest warrants.
4. Explain when warrants are required.
5. Recognize that there are three requirements that must be met before a warrant can be secured.
6. Explain the rules for serving warrants.
7. Discuss the nuances of seven types of warrantless searches and arrests.
8. Summarize electronic surveillance law as it applies to law enforcement officials.
9. Explain the *Miranda v. Arizona* decision.
10. Understand what purpose a lineup serves.
11. Know the exclusionary rule, including its extensions and exceptions.

On August 25, 1999, Rodney Gant was arrested for driving with a suspended license. After he was handcuffed and locked in the back seat of a police car, officers searched the passenger compartment of his car and found cocaine in the pocket of a jacket that was sitting on one of the seats. A trial court denied Gant's request to have the cocaine excluded at trial, but the Arizona Supreme Court reversed that decision, arguing that the search was unreasonable because, since Gant was locked up in the police car, there was no threat to officer safety or risk that the evidence would have been destroyed in the absence of an immediate search. The case then went to the U.S. Supreme Court, which held that the police can search the passenger compartment of a vehicle following a lawful arrest only when it is reasonable to believe that (1) the arrestee may have access to the vehicle at the time of the search or (2) the vehicle contains evidence of the offense of arrest.[1] In essence, the U.S. Supreme Court decided the search of Gant's car was unjustified and in violation of the Fourth Amendment.

The Gant decision altered the Supreme Court's earlier decision in New York v. Belton,[2] a case in which officers were essentially given carte blanche to search vehicle passenger compartments following lawful arrests. Belton was controversial, because even if an arrestee was locked up safely and did not pose any security threat, officers could still search the vehicle passenger compartment without probable cause. They were basically able to avoid the Fourth Amendment's probable cause requirement. Because Gant essentially overturned Belton, it has not been well received by the law enforcement community. Why exactly? It muddies the waters, because the Belton rule gave police clear authority to search, regardless of the offense in question or the arrestee's risk to the officers. Gant makes it more difficult for police to search. Supporters of the Gant decision, however, feel it honors Fourth Amendment rights and protects people from overreaching searches. ■

The *Arizona v. Gant* case reaffirms the delicate balance that always must be struck between effective police work and the rule of law. It is necessary to give law enforcement officials the authority to catch crooks, but when they go too far in this regard, their actions can run afoul of the rights that people enjoy.

Although police want a free hand to search homes and cars for evidence, the Constitution's Fourth Amendment restricts police activities by requiring that they obtain a warrant before conducting a search. When police want to vigorously interrogate a suspect, they must also honor the Fifth Amendment's prohibition against forcing people to incriminate themselves.

## POLICE AND THE COURTS

Once a crime has been committed and an investigation begun, the police may use various means to collect the evidence needed for criminal prosecution. A number of critical decisions must take place:

■ Should surveillance techniques be employed to secure information?

■ How can information be gathered to support a request for a search warrant?

■ If the suspect is driving a vehicle, can the car be searched without a warrant?

■ Can a suspect's phone be tapped or her conversations recorded?

■ Is there reasonable suspicion to justify stopping and frisking a suspect?

■ Can a legal arrest be made?

■ If a suspect has been detained, what constitutes an appropriate interrogation?

■ Can witnesses be brought in to identify the suspect?

The U.S. Supreme Court has taken an active role in answering these questions. Its primary concern has been to balance the law enforcement agent's need for a free hand to investigate crimes with the citizen's constitutional right to be free from illegal searches and interrogations. In some instances, the Supreme Court has expanded police power—for example, by increasing the occasions when police can search without a warrant. In other cases, the Supreme Court has restricted police operations—for example, by ruling that every criminal suspect has a right to an attorney when being interrogated by police. Changes in the law often reflect such factors as the justices' legal philosophy and their concern about the ability of police to control crime, their views on the need to maintain public safety versus their commitment to the civil liberties of criminal defendants, and recent events such as the September 11, 2001, terrorist attacks.

What are the key areas of court involvement with police activities, and how have they been shaped by legal authority? We answer these questions throughout this chapter.

## SEARCH AND SEIZURE

Some of the key elements of police investigation are the search for incriminating evidence, the seizure of that evidence, and its use during a criminal trial. The Fourth Amendment protects criminal suspects against unreasonable searches and seizures by placing limitations on what the police can do in their efforts to catch lawbreakers and collect evidence.

The Fourth Amendment states:

> The right of the people to be secure in their persons, houses, papers, and effects, against unreasonable searches and seizures, shall not be violated, and no warrants shall issue, but upon probable cause, supported by oath or affirmation, and particularly describing the place to be searched, and the persons or things to be seized.

There are two important parts of the Fourth Amendment, called the "reasonable clause" and the "warrants clause." The reasonable clause stops at ". . . shall not be violated." It simply states that searches and seizures must be reasonable. The warrant clause starts at ". . . and no warrants shall issue. . . ." This part of the Fourth Amendment lists warrant requirements. These two Fourth Amendment parts are not necessarily connected. A search can be reasonable without a warrant, but if a warrant is required, it must meet specific requirements.

© AP Images/Mary Altaffer

*A "search" occurs when a government actor infringes on a person's reasonable expectation of privacy. Pictured here are a New York City Police Department surveillance helicopter's cameras, including one for infrared photography. The chopper's arsenal of sophisticated surveillance and tracking equipment is powerful enough to stealthily read license plates, pedestrians' faces, and heat signatures from high above. Should authorities be allowed to use such devices at will? Would doing so raise any Fourth Amendment concerns?*

## Defining a Search

The dictionary definition of "search" is straightforward—namely, to look for something. In the search and seizure context, however, "search" has a very distinct meaning. A Fourth Amendment **search** occurs only when a government actor infringes on a person's reasonable expectation of privacy.[3]

A government actor is most often a police officer, in contrast to a private citizen. As a private citizen, a person could enter someone else's property and search for contraband without triggering the Fourth Amendment prohibitions. This person may commit the offense of criminal trespass, but the Fourth Amendment would not be triggered. Police officers' actions almost always trigger the Fourth Amendment.

Assuming a police officer is the one looking for evidence, then what has to happen for the officer to infringe on someone's reasonable expectation of privacy? The officer must be looking in a place where a person could reasonably expect privacy. Usually this includes private property, such as cars, houses, and personal effects. So if an officer looks for contraband in a person's private home, the officer is conducting a search. In contrast, if the officer looks for evidence in a public park, a search has not occurred because the park is public and does not belong to any one individual. Following are three key examples of actions that are *not* considered searches.

**search**
A government actor's infringement on a person's reasonable expectation of privacy.

*ABANDONED PROPERTY* If a person abandons his or her property, such as by placing trash at the side of the road for pickup, that person cannot continue to assert privacy in the property. In *California v. Greenwood* (1988),[4] investigators found incriminating information in a person's garbage that was set to be picked up. The Supreme Court ruled that this action did not amount to a search. The officers were authorized to seize the evidence.

*OPEN FIELDS* In *Oliver v. United States* (1984),[5] the U.S. Supreme Court distinguished between the privacy granted persons in their own home or its adjacent grounds and fields (curtilage) and the lack of expectation of privacy in open fields. The Court ruled that when the police look for evidence in an **open field**, defined as any unoccupied or undeveloped real property outside the curtilage of a home, a search does not occur. What, then, is **curtilage**? It is defined as the grounds or fields attached to and in close proximity to the house. Concept Summary 8.1 distinguishes between open fields and curtilage in more detail.

**open field**
Any unoccupied or undeveloped real property outside the curtilage of a home.

**curtilage**
Grounds or fields attached to a house.

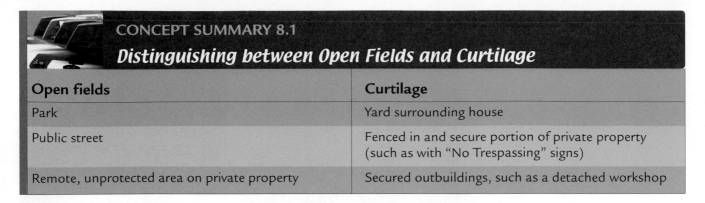

## CONCEPT SUMMARY 8.1
### Distinguishing between Open Fields and Curtilage

| Open fields | Curtilage |
| --- | --- |
| Park | Yard surrounding house |
| Public street | Fenced in and secure portion of private property (such as with "No Trespassing" signs) |
| Remote, unprotected area on private property | Secured outbuildings, such as a detached workshop |

*FLY-OVERS* In *California v. Ciraola* (1986), the police received a tip that marijuana was growing in the defendant's backyard.[6] The yard was surrounded by fences, one of which was 10 feet high. The officers flew over the yard in a private plane at an altitude of 1,000 feet to ascertain whether it contained marijuana plants. On the basis of this information, a search warrant was obtained and executed, and with the evidence against him, the defendant was convicted on drug charges. On appeal, the Supreme Court found that his privacy had not been violated—that a search did not occur. This holding was later expanded in *Florida v. Riley* (1989), when the Court ruled that police do not need a search warrant to conduct even low-altitude helicopter searches of private property.[7] The Court allowed Florida prosecutors to use evidence obtained by a police helicopter that flew 400 feet over a greenhouse in which defendants were growing marijuana plants. The Court said the search was constitutionally permissible because the flight was within airspace legally available to helicopters under federal regulations.

## Defining an Arrest

**arrest**
Occurs when a police officer takes a person into custody or deprives a person of freedom for having allegedly committed a criminal offense.

The Fourth Amendment does not mention arrests, but it does mention seizures. Arrest is one of the most common types of seizures. Some other actions, such as field interrogations, are also considered seizures. Here our concern is with arrest.

*Jellico, Tennessee, police officers remove marijuana plants seized from a remote area of Campbell County. The find is expected to be the largest ever in Tennessee. Officers used a helicopter to transport the marijuana to a nearby state park for destruction in a controlled burn.*

© Wade Payne/Knoxville News Sentinel

The arrest power of the police involves taking a person into custody in accordance with lawful authority and holding that person to answer for a violation of the criminal law. Police officers have complete law enforcement responsibility and unrestricted powers of arrest in their jurisdictions. Private citizens also have the right to make an arrest, generally when a crime is committed in their presence.

An **arrest** occurs when a police officer takes a person into custody or deprives a person of freedom for having allegedly committed a criminal offense. The police stop unlimited numbers of people each day for a variety of reasons, so the time when an arrest occurs may be hard to pinpoint. Some persons are stopped for short periods of questioning, others are informally detained and released, and still others are formally placed under arrest. However, a legal arrest occurs when the following conditions exist:

- The police officer believes that sufficient legal evidence—that is, probable cause—exists that a crime is being or has been committed and intends to restrain the suspect.

- The police officer deprives the individual of freedom.

- The suspect believes that he is in the custody of the police officer and cannot voluntarily leave. He has lost his liberty.

## Search Warrants and Arrest Warrants

There are two varieties of warrants: **search warrants** and **arrest warrants**. A search warrant is an order, issued by a judge, directing officers to conduct a search of specified premises for specified objects. An arrest warrant is an order, issued by a judge, directing officers to arrest a particular individual. Examples of search and arrest warrants appear in Figures 8.1 and 8.2.

## When Warrants Are Necessary

The Fourth Amendment does not necessitate warrants for all searches and arrests. In some situations, however, warrants are necessary. These situations include

- *Arrests and searches in private homes or on specific types of private property.* Subject to some limited exceptions (see the section "Warrantless Searches and Arrests"), warrants are always required for searches and arrests in private homes.[8]

- *Arrests for minor offenses committed out of view of the arresting officer.* There is no clear definition of "minor offense," but generally this includes misdemeanors. Limiting arrests in this fashion is known as the **in-presence requirement**; a misdemeanor needs to occur in the officer's presence for the arrest to be valid.[9]

## WARRANT REQUIREMENTS

There are three requirements that must be satisfied before a warrant can be issued. They are probable cause, a neutral and detached magistrate, and particularity.

**search warrant**
An order, issued by a judge, directing officers to conduct a search of specified premises for specified objects.

**arrest warrant**
An order, issued by a judge, directing officers to arrest a particular individual.

**in-presence requirement**
A police officer cannot arrest someone for a misdemeanor unless the officer sees the crime occur. To make an arrest for a crime the officer did not witness, an arrest warrant must be obtained.

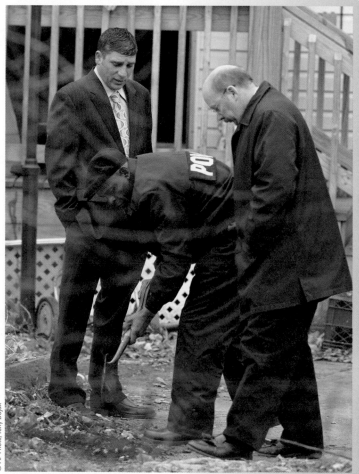

Investigators dig in the backyard of Anthony Sowell's home in Cleveland, Ohio. Sowell, a registered sex offender, was arrested as a suspect in the murder of eleven women whose bodies were discovered at his Cleveland duplex. Investigators, along with the city police and buildings department, the FBI, and the coroner's office, had search warrants to dig by hand in areas of interest identified via FBI thermal-imaging and radar scans.

**FIGURE 8.1**

## A Typical Search Warrant Form

Source: John N. Ferdico, Henry F. Fradella, and Christopher D. Totten, *Criminal Procedure for the Criminal Justice Professional,* 10th ed. (Belmont, Calif.: Cengage Learning, 2008).

**FIGURE 8.2**

## A Typical Arrest Warrant Form

Source: John N. Ferdico, Henry F. Fradella, and Christopher D. Totten, *Criminal Procedure for the Criminal Justice Professional,* 10th ed. (Belmont, Calif.: Cengage Learning, 2008).

**EXHIBIT 8.1**

## Sources of Information for Probable Cause

- A police informant whose reliability has been established because he has provided information in the past.

- Someone who has firsthand knowledge of illegal activities.

- A co-conspirator who implicates herself as well as the suspect.

- An informant whose information can be partially verified by the police.

- A victim of a crime who offers information.

- A witness to the crime related to the search.

- A fellow law enforcement officer.

## Probable Cause

A warrant cannot be issued unless it is based on **probable cause**, which is typically defined as a reasonable belief, based on fact, that a crime has been committed and that the person, place, or object to be searched and/or seized is linked to the crime with a reasonable degree of certainty.

Under normal circumstances, a search warrant cannot be obtained unless the request for it is supported by facts, supplied under oath by a law enforcement officer, that are sufficient to convince the court that a crime has been or is being committed.

To establish probable cause, the police must provide the judge or magistrate with information in the form of written affidavits, which report either their own observations or those of private citizens or police undercover informants. If the magistrate believes that the information is sufficient to establish probable cause to conduct a search, he or she will issue a warrant. Although the suspect is not present when the warrant is issued and therefore cannot contest its issuance, he can later challenge the validity of the warrant before trial.

The Fourth Amendment does not explicitly define probable cause, and its precise meaning still remains unclear. However, police officers have to provide factual evidence to define and identify suspicious activities; they may not simply offer their beliefs or suspicions. In addition, the officers must show how they obtained the information and provide evidence of its reliability. There are several sources of information that officers can use to show probable cause, including firsthand knowledge, informants' statements, anonymous tips, and telephone tips (also see Exhibit 8.1).

*FIRSTHAND KNOWLEDGE*  Police can obtain a warrant if their investigation turns up sufficient evidence to convince a judge that a crime probably has been committed and that the person or place the police wish to search is probably involved materially in that crime. The ideal source of information is the officer's firsthand knowledge. If the officer witnesses a crime being committed, the warrant requirement can often be disposed of altogether and the officer will make a warrantless arrest (we look at warrantless searches and seizures later). If the officer cannot make a particular arrest or engage in a particular search without a warrant, but he or she nevertheless has information that could establish probable cause, then the officer's knowledge will be weighted heavily. For example, if during a drug sting operation an officer buys drugs from a suspect on several occasions, this officer's firsthand information will be important in getting a warrant to search the suspect's property.

*INFORMANTS*  Police often rely on informants. Informants can include victims, witnesses, accomplices, and people familiar with the crime or suspects in question. Unfortunately, many informants often act out of self-interest instead of civic

**probable cause**
The evidentiary criterion necessary to sustain an arrest or the issuance of an arrest or search warrant: a set of facts, information, circumstances, or conditions that would lead a reasonable person to believe that an offense was committed and that the accused committed that offense.

**CourseMate** For more information about the use of **informants**, visit the Criminal Justice CourseMate at CengageBrain.com, then access the "Web Links" for this chapter.

duty, and the reliability of the evidence they provide may be questionable. More-over, their statements reflect only what they have seen and heard and are not substantiated by hard evidence.

The U.S. Supreme Court has been concerned about the reliability of evidence obtained from informants. The Court has determined that hearsay evidence must be corroborated to serve as a basis for probable cause and thereby justify the issuance of a warrant. In the case of *Aguilar v. Texas* (1964), the Court articulated a two-part test for issuing a warrant on the word of an informant. The police had to show (1) why they believed the informant and (2) how the informant acquired personal knowledge of the crime.[10] This ruling restricted informant testimony to people who were in direct contact with police and whose information could be verified.

*ANONYMOUS TIPS* Because the *Aguilar* case required that an informant be known and that his or her information be likely to be reliable, it all but ruled out using anonymous tips to secure a search warrant. This was changed in a critical 1983 ruling, *Illinois v. Gates,* in which the Court eased the process of obtaining search warrants by developing a totality-of-the-circumstances test to determine probable cause for issuing a search warrant. In *Gates,* the police received a knowledgeable and detailed anonymous letter describing the drug-dealing activities of Lance and Sue Gates. On the basis of that tip, the police began surveillance and eventually obtained a warrant to search the Gates' home. The search was later challenged on the grounds that it would be impossible to determine the accuracy of information provided by an anonymous letter, a condition required by the *Aguilar* case. However, the Court ruled that to obtain a warrant, the police must prove to a judge that, considering the totality of the circumstances, an informant has relevant and factual knowledge that a fair probability exists that evidence of a crime will be found in a certain place.[11] The anonymous letter, rich in details, satisfied that demand.

*TELEPHONE TIPS* Can the police conduct a search based on an anonymous tip, such as one that is given via telephone? In *Alabama v. White* (1990), the police received an anonymous tip that a woman was carrying cocaine.[12] Only after police observation showed that the tip had accurately predicted the woman's movements did it become reasonable to believe the tipster had inside knowledge about the suspect and was truthful in his assertion about the cocaine. The Supreme Court ruled that the search based on the tip was legal because it was corroborated by independent police work. In its ruling, the Court stated the following:

> Standing alone, the tip here is completely lacking in the necessary indicia of reliability, since it provides virtually nothing from which one might conclude that the caller is honest or his information reliable and gives no indication of the basis for his predictions regarding [Vanessa] White's criminal activities. However, although it is a close question, the totality of the circumstances demonstrates that significant aspects of the informant's story were sufficiently corroborated by the police to furnish reasonable suspicion. . . . Thus, there was reason to believe that the caller was honest and well informed, and to impart some degree of reliability to his allegation that White was engaged in criminal activity.[13]

The *White* case seemed to give police powers to search someone after corroborating an anonymous tip. However, in *Florida v. J. L.,* the Court narrowed that right. In *J. L.,* an anonymous caller reported to the Miami-Dade police that a young black male standing at a particular bus stop, wearing a plaid shirt, was carrying a gun.[14] The tip was not recorded, and nothing was known about the caller. Two officers went to the bus stop and spotted three black males. One of them, the 15-year-old J. L., was wearing a plaid shirt. Apart from the anonymous tip, the officers had no reason to suspect that any of the males were involved in any criminal activity. The officers did not see a firearm, and J. L. made no threatening or unusual movements. One officer approached J. L., frisked him,

---

**EXHIBIT 8.2**

## *Categories of Evidence*

Warrants are typically issued to search for and seize a variety of evidence:

- Property that represents evidence of the commission of a criminal offense—for example, a bloody glove or shirt.

- Contraband, the fruits of crime, smuggled goods, illegal material, or anything else that is of a criminal nature.

- Property intended for use or which has been used as the means of committing a criminal offense—

for example, burglary tools, safecracking equipment, and drug paraphernalia.

- People may be seized when there is probable cause for their arrest.

- Conversation involving criminal conspiracy and other illegalities can be seized via tape recordings and wiretaps.

---

and seized a gun from his pocket. The Court disallowed the search, ruling that a police officer must have reasonable suspicion that criminal activity is being conducted prior to stopping a person. Because anonymous tips are generally considered less reliable than tips from known informants, they can be used to search only if they include specific information that shows they are reliable. Unlike the *White* case, the police in *J. L.* failed to provide independent corroboration of the tipster's information.

> **CourseMate** For more information about **U.S. Supreme Court decisions on criminal procedure**, visit the Criminal Justice CourseMate at CengageBrain.com, then access the "Web Links" for this chapter.

## Neutral and Detached Magistrate

Warrants can be issued only by neutral and detached magistrates. Any judge is considered a neutral and detached magistrate. Requiring that a judge "sign off" on a warrant brings an element of objectivity to the criminal process. It serves as a check on police officers' decisions concerning who should be arrested and/or searched. The Supreme Court echoed this point over 60 years ago in the important case of *Johnson v. United States* (1948):

> The point of the Fourth Amendment . . . is not that it denies law enforcement the support of the usual inferences reasonable men draw from evidence. Its protection consists in requiring that those inferences be drawn by a neutral and detached magistrate instead of being judged by the officer engaged in the often competitive enterprise of ferreting out crime.[15]

Before a warrant will be issued, a police officer must offer sworn testimony that the facts on which the request for the search warrant is made are trustworthy and true. If the judge issues the warrant, it will authorize police officers to search for particular objects, at a specific location, at a certain time. A warrant may authorize the search of "the premises at 221 Third Avenue, Apt. 6B, between the hours of 8 a.m. and 6 p.m." and direct the police to search for and seize "substances, contraband, paraphernalia, scales, and other items used in connection with the sale of illegal substances." Generally, warrants allow the seizure of a variety of types of evidence, as described in Exhibit 8.2.

## Particularity

Recall that the Fourth Amendment states, in part, that warrants must *particularly* describe "the place to be searched, and the persons or things to be seized." This **particularity** requirement was included in the Fourth Amendment to counteract the use of general warrants by government agents. This was a device used against the colonists by the English crown. British officials had obtained general warrants empowering them to search any suspected places for smuggled goods, placing the liberty of every man in the hands of government officials.[16]

**particularity**
The requirement that a search warrant state precisely where the search is to take place and what items are to be seized.

**CONCEPT SUMMARY 8.2**
*Warrant Requirements*

■ *Probable cause.* Probable cause is determined by whether a police officer has objective, reasonable, and reliable information, based on fact, that the person under investigation has committed or was committing an offense.

■ *Neutral and detached magistrate.* Neither a search warrant nor an arrest warrant can be issued without the signature of a neutral and detached magistrate. Judges are considered neutral and detached.

■ *Particularity.* A search warrant must set forth and precisely specify the places to be searched and the items to be seized so that it can provide reasonable guidance to the police officers and prevent them from having unregulated and unrestricted discretion to search for evidence. An arrest warrant must specify the name of the person to be arrested or provide a sufficiently specific description of the individual.

The particularity requirement is also designed to curtail potential abuse that may result from an officer being allowed to conduct a search with unbridled discretion. If a warrant is issued in violation of the particularity clause, the ensuing search is invalid even if the officers actually exercise proper restraint in executing their search. What and who are to be searched must be clearly spelled out. The police cannot search the basement of a house if the warrant specifies the attic; they cannot look in a desk drawer if the warrant specifies a search for a missing piano. However, this does not mean that police officers can seize only those items listed in the warrant. If, during the course of their search, police officers come across contraband or evidence of a crime that is not listed in the warrant, they can lawfully seize the unlisted items. This is referred to as the plain view exception (see the section "Warrantless Searches and Arrests" for more on plain view). But they cannot look in places that are off-limits within the scope of the warrant.

The particularity requirement applies to arrest warrants, as well. To satisfy this requirement, the police must clearly specify the name of the individual who is to be arrested. If no name is available, they must provide a sufficiently specific description of the individual. Concept Summary 8.2 sums up this and the other two requirements for obtaining a warrant.

## SERVING THE WARRANT

Once a warrant is secured, it needs to be served. There are important procedural steps that must be followed when a warrant is served. The steps are mostly the same for each type of warrant. They include

1. *Knock and announce.* In general, when a warrant is served, officers must knock on the door and announce their presence.[17] Officers must announce their authority and their intentions.[18] When it is likely that an announcement would threaten officer safety, the knock-and-announce rule can be waived. To protect themselves, officers often secure so-called "no-knock" warrants that authorize them in advance to make entry without knocking and announcing. The knock-and-announce rule was recently dealt a blow in the case of *Hudson v. Michigan*, where the Supreme Court held that evidence seized following a violation of the rule does not have to be excluded from trial.[19]

2. *Keep property damage to a minimum.* It may be necessary for officers to forcibly enter the premises if the door is locked or barricaded. Likewise, it could be necessary to damage a person's property when searching for

items named in a warrant. In either case, the standard is "shocks the conscience." If the property damage shocks the conscience, officers may be held liable for the damages they inflict.[20]

3. *Use appropriate force.* It may be necessary for officers to use force during service of either an arrest warrant or a search warrant. An arrestee may resist, or the person whose property is searched could decide to attack the police. In both instances, the standards governing deadly and nondeadly force apply. We discussed these in the previous chapter.

4. *Pay attention to time constraints with search warrants.* Most search warrants require daytime service.[21] The warrant may also limit the amount of time officers can take to search for the evidence they seek. In most jurisdictions, these requirements can be avoided if officers obtain warrants that permit night service or contain other special instructions.

5. *Limit the scope and manner of searches.* The scope and manner of the search must be reasonable in light of what is sought. For example, if a search warrant authorizes police to look for stolen jewelry, then they can look almost anywhere. In contrast, if the warrant names stolen big-screen televisions, then the police cannot look in drawers, cabinets, and other small places where such items could not be stored.[22]

6. *No reporters allowed.* The Supreme Court has held that the police cannot bring members of the media along on the service of search warrants unless they are there to serve a legitimate law enforcement function, such as videotaping the execution of the warrant for training purposes.[23]

## WARRANTLESS SEARCHES AND ARRESTS

Under normal circumstances, the police must obtain a warrant to conduct a search. However, over the years the Supreme Court has carved out some significant exceptions to the warrant requirement of the Fourth Amendment. These include

- Exigent (emergency) circumstances
- Stop and frisk
- Searches incident to lawful arrest
- Automobile searches
- Consent searches
- Searches based on plain view
- Crimes committed in an officer's presence

A warrantless search or arrest must be reasonable. For example, a search would be considered unreasonable if it was conducted simply because of an offender's prior behavior or status. Police officers cannot stop and search a vehicle driven by a known drug dealer unless some other factors support the search. Unless there was something discernible to a police officer that indicated a crime was then being committed, the suspect's past history would not justify an officer's stopping and searching the vehicle. Nor would it be considered reasonable if police decided to search someone simply because he was seen engaging in a pattern of behavior that seemed similar or comparable to the activity of known criminals. A person could not be searched because he was seen driving a flashy new car and making routine stops at the same places each day merely because that is a pattern of behavior typical of drug dealing.

Also, the mere fact that a warrantless arrest is permissible does not mean the officer has complete autonomy to determine whether probable cause is in place. Every person who is subject to warrantless arrest must be brought before a judge, usually within 48 hours, for a **probable cause hearing.**[24]

**probable cause hearing**
If a person is subjected to a warrantless arrest, a hearing is held to determine whether probable cause exists that he committed the crime.

## CRIMINAL JUSTICE AND TECHNOLOGY

# GPS Tagging in Hot-Pursuit Cases

It seems there is an enduring fascination with watching criminals run for their lives. High-speed police pursuits are staples on the evening news. Popular programs such as *World's Wildest Police Chases* quench viewers' thirst for witnessing desperate suspects try to escape the police. All told, some 100,000 high-speed pursuits are recorded each year. Some of the chases end peacefully, others in fiery blazes.

Although most fleeing suspects get caught, there is nothing easy about making the decision to give chase. On the one hand, when a pursuit begins, there is the risk that innocent pedestrians or motorists could be hurt. Officers need to guard against this possibility, especially when the chase could go through a residential neighborhood. On the other hand, if officers gave too much weight to the possibility that others could be hurt and did not give chase, criminals would learn quickly that they can run and avoid apprehension.

Most police departments have policies that guide officers in their decision whether or not to pursue. Some permit pursuit only in cases involving violent felonies. Others are more "generous" and allow officers to commence a pursuit in virtually any situation where a suspect decides to flee. These pursuit policies have been based not just on individual departments' experiences but also on scientific study. Researchers have examined the relationships between various types of pursuit policies and resulting injuries. Others have tried to identify the factors most often associated with injury to innocent third parties and fleeing suspects. In spite of all these efforts, the solution to the pursuit problem has remained elusive—until now. Police officers in several cities are now using GPS-based technology to tag and track fleeing suspects' vehicles.

The pioneer in this area is a company by the name of StarChase. Its Pursuit Management System, reminiscent of a James Bond–like car-mounted rocket launcher, consists of a compressed air launcher affixed to a police cruiser's bumper that fires GPS tagging darts at fleeing vehicles. The darts attach to the fleeing vehicle and send a signal that can be tracked. A dispatcher views the location and movements of the vehicle in real time via a secure Internet connection and relays the information to officers on the ground, who then easily locate the suspect.

LAPD Chief William Bratton has said this about the technology, which *Time* magazine labeled one of the "best innovations of the year":

> Instead of us pushing them doing 70 or 80 miles an hour ... this device allows us not to have to pursue after the car. . . . It allows us to start vectoring where the car is. Even if they bail out of the car, we'll have pretty much instantaneous information where they are.

StarChase is hoping that its technology will make its way into patrol cars across the country. Various police departments are currently partnering with the company to beta test the tracking system. Whether StarChase will deliver on its promises remains to be seen.

### Critical Thinking

1. Is GPS tagging likely to solve the problems that can result from police pursuits? Why or why not?

2. What other options do officers have available for dealing with fleeing motorists? Are they more or less effective than tagging?

Sources: Geoffrey P. Alpert, *Police Pursuit: Policies and Training* (Washington, D.C.: National Institute of Justice, 1997); StarChase, http://starchase.org/ (accessed August 2, 2008); Laurie Sullivan, "L.A. Cops Fight Car Chases with GPS Devices," *Techweb News,* http://tinyurl .com/y2gyyn3 (accessed April 15, 2010).

## Exigent Circumstances

**exigent circumstances**
Emergency or urgent circumstances.

The Supreme Court has identified a number of **exigent circumstances** in which a search warrant might normally have been required but, because of some immediate emergency, police officers can search suspects and places without benefit of a warrant. These include hot pursuit, danger of escape, threats to evidence, and threats to others. In each situation, officers must have probable cause.

The definition of exigent circumstances is not written in stone, and situations that a police officer considers exigent may be later disputed in the courts. In *Kirk v. Louisiana* (2002), police officers observed a suspect engaging in what they believed to be drug deals. Without a warrant, they entered his home, arrested him, frisked him, found a drug vial in his underwear, and seized contraband that was in plain view in the apartment. Only after these actions did the officers obtain a warrant. The Supreme Court ruled that police officers need either a warrant or probable cause plus exigent circumstances to make a lawful entry into a home. Although the Court left unclear the factors that define exigent circumstances, the facts of the *Kirk* case indicate that merely observing a suspect committing what appears to be a nonviolent crime is not enough to justify a warrantless entry of a person's home.[25]

**HOT PURSUIT**    Let's say that police officers become involved in a shoot-out with three suspects who then run into a house. The police would be allowed to enter the premises without a warrant in order to find and arrest the suspects. The warrantless search would be allowed because the police were in **hot pursuit** of the suspects and because failure to search could put citizens in danger, a condition that courts typically view as exigent.[26]

In order to justify a warrantless search by claiming hot pursuit, there are five important requirements that must all be met:

- The police must have probable cause that the suspect is on the premises to be searched.

- The police must have reason to believe that an immediate apprehension is necessary.

- Hot pursuit must be commenced from a lawful vantage point. For example, if officers wrongfully entered private property and commenced a pursuit from there, they could not claim hot pursuit.

- The offense in question must be serious, usually a felony.

- The pursuit must occur prior to or close to apprehension of the suspect. For example, officers cannot justify a search based on hot pursuit if they already have the suspect in custody.[27]

Sometimes hot pursuits end badly, perhaps with an injury to the suspect or an innocent bystander. And sometimes officers are sued for their decisions to pursue, even by the offenders who flee! The Supreme Court recently decided such a case (*Scott v. Harris*) in which the driver of a fleeing vehicle crashed and became a quadriplegic. He sued police, claiming that the force that officers used to bring him to a halt was excessive (an officer rammed Harris's vehicle). The Court held that because Harris posed such a danger to others as he was fleeing, the officer was justified in using force to bring Harris's vehicle to a stop.[28] In response to this and other high-profile pursuit incidents, police departments have adopted policies and acquired technologies intended to help reduce loss of life and injury. See the accompanying Criminal Justice and Technology box for more on this.

**DANGER OF ESCAPE**    If there is a possibility that a suspect will escape if the police have to take time to secure a warrant, they may be able to dispense with the warrant requirement. For example, if the police learn through an informant that a dangerous robbery suspect just entered an apartment complex, they may be able to enter the premises to find the suspect if they cannot secure the property or obtain a warrant in time.[29]

**THREATS TO EVIDENCE**    If the police have probable cause to believe that an individual is about to destroy critical evidence, such as flushing drugs down the toilet, they can enter private property and seize the evidence without first obtaining a warrant. The Supreme Court has also sanctioned the seizure of blood (via a needle) from a man's arm to prove he had been drinking—a practice that continues in some jurisdictions, especially around the holidays.[30]

**hot pursuit**
A legal doctrine that allows police to perform a warrantless search of premises where they suspect a crime has been committed when delay would endanger their lives or the lives of others and lead to the escape of the alleged perpetrator.

# CAREERS IN CRIMINAL JUSTICE

## Postal Inspector

### Duties and Characteristics of the Job

The Postal Inspection Service is a law enforcement body of the U.S. government. Postal inspectors investigate crimes that break postal laws, and they ensure the security of the U.S. Postal Service. The duties of postal inspectors include general law enforcement tasks such as executing warrants, arresting offenders, and testifying in court. However, a large part of a postal inspector's job is investigating crimes perpetrated through the mail, such as mail theft, mail fraud, drug trafficking, child pornography, and identity theft. Postal inspectors conduct investigations using a combination of advanced technology and forensic skills. They investigate harassment and threats against postal employees and the postal service itself. Postal inspectors are also responsible for investigating any threat that involves the mail as a medium. For example, postal inspectors were involved in the 2001 investigation into the envelopes containing anthrax that were mailed to government and news offices.

Postal inspectors are responsible for ensuring that the entire postal service is safe and dependable. Being a postal inspector can be a demanding job; irregular hours and working more than 40 hours per week are common.

### Job Outlook

Unfortunately, opportunities for employment as a postal inspector open at irregular intervals. However, when the postal service is hiring, a diversity of skills and backgrounds is desirable in potential postal inspectors.

### Salary

As with other federal employees, salaries for postal inspectors are determined by the General Pay Scale, and various factors, such as employment qualifications, are used to determine position on the scale. Postal inspectors are exempt from the Fair Labor Standards Act and so cannot earn overtime pay. Entry-level salaries range from $41,563 to $78,355 (not including locality pay, which includes a cost-of-living adjustment in the

The case on which this decision was based, *Breithaupt v. Abram* (1957), predated Breathalyzers, so we are unlikely to see additional cases where needles are used to obtain evidence of intoxication. Regardless of the technique used, the key to the case was that the evidence would have disappeared had the police not obtained it quickly. The suspect would have metabolized the alcohol.

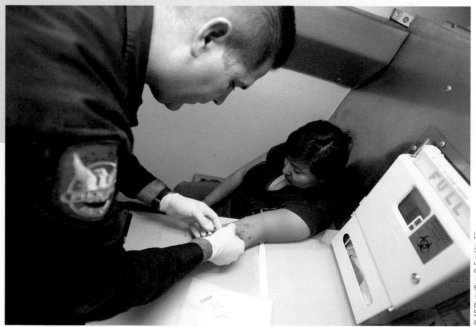

*Phoenix police officer James Lawler, of the agency's DUI Squad, administers a blood test as he works out of a mobile processing van. The Arizona Supreme Court ruled that police must get a search warrant to take a blood sample from a DUI suspect, unless the person clearly consents to providing a sample. Was the Arizona Supreme Court's decision sound?*

© AP Photo/Ross D. Franklin, File

upward direction). A candidate's qualifications and current pay are considered when the initial salary is set.

## Opportunities

Because of the good pay, benefits, prestige, and opportunities that these positions offer, applicants should expect competition. Accounting experience, computer skills, and a law degree are helpful when applying for a position. Law enforcement experience as a detective or even a patrol officer will also be helpful. Finally, good students who earned a bachelor's or an advanced degree with a 3.0 or higher average can qualify for the academic achievement track with or without full-time job experience.

## Qualifications

Candidates must be U.S. citizens 21 or over, but younger than 36½, and they must have a four-year degree, no felony or domestic violence convictions, and a driver's license. A candidate must also be in sound mental and physical health and must pass a hearing test. Qualities such as good communications skills (written and oral), sound decision-making skills, and the ability to follow instructions are also highly valued. Once having satisfied the general requirements, a candidate must qualify for training under one

of several tracks offered: language skills, postal experience, specialized nonpostal experience (includes those with law degrees, certification in auditing or computer systems, law enforcement experience, and others), or academic achievement.

Additionally, applicants must undergo a background check, pass a polygraph, and be interviewed. After completing the proper training, a postal inspector may be relocated, so a willingness to move is also necessary.

## Education and Training

In order to even apply for a position, a potential candidate must have a four-year degree. After successfully moving through the application process and being hired, new employees will be sent to Basic Inspector Training in Potomac, Maryland, where they will learn about the responsibilities of their organization, investigative techniques, firearms proficiency, and physical defense. Those with no postal experience will then be on a six-month probation period before becoming full-time employees.

Sources: "Eligibility," U.S. Postal Inspection Service Employment, retrieved April 15, 2010, from https://postalinspectors.uspis.gov/employment/eligibility.aspx; 2010 Gendental Schedule (Base), www.opm.gov/oca/10tables/pdf/gs.pdf, retrieved April 16, 2010.

**THREATS TO OTHERS** If a suspect poses a risk to others, this also can be considered an exigent circumstance. For example, in a hostage situation, the police can usually dispense with the warrant requirement and storm the property (if it is safe) in order to protect the lives of innocent persons held within. In one recent case, the Supreme Court sanctioned the actions of some officers who, without a warrant, entered a house where a loud party was going on because they observed a fight taking place.[31] The Court stated that "Police may enter a home without a warrant when they have an objectively reasonable basis for believing that an occupant is seriously injured or imminently threatened with such injury."[32]

The same applies, it seems, even if it is not clear whether any one person is being threatened. In *Michigan v. Fisher*,[33] officers arrived at a house and saw Jeremy Fisher, who was screaming and throwing objects, through a window. The officers knocked, but Fisher did not answer. They noticed his hand was bleeding and asked whether he needed medical attention. He ignored the officers' questions and told them to get a warrant. One officer then forced open the door. Fisher drew a gun but was subdued and charged with assault with a dangerous weapon. Fisher sought suppression of the gun at trial, but the Supreme Court decided that his Fourth Amendment rights were not violated.

## Field Interrogation: Stop and Frisk

One important exception to the rule requiring a search warrant is the **stop-and-frisk** procedure. This type of search typically occurs when a police officer encounters a suspicious person on the street and frisks or pats down his outer garments to determine whether he is in possession of a concealed weapon. The police officer need not have probable cause to arrest the suspect but simply must be reasonably suspicious based on the circumstances of the case (that is, time

**stop and frisk**
The situation in which police officers who are suspicious of an individual run their hands lightly over the suspect's outer garments to determine whether the person is carrying a concealed weapon; also called a threshold inquiry or pat-down.

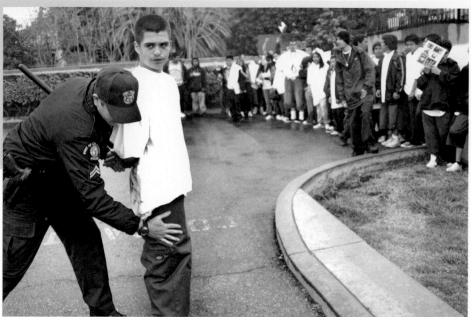

With reasonable suspicion that criminal activity has occurred, a police officer can stop a person and frisk him or her for weapons. Here a San Pedro (California) high school student is frisked by a Los Angeles Port Police officer after students attempted to enter the 110 Harbor Freeway to protest immigration legislation. The students were stopped by the police, ticketed for being truant, and put on a school bus back to school.

© AP Images/Branimir Kvartuc

and place) and her experience as a police officer. The stop-and-frisk search consists of two distinct components:

1.  The stop, in which a police officer wishes to briefly detain a suspicious person in an effort to effect crime prevention and detection.

2.  The frisk, in which an officer pats down, or frisks, a person who is stopped, in order to check for weapons. The purpose of the frisk is protection of the officer making the stop.

The stop and the frisk are separate actions, and each requires its own factual basis. Stopping a suspect allows for brief questioning, and frisking affords the officer an opportunity to avoid the possibility of attack. For instance, a police officer patrolling a high-crime area observes two young men loitering outside a liquor store after dark. The two men confer several times and stop to talk to a third person who pulls up alongside the curb in an automobile. From this observation, the officer may conclude that the men are casing the store for a possible burglary. He can then stop the suspects and ask them for some identification and an explanation of their conduct. However, the facts that support a stop do not automatically allow a frisk. The officer must have reason to believe that the suspect is armed or dangerous. In this instance, if the three men identify themselves as security guards and produce identification, a frisk would not be justified. If they seem nervous and secretive and the officer concludes that they are planning a crime, the suspicion would be enough to justify a pat-down.

The landmark case of *Terry v. Ohio* (1968) shaped the contours of the stop and frisk.[34] In *Terry*, a police officer found a gun in the coat pocket of one of three men he frisked when their suspicious behavior convinced him that they were planning a robbery. At trial, the defendants futilely moved to suppress the gun on the grounds that it was the product of an illegal search. On appeal, the Supreme Court ruled that if a reasonably prudent police officer believes that her safety or that of others is endangered, she may make a reasonable search for weapons on the person, regardless of whether she has probable cause to arrest that individual for a crime or is absolutely certain that the individual is armed. The *Terry* case illustrates the principle that although the police officer must, whenever possible, secure a warrant to make a search and seizure, still, when swift action is called for based upon on-the-spot observations, the need for the warrant is removed.

What kind of behavior can trigger a *Terry* search? How suspicious does a person have to look before the police can legally stop him and pat him down? In *Illinois v. Wardlow* (2000), the defendant was walking on the street in an area known for narcotics trafficking. When he made eye contact with a police officer riding in a marked police car, he ran away. The officer caught up with the defendant on the street, stopped him, and conducted a protective pat-down search for weapons. A handgun was discovered in the frisk, and the defendant was convicted of unlawful use of a weapon by a felon. The Illinois Supreme Court ruled that the frisk violated *Terry v. Ohio* because flight may simply be an exercise of the right to "go on one's way" and does not constitute reasonable suspicion. However, on appeal, the U.S. Supreme Court reversed the state court ruling that a person's presence in a "high crime area," in and of itself, is not enough to support a reasonable, particularized suspicion of criminal activity.[35] It held that a location's characteristics are sufficiently suspicious to warrant further investigation and that, in this case, the additional factor of the defendant's unprovoked flight added up to reasonable suspicion. The officers found that the defendant possessed a handgun, and as a result of the pat-down and search, they had probable cause to arrest him for violation of a state law. The frisk and arrest were thus proper under *Terry v. Ohio*.

The Supreme Court's recent decision in *Arizona v. Johnson*[36] combined the issue of stop and frisk with a vehicle stop. In that case, police officers serving on a gang task force stopped a vehicle for an infraction, but they did not suspect criminal activity. One officer confronted the driver; another questioned one of the passengers, Johnson. After the officer learned that Johnson had a criminal record, he was asked to exit the vehicle, which he did. The officer then frisked Johnson and found a gun. He was arrested, charged, and convicted of illegally carrying a weapon. The Supreme Court sanctioned the search, reinforcing the *Terry* decision's language that police may need to "act instantly if they have reasonable cause to suspect that the persons temporarily detained are armed and dangerous."[37]

## Search Incident to a Lawful Arrest

Traditionally, a search without a warrant is permissible if it is made incident to a lawful arrest. *Incident* means close in time to an arrest, usually right after the arrest. The police officer who searches a suspect incident to a lawful arrest must generally observe two rules: (1) the search must be conducted at the time of or immediately following the arrest, and (2) the police may search only the suspect and the area within the suspect's immediate control. The search may not legally go beyond the area where the person can reach for a weapon or destroy any evidence. For example, if shortly after the armed robbery of a grocery store, officers arrest a suspect hiding in the basement with a briefcase, a search of the suspect's person and of the briefcase would be a proper **search incident to a lawful arrest** without a warrant. The legality of this type of search depends almost entirely on the lawfulness of the arrest. The arrest will be upheld if the police officer observed the crime being committed or had probable cause to believe that the suspect committed the offense. If the arrest is found to have been invalid, then any warrantless search made incident to the arrest would be considered illegal, and the evidence obtained from the search would be excluded from trial.

The U.S. Supreme Court defined the permissible scope of a search incident to a lawful arrest in *Chimel v. California* (1969).[38] According to the *Chimel* doctrine, the police can search a suspect without a warrant after a lawful arrest to protect themselves from danger and to secure evidence. But a search of his home is illegal even if the police find contraband or evidence during the course of that search and if the police would otherwise be forced to obtain a warrant to search the premises.

**search incident to a lawful arrest**
An exception to the search warrant rule, limited to the immediate surrounding area.

## Automobile Searches

The U.S. Supreme Court has also established that certain situations justify the warrantless search of an automobile on a public street or highway. Evidence can be seized from an automobile when a suspect is taken into custody in a lawful

# The Evolution of Carroll v. United States

**Carroll v. United States (1925)**   An automobile can be searched without a warrant if the police have probable cause.[40]

**United States v. Lee (1927)**   An automobile is any conveyance being used for transportation, including even a motor home.[41]

**Cardwell v. Lewis (1974)**   People enjoy a lesser expectation of privacy in their vehicles than in their homes and offices.[42]

**Pennsylvania v. Mimms (1977)**   During routine traffic stops, officers can order drivers out of their cars and frisk them.[43]

**United States v. Ross (1982)**   With probable cause, police can search an automobile without a warrant, including any containers within.[44]

**Michigan v. Long (1983)**   Police can frisk a driver and search the passenger compartment of a vehicle following a valid stop, provided they have reasonable suspicion that the driver poses a danger.[45]

**Michigan Dept. of State Police v. Sitz (1990)**   Suspicionless seizures of motorists are permissible for purposes of detecting drunk driving.[46]

**Whren v. United States (1996)**   The constitutional reasonableness of a traffic stop does not depend on an officer's initial motivation. It depends only on whether there was justification to stop the vehicle.[47]

**Maryland v. Wilson (1997)**   During a routine traffic stop, the officer can order a passenger out of the vehicle and frisk him or her.[48]

**City of Indianapolis v. Edmund (2000)**   The police cannot operate roadblocks for the purpose of detecting illegal drugs.[49]

**Illinois v. Lidster (2004)**   Police are constitutionally authorized to conduct suspicionless vehicle checkpoints for the purpose of gaining information about a crime recently committed in the area.[50]

**Brendlin v. California (2007)**   Passengers, like drivers, are considered "seized" during traffic stops, meaning they enjoy Fourth Amendment protection from unreasonable searches and seizures.[51]

**Arizona v. Gant (2009)**   If a motorist is arrested, police may search the vehicle only if it is reasonable to assume the arrestee could access the vehicle *or* the vehicle contains evidence of the offense of arrest.[52]

arrest. In *Carroll v. United States*, which was decided in 1925, the Supreme Court ruled that distinctions should be made among searches of automobiles, persons, and homes. The Court also concluded that a warrantless search of an automobile is valid if the police have probable cause to believe that the car contains evidence they are seeking.[39] This same rule is in effect today. The accompanying feature, "Evolution of *Carroll v. United States*," summarizes several of the Court's important vehicle search decisions in the wake of *Carroll*, which are discussed further throughout this section.

Because police are now confronting such significant social problems as drug trafficking and terrorist activity, the Supreme Court has given them some additional leeway in terms of making stops. For example, in the 2002 case *United States v. Arvizu*, the Court allowed a stop (and eventual search) of a vehicle based on a pattern of suspicious behavior:

1. A vehicle registration check showing that the vehicle was registered to an address in an area notorious for alien and narcotics smuggling.

2. The patrol officer's personal experience and his knowledge that the suspect had taken a route frequently used by drug smugglers.

3. The driver's route having been designed to pass through the area during a border patrol shift change.

Although each fact alone was insufficient to justify the stop, together they supported the officer's decision to stop the vehicle.[53]

**SCOPE OF THE AUTOMOBILE SEARCH**
The legality of searching automobiles without a warrant has always been a trouble spot for police and the courts. Should the search be limited to the interior of the car, or can the police search the trunk? What about a suitcase in the trunk? What about the glove compartment? Does a traffic citation give the police the right to search an automobile? These questions have produced significant litigation over the years. To clear up the matter, the Supreme Court has focused on two types of situations: "pure" vehicle searches and vehicle searches following driver arrests and/or detentions.

A "pure" vehicle search is one in which the police seek to search a vehicle without regard to whether the vehicle is being driven by a person. In other words, these are searches of the vehicle that do not concern the passenger. In *United States v. Ross* in 1982,[54] the Supreme Court held that if probable cause exists to believe that an automobile contains criminal evidence, a warrantless search by the police is permissible, including a search of closed containers in the vehicle. Probable cause is the all-important requirement. In the absence of probable cause, the search will run afoul of the Fourth Amendment, and any resulting evidence will be inadmissible in court. With probable cause, however, the car may be stopped and searched, contraband can be seized, and the occupant can be arrested, all without violating the Fourth Amendment.

What if, however, a driver is stopped for speeding and the officer has no intent—in advance—to search the vehicle? In *Michigan v. Long*,[55] police officers observed a vehicle swerve into a ditch. When officers approached the vehicle, they noticed that the driver was intoxicated and that there was a large hunting knife on the passenger seat. The officers arrested the driver and searched the passenger compartment of the vehicle. Both actions were sanctioned by the Supreme Court. The search was justified on the grounds that it was necessary to protect officer safety.

More recently, in *Arizona v. Gant*,[56] the case featured in this chapter's opening vignette, the Supreme Court held that a full vehicle search following the driver's arrest is permissible only if it is reasonable to assume the arrestee could access the vehicle *or* the vehicle contains evidence of the offense of arrest. Concerning the latter requirement, if the person was stopped for trafficking in illegal weapons, then with probable cause the police would be authorized to search the vehicle for weapons, even if the driver was arrested, handcuffed, and locked in the back seat of a police car. It is important to note that the *Gant* decision did not overturn *Michigan v. Long*; officers can still search a vehicle's passenger compartment when they have reasonable suspicion that the driver, whether or not he or she is arrested, might gain access to it and obtain a weapon.

*SEARCHING DRIVERS AND PASSENGERS*  Can police officers search drivers and passengers during routine traffic stops? In 1977 the Supreme Court ruled, in *Pennsylvania v. Mimms*, that officers could order drivers out of their cars and frisk them during routine traffic stops. Officers' safety outweighed the intrusion on individual rights.[57] In 1997 the Court held, in *Maryland v. Wilson*, that the police had the same authority with respect to passengers.[58] In the *Wilson* case, a state patrol officer lawfully stopped a vehicle for speeding. While the driver was producing his license, the front-seat passenger, Jerry Lee Wilson, was ordered out of the vehicle. As he exited, crack cocaine dropped to the ground. Wilson was arrested and convicted of drug possession. His attorney moved to suppress the evidence, but the U.S. Supreme Court disagreed and extended the *Mimms* rule to passengers. The Court noted that lawful traffic stops had become progressively more dangerous to police officers and that thousands of officers were assaulted and even killed during such stops. The decision means that passengers must comply when ordered out of a lawfully stopped vehicle.

In 2007 the Supreme Court decided another vehicle search case, this one dealing with searches of passengers. In *Brendlin v. California*,[59] a car was stopped to check its registration. After stopping the vehicle, the officers learned that a passenger, Brendlin, was a parole violator. The officers arrested him, searched him, and found an orange syringe cap on his person. A pat-down search of the driver also revealed contraband. She was also arrested. Then the car was searched incident to the driver's arrest, and methamphetamine paraphernalia was discovered. Brendlin challenged the search, seeking to have the evidence excluded, but the California Supreme Court held that Brendlin was not "seized" in the traffic stop. This meant he could not even challenge his arrest and subsequent search. Not surprisingly, the U.S. Supreme Court disagreed, holding that Brendlin *was* seized. This case was important because the Court held that anyone detained in a traffic stop, not just the driver, is "seized." This means such persons can challenge the police action on constitutional grounds.

*PRETEXT STOPS*  A pretext stop is one in which police officers stop a car because they suspect the driver is involved in a crime such as drug trafficking, but, lacking probable cause, they use a pretext such as a minor traffic violation to stop the car and search its interior. The legality of pretext stops was challenged in

*Whren v. United States* (1996).[60] Two defendants claimed that plainclothes police officers used relatively minor traffic violations as an excuse, or pretext, to stop their vehicle because the officers lacked objective evidence that they were drug couriers. However, the Supreme Court ruled that if probable cause exists to stop a person for a traffic violation, then the actual motivation of the officers is irrelevant; therefore, the search was legal. This point was reiterated in *Arkansas v. Sullivan*, in which the Court ruled that if an officer has a legal basis for making a custodial arrest for a particular crime, it does not matter whether he has suspicions that the suspect is involved in any other criminal activity.[61] Thus, as long as there is a legal basis for making an arrest, officers may do so, even in cases in which they are motivated by a desire to gather evidence of other suspected crimes.

*ROADBLOCK SEARCHES*   Police departments often wish to set up roadblocks to check drivers' licenses or the condition of drivers. Is such a stop an illegal search and seizure? In *Delaware v. Prouse* (1979), the Supreme Court forbade the practice of random stops in the absence of any reasonable suspicion that some traffic or motor vehicle law has been violated.[62] Unless there is at least reasonable belief that a motorist is unlicensed, that an automobile is not registered, or that the occupant is subject to seizure for violation of the law, stopping and detaining a driver to check his or her license violates the Fourth Amendment. In *City of Indianapolis v. Edmond* (2000), the Court ruled that the police may not routinely stop all motorists in the hope of finding a few drug criminals.[63] The general rule is that any seizure must be accompanied by individualized suspicion; the random stopping of cars to search for drugs is illegal.

Although random stops are forbidden, a police department can set up a roadblock to stop cars in some systematic fashion to ensure public safety. As long as the police can demonstrate that the checkpoints are conducted in a uniform manner and that the operating procedures have been determined by someone other than the officer at the scene, roadblocks can be used to uncover violators of even minor traffic regulations. In *Michigan Dept. of State Police v. Sitz* (1990), the Court held that brief, suspicionless seizures at highway checkpoints for the purposes of combating drunk driving were constitutional.[64] Police can stop a predetermined number of cars at a checkpoint and can request each motorist to produce his or her license, registration, and insurance card. While doing so, they can check for outward signs of intoxication. The Court has sanctioned similar stops for purposes of assisting police in a criminal investigation. In *Illinois v. Lidster*, officers briefly detained motorists to ask whether they witnessed a hit-and-run accident that occurred earlier in the same location.[65]

## Consent Searches

Police officers may also undertake warrantless searches when the person in control of the area or object consents to the search. Those who consent to a search essentially waive their constitutional rights under the Fourth Amendment. Ordinarily, courts are reluctant to accept such waivers and require the state to prove that the consent was voluntarily given. In addition, the consent must be given intelligently, and in some jurisdictions, consent searches are valid only after the suspect is informed of the option to refuse consent.

*VOLUNTARINESS*   The major legal issue in most consent searches is whether the police can prove that consent was given voluntarily. In general, consent cannot be the result of "duress or coercion, express or implied."[66] For example, in the case of *Bumper v. North Carolina* (1968), police officers searched the home of an elderly woman after informing her that they possessed a search warrant.[67] At the trial, the prosecutor informed the court that the search was valid because the woman had given her consent. When the government was unable to produce the warrant, the court decided that the search was invalid because the woman's consent was not given voluntarily. On appeal, the U.S. Supreme Court upheld the lower court's finding that the consent had been illegally obtained by the false claim that the police had a search warrant.

In most consent searches, however, voluntariness is a question of fact to be determined from all the circumstances of the case. In *Schneckloth v. Bustamonte* (1973), the defendant helped the police by opening the trunk and glove compartment of the car. The Court said this action demonstrated that the consent was voluntarily given.[68] Furthermore, the police are usually under no obligation to inform a suspect of the right to refuse consent.[69] Failure to tell a suspect of this right does not make the search illegal, but it may be a factor used by the courts to decide whether the suspect gave consent voluntarily.

*THIRD-PARTY CONSENT*   Can a person give consent for someone else? In *United States v. Matlock* (1974), the Court ruled that it is permissible for one co-occupant of an apartment to give consent to the police to search the premises in the absence of the other occupant, as long as the person giving consent shares common authority over the property and no present co-tenant objects.[70] What happens if one party gives consent to a search while another interested party refuses? This is what happened in the 2006 case of *Georgia v. Randolph*. Police were called to Scott Randolph's home because of a domestic dispute. His wife told police that Randolph had been using a lot of cocaine and that drugs were on the premises. One officer asked Randolph whether he could conduct a search of the home, and Randolph said no. Another officer asked his wife for permission, and she not only said yes but also led the officer upstairs to a bedroom where he allegedly found cocaine residue. The Supreme Court held that because Randolph was present when the police came to his home, they were required by the Fourth Amendment to heed his objection to the search; the seizure of the drugs was ruled illegal.[71]

*BUS SWEEPS*   Today, consent searches have additional significance because of their use in drug control programs. On June 20, 1991, the U.S. Supreme Court, in *Florida v. Bostick*, upheld the drug interdiction technique known as the **bus sweep**, in which police board buses and, without suspicion of illegal activity, question passengers, ask for identification, and request permission to search luggage.[72] Police in the Bostick case boarded a bus bound from Miami to Atlanta during a stopover in Fort Lauderdale. Without suspicion, the officers picked out the defendant and asked to inspect his ticket and identification. After identifying themselves as narcotics officers looking for illegal drugs, they asked to inspect the defendant's luggage. Although there was some uncertainty about whether the defendant consented to the search in which contraband was found, and about whether he was informed of his right to refuse consent, the defendant was convicted.

The Supreme Court was faced with deciding whether consent was freely given or the nature of the bus sweep negated the defendant's consent. The Court concluded that drug enforcement officers, after obtaining consent, may search luggage on a crowded bus without meeting the Fourth Amendment requirements for a search warrant or probable cause.

This case raises fundamental questions about the legality of techniques used to discourage drug trafficking. Are they inherently coercive? In *Bostick*, when the officers entered the bus, the driver exited and closed the door, leaving the defendant and other passengers alone with two officers. Furthermore, Terrance Bostick was seated in the rear of the bus, and officers blocked him from exiting. Finally, one of the officers was clearly holding his handgun in full view. In light of these circumstances, was this a consensual or a coercive search? The Supreme Court ruled, despite the coercive circumstances, that the search was appropriate because consent had been given voluntarily.

*"FREE TO GO"*   What if a police officer stops a motorist and asks for consent to search the vehicle? Must the officer inform the driver that he or she is "free to go" before asking consent to search the vehicle? In *Ohio v. Robinette* (1996),

**bus sweep**
Police investigation technique in which officers board a bus or train without suspicion of illegal activity and question passengers, asking for identification and seeking permission to search their baggage.

the Court concluded that no such warning is needed to make consent to a search reasonable. Robert D. Robinette was stopped for speeding. After checking his license, the officer asked whether Robinette was carrying any illegal contraband in the car. When the defendant answered in the negative, the officer asked for and received permission to search the car. The search turned up illegal drugs. The Supreme Court ruled that police officers do not have to inform a driver that he is "free to go" before asking whether they can search the car. According to the Court, the touchstone of the Fourth Amendment is reasonableness, which is assessed by examining the totality of the circumstances.[73] In this case, the search was ruled a reasonable exercise of discretion.

## Plain View

The Supreme Court has also ruled that police can search for and seize evidence without benefit of a warrant if it is in plain view.[74] For example, if a police officer is conducting an investigation and notices, while questioning some individuals, that one has drugs in her pocket, the officer can seize the evidence and arrest the suspect. Or if the police are conducting a search under a warrant authorizing them to look for narcotics in a person's home, and they come upon a gun, the police can seize the gun, even though it is not mentioned in the warrant. The 1986 case of *New York v. Class* illustrates the **plain view doctrine**.[75] A police officer stopped a car for a traffic violation. Wishing to check the vehicle identification number (VIN) on the dashboard, he reached into the car to clear away material that was obstructing his view. While clearing the dash, he noticed a gun under the seat—in plain view. The U.S. Supreme Court upheld the seizure of the gun as evidence because the police officer had the right to check the VIN; therefore, the sighting of the gun was legal.

The doctrine of plain view was applied and further developed in *Arizona v. Hicks* (1987).[76] In that case, the Court held that moving a stereo component in plain view a few inches to record the serial number constituted a search under the Fourth Amendment. When a check with police headquarters revealed that the item had been stolen, the equipment was seized and offered as evidence at James Hicks's trial. The Court held that a plain view search and seizure could be justified only by probable cause, not reasonable suspicion, and suppressed the evidence against the defendant. In this case, the Court decided to take a firm stance on protecting Fourth Amendment rights. The *Hicks* decision is uncharacteristic in an era when most decisions have tended to expand the exceptions to the search warrant requirement.

*PLAIN TOUCH* If the police touch contraband, can they seize it legally? Is "plain touch" like plain view? In the 1993 case of *Minnesota v. Dickerson*, two Minneapolis police officers noticed the defendant acting suspiciously after leaving an apartment building they believed to be a crack house. The officers briefly stopped Timothy Dickerson to question him and conducted a pat-down search for weapons. The search revealed no weapons, but one officer felt a small lump in the pocket of Dickerson's nylon jacket. The lump turned out to be one-fifth of a gram of crack cocaine, and Dickerson was arrested and charged with drug possession. In its decision, the Court added to its plain view doctrine a plain touch or plain feel corollary. However, the pat-down must be limited to a search for weapons, and the officer may not extend the "feel" beyond that necessary to determine whether what is felt is a weapon.[77]

Although *Dickerson* created the plain feel doctrine, the Supreme Court limited its scope in *Bond v. United States*.[78] In that case, a federal border patrol agent boarded a bus near the Texas–Mexico border to check the immigration status of the passengers. As he was leaving the bus, he squeezed the soft luggage that passengers had placed in the overhead storage space. When he squeezed a canvas bag belonging to the defendant, he noticed that it contained a "brick-like" object. The defendant consented to a search of the bag, the agent discovered

**plain view doctrine**
The principle that evidence in plain view of police officers may be seized without a search warrant.

a "brick" of methamphetamine, and the defendant was charged with and convicted of possession. The court of appeals ruled that the agent's manipulation of the bag was not a search under the Fourth Amendment. On appeal, however, the Supreme Court held that the agent's manipulation of the bag violated the Fourth Amendment's rule against unreasonable searches. Personal luggage, according to the Court, is protected under the Fourth Amendment. The defendant had a privacy interest in his bag, and his right to privacy was violated by the police search.

## Crimes Committed in an Officer's Presence

The decision to arrest is often made by the police officer during contact with the suspect and does not rely on a warrant being used. In the case of a felony, most jurisdictions provide that a police officer may arrest a suspect without a warrant when probable cause exists, even though the officer was not present when the offense was committed.

As a general rule, if the police make an arrest without a warrant, the arrestee must be promptly brought before a magistrate for a probable cause hearing. The U.S. Supreme Court dealt with the meaning of "promptly" in the 1991 case of *Riverside County v. McLaughlin*.[79] The Court said that the police may detain an individual arrested without a warrant for up to 48 hours without a court hearing to determine whether the arrest was justified.

*NONCRIMINAL ACTS* Can police arrest someone for a noncriminal act such as a traffic violation? This issue was decided in the case of *Atwater et al. v. City of Lago Vista*.[80] Gail Atwater was stopped for failing to wear a seat belt as she drove her two children home from soccer practice in Lago Vista, near Austin, Texas. She unbuckled for just a moment, she said, to look for a toy that had fallen from the pickup truck onto the street. The Lago Vista patrolman pulled her over, berated her, and arrested her. Under Texas law, she had committed a misdemeanor. Atwater subsequently was found to be driving without a license and to lack proof of insurance.

The standard for determining whether a police action was reasonable under the circumstances in this case is difficult. Some might argue that Atwater's traffic violation was not a breach of the peace, but others might suggest that Atwater's arrest was legal because she had violated a state statute. Whatever your opinion is, in April 2001 the U.S. Supreme Court upheld the right to arrest a suspect for a traffic violation.

In a twist on the *Atwater* case, the Supreme Court recently decided a case where officers in Virginia stopped a motorist for driving with a suspended license. In *Virginia v. Moore*,[81] state law required that the officer issue a citation to the driver, but instead they arrested him. The driver sought to suppress contraband that was seized during a search of the vehicle, arguing that this search violated the Fourth Amendment, but the Court held that police did not violate the Fourth Amendment because the search was based on probable cause. This case raises a really interesting question: Is it fair to allow states to have restrictive laws governing searches but then essentially abandon such laws in favor of a looser standard when it suits the police? This is exactly what happened in the present case. The state of Virginia argued that although the officers' actions violated state law, they did not violate the U.S. Constitution. Is this fair and reasonable?

For a summary of the discussion on warrantless searches, see Concept Summary 8.3.

## ▌ ELECTRONIC SURVEILLANCE

The use of wiretapping to intercept conversations between parties has significantly affected police investigative procedures. Electronic devices enable people to listen to and record the private conversations of other people over telephones, through walls and windows, and even over long-distance phone lines. Using

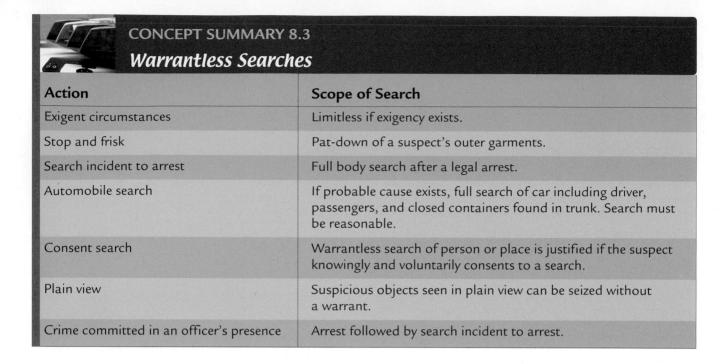

## CONCEPT SUMMARY 8.3
### *Warrantless Searches*

| Action | Scope of Search |
| --- | --- |
| Exigent circumstances | Limitless if exigency exists. |
| Stop and frisk | Pat-down of a suspect's outer garments. |
| Search incident to arrest | Full body search after a legal arrest. |
| Automobile search | If probable cause exists, full search of car including driver, passengers, and closed containers found in trunk. Search must be reasonable. |
| Consent search | Warrantless search of person or place is justified if the suspect knowingly and voluntarily consents to a search. |
| Plain view | Suspicious objects seen in plain view can be seized without a warrant. |
| Crime committed in an officer's presence | Arrest followed by search incident to arrest. |

these devices, police are able to intercept communications secretly and obtain information related to criminal activity.

The oldest and most widely used form of electronic surveillance is wiretapping. With approval from the court and a search warrant, law enforcement officers place listening devices on telephones to overhear oral communications of suspects. Such devices are also often placed in homes and automobiles. The evidence collected is admissible and can be used in the defendant's trial.

Many citizens believe that electronic eavesdropping through hidden microphones, radio transmitters, telephone taps, and bugs represents a grave threat to personal privacy.[82] Although the use of such devices is controversial, the police are generally convinced of their value in investigating criminal activity. However, opponents believe that these techniques are often used beyond their lawful intent to monitor political figures, harass suspects, or investigate cases involving questionable issues of "national security."

In response to concerns about invasions of privacy, the U.S. Supreme Court has increasingly limited the use of electronic eavesdropping in the criminal justice system. In *Katz v. United States* (1967), the Court ruled that when federal agents eavesdropped on a phone conversation using a listening device that could penetrate the walls of a phone booth, they had conducted an illegal search and seizure.[83] The *Katz* doctrine is usually interpreted to mean that the government must obtain a court order if it wishes to listen in on conversations in which the parties have a reasonable expectation of privacy, such as in their own homes or on the telephone. Meanwhile, public utterances or actions are fair game. *Katz* concluded that electronic eavesdropping is a search, even though there is no actual trespass. Therefore, it is unreasonable, and a warrant is needed.

## Surveillance Law

It can be relatively painless to secure a warrant for an ordinary search, but the police have to jump through many more hoops when it comes to electronic surveillance. There are two key laws that restrict government wiretap authority. The first, the Federal Wiretap Act (more formally called Title III of the Omnibus Crime Control and Safe Streets Act), was adopted in 1968 and revised in 1986.[84] It requires court approval of all real-time eavesdropping on electronic communications, including voice, email, fax, Internet, and those connected with criminal investigations. More recently, this authority has been used to support eavesdropping on communications between suspected terrorists. The Patriot Act, the controversial antiterrorism legislation enacted after 9/11, has expanded the number of criminal statutes for which such wiretaps can be authorized.

The second key statute controlling wiretaps and eavesdropping is the Foreign Intelligence Surveillance Act (FISA) of 1978.[85] It authorizes wiretapping of any alien the government believes is a member of a foreign terrorist group or is an agent of a foreign power. In the case of U.S. citizens, there must be probable cause that the person targeted for a wiretap is involved in criminal activity; otherwise, there is no such requirement for aliens. FISA warrants are authorized by the secret Foreign Intelligence Surveillance Court, which meets in a heavily secured room within the U.S. Justice Department. The court is staffed by 11 judges, appointed by the chief justice of the U.S. Supreme Court, who serve seven-year terms.

Just as the Patriot Act altered the Federal Wiretap Act, it also altered FISA. It did so by allowing prosecutors to gather evidence in cases involving national security crimes. In 2007, President Bush signed into law the controversial Protect America Act. It removed the warrant requirement for surveillance of foreign intelligence targets that the government "reasonably believes" are operating outside the United States. The law was especially controversial because it permitted electronic surveillance of all communications, including some domestic ones, that involved foreign targets. Because of a sunset clause, the law expired in early 2008. Even so, in light of recent world events and the ongoing threat of terrorism, changes to federal surveillance law are sure to continue.

## Technologies for Local Law Enforcement

The Federal Wiretap Act and FISA have limited applicability to local law enforcement. Most terrorism investigations and related surveillance activity tend to be federal affairs. For example, most FISA warrants are sought by the FBI. Yet there are plenty of technological advances that have benefited local law enforcement officials. Gone are the days of crude wiretaps outside phone booths and other antiquated devices. Now the police can avail themselves of several technological advances to help them keep tabs on the criminal element. Some devices even permit listening to and looking in on the activities of *everyone*, not just criminals. These devices are controversial because there is no warrant requirement. Examples include surveillance cameras and GPS tracking devices.

*SURVEILLANCE CAMERAS*  Many large cities (including Baltimore, Chicago, Los Angeles, Dallas, Washington, and New York) have installed, in public locations, security cameras that can be monitored by officers from a distance. Since 2006, Washington, D.C., has installed more than 60 cameras across the city. Initially they were used as investigative tools, so that officers could go back through recorded video and find evidence of crimes committed in the cameras' view. Recently, however, police officers have "gone live." A group of officers monitor the cameras for more than 40 hours each week.[86] The cameras have proved helpful on more than one occasion, but critics claim that these "prying eyes" violate people's privacy.

*GPS TRACKING DEVICES*  In *United States v. Garcia*, the Seventh Circuit Court of Appeals held that police officers can use GPS tracking to follow the movements of a suspect's vehicle without a warrant.[87] Officers in that case placed a GPS tracking device on Garcia's vehicle and then monitored its movements from a distance. The device revealed that Garcia had repeatedly traveled to a remote wooded parcel of land. The police obtained permission from the landowner to search the property and found a clandestine methamphetamine lab that Garcia had been using to manufacture speed. The *Garcia* court sided with an earlier Supreme Court decision that gave police the authority to use a "beeper," a less sophisticated tracking device, to monitor a suspect's movements.[88]

# INTERROGATION

After a suspect is taken into custody, it is routine to question him about his involvement in the crime. The police may hope to find out about co-conspirators or even whether the suspect was involved in similar crimes. This is a particularly unsettling time, and the arrestee may feel disoriented, alone, and afraid. Consequently, he may give police harmful information that can be used against him in a court of law. Exacerbating the situation is the fact that the interrogating officers sometimes use extreme pressure to get suspects to talk or to name their accomplices. Because of these concerns, the Supreme Court has issued rulings that protect criminal suspects from police intimidation, the most important of which was set down in the 1966 case of *Miranda v. Arizona*.[89]

## The *Miranda* Warning

In the landmark case of *Miranda v. Arizona* (1966), the Supreme Court held that suspects in custody must be told that they have the following rights:

- They have the right to remain silent.
- If they decide to make a statement, the statement can and will be used against them in a court of law.
- They have the right to have an attorney present at the time of the interrogation, or they will have an opportunity to consult with an attorney.
- If they cannot afford an attorney, one will be appointed for them by the state.

*Miranda* **warning**
The requirement that when a person is custodially interrogated, police inform the individual of the right to remain silent, the consequences of failing to remain silent, and the constitutional right to counsel.

The police must give this information—collectively known as the **Miranda warning**—to a person in custody before questioning begins.

Some suspects choose to remain silent. However, simply remaining silent is not the same as invoking *Miranda* protection. As the Supreme Court recently decided, if a suspect does not assert his or her *Miranda* rights and makes a self-incriminating voluntary statement in response to police questioning, that statement can be used in court.[90] To enjoy the benefits of *Miranda*, then, the suspect must state that he or she intends to remain silent. Also, the suspect can insist on having counsel present.

A suspect's constitutional rights under *Miranda* can be given up (waived). A suspect can choose to talk to the police or sign a confession. However, for the waiver to be effective, the state must first show that it was voluntary and that the defendant was aware of all of his *Miranda* rights. People who cannot understand the *Miranda* warning because of their age, mental handicaps, or language problems may not be legally questioned without an attorney present. If they can understand their rights, they may be questioned.[91]

Once the suspect asks for an attorney, all questioning must stop until the attorney is present. And if the criminal suspect has invoked his or her *Miranda* rights, police officials cannot reinitiate interrogation in the absence of counsel even if the accused has consulted with an attorney in the meantime.[92] This rule was recently modified to some extent; it doesn't apply if the suspect has been released from custody for at least two weeks.[93]

Even if the suspect has invoked his *Miranda* rights and demanded an attorney, the police can question the offender about another, separate crime (as long as they give the *Miranda* warning for the second crime as well). For example, say a person is arrested on burglary charges and requests an attorney. The next day, police question him about a murder after reading the suspect his *Miranda* rights. He decides to waive his rights and confesses to the murder without a lawyer being present. The murder confession would be legal even though the suspect had requested an attorney in the burglary case, because they are two separate legal matters.[94]

**CourseMate** For more information about *Miranda v. Arizona*, visit the Criminal Justice CourseMate at CengageBrain.com, then access the "Web Links" for this chapter.

## The *Miranda* Rule Today

The Supreme Court has used case law to define the boundaries of the *Miranda* warning since its inception. Although statements made by a suspect who was not given the *Miranda* warning or received it improperly cannot be used against him in a court of law, it is possible to use illegally gained statements and the evidence they produce in some well-defined instances:

- If a defendant perjures himself, evidence obtained in violation of the *Miranda* warning can be used by the government to impeach his testimony during trial.[95]
- At trial, the testimony of a witness is permissible even though her identity was revealed by the defendant in violation of the *Miranda* rule.[96]

Initial errors by police in getting statements do not make subsequent statements inadmissible. A subsequent *Miranda* warning that is properly given can cure the condition that made the initial statements inadmissible.[97] However, if police intentionally mislead suspects by questioning them before giving them a *Miranda* warning, their statements made after the warning is given are inadmissible in court. The "*Miranda* rule would be frustrated were the police permitted to undermine its meaning and effect."[98]

Over the years, the Supreme Court has decided a number of cases that have both limited and expanded the reach of *Miranda*. Indeed, a new *Miranda* decision is handed down nearly every term. See the accompanying "Evolution of *Miranda v. Arizona*" feature for a summary of several of these important decisions.

## The Impact of *Miranda*

After *Miranda* was decided, law enforcement officials became concerned that the Supreme Court had gone too far in providing defendants with procedural protections. Subsequent research indicates that the decision has had little effect on the number of confessions obtained by the police and that it has not affected the rate of convictions.[115] It now seems apparent that the police formerly relied too heavily on confessions to prove a defendant's guilt. Other forms of evidence, such as witness statements,

## The Evolution of *Miranda v. Arizona*

***Miranda v. Arizona* (1966)** Any person subjected to custodial interrogation must be advised of his or her Fifth Amendment right to be free from compelled self-incrimination and to have the assistance of counsel.[99]

***Fare v. Michael C.* (1978)** The *Miranda* warning applies only to the right to have an attorney present. The suspect cannot demand to speak to a priest, a probation officer, or any other official.[100]

***New York v. Quarles* (1984)** A suspect can be questioned in the field without a *Miranda* warning if the information the police seek is needed to protect public safety. For example, in an emergency, suspects can be asked where they hid their weapons.[101] This is known as the **public safety doctrine**.

***Oregon v. Elstad* (1985)** Admissions made in the absence of *Miranda* warnings are not admissible at trial, but post-*Miranda* voluntary statements are admissible. A post-*Miranda* voluntary statement is admissible even if an initial incriminating statement was made in the absence of *Miranda* warnings.[102]

***Colorado v. Connelly* (1986)** The admissions of mentally impaired defendants can be admitted in evidence as long as the police acted properly and there is a preponderance of the evidence that the defendants understood the meaning of *Miranda*.[103]

***Moran v. Burbine* (1986)** An attorney's request to see the defendant does not affect the validity of the defendant's waiver of the right to counsel. Police misinformation to an attorney does not affect waiver of *Miranda* rights.[104] For example, a suspect's statements may be used if they are given voluntarily, even though his family has hired an attorney and the statements were made before the attorney arrived. Only the suspect can request an attorney, not his friends or family.

***Colorado v. Spring* (1987)** Suspects need not be aware of all the possible outcomes of waiving their rights for the *Miranda* warning to be considered properly given.[105]

***Minnick v. Mississippi* (1990)** When counsel is requested, interrogation must cease and cannot be resumed until an attorney is present.[106]

***Arizona v. Fulminante* (1991)** The erroneous admission of a coerced confession at trial can be ruled a harmless error that would not automatically result in overturning a conviction.[107]

***Davis v. United States* (1994)** A suspect who makes an ambiguous reference to an attorney during questioning, such as "Maybe I should talk to an attorney," is not protected under *Miranda*. The police may continue their questioning.[108]

***Chavez v. Martinez* (2003)** Failure to give a suspect a *Miranda* warning is not illegal unless the case becomes a criminal issue.[109]

*(continues)*

## The Evolution of Miranda v. Arizona (continued)

**United States v. Patane (2004)**  A voluntary statement given in the absence of a *Miranda* warning can be used to obtain evidence that can be used at trial. Failure to give the warning does not make seizure of evidence illegal per se.[110]

**Missouri v. Seibert (2004)**  *Miranda* warnings must be given before interrogation begins. The accused in this case was interrogated and confessed in the absence of *Miranda* warnings. *Miranda* rights were then read, at which point the accused "re-confessed." The pre-*Miranda* questioning was improper.[111]

**Maryland v. Shatzer (2010)**  *Miranda* protections do not apply if a suspect is released from police custody for at least 14 days and then questioned. However, if the suspect is re-arrested, then *Miranda* warnings must be read.[112]

**Florida v. Powell (2010)**  The *Miranda* warnings do not require that the suspect be advised that he or she has the right to have an attorney present during questioning. It is sufficient to advise the suspect that he or she has the right to talk with a lawyer before questioning and to consult a lawyer at any time during questioning.[113]

**Berghuis v. Thompkins (2010)**  Unless a suspect asserts his or her *Miranda* rights, any subsequent voluntary statements given after the warnings are admissible in court. Simply remaining silent does not imply that a suspect has invoked *Miranda* protection.[114]

physical evidence, and expert testimony, have generally proved adequate to win the prosecution's case. Blaming *Miranda* for increased crime rates in the 1970s and 1980s now seems problematic, given that rates are down and *Miranda* is still the law.[116]

Critics have called the *Miranda* decision incomprehensible and difficult to administer. How can one tell whether a confession is truly voluntary or has been elicited by pressure and coercion? Aren't all police interrogations essentially coercive?[117] These criticisms aside, the Supreme Court is unlikely ever to reverse course. In the 2003 case of *Dickerson v. United States*, for example, the Court made it clear that the *Miranda* ruling is here to stay and has become enmeshed in the prevailing legal system.[118] In that case, the Court invalidated a federal statute enacted shortly after the *Miranda* decision that said any confession could be used against a suspect if it was voluntarily obtained.

Not surprisingly, police administrators who in the past might have been wary of the restrictions imposed by *Miranda* now favor its use.[119] One recent survey found that nearly 60 percent of police chiefs believe that the *Miranda* warning should be retained, and the same number report that abolishing *Miranda* would change the way the police function.[120] To ensure that *Miranda* rules are being followed, many departments now routinely videotape interrogations, although research shows that this procedure is not a sure cure for police intimidation.[121]

With the ongoing war on terrorism, law enforcement officers may find themselves in unique situations involving national security and forced to make an immediate decision about whether the *Miranda* rule applies. It is also important to note that *Miranda* is an American creation. *Miranda*-like warnings are not always required in other countries, as discussed in the accompanying Race, Culture, and Gender in Criminal Justice feature.

**public safety doctrine**
The principle that a suspect can be questioned in the field without a *Miranda* warning if the information the police seek is needed to protect public safety.

## PRETRIAL IDENTIFICATION

After the accused is arrested, he or she is ordinarily brought to the police station, where the police list the possible criminal charges. At the same time, they obtain other information, such as a description of the offender and the circumstances of the offense, for booking purposes. The **booking** process is a police administrative procedure in which the date and time of the arrest are recorded; arrangements are made for bail, detention, or removal to court; and any other information needed for identification is obtained. The defendant may be fingerprinted, photographed, and required to participate in a lineup.

In a **lineup**, a suspect is placed in a group for the purpose of being viewed and identified by a witness. Lineups are one of the primary means that the police have of identifying suspects. Others are show-ups, which occur at the crime scene, and photo displays or mug shots of possible suspects. In accordance with the U.S. Supreme Court decisions in *United States v. Wade* (1967) and

**CourseMate** For more information about **Chief Justice Earl Warren's handwritten notes on the *Miranda* case**, visit the Criminal Justice CourseMate at CengageBrain.com, then access the "Web Links" for this chapter.

*Kirby v. Illinois* (1972), the accused has the right to have counsel present at the post-indictment lineup or in a show-up.[122] There is no right to counsel associated with photographic identification.

In the *Wade* case, the Supreme Court held that a defendant has a right to counsel if the lineup takes place after the suspect has been formally charged with a crime. This decision was based on the Court's belief that the post-indictment lineup procedure is a critical stage of the criminal justice process. In contrast, the suspect does not have a comparable right to counsel at a pretrial lineup when a complaint or indictment has not been issued. Right to counsel does not apply until judicial proceedings have begun and the defendant is formally charged with a crime. When the right to counsel is violated, the evidence of any pretrial identification must be excluded from the trial.

One of the most difficult legal issues in this area is determining whether the identification procedure is suggestive and consequently in violation of the due process clauses of the Fifth and Fourteenth Amendments.[123] In *Simmons v. United States* (1968), the Supreme Court said that "The primary evil to be avoided is a very substantial likelihood of irreparable misidentification."[124] In its decision in *Neil v. Biggers* (1972), the Court established the following general criteria by which to judge the suggestiveness of a pretrial identification procedure:

- The opportunity of the witness to view the criminal at the time of the crime.
- The degree of attention by the witness and the accuracy of the prior description by the witness.
- The level of certainty demonstrated by the witness.
- The length of time between the crime and the confrontation.[125]

Weighing all these factors, the Court determines the substantial likelihood of misidentification.

## THE EXCLUSIONARY RULE

No review of the legal aspects of policing would be complete without a discussion of the **exclusionary rule**, the principal means used to restrain police conduct. The Fourth Amendment guarantees individuals the right to be secure in their persons, homes, papers, and effects against unreasonable searches and seizures. The exclusionary rule provides that all evidence obtained by illegal searches and seizures is inadmissible in criminal trials. Similarly, it excludes the use of illegal confessions under Fifth Amendment prohibitions.

For many years, evidence obtained by unreasonable searches and seizures that consequently should have been considered illegal was admitted by state and federal governments in criminal trials. The only criteria for admissibility were whether the evidence was incriminating and whether it would assist the judge or jury in ascertaining the innocence or guilt of the defendant. How the evidence was obtained was unimportant; its admissibility was determined by its relevance to the criminal case.

In 1914, however, the rules on the admissibility of evidence underwent a change of direction when the Supreme Court decided the case of *Weeks v. United States*.[126] The defendant, Freemont Weeks, was accused by federal law enforcement authorities of using the mail for illegal purposes. After his arrest, the home in which Weeks was staying was searched without a valid search warrant. Evidence in the form of letters and other materials was found in his room and admitted at the trial. Weeks was then convicted of the federal offense based on the incriminating evidence. On appeal, the Supreme Court held that evidence obtained by unreasonable search and seizure must be excluded in a federal criminal trial.

Thus, for the first time, the Court held that the Fourth Amendment barred the use of evidence obtained through illegal search and seizure in a federal

**booking**
The administrative record of an arrest, listing the offender's name, address, physical description, date of birth, and employer, time of arrest, offense, and name of arresting officer; it also includes photographing and fingerprinting of the offender.

**lineup**
Placing a suspect in a group for the purpose of being viewed and identified by a witness.

**exclusionary rule**
The principle that prohibits using illegally obtained evidence in a trial.

## RACE, GENDER, AND CULTURE IN CRIMINAL JUSTICE

# Interrogation Law in Three Other Countries

The Fifth Amendment ensures that those suspected of criminal activity cannot be forced to incriminate themselves and that they have the right to counsel. The Supreme Court's *Miranda* decision requires the police to advise certain criminal suspects of these important protections. In no other area of criminal procedure are the police required to advise suspects of their rights.

*Miranda* and the Fifth Amendment's self-incrimination clause are controversial. On the one hand, they help protect the innocent from being forced to confess. On the other hand, is justice served when the one person who may know most about a particular crime is under no obligation to talk?

To gain an appreciation for the significance of the right to counsel in the United States—and for the *Miranda* decision—it is helpful to take a look at interrogation laws in some other countries. Neither *Miranda*-like warnings nor the right to counsel are uniquely American creations. Several other countries have similar procedures, but to varying degrees. Here we look at three of them: the United Kingdom, France, and China.

### The United Kingdom

The United Kingdom has no single constitutional document as the United States does. Police interrogation is instead governed by the Police and Criminal Evidence Act and the Code of Practice for the Detention, Treatment, and Questioning of Persons by Police Officers.

In the U.K., if a suspect is taken into custody and the police intend to question the suspect, they are required to advise him or her that there is no obligation to talk. The British approach is somewhat stricter than that employed in the United States, because police are required to advise the suspect of the right to silence as soon as there are reasonable grounds to believe he or she has committed an offense. The *Miranda* rule applies only when there is custody and interrogation.

There is also a right to counsel in the U.K., but the suspect generally receives assistance only when he or she asks for it. If a suspect exercises his or her rights and refuses to answer police questions, the court is later permitted to draw adverse inferences from this action. For example, the prosecutor can comment at trial that the suspect failed to answer questions. This can work against him or her at trial.

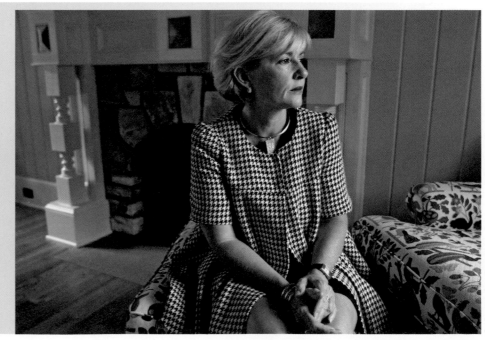

The police occasionally rely on lineups so crime victims can view and identify their attackers. Unfortunately, victims sometimes pick out the wrong person. In the midst of being raped, Jennifer Thompson-Cannino of Winston-Salem, North Carolina, told herself to pay attention to details that would enable her to identify her attacker. She gave police a description that led to a sketch of the suspect. She also identified Ronald Cotton from photographs, picked him out of a lineup, and told jurors she was certain he was the rapist. She was wrong. Cotton was convicted and spent 11 years in prison before he was exonerated on the basis of DNA evidence. Thompson-Cannino and Cotton later met, and their conversation led to forgiveness and understanding. They also coauthored a book about her mistaken identification of him, a book they called Picking Cotton: Our Memoir of Injustice and Redemption

In the United States, the prosecutor *cannot* comment on a defendant's pretrial silence.

## France

In contrast to the United States and the U.K., France is known for long having put society's interest in crime control ahead of individual rights and liberties. France's interrogation law provides evidence of this. First, there is no clear requirement that a suspect be advised that he or she is not required to answer police questions. Second, the right to counsel is limited. Suspects do not have the right to counsel immediately following their detention; the right does not apply until 20 hours after the person has been detained for ordinary offenses. For more serious cases, such as those involving drug rings or terrorism, the right to counsel does not attach for up to 72 hours from the detention. Finally, the accused has the right to consult with counsel only for a limited time; there is no right to have counsel present during police interrogations.

## China

In its earlier days, the People's Republic operated without much regard for individual rights. To this day there are criticisms that its government curtails citizens' freedoms, but legal reforms have brought China's criminal justice system somewhat in line with that of other modernized nations. The 1979 Criminal Procedure Law (CPL), which was significantly amended in 1996, has led to considerable progress in terms of protections afforded to those accused of criminal activity.

The CPL requires that before an interrogation, the police must give the suspect an opportunity to make a statement about his or her involvement (or lack of involvement) in the crime. This presumably protects the suspect from having the police proceed under the assumption that he or she is guilty. Critics have argued that the police routinely ignore this requirement and use psychological pressures to extract confessions. In any case, there is no recognized right to freedom from self-incrimination in China. The CPL prohibits the use of torture, but this does not protect a suspect from incriminating himself or herself. There *is* a right to counsel, but it attaches only after the police have completed their first interrogation.

## Critical Thinking

1. Which country—the United States, the United Kingdom, France, or China—is least concerned with the rights of those who are interrogated? Why?

2. Could the United States improve its interrogation laws vis-à-vis those of other countries? Is there something to be learned from the United Kingdom, France, or China—or from all three?

Sources: Yue Ma, "A Comparative View of the Law of Interrogation," *International Criminal Justice Review* 17 (2007): 5–26; Craig M. Bradley, ed., *Criminal Procedure: A Worldwide Study* (Durham, N.C.: Carolina Academic Press, 1999); Stephen C. Thaman, "*Miranda* in Comparative Law," *Saint Louis University Law Journal* 45 (2001): 581–624.

prosecution. With this ruling, the Court established the exclusionary rule. The rule was based not on legislation but on judicial decision making. Can the criminal go free because the constable blunders? That became the question.

In 1961, the Supreme Court made the exclusionary rule applicable to the state courts in the landmark decision of *Mapp v. Ohio*. In *Mapp*, police officers forcibly searched a home while using a fake warrant. The Court held that although the search had turned up contraband, it violated the Fourth Amendment's prohibition against unreasonable searches and seizures, so the illegally seized evidence could not be used in court. Justice Tom Clark, delivering the majority opinion of the Court, made clear the importance of this constitutional right in the administration of criminal justice:

> There are those who say, as did Justice [then Judge Benjamin] Cardozo, that under our constitutional exclusionary doctrine "[t]he criminal is to go free because the constable has blundered." In some cases this will undoubtedly be the result. But … there is another consideration—the imperative of judicial integrity…. The criminal goes free, if he must, but it is the law that sets him free. Nothing can destroy a government more quickly than its failure to observe its own laws, or worse, its disregard of the charter of its own existence.[127]

The exclusionary rule has also been extended to include derivative, or secondary, evidence, which is also called **fruit of the poisonous tree**.[128] This doctrine applies not only to evidence obtained directly from a violation of the Fourth

**CourseMate** For more information about *Mapp v. Ohio*, visit the Criminal Justice CourseMate at CengageBrain.com, then access the "Web Links" for this chapter.

**fruit of the poisonous tree**
Secondary evidence obtained from a search that violates the exclusionary rule.

Amendment but also to evidence indirectly obtained from such a violation. For example, if the police, without probable cause and a warrant, searched a private home and found a key to a locker at a nearby bus station, a subsequent search of the locker would be considered fruit of the poisonous tree.

## Current Status of the Exclusionary Rule

In the 1980s, a more conservative U.S. Supreme Court gradually began to limit the scope of the exclusionary rule. It created three major exceptions:

1. *Independent source exception.* This rule allows admission of evidence that has been discovered by means wholly independent of any constitutional violation. So if police enter a drug dealer's home with an arrest warrant and, while arresting him, illegally search for and seize evidence such as drug paraphernalia, the illegally seized material may be allowed in court if, independently, a warrant had been issued to search the apartment for the same evidence but had not yet arrived at the scene.[129]

2. *Good faith exception.* In *United States v. Leon* (1984), the Court ruled that evidence seized by police relying on a warrant issued by a detached and neutral magistrate can be used in a court proceeding, even if the judge who issued the warrant erred in drawing up the document.[130] In this case, the Court articulated a **good faith exception** to the exclusionary rule: Evidence obtained with a less than adequate search warrant may be admissible in court if the police officers acted in good faith when obtaining court approval for their search. However, deliberately misleading a judge or using a warrant that the police know is unreasonably deficient would be grounds to invoke the exclusionary rule. In a subsequent case, *Arizona v. Evans*, the Court ruled that the exclusionary rule was designed as a means of deterring police misconduct, not to punish police for honest mistakes; it does not apply when they have acted in objectively reasonable reliance on an apparently valid warrant but later find out it was technically faulty.[131]

   In 2009 the Supreme Court decided *Herring v. United States*,[132] another good faith case. Officers searched Herring based on a warrant listed in a neighboring county's database. Unbeknownst to them, the warrant had been recalled months earlier. The Supreme Court sanctioned the search and further noted that the exclusionary rule will be violated only when there is "systemic error or reckless disregard of constitutional requirements."[133]

3. *Inevitable discovery rule.* This rule holds that evidence obtained through an unlawful search or seizure is admissible in court if it can be established, to a very high degree of probability, that police investigation would be expected to lead to the discovery of the evidence. In the case that established the rule, *Nix v. Williams* (1984), police illegally interrogated a suspect and found the location of his victim's body. The evidence obtained was allowed at trial when the Court ruled that because the body was lying in plain sight and many police officers were searching for the body, it would have been obtained anyway, even without the information provided by the illegal interrogation; this is now referred to as the **inevitable discovery rule**.[134]

In these and other cases, the Supreme Court has made it easier for the police to conduct searches of criminal suspects and their possessions and then use the seized evidence in court proceedings. The Court has indicated that, as a general rule, the protection afforded the individual by the Fourth Amendment may take a back seat to concerns about public safety if criminal actions pose a clear threat to society.

## The Future of the Exclusionary Rule

Should the exclusionary rule be retained? Those who favor retention of the exclusionary rule believe it is justified because it deters illegal searches and seizures. However, the rule appears to result in relatively few case dismissals.

**good faith exception**
The principle that evidence may be used in a criminal trial even though the search warrant used to obtain it was technically faulty, as long as the police acted in good faith when they sought the warrant from a judge.

**inevitable discovery rule**
The principle that evidence can be used in court even though the information that led to its discovery was obtained in violation of the *Miranda* rule if a judge finds it would have been discovered anyway by other means or sources.

Yet the public wants to be protected from overzealous police officers and is concerned with reports that police routinely violate suspects' rights when searching for evidence. Jon Gould and Stephen Mastrofski made direct observations of police searches in a medium-sized U.S. city and found that nearly one-third of searches performed were unconstitutional and that almost none of these illegal searches were recognized as such by the courts. Surprisingly, the majority of illegal searches were made by a relatively small number of otherwise conscientious officers who may have become overzealous in their attempts to enforce the municipality's crackdown on drug offenders.[135]

Supporters believe the rule is fundamentally sound and can be justified on the basis of such legal principles as checks and balances and separation of power. When agents of the executive branch (the police) disregard or sidestep the terms of court-issued search warrants, the judicial branch can respond by overruling the misbehavior. Judges can also react when executive branch prosecutors attempt to introduce illegally seized evidence in court.[136] This power is especially important for warrantless searches, because the judge is not on the scene when a search takes place and becomes aware of the circumstances surrounding the search only when prosecutors are in court seeking to present the evidence that the police acquired. The rule gives the judge the opportunity to correct executive branch excesses before they can influence the outcome of the proceedings.[137]

How can the rule be improved? Suggested approaches to dealing with violations of the exclusionary rule include criminal prosecution of police officers who violate constitutional rights, internal police control, civil lawsuits against state or municipal police officers, and federal lawsuits against the government under the Federal Tort Claims Act.

Law professor Donald Dripps has derived a novel approach for modifying the exclusionary rule.[138] The contingent exclusionary rule would apply when a judge who finds police testimony questionable concludes that the release of the guilty would be unpleasant and unwarranted. Instead of excluding the evidence, she could request that the prosecution or police pay a fee, similar in form to a fine, to use the evidence in court. Exclusion of the evidence would be contingent on the failure of the police department to pay the damages set by the court. Thereby, the judge could uphold the Constitution without freeing the guilty. The contingent exclusionary rule would force the prosecution to decide whether obtaining justice was worth the damages.

The United States is the only nation that applies an exclusionary rule to protect individuals from illegal searches and seizures. Whether the U.S. Supreme Court or legislative bodies adopt any further significant changes to the rule remains to be seen. However, like the *Miranda* warning, the exclusionary rule has been incorporated in modern police procedure and seems to be a permanent fixture.

**CourseMate** For more information about the **exclusionary rule**, visit the Criminal Justice CourseMate at CengageBrain.com, then access the "Web Links" for this chapter.

## PERSPECTIVES ON JUSTICE

### Crime Control

Throughout the past decade, the U.S. Congress has tried to loosen the admissibility of evidence from illegal searches and seizures. Curtailing the use of the exclusionary rule would widen the scope of justice and favor the crime control perspective.

## Ethical Challenges in Criminal Justice: A Writing Assignment

Officer Rodriguez stopped Susan Smart, a motorist, for speeding. After approaching Smart's vehicle to ask for her license and registration, he asked are whether he could search her vehicle. She asked, "Why do you want to search my car?" He said, "We have seen an increase in drug trafficking along this stretch of freeway." She said, "I don't know why you think I would be transporting drugs, and I'm not sure whether this is legal, but okay, go ahead and search." Officer Rodriguez searched Smart's car and found nothing incriminating. He issued her a citation for speeding and sent her on her way.

*(continues)*

Write an essay on the ethics of the behavior presented in this hypothetical situation. Assuming Smart was actually speeding, Officer Rodriguez *was* authorized to ask consent to search her vehicle. What's more, he was under no obligation to tell her she could refuse consent. Even so, Smart seemed a bit apprehensive and uncertain whether she should grant consent. Should Officer Rodriguez have explained the law to her? Why or why not? If a police officer benefits from someone's ignorance of the law, is it just good policing—or is it deviant? See this chapter's "Consent" section for additional information. In what other areas besides consent may law enforcement benefit from citizens' lack of understanding of the law? Answers to this question can be found throughout the chapter.

# Significant Cases in Policing

| Case | Issue | Decision |
|---|---|---|
| *Aguilar v. Texas* (1964) | Informants | If police use informants to develop probable cause to obtain a warrant, they must show why the informant should be believed and how the informant obtained his or her knowledge. |
| *Alabama v. White* (1990) | Anonymous tips | An anonymous phone tip can help formulate probable cause for a warrant, provided the tip it is corroborated by independent police work. |
| *Breithaupt v. Abram* (1957) | Drawing blood from suspects | Police can seize a blood sample from a suspect without a warrant, provided they have probable cause to do so. |
| *Brigham v. Stuart* (2006) | Warrantless search, threats to occupants | If police have an objectively reasonable basis to believe the occupant of a dwelling is seriously injured or threatened with injury, they may enter without a warrant. |
| *California v. Greenwood* (1988) | Abandoned property | Abandoned property does not enjoy Fourth Amendment protection. |
| *Carroll v. United States* (1925) | Automobile searches | The police may search an automobile without a warrant, provided they have probable cause to do so. Also see the "Evolution of *Carroll v. United States*" feature earlier in this chapter for details on post-Carroll decisions. |
| *Chimel v. California* (1969) | Search incident to arrest | The police may search a suspect after a lawful arrest. |
| *Coolidge v. New Hampshire* (1971) | Plain view | The police can search for and seize evidence without benefit of a warrant if it is in plain view. |
| *Florida v. Bostick* (1991) | Consent to search on a bus | Drug enforcement officers, after obtaining consent, may search luggage on a crowded bus without meeting the Fourth Amendment requirements for a search warrant or probable cause. |
| *Harris v. United States* (1947) | Scope of a search based on a search warrant | The scope of a search should be limited to the items named in the search warrant. |
| *Hudson v. Michigan* (2006) | Knock and announce | Evidence need not be excluded because police failed to announce their presence when serving a warrant. |
| *Katz v. United States* (1967) | Definition of a search | A search occurs when a government actor infringes on a person's reasonable expectation of privacy. |

# Significant Cases in Policing (continued)

| Case | Issue | Decision |
| --- | --- | --- |
| *Kirby v. Illinois* (1972) | Right to counsel in lineups | The accused has no right to have counsel present at a pre-indictment lineup. |
| *Mapp v. Ohio* (1961) | Exclusionary rule, states | Evidence obtained in violation of the Fourth Amendment is not admissible in a state criminal trial (the exclusionary rule applies to the states). |
| *Minnesota v. Olson* (1990) | Warrantless search, suspect escape | In the absence of hot pursuit, if there is danger that the suspect will escape, police can enter private property and arrest the suspect without a warrant. |
| *Miranda v. Arizona* (1966) | Custodial interrogation | Suspects subjected to custodial interrogation must be advised of their Fifth Amendment privilege against self-incrimination. Also see the "Evolution of *Miranda v. Arizona*" feature in this chapter for details on post-*Miranda* decisions. |
| *Nix v. Williams* (1984) | Exclusionary rule, inevitable discovery | Evidence obtained through an unlawful search or seizure is admissible in court if it can be established, to a very high degree of probability, that police investigation would be expected to lead to the discovery of the evidence. |
| *Oliver v. United States* (1984) | Search of an open field | Open fields do not enjoy Fourth Amendment protection. |
| *Payton v. New York* (1980) | Search warrant requirement | The Fourth Amendment prohibits warrantless, nonconsensual entry into private property for the purpose of making an arrest. |
| *Schneckloth v. Bustamonte* (1973) | Consent | If a suspect consents to a search, the officer does not need a warrant or probable cause, but such consent must not be the result of duress or coercion. |
| *Segura v. United States* (1984) | Exclusionary rule, independent source | Evidence that has been discovered by means wholly independent of any constitutional violation will be admissible. |
| *Silverthorne Lumber Co. v. United States* (1920) | Fruit of the poisonous tree | The exclusionary rule extends to "fruit of the poisonous tree," or derivative evidence. |
| *Terry v. Ohio* (1968) | Stop and frisk | An officer may stop and frisk a person if he or she has reasonable suspicion that criminal activity is afoot. |
| *United States v. Leon* (1984) | Exclusionary rule, good faith | Evidence obtained with a less than adequate search warrant may be admissible in court if the police officers acted in good faith when obtaining court approval for their search. |
| *United States v. Matlock* (1974) | Co-occupant consent | It is permissible for one co-occupant of a dwelling to give consent to the police to search the premises in the absence of the other occupant, as long as the person giving consent shares "common authority" over the property and no present co-occupant objects. |
| *United States v. Wade* (1967) | Right to counsel in lineups | The accused has the right to have counsel present at a post-indictment lineup. |
| *Warden v. Hayden* (1967) | Hot pursuit | Hot pursuit authorizes the police to dispense with the Fourth Amendment warrant requirement. |
| *Weeks v. United States* | Exclusionary rule, federal court | Evidence obtained in violation of the Fourth Amendment is not admissible in a federal criminal trial (the exclusionary rule is created). |

# SUMMARY

1. **Understand how the Fourth Amendment controls law enforcement officials.**

   ■ The Fourth Amendment controls searches and seizures.

   ■ The Fourth Amendment contains two parts: the reasonableness clause and the warrants clause. Each clause is independent because a search can be reasonable without a warrant, but if a warrant is required, certain steps must be taken.

2. **Define search and arrest.**

   ■ A search occurs when a government actor infringes on a person's reasonable expectation of privacy.

   ■ When police look through abandoned property, look in open fields, or use aerial surveillance, they do not "search."

   ■ An arrest occurs when a police officer takes a person into custody or deprives a person of freedom for having allegedly committed a criminal offense.

3. **Distinguish between search warrants and arrest warrants.**

   ■ A search warrant is an order, issued by a judge, directing officers to conduct a search of specified premises for specified objects.

   ■ An arrest warrant is an order, issued by a judge, directing officers to arrest a particular individual.

4. **Explain when warrants are required.**

   ■ Warrants are required in two key situations: (1) arrests and searches in private homes or on specific types of private property and (2) arrests for minor offenses committed out of view of the arresting officer.

5. **Recognize that there are three requirements that must be met before a warrant can be secured.**

   ■ There are three requirements that must be met before a warrant can be secured: probable cause, neutral and detached magistrate, and particularity.

   ■ Probable cause is usually defined as a reasonable belief, based on fact, that a crime has been committed and that the person, place, or object to be searched and/or seized is linked to the crime with a reasonable degree of certainty.

   ■ Judges are considered be neutral and detached.

   ■ Particularity is concerned with specifically naming the items to be seized pursuant to a search or specifically naming the individual to be arrested pursuant to an arrest warrant.

6. **Explain the rules for serving warrants.**

   ■ There are six general rules governing the service of warrants: Officers should (1) knock and announce their presence, subject to certain exceptions; (2) keep property damage to a minimum; (3) use appropriate force if needed; (4) pay attention to time constraints when serving search warrants; (5) limit the scope and manner of their search to the items named in the search warrant; and (6) not bring reporters along when warrants are served.

7. **Discuss the nuances of seven types of warrantless searches and arrests.**

   ■ The seven types of warrantless searches and arrests are (1) searches based on exigent circumstances; (2) stop and frisk; (3) searches incident to lawful arrest; (4) automobile searches; (5) consent searches; (6) plain view seizures; and (7) arrests committed in an officer's presence.

   ■ Exigent circumstances include hot pursuit, danger of escape, threats to evidence, and threats to others.

   ■ Stop and frisk are two separate acts. Each requires that an officer have reasonable suspicion.

   ■ For a search incident to lawful arrest, the search must be conducted at the time of or immediately following the arrest. Also, the police may search only the suspect and the area within the suspect's immediate control.

   ■ Automobiles can be searched without a warrant, so long as there is probable cause to search.

   ■ Consent searches do not require warrants or probable cause, because the consenting party effectively waives his or her Fourth Amendment rights.

   ■ If an officer is engaged in a lawful search and has probable cause that an item in plain view is subject to seizure, the item can be seized.

   ■ If a person commits a crime in an officer's presence, no warrant is necessary before an arrest is made.

8. **Summarize electronic surveillance law as it applies to law enforcement officials.**

   ■ *Katz v. United States* is the key Supreme Court case dealing with electronic surveillance.

- Important federal legislation governing interception of communication includes the Federal Wiretap Act and the Foreign Intelligence Surveillance Act.

- Recent electronic surveillance technologies that have benefited local law enforcement include GPS tracking devices and video cameras in public areas.

9. **Explain the *Miranda v. Arizona* decision.**

- *Miranda v. Arizona* requires that police officers advise people who are both in custody and interrogated of their constitutional right (from the Fifth Amendment) not to incriminate themselves.

- Suspects who are advised of their *Miranda* rights are told: (1) they have the right to remain silent; (2) if they decide to make a statement, the statement can and will be used against them in a court of law; (3) they have the right to have an attorney present at the time of the interrogation, or they will have an opportunity to consult with an attorney; and (4) if they cannot afford an attorney, one will be appointed for them by the state.

- The Supreme Court has modified the *Miranda* rule to some extent over the years. Mostly, its decisions have relaxed the *Miranda* rule.

- The impact of *Miranda* on law enforcement, such as through lost convictions, has been fairly minimal.

10. **Understand what purpose a lineup serves.**

- In a lineup, a suspect is placed in a group for the purpose of being viewed and identified by a witness.

- Lineups are one of the primary means that the police have of identifying suspects.

- The accused has the right to have counsel present at a post-indictment lineup. This is also true for a show-up, which occurs at the crime scene. There is no right to counsel for photographic identifications.

11. **Know the exclusionary rule, including its extensions and exceptions.**

- The exclusionary rule provides that all evidence obtained by illegal searches and seizures is inadmissible in criminal trials.

- The exclusionary rule has been extended to include "fruit of the poisonous tree," or indirect evidence.

- Exceptions to the exclusionary rule include independent source, good faith, and inevitable discovery.

## KEY TERMS

search, 287
open field, 827
curtilage, 287
arrest, 288
search warrant, 289
arrest warrant, 289
in presence requirement, 289
probable cause, 291

particularity, 293
probable cause hearing, 295
exigent circumstance, 296
hot pursuit, 297
stop and frisk, 299
search incident to lawful arrest, 301
bus sweep, 305
plain view doctrine, 306

*Miranda* warning, 310
public safety doctrine, 312
booking, 313
lineup, 313
exclusionary rule, 313
fruit of the poisonous tree, 315
good faith exception, 316
inevitable discovery rule, 316

## CRITICAL THINKING QUESTIONS

1. Can a search and seizure be reasonable if it is not authorized by a warrant?

2. Should illegally seized evidence be excluded from trial, even though it is conclusive proof of a person's criminal acts?

3. What is a pretext traffic stop? Does it violate a citizen's civil rights?

4. Should a person be put in a lineup without the benefit of counsel?

5. What is the purpose of the *Miranda* warning?

6. Should obviously guilty persons go free because police originally arrested them with less than probable cause?

7. Have criminals been given too many rights? Should courts be more concerned with the rights of the victims or the rights of offenders?

# NOTES

1. *Arizona v. Gant*, No. 07-542 (2009).
2. *New York v. Belton*, 453 U.S. 454 (1981).
3. *Katz v. United States*, 389 U.S. 347 (1967).
4. *California v. Greenwood*, 486 U.S. 35 (1988).
5. *Oliver v. United States*, 466 U.S. 170 (1984).
6. *California v. Ciraola*, 476 U.S. 207 (1986).
7. *Florida v. Riley*, 488 U.S. 445 (1989).
8. *Payton v. New York*, 445 U.S. 573 (1980).
9. *Welsh v. Wisconsin*, 466 U.S. 740 (1984).
10. *Aguilar v. Texas*, 378 U.S. 108 (1964).
11. *Illinois v. Gates*, 462 U.S. 213 (1983).
12. *Alabama v. White*, 496 U.S. 325 (1990).
13. Ibid., at 325, 326.
14. *Florida v. J. L.*, No. 98-1993 (2000).
15. *Johnson v. United States*, 333 U.S. 10 (1948), pp. 13–14.
16. Mark I. Koffsky, "Choppy Waters in the Surveillance Data Stream: The Clipper Scheme and the Particularity Clause," *Berkeley Technology Law Journal* 9 (1994), www.law.berkeley.edu/journals/btlj/articles/vol9/ (accessed April 15, 2010).
17. *Ker v. California*, 374 U.S. 23 (1963); *Wilson v. Arkansas*, 514 U.S. 927 (1995).
18. *Miller v. United States*, 357 U.S. 301 (1958).
19. *Hudson v. Michigan*, 547 U.S. 586 (2006).
20. *County of Sacramento v. Lewis*, 523 U.S. 833 (1998).
21. *Gooding v. United States*, 416 U.S. 430 (1974).
22. *Harris v. United States*, 331 U.S. 145 (1947).
23. *Wilson v. Layne*, 526 U.S. 603 (1999).
24. *Gerstein v. Pugh*, 420 U.S. 103 (1975); *Riverside County v. McLaughlin*, 500 U.S. 44 (1991).
25. *Kirk v. Louisiana*, No. 01-8419, U.S. Supreme Court, per curiam opinion, decided June 24, 2002.
26. *Warden v. Hayden*, 387 U.S. 294 (1967).
27. John L. Worrall, *Criminal Procedure: From First Contact to Appeal*, 2nd ed. (Boston: Allyn & Bacon, 2007), pp. 143–144.
28. *Scott v. Harris*, No. 05-1631 (2007).
29. *Minnesota v. Olson*, 495 U.S. 91 (1990).
30. *Breithaupt v. Abram*, 352 U.S. 432 (1957).
31. *Brigham City v. Utah*, 547 U.S. 398 (2006).
32. Ibid.
33. *Michigan v. Fisher*, No. 09-91 (2009).
34. *Terry v. Ohio*, 392 U.S. 1 (1968).
35. *Illinois v. Wardlow*, 120 S.Ct. 673 (2000).
36. *Arizona v. Johnson*, No. 07-1122 (2009).
37. *Terry v. Ohio*, p. 24.
38. *Chimel v. California*, 395 U.S. 752 (1969).
39. *Carroll v. United States*, 267 U.S. 132 (1925). See also James Rodgers, "Poisoned Fruit: Quest for Consistent Rule on Traffic Stop Searches," *American Bar Association Journal* 81 (1995): 50–51.
40. *Carroll v. United States*, 267 U.S. 132 (1925).
41. *United States v. Lee*, 274 U.S. 559 (1927).
42. *Cardwell v. Lewis*, 417 U.S. 583 (1974).
43. *Pennsylvania v. Mimms*, 434 U.S. 106 (1997).
44. *United States v. Ross*, 456 U.S. 798 (1982).
45. *Michigan v. Long*, 463 U.S. 1032 (1983).
46. *Michigan Dept. of State Police v. Sitz*, 496 U.S. 444 (1990).
47. *Whren v. United States*, 517 U.S. 806 (1996).
48. *Maryland v. Wilson*, 519 U.S. 408 (1997).
49. *City of Indianapolis v. Edmond*, 531 U.S. 32 (2000).
50. *Illinois v. Lidster*, 540 U.S. 419 (2004).
51. *Brendlin v. California*, 551 U.S. 249 (2007).
52. *Arizona v. Gant*, No. 07-542 (2009).
53. *United States v. Arvizu*, 534 U.S. 266 (2002).
54. *United States v. Ross*, 456 U.S. 798 (1982). See also Barry Latzer, "Searching Cars and Their Contents: *U.S. v. Ross*," *Criminal Law*

Bulletin 6 (1982): 220; Joseph Grano, "Rethinking the Fourth Amendment Warrant Requirements," *Criminal Law Review* 19 (1982): 603.
55. *Michigan v. Long*, 463 U.S. 1032 (1983).
56. *Arizona v. Gant*, No. 07-542 (2009); also see *New York v. Belton*, 453 U.S. 454 (1981) and *Thornton v. United States*, 541 U.S. 615 (2004).
57. *Pennsylvania v. Mimms*, 434 U.S. 106 (1977).
58. *Maryland v. Wilson*, 65 U.S.L.W. 4124 (1997).
59. *Brendlin v. California*, 551 U.S. 249 (2007).
60. *Whren v. United States*, 116 S.Ct. 1769 (1996); Mark Hansen, "Rousting Miss Daisy?" *American Bar Association Journal* 83 (1997): 22; *Wyoming v. Houghton*, 526 U.S. 295 (1999).
61. *Arkansas v. Sullivan*, 121 S.Ct. 1876 (2001).
62. *Delaware v. Prouse*, 440 U.S. 648 (1979). See also Lance Rogers, "The Drunk-Driving Roadblock: Random Seizure or Minimal Intrusion?" *Criminal Law Bulletin* 21 (1985): 197–217.
63. *City of Indianapolis v. Edmond*, 531 U.S. 32 (2000).
64. *Michigan v. Sitz*, 496 U.S. 444 (1990).
65. *Illinois v. Lidster*, 540 U.S. 419 (2004).
66. *Schneckloth v. Bustamonte*, 412 U.S. 218 (1973).
67. *Bumper v. North Carolina*, 391 U.S. 543 (1968).
68. *Schneckloth v. Bustamonte*, 412 U.S. 218 (1973).
69. *Ohio v. Robinette*, 519 U.S. 33 (1966).
70. *United States v. Matlock*, 415 U.S. 164 (1974).
71. *Georgia v. Randolph*, No. 04-1067 (2006).
72. *Florida v. Bostick*, 501 U.S. 429 (1991).
73. *Ohio v. Robinette*, 519 U.S. 33 (1996).
74. *Coolidge v. New Hampshire*, 403 U.S. 443 (1971).
75. *New York v. Class*, 475 U.S. 106 (1986).
76. *Arizona v. Hicks*, 480 U.S. 321 (1987).
77. *Minnesota v. Dickerson*, 508 U.S. 366 (1993).
78. *Bond v. United States*, 120 S.Ct. 1462 (2000).
79. *Riverside County v. McLaughlin*, 500 U.S. 44 (1991).
80. *Atwater et al. v. City of Lago Vista*, No. 99-1408 (2001).
81. *Virginia v. Moore*, No. 06-1082 (2008).
82. Gary T. Marx, *Undercover: Police Surveillance in America* (Berkeley: University of California Press, 1988).
83. *Katz v. United States*.
84. 18 U.S.C. Sections 2510–20.
85. 50 U.S.C. §§1801–11, 1821–29, 1841–46, and 1861–62.
86. Allison Keith, "Police Go Live Monitoring D.C. Crime Cameras," *Washington Post*, February 11, 2008, A1.
87. *United States v. Garcia*, 474 F.3d 994 (7th Cir. 2007).
88. *United States v. Knotts*, 460 U.S. 276 (1983).
89. *Miranda v. Arizona*, 384 U.S. 436 (1966).
90. *Berghuis v. Thompkins* 560 U.S. ___ (2010).
91. *Colorado v. Connelly*, 107 S.Ct. 515 (1986).
92. *Minnick v. Mississippi*, 498 U.S. 46 (1990).
93. *Maryland v. Shatzer*, 559 U.S. ___ (2010).
94. *Texas v. Cobb*, No. 99-1702 (2001).
95. *Harris v. New York*, 401 U.S. 222 (1971).
96. *Michigan v. Tucker*, 417 U.S. 433 (1974).
97. *Oregon v. Elstad*, 105 S.Ct. 1285 (1985).
98. *Missouri v. Seibert*, No. 02-1371 (2004).
99. *Miranda v. Arizona*, 384 U.S. 436 (1966).
100. *Fare v. Michael C.*, 439 U.S. 1310 (1978).
101. *New York v. Quarles*, 467 U.S. 649 (1984).
102. *Oregon v. Elstad*, 470 U.S. 298 (1985).
103. *Colorado v. Connelly*, 479 U.S. 157 (1986).
104. *Moran v. Burbine*, 475 U.S. 412 (1986).
105. *Colorado v. Spring*, 479 U.S. 564 (1987).
106. *Minnick v. Mississippi*, 498 U.S. 146 (1990).
107. *Arizona v. Fulminante*, 499 U.S. 279 (1991).
108. *Davis v. United States*, 512 U.S. 452 (1994).

109. *Chavez v. Martinez*, 538 U.S. 760 (2003).

110. *United States v. Patane*, 542 U.S. 630 (2004).

111. *Missouri v. Seibert*, 542 U.S. 600 (2004).

112. *Maryland v. Shatzer*, 559 U.S. ___ (2010).

113. *Florida v. Powell*, 559 U.S. ___ (2010).

114. *Berghuis v. Thompkins* 560 U.S. ___ (2010).

115. Michael Wald and others, "Interrogations in New Haven: The Impact of *Miranda*," *Yale Law Journal* 76 (1967): 1519. See also Walter Lippman, "*Miranda v. Arizona*—Twenty Years Later," *Criminal Justice Journal* 9 (1987): 241; Stephen J. Schulhofer, "Reconsidering *Miranda*," *University of Chicago Law Review* 54 (1987): 435–461; Paul Cassell, "How Many Criminals Has *Miranda* Set Free?" *Wall Street Journal*, March 1, 1995, p. A12.

116. "Don't Blame *Miranda*," *Washington Post*, December 2, 1988, p. A26. See also Scott Lewis, "*Miranda* Today: Death of a Talisman," *Prosecutor* 28 (1994): 18–25; Richard Leo, "The Impact of *Miranda* Revisited," *Journal of Criminal Law and Criminology* 86 (1996): 621–648.

117. Ronald Allen, "*Miranda*'s Hollow Core," *Northwestern University Law Review* 100 (2006): 71–85.

118. *Dickerson v. United States*, 530 U.S. 428 (2000).

119. Marvin Zalman and Brad Smith, "The Attitudes of Police Executives toward *Miranda* and Interrogation Policies," *Journal of Criminal Law and Criminology* 97 (2007): 873–942.

120. Victoria Time and Brian Payne, "Police Chiefs' Perceptions about *Miranda*: An Analysis of Survey Data," *Journal of Criminal Justice* 30 (2002): 77–86.

121. G. Daniel Lassiter, Jennifer Ratcliff, Lezlee Ware, and Clinton Irvin, "Videotaped Confessions: Panacea or Pandora's Box?" *Law and Policy* 28 (2006): 192–210.

122. *United States v. Wade*, 388 U.S. 218 (1967); *Kirby v. Illinois*, 406 U.S. 682 (1972).

123. Marvin Zalman and Larry Siegel, *Key Cases and Comments on Criminal Procedure* (St. Paul, Minn.: West, 1994).

124. *Simmons v. United States*, 390 U.S. 377 (1968).

125. *Neil v. Biggers*, 409 U.S. 188 (1972).

126. *Weaks v. United States*, 232 U.S. 383 (1914).

127. *Mapp v. Ohio*, 367 U.S. 643 (1961).

128. *Silverthorne Lumber Co. v. United States*, 251 U.S. 385 (1920).

129. *Segura v. United States*, 468 U.S. 796 (1984).

130. *United States v. Leon*, 468 U.S. 897 (1984).

131. *Arizona v. Evans*, 514 U.S. 260 (1995).

132. *Herring v. United States*, No. 07-513 (2009).

133. Ibid., p. 11.

134. *Nix v. Williams*, 104 S.Ct. 2501 (1984).

135. Jon Gould and Stephen Mastrofski, "Suspect Searches: Assessing Police Behavior under the U.S. Constitution," *Criminology and Public Policy* 3 (2004): 315–362.

136. Timothy Lynch, *In Defense of the Exclusionary Rule* (Washington, D.C.: Cato Institute, Center for Constitutional Studies, 1998).

137. Ibid.

138. Donald Dripps, "The Case for the Contingent Exclusionary Rule," *American Criminal Law Review* 38 (2001): 1–47.

## PART THREE

# COURTS AND ADJUDICATION

THE ADJUDICATION PHASE OF THE criminal process is intended to ensure that every person charged with a crime is treated according to the applicable rules of legal procedure in an atmosphere of fair play and objectivity. If this process is compromised, the case may be taken to a higher, appellate court, where the trial court proceedings are reexamined. If the defendant's rights have been violated, the appellate court may deem the findings of the original trial improper and either order a new hearing or hold that some other remedy be provided.

Many people work to ensure the court process works as intended, but judges are especially important figures. Judges, as you will see in Chapter 9, preside over trials and ensure that the rules are followed. Becoming a judge is a significant achievement, but the job is not easy. Ruben Andres Martino, presiding justice of the Harlem Community Justice Center, understands the tremendous responsibility judges have as they make decisions that directly affect people's lives. But, he says, "we make these decisions with all of our human limitations. Often, we only have part of the information and hear conflicting versions of the situation. However, we try to do our best to make sure that justice is done and the integrity of our judicial system is upheld."

Judges often rely on the contributions of court reporters, the officials whose job it is to keep an accurate record (or transcript) of the proceedings. Carlos Martinez, an official court reporter who works for the Sonoma County (California) Superior Courts, is but one of many court reporters who are tasked with making a verbatim record of everything that is said in a hearing—trials included. The greatest technical challenges that Carlos faces in a typical day are dealing with rapid speakers and technical jargon. He sometimes has to interrupt the proceedings and ask rapid speakers to slow down so the record can reflect their statements accurately. Also, he finds that he has to read back the record and ask many questions of expert witnesses in order to ensure that no mistakes are made. On a more personal level, Carlos finds some cases, especially those involving murders, molestations, rapes, and abuse, difficult to listen to. "You never get used to it and you never really forget," he says. "You just learn to live with it." Even so, he finds his career especially rewarding and feels he is an integral part of the adjudication process. ∎

THE CHAPTERS IN THIS section cover the court process. Chapter 9 reviews the structure of the courts and the role of the judge. Chapter 10 examines the prosecution and defense. Chapter 11 analyzes both the pretrial stage (including bail and plea bargaining) and the process of the criminal trial (including the legal rules that govern it). Chapter 12 looks at criminal sentencing, including capital punishment.

"You never get used to [some cases] and you never really forget. You just learn to live with it."

"We make these decisions with all of our human limitations. Often, we only have part of the information and hear conflicting versions of the situation. However, we try to do our best to make sure that justice is done and the integrity of our judicial system is upheld."

# CHAPTER 9

# The Courts and the Judiciary

## CHAPTER OBJECTIVES

1. Understand state court structure.
2. Know the differences between limited and general jurisdiction courts.
3. Recognize the function of the state appellate court system.
4. Explain the various levels of federal courts.
5. Describe how a case gets to the U.S. Supreme Court.
6. Know the problems associated with court congestion.
7. Discuss the duties of a judge.
8. Discuss the qualifications of a judge.
9. Explain the different types of judicial alternatives.
10. Summarize the different ways of selecting judges.
11. Identify factors associated with judicial decision making.
12. Explain how technology is changing the process of court administration and management.

© AP Photo/Anchorage Daily News/Bill Roth

O n an evening in March of 1993, two men driving through Anchorage, Alaska, approached a prostitute, soliciting sex. The prostitute, K.G., agreed to a price and got in the car. The three drove around, looking for a place to park. They settled on a quiet area near a park. K.G. demanded cash in advance, but the men refused. Instead, one of them pulled a gun on K.G.. Both raped and assaulted her. She was then ordered to get out of the car and lie face down in the snow. She tried to flee, but the passenger jumped out of the vehicle, beat her with a wooden axe handle, and shot her in the head. Both men tried to cover her body with snow and left her for dead. K.G., however, did not die. The bullet merely grazed her head, and she was able to find her way to a nearby road and flag down a motorist for assistance. After recovering, she accompanied police to the crime scene, where they found a spent shell casing, the axe handle, some of K.G.'s blood-stained clothing, and a used condom.

Six days later, police stopped Dexter Jackson for flashing his high-beams at another vehicle. They discovered a gun that matched the shell casing found earlier—and several items that K.G. reported carrying the night she was attacked. The car also matched the description K.G. gave to the police. Jackson admitted being the driver and told police that William Osborne was the passenger. K.G. identified Osborne in a lineup.

Prior to trial, the state performed "DQ Alpha" DNA testing on the sperm found in the discarded condom. This form of testing is not particularly accurate and has an error rate of approximately 5 percent (meaning that in a group of 100 men, it would identify five of them as suspects). Both Osborne and Jackson were convicted. Osborne received the harsher sentence, because the DNA testing identified him as the perpetrator. He challenged his conviction, claiming that he was entitled to a more accurate form of DNA testing. Eventually, the case worked its way to the U.S. Supreme Court, which held that there is no constitutional right for a convicted individual to access the state's evidence to perform additional DNA testing, even if he or she pays for it.[1] The Court explained in a 5-to-4 decision that legislatures should set rules governing access to DNA evidence for testing. Nearly all the states (but not Alaska, as of the date the Supreme Court reached its decision in this case) had done so, and the Court felt it was not its responsibility to change that. ■

Osborne's case is but one of many that come before the court system on a regular basis. Only a handful of cases ever reach the U.S. Supreme Court, but those accused of crime (defendants) and those convicted of crimes call on the tools of the legal system to provide them with a fair and just hearing, with the burden of proof resting on the state. The court process must render fair, impartial justice in deciding the outcome of a conflict between criminal and victim, law enforcement agents and violators of the law, parent and child, the federal government and violators of governmental regulations, or other parties.

The court is a complex social agency with many independent but interrelated subsystems—clerk, prosecutor, defense attorney, judge, and probation department—each playing a role in the adjudicatory process. Ideally, the entire process, from filing the initial complaint to final sentencing of the defendant, is governed by precise rules of law designed to ensure fairness. No defendant tried before a U.S. court should suffer *or* benefit because of his or her personal characteristics, beliefs, or affiliations.

However, in today's crowded court system, such abstract goals are often impossible to achieve. Discretion accompanies defendants through every step of the process, determining what will happen to them and how their cases will be resolved. Two people committing similar crimes can receive highly dissimilar treatment. For example, most people convicted of homicide receive a prison sentence, but about 4 percent receive probation as their sole sentence. Indeed, more murderers get probation than the death penalty.[2]

The dual curses of overcrowding and underfunding have become standard features of the court system. The nation's court system is chronically under-budgeted, and recent economic downturns have not helped matters.[3] Tax cutting has become a U.S. way of life and has sapped the state and federal budgets that fund the courts. These constraints have a significant impact on the way that courts do justice. The U.S. court system is often the scene of accommodation and "working things out," instead of an arena for a vigorous criminal defense. **Plea negotiations/plea bargaining** and other nonjudicial alternatives, such as diversion, are far more common than the formal trial process.

**plea negotiations/plea bargaining**
Discussions between defense counsel and prosecution in which the accused agrees to plead guilty in exchange for certain considerations, such as reduced charges or a lenient sentence.

## THE CRIMINAL COURT PROCESS

The U.S. court system has evolved over the years into an intricately balanced legal process that has recently come under siege because of the sheer numbers of cases it must consider and the ways in which it is forced to handle such overcrowding.

Overloaded court dockets have given rise to charges of "assembly-line justice," in which a majority of defendants are induced to plead guilty, jury trials are rare, and the speedy trial is highly desired but unattainable. Overcrowding causes the poor to languish in detention while the wealthier go free on bail. An innocent person can be frightened into pleading guilty; conversely, a guilty person can be released because a trial has been delayed too long.[4] Whether providing more judges or new or enlarged courts will solve the problem of overcrowding remains to be seen. Trial alternatives such as mediation, diversion, and bail reform offer other avenues of possible relief. Making court management and administration more efficient is also seen as a step that might ease the congestion of the courts. The introduction of professional trial court managers—administrators, clerks, and judges with management skills—has had a significant influence on court efficiency.

## STATE COURT SYSTEMS

To house this complex process, each state maintains its own state court organization and structure. There are 50 state trial and appellate systems, with separate courts for the District of Columbia, Puerto Rico, and other U.S. territories. Usually three (or more) separate court systems exist within each state jurisdiction. States are free to create as many courts as they wish, to name courts what they like (in New York, felony courts are known as supreme courts!), and to establish specialized courts that handle a single legal matter, such as drug courts and/or domestic courts. Consequently, there is a great deal of diversity in court organization from one state to the next. State courts handle a wide variety of cases and regulate numerous personal behaviors, ranging from homicide to property maintenance. The various state court systems are described below.

### Courts of Limited Jurisdiction

Depending on the jurisdiction in which they are located, state **courts of limited jurisdiction** are known by a variety of names, such as municipal courts, county courts, district courts, and metropolitan courts. The term derives from the fact that the jurisdiction of these courts is limited to minor or less serious civil and criminal cases.

Courts of limited jurisdiction are restricted in the types of cases they may hear. Usually, they will handle misdemeanor criminal infractions, violations of municipal ordinances, traffic violations, and civil suits where the damages involve less than a certain amount of money (usually $1,000). In criminal matters, they hear misdemeanors such as shoplifting, disorderly conduct, or simple assault. Their sanctioning power is also limited. In criminal matters, punishments may be limited to fines, community sentencing, or incarceration in the county jail for up to a year. In addition to their trial work, limited-jurisdiction courts conduct arraignments, preliminary hearings, and bail hearings in felony cases (before they are transferred to superior courts).

Some states separate limited courts into those that handle civil cases only and those that settle criminal cases. Included in the category of courts of limited jurisdiction are special courts, such as juvenile, family, and probate (divorce, estate issues, and custody) courts. State lawmakers may respond to a particular social problem, such as drug use, by creating **specialized courts** that focus on treatment and care for these special-needs offenders. One of the most common is the family or juvenile court, which handles custody cases, delinquency, and other issues involving children (juvenile courts will be discussed further in Chapter 16). Some recent types of specialized courts are discussed in the nearby Analyzing Criminal Justice Issues feature. Also see the Evidence-Based Justice feature on page 329 for a review of the literature concerning the effectiveness of one type of specialized court: the drug court.

The nation's approximately 13,500 limited jurisdiction courts make up 90 percent of all state courts.[5] They are the courts most often accused of providing assembly-line justice. Because the matters they decide involve minor personal confrontations and conflicts—family disputes, divorces, landlord–tenant conflicts, barroom brawls—the rule of the day is "handling the situation" and resolving the dispute.

### Courts of General Jurisdiction

Approximately 2,000 **courts of general jurisdiction** exist in the United States, variously called felony, superior, supreme, county, and circuit courts. Courts of general jurisdiction handle the more serious felony cases (e.g., murder, rape, robbery) and civil cases where damages are over a specified amount, such as $10,000. Courts of general jurisdiction may also be responsible for reviewing cases on appeal from courts of limited jurisdiction. In some instances they base

---

**court of limited jurisdiction**
A court that has jurisdiction over misdemeanors and conducts preliminary investigations of felony charges.

**CourseMate** For more information about the **National Center for State Courts (NCSC)**, visit the Criminal Justice CourseMate at CengageBrain.com, then access the "Web Links" for this chapter.

**specialized court**
A court that has primary jurisdiction over specific types of offenses and that operates differently than a traditional criminal court, such as with a concern over outcomes and extensive judicial monitoring.

**court of general jurisdiction**
A state or federal court that has jurisdiction over felony offenses—serious crimes that carry a penalty of incarceration in a state or federal prison for one year or more.

# ANALYZING CRIMINAL JUSTICE ISSUES

## Specialized Courts

A growing phenomenon in the United States is the creation of specialized courts that focus on one type of criminal act—for example, drug abuse or domestic violence. All cases within the jurisdiction that involve this particular type of crime are funneled to the specialized court, where presumably they will get prompt resolution.

### What Makes Specialized Courts Different?

Specialized courts differ from traditional courts in several key respects. According to the Center for Court Innovation, specialized courts have these six features:

■ *Outcomes are elevated above process.* The main concern is reducing recidivism.

■ *Judicial monitoring is critical.* Judges closely monitor offenders.

■ *Informed decision making is necessary.* Judges hand down sentences with more information about offenders' backgrounds than may be available in traditional sentencing contexts.

■ *Collaboration.* Specialized courts typically collaborate with other public and private agencies, many of which are often housed in the courthouse.

■ *Nontraditional roles.* Specialized court personnel often assume different roles. For example, prosecutors in specialized courts are more interested in helping defendants than in seeing that they are convicted or punished.

■ *Systemic change.* Specialized courts try to change the way the criminal justice system works.

Program supervisor Jeff Schultz (left) presents Brad Zeroni with his diploma upon Zeroni's completion of the Polk County Adult Drug Court program in Des Moines, Iowa. Drug courts are now commonplace in the criminal justice system and appear to be an effective alternative to the traditional court model.

### Drug Courts

The drug court movement began in Florida to address the growing problem of prison overcrowding due in large part to an influx of drug-involved offenders. Drug courts were created to have primary jurisdiction over cases involving substance abuse and drug trafficking. The aim is to place nonviolent first offenders into intensive treatment programs rather than in jail or prison. Today, there are nearly 1,000 drug courts across the United States. Drug courts address the overlap between the public health threats of drug abuse and crime: Crimes are often drug-related, and drug abusers are frequently involved with the criminal justice system. Drug courts provide an ideal setting to address these problems by linking the justice system with health services and drug treatment providers, while easing the burden on the already overtaxed correctional system.

### Mental Health Courts

Based largely on the organization of drug courts, mental health courts focus their attention on mental health treatment to help people with emotional problems reduce their chances of reoffending. By focusing on the need for treatment, along with providing supervision and support from the community, mental health courts provide a venue for those dealing with mental health issues to avoid the trauma of jail or prison, where they will have little if any access to treatment.

Although mental health courts tend to vary in their approach, most share a few basic operating procedures:

■ Most demand active participation by the defendant.

■ The participant must be diagnosed with a mental illness, and a direct link must be established between the illness and the crime committed.

■ Intervention must occur quickly; individuals must be screened and referred to the program either immediately after arrest or within three weeks.

■ Once in the program, participants are closely monitored by case managers.

■ Most provide voluntary outpatient or inpatient mental health treatment, in the least restrictive manner appropriate as determined by the court, that carries with it the possibility of dismissal of charges or reduced sentencing on successful completion of treatment.

■ Centralized case management involves the consolidation of cases that include mentally ill or mentally disabled defendants (including probation violators) and the coordination of mental health treatment plans and social services, including life skills training, placement, health care, and relapse prevention for each participant who requires such services.

■ Supervision of treatment plan compliance continues for a term not to exceed the maximum allowable sentence or probation for the charged or relevant offense, and to the extent practicable, psychiatric care continues at the end of the supervised period.

The mental health court concept seems beneficial, but it has encountered a few operational difficulties. It is hard to get community support for programs and institutions treating mentally ill offenders. Most programs accept only the nonviolent mentally ill; those who are violence prone are still lost in the correctional system without receiving the proper treatment. It is also difficult to assess the benefits of having specialized mental health courts. With other specialized courts, measuring offender improvement is relatively easy. For example, people sent to drug court programs must simply prove they can remain drug free. However, those involved with mental health court programs suffer from complex mental issues, and case managers must ensure that these individuals have gained control over their illness, which can be difficult to determine.

## Community Courts

Community courts are also becoming popular. Rather than targeting specific types of problems such as drugs or mental health, these courts take a more generalized focus. The main concern with community courts is providing "accessible justice" for residents who cannot easily get to downtown courthouses and focusing on quality-of-life offenses that may not be seen as top priority in traditional criminal courts. Community courts often have several on-site services available, as well. The first community court was Manhattan's Midtown Community Court.

## Domestic Violence Courts

Several jurisdictions across the country have created their own domestic violence courts. Brian Ostrom described domestic violence courts in this way: They "seek to coordinate with medical, social service, and treatment providers and establish special procedures and alternative sentencing options to promote effective outcomes. Success necessitates systemwide collaboration and the ongoing commitment of judges, health care professionals, the police, prosecution, and citizens who witness violent acts." Today, there are some 300 domestic violence courts in operation nationwide. Given how new they are, however, not many of them have been evaluated.

## Gun Courts

Rhode Island created the nation's first gun court in 1994. Unlike some of the other specialized courts, this gun court was concerned mainly with minimizing delay and ensuring that gun offenders received the toughest penalties the law allows. Other gun courts emphasize educating defendants about gun violence and safety. Many such courts have focused their efforts on juvenile gun offenders. According to David Sheppard and Patricia Kelly, common features of juvenile gun courts include

■ Early intervention—in many jurisdictions, before resolution of the court proceedings.

■ Short-term (often a single two- to four-hour session), intensive programming.

■ An intensive educational focus, using knowledgeable, concerned adults from the community to show youths the harm that can come from unlawful gun use, the choices they can make about carrying and/or using guns versus nonviolent alternatives for resolving conflicts, and the immediate response by adults in positions of authority that will result when youths are involved with guns.

■ The inclusion of a wide range of court personnel and law enforcement officials—judges, probation officers, prosecutors, defense counsel, and police—working together with community members.

## Other Specialized Courts

There are specialized courts for many different types of crime and social problems. In addition to targeting the above crimes, specialized courts have been formed to deal with everything from homelessness and sex offenses to parole reentry and teen bullying. We have moved well beyond the world of the traditional limited jurisdiction court. Limited jurisdiction courts still exist, but these are often being supplanted by courts whose jurisdiction is not only limited but also very narrow.

## Critical Thinking

1. Do you believe that specialized courts are needed for other types of crimes, such as sex offenses and/or domestic violence?

2. Should a judge preside over a specialized court, or should it be administered by treatment personnel?

Sources: Denise Gottfredson, Stacy Najaka, and Brook Kearley, "Effectiveness of Drug Treatment Courts: Evidence from a Randomized Trial," *Criminology and Public Policy* 2 (2003): 171–197; Greg Berman and John Feinblatt, *Problem-Solving Courts: A Brief Primer* (New York: Center for Court Innovation, 2001); Brian J. Ostrom, "Domestic Violence Courts: Editorial Introduction," *Criminology and Public Policy* 3 (2003).105–108; Office of Juvenile Justice and Delinquency Prevention, *Gun Court—Providence, RI, Profile No. 37* (Washington, D.C.: U.S. Department of Justice, Office of Juvenile Justice and Delinquency Prevention, n.d.), http://ojjdp.ncjrs.org/pubs/gun_violence/profile37.html (accessed August 3, 2008); David Sheppard and Patricia Kelly, *Juvenile Gun Courts: Promoting Accountability and Providing Treatment* (Washington, D.C.: U.S. Department of Justice, Office of Juvenile Justice and Delinquency Prevention, 2002), p. 2.

# EVIDENCE-BASED JUSTICE

## Do Drug Courts Work?

Drug courts have been extensively researched—more than any other type of specialized court—because they have been around the longest. As many studies suggest, they work well. For example, Denise Gottfredson and her colleagues found that drug court judges actually impose harsher sentences, but that they suspend these sentences conditional on compliance with the drug court regimen in drug testing and treatment and attendance at status hearings. Most important, within a 12-month period, 48 percent of drug treatment court clients were arrested for new offenses, compared to 64 percent of the people handled in traditional courts. Among the more serious cases heard, 32 percent of drug court clients were arrested, compared with 57 percent of controls. All things considered, defendants sentenced in a traditional court suffered rearrest at a rate nearly three times that of drug treatment court clients. Another recent study by Jeffrey Bouffard and Katie Richardson found that drug court was able to reduce reoffending for several types of drug users.

One of the problems with drug courts is that many of them are voluntary. This can result in what is known as "selection bias," meaning that the offenders who are most likely to succeed select themselves into drug court treatment. Even so, researchers have recently scoured the literature and attempted to draw general conclusions about the many studies published on drug court effectiveness. In one of the most comprehensive studies to date, Wilson, Mitchell, and MacKenzie reviewed the findings from 55 previous works and concluded that "...drug offenders participating in a drug court are less likely to reoffend than similar offenders sentenced to traditional correctional options."

Sources: Denise Gottfredson and Lyn Exum, "The Baltimore City Drug Treatment Court: One-Year Results from a Randomized Study," *Journal of Research in Crime and Delinquency* 39 (2002): 337–357; Jeffrey A. Bouffard and Katie A. Richardson, "The Effectiveness of Drug Court Programming for Specific Kinds of Offenders: Methamphetamine and DWI Offenders versus Other Drug-Involved Offenders," *Criminal Justice Policy Review* 18 (2007): 274–293; David B. Wilson, Ojmarrh Mitchell, and Doris L. MacKenzie, "A Systematic Review of Drug Court Effects on Recidivism," *Journal of Experimental Criminology* 2 (2006): 459–487, p. 459.

---

their decision on a review of the transcript of the case, whereas in others they can actually grant a new trial; this latter procedure is known as the *trial de novo process.* Changes in the courts of general jurisdiction, such as increases in felony filing rates, are watched closely because serious crime is of great public concern.

Courts of general jurisdiction are typically organized in judicial districts or circuits, based on a political division such as a county or a group of counties (such as Superior Court for the Southern Tier). They then receive cases from the various limited courts located within the county/jurisdiction. Some general courts separate criminal and civil cases so that some specialize in civil matters, whereas others maintain a caseload that is exclusively criminal. In ten states, Washington, D.C., and Puerto Rico, general and limited courts have consolidated their jurisdictions, creating a unified court system.

State criminal appeals are heard in one of the **appellate courts** in the 50 states and the District of Columbia. Each state has at least one court of last resort, usually called a state supreme court, which reviews issues of law and fact appealed from the trial courts. A few states have two high courts, one for civil appeals and the other for criminal cases. In addition, many states have established intermediate appellate courts (IACs) to review decisions by trial courts and administrative agencies before they reach the supreme court stage. Currently, 39 states have at least one permanent IAC.[6] Mississippi was the last state to create an IAC, which began operations in 1995.

Many people believe that criminal appeals clog the nation's court system because so many convicted criminals try to "beat the rap" on a technicality. Actually, criminal appeals represent only about one-quarter of the total number of

**appellate court**
A court to which appeals are made on points of law resulting from the judgment of a lower court; the appellate court may be asked to evaluate the impact of new evidence but more typically decides whether the state or federal constitution was improperly interpreted during a case.

cases processed by the nation's appellate courts.[7] All types of appeals, including criminal ones, continue to inundate the courts, so most courts are having problems processing cases expeditiously.

State courts have witnessed an increase in the number of appellate cases each year.[8] In the meantime, the number of judges and support staff has not kept pace. The resulting imbalance has led to the increased use of intermediate courts to screen cases.

In sum, most states have at least two trial courts and two appellate courts, but they differ about where jurisdiction over such matters as juvenile cases and felony versus misdemeanor offenses is found. Such matters vary from state to state and between the state courts and the federal system.

## Model State Court Structure

Figure 9.1 illustrates the interrelationship of appellate and trial courts in a typical state court structure. Each state's court organization varies from this standard pattern. Every state has a tiered court organization (lower, upper, and appellate courts), but states differ in the way they have delegated responsibility to a particular court system. For example, the court organizations of Texas and New York are complex in comparison with the model court structure (see Figures 9.2 and 9.3). Texas separates its highest appellate divisions into civil and criminal courts. The Texas Supreme Court hears civil, administrative, and juvenile cases, and an independent court of criminal appeals has the final say on criminal matters. New York's unique structure features two separate intermediate appellate courts with different geographic jurisdictions and an independent family court, which handles both domestic relations (such as guardianship and custody, neglect, and abuse) and juvenile delinquency. Surrogates' court handles adoptions and settles disagreements over estate transfers. The court of claims handles civil matters in which the state is a party. In contrast to New York, which has ten independent courts, six states (Idaho, Illinois, Iowa, Massachusetts, Minnesota, and South Dakota) have unified their trial courts into a single system.

## FEDERAL COURTS

The legal basis for the federal court system is contained in Article 3, Section 1, of the U.S. Constitution, which provides that "the judicial power of the United States shall be vested in one Supreme Court, and in such inferior courts as Congress may from time to time ordain and establish." The important clauses in Article 3 indicate that the federal courts have jurisdiction over the laws of the United States, treaties, and cases involving admiralty and maritime jurisdiction, as well as over controversies between two or more states and citizens of different states.[9] This complex language generally means that state courts have jurisdiction over all legal matters, unless they involve a violation of a federal criminal statute or a civil suit between citizens of different states or between a citizen and an agency of the federal government.

Within this authority, the federal government has established a three-tiered hierarchy of court jurisdiction that, in order of ascendancy, consists of the U.S. district courts, the U.S. courts of appeals (circuit courts), and the U.S. Supreme Court (see Figure 9.4).

## District Courts

**U.S. district courts** are the trial courts of the federal system. They have jurisdiction over cases involving violations of federal laws, including civil rights abuses, interstate transportation of stolen vehicles, and kidnappings. They may also hear cases on questions involving citizenship and the rights of aliens. The jurisdiction of the U.S. district court will occasionally overlap that of state courts.

**PERSPECTIVES ON JUSTICE**

*Due Process*

Crime control advocates believe that criminal appeals clog the nation's court system because so many convicted criminals try to get free on a technicality. These advocates may be overstating the case. For example, less than 20 percent of the appeals in federal courts are criminal matters. The right to appeal an unjust conviction lies at the heart of the due process model.

**U.S. district court**
A trial court in the federal court system.

**FIGURE 9.1**
A Model of a State Judicial System

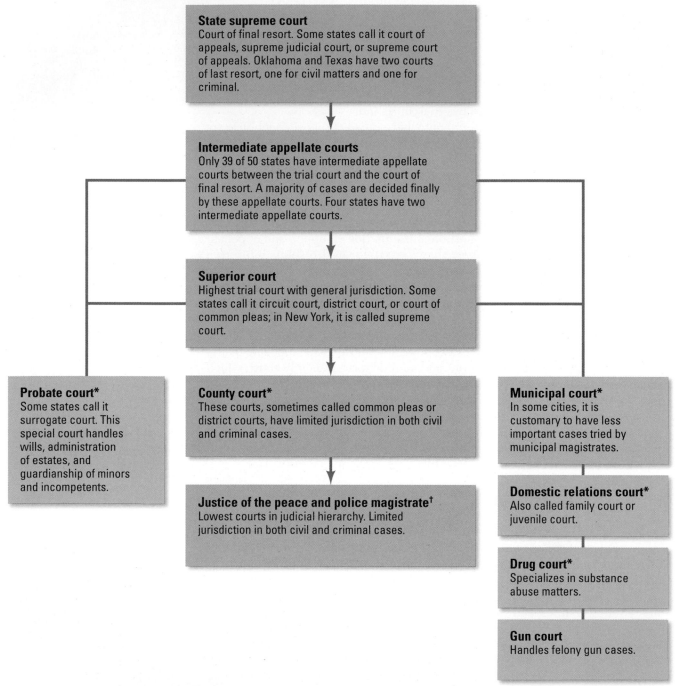

\* Courts of special jurisdictions, such as probate, family, or juvenile courts, and the so-called inferior courts, such as common pleas or municipal courts, may be separate courts or part of the trial court of general jurisdiction.

† Justices of the peace do not exist in all states. Where they do exist, their jurisdictions vary greatly from state to state.

Source: David B. Rottman and Shauna M. Strickland, *State Court Organization, 2004* (Arlington, Va.: National Center for State Courts, 2006), p. 9.

For example, citizens who reside in separate states and are involved in litigation of an amount in excess of $10,000 may choose to have their cases heard in either of the states or in the federal court. Finally, federal district courts hear cases in which one state sues a resident (or firm) in another state, where one state sues another, or where the federal government is a party in a suit. A single judge ordinarily presides over criminal trials; a defendant may also request a jury trial.

**FIGURE 9.2**
Texas Court Structure

**Supreme Court**
9 justices sit en banc
CSP case types:
• Mandatory jurisdiction in civil cases.
• Discretionary jurisdiction in civil, administrative agency, juvenile, certified questions from federal courts, original proceeding cases.

**Court of Criminal Appeals**
9 judges sit en banc
CSP case types:
• Mandatory jurisdiction in capital criminal, criminal, original proceeding cases.
• Discretionary jurisdiction in noncapital criminal, original proceeding cases and certified questions from federal court.

Courts of last resort

**Courts of Appeals** (14 courts)
80 justices sit in panels
CSP case types:
• Mandatory jurisdiction in civil, noncapital criminal, administrative agency, juvenile, original proceeding, interlocutory decision cases.
• No discretionary jurisdiction.

Intermediate appellate courts

**District Courts** (414 courts) 414 judges

**District Court** (404 courts)
404 judges
CSP case types:
• Tort, contract, real property rights ($200/no maximum), domestic relations, estate, miscellaneous civil. Exclusive administrative agency appeals jurisdiction.
• Felony, misdemeanor, DWI/DUI, miscellaneous criminal.
• Juvenile.

Jury trials.

**Criminal District Court** (10 courts)
10 judges
CSP case types:
• Felony, misdemeanor, DWI/DUI, miscellaneous criminal cases.

Jury trials.

Courts of general jurisdiction

**County-Level Courts** (462 courts) 462 judges

**Constitutional County Court**
(254 courts)
254 judges
CSP case types:
• Tort, contract, real property rights ($200/$5,000), domestic relations, estate, mental health, civil trial court appeals, miscellaneous civil.
• Misdemeanor, DWI/DUI, criminal appeals.
• Moving traffic, miscellaneous traffic.
• Juvenile.

Jury trials.

**Probate Court**
(16 courts)
16 judges
CSP case types:
• Estate.
• Mental health.

Jury trials.

**County Court at Law**
(192 courts)
192 judges
CSP case types:
• Tort, contract, real property rights ($200/varies), estate, mental health, civil trial court appeals, miscellaneous civil.
• Misdemeanor, DWI/DUI, criminal appeals.
• Moving traffic, miscellaneous traffic.
• Juvenile.

Jury trials.

**Municipal Court*** (869 courts)
1,294 judges
CSP case types:
• Misdemeanor.
• Moving traffic, parking, miscellaneous traffic. Exclusive ordinance violation jurisdiction.
• Preliminary hearings.

Jury trials.

**Justice of the Peace Court*** (835 courts)
835 judges
CSP case types:
• Tort, contract, real property rights ($0/$5,000), small claims ($5,000), mental health.
• Misdemeanor.
• Moving traffic, parking, miscellaneous traffic.
• Preliminary hearings.

Jury trials.

Courts of limited jurisdiction

*Note: CSP=Court Statistics Project. DWI/DUI = driving while intoxicated/driving under the influence.*
*\* Some municipal and justice of the peace courts may appeal to the district court.*

Source: National Center for State Courts, www.ncsconline.org/D_Research/Ct_Struct/state_inc.asp?STATE=TX (accessed April 20, 2010).

**FIGURE 9.3**
New York Court Structure

Note: *Unless otherwise noted, numbers reflect statutory authorization. Many judges sit in more than one court so the number of judgeships indicated in this chart does not reflect the actual number of judges in the system. Fifty county court judges also serve surrogates' court and six county court judges also serve family court. CSP = Court Statistics Project. DWI/DUI = driving while intoxicated/driving under the influence.*

Source: National Center for State Courts, www.ncsconline.org/D_Research/Ct_Struct/state_inc.asp?STATE=NY (accessed April 20, 2010).

**FIGURE 9.4**
The Federal Judicial System

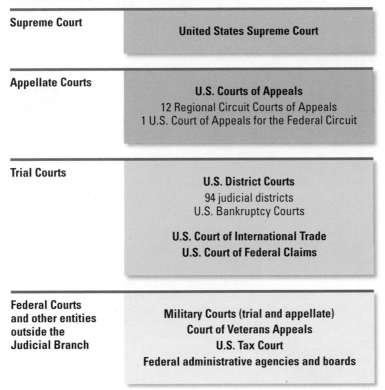

| Supreme Court | **United States Supreme Court** |
|---|---|
| Appellate Courts | **U.S. Courts of Appeals**<br>12 Regional Circuit Courts of Appeals<br>1 U.S. Court of Appeals for the Federal Circuit |
| Trial Courts | **U.S. District Courts**<br>94 judicial districts<br>U.S. Bankruptcy Courts<br><br>**U.S. Court of International Trade**<br>**U.S. Court of Federal Claims** |
| Federal Courts and other entities outside the Judicial Branch | **Military Courts (trial and appellate)**<br>**Court of Veterans Appeals**<br>**U.S. Tax Court**<br>**Federal administrative agencies and boards** |

Source: Administrative Office of the U.S. *Courts, Understanding the Federal Courts,* www.uscourts.gov/understand03/media/UFC03.pdf, p. 9 (accessed April 20, 2010).

Federal district courts were organized by Congress in the Judicial Act of 1789, and today 94 independent courts are in operation. Originally, each state was allowed one court. As the population grew, however, so did the need for courts. Now each state has from one to four district courts, and the District of Columbia has one for itself.

## Federal Appeals Courts

There are 13 **U.S. courts of appeals**, sometimes referred to as U.S. circuit courts. This name is derived from the historical practice of having judges ride the circuit and regularly hear cases in the judicial seats of their various jurisdictions. Today, appellate judges are not required to travel (although some may sit in more than one court), and each federal appellate court jurisdiction contains a number of associate justices who share the caseload. Circuit court offices are usually located in major cities, such as San Francisco and New York, and cases to be heard must be brought to these locations by attorneys.

The circuit court is empowered to review federal and state appellate court cases on substantive and procedural issues involving rights guaranteed by the Constitution. Circuit courts neither retry cases nor determine whether the facts brought out during trial support conviction or dismissal. Instead, they analyze judicial interpretations of the law, such as the charge (or instructions) to the jury, and reflect on the constitutional issues involved in each case they hear.

Although federal court criminal cases make up only a small percentage of appellate cases, they are still of concern to the judiciary. Steps have been taken to make the appeal process more difficult. For example, the U.S. Supreme Court has tried to limit the number of appeals being filed by prison inmates, which often represent a significant number of cases appealed in the federal criminal justice system. For a map of the federal appeals courts (and the districts within them), see Figure 9.5.

**CourseMate** For more information about the **federal courts**, visit the Criminal Justice CourseMate at CengageBrain.com, then access the "Web Links" for this chapter.

**U.S. court of appeals**
An appellate court in the federal court system

**FIGURE 9.5**
U.S. Circuit Map

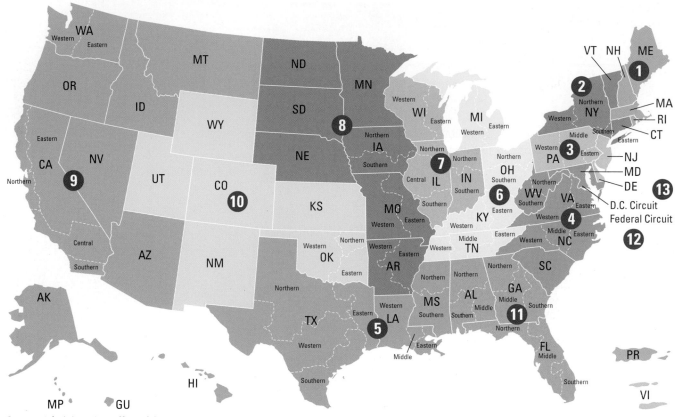

Source: Administrative Office of the U.S. Courts, www.uscourts.gov/courtlinks/ (accessed April 20, 2010).

## The U.S. Supreme Court

**U.S. Supreme Court**
The highest appellate court in the United States

**court of last resort**
A court that handles the final appeal on a matter—in the federal system, the U.S. Supreme Court.

The **U.S. Supreme Court** is the nation's highest appellate body and the **court of last resort** for all cases tried in the various federal and state courts. The Supreme Court is composed of nine members appointed for lifetime terms by the president, with the approval of Congress. (The size of the Court is set by statute.) The Court has discretion over most of the cases it will consider and may choose to hear only those it deems important, appropriate, and worthy of its attention. The Court chooses around 300 of the 5,000 cases that are appealed each year; fewer than half of these typically receive full opinions.

The Supreme Court is unique in several ways. First, it is the only court established by constitutional mandate instead of federal legislation. Second, it decides basic social and political issues of grave consequence and importance to the nation. Third, the justices shape the future meaning of the U.S. Constitution. Their decisions identify the rights and liberties of citizens throughout the United States.

When the Supreme Court rules on a case, usually by majority decision (at least five votes), the outcome becomes a precedent that must be honored by all lower courts. For example, if the Court grants a particular litigant the right to counsel at a police lineup, all similarly situated clients must be given the same right. This type of ruling is usually referred to as a landmark decision. The use of precedent in the legal system gives the Supreme Court power to influence and mold the everyday operating procedures of the police, trial courts, and corrections agencies. This influence became particularly pronounced during the tenure of Chief Justices Earl Warren (1953–1969) and Warren Burger (1969–1986), who greatly amplified and extended the power of the Court to influence criminal justice policies. Under William H. Rehnquist, who was elevated to chief justice in 1986, the Court continued to influence criminal justice matters, ranging from the investigation of crimes to the execution of criminals. The newest chief justice, John Roberts, has also had an influence on the criminal justice system through several recent decisions. The personal legal philosophies of the justices and their orientation toward the civil and personal rights of victims and criminals significantly affect the daily operations of the justice system.

*HOW A CASE GETS TO THE SUPREME COURT* When the nation was first established, the Supreme Court did not review state court decisions involving issues of federal law. Even though Congress had given the Supreme Court jurisdiction to review state decisions, much resistance and controversy surrounded the relationship between the states and the federal government. However, in a famous decision, *Martin v. Hunter's Lessee* (1816), the Court reaffirmed the legitimacy of its jurisdiction over state court decisions when such courts handled issues of federal or constitutional law.[10] This decision allowed the Court to actively review actions by states and their courts and reinforced the Court's power to make the supreme law of the land. Since that time, a defendant who indicates that governmental action—whether state or federal—violates a constitutional law is in a position to have the Court review such action. Today, most cases that come before the Supreme Court involve significant federal questions, usually of a constitutional nature.

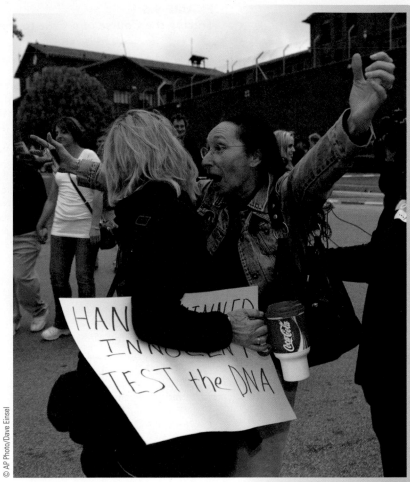

© AP Photo/Dave Einsel

*Sandrine Ageorges, of France, protests the scheduled execution of condemned killer Hank Skinner on March 24, 2010, in Huntsville, Texas. Skinner, who was convicted for killing his girlfriend Twila Busby and her two mentally impaired sons in 1993, married Ageorges in 2008. As Skinner was finishing his final meal, the U.S. Supreme Court issued a stay, blocking his execution. He is still on death row and claims that additional DNA testing could prove his innocence.*

To carry out its responsibilities, the Supreme Court had to develop a method for dealing with the large volume of cases coming from the state and federal courts for final review. In the early years of its history, the Court sought to review every case brought before it. Since the middle of the twentieth century, however, the Court has used the **writ of certiorari** to decide what cases it should hear (*certiorari* is a Latin term meaning to bring the record of a case from a lower court up to a higher court for immediate review). Today, more than 90 percent of the cases heard by the Court are brought by petition for a writ of certiorari.[11] Under this procedure, the justices have discretion to select the cases they will review for a decision. For a writ to be granted, ordinarily four justices must agree to hear the case. This is known as the **rule of four**. However, the Court is required to hear cases in a few instances, such as decisions from a three-judge federal district court on reapportionment and cases involving the Voting Rights Act.

After the Supreme Court decides to hear a case, it reviews written and oral arguments. The written materials are referred to as legal briefs, and oral arguments are normally presented to the justices at the Court in Washington, D.C.

After the material is reviewed and the oral arguments heard, the justices normally meet in what is known as a case conference. At this case conference, they discuss the case and vote to reach a decision. The cases voted on by the Court generally come from the judicial systems of the various states or the U.S. courts of appeals, and they represent the entire spectrum of law.

In reaching a decision, the Supreme Court reevaluates and reinterprets state statutes, the U.S. Constitution, and previous case decisions. Based on a review of the case, the Court either affirms or reverses the decision of the lower court.

**writ of certiorari**
An order of a superior court requesting that a record of an inferior court (or administrative body) be brought forward for review or inspection.

**rule of four**
The convention that four justices must agree to hear a case before a writ of certiorari is granted.

**FIGURE 9.6**
Tracing the Course of a Case to the U.S. Supreme Court

**Full judicial decision by the U.S. Supreme Court**
(majority and dissenting opinions)
The Court affirms or reverses lower-court decisions. (Exception: The decision is not always a final judicial action. Lower courts may try the case again or, as in civil litigation, the case may be retried.) There is no appeal process beyond the U.S. Supreme Court.

**Decision-making conferences by the justices**
Four votes govern the acceptance or rejection of a case: (1) a decision and full opinion; (2) if the case is accepted, there may be a summary decision of a dismissal or affirmation of a lower-court decision (per curiam); (3) if the case is rejected, no explanation (reconsideration is possible); and (4) a rehearing after an unfavorable decision is possible.

**Prescreening**
(discussion of the case list)
The chief justice places cases on a list, including in forma pauperis petitions.

**Discretionary decisions**
(special circumstances)
A writ of certiorari or a writ of habeas corpus.

**Mandatory decisions**
Hears direct statutory appeals in which the state is in conflict with the federal law or Constitution, and original jurisdiction disputes between states.

**Decision making**

**Federal courts**
(U.S. appellate courts)
The U.S. Court of Appeals, the U.S. Court of Claims, and the U.S. Customs Court.

**State Supreme Court**
(State court of last resort)
State supreme court cases that are not an issue of federal law are ineligible for hearing by the Court.

**Federal or state trial court cases**
(processing of case through federal or state court systems)

When the justices reach a decision, the chief justice of the Court assigns someone of the majority group to write the opinion. Another justice normally writes a dissenting, or minority, opinion. When the case is finished, it is submitted to the public and becomes the law of the land. The decision represents the legal precedents that add to the existing body of law on a given subject, change it, and guide its future development. Figure 9.6 shows the course a case takes as it progresses from a federal or state court to the Supreme Court.

In the area of criminal justice, the decisions of the U.S. Supreme Court have had the broadest impact on the reform of the system. The Court's action is the final step in settling constitutional criminal disputes throughout the nation. By discretionary review through a petition for certiorari, the Court requires state courts to accept its interpretation of the Constitution. In doing so, the Court has changed the day-by-day operations of the criminal justice system.

# COURT CONGESTION

The vast U.S. court system has been overloaded by the millions of cases that are brought each year. State court systems now handle about 100 million new cases annually. That total includes

- About 23 million civil and domestic cases
- More than 21 million criminal cases
- More than two million juvenile cases
- More than 56 million traffic and ordinance violations[12]

The number of cases in all state courts, especially limited jurisdiction courts, has been increasing at a steady pace for more than a decade.

Although they are fewer in number, federal courts are equally burdened:

- Approximately 95,000 criminal cases are decided in the district courts each year.[13] See Figure 9.7 for details on criminal cases filed in the district courts between 2005 and 2009.

- The U.S. courts of appeals decide approximately 13,000 criminal appeals each year.[14]

Congestion is undesirable for various reasons. First, it makes people wait too long for resolution. Second, it costs money. For example, it is costly to jail dangerous criminal defendants in the time leading up their court date. Third, too much delay can violate the Sixth Amendment's provisions concerning the right to a speedy trial.

Why has the court system become so congested? Numerous factors produce trial delay and court congestion:[15]

- Rapidly increasing populations in some states, such as Nevada, have outpaced growth in the court system.

**FIGURE 9.7**
Criminal Cased Filed in U.S. District Courts

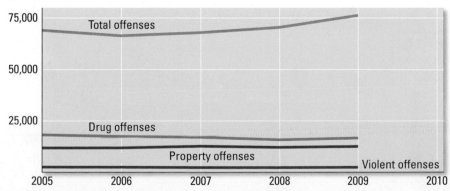

Source: Administrative Office of the United States Courts, *Annual Report of the Director, 2009* (Washington, D.C.: Administrative Office of the United States Courts, 2009), Table D-2, www.uscourts.gov/judbus2009/appendices/D02CSep09.pdf (accessed April 20, 2010).

On March 3, 2010, Lonnie Helms, who has been arrested in Monroe County (Florida) 15 times since 2004, tells Key West police officers he's doing nothing wrong. In the two previous months, Key West police arrested more than 70 vagrants for "quality of life" offenses: aggressive panhandling, trespassing, fighting, public intoxication, defecating on public property, and using residents' outdoor showers and electricity. Such arrests invariably lead to congestion in the courts, and many such offenders are promptly released.

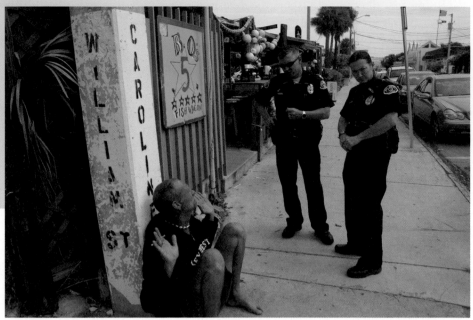

© AP Photo/*Miami Herald*/Cammy Clark

- Some communities have attempted to control crime by aggressively prosecuting petty offenses and nuisance crimes such as panhandling and vagrancy.

- As the law becomes more complex, and involves such technological issues as intellectual property rights concerning computer programs, the need for a more involved court process has escalated.

- Ironically, efforts being made to reform the criminal law may also be helping to overload the courts. The increase of mandatory prison sentences for some crimes may reduce the use of plea bargaining and increase the number of jury trials because defendants fear that a conviction will lead to incarceration and thus must be avoided at all costs.

- Civil litigation has increased as people have come to view the court process as a means of redressing all kinds of personal wrongs. This can result in *frivolous lawsuits*—for example, when overweight people file suit against manufacturers, distributors, or sellers of food products, charging these parties with responsibility for their obesity.[16] Increased civil litigation can add to the backlog because most courts handle both criminal and civil matters.

The courts now handle more than 100 million cases each year, causing congestion and inhibiting case processing. Here criminal defendants chained together are ushered into a Whatcom County courtroom for hearings in Bellingham, Washington. Following a practice that has been routine for nearly 30 years in this county on the Canadian border, federal agents dump scores of drug cases on local officials, clogging the courts and crowding jails. Can anything be done about the congestion in America's courts?

© AP Images/Elaine Thompson

If relief is to be found, it will probably be in the form of better administrative and management techniques that improve the use of existing resources.[17] Another possible method of creating a more efficient court system is to unify existing state courts into a single administrative structure using modern management principles. This has happened already in several states, such as California. In the late 1990s, voters in that state voted to change the state constitution so that municipal and superior courts were unified into a single type of court.

## THE JUDICIARY

The **judge** is the senior officer in a court of law who is authorized to hear and decide cases. A judge's duties are varied and far more extensive than might be expected. During trials, the judge rules on the appropriateness of conduct, settles questions of evidence and procedure, and guides the questioning of witnesses. In a jury trial, the judge must instruct jurors on which evidence is proper to examine and which should be ignored. The judge also formally charges the jury by instructing its members on what points of law and evidence they must consider to reach a verdict of either guilty or not guilty. When a jury trial is waived, the judge must decide whether to hold for the complainant or for the defendant. Finally, if a defendant is found guilty, the judge must decide on the sentence (in some cases, this is legislatively determined), which includes choosing the type of sentence and its length, as well as the conditions under which probation may be revoked.

While carrying out her duties, the judge must be wary of the legal controls placed on the trial process by the appellate court system. If an error is made, the judge's decision may be reversed, causing, at the very least, personal embarrassment. Although some experts believe that fear of reversal shapes judicial decision making, recent research by David Klein and Robert Hume indicates that judges may be more independent than previously believed, especially if they can use their judicial power as a policymaking tool to influence important social policies such as affirmative action or privacy.[18]

### Other Judicial Functions

Beyond these stated duties, the trial judge has extensive control and influence over the other agencies of the court: probation, the court clerk, court reporters, the public defender, and the district attorney's office (see Exhibit 9.1 on page 345). Probation and the clerk may be under the judge's explicit control. In some courts, the operations, philosophy, and procedures of these agencies are within the magistrate's administrative domain. In others—for example, where a state agency controls the probation department—the attitudes of the county or district court judge greatly influence the way a probation department is run and how its decisions are made. Judges often consult with probation staff on treatment decisions, and many judges are interested in providing the most innovative and up-to-date care possible.

Police and prosecutors are also directly influenced by the judge, whose sentencing discretion affects the arrest and charging processes. For example, if a judge usually chooses minimal sentences—such as a fine for a particular offense—the police may be reluctant to arrest offenders for that crime, knowing that doing so will basically be a waste of time. Similarly, if a judge is known to have an open attitude toward police discretion, the local department may be more inclined to engage in practices that border on entrapment or to pursue cases through easily obtained wiretaps. However, a magistrate oriented toward strict use of due process guarantees would stifle such activities by dismissing all cases involving apparent police abuses of personal freedoms. The district attorney's office may also be sensitive to judicial attitudes. The district attorney might forgo indictments in cases that the presiding magistrate expressly considers trivial or quasi-criminal and in which the judge has been known to take only token action, such as the prosecution of pornographers.

**judge**
The senior officer in a court of law, who is authorized to hear and decide cases.

**CourseMate** For more information about the **American Judges Association**, visit the Criminal Justice CourseMate at CengageBrain.com, then access the "Web Links" for this chapter.

Finally, the judge considers requests by police and prosecutors for leniency (or severity) in sentencing. The judge's reaction to these requests is important if the police and the district attorney are to honor the bargains they may have made with defendants to secure information, cooperation, or guilty pleas. For example, when police tell informers that they will try to convince the judge to go easy on them to secure required information, they will often discuss the terms of the promised leniency with representatives of the court. If a judge ignores police demands, the department's bargaining power is severely diminished, and communication within the criminal justice system is impaired.

There is always concern that judges will discriminate against defendants on the basis of their gender, race, or class. Although this issue is of great social concern, most research efforts have failed to find consistent bias in judicial decision making. Judges tend to dismiss cases that they consider weak and less serious.[19]

## Judicial Qualifications

The qualifications for appointment to one of the existing 30,000 judgeships vary from state to state and court to court. Typically, the potential judge must be a resident of the state, licensed to practice law, a member of the state bar association, and at least 25 and less than 70 years of age. However, a significant degree of diversity exists in the basic qualifications, depending on the level of court jurisdiction. Although almost every state requires judges to have a law degree if they are to serve on appellate courts or courts of general jurisdiction, it is not uncommon for municipal or town court judges to lack a legal background, even though they have the power to incarcerate criminal defendants.

Judges are held in high esteem, but they must sacrifice many financial benefits if they shift careers from lucrative private practices to low-paid government positions. Table 9.1 shows the average and median salaries of different kinds of judges (and court administrators) in state courts. Although an average of $155,428 for the chief of the highest court seems substantial, it is relatively modest when compared to corporate salaries and to what partners in top law firms earn. The *starting pay* in some high-powered New York City law firms (e.g., Goodwin Proctor) is now more than what the chief justice of the state's highest court makes![20]

A great deal of concern has been raised about the qualifications of judges. In most states, people appointed to the bench have had little or no training in how to be a judge. Others may have held administrative posts and may not have appeared before a court in years. The relatively low level of judicial salaries may make it difficult to attract the most competent attorneys to the bench.

A number of agencies have been created to improve the quality of the judiciary. For example, the National Conference of State Court Judges, part of the Judicial Division of the American Bar Association,[21] operates judicial training seminars and publishes manuals and guides on state-of-the-art judicial technologies. Its efforts are designed to improve the quality of the nation's judges.

## Judicial Alternatives

Increased judicial caseloads have prompted the use of alternatives to the traditional judge. For example, to expedite matters in civil cases, it has become common for both parties to agree to hire a retired judge or other neutral party and abide by his or her decision.

Other jurisdictions have created new quasi-judicial officers, such as referees or magistrates, to relieve the traditional judge of time-consuming responsibilities. The Magistrate Act of 1968 created a new type of judicial officer in the federal district court system to handle pretrial duties.[22] Federal magistrates also handle civil trials if both parties agree to the arrangement.[23]

Some jurisdictions use part-time judges. Many of these are attorneys who carry out their duties pro bono—for no or limited compensation. These judicial adjuncts assist the courts on a temporary basis while maintaining an active law

EXHIBIT 9.1

## Court Staff

The most visible courtroom personnel include the judge, the prosecutor, and the defense attorney. This chapter looks at judges; the next looks at prosecutors and defense attorneys. But there are many other important court personnel and staff persons. The typical large jurisdiction probably has a mix of the following personnel working in the courtroom or courthouse at any given time.

### CLERK

Court clerks are responsible for a wide range of duties. Their main responsibilities include maintaining court records; receiving, processing, and maintaining judgments; issuing process, such as summonses, subpoenas, and wage garnishments; preserving the court seal; swearing in witnesses, jurors, and grand jurors; collecting fees and fines; handling inquiries from attorneys and other parties; and printing and distributing opinions of the court.

### COURT ADMINISTRATOR

There are two general types of court administrators. The first is a state employee. In each state, these individuals are part of the state administrative office of the court, which is usually under the direction of the state supreme court. Court administrators help develop and implement policies and services for the judicial branch throughout the state. They also conduct research and determine whether judicial needs are identified and incorporated into long-term plans. They establish priorities for the courts, address financial problems and budgeting issues, and manage the use of technology within a state's judicial branch.

The second type of court administrator is a local court administrator. These individuals manage the daily operations of the court, usually under the direction of the presiding judge. They provide administrative support for court programs, help the court establish new programs and evaluate them, and manage purchasing and accounts payable, among other responsibilities.

### COURT SECURITY

The marshal or bailiff for the court is responsible for courthouse security. In some states, such as California, court security is provided by sheriff's deputies who screen people entering the building, provide security during trials, and transport suspects to court from jail. Depending on the jurisdiction, court security personnel may take on additional responsibilities, including some investigation, bond supervising, community service monitoring, and making arrests as needed.

### LEGAL STAFF

The larger and more powerful the court, the more likely it will have a variety of legal staff. These personnel can include legal counsel (prosecutors and defense attorneys), staff attorneys, research attorneys, and law clerks. Law clerks are not to be confused with court clerks. Unlike court clerks, law clerks are often recent law school graduates who assist judges with researching issues before the courts and writing opinions. U.S. Supreme Court law clerks are the cream of the crop, having graduated from many of the nation's top law schools.

### JUDICIAL SUPPORT STAFF

A judge's support staff may include executive assistants, administrative assistants, secretaries, or a mix of all three. Support staff edit and type judicial opinions, create and arrange files, coordinate meetings, coordinate travel arrangements, answer telephone and email inquiries, mail correspondence, and serve as an intermediary between the judge and other outside parties.

### COURT REPORTER

The court reporter records judicial proceedings word for word. See the Careers in Criminal Justice feature in this chapter for more on court reporters.

### JURY STAFF

Many courts have dedicated jury personnel who maintain and review lists of prospective jurors. They may also determine who is eligible to serve, determine the number of jurors needed, issue summonses for jury service, and handle requests by jurors for dismissal, exemption, or disqualification. These individuals may also meet with prospective jurors to explain the process, tell them where to go, and dismiss them from service at the end of the day.

### OTHER OFFICERS

Many courts have representatives on site from other criminal justice agencies. There may be juvenile officers who are vested with the authority to take charge of children who come under the jurisdiction of the juvenile or family court. Representatives from probation may assist judges by performing pre-sentence investigations that can be used during sentencing. In some states, the probation department is part of the judiciary and is thus more closely connected with the court than probation departments in other states.

## CAREERS IN CRIMINAL JUSTICE

# Court Reporter

### Duties and Characteristics of the Job

Court reporters create the official transcripts of legal proceedings such as trials and depositions. These transcripts include all the dialogue as well as other important details, such as emotional reactions. The court reporter records these events as they occur in real time.

Court reporters use three different methods of transcription: voice writing, electronic, and stenographic. Voice writers make an audio record of the proceedings. When making their recording, they speak into a microphone surrounded by a sound-proof mask so that the report cannot be heard by others. Court reporters taking electronic transcription use audio equipment to tape an event and later supplement this recording with notes taken during the proceedings. The most commonly used recording method in legal and courtroom settings is stenography. A modern stenographic court reporter uses a computerized stenotype machine to transcribe spoken words. A court reporter can press multiple keys simultaneously to represent words, sounds, or even phrases. The court reporter will go over the record later to ensure that it is clear, thorough, and accurate. The correctness of this record is important

because it will be the only official record of the event and may be used in future judgments, for trial preparation by attorneys, and during appeals.

Although the court reporter's primary purpose is to record courtroom legal proceedings and depositions, at times a court reporter may do more than just transcription. For example, when a request is made to review the transcript, the court reporter provides the information from the official record. Court reporters may also advise lawyers on legal procedure when necessary. Outside of a strictly legal setting, a court reporter will often also use his or her skills to create real-time translated or closed-captioned transcription for the hearing impaired.

### Job Outlook

The number of jobs available for court reporters is greater than the number of trained professionals entering the field. This means that the job prospects are good and the outlook is favorable for entry-level court reporters, especially those who are certified.

### Salary

A court reporter's pay will depend on several factors, including method of transcription, region of the

practice.[24] Federal judges who are close to retirement age enjoy "senior status" and also work part-time, thus easing the caseload burden on full-time judges.[25]

**alternative dispute resolution**
A means of settling disputes outside the courtroom.

**ALTERNATIVE DISPUTE RESOLUTION**  Every state now has a means of settling disputes with alternatives to litigation. This court-connected **alternative dispute resolution** (ADR) has spread rapidly as court delays remain and legal

### TABLE 9.1

**Judicial Salaries at a Glance**

| | Mean | Median | Range | Average Annual % Change 2003–2008 |
|---|---|---|---|---|
| Chief, highest court | $155,428 | $152,495 | $115,160 to 228,856 | 2.75 |
| Associate justice, court of last resort | 150,633 | 145,984 | 112,530 to 218,237 | 2.83 |
| Judge, intermediate appellate courts | 145,665 | 139,924 | 105,050 to 204,599 | 2.70 |
| Judge, general jurisdiction trial courts | 134,826 | 130,312 | 104,170 to 178,789 | 2.80 |
| State court administrators | 133,562 | 126,738 | 76,500 to 211,272 | 2.69 |

Source: National Center for State Courts, *Survey of Judicial Salaries*, Vol. 34, No. 2, June 30, 2009, http://contentdm.ncsconline.org/cgi-bin/showfile.exe?CISOROOT=/judicial&CISOPTR=288 (accessed April 20, 2010).

United States, type of employer, amount of previous work experience, and level of certification.

Median annual salary for court reporters is $49,710. Half of all court reporters earn between $35,390 and $67,430. The highest paid earn more than $83,500.

### Opportunities

The opportunities for employment as a court reporter are expected to grow at a moderate pace in the next several years. Court reporters are always needed in courtrooms and lawyers' offices across the country, although jobs may be more plentiful in urban areas.

A majority of court reporters work for state and local governments. However, salaried workers such as these often freelance for extra income at attorneys' offices or as closed captioners/real-time translators. Other court reporters work for court reporting agencies or freelance full time. Agency workers and freelancers enjoy the flexibility of setting their own schedules.

### Qualifications

The qualifications necessary to be a practicing court reporter vary by state. In some states, court reporters are required to be notary publics. In others, an individual must become a certified court reporter (CCR) by passing a state certification test. The National Court Reporters Association has several designated levels of certification that a court reporter can achieve, each connoting a higher level of experience and achievement.

Court reporters must continually study and practice their skills. Accuracy is of the utmost importance, and small mistakes can threaten future job opportunities. Because a court reporter must create a record of events as they occur, the ability to listen carefully and work quickly is key. Familiarity with legal terms and practices is necessary, as is a thorough knowledge of grammar, spelling, and vocabulary.

### Education and Training

At minimum a court reporter needs an associate's degree, although a bachelor's degree is more common. A bachelor's degree is useful because it can substitute for several years of work experience when the court reporter is attempting to obtain increasingly higher levels of certification.

In addition to general education, training programs are available at vocational or technical schools. There are 70 National Court Reporters Association–approved programs in the United States and Canada. These programs prepare future court reporters to work with the appropriate technology and meet the standards necessary for certification, such as the minimum 225-words-per-minute capture rate.

Sources: S. E. Lambert and D. Regan, "Court Reporter," in *Great Careers for Criminal Justice Majors* (New York: McGraw-Hill, 2001), pp. 159–161; "Court Reporters" (U.S. Department of Labor: Bureau of Labor Statistics), retrieved April 20, 2010, from www.bls.gov/oco/ocos152.htm.

---

expenses have increased. There is no single definition of ADR, but it typically refers to any means of settling disputes outside the courtroom.[26]

There are two common forms of ADR: arbitration and mediation.[27] **Arbitration** is a simplified version of a trial. There is no discovery and the rules of evidence are simplified. Either both sides select an arbitrator (other than a judge) or each selects one arbitrator and the two select a third to make up a panel of arbitrators. Arbitration hearings are relatively short, unlike trials, and the opinions are not made available to the public. Arbitration is often binding, which means that each side must abide by the arbitrator's decision.

Arbitration is governed by law at both the federal and state levels. Title 9 of the U.S. Code contains federal arbitration law. Nearly every state has adopted its own version of the 1956 Uniform Arbitration Act. The Act was revised in 2000 and adopted by 12 states. These laws generally make arbitration agreements and arbitrators' decisions enforceable by law. In 1970, the United States joined the United Nations Convention on the Recognition and Enforcement of Foreign Arbitral Awards, affirming this country's commitment to the process.

Arbitration can essentially amount to a mini-trial. Such mini-trials have been described as follows:

1. The parties negotiate a set of procedural ground rules (a protocol) that will govern the nonbinding mini-trial.

**arbitration**
A process of dispute resolution in which a neutral third party (arbitrator) renders a decision after a hearing at which both parties agree to be heard.

## PERSPECTIVES ON JUSTICE

### Restorative Justice

The use of mediation is one of the key components of the restorative justice perspective. By removing cases from the court setting, mediation is designed to be both a money-saving device and a forum in which conflicts can be solved in a nonadversarial manner.

2. The time for preparation is relatively short—between six weeks and three months—and the amount of discovery is relatively limited.

3. The hearing itself is sharply abbreviated—usually no more than two days.

4. The hearing is often conducted by a third-party neutral, typically called the "neutral adviser."

5. The case is presented to representatives of the parties with authority to settle; there is no judge or jury.

6. The lawyers present their "best" case; they do not have time to delve into side issues.

7. Immediately after the hearing, the party representatives meet privately to negotiate a settlement.

8. If they cannot reach a settlement, the neutral adviser may render an advisory opinion on how he thinks a judge would rule if the case were to go to court.

9. The proceedings are confidential: the parties generally commit themselves to refrain from disclosing details of the proceedings to any outsider.[28]

**mediation**
An informal dispute resolution process in which a neutral third party (mediator) helps disputing parties reach an agreement.

**Mediation** is an even less formal process than arbitration. Mediators are trained to help disputing parties come together to reach an agreement that is satisfactory to both. Unlike an arbitrator, the mediator has no power to impose a decision on the parties. For this reason, mediation is often used before arbitration. If an agreement cannot be reached, the parties may elect to pursue arbitration.

Still other forms of alternative dispute resolution have emerged. One, advocated by a U.S. district court judge, is a summary jury trial. In this type of trial, people from a real jury pool are selected and asked to decide a matter following a one-day trial. The jurors do not know until after their verdicts are rendered that they are not binding. The verdict gives the parties an impression of what would happen at a real trial, thus giving them an incentive to settle their differences with something less than a full trial. This technique has been used with some regularity at the federal level.

These approaches are more common in the civil context than in the criminal context. For example, many real estate purchase contracts require mediation before the parties can go forward with litigation. In contrast, the preferred (or at least the most common) method of resolving criminal matters is via the formal criminal process. Arbitration and mediation can be—and are—used to settle some criminal disputes, as an alternative to the criminal process.

**CourseMate** For more information about **alternative dispute resolution**, visit the Criminal Justice CourseMate at CengageBrain.com, then access the "Web Links" for this chapter.

## Selecting Judges

Many methods are used to select judges.[29] In some jurisdictions, the governor appoints judges. It is common for the governor's recommendations to be confirmed by the state senate, the governor's council, a special confirmation committee, an executive council elected by the state assembly, or an elected review board. Some states employ a judicial nominating commission that submits names to the governor for approval.

Another form of judicial selection is popular election. In some jurisdictions, judges run as members of the Republican, Democratic, or other parties; in others, they run without party affiliation. In eight states, partisan elections are used for selecting all general jurisdiction court judges.[30] In 20 states, nonpartisan elections are used.[31] A number of other states hold retention elections for judges who are appointed, usually a year or two after appointment. In some of these elections, judges run uncontested.[32] Altogether, about 90 percent of state trial judges face elections of some type and at some time during their tenure on the bench. Elections are less common in the higher-level state courts. Six states have partisan elections for intermediate appellate court judges, and seven states have partisan elections for supreme court justices.

**CourseMate** For more information about **judicial selection**, visit the Criminal Justice CourseMate at CengageBrain.com, then access the "Web Links" for this chapter.

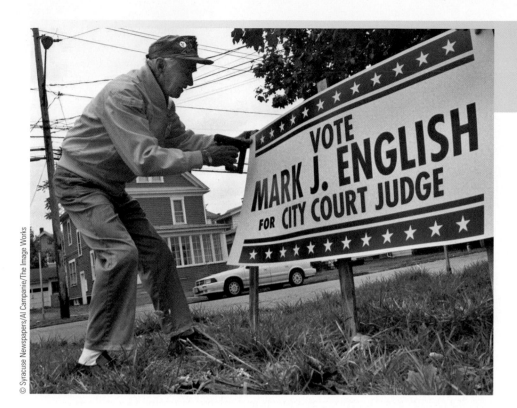

In many states, judges are selected by partisan elections, and campaigning is part of their routine. Here Cliff English, the father of city court candidate Mark J. English, posts a campaign sign for his son.

© Syracuse Newspapers/Al Campanie/The Image Works

Judicial elections are troubling to some because they involve partisan politics in a process to select people who must be nonpolitical and objective. The process itself has been tainted by charges of scandal—for example, when political parties insist that judicial candidates hire favored people or firms to run their campaigns or have them make contributions to the party to obtain an endorsement.[33]

To avoid this problem, a number of states have adopted some form of what is known as the **Missouri Plan** (a form of what has been called "merit selection") to select appellate court judges. This plan consists of three parts: (1) a judicial nominating commission to nominate candidates for the bench, (2) an elected official (usually from the executive branch) to make appointments from the list submitted by the commission, and (3) subsequent nonpartisan and noncompetitive elections in which incumbent judges run on their records and voters can choose either to retain or to dismiss them.[34]

**Missouri Plan**
A method of judicial selection that combines a judicial nominating commission, executive appointment, and nonpartisan confirmation elections.

The quality of the judiciary is a concern. Although merit plans, screening committees, and popular elections are designed to ensure a competent judiciary, it has often been charged that many judicial appointments are made to pay off political debts or to reward cronies and loyal friends. Also not uncommon are charges that those desiring to be nominated for judgeships are required to make significant political contributions. For a review of judicial selection, see Concept Summary 9.1.

## Judicial Decision Making

In an ideal world, judges would base their decisions only on the law and not let personal biases and preferences creep in. Unfortunately, the law is but one factor that appears to influence judges' decisions. Researchers have long found that judges' decisions are influenced by factors such as their ideology, their attitudes toward certain individuals, whether they face reelection, public opinion, and basic demographic characteristics, such as the judge's race or sex.[35] Much of the research has been focused on high-level judges, such as those in appellate and supreme courts.

**CONCEPT SUMMARY 9.1**

*Judicial Selection*

| Type | Process |
|---|---|
| Appointment | Governor selects a candidate, who is confirmed by state senate or other official body. |
| Election | Potential judge runs as partisan politician during regular election. |
| Missouri Plan | Bar committee searches for qualified candidates, governor chooses among them, and the judge runs for reappointment in a nonpartisan election. |

*ATTITUDES, IDEOLOGY, AND OPINIONS* Judges' decisions are influenced by the attitudes and ideology they bring to the bench. This is especially true of U.S. Supreme Court justices. The authors of one important study found that Supreme Court justices' ideology and beliefs were almost perfectly correlated with their decisions.[36] Judges' attitudes and ideology also appear to be shaped by public opinion. One study revealed that Supreme Court decisions aligned with public opinion polls about two-thirds of the time.[37] Other researchers have found strong correlations between people's attitudes on controversial subjects and related Supreme Court decisions.[38]

*DEMOGRAPHIC CHARACTERISTICS* Judges' sex and race may influence their decisions as well. For example, one study of state supreme court justices revealed that female justices voted in a more liberal direction.[39] Indeed, the very presence of a female on a state supreme court appears to influence the probability that male justices will decide liberally.[40] What about race? It is not clear that race is as influential as sex, but it matters to some extent.[41]

*REELECTION* If a judge is facing reelection, to what extent should this factor into his or her decision making? Research shows that election considerations do shape judicial decision making.[42] For example, judges hand down decisions that draw less attention to themselves during election time.[43] The author of another study found that during election time, "a justice will either vote with the majority or will mask his or her disagreement in a concurrence rather than a dissent."[44] Another team of researchers found that "all judges, even the most punitive, increase their sentences as reelection nears."[45] It appears, then, that judges' decisions are based a multitude of factors. The law may be only one of them.[46]

## COURT ADMINISTRATION AND MANAGEMENT

In addition to qualified personnel, the judicial system needs efficient management. Improved court administration may serve as a way to relieve court congestion. Management goals include improving organization and scheduling of cases, devising methods to allocate court resources efficiently, administering fines and monies due the court, preparing budgets, and overseeing personnel.

The federal courts have led the way in creating and organizing court administration. In 1939, Congress passed the Administrative Office Act, which established the Administrative Office of the United States Courts. Its director was charged with gathering statistics on the work of the federal courts and preparing the judicial budget for approval by the Conference of Senior Circuit Judges. One clause of the act created a judicial council with general supervisory responsibilities for the district and circuit courts.

Unlike the federal government, the states have experienced slow and uneven growth in the development and application of court management principles. The first state to establish an administrative office was North Dakota, in 1927. Today, all states employ some form of central administration. The federal government has encouraged the development of state court management through funding assistance to court managers. In addition, the federal judiciary has provided the philosophical impetus for better and more effective court management.

Despite the multitude of problems in reforming court management, some progress is being made. In most jurisdictions today, centralized court administrative services perform numerous functions with the help of sophisticated computers that free the judiciary to fulfill their roles as arbiters of justice.

## Technology and Court Management

Computers and technological advances are becoming staples in the administration and management of courts. Scores of technological advances have been made in areas of

- Case management
- Document management
- Electronic filing of cases
- Integrated justice information systems
- High-tech courtrooms
- Video technologies

Today, all states employ technology for a mix of court-related tasks and duties.[47] What are some other developing areas of court technology?

*CASE MANAGEMENT* In the 1970s, municipal courts installed tracking systems, which used databases to manage court data. These older systems were limited and could not process the complex interrelationships of information pertaining to persons, cases, time, and financial matters that occur in court cases.

*Many courtrooms throughout the country now make liberal use of technology to help prosecutors and defense attorneys to make their cases, judges to ensure that the law is applied properly, and jurors to make sense of the evidence presented. High-tech courts such as the one depicted here are still the exception, however.*

© The Center for Legal and Court Technology's McGlothlin Courtroom at William & Mary Law School

# CRIMINAL JUSTICE AND TECHNOLOGY

## *Using Virtual Reality in the Courtroom*

Just on the horizon is the use of virtual environments (VEs), immersive virtual environments (IVEs), and collaborative virtual environments (CVEs) in the courtroom. These processes employ digital computers to generate images that make possible real-time interaction between a user and the VE. In principle, people can interact with a VE in these modes: visual (by wearing head-mounted digital displays that project objects in the VE), auditory (by wearing earphones with which sounds seem to emanate from a specific point in space in the VE), haptic (by wearing gloves that use mechanical feedback or air blasts toward the hands when a person makes contact with an object in the VE), or olfactory (by wearing a nosepiece that releases different smells when a person approaches different objects in a VE). An IVE is one that perceptually surrounds the user of the system. It enables people to be at the center of the virtual world and to control movement, perception, and so on. An IVE in which numbers of people interact with one another inside the same virtual reality is a CVE.

Current software makes it quite easy to produce digital virtual worlds; consequently, digital VE simulations can be produced to fit almost any specific application effort. So in a courtroom, instead of using maps, charts, and cardboard cutouts, VEs are using computers. Attorneys could employ VEs for a number of tasks, including presenting evidence to the triers of fact (judge or jury) and preparing expert or nonexpert witnesses for the trial process.

VEs can be used to put the trier of fact in the position of the parties and the witnesses to the events surrounding the crime—for example, by recreating crime and accident scenes. Lawyers can create an extremely realistic presentation of the exact site where a crime or accident occurred, including inanimate objects from the scene; witnesses, victims, and suspects from the scene; atmospheric conditions from the scene, such as bright light or fog; background noise such as traffic sounds; and literally any sensory information. Currently, researchers are also exploring the use of IVEs as a mechanism to demonstrate witnesses' identification of suspects in lineups. The use of these technologies in identifying suspects improves on earlier technology by making it possible to gauge degrees of certainty and to better understand the subjective perspective of the witness.

### Critical Thinking

1. VE technology allows for people who are unable to attend the trial to provide useful testimony. Do you believe that virtual trials will someday be conducted, making the physical courtroom a thing of the past?

2. What constitutional principles conflict with the use of VE technology in the courtroom?

Sources: Jeremy Bailenson, Jim Blascovich, Andrew Beall, and Beth Noveck, "Courtroom Applications of Virtual Environments, Immersive Virtual Environments, and Collaborative Virtual Environments," *Law and Policy* 28 (2006): 249–270; Federal Judicial Center, www.fjc.gov/public/pdf.nsf/lookup/CTtech13.pdf/$file/CTtech13.pdf (accessed April 20, 2010).

Contemporary relational databases now provide the flexibility to handle complex case management. To help programmers define the multiplicity of relationships that occur in a court setting, the National Center for State Courts has developed a methodology for structuring a case management system that tracks a person to the case or cases in which he is a defendant, the scheduling of the cases to avoid any conflicts, and (of increasing importance) the fines that have been levied and the accounts to which the money goes. One of the more advanced current approaches to statewide court system automation has been undertaken by Wisconsin, which has developed and implemented an information system called the Circuit Court Automation Program (CCAP) used to improve day-to-day operations of courts, such as case records management and court calendaring, as well as jury selection and financial management.[48]

**COMMUNICATIONS** Court jurisdictions are cooperating with police departments in the installation of communications gear that allows defendants to be arraigned via closed-circuit television while they are in police custody.

Closed-circuit television has been used for judicial conferences and scheduling meetings. Courts are using voice-activated cameras to record all testimony during trials. These provide a convenient means of keeping a record of court proceedings without the need for a court reporter.

Many courts across the country now have videoconferencing capability, which is employed for juvenile detention hearings, expert witness testimony at trial, oral arguments on appeal, and parole hearings. Some courts are also using two-way live, televised remote linkups for first appearance and arraignment. In the usual arrangement, the defendant appears from a special location in the jail where he or she is able to see and hear and to be seen and heard by the presiding magistrate. Such appearances are now being authorized by state statute. Televised appearances minimize delays in prisoner transfer, effect large cost savings through the elimination of transportation and security costs, and reduce escape and assault risks.

**EVIDENCE PRESENTATION** Many high-tech courtrooms are now equipped for real-time transcription and translation, audio-video preservation of the court record, remote witness participation, computer graphics displays, television monitors for jurors, and computers for counsel and judge. For example, several courts have installed digital evidence presentation systems (DEPS). These systems permit counsel from both sides in a case to present evidence electronically to the jury. The DEPS used in the U.S. district court for the District of Utah can display several types of electronic evidence: documents, 3-D objects, photographs, x-rays, negatives, transparencies, and so on.[49]

**INTERNET RECORDS** The Internet has become increasingly involved in the court system. For example, virtual law libraries, including the federal government's J-Net, make it easier for judges and court personnel to receive important information in a timely fashion. The federal court's administrative office has begun sending official correspondence by email, a method that provides instantaneous communication of important information. In 1999, an automated library management system was developed, which meant that judges could access a Web-based virtual law library. An electronic network providing the public with access to court records and other information via the Internet was also implemented. In 2002, 11 federal courts announced that they would allow Internet access to criminal case files. This was the first time the public could gain access to such files. Such technological advances continue to be made.

The federal judiciary's Public Access to Court Electronic Records (PACER)[50] offers an inexpensive, fast, and comprehensive case information service to any individual with a personal computer and Internet access. The PACER system permits people to request information about a particular individual or case. The data is displayed instantly and is simple enough that little user training or documentation is required.

The accompanying Criminal Justice and Technology feature discusses innovative techniques that may be increasingly used in the courtrooms of the future.

**HIGH-TECH COURTS** Certain courts around the country have combined a number of the aforementioned technologies into single high-tech courts, or **e-courtrooms**.[51] These courts perform the same functions as any other court, but they integrate technology seamlessly into daily operations. One such court in the First Judicial District of Pennsylvania contains these features:

> **e-courtroom**
> A court that seamlessly integrates technology into its daily operations.

- A video evidence presentation system with distributed monitors, interactive plasma display, and touch-screen annotation at the podium and witness positions.

- The interactive display featuring a smart overlay mounted on a plasma screen, allowing the easy marking of digital evidence by a witness.

**CourseMate** For more information about **e-courtrooms**, visit the Criminal Justice CourseMate at CengageBrain.com, then access the "Web Links" for this chapter.

■ Touch screens at the witness stand and podium that allow a witness or attorney to easily mark digitally displayed evidence for all in the courtroom to see.

■ Document cameras at both the podium and witness locations to display physical evidence such as documents, pictures, X-rays, and slides.

■ A video player at the podium to display videotapes and DVDs.

■ Computer input connections at the podium, attorney tables, and judge's bench to display computer-generated and scanned materials to the courtroom.

■ A video printer that makes a picture-size representation of the displayed evidence for creating a record of all annotated materials. This does not replace the original material, but simply records its content.

■ A teleconference system that allows clear audio telephone communications for remote audio testimony.

■ A videoconferencing system for remote witness appearances from anywhere in the state, country, or world. Multiple TV cameras automatically switch to the speaker at various locations within the room and do not require any operator control.

■ Stenographic real-time transcription by a court reporter and digital audio recording for a comprehensive record of the proceedings.

■ Foreign-language interpretation transmission through an infrared emitter system, providing translation for all participants in a trial.

■ A sophisticated control system that facilitates simple user operation with a minimum of training.[52]

## Ethical Challenges in Criminal Justice: A Writing Assignment

Judge Eli Sampson, a Republican, has run unopposed—in a largely conservative county—during several past elections. Now he is facing stiff competition from a popular and vocal Democratic rival who seems to have come out of nowhere. In an effort to appeal to his conservative base, Sampson's new campaign slogan is "Tougher than Tough on Crime." His election signs and banners carry the phrase prominently. During debates with his opponent, he repeatedly announces his intentions to "get tough" with criminals, lock up law-breakers, and put them behind bars.

Write an essay on the ethics of Sampson's approach. In doing so, answer these questions: Is it ethical for judicial candidates to run on partisan political platforms? It is most certainly legal in certain jurisdictions, but should it be allowed? What are the possible problems associated with allowing judicial candidates to align themselves with specific political parties? Could party affiliations influence the decision making of these who end up getting elected to the bench? See this chapter's "Selecting Judges" and "Judicial Decision Making" sections for guidance.

## SUMMARY

**1. Understand state court structure.**

■ Each state court system is different.

■ Common state courts include limited jurisdiction courts, general jurisdiction courts, and appellate courts.

■ Each state has at least one court of last resort, usually called a state supreme court.

■ Many states have implemented specialized limited jurisdiction courts, including drug courts, domestic violence courts, mental health courts, and others.

**2. Know the differences between limited and general jurisdiction courts.**

■ Limited jurisdiction courts have jurisdiction over minor or less serious civil and criminal cases.

■ General jurisdiction courts handle the more serious felony cases (e.g., murder, rape, robbery) and civil cases where damages are over a specified amount, such as $10,000.

**3. Recognize the function of the state appellate court system.**

■ State appellate courts (including supreme courts) decide whether the law was properly interpreted or applied during a trial.

■ State appellate courts review decisions by trial courts and administrative agencies before they reach the supreme court stage.

**4. Explain the various levels of federal courts.**

■ There are three levels of courts in the federal system: U.S. district courts, U.S. courts of appeal, and the U.S. Supreme Court.

■ The U.S. district courts are the trial courts of the federal system.

■ The 12 U.S. courts of appeals, sometimes referred to as U.S. circuit courts, are empowered to review federal and state appellate court cases on substantive and procedural issues involving rights guaranteed by the Constitution.

■ The U.S. Supreme Court is the nation's highest appellate body and the court of last resort for all cases tried in the various federal and state courts.

**5. Describe how a case gets to the U.S. Supreme Court.**

■ Most cases that come before the Supreme Court involve significant federal questions, usually of a constitutional nature.

■ When the Supreme Court decides to hear a case, it grants a writ of certiorari, requesting a transcript of the proceedings of the case for review.

■ For a writ to be granted, ordinarily four justices must agree to hear the case. This is known as the rule of four.

**6. Know the problems associated with court congestion.**

■ State court systems now handle about 100 million new cases annually. This has led to significant delay and congestion in the courts.

■ Congestion is time-consuming and costly, and delay can threaten the Sixth Amendment right to a speedy trial.

**7. Discuss the duties of a judge.**

■ The judge is the senior officer in a court of law, who is authorized to hear and decide cases.

■ During trials, the judge rules on the appropriateness of conduct, settles questions of evidence and procedure, and guides the questioning of witnesses.

■ In a jury trial, the judge must instruct jurors on which evidence is proper to examine and which should be ignored.

■ The judge also formally charges the jury by instructing jurors on what points of law and evidence they must consider to reach a verdict of either guilty or not guilty.

■ If a defendant is found guilty, the judge must decide on the sentence.

**8. Discuss the qualifications of a judge.**

■ Typically, a judge must be a resident of the state, licensed to practice law, a member of the state bar association, and at least 25 and less than 70 years of age.

■ Almost every state requires judges to have a law degree if they are to serve on appellate courts or courts of general jurisdiction.

■ Some municipal or town court judges do not need law degrees.

**9. Explain the different types of judicial alternatives.**

■ Alternative dispute resolution (ADR) is a judicial alternative.

■ Arbitration, a type of ADR, is a process of dispute resolution in which a neutral third party (arbitrator) renders a decision following a hearing at which both parties agree to be heard.

■ Mediation, another type of ADR, is an informal dispute resolution process in which a neutral third party (mediator) helps disputing parties reach an agreement.

■ Mediation usually comes before arbitration.

■ Arbitration is usually binding; mediation is not.

**10. Summarize the different ways of selecting judges.**

■ In some jurisdictions, the governor appoints judges.

■ Another form of judicial selection is popular election.

■ The Missouri Plan, another means of selecting judges, consists of three parts: (1) a judicial nominating commission nominates candidates for the bench, (2) an elected official makes the appointment, and (3) retention elections are held.

11. **Identify factors associated with judicial decision making.**

   ■ Researchers have found that in addition to legal considerations, judges base their decisions on ideology, their attitudes toward certain individuals, whether they face reelection, public attitudes, and basic demographic characteristics, such as the judge's race or sex.

12. **Explain how technology is changing the process of court administration and management.**

   ■ Improved court administration may serve as a way to relieve court congestion.

   ■ Computers and technological advances are becoming staples in the administration and management of courts.

   ■ Today, all states employ technology for a mix of court-related tasks and duties.

## KEY TERMS

plea negotiations/plea bargaining, 328
court of limited jurisdiction, 329
specialized court, 329
court of general jurisdiction, 329
appellate court, 332
U.S. district court, 333

U.S. Court of Appeals, 337
U.S. Supreme Court, 338
court of last resort, 338
writ of certiorari, 339
rule of four, 339
judge, 343
alternative dispute resolution, 346

arbitration, 347
mediation, 348
Missouri Plan, 349
e-courtroom, 353

## CRITICAL THINKING QUESTIONS

1. What are the benefits and drawbacks of selecting judges through popular elections? Can a judge who considers herself or himself a Republican or a Democrat render fair and impartial justice?

2. Should more specialized courts be created and, if so, for what?

3. Should all judges be trained as attorneys? If not, what other professions are suitable for consideration?

4. Should a defendant have to be present in the courtroom, or would a virtual courtroom suffice? What about witnesses?

5. What is the Missouri Plan? Do you consider it an ideal way to select judges?

6. The Judiciary Act of 1869 increased the U.S. Supreme Court membership to nine. The judicial workload in the aftermath of the Civil War proved to be more than the seven sitting justices could handle. Considering that the population is now over 300 million, do you think the number of justices should be increased again?

## NOTES

1. *District Attorney's Office v. Osborne*, No. 08-6 (2009).
2. Matthew Durose and Patrick A. Langan, *State Court Sentencing of Convicted Felons, 2002* (Washington, D.C.: Bureau of Justice Statistics, 2005).
3. Kristy Vosky, "State Budget Cuts to Hit Court System Hard," www.wjhg.com/home/headlines/18685719.html (accessed April 20, 2010).
4. Thomas Henderson, *The Significance of Judicial Structure: The Effect of Unification on Trial Court Operations* (Washington, D.C.: National Institute of Justice, 1984).
5. Michael J. Friedman, *Outline of the U.S. Legal System* (Washington, D.C.: U.S. State Department, 2004).
6. David B. Rottman and Shauna M. Strickland, *State Court Organization, 2004* (Arlington, Va.: National Center for State Courts, 2006), p. 9.
7. Robert LaFountain, Richard Schauffler, Shauna Strickland, William Raftery, and Chantal Bromage, *Examining the Work of State Courts, 2006* (Arlington, Va.: National Center for State Courts, 2007), pp. 69–71.
8. Ibid., p. 11.
9. U.S. Constitution, Article 3, Sections 1 and 2.
10. 1 Wharton 304, 4 L.Ed. 97 (1816).
11. Frank R. Baumgartner and Bryan D. Jones, *Policy Dynamics* (Chicago: University of Chicago Press, 2002), p. 272.
12. Robert C. LaFountain, Richard Y. Schauffler, Shauna M. Strickland, Chantal G. Bromage, Sarah A. Gibson, Ashley N. Mason, and William E. Rafferty, *Examining the Work of State Courts: A National Perspective from the Court Statistics Project* (Alexandria, Va.: National Center for State Courts, 2009), p. 2.
13. Administrative Office of the United States Courts, *Annual Report of the Director, 2009* (Washington, D.C.: Administrative Office of the United States Courts, 2009), http://www.uscourts.gov/judbus2009/contents.cfm (accessed April 21, 2010).
14. Ibid.
15. Hans Zeisel, Harry Kalven, Jr., and Bernard Buckholz, *Delay in the Court* (Boston: Little, Brown, 1959); for more recent information, see the National Center for State Court's Caseflow Management Resource Guide, http://www.ncsconline.org/WC/CourTopics/ResourceGuide.asp?topic=CasMan (accessed April 20, 2010).
16. Jason Perez-Dormitzer, "Bill Safeguards Restaurants in Obesity-Related Lawsuits," *Providence Business News*, March 22, 2004, pp. 5–7.
17. Maureen Solomon and Douglas Somerlot, *Caseflow Management in the Trial Court: Now and for the Future* (Chicago: American

Bar Association, 1987); Pamela Casey, "Defining Optimal Court Performance: The Trial Court Performance Standards," *Court Review* (Winter 1998): 24–33.

18. David Klein and Robert Hume, "Fear of Reversal as an Explanation of Lower Court Compliance," *Law and Society Review* 37 (2003): 579–607.

19. Huey-Tsyh Chen, "Dropping In and Dropping Out: Judicial Decisionmaking in the Disposition of Felony Arrests," *Journal of Criminal Justice* 19 (1991): 1–17

20. Starting salaries at New York City firms can be found at www.infirmation.com/shared/search/payscale-compare.tcl?city=New%20York (accessed April 20, 2010). For New York judicial salaries, see http://contentdm.ncsconline.org/cgi-bin/showfile.exe?CISOROOT=/judicial&CISOPTR=84 (accessed April 20, 2010).

21. American Bar Association, Judicial Division, http://new.abanet.org/divisions/Judicial/ncstj/Pages/default.aspx (accessed April 20, 2010).

22. Public Law 90-578, Title I, Sec. 101, 82 Stat. 1113 (1968), amended; Public Law 94-577, Sec. 1, Stat. 2729 (1976); Public Law 96-82, Sec. 2, 93 Stat. 643 (1979).

23. See, generally, Carroll Seron, "The Professional Project of Parajudges: The Case of U.S. Magistrates," *Law and Society Review* 22 (1988): 557–575.

24. Alex Aikman, "Volunteer Lawyer–Judges Bolster Court Resources," *NIJ Report* (January 1986): 2–6.

25. David C. Nixon and J. David Haskin, "Judicial Retirement Strategies," *American Politics Research* 28 (2000): 458–489.

26. Legal Information Institute, http://topics.law.cornell.edu/wex/adr (accessed May 23, 2008).

27. Elena Nosyreva, "Alternative Dispute Resolution in the United States and Russia: A Comparative Evaluation," *Annual Survey of International and Comparative Law* 7 (2001): 7–19.

28. Jethro K. Lieberman and James F. Henry, "Lessons from the Alternative Dispute Resolution Movement," *University of Chicago Law Review* 53 (1986): 424–439.

29. American Bar Association, *Fact Sheet on Judicial Selection Methods in the States*, www.abanet.org/leadership/fact_sheet.pdf (accessed April 20, 2010).

30. Ibid.

31. Ibid.

32. Ibid.

33. Daniel Wise, "Making a Criminal Case over Selection of Judges in Brooklyn," *New York Law Journal* (July 23, 2003): 1.

34. Sari Escovitz with Fred Kurland and Nan Gold, *Judicial Selection and Tenure* (Chicago: American Judicature Society, 1974), pp. 3–16.

35. Lawrence Baum, *The Puzzle of Judicial Behavior* (Ann Arbor: University of Michigan Press, 1998).

36. Jeffrey Segal and Albert Cover, "Ideological Values and the Votes of U.S. Supreme Court Justices," *American Political Science Review* 83 (1989): 557–565.

37. Thomas R. Marshall, *Public Opinion and the Supreme Court* (Boston: Unwin Hyman, 1989).

38. William Mishler and Reginald Sheehan, "The Supreme Court as a Counter-Majoritarian Institution? The Impact of Public Opinion on Supreme Court Decisions," *American Journal of Political Science* 41 (1997): 122–149.

39. Donald R. Songer and Kelley A. Crews-Meyer, "Does Judge Gender Matter? Decision Making in State Supreme Courts," *Social Science Inquiry* 81 (2000): 750–762.

40. Ibid.

41. Cassia Spohn, "Sentencing Decisions of Black and White Judges: Expected and Unexpected Similarities," *Law and Society Review* 24 (1990): 1197–1216.

42. Adam Liptak, "Rendering Justice, with One Eye on Re-election," *New York Times*, May 25, 2008, www.nytimes.com/2008/05/25/us/25exception.html (accessed April 20, 2010).

43. Melinda G. Hall, "Electoral Politics and Strategic Voting in State Supreme Courts," *Journal of Politics* 52 (1992): 427–446.

44. Melinda G. Hall, "Constituent Influence in State Supreme Courts: Conceptual Notes and a Case Study," *Journal of Politics* 49 (1987): 1117–1124, at 1119.

45. Gregory A. Huber and Sanford C. Gordon, "Accountability and Coercion: Is Justice Blind When It Runs for Office?" *American Journal of Political Science* 48 (2004): 247–263, at 258.

46. Howard Gillman, "What's Law Got to Do with It? Judicial Behavioralists Test the 'Legal Model' of Judicial Decision Making," *Law and Social Inquiry* 26 (2001): 465–504.

47. National Center for State Courts, www.ncsconline.org/D_Tech/ (accessed April 20, 2010).

48. Wisconsin Circuit Court Access (WCCA), "Access to the Public Records of the Consolidated Court Automation Programs (CCAP)," http://wcca.wicourts.gov (accessed April 20, 2010).

49. United States District Court for the District of Utah, www.utd.uscourts.gov/documents/depspage.html (accessed April 20, 2010).

50. PACER Service Center, http://pacer.psc.uscourts.gov/ (accessed April 20, 2010).

51. James E. McMillan, "E-Courts: The Times They Are a-Changin'," *Court Review* 42 (2006): 41–42.

52. First Judicial District of Pennsylvania, http://courts.phila.gov/pdf/brochures/625-fact-sheet.pdf (accessed April 20, 2010).

# CHAPTER 10

# The Prosecution and the Defense

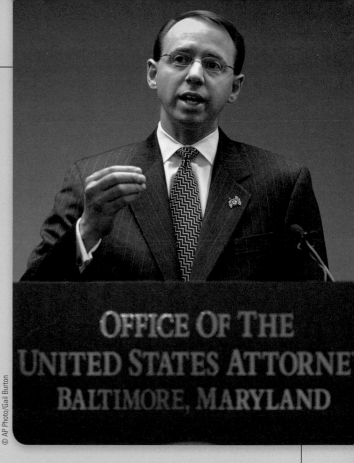

OFFICE OF THE
UNITED STATES ATTORNE
BALTIMORE, MARYLAND

**I**n 2008, police raided George Hayward's Baltimore house and found 1,024 pictures and nearly 200 videos of child pornography on his computer. Hayward was charged in federal court with multiple counts of sexual abuse of a minor, child rape, and sex offenses related to taking pictures and videos of naked children, some as young as 5 years old. He was convicted and, at age 72, sentenced to 20 years in federal prison, effectively a life sentence. But Maryland U.S. attorney Rod Rosenstein (the chief federal prosecutor for that jurisdiction, pictured here) did not stop there. He also took Hayward's house, which he was authorized to do under federal forfeiture laws.

State and federal forfeiture statutes authorize law enforcement officials to seize and then assume ownership of property derived from or used to facilitate various crimes. Forfeiture has historically been used to target drug offenders' property, but it is increasingly being used against other types of offenders. In an effort to send a message to pedophiles, Rosenstein felt that it was necessary to do more than just sentence Hayward to prison. If offenders come to realize that their property can be taken, presumably they will be less inclined to break the law. As of this writing, the house is on the market for $289,500. The proceeds from the sale will go to the federal government, and most of the money will be used for law enforcement purposes. ∎

The traditional image of a prosecutor is that of a hard-charging litigator who argues cases in criminal court. The Hayward case, however, highlights some lesser-known aspects of prosecution in America. First, prosecutors have at their disposal more than just the usual criminal law. Forfeiture statutes—at the federal and state levels—help them go after offenders' assets, hitting them in their pocketbooks. Second, this case highlights some of the out-of-the-box thinking that prosecutors need to engage in to combat crime effectively. It is not always sufficient (nor, in some cases, is it desirable) to seek prison sentences. Forfeiture is an extreme measure reserved for fairly egregious types of criminal behavior, but prosecutors can also seek other alternatives besides the usual "criminal charge" for other varieties of lawbreaking. Prosecutors are all too aware of the "revolving door" problem in criminal justice and are increasingly embarking on creative initiatives in their efforts to fight crime.

# THE PROSECUTOR

**prosecutor**
An appointed or elected member of the practicing bar who is responsible for bringing the state's case against the accused.

The prosecutor is one of the two adversaries who face each other every day in the criminal trial process: the **prosecutor**, who represents the state's interest and serves as the "people's attorney," and the defense attorney, who represents the accused. Although the judge manages the trial process, ensuring that the rules of evidence are obeyed, the prosecution and defense attorneys control the substance of the criminal process. They share the goal and burden of protecting the civil rights of the criminal defendant while they conduct the trial process in a fair and even-handed manner, a difficult task in the current era of vast media coverage and national fascination with high-profile cases.

Depending on the level of government and the jurisdiction in which the prosecutor functions, he or she may be known as a district attorney, a county attorney, a state's attorney, or a U.S. attorney. Whatever the title, the prosecutor is ordinarily a member of the practicing bar who has been appointed or elected to be a public prosecutor responsible for bringing the state's case against the accused. He focuses the power of the state on those who disobey the law by charging them with a crime and eventually bringing them to trial or, conversely, releasing them after deciding that the evidence at hand does not constitute proof of a crime.

**CourseMate** For more information about **standards for prosecution and defense**, visit the Criminal Justice CourseMate at CengageBrain.com, then access the "Web Links" for this chapter.

Although the prosecutor's primary duty is to enforce the criminal law, his fundamental obligation as an attorney is to seek justice as well as convict those who are guilty. If, for example, the prosecutor discovers facts suggesting that the accused is innocent, he must bring this information to the attention of the court.[1] The American Bar Association's *Model Code of Professional Responsibility* requires that prosecutors never bring false or unsupported charges and that they disclose all relevant evidence to the defense.

**CourseMate** For more information about ABA's *Model Code of Professional Responsibility*, visit the Criminal Justice CourseMate at CengageBrain.com, then access the "Web Links" for this chapter.

The senior prosecutor must make policy decisions on the exercise of prosecutorial enforcement powers in a wide range of cases in criminal law, consumer protection, housing, and other areas. In so doing, the prosecutor determines and ultimately shapes the manner in which justice is exercised in society.[2] Although these decisions should be rendered in a fair and objective manner, the prosecutor remains a political figure who has a party affiliation, a constituency of voters and supporters, and a need to respond to community pressures and interest groups.

The political nature of the prosecutor's office can heavily influence decision making. When deciding whether, when, and how to handle a case, the prosecutor cannot forget that he may be up for election soon and may have to answer to an electorate that will scrutinize those decisions. In a murder trial involving a highly charged issue such as child killing, the prosecutor's decision to ask for the death penalty may hinge on his perception of the public's will. Individual prosecutors are often caught between being compelled by their supervisors to do everything

**EXHIBIT 10.1**

## *Prosecutorial Duties*

1. Investigating possible violations of the law
2. Cooperating with police in investigating a crime
3. Determining what the charge will be
4. Interviewing witnesses in criminal cases
5. Reviewing applications for arrest warrants and search warrants
6. Subpoenaing witnesses
7. Representing the government in pretrial hearings and in motion procedures
8. Entering into plea-bargaining negotiations
9. Trying criminal cases
10. Recommending sentences to courts upon conviction
11. Representing the government in appeals

possible to obtain a guilty verdict and acting as a concerned public official to ensure that justice is done.

Today, there are more than 2,300 state court prosecutors' offices employing more than 79,000 attorneys, investigators, and support staff.[3] This represents a 39 percent increase from 1992 and a 13 percent increase from 1996. Most of these offices are relatively small. Half employ nine or fewer people and have a budget of about $300,000 or less.

## Duties of the Prosecutor

The prosecutor is the chief law enforcement officer of a particular jurisdiction. His or her participation spans the entire gamut of the justice system, from the time that search and arrest warrants are issued or a grand jury is impaneled to the final sentencing decision and appeal (Exhibit 10.1). General duties of a prosecutor include enforcing the law, representing the government, maintaining proper standards of conduct as an attorney and court officer, developing programs and legislation for law and criminal justice reform, and being a public spokesperson for the field of law. Of these, representing the government while presenting the state's case to the court is the prosecutor's central activity.

At any given time, prosecutors' offices may be involved in targeting specific types of crime (besides the usual violent and property offenses) that have been particularly difficult to deal with. The following subsections briefly outline some of the leading areas where prosecutors' offices have concentrated their energies recently. Some of the crime problems have become so serious that the American Prosecutors Research Institute has begun to research and identify strategies to deal with them. The institute has shared its findings with prosecutors' offices around the country, at all levels of government.

**CourseMate** For more information about **current research on prosecutorial issues**, visit the Criminal Justice CourseMate at CengageBrain.com, then access the "Web Links" for this chapter.

***CHILD ABUSE AND EXPLOITATION*** Child abuse and exploitation, including work exploitation, has become a serious problem. The Department of Health and Human Services estimates that in any given year, nearly 1,000,000 children are victims of some form of abuse, neglect, or exploitation—in the United States alone.[4] Researchers at the American Prosecutors Research Institute have offered several recommendations for prosecutors who find themselves investigating child abuse cases, including:

■ Limit the number of prosecutors who investigate and prosecute such cases (those who are well versed in and familiar with such cases).

■ Involve the prosecutor early in the case.

■ Set up one or more child-friendly interview rooms. For example, a sketch board and anatomical dolls should be available.

■ Interviewers should be trained in the art/science of questioning possible victims of child abuse.[5]

# EVIDENCE-BASED JUSTICE

## No-Drop Prosecution

Throughout the 1980s and 1990s, prosecutors were faced with a high rate of dismissals in domestic violence cases. The key problem was that victims often refused to participate in the process and testify against their abusers. It sometimes proved difficult for prosecutors to secure convictions without the testimony from victims. In response to this problem, some jurisdictions enacted so-called "no-drop prosecution" policies, which are also referred to as "evidence-based" prosecution. These policies *require* prosecutors to bring charges against domestic abusers regardless of whether the victim participates. Calling them evidence-based means that if there is enough evidence (such as police reports and accounts of witnesses), then the prosecutor will bring charges even without the victim's testimony. No-drop prosecution policies have since "caught on," but do they work? Unfortunately, the evidence is not encouraging.

In a recent evaluation, researchers compared the rearrest rates of abusers in two different jurisdictions in New York: the Bronx and Brooklyn. In the Bronx, domestic violence cases are usually not pursued if the victim does not wish to participate. In Brooklyn, the opposite is true; if there is an arrest, charges are filed, regardless of the victim's wishes. After following defendants for six months, the researchers found basically no difference in rearrest rates. They cautiously concluded that no-drop prosecution does not lead to dramatic reductions in arrest patterns among offenders, and it is important to note that there is not much research in this area because the strategy is relatively new. The researchers *did* find that victims offered some support for evidence-based prosecution because it put the onus for taking a case forward on the prosecutor, not the victim: "Many of those who preferred that their cases not be prosecuted would not have minded if the prosecution proceeded without them; they wanted to avoid confronting the abusers in court and were wary of assuming the responsibility for ensuring that the abusers experienced penalties for their crimes."

Sources: Robert C. Davis, Chris S. O'Sullivan, Donald J. Farole Jr., and Michael Rempel, "A Comparison of Two Prosecution Policies in Cases of Intimate Partner Violence: Mandatory Case Filing versus Following the Victim's Lead," *Criminology and Public Policy* 7(2008): 633–662, quote from p. 658; see also John L. Worrall, *Crime Control in America: What Works?* 2nd ed. (Boston, Mass.: Allyn and Bacon, 2008), pp. 110–111.

**GUN VIOLENCE PROSECUTION** In 2001, President George W. Bush announced Project Safe Neighborhoods (PSN), a gun violence prosecution program that teamed U.S. attorneys' offices with their local counterparts.[6] All federal districts have since created PSN task forces to combat gun violence through aggressive enforcement of federal antigun laws, collaboration, media campaigns, and other strategies. Recent PSN evaluations suggest that such collaborative efforts between federal and local officials can help make significant dents in gun violence, sometimes reducing it as much as 50 percent.[7]

**WHITE-COLLAR CRIME** Well-publicized corporate scandals involving billion-dollar companies such as Enron and WorldCom may be prompting prosecutorial action. In a national survey of prosecutorial practices, Michael Benson and his colleagues found an apparent increase in local prosecution of corporate offenders.[8] According to their research, the federal government historically played a dominant role in controlling white-collar crime, but an increased willingness to prosecute corporate misconduct is evident on a local level if an offense causes substantial harm.

**HIGH-TECH CRIMES** The federal government operates a number of organizations that coordinate efforts to prosecute high-tech crime, including cyber crime. For example, the U.S. Justice Department's Internet Fraud Division brings together representatives of numerous U.S. attorneys' offices and

**CourseMate** For more information about combating **Internet fraud**, visit the Criminal Justice CourseMate at CengageBrain.com, then access the "Web Links" for this chapter.

other law enforcement and regulatory agencies to share information about trends and patterns in Internet fraud schemes and open the door for prosecutions. Because cyber crime is so new, existing laws are sometimes inadequate to address the problem. The Identity Theft and Assumption Act of 1998 was created to help control this emerging form of crime.[9]

***ENVIRONMENTAL CRIMES*** Environmental crime prosecution—a field that mixes elements of law, public health, and science—has also emerged as a new area of specialization. Not only federal prosecutions but also local environmental crime prosecutions have increased dramatically.[10] Approximately half of all U.S. jurisdictions operate special environmental units.

The most common environmental offenses being prosecuted are related to waste disposal. Such cases, often involving the illegal disposal of hazardous wastes, are referred to the prosecutor by local law enforcement and environmental regulatory agencies. The two most important factors in deciding to prosecute these crimes are the degree of harm posed by the offense and the criminal intent of the offender. If the prosecutor decides not to prosecute, it is usually because of a lack of evidence or problems with evidentiary standards and the use of expert witnesses.

***DOMESTIC VIOLENCE*** Another area of priority prosecutions in many jurisdictions is violence against women. For example, bringing the perpetrators of domestic violence to justice has been difficult for prosecutors over the years. Victims do not always want to participate and testify against their abusers, which makes it hard for prosecutors to secure convictions. Increasing attention to this

© AP Photo/Kathy Willens

*Disgraced financier Bernard Madoff leaves U.S. district court after a bail hearing in New York on January 5, 2009. Prosecutors argued that Madoff violated bail conditions by mailing about $1 million worth of jewelry and other assets to relatives and consequently should be jailed without bail.*

© AP Photo/Sara D. Davis

*Crystal Mangum, the alleged victim in the Duke lacrosse rape case, addresses the media during a press conference on the release of Mangum's forthcoming book* The Last Dance for Grace: The Crystal Mangum Story, *while her publisher and coauthor Vincent Clark watches. Mangum, who North Carolina prosecutors determined falsely accused three Duke lacrosse players of raping her at a team party, maintains in her new memoir that she was attacked.*

*Assistant prosecutors conduct investigations into activities that endanger the public health. Although such activities typically involve environmental crimes, this is not always the case. Here Brooklyn, New York, Assistant District Attorney Josh Hanshaft holds a photograph of an X-ray showing the pelvic area of a deceased person with PVC plumbing pipe inserted where bones should have been. This news conference announced the indictment of four individuals, including Michael Mastromarino, head of Biomedical Tissue Services. Mastromarino was convicted in June 2008 of taking body parts from deceased individuals (some of these body parts were diseased) and selling them for profit. He was sentenced to 18 to 54 years in prison. On the table are pieces of PVC piping, illustrating the type of material used to replace bone in cadavers that were looted for body parts.*

problem has resulted in a range of innovate strategies, one of which is described in the accompanying Evidence-Based Justice feature.

*RAPE AND SEXUAL ASSAULT* Local prosecutors' handling of rape crimes continues to undergo changes. In the 1980s, most states imposed a heavy burden on rape victims, such as prompt reporting of the crime to police, corroboration by witnesses, and the need to prove physical resistance. In recent years, many states have removed these restrictions and have also made the victims' sexual history inadmissible as evidence at trial. In addition, the definition of rape has been expanded to include other forms of penetration of the person, and laws now exist making the rape of a woman by her husband a crime. Other areas in which the justice system is expanding its sexual assault prosecution capabilities are the following: more vigorous prosecution of acquaintance rape, testing of defendants for the AIDS virus and for DNA profiling, and improved coordination among police, prosecutors, rape crisis centers, and hospitals.[11]

*PUBLIC HEALTH* Prosecutors have also assumed the role of protector of the public health.[12] They are responsible for such areas as prosecution of physician-assisted suicide, cases in which AIDS transmission is used as a weapon, violence against the elderly, cases in which pregnant women are known drug abusers, and health care fraud cases. Prosecutors are paying special attention to the illegal practices of physicians and other health care professionals who abuse their position of trust. One health-related prosecution that made recent headlines involved a dentist named Michael Mastromarino and three other men who were charged with running a multimillion-dollar body-snatching business. They looted bones and tissue from more than a thousand corpses and sold the body parts to legitimate companies that supplied hospitals around the United States. The tainted tissue was used in such procedures as joint and heart-valve replacements, back surgery, dental implants, and skin grafts.[13]

*TERRORISM* As we will see in detail in Chapter 18, terrorism has altered the criminal justice landscape in a number of respects. Prosecutors have been put in the somewhat difficult position of being forced to respond to a problem that almost never occurs. That is, there have been very few terrorism prosecutions compared to the number of prosecutions for traditional types of crime because terrorist attacks—in this country—are exceptionally uncommon. Not only is terrorism rare, but successful prosecutions are difficult because the resulting attacks often result in the death (suicide) of the suspect. This has forced prosecutors to get creative in their pursuits, for example, by engaging in what is known as "anticipatory prosecution," or prosecuting would-be terrorists because they may soon offend.[14] Other prosecutors have resorted to enforcing statutes that have been rarely used in the past, including those prohibiting mail fraud, obstruction of justice, and racketeering, among others.[15]

## Types of Prosecutors

In the federal system, **United States attorneys** serve as the nation's principal litigators and are appointed by the president. Their subordinates, assistant United States attorneys, are tasked with, among other duties, prosecuting criminal defendants in federal district court. The appointed United States attorney is usually an administrator, whereas assistants normally handle the preparation and trial work. Federal prosecutors are professional civil service employees with reasonable salaries and job security.

At the state and county levels, the **attorney general** and the **district attorney**, respectively, are the chief prosecutorial officers. Again, the bulk of the criminal prosecution and staff work is performed by scores of full-time and part-time attorneys, police investigators, and clerical personnel. Most attorneys who work for prosecutors on the state and county levels are political appointees who earn low salaries, handle many cases, and in some jurisdictions maintain private law practices. Many young lawyers take these staff positions to gain the trial experience that will qualify them for better opportunities. In most state, county, and municipal jurisdictions, however, the attorneys working within the office of the prosecutor can be described as having the proper standards of professional skill and personal integrity.

In urban jurisdictions, the structure of the district attorney's office is often specialized, with separate divisions for felonies, misdemeanors, and trial and appeal assignments. In rural offices, chief prosecutors handle many of the

**United States attorneys**
The nation's principal (federal) litigators, appointed by the president. Assistant United States attorneys are tasked with, among other duties, prosecuting criminal defendants in federal court.

**attorney general**
The chief legal officer and prosecutor of each state and of the United States.

**district attorney**
The county prosecutor who is charged with bringing offenders to justice and enforcing the criminal laws of the state.

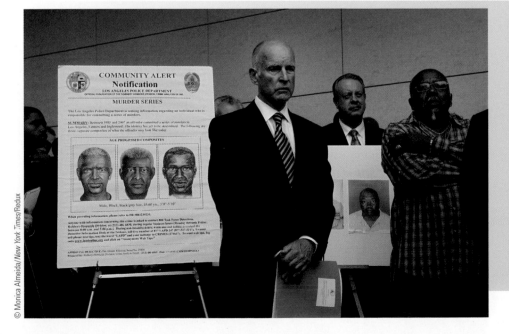

California Attorney General Jerry Brown, left, appears during a press conference held in Los Angeles on July 8, 2010, to discuss the arrest of Lonnie David Franklin Jr., 57. Franklin, dubbed the "grim sleeper" because he apparently took a 14-year break from his crimes, was charged with ten counts of murder for his alleged involvement in a string of southern California slayings. Police determined that DNA left on the victims and DNA from Franklin's son Christopher, who had once been convicted on a felony weapons charge, were sufficiently similar to conclude that the perpetrator was probably one of Christopher's relatives. Only two states, Colorado and California, permit these controversial "familial" DNA searches.

© Monica Almeida/New York Times/Redux

**FIGURE 10.1**
County District Attorney's Office

criminal cases themselves. When assistant prosecutors are employed in such areas, they often work part-time, have limited professional opportunities, and depend on the political patronage of chief prosecutors for their positions. See Figure 10.1 for an organizational chart of a county district attorney's office.

## The Prosecutor within Society

Prosecutors are routinely criticized for bargaining justice away, for using their positions as a stepping-stone to higher political office, and for failing to investigate (or simply dismissing) criminal cases.

In response to these criticisms, during the past decade local, state, and federal prosecutors have become extremely aggressive in attacking particular crime problems. Federal prosecutors have made extraordinary progress in the war against insider trading and securities fraud on Wall Street, using information, wiretaps, and the federal racketeering laws. Some commentators now argue that the government may be going overboard in its efforts to punish white-collar criminals, especially for crimes that are the result of negligent business practices, not intentional criminal conspiracy.[16] Both fines and penalties have been increasing. And even such notorious white-collar criminals as Tyco's Dennis Kozlowski (8 to 25 years in prison) and WorldCom's Bernie Ebbers (a 25-year sentence) have received sympathy because of the severity of their criminal sentences.[17]

In addition, prosecutors are now sharpening their working relationships with both the law enforcement community and the general public. These relationships are key to greater prosecutorial effectiveness.

*PROSECUTORS AND LAW ENFORCEMENT* One of the most important of the prosecutor's many functions involves the relationship between the prosecutor and law enforcement agents. When it comes to processing everyday offenses and minor crimes, the prosecutor often relies on law enforcement officers to provide and initiate the formal complaint. With more serious offenses, such as some felonies, the prosecutor's office may become directly involved in the criminal investigation. Some district attorneys' offices carry out special investigations of organized crime, corruption of public officials, and corporate and white-collar crime, as well as vice and drug offenses. Much of the investigative work is handled by police personnel directly assigned to the prosecutor.

Police and prosecutorial relationships vary from one jurisdiction to another and often depend on whether the police agency is supplying the charge or the district attorney is investigating the matter. In either case, the prosecutor is required to maintain regular contact with the police department to develop the criminal prosecution properly. Some of the areas in which the police officer and the prosecutor work together include the following:

- *The police investigation report.* This report is one of the most important documents in the prosecutor's file. It is basically a statement by the police of the details of the crime, including all the evidence needed to support each element of the offense. It is a critical first step in developing the government's case against a suspect.

- *Providing legal advice.* Often the prosecutor advises the police officer about the legal issues in a given case. The prosecutor may also assist the officer by limiting unnecessary court appearances, informing the officer of the disposition of the case, and preparing the officer for pretrial appearances. As an officer of the court, the prosecutor enjoys civil immunity when assisting the police in criminal cases. This means that she is not liable to a criminal defendant in a civil suit.

- *Training police personnel.* In many jurisdictions, prosecutors help train police officers in securing warrants, making legal arrests, interrogating persons in custody, and conducting legal lineups. Some police departments have police legal advisers who work with the prosecutor in training new and experienced police personnel in legal matters.[18]

**THE PROSECUTOR AND THE COMMUNITY** Today, many prosecutors' offices are improving their working relationship with the community.[19] The concept of **community prosecution** recognizes that crime reduction is built on community partnerships.[20] It is not just a program, but also a new strategy for prosecutors to do their job. Just as police officers no longer simply make arrests, prosecutors need to do more than try cases. They become problem solvers looking to improve the overall safety and well-being of the communities over which they have jurisdiction.[21]

The traditional prosecutorial model is case-oriented and reactive to crime, not problem-oriented and proactive. Prosecutors are centrally located and assigned to teams focusing on specific types of crimes (homicide, narcotics, sex offenses, misdemeanors, and so on), with the most senior prosecutors handling the most serious felonies. Most prosecutions are arrest-generated. There is not much direct interaction among prosecutors, police, and members of the community outside of specific cases.

The lack of direct involvement by prosecutors in the community, when combined with an arrest-generated, case-oriented approach, often leads to an inefficient allocation of criminal justice resources. Frequently, no effort is made to allocate resources on a geographical basis or to assign prosecutors where they are needed. To align resources with community needs, some prosecutors must be in the community daily. In this way, the prosecutors can gauge the seriousness of the crime problem and play a positive role in its solution, along with other law enforcement and community groups. Community prosecution requires that field prosecutors work directly with the police to improve public safety in a particular district.

The main components of such a program include placing prosecutors in selected communities to work at police stations; increasing communication with police and with community groups, schools, and other organizations so prosecutors can be made aware of which cases and problems need the most attention; and using prosecutorial resources to solve community problems, not just to prosecute individual cases.

**community prosecution**
A prosecutorial philosophy that emphasizes community support and cooperation with other agencies in preventing crime, as well as a less centralized and more proactive role for local prosecutors.

**CourseMate** For more information about **community prosecution**, visit the Criminal Justice CourseMate at CengageBrain.com, then access the "Web Links" for this chapter.

What is the role of community prosecutors? They meet with the police daily to discuss law enforcement problems, strategize about the methods used to approach criminal behaviors, attend community meetings to learn about criminal incidents ranging from nuisances to felonies, and screen citizen complaints by diverting those cases that should not be in the criminal justice system. In short, field prosecutors build partnerships with the police, citizen groups, schools, and businesses to ensure public safety for the community.

Community prosecution programs have been started in many jurisdictions, with notable accomplishments. For example, prosecutors working with police and business leaders reduced the incidence of robberies near a local theater by implementing measures to make the area less attractive to criminals (better lighting, removal of pay phones, stricter enforcement of trespass laws, and increased police surveillance). In another example, community prosecutors, police, and housing inspectors closed and condemned a drug house where illegal drug activities were consistently taking place.[22]

Establishing partnerships with the community and law enforcement, as well as strong working relationships with other public and private agencies, is the key to a successful community prosecution approach. Community prosecution is not a new program, but rather an important new philosophy. It is the result of efforts, similar to those involved in community policing, to provide better criminal justice service to the community.

Finally, one of the greatest challenges facing community prosecution is the task of evaluating its effectiveness. What is the best measure of success for a prosecutor? Is it the number of prosecutions? What about the percentage of cases won in court? Is it how many offenders are given prison time? Or is it whether crime is reduced in the community? Each of these factors provides a useful measure for determining the success or failure of community prosecution efforts.

# PROSECUTORIAL DISCRETION

One might expect that after the police make an arrest and bring a suspect to court, the entire criminal court process would be mobilized. This is often not the case, however. For a variety of reasons, a substantial percentage of defendants are never brought to trial. The prosecutor decides whether to bring a case to trial or to dismiss it outright. This is known as **prosecutorial discretion**. Even if the prosecutor decides to pursue a case, the charges may later be dropped, in a process called **nolle prosequi**, if conditions are not favorable for a conviction.

Even in felony cases, the prosecutor ordinarily exercises considerable discretion in deciding whether to charge the accused with a crime.[23] After a police investigation, the prosecutor may be asked to review the sufficiency of the evidence to determine whether a criminal complaint should be filed. In some jurisdictions, this may involve presenting the evidence at a preliminary hearing. In other cases, the prosecutor may decide to seek a criminal complaint through a **grand jury** or other information procedure. These procedures, representing the formal methods of charging the accused with a felony offense, are discussed in Chapter 11.

Prosecutors exercise a great deal of discretion in even the most serious cases. In a classic study of prosecutorial discretion in three counties, Barbara Boland found that prosecutors used their discretion to dismiss a high percentage of the cases before trial.[24] However, when cases were forwarded for trial, few defendants were acquitted, indicating that prosecutorial discretion was exercised to screen out the weakest cases. The reasons why some cases are rejected or dismissed are summarized in Concept Summary 10.1. Evidence problems are the most common reason for rejecting cases; many other cases are dropped because defendants plead guilty to lesser crimes.

**prosecutorial discretion**
The prosecutor's authority to decide whether to bring a case to trial or to dismiss it outright.

**nolle prosequi**
The decision by a prosecutor to drop a case after a complaint has been made because of, for example, insufficient evidence, witness reluctance to testify, police error, or office policy.

**grand jury**
A group of citizens chosen to hear charges against persons accused of crime and to determine whether there is sufficient evidence to bring those persons to trial.

## CONCEPT SUMMARY 10.1
### *Common Reasons for Rejection or Dismissal of a Criminal Case*

Many criminal cases are rejected or dismissed because of:

■ *Insufficient evidence.* A failure to find sufficient physical evidence linking the defendant to the offense.

■ *Witness problems.* For example, when a witness fails to appear, gives unclear or inconsistent statements, is reluctant to testify, or is unsure of the identity of the offender, or when a prior relationship exists between the victim or witness and the offender.

■ *The interests of justice.* Deciding not to prosecute certain types of offenses, particularly those that violate the letter but not the spirit of the law (for example, offenses involving insignificant amounts of property damage).

■ *Due process problems.* Violations of the constitutional requirements for seizing evidence and for questioning the accused.

■ *A plea on another case.* For example, when the accused is charged in several cases and the prosecutor agrees to drop one or more of the cases in exchange for a plea of guilty in another case.

■ *Pretrial diversion.* Agreeing to drop charges when the accused successfully meets the conditions for diversion, such as completion of a treatment program.

■ *Referral for other prosecution.* When there are other offenses, perhaps of a more serious nature, in a different jurisdiction, or deferring to a federal prosecution.

## The Exercise of Discretion

The power to institute or discontinue formal charges against the defendant is the key to the prosecutorial function, representing the control and power that the prosecutor has over an individual's liberty. The prosecutor has broad discretion in the exercise of his or her duties. This discretion is subject to few limitations and often puts the prosecutor in the position of making difficult decisions without appropriate policies and guidelines. Prosecutorial discretion is rarely reviewed by the courts, unless the prosecutor specifically violates a defendant's constitutional rights.[25] As the U.S. Supreme Court stated in *United States v. Armstrong,*

> The Attorney General and the United States Attorneys retain "broad discretion" to enforce the Nation's criminal laws. They have this latitude because they are designated by statute as the President's delegates to help him discharge his constitutional responsibility to "take Care that the Laws be faithfully executed."[26]

As a result, prosecutorial decisions to drop cases are rarely reviewed. More than 70 years ago, legal scholar Newman Baker commented on the problems of prosecutorial decision making:

> "To prosecute or not to prosecute?" is a question which comes to the mind of this official scores of times each day. A law has been contravened and the statute says he is bound to commence proceedings. His legal duty is clear. But what will be the result? Will it be a waste of time? Will it be expensive to the state? Will it be unfair to the defendant (the prosecutor applying his own ideas of justice)? Will it serve any good purpose to society in general? Will it have good publicity value? Will it cause a political squabble? Will it prevent the prosecutor from carrying the offender's home precinct when he, the prosecutor, runs for Congress after his term as prosecutor? Was the law violated a foolish piece of legislation? If the offender is a friend, is it the square thing to do to reward friendship by initiating criminal proceedings? These and many similar considerations are bound to come to the mind of the man responsible for setting the wheels of criminal justice in motion.[27]

Once involved in a case, the prosecutor must also determine the formal charge. Deciding whether to charge a person with a crime is not easy—nor is determining the appropriate charge. Should a 16-year-old boy be charged with burglary or handled as a juvenile offender in the juvenile court? Would it be more appropriate to reduce a drug charge from the sale of marijuana to mere possession? Should an offense be considered mayhem, battery, or simply assault?

*SYSTEM FACTORS*  In determining what course of action to take, the prosecutor has a significant effect on the criminal justice system. Initiating formal charges against all defendants arrested by the police would clog the courts with numerous petty crimes and cases with little chance of conviction. In dealing with minor cases, the prosecutor would waste time that could have been better spent on the investigation and prosecution of more serious crimes. Effective screening by prosecutors can eliminate from the judicial system many cases in which convictions cannot reasonably be obtained or that may be inappropriate for criminal action, such as petty thefts, minor crimes by first offenders, and criminal acts involving offenders in need of special services (such as emotionally disturbed or mentally challenged offenders). The prosecutor can then concentrate on bringing to trial offenders who commit serious personal and property crimes, such as homicide, burglary, rape, and robbery. In meeting this goal, the prosecutor may decide not to press charges in the current case but to rely instead on such mechanisms as revoking the client's probation or, if appropriate, turning the case over to correctional authorities for a parole revocation hearing. As a result, many cases that may look as though they were dropped by the prosecutor conclude with the incarceration of the defendant.[28]

*CASE FACTORS*  Because they are ultimately responsible for deciding whether to prosecute, prosecutors must be aware of the wide variety of circumstances that affect their decisions. Frank Miller, in his classic work *Prosecution: The Decision to Charge a Suspect with a Crime*, identified several factors that affect discretion and the charging decision. Among these factors are the attitude of the victim, the avoidance of undue harm to the suspect, the availability of alternative procedures, the availability of civil sanctions, and the willingness of the suspect to cooperate with law enforcement authorities.[29]

Evidence also indicates that the relationship between the victim and the criminal may greatly influence whether a prosecutor wishes to pursue a case. Barbara Boland found that conviction rates were much lower in cases involving friends (30 percent) or relatives (19 percent) than they were in cases involving strangers (48 percent).[30] Prosecutors who are aware of the lower conviction probability in friend and relative cases may be reluctant to pursue them unless they involve serious offenses. Recent (2006) research by John Worrall and his associates found that case seriousness shapes prosecutorial discretion in domestic violence cases: Charges are more likely to occur if the victim both is a female and is injured in the assault. In some of the cases they studied, police officers could not easily identify a victim and/or a suspect. When the assault seemed to be mutual, prosecutors were much less likely to bring charges than in cases where there was a case with a clear victim and/or suspect. How can this finding be explained? Prosecutors do not move forward if they cannot identify who is responsible.[31]

"Convictability" is another factor that shapes prosecutorial discretion. Prosecutors know that the victim's character and background will be attacked in court and must conclude that their witness and supporting evidence can withstand the attack. When Cassia Spohn and David Holleran studied prosecutors' decisions in rape cases, they found that perception of the victim's character was still a critical factor in the prosecutor's decision to file charges. In cases involving an acquaintance, prosecutors were reluctant to file charges when the victim's character was questioned—for example, when police reports described the victim as sexually active or as being engaged in sexually oriented occupations such as exotic dancing. In cases involving strangers, prosecutors were more likely to take action if a gun or a knife was used. Spohn and Holleran conclude that prosecutors are still influenced by perceptions of what constitutes "real rape" and who are "real victims."

Does increased availability of forensic evidence influence prosecutors' charging decisions? A recent survey of 444 prosecutors revealed that the presence of forensic evidence did not directly affect charging decisions.[32] Only if savvy expert witnesses or jurors can understand and appreciate such evidence does it even play a major role in securing a conviction.

*DISPOSITION FACTORS*  In determining which cases should be eliminated from the criminal process and which should be brought to trial, the prosecutor has the opportunity to select alternative actions if they are more appropriate. Some offenders may be alcoholics or narcotic addicts, they may be mentally ill, or they may have been led into crime by their family situation or their inability to get a job. If they are not helped, they may return to crime. In many cases, only minimal intrusions on defendants' liberty seem necessary. Often it will be enough simply to refer offenders to the appropriate agency in the community and hope that they will take advantage of the help offered. The prosecutor might, for example, be willing to drop charges if a man goes to an employment agency and makes a bona fide effort to get a job, seeks help from a social service agency, or resumes his education. The prosecutor retains legal power to file a charge until the period of limitations has expired, but as a practical matter, unless the offense is repeated, reviewing the initial charge would be unusual.

Today, particularly in those jurisdictions where alternative programs exist, prosecutors often identify and divert offenders to community agencies in cases where the full criminal process does not appear necessary. This may occur in drug, prostitution, and gambling offenses. The American Bar Association recommends the use of social service programs as an appropriate alternative to prosecution.[33]

Dealing with the accused in such a way has come to be known as pretrial **diversion**. In this process, the prosecutor postpones or eliminates criminal prosecution in exchange for the alleged offender's participation in a rehabilitation program.[34] In recent years, the reduced cost and general utility of such programs have made them an important factor in prosecutorial discretion and a major part of the criminal justice system. A more detailed discussion of pretrial diversion is found in Chapter 11.

**diversion**
The use of an alternative to trial, such as referral to treatment or employment programs.

*POLITICAL FACTORS*  The prosecutor is a political figure, typically elected to office, whose discretion may be shaped by prevailing political necessities. If the public is outraged by school shootings, the prosecutor may be under media pressure to do something about children who carry guns to school. Similarly, public interest groups that are interested in curbing particular behaviors, such as domestic violence or possession of handguns, may lobby prosecutors to devote more attention to these social problems. If too successful, however, lobbying efforts may dilute resources and overextend the prosecutor's office. When prosecutors in Milwaukee, Wisconsin, substantially increased the prosecution of domestic violence cases, the time taken to process the cases doubled, convictions declined, pretrial crimes increased, and victim satisfaction with the justice process decreased.[35] For a summary of the many factors that have been linked to prosecutorial decision making, see Concept Summary 10.2.

## The Role of Prosecutorial Discretion

The proper exercise of prosecutorial discretion can improve the criminal justice process, preventing unnecessarily rigid implementation of the criminal law. Discretion enables the prosecutor to consider alternative decisions and humanize the operation of the criminal justice system. If prosecutors had little or no discretion,

# CAREERS IN CRIMINAL JUSTICE

# *Prosecutor*

### Duties and Characteristics of the Job

Prosecutors represent the public in criminal trials and are responsible for proving in court that the accused is guilty of the charges brought against him. Prosecutors work at municipal, state, and federal levels of government. During a trial, a prosecutor is opposed by a defense attorney, who is trying to maintain the innocence of the accused offender. In order to convince the judge or jury of the defendant's guilt, the prosecutor questions witnesses and gives statements using evidence collected during the investigative phase of the case. Prosecutors also decide which cases to bring to trial and have the authority to settle cases out of court. Even though they represent the people, prosecutors often meet with victims of crime and present the case from that point of view when in court.

This job comes with many responsibilities and pressures. Prosecutors must be mindful of their actions and words as representatives of the government body for which they work. Victims of crime and their families, community members, and law enforcement are depending on the prosecutor to prove the guilt of an alleged offender to a jury or judge and gain a conviction. Prosecutors may work long hours, especially during trials. In general, prosecutors may tend to be paid less than their counterparts in private practice; however, many report high personal satisfaction from seeing that justice is served.

### Job Outlook

Crime rates and budgets will dictate the number of job openings. However, job opportunities open up on a regular basis because the position has a high turnover rate. Positions should be more readily available in smaller communities and at lower levels of government.

### Salary

Prosecutors working in federal and state offices tend to earn more than those working at the county and municipal levels. Pay is also higher In larger cities. Entering prosecutors earn an average of approximately $50,000. Senior prosecutors often earn in excess of $100,000 per year.

### Opportunities

There are opportunities for advancement in larger offices, especially in urban areas. A state prosecutor may also wish to seek a position as a federal prosecutor.

A position as a prosecutor is quite often used as a stepping-stone to other prestigious government and law careers. After leaving their position, former prosecutors might open up their own private practice, possibly with the intent of running a lucrative defense attorney business. Prosecutors can also seek appointments to prestigious and well-paying judge positions or choose to leave law practice for a political career.

### Qualifications

The basic qualifications for becoming a prosecutor are the same as those for any successful career as an attorney. This means that in addition to the demanding educational requirements of college and law school, a future lawyer will need to pass the bar exam of the state in which she wants to work.

Like other lawyers, prosecutors need to be comfortable and practiced at public speaking, and they need well-developed analytical skills. There is also a political aspect to being a prosecutor, because in some areas one must be elected or appointed to this position.

### Education and Training

A bachelor's degree with an emphasis on building writing, analytical, and research skills is necessary. In addition to a four-year degree, taking the standardized Law School Admission Test (LSAT) is necessary in order to gain entry into a law school. Entry into law school is very competitive, and the educational requirements are challenging.

Sources: "Lawyer," *Occupational Outlook Handbook*, 2010–2011 edition (Bureau of Labor Statistics, U.S. Department of Labor), retrieved April 23, 2010, from www.bls.gov/oco/ocos053.htm; "Salary Survey Report for Job: District Attorney" (PayScale, Inc.), retrieved April 23, 2010, from www.payscale.com/research/US/Job=District_Attorney/Salary; "Princeton Review Career Profiles: Lawyer," retrieved April 23, 2010, from www.princetonreview.com/cte/profiles/dayInLife.asp?careerID=16.

## CONCEPT SUMMARY 10.2
### Factors Linked to Prosecutorial Decision Making

| System Factors | ■ Cost of trial |
| --- | --- |
| | ■ Court backlog |
| | ■ Serious crime prioritized over less serious crime |
| **Case Factors** | ■ Strength of evidence |
| | ■ Victim–offender relationship |
| | ■ Victim and/or offender background |
| | ■ Victim injury |
| | ■ Victim attitude and/or cooperation |
| | ■ Concern with possible harm to the suspect (perhaps resulting from a prison sentence) |
| | ■ Availability of alternative procedures |
| | ■ Suspect cooperation |
| | ■ Presence and/or use of a weapon |
| **Disposition Factors** | ■ Preference for diversion |
| | ■ Preference for treatment or rehabilitation program |
| **Political Factors** | ■ Elected prosecutor pressuring subordinates or being pressured himself or herself |
| | ■ Public outrage |
| | ■ Media scrutiny |
| | ■ Lobbying efforts |

they would be forced to prosecute all cases brought to their attention. According to Judge Charles Breitel, "If every policeman, every prosecutor, every court, and every postsentence agency performed his or its responsibility in strict accordance with the rules of law, precisely and narrowly laid down, the criminal law would be ordered but intolerable."[36]

On the other hand, too much discretion can lead to abuses that result in the abandonment of law. Prosecutors are political creatures. They are charged with serving the people, but they must also be mindful of their reputations. Losing too many high-profile cases might jeopardize their chances of reelection. Therefore, they may be unwilling to prosecute cases in which the odds of conviction are low. They are worried about *convictability*.[37]

### PERSPECTIVES ON JUSTICE
#### Noninterventionism

Some prosecutors' offices will make liberal use of alternatives such as placing some perpetrators in a community program rather than charging them with a criminal offense. The availability of these community programs is a function of how advocates of nonintervention have shaped the justice process in an effort to reduce stigma and labeling.

## Overzealous Prosecution

Unfortunately, prosecutors sometimes go "too far" in their efforts to secure convictions against criminals. For example, a prosecutor may engage in selective or unfair prosecution, such as by targeting one person for personal reasons rather than making a decision based on the evidence. In *Yick Wo v. Hopkins* (1886), the Supreme Court highlighted this problem:

> Though the law itself be fair on its face and impartial in appearance, yet, if it is applied and administered by public authority with an evil eye and an unequal hand, so as practically to make unjust and illegal discriminations between persons in similar circumstances, material to their rights, the denial of equal justice is still within the prohibition of the Constitution.[38]

Prosecutors have also been known to engage in what is known as pretextual prosecution. This occurs when a prosecutor who lacks evidence to charge a particular person with one crime instead charges the individual with a lesser, unrelated offense. The key here is "unrelated." If, for example, a prosecutor lacks evidence to charge someone with first-degree murder and instead pursues second-degree murder charges, such a decision is perfectly acceptable. In contrast, if a prosecutor lacks evidence to charge a person with racketeering and instead charges the individual with a violation of the Federal Meat Inspection Act, this is a pretextual prosecution.[39]

*PUNISHING OVERZEALOUS PROSECUTORS*   In extreme cases, prosecutors have been known to fabricate evidence, use false statements at trial, withhold potentially favorable evidence from the defense (a violation of due process), influence witnesses, renege on plea agreements, and so on. What can be done? On the one hand, prosecutors cannot be sued for their decisions on whether to press charges or for how they act. Even in the most egregious of cases of flagrant misconduct, a prosecutor cannot be held liable for his or her actions during the judicial stage of a case.[40] This is known as absolute immunity. On the other hand, although prosecutors cannot be sued for misconduct, they can be punished by their superiors and state bar association disciplinary boards. Punishments vary depending on the misconduct in question, but they can include

- Private admonition or reprimand
- Public reprimand
- Suspension from law practice for a designated time period
- Permanent disbarment (that is, losing the authority to practice law)

How often are punishments such as these imposed? The Center for Public Integrity investigated more than 11,000 cases of alleged prosecutorial misconduct that took place over more than three decades.[41] In more than 2,000 of the cases, appellate judges reduced sentences, reversed convictions, or dismissed charges, which suggests there were many cases of serious misconduct. Of 44 cases the Center identified where prosecutors were disciplined, only two were disbarred. The most common sanctions were reprimand and censure. Appellate courts generally uphold convictions when misconduct is not considered serious, so wayward prosecutors are rarely penalized for their behavior.

# THE DEFENSE ATTORNEY

The **defense attorney** is the counterpart of the prosecuting attorney in the criminal process. The accused has a constitutional right to counsel. If the defendant cannot afford an attorney, the state must provide one.

For many years, much of the legal community looked down on the criminal defense attorney and the practice of criminal law. This attitude stemmed from the kinds of legal work a defense attorney was forced to do—working with shady characters, negotiating for the release of known thugs and hoodlums, and often overzealously defending alleged criminals in criminal trials. Lawyers were reluctant to specialize in criminal law because they received comparatively low pay and often provided services without compensation. In addition, law schools in the past seldom offered more than one or two courses in criminal law and trial practice.

In recent years, however, with the implementation of constitutional requirements regarding the right to counsel, interest in criminal law has grown. Almost all law schools today have clinical programs that employ students as voluntary defense attorneys. They also offer courses in trial tactics, brief writing, and appellate procedures. In addition, legal organizations such as the American Bar Association, the National Legal Aid and Defenders Association, and the National Association of Criminal Defense Lawyers have assisted in recruiting able lawyers

---

**CourseMate** For more information about **examples of prosecutorial misconduct**, visit the Criminal Justice CourseMate at CengageBrain.com, then access the "Web Links" for this chapter.

---

**defense attorney**
Legal counsel for the defendant in a criminal case, representing the accused person from arrest to final appeal.

---

**CourseMate** For more information about the **National Legal Aid and Defenders Association (NLADA)**, visit the Criminal Justice CourseMate at CengageBrain.com, then access the "Web Links" for this chapter.

to do criminal defense work. As the American Bar Association has noted, "An almost indispensable condition to fundamental improvement of American criminal justice is the active and knowledgeable support of the bar as a whole."[42]

## The Role of the Criminal Defense Attorney

The defense attorney, like the prosecutor, is an officer of the court. As an attorney, the defense attorney is obligated to uphold the integrity of the legal profession and to observe the requirements of the *Model Rules of Professional Conduct* in the defense of a client. The duties of the lawyer to the adversary system of justice are as follows:

> Our legal system provides for the adjudication of disputes governed by the rules of substantive, evidentiary, and procedural law. An adversary presentation counters the natural human tendency to judge too swiftly in terms of the familiar that which is not yet fully known; the advocate, by his zealous preparation of facts and law, enables the tribunal to come to the hearing with an open and neutral mind to render impartial judgments. The duty of the lawyer to his client and his duty to the legal system are the same: To represent his client zealously within the boundaries of the law.[43]

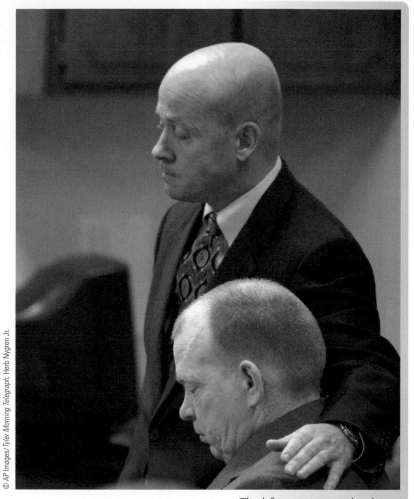

The defense attorney needs to be aware of potential ethical conflicts that could arise from being both an officer of the court and an advocate for her or his client. Here defense attorney Thad Davidson puts his arm on client Patrick "Booger Red" Kelly's shoulder in a courtroom in Tyler, Texas, during a recess on August 21, 2008. Kelly was convicted, in less than two hours of deliberation, of engaging in organized criminal activity for conspiring with other adults to force two young siblings to have sex with each other for a paying audience.

The defense attorney performs many functions while representing the accused in the criminal process. Exhibit 10.2 lists some of the major duties of a defense attorney, whether privately employed by the accused, appointed by the court, or serving as a public defender.

Because of the way the U.S. system of justice operates, criminal defense attorneys face many role conflicts. They are viewed as the prime movers in what is essentially an adversary process. The prosecution and the defense engage in conflict over the facts of the case, with the prosecutor arguing the case for the state and the defense attorney using all the means at her disposal to aid the client. This system can be compared to a sporting event, in which the government and the accused are the players, and the judge and the jury are the referees. As members of the legal profession, defense attorneys must also be aware of their role as officers of the court. As attorneys, defense counsel are obligated to uphold the integrity of the legal profession and to rely on constitutional ideals of fair play and professional ethics to provide adequate representation for a client.

## Ethical Issues

As an officer of the court, along with the judge, prosecutors, and other trial participants, the defense attorney seeks to uncover the basic facts and elements of the criminal act. In this dual capacity as both a defense advocate and an officer of the court, the attorney is often confronted with conflicting obligations to his or her client and profession. In a famous work, Monroe Freedman identified

---

**EXHIBIT 10.2**

## *Functions of the Defense Attorney*

- Investigating the incident
- Interviewing the client, police, and witnesses
- Discussing the matter with the prosecutor
- Representing the defendant at the various pre-trial procedures, such as arrest, interrogation, lineup, and arraignment
- Entering into plea negotiations

- Preparing the case for trial, including developing tactics and strategy
- Filing and arguing legal motions with the court
- Representing the defendant at trial
- Providing assistance at sentencing
- Determining the appropriate basis for appeal

---

three of the most difficult problems involving the professional responsibility of the criminal defense lawyer:

1. Is it proper to cross-examine for the purpose of discrediting the reliability or credibility of an adverse witness whom you know to be telling the truth?

2. Is it proper to put a witness on the stand when you know he will commit perjury?

3. Is it proper to give your client legal advice when you have reason to believe that the knowledge you give him will tempt him to commit perjury?[44]

Other equally important issues confound a lawyer's ethical responsibilities. Lawyers are required to keep their clients' statements confidential—that is, to honor the attorney–client privilege. Suppose a client confides that he is planning to commit a crime. What are the defense attorney's ethical responsibilities? The lawyer would have to counsel the client to obey the law. If the lawyer assisted the client in engaging in illegal behavior, the lawyer would be subject to charges of unprofessional conduct and criminal liability. If the lawyer believed that the danger was imminent, he would have to alert the police. The criminal lawyer needs to be aware of these troublesome situations to properly balance the duties of being an attorney with those of being an officer of the court and a moral person. These decisions are often difficult to make.

What should an attorney do when her client reveals that he committed a murder and that an innocent person has been convicted of the crime and is going to be executed? Should the attorney do the moral thing and reveal the information before a terrible miscarriage of justice occurs? Or should the attorney do the professional thing and maintain her client's confidence? In general, there is no obligation on the defense attorney's part to disclose client confessions—or guilt in the absence of a confession.[45] However, defense attorneys are prohibited from knowingly allowing their clients to take the stand and offer perjured (false) testimony. For example, if a defense attorney knows her client committed the crime, she cannot have the defendant take the witness stand and testify that he was not involved.

In the aftermath of recent terrorist attacks and corporate scandals, the government is pressuring lawyers to breach their clients' confidences. In 2003, the Securities and Exchange Commission adopted a rule requiring lawyers to report potential fraud to corporate boards. The Internal Revenue Service is trying to make law firms disclose which clients bought questionable tax shelters, and the Justice Department has stated that conversations between lawyers and terrorism suspects are subject to eavesdropping.[46]

Because the defense attorney and the prosecutor have different roles, their ethical dilemmas may also differ. The defense attorney must maintain confidentiality and advise his or her client of the constitutional requirements of counsel,

**CourseMate** For more information about the **Southern California Interdisciplinary Law Journal**, visit the Criminal Justice CourseMate at CengageBrain.com, then access the "Web Links" for this chapter.

the privilege against self-incrimination, and the right to trial. The prosecutor represents the public and is not required to abide by such restrictions in the same way. In some cases, the defense attorney may be justified in withholding evidence by keeping the defendant from testifying at the trial. In addition, whereas prosecutors are prohibited from expressing a personal opinion on the defendant's guilt during summation of the case, defense attorneys are not barred from expressing their belief about a client's innocence.

> ## PERSPECTIVES ON JUSTICE
> ### *Due Process*
> The defense attorney's obligation to her client is one of the purest illustrations of the due process perspective, because it mandates fair and equitable treatment of those accused of a crime even if they are personally obnoxious to those representing them in court. The defense attorney cannot let her personal feelings interfere with her obligation to put on a spirited defense.

As a practical matter, therefore, ethical rules may differ because the state is bringing the action against the defendant and must prove the case beyond a reasonable doubt. This is also why a defendant who is found guilty can appeal, whereas a prosecutor must live with an acquittal, and it is why defense lawyers generally have more latitude in performing their duties on behalf of their clients.

Neither side should encourage unethical practices.[47] For example, it would be considered unethical for a prosecutor to withhold exculpatory evidence from the defense or for a defense lawyer to condone perjury by his client during cross-examination.

# DEFENDING THE ACCUSED

Over the past decades, the rules and procedures of criminal justice administration have become extremely complex. Bringing a case to court involves a detailed investigation of the crime, knowledge of court procedures, the use of rules of evidence, and skills in criminal advocacy. Both the state and the defense must have this specialized expertise, particularly when an individual's freedom or life is at stake. Consequently, the right to the assistance of counsel in the criminal justice system is essential if the defendant is to have a fair chance of presenting a case in the adversary process.

The Sixth Amendment right to counsel and the Fifth and Fourteenth Amendments' guarantees of due process of law have been judicially interpreted together to require counsel in all types of criminal proceedings (see Chapter 11 for more on the right to counsel at trial). The right to counsel begins at the earliest stages of the justice system, usually when a criminal suspect is interrogated while in police custody. *Miranda v. Arizona* (1966), a case we looked at closely in Chapter 8, held that any statements made by the accused when in custody are inadmissible at trial unless the accused has been informed of the right to counsel and the right, if indigent, to have an attorney appointed by the state.[48]

The Supreme Court also has extended the right to counsel to postconviction and other collateral proceedings, such as probation and parole revocation and appeal. When, for example, the court intends to revoke a defendant's probation and impose a sentence, the probationer has a right to counsel at the deferred sentence hearing.[49] When the state provides for an appellate review of the criminal conviction, the defendant is entitled to the assistance of counsel for this initial appeal.[50] The Supreme Court has also required states to provide counsel in other proceedings that involve the loss of personal liberty, such as juvenile delinquency hearings and mental health commitments.[51]

Areas still remain in the criminal justice system where the courts have not required assistance of counsel for the accused. These include preindictment lineups; booking procedures, including the taking of fingerprints and other forms of identification; grand jury investigations; appeals beyond the first review; disciplinary proceedings in correctional institutions; and postrelease revocation hearings. Nevertheless, the general rule is that persons cannot be deprived of freedom without representation by counsel if there is a chance that they will lose their

© AP Images/Mario Pinzuoni

*Public defenders are assigned to indigent defendants who cannot afford to pay for their own defense. Here murder suspect John Mark Karr listens with his attorney, deputy public defender Haydeh Takasugi, during an extradition hearing in Los Angeles Superior Court. Karr made national headlines when he confessed to murdering JonBenét Ramsey, but DNA evidence showed that he could not have committed the crime.*

liberty and be incarcerated in a correctional institution. In the next chapter, we look at the leading Supreme Court cases pertaining to criminal defense. Here we focus strictly on the mechanisms by which defense representation is afforded to the accused.

## Legal Services for the Indigent

One of the most critical issues in the justice system has been whether an **indigent defendant** has the right to counsel. Can an accused person who is poor and cannot afford an attorney have a fair trial without the assistance of counsel? Is counsel required at preliminary hearings? Should the convicted indigent offender be given counsel at state expense in appeals of the case? Questions such as these have arisen constantly in recent years. And they are important questions, because as many as 90 percent of criminal defendants are considered indigent.[52]

As far back as 1942, Justice Hugo Black, one of the greatest Supreme Court justices of the twentieth century, acknowledged the need for public defenders when he wrote, "A fair trial is impossible if an indigent is not provided with a free attorney."[53] In 1963, the U.S. Supreme Court took the first major step on the issue of right to counsel by holding that state courts must provide counsel to indigent defendants in felony prosecutions.[54] Nine years later, it extended the obligation to provide counsel to all criminal cases in which the penalty includes imprisonment—regardless of whether the offense is a felony or a misdemeanor.[55]

To satisfy the constitutional requirement that indigent defendants be provided with the assistance of counsel at various stages of the criminal process, the federal government and the states have had to evaluate and expand criminal defense services. Prior to 1963, public defense services were provided mainly by local private attorneys appointed and paid for by the court and called **assigned counsel**, or by limited **public defender** programs. In 1961, for example, public defender services existed in only 3 percent of the counties in the United States, serving only about one-quarter of the country's population.[56] The general lack of defense services for indigents traditionally stemmed from the following causes, among others:

■ Until fairly recently, laws of most jurisdictions did not require the assistance of counsel for felony offenders and others.

■ Only a few attorneys were interested in criminal law practice.

■ The organized legal bar was generally indifferent to the need for criminal defense assistance.

■ The caseloads of lawyers working in public defender agencies were staggering.

■ Financial resources for courts and defense programs were limited.

Over time, the criminal justice system has been forced to increase public defender services. Today, about 3,000 state and local agencies are providing indigent legal services in the United States.

**indigent defendant**
A defendant who lacks the funds to hire a private attorney and is therefore entitled to free counsel.

**assigned counsel**
A private attorney appointed by the court to represent a criminal defendant who cannot afford to pay for a lawyer.

**public defender**
An attorney employed by the government to represent criminal defendants who cannot afford to pay for a lawyer.

**CourseMate** For more information about **indigent defense services**, visit the Criminal Justice CourseMate at CengageBrain.com, then access the "Web Links" for this chapter.

Providing legal services for indigent offenders is a huge undertaking. More than 4.5 million offenders are given free legal services annually. And although most states have a formal set of rules for determining who is indigent, and many require repayment to the state for at least part of their legal services (known as **recoupment**), indigent legal services still cost more than $1.5 billion annually.[57]

Programs providing assistance of counsel to indigent defendants can be divided into three major categories: public defender systems, assigned counsel systems, and contract systems. Other approaches to the delivery of legal services include mixed systems, such as representation by both public defenders and the private bar; law school clinical programs; and prepaid legal services. Of the three major approaches, assigned counsel systems are the most common; a majority of U.S. courts use this method. However, public defender programs seem to be on the increase, and many jurisdictions use a combination of programs statewide.

**recoupment**
Process by which the state later recovers some or all of the cost of providing free legal counsel to an indigent defendant.

*PUBLIC DEFENDERS*  The first public defender program in the United States opened in 1913 in Los Angeles. Over the years, primarily as a result of efforts by judicial leaders and bar groups, the public defender program became the model for the delivery of legal services to indigent defendants in criminal cases throughout the country.

Most public defender offices can be thought of as law firms whose only clients are criminal offenders. However, they are generally administrated at one of two government levels: state or county. About one-third of the states have a statewide public defender's office, headed by a chief public defender who administers the system. In some of these states, the chief defender establishes offices in all counties around the state; in others, the chief defender relies on part-time private attorneys to provide indigent legal services in rural counties. Statewide public defenders may be organized as part of the judicial branch, as part of the executive branch, as an independent state agency, or as a private nonprofit organization.

*ASSIGNED COUNSEL SYSTEM*  In contrast to the public defender system, the assigned counsel system involves the use of private attorneys appointed by the court to represent indigent defendants. The private attorney is selected from a list of attorneys maintained by the court and is reimbursed by the state for any legal services rendered to the client. Assigned counsels are generally used in rural areas, which do not have sufficient caseloads to justify a full-time public defender staff.

There are two main types of assigned counsel systems. In an *ad hoc* assigned counsel system, the presiding judge appoints attorneys on a case-by-case basis. In a *coordinated* assigned counsel system, an administrator oversees the appointment of counsel and sets up guidelines for the administration of indigent legal services. The fees awarded to assigned counsels can vary widely, ranging from a low of $10 per hour for handling a misdemeanor out of court to a high of $100 per hour for a serious felony. Some jurisdictions may establish a maximum allowance per case of $750 for a misdemeanor and $1,500 for a felony. Average rates seem to be between $40 and $80 per hour, depending on the nature of the case. Proposals for higher rates are pending. Restructuring the attorney fee system is undoubtedly needed to maintain fair standards for payment.

The assigned counsel system, unless organized properly, suffers from such problems as unequal assignments, inadequate legal fees, and the lack of supportive or supervisory services. Other disadvantages are the frequent use of inexperienced attorneys and the tendency to use the guilty plea too quickly. Some judicial experts believe that the assigned counsel system is still no more than an ad hoc approach that raises serious questions about the quality of representation. However, the assigned counsel system is simple to operate. It also offers the private bar an important role in providing indigent legal services, because most public defender systems cannot represent all needy criminal defendants.

Thus, the appointed counsel system gives attorneys the opportunity to do criminal defense work.

**contract system**
Provision of legal services to indigent defendants by private attorneys under contract to the state or county.

**CONTRACT SYSTEM** The **contract system** is a relative newcomer in providing legal services to the indigent. It is being used in a small percentage of counties around the United States. In this system, a block grant is given to a lawyer or law firm to handle indigent defense cases. In some instances, the attorney is given a set amount of money and is required to handle all cases assigned. In other jurisdictions, contract lawyers agree to provide legal representation for a set number of cases at a fixed fee. A third system involves representation at an estimated cost per case until the dollar amount of the contract is reached. At that point, the contract may be renegotiated, but the lawyers are not obligated to take new cases.

The contract system is often used in counties that also have public defenders. Such counties may need independent counsel when a conflict of interest arises or when there is a constant overflow of cases. It is also used in sparsely populated states that cannot justify the structure and costs of full-time public defender programs. Experts have found that contract attorneys are at least as effective as assigned counsel and are cost-effective.[58]

The per-case cost in any jurisdiction for indigent defense services is determined largely by the type of program offered. In most public defender programs, funds are obtained through annual appropriations. Assigned counsel costs relate to legal charges for the appointed counsel, and contract programs negotiate a fee for the entire service. No research currently available indicates which is the most effective way to represent the indigent on a cost-per-case basis. However, Lawrence Spears reports that some jurisdictions have adopted the contract model with much success. Advantages include the provision of comprehensive legal services, controlled costs, and improved coordination in counsel programs.[59]

**MIXED SYSTEMS** A mixed system uses both public defenders and private attorneys in an attempt to draw on the strengths of each. In this approach, the public defender system operates simultaneously with the assigned counsel system or contract system to offer total coverage to the indigent defendant. This need occurs when the caseload increases beyond the capacity of the public defender's office. In addition, many counties supply independent counsel to all codefendants in a single case to prevent a conflict of interest. In most others, separate counsel is provided if a codefendant requests it or if the judge or the public defender perceives a conflict of interest.

Other methods of providing counsel to the indigent include the use of law school students and prepaid legal service programs (similar to comprehensive medical insurance). Most jurisdictions have a student practice rule of procedure. Third-year law school students in clinical programs provide supervised counsel to defendants in nonserious offenses. In *Argersinger v. Hamlin*, Supreme Court Justice William Brennan suggested that law students are an important resource in fulfilling constitutional defense requirements.[60]

**COSTS OF DEFENDING THE POOR** Over the past decade, the justice system has faced extreme pressure to provide counsel for all indigent criminal defendants. However, inadequate funding has made implementation of this Sixth Amendment right an impossible task. The chief reasons for underfunded defender programs are caseload problems, lack of available attorneys, and legislative restraints. Increasing numbers of drug cases, mandatory sentencing, and overcharging have put tremendous stress on defender services.

The system is also overloaded with appeals by indigent defendants convicted at the trial level whose representation involves filing complex briefs and making oral arguments. Such postconviction actions often consume a great deal of time and result in additional backlog. Death penalty litigation is another area in which legal resources for the poor are strained.

The indigent defense crisis is a chronic problem. In some jurisdictions, attorneys are just not available to provide defense work. Burnout from heavy caseloads, low salaries, and poor working conditions are generally the major causes for the limited supply of attorneys interested in representing the indigent defendant. Some attorneys refuse to accept appointments in criminal cases because the fees are too low.

Lack of government funding is the most significant problem today. Although the entire justice system is often underfunded, the indigent defense system is usually in the worst shape. Ordinarily, providing funding for indigent criminal defendants is not the most politically popular thing to do. Yet indigent defense services are a critical component of the justice system. If there is growing disparity in the resources allocated to police, courts, and correctional agencies, then few cases will go to trial, and most will have to be settled by informal processing, such as plea bargaining or diversion.[61]

According to Robert Spangenberg and Tessa Schwartz, noted experts on public defense programs, only 3 percent of justice expenditures are devoted to the indigent defense system. All too often, the limited criminal justice resources available are used to place more police officers on the streets and build more prisons, while ignoring prosecution, courts, and public defense.[62]

Current funding for defender programs is ordinarily the responsibility of state and local governments. As a result of an amendment to the Crime Control Act of 1990, however, federal funds are also available through the Drug Control Act of 1988.[63] No effort was made to increase available funds in the 1994–1995 federal crime legislation, but the Anti-Terrorism Act of 1996 authorized $300 million to improve the federal judiciary's public defender program. Since then no significant federal legislation has done much to improve defense representation for indigent defendants.

## The Private Bar

The lawyer whose practice involves a substantial proportion of criminal cases is often considered a specialist in the field. And there is little question that having a preeminent private attorney can help clients prove their innocence. Private defense attorneys can give their full attention to the defendant, whereas public defenders often represent many different clients.

Although a lucky few defendants are able to afford the services of skilled and experienced private counsel, most criminal defendants are represented by lawyers who often accept many cases for minor fees. These lawyers may belong to small law firms or work alone, but a sizable portion of their practice involves representing those accused of crime. Other private practitioners occasionally take on criminal matters as part of their general practice. Criminal lawyers often work on the fringe of the legal business, and they may receive little respect from colleagues or the community as a whole.

All but the most eminent criminal lawyers are bound to spend much of their working lives in overcrowded, physically unpleasant courts, dealing with people who have committed questionable acts, and attempting to put the best possible construction on those acts. It is not the sort of working environment that most people choose. Sometimes a criminal lawyer is identified unjustifiably in the public eye with the client she represents. "How could someone represent a child killer and try to get him off?" is a question that many people may ask.

Another problem associated with the private practice of criminal law is that the fee system can create a conflict of interest. Private attorneys are usually paid in advance and do not expect additional funds whether their client is convicted or acquitted. Many are aware of the guilt of their client before the trial begins, and they earn the greatest profit if they get the case settled as quickly as possible. This usually means bargaining with the prosecutor instead of going to trial. Even if attorneys win the case at trial, they may lose personally because they have only the gratitude of their client to compensate them for the time they have spent. And many criminal defendants cannot afford even a modest legal fee and therefore cannot avail themselves of the services of a private attorney. For these reasons, an elaborate, publicly funded legal system has developed.

## Public versus Private Attorneys

Do criminal defendants who hire their own private lawyers do better in court than those who depend on legal representatives provided by the state? Although having private counsel offers some advantages, national surveys indicate that state-appointed attorneys do well in court. According to data compiled by the federal government:

■ Conviction rates for indigent defendants and those with their own lawyers were about the same in federal and state courts. About 90 percent of the federal defendants and 75 percent of the defendants in the most populous counties were found guilty regardless of what type of attorney represented them.

■ Of defendants found guilty, however, those represented by publicly financed attorneys were incarcerated at a higher rate than those defendants who paid for their own legal representation: 88 percent compared with 77 percent in federal courts, and 71 percent compared with 54 percent in the most populous counties.

■ On average, sentence lengths for defendants sent to jail or prison were shorter for those with publicly financed attorneys than for those who hired counsel. In federal district court, those with publicly financed attorneys were given just under five years on average, and those with private attorneys were given just over five years. In large state courts, those with publicly financed attorneys were sentenced to an average of two and a half years and those with private attorneys to three years.[64]

The data indicates that private counsel may have a slightly better track record in some areas (such as death penalty cases) but that court-appointed lawyers do quite well. This finding was echoed in a recent study by Talia Roitberg Harmon and William Lofquist, who found that having a competent private attorney who puts on a rigorous defense is the single most important factor separating those who are exonerated in murder cases from and those who are executed.[65] The authors of another study examined the outcomes of all felony cases filed in Denver, Colorado, in 2002 and found that, on average, public defenders achieved poorer sentencing outcomes for their clients relative to privately retained attorneys.[66]

## ▌ PROBLEMS OF THE CRIMINAL BAR

The problems of the criminal bar are numerous. Attorneys who specialize in criminal work base their reputation on their power and influence. A good reputation is based on the ability to get obviously guilty offenders acquitted on legal technicalities, to arrange the best deal for clients who cannot hope to evade punishment, and to protect criminals whose illegal activities are shocking to many citizens. Private attorneys are often accused of sacrificing their clients' interests for pursuit of profit. Many have a bad reputation in the legal community because of their unsavory clientele and their reputation as shysters who hang out in court hoping for referrals. Consequently, the private criminal attorney is not often held in high esteem by his or her colleagues.

Public defenders are often young attorneys who are seeking trial practice before going on to high-paying jobs in established law firms. They are in the unenviable position of being paid by the government yet acting in the role of the government's adversary. Generally, they find themselves at the bottom of the legal profession's hierarchy because, for limited wages, they represent clients

Deacon James Cunningham, 76, of Washington, D.C., shares a laugh with Vanessa Buchko, a pro bono lawyer for Legal Council with the Elderly, as she visits him at his apartment in northwest Washington, D.C., on April 23, 2009.

without social prestige. Forced to work under bureaucratic conditions, public defenders can do only routine processing of their cases. Large caseloads prevent them from establishing more than a perfunctory relationship with their clients. To keep their caseload under control, they may push for the quickest and easiest solution to a case—a plea bargain.

Assigned counsel and contract attorneys may also be young lawyers just starting out and hoping to build their practice by taking on indigent cases. Because their livelihood depends on getting referrals from the court, public defender's office, or other government bodies, they risk the problem of conflict of interest. If they pursue too rigorous a defense or handle cases in a way not approved by the presiding judge or other authorities, they may be removed from the assigned counsel lists.

Very often, large firms contribute the services of their newest members for legal aid to indigents; these assignments are referred to as **pro bono** work. Although such efforts may be made in good spirit, they mean that inexperienced lawyers are handling legal cases in which a person's life may be at stake.

## The Informal Justice System

What has emerged is a system in which plea bargaining predominates because little time and insufficient resources are available to give criminal defendants a full-scale defense. Moreover, because prosecutors are under pressure to win their cases, they are often more willing to work out a deal than to pursue a case trial. After all, half a loaf is better than none. Defense attorneys also often find it easier to encourage their clients to plead guilty and secure a reduced sentence or probation instead of seeking an acquittal and risking a long prison term.

These conflicts have helped erode the formal justice process, which is based on the adversary system. Prosecutors and defense attorneys meet in the arena of the courtroom to do battle over the merits of the case. Through the give-and-take of the trial process, the truth of the matter becomes known. Guilty defendants are punished, and the innocent go free. Yet the U.S. legal system seldom works that way. Because of the pressures faced by defense attorneys and prosecutors, the defense and the prosecution more often work together in a spirit of cooperation to get the case over with rather than fighting it out, wasting each other's time, and risking an outright loss. In the process of this working relationship, the personnel in the courtroom—judge, prosecutor, defense attorney—form working

**pro bono**
The practice by private attorneys of taking the cases of indigent offenders without fee as a service to the profession and the community.

## IMAGES OF JUSTICE

# Prosecutors, Defense Attorneys, and the Press

When a high-profile trial is in the news, it is not uncommon to see prosecutors and defense attorneys talking to reporters. What are they allowed to say? What can they not say? A prosecutor who goes too far when talking to the press runs the risk of being disbarred. The same applies to defense attorneys; they have to choose their words carefully when going before the cameras.

### The American Bar Association's Model Rules of Professional Conduct

The American Bar Association's (ABA) *Model Rules of Professional Conduct* guide attorneys' activities. Of particular interest in terms of discussions with the media is Rule 3.6, which provides that

> A lawyer who is participating or has participated in the investigation or litigation of a matter shall not make an extrajudicial statement that a reasonable person would expect to be disseminated by means of public communication if the lawyer knows or reasonably should know that it will have a substantial likelihood of materially prejudicing an adjudicative proceeding in the matter.

Rule 3.6 goes on to list specific types of communications that attorneys are permitted to engage in. These include

1. the claim, offense or defense involved and, except when prohibited by law, the identity of the persons involved;

2. information contained in a public record;

3. that an investigation of a matter is in progress;

4. the scheduling or result of any step in litigation;

5. a request for assistance in obtaining evidence and information necessary thereto;

6. a warning of danger concerning the behavior of a person involved, when there is reason to believe that there exists the likelihood of substantial harm to an individual or to the public interest; and

7. in a criminal case . . . the identity, residence, occupation and family status of the accused; if the accused has not been apprehended, information necessary to aid in apprehension of that person; the fact, time and place of arrest; and the identity of investigating and arresting officers or agencies and the length of the investigation.

---

groups that leave the defendant on the outside. Criminal defendants may find that everyone they encounter in the courtroom seems to be saying "plead guilty," "take the deal," "let's get it over with."

The informal justice system revolves around the common interest of its members to move the case along and settle matters. In today's criminal justice system, defense attorneys share a common history, goals, values, and beliefs with their colleagues in prosecution. They are alienated by class and social background from the clients they defend. Considering the reality of who commits crime, who are its victims, and who defends, prosecutes, and tries the case, it should not be surprising that the adversary system has suffered.

## Relations between Prosecutor and Defense Attorney

In the final analysis, the competence of the prosecutor and the defense attorney depends on their willingness to work together in the interest of the client, the criminal justice system, and the rest of society. However, serious adversarial conflicts have arisen between them in recent years.

The prosecutor, for instance, should exercise discretion in seeking to **subpoena** other lawyers to testify about any relationship with their clients. Although not all communication between a lawyer and his or her client is privileged, confidential information entrusted to a lawyer is ordinarily not available for prosecutorial investigation. Often, however, overzealous prosecutors try to use their subpoena power against lawyers whose clients are involved in drug cases or organized crime cases to obtain as much evidence as possible. Prosecutors interested in confidential information about defendants have subpoenaed

**subpoena**
A court order requiring a witness to appear in court at a specified time and place.

Failure to abide by these and other pertinent ABA rules can result in disbarment and even criminal charges.

## A Balancing Act

Rule 3.6 attempts to achieve a balance between providing a fair trial for the accused and preserving the attorneys' First Amendment right to free speech. Importantly, the First Amendment applies only to *governmental* restrictions on free speech. Since the American Bar Association is a nongovernmental entity, it can take additional steps to restrain speech that the government cannot. Some people feel, however, that a lawyer's duty is to zealously guard his or her client's interests. This can include taking every opportunity available to speak with anyone who is interested, the press included.

## Steven J. Hatfill: A "Person of Interest" in the Post-9/11 Anthrax Scare

The post-9/11 anthrax scare illustrates the possible harmful effects of prosecutorial comments to the media. Steven J. Hatfill, an American physician, virologist, and bioweapons expert, was suspected of sending anthrax-laced envelopes that killed five people. Although he was never charged, a June 28, 2002, news story linked him to the attacks. Then–Attorney General John Ashcroft also identified him as a "person of interest." His name became equated with the anthrax attacks, even though 30 other people were investigated and their names were not released.

Ashcroft's comments may have been offered up as a genuine warning to the public of possible future attacks. This would seem to fit with number six in the list of permissible communications discussed above. But was there really a "likelihood of substantial harm" to the general public once Hatfill was identified? Were Ashcroft's statements potentially prejudicial? Could they affect the prospects for a fair trial if Hatfill were ever charged criminally? The answers are certainly up for debate. Hatfill was never charged, but he did file several lawsuits claiming, among other things, defamation of character. A $10 million lawsuit filed against *Reader's Digest* and *Vanity Fair* was settled. Hatfill's lawsuit against the federal government was settled in June 2008 for $5.82 million, and he was officially cleared of any wrongdoing in August of that year. Hatfill was cleared at about the same time investigators set their sites on Bruce Ivins, another biodefense researcher, who committed suicide as prosecutors prepared to indict him for his involvement in the anthrax attacks.

Sources: Mawiyah Hooker and Elizabeth Lange, "Limiting Extrajudicial Speech in High-Profile Cases: The Duty of the Prosecutor and Defense Attorney in Their Pre-Trial Communications with the Media," *Georgetown Journal of Legal Ethics* 16 (2003): 637–655; Tom Jackman, "Ex-Army Scientist Denies Role in Anthrax Attacks," *Washington Post*, August 11, 2002.

lawyers to testify against them. Court approval should be needed before a lawyer is forced to give information about a client. Otherwise, the defendant is not receiving effective legal counsel under the Sixth Amendment. In addition, prosecutors should refrain from using their grand jury subpoena power to obtain information from private investigators employed by the defense attorney. Judicial remedies for violations of these rules often include suppression of subpoenaed evidence and dismissal of a criminal indictment.

By the same token, some criminal defense lawyers ignore situations in which a client informs them of his or her intention to commit perjury. The purpose of the defense attorney's investigation is to learn the truth from the client. The defense attorney also has a professional responsibility to persuade the defendant not to commit perjury, which is a crime.

It is the duty of the prosecutor to seek justice and not merely to obtain a conviction; this goal also applies to the criminal defense attorney. As legal scholar David G. Bress so aptly put it, "A defense attorney does not promote the attainment of justice when he secures his client's freedom through illegal and improper means."[67]

Often, the public image of prosecutors and defense attorneys is shaped by television programs, movies, and newspaper stories (see the accompanying Images of Justice feature). You may hear of a prosecutor who takes a campaign donation and ignores a politician's crime. A defense attorney may use improper influence in representing a client. Unfortunately, corruption is still a fact of life in the justice system. Doing everything possible to deter such behavior is an important aspect of a fair justice system.

## Ethical Challenges in Criminal Justice: A Writing Assignment

You are a defense attorney. Your client was recently convicted of killing two police officers and sentenced to prison for 25 years. When both of you are conferring about a possible appeal, your client unapologetically admits that he also a murdered a third man, a McDonald's security guard. You discover, however, that an innocent man was convicted of the security guard's murder and was also sentenced to 25 years in prison. You feel bound by attorney–client privilege not to disclose the confession, because doing so would mean a new trial for your client and possibly even more time in prison. Meanwhile, an innocent man was convicted and is now serving a lengthy sentence.

Write an essay on the ethical issues raised in this scenario. In doing so, answer these questions: What should you do? *Can* you do anything? What if your client is unsuccessful in his appeal, serves out his term, and dies in prison? Should you then reveal the confession because it could help free an innocent man? For guidance, consult the subsection on ethics in this chapter's "Defense Attorney" section.

## SUMMARY

**1. Understand the role of the prosecutor.**

- The prosecutor is an appointed or elected member of the practicing bar who is responsible for bringing the state's case against the accused.

- The prosecutor is the chief law enforcement officer of a particular jurisdiction.

- Although the prosecutor's primary duty is to enforce the criminal law, his or her fundamental obligations are to seek justice and convict those who are guilty.

**2. Know the similarities and differences between different types of prosecutors.**

- In the federal system, prosecutors are known as U.S. attorneys and are appointed by the president.

- At the state and county levels, the attorney general and the district attorney, respectively, are the chief prosecutorial officers.

- Most prosecutions take place at the local level.

**3. Recognize the role of prosecutorial discretion in the justice system.**

- The prosecutor, who is the people's attorney, has discretion to decide the criminal charge and disposition.

- The prosecutor retains a great deal of discretion in processing cases.

**4. Identify factors that affect prosecutors' charging decisions.**

- System, case, disposition, and political factors all shape a prosecutor's charging decisions.

- System factors associated with prosecutors' charging decisions include the cost of trial, court backlog, and seriousness of the crime.

- Case factors associated with prosecutors' charging decisions include the strength of evidence, victim–offender relationships, victim and/or offender background, victim injury, victim attitude and/or cooperation, concern with possible harm to the suspect (perhaps resulting from a prison sentence), availability of alternative procedures, suspect cooperation, and the presence and/or use of a weapon.

- Disposition factors associated with prosecutors' charging decisions include preferences for diversion or treatment/rehabilitation.

- Political factors associated with prosecutors' charging decisions include pressure from the elected prosecutor, public outrage, media scrutiny, and lobbying efforts by concerned groups.

**5. Be familiar with the problem of overzealous prosecution.**

- Examples of overzealous prosecution include selective prosecution, pretextual prosecution, fabrication of evidence, use of false statements at trial, withholding potentially favorable evidence from the defense, influencing witnesses, and reneging on plea agreements.

- Prosecutors cannot be held civilly liable for their actions during the judicial phase of a case, but they can be disciplined and/or disbarred for improper behavior.

**6. Understand the role of the defense attorney.**

■ The defense attorney is the counterpart of the prosecuting attorney in the criminal process.

■ Defense attorneys perform several functions while representing the accused. These tasks include investigating the incident; interviewing the client, police, and witnesses; discussing the matter with the prosecutor; representing the defendant at the various pretrial procedures, such as arrest, interrogation, lineup, and arraignment; entering into plea negotiations; preparing the case for trial, including developing tactics and strategy; filing and arguing legal motions with the court; representing the defendant at trial; providing assistance at sentencing; and determining the appropriate basis for appeal.

**7. Explain the importance of defense ethics.**

■ Many ethical issues face defense attorneys, such as whether they should keep their clients' statements confidential even though they know the clients are lying and whether they should defend criminals who they know are guilty.

**8. Discuss the right to counsel.**

■ Today, providing defense services to the indigent criminal defendant is an everyday practice.

■ Under landmark decisions of the U.S. Supreme Court, particularly *Gideon v. Wainwright* and *Argersinger v. Hamlin*, all defendants who can face imprisonment for any offense must be afforded counsel at trial.

**9. Recognize the different types of defender services.**

■ Methods of providing counsel include assigned counsel systems, in which an attorney is selected by the court to represent the accused; public defender programs, in which public employees provide legal services; contract systems, in which legal services to indigent defendants are provided by private attorneys under contract with the state or county; and mixed systems, in which both public defenders and private attorneys are used.

**10. Determine the effectiveness of public versus private attorneys.**

■ Researchers have found that private counsel may have a slightly better track record in some areas (such as death penalty cases) but that court-appointed lawyers do quite well.

**11. Know the problems of the criminal bar.**

■ Private attorneys are often accused of sacrificing their clients' interests for pursuit of profit.

■ Public defenders are often young attorneys who are seeking trial practice before going on to high-paying jobs in established law firms.

■ Plea bargaining is commonplace because little time and insufficient resources are available to give criminal defendants a full-scale defense.

■ The prosecutor and the defense attorney have to work together, despite the presence of adversarial conflicts between the two.

## KEY TERMS

prosecutor, 360
United States attorneys, 365
attorney general, 365
district attorney, 365
community prosecution, 367
prosecutorial discretion, 368

nolle prosequi, 368
grand jury, 368
diversion, 371
defense attorney, 374
indigent defendant, 378
assigned counsel, 378

public defender, 378
recoupment, 379
contract system, 380
pro bono, 383
subpoena, 384

## CRITICAL THINKING QUESTIONS

1. Should attorneys disclose information given them by their clients concerning participation in earlier unsolved crimes?

2. Should defense attorneys cooperate with prosecutors if it means that their clients will go to jail?

3. Should prosecutors have absolute discretion over which cases to proceed on and which to drop? Do you believe prosecutors should have a great deal of discretion? Why?

4. Should potential clients have access to their attorney's track record in court?

5. Does the assigned counsel system present an inherent conflict of interest because attorneys are hired and paid by the institution they are to oppose?

6. Which kinds of cases do you think are most likely to be handled informally?

7. Explain the following: "It is the duty of the prosecutor to seek justice, not merely a conviction."

8. What are the differences between community prosecution and the traditional approach to prosecution?

# NOTES

1. See, for example, *United States v. Ruiz*, 536 U.S. 622 (2002).

2. *Berger v. United States*, 295 U.S. 78 (1935).

3. Steven W. Perry, *Prosecutors in State Courts*, 2005 (Washington, D.C.: U.S. Department of Justice, 2006).

4. Department of Health and Human Services, *Child Maltreatment 2006* (Washington, D.C.: Department of Health and Human Services, Administration for Children and Families, Children's Bureau, 2008).

5. Victor I. Vieth, *Investigating and Prosecuting Cases of Child Abuse* (Alexandria, Va.: American Prosecutors Research Institute, 2005).

6. Project Safe Neighborhoods, http://psn.gov/ (accessed April 23, 2010).

7. Jan Roehl, Dennis P. Rosenbaum, Sandra K. Costello, James R. Coldren Jr., Amie M. Schuck, Laura Kunard, and David R. Forde, *Paving the Way for Project Safe Neighborhoods: SACSI in 10 U.S. Cities* (Washington, D.C.: National Institute of Justice, 2008).

8. Michael Benson, Francis Cullen, and William Maakestad, "Local Prosecutors and Corporate Crime," *Crime and Delinquency* 36 (July 1990): 356–372.

9. Heather Jacobson and Rebecca Green, "Computer Crime," *American Criminal Law Review* 39 (2002): 273–326; Identity Theft and Assumption Act of 1998 (18 U.S.C. §1028(a)(7)).

10. American Prosecutors Research Institute, *Environmental Crime Prosecution: Results of a National Survey*, National Institute of Justice Research in Brief (Washington, D.C.: National Institute of Justice, 1994).

11. Bureau of Justice Statistics, *The Criminal Justice and Community Response to Rape* (Rockville, Md.: National Criminal Justice Reference Service, 1994).

12. Donald Rebovich, "Expanding the Role of Local Prosecution," *National Institute of Justice Journal Research in Action* 28 (1994): 21–24.

13. Michael Powell and David Segal, "In New York, a Grisly Traffic in Body Parts, Illegal Sales Worry Dead's Kin, Tissue Recipients," *Washington Post*, January 28, 2006, p. A3; William Sherman, "Clients Flee Biz Eyed in Ghoul Probe," *New York Daily News*, October 13, 2005.

14. Robert Chesney, "Anticipatory Prosecution in the War on Terror," in John L. Worrall and M. Elaine Nugent-Borakove, *The Changing Role of the American Prosecutor* (Albany, N.Y.: SUNY Press, 2008).

15. Kelly R. Damphouse and Chris Shields, "The Morning After: Assessing the Effect of Major Terrorism Events on Prosecution Strategies and Outcomes," *Journal of Contemporary Criminal Justice* 23 (2007): 174–194.

16. Mark Cohen, "Environmental Crime and Punishment: Legal/Economic Theory and Empirical Evidence on Enforcement of Federal Environmental Statutes," *Journal of Criminal Law and Criminology* 82 (1992): 1054–1109.

17. Grace Wong, "Kozlowski Gets Up to 25 Years," http://money.cnn.com/2005/09/19/news/newsmakers/kozlowski_sentence/ (accessed August 8, 2008).

18. American Bar Association, *Standards for Criminal Justice: Prosecution Function and Defense Function*, 3rd ed. (Washington, D.C.: 1993). See also American Bar Association, *Standards for Criminal Justice: Providing Defense Sources*, 3rd ed. (Washington, D.C.: 1993).

19. John L. Worrall and M. Elaine Nugent-Borakove, eds., *The Changing Role of the American Prosecutor* (Albany, N.Y.: SUNY Press, 2008).

20. Eric Holden, "Community Prosecution," *Prosecutor* 34 (2000): 31.

21. William Scott Cunningham, Brian C. Renauer, and Christy Khalifa, "Sharing the Keys to the Courthouse: Adoption of Community Prosecution by State Court Prosecutors," *Journal of Contemporary Criminal Justice* 22 (2006): 202–219.

22. Douglas Gansler, "Implementing Community Prosecution in Montgomery County, Maryland," *Prosecutor* 34 (2000): 30.

23. Kenneth C. Davis, *Discretionary Justice* (Baton Rouge: Louisiana State University Press, 1969), p. 180. See also James B. Stewart, *The Prosecutor* (New York: Simon and Schuster, 1987).

24. Barbara Boland, *The Prosecution of Felony Arrests* (Washington, D.C.: Government Printing Office, 1983).

25. Leslie Griffin, "The Prudent Prosecutor," *Georgetown Journal of Legal Ethics* 14 (2001): 259–308.

26. *United States v. Armstrong*, 517 U.S. 456 at 464 (1996).

27. Newman Baker, "The Prosecutor—Initiation of Prosecution," *Journal of Criminal Law, Criminology, and Police Science* 23 (1933): 770–771.

28. Rodney F. Kingsworth, Randall C. Macintosh, and Sandra Sutherland, "Criminal Charge or Probation Violation? Prosecutorial Discretion and Implication for Research in Criminal Court Processing," *Criminology* 40 (2002): 553–577.

29. Frank W. Miller, *Prosecution: The Decision to Charge a Suspect with a Crime* (Boston: Little, Brown, 1970). See also Harvey Wallace, "A Prosecutor's Guide to Stalking," *Prosecutor* 29 (1995): 26–30.

30. Boland, *The Prosecution of Felony Arrests*.

31. John Worrall, Jay Ross, and Eric McCord, "Modeling Prosecutors' Charging Decisions in Domestic Violence Cases," *Crime and Delinquency* 52 (2006): 472–503.

32. Dennis J. Stevens, "Forensic Science, Wrongful Convictions, and American Prosecutor Discretion," *Howard Journal of Criminal Justice* 47 (2008): 31–51.

33. American Bar Association, *Standards for Criminal Justice: Prosecution Function and Defense Function*, Standard 3.8, p. 33.

34. Michael Tonry and Richard Frase, *Sentencing and Sanctions in Western Countries* (London: Oxford University Press, 2001).

35. Robert Davis, Barbara Smith, and Bruce Taylor, "Increasing the Proportion of Domestic Violence Arrests That Are Prosecuted: A Natural Experiment in Milwaukee," *Criminology and Public Policy* 2 (2003): 263–282.

36. Charles D. Breitel, "Control in Criminal Law Enforcement," *University of Chicago Law Review* 27 (1960): 427.

37. Cassia Spohn, Dawn Beichner, and Erika Davis-Frenzel, "Prosecutorial Justifications for Sexual Assault Case Rejection: Guarding the 'Gateway to Justice,'" *Social Problems* 48 (2001): 206–235.

38. *Yick Wo v. Hopkins*, 118 U.S. 356 (1886).

39. *United States v. Cammisano*, 413 F.Supp. 886 (1976).

40. *Imbler v. Pachtman*, 424 U.S. 409 (1976); also see *Burns v. Reed*, 500 U.S. 478 (1991) and *Kalina v. Fletcher*, 522 U.S. 118 (1997).

41. Center for Public Integrity, *Harmful Error: Investigative America's Local Prosecutors*, www.publicintegrity.org/pm/ (accessed April 23, 2010).

42. American Bar Association, *Report of Standing Committee on Legal Aid and Indigent Defendants* (Chicago: 1991).

43. See American Bar Association, *Model Rules of Professional Conduct* (Chicago: American Bar Association, 1994), Rule 12.

44. Monroe H. Freedman, "Professional Responsibility of the Criminal Defense Lawyer: The Three Hardest Questions," *Michigan Law Review* 64 (1966): 1468.

45. Michael Asimow and Richard Weisberg, "When the Lawyer Knows the Client Is Guilty: Client Confessions in Legal Ethics, Popular Culture, and Literature," *Southern California Interdisciplinary Law Journal* 18 (2009): 229–258.

46. Jonathan Glater, "Lawyers Pressed to Give Up Ground on Client Secrets," *New York Times*, August 10, 2003, p. 1.

47. Bennett Brummer, *Ethics Resource Guide for Public Defenders* (Chicago: American Bar Association, February 1992).

48. *Miranda v. Arizona*, 384 U.S. 436 (1966).

49. *Mempa v. Rhay*, 389 U.S. 128 (1967).

50. *Douglas v. California*, 372 U.S. 353 (1963).

51. *In re Gault*, 387 U.S. 1 (1967); *Specht v. Patterson*, 386 U.S. 605 (1967).

52. National Center for State Courts, *Indigent Defense FAQs*, www.ncsconline.org/WC/CourTopics/FAQs.asp?topic=IndDef#FAQ533 (accessed April 23, 2010).

53. See *Betts v. Brady*, 316 U.S. 455 (1942). Justice Black subsequently wrote the majority opinion in *Gideon v. Wainwright*, guaranteeing defendants' right to counsel and overruling the *Betts* case.

54. *Gideon v. Wainwright*, 372 U.S. 335 (1963).

55. *Argersinger v. Hamlin*, 407 U.S. 25 (1972).

56. See F. Brownell, *Legal Aid in the United States* (Chicago: National Legal Aid Defender Association, 1961). For an interesting study of the Cook County, Illinois, Office of Public Defenders, see Lisa McIntyre, *Public Defenders: Practice of Law in Shadows of Dispute* (Chicago: University of Chicago Press, 1987).

57. Bureau of Justice Statistics, *Indigent Defense Statistics*, http://bjs.ojp.usdoj.gov/index.cfm?ty=tp&tid=215 (accessed April 23, 2010).

58. Pauline Houlden and Steven Balkin, "Quality and Cost Comparisons of Private Bar Indigent Defense Systems:

Contract vs. Ordered Assigned Counsel," *Journal of Criminal Law and Criminology* 76 (1985): 176–200. See also John Arrango, "Defense Services for the Poor," *American Bar Association Journal on Criminal Justice* 12 (1998): 35.

59. Lawrence Spears, "Contract Counsel: A Different Way to Defend the Poor—How It's Working in North Dakota," *American Bar Association Journal on Criminal Justice* 6 (1991): 24–31.

60. *Argersinger v. Hamlin*.

61. Timothy Murphy, "Indigent Defense and the War on Drugs: The Public Defender's Losing Battle," *American Bar Association Journal on Criminal Justice* 6 (1991): 14–20.

62. Robert Spangenberg and Tessa J. Schwartz, "The Indigent Defense Crisis Is Chronic," *Criminal Justice Journal* 9 (1994): 13–16; *Sourcebook of Criminal Justice Statistics: 1998* (Washington, D.C.: U.S. Department of Justice, 1999).

63. See Drug Control Act of 1988, 42 U.S.C. §375 (G)(10).

64. Data compiled by the Bureau of Justice Statistics, www.ojp.usdoj.gov/bjs/id.htm#conviction (accessed April 23, 2010).

65. Talia Roitberg Harmon and William Lofquist, "Too Late for Luck: A Comparison of Post-*Furman* Exonerations and Executions of the Innocent," *Crime and Delinquency* 51 (2005): 498–520.

66. Morris B. Hoffman, Paul H. Rubin, and Joanna M. Shepherd, "An Empirical Study of Public Defender Effectiveness: Self-Selection by the 'Marginally Indigent,'" *Ohio State Journal of Criminal Law* 3 (2005): 223–251, at 225.

67. David G. Bress, "Professional Ethics in Criminal Trials," *Michigan Law Review* 64 (1966): 1493; John Mitchell, "The Ethics of the Criminal Defense Attorney," *Stanford Law Review* 32 (1980): 325.

# CHAPTER 11

# Pretrial and Trial Procedures

## CHAPTER OBJECTIVES

1. Understand the procedures following arrest.
2. Discuss the legal right to bail.
3. List a variety of bail systems.
4. Recount the history of bail reform.
5. Define pretrial services.
6. List the differences between the indictment process and the information process.
7. Discuss the purpose of arraignment.
8. Explain what is meant by the term "plea bargain."
9. Discuss the pros and cons of plea bargaining.
10. Explain the roles of the prosecutor, defense attorney, judge, and victim in the plea negotiation.
11. Define the term "pretrial diversion."
12. Explain the legal rights of the accused at trial.
13. Summarize the trial process.

**L**ewis Ferrari was found dead in his home on September 5, 2002. The police quickly focused on Jerry Moore, a disgruntled former employee of Ferrari. As they were investigating the case, officers interviewed Jesse Montejo, one of Moore's known associates. Montejo claimed he was with Moore on the day of the murder and eventually admitted that he, not Moore, had shot and killed Ferrari. He even told police that he discarded the murder weapon in a nearby lake. After his admission, Montejo was brought before a judge, formally charged with murder, and assigned a public defender. Later that day, two detectives visited Montejo in his cell and requested that he accompany them so they could locate the gun used to kill Ferrari. Montejo was advised of his Miranda rights, agreed to waive them, and went along with the detectives. While the three were away, Montejo wrote an incriminating letter of apology to Ferrari's widow. Only after coming back to the jail did Montejo have an opportunity to meet his court-appointed attorney, who was more than a little displeased with the detectives' actions.

At trial, the apology letter was admitted over defense objection, and Montejo was convicted and sentenced to death. He later appealed, arguing that his right to counsel was violated when he was questioned by police, after being formally charged, in the absence of his attorney. As part of his argument, he cited an earlier Supreme Court decision, Michigan v. Jackson,[1] in which it was decided that any waiver of Miranda is invalid after a person has been charged, appointed counsel, and later interrogated by police. In other words, Montejo argued that anything he said (and wrote, including the letter) after the detectives began questioning him was not admissible at trial. It seemed Montejo had the weight of Supreme Court precedent to back him up, but the Supreme Court did not agree with his argument. It even went so far as to overturn Jackson. The Court's decision, announced in Montejo v. Louisiana,[2] is an important one. It means that even after counsel is appointed, the police may approach the defendant outside of the presence of counsel and seek to question him or her—even about the charge for which counsel was appointed! ■

**CourseMate** For more information about the **Pretrial Justice Institute**, visit the Criminal Justice CourseMate at CengageBrain.com, then access the "Web Links" for this chapter.

**pretrial procedures**
Legal and administrative actions that take place after arrest and before trial, including grand jury indictments, preliminary hearings, bail, and plea negotiation.

The *Montejo* case highlights many of the intricacies of pretrial and trial procedure. It even raises some of the issues we touched on in Chapter 8 during the discussion of *Miranda v. Arizona*. It is not yet entirely clear what effect *Montejo* will have on pretrial procedures. It will certainly prompt defense attorneys to advise their clients about the possibility of being approached by police for questioning, even after being charged, but will every defendant capably assert his or her right to remain silent? Montejo was in jail when he was questioned, but what if a defendant is released prior to trial? Will the situation differ? This will be an interesting issue to follow.

This chapter reviews the pretrial and trial process, beginning with the pretrial procedures. **Pretrial procedures** are important components of the justice process because the vast majority of all criminal cases are resolved informally at this stage and never come before the courts. Although the media like to focus on the elaborate jury trial with its dramatic elements and impressive setting, formal criminal trials are relatively infrequent. Consequently, understanding the events that take place during the pretrial period is essential in grasping the reality of criminal justice policy.

## PROCEDURES FOLLOWING ARREST

After arrest, the accused is ordinarily taken to the police station, where the police list the possible criminal charges against him and obtain other information for the booking process. This may include recording a description of the suspect and the circumstances of the offense. The suspect may then be fingerprinted, photographed, and required to participate in a lineup.

**complaint**
A sworn written statement addressed to a court or judge by the police, prosecutor, or individual alleging that an individual has committed an offense and requesting indictment and prosecution.

The arrestee is usually detained by the police until it is decided whether a criminal complaint will be filed. The **complaint** is the formal written document identifying the criminal charge, the date and place where the crime occurred, and the circumstances of the arrest. The complaint is sworn to and signed under oath by the complainant, usually a police officer. The complaint will request that the defendant be present at an initial hearing held soon after the arrest is made. In some jurisdictions, this may be referred to by other names, such as arraignment. During **arraignment**, the judge informs the defendant of the charge, ensures that the accused is properly represented by counsel, and determines whether he should be released on bail or some other form of release pending a hearing or trial.

**arraignment**
Initial trial court appearance, at which the accused is read the charges, advised of his or her rights, and asked to enter a plea.

The defendant may plead guilty at the initial hearing, and the case may be disposed of immediately. A defendant who pleads not guilty to a minor offense has been informed of the formal charge, provided with counsel if he is unable to afford a private attorney, and asked to plead guilty or not guilty as charged. A date in the near future is set for trial, and the defendant is generally released on bail or on his own recognizance to await trial. When a felony or a more serious crime is involved, there is usually another step before a person can be tried. This involves proving to an objective body that there is probable cause to believe that a crime has taken place and that the accused should be tried on the matter. This step of the formal charging process is ordinarily an indictment from a grand jury or a charging document known as an information issued by a lower court.

In addition to these steps in the pretrial phase, the defendant is also considered for bail so that he may remain in the community to prepare his criminal defense. Even at this early stage, some may enter court-based treatment programs.

**bail**
The monetary amount required for pretrial release, normally set by a judge at the initial appearance. The purpose of bail is to ensure the return of the accused at subsequent proceedings.

## BAIL

**Bail** is a form of security, usually a sum of money that is put up or exchanged to secure the release of an arrested person before the trial begins. The bail amount serves as a bond, ensuring that the released criminal defendant will return for trial. Failure to appear results in the forfeiting of the bail.

Whether a defendant can be expected to appear at the next stage of the criminal proceedings is a key issue in determining bail.[3] Bail cannot be used to punish an accused, and it cannot be denied or revoked at the indulgence of the court. Bail is a critical stage in the justice process and a key ingredient of a fair and equitable adjudication process: It enables people charged with a crime to be free in the community in order to prepare a defense to the state's criminal charges. It also prevents an innocent person from spending months, if not years, behind bars awaiting trial, only to be freed after a not-guilty verdict is rendered.

## The Legal Right to Bail

Bail is not a new practice. Under English common law, criminal defendants were eligible to be released before trial. Up through the thirteenth century, however, the county shire reeve (sheriff) controlled the release of defendants awaiting trial. The sheriffs were given discretion to determine who would be held and who released and how much bail was required. Because sheriffs sometimes exploited their power, Parliament issued the Statute of Westminster in 1275; it set out the offenses that were bailable and those that were not. Under the new law, the sheriff still retained the authority to determine the amount of bail.

English bail practices were continued in the original colonies. After the Revolution, Congress passed the Judiciary Act of 1789, which set out conditions for bail and limited judicial discretion in setting bail amounts. As the Judiciary Act states, "Upon all arrests in criminal cases, bail shall be admitted, except where punishment may be by death, in which cases it shall not be admitted but by the supreme or a circuit court, or by a justice of the supreme court, or a judge of a district court, who shall exercise their discretion therein."[4]

Bail was also incorporated into the Eighth Amendment of the U.S. Constitution, but only insofar as it prohibits "excessive bail." The Eighth Amendment's excessive bail clause may be interpreted to mean that the sole purpose of bail is to ensure that the defendant returns for trial; bail may not be used as a form of punishment or to coerce or threaten a defendant. In most cases, a defendant has the right to be released on reasonable bail. Many jurisdictions also require a bail review hearing by a higher court in cases in which the initial judge set what might be considered excessive bail.

The U.S. Supreme Court's interpretation of the Eighth Amendment's provisions on bail was set out in the 1951 case of *Stack v. Boyle*.[5] In that case, the

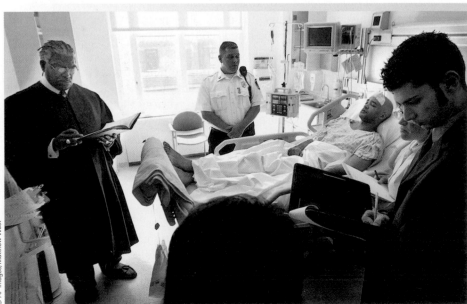

*Bail hearings are generally held in court, but there are always exceptions. At his bail hearing, carjacking suspect John Powell, 30, hospitalized with a gunshot wound to the head, lies on his bed at Boston Medical Center after his arraignment. Judge Edward Redd (left) arraigned Powell in private before opening the room to the media. At center is court officer Michael McCusker. At right are defense attorney Beth Eisenberg and intern Jason Benzahn, from the Roxbury Defenders League.*

Court found bail to be a traditional right to freedom before trial that permits unhampered preparation of a defense and prevents the criminal defendant from being punished prior to conviction. The Court held that bail is excessive when it exceeds an amount reasonably calculated to ensure that the defendant will return for trial. The Court indicated that bail should be in the amount that is generally set for similar offenses. Higher bail can be imposed when evidence supporting the increase is presented at a hearing in which the defendant's constitutional rights can be protected. Although *Stack* did not establish an absolute right to bail, it did set guidelines for state courts to follow: If a crime is bailable, the amount set should not be frivolous, unusual, or beyond a person's ability to pay.

## Making Bail

A majority of criminal defendants are released on bail prior to trial.[6] The most recent surveys of pretrial release practices show that about two-thirds of felony defendants are released prior to the final disposition of their case. As might be expected, defendants charged with the most serious violent offenses are less likely to be released than those charged with less serious public order or drug offenses. Defendants charged with murder are the least likely to be released prior to case disposition. In contrast, defendants charged with misdemeanors and nonviolent felonies are routinely granted bail. All else equal, the less serious the charge, the more likely it is that bail will be granted.

When and how are bail decisions made? Bail is typically considered at a court hearing conducted shortly after a person has been taken into custody. At the hearing, such issues as crime type, flight risk, and dangerousness are considered before a bail amount is set. In jurisdictions with pretrial release programs, program staff often interview arrestees detained at the jail prior to the first hearing, verify the background information, and present recommendations to the court at arraignment. Prior record is an important factor: Fewer than half of defendants with an active criminal justice status, such as parole or probation, at the time of arrest were released, compared to 67 percent of these with no active status. Some jurisdictions have developed bail schedules to make amounts uniform based on the crime and the defendant's criminal history.

## Alternative Bail Release Mechanisms

Although bail is typically granted during a court hearing, there are other stages in the system in which bail may be granted:

■ *Police field citation release.* An arresting officer releases the arrestee on a written promise to appear in court made at or near the actual time and location of the arrest. This procedure is commonly used for misdemeanor charges and is similar to issuing a traffic ticket.

■ *Police station house citation release.* The determination of an arrestee's eligibility and suitability for release and the actual release of the arrestee are deferred until after he or she has been removed from the scene of an arrest and brought to the station house or police headquarters.

■ *Police/pretrial jail citation release.* The determination of an arrestee's eligibility and suitability for citation release and the actual release of the arrestee are deferred until after he or she has been delivered by the arresting department to a jail or other pretrial detention facility for screening, booking, and admission.

■ *Pretrial/court direct release by pretrial bail program.* To streamline release processes and reduce the length of stay in detention, pretrial program courts may authorize pretrial programs to release defendants without direct judicial involvement. When court rules delegate such authority, the practice is generally limited to misdemeanor charges, but felony release authority has been granted in some jurisdictions.

■ *Police/court bail schedule*. An arrestee can post bail at the station house or jail according to amounts specified in a bail schedule. The schedule is a list of all bailable charges and a corresponding dollar amount for each. Schedules may vary widely from jurisdiction to jurisdiction.

## Types of Bail

There are a variety of ways or mechanisms to secure bail, depending on the jurisdiction, the crime, and the defendant:

■ *Full cash bail*. The defendant pays the full bail amount out of pocket. In some jurisdictions, property can be pledged instead of cash.

■ *Deposit bail*. The defendant deposits a percentage of the bail amount, typically 10 percent, with the court. When the defendant appears in court, the deposit is returned, sometimes minus an administrative fee. If the defendant fails to appear, he or she is liable for the full amount of the bail.

■ *Surety bail*. The defendant pays a percentage of the bond, usually 10 percent, to a bonding agent, who posts the full bail. The fee paid to the bonding agent is not returned to the defendant if he or she appears in court. The bonding agent is liable for the full amount of the bond should the defendant fail to appear. Bail bonding agents hire bounty hunters to find defendants who fail to appear for their court dates.

■ *Conditional bail*. The defendant is released after promising to abide by some specified conditions in lieu of cash. For example, she promises to attend a treatment program prior to trial.

■ *Unsecured bond*. The defendant is released with no immediate requirement of payment. However, if the defendant fails to appear, he is liable for the full amount.

■ *Release on recognizance*. Eligible defendants are released without bail upon their promise to return for trial.

As Figure 11.1 shows, surety bond is now the most common type of bail form used with felony defendants, followed by release on recognizance and conditional bail. Relatively few defendants pay full cash bail out of pocket.

## Pretrial Detention

The criminal defendant who is not eligible for bail or release on recognizance is subject to pretrial detention in the local county jail. Unfortunately, the jail has long been a trouble spot for the criminal justice system. Conditions tend to be poor and rehabilitation nonexistent.

In terms of the number of persons affected each year, pretrial custody accounts for more U.S. incarceration than does imprisonment after sentencing. On any given day in the United States, nearly 800,000 people are held in more than 3,500 local jails.[7] Over the course of a year, many times that number pass through the jailhouse door. More than 50 percent of those held in local jails have been accused of crimes but not convicted; they are **pretrial detainees**. In the United States, people are detained at a rate twice that of neighboring Canada and three times that of Great Britain. Hundreds of jails are overcrowded, and many are under court orders to reduce their populations and improve conditions. The national jail-crowding crisis has worsened over the years.

**FIGURE 11.1**
Pretrial Release by Type of Bail Received

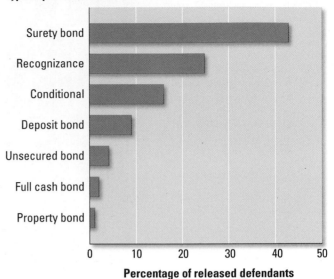

Type of pretrial release

Percentage of released defendants

Source: Tracey Kyckelhahn and Thomas H. Cohen, *Felony Defendants in Large Urban Counties*, 2004 (Washington, D.C.: Bureau of Justice Statistics, 2008).

**CourseMate** For more information about the **Professional Bail Agents**, visit the Criminal Justice CourseMate at CengageBrain.com, then access the "Web Links" for this chapter.

**pretrial detainees**
People who either are denied bail or cannot afford to post bail before trial and are kept in secure confinement.

Jails can be overcrowded and dangerous. Sometimes it takes a court order to improve conditions. Prisoners at Marion County Lockup in Indianapolis sleep on the floor. At least 19 of Indiana's 92 counties have jail populations that are near or beyond their intended capacities. Many have been using some form of early release to reduce the number of inmates. Despite early releases, crowding at the Marion County Lockup is still under scrutiny as its population continues to soar.

© AP Images/Indianapolis Star/Mike Fender

Jails are often considered the weakest link in the criminal justice process. They are frequently dangerous, harmful, decrepit, and filled with the poor and friendless. The costs of holding a person in jail range up to more than $100 per day, or $36,000 per year.[8] In addition, detainees are often confined with those convicted of crimes and those who have been transferred from other institutions because of overcrowding. Many felons are transferred to jails from state prisons to ease crowding. It is possible to have in close quarters a convicted rapist, a father jailed for nonpayment of child support, and a person awaiting trial for a crime that he did not commit. This mix of inmates can lead to violence, brutality, and suicide.

What happens to those who find themselves jailed because they cannot afford to put up bail money? Traditionally, they are more likely to be convicted and get longer prison sentences than those who commit similar crimes but are released on bail. A federally sponsored study of case processing in the nation's largest counties found that about 59 percent of all defendants released prior to their trial were convicted; in contrast, 78 percent of detainees were convicted.[9] Detainees are also more likely than releasees to be convicted of a felony offense and, therefore, are eligible for a long prison sentence instead of the much shorter term of incarceration given misdemeanants. People being held in jails are in a less attractive bargaining position than those released on bail, and prosecutors, knowing their predicament, may be less generous in their negotiations. It is for these reasons that bail reform advocates have tried so hard to eliminate, whenever possible, the detention of nondangerous criminal defendants.

## Bail Reform

Bail has been heavily criticized as one of the most unacceptable aspects of the criminal justice system. Some view it as discriminatory because it works against the poor, who have a much tougher time making bail. Others argue that it is costly because the government must pay to detain those offenders who are unable to make bail but who would otherwise remain in the community. Another problem is the legal effect of detention.

Most states place no precise limit on the amount of bail that a judge may impose. People charged with the most serious crimes usually receive the highest amount of bail. As Table 11.1 shows, about 40 percent of all defendants are given

| TABLE 11.1 | | | | | |
| --- | --- | --- | --- | --- | --- |
| **Bail Amount Set for Felony Defendants** | | | | | |
| Number of defendants | Under $5,000 | $5,000– $9,999 | $10,000– $24,999 | $25,000– $49,999 | $50,000 or more |
| 34,120 | 20% | 19% | 24% | 14% | 23% |

Source: Tracey Kyckelhahn and Thomas H. Cohen, *Felony Defendants in Large Urban Counties, 2004* (Washington, D.C.: Bureau of Justice Statistics, 2008).

bail amounts of under $10,000, and about one-third are asked to put up more than $25,000.

This data troubles experts who believe that the bail system is discriminatory because defendants who are financially well off can make bail, whereas indigent defendants languish in pretrial detention in the county jail. In addition, keeping a person in jail imposes serious financial burdens on local and state governments— and, in turn, on taxpayers, who must pay for the cost of confinement. These factors have given rise to bail reform programs that depend on the defendant's personal promise to appear in court for trial, instead of on financial ability to meet bail. These reforms have enabled many deserving but indigent offenders to go free, but another trend has been to deny people bail on the grounds that they are a danger to themselves or to others in the community.

*RELEASE ON RECOGNIZANCE*  Efforts have been made to reform and even eliminate money bail and reduce the importance of bonding agents. Until the early 1960s, the justice system relied primarily on money bonds as the principal form of pretrial release. Many states now allow defendants to be released without any money bail. This is known as **release on recognizance (ROR)**. ROR programs were popular in the 1960s[10] and resulted in bail reforms that culminated in the enactment of the federal Bail Reform Act of 1966, the first change in federal bail laws since 1789.[11] This legislation sought to ensure that release would be granted in all noncapital cases in which sufficient reason existed to believe that the defendant would return to court. The law clearly established the presumption of ROR that must be overcome before money bail is required, authorized 10 percent deposit bail, introduced the concept of conditional release, and stressed the philosophy that release should be under the least restrictive method adequate to ensure court appearance.

During the 1970s and early 1980s, the pretrial release movement was hampered by public pressure over pretrial increases in crime. As a result, more recent federal legislation, the Bail Reform Act of 1984, mandated that no defendants shall be kept in pretrial detention simply because they cannot afford money bail, established the presumption for ROR in all cases in which a person is bailable, and formalized restrictive preventive detention provisions. The 1984 act required that community safety, as well as the risk of flight, be considered in the release decision. Consequently, such criminal justice factors as the seriousness of the charged offense, the weight of the evidence, the sentence that may be imposed upon conviction, court appearance history, and prior convictions are likely to influence the release decisions of the federal court.

*PREVENTIVE DETENTION*  Whereas bail reform efforts are typically aimed at liberalizing bail, there are also efforts to tighten bail restrictions on the most dangerous offenders. The reason is the fear that serious criminals may reoffend while in the community. These fears are not unfounded. Figure 11.2 shows which arrestees are most likely to engage in misconduct while released on bail.

**release on recognizance (ROR)**
A pretrial release in which a defendant with ties to the community is not required to post bail but promises to appear at all subsequent proceedings.

**CourseMate**  For more information about the **Bail Reform Act of 1984**, visit the Criminal Justice CourseMate at CengageBrain.com, then access the "Web Links" for this chapter.

**FIGURE 11.2**
Released Felony Defendants Committing
Misconduct, by Most Serious Arrest Charge, 2004

| Most serious arrest charge | Released felony defendants in the 75 largest counties | |
| --- | --- | --- |
| | Number | Percentage with misconduct |
| All offenses | 31,540 | 35 |
| Violent offenses | 6,356 | 29 |
| Murder | 41 | 39 |
| Rape | 258 | 15 |
| Robbery | 1,250 | 34 |
| Assault | 3,628 | 30 |
| Other violent | 1,179 | 24 |
| Property offenses | 9,556 | 38 |
| Burglary | 1,997 | 37 |
| Larceny/theft | 2,502 | 37 |
| Motor vehicle theft | 786 | 46 |
| Forgery | 1,437 | 37 |
| Fraud | 1,291 | 36 |
| Other property | 1,545 | 41 |
| Drug offenses | 12,055 | 38 |
| Trafficking | 4,987 | 38 |
| Other drug | 7,068 | 38 |
| Public-order offenses | 3,570 | 31 |
| Weapons | 990 | 32 |
| Driving-related | 1,202 | 32 |
| Other public-order | 1,379 | 28 |

Source: Tracey Kyckelhahn and Thomas H. Cohen, *Felony Defendants in Large Urban Counties, 2004* (Washington, D.C.: Bureau of Justice Statistics, 2008).

For example, 46 percent of suspects arrested for motor vehicle theft committed misconduct (failed to show up for their scheduled court dates, violated release conditions, or were rearrested for a new offense) while out on bail.

As Figure 11.3 shows, nearly 40 percent of released murder defendants were arrested on new charges prior to case disposition. In contrast, only 6 percent of offenders charged with rape were rearrested. Overall, 21 percent of released defendants were rearrested for a new offense allegedly committed while they awaited disposition of their original case. We call these people **avertable recidivists**—their crimes could have been prevented if they had not been given discretionary release and instead had been kept behind bars. Those rearrested tend to be on bail longer, to have a serious prior record, to abuse drugs, and to have a poor work record, and they are disproportionately young, male, and members of minority groups.

One response to the alleged failure of the bail system to protect citizens is the adoption of **preventive detention** statutes. These laws require that certain dangerous defendants be confined before trial for their own protection and that of the community. Preventive detention is an important manifestation of the crime control perspective on justice because it favors the use of incapacitation to control the future behavior of suspected criminals. Often, the key question is whether preventive detention is punishment before trial.

The most striking use of preventive detention can be found in the federal Bail Reform Act of 1984, which

**FIGURE 11.3**
Percentage of People Out on Bail Who Commit New Crimes and Are Rearrested, by Charge and Arrest Type

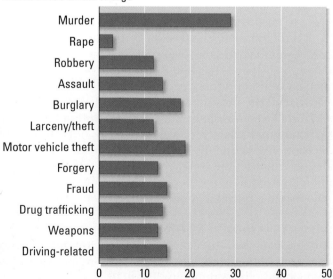

Source: Tracey Kyckelhahn and Thomas H. Cohen, *Felony Defendants in Large Urban Counties, 2004* (Washington, D.C.: Bureau of Justice Statistics, 2008).

contrasted sharply with previous laws.[12] Although the act does contain provisions for ROR, it allows judges to order preventive detention if they determine "that no condition or combination of conditions will reasonably assure the appearance of the person as required and the safety of any other person and the community."[13]

A number of state jurisdictions have incorporated elements of preventive detention into their bail systems. Although most of the restrictions do not constitute outright preventive detention, they serve to narrow the scope of bail eligibility. These provisions include exclusion of certain crimes from bail eligibility, definition of bail to include appearance in court and community safety, and limitations on right to bail for those previously convicted.

Preventive detention has also been a source of concern for civil libertarians who believe it violates the due process clause of the Constitution, because it means that a person will be held in custody before proven guilty. In two important cases, the Supreme Court disagreed with this analysis. In *Schall v. Martin*, the Court upheld the application of preventive detention statutes to juvenile defendants on the grounds that such detention is useful to protect the welfare of the minor and society as a whole.[14] In 1987, the Court upheld the Bail Reform Act's provision on preventive detention for adults in the case of *United States v. Salerno*, when it ruled that the Bail Reform Act's denial of bail to dangerous defendants did not violate the Eighth Amendment.[15]

**avertable recidivist**
A person whose crime would have been prevented if he or she had not been given discretionary release and instead had been kept behind bars.

**preventive detention**
The statutory authorization to deny bail to a particular individual who is considered dangerous or a flight risk.

## PERSPECTIVES ON JUSTICE

### Crime Control

Doesn't preventive detention amount to punishing an individual before he has been brought to trial and found guilty? Crime control advocates argue that even if the defendant is later found not guilty at trial, it is better to err on the side of caution and community safety. Denying defendants the right to bail because they are presumed to be dangerous is at the heart of the crime control perspective.

## PRETRIAL SERVICES

In our overburdened court system, it is critical to determine which defendants can safely be released on bail pending trial.[16] In many jurisdictions, specialized pretrial services help courts deal with this problem. Hundreds of pretrial programs have been established in rural, suburban, and urban jurisdictions; they are typically administered by probation departments, court offices, and local jails or handled by independent county contractors. These programs provide a number of critical services, including the following:

■ Gathering and verifying information about arrestees, including criminal history, current status in the criminal justice system, address, employment, and history of drug and alcohol use, which judicial officers can then take into account in making release/detention decisions.

■ Assessing each arrestee's likelihood of failure to appear and chances of being rearrested.

■ Providing supervision for defendants conditionally released and notifying the court of any failure to comply with release conditions.

Virtually all larger jurisdictions in the United States have pretrial release services in one form or another. Court-administered programs make up the greatest percentage of pretrial programs, although most newer programs are located within probation departments. The general criteria used to assess eligibility for release include the defendant's community ties and prior criminal justice involvement. Many jurisdictions have conditional and supervised release and third-party custody release, in addition to release on a person's own recognizance.

Some pretrial service programs are now being aimed at special needs. One type focuses on defendants suffering from mental illness; almost three-quarters of pretrial service programs now inquire about mental health status and treatment as a regular part of their interview, and about one-quarter report having implemented special supervision procedures for defendants with mental illness.

Another area of concern is domestic violence; about one-quarter of all pretrial programs have developed special risk-assessment procedures for defendants charged with domestic violence offenses, and about one-third have implemented special procedures to supervise such defendants.

## CHARGING THE DEFENDANT

Charging a defendant with a crime is a critical stage in the pretrial process. The charge is selected by the prosecutor, who takes into consideration the facts of the case, strength of the evidence, availability of witnesses, and so on. The process varies depending on whether it occurs via a grand jury or a preliminary hearing.

### The Indictment Process: The Grand Jury

The grand jury was an early development of English common law. Under the Magna Carta (1215), no "freeman" could be seized and imprisoned unless he had been judged by his peers. To determine fairly who was to be tried, a group of freemen from the district where a crime was committed would be brought together to examine the facts of the case and determine whether the charges had merit. Thus, the grand jury was created as a check against arbitrary prosecution by a judge who might be a puppet of the government.

The concept of the grand jury was brought to the American colonies by early settlers and later incorporated into the Fifth Amendment, which states that "no person shall be held to answer for a capital, or otherwise infamous crime, unless on a presentment or indictment of a grand jury." Today, the use of the grand jury is diminishing. Relatively few states require a grand jury indictment to begin all felony proceedings; most allow the prosecutor the option of calling a grand jury or proceeding with a preliminary hearing. The federal government employs both the grand jury and the preliminary hearing systems.

The grand jury today has two roles. First, it has the power to act as an independent investigating body. In this capacity, it examines the possibility of criminal activity within its jurisdiction. These investigative efforts are directed toward general, not individual, criminal conduct. After completing its investigation, the grand jury issues a report called a **presentment,** which contains its findings and (usually) a recommendation of indictment. An **indictment** is a written accusation charging a person with a crime. It is drawn up by a prosecutor and submitted to a grand jury, which—after considering the evidence presented by the prosecutor—votes to endorse or deny the indictment.

The grand jury's second and better-known role is accusatory in nature. In this capacity, the grand jury acts as the community's conscience in determining whether an accusation by the state (the prosecution) justifies a trial. The grand jury relies on the testimony of witnesses called by the prosecution through its subpoena power. After examining the evidence and the testimony of witnesses, the grand jury decides whether probable cause exists for prosecution. If it does, an indictment, or **true bill**, is affirmed. If the grand jury fails to find probable cause, a **no bill** (meaning that the indictment is ignored) is passed. In some states, a prosecutor can present evidence to a different grand jury if a no bill is returned; in other states, this action is prohibited by statute.

A grand jury is ordinarily made up of 16 to 23 individuals, depending on the requirements of the jurisdiction. This group theoretically represents a county. Selection of members varies from state to state, but for the most part, they are chosen at random (for example, from voting lists). To qualify to serve on a grand jury, an individual must be at least 18 years of age, must be a U.S. citizen, must have been a resident of the jurisdiction for one year or more, and must possess sufficient English-speaking skills for communication.

The grand jury usually meets at the request of the prosecution. Hearings are closed and secret. The prosecuting attorney presents the charges and calls witnesses who testify under oath to support the indictment. Usually, the accused

---

**presentment**
The report of a grand jury investigation, which usually includes a recommendation of indictment.

**indictment**
A written accusation returned by a grand jury, charging an individual with a specified crime after determination of probable cause.

**true bill**
The action by a grand jury when it votes to indict an accused suspect.

**no bill**
The action by a grand jury when it votes not to indict an accused suspect.

individuals are not allowed to attend the hearing unless they are asked to testify by the prosecutor or the grand jury.

*REFORMING THE GRAND JURY?* The defense attorney, defendant, and general public are not allowed to attend grand jury proceedings. The prosecuting attorney presents the charges and calls witnesses who testify under oath to support the indictment. This process has been criticized as being a rubber stamp for the prosecution because the presentation of the evidence is shaped by the district attorney, who is not required by law to reveal information that might exonerate the accused.[17]

In the case of *United States v. Williams* (1992), the Supreme Court ruled that no supervisory power in the federal courts requires presentation to a grand jury of **exculpatory evidence** (evidence that can clear a defendant from blame or fault).[18] Some legal scholars find that the Williams decision conflicted with the grand jury's historical purpose of shielding criminal defendants from unwarranted and unfair prosecution and overrode the mandate that it be both informed and independent. An alternative might be to change the rule of criminal procedure so that prosecutors would be obliged to present exculpatory evidence to the grand jury, even if it might result in the issuance of no indictment.[19] Another alternative put forth by defense lawyers is to open the grand jury room to the defense and to hold the government to the same types of constitutional safeguards required to protect defendants that are now used at trial.[20]

## The Information Process: The Preliminary Hearing

The purpose of the **preliminary hearing** is to require the prosecutor to present the case so that the judge can determine whether the defendant should be held to answer the charge against him or her in court. Preliminary hearings are used in about half the states as an alternative to the grand jury. Although the purpose of preliminary hearings and grand jury hearings is the same—to establish whether probable cause is sufficient to merit a trial—the procedures differ significantly.

The preliminary hearing is conducted before a magistrate or lower court judge and, unlike the grand jury hearing, is open to the public unless the defendant requests otherwise. Present at the preliminary hearing are the prosecuting attorney, the defendant, and the defendant's counsel, if already retained. The prosecution presents its evidence and witnesses to the judge. The defendant or the defense counsel then has the right to cross-examine witnesses and to challenge the prosecutor's evidence.

After hearing the evidence, the judge decides whether there is sufficient probable cause to believe that the defendant committed the alleged crime. If so, the defendant is bound over for trial, and the prosecuting attorney's information is filed with the trial court, usually within two weeks. The **information** is the charging document that is brought before a lower court judge in the preliminary hearing. If the judge does not find sufficient probable cause, the charges are dismissed, and the defendant is released from custody.

*WAIVING THE PRELIMINARY HEARING* A unique aspect of the preliminary hearing is the defendant's right to waive the proceeding. In most states, the prosecutor and the judge must agree to this waiver. A waiver has advantages and disadvantages for both the prosecutor and the defendant. In most situations, a prosecutor will agree to a waiver because it avoids the need to reveal evidence to the defense before trial. However, if the state believes it is necessary to obtain a record of witness testimony because of the possibility that a witness or witnesses may be unavailable for the trial or unable to remember the facts clearly, the prosecutor might override the waiver. In this situation, the record of the preliminary hearing can be used at the trial.

The defendant may want to waive the preliminary hearing for one of three reasons: (1) he has already decided to plead guilty, (2) he wants to speed up the

---

**exculpatory evidence**
All information that is material and favorable to the accused defendant because it casts doubt on the defendant's guilt or on the evidence the government intends to use at trial.

**CourseMate** For more information about the **latest news on grand juries**, visit the Criminal Justice CourseMate at CengageBrain.com, then access the "Web Links" for this chapter.

**preliminary hearing**
Hearing before a magistrate to determine whether the government has sufficient evidence to show probable cause that the defendant committed the crime.

**information**
A formal charging document, similar to an indictment, based on probable cause as determined at a preliminary hearing.

**FIGURE 11.4**
Charging the Defendant with a Crime

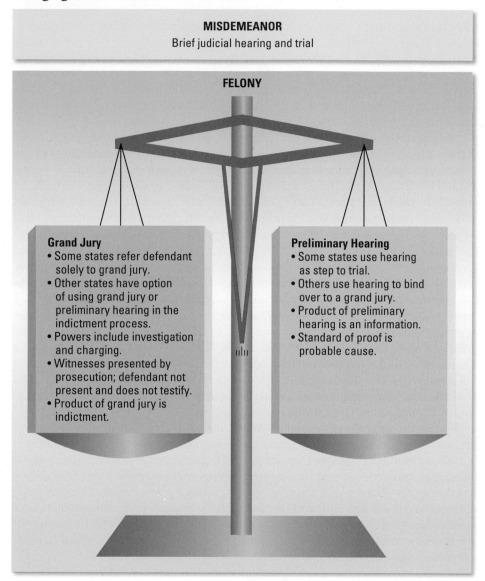

criminal justice process, or (3) he hopes to avoid the negative publicity that might result from the hearing. However, the preliminary hearing is of obvious advantage to the defendant who believes that it will result in a dismissal of the charges. In addition, the preliminary hearing gives the defense the opportunity to learn what evidence the prosecution has. Figure 11.4 outlines the significant differences between the grand jury and the preliminary hearing processes.

## Arraignment

After an indictment or information is filed following a grand jury or preliminary hearing, an arraignment takes place before the court that will try the case. At the arraignment, the judge informs the defendant of the charges against her and appoints counsel if one has not yet been retained. According to the Sixth Amendment, the accused has the right to be informed of the nature and cause of the accusation. Thus, the judge at the arraignment must make sure that the defendant clearly understands the charges.

After the charges are read and explained, the defendant is asked to enter a plea. If a plea of not guilty or not guilty by reason of insanity is entered, a trial date is set. When the defendant pleads guilty or nolo contendere (see below), a date for sentencing is arranged. The magistrate then either sets bail or releases the defendant on personal recognizance.

## The Plea

Ordinarily, a defendant in a criminal trial will enter one of three pleas: guilty, not guilty, or nolo contendere.

*GUILTY* More than 90 percent of defendants appearing before the courts plead guilty prior to the trial stage. A guilty plea has several consequences. It functions not only as an admission of guilt but also as a surrender of the entire array of constitutional rights designed to protect a criminal defendant against unjustified conviction, including the right to remain silent, the right to confront witnesses against him or her, the right to a trial by jury, and the right to be proved guilty by proof beyond a reasonable doubt. For a guilty plea to be valid, however, it must be both understood[21] and voluntary.[22]

The judge must follow certain procedures when accepting a plea of guilty. First, the judge must clearly state to the defendant the constitutional guarantees automatically waived by this plea. Second, the judge must believe that the facts of the case establish a basis for the plea and that the plea is made voluntarily. Third, the defendant must be informed of the right to counsel during the pleading process. The defendant may be required to allocute or admit in open court to having committed the crime. Finally, the judge must inform the defendant of the possible sentencing outcomes, including the maximum sentence that can be imposed.

After a guilty plea has been entered, a sentencing date is arranged. In a majority of states, a guilty plea may be withdrawn and replaced with a not-guilty plea at any time prior to sentencing if good cause is shown.

*NOT GUILTY* At the arraignment or before the trial, a not-guilty plea is entered in two ways: (1) it is orally stated by the defendant or the defense counsel, or (2) it is entered for the defendant by the court when the defendant stands mute before the bench.

Once a plea of not guilty is recorded, a trial date is set. In misdemeanor cases, trials take place in the lower court system, whereas felony cases are normally transferred to the superior court. At this time, a continuance or issuance of bail is once again considered.

*NOLO CONTENDERE* The plea **nolo contendere** ("no contest") is essentially a plea of guilty. This plea has the same consequences as a guilty plea, with one exception: It may not be held against the defendant as proof in a subsequent civil matter because technically no admission of guilt has been made. This plea is accepted at the discretion of the trial court and must be voluntarily and intelligently made by the defendant.

**nolo contendere**
A plea of "no contest"—the defendant submits to sentencing without any formal admission of guilt that could be used against him or her in a subsequent civil suit.

## ▌ PLEA BARGAINING

Plea bargaining is a relatively recent development that took hold late in the nineteenth century. During the first 150 years after the nation's birth, the trial by jury was viewed as the fairest and most reliable method of determining the truth in a criminal matter. Not surprisingly, the Constitution does not mention plea bargaining, nor does the Bill of Rights address the issue. However, by the middle of the nineteenth century, plea negotiations steadily became the dominant method of case disposition in the United States. Today, plea bargaining is one of the most common practices in the criminal justice system and a cornerstone of the informal justice system.[23] Even the Supreme Court has called it an "essential component of the administration of justice."[24]

# ANALYZING CRIMINAL JUSTICE ISSUES

# Strange Plea Agreements

The typical plea agreement results in a reduced charge or a favorable sentencing recommendation by the prosecutor, but some agreements can only be described as strange, or at least outside the box. What follows are some examples identified by law professor and former judge Joseph Colquitt. In exchange for leniency, the defendant agrees to

- Make a charitable contribution
- Relinquish property ownership
- Surrender a professional license
- Undergo sterilization
- Undergo surgical castration
- Enter the military
- Not pursue appeals
- Undertake a shaming punishment, such as carrying a sign that says "I stole from this store"
- Seal the records of a case
- Surrender profits from crime, such as from books written about the crime
- Be banished to another location

These are examples of what Colquitt calls "ad hoc plea bargaining." In his view, ad hoc plea bargaining takes these forms:

(1) the court may impose an extraordinary condition of probation following a guilty plea, (2) the defendant may offer or be required to perform some act as a quid pro quo for a dismissal or more lenient sentence, (3) the court may impose an unauthorized form of punishment as a substitute for a statutorily established method of punishment, (4) the state may offer some unauthorized benefit in return for a plea of guilty, or (5) the defendant may be permitted to plead guilty to an unauthorized offense, such as a "hypothetical" or nonexistent charge, a nonapplicable lesser-included offense, or a nonrelated charge.

Ad hoc plea bargaining is controversial not just because it is unusual. In some cases it can border on unethical. In one case, the prosecutor offered leniency to a drug defendant if he would surrender several thousand dollars in cash that was found during a search of his property. In another case, a defendant was afforded leniency for agreeing to forfeit interest in his vehicle.

## Critical Thinking

1. Are ad hoc plea bargains reasonable? Are they fair?

2. What if the tables were turned and, say, a speeding motorist offered $100 to the officer who stopped her in exchange for leniency? What would happen then?

Sources: Joseph A. Colquitt, "Ad Hoc Plea Bargaining," *Tulane Law Review* 75 (2001): 695–776; Timothy Lynch, *The Case against Plea Bargaining*, www.cato.org/pubs/regulation/regv26n3/v26n3-7.pdf (accessed April 28, 2010).

During this period, criminal case processing came to be seen not primarily as a dispute between two parties that could be resolved through a trial but as a conflict between the state and an individual, controlled by police involvement and prosecutorial discretion. As this change evolved, the court process switched from dispensing individual, carefully considered justice via trials to dispensing mass justice through guilty pleas.[25] At first, judges were reluctant to accept pleas, preferring trials to sharing their power with prosecutors (who make the deal). However, plea bargaining became more attractive at the turn of the twentieth century, when the mechanization of manufacture and transportation prompted a flood of complex civil cases, which persuaded judges that criminal cases had to be settled quickly lest the court system break down.[26] Today, it is estimated that more than 90 percent of criminal convictions result from negotiated pleas of guilty. And, as Figure 11.5 shows, most defendants are likely to plead guilty in even the most serious felony cases.

The data shows that plea bargains benefit both the prosecution, which is assured of a conviction, and the defendant, who is rewarded with a lenient sentence.[27] For example, people who plead guilty to murder are much less likely to get the death penalty or a life sentence than those who are convicted at trial.

## The Nature of the Bargain

Plea bargaining is the exchange of prosecutorial and judicial concessions for pleas of guilty (see Exhibit 11.1). Normally, a bargain can be made between the prosecutor and the defense attorney in four ways: (1) the initial charges may be reduced to those of a lesser offense, thus automatically reducing the sentence imposed; (2) in cases in which many counts are charged, the prosecutor may reduce the number of counts; (3) the prosecutor may promise to recommend a lenient sentence, such as probation; and (4) when the charge imposed has a negative label attached (for example, child molestation), the prosecutor may alter the charge to a more socially acceptable one (such as assault) in exchange for a plea of guilty (see the accompanying Analyzing Criminal Justice Issues box for some interesting exceptions). In a jurisdiction where sentencing disparities exist between judges, the prosecutor may even agree to arrange for a defendant to appear before a lenient judge in exchange for a plea; this practice is known as judge shopping.

**FIGURE 11.5**
Plea Rate by Most Serious Arrest Charge

Source: Tracey Kyckelhahn and Thomas H. Cohen, *Felony Defendants in Large Urban Counties, 2004* (Washington, D.C.: Bureau of Justice Statistics, 2008).

Bargains are rarely a one-shot deal and may be negotiated many times as evidence becomes known and the case unfolds.[28] They are negotiated until the defense believes that it has gotten the best deal for its client and the prosecutor believes that, considering the totality of the circumstances, it has been able to dispense a fair amount of punishment. The defense attorney conducts the bargain as a form of negotiation, putting forth information that will convince the prosecutor that the case is very strong and the chances of an acquittal are quite high. If the defense attorney can magnify the strength of her case, the chances of a favorable plea outcome increase.

## Pros and Cons of Plea Bargaining

Because of excessive criminal court caseloads and the personal and professional needs of the prosecution and the defense (to reach disposition of the case in the least possible time), plea bargaining has become an essential yet controversial part of the administration of justice. Proponents contend that plea bargaining actually benefits both the state and the defendant in the following ways:

- The overall costs of the criminal prosecution are reduced.
- The administrative efficiency of the courts is greatly improved.
- The prosecution can devote more time to more serious cases.
- The defendant avoids possible detention and an extended trial and may receive a reduced sentence.
- Resources can be devoted more efficiently to cases that need greater attention.[29]

Those who favor plea bargaining believe it is appropriate to enter into plea discussions when the interests of the state in the effective administration of justice will be served.

## To Plea or Not to Plea?

Although nearly all cases are settled with a plea, a few proceed to a full-blown trial. What factors influence the decision "to plea or not to plea"?

■ Court-appointed lawyers may want to gain trial experience. They convince their clients not to accept favorable bargains, fearing that the case will be settled out of court and they will lose the opportunity to try the case.

■ Both the prosecution and the defense may be overly optimistic about their skills.

■ The lawyers' overconfidence in their abilities may cloud their judgment, causing them either to refuse to offer a bargain (in the case of the prosecution) or to refuse to accept (in the case of the defense).

■ Some defendants falsely assume that they are so charismatic and appealing that a jury will never reach a conviction.

Source: Stephanos Bibas, "Plea Bargaining outside the Shadow of Trial," *Harvard Law Review* 117 (2004): 2464–2543.

Opponents of the plea bargaining process believe that the negotiated plea should be eliminated for the following reasons:

■ It encourages defendants to waive their constitutional right to trial.

■ Plea bargains allow dangerous offenders to receive lenient sentences. Jesse Timmendequas, a previously convicted sex offender, was given a 10-year plea-bargained sentence for child rape. Upon his release, he raped and killed seven-year-old Megan Kanka in one of the nation's most notorious crimes.[30]

■ Plea bargaining also raises the danger that an innocent person will be convicted of a crime if he or she is convinced that the lighter treatment ensured by a guilty plea is preferable to the risk of conviction and a harsher sentence following a formal trial.

■ Prosecutors are given a free hand to induce or compel defendants to plea bargain, thus circumventing law.[31]

■ It is possible that innocent persons will admit guilt if they believe that the system is biased and that they have little chance of being acquitted.

■ A guilty-plea culture has developed among defense lawyers. Elements of this attitude include the belief that most of their clients are dishonest people who committed the crime with which they have been charged and that getting a "sentence discount" for them is the best and only way to go.[32]

Despite these issues, it is unlikely that plea negotiations will be eliminated or severely curtailed in the near future. Supporters of the total abolition of plea bargaining are in the minority. As a result of abuses, however, efforts are being made to improve plea bargaining operations. Such reforms include development of uniform plea practices, representation of counsel during plea negotiations, and establishment of time limits on plea negotiations.

## The Problem of False Confessions

It is certainly not desirable to have an otherwise innocent offender plead guilty to a crime he or she did not commit, simply to avoid the possibility of being found guilty at trial. Unfortunately, some defendants conclude they will be better off by just admitting to the crime, even if they had nothing at all to do with it. Why take the chance of spending, say, 20 years in prison when they could be home in four? This is the problem of false confessions. How big a problem is it? Researchers have recently found that in approximately 25 percent of the cases where DNA testing resulted in a conviction being overturned, false confessions were given.[33] The testing is providing a window into the world of false confessions, revealing that the problem is perhaps more serious than anyone ever thought.

Why do innocent people confess? According to the Innocence Project, there are several reasons, including

- Duress
- Coercion
- Intoxication
- Diminished capacity
- Mental impairment
- Ignorance of the law
- Fear of violence
- The actual infliction of harm
- The threat of a harsh sentence
- Misunderstanding the situation[34]

## Legal Issues in Plea Bargaining

The U.S. Supreme Court has reviewed the propriety of plea bargaining in several decisions and, while imposing limits on the practice, has upheld its continued use. The Court has ruled in several key cases that

- Defendants are entitled to the effective assistance of counsel to protect them from pressure and influence.[35]
- Pleas must be made voluntarily and without pressure. However, a prosecutor can tell defendants that they may be facing the death penalty if they go to trial.[36]
- Any promise made by the prosecutor during the plea negotiations must be kept after the defendant admits guilt in open court. A prosecutor who promises leniency in private negotiations must stick to that position in court.[37]
- Defendants must also keep their side of the bargain to receive the promised offer of leniency.[38] If they agree to testify against a co-defendant, they must give evidence at trial or forfeit the bargain.
- A defendant's due process rights are not violated when a prosecutor threatens to reindict the accused on more serious charges—for example,

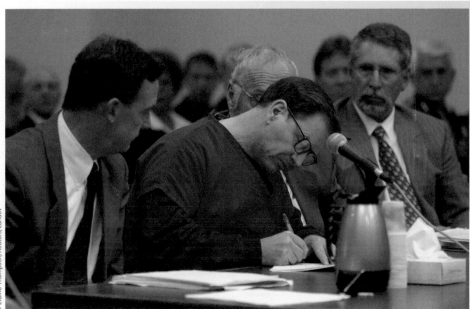

© Elaine Thompson/Reuters/Landov

Plea bargains are used in some of the most notorious violent cases. Gary Leon Ridgway initials the plea agreement in the King County Courthouse in Seattle, where he pleaded guilty to 48 murders. Ridgway added a confession read out by the prosecutor in open court: "I killed so many women I have a hard time keeping them straight." Ridgway pleaded guilty as part of a plea bargain with prosecutors in which his life would be spared. Should a murderer ever be able to escape serious punishment by admitting his guilt?

as a habitual offender—if the defendant does not plead guilty to a lesser offense.[39]

■ Accepting a guilty plea from a defendant who maintains his or her innocence is valid.[40]

■ Statements made during a plea bargain may be used under some circumstances at trial if the negotiations break down. Statements made during a plea negotiation can be used if the defendant (a) admits to a crime during the bargaining process but later testifies in open court that he or she (b) did not do the act and (c) is innocent of the charges.[41]

## The Role of the Prosecutor in Plea Bargaining

The prosecutor in the U.S. system of criminal justice has broad discretion in the exercise of his responsibilities. Such discretion includes deciding whether to initiate a criminal prosecution, determining the nature and number of the criminal charges, and choosing whether to plea bargain a case and under what conditions. Plea bargaining is one of the major tools the prosecutor uses to control and influence the criminal justice system (the other two are the decision to initiate a charge and the ability to take the case to trial).

Few states have placed limits on the discretion of prosecutors in plea bargaining situations. Instead, in making a plea bargaining decision, the prosecutor is generally free to weigh competing alternatives and factors, such as the seriousness of the crime, the attitude of the victim, the police report of the incident, and applicable sentencing provisions. Such factors as the offense, the defendant's prior record and age, and the type, strength, and admissibility of evidence are considered important in the plea bargaining decision.[42] The attitude of the complainant is also an important factor in the decision-making process. For example, in victimless cases, such as heroin possession, the police attitude is most often considered, whereas in victim-related crimes, such as rape, the attitude of the victim is a primary concern. Prosecutors in low-population or rural jurisdictions not only use more information when making their decisions but also seem more likely than their urban counterparts to accept plea bargains, a finding that suggests that case pressure alone is not the incentive for most plea bargains.[43]

Plea bargaining frequently occurs in cases in which the government believes the evidence is weak, such as when a key witness seems unreliable or unwilling to testify. Bargaining permits a compromise settlement in a weak case when the outcome of a criminal trial is in doubt.

Some jurisdictions have established guidelines to provide consistency in plea bargaining cases. They may require the district attorney to define the kinds and types of cases and offenders that may be suitable for plea bargaining. In other jurisdictions, approval to plea bargain may be required. Other controls might include procedures for internally reviewing decisions by the chief prosecutor and the use of written memoranda to document the need for and acceptability of a plea bargain in a given case. In some cases, pleas may be offered on a "take it or leave it" basis. In each case, a special prosecutor, whose job it is to screen cases, sets the bargaining terms. If the defense counsel cannot accept the agreement, there is no negotiation, and the case must go to trial. Only if complications arise in the case, such as witnesses changing their testimony, can negotiations be reopened.[44]

## The Role of the Defense Counsel in Plea Bargaining

Both the U.S. Supreme Court and such organizations as the American Bar Association have established guidelines for the court receiving a guilty plea and for the defense counsel representing the accused in plea negotiations.[45] No court should accept a guilty plea unless the defendant has been properly advised by counsel and the court has determined that the plea is voluntary and has a factual basis. The court has the discretion to reject a plea if it is inappropriately offered.

The defense counsel—a public defender or a private attorney—is required to play an advisory role in plea negotiations. The defendant's counsel is expected to be aware of the facts of the case and of the law and to advise the defendant of the available alternatives. The defense attorney is basically responsible for making certain that the accused understands the nature of the plea bargaining process and the guilty plea. This means that the defense counsel should explain to the defendant that, by pleading guilty, she is waiving certain rights that would be available if the case went to trial. In addition, the defense attorney has the duty to keep the defendant informed of developments and discussions with the prosecutor regarding plea bargaining. While doing so, the attorney for the accused cannot misrepresent evidence or mislead the client into making a detrimental agreement. The defense counsel is not only ethically but also constitutionally required to communicate all plea bargaining offers to a client, even if counsel believes the offers to be unacceptable.[46]

In reality, most plea negotiations occur in the chambers of the judge, in the prosecutor's office, or in the courthouse hallway. Under these conditions, it is often difficult to assess the actual roles played by the prosecutor and the defense attorney. Even so, it is fundamental that a defendant not be required to plead guilty until advised by counsel and that a guilty plea should not be made unless it is done with the consent of the accused.

## The Role of the Judge in Plea Bargaining

One of the most confusing issues in the plea bargaining process has been the proper role of the judge. Should the judge act only in a supervisory capacity or actually enter into the negotiation process? The leading national legal organization, the American Bar Association (ABA), is opposed to judicial participation in plea negotiations.[47] According to ABA standards, judges should not be a party to arrangements for the determination of a sentence, whether as a result of a guilty plea or a finding of guilty based on proof. The perception is that judicial participation in plea negotiations (a) creates the impression in the mind of defendants that they cannot receive a fair trial, (b) lessens the ability of the judge to make an objective determination of the voluntary nature of the plea, (c) is inconsistent with the theory behind the use of pre-sentence investigation reports, and (d) may induce innocent defendants to plead guilty because they are afraid to reject the disposition desired by the judge.[48] To avoid these potential problems, judges generally limit their role to approval or disapproval of the plea agreement.

## The Victim and Plea Bargaining

What role should victims play in plea bargaining? Crime victims are not empowered at the pretrial stage of the criminal process and thus do not play a role in the plea negotiations. Statutes do not require that the prosecutor defer to the victim's wishes, and there are no legal consequences for ignoring the victim in a plea bargaining decision. Even the ABA's *Model Uniform Victims of Crime Act* suggests only that the prosecutor "confer" with the victim.[49] Nonetheless, many prosecutors do confer with crime victims, and some supporters of the victims' rights movements have called for more extensive victim involvement in plea bargaining.[50] Some critics, however, have suggested that the system today is *too* victim-driven—that is, in too many cases prosecutors seek approval for the plea from a victim or family member.

## Plea Bargaining Reform

In recent years, efforts have been made to convert plea bargaining into a more visible, understandable, and fair dispositional process. Many jurisdictions have developed safeguards and guidelines to prevent violations of due process and to

410

ensure that innocent defendants do not plead guilty under coercion. Such safeguards include the following:

1. The judge questions the defendant about the facts of the guilty plea before accepting the plea.
2. The defense counsel is present and can advise the defendant of her rights.
3. The prosecutor and the defense attorney openly discuss the plea.
4. Full and frank information about the defendant and the offenses is made available at this stage of the process. In addition, judicial supervision ensures that plea bargaining is conducted in a fair manner.

What would happen if plea bargaining were banned outright, as its critics advocate? Numerous jurisdictions throughout the United States have experimented with bans on plea bargaining. In 1975, Alaska eliminated the practice. Honolulu, Hawaii, has also attempted to abolish plea bargaining. Other jurisdictions, including Arizona, Delaware, the District of Columbia, and Iowa, have sought to limit the use of plea bargaining.[51] In theory, eliminating plea bargains means that prosecutors in these jurisdictions give no consideration or concessions to a defendant in exchange for a guilty plea.

In reality, however, in these and most jurisdictions, sentence-related concessions, charge-reduction concessions, and alternative methods for prosecution continue to be used in one fashion or another.[52] When plea bargaining is limited or abolished, the number of trials may increase, the sentence severity may change, and more questions regarding the right to a speedy trial may arise. Discretion may also be shifted further up the system. Instead of spending countless hours preparing for and conducting a trial, prosecutors may dismiss more cases outright or decide not to prosecute them after initial action has been taken. Candace McCoy's study of plea reform in California investigated legislative efforts to eliminate the state's plea bargaining process. Instead of achieving a ban on plea bargaining, the process shifted from the superior to the municipal courts. McCoy found that the majority of defendants pleaded guilty after some negotiations and that the new law accelerated the guilty-plea process. McCoy suggests an alternative model of plea bargaining reform that includes emphasizing public scrutiny of plea bargaining, adhering to standards of professionalism, and making a greater commitment to due process procedures.[53] Other researchers have found that plea bargaining can be influenced by state sentencing arrangements. There tends to be less bargaining in states that limit judges' sentencing discretion.[54]

 ## PRETRIAL DIVERSION

Another important feature of the early court process is placing offenders into noncriminal diversion programs before their formal trial or conviction. Pretrial diversion programs were first established in the late 1960s and early 1970s, when it became apparent that a viable alternative to the highly stigmatized criminal sentence was needed. In diversion programs, formal criminal proceedings against an accused are suspended while that person participates in a community treatment program under court supervision. Diversion helps the offender avoid the stigma of a criminal conviction and enables the justice system to reduce costs and alleviate prison overcrowding.

Many diversion programs exist throughout the United States. These programs vary in size and emphasis but generally pursue the same goal: to constructively bypass criminal prosecution by providing a reasonable alternative in the form of treatment, counseling, or employment programs.

The prosecutor often plays the central role in the diversion process. Decisions about nondispositional alternatives are based on the nature of the crime, special characteristics of the offender, whether the defendant is a first-time

© Bob Daemmrich/The Image Works

*Drug courts are often active in the diversion process. In Austin, Texas, a judge presides over the weekly meeting of the Drug Diversion Court, a year-long program for defendants who have been arrested for felony possession of a controlled substance. The program relies on frequent drug screening, offers classes and treatment referrals, and can result in dismissal of charges if the defendant completes the program successfully.*

offender, whether the defendant will cooperate with a diversion program, the impact of diversion on the community, and consideration for the opinion of the victim.[55]

Some diversion programs are separate, independent agencies that were originally set up with federal funds but are now being continued with county or state assistance. Others are organized as part of a police, prosecutor, or probation department's internal structure. Still others are a joint venture between the county government and a private, nonprofit organization that carries out the treatment process.

First viewed as a panacea that could reduce court congestion and help treat minor offenders, diversion programs have come under fire for their alleged failures. Some national evaluations have concluded that diversion programs are no more successful at avoiding stigma and reducing recidivism than traditional justice processing.[56] The most prominent criticism is that they help *widen the net* of the justice system. By this, critics mean that the people placed in diversion programs are the ones most likely to have otherwise been dismissed after a brief hearing with a warning or small fine.[57] Instead of limiting contact with the system, the diversion programs increase it. Not all justice experts agree with this charge, and some have championed diversion as a worthwhile exercise of the criminal justice system's rehabilitation responsibility. Although diversion may not be a cure-all for criminal behavior, it is an important effort that continues to be made in most jurisdictions across the United States. Even if diversion programs were no more successful than traditional court processing, they are certainly less expensive to operate and help reduce court crowding and trial delays.[58]

## THE TRIAL

The criminal trial is an open and public hearing designed to examine the facts of the case brought by the state against the accused. Criminal trials are relatively rare events (most cases are settled by a plea bargain during the pretrial stage), but they are an important and enduring fixture in the criminal justice system. By its very nature, the criminal trial is a symbol of the moral authority of the state. It symbolizes the administration of objective and impartial justice. Regardless of the issues involved, the defendant's presence in a courtroom is designed to guarantee that she will have a hearing conducted under rules of procedure in an atmosphere of fair play and objectivity and that the outcome of the hearing will be clear and definitive. If the defendant believes that her constitutional rights and privileges have been violated, she may appeal the case to a higher court, where the procedures of the original trial will be examined. If, after examining the trial transcript, the appellate court rules that the original trial employed improper and unconstitutional procedures, it may order that a new hearing be held or even that the charges against the defendant be dismissed.

Most formal trials are heard by a jury, although some defendants waive their constitutional right to a jury trial and request a **bench trial**, in which the judge alone renders a **verdict**. In this situation, which occurs daily in the lower criminal courts, the judge may initiate a number of formal or informal dispositions, including dismissing the case, finding the defendant not guilty, finding the defendant guilty and imposing a sentence, or even continuing the case indefinitely. The decision the judge makes often depends on the seriousness of the offense, the background and previous record of the defendant, and the judgment of the court about whether the case can be properly dealt with in the criminal process. The judge may simply continue the case without a finding, in which case the verdict is withheld without a finding of guilt to induce the accused to improve her behavior in the community; if the defendant's behavior does improve, the case is ordinarily closed within a specific amount of time.

This section reviews some of the institutions and processes involved in **adjudication** and trial. We begin with a discussion of the legal rights that structure the trial process.

## Legal Rights during Trial

Underlying every trial are constitutional principles, complex legal procedures, rules of court, and interpretations of statutes—all designed to ensure that the accused will receive a fair trial.

**THE RIGHT TO AN IMPARTIAL JUDGE**  Even though the Constitution does not say so, every criminal defendant enjoys the right to a trial by an impartial judge. The Supreme Court ruled as much way back in the 1927 case of *Tumey v. Ohio*.[59] In that case, a municipal court judge was also the mayor, an executive official. What's more, he received fines and fees that he ordered against defendants who were convicted in his courtroom. The Supreme Court held that it is a violation of due process when a judge "has a direct, personal, substantial pecuniary interest in reaching a conclusion against [a defendant] in his case."[60]

What if a judge is not impartial? How can such a judge be removed? Generally, the judge will excuse himself or herself if there is a conflict of interest. Judicial codes of ethics provide the guidelines judges need to make such decisions. Some jurisdictions, however, permit peremptory removal of judges.[61] These are like the peremptory challenges used in jury selection (covered later in this chapter). When this occurs, one of the attorneys can move to have the judge removed, and another judge will come on board. Usually the peremptory removal can occur only once.

**THE RIGHT TO BE COMPETENT AT TRIAL**  To stand trial, a criminal defendant must be considered mentally competent to understand the nature and extent of the legal proceedings. If a defendant is considered mentally incompetent, his trial must be postponed until treatment renders him capable of participating in his own defense.

Can state authorities force a mentally unfit defendant to be treated so that he can be tried? In *Riggins v. Nevada* (1992), the U.S. Supreme Court ruled that forced treatment does not violate a defendant's due process rights if it is medically appropriate and, considering less intrusive alternatives, is essential for the defendant's own safety or the safety of others.[62]

---

**bench trial**
The trial of a criminal matter by a judge only. The accused waives any constitutional right to a jury trial.

**verdict**
The finding of a jury or a judge on questions of fact at a trial.

**adjudication**
The determination of guilt or innocence—a judgment concerning criminal charges.

***THE RIGHT TO CONFRONT WITNESSES*** The Sixth Amendment states that "In all criminal prosecutions, the accused shall enjoy the right . . . to be confronted with the witnesses against him." The accused enjoys this right not just by being able to confront witnesses in person but also by being allowed to participate in his or her trial. That is, trials cannot be conducted without the accused being afforded the right to appear in person.

The right to confrontation is also violated if out-of-court testimony is used to convict the accused. In *Crawford v. Washington*,[63] the Supreme Court held that it was unconstitutional for a trial court to introduce the defendant's wife's prerecorded statement to police about the stabbing the defendant was accused of. Why? Because he could not cross-examine a video. The Court recently extended this decision to state forensic analyst laboratory reports; such reports are now considered testimonial, meaning the defendant should be allowed to confront and question the analyst at trial.[64] This was a very significant decision because, according to the dissenters, it dispensed with a longstanding rule that scientific evidence could be admitted at trial without the need to require the testimony of the analyst who produced it.

This right can be waived or forfeited through misconduct. The accused may choose not to show up,[65] which is constitutionally permissible, and he or she may forfeit the right to appear by causing significant disruption or distraction in the courtroom.[66] There are also some exceptions, such as in child abuse cases, where it is felt that child victims would suffer irreparable harm be being forced to appear before their abusers.[67] Recently, the Supreme Court decided that if a witness is made unavailable because of the defendant (if, for example, the defendant killed the witness), the confrontation clause will not be violated if that witness cannot appear at trial.[68]

The **confrontation clause** is essential to a fair criminal trial because it restricts and controls the admissibility of **hearsay evidence**. Hearsay evidence is akin to secondhand evidence; rather than being told firsthand, it consists of information related by a second party (it is what one person hears and then says—hence the term "hearsay"). The framers of the Constitution envisioned face-to-face accusations in which the defendant has a right to see and cross-examine all witnesses. The idea is that it is always more difficult to tell lies about people to their face than behind their back is the foundation of the confrontation clause.

**confrontation clause**
The constitutional right of a criminal defendant to see and cross-examine all the witnesses against him or her.

**hearsay evidence**
Testimony that is not firsthand but, rather, relates information told by a second party.

***THE RIGHT TO COMPULSORY PROCESS*** The Sixth Amendment says, in part, that the accused shall "have compulsory process for obtaining witnesses in his favor." **Compulsory process** means to compel the production of witnesses via a subpoena. A subpoena is an order requiring a witness to appear in court at a specified time and place. The Supreme Court decided that compulsory process is a fundamental right in the case of *Washington v. Texas* (1967).[69]

**compulsory process**
Compelling the production of a witness or evidence via a subpoena

***THE RIGHT TO AN IMPARTIAL JURY*** It is no accident that of all the rights guaranteed to the people by the Constitution, only the right to a jury trial in criminal cases appears in both the original Constitution (Article III, Section 2) and the Bill of Rights (the Sixth Amendment). Although they may have disagreed on many points, the Framers did not question the wisdom of the jury trial.

Today, the criminal defendant has the right to choose whether the trial will be before a judge or a jury. Although the Sixth Amendment guarantees the defendant the right to a jury trial, the defendant can and often does waive this right. A substantial proportion of defendants, particularly those charged with misdemeanors, are tried before the court without a jury.

The major legal issue surrounding jury trial has been whether all defendants—those accused of misdemeanors as well as those accused of felonies—have an absolute right to a jury trial. Although the Constitution says that the right to a jury trial exists in *"all criminal prosecutions,"* the U.S. Supreme Court has restricted this right. In *Baldwin v. New York* (1970), the Supreme Court decided

## The Evolution of Gideon v. Wainwright

**Gideon v. Wainwright (1963)**   Indigent felony defendants enjoy the Sixth Amendment right to counsel. The Sixth Amendment right to counsel is fundamental, meaning the states must recognize it.[78]

**Douglas v. California (1963)**   The Fourteenth Amendment guarantees the defendant the right to counsel during his or her first mandatory appeal.[79]

**In re Gault (1967)**   Juveniles enjoy the right to counsel in adjudicatory hearings.[80]

**Coleman v. Alabama (1970)**   The preliminary hearing is a "critical stage," meaning that the defendant enjoys the right to counsel at it.[81]

**Argersinger v. Hamlin (1972)**   The Sixth Amendment right to counsel extends to those accused of committing misdemeanors.[82]

**Morrissey v. Brewer (1972)**   There is no right to counsel in parole revocation hearings.[83]

**Gagnon v. Scarpelli (1973)**   There is no right to counsel in probation revocation hearings.[84]

**Ross v. Moffitt (1974)**   There is no right to counsel provided for the second, discretionary appeal.[85]

**Scott v. Illinois (1979)**   If there is no possibility of confinement, the Sixth Amendment right to counsel does not apply.[86]

**Morris v. Slappy (1983)**   The Sixth Amendment does not require a "meaningful" relationship between the defendant and his or her attorney.[87]

**Wheat v. United States (1988)**   A trial court can deny the defendant's choice of counsel if the attorney's representation carries with it the strong possibility of a conflict of interest.[88]

**United States v. Monsanto (1989)**   It is not unconstitutional for a court to seize a defendant's assets such that it forces him or her to rely on a public defender.[89]

**United States v. Gonzalez-Lopez (2006)**   A convicted defendant has the automatic right to a new trial when a trial judge mistakenly refuses to allow the defendant's paid attorney to represent him.[90]

**Rothgery v. Gillespie County (2008)**   The right to counsel attaches at the initial appearance, shortly after arrest.[91]

that a defendant has a constitutional right to a jury trial when facing a possible prison sentence of six months or more, regardless of whether the crime committed was a felony or a misdemeanor.[70] When the possible sentence is six months or less, the accused is not entitled to a jury trial unless it is authorized by state statute. In most jurisdictions, the more serious the charge, the greater likelihood of trial—and of a trial by jury.

**THE RIGHT TO COUNSEL AT TRIAL**   The right to counsel applies all throughout the criminal process. We say in Chapter 8's discussion of *Miranda v. Arizona* that criminal suspects enjoy the right to counsel during custodial interrogations. The Supreme Court has recently decided that a defendant's very first appearance before a judge also triggers the right to counsel.[71] Our focus in this section, however, is on the right to counsel at trial.

In 1932, the Supreme Court decided in *Powell v. Alabama* that indigent defendants enjoy the right to counsel.[72] The Court limited its decision, however, to "capital case[s], where the defendant is unable to employ counsel, and is incapable adequately of making his own defense because of ignorance, feeble-mindedness, illiteracy, or the like."[73] In *Johnson v. Zerbst,*[74] decided a few years later, the Supreme Court extended the right to counsel to all federal prosecutions. Then, in the 1963 case *Gideon v. Wainwright,*[75] the Court applied the Sixth Amendment right to counsel to the states, meaning that all criminal defendants in felony cases (even the indigent) benefit from it.

Today, state courts must provide counsel at trial to indigent defendants who face even the possibility of incarceration—and who are charged with any type of crime, not just a felony.[76] The threat of incarceration need not be immediate. Even if the defendant might be sentenced to probation in which a prison or jail term is suspended, or might receive any other type of sentence containing a threat of future incarceration, he is afforded the right to counsel at trial.[77]

For a detailed treatment of exactly how and when the right to counsel applies, see the accompanying "Evolution of *Gideon v. Wainwright*" feature. It traces the evolution of right-to-counsel cases since 1963.

What if a defendant wants to serve as his or her own attorney? As a result of a 1975 Supreme Court decision, defendants are now permitted to proceed pro se, or for themselves.[92] When defendants ask to be permitted to represent themselves, the court normally approves their requests. However, these defendants are nearly always cautioned by the court against self-representation.

When pro se defendants' actions are disorderly and disruptive, the court can terminate their right to represent themselves. Also, the state can require representation for those defendants who cannot, because of mental incompetency, effectively represent themselves.[93]

***THE RIGHT TO A SPEEDY TRIAL***   The tactics employed by wary defense attorneys (pretrial motions, complex plea negotiations, delay tactics during trial), along with inefficiencies in the court process (such as the frequent granting of continuances, poor scheduling procedures, and the abuse of time by court personnel), have made delay in criminal cases a serious and constitutional issue. As the American Bar Association states in the *Standards Relating to Speedy Trial,* "Congestion in the trial courts of this country, particularly in urban centers, is currently one of the major problems of judicial administration."[94] Delays in the trial process conflict with the Sixth Amendment's guarantee of a right to a speedy trial.[95]

The Supreme Court has called the right to a speedy trial "as fundamental as any of the rights secured by the Sixth Amendment."[96] Its primary purposes are to

- Improve the credibility of the trial by having witnesses available for testimony as early as possible.
- Help criminal defendants avoid lengthy pretrial detention.
- Avoid extensive pretrial publicity and questionable conduct of public officials that may influence the defendant's right to a fair trial.
- Avoid any delay that could affect the defendant's ability to defend himself or herself against charges.

There is no set time that defines a speedy trial. In *Doggett v. United States,* the Court found that a delay of eight and a half years between indictment and arrest was prejudicial to the defendant and required dismissal of the charges against the defendant.[97] But this is an extreme case. Typically, when a defendant invokes the speedy-trial clause, the appellate court will evaluate the length of delay, the reason for the delay, when the defendant made the claim, and what damage the delay caused. If the prosecution deliberately slows the case down, that may have a greater effect on the appeal process than if the case was delayed because a witness could not be located. And if the defendant agreed to the delay or caused the delay, the speedy-trial right may be lost.

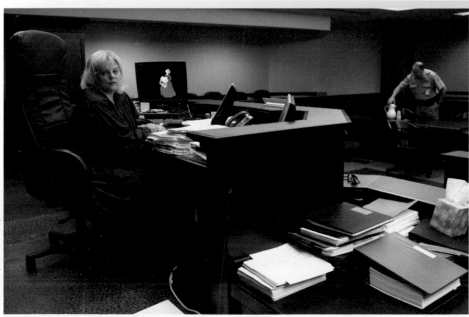

*Judge Susan Criss of the Texas District Court in Galveston discovered on Facebook that a lawyer who had requested a trial delay because of a death was drinking, not grieving, after the funeral.*

© Scott Dalton/*New York Times*/Redux

**THE RIGHT TO A PUBLIC TRIAL** The Sixth Amendment refers to a "public trial." This simply means that all trials must be open to the public. The right to a public trial is generally unrestricted. Anyone who wants to see a criminal trial can do so.

Sometimes having a trial open to the public can cause problems. In the 1966 case of *Sheppard v. Maxwell*, the courtroom was packed with people, including members of the media, for all nine weeks of the trial. Reporters handled evidence and took pictures throughout the trial. The Supreme Court eventually reversed the defendant's conviction, citing the "carnival atmosphere."[98] The case did not lead to the exclusion of cameras from the courtroom, but some judges require that they be kept out. This is why one sometimes see sketches of a case instead of actual photos.

Adverse pretrial publicity can prevent a defendant from getting a fair trial. The release of premature evidence by the prosecutor, extensive and critical reporting by the news media, and vivid and uncalled-for details in indictments can all prejudice a defendant's case. Press coverage can begin early in a criminal case and can even affect the outcome. Judges involved in newsworthy criminal cases have attempted to place restraints on pretrial media coverage to preserve the defendant's right to a fair trial. The Supreme Court has shaped pretrial publicity in several significant cases.[99]

As a general rule, pretrial publicity and reporting cannot be controlled. However, judges may bar the press from some pretrial legal proceedings and hearings, such as preliminary hearings, when police officers make an arrest, or when a warrant is being served, if their presence will infringe on the defendant's right to a fair trial.[100] Other steps can be taken as well. These include changes of venue (moving the trial to another jurisdiction, where there is less press coverage and hence less contamination of the pool of potential jurors) and gag orders (restrictions on what the parties or the media can report), among others.

What about press coverage *during* trial? In the landmark case *Richmond Newspapers, Inc. v. Virginia* (1980), the Supreme Court clearly established that criminal trials must remain open to the press.[101] The Court extended the right of the press to attend trials involving even highly sensitive, sexually related matters in which the victim is under 18 years of age.[102]

More recently, the issue of press coverage has focused on bringing TV cameras into the courtroom. Because of the public interest in high-profile criminal cases, whether jury trials should be televised is one of the most controversial questions in the criminal justice system. The legal community is divided over the use of TV cameras in the courtroom. Today, many state courts permit such coverage, often at the judge's discretion, but federal courts prohibit TV coverage altogether. In 1981, the U.S. Supreme Court in *Chandler v. Florida* removed any constitutional obstacles to the use of electronic media coverage and still photography of public criminal proceedings, over the objections of a criminal defendant.[103] Certainly, the defendant has a constitutional right to a public trial, but it is equally imperative that the media be allowed to exercise their **First Amendment** rights, which include making that public trial truly public.

**THE RIGHT TO BE CONVICTED BY PROOF BEYOND A REASONABLE DOUBT** The standard required to convict a defendant charged with a crime at the adjudicatory stage of the criminal process is **proof beyond a reasonable doubt**. This requirement dates back to early American history and over the years has become the accepted measure of persuasion by which the prosecutor must convince the judge or jury of the defendant's guilt. Many twentieth-century U.S. Supreme Court decisions have reinforced this standard by making "beyond a reasonable doubt a due process and constitutional requirement."[104]

The reasonable-doubt standard is an essential ingredient of the criminal justice process. It is the prime instrument for reducing the risk of convictions based on factual errors.[105] The underlying premise of this standard is that it is better to release a guilty person than to convict someone who is innocent. Because

**First Amendment**
The amendment to the U.S. Constitution that guarantees freedom of speech, religion, press, and assembly, and the right of the people to petition the government for redress of grievances.

**proof beyond a reasonable doubt**
The standard of proof needed to convict in a criminal case. The evidence offered in court does not have to amount to absolute certainty, but it should leave no reasonable doubt that the defendant committed the alleged crime.

**EXHIBIT 11.2**

## Evidentiary Standards of Proof: Degrees of Certainty

| Standard | Definition | Ruling |
|---|---|---|
| Absolute certainty | No possibility of error, 100% certainty | Not used in civil or criminal law |
| Beyond reasonable doubt; moral certainty | Conclusive and complete proof, without leaving any reasonable doubt about the innocence or guilt of the defendant; allows the defendant the benefit of any possibility of innocence | Criminal trial |
| Clear and convincing | Prevailing and persuasive to the trier of fact | Civil commitments, insanity defense evidence |
| Preponderance of the evidence | Greater weight of evidence in terms of credibility; more convincing than an opposite point of view | Civil trial |
| Probable cause | U.S. constitutional standard for arrest and search warrants, requiring existence of facts sufficient to warrant that a crime has been committed | Arrest, preliminary hearing, motions |
| Sufficient evidence | Adequate evidence to reverse a trial court | Appellate review |
| Reasonable suspicion | Rational, reasonable belief that facts warrant investigation of a crime on less than probable cause | Police investigations |
| Less than probable cause | Mere suspicion; less than reasonable belief to conclude criminal activity exists | Prudent police investigation where safety of an officer or others is endangered |

the defendant is presumed innocent until proved guilty, this standard forces the prosecution to overcome this presumption with the highest standard of proof. Unlike the civil law, where a mere **preponderance of the evidence** is the standard, the criminal process requires proof beyond a reasonable doubt for each element of the offense.[106] The various evidentiary standards of proof are analyzed and compared in Exhibit 11.2.

**preponderance of the evidence**
The level of proof in civil cases; more than half the evidence supports the allegations of one side.

## The Trial Process

The trial of a criminal case is a formal process conducted in a specific and orderly fashion in accordance with rules of criminal law, procedure, and evidence. Unlike what transpires in popular TV programs involving lawyers—where witnesses are often asked leading and prejudicial questions and where judges go far beyond their supervisory role—the modern criminal trial is a complicated and often time-consuming, technical affair. It is a structured adversary proceeding in which both prosecution and defense follow specific procedures and argue the merits of their cases before the judge and jury. Each side seeks to present its case in the most favorable light. When possible, the prosecutor and the defense attorney object to evidence they consider damaging to their positions. The prosecutor uses direct testimony, physical evidence, and a confession, if available, to convince the jury that the accused is guilty beyond a reasonable doubt. The defense attorney rebuts the government's case with her own evidence, makes certain that the rights of the criminal defendant under the federal and state constitutions are considered during all phases of the trial, and determines whether an appeal is appropriate if the client is found guilty.

Although each jurisdiction in the United States has its own trial procedures, all jurisdictions conduct criminal trials in a generally similar fashion. The basic steps of the criminal trial, which proceed in an established order, are described in this section and outlined in Figure 11.6.

**FIGURE 11.6**
The Steps in a Jury Trial

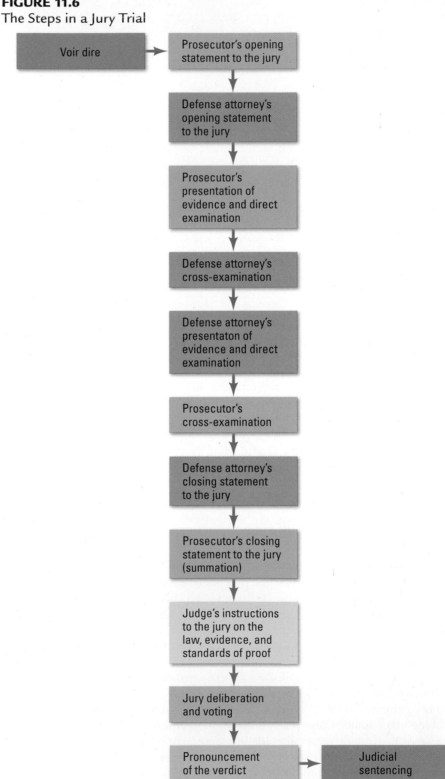

**venire**
The group called for jury duty from which jury panels are selected.

**voir dire**
The process in which a potential jury panel is questioned by the prosecution and the defense in order to select jurors who are unbiased and objective.

Source: Marvin Zalman and Larry Siegel, *Criminal Procedure: Constitution and Society* (St. Paul, Minn.: West Publishing, 1991), p. 655.

**JURY SELECTION** In both civil and criminal cases, jurors are selected randomly from licensing or voter registration lists within each court's jurisdiction. Few states impose qualifications on those called for jury service, although most mandate a residency requirement.[107] There is also little uniformity in the amount of time served by jurors; the term ranges from one day to months, depending on the nature of the trial. In addition, most jurisdictions prohibit convicted felons from serving on juries, as well as others exempted by statute, such as public officials, physicians, and attorneys.

The initial list of persons chosen, which is called a **venire**, or jury array, provides the state with a group of potentially capable citizens able to serve on a jury. Many states, by rule of law, review the venire to eliminate unqualified persons and to exempt those who, by reason of their professions, are not allowed to be jurors. The actual jury selection process begins with those remaining on the list.

The court clerk, who handles the administrative affairs of the court—including the processing of the complaint and other documents—randomly selects what he believes will be enough names to fill the required number of places on the jury. After reporting to a courtroom, the prospective jurors are first required to swear that they will truthfully answer all questions asked about their qualifications to serve. A group of 12 will be asked to sit in the jury box while the remaining group stands by.

Once prospective jurors are chosen, the lengthy process of **voir dire** (from the French for "to tell the truth") starts. To determine their appropriateness to sit on the jury, prospective jurors are examined under oath by the government, the defense, and sometimes the judge about their backgrounds, occupations, residences, and possible knowledge of or interest in the case. A juror who acknowledges any bias for or prejudice against the defendant—if the defendant is a friend or relative, or if the juror has already formed an opinion about the case—may be removed by either the prosecution or the defense with a **challenge for cause** asking the judge to dismiss the biased juror. If the judge accepts the challenge, the juror is removed for cause and replaced with another juror from the remaining panel. Because normally no limit is placed on the number of challenges for cause that can be exercised, it often takes considerable time to select a jury, especially for controversial and highly publicized criminal cases.

Besides challenges for cause, both the prosecution and the defense are allowed **peremptory challenges**, which enable the attorneys to excuse jurors for no particular reason or for undisclosed reasons. A prosecutor might not want a bartender as a juror in a drunk-driving case, believing that a person in that occupation would be sympathetic to the accused. Or the defense attorney might excuse a male prospective juror because the attorney prefers to have a predominantly female jury. The number of peremptory challenges accorded to the prosecution and defense is limited by state statute and often varies by case and jurisdiction.

The peremptory challenge has been criticized by legal experts who question the fairness and propriety with which it has been used.[108] Historically, the

© AP Photo/Sue Ogrocki

*Joshua Durcho, 27, left, who was accused of killing his former girlfriend and her four children, is escorted into the courtroom in El Reno, Oklahoma, on June 23, 2010, to attend a change-of-venue hearing for his murder trial. Durcho's attorneys argued that he could not get a fair trial in the area because widespread publicity about the case had biased potential jurors. The judge denied a motion to move the trial. Should the judge have decided differently?*

**challenge for cause**
Dismissal of a prospective juror by either the prosecution or the defense because he or she is biased, because he or she has prior knowledge about a case, or for other reasons that demonstrate the individual's inability to render a fair and impartial judgment.

**peremptory challenge**
Dismissal of a prospective juror by either the prosecution or the defense for unexplained, discretionary reasons.

## The Evolution of Batson v. Kentucky

**Batson v. Kentucky (1986)**   Prosecutors are barred, under the Fourteenth Amendment, from using peremptory challenges to remove jurors on the basis of race.[110]

**Hernandez v. New York (1991)**   The *Batson* rule extends to Hispanic jurors.[111]

**Powers v. Ohio (1991)**   Defendants can challenge race-based exclusions of jurors through peremptory challenges even if the defendant and the excluded jurors do not share the same race.[112]

**Edmonson v. Leesville Concrete Co. (1991)**   The *Batson* ruling applies to attorneys in civil lawsuits (that is, a private party in a civil action may not use peremptory challenges to exclude jurors on the basis of race).[113]

**Georgia v. McCollum (1992)**   Defense attorneys cannot use peremptory challenges to exclude jurors on the basis of race.[114]

**J.E.B. v. Alabama (1994)**   Peremptory challenges cannot be used to excuse jurors on the basis of their gender.[115]

**Johnson v. California (2005)**   California's "more likely than not" standard for proving that peremptory challenges are being used to exclude prospective jurors on the basis of race is incompatible with *Batson*.[116] In other words, there is no specific test that should be required to prove that peremptory challenges are being used in a discriminatory fashion.

**Miller El v. Dretke (2005)**   A defendant is entitled to a new trial when there is strong evidence of racial bias during the peremptory challenge phase of jury selection.[117]

**Snyder v. Louisiana (2008)**   The state's use of peremptory challenges to dismiss all African American potential jurors violates the Fourteenth Amendment's equal protection clause.[118]

**Rivera v. Illinois (2009)**   A trial court's error in denying the defendant's motion to dismiss a juror (the court wrongfully concluded the dismissal was based on race) does not require automatic reversal of the defendant's conviction.[119]

most significant criticism was that it was used by the prosecution to exclude African Americans from serving on juries in which the defendant was also African American—a policy that seemed to allow legally condoned discrimination against minority group members. In the landmark 1986 case *Batson v. Kentucky*, the Supreme Court held that the use of peremptory challenges against potential jurors by prosecutors in criminal cases violated the U.S. Constitution if the challenges were based solely on race.[109] Since that decision, the issue of race discrimination in the use of peremptory challenges has been raised by defendants in numerous cases. See the accompanying "Evolution of *Batson v. Kentucky*" feature for a summary of cases decided in the wake of *Batson*.

It is becoming increasingly difficult to find impartial jurors, especially in this technological age. Heinous crimes have always been broadcast all over the news, and the result has sometimes been to contaminate the pool of prospective jurors. This still happens, of course, but such crimes are the exception rather than the rule. But now jurors are able to turn to their BlackBerrys and iPhones to seek information about *any* case. By searching the Internet and sharing information (such as on Facebook), they often learn more about cases than is presented in court, which they are expressly forbidden to do. As one article recently noted, this practice is "wreaking havoc on trials around the country, upending deliberations and infuriating judges."[120] Although there is no official tally of the number of cases compromised by jurors' Internet research, the number is certainly growing. For example, a Florida case involving a man accused of illegally selling prescription drugs was upended because one juror researched the case on her own and was able to discover information not presented at trial. After her actions came to light, the judge had no choice but to declare a mistrial.

OPENING STATEMENTS   Once the jury has been selected and the criminal complaint has been read to the jurors by the court clerk, the prosecutor and the defense attorney may each make an opening statement about the case. The purpose of the prosecutor's statement is to acquaint the judge and jury with the particular criminal charges, to outline the facts, and to describe how the government will prove the defendant guilty beyond a reasonable doubt. The defense attorney reviews the case and indicates how the defense intends to show that the accused is not guilty.

Typically, the prosecutor is entitled to offer an opening statement, which is followed by the defense's opening statement. Both sides use the statement to give the jury a concise overview of the evidence that is to follow. Neither attorney is allowed to make prejudicial remarks or inflammatory statements or to mention irrelevant facts. Both are free, however, to identify what they will eventually

## EXHIBIT 11.3

### Types of Evidence Presented at Trial

In general, the primary test for the admissibility of evidence in a criminal proceeding is its relevance; that is, the court must consider whether the gun, tool, or bottle has relevant evidence that shows the defendant to be a known drug user might be relevant. In a prosecution for bribery, photos of the defendant receiving a package from a co-conspirator would clearly be found relevant to the case. There are four main types of evidence:

■ *Testimonial evidence.* Given by police officers, citizens, and experts, this is the most basic form of evidence. The witness must state, under oath, what he or she heard, saw, or experienced.

■ *Real evidence.* Exhibits that can be taken into the jury room for review by the jury constitute real evidence. A revolver that may have been in the defendant's control at the time of a murder, tools in the possession of a suspect charged

with a burglary, and a bottle allegedly holding narcotics are examples of real, or physical, evidence. Photographs, maps diagrams, and crime scene displays are other types for real evidence.

■ *Documentary evidence.* This type of evidence includes writings, government reports, public records, business or hospital records, fingerprint identification, and DNA profiling.

■ *Circumstantial evidence.* In trial proceedings, circumstantial (indirect) evidence is often inferred or indirectly used to prove a fact in question. For example, in a murder case, evidence that carpet fibers found on the body match the carpet in the defendant's home may be used at trial to link the two, even though they do not provide direct evidence that the suspect actually killed the victim.

prove by way of evidence, which includes witnesses, physical evidence, and the use of expert testimony. The opening statements are important because they give both sides an opportunity to sway the jury before the trial begins.

**THE PROSECUTION'S CASE** Following the opening statements, the government begins its case by presenting evidence to the court through its witnesses. Numerous types of evidence are presented at trial (see Exhibit 11.3). Those called as witnesses—such as police officers, victims, or experts—provide testimony via **direct examination**. During direct examination, the prosecutor questions the witness to reveal the facts believed pertinent to the government's case. Testimony involves what the witness actually saw, heard, or touched; it does not include opinions. However, a witness's opinion can be given in certain situations, such as when describing the motion of a vehicle or indicating whether a defendant appeared to act intoxicated or insane. Witnesses may also qualify to give opinions because they are experts on a particular subject relevant to the case. For example, a psychiatrist may testify about a defendant's mental capacity at the time of the crime.

Upon completion of the prosecutor's questioning, the defense usually conducts a **cross-examination** of the witness. During this exchange, the defense attorney may challenge elements of the testimony, such as the witness's accuracy in reporting what was seen or heard. The right to cross-examine witnesses is an essential part of a trial, and unless extremely unusual circumstances exist (such as a person's being hospitalized), witness statements will not be considered unless they are made in court and are open for question. If desired, the prosecutor may seek a second direct examination after the defense attorney has completed cross-examination; this allows the prosecutor to ask additional questions about information brought out during cross-examination. Finally, the defense attorney may then question, or re-cross-examine, the witness once again. All witnesses for the trial are sworn in and questioned in the same basic manner.

**THE CRIMINAL DEFENSE** Once the prosecutor has provided all the government's evidence against a defendant, he informs the court that he rests

**direct examination**
The initial questioning of one's own (prosecution or defense) witness during a trial.

**cross-examination**
The questioning of a prosecution witness by the defense, or of a defense witness by the prosecution.

## IMAGES OF JUSTICE

# The CSI Effect

When *CSI: Crime Scene Investigation* debuted, it was a surprise television hit. At one point, it was labeled the most popular show in the world. Its spinoff programs, *CSI: Miami* and *CSI: New York*, were also popular. *CSI* spawned an entire genre of similar programs, including *Cold Case, Bones,* and *Numb3rs*. In 2006, five of the top ten television programs involved criminal investigations.

The criminal investigations genre is but one in a long line of television programming that has featured (and sensationalized) criminal investigations and courtroom proceedings. More than most other shows, though, *CSI* and its progeny may have started to blur the line between reality and fiction. This may be furthered by the popularity of crime magazine shows such as *48 Hours Mystery, American Justice,* and *Dateline NBC,* which feature real cases.

## The *CSI* Effect

Many attorneys, judges, and journalists have started to claim that *CSI*-like programs have influenced jurors' expectations. Some have alleged that jurors sometimes acquit defendants when no scientific evidence is presented. Others have alleged that jurors have developed unrealistic expectations about just what information scientific investigations can bring to bear on a case. As one prosecutor put it, "Jurors now expect us to have a DNA test for just about every case. They expect us to have the most advanced technology possible, and they expect it to look like it does on television."

## Does a *CSI* Effect Really Exist?

Donald Shelton, a judge, and his colleagues, criminology professors at Eastern Michigan University, surveyed 1,000 prospective jurors in an effort to answer the question: Is there a real *CSI* effect? The survey included questions concerning jurors' expectations and demands for scientific evidence and the television programs they regularly watched. The respondents were asked about several crime types and then asked to report what scientific evidence they would expect to see presented at trial. Choices for the latter ranged from eyewitness testimony and circumstantial evidence to DNA, ballistics, and fingerprint evidence. They were even asked how likely they would be to find the defendant guilty or not guilty based on the evidence presented by the prosecution. The research found that

■ 46 percent expected to see scientific evidence presented in every criminal case.

■ 22 percent expected to see DNA evidence in every criminal case.

■ 36 percent expected to see fingerprint evidence in every criminal case.

■ 32 percent expected to see ballistics or other firearms evidence in every criminal case.

Are these expectations unrealistic? It is far from possible to gather fingerprint evidence in one-third of all criminal cases. It appears, indeed, that the respondents' expectations were driven somewhat by their television-watching habits. For all the categories of evidence, *CSI* viewers tended to have higher expectations of being presented with scientific evidence. This suggests there is evidence of a *CSI* effect, but Shelton and his colleagues also found that respondents were only somewhat likely to alter their verdicts on the basis of the presence or absence of scientific evidence in a trial. They found that

■ *CSI* viewers were more likely than non-*CSI* viewers to convict without scientific evidence if eyewitness testimony was available.

■ In rape cases, *CSI* viewers were less likely to convict if DNA evidence was not presented.

■ In breaking-and-entering and theft scenarios, victim or other testimony was sufficient to convict.

Shelton and his colleagues concluded, in short, that there is a *CSI* effect, but it may not be as influential as previously thought:

> Although *CSI* viewers had higher expectations for scientific evidence than non-*CSI* viewers, these expectations had little, if any, bearing on the respondents' propensity to convict. This, we believe, is an important finding and seemingly very good news for our nation's criminal justice system: that is, differences in expectations about evidence did not translate into important difference in the willingness to convict.

## Critical Thinking

It is said that life imitates art. As the popularity of the CSI profession (as seen on TV) grows, more students will probably be drawn into forensics, and more police and law enforcement agencies are likely to use forensic specialists in their daily operations. Do you think that crime is better solved in the lab or on the beat?

Sources: Young S. Kim, Gregg Barak, and Donald E. Shelton, "Examining the 'CSI-Effect' in the Cases of Circumstantial Evidence and Eyewitness Testimony: Multivariate and Path Analyses," *Journal of Criminal Justice* 37 (2009): 452–460. Donald E. Shelton, "The 'CSI Effect': Does It Really Exist?" *National Institute of Justice Journal* 259 (2008): 1–7; Donald E. Shelton, Young S. Kim, and Gregg Barak, "A Study of Juror Expectation and Demands Concerning Scientific Evidence: Does the 'CSI Effect' Exist?" *Vanderbilt Journal of Entertainment and Technology Law* 9 (2007): 331–368.

the people's case. The defense attorney at this point may enter a motion for a **directed verdict**. This is a procedural device in which the defense attorney asks the judge to order the jury to return a verdict of not guilty. Depending on the weight of the prosecution's case, the judge may either sustain or overrule this motion. In essence, the defense attorney argues in the directed verdict that the prosecutor's case against the defendant is insufficient to support the legal elements needed to prove the defendant guilty beyond a reasonable doubt. If the court sustains the motion, the trial is terminated. If it rejects the motion, the defense begins to legally rebut the prosecution's case.

> **directed verdict**
> A judge's order directing a jury to acquit a defendant because the state has not proved the elements of the crime or otherwise has not established guilt according to law.

The defense attorney has the option of presenting many, some, or no witnesses on behalf of the defendant. The burden of proving guilt is on the prosecution, and if the defense team believes that the burden has not been met, it may feel there is no need to present witnesses of its own. In addition, the defense attorney must decide whether the defendant should take the stand and testify in his own behalf. In a criminal trial, the defendant is protected by the Fifth Amendment right to be free from self-incrimination, which means that a person cannot be forced by the state to testify against himself. However, defendants who choose to tell their side of the story can be subject to cross-examination by the prosecutor.

The defense attorney is charged with putting on a vigorous defense in the adversary system of justice. She presents her own witnesses and introduces evidence to refute the prosecution's allegations. After the defense concludes its case, the government may then present rebuttal evidence. If the judge grants permission, this involves bringing forward evidence to refute, counteract, or disprove evidence introduced by the defense. A prosecutor may not go into new matters or present evidence that further supports or reinforces his own case. At the end of rebuttal, the defense may be allowed so-called surrebuttal—presenting witnesses to respond to issues that were raised for the first time in the prosecutor's rebuttal case. The defense cannot restate its case or introduce new issues during surrebuttal.

**CLOSING ARGUMENTS**  In closing arguments the attorneys review the facts and evidence of the case in a manner favorable to their respective positions. At this stage of the trial, both prosecution and defense are permitted to draw reasonable inferences and to show how the facts prove or refute the defendant's guilt. Often both attorneys have a free hand in arguing about the facts, issues, and evidence, including the applicable law. They cannot comment on matters not in evidence, however, or on the defendant's failure to testify in a criminal case. Normally, the prosecutor makes a closing statement first, followed by the defense, and many jurisdictions allow the prosecution an opportunity for rebuttal. Either party can elect to forgo the right to make a final summation to the jury.

**INSTRUCTIONS TO THE JURY**  In a criminal trial, the judge will instruct, or charge, the jury members on the principles of law that ought to guide and control their decision on the defendant's innocence or guilt. Included in the charge will be information about the elements of the alleged offense, the type of evidence needed to prove each element, and the burden of proof that must be met to obtain a guilty verdict. Although the judge commonly provides this instruction, he or she may ask the prosecutor and the defense attorney to submit instructions for consideration; the judge will then exercise discretion in determining whether to use any of their instructions. The instructions that cover the law applicable to the case are extremely important because they may serve as the basis for a subsequent appeal.

**DELIBERATION AND VERDICT**  Once the charge is given to the jury members, they retire to deliberate on a verdict. In highly publicized and celebrated cases, the judge may sequester the jury, preventing them from having contact

## CAREERS IN CRIMINAL JUSTICE

# *Paralegal*

### *Duties and Characteristics of the Job*

Paralegals assist lawyers by conducting much of the preparation for trials. A paralegal's exact duties vary according to the needs of the office for which he works. However, a paralegal's work typically includes assisting with or carrying out client interviews, drafting legal documents, reviewing pertinent case law, summarizing legal proceedings, and doing some standard office work. Although a paralegal's work may at first be relatively simple, after some experience paralegals are usually given more responsibilities and more complex tasks. Paralegals working outside the law office setting have similar duties but also additional ones that reflect the specialty of their employer.

Paralegals do much of the same work as a lawyer, but there are definite limits on what they can do. For example, paralegals cannot advise on legal issues. Although most paralegals have general legal knowledge, it is becoming more common, especially for long-term or career paralegals, to choose a field of specialization.

A clear majority of paralegals work for law firms, but some find positions with the government, with corporations, or in community service. These paralegals can expect a normal 40-hour workweek, but a paralegal working in a law firm is expected to put in many hours of overtime during busy periods. Increasingly, paralegals are choosing the option of self-employment and working freelance.

### *Job Outlook*

The paralegal profession is expected to grow rapidly in the near future for several reasons, most prominently the fact that some organizations need legal expertise but do not want the extra expense of hiring a lawyer.

### *Salary*

The median (half earn above the amount, half earn below it) annual salary for paralegals ranges from $36,080 to $59,310. Paralegals who work for private firms often receive bonuses for good work.

---

with the outside world. This process is discretionary, and most judges believe that sequestering or "locking up" a jury is needed only in sensational cases.

A review of the case by the jury may take hours or even days. The jurors always meet privately during their deliberations, and in certain lengthy and highly publicized cases, they are kept overnight in a hotel until the verdict is reached. In less sensational cases, the jurors may be allowed to go home, but they are cautioned not to discuss the case with anyone.

If a verdict cannot be reached, the trial may result in a hung jury, after which the prosecutor must bring the defendant to trial again if the prosecution desires a conviction. If found not guilty, the defendant is released from the criminal process. If the defendant is convicted, the judge will normally order a pre-sentence investigation by the probation department before imposing a sentence. Before sentencing, the defense attorney will probably submit a motion for a new trial, alleging that legal errors occurred in the trial proceedings. The judge may deny the motion and impose a sentence immediately—a practice quite common in most misdemeanor offenses. In felony cases, however, the judge will set a date for sentencing, and the defendant will either be placed on bail or be held in custody until that time.

Although jurors are required by law to base their decision on the facts of the case and on the judge's legal instructions, they are sometimes asked by the defense to ignore both and render decisions based on emotion and personal preference.[121] This strategy, called **jury nullification**, has been in practice since 1735 when John Peter Zenger, editor of the *New York Weekly Journal*, was charged with printing libelous statements about the governor of the Colony of New York, William Cosby. Despite the fact that Zenger clearly printed the alleged libels

**jury nullification**
A jury's refusal to render a verdict according to the law and fact regardless of the evidence presented.

## Opportunities

The number of people entering the profession has been steadily increasing, so those entering the paralegal field should expect competition for desirable jobs.

Opportunities for advancement within the field come mainly in the form of supervisory positions, which entail more responsibilities and higher pay. Ultimately, many paralegals use their knowledge and skills to earn a law degree and become a lawyer or judge. They can also move on to better-paying careers where legal experience is useful, such as insurance claims adjuster.

## Qualifications

Much of a paralegal's work is focused on conducting legal research, so skills that aid this process are critical. Because much of this research can now be done using computer programs, databases, and the Internet, up-to-date computer skills confer a distinct advantage. Those with knowledge and experience in a specialized legal field are also in demand, especially for government and corporate positions. Real-world work experience and internship experience can also increase the chances of employment.

Relevant educational experience and certification are useful for gaining employment. Although one can work as a paralegal without certification, it provides a hiring advantage. Various groups such as the National Association of Legal Assistants provide certification if the applicant can pass rigorous exams.

## Education and Training

There are many ways of entering the field. Most paralegals enter their profession with training from a two-year paralegal program approved by the American Bar Association. However, it is possible for people with a liberal arts degree to enter the field by working in legal offices and learning skills on the job. Others with bachelor's degrees enter certification programs or complete a combination bachelor's/paralegal degree. The entrance requirements for these programs vary. Classes in political science may provide useful knowledge for future paralegals. Finally, paralegals must always keep up to date on changes in the law in their area of specialization.

Sources: "Paralegal," *Occupational Outlook Handbook*, 2010-2011 edition (Bureau of Labor Statistics, U.S. Department of Labor), retrieved April 28, 2010, from www.bls.gov/oco/ocos114.htm; "Princeton Review Career Profiles: Paralegal," retrieved April 28, 2010, from www.princetonreview.com/Careers.aspx?page=1&cid=105.

and the trial judge gave the jury clear instructions for a finding of guilt, the jury found Zenger not guilty on all charges. The Zenger case remains one of the most famous examples of jury nullification in the nation's history.

Supporters of jury nullification argue that it is an important safeguard against government oppression and that the function of the jury is to serve as a safety valve against the unjust application of the law. Critics, however, see jury nullification as an abuse of power. Would it be fair if jurors, motivated by racial bias, found a person accused of a hate crime not guilty despite overwhelming evidence of guilt?[122]

There is also some question about what jurors expect when they hear the arguments made by the prosecution and defense and then go into deliberations. According to some critics, popular television programs such as *CSI: Crime Scene Investigation* (and its spinoffs) have caused jurors to have unrealistic expectations concerning what evidence is typically found at crime scenes and introduced at trial. We look at this issue more closely in the accompanying Images of Justice feature.

**THE SENTENCE** Imposing the criminal sentence is normally the responsibility of the trial judge. In some jurisdictions, the jury may determine the sentence or make recommendations involving leniency for certain offenses. Often, the sentencing decision is based on information and recommendations given to the court by the probation department after a pre-sentence investigation of the defendant. The sentence itself is determined by the statutory requirements for the particular crime as established by the legislature; in addition, the judge ordinarily has a

**CourseMate** For more information about the **Sentencing Project**, visit the Criminal Justice CourseMate at CengageBrain.com, then access the "Web Links" for this chapter.

## CONCEPT SUMMARY 11.1
### Stage of the Jury Trial

| | |
|---|---|
| Stage 1<br>Jury Selection | The judge and attorneys question potential jurors until a panel of 12 is agreed upon by all sides. The voir dire process is designed to excuse jurors who might have difficulty in rendering a fair and impartial verdict in that particular case. |
| Stage 2<br>Opening Statements | Brief statements are made by prosecution and defense that outline their view of the facts of the case and what they hope to prove. The prosecutor in a criminal case gives the first statement and the defense attorney follows. |
| Stage 3<br>Presentation of Evidence | Witnesses for the prosecution in a criminal case testify first, witnesses for the defense testify next, and any rebuttal witnesses testify last. The attorney who calls the witness asks questions in direct examination. The attorney for the opposing side then questions the witness in cross-examination. |
| Stage 4<br>Closing Arguments | The prosecutor in a criminal case first attempts to convince the jury to decide in favor of her side of the case. The defense attorney follows with his argument, attempting to do the same. The prosecutor has the opportunity to present a rebuttal to the defense attorney's argument. |
| Stage 5<br>Jury Deliberations | After the judge instructs the jury on the law they must apply in the particular case, they retire from the courtroom to deliberate in secret. When the jurors reach a verdict, they return to the courtroom and the verdict is read aloud to the parties. |
| Stage 6<br>Sentencing | If a guilty verdict is reached, the judge will impose a sentence, choosing the most appropriate sanction from those legislatively available. |

great deal of discretion in reaching a sentencing decision. The different criminal sanctions available include fines, probation, imprisonment, and even commitment to a state hospital. The sentence may be a combination of all these.

The most critical trial stages are reviewed in Concept Summary 11.1.

**APPEALS** Once a verdict has been rendered and a defendant found guilty, the defense may petition an appellate court to review the procedures used during trial. Defendants have two main avenues to challenge such procedures: appeals and habeas corpus. These both give the convicted person an opportunity to appeal to a higher state or federal court on the basis of an error that affected the conviction in the trial court. Extraordinary trial court errors, such as denial of the right to counsel or inability to provide a fair trial, are subject to the plain-error rule of the federal courts.[123] Harmless errors, such as the use of innocuous identification procedures or the denial of counsel at a noncritical stage of the proceeding, would not necessarily result in the overturning of a criminal conviction.

A postconviction **appeal** is a request for an appellate court to examine a lower court's decision in order to determine whether proper procedures were followed. It is important to note that appeals do not give the convicted an opportunity to try the case a second time, only to challenge procedural matters (such as a judge's decision to exclude a witness's testimony). Most defendants benefit from at least one so-called "direct appeal." Direct appeals are guaranteed by law; the result is that most defendants get to appeal at least once, even if they cannot afford it.[124] "Discretionary appeals" are also possible. It is up to the appellate court to decide whether it will hear a discretionary appeal. There is no restriction on the number of discretionary appeals that can be filed.

Through objections made at the pretrial and trial stages of the criminal process, the defense counsel reserves specific legal issues on the record as the basis

**appeal**
A request for an appellate court to examine a lower court's decision in order to determine whether proper procedures were followed.

**writ of habeas corpus**
A judicial order requesting that a person who detains another person produce the body of the prisoner and give reasons for his or her capture and detention. Habeas corpus is a legal device used to request that a judicial body review the reasons for a person's confinement and the conditions of confinement. Habeas corpus is known as "the great writ."

for appeal. A copy of the transcript of these proceedings serves as the basis on which the appellate court will review any errors that may have occurred during the lower-court proceedings.

A **writ of habeas corpus** is the primary means by which state prisoners have their convictions or sentences reviewed in the federal court. A writ of habeas corpus (which means "you have the body") seeks to determine the validity of a detention by asking the court to release the person or give legal reasons for his or her the incarceration.

## Ethical Challenges in Criminal Justice: A Writing Assignment

Shantel is an unemployed former crack addict with an extensive criminal record. When she was actively using, she gave birth to six children, each of whom was taken away by Child Protective Services. She has since put her life back on track, secured a job, stopped using drugs, and given birth to her seventh child, Keisha, who lives with her. When Keisha was two-years-old, Shantel moved back in with her estranged boyfriend, Deshaun, who she thought had also stopped using. Unbeknownst to Shantel, although Deshaun had stopped using crack, he had become hooked on OxyContin and was using the drug on a regular basis. Not long after they moved in together, the police served a search warrant on their property and found a stash of the drug. Both Shantel and Deshaun were charged with drug possession. Shantel's extensive criminal record would probably result in a long-term prison sentence, not to mention the possible loss of Keisha, if she were found guilty at a trial. Surprisingly, during Shantel's pretrial negotiations, the district attorney offered a plea bargain to give Shantel three years *or* probation and no jail time if she agreed to sterilization. Shantel did not want to take the chance of going to trial and getting a long-term prison sentence. She knew she would not have any chance of getting Keisha back if she got a long-term prison sentence. She felt her only option was to agree to the plea negotiation of probation and sterilization.

Write an essay on the ethical issues raised in this plea bargaining scenario. In doing so, answer these questions: Should Shantel plead guilty to a crime she did not commit? Should she subject herself to sterilization for a crime she did not commit? How many other defendants plead guilty to crimes they have not committed? Is it even possible to know? One of the main criticisms of plea bargaining is just this; a guilty plea does not always mean the offender is guilty. What other criticisms of plea bargaining have been raised? Consult this chapter's "Plea Bargaining" section as you answer the questions.

## Significant Cases in the Trial Process

| Case | Issue | Decision |
|------|-------|----------|
| *Baldwin v. New York* (1970) | Right to a jury trial | The defendant has the constitutional right to a jury trial when facing a possible prison sentence of six months or more, regardless of whether the crime committed was a felony or a misdemeanor. |
| *Batson v. Kentucky* (1986) | Peremptory challenges | The use of peremptory challenges based solely on race is unconstitutional. Also see the *"Evolution of Batson v. Kentucky"* feature earlier in this chapter for details on post-Batson decisions. |

*(continues)*

# Significant Cases in the Trial Process *(continued)*

| Case | Issue | Decision |
|---|---|---|
| *Crawford v. Washington* (2004) | Confrontation | The admission at trial of a pre-recorded out-of-court statement violates the confrontation clause. |
| *Faretta v. California* (1975) | Waiver of the right to counsel | The defendant can waive the right to counsel and represent himself or herself (that is, proceed with a *pro se* defense). |
| *Gideon v. Wainwright* (1963) | Right to counsel | The Sixth Amendment right to counsel applies to the states, meaning all criminal defendants benefit from the right to counsel, even if they cannot afford it. Also see the "Evolution of *Gideon v. Wainwright*" feature earlier in this chapter for details on post-*Gideon* decisions. |
| *Illinois v. Allen* (1970) | Confrontation | The defendant can forfeit his or her right to confrontation at trial because of inappropriate conduct (such as being disruptive). |
| *Johnson v. Zerbst* (1938) | Right to counsel | All federal defendants enjoy the Sixth Amendment right to counsel. |
| *Klopfer v. North Carolina* (1967) | Right to a speedy trial | The Sixth Amendment right to a speedy trial is a fundamental right, meaning the states must recognize it. |
| *Melendez-Diaz v. Massachusetts* (2009) | Confrontation | State forensic analyst laboratory reports are considered testimonial evidence and thus require that the defendant be permitted to question the preparer of the report at trial. |
| *Montejo v. Louisiana* (2009) | Right to counsel | Police may approach and question, outside the presence of counsel, a defendant who has been charged with a crime. |
| *Powell v. Alabama* (1932) | Right to counsel | Indigent defendants enjoy the right to counsel, but only in capital cases. |
| *Richmond Newspapers, Inc. v. Virginia* (1980) | Right to a public trial | Criminal trials must remain open to the press. |
| *Riggins v. Nevada* (1992) | Competency at trial | The defendant can be forcibly administered antipsychotic drugs if the procedure is medically appropriate, no alternative is available, and it is necessary for the defendant's safety or the safety of others. |
| *Sheppard v. Maxwell* (1966) | Right to a public trial | A trial can be closed to the public if allowing access to people and/or the press results in a "carnival atmosphere." |
| *Stack v. Boyle* (1951) | Bail | In setting bail, judges should consider the nature and circumstances of the offense charged, the weight of the evidence against the accused, and the accused's ability to pay. |
| *Tumey v. Ohio* (1927) | Impartial judge | A violation of due process occurs when a judge has a personal and/or financial interest in the outcome of a case over which he or she presides. |
| *United States v. Williams* (1992) | Grand juries | The failure to present exculpatory evidence to a grand jury does not make the resulting indictment invalid. |
| *Washington v. Texas* (1967) | Compulsory process | Every defendant enjoys the Sixth Amendment right to compel the production of witnesses and evidence to assist in putting on his or her defense. |

# SUMMARY

**1. Understand the procedures following arrest.**

- Many important decisions about what happens to a defendant are made prior to trial.

- Hearings, such as before the grand jury and the preliminary hearing, are held to determine whether probable cause exists to charge the accused with a crime. If so, the defendant is arraigned, enters a plea, is informed of his constitutional rights (particularly the right to the assistance of counsel), and is considered for pretrial diversion.

**2. Discuss the legal right to bail.**

- Bail is a form of security, usually a sum of money that is put up or exchanged to secure the release of an arrested person before the trial begins.

- A majority of criminal defendants are released on bail prior to trial.

- The Eighth Amendment prohibits both cruel and unusual punishment and excessive bail.

- The Supreme Court has held that bail is excessive when it exceeds an amount reasonably calculated to ensure that the defendant will return for trial.

**3. List a variety of bail systems.**

- There are several types of bail systems, including full cash bail, deposit bail, surety bail, conditional bail, unsecured bonds, and release on recognizance.

**4. Recount the history of bail reform.**

- Bail has been heavily criticized as one of the most unacceptable aspects of the criminal justice system.

- Bail reform has resulted in the use of release on recognizance to replace money bail for nondangerous offenders.

- Whereas release on recognizance is a liberal bail reform, some reform efforts have included preventive detention.

**5. Define pretrial services.**

- Pretrial service programs provide a number of services to those released into the community prior to their trial dates, including (a) gathering and verifying information about arrestees, (b) assessing each arrestee's likelihood of failure to appear and chances of being rearrested, and (c) providing supervision for defendants conditionally released and notifying the court of any failure to comply with release conditions.

**6. List the differences between the indictment process and the information process.**

- There are two primary charging mechanisms in the United States: a grand jury's indictment and a prosecutor's information.

- Grand juries perform two main functions: investigation and accusation.

- The grand jury usually meets, in secret, at the request of the prosecution and decides whether to charge a criminal suspect (that is, to issue an indictment).

- If the prosecutor proceeds by information, then a preliminary hearing is held to determine whether there is enough cause to believe that the defendant committed the crime to warrant a trial.

- Grand jury indictments and preliminary hearings are usually limited to serious offenses. Trials for misdemeanors often occur without either proceeding.

**7. Discuss the purpose of arraignment.**

- At the arraignment, the judge informs the defendant of the charges against her and appoints counsel if one has not yet been retained.

- The accused enters one of three pleas at arraignment: guilty, not guilty, or nolo contendere.

**8. Explain what is meant by the term "plea bargain."**

- Research indicates that most cases never go to trial but, instead, are bargained out of the system.

- Bargains can be made for a plea of guilty in exchange for a reduced sentence, dropping charges, lowering the charge, or substituting a more socially acceptable charge for one with negative connotations.

**9. Discuss the pros and cons of plea bargaining.**

- People who plead guilty generally get lighter sentences than those who go to trial.

- Critics of plea bargaining claim that it results in cynicism and disrespect for the judicial system.

**10. Explain the roles of the prosecutor, defense attorney, judge, and victim in the plea negotiation.**

- The U.S. Supreme Court has shaped the legal contours of the plea system. For example, it has ruled that bargains must be kept on both sides.

- Plea bargains must be accepted and approved by the judge.

- The prosecutor must uphold his or her end of the bargain, but only after the judge accepts the bargain.

- A court will not accept a guilty plea unless the defendant has been properly advised by counsel and the court has determined that the plea is voluntary and has a factual basis.

- Victims have little to no involvement in the plea bargaining process, but some authorities would like to see this change.

## 11. Define the term "pretrial diversion."

- Diversion programs offering a criminal defendant the ability to enter a treatment program instead of a criminal trial continue to be used throughout the United States.

- Most diversion programs have a common goal: to constructively bypass criminal prosecution by providing a reasonable alternative in the form of treatment, counseling, or employment programs.

## 12. Explain the legal rights of the accused at trial.

- Legal rights at trial include the right to an impartial judge, the right to be competent at trial, the right to confront witnesses, the right to compulsory process, the right to an impartial jury, the right to counsel, the right to a speedy trial, the right to a public trial, and the right to be convicted by proof beyond a reasonable doubt.

## 13. Summarize the trial process.

- The trial of a criminal case is a formal process conducted in a specific and orderly fashion in accordance with rules of criminal law, procedure, and evidence.

- In both civil and criminal cases, jurors are selected randomly from licensing or voter registration lists within each court's jurisdiction.

- Once prospective jurors are chosen, the lengthy process of voir dire (from the French for "to tell the truth") starts.

- During voir dire, a juror who acknowledges any bias in favor of or prejudice against the defendant may be removed by either the prosecution or the defense with a challenge for cause.

- During voir dire, both the prosecution and the defense are allowed peremptory challenges, which enables them to excuse jurors for no particular reason or for undisclosed reasons.

- Once the jury has been selected, the prosecutor and the defense attorney may each make an opening statement about the case.

- Following the opening statements, the government begins its case by presenting evidence to the court through its witnesses.

- The central purpose of the direct examination process is to introduce evidence upon which the jury can decide the case.

- Once the prosecution has provided all the government's evidence against a defendant, it informs the court that it rests the people's case. The defense attorney at this point may enter a motion for a directed verdict.

- Closing arguments are used by the attorneys to review the facts and evidence of the case in a manner favorable to their respective positions.

- According to a strategy called jury nullification, jurors are sometimes asked by the defense to ignore the facts of the case and the judge's legal instructions and instead to render decisions based on emotion and personal preference.

- In a criminal trial, the judge instructs, or charges, the jury members on the principles of law that ought to guide and control their decision on the defendant's innocence or guilt.

- Once the charge is given to the jury members, they retire to deliberate on a verdict.

- Imposing the criminal sentence is normally the responsibility of the trial judge.

- Once a verdict has been rendered and a defendant found guilty, that individual may petition an appellate court to review the procedures used during trial.

# KEY TERMS

| | | |
|---|---|---|
| pretrial procedures, 392 | pretrial detainees, 395 | presentment, 400 |
| complaint, 392 | release on recognizance (ROR), 397 | indictment, 400 |
| arraignment, 392 | avertable recidivist, 399 | true bill, 400 |
| bail, 392 | preventive detention, 399 | no bill, 400 |

## CRITICAL THINKING QUESTIONS

1. Should criminal defendants be allowed to bargain for a reduced sentence in exchange for a guilty plea? Should the victim always be included in the plea bargaining process?

2. Should those accused of violent acts be subjected to preventive detention instead of bail, even though they have not been convicted of a crime? Is it fair to the victim to have his alleged attacker running around loose?

3. What purpose does a grand jury or preliminary hearing serve in adjudicating felony offenses?

   Should one of these methods be abandoned? If so, which one?

4. Why should pretrial services be provided for defendants?

5. What are the pros and cons of a jury trial versus a bench trial?

6. Do defendants enjoy too many rights? Why or why not?

7. Is there a "*CSI* effect"? If so, has it caused problems? What kind?

## NOTES

1. *Michigan v. Jackson*, 475 U.S. 625 (1986).
2. *Montejo v. Louisiana*, No. 07-1529 (2009).
3. Christopher Stephens, "Bail," *Georgetown Law Journal* 90 (2002): 1395–1416.
4. The Judiciary Act of 1789, www.constitution.org/uslaw/judiciary_1789.htm (accessed April 27, 2010).
5. *Stack v. Boyle*, 342 U.S. 1 (1951).
6. Data in this section comes from Tracey Kyckelhahn and Thomas H. Cohen, *Felony Defendants in Large Urban Counties, 2004* (Washington, D.C.: Bureau of Justice Statistics, 2008).
7. William J. Sabol, Todd D. Minton, and Paige M. Harrison, *Prison and Jail Inmates at Midyear 2006* (Washington, D.C.: Bureau of Justice Statistics, 2007).
8. James J. Stephan, *State Prison Expenditures, 2001* (Washington, D.C.: Bureau of Justice Statistics, 2004).
9. Kyckelhahn and Cohen, *Felony Defendants in Large Urban Counties, 2004.*
10. *Vera Institute of Justice, 1961–1971: Programs in Criminal Justice* (New York: Vera Institute of Justice, 1972).
11. Public Law 89-465, 18 U.S.C., Sec. 3146 (1966).
12. 18 U.S.C., Sec. 3142 (1984).
13. Fred Cohen, "The New Federal Crime Control Act," *Criminal Law Bulletin* 21 (1985): 330–337.
14. *Schall v. Martin*, 467 U.S. 253 (1984).
15. *United States v. Salerno*, 481 U.S. 739 (1987).
16. This section leans on John Clark and D. Alan Henry, *Pretrial Services Programming at the Start of the 21st Century: A Survey* (Washington, D.C.: Bureau of Justice Assistance, 2003).
17. Ric Simmons, "Reexamining the Grand Jury: Is There Room for Democracy in the Criminal Justice System?" *Boston University Law Review* 82 (2002): 1–76, p. 25; also see *United States v. Williams*, 504 U.S. 36 (1992).
18. *United States v. Williams*, 504 U.S. 36 (1992).
19. Suzanne Roe Neely, "Preserving Justice and Preventing Prejudice: Requiring Disclosure of Substantial Exculpatory Evidence to the Grand Jury," *American Criminal Law Review* 39 (2002): 171–200.
20. John Gibeaut, "Indictment of a System," *ABA Journal* 87 (2001): 34.
21. *Henderson v. Morgan*, 426 U.S. 637 (1976).
22. Federal Rules of Criminal Procedure, Rule 11[d].
23. F. Andrew Hessick and Reshma Saujani, "Plea Bargaining and Convicting the Innocent: The Role of the Prosecutor, the Defense Counsel, and the Judge," *BYU Journal of Public Law* 16 (2002): 189–243.
24. *Brady v. United States*, 397 U.S. 742 (1970).
25. Mike McConville and Chester Mirsky, *Jury Trials and Plea Bargaining: A True History* (Oxford, England: Hart, 2005).
26. George Fisher, "Plea Bargaining's Triumph," *Yale Law Journal* 109 (2000): 857–1058.
27. Matthew Durose and Patrick Langan, *Felony Sentencing in State Courts, 2000* (Washington, D.C.: Bureau of Justice Statistics, 2003).
28. Debra Emmelman, "Trial by Plea Bargain: Case Settlement as a Product of Recursive Decisionmaking," *Law and Society Review* 30 (1996): 335–361.
29. Fred Zacharis, "Justice in Plea Bargaining," *William and Mary Law Review* 39 (1998): 1121–1189.
30. Nathaniel J. Pallone, "Without Plea-Bargaining, Megan Kanka Would Be Alive Today," *Criminology & Public Policy* 3 (2003): 83–96.
31. William Stuntz, "Plea Bargaining and Criminal Law's Disappearing Shadow," *Harvard Law Review* 117 (2004): 2548–2569.
32. Mike McConville, "Plea Bargaining: Ethics and Politics," *Journal of Law & Society* 25 (1998): 526–555.
33. The Innocence Project, *False Confessions*, www.innocenceproject.org/understand/False-Confessions.php (accessed April 28, 2010).
34. Ibid.
35. *Hill v. Lockhart*, 474 U.S. 52 (1985).

36. *Boykin v. Alabama*, 395 U.S. 238 (1969); *Brady v. United States*, 397 U.S. 742 (1970).
37. *Santobello v. New York*, 404 U.S. 257 (1971).
38. *Ricketts v. Adamson*, 483 U.S. 1 (1987).
39. *Bordenkircher v. Hayes*, 434 U.S. 357 (1978).
40. *North Carolina v. Alford*, 400 U.S. 25 (1970).
41. *United States v. Mezzanatto*, 513 U.S. 196 (1995).
42. Jeremy D. Ball, "Is It a Prosecutor's World? Determinants of Court Bargaining Decisions," *Journal of Contemporary Criminal Justice* 22 (2006): 241–260.
43. Stephen P. Lagoy, Joseph J. Senna, and Larry J. Siegel, "An Empirical Study on Information Usage for Prosecutorial Decision Making in Plea Negotiations," *American Criminal Law Review* 13 (1976): 435–471, at 462.
44. Barbara Boland and Brian Forst, *The Prevalence of Guilty Pleas* (Washington, D.C.: Bureau of Justice Statistics, 1984), p. 3. See also Gary Hengstler, "The Troubled Justice System," *American Bar Association Journal* 80 (1994): 44.
45. See American Bar Association, *Standards Relating to Pleas of Guilty*, 2nd ed. (Chicago: 1988). See also *North Carolina v. Alford*, 400 U.S. 25 (1970).
46. Keith Bystrom, "Communicating Plea Offers to the Client," in *Ethical Problems Facing the Criminal Defense Lawyer*, ed. Rodney Uphoff (Chicago: American Bar Association, Section on Criminal Justice, 1995), p. 84.
47. American Bar Association, Standards Relating to Pleas of Guilty, standard 3.3; *National Advisory Commission on Criminal Justice Standards and Goals, Task Force Report on Courts* (Washington, D.C.: U.S. Government Printing Office, 1973), 42.
48. American Bar Association, *Standards Relating to Pleas of Guilty*, 73; see also Alan Alschuler, "The Trial Judge's Role in Plea Bargaining," *Columbia Law Review* 76 (1976): 1059.
49. American Bar Association, *Model Uniform Victims of Crime Act* (Chicago: 1992).
50. Michael M. O'Hear, "Plea Bargaining and Victims: From Consultation to Guidelines," *Marquette Law Review*, forthcoming, http://papers.ssrn.com/sol3/papers.cfm?abstract_id=1005373 (accessed May 30, 2008).
51. National Institute of Law Enforcement and Criminal Justice, *Plea Bargaining in the United States*, pp. 37–40.
52. Gary Blankenship, "Debating the Pros and Cons of Plea Bargaining," *Florida Bar News* 30 (July 15, 2003): 6–7.
53. Candace McCoy, *Politics and Plea Bargaining: Victims' Rights in California* (Philadelphia: University of Pennsylvania Press, 1993).
54. Anne Morrison Piehl and Shawn D. Bushway, "Measuring and Explaining Charge Bargaining," *Journal of Quantitative Criminology* 23 (2007): 105–125.
55. National District Attorneys Association, *National Prosecution Standards*, 2nd ed. (Alexandria, Va.: 1991), p. 130.
56. Franklyn Dunford, D. Wayne Osgood, and Hart Weichselbaum, *National Evaluation of Diversion Programs* (Washington, D.C.: Government Printing Office, 1982).
57. Sharla Rausch and Charles Logan, "Diversion from Juvenile Court: Panacea or Pandora's Box?" in *Evaluating Juvenile Justice*, ed. James Kleugel (Beverly Hills, Calif.: Sage, 1983), pp. 19–30.
58. See Malcolm Feeley, *Court Reform on Trial* (New York: Basic Books, 1983).
59. *Tumey v. Ohio*, 273 U.S. 510 (1927).
60. Ibid., p. 523.
61. See, for example, Minn. R. Crim. P. 26.03, subd. 13(4).
62. *Riggins v. Nevada*, 504 U.S. 127 (1992).
63. *Crawford v. Washington*, 541 U.S. 36 (2004).
64. *Melendez-Diaz v. Massachusetts*, No. 07-591 (2009).
65. *Diaz v. United States*, 223 U.S. 442 (1912); *Taylor v. Illinois*, 484 U.S. 400 (1988).
66. *Illinois v. Allen*, 397 U.S. 337 (1970).

67. *Maryland v. Craig*, 497 U.S. 836 (1990).
68. *Giles v. California*, No. 07-6053 (2008)
69. *Washington v. Texas*, 388 U.S. 14 (1967).
70. *Baldwin v. New York*, 399 U.S. 66 (1970).
71. *Rothgery v. Gillespie County*, No. 07-440 (2008).
72. *Powell v. Alabama*, 287 U.S. 45 (1932).
73. Ibid., p. 71.
74. *Johnson v. Zerbst*, 304 U.S. 458 (1938).
75. *Gideon v. Wainwright*, 372 U.S. 335 (1963).
76. *Scott v. Illinois*, 440 U.S. 367 (1979).
77. *Shelton v. Alabama,* 122 U.S. 1764 (2002).
78. *Gideon v. Wainwright*, 372 U.S. 335 (1963).
79. *Douglas v. California*, 372 U.S. 353 (1963).
80. *In re Gault*, 387 U.S. 1 (1967).
81. *Coleman v. Alabama*, 399 U.S. 1 (1970).
82. *Argersinger v. Hamlin*, 407 U.S. 25 (1972).
83. *Morrissey v. Brewer*, 408 U.S. 471 (1972).
84. *Gagnon v. Scarpelli*, 411 U.S. 778 (1973).
85. *Ross v. Moffitt*, 417 U.S. 600 (1974).
86. *Scott v. Illinois*, 440 U.S. 367 (1979).
87. *Morris v. Slappy*, 461 U.S. 1 (1983).
88. *Wheat v. United States*, 486 U.S. 153 (1988).
89. *United States v. Monsanto*, 491 U.S. 600 (1989)
90. *United States v. Gonzalez-Lopez*, 548 U.S. 140 (2006).
91. *Rochgery v. Gillespie County*, No. 07-440 (2008).
92. *Faretta v. California*, 422 U.S. 806 (1975).
93. *Indiana v. Edwards*, No. 07-208 (2008).
94. See American Bar Association, *Standards Relating to Speedy Trial* (Chicago: ABA, 1995).
95. *Klopfer v. North Carolina*, 386 U.S. 213 (1967).
96. Ibid., at 223, 87 S. Ct. at 993.
97. *Doggett v. United States,* 505 U.S. 162 (1992).
98. *Sheppard v. Maxwell*, 384 U.S. 333 (1966).
99. *Nebraska Press Association v. Stuart*, 427 U.S. 539 (1976); *Gannett Co. v. DePasquale*, 443 U.S. 368 (1979); *Press Enterprise Co. v. Superior Court*, 464 U.S. 501 (1986).
100. *Wilson v. Layne*, 526 U.S. 603 (1999).
101. *Richmond Newspapers, Inc. v. Virginia*, 448 U.S. 555 (1980).
102. *Globe Newspaper Co. v. Superior Court for County of Norfolk*, 457 U.S. 596 (1982).
103. *Chandler v. Florida*, 449 U.S. 560 (1981); see also American Bar Association, *Criminal Justice Standards, Fair Trial, and Free Press* (Washington, D.C.: ABA, 1992).
104. See *Brinegar v. United States,* 338 U.S. 160 (1949); *In re Winship*, 397 U.S. 358, 90 (1970).
105. See *In re Winship*, at 397.
106. Ibid., at 371, 90 S. Ct. at 1076.
107. Brian Kalt, "The Exclusion of Felons from Jury Service," *American University Law Review* 53 (2003): 65–189.
108. George Hayden, Joseph Senna, and Larry Siegel, "Prosecutorial Discretion in Peremptory Challenges: An Empirical Investigation of Information Use in the Massachusetts Jury Selection Process," *New England Law Review* 13 (1978): 768.
109. *Batson v. Kentucky*, 476 U.S. 79 (1986); see also Alan Alschuler and Randall Kennedy, "Equal Justice—Would Color-Conscious Jury Selection Help?" *American Bar Association Journal* 81 (1995): 36–37.
110. *Batson v. Kentucky*, 476 U.S. 79 (1986).
111. *Hernandez v. New York*, 500 U.S. 352 (1991).
112. *Powers v. Ohio*, 499 U.S. 400 (1991).
113. *Edmonson v. Leesvile Concrete Co.*, 500 U.S. 614 (1991).
114. *Georgia v. McCollum*, 505 U.S. 42 (1992).
115. *J.E.B. v. Alabama*, 511 U.S. 127 (1994).
116. *Johnson v. California*, 542 U.S. 162 (2005).
117. *Miller El. v. Dretke*, 545 U.S. 231 (2005). This interpretation is a bit of a simplification. Readers are encouraged to read the

narrative of the case and also this case: *Miller-El v. Cockrell*, 537 U.S. 322 (2003).

118. *Synder v. Louisiana*, 552 U.S. 472 (2008).

119. *Rivera v. Illinois*, No. 07-9995 (2009).

120. John Schwartz, "As Jurors Turn to Web, Mistrials Are Popping Up," *New York Times* (March 17, 2009), www.nytimes.com/2009/03/18/us/18juries.html?_r=1&emc=eta1 (accessed April 28, 2010).

121. Arie Rubenstein, "Verdicts of Conscience: Nullification and the Modern Jury Trial," *Columbia Law Review 106* (2006): 959–993.

122. David Pepper, "Nullifying History: Modern-Day Misuse of the Right to Decide the Law," *Case Western Reserve Law Review 50* (2000): 599–643.

123. *Chapman v. California,* 386 U.S. 18 (1967).

124. *Douglas v. California,* 372 U.S. 353 (1963).

# CHAPTER 12

# Punishment and Sentencing

## CHAPTER OBJECTIVES

1. Outline the historical development of punishment.
2. List the major goals of contemporary sentencing.
3. Distinguish among general and specific deterrence, incapacitation, and retribution.
4. Compare rehabilitation with just desert.
5. Know how sentences are imposed.
6. Classify the various types of sentencing structures.
7. Discuss how people are sentenced today.
8. Demonstrate your knowledge of the nature of capital punishment in the United States and abroad.
9. Be familiar with the arguments for and against capital punishment.
10. Discuss the legality of the death penalty.

**I**n early 2009, the Supreme Court decided whether it should hear an appeal from William Johnson, a man who had been, as of this writing, on death row in Florida for 32 years.[1] In seeking to have the Court hear his case, Johnson argued that the lengthy amount of he spent on death row, not the sentence itself, amounted to cruel and unusual punishment, in violation of the U.S. Constitution's Eighth Amendment.

Johnson's argument was creative, but it lacked merit because he was partly responsible for the delay, having filed many appeals over the years. Calling Johnson out on this, Justice Clarence Thomas said, "I remain unaware of any support in the American constitutional tradition or in this Court's precedent for the proposition that a defendant can avail himself of the panoply of appellate and collateral procedures and then complain when his execution is delayed." On the other hand, something is at least partially awry when a person spends 32 years waiting for a sentence to be carried out. Although he supported the Court's decision not to grant review, Justice John Paul Stevens said, "[O]ur experience during the past three decades has demonstrated that delays in state-sponsored killings are inescapable and that executing defendants after such delays is unacceptably cruel. This inevitable cruelty, coupled with the diminished justification for carrying out an execution after the lapse of so much time, reinforces my opinion that contemporary decisions to retain the death penalty as a part of our law are the product of habit and inattention rather than an acceptable deliberative process." ■

The Supreme Court elected *not* to hear Johnson's case, but its decision sent a signal that there is some concern about the delays between sentencing and execution in capital cases. And although delays like those in Johnson's case are rare, the death penalty is not administered quickly for *any* offenders. According to the Death Penalty Information Center, in 1990 the average time between sentencing and execution was 7 years. That grew to over 12 years in 2008.[2] By all accounts, delays continue to lengthen, prompting death penalty critics to complain about the costs of a drawn-out appeals process. Supporters also express disdain over delays, claiming instead that they undermine the retributive force of death and compromise the penalty's deterrent effect. Both parties agree something must be done.

The death penalty is the most extreme form of punishment, and it is used relatively rarely, but it raises fundamental questions about the nature and extent of punishment: Should the most serious of criminals be executed? What options, if any, are preferable to capital punishment? Is contemporary punishment too harsh or too lenient? Regardless of the penalty in question, is sentencing fair? Is there discrimination in sentencing based on race, gender, or social class? How often are mistakes made? These are but a few of the most significant issues in the realm of punishment and sentencing.

This chapter first examines the history of punishment and then focuses on incarceration and capital punishment, the two most traditional and punitive forms of criminal sanctions used today. Chapter 13 reviews alternative sentences that have been developed to reduce the strain on the overburdened correctional system; these sentences provide intermediate sanctions designed to control people whose behavior and personality make incarceration unnecessary. Such sanctions include probation and other forms of community correction.

# THE HISTORY OF PUNISHMENT

The punishment and correction of criminals has changed considerably through the ages, reflecting custom, economic conditions, and religious and political ideals.[3]

In earlier times, punishment was quite severe. Brutal public punishments, which included beheading and burning, were designed to teach the value of obedience to authority. Even kings, such as Charles I of England, were not immune from execution. Following his conviction on charges of treason during the English Civil War of 1642–1648, Charles was beheaded on January 30, 1649.

© The Granger Collection, New York

## From Exile to Fines, Torture to Forfeiture

In early Greece and Rome, the most common state-administered punishment was banishment or exile. Only slaves were commonly subjected to harsh physical punishment for their misdeeds. Interpersonal violence, even attacks that resulted in death, were viewed as a private matter. These ancient peoples typically used economic punishments, such as fines, for such crimes as assault on a slave, arson, or housebreaking.

During the Middle Ages (the fifth to fifteenth centuries), there was little law or governmental control. Offenses were settled by blood feuds carried out by the families of the injured parties. When possible, the Roman custom of settling disputes by fine or an exchange of property was adopted as a means of resolving interpersonal conflicts with a minimum of bloodshed. After the eleventh century, during the feudal period, forfeiture of land and property was common punishment for persons who violated law and custom or who failed to fulfill their feudal obligations to their lord. The word "felony" has its origins in the twelfth century, when the term "felonia" referred to a breach of faith with one's feudal lord.

During this period the main emphasis of criminal law and punishment was on maintaining public order. If in the heat of passion or while intoxicated a person severely injured or killed his neighbor, freemen in the area would gather to pronounce a judgment and make the culprit do penance or pay compensation, called wergild. The purpose of the fine was to pacify the injured party and ensure that the conflict would not develop into a blood feud and anarchy. The inability of the peasantry to pay fines led to the use of corporal punishment, such as whipping or branding, as a substitute penalty.

The development of the common law in the eleventh century brought some standardization to penal practices. However, corrections remained an amalgam of fines and brutal physical punishments. The criminal wealthy could buy their way out of punishment and into exile, but capital and corporal punishments were used to control the criminal poor, who were executed or mutilated at ever-increasing rates. Execution, banishment, mutilation, branding, and flogging were used on a whole range of offenders, from murderers and robbers to vagrants and Gypsies. Punishments became unmatched in their cruelty, featuring a gruesome variety of physical tortures, often part of a public spectacle, presumably so that the sadistic sanctions would act as deterrents. But the variety and imagination of the tortures inflicted on even minor criminals before their death suggest that retribution, sadism, and spectacle were more important than any presumed deterrent effect.

## Public Work and Transportation to the Colonies

By the end of the sixteenth century, the rise of the city and overseas colonization provided tremendous markets for manufactured goods and spurred the need for labor. Punishment of criminals changed to meet the demands created by these social conditions. Instead of being tortured or executed, many offenders were made to do hard labor for their crimes. "Poor laws," developed at the end of the sixteenth century, required that the poor, vagrants, and vagabonds be put to work in public or private enterprises. Houses of correction were developed to make it convenient to assign petty law violators to work details. In London, a workhouse was developed at Brideswell in 1557; its use became so popular that by 1576 Parliament ordered a Brideswell-type workhouse to be built in every county in England. Many convicted offenders were pressed into sea duty as galley slaves. Galley slavery was considered a fate so loathsome that many convicts mutilated themselves rather than submit to servitude on the high seas.

The constant shortage of labor in the European colonies also prompted authorities to transport convicts overseas. In England, an Order in Council of 1617 granted a reprieve and stay of execution to people convicted of robbery and other felonies who were strong enough to be employed overseas. Similar measures were used in France and Italy to recruit galley slaves and workers.

Transporting convicts to the colonies became popular: It supplied labor, cost little, and was actually profitable for the government, since manufacturers and plantation owners paid for the convicts' services. The Old Bailey Court in London supplied at least 10,000 convicts between 1717 and 1775. Convicts would serve a period as workers and then become free again.

The American Revolution ended the transportation of felons to North America, but it continued in Australia and New Zealand. Between 1787 and 1875, when the practice was finally abandoned, over 135,000 felons were transported to Australia.

Although transportation in lieu of a death sentence may at first glance seem advantageous, transported prisoners endured enormous hardships. Those who were sent to Australia suffered incredible physical abuse, including severe whippings and mutilation. Many of the British prison officials placed in charge of the Australian penal colonies could best be described as sociopaths or sadists.

## The Rise of the Prison

Between the American Revolution in 1776 and the first decades of the nineteenth century, the European and U.S. populations increased rapidly. Transportation of convicts to North America was no longer an option. The increased use of machinery made industry capital intensive, not labor intensive. As a result, there was less need for unskilled laborers in England, and many workers could not find suitable employment.

The gulf between poor workers and wealthy landowners and merchants widened. The crime rate rose significantly, prompting a return to physical punishment and increased use of the death penalty. During the latter part of the eighteenth century, 350 types of crime in England were punishable by death. Although many people sentenced to death for trivial offenses were spared the gallows, the use of capital punishment was common in England during the mid-eighteenth century. Prompted by the excessive use of physical and capital punishment, legal philosophers argued that physical punishment should be replaced by periods of confinement and incapacitation. Jails and workhouses were thus used to hold petty offenders, vagabonds, the homeless, and debtors. However, these institutions were not meant for hard-core criminals. One solution to imprisoning a growing criminal population was to keep prisoners in abandoned ships anchored in rivers and harbors throughout England. In 1777, the degradation under which prisoners lived in these ships inspired John Howard, the sheriff of Bedfordshire, to write *The State of the Prisons in England and Wales*, which led to Parliament's passage of legislation mandating the construction of secure and sanitary structures to house prisoners.

**penitentiary**
A state or federal correctional institution for incarceration of felony offenders for terms of one year or more.

By 1820, long periods of incarceration in walled institutions called reformatories or **penitentiaries** began to replace physical punishment in England and the United States. These institutions were considered liberal reforms during a time when harsh physical punishment and incarceration in filthy holding facilities were the norm. The history of correctional institutions will be discussed further in Chapter 14. Incarceration has remained the primary mode of punishment for serious offenses in the United States since it was introduced in the early nineteenth century. Ironically, in our high-tech society, some of the institutions developed soon after the Revolutionary War are still in use today. In contemporary society, prison as a method of punishment has been supplemented by a sentence to community supervision for less serious offenders, and the death penalty is reserved for those considered to be the most serious and dangerous.

## THE GOALS OF PUNISHMENT

When we hear about a notorious criminal—such as serial killer Jeffrey Dahmer or Oklahoma City bomber Tim McVeigh—receiving a long prison sentence or the death penalty for a particularly heinous crime, each of us has a distinct reaction. Some of us are gratified that a truly evil person "got just what he deserved." Many people feel safer because a dangerous person is now "where he can't harm any other innocent victims." Others hope the punishment serves as a warning to potential criminals that "everyone gets caught in the end." Some may actually feel sorry for the defendant—"he got a raw deal, he needs help, not punishment"—and still others hope that "when he gets out, he'll have learned his lesson." And when an offender is forced to pay a large fine, we say, "What goes around comes around."

Any of these sentiments may be at work when criminal sentences are formulated. After all, punishments are devised and implemented by judges, many of whom are elected officials and share the general public's sentiments and fears. The objectives of criminal sentencing today can usually be grouped into six distinct areas: general deterrence, incapacitation, specific deterrence, retribution/just desert, rehabilitation, and equity/restitution.

### General Deterrence

**general deterrence**
A crime control policy that depends on the fear of criminal penalties. General deterrence measures, such as long prison sentences for violent crimes, are aimed at convincing the potential law violator that the pains associated with the crime outweigh the benefits.

According to the concept of **general deterrence**, people should be punished to set an example for others. If someone is punished severely, others will be too afraid to break the law, knowing that they will face similar treatment. If the state can convince potential criminals that the punishment they face is certain, swift, and severe, they will be to afraid to even contemplate committing criminal offenses. However, punishment cannot be so harsh that it seems disproportionate and unfair. If it did, people would believe they have nothing to lose, and their crimes might escalate in frequency and severity. Thus, if the crime of rape were punished by death, rapists might be encouraged to kill their victims to dispose of the one person who could identify them at trial. Since they would already be facing the death penalty for rape, they would have nothing more to lose.

Some justice experts believe that the recent decline in the crime rate is a result of increasing criminal penalties. Once arrested, people have a greater chance of being convicted today than they did in the past. This phenomenon is referred to as "expected punishment," defined as the number of days in prison a typical criminal can expect to serve per crime.[4] Expected punishment rates are actually still quite low because (a) crime clearance rates remain well under 50 percent, (b) many cases are dropped at the pretrial and trial stages (nolle prosequi), and (c) about one-third of convicted felons are given probationary rather than prison sentences.

Take for instance the crime of burglary. About 2 million burglaries are reported to the police each year, about 300,000 burglars are arrested, 100,000 are convicted, and about 40,000 are sent to prison. Therefore, for every 50 reported burglaries, only one burglar is incarcerated. (Keep in mind that some burglars commit many crimes per year, so we are not talking about 2 million individual burglars but 2 million burglaries.) Such inefficiency limits the deterrent effect of punishment.

Because the justice system is still inefficient, the general deterrent effect of punishment is less than desired. The average prison sentence received by violent felony offenders in state courts decreased from nearly 10 years in 1994 to about 5 years today.[5] Note, however, that the actual time served per sentence has increased somewhat during this period, meaning that inmates are spending more of their sentence behind bars before they are released.[6] On the one hand, deterrence advocates would argue that if prison sentences continue to decline, expected punishments will drop, and as a result crime rates may increase. On the other hand, if the actual time served continues to increase, crime rates may eventually drop because the "cost" of crime (the ratio of punishment to crime) has risen.

### ⚡ Incapacitation

Because criminals will not be able to repeat their criminal acts while they are under state control, **incapacitation** of criminals is another goal of sentencing. For some offenders, this means a period in a high-security state prison where behavior is closely monitored. If dangerous criminals are kept behind bars, they will not be able to repeat their illegal activities.

Does incapacitating criminals help reduce the crime rate? The evidence is mixed. Between 1990 and 2008, the prison population doubled (from 700,000 to more than 1.4 million) and the crime rate dropped dramatically, indicating a significant incarceration effect. However, there have also been periods, such as between 1980 and 1990, when the prison population increased and so did the

**incapacitation**
The policy of keeping dangerous criminals in confinement to eliminate the risk of their repeating their offense in society.

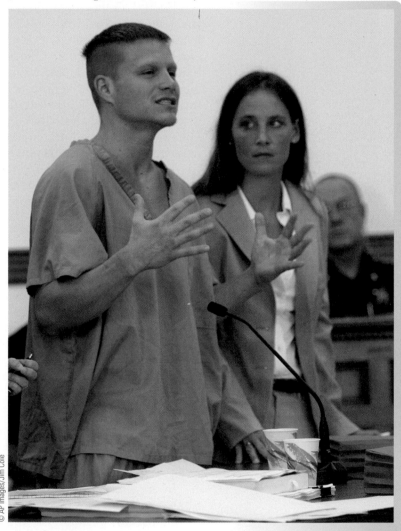

© AP Images/Jim Cole

*One of the goals of criminal sentencing is to ensure that dangerous people are incapacitated, rendering them incapable of hurting others. Sometimes this goal is not met. Here Michael Woodbury speaks to a judge during a hearing in Concord, New Hampshire, on August 17, 2007. Woodbury, an ex-convict, went on a multistate crime spree after leaving prison. He pleaded guilty to killing three men during a botched robbery. The victims' lives would have been spared had Woodbury been incapacitated for a longer period.*

crime rate. This indicates that incarceration trends may influence crime rates but that crime rates may be more closely related to other factors, such as population makeup, police effectiveness, drug use, and the economy.[7]

It is also possible that incarceration can have a short-term effect of reducing crime while the person is behind bars but that this effect quickly ends once the prisoner is released into the community. The prison experience may actually increase the likelihood of reoffending. Many inmates have not engaged in any correctional rehabilitation, and others are exposed to highly dangerous, experienced offenders. This produces a criminogenic effect, increasing the likelihood of their offending once released back into the community.[8]

Even if an incarceration policy were effective, its benefits would diminish as more and more people were put in prison. Think of it this way: If the country had only a single prison cell and only one person could be locked up at a time, chances are that person would be the nation's most dangerous, violent chronic offender. The crime reduction benefit of locking up just that single person would be significant. If we could only incarcerate two, the second inmate would be slightly less dangerous. Each time a person is added to the prison population, the crime reduction benefit is somewhat less than that of jailing the inmate who came before. We now have 1.4 million people behind prison bars. The millionth-plus inmate is far less dangerous than the first, and the incarceration benefits of locking him or her up are significantly less, yet the *cost* of incarcerating each new inmate remains the same as the first![9] Thus, by definition, using incapacitation to reduce crime rates always brings diminishing returns.[10]

## Specific Deterrence

Another goal of punishment is to convince offenders that the pains of punishment are greater than the benefits of crime, so they will not repeat their criminal offending; the experience of suffering punishment should inhibit future law violations.

✴ Does a **specific deterrence** strategy reduce crime rates? A few research efforts have found that experiencing punishment can have a significant specific deterrence effect on future criminality, but these findings are balanced by research that has failed to find specific deterrence effects. For example, some studies have found that punishment reduces the likelihood that spousal abusers will reoffend, but others have failed to get the same positive results.[11]

Claims for a specific deterrent effect are further weakened by data showing that most inmates (more than 80%) who are released from prison have had prior convictions, and the great majority (68%) will reoffend soon after their release.[12]

In some instances, rather than reducing the frequency of crime, severe punishments may actually increase reoffending rates.[13] Some states are now employing high-security "supermax" prisons, which use a bare minimum of treatment and 23-hour-a-day lockdown. Certainly such a harsh regimen should deter future criminality. But a recent study in the state of Washington that matched on a one-to-one basis supermax prisoners with inmates from more traditional prisons showed that upon release, supermax prisoners had significantly higher felony recidivism rates than similar inmates who did their time in less secure institutions.[14]

How is it possible that harsh sentences actually increase the likelihood of future crime?

■ Punishment may bring defiance rather than deterrence. People who are harshly treated may want to show that they cannot be broken by the system.

■ The stigma of harsh treatment labels people and helps lock offenders into a criminal career instead of convincing them to avoid one.

**specific deterrence**
A crime control policy suggesting that punishment should be severe enough to convince convicted offenders never to repeat their criminal activity.

- Criminals who are punished may also believe that the likelihood of getting caught twice for the same type of crime is remote: "Lightning never strikes twice in the same spot," they may reason; no one is that unlucky.[15]

Despite these sketchy results, the goal of specific deterrence remains a fundamental part of sentencing. Some judges and policymakers maintain that a "taste of the bars" should reduce the desire for repeat offending.[16]

## Retribution/Just Desert

According to the retributive goal of sentencing, the essential purpose of the criminal process is to punish offenders—fairly and justly—in a manner that is proportionate to the gravity of their crimes.[17] Offenders are punished simply and solely because they *deserve* to be disciplined for what they have done: "the punishment should fit the crime."[18] It would be wrong to punish people to set an example for others or to deter would-be criminals, as the general deterrence goal demands. Punishment should be no more or less than the offender's actions deserve; it must be based on how **blameworthy** the person is. This is referred to as the concept of **just desert**.[19]

According to this view, punishments must be equally and fairly distributed to all people who commit similar illegal acts. However, determining just punishments can be difficult because there is generally little consensus about the treatment of criminals, the seriousness of crimes, and the proper response to criminal acts. Consequently, there has been an ongoing effort to calculate fair and just sentences and to apply them in an equitable way.

## Rehabilitation

Some sentences are based on the need to treat and/or rehabilitate criminal offenders. Because society has failed them, many offenders have been forced to grow up in disorganized neighborhoods, have been the target of biased police officers, and are disadvantaged at home, at school, and in the job market. To compensate for these deprivations, the justice system is obligated to help these unfortunate people and not simply punish them for their misdeeds.[20] Rehabilitation advocates believe that if the proper treatment is applied, an offender will present no further threat to society.[21] It is not surprising, then, that the general public supports the treatment goal of sentencing and prefers it over policies based on punishment and incarceration.[22]

## Diversion

In some instances, the court process is aimed at sparing nondangerous offenders from the stigma and labeling of a criminal conviction and further involvement with the justice process. Instead of being convicted and sentenced to traditional forms of correction, such as a stay in a county jail, the judge may allow them to be diverted into a community correctional program for treatment. As part of a diversionary sentence, the convicted offender might be asked to make restitution payments to the crime victim or participate in a community-based program that features counseling and/or drug monitoring.

## Equity/Restitution

Because criminals gain from their misdeeds, it seems both fair and just to demand that they reimburse society for its loss caused by their crimes. In the early common law, wergild and fines represented the concept of creating an equitable solution to crime by requiring the convicted offender to make restitution to both the victim and the state. The **equity** goal of punishment means that convicted criminals must pay back their victims for their loss, the justice system for the costs of processing their case, and society for any disruption they may have caused. In a so-called victimless crime such as drug trafficking, the social costs might include the expense

**blameworthy**
Culpable or guilty of participating in a particular criminal offense.

**just desert**
The philosophy of justice asserting that those who violate the rights of others deserve to be punished. The severity of punishment should be commensurate with the seriousness of the crime.

**equity**
The action or practice of awarding each person his or her just due. Sanctions based on equity seek to compensate individual victims and the general society for their losses due to crime.

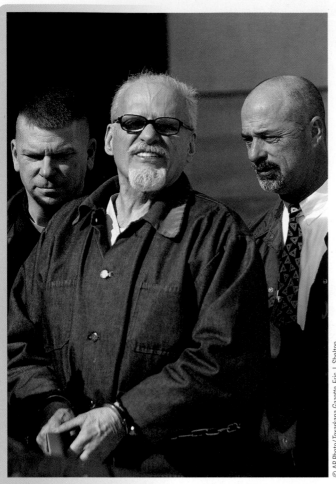

Tony Alamo, founder of Tony Alamo Christian Ministries, is seen leaving a federal courthouse shortly after his restitution hearing in downtown Texarkana, Arkansas, on January 13, 2010. U.S. District Judge Harry Barnes, of the Western District of Arkansas, awarded $500,000 to each of five child-abuse victims for their suffering. A year earlier, Alamo was found guilty on 10 federal counts of child abuse after an investigation turned up evidence of polygamy, underage marriage, and physical and sexual abuse on his 15-acre compound in northeast Texas.

of drug enforcement efforts, drug treatment centers, and care for infants born to drug-addicted mothers. In predatory crimes, the costs might include the services of emergency room doctors, lost workdays and productivity, and treatment for long-term psychological problems. To help defray these costs, convicted offenders might be required to pay a fine, forfeit the property they acquired through illegal gain, do community service work, make financial restitution to their victim, and reimburse the state for the costs of the criminal process. Because the criminals' actions helped expand their personal gains, rights, and privileges at society's expense, justice demands that they lose rights and privileges to restore the social balance.

## Restoration

Defendants may be asked to confront their behavior, the damage they caused the victim, and the shame they brought to their family, friends, and community. A restoration sentence might require that the convicted recognize that he or she caused injury to personal and social relations, along with a determination and acceptance of responsibility, accompanied by a statement of remorse. Restoration involves turning the justice system into a "healing" process rather a distributor of retribution and revenge. The intended result of the sentence is to repair injuries suffered by the victim and the community, while ensuring reintegration of the offender. Among the techniques used are programs that encourage reconciling the conflicts between offenders and victims via victim advocacy, mediation programs, and sentencing circles, in which crime victims and their families are brought together with offenders and their families in an effort to formulate a sanction that addresses the needs of each party. Victims are given a chance to voice their stories, and offenders can help compensate them financially or provide some service (for example, fixing damaged property).[23] The goal is to enable offenders to appreciate the damage they have caused, to make amends, and to be reintegrated into society.

The goals of sentencing are summarized in Concept Summary 12.1.

## IMPOSING THE SENTENCE

In most felony cases, except where the law provides for mandatory prison terms, sentencing is usually based on a variety of information available to the judge. Some jurisdictions allow victims to make impact statements that are considered at sentencing hearings. Most judges also consider a pre-sentence investigation report by the probation department in making a sentencing decision. This report is a social and personal history, as well as an evaluation of the defendant's chances for rehabilitation within the community.

### Concurrent vs. Consecutive Sentences

**concurrent sentences**
Prison sentences for two or more criminal acts, served simultaneously and run together.

In some instances, when an accused is convicted of two or more charges, the judge must decide whether to impose consecutive or **concurrent sentences**. If the sentences are concurrent, they begin the same day and are completed when the longest term has been served. For example, a defendant is convicted of burglarizing an apartment and assaulting its occupant; he is sentenced to 3 years on

## CONCEPT SUMMARY 12.1
### Goals of Criminal Sentencing

| Sentencing Goal | Sentencing Purpose |
|---|---|
| General deterrence | By punishing the known offender for his or her misdeeds, society hopes to convince would-be offenders that the pains of punishment outweigh the potential benefits of criminal behavior. Punishment is based on its effect on others. |
| Specific deterrence | Experiencing harsh criminal punishments should convince convicted offenders that crime does not pay. The suffering caused by punishment should inhibit future law violations. |
| Incapacitation | By incapacitating a convicted offender in a secure facility, such as a prison or jail, the state seeks to reduce or eliminate his or her opportunity to commit future crimes. Offenders are confined not for what they have done but for what it is feared they might do in the future. |
| Rehabilitation | Sentencing is aimed at reducing future criminality by treating and eliminating the underlying causes of crime. |
| Diversion | Sentencing is aimed at sparing nondangerous offenders from the stigma and labeling of a criminal conviction and involvement with the justice process. |
| Retribution/just desert | Because criminals benefit from their misdeeds, they deserve to be punished for their criminal acts. It is only fair that criminals who have committed the most serious crime, murder, receive the most severe penalty, death. |
| Equity/restitution | Because criminals gain from their misdeeds, it seems both fair and just to demand that they reimburse society for the loss(es) it has sustained as a consequence of their crimes. The equity goal of punishment means that convicted criminals must pay back their victims for their loss, the justice system for the costs of processing their case, and society for any disruption they may have caused. |
| Restoration | Defendants may be asked to confront their behavior, the damage they caused the victim, and the shame they brought to their family, friends, and community. The goal is to satisfy everyone's needs and restore the wrongdoer to good standing in society. |

a charge of assault and 10 years for burglary, with the sentences to be served concurrently. After 10 years in prison, the sentences would be completed.

In contrast, receiving a **consecutive sentence** means that on completion of the sentence for one crime, the offender begins serving time for the second of multiple crimes. If the defendant in the previous example had been sentenced consecutively, he would serve 3 years on the assault charge and then 10 years for the burglary. Therefore, the total term on the two charges would be 13 years. Concurrent sentences are the norm; consecutive sentences are requested for the most serious criminals and for those who are unwilling to cooperate with authorities. Figure 12.1 shows the difference between a consecutive and concurrent sentence.

**consecutive sentences**
Prison sentences for two or more criminal acts, served one after the other.

## The Effect of Good Time

When judges impose an incarceration sentence, they know and take into account the fact that the amount of time spent in prison is reduced by the implementation of "time off for good behavior." This concept was first used in 1817 in New York, and it was quickly adopted in most other jurisdictions. Good time is still in use

**FIGURE 12.1**
Consecutive vs. Concurrent Sentences

**Example: In state X**
1. Rape is punishable by 10 years in prison
2. Possession of a handgun by 3 years
3. Possession of heroin by 4 years

**Consecutive sentence**
Rape + possession of a handgun + possession of heroin
10 + 3 + 4 = 17 years
(each sentence served individually)

**Concurrent sentence**
Rape + possession of a handgun + possession of heroin
10 years
(all sentences served simultaneously)

today; state inmates can accrue standard good time at a rate ranging from 10 to 15 days per month. Federal inmates can get as many as 54 days taken off the end of their sentence each year.[24] In addition, some correctional authorities grant earned sentence reductions to inmates who participate in treatment programs, such as educational and vocational training, or who volunteer for experimental medical testing programs. In some jurisdictions, more than half of a determinate sentence (see the following section) can be erased by accumulating both standard and earned good time.

Good-time laws allow inmates to calculate their release date at the time they enter prison by subtracting the expected good time from their sentence. However, good time can be lost if inmates break prison rules, get into fights, or disobey correctional officers. In some jurisdictions, former inmates can be returned to prison to serve the balance of their unexpired sentence when their good time is revoked for failing to conform to conditions set down for their release (for example, not reporting to a postrelease supervisor or abusing drugs).

## SENTENCING MODELS

When a convicted offender is sentenced to prison, the statutes of the jurisdiction in which the crime was committed determine the penalties that may be imposed by the court. Over the years, a variety of sentencing structures have been used in the United States. They include indeterminate sentences, determinate sentences, and mandatory sentences.

### Indeterminate Sentences

In the 1870s, prison reformers Enoch Wines and Zebulon Brockway and others called for creation of **indeterminate sentences** tailored to fit individual needs. Offenders, the argument went, should be confined only until they are rehabilitated and then released on parole. Criminals were believed to be "sick" rather than bad; they could be successfully treated in prison. Rather than holding that "the punishment should fit the crime," reformers believed "the treatment should fit the offender."

The indeterminate sentence is still the most widely used type of sentence in the United States. Convicted offenders are typically given a "light" minimum sentence that must be served and a lengthy maximum sentence that is the outer boundary of the time that can be served. For example, the legislature might set a sentence of a minimum of 2 years and a maximum of 20 years for burglary; the convicted offender must be sentenced to no less than 2 years but to no more than 20 years in prison. Under this scheme, the actual length of time served by the offender is controlled by both the judge and the correctional agency. A judge could sentence a burglar to 5 to 15 years; the inmate then would be paroled from confinement soon after serving the minimum sentence if the correctional authorities believe that she is ready to live in the community. If the inmate accumulates good time, she could be released in as little as 30 months; a troublesome inmate would be forced to do all 15 years.

**indeterminate sentence**
A term of incarceration with a stated minimum and maximum length, such as a sentence to prison for a period of from 3 to 10 years. The prisoner is eligible for parole after the minimum sentence has been served. Based on the belief that sentences should fit the criminal, indeterminate sentences allow individualized sentences and provide for sentencing flexibility. Judges can set a high minimum to override the purpose of the indeterminate sentence.

**PERSPECTIVES ON JUSTICE**

*Rehabilitation Perspective*

The basic purpose of the indeterminate sentence is to individualize each sentence in the interests of rehabilitating the offender. This type of sentencing allows for flexibility not only in the type of sentence to be imposed but also in the length of time to be served. This focus on the offender's needs rather than on society's need for retribution or safety is a key element of the rehabilitation perspective.

Most jurisdictions that use indeterminate sentences employ statutes that specify minimum and maximum terms but allow judicial discretion to fix the actual sentence within those limits. The typical minimum sentence is at least one year; a few state jurisdictions require at least a two-year minimum sentence for felons.[25]

## Determinate Sentences

Dissatisfaction with the disparity and uncertainty of indeterminate sentencing has prompted some states and the federal government to abandon it in favor of determinate sentencing models, or structured sentencing models aimed at curbing judicial discretion (discussed in the next section).

**Determinate sentences** offer a fixed term of years, the maximum set in law by the legislature, to be served by the offender sentenced to prison for a particular crime. If the law provides for a sentence of up to 20 years for robbery, the judge might sentence a repeat offender to a 15-year term; another, less-experienced felon might receive a more lenient sentence of 5 years.

*SENTENCING GUIDELINES* In order to regulate the length of determinate sentences and curb judicial discretion, most jurisdictions that employ them have developed methods to structure and control the sentencing process and make it more rational. To accomplish this task, **sentencing guidelines** have been implemented by determinate sentencing states and the federal government. Guidelines give judges a recommended sentence based on the seriousness of a crime and the background of an offender: The more serious the crime and the more extensive the offender's criminal background, the longer the prison term recommended by the guidelines. For example, guidelines might recommend a sentence of five years for robbery if the offender had no prior offense record and did not use excessive force or violence. For a second offense, the recommended sentence would increase to seven years; those who used force and had a prior record will have three years added to their sentence, and so on. By eliminating judicial discretion, guidelines are designed to reduce racial and gender disparity.[26]

Guidelines were created by appointed sentencing commissions whose members attempted to formulate what an "ideal" sentence would be for a particular crime and offender. In some instances, their decisions were based on empirical analysis of existing sentencing practices; in other instances, sentences were based on the beliefs of the commissioners. Regardless of the formulation, there is a great deal of variation within guidelines. Some coexist with parole release, and some do not. Some deal with all crimes and others only with felonies. Some set narrow sentencing ranges, and some set broad ones. Some address sentences of all types, and some address only state prison sentences.[27] North Carolina, Pennsylvania, and Ohio employ what is known as a "comprehensive structured sentencing system," which sets sentencing standards for felonies and misdemeanors, and for prison, jail, intermediate, and community punishments. They also include mechanisms for tying sentencing policy to correctional capacity and for distributing state funds to stimulate and support local corrections programs.[28]

*THE SENTENCING GRID* One method of guideline creation is to create a grid with prior record and current offense as the two coordinates and set out specific punishments. Figure 12.2 shows Minnesota's guidelines. Note that as prior record and offense severity increase, so does recommended sentence length. After a certain point, probation is no longer an option, and the defendant must do prison time. A burglar with no prior convictions can expect to receive probation for a house break-in; an experienced burglar with six or more prior convictions can get up to 57 months for the same crime. Although it is expected that the guidelines will be followed, they are only recommendations based on typical circumstances. If a case is not typical, the judge can depart from the recommended sentence. If the court does depart, the judge must state the reasons for departure, and either the prosecution or the defense may appeal the pronounced sentence.

**determinate sentence**
A fixed term of incarceration, such as three years' imprisonment. Determinate sentences are felt by many to be too restrictive for rehabilitative purposes; the advantage is that offenders know how much time they have to serve—that is, when they will be released.

**sentencing guidelines**
A set of standards that defines parameters for trial judges to follow in their sentencing decisions.

**FIGURE 12.2**
Minnesota Sentencing Guidelines Grid

| SEVERITY LEVEL OF CONVICTION OFFENSE (Common offenses listed in italics) | | CRIMINAL HISTORY SCORE | | | | | | |
|---|---|---|---|---|---|---|---|---|
| | | **0** | **1** | **2** | **3** | **4** | **5** | **6 or more** |
| *Murder, 2nd Degree (intentional murder; drive-by shootings)* | XI | 306 *261–367* | 326 *278–391* | 346 *295–415* | 366 *312–439* | 386 *329–463* | 406 *346–480[2]* | 426 *363–480[2]* |
| *Murder, 3rd Degree Murder, 2nd Degree (unintentional murder)* | X | 150 *128–180* | 165 *141–198* | 180 *153–216* | 195 *166–234* | 210 *179–252* | 225 *192–270* | 240 *204–288* |
| *Criminal Sexual Conduct, 1st Degree [2] Assault, 1st Degree* | IX | 86 *74–103* | 98 *84–117* | 110 *94–132* | 122 *104–146* | 134 *114–160* | 146 *125–175* | 158 *135–189* |
| *Aggravated Robbery, 1st Degree Criminal Sexual Conduct, 2nd Degree (c),(d),(e),(f),(h)* | VIII | 48 *41–57* | 58 *50–69* | 68 *58–81* | 78 *67–93* | 88 *75–105* | 98 *84–117* | 108 *92–129* |
| *Felony DWI* | VII | 36 | 42 | 48 | 54 *46–64* | 60 *51–72* | 66 *57–79* | 72 *62–84[2]* |
| *Criminal Sexual Conduct, 2nd Degree (a) & (b)* | VI | 21 | 27 | 33 | 39 *34–46* | 45 *39–54* | 51 *44–61* | 57 *49–68* |
| *Residential Burglary Simple Robbery* | V | 18 | 23 | 28 | 33 *29–39* | 38 *33–45* | 43 *37–51* | 48 *41–57* |
| *Nonresidential Burglary* | IV | 12[1] | 15 | 18 | 21 | 24 *21–28* | 27 *23–32* | 30 *26–36* |
| *Theft Crimes (more than $2,500)* | III | 12[1] | 13 | 15 | 17 | 19 *17–22* | 21 *18–25* | 23 *20–27* |
| *Theft Crimes ($2,500 or less) Check Forgery ($200–$2,500)* | II | 12[1] | 12[1] | 13 | 15 | 17 | 19 | 21 *18–25* |
| *Sale of Simulated Controlled Substance* | I | 12[1] | 12[1] | 12[1] | 13 | 15 | 17 | 19 *17–22* |

Presumptive commitment to state imprisonment. First Degree Murder has a mandatory life sentence and is excluded from the guidelines by law. See section II.E., Mandatory Sentences, for policy regarding those sentences controlled by law.

Presumptive stayed sentence; at the discretion of the judge, up to a year in jail and/or other non-jail sanctions can be imposed as conditions of probation. However, certain offenses in this section of the grid always carry a presumptive commitment to state prison. See sections II.C., Presumptive Sentence, and II.E., Mandatory Sentences.

[1]One year and one day

[2]M.S. § 244.09 requires the Sentencing Guidelines to provide a range for sentences which are presumptive commitment to state imprisonment of 15% lower and 20% higher than the fixed duration displayed, provided that the minimum sentence is not less than one year and one day and the maximum sentence is not more than the statutory maximum. See Guidelines Sections II.H., Presumptive Sentence Durations that Exceed the Statutory Maximum Sentence, and II.I., Sentence Ranges for Presumptive Commitment Offenses in Shaded Areas of Grids.

Source: Minnesota Sentencing Guideline Commission, www.msgc.state.mn.us/msgc5/guidelines.htm (accessed September 16, 2008).

**LEGAL CHALLENGES AND THEIR IMPACT** Several recent Supreme Court cases have changed how guidelines can be used. Examples include

- *Apprendi v. New Jersey.* Apprendi pleaded guilty to second-degree possession of a firearm, a charge that carried a prison sentence of between 5 and 10 years. Prosecutors asked the court to impose the state's hate crime law sentencing enhancement provision, which would increase his sentence to between 10 and 20 years. The judge considered the evidence and found it met the hate crime standard. The enhanced prison sentence based on the hate crime statute exceeded the statutory maximum sentence for the underlying offense of weapon possession. The Supreme Court ruled that any factor other than a prior conviction that increases the penalty for the crime beyond the statutory maximum must be submitted to a jury and proved beyond a reasonable doubt.[29]

- *Blakely v. Washington.* Here the Court found that the state of Washington's sentencing guidelines were a violation of a defendant's Sixth Amendment rights because they allowed a judge to consider aggravating factors that would enhance the sentence.[30] The Court ruled that this amounts to a finding of fact without the benefit of a jury trial or personal admission. In *Blakely*, the sentencing judge, acting alone, decided that the offense involved "deliberate cruelty" and enhanced Blakely's sentence. Proving a state of mind such as "deliberate cruelty" must be determined by a jury beyond a reasonable doubt, not by a judge applying guidelines. Here the Court is saying that the right to a jury trial means that a defendant has the right to have a jury, not a judge, make all the factual findings required to impose a sentence in excess of the presumptive sentence guideline, unless the defendant formally admits some or all of the factors or formally waives that right.

- *United States v. Booker.* In *Booker*, the Court ruled that the federal guidelines were unconstitutional, allowing that judges should consider the guideline ranges but must also be permitted to alter sentences in consideration of other factors; sentences could then be subject to appellate review if they were unreasonable.[31] This case may be interpreted as suggesting that guidelines must be used in an advisory capacity alone.

These cases did not outlaw guidelines but, rather, ruled that changes are needed in the way they are administered. For example, the federal guidelines have been heavily criticized for their disparity in the punishment for possessing crack versus powdered cocaine. This differential was a source of irritation to critics who believed that the disparity reflected racism (that is, African Americans were more likely to use crack, while Caucasians favored powdered cocaine). In 2007, the Federal Sentencing Commission revised the guidelines and retroactively considered reducing sentences for people convicted of crack possession.[32] This was partly prompted by the Supreme Court's decision in *Kimbrough v. United States*, where it ruled that the federal cocaine sentencing guidelines, like other federal sentencing guidelines, are advisory.[33] The practical result of these decisions is this: If a sentence departs markedly from the guidelines, it is not necessarily problematic. On the other hand, as a consequence of the Court's decision in *Rita v. United States*, any sentence that falls within the federal sentencing guidelines is presumptively reasonable (meaning that as far as the Court is concerned, the sentence is reasonable).[34]

In a recent and rather ironic twist on all this, the U.S. Sentencing Commission found significant evidence that minorities are being treated *more harshly*, not less harshly, in the wake of the *Booker* decision.[35] Recall that *Booker* made the federal sentencing guidelines advisory. It was hoped that we would see *reduced* sentencing disparities in the years since 2006, when the decision was handed down. Yet the Sentencing Commission found that "Black male offenders received longer sentences than white male offenders . . . [and that] . . . the differences in sentence length have increased steadily since *Booker*."

## EVIDENCE-BASED JUSTICE

# Do Three-Strikes Laws Deter?

In 1994, Washington became the first state to enact a three-strikes law. Other states quickly followed suit. Among the many versions of three-strikes laws, California's is the most punitive. It provides that a person who has two prior convictions for serious felonies and is convicted of *any* third felony can be sent to prison for the rest of his or her life. California's law has been rather controversial, in part because of legal challenges raised by offenders who ended up going to prison for a long time after committing relatively minor third felonies (see the accompanying discussion of *Lockyer v. Andrade* and *Ewing v. California*). Because of the controversial nature of three-strikes laws, researchers have been drawn to them. They have been particularly interested in the general deterrent effects of such laws. Do offenders refrain from committing third felonies for fear of being sentenced to prison for the rest of their lives? Clearly, three-strikes laws have a *specific* deterrent effect because a repeat offender who is in prison cannot harm the community, but do three-strikes laws also discourage would-be offenders from breaking the law? Researchers have focused heavily on California's law because of its harsh nature, but nationwide studies have been published, as well.

It is certainly plausible that three-strikes laws have a general deterrent effect. The very phrase "three strikes" is catchy and easy to remember. Unfortunately, though, precious little research supports any kind of deterrent effect. Joanna Shepherd, an economist, published a 2002 study wherein she found that California's three-strikes law led to significant reductions in serious crime, but her findings have been largely drowned out by a number of more recent studies that have detected little if any deterrent effect. John Worrall replicated Shepherd's approach and found no evidence that three strikes deters. Interestingly, two teams of researchers have found that three-strikes laws may actually *increase* crime, particularly homicide, as offenders who face possible life terms go to lethal lengths (that is, they kill their pursuers) to resist apprehension. We cannot definitively state that three-strikes laws do nothing to deter crime, but we can certainly conclude that the jury is still out.

Sources: Joanna M. Shepherd, "Fear of the First Strike: The Full Deterrent Effect of California's Two- and Three-Strikes Legislation," *Journal of Legal Studies* 31 (2002): 159–201; John L. Worrall, "The Effect of Three-Strikes Legislation on Serious Crime in California," *Journal of Criminal Justice* 32 (2004): 283–296; Thomas B. Marvell and Carlisle E. Moody, "The Lethal Effects of Three-Strikes Laws," *Journal of Legal Studies* 30 (2001): 89–106; Tomislav Kovandzic, John J. Sloan III, and Lynne M. Vieraitis, "Unintended Consequences of Politically Popular Sentencing Policy: The Homicide-Promoting Effects of Three Strikes in U.S. Cities (1980–1999), *Criminology and Public Policy* 1 (2002): 399–424.

## Mandatory Sentences

Another effort to limit judicial discretion and at the same time get tough on crime has been the development of the **mandatory sentence**. Some states have passed legislation prohibiting people convicted of certain offenses, such as violent crimes or drug trafficking, from being placed on probation; they must serve at least some time in prison. Other statutes are aimed at chronic recidivists. Mandatory sentencing legislation may impose minimum and maximum terms, but usually it requires a fixed prison sentence.

Mandatory sentencing generally limits the judge's discretionary power to impose any disposition but that authorized by the legislature; as a result, it limits individualized sentencing and restricts sentencing disparity. More than 35 states have already replaced discretionary sentencing with fixed-term mandatory sentences for such crimes as the sale of hard drugs, kidnapping, gun possession, and arson. The results have been mixed. Mandatory sentences have contributed to the recent increase in the size of the correctional population to record levels. Because of mandatory sentences, many offenders who in the past might have

**mandatory sentence**
A statutory requirement that a certain penalty shall be set and carried out in all cases upon conviction for a specified offense or series of offenses.

## PERSPECTIVES ON JUSTICE

### Crime Control Perspective

It goes without saying that mandatory sentences are a direct manifestation of the crime control perspective. They are designed both to deter would-be criminals by ensuring that they cannot expect a "break" and to punish those who have flouted the law, teaching them the lesson that crime certainly does not pay.

received probation are being incarcerated. The Supreme Court has sanctioned certain mandatory sentences, holding that they do not violate the Eighth Amendment's prohibition against cruel and unusual punishment.[36]

**THREE-STRIKES LAWS** Three-strikes (and you're out) laws provide lengthy terms for any person convicted of three felony offenses, even if the third crime is relatively trivial. The law is applied differently in different state jurisdictions. Some require all three felony convictions to be for violent crimes in order for the mandatory sentence to be pronounced, whereas others provide enhanced sentencing for any third felony conviction as long as the first two felonies were deemed to be either violent or serious, or both. California's three-strikes law is aimed at getting habitual criminals off the street. Anyone convicted of a third felony must do a minimum term of 25 years to life; the third felony does not have to be serious or violent. The Federal Crime Act of 1994 also adopted a three-strikes provision, requiring a mandatory life sentence for any offender convicted of three felony offenses; 26 states have so far followed suit and passed some form of the three-strikes law.

Although welcomed by conservatives seeking a remedy for violent crime, the three-strikes policy is controversial because a person convicted of a minor felony can receive a life sentence. In two well-known California cases, defendants received life sentences for (a) stealing a slice of pizza and (b) stealing some chocolate chip cookies.[37] The pizza thief, Jerry Dewayne Williams, later had his sentence reduced to "only" six years.

Three-strikes laws have undeniable political appeal to legislators being pressured by their constituents to "do something about crime." But even if such laws are possibly effective against crime (see the accompanying Evidence-Based Justice feature), any effort to deter criminal behavior through tough laws is not without costs. Criminologist Marc Mauer, a leading opponent of the three-strikes law, finds that the approach may satisfy the public's hunger for retribution but makes little practical sense. First, many "three-time losers" are on the brink of aging out of crime; locking them up for life should have little effect on the crime rate. In addition, current sentences for chronic violent offenders are already severe, yet their punishment seems to have had little effect in reducing national violence rates. The efficacy of a three-strikes policy also suffers because criminals typically underestimate their risk of apprehension, while overestimating the rewards of crime. Given their inflated view of the benefits of crime, coupled with a seeming disregard of the risks of apprehension and punishment, it is unlikely a three-strikes policy can have a measurable effect on the crime rate.

Even if such a policy could reduce the number of career offenders on the street, the drain in economic resources that might have gone for education and social welfare ensures that a new generation of young criminals will fill the offending shoes of their incarcerated brethren. Mauer also suggests that a three-strikes policy severely stresses an already overburdened prison system, driving up costs, and, presumably, reducing resources available to house other inmates. Mauer warns too that African Americans face an increased risk of being sentenced under three-strikes statutes, expanding the racial disparity in sentencing. More ominous is the fact that police officers may be put at risk because two-time offenders would violently resist arrest, knowing that they face a life sentence.

**LEGAL CONTROLS** Is it fair to give someone a life sentence for a petty crime merely because she or he has prior convictions? On March 6, 2003, the Supreme Court in *Lockyer v. Andrade* upheld the three-strikes sentence of Leandro Andrade, a man sentenced to prison in California for 50 years for stealing $153 worth of videotapes.[38] It also upheld the conviction of Gary Ewing, who appealed his 25-year sentence for stealing a set of golf clubs.[39] In both cases the Court ruled that the challenged sentences were not so grossly disproportionate as to violate the Eighth Amendment's prohibition against cruel and unusual punishment. In her majority decision, Justice Sandra Day O'Connor added that any criticism of the law "is appropriately directed at the legislature" and is not a judicial matter. Four judges dissented in the case, arguing that the Court's test for sentence disproportionality had been met. Writing in the *Andrade* case, Justice David Souter said, "If Andrade's sentence is not grossly disproportionate, the principle has no meaning."

## Truth in Sentencing

As you may recall, even though criminal sentences are getting shorter, people are spending more of their sentence behind bars. One reason is a get-tough measure designed to fight a rising crime rate: **truth in sentencing**. These laws require offenders to serve a substantial portion of their prison sentence behind bars.[40] Parole eligibility and good-time credits are restricted or eliminated. The movement was encouraged by the Violent Offender Incarceration and Truth-in-Sentencing Incentive Grants Program, part of the federal government's 1994 crime act, which offered funds to help the states pay the costs involved with creating longer sentences. To qualify for federal funds, states must require persons convicted of a violent felony crime to serve not less than 85 percent of their prison sentence. The provision is already having an effect: Violent offenders released from prison in 1996 served slightly more than half of their prison sentence, or 45 months. Under truth-in-sentencing laws, violent inmates entering prison today will serve an average of 88 months behind bars. Today, more than half the states and the District of Columbia meet the federal Truth-in-Sentencing Incentive Grants Program eligibility criteria, and another 13 have adopted some form of truth-in-sentencing program.

## ■ HOW PEOPLE ARE SENTENCED

The federal government conducts surveys on sentencing practices in state and federal courts.[41] The most recent survey found that more than 1.1 million adults are convicted of felonies in a single year. What happens after conviction? About 70 percent of all felons convicted in state courts are sentenced to a period of confinement—41 percent to state prisons and 28 percent to local jails.[42] The rest are sentenced to straight probation with no jail or prison time to serve.

The average felony sentence is approximately five years, but most offenders are likely to serve only half of that sentence before release.[43] Besides being sentenced to incarceration (in prison or jail), about one-third of all sentenced felons are put on probation or expected to pay a fine, pay victim restitution, receive treatment, perform community service, or comply with some other additional penalty. As Table 12.1 shows, violent felons who are given a prison sentence average about eight years, while property offenders are typically sentenced to about four years. If they receive a jail sentence, their period of confinement is considerably less.

## What Factors Affect Sentencing?

What factors influence judges when they decide on criminal sentences? State sentencing codes usually include various factors that can legitimately influence the length of prison sentences. These factors include

- The severity of the offense
- The offender's prior criminal record
- Whether the offender used violence
- Whether the offender used weapons
- Whether the crime was committed for money

Research does in fact show a strong correlation between these legal variables and the type and length of sentence meted out. Judges sentence more severely in cases involving the most serious criminal charges, such as terrorism, while being

## TABLE 12.1

### Lengths of Felony Sentences Imposed by State Courts

| Most Serious Conviction Offense | Average Maximum Sentence Length (in Months) for Felons Sentenced to: | | | |
|---|---|---|---|---|
| | Incarceration | | | |
| | Total | Prison | Jail | Probation |
| All offenses | 38 | 57 | 6 | 38 |
| Violent offenses | 71 | 96 | 7 | 44 |
| Property offenses | 30 | 47 | 6 | 38 |
| Drug offenses | 31 | 50 | 5 | 37 |
| Weapon offenses | 32 | 48 | 6 | 37 |
| Other offenses | 24 | 41 | 5 | 36 |

Source: Sean Rosenmerkel, Matthew Durose, and Donald Farole Jr., *Felony Sentences in State Courts, 2006—Statistical Tables* (Washington, D.C.: Bureau of Justice Statistics, 2007), Table 1.3, http://bjs.ojp.usdoj.gov/content/pub/pdf/fssc06st.pdf (accessed May 3, 2010).

more lenient in low-severity cases.[44] As Figure 12.3 shows, people with prior convictions are much more likely to receive prison time than those convicted of similar offenses without a prior record.

Besides these legally appropriate factors, sentencing experts suspect that judges are also influenced by the defendant's age, race, gender, and income. Consideration of such variables would be a direct violation of constitutional due process and equal protection, as well as of federal statutes, such as the Civil Rights Act. Limiting judicial bias is one reason why states have adopted determinate and mandatory sentencing statutes. Do extralegal factors actually influence judges when they make sentencing decisions?

## FIGURE 12.3
### The Association between Prior Offense Record and Sentencing Outcome

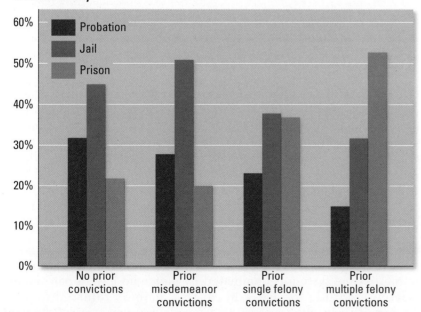

Source: Tracey Kyckelhahn and Thomas Cohen, *Felony Defendants in Large Urban Counties, 2004* (Washington, D.C.: Bureau of Justice Statistics, 2008), www.ojp.usdoj.gov/bjs/pub/pdf/fdluc04.pdf (accessed August 26, 2008).

## CAREERS IN CRIMINAL JUSTICE

# Forensic Psychologist

### Duties and Characteristics of the Job

Forensic psychologists apply the knowledge and scientific methods that are characteristic of the field of psychology in legal settings. They evaluate the mental health of parolees, run inmate mental health programs, and provide counseling to victims. In the court system, forensic psychologists consult with attorneys to assess individuals' mental health to determine what bearing, if any, their mental state has on the trial. They may help in crafting sentences based on the clinical needs of the criminal defendant. They consult with law enforcement at all levels in order to apprehend criminals. They might create a psychological model of a suspect to predict her behavior.

### Job Outlook

The employment outlook for forensic psychologists is good. Because recognition of the importance of psychological factors in behavior and functioning is increasing, the need for forensic psychologists should expand.

### Salary

Like that of other psychologists, a forensic psychologist's mean annual salary is approximately $70,000. The majority of these psychologists make between $54,100 and $115,720 a year. Some will earn less than $40,000, and others will earn as much or more than $150,000 a year.

### Opportunities

The number of educational institutions that offer graduate programs in forensic science is relatively small, so entry into a program is competitive.

### Qualifications

The primary qualifier for a position as a forensic psychologist is educational.

### Education and Training

A forensic psychologist will have to gain entrance into one of a select number of master's or doctorate programs. A master's degree will prepare future forensic psychologists for entry-level work in places such as police departments, prisons and jails, and mental health centers. The two most advanced programs lead to a Ph.D. in psychology and a Psy.D. in forensic psychology, respectively. Some states require certification. A doctoral program prepares students primarily for administrative or management positions at law enforcement and health organizations and enables them to provide services such as mediation and research for organizations. Psy.D. training prepares students for an applied focus in jobs, such as providing mental health treatment and being an expert court witness.

Sources: The British Psychological Society, Forensic Psychology, www .bps.org.uk/careers/what-do-psychologists-do/areas/forensic.cfm (accessed May 3, 2010); Bureau of Labor Statistics, U.S. Department of Labor, "Psychologists," *Occupational Outlook Handbook, 2010–11 Edition*, www.bls.gov/oco/ocos056.htm (accessed May 3, 2010).

**SOCIAL CLASS** Evidence supports an association between social class and sentencing outcomes: Members of the lower class may expect to get longer prison sentences than more affluent defendants. One reason is that defendants who are poor may be unable to obtain quality legal representation or to make bail, factors that influence sentencing.[45] Not all research efforts have found a consistent relationship between social class and sentence length. The relationship may be more robust for some crime patterns than for others. Nonetheless, the consensus is that affluent defendants are more likely than the indigent to receive lenient sentences.[46]

**GENDER** Does a defendant's gender influence how he or she is sentenced? Some theorists believe that women benefit from sentence disparity because the criminal justice system is dominated by men who have a paternalistic, or protective, attitude toward women; this claim is referred to as the **chivalry hypothesis**. Others argue that female criminals can be the victim of bias because their behavior violates what men believe is "proper" female behavior.[47]

**chivalry hypothesis**
The view that the low rates of crime and delinquency among females reflect the leniency with which female offenders are treated.

Most research indicates that women receive more favorable outcomes the further they go in the criminal justice system: They are more likely to receive preferential treatment from a judge at sentencing than they are from the police officer making the arrest or the prosecutor seeking the indictment.[48] Favoritism crosses both racial and ethnic lines, benefiting African American, white, and Hispanic women.[49] Gender bias may be present because judges perceive women as better risks than men. Women have been granted more lenient pretrial release conditions and lower bail amounts than men; women are also more likely to spend less time in pretrial detention.[50] Ironically, mandatory and structured sentences, designed originally to limit bias and discretion, have resulted in harsher sentences for women. Because these methods are "gender neutral," they reverse any advantage women may have had in sentencing decisions. Some women who are peripherally involved in drug trafficking through association with boyfriends and husbands have received very long sentences.[51]

*AGE* Another extralegal factor that may play a role in sentencing is age. It should be expected that older people will be punished more harshly than younger ones because they have had a greater opportunity to accumulate a criminal record and most state laws increase penalties for multiple offenders. Of course, this creates the dilemma whereby an older offender, because of crimes he might have committed years ago, is punished more severely than a younger offender who is more dangerous or is committing more crimes in the present.[52]

This association is not necessarily linear. On the one hand, some judges may actually be more lenient with older defendants and more punitive toward younger ones.[53] Although sentencing leniency may result from judges' perception that the elderly pose little risk to society, such practices are a violation of the civil rights of younger defendants.[54] On the other hand, some judges may also wish to protect the youngest defendants, sparing them the pains of a prison experience.[55]

*VICTIM CHARACTERISTICS* Victim characteristics may also influence sentencing. Victims may be asked or allowed to make a **victim impact statement** before the sentencing judge, giving them the opportunity to tell of their experiences and describe their ordeal. In a murder case, the surviving family can recount the effect the crime has had on their lives and well-being.[56] The effect of victim and witness statements on sentencing has been the topic of some debate. Some research finds that victim statements result in a higher rate of incarceration, but other studies suggest that the effects of victim and witness statements are insignificant.[57]

Sentences may be reduced when victims have "negative" personal characteristics or qualities. For example, people convicted of raping prostitutes or substance abusers receive much shorter sentences than those who assault women without these characteristics.[58]

Sentences may also be tailored to the needs of offenders, especially when they have severe psychological deficits. In making their decision, judges may rely on the opinion of a forensic psychologist, who may be asked to clinically evaluate the defendant before sentencing. The Careers in Criminal Justice feature discusses forensic psychologists.

**victim impact statement**
A postconviction statement by the victim of crime or the victim's family that may be used to guide sentencing decisions.

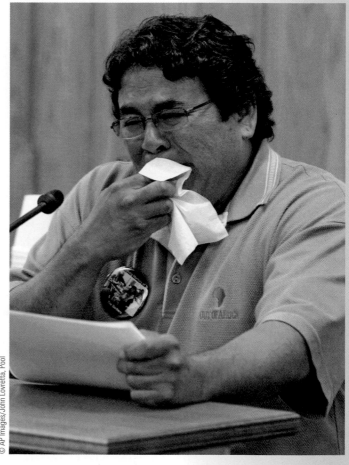

© AP Images/John Lowretta, Pool

*Victim impact statements give surviving family members an opportunity to tell the court about the effect the crime had on their lives and well-being. On June 19, 2007, at the Van Buren County Courthouse in Keosauqua, Iowa, Mario Mendez, brother of murder victim Sandra Bentler, is overcome with emotion as he reads his victim impact statement during the sentencing of Shawn Bentler, who was found guilty of killing his parents and three teenage sisters. A judge later sentenced Bentler to five life sentences, bringing to an end one of the most grisly murder trials in Iowa history.*

## RACE, GENDER, AND CULTURE IN CRIMINAL JUSTICE

# Does Race Matter?

There are more minorities in prison per capita than whites, a condition that suggests to some the existence of a racial bias in sentencing. The problem of race-based disparity is disturbing because of the impact the justice system has on the minority community. As sociologist Bruce Western points out, by the time they reach their mid-thirties, 60 percent of black high school dropouts are either prisoners or ex-cons. This, Western warns, has resulted in "a collective experience for young black men that is wholly different from the rest of American society." Is Western's analysis correct? Does race still matter in the sentencing process?

A number of research studies (far too many to list here) do find that race bias still exists in the judicial process. In one recent study of federal sentencing, Jill Doerner and Stephen Demuth found, like many before them, that Hispanics and blacks receive harsher sentences on the whole than white defendants. Shawn Bushway and Anne Morrison Piehl studied sentencing outcomes in Maryland and found that, on average, African Americans receive 20 percent longer sentences than whites, even when

age, gender, and recommended sentence length are held constant. So the nagging issue of racial disparity in sentencing still haunts the justice process. In a review of over 70 published studies, Ojmarrh Mitchell found that, indeed, African Americans are sentenced more harshly than similarly situated white offenders.

Although evidence of unequal treatment exists, research has failed to show a definitive pattern of racial *discrimination*. Although some research does indicate that a defendant's race has a direct impact on sentencing outcomes, other efforts show that the influence of race on sentencing is less clear, and, as John Wooldredge has found recently, in some contexts minority group members actually get lesser sentences than whites. It is possible, the counterargument goes, that the disproportionate number of minority group members in prison is not a function of racial bias by judges but, rather, reflects actual racial and ethnic differences in the crime rate: Minority group members go to prison more often simply because they commit more crime.

Why does the critical issue of racial disparity remain so murky? One reason is that it may involve

**RACE**  No issue concerning personal factors in sentencing is more important than the suspicion that race influences sentencing outcomes. Racial disparity in sentencing has been suspected because a disproportionate number of African American inmates are in state prisons and on death row. Minorities seem to receive longer sentences than Caucasians, especially those who are indigent or unemployed.[59] Young black men are more likely to be imprisoned for drug offenses, a practice (says sentencing expert Michael Tonry) that places the entire cohort of young African American males in jeopardy.[60] Because this issue is so important, it is the focus of the accompanying Race, Gender, and Ethnicity in Criminal Justice feature.

## CAPITAL PUNISHMENT

The most severe sentence used in the United States is capital punishment, or execution. More than 14,500 confirmed executions have been carried out in America under civil authority, starting with the execution of Captain George Kendall in 1608; today there are more than 3,200 people on death row, and about 40 to 50 are executed each year (see Figure 12.4). Most of these executions have been for murder and rape. However, federal, state, and military laws have imposed the death penalty for other crimes, including robbery, kidnapping, treason (offenses against the federal government), espionage, and desertion from military service.

multiple factors that lie outside judicial sentencing practices:

- African Americans are more likely to be detained before trial than whites.

- Prosecutors are less likely to divert minorities from the legal system than they are whites.

- Minorities have less money for bail and private attorneys.

- Minorities live in poor communities, and people living in poor areas get harsher sentences, regardless of their race.

- African Americans receive longer sentences for drug crimes than whites because (a) they are more likely to be arrested for crack possession and sales, and (b) crack dealing is more severely punished by state and federal laws than other drug crimes.

Other factors may also obscure the associations. For example, ample research indicates that it is the victim's race, rather than the offender's, that structures sentencing outcomes. Minority defendants are sanctioned more severely if their victim is white than if their target is a fellow minority group member; minorities who kill whites are more likely to get the death penalty than are those who kill other minorities.

In sum, even though the true association between race and sentencing remains to be established, there is little question that issues of ethnicity and race help shape the contours of justice. Whatever the cause, the effects can be devastating. As Bruce Western warns, marginalizing and incarcerating so many African American men has destabilized whole communities. And doing prison time, Western warns, can turn minor offenders into hardened criminals, which removes any chance of rehabilitation and later opportunities. The prison boom, Western writes, "may be a self-defeating strategy for crime control."

## Critical Thinking

1. Because of the lingering problem of racial and class bias in the sentencing process, one primary goal of the criminal justice system has been to reduce disparity by creating new forms of criminal sentences that limit judicial discretion and are aimed at uniformity and fairness. Can such measures as sentencing guidelines and mandatory sentences reduce race-based disparity?

2. What is the difference between unequal treatment and racial discrimination? Which term better characterizes sentencing in the United States?

Sources: Bruce Western, *Punishment and Inequality in America* (New York: Russell Sage Foundation, 2006); Jill K. Doerner and Stephen Demuth, "Independent and Joint Effects of Race/Ethnicity, Gender, and Age on Sentencing Outcomes in U.S. Federal Courts," *Justice Quarterly* 27 (2010): 1–27; Shawn Bushway and Anne Morrison Piehl, "Judging Judicial Discretion: Legal Factors and Racial Discrimination in Sentencing," *Law and Society Review* 35 (2001): 733–765; Ojmarrh Mitchell, "Meta-Analysis of Race and Sentencing Research: Explaining the Inconsistencies," *Journal of Quantitative Criminology* 21 (2005): 439–466; John Wooldredge, "Neighborhood Effects on Felony Sentencing," *Journal of Research in Crime and Delinquency* 44 (2007): 238–263.

**FIGURE 12.4**
Yearly Executions in the United States

**Number of executions**

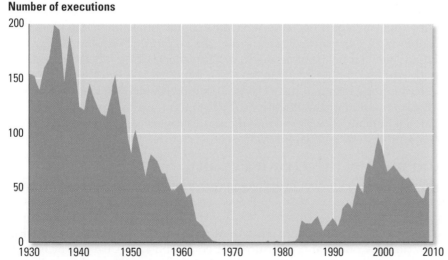

Source: Bureau of Justice Statistics, http://bjs.ojp.usdoj.gov/content/glance/exe.cfm (accessed May 3, 2010).

*Marianne Connelly reacts after hearing that serial killer Rodney Alcala received the death sentence for killing her 12-year-old daughter, Robin Samsoe. Alcala was found guilty of the kidnapping and murder of the 12-year-old and of the murder of four women in Los Angeles County.*

© AP Photo/Michael Goulding, Pool

In recent years, the Supreme Court has limited the death penalty to first-degree murder, and even then it is available only when aggravating circumstances, such as murder for profit or murder using extreme cruelty, are present.[61] The federal government still has provisions for imposing the death penalty for espionage by a member of the armed forces, treason, and killing during a criminal conspiracy, such as drug trafficking. Some states have laws permitting capital punishment for such crimes as aircraft piracy, ransom kidnapping, and the aggravated rape of a child, but it remains to be seen whether the courts will allow criminals to be executed today for any crime less serious than aggravated first-degree murder. The most recent death penalty data are included in Exhibit 12.1.

Despite its continued use and public acceptance, there seems to be growing unease with administration of the death penalty, and the recent use of scientific evidence based on DNA has resulted in numerous exonerations of death row inmates. On January 11, 2003, Illinois Governor George Ryan announced his decision to commute all Illinois death sentences—a gesture that spared the lives of 163 men and 4 women who have served a collective 2,000 years for the murders of more than 250 people. In the case of *People v. Stephen LaValle* (2004), a New York appellate court declared the state's capital punishment law unconstitutional, placing a moratorium on its use for the near term.[62] And in 2007, as we have noted, New Jersey became the first state since 1976 to abolish the death penalty by law.

No issue in the criminal justice system is more controversial or emotional than implementation of the death penalty.[63] Opponents and proponents have formulated a number of powerful arguments in support of their positions; these arguments are reviewed in the following sections.

## Arguments for the Death Penalty

Supporters advance a number of arguments for retaining the death penalty in the United States.

***INCAPACITATION*** Supporters argue that death is the "ultimate incapacitation" and the only one that can ensure that convicted killers can never be pardoned, be paroled, or escape. Most states that do not have capital punishment provide the sentence of "life in prison without the chance of parole." However,

## EXHIBIT 12.1

# Death Penalty Facts and Trends

- In 2009, 52 inmates were executed, 15 more than in 2008.

- Of the 52 executions carried out in the United States in 2009, there were 24 in Texas; 6 in Alabama; 5 in Ohio; 3 each in Virginia, Oklahoma, and Georgia; 2 each in Florida, South Carolina, and Tennessee; and 1 each in Missouri and Indiana.

- Of the 52 persons executed in 2009, 23 were white, 22 were black, and 7 were Hispanic.

- All 52 inmates executed in 2009 were men.

- Lethal injection was used in 51 executions in 2009; 1 execution was by electrocution.

- Thirty-five states and the federal government retain the death penalty as a form of punishment, although some have not used it in decades.

  - The states that currently can impose the death penalty are Alabama, Arizona, Arkansas, California, Colorado, Connecticut, Delaware, Florida, Georgia, Idaho, Indiana, Illinois, Kansas, Kentucky, Louisiana, Maryland, Mississippi, Missouri, Montana, Nebraska, Nevada, New Hampshire, North Carolina, Ohio, Oklahoma, Oregon, Pennsylvania, South Carolina, South Dakota, Tennessee, Texas, Utah, Virginia, Washington, and Wyoming.

  - The states that currently cannot impose the death penalty states are Alaska, Hawaii, Iowa, Maine, Massachusetts, Michigan, Minnesota, North Dakota, New Jersey, New Mexico, New York, Rhode Island, Vermont, West Virginia, and Wisconsin (plus the District of Columbia).

- In 2007, New Jersey was the first U.S. state to abolish capital punishment by law since the death penalty was reintroduced in the United States in 1972. In 2009, New Mexico voted to abolish the death penalty.

- Between 1977 and 2008, 7,658 people have been under sentence of death. Of these, 15 percent were executed, 5 percent died from other causes, and 38 percent received other dispositions.

- During 2008, 3,207 persons were sentenced to death.

  - 98.2 percent were male.
  - 56.1 percent were white.
  - 41.7 percent were African American.
  - 2.2 percent were neither white nor African American (for example, American Indian).
  - 13.2 percent were Hispanic.
  - 40.8 percent had the equivalent of a high school diploma or less.
  - 22.2 percent were married.

- Among inmates under sentence of death and with available criminal histories (as of 2008):
  - Nearly 2 in 3 had a prior felony conviction.
  - 1 in 12 had a prior homicide conviction.

- Among persons for whom arrest information was available during 2008, the average age at time of arrest was 29; approximately 10 percent were age 19 or younger at the time of arrest.

- The youngest person sentenced to death in 2008 was 20 years old.

Source: Death Penalty Information Center, http://deathpenaltyinfo.org/executions (accessed May 3, 2010); Tracy L. Snell, *Capital Punishment, 2008—Statistical Tables* (Washington, D.C.: Bureau of Justice Statistics), http://bjs.ojp.usdoj.gov/content/pub/pdf/cp08st.pdf (accessed May 3, 2010).

48 states (a) give their chief executive the right to grant clemency and commute a life sentence and (b) may give "lifers" eligibility for various furlough and release programs.

Death penalty advocates believe that the potential for recidivism is a serious enough threat to require that murderers be denied further access to the public.[64] About 8 percent of prisoners under a sentence of death have prior homicide convictions; if they had been executed for their first offense, their victims would still be alive.[65]

**DETERRENCE**  Proponents of capital punishment argue that executions serve as a strong deterrent for serious crimes. Although capital punishment would probably not deter the few mentally unstable criminals, it could have an effect on the cold, calculating murderer, such as the hired killer or someone who kills for profit. The fear of death may also convince felons not to risk using handguns during robberies.

Proponents argue that the deterrent effect of an execution can produce a substantial decline in the murder rate.[66] They argue, for example, that homicide rates increased dramatically in the 1960s and 1970s when executions were halted by the courts and death penalty laws were subsequently abolished. It is not a coincidence that murder rates have dropped since the death penalty was reinstated; murder rates would actually be much higher if capital punishment were not being used.[67] The death penalty scares would-be criminals, and not surprisingly, homicide rates drop after a well-publicized execution.[68]

Some recent research supports these claims. James Yunker, using a national data set, has found evidence that capital punishment has a deterrent effect now that the pace of executions has accelerated.[69] Economists Hashem Dezhbakhsh, Paul H. Rubin, and Joanna M. Shepherd performed an advanced statistical analysis on county-level homicide data in order to calculate the effect of each execution on the number of homicides that would otherwise have occurred.[70] Using a variety of models (such as the long-term effect of an execution), they found that each execution leads to an average of 18 fewer murders. In another study, Shepherd found that capital punishment may have differing influence depending on where and how it is used.[71] The death penalty may influence each state's murder rate differently, and lumping all state data together masks the deterrent effect of the death penalty. She found that the use of capital punishment deterred murder in states that conducted more executions than the norm. In contrast, in states that conducted relatively few executions (one or two per year), the average execution either increased the murder rate or had no effect. Shepherd concludes that only if a state routinely uses executions does the deterrent effect take place; only then do potential criminals become convinced that the state is serious about the use of capital punishment.

**MORALLY CORRECT** This argument contends that the death penalty is morally correct: It is mentioned in the Bible and other religious works. Although the U.S. Constitution forbids "cruel and unusual punishments," this prohibition does not include the death penalty because capital punishment was widely used at the time the Constitution was drafted. The "original intent" of the founding fathers was to allow the states to use the death penalty; capital punishment may be cruel, but it is not unusual.

The death penalty is morally correct because it provides the greatest justice for the victim and helps alleviate the psychic pain of the victim's family and friends. The death penalty makes a moral statement: There is behavior that is so unacceptable to a community of human beings that one who engages in such behavior forfeits his right to live.[72]

**PROPORTIONAL TO THE CRIME** Putting dangerous criminals to death also conforms to the requirement that the punishment must be proportional to the seriousness of the crime. Since we use a system of escalating punishments, it follows that the most serious punishment should be used to sanction the most serious crime. Before the brutality of the death penalty is considered, the cruelty with which the victim was treated must not be forgotten.

**REFLECTS PUBLIC OPINION** The death penalty is justified because it represents the will of the people. A majority of the general public believe that criminals who kill innocent victims should forfeit their own lives. Public opinion polls show that Americans favor the use of the death penalty by a wide majority.[73] Public approval rests on the belief that the death penalty is an important instrument of social control, can deter crime, and is less costly than maintaining a murderer in prison for life.[74] Research by Alexis Durham and his associates found that almost everyone (95%) would give criminals the death penalty under some circumstances, and the most heinous crimes are those for which the public is most likely to approve capital punishment.[75]

**UNLIKELY CHANCE OF ERROR** The many legal controls and appeals currently in use make it almost impossible for an innocent person to be executed or for the death penalty to be used in a racist or capricious manner. Although some unfortunate mistakes have been made in the past, the current system makes it virtually impossible to execute an innocent person. Federal courts closely scrutinize all death penalty cases and rule for the defendant in an estimated 60 to 70 percent of the appeals. Such judicial care should ensure that only those who are both truly guilty and deserving of death are executed.

In sum, those who favor the death penalty find it to be a traditional punishment for serious crimes and one that can help prevent criminality, is in keeping with the traditional moral values of fairness and equity, and is highly favored by the public.

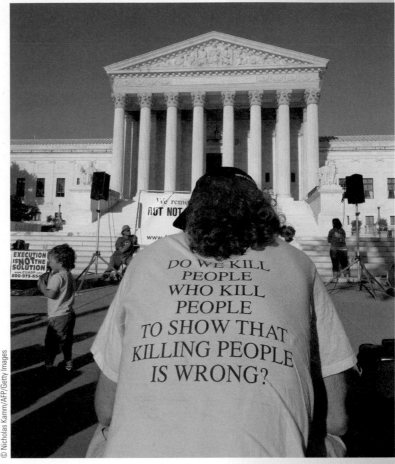

© Nicholas Kamm/AFP/Getty Images

*A great deal of research shows that the death penalty has little effect on crime and is therefore not a deterrent to murder. The lack of a clear-cut deterrent effect has encouraged abolitionists to campaign against capital punishment: If it does not stop crime, why have it? Here an opponent of the death penalty attends the 15th Annual Fast and Vigil to Abolish the Death Penalty in front of the Supreme Court in Washington on July 2, 2008. Organized by the Abolition Action Committee (ABA) and the National Coalition to Abolish the Death Penalty (NCADP), the event commemorates the historic 1972 Supreme Court ruling that suspended the death penalty in the United States. Four years later, however, the court ruled that executions could resume.*

## Arguments against the Death Penalty

These arguments for the death penalty are countered as follows by those who support its abolition.

**POSSIBILITY OF ERROR** Critics of the death penalty believe capital punishment has no place in a mature democratic society.[76] They point to the finality of the act and to the real possibility that innocent persons can be executed. Examples of people wrongfully convicted of murder abound. According to classic research by Michael Radelet and Hugo Bedeau, there have been about 350 wrongful murder convictions since 1900, of which 23 led to executions. They estimate that about three death sentences are returned every two years in cases where the defendant has been falsely accused. More than half the errors stem from perjured testimony, false identifications, coerced confessions, and suppression of evidence. In addition to the 23 who were executed, 128 of the falsely convicted served more than 6 years in prison, 39 served more than 16 years in confinement, and 8 died while serving their sentence.[77]

An important congressional report cited 48 cases in which people who served time on death row were released because of new evidence proving their innocence; one Maryland man served nine years on death row before DNA testing proved that he could not have committed the crime.[78] These findings show that even with the best intentions, there is grave risk that an innocent person can be executed.[79] The nearby Analyzing Criminal Justice Issues feature addresses wrongful convictions in more depth.

Because of the chances of error, a number of states have placed a moratorium on executions until the issue of errors in the process can be adequately

## ANALYZING CRIMINAL JUSTICE ISSUES

# *Reducing Wrongful Convictions*

Some 250 wrongfully convicted criminals have been exonerated in recent years thanks to DNA evidence. Growing awareness of wrongful convictions raises many questions. Why are these cases coming to light? How often are innocent people imprisoned? Has an innocent person been executed in the last 40 years? Why do wrongful convictions occur? What can be done to reduce justice system errors?

In the early 1990s, only two organizations existed to take on cases of prisoners claiming to be factually innocent. Today, more than 50 innocence projects exist. Collectively, as an Innocence Network, they screen claims of innocence, work to exonerate the factually innocent, promote policies to reduce errors of justice, and provide support for exonerees.

According to the Innocence Project, more than 250 DNA exonerees have been released after being convicted of crimes they did not commit. Almost all of these exonerations were for the crimes of murder and rape. Experts and criminal justice officials estimate that at least one-half of 1 percent of all types of felony convictions are "wrong-person convictions." This would mean that of the 1.1 million convictions each year, at least 5,500 people suffer the humiliation of being wrongly convicted, and 3,800 of them the anguish of being jailed or imprisoned for a crime they did not commit.

The pressures to ensure convictions in homicide cases may lead to a higher rate of wrongful convictions in murder cases. There have been no official exonerations of an innocent person executed since 1973, but intensive investigations provide strong evidence that at least some people have been executed for murders they did not commit.

## Why Do Errors Occur?

There are several reasons why the criminal justice system produces a steady stream of such serious errors. As many as 25 percent of all eyewitness identifications may be wrong; many of these errors are caused by suggestive police lineups. Once a person is misidentified, police may develop "tunnel vision"—an unshakeable belief that the suspect is the real criminal. Tunnel vision can lead police to become overly aggressive during interrogations, causing innocent persons to confess in order to escape the enormous psychological strain of high-pressure interrogation. This is a special problem with suspects who are more easily manipulated, such as teenagers and mentally challenged suspects. Police often rely on informants, especially jailhouse snitches claiming that a suspect confessed. These snitches may be pathological liars willing to say anything to get a break in their cases.

Police are also not required to include exculpatory evidence—evidence that favors innocence—in their investigative reports. Even if they do, many prosecutors fail to turn over exculpatory evidence to defense lawyers, although required to do so by law. Overworked or incompetent defense attorneys often fail to provide a competent defense. Judges and appellate courts tend to favor the prosecution and, in a large

addressed.[80] Because these errors may occur, some commentators have called for a new evidentiary standard of "absolute certainty" to replace "beyond a reasonable doubt" in death penalty cases. Others argue that such a standard would end guilty verdicts because at least one juror would always have some uncertainty.[81]

*UNFAIR USE OF DISCRETION* Critics also frown on the tremendous discretion used in seeking the death penalty and on the arbitrary manner in which it is imposed. Of the approximately 10,000 persons convicted each year on homicide charges, only 250 to 300 are sentenced to death, while an equal number receive a sentence of probation or community supervision only. It is true that many convicted murderers do not commit first-degree murder and therefore are ineligible for execution, but it is also likely that many serious criminals who could have received the death penalty are not sentenced to death because of prosecutorial discretion. Some escape death by cooperating or giving testimony against their proportion of cases, simply overlook serious errors. In a number of cases, junk science, substandard forensic laboratories, or fraudulent forensic scientists have presented juries with completely erroneous conclusions.

## Reform Efforts

In the last few years, a number of reform efforts have begun to percolate through several cities and states in response to the crisis of convicting the innocent. In 2006, North Carolina became the first state to establish an Innocence Inquiry Commission to review and investigate prisoners' claims that they were wrongly convicted. Several states and a large number of police departments have started videotaping the entire interrogation of suspects, not just the confession. This reform is well liked by police, because confessions by guilty suspects provide strong proof at trial, and the videotape can be used to confirm that they used proper procedures.

A number of lineup reforms are shown by psychological experiments to reduce eyewitness errors. The most important include "double-blind" lineup administration, where the officer running the lineup does not know the identity of the suspect. Other procedures to ensure lineup accuracy include carefully documenting the identification, telling eyewitnesses that the perpetrator may or may not be included in the lineup, and picking "fillers" from witnesses' verbal descriptions and not the likeness of the suspect (who might be innocent). Somewhat more controversial is the recommendation to replace the traditional side-by-side live or photographic simultaneous lineups with a one-at-a-time, or sequential, lineup.

In addition to these and many other suggested reforms, there has been a call for all states to provide monetary compensation and psychological and other support for the wrongly convicted, many of whom suffer serious psychological damage from their ordeals. The conviction of a factually innocent person creates multiple victims: the wrongly convicted person who does time for another person's crime; the original crime victims, who later learn that instead of providing closure, the criminal justice system compounded their woes; and those people later victimized by the real criminal who was not caught in the first place. Knowledge about wrongful convictions should be viewed as an important topic in criminal justice and an opportunity to create a more professional criminal justice system.

## Critical Thinking

1. Describe how the conviction of an innocent person actually creates multiple victims, and see whether you can cite other people or institutions that are damaged by a wrongful conviction.

2. Apply what you know about criminal justice to create an innovative approach that might help reduce wrongful convictions. What role, if any, does technology play in your plan to reduce wrongful convictions?

Sources: *The Innocence Project*, available at www.innocenceproject.org (accessed May 5, 2010); *The Innocence Network*, available at www.innocencenetwork.org (accessed May 3, 2010; D. Michael Risinger, "Innocents Convicted: An Empirically Justified Factual Wrongful Conviction Rate," *Journal of Criminal Law and Criminology* 97 (2007): 761–806; Barry Scheck, Peter Neufeld, and Jim Dwyer, *Actual Innocence: When Justice Goes Wrong and How to Make It Right* (New York: Penguin/New American Library, 2003); The Justice Project, "Eyewitness Identification: A Policy Review," www.thejusticeproject.org (accessed May 3, 2010); Samuel R. Gross, Kristen Jacoby, Daniel J. Matheson, Nicholas Montgomery, and Sujata Patil, "Exonerations in the United States, 1989 through 2003," *Journal of Criminal Law and Criminology* 95 (2005): 523–560.

partners in the crime. A person who commits a particularly heinous crime and knows full well that he will receive the death penalty if convicted may be the one most likely to plea bargain to avoid capital punishment. Is it fair to spare the life of a dangerous killer who cooperates with the prosecutor, while executing another who does not?

Abolitionists also argue that juries use inappropriate discretion when they make capital punishment recommendations. The ongoing Capital Jury Project has been interviewing members of juries involved in making death penalty decisions and finds that many are motivated by ignorance and error.

Those who abhor the use of discretion in capital cases also point to instances where offenders who killed on the spur of the moment are executed, while truly vicious criminals who grievously injure victims during murder attempts are spared the death penalty. Some particularly heinous crimes are not punished with death simply because a physician's skill saved the victim. Some notable cases come to mind. Lawrence Singleton used an axe to cut off the arms of a

**CourseMate** For more information about **capital punishment**, visit the Criminal Justice CourseMate at CengageBrain.com, then access the "Web Links" for this chapter.

woman he raped, yet he served only eight years in prison because the victim's life was saved by prompt medical care (after being released from prison, Single-ton killed a female companion in 1997). In another case, "David," a boy severely burned in a murder attempt, lives in fear because his assailant—his father, Charles Rothenberg—was paroled from prison after serving a short sentence.[82] Although these horrific crimes received national attention and the intent to kill the victim was present, the death penalty could not be applied because of the availability of effective medical treatment. Areas that have superior medical resources actually have lower murder rates than less well-equipped areas; for example, ambulance response time can reduce the death rate by expeditiously transporting victims to an appropriate treatment center.[83] It makes little sense to punish someone for an impulsive murder while sparing the life of those who intentionally maim and torture victims who happen by chance to live because of prompt medical care.

*MISPLACED VENGEANCE*   Although critics acknowledge that the general public approves of the death penalty, they maintain that prevailing attitudes reflect a primitive desire for revenge and not just desert. Public acceptance of capital punishment has been compared to the approval of human sacrifices practiced by the Aztecs in Mexico 500 years ago.[84] It is ironic that many death penalty advocates also oppose abortion on the grounds that it is the taking of human life.[85] The desire to be vengeful and punitive outweighs their concern about taking life.

At least 30 states now have a sentence of life in prison without parole, and this can more than make up for an execution. Being locked up in a hellish prison without any chance of release (barring a rare executive reprieve) may be a worse punishment than a painless death by lethal injection. If vengeance is the goal, life without parole may eliminate the need for capital punishment.

*WEAK PUBLIC SUPPORT*   Some politicians endorse the death penalty in the mistaken belief that the public favors such harsh punishment for criminal offenders.[86] But approval ratings have been in decline for the past decade.[87] When surveys give respondents a choice of punishments, such as life without parole, support for the death penalty declines to the 50 percent level. Well-publicized incidents of innocent people being sentenced to death have helped erode support for capital punishment.[88] So even though a majority of the public still support the death penalty in principle, a substantial proportion lack confidence in its use and believe that executions should be halted until the system can be made foolproof.[89]

Public opinion in favor of the death penalty is not solid and may be influenced by such factors as the personal characteristics of the offender and the circumstances of the offense.[90] People who generally support the death penalty may not want to see it used with juveniles, the mentally challenged, or the mentally ill.[91] And even if a majority support capital punishment, their motives must be closely examined: Is it possible that support for the death penalty is a function of racist attitudes and the belief that capital punishment helps control and hold back the minority population?[92]

*LITTLE DETERRENT EFFECT*   Those opposed to the death penalty also find little merit in the argument that capital punishment deters crime.[93] They charge that there is little hard evidence that the threat of a death sentence can convince potential murderers to forgo their criminal activity. Three methods are typically used to determine whether capital punishment reduced the murder rate:

■   *Immediate-impact studies*, which calculate the effect a well-publicized execution has on the short-term murder rate

- *Time-series analysis*, which compares long-term trends in murder and capital punishment rates

- *Contiguous-state analysis*, which compares murder rates in states that have the death penalty with a similar state that has abolished capital punishment

Using these three methods over a 60-year period, most researchers have failed to show any deterrent effect of capital punishment.[94] These studies show that murder rates do not seem to rise when a state abolishes capital punishment any more than they decrease when the death penalty is adopted. The murder rate is also quite similar both in states that use the death penalty and neighboring states that have abolished capital punishment. Finally, little evidence shows that executions can lower the murder rate. One test of the deterrent effect of the death penalty in Texas found no association between the frequency of execution during the years 1984 to 1997 and murder rates.[95] International studies show that homicide rates in countries that routinely employ the death penalty are no lower than rates in countries that rarely if ever use capital punishment.[96] A recent study by Kenneth Land and his colleagues offers a different perspective, but they were able to find only a *very minor* deterrent effect associated with capital punishment.[97]

Why doesn't the death penalty deter murder? According to abolitionists, most murders involve people who knew each other, very often friends and family members. Because murderers are often under the influence of alcohol or drugs or are suffering severe psychological turmoil, no penalty is likely to be a deterrent. Another problem is that the death penalty is rarely applied outside of certain states, notably Texas and Virginia. This makes it exceedingly difficult to detect a deterrent effect.[98]

*NO HOPE OF REHABILITATION*  The death sentence rules out any hope of offender rehabilitation. There is evidence that convicted killers often make good parole risks; convicted murderers are often model inmates and, once released, commit fewer crimes than other parolees. It is possible that the general public, including people who sit on juries, overestimate the dangerousness of people who commit murder. In reality, those people who are given a life sentence for capital murder have a *less than 1 percent* (0.2%) chance of committing another homicide over a 40-year term; the risk of their committing an assault is about 16 percent.[99]

*RACE, GENDER, AND OTHER BIAS*  Capital punishment may be tarnished by gender, racial, ethnic, and other biases. More people are sentenced to death, and the death penalty is used more often, in nations with a large minority population. This is referred to as the "minority group–threat hypothesis" (in other words, use of extreme punishment is related to the regulation of groups that are racially, culturally, or ethnically different).[100]

- There is evidence that homicides with male offenders and female victims are more likely to result in a death sentence than homicides involving female offenders and male victims.[101]

- Homicides involving strangers are more likely to result in a death sentence than homicides involving nonstrangers or acquaintances.

- Prosecutors are more likely to recommend the death sentence for people who kill white victims than they are in any other racial combination of victim and criminal.[102] Prosecutors are less likely to seek the death penalty if the victim is a minority group member.[103] Killing a white female is more likely to result in the death penalty than any other combination of race/gender.[104]

Since the death penalty was first instituted in the United States, disproportionate numbers of minorities have been executed. Charges of racial bias are supported by the disproportionate numbers of African Americans who have received the death sentence, who are currently on death row, and who have been executed (54% of all executions). Racism was particularly blatant when the death penalty was invoked in rape cases: Of those receiving the death penalty for rape, 90 percent in the South and 63 percent in the North and West were African American.[105] Today, about 40 percent of the inmates on death row are African American, a number disproportionate to the minority representation in the population. When a black criminal kills a white victim, the likelihood of the death penalty being invoked is far greater than when a white kills a black victim.[106] In contrast, since 1976 only two white criminals have been executed for murdering a black victim, the most recent being Kermit Smith, who was executed on January 24, 1995, in North Carolina for the kidnapping, rape, and murder of a 20-year-old college cheerleader.[107] It is not surprising, considering these patterns, that support for the death penalty in the minority community is significantly lower than among European Americans.[108]

*CAUSES MORE CRIME THAN IT DETERS*  Some critics fear that the introduction of capital punishment will encourage criminals to escalate their violent behavior, consequently putting police officers at risk. A suspect who kills someone during a botched robbery may be inclined to "fire away" upon encountering police rather than to surrender peacefully; the killer faces the death penalty already, so what does he have to lose? Geoffrey Rapp studied the effect of capital punishment on the killings of police and found that, all other things being equal, the greater the number of new inmates on death row, the greater the number of police officers killed by citizens.[109] Rapp concluded that what the death penalty seems to do is create an extremely dangerous environment for law enforcement officers because it does not deter criminals and may lull officers into a false sense of security, leading them to believe that the death penalty will deter violence directed against them and causing them to let their guard down.

*IT IS BRUTAL*  Abolitionists believe that executions are unnecessarily cruel and inhuman and come at a high moral and social cost. Even death by lethal injection, considered relatively painless by advocates, has been challenged because it may cause extreme pain and can take much longer to cause death than was originally believed.[110] Our society does not punish criminals by subjecting them to the same acts they themselves committed. Rapists are not sexually assaulted, and arsonists do not have their houses burned down. Why, then, should murderers be killed?

Robert Johnson has described the execution process as a form of torture in which the condemned are first tormented psychologically by being made to feel powerless and alone while on death row; suicide is a constant problem among those on death row.[111] The execution itself is a barbaric affair marked by the smell of burning flesh and stiffened bodies. The executioners suffer from delayed stress reactions, including anxiety and a dehumanized personal identity.

The brutality of the death penalty may actually produce more violence than it prevents—the so-called **brutalization effect**.[112] Executions may increase murder rates because they raise the general violence level in society and because violence-prone people actually identify with the executioner, not with the target of the death penalty. When someone gets in a conflict with such violence-prone individuals or challenges their authority, these individuals may execute them in the same manner the state executes people who violate its rules.[113] There is evidence that the brutalization effect does influence murder rates: Homicides of strangers increase after an execution.[114] People may be more inclined to settle conflicts with violence after a state executes a criminal—"If they can do it, why can't I?"[115]

Because of its brutality, many enlightened countries, including Denmark and Sweden, have long since abandoned the death penalty, and 40 percent of the countries with a death penalty have active abolitionist movements.[116] It is ironic that citizens of countries that have eliminated the death penalty sometimes find themselves on death row in the United States.

**brutalization effect**
The belief that capital punishment creates an atmosphere of brutality that enhances, rather than reduces, the level of violence in society. The death penalty reinforces the view that violence is an appropriate response to provocation.

*IT IS EXPENSIVE* Some people complain that they do not want to support "some killer in prison for 30 years." Abolitionists counter that legal appeals drive the cost of executions far higher than the cost of years of incarceration. If the money spent on the judicial process were invested, the interest would more than pay for the lifetime upkeep of death row inmates. Because of numerous appeals, the median time between conviction by a jury, sentencing by a judge, and execution averages 14 years in California; the state spends more than $5 million per year on death row appeals.[117]

*MORALLY WRONG* The death penalty is brutal and demeaning. Even if the general public voices approval of the death penalty, abolitionists argue, "social vengeance by death is a primitive way of revenge which stands in the way of moral progress."[118] And although early religious leaders accepted the death penalty, today others such, as the Catholic Church, condemn the practice.[119] In his recent book *The Contradictions of American Capital Punishment*, Franklin Zimring links America's obsession with the death penalty—unique among Westernized nations—with its vigilante tradition, in which people on the frontier took justice into their own hands, assuming that their targets were always guilty as charged.[120] The death penalty was widely practiced against slaves, and at one time, mass executions were a brutal and common practice to stifle any thought of escapes and/or revolts.[121]

While the debate continues, there seems to be little question that the public's support for the death penalty has weakened, and, concomitantly, the number of death sentences being handed down is in sharp decline.[122] Whether these developments are harbingers of the demise of capital punishment remains to be seen.

## Legal Issues in Capital Punishment

The constitutionality of the death penalty has been a major concern to both the nation's courts and its social scientists. In 1972 the U.S. Supreme Court decided, in *Furman v. Georgia*,[123] that the discretionary imposition of the death penalty was cruel and unusual punishment under the Eighth and Fourteenth Amendments of the U.S. Constitution. The Supreme Court did not completely rule out the use of capital punishment as a penalty; rather, it objected to the arbitrary and capricious manner in which it was imposed. After *Furman*, many states changed statutes that had allowed jury discretion in imposing the death penalty. Then, in July 1976, the Supreme Court ruled on the constitutionality of five state death penalty statutes. In the first case, *Gregg v. Georgia*,[124] the Court found valid the Georgia statute holding that a finding by the jury of at least one "aggravating circumstance" out of ten is required in pronouncing the death penalty in murder cases. In the *Gregg* case, the jury imposed the death penalty after finding beyond a reasonable doubt two aggravating circumstances: (1) the offender was engaged in the commission of two other capital felonies, and (2) the offender committed the offense of murder for the purpose of receiving money and other financial gains (an automobile).[125] The *Gregg* case signaled the return of capital punishment as a sentencing option.

Although the Court has generally supported the death penalty, it has also placed some limitations on its use. Rulings have promoted procedural fairness in the capital sentencing process. In *Ring v. Arizona*, the Court found that juries, not judges, must make the critical findings that send convicted killers to death row. The Court reasoned that the Sixth Amendment's right to a jury trial would be "senselessly diminished" if it did not allow jurors to decide whether a person deserves the death penalty.[126] The Court has also limited who may be eligible for death:

■ The Court has limited the crimes for which the death penalty can be employed by ruling that it is not permissible to punish rapists with death.[127] Only people who commit intentional or felony murder may be executed.

■ People who are mentally ill may not be executed.[128] In a 2002 case, *Atkins v. Virginia*, the Court ruled that execution of mentally retarded criminals is "cruel and unusual punishment" prohibited by the Eighth Amendment.[129]

## The Evolution of Furman v. Georgia

**Furman v. Georgia (1972)** The death penalty (in three Georgia cases) amounts to cruel and unusual punishment in violation of the Eighth Amendment. Furman led to a de facto moratorium on capital punishment.[134]

**Gregg v. Georgia (1976)** The punishment of death for the crime of murder does not violate the Eighth Amendment under all circumstances.[135]

**Woodson v. North Carolina (1976)** Mandatory death penalty laws (those that do not take into account aggravating and mitigating circumstances) violate the Eighth Amendment and are thus unconstitutional.[136]

**Coker v. Georgia (1977)** Rapists cannot be sentenced to death.[137]

**Lockett v. Ohio (1978)** The defendant must be allowed to present all mitigating evidence pertaining to his or her "character, record, and circumstances of the crime."[138]

**Enmund v. Florida (1982)** It is a violation of the Eighth Amendment to impose the death penalty on a person who commits a felony that results in murder without considering the person's level of intent.[139]

**Glass v. Louisiana (1985)** Death by electrocution is not cruel and unusual punishment.[140]

**Cabana v. Bullock (1986)** The death penalty cannot be imposed on an accomplice unless it is proved that the accomplice killed, attempted to kill, or intended to kill.[141]

**Ford v. Wainwright (1986)** It is a violation of the Eighth Amendment to execute a person who is insane (or was insane at the time of the crime).[142]

**Atkins v. Virginia (2002)** The execution of a mentally retarded individual violates the Eighth Amendment.[143]

**Ring v. Arizona (2002)** It is a violation of the Sixth Amendment's jury trial provision to allow a judge, rather than a jury, to find aggravating circumstances necessary for imposition of the death penalty.[144]

**Roper v. Simmons (2005)** It is a violation of the Eighth Amendment to sentence to death a defendant who committed his or her capital crime under the age of 18.[145]

**Deck v. Missouri (2005)** It is unconstitutional to force the defendant to wear visible shackles during the sentencing phase of a capital trial.[146]

**Oregon v. Guzek (2006)** Death penalty defendants may not present new evidence during the sentencing phase of the criminal process.[147]

**Baze v. Rees (2008)** A three-drug lethal injection procedure does not violate the Eighth Amendment.[148]

**Kennedy v. Louisiana (2008)** A child rapist cannot be sentenced to death if the crime did not result in (or was not intended to result in) the child's death.[149]

■ In *Roper v. Simmons* (2005), the Court set 18 years as the minimum age of defendants who could be sentenced to death.[130] The Court said that executing young teens violates "the evolving standards of decency that mark the progress of a maturing society" and that American society regards juveniles as less responsible than adult criminals. Although 19 states had allowed the execution of juvenile murderers prior to *Simmons*, only Texas, Virginia, and Oklahoma have executed any in the past decade.

■ In *Kennedy v. Louisiana* (2008), the Court barred capital punishment for child rapists—unless the rape resulted in (or was intended to result in) the death of the child.[131]

In an important 2008 case, *Baze v. Rees*, the Supreme Court settled the issue of whether lethal injection was cruel and unusual punishment.[132] Two death row inmates, Ralph Baze and Thomas C. Bowling, had argued that the combination of drugs used to execute prisoners in Kentucky, and in at least 29 other states with the same procedure, carried an "unnecessary risk" of inflicting cruel and unusual punishment, in violation of the Eighth Amendment. The inmates did not challenge the death penalty itself. Chief Justice John Roberts, writing a lead opinion, said the mere fact that there may be a safer alternative to Kentucky's protocol doesn't mean that the current regimen is unconstitutional. The inmates had argued that a single drug could be administered to the condemned, similar to the process used to euthanize animals, to reduce the risk of agonizing pain. However, the Court ruled that capital punishment is constitutional, and so there must be a means for its implementation.

The accompanying "Evolution of *Furman v. Georgia*" feature highlights the key death penalty decisions since 1972. Note that in the wake of the *Gregg* decision, the Supreme Court has become more and more restrictive with respect to application of the death penalty.[133]

## Significant Cases in Punishment and Sentencing

| Case | Issue | Decision |
| --- | --- | --- |
| *Apprendi v. New Jersey* (2000) | Sentencing guidelines | Any factor other than a prior conviction that increases the penalty for the crime beyond the statutory minimum must be submitted to a jury and proved beyond a reasonable doubt. |
| *Blakely v. Washington* (2004) | Sentencing guidelines | Washington's sentencing guidelines are unconstitutional because they permit a judge, not a jury, to consider aggravating factors that would enhance the sentence. |
| *Ewing v. California* (2003) | Three strikes | A sentence of 25 years to life resulting from California's three-strikes law does not violate the Eighth Amendment's prohibition against cruel and unusual punishment. |
| *Furman v. Georgia* (1972) | Death penalty | The death penalty as applied in three Georgia cases is unconstitutional. For review of additional death penalty cases, see the "Evolution of *Furman v. Georgia*" feature in this chapter. |
| *Gregg v. Georgia* (1976) | Death penalty | The death penalty does not constitute cruel and unusual punishment in all circumstances. For review of additional death penalty cases, see the "Evolution of *Furman v. Georgia*" feature in this chapter. |
| *Harmelin v. Michigan* (1991) | Mandatory sentencing | A statutorily mandated sentence that does not take into account mitigating circumstances does not violate the Eighth Amendment's cruel and unusual punishment clause. |
| *Kimbrough v. United States* (2007) | Sentencing guidelines, cocaine | The federal cocaine sentencing guidelines are advisory. |
| *Lockyer v. Andrade* (2003) | Three strikes | There is no habeas corpus relief from a sentence imposed under California's three-strikes law. |
| *Payne v. Tennessee* (1991) | Victim impact statements | The Eighth Amendment is not violated if a capital sentencing jury hears a victim impact statement from surviving family members. |
| *Ring v. Arizona* (2002) | Death penalty | Juries, not judges, must make the critical findings (aggravating circumstances) that send killers to death row. For review of additional death penalty cases, see the "Evolution of *Furman v. Georgia*" feature in this chapter. |
| *Rita v. United States* (2007) | Sentencing guidelines | Any sentence that falls within the federal sentencing guidelines is presumptively reasonable. |
| *United States v. Booker* (2005) | Sentencing guidelines | The federal sentencing guidelines are advisory, not mandatory. |

## Ethical Challenges in Criminal Justice: A Writing Assignment

You are a defense attorney who, last year, represented Sam Smith in his capital murder trial. The jury found Smith guilty of the brutal killing of a young girl and sentenced him to death. You also represented him in his first appeal, arguing that the prosecutor intentionally withheld exculpatory evidence, but the verdict was affirmed. You have now decided to volunteer your services for one more appeal because you are not convinced Smith is guilty and you believe the death penalty is a cruel form of punishment, but Smith declines your assistance, saying he wants to die. He does not want to grow old on death row, fears what he is convinced will be a dehumanizing experience on death row, thinks the likely roller coaster of appeals won't be worth the ride, and wants to spare his family the pain of not knowing his fate. Smith is what some would call a "death row volunteer."[150]

Write an essay on the ethical dilemmas posed in this scenario. In doing so, answer these questions: Should you let Smith go to his death? What could you do to persuade him to change his mind, if anything? If Smith opts for one more appeal, what other arguments could you raise in that appeal? Could any of the common criticisms of the death penalty serve as a basis for an appeal? If so, which ones? In answering these questions, refer to this chapter's "Capital Punishment" section—and particularly to the subsections "Arguments against the Death Penalty" and "Legal Issues in Capital Punishment."

## SUMMARY

1. **Outline the historical development of punishment.**

   ■ Historically, people who violated the law were considered morally corrupt and in need of strong discipline.

   ■ In early Greece and Rome, the most common state-administered punishment was banishment or exile.

   ■ During the Middle Ages, people found guilty of crime faced a wide range of punishments, including physical torture, branding, whipping, and (for most felony offenses) death. The main emphasis of criminal law and punishment was on maintaining public order.

   ■ The development of the common law in the eleventh century brought some standardization to penal practices.

   ■ By the end of the sixteenth century, many offenders were made to do hard labor for their crimes.

   ■ In England, transporting convicts to the colonies became popular.

   ■ By 1820, long periods of incarceration in walled institutions called reformatories or penitentiaries began to replace physical punishment in England and the United States.

2. **List the major goals of contemporary sentencing.**

   ■ The objectives of criminal sentencing today can be grouped into six distinct areas: general deterrence, incapacitation, specific deterrence, retribution/just desert, rehabilitation, and equity/restitution.

3. **Distinguish among general and specific deterrence, incapacitation, and retribution.**

   ■ According to the concept of general deterrence, people will be too afraid to break the law if they believe that they will be caught and punished severely.

   ■ The purpose of specific deterrence, another goal of punishment, is to convince offenders that the pains of punishment are greater than the potential benefits of crime.

   ■ Incapacitation is intended to keep criminals from repeating their criminal acts while they are under state control.

   ■ According to the retributive goal of sentencing, the essential purpose of the criminal process is to punish offenders—fairly and justly—in a manner that is proportionate to the gravity of their crimes.

**4. Compare rehabilitation with just desert.**

- Rehabilitation, or treatment, is built on the view that the justice system is obligated to *help* criminals, not just to punish them for their misdeeds.

- According to just desert, punishment should be no more or less than the offender's actions warrant.

**5. Know how sentences are imposed.**

- In some instances, when an accused is convicted of two or more charges, the judge must decide whether to impose consecutive (back-to-back) or concurrent (overlapping) sentences.

- When judges impose an incarceration sentence, they know and take into account the fact that the amount of time spent in prison is reduced by the implementation of "time off for good behavior."

**6. Classify the various types of sentencing structures.**

- Indeterminate sentences are tailored to fit individual needs. Convicted offenders are typically given a "light" minimum sentence that must be served and a lengthy maximum sentence that is the outer boundary of the time that can be served.

- Determinate sentences offer a fixed term of years, the maximum set in law by the legislature, to be served by the offender sentenced to prison for a particular crime.

- Sentencing guidelines have been implemented to provide judges with a recommended sentence based on the seriousness of a crime and the background of an offender.

- Some states have passed mandatory sentence legislation prohibiting people convicted of certain offenses, such as violent crimes and drug trafficking, from being placed on probation; they must serve at least some time in prison.

- Three-strikes (and you're out) laws provide lengthy terms for any person convicted of three felony offenses, even if the third crime is relatively trivial.

- Truth-in-sentencing laws require offenders to serve a substantial portion of their prison sentence behind bars.

**7. Discuss how people are sentenced today.**

- About 70 percent of all felons convicted in state courts are sentenced to a period of confinement—41 percent to state prisons and 28 percent to local jails. The remaining third are sentenced to straight probation with no jail or prison time to serve.

- State sentencing codes usually include various factors that can legitimately influence the length of prison sentences, including the severity of the offense, the offender's prior criminal record, whether the offender used violence, whether the offender used weapons, and whether the crime was committed for money.

- Evidence supports an association between social class and sentencing outcomes: Members of the lower class may expect to get longer prison sentences than more affluent defendants.

- Most research indicates that women receive more favorable outcomes the further they go in the criminal justice system.

- Older people will be punished more harshly than younger ones because they have had a greater opportunity to accumulate a criminal record and most state laws increase penalties for multiple offenders.

- Minorities seem to receive longer sentences than Caucasians, especially those who are indigent or unemployed.

**8. Demonstrate your knowledge of the nature of capital punishment in the United States and abroad.**

- The most severe sentence used in the United States is capital punishment, or execution.

- The United States is not alone in using the death penalty, but over half the countries in the world have now abolished the death penalty in law or practice.

- Despite its continued use and public acceptance, there seems to be growing unease with the administration of the death penalty, and the recent use of scientific evidence based on DNA has resulted in numerous exonerations of death row inmates.

**9. Be familiar with the arguments for and against capital punishment.**

- Supporters argue that death is the "ultimate incapacitation" and the only one that can ensure that convicted killers can never be pardoned, be paroled, or escape.

- Proponents of capital punishment argue that executions serve as a strong deterrent for serious crimes.

- Putting dangerous criminals to death also conforms to the requirement that the punishment be proportional to the seriousness of the crime.

- The death penalty is justified because it represents the will of the people.

- The many legal controls and appeals currently in use make it almost impossible for an innocent person to be executed or for the death penalty to be used in a racist or capricious manner.

- Critics of the death penalty believe capital punishment has no place in a mature democratic society.

- Because of the chances of error, a number of states have placed a moratorium on executions until the issue of errors in the process can be adequately addressed.

- The pressures to ensure convictions in homicide cases may lead to a higher rate of wrongful convictions in murder cases.

- Critics frown on the tremendous discretion used in seeking the death penalty and on the arbitrary manner in which it is imposed.

- Politicians favor the death penalty in the mistaken belief that the public favors such harsh punishment for criminal offenders.

- Capital punishment may be tarnished by gender, racial, ethnic, and other biases.

- Abolitionists believe that executions are unnecessarily cruel and inhuman and come at a high moral and social cost.

- The constitutionality of the death penalty has been a major concern to both the nation's courts and its social scientists.

**10. Discuss the legality of the death penalty.**

- In *Gregg v. Georgia*, the Court found valid the Georgia statute holding that a finding by the jury of at least one "aggravating circumstance" out of ten is required in pronouncing the death penalty in murder cases.

- The Court has limited the crimes for which the death penalty can be employed by ruling that it is not permissible to punish rapists with death.

- People who are mentally ill may not be executed.

- In *Roper v. Simmons* (2005), the Court set a limit of 18 years as the age of defendants who could be sentenced to death.

## KEY TERMS

penitentiary, 438
general deterrence, 438
incapacitation, 439
specific deterrence, 440
blameworthy, 441
just desert, 441

equity, 441
concurrent sentences, 442
consecutive sentences, 443
indeterminate sentence, 444
determinate sentence, 445
sentencing guidelines, 445

mandatory sentence, 448
truth in sentencing, 450
chivalry hypothesis, 452
victim impact statement, 453
brutalization effect, 454

## CRITICAL THINKING QUESTIONS

1. Discuss the sentencing dispositions in your jurisdiction. What are the pros and cons of each?

2. Compare the various types of incarceration sentences. What are the similarities and differences?

3. What are the arguments for and against three-strikes laws? Who is more persuasive, the supporters or the critics?

4. Summarize the arguments for and against capital punishment. Who is more persuasive, the supporters or the critics?

5. Why does sentencing disparity exist? Are there programs that can reduce disparity in sentencing? If so, what are they? Should all people who commit the same crime receive the same sentence? Explain.

## NOTES

1. *Thompson v. McNeil*, No. 08-7369 (2009), cert denied.
2. Death Penalty Information Center, *The Death Penalty in 2008: Year End Report*, available at www.deathpenaltyinfo .org/2008YearEnd.pdf (accessed May 5, 2010); see also www .deathpenaltyinfo.org/time-death-row (accessed May 6, 2010).
3. Among the most helpful sources for this section were Benedict Alper, *Prisons Inside-Out* (Cambridge, Mass.: Ballinger, 1974); Gustave de Beaumont and Alexis de Tocqueville, *On the*

*Penitentiary System in the United States and Its Applications in France* (Carbondale, Ill.: Southern Illinois University Press, 1964, originally published in 1833); Orlando Lewis, *The Development of American Prisons and Prison Customs, 1776–1845* (Montclair, N.J.: Patterson-Smith, 1967); Leonard Orland, ed., *Justice, Punishment, and Treatment* (New York: Free Press, 1973); J. Goebel, *Felony and Misdemeanor* (Philadelphia: University of Pennsylvania Press, 1976); George Rusche and Otto Kircheimer, *Punishment and*

*Social Structure* (New York: Russell & Russell, 1939); Samuel Walker, *Popular Justice* (New York: Oxford University Press, 1980); Newman, *The Punishment Response*; David Rothman, *Conscience and Convenience* (Boston: Little, Brown, 1980); George Ives, *A History of Penal Methods* (Montclair, N.J.: Patterson-Smith, 1970); Robert Hughes, *The Fatal Shore* (New York: Knopf, 1986); Leon Radzinowicz, *A History of English Criminal Law*, vol. 1 (London: Stevens, 1943), p. 5.

4.  *Crime and Punishment in America, 1999*, Report 229 (Washington, D.C.: National Center for Policy Analysis, 1999).

5.  Sean Rosenmerkel, Matthew Durose, and Donald Farole Jr., *Felony Sentences in State Courts, 2006–Statistical Tables* (Washington, D.C.: Bureau of Justice Statistics, 2009), p. 1.

6.  Matthew Durose and Patrick Langan, *Felony Sentences in State Courts, 2004* (Washington, D.C.: Bureau of Justice Statistics, 2007).

7.  Tomislav Kovandzic and Lynne Vieraitis, "The Effect of County-level Prison Population Growth on Crime Rates," *Criminology and Public Policy* 5 (2006): 213–244.

8.  Lynne Vieraitis, Tomislav Kovandzic, and Thomas Marvell, "The Criminogenic Effects of Imprisonment: Evidence from State Panel Data, 1974–2002," *Criminology and Public Policy* 6 (2007): 589–622.

9.  Raymond Liedka, Anne Morrison Piehl, and Bert Useem, "The Crime-Control Effect of Incarceration: Does Scale Matter?" *Criminology and Public Policy* 5 (2006): 245–276.

10.  Ibid.

11.  Positive results were achieved by Lawrence Sherman and Richard Berk, "The Specific Deterrent Effects of Arrest for Domestic Assault," *American Sociological Review* 49 (1984): 261–272; negative by Christopher Maxwell, Joel Garner, and Jeffrey Fagan, *The Effects of Arrest in Intimate Partner Violence: New Evidence from the Spouse Assault Replication Program* (Washington, D.C.: National Institute of Justice, 2001); Robert Davis, Barbara Smith, and Laura Nickles, "The Deterrent Effect of Prosecuting Domestic Violence Misdemeanors," *Crime and Delinquency* 44 (1998): 434–442.

12.  Patrick Langan and David Levin, *Recidivism of Prisoners Released in 1994* (Washington, D.C.: Bureau of Justice Statistics, 2002).

13.  Christina Dejong, "Survival Analysis and Specific Deterrence," *Criminology* 35 (2006): 561–576; Raymond Paternoster and Alex Piquero, "Reconceptualizing Deterrence: An Empirical Test of Personal and Vicarious Experiences," *Journal of Research in Crime and Delinquency* 32 (1995): 251–258.

14.  David Lovell, L. Clark Johnson, and Kevin Cain, "Recidivism of Supermax Prisoners in Washington State," *Crime and Delinquency* 53 (2007): 633–656.

15.  Greg Pogarsky and Alex R. Piquero, "Can Punishment Encourage Offending? Investigating the 'Resetting' Effect," *Journal of Research in Crime and Delinquency* 40 (2003): 92–117.

16.  Faith Lutze, "The Influence of Shock Incarceration Program on Inmate Adjustment and Attitudinal Change," *Journal of Criminal Justice* 29 (2001): 255–266.

17.  Charles Logan, *Criminal Justice Performance Measures for Prisons* (Washington, D.C.: Bureau of Justice Statistics, 1993), p. 3.

18.  Alexis Durham, "The Justice Model in Historical Context: Early Law, the Emergence of Science, and the Rise of Incarceration," *Journal of Criminal Justice* 16 (1988): 331–346.

19.  Andrew von Hirsh, *Doing Justice: The Choice of Punishments* (New York: Hill and Wang, 1976).

20.  Shawn Bushway, "The Impact of an Arrest on the Job Stability of Young White American Men," *Journal of Research in Crime and Delinquency* 35 (1998): 454–479.

21.  Lawrence W. Sherman, David P. Farrington, Doris Layton MacKenzie, Brandon Walsh, Denise Gottfredson, John Eck, Shawn Bushway, and Peter Reuter, *Evidence-Based Crime Prevention* (London: Routledge and Kegan Paul, 2002); see also Arnulf Kolstad, "Imprisonment as Rehabilitation: Offenders' Assessment of Why It Does Not Work," *Journal of Criminal Justice* 24 (1996): 323–335.

22.  Francis Cullen, John Paul Wright, Shayna Brown, Melissa Moon, and Brandon Applegate, "Public Support for Early Intervention Programs: Implications for a Progressive Policy Agenda," *Crime and Delinquency* 44 (1998): 187–204; Richard McCorkle, "Research Note: Punish and Rehabilitate? Public Attitudes toward Six Common Crimes," *Crime and Delinquency* 39 (1993): 240–252; D. A. Andrews, Ivan Zinger, Robert Hoge, James Bonta, Paul Gendreau, and Francis Cullen, "Does Correctional Treatment Work? A Clinically Relevant and Psychologically Informed Meta-Analysis," *Criminology* 28 (1990): 369–404.

23.  Gordon Bazemore and Curt Taylor Griffiths, "Conferences, Circles, Boards, and Mediations: The 'New Wave' of Community Justice Decision Making," *Federal Probation* 61 (1997): 25–37.

24.  See *Barber v. Thomas*, 09-5201 (2010) for a case illustrating some of the controversy in the calculation of credit for good time.

25.  Paula Ditton and Doris James Wilson, *Truth in Sentencing in State Prisons* (Washington, D.C.: Bureau of Justice Statistics, 1999).

26.  Jo Dixon, "The Organizational Context of Criminal Sentencing," *American Journal of Sociology* 100 (1995): 1157–1198.

27.  Michael Tonry, *The Fragmentation of Sentencing and Corrections in America* (Washington, DC: National Institute of Justice, 1999).

28.  Ibid., p. 11.

29.  *Apprendi v. New Jersey*, 530 U.S. 466 (2000).

30.  *Blakely v. Washington*, 124 S.Ct. 2531 (2004).

31.  *United States v. Booker*, No. 04-104 (2005).

32.  News Release, "U.S. Sentencing Commission Votes Unanimously to Apply Amendment Retroactively for Crack Cocaine Offenses, Effective Date for Retroactivity Set for March 3, 2008," www.ussc .gov/PRESS/rel121107.htm (accessed May 3, 2010).

33.  *Kimbrough v. United States*, 552 U.S. 85 (2007).

34.  *Rita v. United States*, 551 U.S. 338 (2007).

35.  United States Sentencing Commission, *Demographic Differences in Federal Sentencing Practices: An Update of the* Booker *Report's Multivariate Regression Analysis* (Washington, DC: U.S. Sentencing Commission), www.ussc.gov/general/Multivariate_ Regression_Analysis_Report_1.pdf (accessed May 5, 2010), p. 2.

36.  *Harmelin v. Michigan*, 501 U.S. 957 (1991).

37.  "Man Who Stole Slice of Pizza Sentenced to 25 Years to Life in California," *New York Times*, March 5, 1995, http://findarticles .com/p/articles/mi_m1355/is_n20_v87/ai_16709220 (accessed May 3, 2010); "Cookie Burglar Gets at Least 25 Years," www.cnn.com/ US/Newsbriefs/9510/10-27/ (accessed May 3, 2010).

38.  *Lockyer v. Andrade*, 538 U.S. 63 (2003).

39.  *Ewing v. California*, 538 U.S. 11 (2003).

40.  Ditton and Wilson, *Truth in Sentencing in State Prisons*.

41.  Rosenmerkel, Durose, and Farole Jr., *Felony Sentences in State Courts*.

42.  Ibid.

43.  Matthew Durose and Patrick Langan, *Felony Sentences in State Courts, 2004* (Washington, D.C.: Bureau of Justice Statistics, 2007).

44.  Brent Smith and Kelly Damphouse, "Terrorism, Politics, and Punishment: A Test of Structural-Contextual Theory and the Liberation Hypothesis," *Criminology* 36 (1998): 67–92.

45.  For a general look at the factors that affect sentencing, see Susan Welch, Cassia Spohn, and John Gruhl, "Convicting and Sentencing Differences among Black, Hispanic, and White Males in Six Localities," *Justice Quarterly* 2 (1985): 67–80.

46.  Stewart D'Alessio and Lisa Stolzenberg, "Socioeconomic Status and the Sentencing of the Traditional Offender," *Journal of Criminal Justice* 21 (1993): 61–77.

47.  Cecilia Saulters-Tubbs, "Prosecutorial and Judicial Treatment of Female Offenders," *Federal Probation* 57 (1993): 37–41.

48.  See, generally, Janet Johnston, Thomas Kennedy, and I. Gayle Shuman, "Gender Differences in the Sentencing of Felony Offenders," *Federal Probation* 49 (1987): 49–56; Cassia Spohn and Susan Welch, "The Effect of Prior Record in Sentencing Research: An Examination of the Assumption That Any Measure

Is Adequate," *Justice Quarterly* 4 (1987): 286–302; David Willison, "The Effects of Counsel on the Severity of Criminal Sentences: A Statistical Assessment," *Justice System Journal* 9 (1984): 87–101.

49. Cassia Spohn, Miriam DeLone, and Jeffrey Spears, "Race/Ethnicity, Gender, and Sentence Severity in Dade County, Florida: An Examination of the Decision to Withhold Adjudication," *Journal of Crime and Justice* 21 (1998): 111–132.

50. Ellen Hochstedler Steury and Nancy Frank, "Gender Bias and Pretrial Release: More Pieces of the Puzzle," *Journal of Criminal Justice* 18 (1990): 417–432.

51. Shimica Gaskins, "Women of Circumstance—The Effects of Mandatory Minimum Sentencing on Women Minimally Involved in Drug Crimes," *American Criminal Law Review* 41 (2004): 1533–1563.

52. Shawn Bushway and Anne Morrison Piehl, "The Inextricable Link between Age and Criminal History in Sentencing," *Crime and Delinquency* 53 (2007): 156–183.

53. Dean Champion, "Elderly Felons and Sentencing Severity: Interregional Variations in Leniency and Sentencing Trends," *Criminal Justice Review* 12 (1987): 7–15.

54. Darrell Steffensmeier, John Kramer, and Jeffery Ulmer, "Age Differences in Sentencing," *Justice Quarterly* 12 (1995): 583–601.

55. Darrell Steffensmeier, Jeffery Ulmer, and John Kramer, "The Interaction of Race, Gender, and Age in Criminal Sentencing: The Punishment Cost of Being Young, Black, and Male," *Criminology* 36 (1998): 763–798.

56. *Payne v. Tennessee*, 501 U.S. 808 (1991).

57. Robert Davis and Barbara Smith, "The Effects of Victim Impact Statements on Sentencing Decisions: A Test in an Urban Setting," *Justice Quarterly* 11 (1994): 453–469; Edna Erez and Pamela Tontodonato, "The Effect of Victim Participation in Sentencing on Sentence Outcome," *Criminology* 28 (1990): 451–474.

58. Rodney Kingsworth, Randall MacIntosh, and Jennifer Wentworth, "Sexual Assault: The Role of Prior Relationship and Victim Characteristics in Case Processing," *Justice Quarterly* 16 (1999): 276–302.

59. Tracy Nobiling, Cassia Spohn, and Miriam DeLone, "A Tale of Two Counties: Unemployment and Sentence Severity," *Justice Quarterly* 15 (1998): 459–486.

60. Michael Tonry, *Malign Neglect: Race, Crime, and Punishment in America* (New York: Oxford University Press, 1995), 105–109.

61. *Coker v. Georgia*, 433 U.S. 584 (1977).

62. *People v. Stephen LaValle*, Sup.C. #71 (2004).

63. For more on this issue, read Hugo Adam Bedeau and Paul Cassell, *Debating the Death Penalty: Should America Have Capital Punishment? The Experts on Both Sides Make Their Best Case* (London: Oxford University Press, 2003).

64. Stephen Markman and Paul Cassell, "Protecting the Innocent: A Response to the Bedeau-Radelet Study," *Stanford Law Review* 41 (1988): 121–170.

65. Tracy L. Snell, *Capital Punishment, 2008—Statistical Tables* (Washington, D.C.: Bureau of Justice Statistics), http://bjs.ojp.usdoj.gov/content/pub/pdf/cp08st.pdf (accessed May 3, 2010).

66. Stephen Layson, "United States Time-Series Homicide Regressions with Adaptive Expectations," *Bulletin of the New York Academy of Medicine* 62 (1986): 589–619.

67. James Galliher and John Galliher, "A 'Commonsense' Theory of Deterrence and the 'Ideology' of Science: The New York State Death Penalty Debate," *Journal of Criminal Law and Criminology* 92 (2002): 307.

68. Steven Stack, "The Effect of Well-Publicized Executions on Homicide in California," *Journal of Crime and Justice* 21 (1998): 1–12.

69. James Yunker, "A New Statistical Analysis of Capital Punishment Incorporating U.S. Postmoratorium Data," *Social Science Quarterly* 82 (2001): 297–312.

70. Hashem Dezhbakhsh, Paul H. Rubin, and Joanna M. Shepherd, "Does Capital Punishment Have a Deterrent Effect? New Evidence from Postmoratorium Panel Data," *American Law and Economics Review* 5 (2003): 344–376.

71. Joanna Shepherd, "Deterrence versus Brutalization: Capital Punishment's Differing Impacts among States," *Michigan Law Review* 104 (2005): 203–253.

72. David Friedrichs, "Comment—Humanism and the Death Penalty: An Alternative Perspective," *Justice Quarterly* 6 (1989): 197–209.

73. *Sourcebook of Criminal Justice Statistics, 2003*, www.albany.edu/sourcebook/pdf/t253.pdf (accessed May 3, 2010).

74. For an analysis of the formation of public opinion on the death penalty, see Kimberly Cook, "Public Support for the Death Penalty: A Cultural Analysis," paper presented at the annual meeting of the American Society of Criminology, San Francisco, November 1991.

75. Alexis Durham, H. Preston Elrod, and Patrick Kinkade, "Public Support to the Death Penalty: Beyond Gallup," *Justice Quarterly* 13 (1996): 705–736.

76. See, generally, Hugo Bedeau, *Death Is Different: Studies in the Morality, Law, and Politics of Capital Punishment* (Boston: Northeastern University Press, 1987); Keith Otterbein, *The Ultimate Coercive Sanction* (New Haven, Conn.: HRAF Press, 1986).

77. Michael Radelet and Hugo Bedeau, "Miscarriages of Justice in Potentially Capital Cases," *Stanford Law Review* 40 (1987): 121–181.

78. House Subcommittee on Civil and Constitutional Rights, *Innocence and the Death Penalty: Assessing the Danger of Mistaken Executions* (Washington, D.C.: Government Printing Office, 1993).

79. David Stewart, "Dealing with Death," *American Bar Association Journal* 80 (1994): 53.

80. "The Innocence Protection Act," editorial, *America* 187 (2002): 2–3.

81. Erik Lillquist, "Absolute Certainty and the Death Penalty," *American Criminal Law Review* 42 (2005): 45–92.

82. "A Victim's Progress," *Newsweek* (June 12, 1989): 5.

83. William Doerner, "The Impact of Medical Resources on Criminally Induced Lethality: A Further Examination," *Criminology* 26 (1988): 171–177.

84. Elizabeth Purdom and J. Anthony Paredes, "Capital Punishment and Human Sacrifice," in *Facing the Death Penalty: Essays on Cruel and Unusual Punishment*, ed. Michael Radelet (Philadelphia: Temple University Press, 1989), pp. 152–153.

85. Kimberly Cook, "A Passion to Punish: Abortion Opponents Who Favor the Death Penalty," *Justice Quarterly* 15 (1998): 329–346.

86. John Whitehead, Michael Blankenship, and John Paul Wright, "Elite versus Citizen Attitudes on Capital Punishment: Incongruity between the Public and Policy Makers," *Journal of Criminal Justice* 27 (1999): 249–258.

87. Julian Roberts, "Capital Punishment, Innocence, and Public Opinion," *Criminology and Public Policy* 4 (2005): 1–3.

88. James Unnever and Francis Cullen, "Executing the Innocent and Support for Capital Punishment: Implications for Public Policy," *Criminology and Public Policy* 4 (2005): 3–37.

89. Scott Vollum, Dennis Longmire, and Jacqueline Buffington-Vollum, "Confidence in the Death Penalty and Support for Its Use: Exploring the Value-Expressive Dimension of Death Penalty Attitudes," *JQ: Justice Quarterly* 21 (2004): 521–546.

90. Gennaro Vito and Thomas Keil, "Elements of Support for Capital Punishment: An Examination of Changing Attitudes," *Journal of Crime and Justice* 21 (1998): 17–25.

91. Denise Paquette Boots, Kathleen Heide, and John Cochran, "Death Penalty Support for Special Offender Populations of Legally Convicted Murderers: Juveniles, the Mentally Retarded, and the Mentally Incompetent," *Behavioral Sciences and the Law* 22 (2004): 223–238.

92. James Unnever and Francis Cullen, "The Racial Divide in Support for the Death Penalty: Does White Racism Matter?" *Social Forces* 85 (2007): 1281–1301.

93. John Donohue and Justin Wolfers, "Uses and Abuses of Empirical Evidence in the Death Penalty Debate," *Stanford Law Review* 58 (2005): 791–845.

94. Walter C. Reckless, "Use of the Death Penalty," *Crime and Delinquency* 15 (1969): 43; Thorsten Sellin, "Effect of Repeal and Reintroduction of the Death Penalty on Homicide Rates," in *The Death Penalty*, ed. Thorsten Sellin (Philadelphia: American Law Institute, 1959); Robert H. Dann, "The Deterrent Effect of Capital Punishment," *Friends Social Service Series* 29 (1935): 1; William Bailey and Ruth Peterson, "Murder and Capital Punishment: A Monthly Time-Series Analysis of Execution Publicity," *American Sociological Review* 54 (1989): 722–743; David Phillips, "The Deterrent Effect of Capital Punishment," *American Journal of Sociology* 86 (1980): 139–148; Sam McFarland, "Is Capital Punishment a Short-Term Deterrent to Homicide? A Study of the Effects of Four Recent American Executions," *Journal of Criminal Law and Criminology* 74 (1984): 1014–1032; Richard Lempert, "The Effect of Executions on Homicides: A New Look in an Old Light," *Crime and Delinquency* 29 (1983): 88–115.

95. Jon Sorenson, Robert Wrinkle, Victoria Brewer, and James Marquart, "Capital Punishment and Deterrence: Examining the Effect of Executions on Murder in Texas," *Crime and Delinquency* 45 (1999): 481–493.

96. Keith Harries and Derral Cheatwood, *The Geography of Executions: The Capital Punishment Quagmire in America* (Lanham, Md.: Rowman and Littlefield, 1997).

97. Kenneth C. Land, Raymond H.C. Teske Jr., and Hui Zheng, "The Short-Term Effects of Executions on Homicides: Deterrence, Displacement, or Both?" *Criminology* 47 (2009): 1009–1043.

98. Ibid., pp. 1012–1013.

99. Jonathan R. Sorensen and Rocky L. Pilgrim, "An Actuarial Risk of Assessment of Violence Posed by Murder Defendants," *Journal of Criminal Law and Criminology* 90 (2000): 1251–1271.

100. Rick Ruddell and Martin Urbina, "Minority Threat and Punishment: A Cross-National Analysis," *JQ: Justice Quarterly* 21 (2004): 903–931.

101. Marian Williams and Jefferson Holcomb, "Racial Disparity and Death Sentences in Ohio," *Journal of Criminal Justice* 29 (2001): 207–218.

102. Jon Sorenson and Donald Wallace, "Prosecutorial Discretion in Seeking Death: An Analysis of Racial Disparity in the Pretrial Stages of Case Processing in a Midwestern County," *JQ: Justice Quarterly* 16 (1999): 559–578.

103. Catherine Lee, "Hispanics and the Death Penalty: Discriminatory Charging Practices in San Joaquin County, California," *Journal of Criminal Justice* 35 (2007): 17–27.

104. Jefferson Holcomb, Marian Williams, and Stephen Demuth, "White Female Victims and Death Penalty Disparity Research," *JQ: Justice Quarterly* 21 (2004): 877–902.

105. Lawrence Greenfield and David Hinners, *Capital Punishment, 1984* (Washington, D.C.: Bureau of Justice Statistics, 1985).

106. Gennaro Vito and Thomas Keil, "Capital Sentencing in Kentucky: An Analysis of the Factors Influencing Decision Making in the Post-Gregg Period," *Journal of Criminal Law and Criminology* 79 (1988): 483–508.

107. David Brown, "Man Is Executed in Carolina: Second of a White Who Killed a Black," *Boston Globe*, January 25, 1995, p. 3.

108. James Unnever and Francis Cullen, "Reassessing the Racial Divide in Support for Capital Punishment: The Continuing Significance of Race," *Journal of Research in Crime and Delinquency* 44 (2007): 124–158.

109. Geoffrey Rapp, "The Economics of Shootouts: Does the Passage of Capital Punishment Laws Protect or Endanger Police Officers?" *Albany Law Review* 65 (2002): 1051–1084.

110. *Hill v. McDonough*, 547 U.S. 573 (2006).

111. Robert Johnson, *Death Work: A Study of the Modern Execution Process* (Pacific Grove, Calif.: Brooks/Cole, 1990).

112. William Bailey, "Disaggregation in Deterrence and Death Penalty Research: The Case of Murder in Chicago," *Journal of Criminal Law and Criminology* 74 (1986): 827–859.

113. Gennaro Vito, Pat Koester, and Deborah Wilson, "Return of the Dead: An Update on the Status of Furman-Commuted Death Row Inmates," in *The Death Penalty in America: Current Research*, ed. Robert Bohm (Cincinnati, Ohio: Anderson, 1991), 89–100; Gennaro Vito, Deborah Wilson, and Edward Latessa, "Comparison of the Dead: Attributes and Outcomes of Furman-Commuted Death Row Inmates in Kentucky and Ohio," in *The Death Penalty in America: Current Research*, ed. Robert Bohm (Cincinnati, Ohio: Anderson, 1991), 101–112.

114. John Cochran, Mitchell Chamlin, and Mark Seth, "Deterrence or Brutalization? An Impact Assessment of Oklahoma's Return to Capital Punishment," *Criminology* 32 (1994): 107–134.

115. William Bailey, "Deterrence, Brutalization, and the Death Penalty: Another Examination of Oklahoma's Return to Capital Punishment," *Justice Quarterly* 36 (1998): 711–734.

116. Joseph Schumacher, "An International Look at the Death Penalty," *International Journal of Comparative and Applied Criminal Justice* 14 (1990): 307–315.

117. Don Terry, "California Prepares for Faster Execution Pace," *New York Times*, October 17, 1998, p. A7.

118. See, for example, Ernest Van Den Haag, *Punishing Criminals: Concerning a Very Old and Painful Question* (New York: Basic Books, 1975), 209–211; Walter Berns, "Defending the Death Penalty," *Crime and Delinquency* 26 (1980): 503–511.

119. Thoroddur Bjarnason and Michael Welch, "Father Knows Best: Parishes, Priests, and American Catholic Parishioners' Attitudes toward Capital Punishment," *Journal for the Scientific Study of Religion* 43 (2004): 103–118.

120. Franklin Zimring, *The Contradictions of American Capital Punishment* (London: Oxford University Press, 2003).

121. Vance McLaughlin and Paul Blackman, "Mass Legal Executions in Georgia," *Georgia Historical Quarterly* 88 (2004): 66–84.

122. Austin Sarat, "Innocence, Error, and the 'New Abolitionism': A Commentary," *Criminology and Public Policy* 4 (2005): 45–53.

123. *Furman v. Georgia*, 408 U.S. 238 (1972).

124. *Gregg v. Georgia*, 428 U.S. 153 (1976).

125. Ibid.

126. *Ring v. Arizona*, 536 U.S. 584 (2002).

127. *Coker v. Georgia*, 430 U.S. 349 (1977).

128. *Ford v. Wainwright*, 477 U.S. 399 (1986).

129. *Atkins v. Virginia*, 536 U.S. 304 (2002).

130. *Roper v. Simmons*, 543 U.S. 551 (2005).

131. *Kennedy v. Louisiana*, 128 S.Ct. 2641 (2008).

132. *Baze v. Rees*, 553 U.S. 35 (2008).

133. See also Adam. S. Goldstone, "The Death Penalty: How America's Highest Court Is Narrowing Its Application," *Criminal Law Brief* 4 (2009): 23–39.

134. *Furman v. Georgia*, 408 U.S. 238 (1972).

135. *Gregg v. Georgia*, 428 U.S. 153 (1976).

136. *Woodson v. North Carolina*, 428 U.S. 280 (1976).

137. *Coker v. Georgia*, 430 U.S. 349 (1977).

138. *Lockett v. Ohio*, 438 U.S. 586 (1978).

139. *Enmund v. Florida*, 458 U.S. 782 (1982).

140. *Glass v. Louisiana*, 471 U.S. 1080 (1985).

141. *Cabana v. Bullock*, 474 U.S. 376 (1986).

142. *Ford v. Wainwright*, 477 U.S. 399 (1986).

143. *Atkins v. Virginia*, 536 U.S. 304 (2002).

144. *Ring v. Arizona*, 536 U.S. 584 (2002).

145. *Roper v. Simmons*, 543 U.S. 551 (2005).

146. *Deck v. Missouri*, 544 U.S. 622 (2005).

147. *Oregon v. Guzek*, 546 U.S. 517 (2006).

148. *Baze v. Rees*, 553 U.S. 35 (2008).

149. *Kennedy v. Louisiana*, 128 S.Ct. 2641 (2008).

150. C. Lee Harrington, "A Community Divided: Defense Attorneys and the Ethics of Death Row Volunteering," *Law and Social Inquiry* 25 (2000): 849–881.

## PART FOUR

# CORRECTIONS

CORRECTIONS IS A SIGNIFICANT PART of the criminal justice system, employing more than half a million people and costing taxpayers close to $70 billion per year. Though challenging, correctional work can also be rewarding. Many correctional employees work in community corrections and attempt to help their clients turn their lives around without need for a term in a secure prison facility. Take, for instance, the career of probation officer Ann Beranis, who first became interested in the justice system while a student of clinical psychology. After receiving a master's degree, she decided to work as a probation officer. Ann finds the job both challenging and rewarding. She believes that most people she meets do not understand that community corrections is not about punishing offenders but about helping them change their thinking and behavior. She says, "Most of a probation officer's time is spent diagnosing the cause of an individual's antisocial behavior and then devising strategies for behavior change. It is challenging when clients are resistant to change. But while difficult, accurate assessments can be made and techniques applied to increase the client's motivation." Ann finds that probation officers must learn to tap into community resources, such as employment opportunities, and create strong partnerships with service providers. Her greatest reward on the job is seeing clients turn their lives around and leave probation with confidence in themselves and hope for the future. "It is also rewarding," she says, "knowing that [my] hard work helps crime victims and protects the community from further victimization."

Just as working in community corrections is a challenge, so is working in secure correctional facilities. Rachel Anita Jung, executive development program manager in the Arizona Department of Corrections, always knew she would be in a helping/public service profession. She channeled her basic curiosity about human behavior into a career in corrections, which has included stints as a jail screener, as a case manager for a treatment and referral program for substance abusers, and as an adult probation officer. Most recently, Rachel has managed executive development for the corrections staff. She relishes the opportunity to develop in-service programming that not only influences leadership practices but also affects the way staff interact with inmates throughout the entire state system. ■

*ANN BERANIS AND RACHEL ANITA JUNG have made a career in the contemporary correctional system, which is today charged with the supervision and treatment of 7 million people. The chapters in this section attempt to describe the operations, philosophies, and programs of this immense system. Chapter 13 looks at community sentences such as probation, alternative sanctions, and restorative justice. Chapters 14 and 15 explore secure correctional institutions, including prisons and jails. A number of important issues are analyzed, ranging from the development of new-generation jails to the reentry of prisoners into society.*

*"Most of a probation officer's time is spent diagnosing the cause of an individual's antisocial behavior and then devising strategies for behavior change. It is challenging when clients are resistant to change. But while difficult, accurate assessments can be made and techniques applied to increase the client's motivation. It is also rewarding, knowing that [my] hard work helps crime victims and protects the community from further victimization."*

# CHAPTER 13

# Community Sentences: Probation, Intermediate Sanctions, and Restorative Justice

## CHAPTER OBJECTIVES

1. Be familiar with the concept of community sentencing.
2. Know the history of community sentences.
3. Recognize the different types of probation sentences.
4. Be familiar with the rules of probation.
5. Discuss the organization and administration of probation services.
6. Define and discuss the term *"risk classification."*
7. Be familiar with the legal issues related to probation.
8. Debate the effectiveness of probation.
9. Know what is meant by intermediate sanctions.
10. Explain the concept of restorative justice and discuss its merits.

**W**ho can forget the image of pop singer Rihanna beaten and bruised after an altercation with her rapper boyfriend Chris Brown? Brown later released a statement saying, "Words cannot begin to express how sorry and saddened I am over what transpired." He continued to apologize for the incident on a number of national TV shows. After being charged with felony assault, the R&B singer pled guilty in a Los Angeles court on March 22, 2009, to one count of felony assault. Instead of going to prison, Brown received five years of supervised probation and six months of community labor. He was allowed to complete his community service in his home state of Virginia but would have to return to California for updates every three months. The judge also imposed a stay-away order, requiring that Brown and Rihanna stay at least 50 yards from each other, except at industry events, when the distance is reduced to 10 yards. Rihanna was also told that she would be held in violation of the order if she gets closer to Mr. Brown than its terms allow.[1] ■

Chris Brown's community sentence is neither uncommon nor reserved for celebrities. Community sentencing is the most common form of correctional treatment because it makes no sense to lock up nondangerous, repentant offenders in an overcrowded and dangerous correctional system, which can damage them and lock them into a life of crime. It may be both more effective and less costly to have them remain in the community under the supervision of a trained court officer, where they can receive treatment that will help them turn their lives around. Rehabilitation would be aided immensely if those who commit crime could be made to understand the problems their actions cause their family, friends, and community.

Although community sentencing has its benefits, some might argue that merely releasing someone like Chris Brown, a man who committed a violent assault, on his promise that he will never repeat his criminal behavior, is too lenient a sentence—that he "deserves' more punishment. Therefore, additional sanctions have been developed as an add-on to community sentencing; in this case, Chris Brown had to complete a term of community service. Considering the potential benefits and cost-effectiveness of community sentences, it is not surprising that a great variety of these alternative sanctions have been developed, ranging from traditional probation to house arrest and placement in community correctional centers. These newer forms of community sentences have the potential to become reasonable solutions to many of the economic and social problems faced by correctional administrators, as well as contributing to more positive outcomes for offenders:

- They are less costly than jail or prison sentences.
- They help the offender maintain family and community ties.
- They can be structured to maximize security and maintain public safety.
- They can be scaled in severity to correspond to the seriousness of the crime.
- They can feature restoration and reintegration rather than punishment and ostracism.
- They give convicted offenders a "second chance" that can enable them to resume a more productive lifestyle.[2]

In a tight economic environment, such as the one that now grips the United States, cost-effective programming such as probation makes economic sense. It is not surprising that a growing number of convicted offenders are being offered community sentences ranging from traditional probation to house arrest and placement in community correctional centers. Chris Brown's case shows that this approach can be successful: Rather than languishing in prison, he has continued his successful recording career, while also appearing in the 2010 film *Takers* and serving as its executive producer.

This chapter reviews these criminal sanctions. It begins by discussing the role of traditional probation as a community-based correctional practice. It then turns to a brief history of community sentencing. Then it focuses on so-called alternative or intermediate sanctions, such as intensive supervision, house arrest, and electronic monitoring. Finally, the chapter turns to a discussion of the concept of restorative justice and programs based on its principles.

## ▌ PROBATION

**Probation** is a criminal sentence that suspends or delays a correctional term in a prison or jail in return for a period of community supervision during which the probationers must abide by certain conditions set forth by the court, under the supervision of a probation officer.

The philosophy of probation today rests on the assumption that the typical offender is not a dangerous criminal or a "menace to society," but someone who has made a mistake and has the ability and potential to reform. When such

**probation**
A sentence entailing the conditional release of a convicted offender into the community under the supervision of the court (in the form of a probation officer), subject to certain conditions for a specified time. The conditions are usually similar to those of parole. (Note: Probation is a sentence, an alternative to incarceration; parole is administrative release from incarceration.) Violation of the conditions of probation may result in revocation of probation.

offenders are institutionalized instead of being granted community release, the prison community becomes their new reference point, they are forced to interact with hardened criminals, and they develop an "ex-con" label that interferes with successful adjustments to society—all conditions that both impede their successful rehabilitation and increase the likelihood of recidivism. For example, it is widely assumed that the opportunity to avoid stigma and negative labels can be critical to rehabilitation. When Ted Chiricos and his associates examined a Florida law that allows judges to withhold a formal adjudication of guilt for individuals who have been convicted of a felony and sentenced to probation, they found that those offenders who were able to avoid official criminal labels are significantly less likely to recidivate than those branded with official criminal labels.[3] Following this logic, it is evident that the stigma of a prison sentence would have far more devastating effects than a community sentence.

***EXTENT OF PROBATION*** Probation provides offenders with the opportunity to prove themselves, gives them a second chance, and allows them to be closely supervised by trained personnel who can help them reestablish proper forms of behavior in the community. Even dangerous offenders who might normally be sent to a penal institution can be successfully rehabilitated in the community if given the proper balance of supervision, treatment, and control.

Considering these benefits, it's not surprising that the probation population has undergone continual growth. Over 4.2 million people are currently on probation, and the adult probation population has grown significantly during the past decade (see Figure 13.1). Growth in the probation population has slowed in recent years to an average of 0.7% annually between 2003 and 2008 from an average of 2.5% annually between 2000 and 2003. Although expansion has slowed, more than 2 million people are still being placed on probation annually, and a slightly smaller number exit their probation sentence, causing an ongoing increase in the number of people on probation. Without probation, the correctional system would rapidly become even more overcrowded, overly expensive, and unmanageable.

# The History of Community Sentencing

How did this idea of community supervision and control begin? The roots of probation can be traced back to the traditions of the English common law. During the Middle Ages, judges who wished to spare deserving offenders from commonly used punishments such as torture, mutilation, and death used their power to grant

**FIGURE 13.1**
National Estimates of Probation Entries and Exits

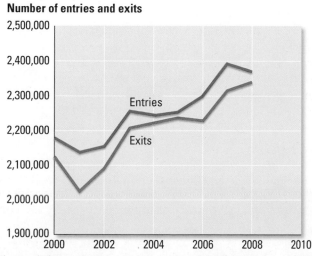

Source: Lauren Glaze and Thomas Bonczar, *Probation and Parole in the United States, 2008* (Washington, D.C: Bureau of Justice Statistics, 2009).

**judicial reprieve**
The common-law practice that allowed judges to suspend punishment so that convicted offenders could seek a pardon, gather new evidence, or demonstrate that they had reformed their behavior.

**recognizance**
The medieval practice of allowing convicted offenders to go unpunished if they agreed to refrain from any further criminal behavior.

 **CourseMate** For more information about **John Augustus**, visit the Criminal Justice CourseMate at CengageBrain.com, then access the "Web Links" for this chapter.

**probation rules**
Conditions or restrictions mandated by the court that must be obeyed by a probationer.

clemency and stays of execution. The common-law practice of **judicial reprieve** allowed judges to suspend punishment so that convicted offenders could seek a pardon, gather new evidence, or demonstrate that they had reformed their behavior. Similarly, the practice of **recognizance** enabled convicted offenders to remain free if they agreed to enter into a debt obligation with the state. The debt would have to be paid only if the offender was caught engaging in further criminal behavior. Sometimes sureties were required—these were people who made themselves responsible for the behavior of an offender after he was released.

*JOHN AUGUSTUS*  Early U.S. courts continued the practice of indefinitely suspending sentences of criminals who seemed deserving of a second chance, but it was John Augustus of Boston who is usually credited with originating the modern probation concept.[4] As a private citizen, Augustus began in 1841 to supervise offenders released to his custody by a Boston judge. Over an 18-year period, Augustus supervised close to 2,000 probationers and helped them get jobs and establish themselves in the community. Augustus had an amazingly high success rate, and few of his charges became involved in crime again.

In 1878, Augustus's work inspired the Massachusetts legislature to pass a law authorizing the appointment of a paid probation officer for the city of Boston. In 1880 probation was extended to other jurisdictions in Massachusetts, and by 1898 the probation movement had spread to the superior (felony) courts.[5] The Massachusetts experience was copied by Missouri (1887) and Vermont (1898), and soon after by most other states. In 1925, the federal government established a probation system for the U.S. district courts. The probation concept soon became the most widely used correctional mechanism in the United States.[6]

## Contemporary Probation

Although the term today has many meanings, probation usually entails a nonpunitive form of sentencing for convicted criminal offenders and delinquent youths, emphasizing maintenance in the community and treatment without institutionalization or other forms of punishment.[7] Once on probation, the offender is subject to certain rules and conditions that she or he must follow in order to remain in the community.

Most probation orders involve a contract between the court and the offender in which a prison or jail term is suspended and the probationer promises to obey a set of **probation rules**, or conditions, mandated by the court. If the rules

*David Jacobs pled guilty in 2004 to conspiring to distribute anabolic steroids and was sentenced to three years of probation. For more than a year, Jacobs operated a makeshift pharmaceutical lab out of the kitchen in his one-story suburban home in Plano, Texas. Each month, he said, he sold about a thousand of his own bottles of steroids, and another thousand kits of human growth hormone smuggled from China, to dealers across the United States. Among the dealers he supplied, Jacobs said, were two NFL players, who would then supply a handful of other NFL players with the banned substances. Was probation, rather than prison, an appropriate sentence for Jacobs?*

**EXHIBIT 13.1**

## California Rules of Court: Criteria Affecting Probation

Facts related to the crime:

1. The nature, seriousness, and circumstances of the crime as compared to other instances of the same crime
2. Whether the defendant was armed with or used a weapon
3. The vulnerability of the victim
4. Whether the defendant inflicted physical or emotional injury
5. The degree of monetary loss to the victim
6. Whether the defendant was an active or a passive participant
7. Whether the crime was committed because of an unusual circumstance, such as great provocation, that is unlikely to recur
8. Whether the manner in which the crime was carried out demonstrated criminal sophistication or professionalism on the part of the defendant
9. Whether the defendant took advantage of a position of trust or confidence to commit the crime

Facts related to the defendant:

1. Prior record of criminal conduct, whether as an adult or a juvenile, including the recency and frequency of prior crimes; and whether the prior record indicates a pattern of regular or increasingly serious criminal conduct
2. Prior performance on probation or parole and present probation or parole status
3. Willingness to comply with the terms of probation
4. Ability to comply with reasonable terms of probation as indicated by the defendant's age, education, health, mental faculties, history of alcohol or other substance abuse, family background and ties, employment and military service history, and other relevant factors
5. The likely effect of imprisonment on the defendant and his or her dependents
6. The adverse collateral consequences on the defendant's life resulting from the felony conviction
7. Whether the defendant is remorseful
8. The likelihood that, if not imprisoned, the defendant will be a danger to others

Source: California Rules of Court, Rule 4.414. Criteria affecting probation, www.courtinfo.ca.gov/rules/index.cfm?title=four&linkid=rule4_414 Accessed on April 15, 2010.

are violated (technical violation), or if the probationer commits a subsequent criminal offense (legal violation), then probation may be revoked. **Revocation** means that the community sentence is terminated and the original sentence of incarceration is enforced. If an offender on probation commits a second offense that is more serious than the first, he or she may also be indicted, tried, and sentenced on the second offense. However, probation may be revoked simply because the conditions of probation have not been met; it is not necessary for the offender to commit another crime.

## Awarding Probation

Probationary sentences may be granted by state and federal district courts and state superior (felony) courts. In some states, juries may recommend probation if the case meets certain legally regulated criteria (for example, if it falls within a certain class of offenses as determined by statute). Even in those jurisdictions that allow juries to recommend probation, judges have the final say in the matter and may grant probation at their discretion. In nonjury trials, probation is granted solely by judicial mandate. Some states have attempted to shape judicial discretion by creating guidelines for granting probation. California's probation statute directs judges to use the criteria set out in Exhibit 13.1 in deciding whether to award probation.

### PERSPECTIVES ON JUSTICE

#### Rehabilitation versus Crime Control

The revocation of probation represents the inherent conflict between its rehabilitation and its crime control aspects. On the one hand, probation is viewed as a second chance that enables deserving offenders to rehabilitate themselves in the community. On the other hand, probationers are convicted offenders who must obey stringent rules unless they want to be sent to prison. Rehabilitation advocates may not want to pull the revocation trigger unless it is absolutely necessary, whereas those who espouse a crime control approach may be less charitable to offenders who break probation rules.

**revocation**
An administrative act performed by a parole authority that removes a person from parole, or a judicial order by a court removing a person from parole or probation, in response to a violation on the part of the parolee or probationer.

**suspended sentence**
A prison term that is delayed while the defendant undergoes a period of community treatment. If the treatment is successful, the prison sentence is terminated.

More than half of all cases involve a direct sentence to probation without a prison term being suspended or delayed. In slightly more than 20 percent of sentences, judges formulate a prison sentence and then suspend it if the offender agrees to obey the rules of probation while living in the community (a **suspended sentence**).[8] Some offenders (about 10%) receive some form of split sentence in which they must first serve a jail term before being released on probation; in about 9 percent of cases, the imposition of the sentence is suspended and the case continued, without a finding, until further notice.

The term of a probationary sentence may simply extend to the limit of the suspended prison term, but in most cases the judge will devise a specific probationary period. For misdemeanors, probation usually extends for the entire period of the jail sentence, whereas felonies are more likely to warrant probationary periods that are actually shorter than the suspended prison sentences. The typical probation sentence in urban courts is about 38 months for violent offenses, 32 months for property offenses, and 32 months for drug crimes.[9]

## Probation Eligibility

Although originally conceived as a way to provide a second chance for young offenders who committed nonserious crimes, probation today is also a means of reducing the population overload in an overcrowded and underfunded correctional system. Probation is not restricted to petty or first-time criminals: Most people convicted of felonies do receive some form of incarceration, in either prison or jail, but more than 30 percent of first-time felons are sentenced to probation, and about 17 percent of repeat felony offenders are given community sentences.[10] This means that 17 percent of criminal defendants convicted of multiple prior felonies still receive a community sentence rather than having to spend time behind bars!

Thus there are two distinct sides to probation, one involving the treatment and rehabilitation of nondangerous offenders deserving of a "second chance," and the other involving the supervision and control of criminals who might otherwise be incarcerated.

## Conditions of Probation

When granting probation, the court sets down certain conditions or rules of behavior that the probationer is bound to obey. Although probation officers themselves can later set some conditions, courts have typically ruled that the most restrictive ones must be approved by the sentencing judge and that probation officers' instructions or directives cannot require the defendant to adhere to new requirements of supervision about which he or she did not have reasonable notice.[11]

Some conditions (such as "Do not leave the jurisdiction") are standard and are applied in every probation case, but the sentencing judge usually has broad discretion to set specific conditions on a case-by-case basis. Sometimes an individual probationer is given specific rules related to his or her particular circumstances, such as the requirement to enroll in an anger management or drug treatment program, make a personal apology to the victim, or have no contact with his or her ex-spouse.[12] A presiding judge may not impose capricious or cruel conditions, of course, such as requiring an offender to make restitution out of proportion to the seriousness of the criminal act.[13] Judges may, however, legally impose restrictions tailored to fit the probationer's individual needs and/or to protect society from additional harm.

## Probation Conditions in the Internet Age

Because the personal computer and the Internet are commonplace, probation orders now account for Internet use, including entry into chat rooms, visits to adult entertainment websites, purchasing of drugs via the Web, and so on. One area of concern is that the Internet has made it easier for sex offenders to search for pornography sites—or their next victim. As a result, probationers may be ordered either to avoid certain sites or to allow probation officers to monitor what they are viewing. Probation authorities have worked with social networking sites such as MySpace to identify and remove registered sex offenders and have asked the sites to turn over the identities of registered sex offenders who may be using the service.[14] This approach is not without controversy. Court rulings say Internet use is so broadly ingrained in today's society that restricting access would be like barring individuals from all telephone use because they used the telephone to commit fraud.

The American Probation and Parole Association believes that by checking an offender's hard drive, the supervising officer can create a baseline for helping the offender get proper treatment. The computer check is now equated to a drug test: Offenders may beat a particular drug test, but anyone who is still a user will eventually get caught. The same principle applies to Internet offenders: They might get around monitoring a couple of times, but not forever.[15]

Whereas the Probation and Parole Association believes that monitoring the Internet habits of offenders can be productive, the American Civil Liberties Union is fighting such practices on the grounds that they violate an individual's right to privacy. One successful ACLU effort occurred in Indiana, where a federal judge ruled unconstitutional a law that allowed police to monitor the Internet use of sex offenders and also required convicted offenders to install, on their computer, software that enabled police to keep tabs on their Internet activity 24 hours a day, seven days a week. In its decision, the Court stated, "The new law forces an unconstitutional choice upon these plaintiffs. They must choose now between committing a new crime by refusing to consent and giving up their Fourth Amendment rights to privacy and security in their homes, their 'papers,' and their effects. The unprecedented new law, however well-intentioned it may be, violates the Fourth Amendment rights of the plaintiff class, who have completed their sentences and are no longer on probation, parole, or any other kind of court supervision."[16]

## Administration of Probation Services

The United States has approximately 2,000 adult probation agencies. More than half are associated with a state-level agency. In the rest of the states, probation is primarily a local responsibility; probation departments in these jurisdictions are housed within the local court and controlled by judicial authorities. About 30 states combine probation and parole supervision into a single agency. A number of states have also permitted the private sector to administer probation supervision.

*STATE VS. LOCAL CONTROL* There is an ongoing debate over the most effective method of probation administration. Some experts believe that probation should be a local institution and that state involvement should be limited to providing financial support, setting standards, and arranging training courses.

One of the most persuasive arguments for local administration is that citizens and agencies of the community more readily support programs that are open to their participation and are responsive to local needs and problems. Locally controlled departments tend to be smaller and more flexible, able to adjust more quickly to change, and less encumbered by bureaucratic rigidity.

Although these arguments are persuasive, some policymakers believe that

- A state-administered probation system can set standards of service, thereby ensuring uniformity of procedures, policies, and services.

- A larger agency can make more effective use of funds and personnel.

- Greater efficiency in the disposition of resources is possible when all probation officers are state employees.

*PROBATION DEPARTMENTAL ORGANIZATION* Whether it be state or locally controlled and administered, the typical probation department is situated in a single court district, such as juvenile, superior, district, or municipal court.

# CAREERS IN CRIMINAL JUSTICE

# *Probation Officer*

## *Duties and Characteristics of the Job*

Probation officers monitor offenders' behavior through personal contact with the offenders and their families. Another part of the probation officer's job involves working in the courts. The number of cases a probation officer has depends on both the counseling needs of offenders and the risks they pose to society. Probation officers may find their jobs stressful because they work with convicted criminals and interact with many other individuals, including family members and friends of their clients, who may be angry, upset, or uncooperative. Although stress makes these jobs difficult at times, the work also can be rewarding. Many probation officers gain personal satisfaction from counseling members of their community and helping them become productive citizens.

## *Job Outlook*

Jobs for probation officers are more plentiful in urban areas. There are also more jobs in states that have many men and women on probation.

## *Salary*

Median annual wages of probation officers and correctional treatment specialists is now about $45,910. The middle 50 percent earned between $35,990 and $60,430. The lowest 10 percent earned less than $29,490, and the highest 10 percent earned more than $78,210. Median annual wages for probation officers and correctional treatment specialists employed in state government were $46,580; those employed in local government earned $46,420. Higher wages tend to be found in urban areas

## *Opportunities*

Employment of probation officers and correctional treatment specialists is projected to grow about 19 percent between 2008 and 2018, faster than the average for all occupations. Overcrowding in prisons also has swelled the probation population as judges and prosecutors search for alternative forms of punishment, such as electronic monitoring and day reporting centers. Although community supervision is far less expensive than keeping offenders in prison, a change in political trends toward more imprisonment and away from community supervision could result in reduced employment opportunities. Other openings will result from the need to replace workers who leave the occupation permanently—including the large number expected to retire over the next several years.

## *Qualifications*

Prospective probation officers must be in good physical condition and be emotionally stable. Most agencies require applicants to be at least 21 years old and, for federal employment, not older than 37. Those convicted of felonies may not be eligible for employment in these occupations. Probation officers need strong writing skills because of the large number of reports they must prepare. Familiarity with computers is often required. Job candidates also should be knowledgeable about laws and regulations pertaining to corrections.

## *Education and Training*

Educational requirements for probation officers vary by state, but a bachelor's degree in social work or criminal justice is usually required. Some states require probation officers to have one year of work experience in a related field or one year of graduate study in criminal justice, social work, or psychology. Most probation officers must complete a training program and work as trainees for about six months. Candidates who successfully complete the training period obtain a permanent position. Some states require applicants to take a certification test during or after training. Applicants usually must also pass written, oral, psychological, and physical examinations.

Source: Bureau of Labor Statistics, *Occupational Outlook Handbook, 2010–11 Edition* "Probation Officers and Correctional Treatment Specialists," www.bls.gov/oco/ocos265.htm (accessed April 15, 2010).

---

The relationship between the department and court personnel (especially the judge) is extremely close.

In the typical department, the chief probation officer (CPO) sets policy, supervises hiring, determines training needs, and may personally discuss sentencing with the judge or even make sentencing recommendations. In state-controlled departments, some of the CPO's duties are mandated by the central office; training guidelines, for example, may be determined at the state level. If the department is locally controlled, the CPO has great discretion in the management of the department.

The line staff, or the probation officers (POs), may be in direct and personal contact with the entire supervisory staff, or they may be independent of the CPO and answer mainly to the assistant chiefs. Line staff perform the following major functions:

- Supervise or monitor cases assigned to them to ensure that the rules of probation are followed.

- Attempt to rehabilitate their cases through specialized treatment techniques.

- Investigate the lives of convicted offenders to enable the court to make intelligent sentencing decisions.

- Occasionally collect fines due the court or oversee the collection of delinquent payments, such as child support.

- Interview complainants and defendants to determine whether criminal action should be taken, whether cases can be decided informally, whether diversion should be advocated, and so on. This last procedure, called **intake**, is common in juvenile probation.

**intake**
The process in which a probation officer settles cases at the initial appearance before the onset of formal criminal proceedings. Also, the process in which a juvenile referral is received and a decision is made to file a petition in the juvenile court, release the juvenile, or refer the juvenile elsewhere.

How probation officers carry out these tasks may be a function of their self-image and professional orientation. Some POs view themselves as "social workers" and maintain a treatment orientation; their goal is to help offenders adjust in the community. Others are "law enforcers" who are more concerned with supervision, control, and public safety. Ironically, younger officers appear to be more control- and safety-oriented than older officers, who are more likely to embrace the rehabilitation ideal. As these older officers retire, probation may adopt a more conservative focus.[17]

Like other criminal justice professionals, probation officers have a great deal of personal discretion when they carry out their monitoring and supervision duties. They may choose to ignore an infraction, issue a warning, or take some sort of formal action. A recent survey by Mark Jones and John Kerbs finds that probation officers are more likely to take formal action—that is, seek to revoke probation—when their client commits a new offense or directly disobeys an officer's verbal warnings to avoid associations with a codefendant or refuses to attend substance abuse treatment after testing positively for marijuana.[18]

An officer's use of discretion and her or his supervision style are influenced by personal values, caseload pressure and makeup, and the probation department's general policies and orientation.[19] A recent analysis of probationers in California shows that the probation population is getting older, more experienced, and more violent. Since 1980, the proportion of violent offenders in the California probation population has increased 36 percent, the proportion of drug offenders has increased 15 percent, and property offenders as a share of the probation population have declined 38 percent.[20] The change in caseload composition has influenced the daily activities of supervising officers. New York City probation officers are now authorized to carry handguns in order to enhance the supervision of their clients, the majority of whom are felons. Carrying weapons became necessary because New York probation officers are required to spend more time visiting their clients in their neighborhoods and homes. Other departments have armed their officers as the number of probationers has increased and the officers' duties have become more dangerous.[21] It is not surprising, then, that research shows that many probation officers undergo job-related stress, especially those who feel educationally underprepared.[22]

Despite these problems, being a probation officer is a highly sought-after career. For more on a career as a probation officer, see the Careers in Criminal Justice feature.

## Duties of Probation Officers

Staff officers in probation departments are usually charged with five primary tasks: investigation, intake, diagnosis, treatment supervision, and risk classification.

# CRIMINAL JUSTICE AND TECHNOLOGY

## Monitoring Probationers with Technology

Technology is now being used to improve the effectivenes and efficiency of probation supervision. A number of new methods are now being tried.

### Electronic Reporting

To improve efficiency, probation departments are allowing clients to report in without appearing personally. New York City is now employing a kiosk system that allows low-risk offenders to report in electronically, using hand biometrics as identification, instead of meeting with the officer assigned. This innovation helps probation officers to focus their attention on the high-risk offenders, automates the offender reporting process, and also permits real-time information exchange. Designed for flexibility and portability, the kiosk system can be used as a stand-alone system or as part of a larger case management system. Currently, 22,700 probationers report to kiosks located in department offices citywide.

### Sleep Pattern Analysis

Sleep pattern analysis technology, already used by some jurisdictions, can provide preliminary indications of substance abuse and help community corrections officials determine whether more testing is warranted. Sleep disruption due to substance abuse can occur in several ways, including altering the sequence and duration of various stages of sleep, total sleep time, and the amount of time needed to fall asleep. The technology consists of a small device, secured to an offender's wrist with a tamper-evident band, that measures sleep quality by recording gross motor activity. Analysis of the data collected may indicate sleep disorders, which could be caused by substance abuse. The device passively collects and records body movement information, and when the offender reports to the probation office or drug court, data can be downloaded and analyzed in a matter of minutes. If data analysis indicates possible substance abuse, the offender can be required to immediately provide a urine specimen for further testing.

### Infrared Spectroscopy

Currently in field tests, this technology seeks to modify a glucose-monitoring device into an alcohol-testing product. The device uses a light source, an optical detector, and spectrometers to conduct chemical analysis of tissue and measure alcohol levels. Results, available

---

**pre-sentence investigation**
An investigation performed by a probation officer attached to a trial court after the conviction of a defendant. The report contains information about the defendant's background, education, previous employment, and family; his or her own statement concerning the offense; prior criminal record; interviews with neighbors or acquaintances; and his or her mental and physical condition (that is, information that would not be made public record in the case of guilty plea or that would be inadmissible as evidence at a trial but could be influential and important at the sentencing stage).

**INVESTIGATION** In the investigative stage, the supervising probation officer accumulates important information on the background and activities of the offender being considered for probation. This **pre-sentence investigation** serves as the basis for sentencing and controls whether the convicted defendant will be granted community release or sentenced to secure confinement. In the event that the offender is placed on probation, the investigation becomes useful as a tool to shape treatment and supervision efforts.

The style and content of pre-sentence investigations may vary among jurisdictions and also among individual POs within the same jurisdiction. Some departments require voluminous reports covering every aspect of the defendant's life; other departments, which may be rule oriented, require that officers stick to the basic facts, such as the defendant's age, race, sex, and previous offense record. Each department also has its own standards for pre-sentence investigations.

At the conclusion of most pre-sentence investigations, a recommendation is made. the presiding judge that reflects the department's sentencing posture on the case Among the most critical factors that contribute to a recommendation of community treatment are the probationer's demeanor, amenability to treatment, and willingness to abide by both legal and probationary rules.[23] Under normal circumstances, the department's recommendation is accepted by the judge when they hand down the actual sentence.

**INTAKE** Probation officers who conduct intake interviews may be looking to settle the case without the necessity of a court hearing. The probation officer works with all parties involved in the case—offender, victim, police officer, and so on—to design an equitable resolution of the case. If the intake process is successful, the within just one minute, have accuracy comparable to that of Breathalyzers and blood tests. The technology uses infrared spectroscopy to make a nonintrusive examination of a subject's inner forearm; the device also could be modified to examine other parts of the body. The analysis process incorporates a biometric component that identifies an individual's unique tissue structure and tissue chemistry, thus ensuring accurate identification of the person being tested.

### Driver Monitoring and Surveillance

This surveillance technology consists of a pair of ankle bracelets that collect data on the unique patterns of movement associated with foot-to-brake, foot-to-gas-pedal, acceleration, and deceleration of a motor vehicle. Data analysis can then indicate whether and when a subject has been driving. In the case of an individual whose license is restricted, rather than suspended, it can also indicate whether the driving took place during a prohibited time (such as outside the normal workday). The bracelets can store and process data for up to 30 days, allowing a community corrections officer to upload data during a scheduled monthly visit. This technology would help community corrections professionals deal with a widespread and long-standing problem, because research indicates that up to 75 percent of all drivers with suspended or restricted licenses continue to drive.

### Long-Distance Alcohol Monitoring

It is possible to monitor probationer alcohol intake through transdermal measuring devices—the Wrist Transdermal Alcohol Sensor (WrisTAS) and the Secure Continuous Remote Alcohol Monitor (SCRAM) bracelet. Worn by the probationers, these devices detect alcohol from continuous samples of vaporous or insensible perspiration (sweat) collected from the air above the skin and transmit that data via the Internet. The SCRAM device achieved noteriety in California when actress Lindsay Lohan wore the alcohol-monitoring ankle bracelet in 2007 after her release from a rehabilitation clinic.

### Critical Thinking

Would you place limits on the electronic monitoring of probationers? On the one hand, some of these methods seem awfully intrusive. On the other hand, should community safety be sacrificed in order to maintain an individual's dignity and privacy? After all, probationers have been convicted of a crime, sometimes even of a felony offense.

Source: National Law Enforcement and Corrections Technology Center, "The Greening of Probation," *Tech Beat*, Fall 2009 (accessed April 31, 2010), http://www.justnet.org/TechBeat%20Files/The%20 Greening%20of%20Probation.pdf National Law Enforcement and Corrections Technology Center, "Community Corrections Directions," *Tech Beat*, Spring 2007, www.justnet.org/TechBeat%20Files/ CommunityCorrections.pdf (accessed April 31, 2010).

probation officer may settle the case without further court action, recommend restitution or other compensation, or recommend unofficial or informal probation. If an equitable solution cannot be found, the case is filed for a court hearing.

*DIAGNOSIS*  In order to select appropriate treatment modes, probation officers—using their training in counseling, social work, or psychology—analyze the probationer's character, attitudes, and behavior. The goal of diagnosis is to develop a personality profile that may be helpful in treating the offender. An effective diagnosis integrates all that has been learned about the individual, organized in such a way as to provide a means for the establishment of future treatment goals. The emergence of standardized diagnostic tools and tests has diminished the probationer officer's individual role in diagnosis. To some commentators, this is problematic because it removes the human element from diagnosis and treatment.[24]

*TREATMENT SUPERVISION*  After the diagnosis has been completed, the probation staff is asked to carry out the treatment supervision, a program of therapy designed to help the client deal with the problems that resulted in her or his antisocial behavior. In years past, the probation staff had primary responsibility for supervision and treatment, but today's large caseloads limit opportunities for hands-on treatment; most probation treatment efforts rely on community resources.

A PO who discovers that a client has a drinking problem may place the client in a detoxification program. A spousal abuser may be required to enroll in an anger management or drug treatment program, to make a personal apology to the victim, or to have no contact with his or her ex-spouse.[25] In the case of juvenile delinquency, a PO may work with teachers and other school officials to help a young offender stay in school. The need for treatment is critical, and the vast size of probation caseloads, especially the large numbers of narcotics abusers, can be a formidable challenge to community-based substance abuse programs.[26]

Effective supervision is critical for another reason: It protects the probation department from civil liability. Failure to supervise probationers adequately and determine whether they are obeying the rules of probation can result in the officer and the department being held legally liable for civil damages. If, for example, a probationer with a history of child molestation attacks a child while working as a school custodian, the probationer's case supervisor could be held legally responsible for failing to check on the probationer's employment activities.[27] The accompanying Criminal Justice and Technology feature describes how probation officers are using technology to monitor offender activities.

**risk classification**
Classifying probationers so that they may receive an appropriate level of treatment and control.

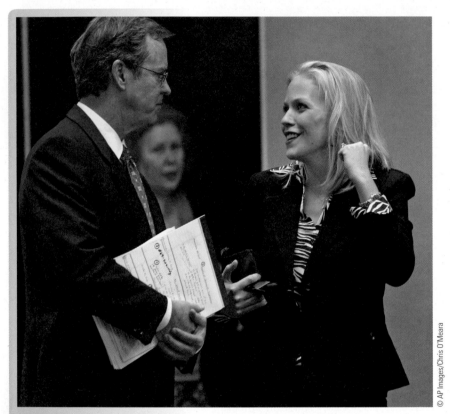

Risk classification is used to determine the level of control imposed on probationers in the community. Some probationers are more dangerous and require greater security than others. Here former schoolteacher Debra Lafave raises her fist as she talks with her attorney John Fitzgibbons during a probation violation hearing on January 10, 2008, at the Hillsborough County Courthouse in Tampa, Florida. Circuit Judge J. Rogers Padgett found Lafave guilty of violating her probation by talking to a 17-year-old former coworker about sex, but she faced no additional penalties. She was originally arrested in 2002 for having sex with a 14-year-old student. Would you consider someone like Lafave a dangerous person in need of close supervision?

**RISK CLASSIFICATION** As part of clients' entry into probation, an assessment is made about the risk level they pose to the community and themselves. Based on this assessment, offenders are assigned to specific supervision levels, where a variety of tools and techniques will be applied in an attempt to manage the risk they pose to the community and to themselves. Because more than 4 million people must now be managed, experts argue that risk assessment is the single most important decision being made by probation officers today.[28]

Probationers typically receive a **risk classification** that assigns them to a level and type of supervision on the basis of their particular needs and the risks they present to the community. Some clients may receive frequent (intensive) supervision in which they are contacted by their supervising probation officer almost every day, whereas other, minor offenders are assigned to minimum monitoring by a PO. A number of risk assessment classification approaches are used, but most employ such objective measures as the offender's age, employment status, drug abuse history, prior felony convictions, and number of address changes in the year before sentencing. Some departments are using standardized tests to predict failure and assign treatment. One of the most widely advertised systems is the Level of Service Inventory—Revised (or LSI-R), which was first developed in Canada and has now been adopted by a number of U.S. correctional agencies. The LSI-R consists of 54 items that are sorted into the following substantive areas, which are believed to be related to future criminal behavior.

1. Criminal history (10 items)
2. Education and employment (10 items)
3. Financial (2 items)
4. Family and marital (4 items)
5. Accommodations (3 items)
6. Leisure and recreation (2 items)
7. Companions (5 items)

8. Alcohol and drugs (9 items)

9. Emotional and personal (5 items)

10. Attitude and orientation (4 items)[29]

Developing effective risk assessment instruments takes on greater importance when we consider that probation is now routinely employed with felons, even some who have been convicted of extremely violent crimes such as rape and murder. Data shows that many of these clients have a significant likelihood of killing or being killed and that many murders in the United States are committed by people who are community corrections clients. It is critical to identify and treat these at-risk clients, who may be suffering from emotional disorders such as depression and post-traumatic stress disorder.[30]

Evaluations of risk assessment instruments show that when they are used properly, they can be highly valid and effective.[31] However, there is room for further improvement. Simpler, easier-to-score measurement devices should be created. And because some communities present greater risks than others, the neighborhood where probationers reside must be considered in their individual risk classification.[32] Finally, the validity of measurement devices must be improved. Can they really predict dangerousness and future crime? Or are they merely indicators of the probability that the client will succeed on probation?[33]

## Legal Rights of Probationers

What are the legal rights of probationers? How has the U.S. Supreme Court set limits on the probation process? A number of important legal issues surround probation, one set involving the civil rights of probationers and another involving the rights of probationers during the revocation process.

*CIVIL RIGHTS*    The Court has ruled that probationers have a unique status and therefore are entitled to fewer constitutional protections than other citizens.

- *Minnesota v. Murphy* (1984). In *Murphy,* the Supreme Court ruled that the probation officer–client relationship is not confidential, as physician–patient and attorney–client relationships are. If a probationer admits to committing a crime to his or her probation supervisor, that information can be passed on to the police or district attorney. Furthermore, the *Murphy* decision held that a probation officer could even use trickery or psychological pressure to get information and turn it over to the police.[34]

- *Griffin v. Wisconsin* (1987). In *Griffin,* the Supreme Court held that a probationer's home may be searched without a warrant on the grounds that probation departments "have in mind the welfare of the probationer" and must "respond quickly to evidence of misconduct."[35]

- *United States v. Knights* (2001). In *Knights,* the Supreme Court upheld the legality of a warrantless search of a probationer's home for the purposes of gathering criminal evidence. The Court ruled that the home of a probationer who is suspected of a crime can be searched without a warrant if (a) the search is based on reasonable suspicion that he had committed another crime while on probation and (b) a condition of his previous probation was that he would submit to searches. The Court reasoned that the government's interest in preventing crime, combined with *Knights*'s diminished expectation of privacy, required only a *reasonable suspicion* to make the search legal, rather than a violation of the probationer's Fourth Amendment right to privacy.[36]

*REVOCATION RIGHTS*    During the course of a probationary term, a violation of the rules or terms of probation or the committing of a new crime can result in probation being revoked, at which time the offender may be placed in an institution. Revocation is not often an easy decision, because it conflicts with the treatment philosophy of many probation departments.

**CourseMate** For more information about **using risk assessment instruments to guide justice decisions**, visit the Criminal Justice CourseMate at CengageBrain.com, then access the "Web Links" for this chapter.

**CourseMate** For more information about **the LIS-R**, visit the Criminal Justice CourseMate at CengageBrain. com, then access the "Web Links" for this chapter.

When revocation is chosen, the offender is notified, and a formal hearing is scheduled. If the charges against the probationer are upheld, the offender can then be placed in an institution to serve the remainder of the sentence. Most departments will not revoke probation unless the offender commits another crime or seriously violates the rules of probation.

Because placing a person on probation implies that probation will continue unless the probationer commits some major violation, the defendant has been given certain procedural due process rights at this stage of the criminal process. In some significant decisions, the U.S. Supreme Court provided procedural safeguards to apply at proceedings to revoke probation (and parole):

■ *Mempa v. Rhay* (1967). In *Mempa,* the Court unanimously held that a probationer was constitutionally entitled to counsel in a revocation-of-probation proceeding where the imposition of sentence had been suspended.[37]

■ *Morrissey v. Brewer* (1972). In *Morrissey*, the Supreme Court required an informal inquiry to determine whether there was probable cause to believe the arrested parolee had violated the conditions of parole, as well as a formal revocation hearing with minimum due process requirements. Because the revocations of probation and parole are similar, the standards in the *Morrissey* case affected the probation process as well.[38]

■ *Gagnon v. Scarpelli* (1973). In *Gagnon*, the Supreme Court held that both probationers and parolees have a constitutionally limited right to counsel in revocation proceedings.[39] This means that during a probation revocation hearing, the defendant must be given counsel if it is required for an effective defense. A judge may deny counsel under some circumstances, such as when probation will be continued despite the violation. The *Gagnon* case can be viewed as a step forward in the application of constitutional safeguards to the correctional process. The provision of counsel helped establish some control over the unlimited discretion exercised in the past by probation and parole personnel in revocation proceedings.

■ *Beardon v. Georgia* (1983). In *Beardon*, the U.S. Supreme Court ruled that a judge cannot revoke a defendant's probation for failure to pay a fine and make restitution, unless the probation is somehow responsible for the failure or the alternative forms of punishment are inadequate to meet the state's interest in punishment and deterrence. *Beardon* involved a Georgia defendant who was unable to pay his restitution because he lost his job and could not find another. The trial court revoked probation, and the defendant was sent to prison. On appeal, the Supreme Court ruled that if a state determines a fine or restitution to be appropriate and an adequate penalty for the crime, it may not thereafter imprison a defendant solely because he or she lacks the resources to pay, because this would be a violation of a probationer's right to equal protection.[40]

■ *United States v. Granderson* (1994). In *Granderson*, the Supreme Court helped clarify what can happen to a probationer whose community sentence is revoked. Granderson was eligible for a 6-month prison sentence but instead was given 60 months of probation. When he tested positive for drugs, his probation was revoked. The statute he was sentenced under required that he serve one-third of his original sentence in prison. When the trial court sentenced him to 20 months, he appealed. Was his original sentence 6 months or 60 months? The Supreme Court found that it would be unfair to force a probationer to serve more time in prison than he would have served if originally incarcerated and ruled that the proper term should have been one-third of the 6 months, or 2 months.[41]

## How Successful Is Probation?

Probation is the most commonly used alternative sentence for a number of reasons: It is humane, it helps offenders maintain community and family ties, and

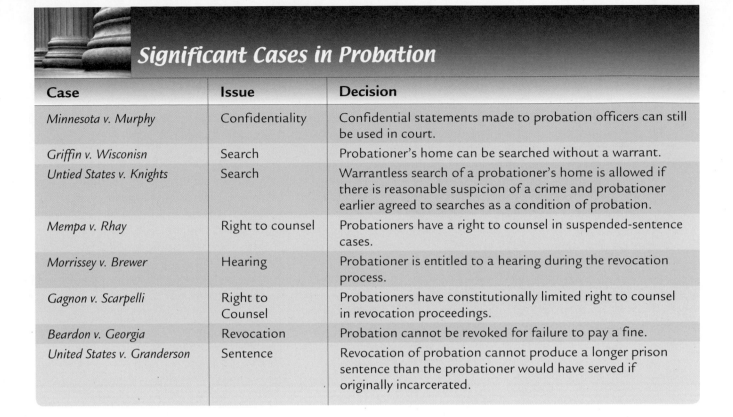

## Significant Cases in Probation

| Case | Issue | Decision |
|------|-------|----------|
| *Minnesota v. Murphy* | Confidentiality | Confidential statements made to probation officers can still be used in court. |
| *Griffin v. Wisconisn* | Search | Probationer's home can be searched without a warrant. |
| *Untied States v. Knights* | Search | Warrantless search of a probationer's home is allowed if there is reasonable suspicion of a crime and probationer earlier agreed to searches as a condition of probation. |
| *Mempa v. Rhay* | Right to counsel | Probationers have a right to counsel in suspended-sentence cases. |
| *Morrissey v. Brewer* | Hearing | Probationer is entitled to a hearing during the revocation process. |
| *Gagnon v. Scarpelli* | Right to Counsel | Probationers have constitutionally limited right to counsel in revocation proceedings. |
| *Beardon v. Georgia* | Revocation | Probation cannot be revoked for failure to pay a fine. |
| *United States v. Granderson* | Sentence | Revocation of probation cannot produce a longer prison sentence than the probationer would have served if originally incarcerated. |

it is cost-effective. Incarcerating an inmate typically costs over $25,000 per year, whereas probation costs about $2,000 per year.

Although unquestionably inexpensive, is probation successful? If most probation orders fail, the costs of repeated criminality would certainly outweigh the cost savings of a probation sentence. National data indicates that almost 60 percent of probationers successfully complete their probationary sentence, whereas about 40 percent are rearrested, violate probation rules, or abscond.[42]

Most revocations occur for technical violations during the first three months of the probation sentence.[43] Studies of federal probationers show even better results (30 percent failure rate).[44] Although a 30 to 40 percent failure rate may seem high, even the most serious criminals who receive probation are less likely to recidivate than those who are sent to prison or jail for committing similar crimes.[45] The following Evidence-Based Justice feature examines the utility of community-based treatment.

> **CourseMate** For more information about the **Los Angeles County Probation Department**, visit the Criminal Justice CourseMate at CengageBrain.com, then access the "Web Links" for this chapter.

## How Successful Is Felony Probation?

Many convicted felons receive probation, including rapists and murderers. How do these more dangerous criminals fair in their community sentence? Are they as successful as petty criminals and/or misdemeanants? In a now classic study, Joan Petersilia and her colleagues at the RAND Corporation, a private think tank, traced 1,672 men convicted of felonies who had been granted probation in Los Angeles and Alameda Counties in California.[46] Petersilia found that 1,087 (65%) were rearrested; of those rearrested, 853 (51%) were convicted; and of those convicted, 568 (34%) were sentenced to jail or prison. Of the probationers who had new charges filed against them, 75 percent were charged with burglary, theft, robbery, and other predatory crimes; 18 percent were convicted of serious violent crimes.

Upon further analysis, Petersilia found that the crimes and criminal records of about 25 percent of all probationers are indistinguishable from those of offenders who go to prison. Many people given prison sentences could just as easily have been granted community sentences, and vice versa. Although the felony

> **CourseMate** For more information about **felony probation in Florida**, visit the Criminal Justice CourseMate at CengageBrain.com, then access the "Web Links" for this chapter.

## EVIDENCE-BASED JUSTICE

# Prison versus Probation?

Probation advocates believe that treating offenders in the community may be more effective than institutional programs. Is that wishful thinking, or does community treatment more effectively reduce the chances of recidivism? To test this hypothesis, Christopher Krebs, Kevin Strom, Willem Koetse, and Pamela Lattimore carefully compared treatment outcomes of large groups of drug-involved offenders in the state of Florida. Three groups were involved: (a) those who received community-based treatment, (b) those who received institutional treatment, and (c) those who received no treatment. Using sophisticated analytic tools, Krebs found that compared with no treatment, nonresidential drug treatment reduced the chances for a subsequent arrest for a felony by 22 percent. Institutional treatment, which cost three times as much as community-based treatment, did not have similar success, and inmates showed no particular improvement from their institutional drug treatment program. Considering that there are more than 4 million people now on probation, many of whom have substance abuse problems, the use of community-based treatment can result in significant public safety and justice system cost savings at far less cost than either doing nothing or locking up offenders. At a time of declining budgets and high caseloads, the effectiveness of relatively inexpensive community treatment can be critical.

Source: Christopher Krebs, Kevin Strom, Willem Koetse, and Pamela Lattimore, "The Impact of Residential and Nonresidential Drug Treatment on Recidivism among Drug-Involved Probationers: A Survival Analysis," *Crime & Delinquency* 55 (2009): 442–471.

---

probation failure rate that Petersilia found seems disturbingly high, her findings still support the continued use of probation because people with similar criminal backgrounds who are sentenced to incarceration are more likely to recidivate than the community treatment group.[47]

## Probation Success and Failure

What does it take to succeed on probation and what causes people to fail? Stability helps: Probationers who are married with children, have lived in the area for two or more years, and are adequately employed are the most likely to be successful on probation.[48] Conviction offense also matters. People with long histories of substance abuse do not fare well; surprisingly, people convicted on sexual offenses seem to do quite well on probation.[49] Among female probationers, those who have stable marriages, are better educated, and are employed full-time or part-time are more likely to complete probation orders.[50]

Not all probation sentences are successful, and many probationers recidivate. Probationers bring with them a lot of emotional baggage that may reduce their chances of successful rehabilitation. Many are felons who have long histories of offending; more than 75 percent of all probationers have had prior convictions. Others suffer from a variety of social and psychological disabilities. Surveys indicate that almost 20 percent suffer from mental illness.[51] The increase in the use of probation for felony offenders means that caseloads now include significant numbers of serious sex offenders, a group that demands a great deal of attention.[52] Ironically, many failures are linked to probationers' avoiding required treatment programs originally created to help them stay out of trouble and succeed on probation.[53]

Whether mentally ill or mentally sound, probationers are likely to have grown up in households in which family members were incarcerated, so they have lived part of their lives in foster homes or state institutions. Many had parents or guardians who abused drugs; they also suffered high rates of physical and sexual abuse. They are now unemployed or underemployed, and almost half are substance abusers. Considering their harsh and abusive backgrounds and their current economic distress and psychological stresses and strains, it is not surprising that many find it difficult to comply with the rules of probation and forgo criminal activity. As for individual characteristics, young males who are unemployed or who have a very low income, a prior criminal record, and a history of instability are most likely to be rearrested.[54]

## The Future of Probation

Some critics are worried that probation is now undergoing a shift from traditional casework methods that featured diagnosis and treatment to an emphasis on risk assessment and control.[55] To improve the effectiveness of probation even more (what Petersilia calls "reforming, reinvesting, and restructuring"), several steps appear to be necessary.[56] More financial resources must be provided to implement quality programming for appropriate probation target groups. The credibility of probation with the public and the judiciary must be improved. Support is needed from a public that views the probation sanction as sufficiently punitive to make up for the harm of criminal behavior and from a judiciary that is convinced offenders should be held accountable for their behavior. A number of initiatives are now ongoing or being suggested that may help shape the future of probation:

© Mark Ralston/AFP/Getty Images

*People fail on probation for many reasons. Many are drug and alcohol abusers who find it difficult to confront their habits. On July 20, 2010, Lindsay Lohan arrives at the courthouse in Beverly Hills, California, with her lawyer Shawn Chapman Holly, right, to begin a 90-day jail sentence. Lohan was arrested for driving under the influence and thereby violating the terms of her probation in connection with a prior (2007) DUI conviction. In accordance with a policy of early release of nonviolent offenders to reduce jail overcrowding, however, she was released after serving 14 days of the sentence. She was immediately taken to an inpatient rehabilitation facility, where she was expected to stay another 90 days. Lohan was instead released after serving 23 days, but she was required to undergo outpatient therapy, to submit to random drug and alcohol screenings, and to attend psychotherapy and behavior therapy twice a week.*

- *Making probationers pay.* At least 25 states now impose some form of fee on probationers to defray the cost of community corrections. Massachusetts initiated **day fees**, which are based on the probationer's wages (the usual fee is between one and three days' wages each month).[57] Texas requires judges to impose supervision fees unless the offender is truly unable to pay; fees make up more than half the probation department's annual budget.[58]

- *HotSpot probation.* Maryland's HotSpot probation initiative involves police officers, probation agents, neighbors, and social service professionals to form community probation supervision teams. Using a team approach, they provide increased monitoring of offenders through home visits and drug testing. They also work with the offenders to ease reentry through offender creation of work crews that participate in community cleanups, work on vacant houses, and participate in other projects. Evaluations find that the recidivism rates of HotSpot probationers were not significantly different from those of traditional probation, but the initiative seems to have a great deal of utility and warrants further study.[59]

- *Area needs.* Some experts suggest that probation caseloads be organized around area rather than client needs. Research shows that probationers' residences are concentrated in certain locations. In the future, probation officers may be assigned cases on the basis of where they live in order to develop a working knowledge of community issues and develop expertise on how to best serve their clients' interests and needs.[60]

**day fees**
A program requiring probationers to pay in part for the costs of their treatment.

**SPECIALIZED PROBATION** Some probation departments are experimenting with focused or specialized probation. Teams of probation officers take on clients convicted of one specific type of crime, such as drug offenses or domestic violence, rather than treating a mixed bag of offenders. Focusing on specialized caseloads enables probation officers to develop specific treatment and control skills. This approach may have utility: A recent examination of specialized supervision of domestic violence probation found that clients, especially lower-risk abusers, were significantly less likely to be rearrested for domestic violence and nondomestic violence crimes than were those supervised in the traditional mixed caseloads.[61]

*PRIVATIZATION* Probation services have been privatized in some jurisdictions for more than 30 years, and the practice is now being used in least ten states, including Colorado and Missouri. The Private Probation Services company (established in 2003) specializes in providing offender supervision; it serves the courts and communities of northwest Missouri. For a fee, Private Probation Services performs many typical probation activities:

■ Probation supervision
■ Bond supervision
■ Electronic monitoring (house arrest)
■ Secure continuous remote alcohol monitoring (SCRAM)
■ Ignition interlock
■ On-site urinalysis testing
■ Alcohol Breathalyzer testing
■ Timely and informative reports to the court[62]

Privatization can help alleviate the burden of providing effective probation services. By utilizing private probation for low-risk offenders, state probation departments can commit more resources to high-risk offenders. However, some reviews suggest that existing statutory guidelines are currently insufficient to monitor and control the operations of private probation supervision agencies and that greater state oversight is needed to maintain quality.[63]

*SWIFT AND SURE PUNISHMENT* The threat of swift and sure punishment that is somewhat less than a full revocation of probation may help reduce rule violations. Hawaii has been experimenting with a system that provides immediate punishment for any probationers found in violation of their court orders. Probations are warned during a court hearing that if they violate the conditions of probation, they will be immediately arrested, will appear in court within hours, and will have the terms of their supervision modified to include a short stay in jail. The jail terms imposed are usually only a few days, but sentence length increases for successive violations. The program appears to be highly successful in reducing violations.[64]

Probation is unquestionably undergoing dramatic changes. In many jurisdictions, traditional probation is being supplemented by intermediate sanctions, which are penalties that fall between traditional community supervision and confinement in jail or prison. These new correctional services are discussed in the following section.

## INTERMEDIATE SANCTIONS

In 2005, Jennifer Wilbanks became notorious for having run away just before her wedding and claiming to have been abducted. When the truth was revealed, she pled guilty to charges of filing a false police report. At her hearing she told the court, "I'm truly sorry for my actions and I just want to thank Gwinnett County and the city of Duluth." The judge, Ronnie Batchelor, then sentenced Jennifer, AKA "The Runaway Bride," to two years of probation and 120 hours of community service. He also ordered her to continue mental health treatment and pay the sheriff's office $2,550 in addition to the $13,250 she had already agreed to pay the city of Duluth, Georgia, to help cover the overtime costs incurred in searching for her.[65]

Wilbanks's sentence reflects the growing trend to add sanctions to traditional probation sentences; in her case, those sanctions were monetary fines and community service. These programs can be viewed as "probation plus," since they add restrictive penalties and

© AP Images/Ric Feld

conditions to traditional community service orders, which emphasized treatment and rehabilitation more than control and restraint.[66] They can therefore range from the barely intrusive, such as restitution orders, to the highly restrictive, such as house arrest accompanied by electronic monitoring and a stay in a community correctional center. Today, **intermediate sanctions** include programs that are usually administered by probation departments: intensive probation supervision, house arrest, electronic monitoring, restitution orders, shock probation or split sentences, and residential community corrections.[67]

## Advantages of Intermediate Sanctions

Although some worry that intermediate sanctions will "widen the net" of justice and involve probationers in new, more intrusive and extensive programs, they also provide a number of benefits not offered in either traditional probation or incarceration sentences:

■ *Cost benefits.* Intermediate sanctions provide cost benefits. Though somewhat more costly than traditional probation, intermediate sanctions are far less expensive to run than prisons or jails. If those offenders who are given alternative sanctions would otherwise have been incarcerated, the extra cost would have been significant. In addition, offenders given intermediate sanctions generate income, pay taxes, reimburse victims, perform community service, and generate other cost savings that would be nonexistent had they been incarcerated. They also reduce the need for costly future prison and jail construction.

■ *Equitable community sentences.* Intermediate sanctions help meet the need for developing community sentences that are fair, equitable, and proportional.[68] It seems unfair to treat both a rapist and a shoplifter with the same type of probationary sentence, considering the differences in their crimes. As Figure 13.2 illustrates, intermediate sanctions can form the successive steps of a meaningful "ladder" of scaled punishments outside of prison, thereby restoring fairness and equity to nonincarceration sentences.[69] Forgers may be ordered to make restitution to their victims, and rapists can be placed in a community facility and receive counseling at a local clinic. This feature of intermediate sanctions allows judges to fit the punishment to the crime without resorting to a prison sentence.

■ *Increased control.* Intermediate sanctions can be designed to increase control over probationers whose serious or repeat crimes make a straight probation sentence inappropriate, yet for whom a prison sentence would be unduly harsh and counterproductive.[70] Some forms, such as electronic

Intermediate sanctions have been employed in some high-profile cases. This billboard, photographed in Duluth, Georgia, on May 3, 2005, shows the likeness of runaway bride Jennifer Wilbanks, who had vanished April 26 after saying she was going out jogging, initially told authorities she had been abducted. She later admitted she took a cross-country bus trip to Albuquerque, New Mexico, to avoid her lavish 600-guest wedding, which was to have taken place that Saturday. Charged with making false statements, she pled guilty and was sentenced to two years on probation and 120 hours of community service (including mowing lawns and cleaning toilets in government buildings). She was also ordered to pay $2,250 in restitution to the Gwinnett County Sheriff's Department and to reimburse the city of Duluth $13,250 to cover its costs in the case.

**intermediate sanctions**
The group of punishments falling between probation and prison ("probation plus"). Community-based sanctions, including house arrest and intensive supervision, serve as alternatives to incarceration.

**FIGURE 13.2**
Punishment Ladder

Death penalty

Prison

Shock probation

Residential community center

Electronic monitoring

House arrest

Intensive probation

Restitution

Probation

Forfeiture

Fines

Pretrial release

Restorative justice

**fine**
Levying a money payment on offenders to compensate society for their misdeeds.

monitoring, provide increased surveillance for probationers who might otherwise continue to commit crimes while in the community. Self-report surveys suggest that about half of probationers commit at least one offense while they are on probation and that about a third report committing more than four offenses during this same time.[71] Intermediate sanctions may help reduce this hidden recidivism.

■ *Reduced overcrowding.* Intermediate sanctions can reduce the number of convicted criminals who might otherwise be given an incarceration sentence but who either pose a low risk of recidivism or are of little threat to society (such as nonviolent property offenders). For example, overcrowding in jails can be reduced by providing alternatives to incarceration for misdemeanants and cutting the number of pretrial detainees, who currently make up about half of the inmate population.[72] Some forms of bail require conditions such as supervision by court officers and periods of home confinement (conditional bail).

■ *Use with different classes of offenders.* Intermediate sanctions can potentially be used as halfway-back strategies for probation and parole violators. Probationers who violate the conditions of their community release could be placed under increasingly intensive supervision before actual incarceration was required. Parolees who pose the greatest risk of recidivism might receive conditions that require close monitoring or home confinement. Parole violators could be returned to a community correctional center rather than a walled institution.

In sum, rather than being a net-widening measure, intermediate sanctions can act as a "net-repairing" strategy.[73] The various types of intermediate sanctions currently in use are more thoroughly discussed in the following sections.

## Fines

Monetary payments, or **fines,** can be imposed on offenders as an intermediate punishment for their criminal acts. Fines are a direct offshoot of the early common-law practice of requiring that compensation be paid to the victim and the state (*wergild*) for criminal acts. Fines are still commonly used in Europe, where they are often the sole penalty, even in cases involving chronic offenders who commit fairly serious crimes.

In the United States, fines are most commonly used in cases involving misdemeanors and lesser offenses. Fines are also frequently used in felony cases where the offender benefited financially. Fines may be used as a sole sanction but are typically combined with other punishments such as probation. Judges commonly supplement fines with other monetary sanctions (such as court costs, public defender fees, probation and treatment fees, and victim restitution) to increase the force of the financial punishment. However, there is evidence that many offenders fail to pay fines and that courts are negligent in their efforts to collect unpaid fees.[74]

In most jurisdictions, little guidance is given to the sentencing judge who directs the imposition of the fine. Judges often have inadequate information on the offender's ability to pay, and this results in defaults and contempt charges. Because the standard sanction for nonpayment is incarceration, many offenders held in local jails are confined for nonpayment of criminal fines. Even though the U.S. Supreme Court in *Tate v. Short* (1971) recognized that incarcerating a person who is financially unable to pay a fine discriminates against the poor, many judges continue to incarcerate offenders for noncompliance with financial orders.[75]

**DAY FINES** Because judges rely so heavily on offense seriousness to fix the level of fines, financial penalties may have a negative impact on success rates. The more serious the offense and the higher the fine, the greater the chances that the offender will fail to pay the fine and risk probation revocation. To overcome this sort of problem, justice systems in European nations such as Finland and

Sweden have employed the concept of **day fines** geared to an offender's net daily income. In an effort to make them equitable and fairly distributed, fines are based on the severity of the crime, weighted by a daily-income value taken from a chart similar to an income tax table; the number of the offender's dependents is also taken into account. The day fine concept means that the severity of punishment is geared to the offender's ability to pay.[76]

Although they are not widely used in the United States, some jurisdictions have experimented with day fines. The first day fines pilot program in the United States was designed and operated by the Vera Institute of Justice in Staten Island, New York, between 1987 and 1989. Since then, similar structured-fine systems have been tried experimentally in Arizona, Connecticut, Iowa, and Oregon.[77]

## Forfeiture

Criminal (in personam) and civil (in rem) **forfeiture** may be considered a form of intermediate sanction. Both involve the seizure of goods and instrumentalities related to the commission or outcome of a criminal act. The difference is that criminal forfeiture proceedings target criminal defendants and can only follow a criminal conviction. In contrast, civil forfeiture proceedings target property used in a crime and do not require that formal criminal proceedings be initiated against a person or that the person be proved guilty of a crime.[78] Federal law provides that after arresting drug traffickers, the government may seize the boats they used to import the narcotics, the cars they used to carry the drugs overland, the warehouses in which the drugs were stored, and the homes paid for with the drug profits; upon their conviction, the drug dealers permanently lose ownership of these "instrumentalities" of crime.

Forfeiture is not a new sanction. During the Middle Ages, "forfeiture of estate" was a mandatory result of most felony convictions. The Crown could seize all of a felon's real and personal property. Forfeiture derived from the common-law concept of "corruption of blood" or "attaint," which prohibited a felon's family from inheriting or receiving his property or estate. The common law mandated that descendants could not inherit property from a relative who might have acquired the property illegally: "[T]he Corruption of Blood stops the Course of Regular Descent, as to Estates, over which the Criminal could have no Power, because he never enjoyed them."[79]

Forfeiture was reintroduced into U.S. law with passage of the Racketeer Influenced and Corrupt Organization (RICO) Act and the Continuing Criminal Enterprises Act, both of which allow the seizure of any property derived from illegal enterprises or conspiracies. Although these acts were designed to apply to ongoing criminal conspiracies, such as drug or pornography rings, they are now being applied to a far-ranging series of criminal acts, including white-collar crimes. More than 100 federal statutes use forfeiture of property as a punishment.

*ZERO TOLERANCE.* Although law enforcement officials at first applauded the use of forfeiture as a hard-hitting way of seizing the illegal profits of drug law violators, the practice has been criticized because the government has often been overzealous in its application. Million-dollar yachts have been seized because someone aboard possessed a small amount of marijuana; this confiscatory practice is referred to as **zero tolerance**. This strict interpretation of the forfeiture statutes has come under fire because it is often used capriciously, the penalty is sometimes disproportionate to the crime involved, and it makes the government a "partner in crime."[80] It is also alleged that forfeiture unfairly targets a narrow range of offenders. For example, it is common for government employees involved in corruption to forfeit their pensions, whereas employees of public companies are exempt from such punishment.[81] There is also the issue of conflict of interest: Because law enforcement agencies can use forfeited assets to supplement their budgets, they may direct their efforts to cases that promise the greatest

**day fine**
A fine geared to the average daily income of the convicted offender in an effort to bring equity to the sentencing process.

**forfeiture**
The seizure of personal property by the state as a civil or criminal penalty.

**zero tolerance**
The practice of seizing all instrumentalities of a crime, including homes, boats, and cars. It is an extreme example of the law of forfeiture.

**restitution**
A condition of probation in which the offender repays society or the victim of crime for the trouble the offender caused.

**monetary restitution**
A sanction requiring that convicted offenders compensate crime victims by reimbursing them for out-of-pocket losses caused by the crime. Losses can include property damage, lost wages, and medical costs.

"payoff" rather than to cases that have the highest law enforcement priority.[82] As a result of these and other criticisms, the government has backed off its zero tolerance approach to drug-related seizures. Nonetheless, law enforcement agencies continue to seize property that has been used to facilitate crimes. Recently, for example, a Hartford County, Maryland, home was listed on the market at a bargain price almost $200,000 under its assessed value. Why the discount? The home had been seized by the U.S. Marshals Service after its previous owner, George K. Hayward, was sentenced to 20 years in federal prison for taking pornographic pictures of children, some as young as 5 years old, inside the house.[83]

## Restitution

Another popular intermediate sanction is **restitution**, which can take the form of requiring offenders to either pay back the victims of crime (**monetary restitution**) or serve the community to compensate for their criminal acts (**community service restitution**).[84] Restitution programs offer offenders a chance to avoid a jail or prison sentence or a lengthier probation period. The programs may help them develop a sense of allegiance to society, better work habits, and some degree of gratitude for being given a second chance. Restitution serves many other purposes, including giving the community something of value without asking it to foot the bill for an incarceration stay and helping victims regain lost property and income.

If a defendant is sentenced to pay monetary restitution as part of her probation order, a determination of victim loss is made and a plan for paying fair compensation developed. To avoid the situation in which a wealthy offender can fill a restitution order by merely writing a check, judges will sometimes order that compensation be paid out of income derived from a low-paid social service or public works job.

Community service orders usually require duty in a public nursing home, shelter, hospital, drug treatment unit, or public works program; some young vandals may find that they must clean up the damage they caused to the school or the park. Judges and probation officers have embraced the concept of restitution because it appears to benefit the victim, the offender, the criminal justice system, and society.[85] Financial restitution is inexpensive to administer, helps avoid stigma, and provides compensation for victims of crime. Offenders ordered to do community service work have been placed in schools, hospitals, and nursing homes. Helping them avoid a jail sentence can mean saving the public thousands of dollars that would have gone to maintaining them in a secure institution, freeing up needed resources, and giving the community the feeling that equity has been returned to the justice system.

Does restitution work? Most reviews rate it as a qualified success. An evaluation of community service in Texas found that nearly three-fourths of offenders with community service orders met their obligations and completed community service work.[86] The Texas experience is not atypical; most restitution clients successfully complete their orders and have no subsequent contact with the justice system.[87]

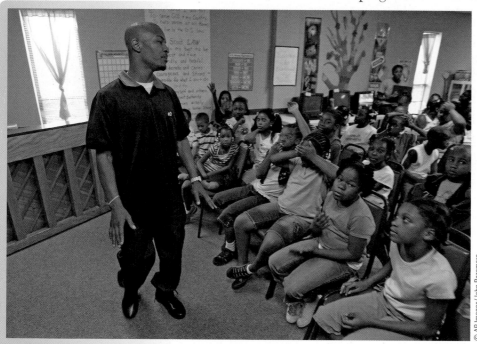

© AP Images/John Bazemore

Community services restitution requires offenders to provide service to the community to help compensate it for the trouble they caused or the damage they did. On June 17, 2008, rap star T.I., whose real name is Clifford Harris, talks with children at a day camp in Decatur, Georgia. In a deal worked out with prosecutors, Harris was sentenced to spend at least 1,000 hours talking to youth groups about the pitfalls of guns, gangs, and drugs before reporting for about a year in prison. He was arrested on October 13, 2007, and charged with possession of unregistered machine guns and silencers, as well as possession of firearms by a convicted felon. Which part of Harris's sentence—helping kids or doing time in prison—do you think will have a better outcome for the community? Which will do more to solve Harris's own problems?

## Shock Probation and Split Sentencing

Shock probation and split sentences are alternative sanctions designed to allow judges to grant offenders community release only after they have sampled prison life. These sanctions are based on the premise that if offenders are given a taste of incarceration sufficient to shock them into law-abiding behavior, they will be reluctant to violate the rules of probation or commit another crime.

In a number of states and in the U.S. Criminal Code, a jail term can actually be a condition of probation; this practice is known as split sentencing. About 10 percent of probationers are now given **split sentences**. The **shock probation** approach involves resentencing an offender to probation after a short prison stay. The shock comes because the offender originally received a long maximum sentence but is then eligible for release to community supervision at the discretion of the judge (usually within 90 days of incarceration).

Some states have linked the short prison stay with a boot camp experience referred to as shock incarceration, in which young inmates undergo a brief but intense period of military-like training and hard labor designed to impress them with the rigors of prison life.[88] (Boot camp programs are discussed in greater detail in Chapter 15.) Shock probation and split sentencing have been praised as ways to limit prison time, reintegrate the client quickly into the community, maintain family ties, and reduce prison populations and the costs of corrections.[89] An initial jail sentence probably makes offenders more receptive to the conditions of probation, because it amply illustrates the problems they will face if probation is violated.

But split sentences and shock probation programs have been criticized by those who believe that even a brief period of incarceration can interfere with the purpose of probation, which is to provide the offender with nonstigmatizing, community-based treatment. Even a short-term commitment subjects probationers to the destructive effects of institutionalization, disrupts their life in the community, and stigmatizes them for having been in jail.

## Intensive Probation Supervision

**Intensive probation supervision (IPS)** programs, also referred to as intensive supervision programs, have been implemented in some form in about 40 states and today include about 100,000 clients. IPS programs involve small caseloads of 15 to 40 clients who are kept under close watch by probation officers.[90] IPS programs typically have three primary goals:

■ *Decarceration.* Without intensive supervision, clients would normally be sent to already overcrowded prisons or jails.

■ *Control.* High-risk offenders can be maintained in the community under much closer security than traditional probation efforts can provide.

■ *Reintegration.* Offenders can maintain community ties and be reoriented toward a more productive life, while avoiding the pains of imprisonment.

In general, IPS programs rely on a great degree of client contact to achieve the goals of decarceration, control, and reintegration. Most programs have admissions criteria based on the nature of the offense and the offender's criminal background. Some programs exclude violent offenders; others will not take substance abusers. Other jurisdictions do not exclude offenders on the basis of their prior criminal history.

IPS programs are used in several ways. In some states, IPS is a direct sentence imposed by a judge; in others, it is a post-sentencing alternative used to divert offenders from the correctional system. A third practice is to use IPS as a case management tool to give the local probation staff flexibility in dealing with clients. Other jurisdictions use IPS in all three ways, in addition to applying it to probation violators to bring them halfway back into the community without resorting to a prison term.

---

**community service restitution**
An alternative sanction that requires an offender to work in the community at such tasks as cleaning public parks or working with disabled children in lieu of an incarceration sentence.

**split sentence**
A practice that requires convicted criminals to spend a portion of their sentence behind bars and the remainder in the community.

**shock probation**
A sentence in which offenders serve a short prison term before they begin probation, to impress them with the pains of imprisonment.

**intensive probation supervision (IPS)**
A type of intermediate sanction involving small probation caseloads and strict monitoring on a daily or weekly basis.

*IS IPS EFFECTIVE?* There are indications that the failure rate in IPS caseloads is high, in some cases approaching 50 percent; IPS clients have a higher rearrest rate than other probationers.[91] It should come as no surprise that IPS clients fail more often because, after all, they are more serious criminals who might otherwise have been incarcerated and are now being watched and supervised more closely than probationers. Probation officers may also be more willing to revoke the probation of IPS clients because they believe the clients are a risk to the community and, under normal circumstances, would have been incarcerated. Why risk the program to save a few "bad apples"?

IPS seems to work better for some offenders than for others. Those with good employment records seem to do better than the underemployed or unemployed. Younger offenders who commit petty crimes are the most likely to fail on IPS; ironically, people with these characteristics are the ones most likely to be included in IPS programs.[92]

IPS may also be more effective when combined with particular treatment modalities such as cognitive-behavioral treatment, which stresses such life skills as problem solving, social skills, negotiation skills, management of emotion, and values enhancement.[93]

## House Arrest

On March 14, 2009, a car driven by pro football player Donte Stallworth struck and killed Mario Reyes, 59, in Miami Beach, Florida. Stallworth later admitted to drinking the night prior to the accident. Police estimated Stallworth was driving about 50 mph in a 40 mph zone. On April 1, 2009, Stallworth was charged with DUI and second-degree manslaughter. He pled guilty and received a sentence of 30 days in jail, plus 1,000 hours of community service, two years of house arrest, and eight years on probation and a life-time suspension of his Florida state driver's license. On July 10, 2009, Stallworth was released from jail after serving 24 days of a 30-day sentence and began his house arrest.[94]

Donte Stallworth is one of thousands of convicted offenders now serving time under **house arrest**. This intermediate sanction requires convicted offenders to spend extended periods of time in their own home as an alternative to an incarceration sentence. For example, persons convicted on a drunk-driving charge might be sentenced to spend between 6:00 P.M. Friday and 8:00 A.M. Monday and every weekday after 5:30 P.M. in their home for six months. House

**house arrest**
A form of intermediate sanction that requires that the convicted offender spend a designated amount of time per week in his or her own home—such as from 6:00 P.M. Friday until 8:00 A.M. Monday.

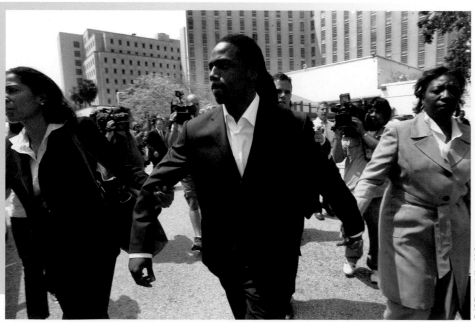

*House arrest is typically used in conjunction with other types of intermediate sanctions. Here Cleveland Browns football player Donte Stallworth, center, leaves Dade County Pretrial Detention Center along with his mother Donna, right, after posting a $200,000 bond on April 2, 2009, in Miami. On the morning of March 14, 2009, a 2005 Bentley coupé driven by Stallworth struck and killed Mario Reyes, 59. Stallworth was driving about 50 mph in a 40 mph zone and had been drinking prior to the incident. Charged with DUI and second-degree manslaughter, he pled guilty and received a sentence of 30 days in jail, plus 1,000 hours of community service, 2 years of house arrest, and 8 years on probation. His Florida state driver's license was also suspended for life.*

© AP Photo/Jeffrey M. Boan

arrest initiatives can vary in administration, client services, and goals. Some are administered by probation departments, while others are simply judicial sentences monitored by surveillance officers. Some check clients 20 or more times a month, while others do only a few curfew checks. Some impose 24-hour confinement, while others allow offenders to attend work or school.

No definitive data indicates that house arrest is an effective crime deterrent, nor is there sufficient evidence to conclude that it has utility as a device to lower the recidivism rate. One evaluation found that nearly 10 percent of the house arrest sample had their probation revoked for technical violations within 18 months of their sentencing.[95] Another found that recidivism rates were almost identical to those of a matched sample of inmates released from secure correctional facilities; four out of five offenders in both forms of correction recidivated within five years.[96] Although these findings are troublesome, the advantages of house arrest in reducing costs and overcrowding in the correctional system probably make further experimentation inevitable.

## Electronic Monitoring

For house arrest to work, sentencing authorities must be assured that arrestees are actually at home during their assigned times. Random calls and visits are one way to check on compliance with house arrest orders. However, one of the more interesting developments in the criminal justice system has been the introduction of **electronic monitoring (EM)** devices to manage offender obedience to home confinement orders.[97]

Electronically monitored offenders wear devices that send signals to a control office; the devices are worn around their ankles, wrists, or necks. Two basic types of systems are used: active and passive. Active systems constantly monitor offenders by continuously sending a signal to the central office. If offenders leave their home at an unauthorized time, the signal is broken, and the "failure" is recorded. In some cases, the control officer is automatically notified electronically through a beeper. In contrast, passive systems usually involve random phone calls generated by computers to which the offenders must respond within a particular time (such as 30 seconds). EM can also be used at the front end of the system with bailees and at the back end with parolees.

The most commonly used EM devices are described in Exhibit 13.2 However, electronic monitoring systems are now being developed by private industry. Many systems now employ global positioning satellite (GPS) technology to keep tabs on probationers even when they leave home. For example, Omnilink Systems of Alpharetta, Georgia, has developed an EM system that employs cellular technology to locate a tracking device even when it's indoors. A single-unit ankle monitoring device is paired with monitoring software that gives law enforcement administrators the ability to set up offender profiles and then configure inclusion and exclusion zones for each one. If an offender violates a zone, an alert is immediately sent to appropriate individuals.

In addition, a wireless tracking device alerts potential victims when a monitored offender is in the victim's vicinity in violation of a court restraining or protection order.[98] This is done by linking the wireless device to the victim's cell phone; if the offender comes within a certain distance of the cell phone, the victim is notified via phone and can seek safety until the police arrive. The Omnilink monitoring device can be programmed to perform various types of monitoring, including time-related curfews, prohibitions against monitored offenders being in certain areas (for example, against pedophiles being in specified areas frequented by children), and continuous tracking no matter where the offender is located.[99] These services are particularly important in domestic violence cases, where victims may not feel safe in their own home and are forced to flee to shelters.[100] A number of states, including Massachusetts, routinely use GPS systems with certain classes of probationers (such as sex offenders) to monitor their whereabouts and ensure that they obey their probation orders (such as staying at least 1,000 yards away from a school).

**electronic monitoring (EM)**
Requiring convicted offenders to wear a monitoring device as part of their community sentence. Typically part of a house arrest order, this enables the probation department to ensure that offenders are complying with court-ordered limitations on their freedom.

EXHIBIT 13.2

## Electronic Monitoring Systems

■ *Identity verification devices* range from personal identification numbers to biometric verification that recognizes different parts of the human body to ensure that the reporting person is the intended offender.

■ *Remote alcohol detection devices* require users to blow into a device, usually located in the offender's home, that measures blood alcohol content. The results are recorded by a computer to determine compliance with conditions of alcohol consumption.

■ *Ignition interlock devices* are linked to the electrical systems of automobiles. The driver must expel deep lung air into the device to operate the vehicle. If the driver's blood alcohol content registers above a predetermined level at which it is deemed unsafe for the operator to drive, the vehicle will not start.

■ *Programmed contact systems* are used to contact and verify the location of offenders in their homes or elsewhere. They use a central computer that either receives telephone calls from offenders or makes calls to them in one or more locations.

■ *Continuous signaling devices* are battery-powered and transmit a radio signal two or more times per minute. They are placed on the offender's wrist or ankle with a tamper-resistant strap and must be worn at all times. A receiver detects the transmitter's signals and conveys a message, via telephone, to a central computer when either it stops receiving the radio frequency or the signal resumes. Receivers can detect transmitter signals from a distance of about 150 feet when installed in a typical home environment.

■ *Victim notification systems* alert the victim when the offender is approaching that person's residence.

A transmitter is worn by both the offender and the victim, and a receiver is placed at both residences.

■ *Field monitoring devices,* or "drive-by" units, are another type of continuous signaling technology. Probation or parole officers or other authorities use a portable device that can be handheld or used in a vehicle with a roof-mounted antenna. When within 200 to 800 feet of an offender's ankle or wrist transmitter, the portable device can detect the radio signals of the offender's transmitter.

■ *Group monitoring units* enable supervisors to monitor several offenders in the same location. They are used for such purposes as verifying attendance of multiple offenders in a day reporting program and monitoring offenders confined in a residential group setting.

■ *Location tracking systems,* also known as global positioning systems, offer yet another way to monitor offenders. Receivers detect satellite signals that include the exact time the signal is sent and the identity of the satellite sending the signal. This information is processed to determine the person's location. This more expensive technology is generally reserved for high-risk offenders. It can determine when offenders leave an area where they are supposed to be (inclusion zone) or enter an area where they are not allowed to be (exclusion zone).

Sources: William Burrell and Robert Gable, "From B. F. Skinner to Spiderman to Martha Stewart: The Past, Present and Future of Electronic Monitoring of Offenders," *Journal of Offender Rehabilitation 46* (2008): 101–118; Hugh Downing, "Emergence of Global Positioning Satellite (GPS) Systems in Correctional Applications," *Corrections Today* 68 (2006): 42–45; Ann Crowe, "Electronic Supervision: From Decision Making to Implementation," *Corrections Today* 64 (2002): 131–132.

Electronic monitoring supporters claim EM has the benefits of relatively low cost and high security, while helping offenders avoid the pains of imprisonment in overcrowded, dangerous state facilities. Electronic monitoring is capital-intensive rather than labor-intensive. Because offenders are monitored by computers, an initial investment in hardware rules out the need to hire many more supervisory officers to handle large numbers of clients.

There are some indications that EM can be an effective addition to the roster of intermediate sanctions and provide the judiciary with an enhanced supervision tool. EM can be used as part of a pretrial diversionary program, to enhance probation, or as a post-incarceration security measure. Surveys of offenders reveal that they find EM preferable to incarceration.[101] Programs save money and avoid new construction costs without widening the net of social control.[102] Because of its low cost and assumed effectiveness, EM is now being used with a wide variety of offenders, even those who have committed serious felony sex offenses.[103]

Evaluations of the ability of EM programs to reduce recidivism have yielded mixed results. Some evaluations indicate that offenders monitored via EM misunderstand its purpose and are just as likely to recidivate as those released without such supervision.[104] Other evaluations have achieved much better results. In one extensive effort, Kathy Padgett and her associates evaluated data on more than 75,000 offenders placed on home confinement in Florida from 1998 to 2002. They found that EM significantly reduced the likelihood of technical violations, reoffending, and absconding. Probationers placed on home confinement with EM had been previously involved in significantly more serious crimes than those placed on home confinement without EM, indicating that the procedure is being used with the appropriate offender population—that is, the most serious probation population.[105] Thus the EM program produced little "net widening." However, some critics argue that the evidence that EM can lower recidivism rates is thin and that it may not work well as a stand-alone program. Instead, EM can improve public safety when it is combined with some other treatment modality, such as social interventions and counseling.[106]

## Residential Community Corrections

The most secure intermediate sanction is a sentence to a **residential community corrections (RCC)** facility. Such facilities house offenders at night but allow them the freedom to work, attend school, and/or participate in community-based treatment activities and programs during the day.

Traditionally, the role of residential community corrections was to reintegrate soon-to-be-paroled prison inmates into the community. Inmates spent the last few months of their sentence in the halfway house, finding suitable employment, building up cash reserves, obtaining an apartment, and acquiring a job-related wardrobe.

The traditional concept of community corrections has expanded, and it is now a direct-sentencing option for judges who believe particular offenders need a correctional alternative halfway between traditional probation and a stay in prison. Placement in an RCC center can be used as a condition of probation for offenders who need a nonsecure community facility that provides a more structured treatment environment than traditional probation. One example is California's Substance Abuse and Crime Prevention Act (SACPA), which allows adults convicted of nonviolent drug-possession offenses to participate in community-based drug treatment programs. Evaluations of the program found that SACPA clients were likely to be rearrested for drug crimes, undercutting the effectiveness of the treatment initiative.[107] One reason for the failure may have been that the sudden influx of offenders overwhelmed the treatment resources of an already strained community treatment system; many clients were simply "undertreated."

Some RCC centers are operated by private nonprofit groups that receive referrals from the county or district courts and from probation or parole departments. Two successful programs are described in Exhibit 13.3.

Besides acting as sole sentences and halfway houses, RCC facilities have also been used as residential pretrial release centers for offenders who are in immediate need of social services before their trial and as halfway-back alternatives for both parole and probation violators who might otherwise have to be imprisoned. In this capacity, RCC programs serve as a base from which offenders can be placed in outpatient psychiatric facilities, drug and alcohol treatment programs, job training, and so on. Some programs make use of both inpatient and outpatient programs to provide clients with specialized treatment, such as substance abuse management.[109]

More than 2,000 state-run community-based facilities are in use today. In addition, up to 2,500 private nonprofit RCC programs operate in the United States. About half also house inmates who have been released from prison (halfway houses) and who use the RCC placement as a way to ease back into society. The remainder are true intermediate sanctions, including about 400 federally sponsored programs.

**CourseMate** For more information about the Massachusetts Probation Service's program to track sex offenders via GPS, visit the Criminal Justice CourseMate at CengageBrain.com, then access the "Web Links" for this chapter.

**residential community corrections (RCC)**
A nonsecure facility, located in the community, that houses probationers who need a more secure environment. Typically, residents are free during the day to go to work, school, or treatment, and return in the evening for counseling sessions and meals.

**EXHIBIT 13.3**

## Two Successful RCC Programs

### THE HOUSE OF HEALING (HOH)

The House of Healing (HOH) is a community-living residential program located in Erie, Pennsylvania, that at any one time cares for a maximum of eight female offenders and their children. HOH relies on *relational theory*—the view that a woman's primary motivation is to build a sense of connection with others. In order to develop the clients' sense of self and self-worth, HOH emphasizes building and maintaining relationships by encouraging contact visitation with family and friends and applying extremely liberal telephone policies. Most important, children under 12 years old of female offenders reside at the facility and remain in the care of their mother, and children over age 12 are permitted overnight visits. When kids cannot stay with their mother, day visits are invited and phone calls are encouraged and permitted for nominal or no fees. The core program includes classes in parenting and communication skills, self-esteem, anger management, and budgeting. Counseling for chemical addictions, domestic violence, sexual abuse, and mental health issues is also a critical part of the program, as are health care referrals and job placement assistance. The programming conducted within HOH is designed to keep families together, stop the cycle of crime, and teach women and children the skills and appropriate behaviors they need to reintegrate successfully into society. Residents participate in both on-site and off-site recreational and cultural activities. Community service is required of participants until they obtain paid employment. Residents are encouraged to develop their spirituality, cultivate a positive support system, and participate in an active 12-step recovery program.

### PORTLAND HOUSE

Portland House, a private residential center in Minneapolis, operates as an alternative to incarceration for young adult offenders. Since 1973, it has served thousands of men and helped them develop meaningful employment and community interaction, as well as social, money management, chemical health, and positive goal-setting skills. This is achieved through processes of self-analysis and group dynamics that challenge residents to reverse criminal behavior and develop responsible behaviors, clear direction, and goals.[108] The 25 residents regularly receive group therapy and financial, vocational, educational, family, and personal counseling. Residents may work to earn a high school equivalency degree. With funds withheld from their earnings at work-release employment, residents pay room and board, family and self-support, and income taxes. Portland House appears to be successful. It is significantly cheaper to run than a state institution, and the recidivism rate of clients is much lower than that of those who have gone through traditional correctional programs.

Source: Sara Lichtenwalter, Maria Garase, and David Barker, "Evaluation of the House of Healing: An Alternative to Female Incarceration," *Journal of Sociology & Social Welfare* 37 (2010): 75–94. Information provided by Portland House, www.lssmn.org/portland.htm.

---

**day reporting center (DRC)**

A nonresidential community-based treatment program.

**DAY REPORTING CENTERS** A number of states have set up a system of **day reporting centers (DRCs)** to oversee intermediate sanctions and treatment placements. These provide a single location to which a variety of clients can report for supervision and treatment. In Georgia, Delaware, Utah, Massachuasetts, and other jurisdictions, DRCs serve nonresidential clients using RCC facilities. They can be used as a step up in security for probationers who have failed in the community and as a step down in security for jail or prison inmates. For example, 13 DRCs are now operating throughout Georgia, providing intensive substance abuse treatment for up to one hundred offenders sentenced by the Courts and also supervising probationers who have not responded to more traditional supervision and treatment efforts. Failure at a DRC results in revocation proceedings against the offender. Although the cost is greater than that of field probation, a DRC placement can be made at only a fraction of the cost of a residential alternative.[110] The program includes substance abuse counseling, cognitive restructuring, adult basic education, employment enhancement, intensive supervision, and community service. An aftercare component follows the on-site programming. Offenders assigned to the program are required to be employed

## CONCEPT SUMMARY 13.1
### *Intermediate Sanctions*

| Sanction | Goal | Problems |
|---|---|---|
| Fines | Monetary sanction | Overburdens the poor |
| Forfeiture | Monetary sanction, equity | Can be overreaching |
| Restitution | Pay back victim | Does not reduce recidivism |
| Shock incarceration and split sentence | "Taste of bars" as a deterrent | Can cause labeling and stigma |
| Intensive probation | Small caseloads, more supervision | High failure rate |
| House arrest | Avoids jail | Lacks treatment possibility |
| Electronic monitoring | Supervision by computer | Technology-dependent, no treatment |
| Residential community | Less secure than prison | Expensive, high failure rate |

as soon as they have completed the initial orientation, assessment, diagnostics, and programming.

In a program that closely resembles DRCs, Massachusetts has developed a network of 26 nonresidential community corrections centers—community-based, intensive supervision sites that deliver bundled sanctions and services, including treatment and education, to high-risk offenders who might otherwise face incarceration. Among the sanctions delivered at community corrections centers are

- Electronic monitoring
- Community service
- Drug and alcohol testing
- Day reporting

    Among the services provided at community corrections centers are

- Substance abuse treatment
- GED/ABE/ESL or a comparable educational component
- Communicable disease prevention education
- Job readiness training and placement
- Referral to Department of Public Health or Department of Mental Health service providers
- Women's services[111]

The goal of the Massachusetts community corrections centers is to provide targeted treatment to a specific group of offenders who may be on probation but who have a serious criminal history and are chronic substance abusers; members of this group are typically underemployed or unemployed.

Evaluations show that DRCs can be successful at reducing recidivism.[112] DRCs seem to work better with certain types of offenders, such as those who are older and more experienced, than with others, such as younger offenders.[113] DRC participants with alcohol problems, criminal companions, and poor living situations are also more likely to fail. In contrast, those who receive counseling seem to do better.[114]

Concept Summary 13.1 sets out the goals and problems of the various forms of intermediate sanctions.

# EVIDENCE-BASED JUSTICE

## Drug Treatment Alternative-to-Prison (DTAP) Program

The Brooklyn-based Drug Treatment Alternative-to-Prison (DTAP) Program incorporates drug treatment in place of incarceration for repeat felony offenders who were drug users or drug dealers of heroin, crack, and powder cocaine, among other dangerous drugs.

All candidates must apply for the program, and the district attorney's office chooses who will be permitted into the program after close scrutiny of all applicants. The DTAP program provides 15 to 24 months of residential drug treatment, educational classes, vocational training, employment strategies, and social, mental health, and family services. The average stay is about 18 months. Participants plead guilty to a felony, thereby ensuring a mandatory prison sentence if they abscond from the program. Sentencing is deferred upon program participation. If participants complete the program, their guilty plea is withdrawn and the charges dismissed. If at any time an individual does not comply with the rigid rules established by the program, by either using drugs or partaking in violent behavior, he faces being kicked out of the program and will begin the incarceration sentence.

The program has an employer counselor who works with the participants to help them develop skills in gaining employment. After release from the program, it is important that the individual have legitimate activities to participate in so he will not be as likely to return to drug use or to reliance on drug dealing to make a living. Vocational training with the employer counselor considerably increases his chances of success.

### Does It Work?

The Center on Addiction and Substance Abuse at Columbia University closely analyzed the records of 280 DTAP participants and compared them with 130 individuals who went through the regular process of incarceration. Findings suggest that the program is very beneficial. In fact, DTAP graduates experienced a 26 percent lower rearrest rate and a 36 percent lower reconviction rate, and they were 67 percent less likely to return to prison than members of the control/comparison group.

The research also shows that those who participated in the program are three times more likely to be employed after release from the program, compared with their employment rates when they entered the program. Ninety-one percent of DTAP's graduates who are able to work are employed. Another plus discovered in the research evidence was that DTAP is highly cost-effective. Analysis of the savings realized on corrections, health care, public assistance, and recidivism costs, combined with the tax revenues generated by the DTAP graduates, reveals that diversion to DTAP has resulted in economic benefits of approximately $40,000 per graduate. As of April 1, 2010, 2,862 defendants had been accepted into the program, 382 were still in treatment, and 1,215 had completed the program and had their charges dismissed. In all, more than $48 million has been saved through DTAP

Sources: DTAP (Drug Treatment Alternative-to-Prison) Program, www.brooklynda.org/dtap/DTAP.htm (accessed April 15, 2010); Columbia University, National Center on Addiction and Substance Abuse, *Crossing the Bridge: An Evaluation of the Drug Treatment Alternative-to-Prison (DTAP) Program* (New York: 2003).

## RESTORATIVE JUSTICE

**restorative justice**
A view of criminal justice that focuses on crime as an act against the community rather than the state. Justice should involve all parties affected by crime—victims, criminals, law enforcement, and the community.

As you may recall, one of the goals of contemporary sentencing is to "restore" offenders into society. This goal has particular relevance today because many crime experts believe that, ironically, rather than reducing crime and recidivism, policies based on "getting tough on crime," even intermediate sanctions, can cause crime rates to fluctuate higher and offenders to commit more crime. Punishment may not work because it both carries hard-to-erase stigma and destroys the offender's dignity and peace of mind. When traditional community-based correctional models such as probation are supplemented by the new alternative/intermediate sanctions, the effect is to add a punitive aspect that can further hinder rehabilitation efforts. Instead, **restorative justice** advocates suggest a policy based on restoring the damage caused by crime and creating a system of justice that includes all the parties harmed by the criminal act: the victim, the offender, the community, and society.[115]

Restorative justice models jibe with the thoughts of Australian justice expert John Braithwaite, who argues that crime control today involves shaming and stigmatizing offenders. This helps set them apart from normative society and undermines their potential for change. He calls instead for a policy of "reintegrative shaming." Here disapproval is limited to the offender's evil deeds; it is not direct at the offender himself. Law violators must be made to realize that even though their actions have caused harm, they are still valuable people—people who can be reaccepted by society. A critical element of reintegrative shaming occurs when the offenders themselves begin to understand and recognize their wrongdoing and shame. To be reintegrative, shaming must be brief and controlled and must be promptly followed by ceremonies of forgiveness, apology, and repentance.[116] Braithwaite's work is at the core of the restorative justice movement.

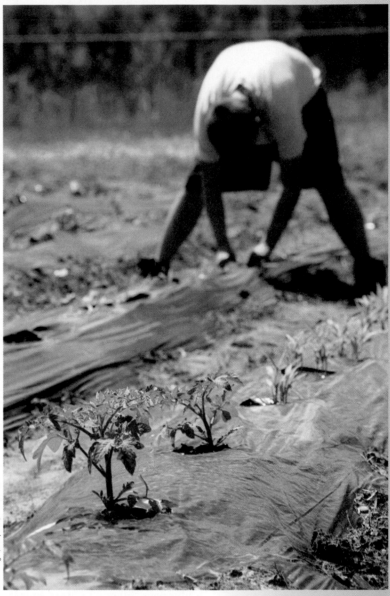

## The Concept of Restoration

According to the restorative view, even though crimes can seem quite different, ranging from a violent assault to a white-collar fraud scheme, they all share one common trait: They inflict harm on the community in which they occur. And yet, the traditional justice system has done little to involve the community in the justice process. What has developed is a system of coercive punishments administered by bureaucrats that is inherently harmful to offenders and reduces the likelihood that they will ever again be productive members of society. This system relies on punishment, stigma, and disgrace. What is needed instead is a justice policy that repairs the harm caused by crime and comprises all parties that have suffered from that harm, including the victim, the community, and the offender. Exhibit 13.4 sets out the principles of the restorative justice approach.

An important aspect of achieving these goals is that offenders accept accountability for their actions and responsibility for the harm their actions caused. Only then can they be restored as productive members of their community. Restoration involves turning the justice system into a "healing" process rather than a distributor of retribution and revenge.

Most people involved in offender–victim relationships actually know one another or were related in some way before the criminal incident took place. Instead of treating one of the involved parties as a victim deserving sympathy and the other as a criminal deserving punishment, it is more productive to address the issues that produced the conflict between these people. Rather than take sides and choose whom to isolate and punish, society should try to

*A Florida Parishes Juvenile Detention Center detainee works in the center's garden in Goodbee, Louisiana. Detainees contribute time and effort for the benefit of the community, harvesting the produce and donating it to a local food pantry. Juvenile detainees are learning restorative justice with programs such as these that teach new skills and encourage them to share the benefits of what they have learned with the larger community.*

© AP Images/*Daily Star*, Kari Wheeler

**EXHIBIT 13.4**

## *Basic Principles of Restorative Justice*

- Crime is an offense against human relationships.
- Victims and the community are central to justice processes.
- The first priority of justice processes is to assist victims.
- The second priority is to restore the community, to the degree possible.
- The offender has a personal responsibility to victims and to the community for crimes committed.

- The offender will develop improved competency and understanding as a result of the restorative justice experience.
- Stakeholders share responsibilities for restorative justice through partnerships for action.

Source: Anne Seymour, "Restorative Justice/Community Justice," in the *National Victim Assistance Academy* textbook (Washington, D.C.: National Victim Assistance Academy, 2001.

reconcile the parties involved in conflict.[117] The effectiveness of justice ultimately depends on the stake a person has in the community (or a particular social group). If a person does not value her membership in the group, she will be unlikely to accept responsibility, show remorse, or repair the injuries caused by her actions.

## Restoration Programs

Restoration programs try to include all the parties involved in a criminal act: the victim, the offender, and the community. Although processes differ in structure and style, they generally include the following:

- Recognition by offenders that they have caused injury to personal and social relations, and a determination and acceptance of responsibility (ideally accompanied by a statement of remorse)
- A commitment to both material reparation (such as monetary restitution) and symbolic reparation (such as an apology)
- A determination of community support and assistance for both victim and offender

The intended result of the process is to repair injuries suffered by the victim and the community, while ensuring reintegration of the offender.

Negotiation, mediation, consensus building, and peacemaking have been part of the dispute resolution process in European and Asian communities for centuries.[118] Native American and Native Canadian people have long used (in sentencing circles, sentencing panels, and elders panels) the type of community participation in the adjudication process that restorative justice advocates are now embracing.[119]

In some Native American communities, people accused of breaking the law meet with community members, victims (if any), village elders, and agents of the justice system in a **sentencing circle**. All members of the circle express their feelings about the act that was committed and raise questions or concerns. The accused can express regret about his or her actions and a desire to change the harmful behavior. People may suggest ways in which the offender can make things up to the community and to those who were harmed. A treatment program such as Alcoholics Anonymous may be suggested, if appropriate.

## Restoration in Practice

Restorative justice policies and practices are now being adapted around the world. Legislation in 19 states includes reference to the use of victim–offender mediation. There are more than 1,400 victim–offender mediation programs in North America and Europe.[120] Restorative justice is being embraced on many levels in the justice system.

**sentencing circles**
A type of sentencing in which victims, family members, community members, and the offender participate in an effort to devise fair and reasonable sanctions that are ultimately aimed at reintegrating the offender into the community.

*SCHOOLS* Some schools have employed restorative justice practices to avoid more punitive measures such as expulsion in dealing with students involved in drug and alcohol abuse. Schools in Minnesota, Colorado, and elsewhere are now trying to involve students in "relational rehabilitation" programs, which strive to improve offenders' relationships with key figures in the community who may have been harmed by their actions.[121]

*POLICE* Restorative justice has also been implemented when crime is first encountered by police. The new community policing models can be viewed as an attempt to bring restorative concepts into law enforcement. Restorative justice relies on criminal justice policymakers listening to and responding to the needs of those who will be affected by their actions, and community policing relies on policies established with input and exchanges between officers and citizens.[122] The technique is also being used by police around the world. In England, police are using a format called restorative cautioning. After an arrest is made, police in England and Wales traditionally had four procedures they could follow: (1) take no further action, (2) give an informal warning, (3) administer a formal police caution, or (4) decide to prosecute by sending the case to the Crown Prosecution Service. English police forces are now experimenting with a form of restorative cautioning. This uses a trained police facilitator with a script to encourage an offender to take responsibility for repairing the harm caused by the offense. Sometimes the victim is present, in which case the meeting is called a restorative conference; usually, however, the victim is not present. Traditional cautioning, on the other hand, lasts only a few minutes, requires no special training, and focuses on the officer explaining the possible consequences of future offending. Although the police report that the new system seems to be working quite well, with crime rates down as much as 30 percent), some experts have questioned whether restorative cautioning can produce the results being claimed.[123]

*COURTS* In the court system, restorative programs usually involve diverting offenders from the formal court process. Instead, these programs encourage meeting and reconciling the conflicts between offenders and victims via victim advocacy, mediation programs, or sentencing circles, in which crime victims and their families are brought together with offenders and their families in an effort to formulate a sanction that addresses the needs of each party. Victims are given a chance to voice their stories, and offenders can help compensate them financially or provide some service (such as repairing damaged property).[124] Again, the goal is to enable offenders to appreciate the damage they have caused, make amends, and be reintegrated into society.

Restorative justice has found a niche all over the world. It is even being used to resolve cases in the Middle East involving Arabs and Israelis![125] The accompanying Race, Gender, and Culture in Criminal Justice feature discusses restorative justice in New Zealand and Australia.

## The Challenge of Restorative Justice

Although restorative justice holds great promise, there are also some concerns.[126] One issue is whether programs reach out to all members of the community. Research indicates that entry into programs may be more readily available to white offenders than to minorities, a condition that would defeat the purpose of the restorative movement.[127]

Restorative justice programs must be wary of cultural and social differences, which can be found throughout America's heterogeneous society.[128] What may be considered restorative in one subculture may be considered insulting and damaging in another.[129] Furthermore, so many diverse programs call themselves restorative that evaluating them is difficult. Each one may be pursuing a unique objective. In other words, no single definition of "restorative justice" has emerged.[130]

# RACE, GENDER, AND CULTURE IN CRIMINAL JUSTICE

## Restoration in Australia and New Zealand

Australia and New Zealand have been leaders in adopting restoration programs. One innovative effort in New Zealand, Family Group Conferences, is based in part on native Maori practices and aims to give families a greater say in the resolution of both child protection and juvenile justice matters. The Children, Young Persons and Their Families Act in 1989 made conferencing the primary decision-making process within the child protection system. If official action is to be taken after an investigation, a conference is convened, and support is made available if family members lack the financial resources to travel. Conferences are arranged and facilitated in New Zealand by specialist care and protection coordinators, who are employed directly by Child, Youth and Family, the child protection agency in New Zealand. Coordinators work with the family to bring together the conference. This usually includes the child/young person, his or her advocate and/or legal representative, the parents, extended family members, any other support person the family wishes, and the referring care and protection worker. These people are all entitled by law to attend the conference. Other professionals who are not involved in the decision making may be invited to provide information. The purpose of the conference is for the family to hear the child protection concerns, to decide whether the child is in need of care and protection, and to make plans that can address these concerns.

Conferences occur in three stages. In the first stage, child protection workers and other professionals share information with the family. The second stage involves the family having time on their own to deliberate and agree on possible solutions. In the final phase of the conference, the aim is to arrive at agreement on (1) whether the child is in need of care and protection, and (2) a plan that will address these concerns. This may involve negotiation among the family, care and protection workers, and other agencies about the services and supports that can be provided. For a conference agreement to go into effect, it is necessary that all participants agree. Recent estimates suggest that more than 50,000 conferences have been convened during the past 20 years, a number that reflects the central role that conferences play in New Zealand's child protection system.

Possibly the greatest challenge to restorative justice is the difficult task of balancing the needs of offenders with those of their victims. If programs focus solely on reconciliation of the victim's needs, they may risk ignoring the offender's needs and increasing the likelihood of reoffending. Sharon Levrant and her colleagues suggest that restorative justice programs featuring short-term interactions with victims fail to help offenders learn prosocial ways of behaving. Restorative justice advocates may falsely assume that relatively brief interludes of public shaming will change deeply rooted criminal predispositions.[131] Yet, is it reasonable to include any form of punishment or sanction in a restorative-based program?[132]

In contrast, programs focusing on the offender may turn off victims and their advocates. Some victim advocacy groups have voiced concerns about the focus of restorative justice programs. Some believe that victims' rights are threatened by features of the restorative justice process, such as respectful listening to the offender's story and consensual dispositions. These features seem affronts to a victim's claim of the right to be seen as a victim, to insist on the offender being branded a criminal, to blame the offender, and not to be "victimized all over again by the process." Many victims do want an apology, if it is heartfelt and easy to get. But some want even more to put the traumatic incident behind them, to retrieve stolen property being held for use at trial, and to be assured that the offender will receive treatment he is thought to need if he is not to victimize

## Conferencing in Australia

Conferencing was introduced into the Australian criminal justice systems in the early 1990s by police in the city of Wagga Wagga, New South Wales. Other police experimented with the idea, and between 1992 and 1995, police-run conferences were established in the Australian Capital Territory (ACT) and were tried on a pilot basis in Western Australia, the Northern Territory, Queensland, and Tasmania. Since 1994, other applications of the conferencing idea have been launched in schools and workplaces in New South Wales and Queensland, and these continue to operate.

Conferencing is not offered when offenders wish to contest their guilt. Those who do not are referred to the conference, which normally lasts one to two hours and is attended by the victims and their supporters, the offenders and their supporters, and other relevant parties. The conference coordinator focuses the discussion on condemning the act without condemning the character of the actor. Offenders are asked to explain what happened, how they have felt about the crime, and what they think should be done. The victims and others are asked to describe the physical, financial, and emotional consequences of the crime. This discussion may lead the offenders, their families, and their friends to experience the shame of the act, prompting an apology to the victim. A plan of action is developed and signed by key participants. The plan may include the offender paying compensation to the victim, doing work for the victim or the community, or any other undertaking the participants may agree upon. It is the responsibility of the conference participants to determine the outcomes that are most appropriate for these particular victims and these particular offenders.

### Critical Thinking

1.  How can this essentially humanistic approach be sold to the general public, who now support more punitive sanctions? Would it be feasible to claim that using restorative justice with nonviolent offenders frees resources for dealing with the relatively few dangerous people in the criminal population?

2.  Would a method that works in New Zealand and/or Australia also have utility in the United States, with its more heterogeneous population, greater social problems, and more violent crime?

Sources: Nathan Harris, "Family Group Conferencing in Australia 15 Years On," Australian Institute of Family Studies, www.aifs.gov.au/nch/pubs/issues/issues27/issues27.html (accessed May 1, 2010); Australian Institute of Criminology, "Restorative Justice: An Australian Perspective," www.aic.gov.au/rjustice/australia.html (accessed August 31, 2008); Kathleen Daly and Hennessey Hayes, *Restorative Justice and Conferencing in Australia*, http://www.aic.gov.au/documents/5/3/D/%7B53D95879-0B21-40BC-B716-3DACF695FA3B%7Dti186.pdf (accessed August 31, 2010); Hennessey Hayes, "Assessing Reoffending in Restorative Justice Conferences," *Australian and New Zealand Journal of Criminology* 38 (2005): 77–101.

someone else. For victims such as these, restorative justice processes can seem unnecessary at best.[133]

These are a few of the obstacles that restorative justice programs must overcome in order to be successful and productive. But because the method holds so much promise, criminologists are conducting numerous demonstration projects to find the most effective means of returning ownership of justice to the people and the community.

## Ethical Challenges in Criminal Justice: A Writing Assignment

Y**ou are an appellate court judge. Before you is the case of a famous 26-year-old party-girl/model/hotel-heiress named London Marriott who was arrested for reckless driving at 2:00 A.M., even though she was under a probation order forbidding any misbehavior and imposing an 11:00 P.M. curfew. The sentencing judge sentenced her to 45 days in county jail, reminding her that she had been warned against any further violations and it had been made clear that violating the conditions of probation would not be tolerated. The day she arrived in jail, however, the county sheriff signed orders reassigning Ms. Marriott to 40 days of home confinement**

and electronic monitoring. The sheriff commented, "My message to those who don't like celebrities is that punishing celebrities more than the average American is not justice." He stated that under normal circumstances, Marriott would not have served any time in jail, and he added that "The special treatment, in a sense, appears to be because of her celebrity status. . . . She got more time in jail." But the sentencing judge then summoned Marriott to reappear in court the following morning and ordered her to serve her original sentence behind bars with "No work furlough. No work release. No electronic monitoring."

Ms. Marriott's lawyers have filed an emergency appeal, asking you, the appellate court judge, to grant her relief and suggesting that the original sentence was overly harsh and a violation of her due process rights. Write an essay on how you would you deal with the case. In your paper, address whether you think London should be jailed for her behavior or believe, along with the sheriff, that more appropriate, alternative sanctions are available. In formulating your answer, you may want to refer to the sections on alternative sanctions. You may also want to address this issue: Would it be fair to give a wealthy celebrity a lenient sentence while indigent women go to jail for the same crime?

# SUMMARY

### 1. Be familiar with the concept of community sentencing.

- Many of those convicted in criminal courts can be reintegrated into the community and, if given the proper treatment, are unlikely to recidivate.

- There are now a great variety of community sentences, ranging from traditional probation to house arrest and placement in community correctional centers.

- Community sentences can be structured to maximize security and maintain public safety.

### 2. Know the history of community sentences.

- The roots of community sentencing can be traced to the traditions of the English common law. During the Middle Ages, judges who wanted to spare deserving offenders from the pains of (sometimes horrific) punishment granted clemency and stays of execution.

- The common-law practice of judicial reprieve allowed judges to suspend punishment so that convicted offenders could seek a pardon, gather new evidence, or demonstrate that they had reformed their behavior.

- John Augustus of Boston is usually credited with originating the modern probation concept.

### 3. Recognize the different types of probation sentences.

- Most probation orders involve a contract between the court and the offender in which a prison or jail term is suspended and the probationer promises to obey a set of probation rules or conditions mandated by the court.

- Offenders who are on probation have been convicted of a crime, but instead of being incarcerated, they are returned to the community for a period during which they must abide by certain conditions set forth by the court under the supervision of a probation officer.

- Probationary sentences may be granted by state and federal district courts and state superior (felony) courts.

### 4. Be familiar with the rules of probation.

- When granting probation, the court sets down certain conditions or rules of behavior that the probationer is bound to obey.

- Rules can set curfews, prohibit behaviors such as drinking or owning a gun, and/or mandate that the probationer hold a job and not leave the jurisdiction without permission.

■ Probation may be revoked if clients fail to comply with rules or disobey reasonable requests to meet their treatment obligations.

**5. Discuss the organization and administration of probation services.**

■ In some states, there is a statewide probation service, but each court jurisdiction controls its local department. Other states maintain a strong statewide authority with centralized control and administration.

■ Staff officers in probation departments are usually charged with five primary tasks: investigation, intake, diagnosis, treatment supervision, and risk classification.

**6. Define and discuss the term "risk classification."**

■ As part of clients' entry into probation, an assessment is made about the risk level they pose to the community and themselves.

■ On the basis of this assessment, offenders are assigned to a specific supervision level.

**7. Be familiar with the legal issues related to probation.**

■ The U.S. Supreme Court has ruled that probationers have a unique status and therefore are entitled to fewer constitutional protections than other citizens.

■ During the course of a probationary term, violating the rules or terms of probation or committing a new crime can result in probation being revoked.

■ In some significant decisions, the Supreme Court has provided procedural safeguards to apply at proceedings convened to consider revoking probation.

**8. Debate the effectiveness of probation.**

■ Probation is cost-effective. Incarcerating an inmate typically costs over $25,000 per year, whereas probation costs about $2,000 per year.

■ National data indicates that almost 60 percent of probationers successfully complete their probationary sentence, while more than 40 percent are rearrested, violate probation rules, or abscond.

■ Although the failure rate seems disturbingly high, even the most serious criminals who receive probation are less likely to recidivate than those who are sent to prison for committing similar crimes.

**9. Know what is meant by intermediate sanctions.**

■ Intermediate sanctions include programs that are usually administered by probation departments: intensive probation supervision, house arrest, electronic monitoring, restitution orders, shock probation or split sentences, and residential community corrections.

■ Intermediate sanctions offer effective alternatives to prisons and jails.

■ They also have the potential to save money; although they are more expensive than traditional probation, they are far less costly than incarceration.

**10. Explain the concept of restorative justice and discuss its merits.**

■ Restorative justice advocates suggest a policy based on restoring the damage caused by crime and creating a system of justice that includes all the parties harmed by the criminal act: the victim, the offender, the community, and society.

■ Restorative justice advocates believe what is needed is a justice policy that repairs the harm caused by crime and includes all parties that have suffered from that harm.

■ Restorative justice programs stress healing and redemption rather than punishment and deterrence.

## KEY TERMS

probation, 478
judicial reprieve, 480
recognizance, 480
probation rules, 480
revocation, 481
suspended sentence, 482
intake, 485
pre-sentence investigation, 486
risk classification, 488
day fees, 493

intermediate sanctions, 495
fine, 496
day fine, 497
forfeiture, 497
zero tolerance, 497
restitution, 498
monetary restitution, 498
community service restitution, 499
shock probation, 499
split sentence, 499

intensive probation supervision (IPS), 499
house arrest, 500
electronic monitoring (EM), 501
residential community corrections (RCC), 503
day reporting center (DRC), 504
restorative justice, 506
sentencing circles, 508

## CRITICAL THINKING QUESTIONS

1. What is the purpose of probation? Identify some conditions of probation, and discuss the responsibilities of the probation officer.

2. Discuss the procedures involved in probation revocation. What are the rights of the probationer? Is probation a privilege or a right? Explain.

3. Should a convicted criminal make restitution to the victim? Why or why not? When is restitution inappropriate?

4. Should offenders be fined on the basis of the severity of what they did or according to their ability to pay? Is it fair to base day fines on wages? Why or why not? Should offenders be punished

more severely because they are financially successful? Explain.

5. Does house arrest involve a violation of personal freedom? Does wearing an ankle bracelet smack of "Big Brother"? Would you want the government monitoring your daily activities? Could this be expanded, for example, to monitoring the whereabouts of AIDS patients? Explain.

6. Do you agree that criminals can be restored through community interaction? Considering the fact that recidivism rates are so high, are traditional sanctions a waste of time and restorative ones the wave of the future?

## NOTES

1. Dave Itzkoff, "Chris Brown Pleads Guilty in Deal," *New York Times*, June 22, 2009, http://artsbeat.blogs.nytimes.com/2009/06/22/chris-brown-pleads-guilty-in-deal/.

2. Brandon Applegate, Hayden Smith, Alicia Sitren, and Nicolette Fariello Springer, "From the Inside: The Meaning of Probation to Probationers," Criminal Justice Review 34 (2009): 80–95.

3. Ted Chiricos, Kelle Barrick, William Bales, and Stephanie Bontrager, "The Labeling of Convicted Felons and Its Consequences for Recidivism, *Criminology* 45 (2007): 547–581).

4. For a history of probation, see Edward Sieh, "From Augustus to the Progressives: A Study of Probation's Formative Years," *Federal Probation* 57 (1993): 67–72.

5. Ibid.

6. David Rothman, *Conscience and Convenience* (Boston: Little, Brown, 1980), pp. 82–117.

7. See, generally, Todd Clear and Vincent O'Leary, *Controlling the Offender in the Community* (Lexington, Mass.: Lexington Books, 1983).

8. Lauren Glaze and Thomas Bonczar, *Probation and Parole, 2008* (Washington, D.C.: Bureau of Justice Statistics, 2010), http://bjs.ojp.usdoj.gov/content/pub/ascii/ppus08.txt. Data on probation comes from this source.

9. Thomas Cohen and Tracey Kyckelhahn , *Felony Sentences in Large Urban Courts*, 2006 (Washington, D.C.: Bureau of Justice Statistics, 2010).

10. Ibid.

11. Heather Barklage, Dane Miller, and Gene Bonham Jr., "Probation Conditions vs. Probation Officer Directives," *Federal Probation* 70 (2006), www.uscourts.gov/fedprob/December_2006/probationconditions.html (accessed August 30, 2008).

12. Karl Hanson and Suzanne Wallace-Carpretta, "Predictors of Criminal Recidivism among Male Batterers," *Psychology, Crime and Law* 10 (2004): 413–427.

13. *Higdon v. United States*, 627 F.2d 893 (1980).

14. Elinor Mills, "Conn. AG to MySpace: Turn over sex offender data," *Digital Media*, January 23, 2009, http://news.cnet.com/8301-1023_3-10149435-93.html (accessed April 5, 2010).

15. Techbeat, "'Monitoring' the Sex Offender," National Law Enforcement and Corrections Technology Center (2005), http://www.justnet.org/TechBeat%20Files/MonitorSexOffender.pdf (accessed May 1, 2010).

16. *John Doe and Steve Morris vs. Prosecutor, Marion County, Indiana*, CASE NO. 1:08-cv-0436-DFH-TAB (2008), http://media.courierpress.com/media/static/federal_court_ruling.pdf.

17. Geoff Ward and Aaron Kupchik, "What Drives Juvenile Probation Officers? Relating Organizational Contexts, Status Characteristics, and Personal Convictions to Treatment and Punishment Orientations," Crime & Delinquency 56 ( 2010): 35–69.

18. Mark Jones and John Kerbs, "Probation and Parole Officers and Discretionary Decision-Making: Responses to Technical and Criminal Violations," *Federal Probation* 71 (2007): 9–15.

19. Todd Clear and Edward Latessa, "Probation Officers' Roles in Intensive Supervision: Surveillance versus Treatment," *Justice Quarterly* 10 (1993): 441–462.

20. Kathleen Auerhahn, "Do You Know Who Your Probationers Are? Using Simulation Modeling to Estimate the Composition of California's Felony Probation Population, 1980–2000," *Justice Quarterly* 24 (2007): 28–48.

21. Paul von Zielbauer, "Probation Dept. Is Now Arming Officers Supervising Criminals," *New York Times*, August 7, 2003, p. 5.

22. Wayne Pitts, "Educational Competency as an Indicator of Occupational Stress for Probation and Parole Officers," *American Journal of Criminal Justice* 32 (2007): 57–73.

23. Jeffrey Lin, Joel Miller, and Mayumi Fukushima, "Juvenile Probation Officers Dispositional Recommendations: Predictive Factors and Their Alignment with Predictors of Recidivism, Journal of Crime & Justice 31 (2008): 1–34.

24. Diana Wendy Fitzgibbon, "Deconstructing Probation: Risk and Developments in Practice," *Journal of Social Work Practice* 22 (2008): 85–101.

25. Hanson and Wallace-Carpretta, "Predictors of Criminal Recidivism among Male Batterers."

26. David Duffee and Bonnie Carlson, "Competing Value Premises for the Provision of Drug Treatment to Probationers," *Crime and Delinquency* 42 (1996): 574–592.

27. Richard Sluder and Rolando Del Carmen, "Are Probation and Parole Officers Liable for Injuries Caused by Probationers and Parolees?" *Federal Probation* 54 (1990): 3–12.

28. James Byrne, "Introduction to Special Issue on Risk Assessment," *Federal Probation* 70 (2006), www.uscourts.gov/fedprob/September_2006/ (accessed August 30, 2008).

29. James Austin, "How Much Risk Can We Take? The Misuse of Risk Assessment in Corrections," *Federal Probation* 70 (2006), www.uscourts.gov/fedprob/September_2006/risk.html (accessed August 30, 2008).

30. Lawrence W. Sherman, "Use Probation to Prevent Murder," *Criminology and Public Policy* 6 (2007): 843–849.

31. Carolin Kröner, Cornelis Stadtland, Matthias Eidt, and Norbert Nedopil, "The Validity of the Violence Risk Appraisal Guide (VRAG) in Predicting Criminal Recidivism," *Criminal Behaviour and Mental Health* 17 (2007): 89–100.

32. James Byrne and April Pattavina, "Assessing the Role of Clinical and Actuarial Risk Assessment in an Evidence-Based Community Corrections System: Issues to Consider," *Federal Probation* 70 (2006), www.uscourts.gov/fedprob/September_2006/issues.html (accessed August 30, 2008).

33. Kathleen Auerhahn, "Conceptual and Methodological Issues in the Prediction of Dangerous Behavior," *Criminology and Public Policy* 5 (2006): 771–778.

34. *Minnesota v. Murphy*, 465 U.S. 420 (1984).

35. *Griffin v. Wisconsin*, 483 U.S. 868 (1987).

36. *United States v. Knights*, 122 S.Ct. 587 (2001).

37. *Mempa v. Rhay*, 389 U.S. 128 (1967).

38. *Morrissey v. Brewer*, 408 U.S. 471 (1972).

39. *Gagnon v. Scarpelli*, 411 U.S. 778 (1973).

40. *Beardon v. Georgia*, 33 CrL 3101 (1983).

41. *United States v. Granderson*, 511 U.S. 39 (1994).

42. Glaze and Bonczar, *Probation 2008.*

43. M. Kevin Gray, Monique Fields, and Sheila Royo Maxwell, "Examining Probation Violations: Who, What, and When," *Crime and Delinquency* 47 (2001): 537–557.

44. Kevin Minor, James Wells, and Crissy Sims, "Recidivism among Federal Probationers—Predicting Sentence Violations," *Federal Probation* 67 (2003): 31–37.

45. Cassia Spohn and David Holleran, "The Effect of Imprisonment on Recidivism Rates of Felony Offenders: A Focus on Drug Offenders," *Criminology* 40 (2002): 329–359.

46. Joan Petersilia, Susan Turner, James Kahan, and Joyce Peterson, *Granting Felons Probation: Public Risks and Alternatives* (Santa Monica, Calif.: RAND, 1985).

47. Spohn and Holleran, "The Effect of Imprisonment."

48. Kathryn Morgan, "Factors Influencing Probation Outcome: A Review of the Literature," *Federal Probation* 57 (1993): 23–29.

49. Michelle Meloy, "The Sex Offender Next Door: An Analysis of Recidivism, Risk Factors, and Deterrence of Sex Offenders on Probation," *Criminal Justice Policy Review* 16 (2005): 211–236.

50. Kathryn Morgan, "Factors Associated with Probation Outcome," *Journal of Criminal Justice* 22 (1994): 341–353.

51. Paula M. Ditton, *Mental Health and Treatment of Inmates and Probationers* (Washington, D.C.: Bureau of Justice Statistics, 1999).

52. Naomi Freeman, "Predictors of Rearrest for Rapists and Child Molesters on Probation," *Criminal Justice and Behavior* 34 (2007): 752–768.

53. Nancy Rodriguez and Vincent Webb, "Probation Violations, Revocations, and Imprisonment: The Decisions of Probation Officers, Prosecutors, and Judges Pre- and Post-Mandatory Drug Treatment," *Criminal Justice Policy Review* 18 (2007): 3–30.

54. Kathryn Morgan, "Factors Associated with Probation Outcome."

55. Diana Wendy Fitzgibbon, "Deconstructing Probation."

56. Joan Petersilia, "Probation in the United States," in *Crime and Justice: A Review of Research* 21, ed. Michael Tonry (Chicago: University of Chicago Press, 1997), p. 185.

57. "Law in Massachusetts Requires Probationers to Pay 'Day Fees,'" *Criminal Justice Newsletter*, September 15, 1988, p. 1.

58. Peter Finn and Dale Parent, *Making the Offender Foot the Bill: A Texas Program* (Washington, D.C.: National Institute of Justice, 1992).

59. Nicole Leeper Piquero, "A Recidivism Analysis of Maryland's Community Probation Program," *Journal of Criminal Justice* 31 (2003): 295–308.

60. Todd R. Clear, "Places Not Cases: Rethinking the Probation Focus," *Howard Journal of Criminal Justice* 44 (2005): 172–184.

61. Andrew Klein and Ann Crowe, "Findings from an Outcome Examination of Rhode Island's Specialized Domestic Violence Probation Supervision Program," *Violence Against Women* 14 (2008): 226–246.

62. Private Probation Services, www.privateprobationservices.com (accessed August 30, 2010).

63. Christine Schloss and Leanne Alarid, "Standards in the Privatization of Probation Services: A Statutory Analysis," *Criminal Justice Review* 32 (2007): 233–245.

64. "HOPE in Hawaii: Swift and Sure Changes in Probation" (government monograph), National Institute of Justice, 2008, www.ncjrs.gov/pdffiles1/nij/222758.pdf.

65. Ariel Hart, "Runaway Bride Enters Plea and Is Sentenced to Probation," *New York Times*, June 3, 2005, p. A14.

66. Todd Clear and Patricia Hardyman, "The New Intensive Supervision Movement," *Crime and Delinquency* 36 (1990): 42–60.

67. For a thorough review of these programs, see James Byrne, Arthur Lurigio, and Joan Petersilia, eds., *Smart Sentencing: The Emergence of Intermediate Sanctions* (Newbury Park, Calif.: Sage, 1993). Hereinafter cited as *Smart Sentencing*.

68. Norval Morris and Michael Tonry, *Between Prison and Probation: Intermediate Punishments in a Rational Sentencing System* (New York: Oxford University Press, 1990).

69. Michael Tonry and Richard Will, *Intermediate Sanctions* (Washington, D.C.: National Institute of Justice, 1990).

70. Ibid., p. 8.

71. Stephen Farrall, "Officially Recorded Convictions for Probationers: The Relationship with Self-Report and Supervisory Observations," *Legal and Criminological Psychology* 10 (2005): 121–132.

72. Michael Maxfield and Terry Baumer, "Home Detention with Electronic Monitoring: Comparing Pretrial and Postconviction Programs," *Crime and Delinquency* 36 (1990): 521–556.

73. Robert Homant and Mark DeMercurio, "Intermediate Sanctions in Probation Officers' Sentencing Recommendations: Consistency, Net Widening, and Net Repairing," The Prison Journal 89 (2009): 426–439.

74. George Cole, "Monetary Sanctions: The Problem of Compliance," in *Smart Sentencing*, 51–64.

75. *Tate v. Short*, 401 U.S. 395 (1971).

76. Lina Eriksson and Robert Goodin, "The Measuring Rod of Time: The Example of Swedish Day-fines," *Journal of Applied Philosophy* 24 (2007): 125–136.

77. Pennsylvania Department of Corrections, *Day Fines, 2003*, www.cor.state.pa.us/stats/lib/stats/Day_Fines.pdf (accessed August 30, 2008).

78. John L. Worrall, "Addicted to the Drug War: The Role of Civil Asset Forfeiture as a Budgetary Necessity in Contemporary Law Enforcement," *Journal of Criminal Justice* 29 (2001): 171–187.

79. C. Yorke, *Some Consideration on the Law of Forfeiture for High Treason*, 2d ed. (1746), p. 26; cited in David Fried, "Rationalizing Criminal Forfeiture," *Journal of Criminal Law and Criminology* 79 (1988): 328–436.

80. Fried, "Rationalizing Criminal Forfeiture," p. 436.

81. James B. Jacobs, Coleen Friel, and Edward O'Callaghan, "Pension Forfeiture: A Problematic Sanction for Public Corruption," *American Criminal Law Review* 35 (1997): 57–92.

82. Worrall, "Addicted to the Drug War."

83. Peter Hermann, "Feds Start Seizing Homes of Child Pornographers," *Baltimore Sun*, April 21, 2010, http://articles.baltimoresun.com/2010-04-21/news/bs-md-hermann-porn-20100421_1_child-pornography-house-seizures-harford-county-house.

84. For a general review, see Burt Galaway and Joe Hudson, *Criminal Justice, Restitution, and Reconciliation* (New York: Criminal Justice Press, 1990)

85. Frederick Allen and Harvey Treger, "Community Service Orders in Federal Probation: Perceptions of Probationers and Host Agencies," *Federal Probation* 54 (1990): 8–14.

86. Gail Caputo, "Community Service in Texas: Results of a Probation Survey," *Corrections Compendium* 30 (2005): 8–12.

87. Sudipto Roy, "Two Types of Juvenile Restitution Programs in Two Midwestern Counties: A Comparative Study," *Federal Probation* 57 (1993): 48–53.

88. Joan Petersilia, *The Influence of Criminal Justice Research* (Santa Monica, Calif.: RAND, 1987).

89. Ibid.

90. Jodi Brown, *Correctional Populations in the United States, 1996* (Washington, D.C.: Bureau of Justice Statistics, 1999), p. 39.

91. Joan Petersilia and Susan Turner, "Evaluating Intensive Supervision Probation/Parole: Results of a Nationwide Experiment," National Institute of Justice, Research in Brief (Washington, D.C.: National Institute of Justice, 1993).

92. James Ryan, "Who Gets Revoked? A Comparison of Intensive Supervision Successes and Failures in Vermont," *Crime and Delinquency* 43 (1997): 104–118.

93. Angela Robertson, Paul Grimes, and Kevin Rogers, "A Short-Run Cost–Benefit Analysis of Community-Based Interventions for Juvenile Offenders," *Crime and Delinquency* 47 (2001): 265–284.

94. UPI. com, Stallworth pleads guilty to manslaughter, June 16, 2009, www.upi.com/Sports_News/2009/06/16/Stallworth-pleads-guilty-to-manslaughter/UPI-64531245170350/.

95. S. Christopher Baird and Dennis Wagner, "Measuring Diversion: The Florida Community Control Program," *Crime and Delinquency* 36 (1990): 112–125.

96. Linda Smith and Ronald Akers, "A Comparison of Recidivism of Florida's Community Control and Prison: A Five-Year Survival Analysis," *Journal of Research in Crime and Delinquency* 30 (1993): 267–292.

97. Robert N. Altman, Robert E. Murray, and Evey B. Wooten, "Home Confinement: A '90s Approach to Community Supervision," *Federal Probation* 61 (1997): 30–32.

98. Ronnie Garrett, "Home Monitoring System Boosts Victim and Community Safety," *Law Enforcement Technology* 34 (2007): 120, 122–124.

99. Omnilink Systems, www.omnilink.com (accessed May 1, 2010).

100. Edna Erez and Peter Ibarra, "Making Your Home a Shelter: Electronic Monitoring and Victim Re-entry in Domestic Violence Cases," *British Journal of Criminology* 47 (2007): 100–120.

101. Brian Payne and Randy Gainey, "The Electronic Monitoring of Offenders Released from Jail or Prison: Safety, Control, and Comparisons to the Incarceration Experience," *Prison Journal* 84 (2004): 413–435.

102. Kevin E. Courtright, Bruce L. Berg, and Robert J. Mutchnick, "The Cost-Effectiveness of Using House Arrest with Electronic Monitoring for Drunk Drivers," *Federal Probation* 61 (1997): 19–22.

103. Matthew DeMichele, Brian Payne, and Deeanna Button, "Electronic Monitoring of Sex Offenders: Identifying Unanticipated Consequences and Implications, Journal of Offender Rehabilitation 46 (2008): 119–135.

104. Payne and Gainey, "The Electronic Monitoring of Offenders Released from Jail or Prison"; Mary Finn and Suzanne Muirhead-Steves, "The Effectiveness of Electronic Monitoring with Male Parolees," *Justice Quarterly* 19 (2002): 293–313.

105. Kathy Padgett, William Bales, and Thomas Blomberg, "Under Surveillance: An Empirical Test of the Effectiveness and Consequences of Electronic Monitoring," *Criminology and Public Policy* 5 (2006): 61–91.

106. William Burrell and Robert Gable, "From B. F. Skinner to Spiderman to Martha Stewart: The Past, Present and Future of Electronic Monitoring of Offenders," Journal of Offender Rehabilitation 46 (2008): 101–118.

107. David Farabee, Yih-Ing Hser, Douglas Anglin, and David Huang, "Recidivism among an Early Cohort of California's Proposition 36 Offenders," *Criminology and Public Policy* 3 (2004): 563–583.

108. Portland House, www.lssmn.org/portland.htm (accessed August 30, 2008).

109. Harvey Siegal, James Fisher, Richard Rapp, Casey Kelliher, Joseph Wagner, William O'Brien, and Phyllis Cole, "Enhancing Substance Abuse Treatment with Case Management," *Journal of Substance Abuse Treatment* 13 (1996): 93–98.

110. Georgia Department of Corrections, Day Reporting Centers, www.dcor.state.ga.us/Divisions/Corrections/ProbationSupervision/DayReporting.html (accessed April 18, 2010).

111. The Commonwealth of Massachusetts Trial Court Office of Community Corrections, Utilization of Community Corrections Centers Statistical Report, 2009, http://www.mass.gov/courts/admin/occ/fy2009report.pdf (accessed April 18, 2010).

112. Michael Ostermann, "An Analysis of New Jersey's Day Reporting Center and Halfway Back Programs: Embracing the Rehabilitative Ideal through Evidence-Based Practices," Journal of Offender Rehabilitation 48 (2009): 139–153.

113. Dae-Young Kim, Hee-Jong Joo, and William McCarty, "Risk Assessment and Classification of Day Reporting Center Clients: An Actuarial Approach,⬛ Criminal Justice and Behavior 35 (2008): 792–812.

114. Amy Craddock, "Day Reporting Center Completion: Comparison of Individual and Multilevel Models," Crime and Delinquency 55 (2009): 105–133; Sudipto Roy and Shannon Barton, "Convicted Drunk Drivers in Electronic Monitoring Home Detention and Day Reporting Centers," *Federal Probation* 70 (2006), www.uscourts .gov/fedprob/June_2006/drunkdrivers.html (accessed June 20, 2007).

115. Kathleen Daly and Russ Immarigeon, "The Past, Present, and Future of Restorative Justice: Some Critical Reflections," *Contemporary Justice Review* 1 (1998): 21–45.

116. John Braithwaite, *Crime, Shame, and Reintegration* (Melbourne, Australia: Cambridge University Press, 1989).

117. Gene Stephens, "The Future of Policing: From a War Model to a Peace Model," in *The Past, Present and Future of American Criminal Justice,* ed. Brendan Maguire and Polly Radosh (Dix Hills, N.Y.: General Hall, 1996), pp. 77–93.

118. Kay Pranis, "Peacemaking Circles: Restorative Justice in Practice Allows Victims and Offenders to Begin Repairing the Harm," *Corrections Today* 59 (1997): 74.

119. Carol LaPrairie, "The 'New' Justice: Some Implications for Aboriginal Communities," *Canadian Journal of Criminology* 40 (1998): 61–79.

120. Robert Coates, Mark Umbreit, and Betty Vos, "Restorative Justice Systemic Change: The Washington County Experience," *Federal Probation* 68 (2004): 16–23.

121. David R. Karp and Beau Breslin, "Restorative Justice in School Communities," *Youth and Society* 33 (2001): 249–272.

122. Paul Jesilow and Deborah Parsons, "Community Policing as Peacemaking," *Policing and Society* 10 (2000): 163–183.

123. Aidan Wilcox, Richard Young, and Carolyn Hoyle, "Two-Year Resanctioning Study: A Comparison of Restorative and Traditional Cautions" (British Home Office: 2004), www.homeoffice.gov.uk/rds/pdfs04/rdsolr5704.pdf (accessed August 30, 2008); Lynette Parker, "Evaluating Restorative Programmes: Reports from Two Countries" (Restorative Justice.org: June 2005), www.restorativejustice.org/editions/2005/june05/evaluations (accessed August 30, 2008); Aidan Wilcox and Richard Young, "How Green Was Thames Valley? Policing the Image of Restorative Justice Cautions," *Policing and Society* 17 (2007): 141–163.

124. Gordon Bazemore and Curt Taylor Griffiths, "Conferences, Circles, Boards, and Mediations: The 'New Wave' of Community Justice Decision Making," *Federal Probation* 61 (1997): 25–37.

125. Mark Umbreit and Rina Ritter, "Arab Offenders Meet Jewish Victim: Restorative Family Dialogue in Israel," *Conflict Resolution Quarterly* 24 (2006): 99–109.

126. John Braithwaite, "Setting Standards for Restorative Justice," *British Journal of Criminology* 42 (2002): 563–577.

127. Nancy Rodriguez, "Restorative Justice, Communities, and Delinquency: Whom Do We Reintegrate?" *Criminology and Public Policy* 4 (2005): 103–130.

128. John Braithwaite, "Setting Standards for Restorative Justice," *British Journal of Criminology* 42 (2002): 563–577.

129. David Altschuler, "Community Justice Initiatives: Issues and Challenges in the U.S. Context," *Federal Probation* 65 (2001): 28–33.

130. Lois Presser and Patricia Van Voorhis, "Values and Evaluation: Assessing Processes and Outcomes of Restorative Justice Programs," *Crime and Delinquency* 48 (2002): 162–189.

131. Sharon Levrant, Francis Cullen, Betsy Fulton, and John Wozniak, "Reconsidering Restorative Justice: The Corruption of Benevolence Revisited?" *Crime and Delinquency* 45 (1999): 3–28.

132. Dean Gromet and John Darley, "Restoration and Retribution: How Including Retributive Components Affects the Acceptability of Restorative Justice Procedures," *Social Justice Research* 19 (2006): 395–432.

133. Michael E. Smith, *What Future for "Public Safety" and "Restorative Justice" in Community Corrections?* (Washington, D.C.: National Institute of Justice, (2001).

# CHAPTER 14

# Corrections: History, Institutions, and Populations

## CHAPTER OBJECTIVES

1. Identify the various components of the correctional institution system.
2. Discuss some of the most significant problems facing the correctional system.
3. Be able to articulate how the first penal institutions developed in Europe.
4. Explain how William Penn revolutionized corrections.
5. Compare the early New York and Pennsylvania prison models.
6. Chart the development of penal reform.
7. List the purposes of jails, and understand the characteristic makeup of jail populations.
8. Be familiar with the term "new-generation jail."
9. Classify the different types of federal and state penal institutions.
10. Discuss prison population trends.

© Joshua Lott/New York Times/Redux

**A**rizona's Maricopa County (Phoenix) Sheriff Joe Arpaio enthusiastically promotes himself as "America's Toughest Sheriff." Accordingly, he created Tent City, which is considered the nation's toughest *jail*. Here 2,000 inmates live in tents surrounded by 25-foot barbed wire fences, baking in temperatures of 122 degrees in summer and freezing in winter. As new inmates enter, more tents are constructed. In addition to banning salt and pepper and coffee, Tent City now has two sky watchtowers for security, stun fences around the perimeter, and facial recognition computer software for inmate identification. K-9 units and patrol deputies have been added for additional security. Recently, Arpaio announced that Maricopa County jail inmates will start paying for their own meals. The policy will be to charge inmates $1.25 per day for their meals and will apply only to those inmates who have money in personal accounts, "on their books." Those who can't afford to pay will still receive food but will run "a tab" and will be forced to pay their accumulated charges if they are arrested again and returned to one of the county facilities. According to Arpaio, "If [family members] send money in to buy chocolate bars, it's going to go to food first instead of chocolate bars."[1] Arpaio believes that inmates should live no better than servicemen and women serving in Iraq and Afghanistan and refuses to provide them amenities found in less rigorous correctional facilities. Inmates have filed suit against Arpaio's harsh tactics, and one former inmate (Shaun Attwood) has issued a guidebook for survival in Tent City. It contains the following tips:[2]

■ If you don't want to end up with the mystery-meat slop the inmates call "red death," then when you first enter the jail, tell the booking officer you need a religious diet. Claiming Hindu will get you vegetarian food. The Jewish food is considered the best, but you'll have some explaining to do to the Aryan Brotherhood.

■ When you get your first chow, sit down last because you don't want to sit on the seat of someone who likes to knock people out for the slightest affront. Find out who sits where, and ask someone where it's safe for you to sit.

■ If you must do drugs, clean the works. There are hundreds of men sharing one dirty syringe throughout Arpaio's jail system. Hepatitis C is rampant, and TB not uncommon. The way Arpaio runs the jail constitutes a public-health risk.

**jail**
A correctional facility designed to hold pretrial detainees and misdemeanants serving their criminal sentence.

**prison**
A correctional facility designed to hold convicted felons while they serve their criminal sentence.

Sheriff Joe Arpaio is the nation's most notorious practitioner of "no frills" corrections. According to this view, inmates should not be coddled but should be punished so they will choose never to repeat their crimes.[3] Although this get-tough approach sounds attractive to some, many wardens and **prison** administrators are wary of a policy that restricts inmate activities, increases boredom, and threatens their control over inmates. Obviously, there is still great debate over the true role of secure corrections. Some penal experts maintain that prisons and jails should be used to help treat and rehabilitate convicted offenders in "therapeutic communities."[4] In contrast, other correctional experts believe secure facilities should be designed to deter would-be criminals and keep those convicted of crime apart from society.[5] Under this latter model, prison success would be measured by such factors as physical security, length of incapacitation, a lower crime rate, and the fear of criminal sanctions.

On the surface, this get-tough approach appears to be effective: After all, the crime rate has declined as the number of people under lock and key has risen.[6] Nonetheless, the association between the use of secure confinements and the falling crime rate may be spurious: It is also possible that the recent crime drop has little to do with the prison boom and more to do with police effectiveness or sentencing policy. Locking people up may have less influence on present and future crime rates than those in the get-tough camp believe.[7] Consequently, correctional rehabilitation and treatment efforts have not been abandoned, and numerous examples of successful programs still flourish in prisons. Educational programs allow inmates to get college credits, vocational training has become more sophisticated, counseling and substance-abuse programs are almost universal, and some states now provide faith-based programs that allow religious organizations into the prison to help inmates adjust and reform.

While the debate over correctional rehabilitation rages on, there is no question that the nation's vast secure corrections system, with branches in the federal, state, and county levels of government, has not met its stated goals. Although the majority of inmates yearn for freedom, one of the great tragedies of our time is that correctional institutions do not seem to correct: The majority of former inmates offend again soon after reentering society. This means that each year, hundreds of thousands of former inmates return to prison because they have failed to resist the temptation to commit further crimes after returning to the community.

Although the debate still rages between those who emphasize punishment and those who promote treatment, there is no question that the contemporary correctional system has become quite complex and now contains a variety of different types of institutions designed to house and correct different classes of offenders. Felons are housed in high-security prisons while misdemeanants are housed in county jails, which are sometimes called reformatories or houses of correction. Juvenile offenders have their own institutions, called schools, camps, ranches, or homes. There are also prison farms for adult offenders, and there are community correctional centers, such as halfway houses, for inmates who are about to return to society.

In this chapter, we explore the correctional system, beginning with the history and nature of correctional institutions. Then, in Chapter 15 we examine institutional life in some detail.

## THE HISTORY OF CORRECTIONAL INSTITUTIONS

The original legal punishments were typically banishment or slavery, restitution, corporal punishment, and execution. The concept of incarcerating convicted offenders for long periods of time as a punishment for their misdeeds did not become the norm in corrections until the nineteenth century.[8]

Although the use of incarceration as a routine punishment began much later, some early European institutions were created specifically to detain and control criminal offenders. Penal institutions were constructed in England during the tenth century to hold pretrial detainees and those waiting for their sentence to be carried out.[9] During the twelfth century, King Henry II constructed a series of county jails to hold thieves and vagrants prior to the disposition of their sentence. In 1557, the workhouse in Brideswell was built to hold people convicted of relatively minor offenses who would work to pay their debt to society. Those who had committed more serious offenses were held there pending execution.

Le Stinche, a prison in Florence, Italy, was used to punish offenders as early as 1301.[10] Prisoners were enclosed in separate cells, classified on the basis of gender, age, mental state, and crime seriousness.

### PERSPECTIVES ON JUSTICE

#### Crime Control

Prison reform challenged the crime control orientation of prisons. Opposed to the reformers were conservative prison administrators and state officials who believed that stern disciplinary measures were needed to control dangerous prison inmates. They continued the time-honored system of regimentation and discipline. Although the whip and the lash were eventually abolished, solitary confinement in dark, bare cells became a common penal practice.

© Vincent van Gogh, Prisoner's Round (detail), 1890. Pushkin Museum of Fine Arts, Moscow. Scala/Art Resource, New York.

Even though he himself was voluntarily committed to the asylum shown here, Vincent van Gogh captured the despair of the nineteenth-century penal institution in this detail from an 1890 painting sometimes titled *Prisoners Exercising*. The face of the prisoner near the center of the picture looking at the viewer is van Gogh's.

## CAREERS IN CRIMINAL JUSTICE

# *Corrections Counselor*

### Duties and Characteristics of the Job

The responsibility of corrections counselors is to review the situation of individual offenders and determine the most effective method of rehabilitation. They create, enact, manage, and sometimes evaluate programs designed to improve the psychosocial functions of offenders. Corrections counselors also provide counseling and educational sessions, survey the needs of offenders, and prepare reports for court. Counselors may choose a field of specialization, such as substance abuse or juvenile rehabilitation. They most often work in an office setting. Counseling can be a stressful job, given the population being served, the often serious nature of inmate problems, and the pressure for immediate results.

### Job Outlook

The employment of counselors is expected to grow at a faster than average rate in the near future. The expansion of the prison system means that opportunities for employment as a corrections counselor are good.

### Salary

The median annual wages of correctional treatment specialists are about $46,000; the highest 10 percent recently earned more than $78,000 per year. Higher wages tend to be found in urban areas, and those with graduate-level education are also more likely to have higher salaries and greater opportunities for advancement.

### Opportunities

Thanks to high rates of turnover within the field, prospects for employment are very good. A corrections counselor with the proper education and training has the potential to find employment readily and to be promoted to administrative and supervisory positions.

### Qualifications

Qualifications for higher-paid positions are more demanding. A corrections counselor's education and work experience should familiarize him or her with the criminal justice system and prepare him or her for determining how to reduce a client's chances of recidivism, as well as how to deal with unwilling clients. The ability to speak more than one language is also an advantage. Personality characteristics and skills such as the desire to help others and the ability to communicate well are important. Because of the settings and populations counselors work with, a future counselor will need to pass a background check and gain security clearance of the appropriate level. Some states also require certification before a corrections counselor can work in that state.

### Education and Training

Future corrections counselors should have a bachelor's degree in a field such as social work, criminal justice, or psychology. However, additional education at the master's level in these fields may be necessary to advance or to get certain positions. For some positions, clinical training can take the place of experience. Specialized skills such as expertise working with drug addiction or violent offenders can also lead to a higher-paying position. In addition to educational requirements, many entry-level jobs require some previous work experience, such as substance abuse counseling or corrections casework.

Sources: Bureau of Labor Statistics, United States Department of Labor, *Correctional Treatment Specialists Occupational Outlook Handbook, 2010–2011*, www.bls.gov/oco/ocos265.htm (accessed May 1, 2010).

---

Furloughs and conditional release were permitted, and—perhaps for the first time—a period of incarceration replaced corporal punishment for some offenses. Although Le Stinche existed for 500 years, relatively little is known about its administration or whether this early example of incarceration was unique to Florence.

The first penal institutions were foul places devoid of proper care, food, or medical treatment. The jailer, usually a shire reeve (sheriff)—an official appointed by the king or a noble landholder as chief law enforcement official of a county—ran the jail under a fee system, whereby inmates were required to pay for their own food and services. Those who could not pay were fed scraps until they starved to death:

> In 1748, the admission to Southwark prison was eleven shillings and four pence. Having got in, the prisoner had to pay for having himself put in irons, for his bed, of whatever sort, for his room if he was able to afford a separate room. He had to pay for his food, and when he had paid his debts and was ready to go out, he had to pay for having his irons struck off, and [he was charged] a discharge fee. . . . The gaolers [jailers] were usually "low bred, mercenary and oppressive, barbarous fellows, who think of nothing but enriching themselves by the most cruel extortion, and have less regard for the life of a poor prisoner than for the life of a brute."[11]

Jail conditions were deplorable because jailers ran them for personal gain. The fewer services provided, the greater their profit. Early jails were catchall institutions that held not only criminal offenders awaiting trial but also vagabonds, debtors, the mentally ill, and assorted others.

From 1776 to 1785, a growing inmate population that could no longer be transported to North America forced the English to house prisoners on **hulks**, abandoned ships anchored in harbors. The hulks became infamous for their degrading conditions and brutal punishments but were not abandoned until 1858. The writings of John Howard, the reform-oriented sheriff of Bedfordshire, drew attention to the squalid conditions in British penal institutions. His famous book *The State of the Prisons* (1777) condemned the lack of basic care given English inmates awaiting trial or serving sentences.[12] Howard's efforts to create humane standards in the British penal system resulted in the Penitentiary Act, by which Parliament established a more orderly penal system, with periodic inspections, elimination of the fee system, and greater consideration for inmates.

**hulk**
Mothballed ship used to house prisoners in eighteenth-century England.

## The Origin of Corrections in the United States

Although Europe had jails and a variety of other penal facilities, correctional reform was first instituted in the United States. The first American jail was built in James City in the Virginia colony in the early seventeenth century. However, the modern American correctional system had its origin in Pennsylvania under the leadership of William Penn.

At the end of the seventeenth century, Penn revised Pennsylvania's criminal code to forbid torture and the capricious use of mutilation and physical punishment. These penalties were replaced with imprisonment at hard labor, moderate flogging, fines, and forfeiture of property. All lands and goods belonging to felons were used to make restitution to the victims of their crimes, with restitution limited to twice the value of the damages. Felons who owned no property were assigned by law to the prison workhouse until the victim was compensated.

Penn ordered that a new type of institution be built to replace the widely used public forms of punishment—stocks, pillories, gallows, and branding irons. Each county was instructed to build a house of corrections similar to today's jails. County trustees or commissioners were responsible for raising money to build the jails and providing for their maintenance, although they were operated by the local sheriff. Penn's reforms remained in effect until his death in 1718, when the criminal penal code was changed back to open public punishment and harsh brutality.

Identifying the first American prison is difficult. Alexis Durham has described the 1773 opening of the Newgate Prison of Connecticut on the site of an abandoned copper mine. However, Newgate, which closed in the 1820s, is often ignored by correctional historians.[13] In 1785, Castle Island Prison was opened in Massachusetts and operated for about 15 years.

## Creating a Correctional System

The origin of the modern correctional system is usually traced to eighteenth-century developments in Pennsylvania. In 1776, post-revolutionary Pennsylvania again adopted William Penn's code, and in 1787, a group of Quakers led by

Benjamin Rush formed the Philadelphia Society for Alleviating the Miseries of Public Prisons. The aim of the society was to bring some degree of humane and orderly treatment to the growing penal system. The Quakers' influence on the legislature resulted in limiting the use of the death penalty to cases involving treason, murder, rape, and arson. Their next step was to reform the institutional system so that the prison could serve as a suitable alternative to physical punishment.

The only models of custodial institutions at that time were the local county jails that Penn had established. These facilities were designed to detain offenders, to securely incarcerate convicts awaiting other punishment, or to hold offenders who were working off their crimes. The Pennsylvania jails placed men, women, and children of all ages indiscriminately in one room. Liquor was often freely sold.

Under pressure from the Quakers to improve these conditions, the Pennsylvania legislature in 1790 called for renovation of the prison system. The eventual result was the creation of a separate wing of Philadelphia's **Walnut Street Jail** to house convicted felons (except those sentenced to death). Prisoners were placed in solitary cells, where they remained in isolation and did not have the right to work.[14] Quarters that contained the solitary or separate cells were called **penitentiary houses**, as was already the custom in England.

The new Pennsylvania prison system took credit for a rapid decrease in the crime rate—from 131 convictions in 1789 to 45 in 1793.[15] The prison became known as a school for reform and a place for public labor. The Walnut Street Jail's equitable conditions were credited with reducing escapes to none in the first four years of its existence (except for 14 on opening day). However, the Walnut Street Jail was not a total success. Isolation had a terrible psychological effect on inmates, and eventually inmates were given in-cell piecework on which they worked up to eight hours a day. Overcrowding undermined the goal of solitary confinement of serious offenders, and soon more than one inmate was placed in each cell. Despite these difficulties, similar institutions were erected in New York (Newgate in 1791) and New Jersey (Trenton in 1798).

## The Pennsylvania System

In 1818, Pennsylvania took the radical step of establishing a prison that placed each inmate in a single cell for the duration of his sentence. Classifications were abolished because each cell was intended as a miniature prison that would prevent inmates from associating with one another. In 1827, the Western State Penitentiary was built in Allegheny County. It took the form of a semicircle, with the cells positioned along its circumference. Built back to back, some cells faced the boundary wall and others faced the internal area of the circle. Inmates were kept at hard labor in solitary confinement, being allowed out for about an hour a day for exercise. The Western Penitentiary solitary system soon failed, because the small cells lacked adequate air and light, making solitary work impossible. The entire building had to be demolished in the 1830s and rebuilt in 1882 with larger individual cells. Known as Riverside, it survives and is still in use.

Two years later, in 1829, the Eastern State Penitentiary was built outside Philadelphia. Eastern State abandoned the use of corporal punishment and ill treatment of inmates that was common during that period. This new-style penitentiary was intended not merely to punish but also to move the criminal toward spiritual reflection and change. The method was a Quaker-inspired system of isolation from other prisoners, with labor. The early system was strict: inmates were hooded whenever they were outside their cells. But the proponents of the system believed strongly that the criminals, induced, in silence, to ponder their behavior and the ugliness of their crimes, would become genuinely penitent. The building's design was quite radical: Seven cell blocks radiated from a central surveillance rotunda. Each prisoner had his or her own private cell, centrally heated, with running water, a flush toilet (conveniences not available to the president in the White House at the time), and a skylight. Adjacent to the cell was a private

**Walnut Street Jail**
The birthplace of the modern prison system and of the Pennsylvania system of solitary confinement

**penitentiary house**
A correctional institution for those convicted of major crimes.

© Courtesy of the Library Company of Philadelphia

*Eastern State Penitentiary, built in 1829, was at the time the largest and most expensive public structure in the country. Designed by John Haviland, it consisted of an octagonal center connected by corridors to seven radiating single-story cell blocks. Each cell had hot water heating, a water tap, toilet, and an individual exercise yard the same width as the cell. There were rectangular openings in the cell wall through which food and work materials could be passed to the prisoner, as well as peepholes for guards to observe prisoners without being seen. Each cell contained a skylight so that the inmate could look to the heavens.*

outdoor exercise yard surrounded by a ten-foot wall. Each inmate was given a Bible to read and honest work (including shoemaking and weaving), thought to lead to penitence.[16]

Supporters of the **Pennsylvania system** believed that the penitentiary was truly a place to do penance. By removing sinners from society and allowing them a period of isolation in which to consider the evils of crime, the Pennsylvania system reflected the influence of religion and religious philosophy on corrections. Its supporters believed that solitary confinement with in-cell labor would make work so attractive that, upon release, the inmate would be well suited to resume a productive existence in society.

The Pennsylvania system eliminated the need for large numbers of guards or disciplinary measures. Isolated from one another, inmates could not plan escapes or collectively break rules. When discipline was a problem, however, the whip and the iron gag were used.

## The Auburn System

In 1816, New York built a new prison at Auburn, hoping to alleviate some of the overcrowding at Newgate. The Auburn Prison design became known as the **tier system** because cells were built vertically on five floors of the structure. It was also referred to as the **congregate system** because most prisoners ate and worked in groups. In 1819, construction began on a wing of solitary cells to house unruly prisoners. Three classes of prisoners were then created. One group remained continually in solitary confinement as a result of breaches of prison discipline, the second group was allowed labor as an occasional form of recreation, and the third and largest class worked and ate together during the day and was separated only at night.

The philosophy of the **Auburn system** was crime prevention through fear of punishment and silent confinement. The worst felons were to be cut off from all contact with other prisoners, and although they were treated and fed relatively well, they had no hope of pardon to relieve their solitude or isolation. For a time, some of the most dangerous convicts were forced to remain alone and silent during the entire day. This practice, which led to mental breakdowns, suicides, and self-mutilations, was abolished in 1823.

The combination of silence and solitude as a method of punishment was not abandoned easily. Prison officials sought to overcome the side effects of total isolation while maintaining the penitentiary system. The solution adopted at Auburn was to keep convicts in separate cells at night but allow them to work together during the day under enforced silence. Hard work and silence became

**Pennsylvania system**
A prison system, developed in Pennsylvania during the nineteenth century, based on total isolation and individual penitence.

**tier system**
A type of prison in which cells are located along corridors in multiple layers or levels.

**congregate system**
A prison system, originated in New York, in which inmates worked and ate together during the day and then slept in solitary cells at night.

**Auburn system**
A prison system, developed in New York during the nineteenth century, based on congregate (group) work during the day and separation at night.

the foundation of the Auburn system wherever it was adopted. Silence was the key to prison discipline. It prohibited the formulation of escape plans, it prevented plots and riots, and it allowed prisoners to contemplate their infractions.

Many fiery debates occurred between advocates of the Pennsylvania system and adherents of the Auburn system. Those supporting Auburn's congregate system claimed that it was the cheapest and most productive way to reform prisoners. They criticized the Pennsylvania system as cruel and inhumane, suggesting that solitary confinement was both physically and mentally damaging. The Pennsylvania system's supporters argued that their system was quiet, efficient, humane, and well ordered, providing the ultimate correctional facility. They chided the Auburn system for tempting inmates to talk by putting them together for meals and work and then punishing them when they did talk. Finally, the Auburn system was accused of becoming a breeding place for criminal associations by allowing inmates to get to know one another.

The Auburn system eventually prevailed and spread throughout the United States. Many of its features are still used today. Its innovations included congregate working conditions, the use of solitary confinement to punish unruly inmates, military regimentation, and discipline. In Auburn-like institutions, prisoners were marched from place to place. Their time was regulated by bells telling them when to wake up, sleep, and work. The system was so like the military that many of its early administrators were recruited from the armed services.

## Why Did Prisons Develop?

Why did prisons develop at this time? One reason was that during this period of enlightenment, a concerted effort was made to alleviate the harsh punishments and torture that had been the norm. The interest of religious groups, such as the Quakers, in prison reform was prompted in part by humanitarian ideals. Another factor was the economic potential of prison industry, which was viewed as a valuable economic asset in times of short labor supply.[17]

The concept of using harsh discipline and control to retrain the heart and soul of offenders was the subject of an important book on penal philosophy, *Discipline and Punish* (1978), by French sociologist Michel Foucault.[18] Foucault's thesis was that as societies evolve and become more complex, they create increasingly elaborate mechanisms to discipline their recalcitrant members and make them docile enough to obey social rules. In the seventeenth and eighteenth centuries, discipline was directed toward the human body itself, through torture. However, physical punishment and torture turned some condemned men into heroes and martyrs. Prisons presented the opportunity to rearrange, not diminish, punishment—to make it more effective and regulated. In the development of the nineteenth-century prison, the objective was to discipline the offender psychologically: "[T]he expiation that once rained down on the body must be replaced by a punishment that acts in the depths of the heart."[19]

Regimentation became the standard mode of prison life. Convicts did not simply walk from place to place; instead, they went in close order and single file, each looking over the shoulder of the preceding person, faces inclined to the right, feet moving in unison. The lockstep prison shuffle was developed at Auburn and is still used in some institutions today.[20]

When discipline was breached in the Auburn system, punishment was applied in the form of a rawhide whip on the inmate's back. Immediate and effective, Auburn discipline was so successful that when 100 inmates were used to build the famous Sing Sing Prison in 1825, not one dared try to escape, even though they were housed in an open field with only minimal supervision.[21]

Although the prison was viewed as an improvement over capital and corporal punishment, it quickly became the scene of depressed conditions. Inmates were treated harshly and were routinely whipped and tortured. Prison brutality flourished in these institutions, which had originally been devised as a more humane

**contract system**
A prison industry system, widely employed until after the Civil War, in which officials sold the labor of prison inmates to private businesses, for use either inside or outside the prison.

**convict-lease system**
A contract system in which a private business leased prisoners from the state for a fixed annual fee and assumed full responsibility for their supervision and control.

## CONCEPT SUMMARY 14.1
### Early Correctional Systems

| Prison | Structure | Living Conditions | Activities | Discipline |
|---|---|---|---|---|
| Auburn system | Tiered cells | Congregate | Group work | Silence, harsh punishment |
| Pennsylvania system | Single cells set in semicircle | Isolated | In-cell work, Bible study | Silence, harsh punishment |

correctional alternative. In these early penal institutions, brutal corporal punishment took place indoors where, hidden from public view, it could become even more savage (see Concept Summary 14.1).[22]

## Creating Prison Industry

Prison industry developed and became the predominant theme around which institutions were organized. Some prisons used the **contract system**, in which officials sold the labor of inmates to private businesses. Sometimes the contractor supervised the inmates inside the prison itself. Under the **convict-lease system**, the state leased its prisoners to a business for a fixed annual fee and gave up supervision and control. Finally, some institutions had prisoners produce goods for the prison's own use.[23]

The development of prison industry quickly led to the abuse of inmates, who were forced to work for almost no wages, and to profiteering by dishonest administrators and business owners. During the Civil War era, prisons were major manufacturers of clothes, shoes, boots, furniture, and the like. Beginning in the 1870s, opposition by trade unions sparked restrictions on interstate commerce in prison goods. After the Civil War, a number of states abandoned the contract system and introduced the **public account system**, under which employment was directed by the state and the products of the prisoners' labor were sold for the benefit of the state. Some correctional jurisdictions compensated prisoners for their labor but deducted funds for room, board, clothing, and the costs of trial; remaining funds were sent to the inmates' families and dependents. For inmates who had no family and/or dependents, their earnings accumulated and were paid to them upon their release.

**public account system**
A prison industry system, popular after the Civil War, in which employment was directed by the state and the products of the prisoners' labor were sold for the benefit of the state.

© The Granger Collection, New York

*Prison in the late nineteenth century was a brutal place. This line engraving from 1869 shows an inmate undergoing water torture in New York's Sing Sing Prison.*

## Prison Reform Efforts

The prisons of the late nineteenth century were overcrowded, and the single-cell principle was often ignored. The prison, like the police department, became the scene of political intrigue and efforts by political administrators to control the hiring of personnel and the dispensing of patronage.

The National Congress of Penitentiary and Reformatory Discipline, held in Cincinnati in 1870, heralded a new era of prison reform. Organized by penologists Enoch Wines and Theodore Dwight, the congress provided a forum for corrections experts from around the nation to call for better treatment, education, and training of inmates. Overseas, another penal reform was being developed in which inmates could earn early release and serve out their sentence in the community; this innovation was called parole and is discussed below.

One of the most famous people to attend the congress, Zebulon Brockway, warden of the Elmira Reformatory in New York, advocated individualized treatment, the indeterminate sentence, and parole. The reformatory program initiated by Brockway included elementary education for illiterates, designated library hours, lectures by faculty members of the local Elmira College, and a group of vocational training shops. From 1888 to 1920, Elmira administrators used military-like training to discipline the inmates and organize the institution. The military organization could be seen in every aspect of the institution: schooling, manual training, sports, supervision of inmates, and even parole decisions.[24] The cost to the state of the institution's operations was to be held to a minimum.

Although Brockway proclaimed Elmira to be an ideal reformatory, his achievements were limited. The greatest significance of his contribution was the injection of a degree of humanitarianism into the industrial prisons of that day (although accusations were made that excessive corporal punishment was used and that Brockway personally administered whippings).[25] Many institutions were constructed across the nation and labeled reformatories based on the Elmira model, but most of them continued to be industrially oriented.[26]

## Prisons in the Twentieth Century

The early twentieth century was a time of contrasts in the U.S. prison system.[27] At one extreme were those who advocated reform, such as the Mutual Welfare League, led by Thomas Mott Osborne. Prison reform groups proposed better treatment for inmates, an end to harsh corporal punishment, the creation of meaningful prison industries, and educational programs. Reformers argued that prisoners should not be isolated from society and that the best elements of society—education, religion, meaningful work, and self-governance—should be brought to the prison. Osborne went so far as to spend a week in New York's notorious Sing Sing Prison to learn firsthand about its conditions.

In time, some of the more rigid prison rules gave way to liberal reform. By the mid-1930s, few prisons required inmates to wear the red-and-white-striped convict suit; nondescript gray uniforms were substituted. The code of silence ended, as did the lockstep shuffle. Prisoners were allowed "the freedom of the yard" to mingle and exercise an hour or two each day.[28] Movies and radio appeared in the 1930s. Visiting policies and mail privileges were liberalized.

A more important trend was the development of specialized prisons designed to treat particular types of offenders. In New York, for example, the prisons at Clinton and Auburn were viewed as industrial facilities for hard-core inmates, Great Meadow was an agricultural center for nondangerous offenders, and

*Elmira Reformatory, training course in drafting, 1909. Inmates stand at drafting tables as guards watch and a supervisor sits at a fenced-off desk at the front of the hall. Elmira was one of the first penal institutions to employ education and training programs.*

© American Correctional Association

Dannemora was a facility for the criminally insane. In California, San Quentin housed inmates whom correctional authorities considered salvageable, and Folsom was reserved for hard-core offenders.[29]

Prison industry also evolved. Opposition by organized labor helped put an end to the convict-lease system and forced inmate labor. By 1900, a number of states had restricted the sale of prisoner-made goods on the open market. The worldwide Great Depression, which began in 1929, prompted industry and union leaders to further pressure state legislators to reduce competition from prison industries. A series of ever more restrictive federal legislative initiatives led to the Sumners-Ashurst Act (1940), which made it a federal offense to transport interstate commerce goods made in prison for private use, regardless of the laws of the state receiving the goods.[30] The restrictions imposed by the federal government helped to severely curtail prison industry for 40 years. Private entrepreneurs shunned prison investments because they were no longer profitable. The result was inmate idleness and make-work jobs.[31]

Despite some changes and reforms, the prison in the mid-twentieth century remained a destructive total institution. Although some aspects of inmate life improved, severe discipline, harsh rules, and solitary confinement were the way of life in prison.

## The Development of Parole

While the prison is an American invention, parole was a concept that developed overseas and was later brought to the United States.[32] The term "parole" itself comes from the French for "promise," referring to the practice of releasing captured enemy soldiers if they promised (or gave their word) not to fight again, with the threat that they would be executed if recaptured.

In the early seventeenth century, English judges began to spare the lives of offenders by banishing them to the newly formed overseas colonies. In 1617, the Privy Counsel of the British Parliament standardized this practice by passing an order granting reprieves and stays of execution to convicts willing to be transported to the colonies. Such *transportation* was viewed as an answer to labor shortages caused by war, disease, and the opening of new commercial markets.

By 1665, transportation orders were modified to include specific conditions of employment and to provide for reconsideration of punishment if the conditions were not met—for example, if the person returned to England before the expiration of the sentence. In 1717, the British Parliament passed legislation creating the concept of *property in service,* which transferred control of prisoners to a contractor or shipmaster until the expiration of their sentences. When the prisoners arrived in the colonies, their services could be resold to the highest bidder. After sale, an offender's status changed from convict to indentured servant.

Transportation quickly became the most common sentence for theft offenders. In the American colonies, property in service had to be abandoned after the revolution. Thereafter, Australia, which had been claimed as a British colony in 1770, became the destination for most transported felons. From 1815 to 1850, large numbers of inmates were shipped to Australia to serve as indentured servants working for plantation owners, in mines, or on sheep stations.

In England, opposition to penal servitude and the deprivations associated with transportation produced such organizations as the Society for the Improvement of Prison Discipline. This group asked the famous reformer Alexander Maconochie to investigate conditions in Australia. Maconochie condemned transportation and eventually helped end the practice. Later, when appointed director of the infamous Australian prison on Norfolk Island, Maconochie instituted reforms, such as classification and rehabilitation programs, that became models for the treatment of convicted offenders. Recalled from Australia, Maconochie returned to England, where his efforts led to the English Penal Servitude Act of 1853, which all but ended transportation and substituted imprisonment as a punishment.

Part of this act made it possible to grant a *ticket-of-leave* to those who had served a sufficient portion of their prison sentence. This form of conditional release permitted former prisoners to be at large in specified areas. The conditions of their release were written on a license that the former inmates were required to carry with them at all times. Conditions usually included sobriety, lawful behavior, and hard work. Many releasees violated these provisions, prompting criticism of the system. Eventually, prisoner aid society members helped supervise and care for releasees.

In Ireland, Sir Walter Crofton, a disciple of Maconochie's reforms, liberalized Irish prisons. He instituted a mark system in which inmates could earn their ticket-of-leave by accumulating credits for good conduct and hard work in prison. Crofton also instituted a system in which private volunteers or police agents could monitor ticket-of-leave offenders in the community. Crofton's work is considered an early form of parole.

The concept of parole spread to the United States. As early as 1822, volunteers from the Philadelphia-based Society for Alleviating the Miseries of Public Prisons began to help offenders once they were released from prison. In 1851, the society appointed two agents to work with inmates discharged from Pennsylvania penal institutions. Massachusetts appointed an agent in 1845 to help released inmates obtain jobs, clothing, and transportation.

In the 1870s, using a carefully weighted screening procedure, Zebulon Brockway selected rehabilitated offenders from Elmira Reformatory for early release under the supervision of citizen volunteers known as *guardians*. The guardians met with the parolees at least once a month and submitted written reports on their progress. The parole concept spread rapidly. Ohio created the first parole agency in 1884. By 1901, as many as 20 states had created some type of parole agency. By 1927, only three states (Florida, Mississippi, and Virginia) had not established some sort of parole release. Parole had become institutionalized as the primary method of release for prison inmates, and half of all inmates released in the United States were paroled.

## Contemporary Correctional Institutions

The modern era has been a period of change and turmoil in the nation's correctional system. Three trends stand out. First, between 1960 and 1980, came the prisoners' rights movement. After many years of indifference (the so-called hands-off doctrine), state and federal courts ruled in case after case that institutionalized inmates had rights to freedom of religion and speech, medical care, procedural due process, and proper living conditions. Inmates won rights unheard of in the nineteenth and early twentieth centuries. Since 1980, however, an increasingly conservative judiciary has curtailed the growth of inmate rights.

Second, violence within the correctional system became a national concern. Well-publicized riots at New York's Attica Prison and the New Mexico State Penitentiary drew attention to the potential for death and destruction that lurks in every prison. Prison rapes and killings have become commonplace. The locus of control in many prisons has shifted from the correctional staff to violent inmate gangs. In reaction, some administrators have tried to improve conditions and provide innovative programs that give inmates a voice in running the institution. Another reaction has been to tighten discipline and build new super-maximum-security prisons to control the most dangerous offenders. Prison overcrowding has made attempts to improve conditions extremely difficult.

Third, the view that traditional correctional rehabilitation efforts have failed has prompted many penologists to reconsider the purpose of incarcerating criminals. Between 1960 and 1980, it was common for correctional administrators to cling to the **medical model**, which viewed inmates as sick people who were suffering from some social malady that prevented them from adjusting to society. It was assumed that correctional treatment could help cure them and enable them to live productive lives once they returned to the community. In the 1970s,

**medical model**
A view of corrections holding that convicted offenders are victims of their environment who need care and treatment to transform them into valuable members of society.

efforts were also made to help offenders become reintegrated into society by providing them with new career opportunities that relied on work release programs. Inmates were allowed to work outside the institution during the day and return in the evening. Some were given extended furloughs in the community. Work release became a political issue when, in a famous incident, Willie Horton, a furloughed inmate from Massachusetts, raped a young woman. Criticism of the state's "liberal" furlough program helped Vice President George Bush defeat Massachusetts Governor Michael S. Dukakis for the U.S. presidency in 1988. In the aftermath of the Horton case, a number of states, including Massachusetts, restricted their furlough policies.

Since the 1980s, as the nation moved toward a more conservative political outlook, prisons came to be viewed as places for control, incapacitation, and punishment, rather than as sites for rehabilitation and reform. As you may recall, advocates of the "no frills," or **penal harm,** movement argue that if prison is a punishing experience, criminals will be deterred from crime, and current inmates will be encouraged to go straight. Besides, why should people who have engaged in antisocial activities receive benefits behind bars that are sometimes unavailable to the honest and law-abiding citizen, such as higher-education courses? Although historians find conditions in early prisons to be overly severe, some modern administrators have sought to copy the harsh regimes in an effort to convince inmates that their institution is no country club and that they had better not return.

This conservative approach is currently dominant, but those who believe that correctional institutions could be used as treatment facilities still support a rehabilitation approach. And although public support for rehabilitation has declined somewhat, the general public still believes that treatment is a legitimate correctional objective for certain population classes, such as juvenile and nonviolent offenders.[33]

The alleged failure of correctional treatment, coupled with constantly increasing correctional costs, has prompted the development of alternatives to incarceration, such as intensive probation supervision, house arrest, and electronic monitoring (see Chapter 13). What has developed is a dual correctional policy: Keep as many nonviolent offenders out of the correctional system as possible by means of community-based programs; incarcerate dangerous, violent offenders for long periods of time.[34] These efforts have been compromised by a growing get-tough stance in judicial and legislative sentencing policy, accented by mandatory minimum sentences for gun crimes and drug trafficking. Despite the development of alternatives to incarceration, the number of people under lock and key has skyrocketed.

The following sections review the most prominent types of correctional facilities in operation today.

**penal harm**
The belief that during their incarceration inmates should endure pain and suffering, in order to make the punishment deliberately harder so they will not dare recidivate.

## PERSPECTIVES ON JUSTICE
### *Noninterventionism versus Crime Control*
Advocates of the nonintervention perspective have sought to develop alternatives to incarceration, such as intensive probation supervision, house arrest, and electronic monitoring, because prisons and incarceration do not seem to work. However, crime control advocates question the wisdom of alternative sanctions and have countered them with tougher sentencing policies, including mandatory minimum sentences for gun crimes and drug trafficking.

## JAILS

The nation's jails are institutional facilities with five primary purposes:

- They detain accused offenders who cannot make or are not eligible for bail prior to trial.
- They hold convicted offenders awaiting sentence.
- They serve as the principal institution of secure confinement for offenders convicted of misdemeanors.
- They hold probationers and parolees picked up for violations and waiting for a hearing.
- They house felons when state prisons are overcrowded.

## EXHIBIT 14.1

### Jail Functions and Services

- Receive individuals pending arraignment and hold them while they are awaiting trial, conviction, or sentencing.

- Readmit probation, parole, and bail-bond violators and absconders.

- Temporarily detain juveniles pending transfer to juvenile authorities.

- Hold mentally ill persons pending their movement to appropriate health facilities.

- Hold individuals for the military, for protective custody, for contempt, and for the courts as witnesses.

- Release convicted inmates to the community upon completion of their sentence.

- Transfer inmates to federal, state, or other authorities.

- House inmates for federal, state, or other authorities because of crowding of their facilities.

- Sometimes operate community-based programs as alternatives to incarceration.

- Hold inmates sentenced to short terms (generally under one year).

Source: Bureau of Justice Statistics, 2010, http://bjs.ojp.usdoj.gov/index.cfm?ty=tp&tid=12.

## TABLE 14.1

### Number of People in Jail and Jail Incarceration Rate

| Year | Number Held in Jail | Jail Incarceration Rate* |
|------|---------------------|--------------------------|
| 2009 | 767,992 | 250 |
| 2008 | 785,556 | 258 |
| 2007 | 780,582 | 259 |
| 2006 | 766,010 | 256 |
| 2005 | 747,529 | 252 |
| 2004 | 713,990 | 243 |
| 2003 | 691,301 | 238 |
| 2002 | 665,475 | 231 |
| 2001 | 631,240 | 222 |
| 2000 | 621,149 | 220 |
| 1995 | 507,044 | 193 |

*Number of jail inmates per 100,000 U.S. residents on July 1 of each year.

Sources: Paige M. Harrison and Allen J. Beck, *Prison and Jail Inmates at Midyear 2005* (Washington, D.C.: Bureau of Justice Statistics, 2006); William Sabol, Heather West, Todd Minton, and William J. Sabol *Prison and Jail Inmates at Midyear 2008* (Washington, D.C.: Bureau of Justice Statistics, 2009). Updated 2010.

A number of formats are used to jail offenders. About 15,000 local jurisdictions maintain short-term police or municipal lockups that house offenders for no more than 48 hours before a bail hearing can be held; thereafter, detainees are kept in the county jail In some jurisdictions, such as Massachusetts, a house of corrections holds convicted misdemeanants, and a county jail holds pretrial detainees. Today, jails are multipurpose correctional institutions—Exhibit 14.1 sets out their main functions.

## Jail Populations and Trends

As you may recall, there has been a national movement to help criminal defendants remain in the community through the adoption of both bail reform measures and pretrial diversion. Nonetheless, as Table 14.1 shows, not only has the number of people in jail been increasing, but so has the jail incarceration rate—the percentage of the population in jail. During a period when the crime rate has been in decline (1995–2009), the incarceration rate has increased almost 30 percent. There are now about 767,000 jail inmates—more than 250 inmates for every 100,000 U.S. residents. Jail populations declined slightly in 2009, the first time in many years that the incarceration rate dropped.

Considering these measures and the declining crime rate, why do jail populations continue to increase? As prisons become more overcrowded, prison correctional officials use local jails to house inmates for whom there is no room in state prisons. Jail populations also respond to the efforts being made to reduce or control particular crime problems, including substance abuse, spousal abuse, and driving while intoxicated (DWI). Some jurisdictions have passed legislation requiring that people arrested on suspicion of domestic violence be held in confinement for a number of hours to "cool off" before becoming eligible for bail. Other jurisdictions have attempted to deter drunk driving by passing mandatory jail sentences for people convicted of DWI; such legislation can quickly result in overcrowded jails.[35]

However, the rate of increase in the jail population has been slowing, reflecting a declining U.S. crime rate and greater reliance on alternatives to incarceration such as probation, electronic monitoring, and house arrest. It is possible that in the future, jail populations may stabilize or begin to decline.

## Jail Populations

Almost nine out of every ten jail inmates are adult males, and although whites make up more than 40 percent of the jail population, minority overrepresentation is still a significant problem (Figure 14.1). Members of ethnic and racial minorities make up a disproportionate number of the jail population, presumably reflecting such factors as overrepresentation in the arrest statistics, failure to secure bail, inferior legal representation, and racial/ethnic bias in the justice system. Between 1990 and 2008, the number of Hispanic jail inmates increased at a greater average annual rate of growth (4.5%) than the numbers of white (3.8%) and black inmates (3.3%).

At one time many thousands of minor children were held in jails as runaways, truants, and so on. The number of juveniles held in adult jails has been in decline since 1995, a result of ongoing government initiatives to remove juveniles from adult facilities. Nonetheless, about 7,500 minors are still being held in adult jails each day (down from a high of 9,100).

*FEMALE JAIL INMATES* As Figure 14.2 shows, about 10 percent of jail inmates are women. However, even though men make up 90 percent of the jail population, during the past two decades the percentage of adult females in jail increased at a faster pace than that of males. Female jail inmates face many challenges. Most come from significantly disadvantaged backgrounds. Many have suffered abuse and severe economic disadvantage. One recent study of 100 female inmates found extremely high rates of lifetime trauma exposure (98%), current mental disorders (36%), and drug/alcohol problems (74%).[36]

**FIGURE 14.1**
Jail Populations by Race and Ethnicity

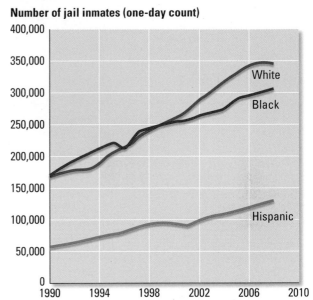

Source: Bureau of Justice Statistics Correctional Surveys, www.ojp.usdoj.gov/bjs/glance/jailrace.htm.

**FIGURE 14.2**
Jail Population Trends by Age and Gender

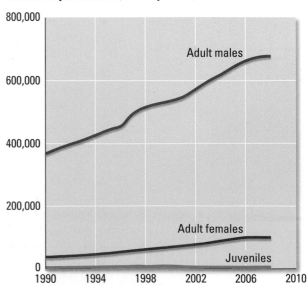

Source: Bureau of Justice Statistics Correctional Surveys, www.ojp.usdoj.gov/bjs/glance/jailag.htm.

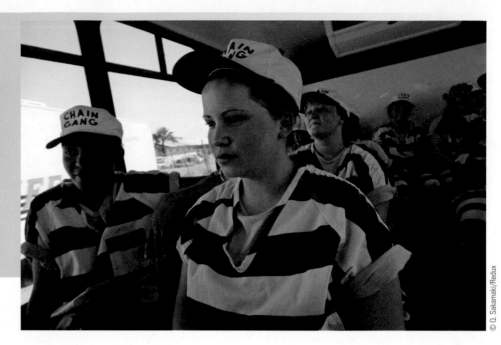

Sheriff Arpaio's tough penal regime is not restricted to men only. After finishing their work for the day, a female chain gang from the Estrella Jail boards a bus to go back to the high-security prison compound. Most inmates of the county jail system, which includes Estrella, are serving time for relatively minor crimes; in some cases, they are merely awaiting trial because they could not make bail. Yet under Arpaio, the local sheriff, the 8,000 inmates in the county work seven days a week and are fed only twice a day. They get no coffee; no cigarettes; no salt, pepper, or ketchup; and no organized recreation. Human rights groups regard it as the harshest jail system in the United States.

© O. Sakamaki/Redux

Given this background, how can female inmates make a successful reentry into society? Employment seems to be a key issue. Those who have worked recently before their incarceration are most likely to have other survival skills and assets: They are more likely to have a high school education, to have a skill, and to have a driver's license with access to a car.[37]

## Jail Conditions

Jails are usually a low-priority item in the criminal justice system. Because they are often administered on a county level, jail services have not been sufficiently regulated, nor has a unified national policy been developed to mandate what constitutes adequate jail conditions. Consequently, jails in some counties are physically deteriorated, holding dangerous and troubled people, many of whom suffer emotional problems that remain untreated. Not atypical was a recent (2009) review of the Dallas, Texas, jail system by federal inspectors, who found the following problems, among many others.

■ The inspectors noted delays in issuing medications, a lack of medical evaluations, inconsistent care, and a lack of medical care for mental health patients.

■ The jail kitchen was found to have moldy ceilings that dripped water, live wires next to standing water, and condensation so thick it was almost impossible to see across the room.

■ Maintenance and sanitation problems still exist, including broken intercoms, inadequate shower temperatures, sinks without hot water, clogged sinks and shower drains, and broken toilets.[38]

Many inmates have been victims of prior physical and sexual abuse, including more than 10 percent of male inmates and nearly 50 percent of female inmates.[39] About two-thirds of all jail inmates report having a mental health problem, including more than 15 percent who display psychotic symptoms. That means more than 100,000 people in jail today are suffering from severe psychosis, and more than 400,000 have some form of mental disorder.[40] It is not surprising then that some counties report that inmate suicides are their biggest concern.[41] Although the jail suicide rate has declined significantly, the percentage of jail inmates who take their own lives is higher than that of the general population.

Because being warehoused in local jails does little to alleviate social and individual problems, jails are considered the revolving door of the justice system. Millions of people enter jail each year and millions are released, only to be rearrested and incarcerated again soon after returning to their communities.

## New-Generation Jails

To relieve overcrowding and improve effectiveness, a jail-building boom has been under way. Many of the new jails are using modern designs to improve effectiveness; these are referred to as new-generation jails.[42] Traditional jails are constructed on what is referred to as the linear/intermittent surveillance model. Jails designed this way are rectangular, with corridors leading to either single- or multiple-occupancy cells arranged at right angles to the corridor. Correctional officers must patrol to see into cells or housing areas, and when they are in a position to observe one cell, they cannot observe others; unobserved inmates are essentially unsupervised.

In contrast, new-generation jails allow for continuous observation of residents. There are two types: direct-supervision and indirect-supervision jails. Direct-supervision jails contain a cluster of cells surrounding a living area or "pod," which contains tables, chairs, and televisions. A correctional officer is stationed within the pod. The officer has visual observation of inmates and maintains the ability to relate to them on a personal level. Placing the officer in the pod increases the officer's awareness of the behaviors and needs of the inmates. This results in a safer environment for both staff and inmates. Because interaction between inmates is constantly and closely monitored, dissension can be quickly detected before it escalates. During the day, inmates stay in the open area (dayroom) and typically are not permitted to go into their rooms except with permission of the officer in charge.

The officer controls door locks to cells from the control panel. In case of trouble or if the officer leaves the station for an extended period of time, command of this panel can be switched to a panel at a remote location, known as central control. The officer usually wears a device that permits immediate communication with central control in case of trouble, and the area is also covered by a video camera monitored by an officer in the central control room.

Indirect-supervision jails use similar construction; however, the correctional officer's station is located inside a secure room. Microphones and speakers inside the living unit permit the officer to hear and communicate with inmates. Although these institutions have not yet undergone extensive evaluation, research shows that they may help reduce postrelease offending in some situations.[43] However, some critics suggest new-generation jails have failed to live up to their promise because they lack important components, such as a normalized living environment, in their facilities.[44]

CourseMate For more information about the **new-generation jail philosophy**, visit the Criminal Justice CourseMate at CengageBrain.com, then access the "Web Links" for this chapter.

## PRISONS

There are about 1,800 secure public and private adult correctional facilities housing more than 1.6 million state and federal prisoners. Usually, prisons are organized or classified on three levels—maximum, medium, and minimum security—and each has distinct characteristics.

*MAXIMUM-SECURITY PRISONS*  Housing the most notorious criminals, and the subject of numerous films and stories, **maximum-security prisons** are probably the incarceration institutions most familiar to the public. Famous "max prisons" have included Sing Sing, Joliet, Attica, Walpole, and the most fearsome prison of all, the now-closed federal facility on Alcatraz Island known as The Rock.

A typical maximum-security facility is fortress-like, surrounded by stone walls with guard towers at strategic places. These walls may be 25 feet high, and sometimes inner and outer walls divide the prison into courtyards. Barbed wire or electrified fences are used to discourage escapes. High security, armed guards,

**maximum-security prison**
A correctional institution that houses dangerous felons and maintains strict security measures, high walls, and limited contact with the outside world.

## CRIMINAL JUSTICE AND TECHNOLOGY

# Increasing Security/Reducing Escapes

Technical experts have identified numerous areas of correctional management that can be aided by information technology (IT), including reception and commitment, sentence and time accounting, classification, caseload management, security, discipline, housing/bed management, medical, grievances, programs, scheduling, investigations/gang management, property, deposits into inmates' bank accounts, visitation, release and discharge, and community supervision. Because there are so many areas in which IT can be applied within correctional establishments, prison administrators have begun to take advantage of the potential offered by the new technologies. How has IT been applied within prison walls? Following are a few examples of efforts that have been made to improve institutional security and reduce the chance of escapes.

### Ground-Penetrating Radar

Ground-penetrating radar (GPR) can locate tunnels that inmates use to escape. GPR works almost like an old-fashioned Geiger counter, but instead of detecting radiation, the system detects changes in ground composition, including voids such as those created by a tunnel.

### Heartbeat Monitoring

Now it is possible to prevent escapes by monitoring inmates' heartbeats! The Advanced Vehicle Interrogation and Notification (AVIAN) System detects the presence of persons who try to escape by hiding in vehicles. Using data from seismic sensors that are placed on the vehicle, AVIAN reads the shock wave generated by the beating heart, which couples to any surface or object with which the body is in contact. It collects the data and analyzes it using advanced signal-processing algorithms to detect a person hiding in a vehicle, such as a large truck, in less than two minutes. The system works by accounting for all the frequencies of movement in the vehicle, such as the expansion and contraction of an engine or rain hitting the roof.

### Nonlethal Electrified Fences

Nonlethal electrified containment fences stop inmates from trying to escape by climbing prison security fences without causing severe harm or death. If an inmate tries to climb or cut through the perimeter fence, he or she will receive a nonlethal jolt of electricity, which causes temporary immobilization. At the

and stone walls give the inmate the sense that the facility is impregnable and reassure the citizens outside that convicts will be completely incapacitated. Because they fear that violence may flare up at any moment, prison administrators have been quick to adopt the latest high-tech security measures. Today, prison administrators rely on technology to help them maintain security, a topic covered in the accompanying Criminal Justice and Technology feature.

Inmates live in interior, metal-barred cells that contain their own plumbing and sanitary facilities and are locked securely by either key or electronic device. Cells are organized in sections called blocks, and in large prisons a number of cell blocks make up a wing. During the day, the inmates engage in closely controlled activities: meals, workshops, education, and so on. Rule violators may be confined to their cells, and working and other shared recreational activities are viewed as privileges.

The byword of the maximum-security prison is "security." Correctional workers are made aware that each inmate may be a dangerous criminal or violent, and that as a result, the utmost security must be maintained. These prisons are designed to eliminate hidden corners where people can congregate, and passages are constructed so that they can be easily blocked off to quell disturbances.

**super-maximum-security prison**
The newest form of a maximum-security prison, which uses high-level security measures to incapacitate the nation's most dangerous criminals. Most inmates are in lockdown 23 hours per day.

SUPER-MAXIMUM-SECURITY PRISONS Some states have constructed **super-maximum-security prisons** (supermax prisons) to house the most predatory criminals. These high-security institutions can be independent correctional centers or locked wings of existing prisons.[45] Some supermax prisons lock inmates in their cells 22 to 24 hours a day, never allowing them out unless they are shackled.[46] According to Jody Sundt and her associates, the supermax model same time, the system alerts prison staff that an escape attempt has occurred and identifies its location.

## Transmitter Wristbands

These wristbands broadcast a unique serial number via radio frequency every two seconds so that antennas throughout the prison can pick up the signals and pass the data via a local area network to a central monitoring station PC. The wristbands can sound an alert when a prisoner gets close to the perimeter fence or when an inmate doesn't return from a furlough on time; they can even tag gang members and notify guards when rivals come in contact with each other.

## Under-Vehicle Surveillance System

An under-vehicle surveillance system uses a drive-over camera that records a video image of the license plate and the underside of any vehicle entering or leaving the secure perimeter of the prison. This system enables prison staff to check each vehicle for possible escape attempts and keeps a digital recording of every vehicle that enters or exits the prison.

## Radar Vital Signs Monitor/Radar Flashlight

The handheld radar flashlight can detect the respiration of a human in a cell from behind a 20-centimeter hollow-core concrete wall or an eight-inch cinder block wall. It instantly gives the user a bar-graph readout that is viewed on the apparatus itself. Other miniature radar detectors give the user heartbeat and respiration readings. The equipment is expected to be a useful tool in searches for people who are hiding, because the only thing that successfully blocks its functioning is a wall made of metal or conductive material.

## Critical Thinking

1. Some elements of information technology intrude on the privacy of inmates. Should the need for security outweigh an inmate's right to privacy?

2. Should probationers and parolees be monitored with modern technology? Do they deserve more privacy than incarcerated inmates?

Sources: Philip Bulman, "Using Technology to Make Prisons and Jails Safer," *NIJ Journal* 262 (March 2009), www.ojp.usdoj.gov/nij/journals/262/corrections-technology.htm; John Ward, "Jump-Starting Projects to Automate Correctional Processes," *Corrections Today* 68 (2006): 82–83; Debbie Mahaffey, "Security and Technology: The Human Side," *Corrections Today* 66 (2004): 8; Frank Lu and Laurence Wolfe, "Automated Record Tracking (SMART) Application," *Corrections Today* 66 (2004): 78–81.

is based on the assumption that prison disorder is primarily the result of a handful of disruptive, violent inmates and that if these few can be strictly controlled, the violence level in the entire correctional system can be reduced.

The 484-bed facility in Florence, Colorado, has the most sophisticated security measures in the United States, including 168 video cameras and 1,400 electronically controlled gates. Inside the cells, all furniture is unmovable; the desk, bed, and TV stand are made of cement. All potential weapons, including soap dishes, toilet seats, and toilet handles, have been removed. The cement walls are 5,000-pound quality, and steel bars crisscross every eight inches inside the walls. Cells are angled so that inmates can see neither each other nor the outside. This cuts down on communication and denies inmates a sense of location, to prevent escapes.

A number of experts have given supermax prisons mixed reviews. Although they can achieve correctional benefits by enhancing security and quality of life, critics believe that they infringe directly on the right of inmates to due process because they deprive them of such basic rights such as human contact; they also eliminate any opportunity for rehabilitation.[47] Civil rights watchdog groups charge that these supermax prisons violate the United Nations standards for the treatment of inmates. They are typically located in rural areas, which makes staffing difficult in the professional areas of dentistry, medicine, and counseling. Senior officers prefer not to work in these institutions, so the most difficult inmates are often in the hands of the least experienced correctional officers. These fears are not ungrounded. One survey by Leena Kurki and Norval Morris found that, although conditions vary from state to state, many supermax prisons subject inmates to nearly complete isolation and deprivation of sensory stimuli. Although the long-term effects of such conditions on inmates are still uncertain, Kurki and Morris believe that they are likely to have extremely harmful effects, especially on those who suffer from preexisting mental illness and those with subnormal intelligence.[48]

Some recent research by Daniel Mears and his colleagues on the effectiveness of supermax prisons yielded mixed results. Mears, along with Jamie Watson, conducted surveys of correctional officials and found that on the one hand, supermax prisons may actually enhance the quality of life of inmates and consequently improve their mental health.[49] They increase privacy, reduce danger, and even provide creature comforts (such as TV sets) that are unavailable in general-population prisons. Staff report less stress and fear because they have to contend with fewer disruptive inmates.

On the other hand, Mears and Watson found that supermax prisons also have some unintended negative consequences. Staff may have too much control over inmates—a condition that damages staff–inmate relationships. Long hours of isolation may be associated with mental illness and psychological disturbances. Supermax inmates seem to have a more difficult time readjusting upon release. A stay in a supermax prison inhibits reintegration into other prisons, communities, and families. In another study, Mears and Jennifer Castro surveyed wardens and found that even though they seem to favor supermax prisons, they also expressed concern that the general public considers supermax institutions inhumane, that they drain limited funds from state budgets, and that they produce increases in litigation and court interventions, as well as increased recidivism and reentry failure among released inmates.[50]

**medium-security prison**
A less secure institution that houses nonviolent offenders and provides more opportunities for contact with the outside world.

*MEDIUM-SECURITY PRISONS*  Although **medium-security prisons** are similar in appearance to maximum-security prisons, the security is not so tight or the atmosphere so tense. Medium-security prisons are also surrounded by walls, but there may be fewer guard towers or other security precautions; visitations with personal contact may be allowed. Although most prisoners are housed in cells, individual honor rooms in medium-security prisons are used to reward those who make exemplary rehabilitation efforts. Finally, medium-security prisons promote greater treatment efforts, and the relaxed atmosphere allows freedom of movement for rehabilitation workers and other therapeutic personnel.

**minimum-security prison**
The least secure correctional institution, which houses white-collar and nonviolent offenders, maintains few security measures, and has liberal furlough and visitation policies.

*MINIMUM-SECURITY PRISONS*  Operating without armed guards or perimeter walls, **minimum-security prisons** usually house the most trustworthy and least violent offenders; white-collar criminals may be their most common occupants. Inmates are allowed a great deal of personal freedom. Instead of being marched to activities by guards, they are summoned by bells or loudspeaker announcements, and they assemble on their own. Work furloughs and educational releases are encouraged, and vocational training is of the highest level. Dress codes are lax, and inmates are allowed to grow beards or mustaches or demonstrate other individual characteristics.

Minimum-security facilities may have dormitories or small private rooms for inmates. Prisoners are allowed to own personal possessions that might be deemed dangerous in a maximum-security prison, such as radios. Minimum-security prisons have been criticized for being like "country clubs"; at one time some federal facilities even had tennis courts and pools (they are derisively called "Club Fed"). Yet they remain prisons, and the isolation and loneliness of prison life deeply affect the inmates.

## ALTERNATIVE CORRECTIONAL INSTITUTIONS

In addition to prisons and jails, a number of other correctional institutions are operating within the United States. Some have been in use for quite a while, whereas others have been developed more recently as part of innovative or experimental programs.

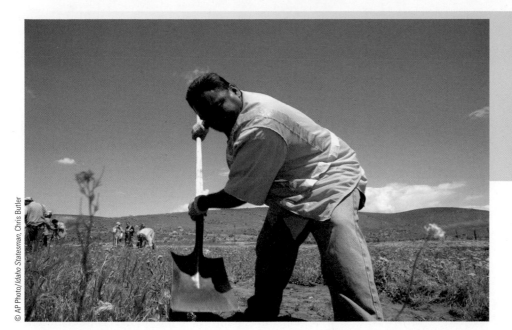

Prison farms and camps are quite common in the South and West. On May 13, 2010, Anthony Velenzuela, an inmate at the South Idaho Correctional Institution, begins clearing land that will be used as a six-acre farm south of Boise, Idaho. Idaho prisoners are growing produce for a food bank on cropland in the desert south of Boise—a project designed to give inmates something to do and the needy something to eat.

## Prison Farms and Camps

Prison farms and camps are used to detain offenders. These types of facilities are found primarily in the South and the West and have been in operation since the nineteenth century. Today, about 40 farms, 40 forest camps, 80 road camps, and more than 60 similar facilities (vocational training centers, ranches, and so on) exist in the nation. Prisoners on farms produce dairy products, grain, and vegetable crops that are used in the state correctional system and other governmental facilities, such as hospitals and schools. Forestry camp inmates maintain state parks, fight forest fires, and do reforestation work. Ranches, primarily a western phenomenon, employ inmates in cattle raising and horse breeding, among other activities. Road gangs repair roads and state highways.

## Shock Incarceration in Boot Camps

Another correctional innovation that gained popularity in the 1980s and 1990s, **boot camp** involves youthful, first-time offenders in military discipline and physical training. The concept is that short periods (90 to 180 days) of high-intensity exercise and work will "shock" the inmate into going straight. Tough physical training is designed to promote responsibility and improve decision-making skills, build self-confidence, and teach socialization skills. Inmates are treated with rough intensity by drillmasters who may call them names and punish the entire group for the failure of one member.[51]

Some programs also include educational and training components, counseling sessions, and treatment for special-needs populations, whereas others devote little or no time to therapeutic activities. Some receive program participants directly from court sentencing, whereas others choose potential candidates from the general inmate population. Some allow voluntary participation and others voluntary termination.[52]

Is **shock incarceration** a correctional panacea or another fad doomed to failure? Those who advocate shock incarceration portray it as a lower-cost alternative to overcrowded prisons. Both staff and inmates report benefiting from the experience.[53] The daily costs of boot camps are no lower than those of traditional prisons, but because sentences are shorter, they provide long-term savings. A number of states, including New York, make extensive use of shock incarceration facilities.

Despite such support, empirical research (the majority of it contributed by Doris Layton MacKenzie, a criminologist who has been involved in many

**boot camp**
A short-term, militaristic correction facility in which inmates undergo intensive physical conditioning and discipline.

**shock incarceration**
A short prison sentence served in boot camp–type facilities.

**community treatment**
The attempt by correctional agencies to maintain convicted offenders in the community rather than in a secure facility; it includes probation, parole, and residential programs.

**halfway house**
A community-based correctional facility that houses inmates before their outright release so that they can become gradually acclimated to conventional society.

evaluations of boot camp) has yielded disappointing results. She finds that clients leaving boot camps often have higher rates of technical violations and revocations than traditional probationers and parolees.[54] MacKenzie's extensive evaluations of the boot camp experience generate little evidence that they can significantly lower recidivism rates. Those few programs that seem to work best stress treatment and therapeutic activities, are voluntary, and are longer in duration.[55] Because of these sketchy results, the future of the boot camp approach is clouded. Many state programs, including those in Georgia and Florida, have been canceled, and in 2005, the federal government decided to close its boot camp program.[56]

## Community Correctional Facilities

One goal of correctional treatment is to help reintegrate the offender into society. Placing offenders in a prison makes them more likely to adopt an inmate lifestyle than to reassimilate conventional social norms. As a result, the **community treatment** concept began to take off in the 1960s. State and federal correctional systems created community-based correctional models as an alternative to closed institutions. Many are **halfway houses** to which inmates are transferred just before their release into the community. These facilities are designed to bridge the gap between institutional living and the community. However, commitment to a community correctional center may also be used as an intermediate sanction and sole mode of treatment. An offender may be assigned to a community treatment center operated by the state department of corrections or to probation. Alternatively, the corrections department can contract with a private community center. Community corrections programs often offer specialized treatment or focus on specific groups of offenders, helping residents use the experience to cushion the shock of reentering society. This practice is common in the treatment of drug abusers and other nonviolent offenders whose special needs can be met in a self-contained community setting that specializes in specific types of treatment.

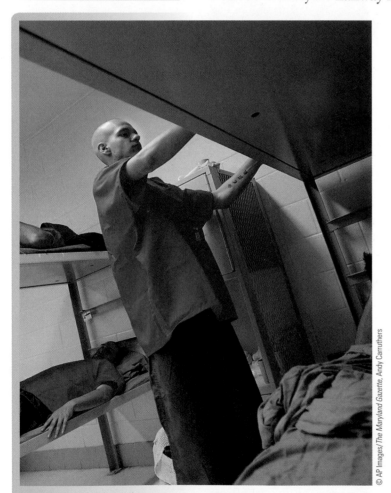

Inside the Ordnance Road Correctional Center in Glen Burnie, Maryland, 19-year-old inmate Kenneth Lee puts sheets on his plastic covered mattress. He serves his prison sentence one weekend at a time, living in a dormitory-style room housing a dozen men. Alternative correctional institutions have sprung up around the nation as a response to overcrowding and high recidivism rates.

© AP Images/*The Maryland Gazette*, Andy Carruthers

## Private Prisons

About 450 correctional facilities are now being run by private firms as business enterprises housing more than 100,000 inmates.[57] In some instances, a private corporation will finance and build an institution and then contract with correctional authorities to provide services for convicted criminals. Sometimes the private concern will finance and build the institution and then lease it outright to the government. This model has the advantage of allowing the government to circumvent the usually difficult process of getting voters to approve a bond issue and raising funds for prison construction. Another common method of private involvement is with specific service contracts; for example, a private concern might be hired to manage the prison health-care system, food services, or staff training.

On January 6, 1986, the U.S. Corrections Corporation opened the first private state prison in Marion, Kentucky—a 300-bed minimum-security facility for inmates who are within three years of parole. Today, private companies in the United States operate more than 400 correctional facilities, which now hold about 120,000 people.[58] Private prisons play an important correctional role in the

United States, Australia, and the United Kingdom.[59] One industry leader, Corrections Corporation of America (CCA), houses approximately 75,000 offenders and detainees in 65 facilities, more than 40 of which are company-owned, with a total bed capacity of nearly 80,000. CCA currently partners with all three federal corrections agencies (the Federal Bureau of Prisons, the U.S. Marshals Service, and Immigration and Customs Enforcement), with nearly half of all states, and with more than a dozen local municipalities.[60] A competitor, the GEO Group, runs facilities in Australia, New Zealand, and South Africa as well as in the United States; GEO manages more than 60,000 offenders in over 60 facilities around the globe. GEO runs the Arizona State Prison at Florence West, an institution specifically designed for return-to-custody (RTC) inmates and those convicted of driving under the influence (DUI). The GEO Group offers employment skills, parenting classes, substance abuse education and counseling, nutrition/diet education, GED classes, case management, individual and group counseling, stress management, facility work programs, job placement, and prison works/prison labor.[61]

*DO PRIVATE PRISONS WORK?* The most thorough evaluations of recidivism rate differences between private and public facilities find little difference in the recidivism rates of inmates released from the two different types of institutions.[62] There is some evidence that inmates released from private prisons who do reoffend may commit less serious offenses than those released from public institutions, and even though private and state institutions cost about the same to operate, private prisons seem cheaper to construct.[63]

These findings help support the concept of the private correctional institution, but some experts question reliance on private prisons, believing that their use raises a number of vexing problems: Will private providers be able to evaluate programs effectively when they know that a negative evaluation might cause them to lose their contract? Will they skimp on services and programs in order to reduce costs? Might they not skim off the "easy" cases and leave the hard-core inmate to the state's care? And will the need to keep business booming require widening the net to fill empty cells? Must they maintain state-mandated liability insurance to cover inmate claims?[64] Some private service providers have been sued because their services were inadequate, causing harm to inmates.[65]

Private corrections firms also run into opposition from existing state correctional staff and management, who fear the loss of jobs and autonomy. Moreover, the public may be skeptical about an untested private concern's ability to provide security and protection. Private corrections also face administrative problems: How will program quality be controlled? To compete on price, a private facility may have to cut corners to beat the competition. Determining accountability for problems and mishaps will be difficult when state authorities are dealing with a corporation whose managers and officers are legally protected from personal responsibility for their actions.

*LEGAL ISSUES* There are also unresolved legal problems: Can privately employed guards patrol the perimeter and use deadly force to stop escape attempts? Do private correctional officers have less immunity from lawsuits than state employees? In *Richardson v. McKnight*, the Supreme Court held that prison guards employed by a private firm are not entitled to a qualified immunity from suit by prisoners charging a section 1983 violation. Emphasizing that a private firm was systematically organized to manage the prison, the majority opinion said, "Our examination of history and purpose . . . reveals nothing special enough about the job or about its organizational structure that would warrant providing these private prison guards with a governmental immunity."[66]

The case of *Correctional Services Corp. v. Malesko* helps define the rights and protections of inmates in private correctional facilities. Malesko had a heart condition but was forced to walk up stairs rather than take an elevator. When he suffered a heart attack, he sued the Correctional Services Corporation (CSC),

**CourseMate** For more information about the **Corrections Corporation of America (CCA)**, visit the Criminal Justice CourseMate at CengageBrain.com, then access the "Web Links" for this chapter.

which was operating the prison, under the federal Civil Rights Act, alleging that the denial of proper medical care violated his civil rights. Citizens are generally allowed to seek damages against federal agents who violate their civil rights. However, the Court ruled that although Malesko could sue an individual employee of the private correctional corporation for allegedly violating his constitutional rights, he could not sue the correctional corporation itself. This decision shields the private prison corporation from suits brought under the federal civil rights statute. The *Malesko* decision lends credence to the concerns of some critics, who view the private prison as an insidious expansion of state control over citizens: a state-supported entity that actually has more freedom to exert control than the state itself.[67]

In the abstract, a private correctional enterprise may be an attractive alternative to a costly correctional system, but these legal, administrative, and cost issues need to be resolved before the use of private prisons can become widespread.[68] A balance must be reached between the need for a private business to make a profit and the integrity of a prison administration that must be concerned with such complex issues as security, rehabilitation, and dealing with highly dangerous people in a closed environment.[69] And unlike state institutions, private prisons, like all private enterprise systems, must conform to the whims of the marketplace. The private prison industry expanded rapidly during a time when mushrooming inmate populations strained the capacities of existing public institutions to house the inmate population. Now that demand has leveled off, so too has the need for private prisons. In addition, government regulation of the industry has produced conditions in which private prisons have been molded into mirror images of their public-sector counterparts. There has also been an antiprivatization movement conducted by faith-based groups competing for funding, which has further limited the growth of prisons.[70]

# INMATE POPULATIONS

This vast correctional system, with more than 1,800 public and private institutions on both the state and the federal level, now contains more than 1.6 million prison inmates. The background and characteristics of inmates reflect arrest data and are similar to those of the jail population: disproportionately young, male, minority, and poor. Minority males make up a disproportionate percentage of the prison population: Recently, the custody incarceration rate for black males was 4,618 per 100,000. Hispanic males were incarcerated at a rate of 1,747 per 100,000; in contrast, the estimated incarceration rate of white males was 773 per 100,000. Compared to the estimated numbers of black, white, and Hispanic males in the U.S. resident population, black males were six times as likely, and Hispanic males twice as likely, as white males to be held in custody.[71] Women still make up less than 10 percent of the total prison population.

Many inmates suffer from multiple social problems. Inmates are undereducated, are underemployed, and come from abusive homes. Recent research found that a disproportionate number had experienced homelessness (living on the street or in a homeless shelter) and other, associated social problems, including mental illness, substance abuse, and unemployment. Nine percent of inmates reported an episode of homelessness in the year prior to arrest, four to six times the estimated rate in the general U.S. adult population.[72] About one-third of current inmates had received a high school diploma, compared with more than 80 percent of the general population.[73] It is not surprising, then, that surveys show that inmates suffer from serious psychological and emotional problems, including psychosis and major depression.[74]

## Growth Trends

Why has the prison population continued to grow, even though the crime rate has fallen? One reason is that so many people who are released from prison soon return after failing on parole and other forms of early release. Another may be that public concern about drugs and violent crime has not been lost on state lawmakers. Tough new criminal legislation, including mandatory sentencing laws, increases the chances that a convicted offender will be incarcerated and thus limits the availability of early release via parole. Almost half of the prison growth during the past decade was for violent crimes. Although probation and community sentences still predominate, structural changes in criminal codes and crime rates have helped produce an expanding correctional population. The amount of time served in prison has increased because of such developments as truth-in-sentencing laws that require inmates to serve at least 85 percent of their sentences behind bars.[75] In addition, get-tough policies have curtailed the use of parole and have reduced judicial discretion to impose nonincarceration sentences.[76]

So many people are now going to prison that the federal government estimates that a significant portion of the nation's population will at one time or another be behind prison gates. About 5 percent of the population, or more than 13 million people, will serve a prison sentence some time during their lives. Men are over eight times more likely than women to be incarcerated in prison at least once during their lives. Among men, African Americans (28.5%) are about twice as likely as Hispanics (16.0%) and six times as likely as whites (4.4%) to be admitted to prison during their lives. Among women, 3.6 percent of African Americans, 1.5 percent of Hispanics, and 0.5 percent of whites will enter prison at least once.[77]

As more people go to prison and are forced to serve more of their sentence, the prison population will age, bringing additional costs in terms of health care and special programming.

## Future Trends

Despite such ominous signs, the nation's prison population may be "maxing out," and the rate of increase has slowed markedly. Budget cutbacks and belt tightening may halt the expansion of prison construction and cause the housing of ever more prisoners in already crowded prison facilities. Some rural communities that welcomed prison construction as a means of juicing up the economy and creating jobs may now be regretting their decision: Although prison construction may produce a short-term gain, in the long run it may actually impede economic development and retard job growth.[78]

Although new modular construction techniques and double- and triple-bunking of inmates make existing prisons expandable, the secure population probably cannot expand endlessly; declining crime rates will eventually reduce the number of inmates. As costs sharply increase, some states are now spending more on prisons than on higher education. The public may begin to question the wisdom of a strict incarceration policy. There may also be fewer criminals to incarcerate. The waning of the crack cocaine epidemic in large cities may hasten this decline, because street crimes will decline and fewer offenders will be eligible for the long penalties associated with the possession of crack.[79] As noted earlier, people are now receiving shorter prison sentences than five years ago (even though the time they serve is increasing), and if this trend holds, the prison population may eventually decline. However, if violence rates tick upward, increasing levels of serious crime will eventually reverse any reduction in the prison population.

In the final analysis, change in the correctional population may depend on the faith that judges and legislators place in incarceration as a crime control policy. As long as policymakers believe that incarcerating predatory criminals can bring down crime rates, the likelihood of a significant decrease in the institutional population seems remote. If there is little evidence that this costly system does lower crime rates, then less costly and equally effective alternatives may be sought.

## Ethical Challenges in Criminal Justice: A Writing Assignment

The governor of your state is running for reelection and wants to build a supermax prison to show her willingness to crack down on crime. She also wants to increase the use of mandatory sentences for drug and violent offenders and to put the worst ones in the supermax prison. She has asked you, as a criminal justice expert, to write a paper outlining the pros and cons (no pun intended) of this correctional policy and to come up with alternative models if you disapprove of her plan. What would you say to her? Before you answer, you may want to review the section on super-maximum-security prisons. Think about this topic: Should nonviolent drug offenders be placed in high-security prisons, or would you reserve these institutions for violent predators?

## SUMMARY

**1. Identify the various components of the correctional institution system.**

- The contemporary correctional system has branches in the federal, state, and county levels of government. Felons may be placed in state or federal penitentiaries (prisons), which are usually isolated, high-security structures. Misdemeanants are housed in county jails, sometimes called reformatories or houses of correction.

- Other types of correctional institutions include ranches and farms for adult offenders and community correctional settings, such as halfway houses, for inmates who are about to return to society.

**2. Discuss some of the most significant problems facing the correctional system.**

- Many former inmates recidivate soon after reentering society.

- There is still great debate over the true role of secure corrections.

**3. Be able to articulate how the first penal institutions developed in Europe.**

- The first penal institutions were foul places devoid of proper care, food, and medical treatment.

- From 1776 to 1785, a growing inmate population forced the English to house prisoners on hulks—abandoned ships anchored in harbors.

- The first American jail was built in James City in the Virginia colonies in the early seventeenth century.

**4. Explain how William Penn revolutionized corrections.**

- The "modern" American correctional system had its origins in Pennsylvania under the leadership of William Penn.

- Philadelphia's Walnut Street Jail was used to house convicted felons, except those sentenced to death.

**5. Compare the early New York and Pennsylvania prison models.**

- In 1816, Auburn Prison design was referred to as the congregate system since most prisoners ate and worked in groups.

- Pennsylvania established a prison that placed each inmate in a single cell for the duration of his sentence. Each cell was intended as a miniature prison that would prevent the inmates from contaminating one another.

**6. Chart the development of penal reform.**

- The National Congress of Penitentiary and Reformatory Discipline, held in Cincinnati in 1870, heralded a new era of prison reform.

- Prison reform groups proposed better treatment for inmates, an end to harsh corporal punishment, the creation of meaningful prison industries, and educational programs.

- Another important trend was the development of specialized prisons designed to treat particular types of offenders.

**7. List the purposes of jails, and understand the characteristic makeup of jail populations.**

- Jails are used to detain accused offenders who cannot make or are not eligible for bail prior to trial; they hold convicted offenders awaiting sentence; they serve as the principal institution of secure confinement for offenders convicted of misdemeanors.

- Almost nine out of every ten jail inmates are adult males, but the number of adult females in jail has been increasing faster than the number of males.

- Characteristics of jail inmates tend to reflect arrest data: Men, the poor, and racial and ethnic minorities are overrepresented.

**8. Be familiar with the term "new-generation jail."**

- New-generation jails allow for continuous observation of residents.
- Correctional officers have closer contact with inmates.
- Research shows that such jails may help reduce postrelease offending and recidivism.

**9. Classify the different types of federal and state penal institutions.**

- Maximum-security prisons, which house the most notorious criminals, are fortress-like, surrounded by stone walls with guard towers at strategic places. These walls may be 25 feet high, and sometimes inner and outer walls divide the prison into courtyards.

- Medium-security prisons are similar in appearance to maximum-security prisons, but security is not quite so tight, and the atmosphere is less tense.
- Operating without armed guards or perimeter walls, minimum-security prisons usually house the most trustworthy and least violent offenders.

**10. Discuss prison population trends.**

- This vast correctional system, with more than 1,800 institutions, now contains about 1.6 million prison inmates.
- The inmate population has continued to increase despite a decade-long drop in crime.
- One reason for the increase: Tough new criminal legislation, including mandatory sentencing laws, increases the chances that a convicted offender will be incarcerated and limits the availability of early release via parole.

## KEY TERMS

jail, 520
prison, 520
hulk, 523
Walnut Street Jail, 524
penitentiary house, 524
Pennsylvania system, 525
tier system, 525
congregate system, 525

Auburn system, 525
contract system (convict), 526
convict-lease system, 526
public account system, 527
medical model, 530
penal harm, 531
maximum-security prison, 535
super-maximum-security prison, 536

medium-security prison, 538
minimum-security prison, 538
boot camp, 539
shock incarceration, 539
community treatment, 540
halfway house, 540

## CRITICAL THINKING QUESTIONS

1. Would you want a community correctional center to be built in your neighborhood? Why or why not?
2. Should pretrial detainees and convicted offenders be kept in the same institution? Explain.
3. What can be done to reduce overcrowding in correctional facilities?
4. Should private companies be allowed to run correctional institutions? Why or why not?
5. What are the drawbacks of shock incarceration?

## NOTES

1. J. J. Hensley, "Arpaio Will Begin Charging Prisoners for Meals, *The Arizona Republic*, December 12, 2008, www.azcentral.com/arizonarepublic/news/articles/2008/12/12/20081212mcsofood1212.html.
2. http://abouttentcity.com/forum/tent-city-tips/how-to-survive-sheriff-joe-arpaio%e2%80%99s-jail-system/#p6.
3. W. Wesley Johnson, Katherine Bennett, and Timothy Flanagan, "Getting Tough on Prisoners: Results from the National Corrections Executive Survey, 1995," *Crime and Delinquency* 43 (1997): 24–41; Peter Kilborn, "Revival of Chain Gangs Takes a Twist," *New York Times*, March 11, 1997, p. A18.
4. Francis Cullen, "The Twelve People Who Saved Rehabilitation: How the Science of Criminology Made a Difference," *Criminology* 43 (2005): 1–42.

5. See David Fogel, *We Are the Living Proof*, 2d ed. (Cincinnati, Ohio: Anderson, 1978); Andrew von Hirsch, *Doing Justice: The Choice of Punishments* (New York: Hill and Wang, 1976); R. G. Singer, *Just Deserts—Sentencing Based on Equality and Desert* (Cambridge, Mass.: Ballinger, 1979). The most widely cited source on the failure of rehabilitation is Robert Martinson; see Douglas Lipton, Robert Martinson, and Judith Wilks, *The Effectiveness of Correctional Treatment: A Survey of Treatment Evaluation Studies* (New York: Praeger, 1975).
6. Thomas Stucky, Karen Heimer, and Joseph Lang, "Partisan Politics, Electoral Competition, and Imprisonment: An Analysis of States over Time," *Criminology* 43 (2005): 211–247.
7. Paul Schupp and Craig Rivera, "Identifying Imprisonment Patterns and Their Relation to Crime among New York

Counties 1990–2000," *Criminal Justice Policy Review* 21 (2010): 50–75.

8. Among the most helpful sources in developing this section were Mark Colvin, *Penitentiaries, Reformatories, and Chain Gangs* (New York: St. Martin's, 1997); David Duffee, *Corrections: Practice and Policy* (New York: Random House, 1989); Harry Allen and Clifford Simonsen, *Correction in America*, 5th ed. (New York: Macmillan, 1989); Benedict Alper, *Prisons Inside-Out* (Cambridge, Mass.: Ballinger, 1974); Harry Elmer Barnes, *The Story of Punishment*, 2d ed. (Montclair, N.J.: Patterson-Smith, 1972); Gustave de Beaumont and Alexis de Tocqueville, *On the Penitentiary System in the United States and Its Applications in France* (Carbondale: Southern Illinois University Press, 1964); Orlando Lewis, *The Development of American Prisons and Prison Customs, 1776–1845* (Montclair, N.J.: Patterson-Smith, 1967); Leonard Orland, ed., *Justice, Punishment, and Treatment* (New York: Free Press, 1973); J. Goebel, *Felony and Misdemeanor* (Philadelphia: University of Pennsylvania Press, 1976); Georg Rusche and Otto Kircheimer, *Punishment and Social Structure* (New York: Russell and Russell, 1939); Samuel Walker, *Popular Justice* (New York: Oxford University Press, 1980); Graeme Newman, *The Punishment Response* (Philadelphia: J. B. Lippincott, 1978); David Rothman, *Conscience and Convenience* (Boston: Little, Brown, 1980).

9. F. Pollock and F. Maitland, *History of English Law* (London: Cambridge University Press, 1952).

10. Marvin Wolfgang, "Crime and Punishment in Renaissance Florence," *Journal of Criminal Law and Criminology* 81 (1990): 567–584.

11. Margaret Wilson, *The Crime of Punishment, Life and Letters Series*, no. 64 (London: Jonathan Cape, 1934), p. 186.

12. John Howard, *The State of Prisons*, 4th ed. (1792; reprint, Montclair, N.J.: Patterson-Smith, 1973).

13. Alexis Durham III, "Newgate of Connecticut: Origins and Early Days of an Early American Prison," *Justice Quarterly* 6 (1989): 89–116.

14. Lewis, *The Development of American Prisons and Prison Customs*, p. 17.

15. Ibid., p. 29.

16. "Pennsylvania Correctional Industries, The Pioneer in United States Prison Labor," www.pci.state.pa.us/portal/server.pt/community/history_of_pci/17812.

17. Dario Melossi and Massimo Pavarini, *The Prison and the Factory: Origins of the Penitentiary System* (Totowa, N.J.: Barnes and Noble, 1981).

18. Michel Foucault, *Discipline and Punish* (New York: Vintage, 1978).

19. Ibid., p. 16.

20. David Rothman, *The Discovery of the Asylum* (Boston: Little, Brown, 1970).

21. Orland, *Justice, Punishment, and Treatment*, p. 143.

22. Walker, *Popular Justice*, p. 70

23. Ibid., p. 71.

24. Beverly Smith, "Military Training at New York's Elmira Reformatory, 1880–1920," *Federal Probation* 52 (1988): 33–41.

25. Ibid.

26. See Z. R. Brockway, "The Ideal of a True Prison System for a State," in *Transactions of the National Congress on Penitentiary and Reformatory Discipline* (reprint, Washington, D.C.: American Correctional Association, 1970), pp. 38–65.

27. This section leans heavily on Rothman, *Conscience and Convenience*.

28. Ibid., p. 23.

29. Ibid., p. 133.

30. 18 U.S.C. 1761.

31. Barbara Auerbach, George Sexton, Franlin Farrow, and Robert Lawson, *Work in American Prisons: The Private Sector Gets Involved* (Washington, D.C.: National Institute of Justice, 1988), p. 72.

32. This section relies heavily on William Parker, *Parole: Origins, Development, Current Practices, and Statutes* (College Park, Md.: American Correctional Association, 1972); Samuel Walker, *Popular Justice* (New York: Oxford University Press, 1980).

33. Jody Sundt, Francis Cullen, Brandon Applegate, and Michael Turner, "The Tenacity of the Rehabilitative Ideal Revisited: Have Attitudes toward Offender Treatment Changed?" *Criminal Justice and Behavior* 25 (1998): 426–481.

34. See, generally, Jameson Doig, *Criminal Corrections: Ideals and Realities* (Lexington, Mass.: Lexington Books, 1983).

35. Fred Heinzlemann, W. Robert Burkhart, Bernard Gropper, Cheryl Martorana, Lois Felson Mock, Maureen O'Connor, and Walter Philip Travers, *Jailing Drunk Drivers: Impact on the Criminal Justice System* (Washington, D.C.: National Institute of Justice, 1984).

36. Bonnie Green, Jeanne Miranda, Anahita Daroowalla, and Juned Siddique, "Trauma Exposure, Mental Health Functioning, and Program Needs of Women in Jail," *Crime and Delinquency* 51 (2005): 133–151.

37. Sonia Alemagno and Jill Dickie, "Employment Issues of Women in Jail," *Journal of Employment Counseling* 42 (2005): 67–74.

38. Kevin Krause, "Inspectors Fault Medical Care at Dallas County Jail," *Dallas Morning News*, February 4, 2009, www.dallasnews.com/sharedcontent/dws/news/localnews/stories/DN-jailreport_05met.ART.State.Edition1.4c50f36.html (accessed March 1, 2009).

39. Caroline Wolf Harlow, *Prior Abuse Reported by Inmates and Probationers* (Washington, D.C.: Bureau of Justice Statistics, 1999).

40. Doris James and Lauren Glaze, *Mental Health Problems of Prison and Jail Inmates* (Washington, D.C.: Bureau of Justice Statistics, 2006).

41. NBC5.com, Chicago, "Suicides Top List of Lake County Jail's Problems, Federal Report: Inmates Killing Themselves at Alarming Rate," May 20, 2007, www.nbc5.com/news/13354500/detail.html (accessed September 4, 2008).

42. Brandon Applegate, Ray Surette, and Bernard McCarthy, "Detention and Desistance from Crime: Evaluating the Influence of a New Generation of Jail on Recidivism," *Journal of Criminal Justice* 27 (1999): 539–548.

43. Ibid.

44. Christine Tartaro, "Watered Down: Partial Implementation of the New Generation Jail Philosophy," *Prison Journal* 86 (2006): 284–300.

45. Human Rights Watch, *Prison Conditions in the United States*, www.hrw.org/wr2k2/prisons.html (accessed September 14, 2005).

46. "Suit Alleges Violations in California's 'Super-Max' Prison," *Criminal Justice Newsletter*, September 1, 1993, p. 2.

47. Jody Sundt, Thomas Castellano, and Chad Briggs, "The Sociopolitical Context of Prison Violence and Its Control: A Case Study of Supermax and Its Effect in Illinois," *The Prison Journal* 88 (2008): 94–122.

48. Leena Kurki and Norval Morris, "The Purpose, Practices, and Problems of Supermax Prisons," in *Crime and Justice: An Annual Edition*, ed. Michael Tonry (Chicago: University of Chicago Press, 2001), pp. 385–422.

49. Daniel Mears and Jamie Watson, "Towards a Fair and Balanced Assessment of Supermax Prisons," *Justice Quarterly* 23 (2006): 232–270.

50. Daniel Mears, "An Assessment of Supermax Prisons Using an Evaluation Research Framework," *The Prison Journal* 88 (2008): 43–68; Daniel Mears and Jennifer Castro, "Wardens' Views on the Wisdom of Supermax Prisons," *Crime and Delinquency* 52 (2006): 398–431; Daniel Mears and Jamie Watson, "Towards a Fair and Balanced Assessment of Supermax Prisons."

51. James Anderson, Laronistine Dyson, and Jerald Burns, *Boot Camps: An Intermediate Sanction* (Lanham, Md.: University Press of America, 1999), pp. 1–17.

52. Ibid., pp. 328–329.

53. Doris Layton MacKenzie, "Boot Camp Prisons: Components, Evaluations, and Empirical Issues," *Federal Probation* 54 (1990): 44–52; see also "Boot Camp Programs Grow in Number and Scope," *NIJ Reports* (November/December 1990): 6–8.

54. Doris Layton MacKenzie and James Shaw, "The Impact of Shock Incarceration on Technical Violations and New Criminal Activities," *Justice Quarterly* 10 (1993): 463–487.

55. Doris Layton MacKenzie, Robert Brame, David McDowall, and Claire Souryal, "Boot Camp Prisons and Recidivism in Eight States," *Criminology* 33 (1995): 327–358.

56. Vanessa St. Gerard, "Federal Prisons to Eliminate Boot Camps," *Corrections Today* 67 (2005): 13–16.

57. James Stephan, *Census of Federal and State Correctional Facilities, 2005* (Washington, D.C.: Bureau of Justice Statistics, 2008).

58. William J. Sabol, Heather Couture, and Paige M. Harrison, *Prisoners in 2006* (Washington, D.C.: Bureau of Justice Statistics, 2007).

59. Richard Harding, "Private Prisons," in *Crime and Justice: An Annual Edition*, ed. Michael Tonry (Chicago: University of Chicago Press, 2001), pp. 265–347.

60. Corrections Corporation of America, www.correctionscorp.com/about/ (accessed September 4, 2008); Palash Ghosh, "Private Prisons Have a Lock on Growth," *Business Week Online*, www.businessweek.com/investor/content/jul2006/pi20060706_849785.htm, July 7, 2006.

61. The GEO Group Homepage, www.thegeogroupinc.com/index.asp (accessed May 1, 2010).

62. William Bales, Laura Bedard, Susan Quinn, David Ensley, and Glen Holley, "Recidivism of Public and Private State Prison Inmates in Florida," *Criminology and Public Policy* 4 (2005): 57–82; Lonn Lanza-Kaduce, Karen Parker, and Charles Thomas, "A Comparative Recidivism Analysis of Releases from Private and Public Prisons," *Crime and Delinquency* 45 (1999): 28–47.

63. Charles Thomas, "Recidivism of Public and Private State Prison Inmates in Florida: Issues and Unanswered Questions," *Criminology and Public Policy* 4 (2005): 89–99; Travis Pratt and Jeff Maahs, "Are Private Prisons More Cost-Effective Than Public Prisons? A Meta-Analysis of Evaluation Research Studies," *Crime and Delinquency* 45 (1999): 358–371.

64. Ira Robbins, *The Legal Dimensions of Private Incarceration* (Chicago: American Bar Association, 1988).

65. Danica Coto, "Medical Care Company Named in Numerous Jail Lawsuits," *Charlotte Observer*, August 30, 2004.

66. *Richardson v. McKnight*, 521 U.S. 399 (1997).

67. Ahmed A. White, "Rule of Law and the Limits of Sovereignty: The Private Prison in Jurisprudential Perspective," *American Criminal Law Review* 38 (2001): 111–147; *Correctional Services Corp. v. Malesko*, 534 U.S. 61 (2001).

68. Lawrence Travis, Edward Latessa, and Gennaro Vito, "Private Enterprise and Institutional Corrections: A Call for Caution," *Federal Probation* 49 (1985): 11–17.

69. Patrick Anderson, Charles Davoli, and Laura Moriarty, "Private Corrections: Feast or Fiasco?" *Prison Journal* 65 (1985): 32–41.

70. Richard Culp, "The Rise and Stall of Prison Privatization: An Integration of Policy Analysis Perspectives," *Criminal Justice Policy Review* 16 (2005): 412–442.

71. Heather Couture and William J. Sabol, *Prison Inmates at Midyear 2007* (Washington, D.C.: Bureau of Justice Statistics, 2008).

72. Greg Greenberg and Robert Rosenheck, "Homelessness in the State and Federal Prison Population," *Criminal Behaviour and Mental Health* 18 (2008): 88–103.

73. Caroline Wolf Harlow, *Education and Correctional Populations* (Washington, D.C.: Bureau of Justice Statistics, 2003).

74. Seena Fazel and John Danesh, "Serious Mental Disorder in 23,000 Prisoners: A Systematic Review of Sixty-Two Surveys," *Lancet* 359 (2002): 545–561.

75. Todd Clear, *Harm in American Penology: Offenders, Victims, and Their Communities* (Albany: State University of New York Press, 1994).

76. Daniel Nagin, "Criminal Deterrence Research: A Review of the Evidence and a Research Agenda for the Outset of the 21st Century," in *Crime and Justice: An Annual Review*, ed. Michael Tonry (Chicago: University of Chicago Press, 1997).

77. Thomas P. Bonczar and Allen J. Beck, *Lifetime Likelihood of Going to State or Federal Prison* (Washington, D.C.: Bureau of Justice Statistics, 1997).

78. Gregory Hooks, Clayton Mosher, Shaun Genter, Thomas Rotolo, Thomas, and Linda Lobao, "Revisiting the Impact of Prison Building on Job Growth: Education, Incarceration, and County-Level Employment, 1976–2004," *Social Science Quarterly* 91 (2010): 228–244.

79. Andrew Lang Golub, Farrukh Hakeem, and Bruce Johnson, *Monitoring the Decline in the Crack Epidemic with Data from the Drug Use Forecasting Program, Final Report* (Washington, D.C.: National Institute of Justice, 1996).

# CHAPTER 15

# Prison Life: Living in and Leaving Prison

## CHAPTER OBJECTIVES

1. Discuss the problems of the adult correctional system.
2. Know what is meant by the term "total institution."
3. Differentiate between a no-frills philosophy and a rehabilitation philosophy.
4. Chart the "prisonization" process and the development of the inmate social code.
5. Compare the lives and cultures of male and female inmates.
6. Be familiar with the different forms of correctional treatment.
7. Discuss the world of correctional officers.
8. Understand the causes of prison violence.
9. Know what is meant by prisoners' rights, and discuss some key privileges that have been granted to inmates.
10. Be familiar with the problems of prisoner reentry.

© Joyce Dopkeen/New York Times/Redux

**K**athy Boudin served 20 years in prison at the Bedford Hills Correctional Facility for her role in the October 20, 1981, robbery of a Brinks truck at the Nanuet Mall in Rockland County, New York. During the robbery Peter Paige, a Brinks employee, was killed. Boudin, then a member of the 1960s radical group the Weathermen, drove the getaway truck in what was considered a terrorist act by members of the Black Revolutionary Army. After the police closed in, Boudin surrendered, but two officers were killed in the subsequent shootout with the other robbers. At trial it was determined that she was unarmed and unaware that the conspirators would use violence. However, under New York's felony murder law, Boudin was liable for any death that occurred during the course of the robbery. The jury did not buy her defense that she could not be held legally responsible for the killings of the officers because she had already surrendered and was in custody.

While she was in prison, Boudin's behavior was exemplary. She worked with AIDS patients, supported incarcerated parents and their children, and taught educational programs for inmates. She earned a master's degree and started on a doctorate. Boudin also wrote and published poetry and scholarly articles. After twice being denied parole, she was granted release on August 20, 2003. Her victims' surviving relatives treated the decision with bitterness, questioning whether she was at all remorseful. However, a letter she wrote to her college (Bryn Mawr) journal while still incarcerated expresses both her profound regrets and her considerable personal change:

> For the last 19 years I have lived in prison, quietly making a personal journey that has helped me to face the tragedy I am responsible for, understanding what allowed me to be involved, and building a new sense of life and what is worth doing. I want to thank you who have been with me throughout, who have helped me survive and learn to rebuild. When I stood in front of the judge almost two decades ago, I expressed my remorse. That was the beginning of a long process of facing what I had done. I want to describe some of what I have learned.
>
> Do I feel what I did was wrong? Yes. I want to be clear. I know that I am responsible for a terrible thing. I feel nothing but remorse and shame about my involvement. I will live with this for the rest of my life. . . .

At Bedford Hills I began to create a new life. I dedicated myself to working with our Children's Center. With women here, I've learned about how to love and support our children from a distance and how to help other mothers do this. I went through years when our whole community faced fear, loss, and death caused by AIDS. Together, we developed a peer community health program to cope with the AIDS epidemic. I have worked with women committed to acquir[ing] a college education, and with them moved educators on the outside to help build a wonderful four-year college program. I find satisfaction in the day-to-day ways that people find strength in their abilities, and being part of this: teaching women to read and write, to communicate with their children, and learning about dying and living with dignity. I have known wonderful people—inmates and staff—and learned from them and with them.

Fortunately, I've been in a prison that believes people can change, and can make a difference. Here, I live with many other inmates who, like myself, have grown to become teachers and peer counselors, coming together to solve shared problems. It is through these experiences and relationships that my own change and growth have come about. My experience at Bedford leaves me both hopeful and inspired by the enormous potential of people. I believe that there are lessons from our work here that would be useful in the broader society. My opportunities to learn, to get a master's degree in adult education, to study psychology and social work, have helped me reorient myself and my goals.

I know it is impossible to make up for the suffering I helped to cause; I have tried to give back to a community of people, to live my life in a life-giving way.

My work, while the source of much hope, has also taken me in another direction. It deepens over and over my grasp of the human sorrow and loss that I am tied to. Sitting with young women dying of AIDS, creating a quilt for those in our community who are no longer with us, I face the deaths for which I am responsible. As I work with mothers on rebuilding their relationships with the children they left, I am overwhelmed by my own responsibility for leaving a group of children with no hope of ever seeing their own fathers again. Now I can ask: What if it were my father, my husband, or my son who had been killed or hurt? What would I feel? I understand the rage that the victims' families may feel towards me. If I could just turn the clock back and make things different; if only I could do that.[1]

Her supporters endorsed her release, proclaiming that she was ashamed and contrite about her earlier life. Barbara Hanson Treen, a former member of the New York State Division of Parole who got to know Boudin, told the media the following:

Kathy is really an example of the best that prison could provide for people. . . . People are so much more complex than that one crime that defines them. The best thing for people coming home is to treat them with dignity, as individual human beings, and to get them ready.[2]

Three other surviving participants in the robbery, including Boudin's estranged husband, David Gilbert, cannot be considered for parole before 2056. A fourth defendant, Abdul Majid, is up for parole in 2015. A fifth defendant, Kuwasi Balagoon, died in prison in 1986. ∎

Kathy Boudin's story reveals a number of important issues surrounding the prison experience. It illustrates the fact that most inmates, even those involved in notorious crimes, do not serve their entire sentence in prison but are released on parole or other early-release mechanisms. It also shows how many inmates try to turn their lives around while inside prison walls, entering treatment programs and even earning graduate degrees. It raises the question: Are prisons places of punishment and incapacitation or communities where people can be successfully treated and rehabilitated, like Kathy Boudin?

Unfortunately, most inmates are not rehabilitated, and a majority return to prison soon after their release, helping to swell the number of people behind bars. As the prison population increases in size, corrections officials have responded by constructing new facilities at a record pace. During the past 25 years, the number of secure correctional facilities increased from just under 600 to over 1,800. In other words, most prisons in operation today were opened in the last 25 years.[3] These facilities take a variety of forms, including prisons, prison hospitals, prison farms, boot camps, work release centers, and centers for reception, classification, or alcohol and drug treatment.[4] Although many facilities have a recent pedigree, a significant number are old, decrepit, archaic structures: 25 were built before 1875, 79 between 1875 and 1924, and 141 between 1925 and 1949. In fact, some of the first prisons ever constructed, such as the Concord Reformatory in Massachusetts, which first opened in 1878, are still in operation.

Although most prisons are classified as medium-security, more than half of all inmates are held in large maximum-security institutions. Despite the continuous outcry by penologists against the use of fortress-like prisons, institutions holding 1,000 or more inmates still predominate. Prison overcrowding is a significant problem. Many institutions are operating above stated capacity. Recreation and workshop space has been turned into dormitories housing 30 or more inmates in a single room. Most prison experts agree that a minimum of 60 square feet is needed for each inmate, but many prisons fail to meet this standard.

This giant system designed to reform and rehabilitate offenders is instead undergoing a crisis of massive proportions. Institutions are so overcrowded that meaningful treatment efforts are often a matter of wishful thinking; recidivism rates are shockingly high. Inmates are resentful of the deteriorated conditions, and correctional officers fear that the institution is ready to explode. Rather than deterring people from future criminality, a prison stay may actually reinforce and/or encourage their criminal offending.[5] This lack of success is not lost on the general public. It might surprise some "get tough" politicians, but the general public is not ready to embrace a prison-building boom at the expense of rehabilitation efforts.[6] And, rather than rehabilitating their residents, penal institutions seem to exacerbate their criminal tendencies. It is popular to describe the typical prison as a "school for crime" in which young offenders are taught by older cons to become sophisticated criminals. The "school for crime" may not be some form of urban myth. Why spend millions on prisons if they really do not work?

This chapter presents a brief review of some of the most important issues confronting the nation's troubled correctional system.

## MEN IMPRISONED

According to the prevailing wisdom, prisons in the United States are **total institutions**. This means that inmates locked within their walls are segregated from the outside world, kept under constant scrutiny and surveillance, and forced to obey strict official rules to avoid facing formal sanctions. Their personal possessions are taken from them, and they must conform to institutional dress and personal appearance norms. Many human functions are strictly curtailed; heterosexual sex, friendships, family relationships, education, and participation in groups become privileges of the past. As you may recall, some institutions employ a **"no-frills policy,"** which means that inmates receive the bare minimum of

**total institution**
A regimented, dehumanizing institution, such as a prison, in which like-situated people are kept in social isolation, cut off from the world at large.

**no-frills policy**
A correctional policy that stipulates that prisons are intended to punish, not coddle, inmates. This usually means a strict regimen of work and discipline and reduced opportunities for recreation and education.

food, services, and medical care required by law. The purpose: Convince them that prison is no place to be, and they'd better not return.

## Living in Prison

Inmates quickly learn what the term "total institution" really means. When they arrive at prison, they are stripped, searched, shorn, and assigned living quarters. Before they get there, though, their first experience occurs in a classification or reception center, where they are given a series of psychological and other tests and evaluated on the basis of their personality, background, offense history, and treatment needs. Based on the classification they are given, they will be assigned to a permanent facility. Hard-core, repeat, and violent offenders go to the maximum-security unit. Offenders with learning disabilities may be assigned to an institution that specializes in educational services. Mentally disordered offenders will be held in a facility that can provide psychiatric care. Some states have instituted rigorous classification instruments designed to maximize the effectiveness of placements, thereby cutting down on the cost of incarceration. If classification can be conducted in an efficient and effective manner, nondangerous offenders will not needlessly be kept in expensive, high-security facilities.[7]

All previous concepts of personal privacy and dignity are soon forgotten. Inmate turned author James A. Paluch Jr. calls prison cells "cold coffin[s] . . . leaving a chilling effect on anyone forced to live inside them." Serving a life term without hope of parole, Paluch views prison life as one of constant manipulation and deceit both by guards and by other inmates. Trusting anyone can bring personal hardship and victimization.[8] Personal losses include the deprivation of liberty, goods and services, heterosexual relationships, autonomy, and security.[9] Newcomers may be subject to verbal and physical attack and threats from older cons, with little chance of legal redress. Even if they are not abused, the staff may be quick to warn them about the danger of violence and sexual coercion they now face. The threats are not lost on them: Interview data from a national study of prison sexual violence conducted by Mark Fleisher and Jessie Krienert revealed that scared or naive inmates often refuse to participate in social activities, such as watching television in a day room or playing cards.[10]

Overcrowded prisons are filled with young, aggressive men who are responsible for the majority of inmate-on-inmate assaults.[11] Although criminal law applies to inmates, just as to any other citizen, it is rarely enforced within prison walls.[12] Therefore, part of living in prison involves learning to protect oneself and developing survival instincts. Frightened inmates remain in close proximity

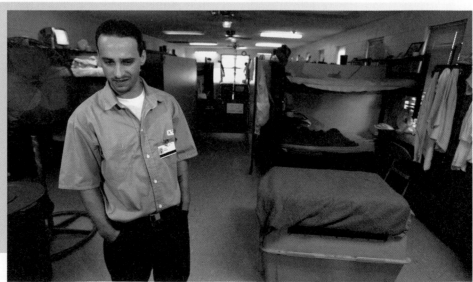

*Prisons are total institutions, and adjustment can be difficult. Many inmates have long histories of offending and move in and out of correctional institutions on a regular basis. Some have failed in community corrections and/or are parole violators. Here Elijah Corum talks about prison life in his living quarters at Lansing Correctional Facility in Lansing, Kansas, on August 3, 2007. Corum, who is behind bars because his probation on a drug charge was revoked, is representative of the type of offender targeted by a new program aimed at keeping convicts from violating probation and ending up in prison.*

© AP Images/Charlie Riedel

to their cells or to the sleeping area in dorms. Victims of physical and/or sexual violence may not use shower facilities out of fear of further such attacks.[13]

Inmates in large, inaccessible prisons may find themselves physically cut off from families, friends, and associates. Visitors may find it difficult to travel great distances to see them; mail is censored and sometimes destroyed. And while incarcerated, inmates are forced to associate with a peer group who bring with them a disproportionate share of mental and physical problems. Various communicable diseases are commonly found, such as hepatitis C virus, HIV, and syphilis. Not surprisingly, inmate health is significantly worse than that of the general population.[14]

**CourseMate** For more information about **PrisonerLife.com**, visit the Criminal Justice CourseMate at CengageBrain.com, then access the "Web Links" for this chapter.

## Adjusting to Prison

Inmates go through a variety of attitude and behavior changes, or cycles, as their sentence unfolds. During the early part of their prison stay, inmates may become easily depressed as they consider the long duration of the sentence and the loneliness and dangers of prison life. They must learn the ins and outs of survival in the institution: Which persons can be befriended, and which are best avoided? Who will grant favors and for what repayment? To avoid victimization, inmates must learn to adopt a defensive lifestyle.[15] They must discover areas of safety and danger. Sex offenders in particular often find it difficult to adjust to prison, and some try to create new identities and secure niches that enable them to survive in the prison's general population. Ironically, these new identities and protective niches are jeopardized when they enter a sex offender treatment program that, although designed to help them, gives them away to the other inmates.[16]

Some learn how to fight back to prove they are not people who can be bullied. People who viewed violence as an acceptable method of settling disputes before entering prison are the ones most likely to use violence while they are inmates.[17] Research shows that inmates who have a history of pre-arrest drug use and have been incarcerated for violent crimes are the ones most likely to get involved in assaults and drug/alcohol offenses while they are incarcerated.[18] Rule violations may be more common among inmates who, having lived in a subculture of violence on the outside, bring their beliefs regarding crime and violence into the prison environment. Survival in prison may depend on one's ability to identify troubled inmates and avoid contact.

Whereas some kill their attackers and get even longer sentences, others join cliques and gangs that provide protection and the ability to acquire power within the institution. Gangs are powerful in the larger prison systems, especially in California. Some inmates seek transfers to a different cell block or prison, ask for protective custody, or simply remain in their cells all the time.

Inmates may find that some prisoners have formed cliques, or groups, based on ethnic backgrounds or personal interests; they are also likely to encounter Mafia-like or racial terror groups that must be dealt with. Inmates may find that power in the prison is shared by correctional officers and inmate gangs; the only way to avoid being beaten and raped may be to learn how to beat and rape. If they are weak and unable to defend themselves, new inmates may find that they are considered "punks"; if they ask a guard for help, they are labeled "snitches." Those most likely to be targets of sexual assaults may spend their sentence in protective custody, sacrificing the "freedom of the yard" and rehabilitation services for personal protection.[19]

As the prison population expands, the violence and danger of the streets will be imported into the prison culture. A recent report from the Commission on Safety and Abuse in America's Prisons, funded by New York's Vera Foundation, found that violence, medical problems, and segregation of inmates still plague the nation's prisons (see Exhibit 15.1).[20]

Despite all these hardships, many inmates learn to adapt to the prison routine. Each prisoner has his own method of coping. He may stay alone, become friends with another inmate, join a group, or seek the advice of treatment personnel.

**EXHIBIT 15.1**

## Report of the Commission on Safety and Abuse in America's Prisons

### VIOLENCE

There is disturbing evidence of individual assaults and patterns of violence in some U.S. prisons and jails. Corrections officers told the commission about a near-constant fear of being assaulted. Former prisoners recounted gang violence, rape, beatings by officers, and (in one large jail) a pattern of illegal and humiliating strip searches. Former Florida warden Ron McAndrew described small groups of officers operating as "goon squads" to abuse prisoners and intimidate other staff. Inmate-on-inmate violence is common, even if the prison death rate has been in sharp decline.

### MEDICAL PROBLEMS

High rates of disease and illness among prisoners, coupled with inadequate funding for correctional health care, endanger prisoners, staff, and the public. Much of the public dismiss jails and prisons as sealed institutions, where what happens inside remains inside. In the context of disease and illness, which travel naturally from one environment to another, that view is clearly wrong. Left untreated, staph infections and diseases such as tuberculosis, hepatitis C, and HIV directly affect our families, neighborhoods, and communities. As a result of poverty, substance abuse, and years of poor health care, prisoners as a group are much less healthy than average Americans. Every year, more than 1.5 million people are released from jail and prison carrying a life-threatening contagious disease. At least 350,000 prisoners have a serious mental illness.

### SEGREGATION

Separating dangerous or vulnerable individuals from the general prison population is now commonplace. In some systems, prisoners who should be housed at safe distances from particular individuals or groups of prisoners end up locked in their cells 23 hours a day, every day, with little opportunity to be productive and prepare for release. People who pose no real threat to anyone and also those who are mentally ill are placed for months or years in high-security units and supermax prisons. In some places, the environment is so severe that people end up completely isolated, confined in constantly bright or constantly dim spaces without any meaningful human contact—torturous conditions that have been proved to cause mental deterioration. Prisoners often are released from solitary confinement and other high-security units directly to the streets, despite the clear dangers of this practice.

Source: John Gibbons and Nicholas de B. Katzenbach, *Confronting Confinement: A Report of the Commission on Safety and Abuse in America's Prisons* (New York: Vera Institute of Justice, 2006).

---

Inmates soon learn that their lifestyle and activities can contribute to their being victimized by more aggressive inmates. The more time they spend in closely guarded activities, the less likely they are to become the victims of violence. The more they isolate themselves from others who might protect them, the greater their vulnerability to attack. The more visitors they receive, the more likely they are to be attacked by fellow inmates jealous of their relationships with the outside world.[21]

Of course, not all inmates learn to cope. Some inmates repeatedly violate institutional rules. Predicting who will become an institutional troublemaker is difficult, but rule-breaking behavior has been associated with being a younger inmate with a low IQ, with having had numerous juvenile convictions, with being a repeat offender, and with having victimized a stranger. Inmates who have limited intelligence and little self-control may not be able to form adaptive coping mechanisms and manage the stress of being in prison.[22]

## The Inmate Social Code

For many years, criminal justice experts maintained that inmates formed their own world with a unique set of norms and rules known as the **inmate subculture**.[23] A significant aspect of the inmate subculture was a unique **inmate social code**—unwritten guidelines that expressed the values, attitudes, and type of behavior that older inmates demanded of young ones. Passed on from one generation of inmates to another, the inmate social code represented the values of interpersonal relations in the prison.

**inmate subculture**
The loosely defined culture that pervades prisons and has its own norms, rules, and language.

**inmate social code**
An unwritten code of behavior, passed from older inmates to younger ones, that serves as a guideline for appropriate inmate behavior within the correctional institution.

## EXHIBIT 15.2

## Elements of the Inmate Social Code

■ *Don't interfere with inmates' interests.* Within this area of the code are maxims concerning serving the least amount of time in the greatest possible comfort. For example, inmates are warned never to betray another inmate to authorities; in other words, grievances must be handled personally. Other aspects of the noninterference doctrine include "Don't be nosy," "Don't have a loose lip," "Keep off the other inmates' backs," and "Don't put another inmate on the spot."

■ *Don't lose your head.* Inmates are also cautioned to refrain from arguing, quarreling, or engaging in other emotional displays with fellow inmates. The novice may hear such warnings as "Play it cool," and "Do your own time."

■ *Don't exploit inmates.* Prisoners are warned not to take advantage of one another—"Don't steal from cons," "Don't welsh on a debt," and "Be right."

■ *Be tough and don't lose your dignity.* Although the second rule forbids conflict, once it starts an inmate must be prepared to deal with it effectively and thoroughly. Maxims include "Don't cop out," "Don't weaken," and "Be tough; be a man."

■ *Don't be a sucker.* Inmates are cautioned not to make fools of themselves and support the guards or prison administration over the interest of the inmates—"Be sharp."

Source: Gresham Sykes, *The Society of Captives* (Princeton, N.J.: Princeton University Press, 1958).

National attention was first drawn to the inmate social code and subculture by Donald Clemmer's classic book *The Prison Community*, in which he presented a detailed sociological study of life in a maximum-security prison.[24] Clemmer was able to identify a unique language, or argot, that prisoners use. He found that prisoners tend to group themselves into cliques on the basis of such personal criteria as sexual preference, political beliefs, and offense history. He found complex sexual relationships in prison and concluded that many heterosexual men will turn to homosexual relationships when faced with long sentences and the loneliness of prison life.

Clemmer's most important contribution may have been his identification of what he called the **prisonization** process. This he defined as the inmate's assimilation into the existing prison culture through acceptance of its language, sexual code, and norms of behavior. Those who become the most "prisonized" will be the least likely to reform on the outside.

Using Clemmer's work as a jumping-off point, a number of prominent sociologists have set out to explore more fully the various roles in the prison community. The most important principles of the dominant inmate culture are listed in Exhibit 15.2.

Although some inmates violate the code and exploit their peers, the "right guy" is someone who uses the inmate social code as his personal behavior guide. He is always loyal to his fellow prisoners, keeps his promises, is dependable and trustworthy, and never interferes with inmates who are conniving against the officials.[25] The right guy does not go around looking for a fight, but he never runs away from one; he acts like a man. In contrast, the exploiter is shunned by his peers. Rapists, for example, are unwelcome in mainstream inmate society; they have few companions, and their social life rests precariously on the margin of inmate society.[26]

The effects of prisonization may be long-term and destructive. Many inmates become hostile to the legal system, learning to use violence as a means of solving problems and to value criminal peers.[27] For some this change may be permanent; for others it is temporary, and they may revert to their "normal" life after release.

**prisonization**
Assimilation into the separate culture of the prison. This loosely defined culture that pervades prisons has its own norms, rules, and language. The traditional prison culture is now being replaced by a violent gang culture.

## The New Inmate Culture

The importation of outside values into the inmate culture has had a dramatic effect on prison life. Although the "old" inmate subculture may have been harmful because its norms and values insulated the inmate from change efforts, it also helped maintain order in the institution and prevented violence among the inmates. People who violated the code and victimized others were sanctioned by their peers. An understanding developed between guards and inmate leaders: The guards would let the inmates have things their own way, and the inmates would not let things get out of hand and draw the attention of the administration.

The old system may be dying or already dead in most institutions. The change seems to have been precipitated by the black power movement in the 1960s and 1970s. Black inmates were no longer content to play a subservient role and challenged the power of established white inmates. As the black power movement gained prominence, racial tension in prisons created divisions that severely altered the inmate subculture. Older, respected inmates could no longer cross racial lines to mediate disputes. Predatory inmates could victimize others without fear of retaliation. Consequently, more inmates than ever are now assigned to protective custody for their own safety.

In the new culture, African American and Latino inmates are much more cohesively organized than whites.[28] Their groups sometimes form out of religious or political affiliations, such as the Black Muslims; out of efforts to combat discrimination in prison, such as the Latino group La Nuestra Familia; or from street gangs, such as the Vice Lords or Gangster Disciples in the Illinois prison system and the Crips in California. Where white inmates have successfully organized, it is in the form of a neo-Nazi group called the Aryan Brotherhood. Racially homogeneous gangs are so cohesive and powerful that they are able to supplant the original inmate code with one of their own.

## WOMEN IMPRISONED

Before 1960, few women were in prison. Women's prisons were relatively rare and were usually an outgrowth of male institutions. Only four institutions for women were built between 1930 and 1950; in comparison, 34 women's prisons were constructed during the 1980s as crime rates soared.

At the turn of the twentieth century, female inmates were viewed as morally depraved people who flouted conventional rules of female behavior. The treatment of white and African American women differed significantly. In some states, white women were placed in female-only reformatories designed to improve their deportment; black women were placed in male prisons, where they were put on chain gangs and were subject to beatings.[29]

As you may recall (Chapter 14), the female offender population has increased more rapidly than the male population. There are a number of reasons for this growth. Women have accelerated their crime rate at a faster pace than men. The "get tough" policies that produced mandatory and determinate sentencing statutes have also helped reduce the judicial discretion that has traditionally benefited women; women are now less likely to be granted lenient gender-based sentences.

### Female Institutions

State jurisdictions have been responding to the influx of female offenders into the correctional system by expanding the facilities for housing and treating them. Women's prisons tend to be smaller than those housing male inmates. Although some female institutions are strictly penal, with steel bars, concrete floors, and other security measures, the majority are nonsecure institutions similar to college dormitories and group homes in the community. Women's facilities, especially those in the community, commonly offer inmates a great deal of autonomy and allow them to make decisions affecting their daily lives.

However, like men's prisons, women's prisons suffer from a lack of adequate training, health, treatment, and educational facilities. Psychological counseling often takes the form of group sessions conducted by laypeople, such as correctional officers. Most trained psychologists and psychiatrists restrict themselves to such activities as conducting intake classifications and court-ordered examinations

**CourseMate** For more information about the **Women's Prison Association**, visit the Criminal Justice CourseMate at CengageBrain.com, then access the "Web Links" for this chapter.

and prescribing mood-controlling medication. Although many female inmates are parents and had custody of their children before incarceration, little effort is made to help them develop better parenting skills. Although most female (and male) inmates have at least one child, less than a quarter actually get an annual visit. Who takes care of these children while their mothers are incarcerated? Most children of incarcerated women are placed with their father, a grandparent, another relative, or a family friend. About 10 percent wind up in foster homes or state facilities.[30]

Job-training opportunities are also a problem. Where vocational training exists, it is in areas where income is likely to be low, which hinders adjustment on release. Female inmates, many of whom were on the economic margin before their incarceration began, find little room for improvement during their prison experience.[31] Surveys also indicate that the prison experience does little to prepare women to reenter the workforce after they complete their sentence. Gender stereotypes still shape vocational opportunities.[32] Female inmates are still being trained for "women's roles," such as child rearing, and are not offered a course of study designed to help them make successful adjustments in the community.[33]

## Female Inmates

Like their male counterparts, female inmates are disproportionately more likely to be young (most are under age 30), minority group members, unmarried, undereducated, and either unemployed or underemployed. The typical woman behind bars is a poor, unskilled woman of color with small children who has health problems, has a history of abuse, and is incarcerated for low-level drug or property offenses.[34]

Incarcerated women also have had a troubled family life. Significant numbers were at-risk children, products of broken homes and the welfare system; over half have received welfare at some time during their adult lives. Many claim to have been physically or sexually abused at some point in their lives. This pattern continued in adult life: Many female inmates were victims of domestic violence. It is not surprising that many display psychological problems.[35]

A significant number of female inmates report having substance abuse problems. About three-fourths have used drugs at some time in their lives, and almost half were involved with addictive drugs, such as cocaine, heroin, or PCP. The incarceration of so many women who are low criminal risks, yet face a high risk of exposure to HIV (human immunodeficiency virus, which causes AIDS) and other health issues because of their prior history of drug abuse, presents a significant problem. One recent study of incarcerated women found that one-third of the sample reported that before their arrest, they had traded sex for money or drugs; 24 percent of the women reported trading sex for money or drugs "weekly or more often."[36] Such risky behavior significantly increases the likelihood of their carrying the AIDS virus or other sexually transmitted diseases.

The picture that emerges of the female inmate is troubling. After a lifetime of emotional turmoil, physical and sexual abuse, and drug use, it seems improbable that overcrowded, underfunded correctional institutions can forge a dramatic turnaround in the behavior of at-risk female inmates. Many have lost custody of their children, a trauma that is more likely to afflict those who are already

© AP Images/James MacPherson

*Incarcerated women inhabit a distinct social world that is quite different from that of male inmates. Amanda Espinoza stands in the Dakota Women's Correctional Rehabilitation Center in New England, North Dakota, on May 10, 2006. The 21-year-old Grand Forks native said she wants to raise her son and attend college once she completes her three-year prison term for failing to comply with the terms of her probation on an auto theft conviction. Oklahoma, Mississippi, and the mountain states have set the pace in increasing the imprisonment of women, while several northeastern states have reduced the number of women behind bars.*

---

**EXHIBIT 15.3**

## Problems Encountered in Female Institutions

■ *Failure to refer seriously ill inmates for treatment and delays in treatment.* Women inmates suffering from treatable diseases such as asthma, diabetes, sickle cell anemia, cancer, late-term miscarriages, and seizures have little or no access to medical attention; such conditions sometimes result in death or permanent injury. Instances of failure to deliver life-saving drugs for inmates with HIV/ AIDS has also been noted.

■ *Lack of qualified personnel and resources and use of nonmedical staff.* There are too few staff to meet physical and mental health needs. This often results in long delays in obtaining medical attention; disrupted and low-quality treatment causing physical deterioration of prisoners with chronic and degenerative diseases such as cancer; overmedication of prisoners with psychotropic drugs; and lack of mental health treatment. The use of nonmedical staff to screen requests for treatment is also common.

■ *Charges for medical attention.* In violation of international standards, many prisons/jails charge inmates for medical attention, on the grounds that charging for health-care services deters prisoners from seeking medical attention for minor matters or because they want to avoid work. The U.S. Justice Department has expressed concern that in some super-maximum-security prisons, where prisoners cannot work at all, charging prisoners impedes their access to health care.

■ *Inadequate reproductive health care.* In 1994, the National Institute of Corrections stated that provision of gynecological services for women in prison is inadequate. Only half of the state prison systems surveyed offered female-specific services such as mammograms and Pap smears, and women often had to wait a long time to be seen.

■ *Shackling during pregnancy.* Shackling of all prisoners, including pregnant prisoners, is policy in federal prisons and the U.S. Marshals Service, and it occurs in nearly all state prisons. Only two states have legislation regulating the use of restraints (belly chain, leg irons, and handcuffs). Shackling during labor may cause complications during delivery, such as hemorrhage or decreased fetal heart rate. If a caesarian section is needed, a delay of even five minutes may result in permanent brain damage to the baby.

■ *Lack of treatment for substance abuse.* The gap between services available and treatment needs continues to grow. The number of prisoners with histories of drug abuse is growing, but the proportion of prisoners receiving treatment declined from 40 percent in 1991 to 18 percent today.

■ *Lack of adequate or appropriate mental health services.* From 48 to 88 percent of women inmates experienced sexual or physical abuse before coming to prison (as many as 90 percent in New York and Ohio prisons) and suffer post-traumatic stress disorder. Very few prison systems provide counseling. Women attempting to access mental health services are routinely given medication without any opportunity to undergo psychotherapeutic treatment.

Source: Amnesty International, www.amnestyusa.org/abuse-of-women-in-custody/fact-sheet-women-in-prison/page.do?id=1108246 (accessed May 1, 2010).

---

substance abusers and suffer from depression.[37] Many female inmates feel strain and conflict, which are psychological conditions related to violent episodes.[38] It is not surprising that these conditions also produce high suicide rates in the female prison population.[39]

Exhibit 15.3 lists some of the many problems experienced in female institutions.

## Adapting to the Female Institution

Daily life in women's prisons differs somewhat from that in male institutions. For one thing, unlike male inmates, women usually do not present an immediate physical danger to staff and fellow inmates. Relatively few engage in violent behavior, and incidents of inmate-initiated sexual aggression, so common in male institutions, are rare in women's prisons.[40] Few female inmates experience the violent atmosphere common in male institutions or suffer the same racial and ethnic conflict and divisiveness.[41] Although female inmates may experience less discomfort than males, that does not mean their experience is a bed of roses. Many still experience fear and are forced to undergo a process of socialization fraught with danger and volatile situations.[42] However, female inmates seem to receive more social support from both internal sources (e.g., inmate peers, correctional staff) and external sources (e.g., families, peers), a factor that may help lessen the pains of prison life, help them adjust, and improve the social climate within female institutions.[43] A number of studies have documented the existence of same-sex relations in women's prisons. One conducted in the Louisiana Correctional Institute for Women (LCW) found that the majority of inmates were involved in some degree of lesbian relationships.[44] Theresa Severance's study of a women's prison concluded that about one-third of women inmates are sexually active with other inmates. Some of the respondents who were sexually involved saw their involvements as limited to prison, whereas others were questioning their sexual identity and thought they might continue the same or other same-sex relationships on the outside. The reasons given for their sexual involvement were loneliness, curiosity, deprivation of sexual contact, and reaction to the abusive relationships they had had with men.[45]

The rigid, anti-authority inmate social code found in many male institutions does not exist in female institutions.[46] Confinement for women, however, may produce severe anxiety and anger because of separation from families and loved ones and the inability to function in normal female roles. Unlike men, who direct their anger outward, female prisoners may turn to more self-destructive acts to cope with their problems. Female inmates are more likely than males to harm their own bodies and attempt suicide. For example, one common practice among female inmates is self-mutilation, or "carving." This ranges from simple scratches to carving the name of their boyfriend on their body or even complex statements or sentences ("To mother, with hate").[47]

Another form of adaptation to prison used by women is the **make-believe family**. This group contains masculine and feminine figures acting as fathers and mothers; some even act as children and take on the role of brother or sister. Formalized marriages and divorces may be conducted. Sometimes one inmate plays multiple roles, so that a "sister" in one family may "marry" and become the "wife" of another inmate. It is estimated that about half of all female inmates are members of make-believe families.[48]

Why do make-believe families exist? Experts suggest that they provide the warm, stable relationships that are otherwise unobtainable in the prison environment. People both in and out of prison have needs for security, companionship, affection, attention, status, prestige, and acceptance that can be filled only by having primary group relationships. Friends fill many of these needs, but the family better represents the ideal of, or desire for, these things in a stable relationship.

Some prison officials find make-believe families disruptive, but their attitudes may stem from preconceived notions rather than from any real harm caused by such pairings.[49]

**make-believe families**
In female prisons, substitute family groups with a faux father, mother, and siblings.

## The Changing Culture of Women's Prisons

Candace Kruttschnitt and Rosemary Gartner observed women's interactions in two California women's prisons: the Central Institution for Women (CIW) and Valley State Prison for Women (VSPW), a new high-security facility.[50] They found that imprisonment for women has changed over the past 40 years. Today administrators place greater emphasis on custody and security, while paying less attention to individual needs. As a result, less is expected of prisoners and inmates, who, in turn, expect less from the prison administration and more from each other. Because administrators are now preoccupied with the security and management of prisoners rather than with rehabilitation, female inmates have become disaffected, suspicious, and isolated.[51]

Although the structure of female social relations may be changing, Kruttschnitt and Gartner's study found that sexual relationships were still very

# IMAGES OF JUSTICE

## *World Apart: Life in a Female Prison*

Cristina Rathbone has dedicated her journalistic career to exposing myths about women's prisons and telling the life story of women behind bars. She is appalled at the conditions they are forced to endure, their exploitation by correctional officers, and their struggles to maintain ties to family and friends. Rather than a violent and aggressive career criminal, the female inmate she encounters is more likely to be a 35-year-old single mother with three children serving a five-year mandatory sentence for a first-time, nonviolent drug offense.

A great deal of Rathbone's research was conducted in a women's prison in Massachusetts, MCI-Framingham. There, after years of battling authorities for entry, she was able to meet and interview female inmates in the visitors' rooms. She finds that, in contrast to the men's prisons in the state, where most inmates are serving time for violent crimes, almost two-thirds of incarcerated women—63 percent—are serving time for nonviolent offenses. Most are drug and alcohol addicts; about a third are seriously mentally ill; more than 70 percent are mothers.

Rathbone finds that female inmates are cut off from their families and are given little help in maintaining contact with their children. Behind prison walls, they are offered a minimum of education and job-training programs. It is not surprising that more than 60 percent of the women in Framingham receive some kind of mental health services. The truth, Rathbone finds, is that the air in a woman's prison is filled more with despair than with depravity.

Rathbone finds that women's prisons have not changed as much as we would like to believe since they were instituted more than 100 years ago. When MCI-Framingham first opened its doors in 1877, the prison held just three women convicted of violent acts and more than 240 incarcerated for nonviolent crimes, including a majority imprisoned for being drunk or promiscuous. Many had been sentenced for being "lewd," "stubborn," "intemperate," or "idle." At the time, living and sleeping with a man outside marriage was punishable by prison terms of up to five years. The first inmates were almost exclusively poor, first-generation immigrants; the law applied to some people more than to others. Despite their shortcomings, women's prisons such as Framingham were

*Many incarcerated women are mothers, and keeping them in contact with their children is considered important for their rehabilitation. Alicia Stenzel stands with her child at the fence of the Indiana Women's Prison, where she is currently incarcerated. Her child's visit is made possible by to the Family Preservation Program. The program has expanded to include the Wee Ones Nursery, which enables eligible offenders who deliver while incarcerated at IWP to reside with their infant at the facility for up to 18 months or until the mother's earliest possible release date, whichever is sooner.*

considered an improvement over prior practices, in which women were simply sent to the basements or attics of men's prisons, where they had no opportunities for exercise or education. Rape—at the hands of both guards and male inmates—was common. Women's prisons had programs that taught inmates how to read, gave them job training, and provided instruction in "domestic skills" such as knitting and sewing.

Rathbone spent more than four years investigating the prison, including her legal fight to gain access to inmates. Even then she was harassed, made to wait hours to enter the visitors' area, and subjected to random searches. She met Denise, a 32-year-old crack addict serving time for an illegal drug purchase. Denise was terrified when she arrived in prison and was befriended by older, more experienced inmates. She despaired for her 9-year-old son, Pat, who had been left in the care of his abusive father. Denise's fears were well founded; by the time she left prison, Pat had been incarcerated for petty theft.

Denise's story is not unique. Framingham inmates are the daughters of abuse and abandonment. Some are given long sentences for acting as drug mules and traffickers for their boyfriends, who go free. Others have been ignored by their parents and forced to fend for themselves on the streets. Many of the inmates engage in sexual relationships with correctional officers, even though it is a felony under state law. Some are seeking favors and special treatment; others are simply bored and looking for ways to pass the time. Those who do not wish such intimacies can still be victimized: Inmates are defenseless against sexual abuse and rape. Relatively few cases are prosecuted, and even fewer result in convictions.

Rathbone calls for the reform of women's prisons. Sentences should be geared to the special status of women. Mothers should have better access to their children. Meaningful programming is needed. Women must be protected from predatory guards. Despite the problems, she is convinced that dedicated and sensitive prison administrators can make a meaningful difference.

## Critical Thinking

Should women be allowed to raise children behind bars? What would be the benefits of this policy, and what would be the drawbacks? If you endorse such a policy, would you recommend a point at which the practice should end, such as when the chid was 2 years old, or 3, or 4? What might happen if a child were taken from his or her mother after they had been attached for years?

Sources: Cristina Rathbone, *World Apart: Women, Prison, and Life behind Bars* (New York: Random House, 2005); Cristina Rathbone, "Locked In," *Boston Globe*, May 29, 2005.

much a part of life in prison. The researchers reason that because of the public's greater acceptance of same-sex relationships, there is now less regulation of prisoners' personal lives.[52]

Kruttschnitt and Gartner found that the prisoners in the two prisons they studied had three major ways of negotiating, or coping with, prison life:

■ *Adopted style.* In this model, women associate with other prisoners and enjoy their associations. Few of these women report having problems with correctional officers.

■ *Convict style.* This involves spending time with only one or two others, or alone, and, like the adopted class, these women enjoy their associations with other inmates. However, unlike the adopted class, they are very likely to have difficulty dealing with correctional officers.[53]

■ *Isolate style.* Characterized by preferring to be alone when not locked up in cells and alienated from other prisoners, this negative and singular style gives female inmates the feeling that they have no control over their prison environment.

In more punitive environments, women prisoners were least likely to approach their confinement in an adapted, as opposed to an isolate, manner. Women prisoners were also far more outspoken about what they saw as inhumane treatment and abuse from staff and about arbitrary restrictions. The accompanying Images of Justice feature gives a picture of life in a woman's prison.

There may also be changes taking place in the treatment women receive behind bars. Critics have charged that female correctional institutions do not get the same level of support as male facilities and that, as a result, educational and vocational programs are deficient. Female inmates were not provided with the tools needed to succeed on the outside because the limited vocational training stressed what was considered traditional "women's work": cosmetology, secretarial work, and food services.

To remedy this situation, most state correctional agencies have instituted some sort of vocational training programs for women. Although the traditional vocation of sewing is the most common industrial program, correctional authorities are beginning to teach data processing, and female inmates are involved in other industries such as farming, printing, telemarketing, and furniture repair. Clearly, greater efforts are needed to improve the quality of work experiences for female inmates.

## PRISON VIOLENCE

Conflict, violence, and brutality are sad but ever-present facts of institutional life for both male and female inmates. Violence can involve individual conflict: inmate versus inmate, inmate versus staff, staff versus inmate. Violence can be sexual in nature, involving rape and coercion. Violence can also involve collective prison riots; more than 300 have occurred since the first one in 1774.[54]

### Individual Violence

Each year in U.S. prisons, about 75 to 100 inmates are killed by their peers, 6 or 7 staff members are murdered, and some 120 suicides are recorded. What are the causes of prison violence? The motives for individual violence vary widely. They include sexual dominance and coercion; the aggressor's desire to shake down the victim for money and personal favors; racial conflict; and the need to establish power within the institution. Although there is no single cause of individual prison violence, a number of explanations have been suggested.[55]

■  *History of prior violence.* Younger inmates, especially those with histories of violence, are the ones most likely to be aggressive behind bars. Some are former gang members, who routinely used force to get their own way on the outside and who quickly join inmate gangs.[56] In many instances, street gangs maintain prison branches that unite the inmate with their former violence-prone peers. Having this connection supports and protects gang members while they are in prison, and it assists in supporting gang members' families and associates outside the wall.[57]

  Although the association between a history of violence and aggression behind bars is significant, some recent research by Jon Sorenson and Mark Cunningham found that people convicted of murder are no more violent than others members of the inmate population. This finding is important because it runs counter to the argument that murderers are dangerous people with a "propensity for murder." Sorenson and Cunningham's conclusion that a murder conviction is no more reliable a predictor of prison violence than a conviction for some other offense counters an important argument for the use of capital punishment.[58]

■  *Psychological malady.* Many inmates suffer from personality disorders. Recent research shows that among institutionalized offenders, psychopathy is the strongest predictor of violent recidivism and indifferent response to treatment.[59] In the crowded, dehumanizing world of the prison, it is not surprising that people suffering extreme psychological distress may resort to violence to dominate others.[60]

■  *Prison conditions.* The prison experience itself causes people to become violent. Inhuman conditions, including overcrowding, depersonalization, and the threat of sexual assault, are violence-producing conditions. Even in the most humane prisons, life is a constant put-down, and prison conditions are a threat to the inmates' sense of self-worth; violence may be a not-unexpected consequence of these conditions.[61]

Just as prison conditions may produce violence, effective prison administration may reduce it: Consistent and firm disciplinary actions may help disruptive inmates realize that repeated violent incidents are punished by long-term stays in segregation and other negative consequences.[62]

- *Lack of dispute resolution mechanisms.* Many prisons lack effective mechanisms for handling inmate grievances against either prison officials or other inmates fairly and equitably. Prisoners who complain about other inmates are viewed as "rats" or "snitches" and may be marked for death by their enemies. Similarly, inmates' complaints or lawsuits filed against the prison administration may result in the inmate being placed in solitary confinement—"the hole."

- *Basic survival.* Inmates resort to violence in order to survive. The lack of physical security, inadequate mechanisms for resolving complaints, and the code of silence promote individual violence by inmates who might otherwise be much less dangerous.

## Collective Violence

Collective violence also is an ever-present danger in the prison community, and prison riots have become routine. The most famous of these outbreaks include the infamous Attica riot in 1971, which claimed 39 lives, and the New Mexico State Penitentiary riot of February 1980, in which the death toll was 33. The 1980 New Mexico State Penitentiary riot drew national attention to the problem of prison overcrowding and the conflict it produced. The prison was designed for 800 prisoners but actually held 1,135; overcrowding, squalor, poor food, and lack of medical treatment were chronic conditions. The state government had been called on to improve guard training, upgrade physical plant quality, and relieve the overcrowding, but it was reluctant to spend the necessary money. Even though conditions have improved in most facilities, the prison riot still remains a threat. For example, on March 28, 2008, a riot at the federal penitentiary in Three Rivers, Texas, left one prisoner dead and 22 others injured. Intelligence sources said they believe the riot began when tensions over prison leadership developed between Mexican American inmates who consider themselves Chicanos and inmates who have closer ties to Mexico.[63]

The suggested causes of collective prison violence include

- *Inmate-balance theory.* Riots and other forms of collective violence occur when prison officials make an abrupt effort to take control of the prison and limit freedoms. Crackdowns occur when officials perceive that inmate leaders have too much power and take measures to control their illicit privileges, such as gambling or stealing food.[64]

- *Administrative-control theory.* Collective violence is caused by prison mismanagement, lack of strong security, and inadequate control by prison officials. Poor management may inhibit conflict management and set the stage for violence. Repressive administrations give inmates the feeling that nothing will ever change, that they have nothing to lose, and that violence is the only means for change.

- *Prison overcrowding theory.* As the prison population continues to climb, unmatched by expanded capacity, prison violence may increase. Overcrowding caused by the rapid increases in the prison population has also been linked to increases in both inmate substance abuse and prison violence.[65]

To reduce violence and monitor inmates more closely, correctional authorities are relying on developing forms of technology. The accompanying Criminal Justice and Technology feature describes some of these efforts.

## CRIMINAL JUSTICE AND TECHNOLOGY

# Using Technology to Improve Prison Life and Security

Technology is now being used to improve security within prison walls and reduce violence. The following are among the technological aids being used or developed for this purpose.

### Backscatter Imaging System for Concealed Weapons

This system uses a backscatter imager to detect weapons and contraband. The primary advantage of this device over current walk-through portals is that it can detect nonmetallic as well as metallic weapons. It uses low-power X-rays equal to about five minutes of exposure to the sun at sea level. Although these X-rays penetrate clothing, they do not penetrate the body.

### Personal Health Status Monitor

The personal health status monitor uses acoustics to track the heartbeat and respiration of a person in a cell. More advanced health status monitors are now being developed that can monitor five or more vital signs at once and, based on the combination of findings, can produce an assessment of an inmate's state of health. This more advanced version of the personal

health status monitor may take another decade to develop, but the version currently available may have already helped save lives that would otherwise have been lost to suicide.

### All-in-One Drug Detection Spray

Drug detection sprays detect whether someone possesses marijuana, methamphetamines, heroin, or cocaine. A specially made piece of paper is wiped on a surface; when sprayed with one of the aerosol sprays, it changes color within 15 seconds if as little as 4 to 20 micrograms of the drug are present. A new detection device that is now being developed uses a single spray to test for all drugs at once. The test paper will turn different colors, depending on which drugs the spray contacts, and several positive results will be possible with a single use of the spray.

### Personal Alarm Location System

It is now possible for prison employees to carry a tiny transmitter linking them with a computer in a central control room. In an emergency, they can hit an alarm button, and that computer automatically records whose distress button has been pushed. An architectural map of the facility instantly appears on screen,

## Sexual Violence

One of the most common visions of prison life is the routine threat of sexual coercion and violence. The problem appears so severe that Congress enacted the Prison Rape Reduction Act of 2003, which established three programs in the Department of Justice:

- A program dedicated to collecting national prison rape statistics and to conducting research
- A program dedicated to disseminating information and procedures for combating prison rape
- A program to assist in funding state programs[66]

Recognizing the problem is a good first step, but the most recent data indicates that sexual assault and coercion are still a serious problem. Who are the targets of prison sexual violence? Young males may be raped and kept as sexual slaves by older, more aggressive inmates. When these "slave holders" are released, they may sell their "prison wives" to other inmates.[67] Some inmates demand that regular sexual payments be made to them in exchange for protection from even more violent inmates who threaten rape and beatings.[68] The weaker inmates who agree to such arrangements in return for protection are called "punks" and occupy the bottom of the inmate sexual hierarchy. Straight inmates are more likely to showing the exact location of the staff member in need of assistance.

## Millimeter Wave Imaging

This imaging system can look through clothing to detect weapons, cell phones, and nonmetallic objects. Developed by the Transportation Security Administration (TSA) to scan passengers at an increasing number of airports, the system was tested and evaluated at Graterford State Correctional Institution in Pennsylvania, a maximum-security facility that houses about 3,100 inmates outside Philadelphia. A person steps into a "portal," which looks like a booth. The system beams radio energy in the millimeter wave spectrum from antennas that rotate around the person. The energy is reflected, and scanners produce an image of the body and any objects hidden beneath the clothing. According to the manufacturer, L-3 Communications, the system produces less radiation than a cell phone transmission.

## Pinpointing Trouble Hotspots

Corrections officials are beginning to test radio frequency identification (RFID) technology that uses small transponders called "tags" to track movements. Each tag has an integrated circuit and a tiny antenna to handle radio signals and can be used with a network of sensors—called RFID readers—to track movements. For example, a few correctional institutions have used such a system to provide information on prisoners' movements and to alert staff if there is an unusual concentration of people in a certain area. Movement information can be stored in computers and could prove useful in investigations to determine who was present in a certain part of a building at a particular time.

## Risk Prediction

By employing existing crime-mapping tools to develop a web-based trend analysis system, the Florida Department of Corrections is creating a correctional crime-mapping and information management system to monitor daily operations and to identify trends, patterns, hotspots, and areas of concern for correctional managers. Called COTAS (Correctional Operational Trend Analysis System), the project uses archived data to look for patterns in such areas as inmate health and conduct. The creation of analytical tools using statistics, data-modeling techniques, and mapping will help identify key indicators of disruption, violence, and institutional risk, which in turn will help administrators proactively minimize negative impacts. COTAS will be implemented first in Florida, which is in the vanguard of development and application of technology in correctional operations.

Source: Philip Bulman, "Using Technology to Make Prisons and Jails Safer," *NIJ Journal* 262 (March 2009), www.ojp.usdoj.gov/nij/journals/262/corrections-technology.htm; "Corrections Assistance," *TechBeat* (Winter 2008), Office of Justice Programs' National Institute of Justice (NIJ), www.nlectc.org/TECHBeat/winter2008/Corrections Assistance.pdf.

respect "true" homosexuals, because they were gay before entering prison and are therefore "true to themselves," whereas punks are despised because they are weak: they did not want to have sex with other men but were too weak to resist or not brave enough to stand up to sexual predators. Even "queens" (inmates who look and act as women) get more respect than punks, because they chose their lifestyle and did not have it forced upon them by others.[69]

*HOW COMMON IS PRISON RAPE?* Even though urban legend and media exposés typically suggest that prison rape is an everyday occurrence, it is actually very difficult to get an accurate reading of the true incidence of prison rape. Some research efforts indicate that rape is very rare, whereas others find that nearly half of all inmates experience some form of sexual coercion.[70] What explains the difficulty in getting an accurate count? Inmates are reluctant to report rape either to researchers or to prison administrators. When Kristine Levan Miller surveyed inmates, she found that the following reasons were given for not reporting prison rape.

■ *Embarrassment.* The inmate social code demands that inmates be strong and show no sign of weakness. Although the assailant in a sexual assault gains respect and status, victims may fear that their fellow inmates perceive them as weak and vulnerable to further attacks.

- *Fear of harassment.* Inmates fear that if they report sexual assault, they will be harassed by other inmates.

- *Retaliation from perpetrator.* Inmates do not want to report rape because they fear retaliation from their attacker.

- *Personal matter/no one else's business.* Inmates may believe that sexual assault is a personal matter and nobody else's business.

- *Don't want to be put in safekeeping.* Victims may want to stay in the general population and fear that reporting victimization may result in their being placed in segregation.[71]

Surveys show that prison administrators deny or downplay the occurrence of rape.[72] For example, one cross-national study of prison administrative records of sexual assaults reported to prison staff found that slightly more than 8,000 male, female, and juvenile inmates—or 0.005 percent of the total incarcerated population—reported that they had been victims of sexual violence while incarcerated; an even smaller percentage of these claims were substantiated.[73] However, self-report surveys of the inmates themselves found evidence that at least 60,000 attacks occur each year. That amounts to an estimated 123 incidents of sexual victimization per 1,000 inmates held in state and federal prisons, or about 12 percent of all inmates. Thus it is evident that far more attacks occur than are reported to prison authorities. One reason may be that prison staff members are viewed as "the enemy": Inmates report that they are more likely to be sexually abused by prison staff members than by other inmates.[74]

**WHAT FACTORS LEAD TO SEXUAL VICTIMIZATION?**  Studies show that institutions with the highest sexual coercion rates had several things in common, including barrack-style housing, large prison populations, and lenient security.[75] In these institutions, sexual harassment leads to fights, social isolation, fear, anxiety, and crisis. When James Austin studied sexual violence in the Texas prison system, he made the following discoveries:

- *White inmates are attacked more than any other race.* Nearly 60 percent of the 43 "sustained" incidents—those proved to be true by an investigation—involved a white victim.

- *Victims are generally younger than their assailants.* The average age of victims in "sustained" cases was 3 years younger than the average age of the assailants.

- *Mentally ill or intellectually impaired inmates are more likely to be victimized.* Although only 12 percent of the allegations involved a mentally ill or intellectually impaired prisoner, this percentage is 8 times the proportion of mentally ill inmates in the general prisoner population (1.6 percent).

- *Cellblocks with solid cell fronts may contribute to sexual assault.* Solid cell fronts, while permitting privacy for the inmates and reducing noise within the unit, also provide the degree of privacy that permits sexual assaults to occur. Unlike older prison designs, in which the cell fronts consist of bars, solid doors limit visual observation by staff and soundproof the cells enough so that staff have difficulty hearing what is going on in individual cells.[76]

**SEXUAL VIOLENCE IN WOMEN'S PRISONS**  There are numerous reports of female prisoners being sexually abused and exploited by male correctional workers who either use brute force or psychological coercion to gain sexual control over inmates. Staff-on-inmate sexual misconduct covers a wide range of behaviors, from lewd remarks to voyeurism, to assault and rape. Few if any of these incidents are reported, and perpetrators rarely go to trial. Institutional workers cover for each other, and women who file complaints are offered little protection from vengeful guards.[77] Because this situation persists, more than 40 states and the District of Columbia have been forced to pass laws criminalizing some types of staff sexual misconduct in prisons.[78] However, not all sexual liaisons in women's prisons are unwanted, and when Rebecca Trammell conducted interviews with former female inmates, she learned that some inmates fight over correctional officers as the only men in their lives.[79]

## CORRECTIONAL REHABILITATION

Almost every prison facility uses some mode of treatment to help in inmate rehabilitation. This may come in the form of individual or group therapy programs, drug counseling, anger management, and/ or educational or vocational training. This section presents a selected number of therapeutic methods that have been used nationally in correctional settings and identifies some of their salient features.

> **PERSPECTIVES ON JUSTICE**
>
> *Rehabilitation Perspective*
>
> The fact that correctional rehabilitation still flourishes behind prison walls indicates that the rehabilitation perspective still has its advocates, despite a shift toward crime control during the past decade.

### Individual and Group Counseling

Prison inmates typically suffer from a variety of cognitive and psychosocial deficits, such as poor emotional control, social skills, and interpersonal problem solving. Modern counseling programs help inmates to control emotions (e.g., understanding why they feel the way they do, dealing with nervousness or anxiety, solving their problems creatively); to communicate with others (e.g., understanding what people tell them, communicating clearly when they write); to deal with legal concerns (e.g., keeping out of legal trouble, avoiding breaking laws); to manage general life issues (e.g., finding a job, dealing with difficult coworkers, being a good parent); and to develop and maintain social relationships (e.g., having good relations with others, making others happy, making others proud).[80] Some counseling programs use traditional techniques such as group therapy, whereas others employ nontraditional artistic and spiritual activities, such as visual and performance arts, meditation, and yoga.[81]

One popular approach has been to aim counseling efforts at inmates whose anger and lack of self-control have been linked to violent criminal behavior both in the institution and upon release in the community. As a result, **anger management** programs have been developed to help inmates cope with their violent behavioral urges and tendencies. One survey of group psychotherapy services in correctional facilities indicated that anger therapy may be the type of group therapy most frequently offered within prison settings today.[82] Anger management is often combined with other group techniques as part of drug treatment and sex offender treatment programs. Anger management or violence programs have also been implemented in other countries; for example, violence management programs are widely used in Australia.[83]

**anger management**
Programs designed to help people who have become dependent on anger as a primary means of expressing themselves and those who inappropriately use anger or the threat of violence to get their way.

Anger management programs often rely on cognitive-behavioral therapy (CBT), a technique used to help restructure distorted thinking and perception. A recent evaluation of CBT programs provides valuable insight into their effectiveness and is the subject of the accompanying Evidence-Based Justice feature.

### Faith-Based Programs

Research has shown that inmates involved in religious programs and education do better following release than those in comparison groups, but differences quickly erode.[84] Nonetheless, under the George W. Bush administration, religion-oriented rehabilitation efforts flourished.[85] In 2003, then-governor Jeb Bush dedicated the first faith-based prison in the United States, a 750-bed medium-security facility for males in Lawtey, Florida. Governor Bush claimed that the only way to achieve the rehabilitation of criminals and to reduce recidivism is to "lead them to God."[86] In 2004, Florida converted what was then the all-male Hillsborough Correctional Institution into the nation's first faith-based

# EVIDENCE-BASED JUSTICE

## Cognitive-Behavioral Therapy

One of the most notable characteristics of criminal offenders is distorted cognition, which involves such traits as misinterpretation of social cues, displacement of blame, deficient moral reasoning, and belief in dominance and entitlement. Offenders with such distorted thinking may perceive harmless situations as threats and casual remarks as disrespectful or deliberately provocative. Among the personality traits and thinking patterns of cognitively impaired individuals are

■ Immature or developmentally arrested thoughts

■ Poor problem solving and decision making

■ An inability to consider the effects of one's behavior

■ An egocentric viewpoint with a negative view or lack of trust in other people

■ A hampered ability to reason and accept blame for wrongdoing

■ A distorted sense of entitlement, which may include being unable to delay gratification, confusing wants and needs, and ignoring the rights of other people

■ A tendency to act on impulse, including a lack of self-control and empathy

■ An inability to manage feelings of anger

Social scientists Mark Lipsey, Nana Landenberger, and Sandra Wilson conducted a national study of cognitive-behavioral therapy programs in the prison setting. They found that most programs are based on the assumption that offenders' distorted thinking patterns are learned. Prison-based cognitive-behavioral therapy programs emphasize individual accountability and attempt to teach offenders to understand the thinking processes and choices that resulted in their antisocial activities. The therapy teaches them to self-monitor their thinking and helps them identify and correct biased, risky, or deficient thinking patterns. Offenders learn a set of standard techniques for building cognitive skills and techniques related to anger management, social skills, moral development, and relapse prevention.

Do these programs work? When Lipsey, Landenberger, and Wilson evaluated various cognitive-behavioral therapy programs used in prisons around the country, they found them highly successful. The programs that worked best had three components:

■ The inclusion of anger control and interpersonal problem solving in the treatment program's intended effects.

■ High-quality implementation. This means that there were a low proportion of treatment dropouts, close monitoring of the quality and fidelity of the treatment implementation, and adequate training for the providers.

■ Use with high-risk offenders.

That last element is surprising. Cognitive-behavioral therapy seems to be more effective with more dangerous, hard-core offenders than with less dangerous subjects. The best results occur when higher-risk offenders receive more intensive services that target criminogenic characteristics such as criminal thinking patterns, using cognitive-behavioral and social learning approaches.

Source: Mark Lipsey, Nana Landenberger, and Sandra Wilson, "Effects of Cognitive-Behavioral Programs for Criminal Offenders," *Campbell Systematic Reviews* (2007): 6, www.campbellcollaboration.org/lib/download/143/.

correctional facility for women. At least five states—Texas, Kansas, Minnesota, Florida, and Iowa—have opened new prison facilities in which the central philosophy involves religious teaching. The privately run Corrections Corporation of America (CCA) announced its interest in developing faith-based correctional facilities in partnership with Basic-Life Principles, a Chicago-based prison ministry group, to develop faith-based programming that would eventually be extended to all 64 CCA jails, detention centers, and prisons throughout the United States. Missouri and Florida also opened facilities for youthful offenders founded on faith-based principles.[87]

Can faith-based programs work or are they a fad destined to fade away with change in the political winds? The Urban Institute's evaluation of both Lawtey and Hillsborough, the two Florida faith- and character-based correctional institutions, revealed that staff, inmates, and volunteers overwhelmingly find value in the model and believe that it is achieving its goals of changing inmate behaviors, preparing inmates for successful reentry in society, and ultimately reducing recidivism. The researchers concluded that faith-based programs promote family reunification and inmates' employment prospects upon release, while also improving the prison environment for inmates, volunteers, and staff.[88] Despite these favorable reviews, there were concerns about security and safety within the facility. Considering the high levels of inmate–civilian interaction, volunteers may be vulnerable to manipulation and may undermine correctional officers' efforts to maintain a safe and secure environment.

## Drug Treatment Programs

Most prisons have programs designed to help inmates suffering from alcohol and substance abuse. Some institutions use 12-step meetings, group and/or individual counseling, and recovery training to try to provide a psychological climate conducive to change. Another approach is multisystemic treatment that relies on a combination of services, including psychological treatment, medical care, vocational training, educational enhancement, family therapy, and so on. Another approach is to provide abusers with the long-term administration of a medication that either replaces the illicit drug or blocks its actions. Pharmacological treatment may include the following medications, among others.

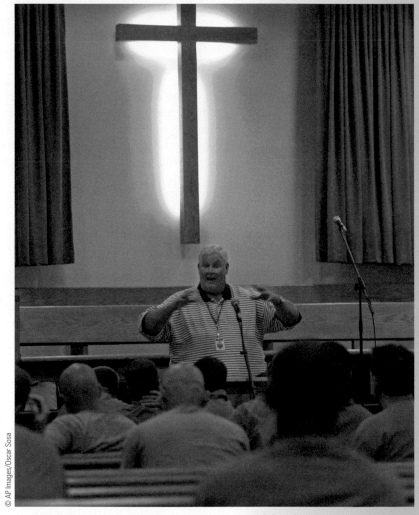

© AP Images/Oscar Sosa

*Faith-based treatment programs are becoming more common in prison, and some are used to deal with issues such as anger management. Here Steve McCoy, senior pastor at Beaches Chapel Church in Jacksonville, Florida, conducts an anger management class in the chapel of Lawtey Correctional Institution in Lawtey, Florida. Along with regular prayer sessions, the Lawtey Correctional Institution offers religious studies, choir practice, religious counseling, and other spiritual activities seven days a week.*

- Methadone: a narcotic analgesic that is an effective substitute for heroin, morphine, codeine, and other opiate derivatives
- Naltrexone: an opioid antagonist that blocks the effects of opioids, such as heroin, thereby discouraging their use[89]

Because substance abuse is so prevalent among correctional clients, some correctional facilities have been reformulated into treatment-dispensing total institutions referred to as "therapeutic communities" (TC) in order to best serve their clientele.[90] TC uses a psychosocial, experiential learning process that relies on positive peer pressure within a highly structured social environment. The community itself, including staff and program participants, becomes the primary method of change. All work together as members of a "family" in order to create a culture where community members confront each other's negative behavior and attitudes and establish an open, trusting, and safe environment.

An example of a therapeutic community program that has been implemented to help substance-abusing inmates is the Residential Substance Abuse Treatment (RSAT).[91] RSAT consists of 9 to 12 months of rigorous drug treatment provided by a private contractor. Clients are low-risk offenders with a habitual substance abuse problem, a desire to change, a positive attitude, and legitimate resources on the outside that will assist them when released. During their treatment, participants are to better themselves by learning to think before they act, in order to change their ways of decision making. They are required to write down their thoughts and feelings, expressing why they engage in destructive behavior and how they expect to change their ways with more constructive choices. Participants work on their social, behavioral, and vocational skills as well. Clients are also part of a 12-step model similar to the programs used by Alcoholics Anonymous and Narcotics Anonymous, and they engage in group counseling, individual counseling, group meetings, and physical activity.

There is evidence that those inmates who successfully complete programs have significantly lower recidivism rates than nonattendees and are more likely to seek treatment once they return to the community; in additon, TC programs seem to be effective in reducing rearrest and reincarceration rates.[92]

## Treating the AIDS-Infected Inmate

The AIDS-infected inmate has been the subject of great concern. Two groups of people at high risk of contracting HIV are intravenous drug users who share needles and males who engage in same-sex relations, two lifestyles common in prison. Because drug use is common and syringes scarce, many high-risk inmates share drug paraphernalia, increasing the danger of HIV transmission.[93] Although the numbers are constantly changing, the rate of HIV infection among state and federal prisoners has stabilized at around 2 percent, and there are about 25,000 HIV-infected inmates.

Correctional administrators have found it difficult to arrive at effective policies to confront AIDS. Even though all state and federal jurisdictions do some AIDS testing, only 18 states and the Federal Bureau of Prisons conduct mass screenings of all inmates. Most states test inmates only if there are significant indications that they are HIV-positive. About 40 percent of all state prison inmates have never been tested for AIDS.

Most correctional systems are now training staff about AIDS. But educational programs for inmates are often inadequate, because administrators are reluctant to give them information on the proper cleaning of drug paraphernalia and safe sex (since both drug use and sexual relations are forbidden in prison).

## Educational and Vocational Programs

Besides treatment programs stressing personal growth through individual analysis or group process, inmate rehabilitation is also pursued through vocational and educational training. Although these two kinds of training sometimes differ in style and content, they can also overlap when, for example, education involves practical job-related study.

The first prison treatment programs were in fact educational. A prison school was opened at the Walnut Street Jail in 1784. Elementary courses were offered in New York's prison system in 1801 and in Pennsylvania's in 1844. An actual school system was established in Detroit's House of Corrections in 1870, and the Elmira Reformatory opened a vocational trade school in 1876. Today, most institutions provide some type of educational program. At some prisons, inmates can obtain a high school diploma or a General Educational Development (GED) certificate through equivalency exams. Other institutions provide an actual classroom education, in programs usually staffed by certified teachers employed full-time at the prison or by part-time teachers who also teach full-time at nearby public schools.

The number of hours devoted to educational programs and the quality and intensity of these efforts vary greatly. Some are full-time programs employing highly qualified and concerned educators, whereas others are part-time programs without any real goals or objectives. Although worthwhile attempts are being made, prison educational programs often suffer from inadequate funding and administration. The picture is not totally bleak, however. In some institutions, programs have been designed to circumvent the difficulties inherent in the prison structure. They encourage volunteers from the community and local schools to tutor willing and motivated inmates. Some prison administrators have arranged flexible schedules for inmate students and actively encourage their participation in these programs. In several states, statewide school districts serving prisons have been created. Forming such districts can make better-qualified staff available and provide the materials and resources necessary for meaningful educational programs.

Every state correctional system also has some job-related services for inmates. Some have elaborate training programs inside the institution, whereas others have instituted prerelease and postrelease employment services. Inmates who hope to obtain parole need to participate in prison industry. Documenting a history of stable employment in prison is essential if parole agents are to convince prospective employers that the ex-offender is a good risk, and postrelease employment is usually required for parole eligibility.[94]

A few of the more important work-related services are discussed in the following sections.

*VOCATIONAL TRAINING* Most institutions provide vocational training programs. On the federal level, the Federal Prison Industries, more commonly known as UNICOR, teach inmates to produce goods and services such as the following for sale to government agencies only.

- *Clothing and textiles*. This encompasses about 65 products, from mailbag repair to the production of towels.
- *Corporate services*. These contracts include materials, equipment, construction, IT, lease agreements, partnerships, and joint ventures.
- *Electronics*. This includes such items as cable assemblies, wiring harnesses, circuit card assemblies, battery boxes, military connectors, power distribution systems, portable light systems, and specialty cables.
- *Fleet management/vehicular components*. These contracts include items such as retrofit, vehicle components, remanufacturing of engines, and forklifts.
- *Industrial products*. This category encompasses a diverse array of metal fabrication capabilities, including stamping, machining, welding, coating-finishing systems, and tool and die operations.
- *Office furniture*. Inmates manufacture a wide variety of furniture products, including dorm and quarters furniture, office furniture, office seating, systems furniture, and case goods.

About 25 percent of federal prisoners work in 100 or so factories within federal prisons. The minimum UNICOR wage is 23 cents an hour, and the maximum wage is $1.15. UNICOR sales average about $800 million a year, and they turn a profit of $120 million a year—making UNICOR the most profitable line of business in the United States.[95]

State institutions maintain similar programs. In New York, more than 42 trade and technical courses are provided in organized training shops under qualified civilian instructors. Some of these courses not only benefit the inmate but also provide services for the institution. New York has trained inmates to become dental laboratory technicians; this program provides dentures for inmates and saves the state money. Another New York program trains inmates to become optical technicians and has the added benefit of providing eyeglasses for inmates. Other New York correctional training programs include barber training, computer programming, auto mechanics, auto body work, and radio and television repair. The products of most of these programs save the taxpayers money, and the programs provide the inmates with practical experience. Many other states offer this type of vocational programming.

Despite the promising aspects of such programs, they have also been seriously criticized. Upon their release, inmates often have trouble finding skill-related, high-paying jobs. Equipment in prisons is often secondhand, obsolete, and hard to come by. Some programs are thinly disguised excuses for prison upkeep and maintenance, and unions and other groups resent the intrusion of prison labor into their markets.

**WORK RELEASE**  To supplement programs stressing rehabilitation via in-house job training or education, more than 40 states have attempted to implement **work release** or **furlough** programs. These allow deserving inmates to leave the institution and hold regular jobs in the community.

Inmates enrolled in work release may live at the institution at night while working in the community during the day. However, security problems (for instance, contraband may be brought in), combined with the fact that prisons are often located in remote areas, often make this arrangement difficult. More typical is the extended work release, where prisoners are allowed to remain in the community for significant periods of time. To help inmates adjust, some states operate community-based prerelease centers where inmates live while working. Some inmates may work at their previous jobs, whereas others seek new employment.

Like other programs, work release has its good and bad points. On the one hand, inmates are sometimes reluctantly received in the community and find that certain areas of employment are closed to them. Citizens are often concerned about prisoners "stealing" jobs or working for lower than normal wages; consequently, such practices are prohibited by Public Law 89-176, which controls the federal work release program.

On the other hand, inmates gain many benefits from work release, including the ability to hone work skills, to maintain community ties, and to make an easier transition from prison to the outside world. For those who have learned a skill in the institution, work release offers an excellent opportunity to test a new occupation. For others, the job may be a training situation in which new skills are acquired. A number of states have reported that few work release inmates abscond while in the community.

**PRIVATE PRISON ENTERPRISE**  Opposition from organized labor ended the profitability of commercial prison industries, but a number of interesting efforts have been made to vary the type and productivity of prison labor. The federal government helped put private industry into prisons when it approved the Free Venture Program in 1976. Seven states, including Connecticut, South Carolina, and Minnesota, were given grants to implement private industries inside prison walls. This successful program led to the Percy Amendment (1979), federal legislation that allowed prison-made goods to be sold across state lines if the projects complied with strict rules, such as making sure unions were consulted and preventing manufacturers from undercutting the existing wage structure.[96] The new law authorized a number of prison industry enhancement pilot projects. These were certified as meeting the Percy Amendment operating rules and were therefore free to ship goods out of state; by 1987, 15 projects had been certified.

Today, private prison industries use a number of models. One approach, the state-use model, makes the correctional system a supplier of goods and services that serves state-run institutions. The California Prison Industry Authority (PIA) is an inmate work program that provides work assignments for approximately 7,000 inmates and operates 70 service, manufacturing, and agricultural industries in 23 prisons. These industries produce a variety of goods and services, including flags, printing services, signs, binders, eyewear, gloves, office furniture, clothing, and cell equipment. PIA products and services are available to government entities, including federal, state, and local government agencies. Court-ordered

**work release**
A prison treatment program that allows inmates to be released during the day to work in the community, returning to prison at night.

**furlough**
A correctional policy that allows inmates to leave the institution for vocational or educational training, for employment, or to maintain family ties.

restitutions or fines are deducted from the wages earned by PIA inmates and are transferred to the Crime Victims' Restitution Fund. PIA inmates receive wages of between 30 cents and 95 cents per hour, before deductions.[97]

In another approach, the free-enterprise model, private companies set up manufacturing units on prison grounds or purchase goods made by inmates in shops owned and operated by the corrections department. In the corporate model, a semi-independent business is created on prison grounds; its profits go to the state government and inmate laborers.[98] Despite widespread publicity, the partnership between private enterprise and the prison community has been limited to a few experimental programs. However, it is likely to grow in the future.

*POSTRELEASE PROGRAMS* A final element of job-related programming involves helping inmates to obtain jobs before they are released and to keep them once they are on the outside. A number of correctional departments have set up employment services designed to ease the transition between institution and community. Employment program staff assess inmates' backgrounds to determine their abilities, interests, goals, and capabilities. They also help inmates create job plans essential to receiving early release (parole) and successfully reintegrating into the community. Some programs maintain community correctional placements in sheltered environments that help inmates bridge the gap between institutions and the outside world. Services include job placement, skill development, family counseling, and legal and medical assistance.

## Can Rehabilitation Work?

Despite the variety and number of treatment programs in operation, questions remain about their effectiveness. In their oft-cited research, Robert Martinson and his associates (1975) found that a majority of treatment programs were failures, giving birth to the generalization that "nothing works" in prison rehabilitations.[99] Martinson's work was followed by efforts showing that some high-risk offenders were more likely to commit crimes after they had been placed in treatment programs than before the onset of rehabilitation efforts.[100] A slew of reviews have claimed that correctional treatment efforts aimed at youthful offenders provide little evidence that rehabilitation can occur within correctional settings. Evidence gathered at that time suggested that treatment efforts—even those that include vocational, educational, and mental health services—can consistently lower recidivism rates.[101]

In the decades since Martinson's work was published, there has been considerable debate about the effectiveness of correctional treatment. Even some of the most carefully crafted treatment efforts, using the most up-to-date rehabilitation modalities such as cognitive-behavioral therapy, have failed to show that treatment has a positive impact on inmates returning to the community.[102] In contrast, treatment proponents have dismissed the "nothing works" philosophy as exaggerated and, using sophisticated data analysis techniques, have found evidence that correctional rehabilitation can be effective.[103] When Paul Gendreau and Robert R. Ross reviewed the published work on correctional rehabilitation programs, they found that many intervention programs reported success.[104] According to Gendreau and Ross, there is now "convincing evidence that some treatment programs, when they are applied with integrity by competent practitioners in appropriate target populations, can be effective in preventing crime or reducing recidivism."[105] Martinson eventually conceded that "contrary to [his] previous position, some treatment programs *do* have an appreciable effect on recidivism. Some programs are indeed beneficial."[106] More recently, Mark Lipsey and Francis Cullen's comprehensive review of the studies of correctional rehabilitation found consistently positive effects on reducing recidivism. However, even they recognize that considerable variability exists in those effects, depending on the type of treatment, its implementation, and the nature of offenders to which it is applied.[107]

**CourseMate** For more information about **Connecticut's prison enterprise**, visit the Criminal Justice CourseMate at CengageBrain.com, then access the "Web Links" for this chapter.

# CAREERS IN CRIMINAL JUSTICE

## Correctional Officer

### Duties and Characteristics

In maximum- and most medium-security cell houses, the correctional officer is required to do the following: (a) open and close the steel-barred door that allows entrance and exit to cell houses; (b) conduct an inmate count several times a day; (c) distribute medicine, mail, and laundry; (d) supervise maintenance activities; and (e) answer the telephone.

The inmates' daily showers must also be supervised. If violations of rules occur, the cell house guard must write disciplinary tickets. During the day shift, the majority of correctional officers are assigned to work areas, such as the metal factory, the furniture factory, the yard, the canteen, or some other prison industry. Officers primarily enforce regulations through communication skills and moral authority and attempt to avoid conflict at all costs. Most officers attend to their duties unarmed, but a few officers hold positions in lookout towers, armed with high-powered rifles. In addition to the custodial duties they perform in more secure facilities, correctional officers in federal institutions and some minimum-security state facilities are also responsible for providing rehabilitative services.

### Job Outlook

With the continued construction of federal, state, and private prisons, there are jobs available for those who are interested in becoming correctional officers. With so many existing prisons in small towns and in isolated areas, applicants may need to be willing to relocate for these positions.

### Salary

Recently, median annual wages of correctional officers and jailers were about $38,000; the highest-paid 10 percent earned more than $64,110. Median annual wages in the public sector were $50,830 in the federal government, $38,850 in state government, and $37,510 in local government. In the facilities support services industry, where the relatively small number of officers employed

---

**REHABILITATION DOES WORK** Despite challenges to the efficacy of rehabilitation, many experts still believe in the rehabilitative ideal.[108] They view it as not only humanistic but also cost-effective: Even though treatment programs may be expensive, if they reduce crime, the savings in suffering and loss will more than offset their costs.[109] And some reviews have found evidence that the right mix of behavioral adjustment programs can produce large reductions in misconduct within the institution that may carry over into reductions in recidivism in the community.[110]

Some evaluations of education, vocation, and work programs indicate that they may be able to lower recidivism rates and increase postrelease employment.[111] Inmates who have completed higher levels of education find it easier to gain employment upon release and consequently are less likely to recidivate over long periods.[112] The programs that have produced positive results both in the community and inside correctional institutions

- Teach interpersonal skills
- Provide individual counseling
- Make use of behavior modification techniques
- Use cognitive-behavioral therapy
- Stress improving moral reasoning
- Combine in-prison therapeutic communities with follow-up community treatment[113]

It is also possible that a combination of efforts rather than a singular approach can have beneficial results; an example might be combining institutional treatment with postrelease aftercare.[114] Thus, even though not all programs are by privately operated prisons is classified, median annual wages were $28,790.

### Opportunities

Job opportunities for correctional officers are expected to be excellent. The need to replace correctional officers who transfer to other occupations, retire, or leave the labor force, coupled with rising employment demand, will generate thousands of job openings each year. Employment for correctional officers is expected to grow 16 percent between 2006 and 2016, faster than the average for all occupations. Some employment opportunities also will arise in the private sector, as public authorities contract with private companies to provide and staff corrections facilities. Both state and federal corrections agencies are increasingly using private prisons.

### Qualifications

Most correctional officer positions require that the applicant have a high school education or its equivalent, be at least 18 or 21 years of age, be a U.S. citizen, and have no felony convictions. A potential corrections officer must also be in excellent health and must meet formal standards for physical fitness, eyesight, and hearing. Drug testing and background checks of applicants are usually done.

### Education and Training

A high school diploma or graduation equivalency degree is required. Some state and local corrections agencies require some college credits, but law enforcement or military experience may be substituted to fulfill this requirement. In the Federal Bureau of Prisons and many state facilities, the salaries offered for new officers are sufficient to attract a large applicant pool. As a result, most of those selected have college educations or at least degrees from two-year institutions. Federal, state, and some local departments of corrections provide training for correctional officers. Some states have regional training academies that are available to local agencies. State and local correctional agencies also provide on-the-job training, including training on legal restrictions and interpersonal relations. Officer trainees typically receive several weeks or months of training in an actual job setting under the supervision of an experienced officer. However, on-the-job training varies widely from agency to agency.

Sources: Bureau of Labor Statistics, U.S. Department of Labor, "Correctional Officers," *Occupational Outlook Handbook, 2010–2011 Edition*, www.bls.gov/oco/ocos156.htm (accessed May 1, 2010).

---

successful for all inmates, many treatment programs are effective, and some participants, especially younger clients, have a better chance of success on the outside than those who forgo treatment.[115]

## GUARDING THE INSTITUTION

Control of a prison is a complex task. On the one hand, a tough, high-security environment may meet the goals of punishment and control but fail to reinforce positive behavior changes. On the other hand, too liberal an administrative stance can lower staff morale and place inmates in charge of the institution. For many years, prison guards were viewed as ruthless people who enjoyed their power over inmates, fought rehabilitation efforts, were racist, and had a "lock psychosis" developed over their years of counting, numbering, and checking on inmates. This view has changed in recent years. Correctional officers are now viewed as public servants who are seeking the security and financial rewards of a civil service position.[116] Most are in favor of rehabilitation efforts and do not hold any particular animosity toward the inmates. The correctional officer has been characterized as both a "people worker" who must be prepared to deal with the problems of inmates on a personal level and a member of a complex bureaucracy who must be able to cope with its demands.

Corrections officers play a number of roles in the institution. They supervise cell houses, dining areas, shops, and other facilities, as well as perching on the walls, armed with rifles, to oversee the yard and prevent escapes. Corrections officers also sit on disciplinary boards and escort inmates to hospitals and court appearances.

The greatest problem that correctional officers face is the duality of their role: maintainers of order and security and advocates of treatment and rehabilitation.

Added to this basic dilemma is the changing inmate role. In earlier times, corrections officers could count on inmate leaders to help them maintain order, but now they are confronted by a racially charged atmosphere in which violence is a way of life. Today, correctional work in some institutions can be filled with danger, tension, boredom, and little evidence that efforts to help inmates lead to success. Research indicates that correctional work is extremely high risk.[117] And unlike police officers, correctional officers apparently do not form a close-knit subculture with unique values and a sense of intergroup loyalty. Correctional officers experience alienation and isolation from inmates, from the administration, and from each other. Interestingly, this sense of alienation seems greatest in younger officers; evidence exists that later in their careers, officers enjoy a revival of interest in their work and take great pride in providing human services to inmates.[118] It is not surprising that correctional officers experience significant stress related to such job factors as lack of safety, inadequate career opportunities, and work overload.[119] Eric Lambert and his associates found that the stress of the prison experience can lead to emotional exhaustion, a powerful dimension of job burnout that, if left unchecked, is associated with high levels of turnover and absenteeism and with general job dissatisfaction.[120]

However, correctional officers who have high levels of job satisfaction, good relations with their coworkers, and high levels of social support seem to be better able to deal with the stress of the correctional setting.[121] Mike Vuolo and Candace Kruttschnitt found that correctional officers can have a sizable impact on prisoners' ability to adjust to prison life. Correctional staff members who conduct themselves professionally and gain the respect and cooperation of the inmates are able to have a very positive influence on these inmates' later readjustment to society. In contrast, those who fail miserably on both counts may be contributing the nation's high recidivism rates.[122] For more on a career as a correctional officer, read the Careers in Criminal Justice feature.

## Female Correctional Officers

The issue of female correctional officers in male institutions comes up repeatedly. Research finds that they differ little from their male colleagues in their behavior or their use of aggressive tactics.[123]

The employment of women as guards in close contact with male inmates has raised many questions of privacy and safety and spawned a number of legal cases. In one important case, *Dothard v. Rawlinson* (1977), the U.S. Supreme Court upheld Alabama's refusal to hire female correctional officers on the grounds that it would put them in significant danger from the male inmates.[124] Despite such setbacks, women now work side by side with male guards in almost every state, performing the same duties. Research indicates that discipline has not suffered because of the inclusion of women in the guard force. Sexual assaults have been rare, and more negative attitudes have been expressed by the female guards' male peers than by inmates. Most commentators believe that the presence of female guards can have an important beneficial effect on the self-image of inmates and improve the guard–inmate working relationship.

Ironically, female correctional officers may find that an assignment to a male institution can boost their career. Recent restrictions on male staff in women's prisons, in the wake of well-publicized sex scandals, have forced administrators to assign women officers to the dormitory areas, the least desirable areas in which to work. Women officers are not similarly restricted in male-only facilities.[125]

## ▌ PRISONERS' RIGHTS

Before the early 1960s, it was accepted that upon conviction, an individual forfeited all rights not expressly granted by statutory law or correctional policy; in other words, inmates were civilly dead. The U.S. Supreme Court held that convicted offenders should expect to be penalized for their misdeeds and that part of their punishment was the loss of freedoms that ordinary citizens take for granted.

One reason why inmates lacked rights was that state and federal courts were reluctant to intervene in the administration of prisons unless the circumstances of a case clearly indicated a serious breach of the Eighth Amendment protection against cruel and unusual punishment. This judicial policy is referred to as the **hands-off doctrine**. The courts used three basic justifications for their neglect of prison conditions:

1. Correctional administration was a technical matter best left to experts rather than to courts ill equipped to make appropriate evaluations.

2. Society as a whole was apathetic to what went on in prisons, and most individuals preferred not to associate with or know about the offenders.

3. Prisoners' complaints involved privileges rather than rights. Prisoners were considered to have fewer constitutional rights than other members of society.[126]

As the 1960s drew to a close, the hands-off doctrine was eroded. Federal district courts began seriously considering prisoners' claims about conditions in the various state and federal institutions and used their power to intervene on behalf of the inmates. In some ways, this concern reflected the spirit of the times, which saw the onset of the civil rights movement, and subsequently was paralleled in such areas as student rights, public welfare, mental institutions, juvenile court systems, and military justice.

Beginning in the late 1960s, such activist groups as the NAACP Legal Defense Fund and the American Civil Liberties Union's National Prison Project began to search for appropriate legal vehicles to bring prisoners' complaints before state and federal courts. The most widely used device was the federal Civil Rights Act, 42 U.S.C. 1983:

> Every person who, under color of any statute, ordinance, regulation, custom, or usage of any State or Territory[,] subjects, or causes to be subjected, any citizen of the United States or other person within the jurisdiction thereof to the deprivation of any rights, privileges, or immunities secured by the Constitution and laws shall be liable to the party injured in an action at law, suit in equity, or other proper proceeding for redress.

The legal argument went that, as U.S. citizens, prison inmates could sue state officials if their civil rights were violated—for example, if they were the victims of racial or religious discrimination.

The U.S. Supreme Court first recognized the right of prisoners to sue for civil rights violations in cases involving religious freedom brought by the Black Muslims. This well-organized group had been frustrated by prison administrators who feared its growing power and wanted to limit its recruitment activities. In the 1964 case of *Cooper v. Pate*, however, the Supreme Court ruled that inmates who were being denied the right to practice their religion were entitled to legal redress under 42 U.S.C. 1983.[127] Although *Cooper* applied to the narrow issue of religious freedom, it opened the door to providing other rights for inmates.

The subsequent prisoners' rights crusade, stretching from 1964 to 1980, paralleled the civil rights and women's movements. Battle lines were drawn between prison officials, who hoped to maintain their power and resented interference by the courts, and inmate groups and their sympathizers, who used state and federal courts as a forum for demanding better living conditions for prisoners and recognition of their personal rights. Each decision handed down by the courts was viewed as a victory for one side or the other. To slow down prison litigation, which had been clogging the federal courts, Congress passed the Prison Litigation Reform Act in 1996.[128] The most important provision of this act requires prisoners to exhaust *all* internal administrative grievance procedures before they can file a civil rights case in federal court. It also

**hands-off doctrine**
The legal practice of allowing prison administrators a free hand in running the institution, even if correctional practices violate inmates' constitutional rights; this practice ended with the onset of the prisoners' rights movement in the 1960s.

**CourseMate** For more information about the **ACLU's National Prison Project**, visit the Criminal Justice CourseMate at CengageBrain.com, then access the "Web Links" for this chapter.

bars litigation if a prisoner has not suffered a physical injury in addition to a violation of his or her constitutional rights. There is a limit on the number of times an appeal can be filed, and if a judge decides that an appeal is frivolous, is malicious, or does not state a proper claim, that appeal counts as a "strike." After getting three strikes, an inmate who wants to file another lawsuit must pay the entire court filing fee up-front. The U.S. Supreme Court has upheld the provisions of the act in two cases—one dealing with a request for monetary relief and the other dealing with allegations of excessive use of force. In *Booth v. Churner* (2001) and *Porter v. Nussle* (2002), the Court ruled that it is constitutional to require that an inmate go through all administrative processes before a case can be brought to the courts.[129] Civil rights groups believe that the Reform Act has a chilling affect on inmate litigation and has asked Congress to amend its provisions.[130]

While the prisoner's movement may have slowed, it has not ended. Below, some of the most important substantive and procedural rights of inmates

## Substantive Rights

Through a slow process of legal review, the courts have granted inmates a number of **substantive rights** that have significantly influenced the entire correctional system. The most important of these rights are discussed in the following sections.

***ACCESS TO COURTS, LEGAL SERVICES, AND MATERIALS*** Without the ability to seek judicial review of conditions that cause discomfort or violate constitutional rights, the inmate must depend solely on the slow and often insensitive administrative mechanism of relief within the prison system. Therefore, the right of easy access to the courts gives inmates hope that their rights will be protected during incarceration. Courts have held that inmates are entitled to have legal materials available and to be provided with assistance in drawing up and filing complaints. Inmates who help others, so-called **jailhouse lawyers**, cannot be interfered with or harassed by prison administrators.

***FREEDOM OF THE PRESS AND OF EXPRESSION*** Correctional administrators traditionally placed severe limitations on prisoners' speech and expression. For example, they read and censored inmate mail and restricted inmates' reading material. With the lifting of the hands-off doctrine, courts have consistently ruled that only when a compelling state interest exists can prisoners' First Amendment rights be modified. Correctional authorities must justify the limiting of free speech by showing that granting it would threaten institutional security. In a 2001 case, *Shaw v. Murphy*, the Supreme Court ruled that inmates do not have an absolute right to correspond with other inmates, even if it concerns legal advice. If prison administrators believe such correspondence undermines prison security, the First Amendment rights of inmates can be curtailed.[131]

***FREEDOM OF RELIGION*** Freedom of religion is a fundamental right guaranteed by the First Amendment. In general, the courts have ruled that inmates have the right to assemble and pray in the religion of their choice, but that religious symbols and practices that interfere with institutional security can be restricted. Administrators can draw the line if religious needs become cumbersome or impossible to carry out for reason of cost or security. Granting special privileges can also be denied on the grounds that they will cause other groups to make similar demands. Although the Court recognized the right to practice religion, the most important case on this issue limited absolute religious freedom and placed the security of an institution above the right to attend religious services. In *O'Lone v. Estate of Shabazz*, Muslim inmates in a minimum-security classification requested permission to attend services held in another portion of the prison.[132] They argued that these services were essential to the practice of

---

**substantive rights**
Civil rights that include the right of inmates to receive mail and medical benefits and to practice their religion.

**jailhouse lawyer**
An inmate trained in law, or otherwise educated, who helps other inmates prepare legal briefs and appeals.

their religion. The request was denied on the basis of security. The Supreme Court upheld the denial, holding that "[w]hen a prison regulation impinges on inmates' constitutional rights, the regulation is valid if it is reasonably related to legitimate penological interests."[133] To determine whether there was such a relationship, the trial court should consider

- Whether there is a logical connection between the restriction and the governmental interests invoked to justify it
- The availability of alternative means to exercise the restricted right
- The impact that accommodation of the right might have on other inmates, on prison personnel, and on allocation of prison resources generally
- Whether there are "obvious, easy alternatives" to the policy that could be adopted at a minimal cost

In an important 2005 case, *Cutter v. Wilkinson*, the Court ruled that the Religious Land Use and Institutionalized Persons Act of 2000, which was intended to protect the rights of prisoners, is not an unconstitutional government promotion of religion.[134] Writing for the majority, Justice Ruth Bader Ginsburg stated, "It confers no privileged status on any particular religious sect, and singles out no bona fide faith for disadvantageous treatment." *Cutter* allows inmates to practice their own religion unless their practices clearly undermine prison security and safety.

*MEDICAL RIGHTS* In early prisons, inmates' right to medical treatment was restricted through the "exceptional circumstances doctrine." Using this policy, the courts would hear only those cases in which the circumstances totally disregarded human dignity, while denying hearings to less serious cases. The cases that were allowed access to the courts usually represented a situation of total denial of medical care.

To gain their medical rights, prisoners have resorted to class action suits (suits brought on behalf of all individuals affected by similar circumstances—in this case, poor medical attention). In the most significant case, *Newman v. Alabama* (1972), the entire Alabama prison system's medical facilities were declared inadequate.[135] The Supreme Court cited the following factors as contributing to inadequate care: insufficient physician and nurse resources, reliance on untrained inmates for paramedical work, intentional failure in treating the sick and injured, and failure to conform to proper medical standards. The *Newman* case forced corrections departments to upgrade prison medical facilities.

It was not until 1976, in *Estelle v. Gamble*, that the Supreme Court clearly mandated an inmate's right to have medical care.[136] Gamble had hurt his back in a Texas prison and filed suit because he contested the type of treatment he had received and questioned the lack of interest that prison guards had shown in his case. The Supreme Court said, "Deliberate indifference to serious medical needs of prisoners constitutes the 'unnecessary and wanton infliction of pain' proscribed by the Eighth Amendment."[137] Gamble was allowed to collect monetary damages for his injuries. Consequently, correctional administrators must consider access, quality, and cost of health care as part of the prison regime.[138]

*CRUEL AND UNUSUAL PUNISHMENT* The concept of **cruel and unusual punishment** is founded in the Eighth Amendment of the Constitution. The term itself has not been specifically defined by the Supreme Court, but the Court has held that treatment constitutes cruel and unusual punishment when it does the following:

- Degrades the dignity of human beings[139]
- Is more severe than (disproportionate to) the offense for which it has been given[140]
- Shocks the general conscience and is fundamentally unfair[141]

**cruel and unusual punishment**
Physical punishment or punishment that far exceeds that given to people under similar circumstances and is therefore banned by the Eighth Amendment. The death penalty has so far not been considered cruel and unusual if it is administered in a fair and nondiscriminatory fashion.

- Is deliberately indifferent to a person's safety and well-being[142]
- Punishes people because of their status, such as race, religion, and mental state[143]
- Is in flagrant disregard of due process of law, such as punishment that is capriciously applied[144]

State and federal courts have placed strict limits on disciplinary methods that may be considered inhumane. Corporal punishment all but ended after the practice was condemned in *Jackson v. Bishop* (1968).[145] Although the solitary confinement of disruptive inmates continues, its prolonged use under barbaric conditions has been held to be in violation of the Eighth Amendment. Courts have found that inmates placed in solitary have the right to adequate personal hygiene, exercise, mattresses, ventilation, and rules specifying how they can earn their release.

*PHYSICAL ABUSE* There are two critical contexts in which physical abuse occurs in prisons: inmate-on-inmate abuse and guard-on-inmate abuse.

The courts have generally been unwilling to impose liability on prison officials for failing to protect prisoners from physical abuse and sexual assault by other inmates. However, the courts have ruled that prison officials are liable for damages if they display indifference to attacks on inmates occurring inside the prison. The most important case in this area is *Farmer v. Brennan*.[146] In *Farmer*, a biological male who had undergone sex change treatment was transferred to a male high-security prison and placed in the general population. Within two weeks, he was beaten and raped by another prisoner. He sued for damages, alleging that his transfer violated the Eighth Amendment. The Court held that prisoners, in the presence of other prisoners, some of whom are very dangerous, have no real means to protect themselves. Prison officials cannot close their eyes to the inevitable and are liable for their care and protection. The test of liability is "deliberate indifference," which requires something more than mere negligence but less than deliberate indifference: If prison officials were aware of a serious risk to an inmate's safety, they are liable for injuries suffered, even though they did not know for certain that the inmate would be harmed. Prison officials may be liable if they had knowledge of the risk of harm but failed to take reasonable steps for its prevention. Thus, the Court stated that in these circumstances, a prison official cannot escape liability by arguing that "he merely refused to verify underlying factors that he strongly suspected to be true, or declined to confirm inferences of risk that he strongly suspect[ed] to exist."[147]

In *Hudson v. McMillian* (1992), a Louisiana prison inmate testified that he had suffered minor bruises, facial swelling, loosened teeth, and a cracked dental plate after receiving a beating by two prison guards. A supervisor on duty watched the beating but merely told the officers "not to have too much fun." The magistrate hearing the case ruled that the staff had violated the Eighth Amendment's prohibition on cruel and unusual punishments, and Hudson was awarded damages. The case was appealed to the Supreme Court, which ruled that as long as force is used in a good-faith effort to maintain control, there is no liability. It is only in instances when prisoners can provide evidence that correctional officers acted maliciously that liability is held.[148]

In a 2002 case, *Hope v. Pelzer*, the Supreme Court ruled that correctional officials who knowingly violate the Eighth Amendment rights of inmates can be held liable for damages.[149] Larry Hope, an Alabama prison inmate, was twice handcuffed to a hitching post for disruptive conduct while he was working outside the prison on a chain gang. He was handcuffed above shoulder height, and when he tried moving his arms to improve circulation, the handcuffs cut into his wrists, causing pain and discomfort. He spent seven hours on the hitching post, during which he was given one or two water breaks but no bathroom breaks, and a guard taunted him about his thirst. Hope filed a suit against three guards, charging them with violating his civil rights. The guards argued that they were entitled to **qualified immunity** from lawsuits, a legal doctrine that protects government officials from liability from civil damages if their conduct did not violate clearly established statutory or constitutional rights of which a reasonable person would have been aware.

The Supreme Court ruled that Hope's allegations established an Eighth Amendment violation. It ruled that among the "'unnecessary and wanton' inflictions of pain [constituting cruel and unusual punishment forbidden by the amendment] are those that are 'totally without penological justification.'" In the context of prison conditions, this determination is made by ascertaining whether an official acted with "deliberate indifference" to the inmate's health or safety, a state of mind that can be inferred from the fact that the risk of harm is obvious. The Court reasoned that any safety concerns had long since ended by the time Hope was handcuffed to the hitching post, because he had already been subdued, handcuffed, placed in leg irons, and transported back to prison. The *Hope* case shows that correctional officials can be successfully sued if their behavior violates an inmate's constitutional rights and if they or any reasonable person should have surmised that the behavior was in violation of accepted practices.

*RACIAL SEGREGATION* On August 8, 2009, a riot in the California prison at Chino left hundreds injured, buildings burnt, and property destroyed.[150] The disturbance was sparked by racial tensions between Latino and black inmates, and it later generated a great deal of controversy over the issue of racial segregation in prison. Should prisons be segregated to prevent violence among gangs such as the Aryan Brotherhood, the Mexican Mafia, and the Black Guerrilla Family? Or, as in other institutions, are inmates entitled to equal treatment under the law such that any form of segregation is considered inherently unconstitutional?

In a 2005 case, *Johnson v. California*, the Supreme Court ruled that the segregation of prison inmates on the basis of race, in their cells or anywhere on prison grounds, is an inappropriate form of racial classification.[151] However, it left it open for lower courts to decide, using a standard of *strict scrutiny*, when segregation is inappropriate and unconstitutional. *Johnson* focused on the policy of segregating inmates upon their arrival at a prison. However, the Court's ruling seemed to suggest that if racial segregation were allowed for incoming inmates, there was a danger that it might also be imposed "in the dining halls, yards, and

**qualified immunity**
A legal doctrine that shields government officials from liability if their conduct did not violate clearly established civil rights that a reasonable person would have known about.

Racial conflict is an ever-present danger in the nation's prison system. Consequently, in some institutions inmates prefer segregated housing units. On January 28, 2009, inmates Tim Heffernan, left, and Daniel Mabson talk while sitting on their adjacent bunks at the Sierra Conservation Center in Jamestown, California. Despite efforts by California prison officials to end institutionalized, government-mandated racial segregation, powerful race-based gangs violently oppose desegregation in prison housing units. Blacks, whites, and Hispanics are willing to sleep side by side in bunk beds spaced an arm's length apart, but they would brawl or risk longer sentences rather than accept an inmate of another race in a bed above or below them in the same bunk bed stack.

© AP Photo/Rich Pedroncelli

# Significant Constitutional Cases on Correctional Matters

| Case | Issue | Decision |
|------|-------|----------|
| *Bell v. Wolfish* (1979) | Cruel and unusual punishment | Although people are sent to prison for punishment, it does not mean that prison should be a punishing experience. |
| *Cooper v. Pate* (1964) | Freedom of religion | Inmates who were being denied the right to practice their religion were entitled to legal redress. |
| *Cutter v. Wilkinson* (2005) | | Inmates may practice their own religion unless their practices clearly undermine prison security and safety. |
| *Estelle v. Gamble* (1976) | Medical care | Inmates have a right to have medical care. Access to quality health care is part of the prison regime. |
| *Farmer v. Brennan* (1994) | | If prison officials were aware of a serious risk to an inmate's safety, but failed to take reasonable steps for its prevention, they are liable for injuries suffered. |
| *Hope v. Pelzer* (2002) | | Correctional officials who knowingly violate the Eighth Amendment rights of inmates can be held liable for damages if their actions are "totally without penological justification." |
| *Hudson v. McMillian* (1992) | Use of force in prison | As long as force is used in a good-faith effort to maintain control, there is no liability. To be liable, correctional officers must act maliciously. |
| *Jackson v. Bishop* (1968) | Physical punishment | The use of corporal punishment is forbidden in prison. |
| *Johnson v. California* (2005) | Racial segregation | The segregation of prison inmates based on race, in their cells or anywhere on prison grounds, is an inappropriate form of racial classification. |
| *Newman v. Alabama* (1972) | Medical care in prisons | An entire state prison system's medical facilities are inadequate if they provide insufficient physician and nurse resources, rely on untrained inmates for paramedical work, intentionally fail to treat the sick and injured, and fail to conform to proper medical standards. |
| *O'Lone v. Estate of Shabazz* (1987) | Prison regulations | A prison regulation is valid if it is reasonably related to legitimate penological interests. |
| *Rhodes v. Chapman* (1981) | Prison care and conditions | If there is a legitimate purpose for the use of governmental restrictions, they may be considered constitutional. |
| *Shaw v. Murphy* (2001) | Correspondence | Inmates do not have an absolute right to correspond with other inmates, even if it concerns legal advice. |

general housing areas. . . ." Segregation should be allowed, the judges reasoned, only when a prison administrator could prove that it served a compelling interest to promote prison safety. The Court recognized that "prisons are dangerous places, and the special circumstances they present may justify racial classifications in some contexts." Because the Chino riot occurred after California began to integrate prison entry centers, it is possible that future efforts to racially integrate prisons will be frustrated. State courts, even when using a "strict scrutiny" standard, may conclude that racial integration, in some instances, is just too dangerous.

*OVERALL PRISON CONDITIONS* Prisoners have long had the right to the minimal conditions necessary for human survival, such as the food, clothing, shelter, and medical care necessary to sustain human life. A number of attempts have been made to articulate reasonable standards of prison care and to make sure they are applied. Courts have held that although people are sent to prison for punishment, it does not mean that prison should be a punishing experience.[152] As explained earlier, in the 1994 case of *Farmer v. Brennan*, the court ruled that prison officials are legally liable if, knowing that an inmate faces a serious risk of harm, they disregard that risk by failing to take measures to avoid or reduce it. Furthermore, prison officials should be able to infer the risk from the evidence at hand; it is not necessary for them to have been warned or told.[153]

Although inmates retain the right to reasonable care, if there is a legitimate purpose for the use of governmental restrictions, they may be considered constitutional. Thus, it might be possible to restrict reading material, allow strip searches, and prohibit inmates from receiving packages from the outside if the restrictions are legitimate security measures. If overcrowded conditions require it, inmates may be double-bunked in cells designed for a single inmate.[154]

The accompanying table reviews the most significant cases in the clarification of inmates' constitutional rights.

# LEAVING PRISON

At the expiration of their prison term, most inmates return to society and try to resume their lives. As Figure 15.1 shows, around 600,000 inmates are released on **parole** each year, and slightly less complete their parole order. Thus the total number of people on parole (860,000) continues to rise, though at a slower pace than earlier in the decade.

> **parole**
> The early release of a prisoner from imprisonment subject to conditions set by correctional authorities.

About 35 percent of inmates who enter parole supervision go before a parole board, a group of correctional officials who determine whether an inmate is eligible for and/or worthy of early release.[155] The board is a duly constituted body of men and women who review inmate cases and determine whether offenders have reached a rehabilitative level sufficient to deal with the outside world. The board also dictates what specific parole rules parolees must obey.

In states where determinate-sentencing statutes have eliminated discretionary parole, offenders are released after having served their determinate sentence, minus time off for good behavior and any other credits by which the term of incarceration can be reduced. Their release may involve supervision in the community, and rule violations can result in return to prison for the balance of their unexpired sentence. In these jurisdictions, the amount of time a person must remain in prison is a predetermined percentage of the inmate's sentence, assuming that there are no infractions or escape attempts. With mandatory parole release, the inmate is released when the unserved portion of the maximum prison term equals the inmate's earned good time (less time served in jail awaiting trial). In some states, sentences can be reduced by more than half with a combination of statutory and earned good time. If the conditions of their release are violated, mandatory releasees can have their good time revoked and be returned to the institution to serve the remainder of their unexpired term. More than half of all parolees are now released in this fashion.

The remaining inmates are released for a variety of reasons, including expiration of their term, commutation of their sentence, and court orders to relieve overcrowding in prisons.

**FIGURE 15.1**

**National Estimates of Parole Entries and Exits**

**Number of entries and exits**

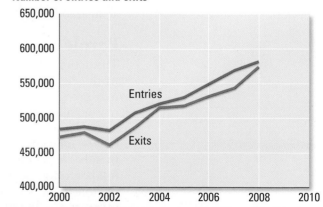

Source: Lauren Glaze and Thomas Bonczar, *Probation and Parole in the United States*, 2008 (Washington, D.C.: Bureau of Justice Statistics, 2009), http://bjs.ojp.usdoj.gov/content/pub/pdf/ppus08.pdf.

**PERSPECTIVES ON JUSTICE**

*Perspectives on Justice*

Mandatory parole release is consistent with the justice perspective of fairness and the elimination of discretion from justice system decision making. It is a cornerstone of the justice perspective, because it removes an important source of unfairness perceived by inmates who are denied discretionary parole only to see others granted early release whom they consider no more deserving.

Depending on the jurisdiction, inmates must serve a certain portion of their sentences before becoming eligible for parole. The conditions of parole may require the individual to report regularly to a parole officer, to refrain from criminal conduct, to maintain and support his or her family, to avoid contact with other convicted criminals, to abstain from using alcohol and drugs, to remain within the jurisdiction, and so on. Violations of the conditions of parole may result in revocation, in which case the individual will be returned to prison. The concept behind parole is to allow the release of the offender to community supervision, where rehabilitation and readjustment can be facilitated.

In a few instances, inmates are released after their sentences have been commuted by a board of pardons or directly by a governor or even the president. About 15 percent of prison inmates are released after serving their entire maximum sentence, without any time excused or forgiven. Regardless of the method of their release, former inmates face the formidable task of readjusting to society. This means regaining legal rights they may have lost on their conviction, reestablishing community and family ties, and finding employment. After being in prison, these goals are often difficult to achieve.

## The Parole Board

In those states that have maintained discretionary parole, the authority to release inmates is usually vested in the parole board. State parole boards have four primary functions:

1.  To select and place prisoners on parole
2.  To aid, supervise, and provide continuing control of parolees in the community
3.  To determine when the parole function is completed and to discharge parolees
4.  To determine whether parole should be revoked if violations of conditions occur

Most parole authorities are independent agencies with their own staff and administration, and a few parole boards are part of the state department of corrections. Arguments for keeping the board within a corrections department usually include improved communication and the availability of more intimate knowledge about offenders.

Most boards are relatively small, usually numbering fewer than ten members. Their size, coupled with their large caseloads and the varied activities they are expected to perform, can prevent board members from becoming as well acquainted with the individual inmates as might be desired.

## Parole Hearings

The actual (discretionary) parole decision is made at a parole-granting hearing. At this hearing the full board or a selected subcommittee reviews information, may meet with the offender, and then decides whether the parole applicant has a reasonable probability of succeeding outside of prison. Each parole board has its own way of reviewing cases. In some, the full board meets with the applicant; in others, only a few members do that. In a number of jurisdictions, a single board member can conduct a personal investigation and submit the findings to the full board for a decision. Whether in an individual or group format, face-to-face meetings can be beneficial, because the panel can get feedback from inmates to more thoroughly evaluate parole readiness. Parole board officials, many of whom have had varied professional training and experience, can use these meetings to assess an inmate's sincerity and readiness for release.[156]

When parole is discretionary, most parole boards look at the inmate's crime, institutional record, and willingness to accept responsibility before making the release decision. Some jurisdictions rely on standardized tests that predict whether a potential parolee will recidivate upon release.[157] Letters may be solicited from the inmate's friends and family members. In some jurisdictions, victims may appear and make statements about the losses they suffered. By speaking directly to the applicant, the board can also promote and emphasize the specific types of behavior and behavior changes it expects to see if the inmate is to eventually qualify for or effectively serve parole. Inmates who maintain their innocence may find that denying responsibility for their crimes places their release date in jeopardy. The requirement that they admit guilt or culpability is especially vexing for those inmates who actually are innocent and who actively refuse to accept their institutional label of "convicted criminal."[158]

The inmate's specific rights at a parole-granting hearing also vary from jurisdiction to jurisdiction. In about half of the parole-granting jurisdictions, inmates are permitted counsel or are allowed to present witnesses on their behalf; other jurisdictions do not permit these privileges. Because the federal courts have declared that the parole applicant is not entitled to any form of legal representation, the inmate may have to pay for legal services when this privilege is allowed. In almost all discretionary parole-granting jurisdictions, the reasons for the parole decision must be given in writing, and in about half of the jurisdictions, a verbatim record of the hearing is made.

In the case of *Pennsylvania Board of Probation and Parole v. Scott*, the U.S. Supreme Court held that the exclusionary rule for illegally obtained evidence does not apply to parole revocation proceedings. The Court reasoned that the social costs of excluding incriminating evidence outweigh any benefits of protecting parolees from invasion of their privacy. *Scott* thus allows evidence to be used in a parole revocation hearing that would be excluded from a criminal prosecution.[159]

## The Parolee in the Community

Once released into the community, a parolee is given a standard set of rules and conditions that must be obeyed. Today, parole officers, as the accompanying Criminal Justice and Technology feature shows, are using technology to ensure that these rules are being obeyed.

As with probation, the offender who violates these rules may have parole revoked and be sent back to the institution to serve the remainder of the sentence. Once in the community, the parolee is supervised by a trained staff of parole officers who help the offender search for employment and monitor the parolee's behavior and activities to ensure that the conditions of parole are met.

Parole is generally viewed as a privilege granted to deserving inmates on the basis of their good behavior while in prison. Parole has two conflicting sides, however. On one hand, the paroled offender is allowed to serve part of the sentence in the community, an obvious benefit for the deserving offender. On the other hand, because parole is a privilege and not a right, the parolee is viewed as a dangerous criminal who must be carefully watched and supervised. The conflict between the treatment and enforcement aspects of parole has not been reconciled by the criminal justice system, and the parole process still contains elements of both.

To overcome these roadblocks to success, the parole officer may have to play a much greater role than the probation officer in directing and supervising clients' lives. In some instances, parole programs have become active in creating new postrelease treatment-oriented programs designed to increase the chances of parole success. For example, the Kansas Parole Department has adopted a restorative justice approach and is now having parolees work in community service settings upon their release. Jobs may include work at soup kitchens, homeless shelters, and halfway houses. Reports indicate that the program is quite successful.[160] In other instances, parole agencies have implemented law enforcement–oriented

## CRIMINAL JUSTICE AND TECHNOLOGY

# Monitoring Parolees with GPS technology

Global positioning satellite (GPS) technology is now being used to monitor offenders in the community, not only to protect the public from repeat offenders but also to clear offenders who may be suspects because of their past activities. Take, for instance, a case that occurred recently in Florida. A local 11-year-old boy disappeared from his home in Pinellas County, and his mother reported his absence to the police. Five days later, the boy returned home and said he had become friends with an older man who gave him a place to live, took him shopping, and so on. The boy refused to identify his abductor. Extremely concerned, his mother searched the database of sex offenders made public by the Florida Department of Law Enforcement (FDLE). The user-friendly mapping tools and search functions on this website enabled her to identify a likely suspect named "Joshua," a parolee who lived in the vicinity of the school her son attended. She reported her suspicions to the authorities. Was Joshua the culprit?

The subsequent investigation was aided by Florida's use of mapping and monitoring devices that enable law enforcement agencies to keep tabs on sex offenders who have been released back into the community. These offenders must follow a specific set of parole conditions and residency restrictions. Now, parole officers can use global positioning system (GPS) and mapping applications to monitor their whereabouts and enforce sanctions if they violate rules. Florida sex offenders such as Joshua must obey residency restriction laws that prohibit their living within 1,000 feet of a day care center, school, park, or playground and their being near school bus stops or in other locations where children congregate.

This case could have presented a thorny problem for authorities, but the use of technology helped ease the process. Following his release, Joshua had been under Florida Department of Corrections (FDOC) supervision with special restrictions. He had found a residence in a location that complied with his release conditions and had begun working as a flight mechanic. As he reintegrated into society, he was required to wear a GPS tracking device, so his movements could be monitored and the 1,000-foot buffer rule enforced.

Joshua also reported to FDOC intake to receive the details of his release and the type of supervision imposed. His address was checked again, and the report was printed and placed in his file. Joshua's sanctions included routine polygraph and drug tests, regular attendance in a sex offender treatment program, monthly checks for new arrests, a requirement to maintain a driving log, random computer checks, provision of all email addresses and Instant Message logins, adherence to a curfew, and a requirement that he have an evacuation plan in the event of an emergency. Joshua was registered with the Pinellas County Sheriff's Office Sexual Predator and Offender Tracking (SPOT) Unit. Joshua's picture was taken and his information updated. Joshua was then instructed on how to maintain connection to the satellite transmission. Settings were adjusted to adhere to Joshua's restrictions, while accommodating his schedule for attending sex offender treatment and work hours.

Although these restrictions seem cumbersome, they may also help offenders avoid unfounded accusations. In this case, Joshua's GPS displays (or tracks) for the period that the 11-year-old boy was missing from his home showed that it was impossible for Joshua to have been the culprit. After interviewing and getting confirming evidence from Joshua's employer and other witnesses, the officer determined that he was not involved in the boy's disappearance.

The mapping tools enable both county and state agencies to validate sex offenders' activities. Automated notification and placement tools analyze distance from the offender's residence and provide a list of locations that may suggest the potential for a violation. With these tools and investigative techniques, offenders can be included as suspects or, as in Joshua's case, proved innocent.

Source: Kristin Preston, "Right Place, Right Time: GPS Monitoring in Pinellas County," *Geography and Public Safety* 2 (2009): 3–5, www.ojp .usdoj.gov/nij/maps/gps-bulletin-v2i1.pdf.

services that work with local police agencies to identify and apprehend parolees who may have been involved in criminal activity. The California Department of Corrections has established the Special Service Unit, which (among its other tasks) acts as a liaison to help local police agencies solve major crimes when inmates or state parolees are the known or suspected offenders.[161]

*INTENSIVE SUPERVISION PAROLE* To aid supervision, some jurisdictions are implementing systems that classify offenders on the basis of their supervision needs. Typically, a point or guideline system (sometimes called a salient factor score) based on prior record and prison adjustment divides parolees into three groups: (1) those who require intensive surveillance, (2) those who require social services instead of surveillance, and (3) those who require limited supervision.

In some jurisdictions, parolees in need of closer surveillance are placed on **intensive supervision parole (ISP)**. These programs use limited caseload sizes, treatment facilities, the matching of parolee and supervisor by personality, and shock parole (which involves immediate short-term incarceration for parole violators to impress them with the seriousness of a violation). ISP clients are required to attend more office and home visits than routine parolees. ISP may also require frequent drug testing, a term in a community correctional center, and electronic monitoring in the home. More than 17,000 parolees are under intensive supervision, 1,400 of whom are monitored electronically by computer.

Evaluations of ISP programs have yielded mixed results. Some show that ISP may actually produce a higher violation rate than traditional parole supervision, because limiting caseload size enables parole officers to supervise their clients more closely and spot infractions more easily.[162] Some recent research shows that under some conditions, a properly run ISP program can significantly reduce recidivism upon release. The key factors may be parole officer orientation (a balance between social service and law enforcement seems to work best) and a supportive organizational environment in which the program is being run.[163]

**intensive supervision parole (ISP)**
A form of parole characterized by smaller caseloads and closer surveillance; it may include frequent drug testing and, in some cases, electronic monitoring.

## The Effectiveness of Parole

According to justice expert Joan Petersilia,

> Persons released from prison face a multitude of difficulties. They remain largely uneducated, unskilled, and usually without solid family support systems—to which are added the burdens of a prison record. Not surprisingly, most parolees fail, and rather quickly—rearrests are most common in the first six months after release.[164]

Despite all efforts to treat, correct, and rehabilitate incarcerated offenders, a majority still return to prison shortly after their release. About 45 percent of all parolees successfully complete their sentence in the community, and the rest commit new crimes, abscond, or violate parole conditions.[165]

An important study of more than 270,000 prisoners released in 15 states provides data that underscores the problem. Of the total number of releasees, 67.5 percent were rearrested within three years of leaving prison for a felony or serious misdemeanor.[166] About 47 percent were reconvicted for a new crime, and 25 percent were resentenced to prison for a new crime. Within three years, about 52 percent were back in prison, serving time for a new prison sentence or for a technical violation of their release, such as failing a drug test, missing an appointment with their parole officer, or being arrested for a new crime. The cost of recidivism is acute. The 272,111 offenders discharged in 1994 had accumulated 744,000 charges within three years of release. To put it another way, about a quarter of a million U.S. citizens are victimized each year by people released on parole in just 15 states. Another federal survey of 156,000 parole violators serving time in the nation's prison system estimated that these offenders had committed at least 6,800 murders, 5,500 rapes, 8,800 assaults, and 22,500 robberies while under supervision in the community an average of 13 months.[167]

## Who Fails on Parole?

It may come as no surprise that those who violate parole are typically younger, less well educated inmates who have histories of criminal activity and drug dependence and who live in deteriorated, crime-ridden communities. These social problems reduce the likelihood of post-prison success for both male and female offenders.[168] The released prisoners with the highest rearrest rates were robbers, burglars, larcenists, motor vehicle thieves, those convicted of possessing or selling stolen property, and those convicted of possessing illegal weapons. Ironically, those who might be considered the most dangerous criminals—murderers and rapists—have the lowest recidivism rates.

Those most likely to fail on parole are also those who maintain criminal peer associations, carry weapons, abuse alcohol, and harbor aggressive feelings.[169] In contrast, those who are employed, have stable living arrangements, and are receiving some type of drug and/or alcohol program intervention are far less likely to fail on parole.[170]

In a recent study of substance use, sexual behavior, and reincarceration among men released from five state prisons across the United States, David Seal and his associates identified the important role that social and economic support plays in parole success.[171] The men used one of three methods in trying to reintegrate into society: (1) moving toward successful reintegration into social life, (2) resuming the behaviors that got them into prison in the first place and behavioral patterns that preceded incarceration, and (3) withdrawing or isolating themselves from society. Their choice of coping mechanism was shaped by the strength of their social relationships, the nature of the social support they received on the outside from friends and family, and the degree of structural stability they could achieve, such as gaining stable employment and housing. Collectively, these factors were related to the prevalence and frequency of substance use, patterns of sexual behavior, and incidence of reincarceration. For example, those men with less consistent and more negative social relationships were more likely to use drugs, to have multiple sexual partners, and eventually to return to prison. In sum, what greets former inmates on the outside plays a significant role in their ability to adjust.

*PERSONAL DEFICITS* Parole failure can also be tied to the releasee's own personal deficits. Most research efforts indicate that a long history of criminal behavior, an antisocial personality, and childhood experiences with family dysfunction are all correlated with postrelease recidivism.[172] Many releasees have suffered from a lifetime of substance abuse or dependence.[173] A history of physical and sexual abuse has also been linked to recidivism.[174] Other parolees have substance abuse or mental health problems, and more than 10 percent exhibit both mental illness and substance abuse. One study of 400 Texas inmates found that almost 75 percent suffered from lifetime substance abuse or dependence disorder.[175]

The prison experience probably does little to improve offenders' personality or behavior. And when offenders return to society, it may be to the same destructive neighborhoods and social groups that they left for prison. Some ex-inmates may have to prove that the prison experience has not changed them: Taking drugs or being sexually aggressive may show friends that they have not lost their "heart."[176]

One study of youthful ex-offenders trying to make it on the outside found that many experience delayed emotional and cognitive development because of early drug use. Most have never learned to use problem-solving or coping skills outside the correctional setting, and most remain drug dependent.[177] Sensitive to these problems, some states have instituted support groups designed to help inmates' families deal with their loneliness and despair.[178]

*ECONOMIC DEFICITS* Former inmates soon find that imprisonment reduces their income and employment opportunities.[179] By law, ex-convicts are denied the right to work in certain occupations. And even if a criminal record does not automatically prohibit employment, many employers are reluctant to hire people who have served time. Why would someone hire an ex-con when other applicants are available? Many find that it is difficult to get jobs because potential employers are unconvinced that reform is possible or doubt that former inmates have the "people skills" that will enable them to succeed in the workplace. Some business owners are concerned about customers' reactions if they know that an employee is an ex-inmate.[180] If ex-offenders lie about their prison experience and are later found out, they can be dismissed for misrepresentation. The stress of economic deprivation, in turn, can lead to family breakup and to less involvement with children.[181] Research shows that former inmates who gain and keep meaningful employment are more likely to succeed on parole than those who are unemployed or underemployed.[182]

*MARRIAGE AND FAMILY DEFICITS* Recidivism may be a by-product of the disruptive effect a prison experience has on personal relationships. Ex-inmates may find their home life torn and disrupted when they are finally released. Recent research by Beth Heubner shows that incarceration significantly reduces the chances of marriage for all men. Although whites were most likely to be married overall, incarceration was associated with a 59 percent decline in the odds of marriage for whites, and the odds of marriage decreased 30 percent for blacks and 41 percent for Hispanics. Since marriage has proved to be a significant neutralizer of future criminality, the suppression effect on marriage that a prison sentence inflicts may help explain high recidivism rates.[183] And even if they do marry, former inmates may be restricted in their choice of mates. Their circumstances may force them to choose partners with equally checkered backgrounds, a circumstance that may enhance rather than depress the likelihood of future criminality.

What about men who are married and then go to prison? Wives of inmates report that they had to face the shame and stigmatization of having an incarcerated spouse while withstanding a barrage of calls from their jealous husbands on the "inside," who tried to monitor their behavior and control their lives. Family visits to the inmate became traumatic, and they also strained relationships because they often involved strip searches and other invasions of privacy.[184] Once the offender is on the outside, immersion in family life can have mixed effects. Beth Heubner and Mark Berg found that inmates with children were the most likely to desist from crime; bonds to children can be a part of long-term offender change. However, children can put a strain on some releasees, especially those who did not live with their families before incarceration and those who suffer separation upon release. Being asked to pay child support exacerbates the financial problems faced by parolees and heightens their chances of failure, particularly when they are under the close supervision of a parole officer.[185]

## The Problems of Reentry

The specter of recidivism is especially frustrating to the U.S. public. It is so difficult to apprehend and successfully prosecute criminal offenders that it seems foolish to grant them early release so they can prey on more victims. This problem is exacerbated when the parolee is a chronic, frequent offender. Research indicates that many of these returning prisoners are *less* prepared for reintegration and less connected to community-based social structures than in the past.[186] There seems to be a strong association between prior and future offending: The parolees most likely to fail on release are the ones who have failed in the past; chronic offenders are the ones most likely to reoffend.

The problems of reentry are exacerbated now because of America's two-decade-long imprisonment boom, which has resulted in more than 700,000 inmates being released into the community each year. As criminologist Joan Petersilia warns, many of those being released have not received adequate treatment and are ill prepared for life in conventional society.[187] The risks they present to the community include increases in child abuse, family violence, the spread of infectious diseases, homelessness, and community disorganization. Many have no way to cope and wind up in homeless shelters. One study of shelters in New York City found that 23 percent of the occupants had been released from New York prisons and jails in the past two years.[188]

The increased reentry risks can be tied to legal changes in how people are released from prison. In the past, offenders were granted early release only if a parole board believed they were rehabilitated and had ties to the community—such as a family or a job. Inmates were encouraged to enter treatment programs to earn parole. Changes in sentencing laws have resulted in the growth of mandatory release and limits on discretionary parole. People now serve a fixed sentence, and the discretion of parole boards has been blunted. Inmates may be discouraged from seeking involvement in rehabilitation programs (they do not influence the chance of parole), and this lack of incentive means that fewer inmates leaving prison have participated in programs to address work, education, and substance use deficiencies. Nor does the situation improve upon release. Many inmates are not assigned to supervision caseloads once back in the community. About 200,000 released inmates go unsupervised each year, three-quarters of whom have been released after completing their maximum sentence and are therefore not obligated to be supervised.

Petersilia argues that most leave prison with no savings, no immediate entitlement to unemployment benefits, and few employment prospects.[189] Upon release, some find that they are no longer welcome in subsidized public housing complexes because of the U.S. Department of Housing and Urban Development's "one strike and you're out" policy, where all members of the household are evicted if one member is involved in crime. A year after release, as many as 60 percent of former inmates are not employed in the regular labor market, and employers are increasingly reluctant to hire ex-offenders. Ex-offenders are commonly barred from working in the fields in which most jobs are being created, such as child care, education, security, nursing, and home health care. More jobs are also now unionized, and many unions exclude ex-offenders.

Being barred from work opportunities produces chronic unemployment, a status closely related to drug and alcohol abuse. Losing a job can lead to substance abuse, which in turn is related to child and family violence. Children of incarcerated and released parents may suffer confusion, sadness, and social stigma, and these feelings often result in difficulties in school, low self-esteem, aggressive behavior, and general emotional dysfunction. When the parents are negative role models, children fail to develop positive attitudes about work and responsibility. Children of incarcerated parents are five times more likely to serve time in prison than children whose parents are not incarcerated.

Prisoners have significantly more physical and mental health problems than the general population. More than three-fourths of the inmates leaving prison report drug and/or alcohol abuse in the year following their release. Inmates with mental illness are also increasingly being imprisoned—and then released. One recent study in New York State (2008) found that the number of prison inmates receiving mental health services had grown steadily, almost doubling from 4,500 in 1990 to 8,600 in 2008. In the same period there was a 22 percent increase in inmates who had a diagnosis of serious mental illness.[190]

Even when public mental health services are available, many mentally ill individuals fail to use them because they fear institutionalization, deny they are mentally ill, or distrust the mental health system. The situation will become more serious as more and more parolees are released into the disorganized communities whose deteriorated conditions may have prompted their original crimes. Because of these issues, some state jurisdictions are creating programs that ease the reentry process. Some private groups have attained funding to provide postrelease counseling and support. One promising Virginia program, Women Inspired to Transform (WIT), uses volunteers to teach female returnees about anger management, job interviewing, communication, relationships, and parenting.[191] Yet the large number of parolees strains the system of public and private providers and has made the problem of returning inmates a national issue. Crime experts believe that the large numbers of former inmates returning to their neighborhoods can destabilize areas and increase existing crime rates.

Fear of a prison stay has less of an effect on behavior than ever before. As the prison population grows, the negative impact of incarceration may be lessening. In neighborhoods where "doing time" is more the rule than the exception, it becomes less of a stigma and more of a badge of acceptance. However, it also becomes a way of life from which some ex-convicts do rebound. Teens may encounter older men who have gone to prison and have returned to begin their lives again. With the proper skills and survival techniques, prison is considered "manageable." Although a prison stay is still unpleasant, it has lost its aura of shame and fear. By becoming commonplace and mundane, the "myth" of the prison experience has been exposed and its deterrent power reduced.

*THE SPECIAL PROBLEMS OF FEMALE INMATES*  Women released from prison face special challenges, and nearly half are either reconvicted or reincarcerated soon after parole release. Which women have the most trouble making it on the outside? As might be expected, those who were drug dependent, live in disorganized areas, and lack close personal relationships are the ones most likely to fail on parole. Having a history of drug abuse is particularly harmful. According to recent research conducted by Beth Heubner and her associates, substance abuse makes it very difficult to readjust.[192] It compromises returning women's employment opportunities, relationships with children, and social support. The impact of drug abuse is felt most acutely by minority women who must balance the demands of substance abuse treatment, employment, and family responsibilities, all the while living in disorganized areas with little access to services or social support. Drug convictions may close doors to both social service providers and employers, who have little interest in helping or employing abusers. For example, recent welfare reform acts deny government benefits to people convicted of drug offenses and/or their families, a policy that has a significant impact on African American and Hispanic mothers, who are disproportionately represented in the welfare system. And although being a mother seems to be a deterrent to recidivism, women in prison who are substance abusers and are marginally employed may face loss of parental rights upon release, further undermining their chances of successful reintegration.

*THE EFFECT ON COMMUNITIES*  Parole expert Richard Seiter notes that when there were only a few hundred thousand prisoners, and a few thousand releasees per year, the issues surrounding the release of offenders did not overwhelm communities.[193] Families could house ex-inmates, job-search organizations could find them jobs, and community social service agencies could respond to their individual needs for mental health or substance abuse treatment. Today, the sheer number of reentering inmates has taxed the communities to which they are returning. Charis Kubrin and Eric Stewart have found that communities that already face the greatest social and economic disadvantages are those where the highest recidivism rates occur.[194] Obviously, the influx of returning inmates can magnify their problems.

Research shows that high rates of prison admissions produce high crime rates. Clearly, the national policy of relying on prison as a deterrent to crime may produce results that policymakers had not expected or wanted.

*IMPROVING CHANCES ON REENTRY*  Can something be done to ease reentry? Now that the scope of the problem has been recognized, both the federal and state governments have devoted energy to improving reentry success. On April 9, 2008, the Second Chance Act was signed into law. This federal legislation authorized various grants to government agencies and nonprofit groups to provide a variety of services, including employment assistance, housing, substance abuse treatment, and family programming, that can help to reduce reoffending and violations of probation and parole. The key provisions of the act are set out in Exhibit 15.4.

At the federal level, a number of initiatives have been taken to help prepare inmates for reentry. The emphasis on release preparation intensifies at least 18 months prior to the end of the prison stay when inmates enter the Release Preparation Program, which includes classes in areas such as résumé writing, job search, and job retention. The program also includes presentations by members of community-based organizations that help ex-inmates find jobs and training

**EXHIBIT 15.4**

## Key Provisions of the Second Chance Act

- *Demonstration Grants.* Provides funds to states and local governments to be used to promote reintegration into the community of individuals who have been incarcerated. Funds for employment services, substance abuse treatment, housing, family programming, mentoring, victims services, and methods to improve release and revocation decisions using risk assessment tools.

- *Mentoring Grants.* Provides funds to nonprofit organizations that may be used for mentoring adult offenders or offering transitional services for reintegration into the community.

- *Offender Reentry Substance Abuse Treatment.* Provides funds for drug treatment to offenders in prisons, jails, and juvenile facilities.

- *Family Drug Treatment Programs.* Authorizes states, local governments, and Indian tribes to develop and implement grants for family-based treatment programs for incarcerated parents who have minor children.

- *Federal Reentry Initiative.* Provides guidance to the Bureau of Prisons for enhanced reentry planning procedures. Provides information on health, employment, personal finance, release requirements, and community resources to each inmate released.

- *Reentry Research.* Requests that U.S. Justice Department's National Institute of Justice and the Bureau of Justice Statistics to conduct reentry-related research.

- *National Adult and Juvenile Offender Reentry Resource Center.* Establishes a national resource center to collect and disseminate information and to provide training on and support for reentry efforts.

Source: The Second Chance Act of 2007, H.R. 1593, § 1060, www.fedcure.org/information/HR1593.shtml (accessed September 8, 2008).

opportunities after release. The Federal Bureau of Prisons then places appropriate inmates in halfway houses prior to release to help them adjust to life in the community and find employment. Some inmates become eligible for a release gratuity, clothing, or money for transportation to their release destination.[195] The Inmate Transition Branch also provides additional prerelease employment assistance. Many institutions hold mock job fairs to give inmates an opportunity to practice job interview skills and to acquaint community recruiters with the skills available among inmates being released. Qualified inmates may apply for jobs with companies that have posted job openings. This branch also helps inmates prepare release folders that include a résumé; education certificates, diplomas, and transcripts; and other significant documents needed for a successful job interview.

There have also been a number of initiatives on the state level:[196]

- *Offender notification forums.* As part of its Project Safe Neighborhood (PSN) initiative, the city of Chicago launched an offender notification forum. In designated neighborhoods, individuals recently assigned to parole or probation who had a history of gun violence and gang participation attended a forum hosted by the PSN team. In these forums, the individual met with representatives from state and local law enforcement agencies, community representatives, and service providers. The meetings focused on the consequences of gun crimes and the choices individuals can make based on alternatives that are available, including job training, education programs, drug treatment, temporary shelter, and counseling. An evaluation of the PSN initiative indicates that the forums have been "remarkably effective in reducing neighborhood crime rates."[197]

- *Reentry courts.* The concept of a reentry court, first proposed nearly a decade ago, is taking hold in state and federal systems. By placing a judge (or magistrate) in the role of reentry manager, these courts, inspired by the successes of drug courts and other problem-solving courts, create a different relationship between returning prison inmates and the criminal justice system. They provide for coordinated services in ways that are not possible in traditional parole systems.

## EXHIBIT 15.5

# Rights Lost upon Release from Prison

- Fourteen states permanently deny felons the right to vote; 18 states suspend the right to vote until after the correctional sentence has been completed.

- Nineteen states terminate parental rights.

- Twenty-nine states consider a felony conviction legal grounds for a divorce.

- Six states deny felons the opportunity for public employment.

- Thirty-one states disallow convicted felons the right to serve on juries.

- Twenty-five states prohibit convicted felons from holding public office.

- Federal law denies ex-convicts the right to own guns. In addition, all states except Vermont employ additional legal measures to prevent felons from possessing firearms.

- Forty-six states require that felons register with law enforcement agencies. This requirement is up sharply in recent years; in 1986 only eight states required felons to register.

- Civil death, or the denial of all civil rights, is still practiced in four states.

Source: Kathleen Olivares, Velmer Burton, and Francis Cullen, "The Collateral Consequences of a Felony Conviction: A National Study of State Legal Codes Ten Years Later," Federal Probation 60 (1996): 10–17.

- *Community-based interventions.* Recognizing that some communities are experiencing high rates of incarceration and reentry, these projects approach reentry as a community phenomenon. They create coalitions of community organizations to interact with every person returning home from prison. The NYC Justice Corps provides transitional employment for young adults returning home from prison and jail in two New York City neighborhoods most impacted by incarceration and reentry. In each location, a local organization brings together young people and their community to identify community improvement projects that NYC Justice Corps members can execute while developing valuable skills that help ready them for the labor market.

The accompanying Evidence-Based Justice feature reviews a well-known Boston-based program designed to assist with the reentry process.

**LEGAL RESTRICTIONS** Ex-inmates may also find that going straight is an economic impossibility. Research shows that former inmates who gain and keep meaningful employment are more likely to succeed on parole than those who are unemployed or underemployed.[198] One reason why ex-inmates find it so difficult to make it on the outside is the legal restrictions they are forced to endure. These may include prohibitions on certain kinds of employment, limits on obtaining licenses, and restrictions on their freedom of movement. One survey found that a significant number of states still restrict the activities of former felons.[199] Some of the more important findings are listed in Exhibit 15.5.

In general, states have placed greater restrictions on former felons, part of the "get tough" movement. However, courts have considered individual requests by convicted felons to have their rights restored. It is common for courts to look at such issues as how recently the criminal offense took place and its relationship to the right in question before deciding whether to restore it.

A number of experts and national commissions have condemned the loss of rights of convicted offenders as a significant cause of recidivism. Consequently, courts have generally moved to eliminate the most restrictive elements of post-conviction restrictions.[200]

**MAKING GOOD** Although most inmates recidivate soon after they are released, some do not and somehow are able to turn their lives around. What helps them go straight when so many others fail? One reason may be tied to the social and economic support that inmates receive on the outside. Maintaining family ties and gaining steady employment may help.

# EVIDENCE-BASED JUSTICE

## The Boston Reentry Initiative

Recidivism rates are extremely high, and most released inmates fail soon after reentry. Can anything be done to improve the chances of inmates upon release? One well-known effort, the Boston Reentry Initiative (BRI) seems to do just that. The BRI is a partnership enter into by the Suffolk County Sheriff's Department, the Boston Police Department, the U.S. Attorney's Office, and the District Attorney's Office. Its aim is to serve as an interagency support system for inmates both before and after their release from the House of Correction, the facility that houses incarcerated misdemeanants in the Boston area.

The BRI program is actually set in motion while inmates are still at the House of Correction. First, the BRI team targets a group of younger male inmates (aged 18 to 32) who are considered to be at high risk for failure for a variety of reasons: Perhaps they have been gang members or associates, have engaged in violent gang conflicts, have been the target of violent threats by other inmates or made threats themselves, or have a background of firearm offenses. In the first few months of incarceration, a panel made up of the U.S. Attorney's Office, the District Attorney's Office, parole, probation, community agencies, and faith-based organizations meets with offenders and discusses issues that may affect whether their transition back into the community is successful.

Within 45 days of their initial booking into the House of Correction, selected inmates are chosen to participate in panels of 12, which are convened monthly. The panel is used to impart two messages: First, the law enforcement community is aware of the offenders' past criminal activities and is prepared to act quickly and decisively should the offender resume those activities upon release. Second, there are significant resources—employment, housing, educational, and other support services—available to aid their transition back into community life. Every inmate is assigned a mentor from a faith-based organization or community service provider who assists them in implementing the discharge plan they receive upon release. Each of the panel members addresses the inmates and describes the resources and support that his or her organization or agency can provide to assist inmates with their transition back into the community, both while they are in the jail and after their release. All the speakers convey a unified message that the inmates have the power to choose their own destiny.

Following the panel, inmates are assigned jail-staff caseworkers and faith-based mentors from the community. They are enrolled in education, substance abuse, and other institutional programs that are customized to address their individual needs.

On the day of release, the institution arranges for either a family member or a mentor to meet each BRI client. The released prisoners are encouraged to continue to work with their caseworkers, mentors, and social service providers during their reentry periods. A typical BRI participant has about seven contacts with his mentors in the community and participates in 40 hours of treatment programming, including social service assistance (such as substance abuse and mental health treatment) and vocational development (such as the training, education, and résumé preparation necessary to secure employment). A recent evaluation of the BRI by Anthony Braga and his associates found that it reached its target audience: younger inmates with violent criminal histories. Most encouraging was the fact that BRI participants had 30 percent lower rates of recidivism than subjects in a comparison group.

The conclusion: Not only is it possible to provide services to an extremely high-risk population, but it is possible to do so effectively. If prison reentry is to be dealt with in an effective manner, it will take the cooperation of a variety of treatment and law enforcement agencies working together in an integrated fashion with a common goal.

Source: Anthony Braga, Anne Piehl, and David Hureau, "Controlling Violent Offenders Released to the Community: An Evaluation of the Boston Reentry Initiative," *Journal of Research in Crime and Delinquency* 46 (2009): 411–436

Parolees who had a good employment record before their incarceration and who are able to find jobs after their release are the ones most likely to avoid recidivating.[201] A recent four-state survey conducted by Paul Hirschfield and Alex Piquero found that although some people regard ex-offenders as dangerous and dishonest, many reject these stereotypes, and a majority say they would be willing to work and associate with people who had been incarcerated *recently*. Employers may view ex-offenders with caution, but workers may be more

© AP Images/Oscar Sosa

Many inmates fail on parole, and making good is often a challenge. One way to ease reentry is through restoration programs. Here Glen Mitchell (left), founder of Compassionate Families, and Ellis Curry talk on August 15, 2006, in Mitchell's Jacksonville, Florida, office, where photos of murder victims hang on the wall. Mitchell's 14-year-old son Jeff was shot and killed by Curry and three other young men 13 years ago. But Mitchell harbors no ill feelings toward Curry, because he has expressed remorse for causing Jeff Mitchell's death. Curry is now out of prison and is making joint appearances with Mitchell, spreading the message that violence is not the answer.

comfortable working alongside ex-offenders than their more conservative supervisors realize. One reason, the survey showed, was that the less faith people have in the fairness of the justice system, the more likely they are to espouse notions of redeemability and compassion toward ex-offenders. Even people who believe in harsh punishment may be willing to work alongside people who have paid their debt to society. If more people were acquainted with ex-offenders, more would be willing to hire them and give them the economic opportunity to succeed.[202]

In the final analysis, successful reentry may rely on a willingness to accept personal deficits and to change. When justice expert Shadd Maruna interviewed a group of serious criminals to understand how they were able to reform their lives, he found that going straight was a long process, not an instantaneous event.[203] Those who do well after prison have undergone a long-term cognitive change in which they begin to see themselves as a new person or adopt a new outlook on life. They begin to try to understand their past and develop insights into why they behaved the way they did and why and how things went wrong. Those who leave a life of crime begin to feel a sense of fulfillment in engaging in productive behaviors, and in so doing, they become agents of their own change. They start feeling in control of their future and have a newfound purpose in life. Instead of running from the past, they view their prior history as a learning experience, finding a silver lining on an otherwise dark horizon.

## Ethical Challenges in Criminal Justice: A Writing Assignment

Some prison administrators and politicians believe that prisoners are being coddled and have too many privileges. They want to adopt a no-frills policy designed to convince inmates never to repeat their criminal acts. Prisons, they believe, are places of confinement and nothing more. Write an essay that challenges their beliefs. You may want to refer to the sections on rehabilitation and treatment to point out that successful programs do exist and to the sections on prisoners' rights to show that certain kinds of care may be a legal right of inmates, rather than a privilege. *Note:* If you prefer to support aspects of the no-frills policy, please do so, but be sure to acknowledge the information provided in the sections mentioned here.

## SUMMARY

**1. Discuss the problems of the adult correctional system.**

- A significant number of facilities are old and in ill repair.

- More than half of all inmates are held in large, maximum-security institutions.

- Institutions are overcrowded, and meaningful treatment efforts are often a matter of wishful thinking.

**2. Know what is meant by the term "total institution."**

- Prisons in the United States are referred to as total institutions.

- Inmates locked within their walls are segregated from the outside world, kept under constant surveillance, and forced to obey strict official rules to avoid facing formal sanctions.

**3. Differentiate between a no-frills philosophy and a rehabilitation philosophy.**

- Most correctional institutions attempt to help inmates deal with their problems so that they can be rehabilitated and go straight.

- Some correctional administrators refuse to coddle inmates. They employ a no-frills policy, which means that inmates receive the bare minimum of food, services, and medical care required by law.

**4. Chart the "prisonization" process and the development of the inmate social code.**

- Inmates go through a variety of attitude and behavior changes, or cycles, as their sentence unfolds.

- Inmates form their own world, known as the inmate subculture, which has a unique set of norms and rules.

- The traditional inmate subculture included a unique inmate social code—unwritten guidelines that expressed the values, attitudes, and type of behavior that older inmates demanded of young ones.

- The traditional inmate culture has given way to one dominated by race and ethnicity based gangs.

- Those who become the most "prisonized" will be the least likely to reform on the outside.

**5. Compare the lives and cultures of male and female inmates.**

- Unlike male inmates, women usually do not present an immediate physical danger to staff and fellow inmates.

- Make-believe family groups in women's prisons consist of masculine and feminine figures acting as fathers and mothers; some prisoners even act as children and take on the role of brother or sister in these families.

- Female correctional institutions do not get the same level of support as male facilities, and as a result, educational and vocational programs are deficient.

**6. Be familiar with the different forms of correctional treatment.**

- Counseling programs help inmates to control emotions, communicate with others, deal with legal concerns, manage general life issues, and develop and maintain social relationships.

- Most prisons have programs designed to help inmates suffering from alcohol and substance abuse.

- The AIDS-infected inmate has been the subject of great concern.

- Inmate rehabilitation is also pursued through vocational and educational training.

**7. Discuss the world of correctional officers.**

- For many years, prison guards were viewed as ruthless people who enjoyed and exploited their power over inmates, fought rehabilitation efforts, were racist, and had a "lock psychosis" developed over years of counting, numbering, and checking on inmates.

- Correctional officers are now viewed more as dedicated public servants.

- There are few gender differences in the behavior of correctional officers.

**8. Understand the causes of prison violence.**

- Conflict, violence, and brutality are sad but ever-present facts of institutional life.

- Violence can involve individual conflict: inmate versus inmate, inmate versus staff, or staff versus inmate.

- Prison violence has been linked to overcrowding, lack of effective dispute resolution mechanisms, individual inmate history of violence, and poor prison conditions.

**9. Know what is meant by prisoners' rights, and discuss some key privileges that have been granted to inmates.**

- Before the early 1960s, it was accepted that upon conviction, an individual forfeited all legal rights.

- As the 1960s drew to a close, inmates began to be granted legal rights.
- Today inmates have the right to medical care, freedom from cruel and unusual treatment, the right to an attorney, and the right to practice their religion.

**10. Be familiar with the problems of prisoner reentry.**

- Despite all efforts to treat, correct, and rehabilitate incarcerated offenders, more than half return to prison shortly after their release.
- Recidivism may be a by-product of the disruptive effect a prison experience has on personal relationships.
- Ex-inmates may find their home life torn and disrupted when they are finally released.
- Parole failure has been linked to being barred from work opportunities.

## KEY TERMS

total institution, 551
no-frills policy, 551
inmate subculture, 554
inmate social code, 554
prisonization, 555
make-believe family, 559

anger management, 567
work release, 572
furlough, 572
hands-off doctrine, 577
substantive rights, 578
jailhouse lawyer, 578

cruel and unusual punishment, 579
qualified immunity, 581
parole, 583
intensive supervision parole (ISP), 587

## CRITICAL THINKING QUESTIONS

1. Considering the dangers that men face during their prison stay, should nonviolent inmates be placed in separate institutions to protect them from harm?
2. Should women be allowed to work as guards in male prisons? What about male guards in female prisons? Why or why not?
3. Should prison inmates be allowed a free college education while noncriminals must pay tuition? Why or why not? Do you believe in less parole eligibility for prisoners?
4. Define parole, including its purposes and objectives. How does it differ from probation?
5. What is the role of the parole board?
6. Should a former prisoner have all the civil rights afforded the average citizen? Explain.
7. Should people be further penalized after they have paid their debt to society? Why or why not?

## NOTES

1. Letter to *Bryn Mawr Journal*, Winter 2000, www.brynmawr.edu/alumnae/bulletin/letsu01.htm (accessed September 9, 2008).
2. Darryl McGrath, "Brinks Case Decision: Ex-Militant's Parole Buoys Son, Angers Bereaved," *Boston Globe*, September 1, 2003, p. 1.
3. Sarah Lawrence and Jeremy Travis, *The New Landscape of Imprisonment: Mapping America's Prison Expansion* (Washington, D.C.: Urban Institute, 2004), www.urban.org/UploadedPDF/410994_mapping_prisons.pdf (accessed September 9, 2008).
4. James Stephan and Jennifer Karberg, *Census of State and Federal Correctional Facilities, 2000* (Washington, D.C.: Bureau of Justice Statistics, 2003). Updated 2007.
5. Ros Burnett and Shadd Maruna, "So 'Prison Works,' Does It? The Criminal Careers of 130 Men Released from Prison under Home Secretary Michael Howard," *Howard Journal of Criminal Justice* 43 (2004): 390–404.
6. Barbara Sims and Eric Johnston, "Examining Public Opinion about Crime and Justice: A Statewide Study," *Criminal Justice Policy Review* 15 (2004): 270–294.
7. Richard Berk, Heather Ladd, Heidi Graziano, and Jong-Ho Baek, "A Randomized Experiment Testing Inmate Classification Systems," *Criminology and Public Policy* 2 (2003): 215–242.
8. James A. Paluch Jr., *A Life for a Life, Life Imprisonment (America's Other Death Penalty)* (Los Angeles: Roxbury Press, 2004), p. 4.
9. Gresham Sykes, *The Society of Captives* (Princeton, N.J.: Princeton University Press, 1958).
10. Mark Fleisher and Jessie Krienert, "The Culture of Prison Sexual Violence," final report submitted to the National Institute of Justice, November 2006, www.ncjrs.gov/pdffiles1/nij/grants/216515.pdf.
11. Karen Lahm, "Inmate-on-Inmate Assault: A Multilevel Examination of Prison Violence," *Criminal Justice and Behavior* 35 (2008): 120–137.
12. David Eichenthal and James Jacobs, "Enforcing the Criminal Law in State Prisons," *Justice Quarterly* 8 (1991): 283–303.
13. Mark Fleisher and Jessie Krienert, "The Culture of Prison Sexual Violence."
14. Manop Kanato, "Drug Use and Health among Prison Inmates," *Current Opinion in Psychiatry* 21 (2008): 252–254.
15. John Wooldredge, "Inmate Lifestyles and Opportunities for Victimization," *Journal of Research in Crime and Delinquency* 35 (1998): 480–502.
16. Charles Schwaebe, "Learning to Pass: Sex Offenders' Strategies for Establishing a Viable Identity in the Prison General Population,"

*International Journal of Offender Therapy and Comparative Criminology* 49 (2005): 614–625.

17. Mark Kellar and Hsiao-Ming Wang, "Inmate Assaults in Texas County Jails," *Prison Journal* 85 (2005): 515–534.

18. Benjamin Steiner and John Wooldredge, "Inmate versus Environmental Effects on Prison Rule Violations," *Criminal Justice and Behavior* 35 (2008): 438–456.

19. Robert Johnson, *Hard Time: Understanding and Reforming the Prison* (Monterey, Calif.: Brooks/Cole, 1987), p. 115.

20. John Gibbons and Nicholas de B. Katzenbach, *Confronting Confinement: A Report of the Commission on Safety and Abuse in America's Prisons* (New York: Vera Institute of Justice, 2006).

21. Wooldredge, "Inmate Lifestyles and Opportunities for Victimization."

22. Leonore Simon, "Prison Behavior and Victim-Offender Relationships among Violent Offenders," paper presented at the annual meeting of the American Society of Criminology, San Francisco, November 1991.

23. John Irwin, "Adaptation to Being Corrected: Corrections from the Convict's Perspective," in *Handbook of Criminology*, ed. Daniel Glazer (Chicago: Rand McNally, 1974), pp. 971–993.

24. Donald Clemmer, *The Prison Community* (New York: Holt, Rinehart & Winston, 1958).

25. Gresham Sykes and Sheldon Messinger, "The Inmate Social Code," in *The Sociology of Punishment and Corrections*, ed. Norman Johnston, Leonard Savitz, and Marvin Wolfgang (New York: Wiley, 1970), pp. 401–408.

26. Mark Fleisher and Jessie Krienert, "The Culture of Prison Sexual Violence."

27. Ibid.

28. James B. Jacobs, ed., *New Perspectives on Prisons and Imprisonment* (Ithaca, N.Y.: Cornell University Press, 1983); Jacobs, "Street Gangs behind Bars," *Social Problems* 21 (1974): 395–409; Jacobs, "Race Relations and the Prison Subculture," in *Crime and Justice*, vol. 1, ed. Norval Morris and Michael Tonry (Chicago: University of Chicago Press, 1979), pp. 1–28.

29. Nicole Hahn Rafter, *Partial Justice* (New Brunswick, N.J.: Transaction Books, 1990), pp. 181–182.

30. Kathryn Watterson and Meda Chesney-Lind, *Women in Prison: Inside the Concrete Womb* (Boston: Northeastern University Press, 1996).

31. Merry Morash, Robin Harr, and Lila Rucker, "A Comparison of Programming for Women and Men in U.S. Prisons in the 1980s," *Crime and Delinquency* 40 (1994): 197–221.

32. Pamela Schram, "Stereotypes about Vocational Programming for Female Inmates," *Prison Journal* 78 (1998): 244–271.

33. Morash, Harr, and Rucker, "A Comparison of Programming for Women and Men in U.S. Prisons in the 1980s."

34. Vernetta Young and Rebecca Reviere, *Women behind Bars: Gender and Race in U.S. Prisons* (Boulder, Colo.: Lynne Rienner Publishers, 2006).

35. Seena Fazel and John Danesh, "Serious Mental Disorder in 23,000 Prisoners: A Systematic Review of 62 Surveys," *Lancet* 359 (2002): 545–561.

36. Gary Michael McClelland, Linda Teplin, Karen Abram, and Naomi Jacobs, "HIV and AIDS Risk Behaviors among Female Jail Detainees: Implications for Public Health Policy," *American Journal of Public Health* 92 (2002): 818–826.

37. Christine Grella and Lisa Greenwell, "Correlates of Parental Status and Attitudes toward Parenting among Substance-Abusing Women Offenders," *Prison Journal* 86 (2006): 89–113.

38. Lee Ann Slocum, Sally Simpson, and Douglas Smith, "Strained Lives and Crime: Examining Intra-Individual Variation in Strain and Offending in a Sample of Incarcerated Women," *Criminology* 43 (2005): 1067–1110.

39. Lauren Sharkey, "Does Overcrowding in Prisons Exacerbate the Risk of Suicide among Women Prisoners?" *Howard Journal of Criminal Justice* 49 (2010): 111–124.

40. Candace Kruttschnitt and Sharon Krmpotich, "Aggressive Behavior among Female Inmates: An Exploratory Study," *Justice Quarterly* 7 (1990): 370–389.

41. Candace Kruttschnitt, Rosemary Gartner, and Amy Miller, "Doing Her Own Time? Women's Responses to Prison in the Context of the Old and New Penology," *Criminology* 38 (2000): 681–718.

42. Mark Pogrebin and Mary Dodge, "Women's Accounts of Their Prison Experiences: A Retrospective View of Their Subjective Realities," *Journal of Criminal Justice* 29 (2001): 531–541.

43. Shanhe Jiang and L. Thomas Winfree Jr., "Social Support, Gender, and Inmate Adjustment to Prison Life," *Prison Journal* 86 (2006): 32–55.

44. Craig J. Forsyth, Rhonda D. Evans, and D. Buck Foster, "An Analysis of Inmate Explanations for Lesbian Relationships in Prison," *International Journal of Sociology of the Family* 30 (2002): 66–77.

45. Theresa A. Severance, "The Prison Lesbian Revisited," *Journal of Gay and Lesbian Social Services* 17 (2004): 39–57.

46. Edna Erez, "The Myth of the New Female Offender: Some Evidence from Attitudes toward Law and Justice," *Journal of Criminal Justice* 16 (1988): 499–509.

47. Robert Ross and Hugh McKay, *Self-Mutilation* (Lexington, Mass.: Lexington Books, 1979).

48. Alice Propper, *Prison Homosexuality* (Lexington, Mass.: Lexington Books, 1981).

49. Denise Huggins, Loretta Capeheart, and Elizabeth Newman, "Deviants or Scapegoats: An Examination of Pseudofamily Groups and Dyads in Two Texas Prisons," *Prison Journal* 86 (2006): 114–139.

50. Candace Kruttschnitt and Rosemary Gartner, *Marking Time in the Golden State: Women's Imprisonment in California* (Cambridge, England: Cambridge University Press, 2005).

51. Ibid., p. 118.

52. Ibid., p. 92.

53. Ibid., pp. 133–134

54. David Duffee, *Corrections, Practice and Policy* (New York: Random House, 1989), p. 305.

55. Randy Martin and Sherwood Zimmerman, "A Typology of the Causes of Prison Riots and an Analytical Extension to the 1986 West Virginia Riot," *Justice Quarterly* 7 (1990): 711–737.

56. David Allender and Frank Marcell, "Career Criminals, Security Threat Groups, and Prison Gangs," *FBI Law Enforcement Bulletin* 72 (2003): 8–12.

57. Terri Compton and Mike Meacham, "Prison Gangs: Descriptions and Selected Intervention," *Forensic Examiner* 14 (2005): 26–31.

58. Jon Sorensen and Mark Cunningham, "Conviction Offense and Prison Violence: A Comparative Study of Murderers and Other Offenders," *Crime & Delinquency* 56 (2010): 103–125.

59. Grant Harris, Tracey Skilling, and Marnie Rice, "The Construct of Psychopathy," in *Crime and Justice: An Annual Edition*, ed. Michael Tonry (Chicago: University of Chicago Press, 2001), pp. 197–265.

60. For a series of papers on the position, see A. Cohen, G. Cole, and R. Baily, eds., *Prison Violence* (Lexington, Mass.: Lexington Books, 1976).

61. Scott Camp and Gerald Gaes, "Criminogenic Effects of the Prison Environment on Inmate Behavior: Some Experimental Evidence," *Crime and Delinquency* 51 (2005): 425–442.

62. Hans Toch, "Cumulative Default: The Cost of Disruptive Prison Careers," *Criminal Justice and Behavior* 35 (2008): 943–955.

63. *San Antonio Express News*, March 28, 2008.

64. Bert Useem and Michael Resig, "Collective Action in Prisons: Protests, Disturbances, and Riots," *Criminology* 37 (1999): 735–760.

65. Wayne Gillespie, "A Multilevel Model of Drug Abuse inside Prison," *Prison Journal* 85 (2005): 223–246.

66. Section 1435[108]: Prison Rape Elimination Act of 2003; Public Law 108-79 (2003).

67. Wilbert Rideau and Ron Wikberg, *Life Sentences: Rage and Survival Behind Bars* (New York: Times Books, 1992), pp. 78–80.

68. Christopher Hensley, Mary Koscheski, and Richard Tewksbury, "Examining the Characteristics of Male Sexual Assault Targets in a Southern Maximum-Security Prison," *Journal of Interpersonal Violence* 20 (2005): 667–679.

69. Mark Fleisher and Jessie Krienert, *The Myth of Prison Rape: Sexual Culture in American Prisons* (Lanham, Md.: Rowman & Littlefield, 2009),

70. Tonisha Jones and Travis Pratt, "The Prevalence of Sexual Violence in Prison," *International Journal of Offender Therapy and Comparative Criminology* 52 (2008): 280–295.

71. Kristine Levan Miller, "The Darkest Figure of Crime: Perceptions of Reasons for Male Inmates to Not Report Sexual Assault," *Justice Quarterly* (2009): 1–21(online version), http://pdfserve.informaworld.com.libproxy.uml.edu/832253_731219438._915759575.pdf.

72. Christopher Hensley and Richard Tewksbury, "Wardens' Perceptions of Prison Sex," Prison Journal 85 (2005): 186–197.

73. Allen J. Beck and Timothy A. Hughes, *Sexual Violence Reported by Correctional Authorities, 2004* (Washington, D.C.: Bureau of Justice Statistics, 2005).

74. Allen J. Beck and Paige M. Harrison, *Sexual Victimization in State and Federal Prisons Reported by Inmates, 2007* (Washington, D.C.: Bureau of Justice Statistics, 2007), www.ojp.usdoj.gov/bjs/pub/pdf/svsfpri07.pdf.

75. Thomas Noll, "Sexual Violence in Prison," *International Journal of Offender Therapy and Comparative Criminology* 52 (2008): 251–252.

76. James Austin, Tony Fabelo, Angela Gunter, and Ken McGinnis, *Sexual Violence in the Texas Prison System*, final report submitted to the National Institute of Justice, September 2006, www.ncjrs.gov/pdffiles1/nij/grants/215774.pdf (accessed April 28, 2010).

77. Meda Chesney-Lind, "Vengeful Equity: Sentencing Women to Prison," in *The Female Offender: Girls, Women, and Crime*, ed. Medea Chesney-Lind and Lisa J. Pasko (Thousand Oaks, Calif.: Sage, 1997).

78. General Accounting Office, *Women in Prison: Sexual Misconduct by Correctional Staff* (Washington, D.C.: U.S. Government Printing Office, 1999).

79. Rebecca Trammell, "Relational Violence in Women's Prison: How Women Describe Interpersonal Violence and Gender," *Women & Criminal Justice* 19 (2009): 267–285.

80. Dianna Newbern, Donald Dansereau, and Urvashi Pitre, "Positive Effects on Life Skills Motivation and Self-Efficacy: Node-Link Maps in a Modified Therapeutic Community," *American Journal of Drug and Alcohol Abuse* 25 (1999): 407–410.

81. Rose Parkes and Charlotte Bilby, "The Courage to Create: The Role of Artistic and Spiritual Activities in Prisons," *Howard Journal of Criminal Justice* 49 (2010): 97–110.

82. Steven D. Vannoy and William T. Hoyt, "Evaluation of an Anger Therapy Intervention for Incarcerated Adult Males," *Journal of Offender Rehabilitation* 39 (2004): 40.

83. University of South Australia, School of Psychology, www.unisa.edu.au/psychology/research/CAPR/FPRG.asp (accessed September 9, 2008).

84. Byron R. Johnson, "Religious Programming, Institutional Adjustment and Recidivism among Former Inmates in Prison Fellowship Programs," *Justice Quarterly* 21 (2004): 329–354.

85. Charles McDaniel, Derek Davis, and Sabrina Neff, "Charitable Choice and Prison Ministries: Constitutional and Institutional Challenges to Rehabilitating the American Penal System," *Criminal Justice Policy Review* 16 (2005): 164–189.

86. Lawrence T. Jablecki, "A Critique of Faith-Based Prison Programs," *Humanist* 65 (2005): 11–16.

87. Ibid.

88. Nancy G. LaVigne, Diana Brazzell, and Kevonne Small, *Evaluation of Florida's Faith- and Character-Based Institutions: Final Report* (Washington, D.C.: Urban Institute, 2007).

89. Kate Dolan, James Shearer, Bethany White, Zhou Jialun, John Kaldor, and Alex Wodak, "Four-Year Follow-up of Imprisoned Male Heroin Users and Methadone Treatment: Mortality, Re-incarceration and Hepatitis C Infection," *Addiction* 100 (2005): 820–828.

90. James Inciardi, Steven Martin, and Clifford Butzin, "Five-Year Outcomes of Therapeutic Community Treatment of Drug-Involved Offenders after Release from Prison," *Crime and Delinquency* 50 (2004): 88–107; Clayton Mosher and Dretha Phillips, "The Dynamics of a Prison-Based Therapeutic Community for Women Offenders: Retention, Completion, and Outcomes," *Prison Journal* 86 (2006): 6–31.

91. Mary Stohr, Craig Hemmens, Diane Baune, Jed Dayley, Mark Gornik, Kirstin Kjaer, and Cindy Noon, *Residential Substance Abuse Treatment for State Prisoners: Breaking the Drug-Crime Cycle among Parole Violators* (Washington, D.C.: National Institute for Justice, 2003).

92. Wayne Welsh, "A Multisite Evaluation of Prison-Based Therapeutic Community Drug Treatment," *Criminal Justice and Behavior* 34 (2007): 1481–1498.

93. Daniel Werb, Thomas Kerr, Will Small, Kathy Li, Julio Montaner, and Evan Wood, "HIV Risks Associated with Incarceration among Injection Drug Users: Implications for Prison-Based Public Health Strategies," *Journal of Public Health* 30 (2008): 126–132; Will Small, S. Kain, Nancy Laliberte, Martin Schechter, Michael O'Shaughnessy, and Patricia Spittal, "Incarceration, Addiction and Harm Reduction: Inmates Experience Injecting Drugs in Prison," *Substance Use and Misuse* 40 (2005): 831–843.

94. Howard Skolnik and John Slansky, "A First Step in Helping Inmates Get Good Jobs after Release," *Corrections Today* 53 (1991): 92.

95. Federal Bureau of Prisons web page concerning UNICOR Federal Prison Industries, Inc., retrieved September 9, 2008, from www.unicor.gov/fpi_contracting/.

96. Public Law 96-157, Sec. 827, codified as 18 U.S.C., Sec. 1761(c).

97. Courtesy of the Prison Industry Authority, 560 East Natoma Street, Folsom, California 95630-2200.

98. Diane Dwyer and Roger McNally, "Public Policy, Prison Industries, and Business: An Equitable Balance for the 1990s," *Federal Probation* 57 (1993): 30–35.

99. Douglas Lipton, Robert Martinson, and Judith Wilks, *The Effectiveness of Correctional Treatment: A Survey of Treatment Evaluation Studies* (New York: Praeger, 1975).

100. Charles Murray and Louis Cox, *Beyond Probation: Juvenile Corrections and the Chronic Delinquent* (Beverly Hills, Calif.: Sage, 1979).

101. Steven Lab and John Whitehead, "An Analysis of Juvenile Correctional Treatment," *Crime and Delinquency* 34 (1988): 60–83.

102. James Wilson and Robert Davis, "Good Intentions Meet Hard Realities: An Evaluation of the Project Greenlight Reentry Program," *Criminology and Public Policy* 5 (2006): 303–338.

103. Paula Smith, Paul Gendreau, and Kristin Swartz, "Validating the Principles of Effective Intervention: A Systematic Review of the Contributions of Meta-Analysis in the Field of Corrections," *Victims & Offenders* 4 (2009): 148–169.

104. Paul Gendreau and Robert Ross, "Effective Correctional Treatment: Bibliotherapy for Cynics," *Crime and Delinquency* 27 (1979): 463–489.

105. Robert R. Ross and Paul Gendreau, eds., *Effective Correctional Treatment* (Toronto: Butterworth, 1980), p. viii; Paul Gendreau and Robert R. Ross, "Revivification or Rehabilitative Evidence," *Justice Quarterly* 4 (1987): 349–407.

106. Robert Martinson, "New Findings, New Views: A Note of Caution Regarding Sentencing Reform," *Hofstra Law Review* 7 (Winter 1979): 244.

107. Mark W. Lipsey and Francis T. Cullen, "The Effectiveness of Correctional Rehabilitation: A Review of Systematic Reviews," *Annual Review of Law and Social Science* 3 (2007): 297–320.

108. Francis Cullen and Karen Gilbert, *Reaffirming Rehabilitation* (Cincinnati, Ohio: Anderson Publications, 1982).

109. Michael Caldwell, Michael Vitacco, and Gregory Van Rybroek, "Are Violent Delinquents Worth Treating? A Cost–Benefit Analysis," *Journal of Research in Crime and Delinquency* 43 (2006): 148–168.

110. Sheila French and Paul Gendreau, "Reducing Prison Misconducts: What Works!" *Criminal Justice and Behavior* 33 (2006): 185–218.

111. David Wilson, Catherine Gallagher, and Doris MacKenzie, "A Meta-Analysis of Corrections-Based Education, Vocation, and Work Programs for Adult Offenders," *Journal of Research in Crime and Delinquency* 37 (2000): 347–368.

112. Mary Ellen Batiuk, Paul Moke, and Pamela Wilcox Rountree, "Crime and Rehabilitation: Correctional Education as an Agent of Change—A Research Note," *Justice Quarterly* 14 (1997): 167–180.

113. David Wilson, Leana Bouffard, and Doris MacKenzie, "A Quantitative Review of Structured, Group-Oriented, Cognitive-Behavioral Programs for Offenders," *Criminal Justice and Behavior* 32 (2005): 172–204; Mark Lipsey and David Wilson, "Effective Intervention for Serious Juvenile Offenders: A Synthesis of Research," in *Serious and Violent Juvenile Offenders: Risk Factors and Successful Interventions*, ed. Rolf Loeber and David Farrington (Thousand Oaks, Calif.: Sage, 1998).

114. Megan Kurlychek and Cynthia Kempinen, "Beyond Boot Camp: The Impact of Aftercare on Offender Reentry," *Criminology and Public Policy* 5 (2006): 363–388.

115. David Farrington and Brandon Welsh, "Randomized Experiments in Criminology: What Have We Learned in the Last Two Decades?" *Journal of Experimental Criminology* 1 (2005): 9–38.

116. Lucien X. Lombardo, *Guards Imprisoned* (New York: Elsevier, 1981); James Jacobs and Norma Crotty, "The Guard's World," in *New Perspectives on Prisons and Imprisonment*, ed. James Jacobs (Ithaca, N.Y.: Cornell University Press, 1983), 133–141.

117. Claire Mayhew and Duncan Chappell, "An Overview of Occupational Violence," *Australian Nursing Journal* 9 (2002): 34–35.

118. John Klofas and Hans Toch, "The Guard Subculture Myth," *Journal of Research in Crime and Delinquency* 19 (1982): 238–254.

119. Ruth Triplett and Janet Mullings, "Work-Related Stress and Coping among Correctional Officers: Implications from the Organizational Literature," *Journal of Criminal Justice* 24 (1996): 291–308.

120. Eric Lambert, Nancy Hogan, and Irshad Altheimer, "An Exploratory Examination of the Consequences of Burnout in Terms of Life Satisfaction, Turnover Intent, and Absenteeism among Private Correctional Staff," *The Prison Journal* 90 (2010): 94–114.

121. Stephen Owen, "Occupational Stress among Correctional Supervisors," *Prison Journal* 86 (2006): 164–181; Eugene Paoline, Eric Lambert, and Nancy Hogan, "A Calm and Happy Keeper of the Keys: The Impact of ACA Views, Relations with Coworkers, and Policy Views on the Job Stress and Job Satisfaction of Jail Staff," *Prison Journal* 86 (2006): 182–205.

122. Mike Vuolo and Candace Kruttschnitt, "Prisoners' Adjustment, Correctional Officers, and Context: The Foreground and Background of Punishment in Late Modernity," *Law & Society Review* 42 (2008): 307–335.

123. Richard Tewksbury and Sue Caner Collins, "Aggression Levels among Correctional Officers: Reassessing Sex Differences," *Prison Journal* 86 (2006): 327–343.

124. *Dothard v. Rawlinson*, 433 U.S. 321 (1977).

125. Dana Britton, *At Work in the Iron Cage: The Prison as Gendered Organization* (New York: New York University Press, 2003), Ch. 6.

126. National Advisory Commission on Criminal Justice Standards and Goals, *Corrections* (Washington, D.C.: U.S. Government Printing Office, 1973), p. 18.

127. *Cooper v. Pate*, 378 U.S. 546 (1964).

128. Prison Litigation Reform Act P.L. 104-134, 110 Stat. 1321 (2006); 42 U.S.C. § 1997e (1994 ed. & Supp. II).

129. *Booth v. Churner*, U.S. 731 (2001); *Porter v. Nussle*, 534 U.S. 516 (2002).

130. ACLU, "Know Your Rights: The Prison Litigation Reform Act (PLRA)," www.aclu.org/images/asset_upload_file79_25805.pdf (accessed May 1, 2010).

131. *Shaw v. Murphy* No. 99-1613 (2007).

132. *O'Lone v. Estate of Shabazz*, 482 U.S. 342 (1987).

133. Ibid., p. 349.

134. *Cutter v. Wilkinson* No. 03-9877 (2005).

135. *Newman v. Alabama*, 92 S.Ct. 1079 (1972).

136. *Estelle v. Gamble*, 429 U.S. 97 (1976).

137. Ibid.

138. Lester Wright, "*Health Care in Prison Thirty Years after Estelle v. Gamble*," *Journal of Correctional Health Care* 14 (2008): 31–35.

139. *Trop v. Dulles*, 356 U.S. 86 (1958); see also *Furman v. Georgia*, 408 U.S. 238 (1972).

140. *Weems v. United States*, 217 U.S. 349 (1910).

141. *Lee v. Tahash*, 352 F.2d 970 (1965).

142. *Estelle v. Gamble*, 429 U.S. 97 (1976).

143. *Robinson v. California*, 370 U.S. 660 (1962).

144. *Gregg v. Georgia*, 428 U.S. 153 (1976).

145. *Jackson v. Bishop*, 404 F.2d 571 (1968).

146. *Farmer v. Brennan*, 511 U.S. 825 (1994).

147. Ibid., at 843 n. 8.

148. *Hudson v. McMillian*, U.S. 1 (1992).

149. *Hope v. Pelzer* et al., 536 U.S. 730 (2002).

150. *L.A. Times*, "Report Predicted Violence at Chino Prison Dorm Hit by Race Riots," August 10, 2009, http://latimesblogs.latimes.com/lanow/2009/08/report-warned-of-violence-at-chino-prison-baracks-hit-by-race-riots.html (accessed August 11, 2009).

151. *Johnson v. California*, 543 U.S. 499 (2005).

152. *Bell v. Wolfish*, 99 S.Ct. 1873-1974 (1979); see "*Bell v. Wolfish: The Rights of Pretrial Detainees*," *New England Journal of Prison Law* 6 (1979): 134.

153. *Farmer v. Brennan*, 511 U.S. 825 (1994).

154. *Rhodes v. Chapman*, 452 U.S. 337 (1981); for further analysis of *Rhodes*, see Randall Pooler, "Prison Overcrowding and the Eighth Amendment: The Rhodes Not Taken," *New England Journal on Criminal and Civil Confinement* 8 (1983): 1–28.

155. Lauren Glaze and Thomas Bonczar, *Probation and Parole in the United States, 2006* (Washington, D.C.: Bureau of Justice Statistics, 2007).

156. Sandra Crockett Mack and Khalil Osiris, "Successful Reentry, One Case at a Time," *Corrections Today* 69 (2007): 50–55.

157. Carolin Kröner, Cornelis Stadtland, Matthias Eidt, and Norbert Nedopil, "The Validity of the Violence Risk Appraisal Guide (VRAG) in Predicting Criminal Recidivism," *Criminal Behaviour and Mental Health* 17 (2007): 89–100.

158. Kathryn Campbell and Myriam Denov, "The Burden of Innocence: Coping with a Wrongful Imprisonment," *Canadian Journal of Criminology and Criminal Justice* 46 (2004): 139–164.

159. *Pennsylvania Board of Probation and Parole v. Scott*, 524 U.S. 357 (1998); Duncan N. Stevens, "Off the Mapp: Parole Revocation Hearings and the Fourth Amendment," *Journal of Criminal Law and Criminology* 89 (1999): 1047–1060.

160. Gregg Etter and Judy Hammond, "Community Service Work as Part of Offender Rehabilitation," *Corrections Today* 63 (2001): 114–117.

161. Brian Parry, "Special Service Unit: Dedicated to Investigating and Apprehending Violent Offenders," *Corrections Today* 63 (2001): 120.

162. Thomas Hanlon, David N. Nurco, Richard W. Bateman, and Kevin E. O'Grady, "The Response of Drug Abuser Parolees to a Combination of Treatment and Intensive Supervision," *Prison Journal* 78 (1998): 31–44; Susan Turner and Joan Petersilia, "Focusing on High-Risk Parolees: An Experiment to Reduce Commitments to the Texas Department of Corrections," *Journal of Research in Crime and Delinquency* 29 (1992): 34–61.

163. Mario Paparozzi and Paul Gendreau, "An Intensive Supervision Program That Worked: Service Delivery, Professional Orientation, and Organizational Supportiveness," *Prison Journal* 85 (2005): 445–466.

164. Joan Petersilia, "When Prisoners Return to Communities: Political, Economic, and Social Consequences," *Federal Probation* 65 (2001): 3–9.

165. Lauren Glaze and Thomas Bonczar, *Probation and Parole in the United States, 2008* (Washington, D.C.: Bureau of Justice Statistics, 2009), http://bjs.ojp.usdoj.gov/content/pub/pdf/ppus08 .pdf

166. Patrick A. Langan and David J. Levin, *Recidivism of Prisoners Released in 1994* (Washington, D.C.: Bureau of Justice Statistics, 2002).

167. Robyn L. Cohen, *Probation and Parole Violators in State Prison, 1991: Survey of State Prison Inmates, 1991* (Washington, D.C.: Bureau of Justice Statistics, 1995).

168. Beth Huebner, Christina DeJong, and Jennifer Cobbina, "Women Coming Home: Long-Term Patterns of Recidivism," Justice Quarterly 27 (2010): 225–254.

169. Brent Benda, "Gender Differences in Life-Course Theory of Recidivism: A Survival Analysis," *International Journal of Offender Therapy and Comparative Criminology* 49 (2005): 325–342.

170. Pamela Schram, Barbara Koons-Witt, Frank Williams, and Marilyn Mcshane, "Supervision Strategies and Approaches for Female Parolees: Examining the Link between Unmet Needs and Parolee Outcome," *Crime and Delinquency* 52 (2006): 450–471.

171. D. W. Seal, G. D. Eldrige, D. Kacanek, D. Binson, R. J. MacGowan and the Project START Study Group, "A Longitudinal, Qualitative Analysis of the Context of Substance Use and Sexual Behavior among 18- to 29-Year-Old Men after Their Release from Prison," *Social Science and Medicine* 65 (2007): 2394–2406.

172. James Bonta, Moira Law, and Karl Hanson, "The Prediction of Criminal and Violent Recidivism among Mentally Disordered Offenders: A Meta-analysis," *Psychological Bulletin* 123 (1998): 123–142.

173. Roger Peters, Paul Greenbaum, John Edens, Chris Carter, and Madeline Ortiz, "Prevalence of DSM-IV Substance Abuse and Dependence Disorders among Prison Inmates," *American Journal of Drug and Alcohol Abuse* 24 (1998): 573–580.

174. Catherine Hamilton, Louise Falshaw, and Kevin D. Browne, "The Link between Recurrent Maltreatment and Offending Behavior," *International Journal of Offender Therapy and Comparative Criminology* 46 (2002): 75–95.

175. Peters, Greenbaum, Edens, Carter, and Ortiz, "Prevalence of DSM-IV Substance Abuse and Dependence Disorders among Prison Inmates."

176. J. E. Ryan, "Who Gets Revoked? A Comparison of Intensive Supervision Successes and Failures in Vermont," *Crime and Delinquency* 43 (1997): 104–118.

177. Bonnie Todis, Michael Bullis, Miriam Waintrup, Robert Schultz, and Ryan D'Ambrosio, "Overcoming the Odds: Qualitative Examination of Resilience among Formerly Incarcerated Adolescents," *Exceptional Children* 68 (2001): 119–140.

178. Leslee Goodman Hornick, "Volunteer Program Helps Make Inmates' Families Feel Welcome," *Corrections Today* 53 (1991): 184–186.

179. Jeffrey Fagan and Richard Freeman, "Crime and Work," in *Crime and Justice: A Review of Research*, vol. 25, ed. Michael Tonry (Chicago: University of Chicago Press, 1999), pp. 211–229.

180. Rachelle Giguere and Lauren Dundes, "Help Wanted: A Survey of Employer Concerns about Hiring Ex-Convicts," *Criminal Justice Policy Review* 13 (2002): 396–408.

181. John Hagan and Ronit Dinovitzer, "Collateral Consequences of Imprisonment for Children, Communities, and Prisoners," in *Crime and Justice: A Review of Research*, vol. 26, ed. Michael Tonry and Joan Petersilia (Chicago: University of Chicago Press, 1999), pp. 89–107.

182. Thomas Hanlon, David Nurco, Richard Bateman, and Kevin O'Grady, "The Response of Drug Abuser Parolees to a Combination of Treatment and Intensive Supervision." The Prison Journal 78 (1998): 31–44

183. Beth Huebner, "Racial and Ethnic Differences in the Likelihood of Marriage: The Effect of Incarceration," *Justice Quarterly* 24 (2007): 156–183.

184. Laura Fishman, *Women at the Wall: A Study of Prisoners' Wives Doing Time on the Outside* (New York: State University of New York Press, 1990).

185. *Beth Huebner and Mark Berg,* "Examining the Sources of Variation in Risk for Recidivism," *Justice Quarterly* (online version), November 25, 2009, www.informaworld.com.libproxy.uml .edu/smpp/content~db=all~content=a917141588.

186. Jeremy Travis and Joan Petersilia, "Reentry Reconsidered: A New Look at an Old Question," *Crime and Delinquency* 47 (2001): 291–313.

187. Joan Petersilia, *When Prisoners Come Home: Parole and Prisoner Reentry* (New York: Oxford University Press, 2003); Petersilia, "Hard Time Ex-Offenders Returning Home after Prison," *Corrections Today* 67 (2005): 66–72; Petersilia, "When Prisoners Return to Communities."

188. Stephen Metraux and Dennis Culhane, "Recent Incarceration History among a Sheltered Homeless Population," *Crime and Delinquency* 52 (2006): 504–517.

189. Petersilia, "Hard Time Ex-Offenders Returning Home after Prison."

190. Bruce Way, Donald Sawyer, Stephanie Lilly, Catherine Moffitt, and Barbara Stapholz, "Characteristics of Inmates Who Received a Diagnosis of Serious Mental Illness upon Entry to New York State Prison," *Psychiatric Services* 59 (2008): 1335–1337.

191. Stacy Adams, "Richmond Program Helps Former Female Inmates," *Crisis* 113 (2006): 8.

192. *Beth Huebner, Christina DeJong and Jennifer Cobbina,* "Women Coming Home: Long-Term Patterns of Recidivism," *Justice Quarterly* 27 (2020): 225–254.

193. Richard Seiter, "Prisoner Reentry and the Role of Parole Officers," *Federal Probation* 66 (2002). 50–54.

194. Charis Kubrin and Eric Stewart, "Predicting Who Reoffends: The Neglected Role of Neighborhood Context in Recidivism Studies," *Criminology* 44 (2006): 165–197.

195. Federal Bureau of Prisons, "Release Preperation," www.bop.gov/ inmate_programs/release_emp.jsp (accessed April 22, 2010).

196. This section relies on Jeremy Travis, Anna Crayton, and Debbie Mukamal, "*A New Era in Inmate Reentry*," *Corrections Today* 71 (2009): 38–41.

197. Project Safe Neighborhoods, http://www.psn.gov/

198. Hanlon, Nurco, Bateman, and O'Grady, "The Response of Drug Abuser Parolees to a Combination of Treatment and Intensive Supervision."

199. Kathleen Olivares, Velmer Burton, and Francis Cullen, "The Collateral Consequences of a Felony Conviction: A National Study of State Legal Codes Ten Years Later," *Federal Probation* 60 (1996): 10–17.

200. See, for example, *Bush v. Reid*, 516 P.2d 1215 (Alaska, 1973); *Thompson v. Bond*, 421 F.Supp. 878 (W.D. Mo., 1976); *Delorne v. Pierce Freightlines Co.*, 353 F.Supp. 258 (D. Or., 1973); and *Beyer v. Werner*, 299 F.Supp. 967 (E.D. N.Y., 1969).

201. Hanlon, Nurco, Bateman, and O'Grady, "The Response of Drug Abuser Parolees to a Combination of Treatment and Intensive Supervision."

202. Paul Hirschfield and Alex Piquero, "Normalization and Legitimation: Modeling Stigmatizing Attitudes toward Ex-Offenders," *Criminology* 48 (2010): 27–55.

203. Shadd Maruna, *Making Good: How Ex-Convicts Reform and Rebuild Their Lives* (Washington, D.C.: American Psychological Association, 2000).

## PART FIVE

# CONTEMPORARY CHALLENGES IN CRIMINAL JUSTICE

WHEN ASKED WHAT CRIMES SCARE THEM, most people express fear over murders, rapes, assaults, and other "traditional" crimes that make newspaper headlines and are featured on the evening news. It is not often that someone worries about being killed by a child in a mass shooting at a public school, being caught in the crossfire of rival camps in an international criminal syndicate, or being the victim of a terrorist attack. These problems, heinous as they are, are uncommon, relatively isolated, and therefore not on most people's minds as they go about their daily lives. But such problems are of great interest to criminal justice practitioners, because they are among those who serve on the front lines of the battle to keep us free and safe from dangers of this kind.

Juvenile crime is one of those harms that does not necessarily benefit from the traditional approach of locking up offenders and throwing away the keys. Sometimes a more delicate approach is needed, especially in the case of kids who have not yet chosen a life of crime. Kevin Kellems, a juvenile probation officer in Calhoun County, Michigan, says that "the goal of the juvenile system is treatment. The law requires that treatment be attempted in the home and community if possible." Of course, a treatment-oriented (rather than enforcement-oriented) approach can be difficult to plan and apply, because not everyone is amenable to change. Kevin's job is also challenging because much of his time is spent "working with a population of young people and their families, which are often highly chaotic and dysfunctional."

Terrorism, too, is a difficult problem that has only recently become a priority for the criminal justice system. The September 11, 2001, terrorist attacks caused a dramatic change in the priorities of the federal government. The Department of Homeland Security was created, and the priorities of several law enforcement agencies were changed to emphasize the prevention of terrorist attacks. Mark O., a special agent with the Department of Homeland Security, is one of many people who was moved by the 9/11 attacks and decided to do something to help protect his country. He became a special agent with Immigration and Customs Enforcement (ICE), conducting criminal investigations into suspected, alleged, and known violations of federal law. Because of the nature of his work, we cannot divulge his identity. He does say, however, that in his line of work it can take years to make a case, that there are rarely any "smoking guns," and that convictions are secured after the painstaking accumulation of a great deal of evidence. "Investigations require patience, and answers aren't always clear-cut, so an investigator must maintain a high level of alertness, flexibility, and focus." ∎

*THE FOLLOWING THREE CHAPTERS explore special topics in criminal justice. Chapter 16 covers juvenile justice. Chapter 17, a new chapter, focuses on crimes that have arisen in the wake of the technological revolution, including corporate enterprise crime, cyber crime, and transnational organized crime. Chapter 18, another new chapter, considers the criminal justice response to terrorism. Although at first glance these chapters may seem to address very different topics, they share a unifying theme: Each examines a set of issues and problems that the traditional tools of the criminal justice system (those introduced in the last four sections of this book) are not always equipped to handle.*

*"The goal of the juvenile system is treatment. The law requires that treatment be attempted in the home and community if possible."*

# CHAPTER 16

# Juvenile Justice

## CHAPTER OBJECTIVES

1. Describe the nature and purpose of the juvenile justice system.
2. Be familiar with the history and development of juvenile justice.
3. Discuss the child savers and their vision of juvenile justice.
4. Describe the beginnings of the independent juvenile court.
5. Cite the changes in juvenile justice that began in the 1960s and continue today.
6. Describe police processing of juvenile offenders.
7. Discuss the detention of juveniles.
8. Discuss the problems and legal issues surrounding the waiver decision.
9. Chart the juvenile trial and sentencing process.
10. Discuss efforts to treat troubled kids in the juvenile justice system. Next outline the arguments of those who believe that treatment in the juvenile justice system is ineffective and should be abolished. Then cite the arguments of those who believe it should be retained.

**I**t was a case that shook the Commonwealth of Massachusetts to its core: On January 19, 2007, 16-year-old John Odgren followed James Alenson, a young boy he had never met, into the bathroom at Lincoln-Sudbury Regional High School, drew out a long knife, and stabbed him to death. Because he was 16 at the time, Massachusetts law required that Odgren be charged as an adult, and he was tried on a charge of first-degree murder before a jury in Middlesex Superior Court. Odgren's attorney, Jonathan Shapiro, defended him by suggesting that he was delusional and psychotic at the time of the murder: "Why did a geeky, uncoordinated, awkward 16-year-old who had never been in any trouble with the law suddenly and without provocation ferociously stab to death a 15-year-old classmate who he did not even know?" Shapiro said. "The illnesses that John Odgren suffers from made him lose touch with reality." According to the defense, Odgren has attention-deficit/hyperactivity disorder, depression, anxiety, and possibly bipolar disorder and also suffers from Asperger syndrome, a form of autism whose symptoms include significant difficulties in social interaction, repetitive patterns of behavior and interests, physical clumsiness, and atypical use of language. Odgren was reportedly obsessed with the number 19, and the fact that he committed his crime on the 19th day of the month was not viewed as a coincidence. The prosecution did not deny that Odgren had a history of mental illness but maintained that his condition was not serious enough to be considered legal insanity; he was not delusional and knew that his actions were a crime. The jury heard that Odgren had a history of secretly bringing knives to school and enjoying violent novels, as if he were carefully planning "the perfect murder." After two weeks of testimony, the jurors rejected the defense argument that Odgren was criminally insane when he randomly selected Alenson as his target. The jury also rejected the option of the lesser offense of second-degree murder, which would have made Odgren eligible for parole after 15 years. Under state law, Odgren's first-degree murder conviction was automatically reviewed and upheld by the State Supreme Judicial Court.[1] ■

The Odgren case is representative of the difficult choices that agents of the juvenile justice system are continually asked to make: How should troubled children be treated? What can be done to treat dangerous young offenders? Should youthful law violators be given special treatment because of their age, or should they be treated in a similar fashion to an adult committing the same crime? Is it fair to place a troubled youth such as John Odgren in prison for the rest of his life without the possibility of parole (more on this later)? But what about the victim, in this case James Alenson? Doesn't he deserve justice also? He did nothing to prompt his attacker. Why should his death go unpunished? And if Odgren's attack was the product of a mental defect, is the juvenile justice system really equipped to help him, and if not, how can we ever be sure that he is "cured"?

Independent of (yet interrelated with) the adult criminal justice system, the juvenile justice system is primarily responsible for dealing with juvenile and youth crime, as well as with incorrigible and truant children and runaways. Conceived at the turn of the twentieth century, the juvenile justice system was originally viewed as a quasi–social welfare agency that was to act as a surrogate parent in the interests of the child; this is referred to as the **parens patriae** philosophy. Many people who work in the system still adhere to the original social welfare principles of the juvenile justice system. In contrast, those who take a crime control orientation suggest that the juvenile justice system's parens patriae philosophy is outdated. They question whether the system really is designed to handle youths who commit serious violent acts, such as John Odgren, whose acts were brutal but certainly not unique. They point to nationally publicized incidents of juvenile violence, such as the shootings at Columbine High School in Colorado, as indicators that serious juvenile offenders are out there and that something must be done to protect society from their depraved and violent acts. In the Odgren case, this meant trying him as an adult and giving him a life sentence. Violent young criminals, they suggest, should be punished and disciplined rather than treated and rehabilitated. "Why should we give special treatment to violent young juveniles?" they ask. "After all, juveniles commit 10 percent of all the murders and 15 percent of all rapes."[2]

It remains to be seen whether the juvenile justice system will continue on its path toward deterrence, punishment, and control or return to its former role as a treatment-dispensing agency. This chapter reviews the history of juvenile justice and discusses the justice system's processing of youthful offenders.

## THE HISTORY OF JUVENILE JUSTICE

The modern practice of legally separating adult and juvenile offenders can be traced to two developments in English custom and law: poor laws and chancery courts. Both were designed to allow the state to take control of the lives of needy, but not necessarily criminal, children.[3] They set the precedent for later American developments.

As early as 1535, the English passed statutes known as **poor laws,** which in part mandated the appointment of overseers who placed destitute or neglected children with families who then trained them in agricultural, trade, or domestic services; this practice was referred to as indenture. The Elizabethan poor laws of 1601 created a system of church wardens and overseers who, with the consent of justices of the peace, identified vagrant, delinquent, and neglected children and took measures to put them to work. Often this meant placing them in poorhouses or workhouses or, more commonly, apprenticing them until their adulthood. The indenture, or involuntary apprentice, system set the precedent, which continues today, of allowing the government to take control of youths who have committed no illegal acts but are deemed unable to care for themselves.

In contrast, **chancery courts** protected the property rights and welfare of more affluent minor children who could not care for themselves—children whose position and property were of direct concern to the monarch. They dealt with issues of guardianship and the use and control of property. Chancery courts

**parens patriae**
Latin term meaning "father of his country." According to this legal philosophy, the government is the true guardian of the needy and infirm including dependent children. It refers to the power of the state to act on behalf of a child and provide care and protection equivalent to that of a parent.

**poor laws**
Sixteenth-century English laws under which vagrants and abandoned and neglected children were bound to masters as indentured servants.

**chancery courts**
Early English courts established to protect the property rights and welfare of the minor children of affluent families.

operated under the parens patriae philosophy, which held that children were under the protective control of the state and that its rulers were justified in intervening in their lives.[4] In the famous English case *Wellesley v. Wellesley*, a duke's children were taken from him in the name of parens patriae because of his scandalous behavior.[5]

The concept of parens patriae came to represent the primacy of the state and its power to act in "the best interests of the child." In the twentieth century, the idea that the state was legally obligated to protect the immature, the incompetent, the neglected, and the delinquent became a major influence on the development of the U.S. juvenile justice system.

## Care of Children in Early America

The forced apprenticeship system and the poor laws were brought from England to colonial America. Poor laws were passed in Virginia in 1646 and in Connecticut and Massachusetts in 1678, and they continued in force until the early nineteenth century. They mandated care for wayward and destitute children. However, those youths who committed serious criminal offenses were tried in the same courts as adults.

To accommodate dependent youths, local jurisdictions developed almshouses, poorhouses, and workhouses. Crowded and unhealthy, these accepted the poor, the insane, the diseased, and vagrant and destitute children. Middle-class civic leaders, who referred to themselves as **child savers,** began to develop organizations and groups to help alleviate the burdens of the poor and immigrants by sponsoring shelter care for youths, educational and social activities, and the development of settlement houses. In retrospect, their main focus seems to have been on extending government control over a whole range of youthful activities that previously had been left to private or family control, including idleness, drinking, vagrancy, and delinquency.[6]

## The Child-Saving Movement

The child savers were responsible for creating a number of programs for indigent youths, including the New York House of Refuge, which began operations in 1825.[7] Its creation was effected by prominent Quakers and influential political leaders, such as Cadwallader Colden and Stephen Allen. In 1816 they formed the Society for the Prevention of Pauperism, which was devoted to protecting indigent youths who were at risk of leading a life of crime by taking them off the streets and reforming them in a family-like environment.[8]

The first House of Refuge constructed in New York City was the product of their reform efforts. Although the program was privately managed, the state legislature began providing funds partly through a head tax on arriving transatlantic passengers and seamen, plus the proceeds from license fees for New York City's taverns, theaters, and circuses. These revenue sources were deemed appropriate, given that supporters blamed immigration, intemperance, and commercial entertainment for juvenile crime.

The reformatory opened on January 1, 1825, with only six boys and three girls. However, within the first decade of its operation, 1,678 youths were admitted. Most kids were sent to the reformatory because of vagrancy and petty crimes and were sentenced or committed indefinitely until they reached adulthood. Originally, the institution accepted inmates from across the state, but when a Western House of Refuge was opened in Rochester, New York, in 1849, residents of the original reformatory came only from the eastern quarters.

In the reformatory, a large part of the adolescent's daily schedule was devoted to supervised labor, which was regarded as beneficial to education and

© The Granger Collection, New York

*This nineteenth century photo shows indigent boys sleeping on the front door landing of an abandoned tenement building in New York City. The child savers were concerned that if left alone, children such as these would enter a life of crime. Critics, however, accused the child savers of class and race discrimination and thought they sought to maintain control over the political system.*

**child savers**
Civic leaders who focused their attention on the misdeeds of poor children to control their behavior.

discipline. Inmate labor also supported operating expenses for the reformatory. Male inmates worked in shops that produced brushes, cane chairs, brass nails, and shoes. Female inmates sewed uniforms, did laundry, and carried out other domestic work. A badge system was used to segregate inmates according to their behavior. Although students acquired a rudimentary education, greater emphasis was placed on evangelical religious instruction; non-Protestant clergy were excluded. The reformatory had the authority to commit inmates to indenture agreements with private employers. Most males became farm workers; most females became domestic laborers.

## The Reform Movement Spreads

When the House of Refuge opened, the majority of children admitted were status offenders placed there because of vagrancy or neglect. Children were put in the institution by court order, sometimes over parents' objections. Their length of stay depended on need, age, and skill. Critics complained that the institution was run like a prison, with strict discipline and absolute separation of the sexes. Such a harsh program drove many children to run away, and the House of Refuge was forced to take a more lenient approach. Despite criticism, the concept enjoyed expanding popularity. In 1826 the Boston City Council founded the House of Reformation for juvenile offenders.[9] The courts committed children found guilty of criminal violations, or found to be beyond the control of their parents, to these schools. Because the child savers considered parents of delinquent children to be as guilty as convicted offenders, they sought to have the reform schools assume control over the children. Refuge managers believed they were preventing poverty and crime by separating destitute and delinquent children from their parents and placing them in an institution.[10]

The child savers also influenced state and local governments to create independent correctional institutions to house minors. The first of these reform schools opened in Westboro, Massachusetts, in 1848 and in Rochester, New York, in 1849. Other states soon followed suit—Ohio in 1850 and Maine, Michigan, and Rhode Island in 1860. Children lived in congregate conditions and spent their days working at institutional jobs, learning a trade when possible, and receiving some basic education. They were racially and sexually segregated, discipline was harsh and often involved whipping and isolation, and the physical care was of poor quality.

In 1853 New York philanthropist Charles Loring Brace helped develop the **Children's Aid Society** as an alternative for dealing with neglected and delinquent youths. Brace proposed rescuing wayward youths from the harsh environment of the city and providing them with temporary shelter and care. He then sought to place them in private homes in rural communities where they could engage in farming and agricultural work outside the harsh influence of the city.

Although some placements proved successful, others resulted in the exploitation of children in a strange environment with few avenues of escape.

## Establishment of the Juvenile Court

As the nation expanded, it became evident that private charities and public organizations were not caring adequately for the growing number of troubled youths. The child savers lobbied for an independent, state-supported **juvenile court**, and their efforts prompted the development of the first comprehensive juvenile court in Illinois in 1899. The Illinois Juvenile Court Act set up an independent court to handle criminal law violations by children under 16 years of age, as well as to care for neglected, dependent, and wayward youths. The act also created a probation department to monitor youths in the community and to direct juvenile court judges to place serious offenders in secure schools for boys and industrial schools for girls. The ostensible purpose of the act was to separate juveniles from adult offenders and provide a legal framework in which juveniles could get

**Children's Aid Society**
A group created by Charles Loring Brace to place indigent city children with farm families.

**juvenile court**
A court that has original jurisdiction over persons defined by statute as legal minors and alleged to be involved in juvenile delinquency or status offenses. In some jurisdictions, these are family courts that also deal with custody and neglect issues.

adequate care and custody. By 1925, most states had developed juvenile courts. Enactment of the Juvenile Court Act of 1899 was a major event in the history of the juvenile justice movement in the United States.

Although the creation of the first independent juvenile courts were originally seen as liberal reforms, modern scholars commonly view them as the product of the upper classes' attempt to control and punish those in the lower classes of society.[11] Thus, according to this revisionist approach, the reformers applied the concept of parens patriae for their own purposes, which included the perpetuation of middle- and upper-class values, control over the political system, and the maintenance of a child labor system that exploited lower-class workers with marginal skills.

The juvenile court movement quickly spread across the United States. In its early form it provided youths with quasi-legal, quasi-therapeutic, personalized justice. The main concern was the "best interests of the child," not strict adherence to legal doctrine, constitutional rights, or due process of law. The court was paternalistic, not adversarial. For example, attorneys were not required. Hearsay evidence, inadmissible in criminal trials, was commonly employed in the adjudication of juvenile offenders. Children were encouraged to admit their guilt in open court in violation of their Fifth Amendment rights. Verdicts were based on a "preponderance of the evidence" instead of "beyond a reasonable doubt." Juvenile courts functioned as quasi–social service agencies.

**REFORM SCHOOLS** Youngsters who were found delinquent in juvenile court could spend years in a state training school. Though priding themselves on not being punitive, these early reform schools were generally aimed at punishment and were based on the concept of reform through hard work and discipline. In the second half of the nineteenth century, the emphasis shifted from massive industrial schools to the cottage system. Juvenile offenders were housed in a series of small cabins, each one holding 20 to 40 children, run by "cottage parents" who attempted to create a home-like atmosphere. The first cottage system was established in Massachusetts, the second in Ohio. The system was generally applauded as a great improvement over the industrial training schools. It represented a general movement away from punishment and toward rehabilitation by attending to the needs of the individual and by implementing complex programs of diagnosis and treatment.[12] In the 1950s, the influence of such therapists as Karen Horney and Carl Rogers promoted the introduction of psychological treatment in juvenile corrections. Group counseling techniques became standard procedure in most juvenile institutions.

**JUVENILE JUSTICE 1960–1980** In the 1960s and 1970s the U.S. Supreme Court radically altered the juvenile justice system when it issued a series of decisions that established the right of juveniles to due process of law.[13] The Court ruled that juveniles had the same rights as adults in important areas of trial process, including the right to confront witnesses, notice of charges, and the right to counsel (These cases are set out on page 632). That brought procedural due process to the juvenile justice system. Also during this period, Congress passed the Juvenile Justice and Delinquency Prevention Act of 1974 (the JJDP Act), which established the federal Office of Juvenile Justice and Delinquency Prevention (OJJDP).[14] This legislation was enacted to identify the needs of youths and to fund programs in the juvenile justice system. Some of the most important provisions of the act were to insulate juveniles from contact with more dangerous and/or older offenders. In practice, this meant that juveniles who were being held by the state for noncriminal actions such as cutting school or running away from home (referred to as **status offenders**) could not be detained in the same institutions with delinquent youths who had committed actual crimes. The *deinstitutionalization of status offenders and nonoffenders*

**status offender**
A noncriminal youth who falls under the jurisdiction of the juvenile court by reason of having engaged in behavior prohibited to minors, such as being truant from school, running away from home, or being habitually disobedient and ungovernable.

## CONCEPT SUMMARY 16.1
### *Shifting Philosophies of Juvenile Justice*

■ Before 1899: Juveniles treated similarly to adult offenders. Little distinction by age was made between youth and adults who committed criminal acts.

■ 1899–1950s: Children treated differently, beginning with the Illinois Juvenile Court Act of 1899. By 1925, juvenile court acts established in virtually every state. Parens patriae philosophy dominates.

■ 1950–1970: Recognition by experts that the rehabilitation model and the protective nature of parens patriae had failed to prevent delinquency.

■ 1970–1980: Introduction of constitutional due process into the juvenile justice system. Experimentation with diversion and concern about stigma and labeling. Juvenile Justice and Delinquency Prevention Act of 1974 enacted.

■ 1980–2000: Rising juvenile crime rates coupled with the perceived failure of rehabilitation to control delinquency led to a shift to a crime control and punishment philosophy similar to that of the adult criminal justice system. Focus on expanding the crime control capabilities of the juvenile justice system so that it resembles the adult system.

■ 2000–today: Balanced approach. Attempt to provide treatment to needy youth and get tough with dangerous repeat offenders. Restorative justice.

provision of the JJDP Act mandated that juveniles not charged with conduct that would be crimes for adults "shall not be placed in secure detention facilities or secure correctional facilities." In addition, delinquents were expected to be removed from facilities housing adults and, failing that, were protected from having any sight or sound contact with adult inmates who were in custody because they were awaiting trial on criminal charges or had been convicted of a crime. The "sight and sound" provision requires that juvenile and adult inmates not be able to see each other and that no conversation between them be possible.

*JUVENILE JUSTICE 1980–2000* During the last two decades of the twentieth century, public concern over juvenile crime helped reshape the philosophy of the juvenile justice system. The media picked up on stories of violent juvenile gangs, school shootings, and juvenile predators. Media frenzy helped fuel legislative change. States began to pass laws that made it easier to exclude from juvenile court jurisdiction juveniles who commit serious crimes such as violent acts or drug trafficking. Some states gave prosecutors greater discretion to prosecute cases directly in criminal court rather than in juvenile court, and other states passed laws making it easier to transfer juvenile offenders to the criminal justice system, where they could be treated as adults. Many states increased the length and severity of sentences allowed for juvenile offenders. There was also an effort to make juvenile proceedings more open, an effort that included making juvenile records and court proceedings, which had historically been kept confidential, more easily accessible to the public. The victims' rights movement invaded the juvenile court, and the victims of juvenile crime were now being heard during court proceedings. In sum, as a reaction to a rising tide of juvenile crime, the juvenile justice system was modified to look and act more like the adult system.[15]

The various stages in juvenile justice history are set out in Concept Summary 16.1.

**FIGURE 16.1**
Chart of Juvenile Justice Case Flow

Source: Office of Juvenile Justice and Delinquency Prevention, http://ojjdp.ncjrs.gov/ojstatbb/structure_process/case.html.

## Juvenile Justice Today

Today, the juvenile justice system has jurisdiction over two distinct categories of offenders: delinquents and status offenders.[16] The term **juvenile delinquency** refers to children who fall under a jurisdictional age limit, which varies from state to state, and who commit an act in violation of the penal code. Status offenders, in contrast, commit acts forbidden to minors, which include truancy and being a habitually disobedient and ungovernable child (see Figure 16.1). They are commonly characterized in state statutes as persons or children in need of supervision (PINS or CHINS). Most states distinguish such behavior from delinquent conduct to reduce the effect of any stigma on children, although in most jurisdictions status offenders can be placed on probation, much as delinquent offenders can. In most instances, however, they cannot be placed in secure facilities that hold delinquent offenders. In addition, juvenile courts generally have jurisdiction over situations involving conduct directed at (rather than committed by) juveniles, such as parental neglect, deprivation, abandonment, and abuse.

> **juvenile delinquency**
> Participation in illegal behavior by a minor who falls under a statutory age limit.

The states have also set different maximum ages below which children fall under the jurisdiction of the juvenile court. Many states include all children under 18 years of age, others set the limit at 17, and still others at 16.

Some states exclude certain classes of offenders or offenses from the juvenile justice system. Those youths who commit serious violent offenses such as rape or murder may be automatically excluded from the juvenile justice system and treated as adults on the premise that they stand little chance of rehabilitation within the confines of the juvenile system. Juvenile court judges may also waive, or transfer to the adult justice system, repeat offenders whom they deem untreatable by the juvenile authorities.

Another trend has been to create family courts, which include a broad range of family- and child-related issues within their jurisdictions. Family courts are in use or are being considered in more than half of U.S. states. These are designed to provide more individualized, client-focused treatment than traditional juvenile courts and to bring a holistic approach to helping kids and their families rather than focusing on punishing and/or controlling delinquency.[17]

**EXHIBIT 16.1**

## Similarities and Differences between Juvenile and Adult Justice Systems

| Similarities | Differences |
|---|---|
| ■ Discretion used by police officers, judges, and correctional personnel | ■ The primary purpose of juvenile procedures is protection and treatment; with adults, the aim is to punish the guilty. |
| ■ Right to receive *Miranda* warning | ■ Jurisdiction is determined by age in the juvenile system, by the nature of the offense in the adult system. |
| ■ Protection from prejudicial lineups or other identification procedures | ■ Juveniles can be apprehended for acts that would not be criminal if committed by an adult (status offenses). |
| ■ Procedural safeguards when making an admission of guilt | ■ Juvenile proceedings are not considered criminal; adult proceedings are criminal matters. |
| ■ Advocacy roles of prosecutors and defense attorneys | ■ Juvenile court proceedings are generally informal and private; adult court proceedings are more formal and are open to the public. |
| ■ Right to counsel at most key stages of the court process | ■ Courts cannot release to the press identifying information about a juvenile. |
| ■ Availability of pretrial motions | ■ Parents are highly involved in the juvenile process but not in the adult process. |
| ■ Plea negotiation/plea bargaining | ■ The standard of arrest is more stringent for adults than for juveniles. |
| ■ Right to a hearing and an appeal | ■ Juveniles are released into parental custody; adults are generally given bail. |
| ■ Standard of proof beyond a reasonable doubt | ■ Juveniles have no constitutional right to a jury trial in school without probable cause or a warrant. |
| ■ Pretrial detention possible | ■ A juvenile's record is generally sealed when the age of majority is reached; an adult's record is permanent. |
| ■ Detention without bail if considered dangerous | ■ A juvenile court cannot sentence juveniles to county jails or state prisons. |
| ■ Probation as a sentencing option | ■ The U.S. Supreme Court has declared that the Eighth Amendment prohibits the death penalty for juveniles under age 18. |
| ■ Community treatment as a sentencing option | ■ Juveniles waived to adult court cannot get a life sentence for a non-capital crime. |

The juvenile justice system has evolved into a parallel yet independent system of justice with its own terminology and rules of procedure. Exhibit 16.1 describes the basic similarities and differences between the juvenile and adult justice systems. Exhibit 16.2 points out how the language used in the juvenile court differs from that used in the adult system.

Today, the juvenile justice system is responsible for processing and treating almost 2 million cases of youthful misbehavior annually. Each state's system is unique, so it is difficult to give a precise accounting of the justice process. Keeping this in mind, the following sections offer a general description of some key processes and decision points in juvenile justice. Figure 16.1 shows a model of the juvenile justice process.

**EXHIBIT 16.2**

## Comparison of Terms Used in Adult and Juvenile Justice Systems

| | Juvenile Terms | Adult Terms |
|---|---|---|
| The person and the act | Delinquent child | Criminal |
| | Delinquent act | Crime |
| Preadjudicatory stage | Take into custody | Arrest |
| | Petition | Indictment |
| | Agree to a finding | Plead guilty |
| | Deny the petition | Plead not guilty |
| | Adjustment | Plea bargain |
| | Detention facility; child-care shelter | Jail |
| Adjudicatory stage | Substitution | Reduction of charges |
| | Adjudicatory or fact-finding hearing | Trial |
| | Adjudication | Sentencing hearing |
| Postadjudicatory stage | Dispositional hearing | Sentence |
| | Disposition | Incarceration |
| | Commitment | Prison |
| | Youth development center; treatment center; training school | |
| | Residential child-care facility | Halfway house |
| | Aftercare | Parole |

## POLICE PROCESSING OF THE JUVENILE OFFENDER

According to the Uniform Crime Reports, police officers arrest more than 1.5 million juveniles ages each year, including about 400,000 under age 15.[18] Most large police departments have detectives who handle only juvenile delinquency cases and focus their attention on the problems of youth. In addition to conducting their own investigations, they typically take control of cases after an arrest is made by a uniformed officer.

Most states do not have specific statutory provisions distinguishing the arrest process for children from that for adults. Some jurisdictions, however, give broad arrest powers to the police in juvenile cases by authorizing the officer to make an arrest whenever he or she believes the child's behavior falls within the jurisdiction of the juvenile court. Consequently, police may arrest youths for behavior considered legal for adults, including running away, curfew violations, and being in possession of alcohol.

### Use of Discretion

When a juvenile is found to have engaged in delinquent or incorrigible behavior, police agencies are charged with deciding whether to release or to detain the child and refer her to juvenile court.

Because of the state's interest in the child, the police generally have more discretion in the investigatory and arrest stages of the juvenile process than they do when dealing with adult offenders. This discretionary decision—to release or to detain—is based not only on the nature of the offense but also

## RACE, GENDER, AND CULTURE IN CRIMINAL JUSTICE

# Minority Overrepresentation in Juvenile Justice

It has long been charged that police are more likely to act formally with African American suspects and to use their discretion to benefit European Americans. Many studies have found that African Americans are disproportionately stopped by police and that race is the primary reason for this practice. African American youths are arrested at a rate disproportionate to their representation in the population.

One reason for this phenomenon is that minority and lower-class neighborhoods experience much greater police scrutiny than white, middle-class areas, and their residents face a greater chance of arrest. For example, a significant body of literature shows that police are more likely to "hassle" or arrest African American males in poor neighborhoods. It is therefore not surprising that, as Harvard criminologist Robert Sampson has found, teenage residents of neighborhoods with low socioeconomic status (SES) have a significantly greater chance of acquiring police records than youths living in higher-SES areas, regardless of the actual crime rates in these areas. Sampson's research indicates that even though police officers may not discriminate on an individual level, departmental policy that focuses on lower-class areas may result in class and racial bias in the police processing of delinquent youth.

Once arrested, minority youths face other problems as they are processed through the system. Those accused of delinquent acts are less likely than European American youths to be diverted from the court system into informal sanctions and are more likely to receive sentences involving incarceration. Today, more than six in ten juveniles in custody belong to racial or ethnic minorities. In some states, the ratio of minority custody to white custody is four or more to one. Minority youths are also waived to the adult justice system at a rate that is greater than their representation in the population. About 40 percent of all waived youths are African Americans, even though they represent less than a third of the juvenile court population.

Racial disparity in juvenile disposition is an ongoing problem that demands immediate public scrutiny. In response, many jurisdictions have initiated studies of racial disproportion in their juvenile justice systems, along with responding to federal requirements to reduce disproportionate minority confinement (DMC), as contained in the Juvenile Justice and Delinquency Prevention Act of 2002. The most recent federal government report on state compliance to reduce DMC demonstrates that some progress has been made but that many challenges remain, including the basic need to identify factors that contribute to DMC (at least 18 states have yet to initiate this process), incomplete and inconsistent data systems, and the need for ongoing evaluation of focused interventions and system-wide efforts to reduce DMC.

The disproportionate minority representation in juvenile correctional facilities is a very serious matter, but it also reflects the racial disparity that occurs at every stage of the juvenile justice process. A disproportionate number of minority youths suffer arrest, detention, waivers, and so on. It is not surprising then that they also face disparity in the probability of incarceration.

The National Council on Crime and Delinquency report "Treatment of Youth of Color in the Justice System" describes how minority youths receive differential treatment at every stage of the justice process. Among the findings from the council's report are these:

■ Although African American youths make up 16 percent of the adolescent population in the United States, they constitute 38 percent of the almost 100,000 youths confined in local detention and state correctional systems. They are overrepresented in all offense categories.

■ Youths of color make up the majority of young people held in both public and private facilities.

■ Youths of color, especially Latino youths, are a much larger proportion of the young in public

## Overrepresentation of Minority Youth in the Justice System

From 2002 to 2004 African Americans were represented in the following proportions:

- 16% of youths in the United States
- 28% of juvenile arrests
- 30% of referrals to juvenile court
- 37% of the detained population
- 34% of youths formally processed by the juvenile court

- 30% of adjudicated youths
- 35% of youths judicially waived to criminal court
- 38% of youths in residential placement
- 58% of youths admitted to state adult prison

Source: National Council on Crime and Delinquency, "*And Justice for Some: Differential Treatment of Minority Youth in the Justice System*," January 2007.

facilities than in private facilities, which tend to be less harsh environments.

- Although they represent just 34 percent of the U.S. population, youths of color are 62 percent of young people in detention, 66 percent of those committed to public facilities, and 55 percent of those committed to private facilities.

- Nationwide, youths of color are represented in the detained population at 3.1 times the rate of white youths, are committed to public facilities at 2.9 times the rate of white youths, and are committed to private institutions at 2.0 times the rate of white youths.

- Overall, custody rates are four times greater for African American youths than for white youths. Custody rates for Latino and Native American youths are 1.8 and 2.6 times the custody rate for white youths, respectively (See Exhibit A).

The council report concludes with this statement:

Even though "Equal Justice Under the Law" is the foundation of our legal system, and is carved on the front of the U.S. Supreme Court building, the juvenile justice system is anything but equal for all. Throughout the system, youths of color—especially African American youths—receive different and harsher treatment. This is true even when white youths and youths of color are charged with similar offenses. This report documents a juvenile justice system that is "separate and unequal." It is time for a nationwide effort to identify the causes of this differential treatment of youths of color and to mount a concerted campaign to provide a fair and equal justice system for juveniles in this country.

To try to alleviate this problem, since 1988 the Juvenile Justice and Delinquency Prevention Act has required that in order to receive certain funding, states must monitor whether the proportion of juvenile minorities in confinement exceeds their proportion in the general population.[19] Achieving the goal of proportional representation has been elusive in actual practice. A number of strategies have been attempted, ranging from cultural competency training to providing increasing community-based detention alternatives.[20] But, as the National Council report indicates, the problem of racial disparity has proved difficult to overcome.

Sources: Mark Soler and Lisa M. Garry, *Reducing Disproportionate Minority Contact: Preparation at the Local Level* (Washington, D.C.: Office of Juvenile Justice and Delinquency Prevention, 2009), www.ncjrs.gov/pdffiles1/ojjdp/218861.pdf; Emily Cabaniss, James Frabutt, Mary Kendrick, and Margaret Arbuckle, "Reducing Disproportionate Minority Contact in the Juvenile Justice System: Promising Practices," *Aggression & Violent Behavior* 12 (2007): 393–401; Howard N. Snyder and Melissa Sickmund, *Juvenile Offenders and Victims: 2006 National Report* (Washington, D.C.: Office of Juvenile Justice and Delinquency Prevention, 2006), available online at http://ojjdp.ncjrs.gov/ojstatbb/nr2006/downloads/NR2006.pdf (accessed March 26, 2009); John F. Chapman, Rani A. Desai, Paul R. Falzer, and Randy Borum, "Violence Risk and Race in a Sample of Youth in Juvenile Detention: The Potential to Reduce Disproportionate Minority Confinement," *Youth Violence and Juvenile Justice* 4 (2006): 170–184; Robert Sampson, "Effects of Socioeconomic Context on Official Reaction to Juvenile Delinquency," *American Sociological Review* 51 (1986): 876–885; Heidi M. Hsia, George S. Bridges, and Rosalie McHale, *Disproportionate Minority Confinement: 2002 Update: Summary* (Washington, D.C.: Office of Juvenile Justice and Delinquency Prevention, 2004): National Council on Crime and Delinquency, *And Justice for Some: Differential Treatment of Minority Youth in the Justice System*, January 2007, www.nccd-crc.org/nccd/pubs/2007jan_justice_for_some.pdf (accessed March 26, 2009), Public Law 93-415, 42 USC 5601 et seq., amended 1992.

on police attitudes and the child's social and personal conditions at the time of the arrest:

- The type and seriousness of the child's offense
- The ability of the parents to be of assistance in disciplining the child
- The child's past contacts with police
- The degree of cooperation obtained from the child and parents and their demeanor, attitude, and personal characteristics
- Whether the child denies the allegations in the petition and insists on a court hearing[21]

Whereas police officers' actions in cases involving adults are usually controlled by the law and their own judgment or discretion, cases involving a juvenile demand that the officer consider the "best interests of the child" and how the officer's actions will influence the child's future well-being.[22] A recent study found that although young people are significantly more likely to be arrested than adults, a disrespectful demeanor on the part of juveniles did not increase the likelihood of their arrest.[23] This research may indicate that police are more willing to arrest juveniles if they perceive the youths are in need of services and not if they are disrespectful. Two-thirds (66 percent) of all juvenile arrests are now being referred to juvenile court for treatment and supervision; most of the rest are handled informally at the station or sent to social services. Police today may be more cautious with juveniles and more willing to refer them to juvenile court services than in the past.

One of the more troubling issues of discretion is whether race plays a role in decision making and, if it does, how that affects the entire system of juvenile justice. This is the topic of the accompanying Race, Gender, and Culture in Criminal Justice feature.

## Legal Rights of Juveniles in Custody

Once a juvenile has been taken into custody, the child has the same Fourth Amendment right as an adult to be free from unreasonable searches and seizures. Children in police custody can be detained prior to trial, interrogated, and placed in lineups. However, because of their youth and inexperience, children are generally afforded more protections than adults. Police must be careful that the juvenile suspect understands his constitutional rights and, if there is some question, must provide access to a parent or guardian to protect the child's legal interests. In the past, police often questioned juveniles in the absence of their parents or an attorney. Any incriminatory statements or confessions made by juveniles could be placed in evidence at their trials. That is no longer permissible, and children have the same (or more) *Miranda* rights as adults, which was confirmed in the case of *Fare v. Michael C.* (1979).[24] Today, police will interrogate a juvenile without an adult present only if they believe that the youth is unquestionably mature and experienced enough to understand her legal rights.[25]

Legal expert Barry Feld finds that police interrogation tactics with juveniles are quite similar to their questioning of adults. Once juveniles waive their *Miranda* rights, police used the same strategies and tactics to question them, including the use of false statements and evidence. Juveniles responded to those tactics, cooperated or resisted, and provided incriminating evidence at about the same rate as did adults. Feld's conclusion: The law treats juveniles just like adults, and police question them just as they do older suspects. Although the questioning was somewhat more benign than Feld had expected, the danger of false confessions and convictions still exists.[26]

## Legal Rights in the School Setting

Because a great deal of juvenile crime occurs on school grounds, police departments have been stationing officers within schools. These police officers are generally referred to as school resource officers (SROs). The increased presence of

**CourseMate** For more information about a **police juvenile division**, visit the Criminal Justice CourseMate at CengageBrain. com, then access the "Web Links" for this chapter.

© Thomas Barwick/The Image Bank/Getty Images

*Students do not lose their rights at the schoolhouse door. However, they do not have the same protections as adults in society. For example, they can be searched without a warrant if they violate school rules, even if their behavior does not amount to a crime. And although they have the right to limited, passive free speech, such as wearing a peace symbol, they can be suspended if school officials believe that their behavior constitutes a security risk. For example, writing an article in the school newspaper explaining how to smoke marijuana might not be allowed.*

law enforcement officers within schools raises the question of the legal rights of students in the educational environment. The issue of student privacy relates not only to police but also to school officials, who often assume quasi-police powers over children. Both police officers and school officials may wish to search students to determine whether they are in possession of contraband, such as drugs or weapons; to search their lockers and desks; and to interrogate them about illegal activities.

In *New Jersey v. T.L.O.* (1985), the U.S. Supreme Court held that a school official had the authority to search a student's purse even though no warrant had been was issued and no probable cause existed that a crime had been committed, only a suspicion that T.L.O. had violated school rules.[27] This case involved an assistant principal's search of the purse of a 14-year-old female student who had been observed smoking a cigarette in a school lavatory. The assistant principal found cigarette-rolling papers when a pack of cigarettes was removed from the purse. A further search revealed marijuana and several items indicating marijuana selling. As a result, T.L.O. was adjudicated as a delinquent. The Supreme Court held that the Fourth Amendment protections against unreasonable searches and seizures apply to students but that the need to maintain an orderly educational environment modified the usual Fourth Amendment requirements of warrants and probable cause. The Court relaxed the usual probable cause standard and found the search to be reasonable. It declared that the school's right to maintain discipline on school grounds allowed it to search students and their possessions as a safety precaution. The Court, which had guarded the warrant requirement and its exceptions in the past, now permits warrantless searches in school, based on the lesser standard of "reasonable suspicion." This landmark decision did not deal with other thorny issues, however, such as the search and seizure of contraband from a student's locker or desk.

**SEARCHING FOR DRUGS**  Faced with crime by students in public schools, particularly illicit drug use, school administrators have gone to extreme measures to enforce drug-control statutes and administrative rules. Some urban schools routinely employ breathalyzers, drug-sniffing dogs, hidden video cameras, and

**CourseMate**  For more information about **juveniles and the law**, visit the Criminal Justice CourseMate at CengageBrain.com, then access the "Web Links" for this chapter.

routine searches of students' pockets, purses, lockers, and cars. In general, courts consider such searches permissible when they are not overly offensive and when reasonable grounds are found to suspect that the student has violated the law. School administrators are walking a tightrope between a student's constitutional right to privacy and school safety. The Supreme Court has allowed school authorities to conduct random drug tests on the grounds that these are less intrusive than a search of a student's body. In the 1995 case *Vernonia School District 47J v. Acton*, the Court allowed the testing of student athletes who were going off campus to engage in events.[28] Underlying this decision is the recognition that drug use is a serious threat to public safety that interferes with the right of children to receive a decent and safe education. Although drug tests are intrusive, maintaining school safety was viewed as outweighing the attendant minor inconvenience and loss of personal privacy. In a subsequent case, *Board of Education of Independent School District No. 92 of Pottawatomie County et al. v. Earls et al.*, the Court extended the right to test for drugs without probable cause to all students as long as the drug-testing policies were "reasonable." In this instance, the need for applying swift and informal disciplinary procedures to maintain order in a public school outweighs the right to personal privacy. Because the school's responsibility for children cannot be disregarded, it would not be unreasonable to search students for evidence of drug usage even if no single student was suspected of abusing drugs.

The Court also ruled that, within this context, students have a limited expectation of privacy. In their complaint, the students argued that children participating in nonathletic extracurricular activities have a stronger expectation of privacy than athletes who regularly undergo physicals as part of their participation in sports. The Court disagreed, however, maintaining that students who participate in competitive extracurricular activities voluntarily subject themselves to many of the same intrusions on their privacy as do athletes.[29]

**LIMITING DRUG SEARCHES**   How far can school officials go in their efforts to preserve a safe school environment? The Court clarified this issue in *Safford Unified School District v. Redding*, a 2009 case that drew national headlines. Savana Redding was a 13-year-old eighth-grade honors student at Safford Middle School, located about 127 miles from Tucson, Arizona, when on October 3, 2003, she was taken out of class by the school's vice principal.

Savana Redding is flanked by her mother, April Redding, and her attorney, Adam Wolf, as she speaks to reporters outside the Supreme Court in Washington on April 21, 2009. Redding was 13 when Safford (Arizona) Middle School officials, on a tip from another student, ordered her to remove her clothes and shake out her underwear. They were looking for ibuprofen pills because the school had banned prescription and over-the-counter drugs from campus. The Supreme Court ruled that the search was humiliating and unjustified by the circumstances, a ruling that set a precedent limiting the right of schools to conduct drug-related searches.

© Jim Wilson/*New York Times*/Redux

It seems that one of Redding's classmates had been caught possessing four prescription-strength ibuprofen pills (400 mg, the strength of two Advils), and when asked where she got the pills, she blamed Redding, who had no history of disciplinary issues or drug abuse. Although Redding claimed that she had no knowledge of the pills, she was subjected to a strip search by the school nurse and another female employee, because the school has a zero-tolerance policy for all over-the-counter medication (which students could not possess without prior written permission). During the search, Redding was forced to strip to her underwear and her bra, and her underpants were pulled away from her body.[30] On June, 25, 2009, the Supreme Court held that Redding's Fourth Amendment rights were indeed violated by the search. With Justice David Souter writing for the majority, the Court agreed that search measures used by school officials to root out contraband must be "reasonably related to the objectives of the search and not excessively intrusive in light of the age and sex of the student and the nature of the infraction."

## THE JUVENILE COURT PROCESS

After the police have determined that a case warrants further attention, they bind it over to the prosecutor's office, which then is responsible for channeling the case through the juvenile court. In addition, cases may be petitioned to the court from other than law enforcement sources, such as when educational authorities ask the court to intervene in cases of truancy or parents directly petition the court asking that their child be considered a status offender. The juvenile court plays a major role in controlling juvenile behavior and delivering social services to children in need.

U.S. juvenile courts process an estimated 1.6 million delinquency cases each year. The juvenile court delinquency caseload today is four times as large as it was in 1960.

**CourseMate** For more information about the **juvenile justice process**, visit the Criminal Justice CourseMate at CengageBrain.com, then access the "Web Links" for this chapter.

### The Intake Process

After police processing, the juvenile offender is usually remanded to the local juvenile court's intake division. At this juncture, court intake officers or probation personnel review and initially screen the child and the family to determine whether the child needs to be handled formally or the case can be settled without the necessity of costly and intrusive official intervention. Their report helps the prosecutor decide whether to handle the case informally or bind it over for trial. The intake stage represents an opportunity to place a child in informal programs both within the court and in the community. The intake process also is critically important because more than half of the referrals to the juvenile courts never go beyond this stage.

### The Detention Process

After a juvenile is formally taken into custody, either as a delinquent or as a status offender, the prosecutor usually decides whether to release the child to the parent or guardian or to detain the child in a secure shelter pending trial.

**Detention** has always been a controversial area of juvenile justice. Far too many children have been routinely placed in detention while awaiting court appearances. Status offenders and delinquents have been held in the same facility, and in many parts of the country, adult county jails were used to detain juvenile offenders. The Juvenile Justice Act of 1974 emphasized reducing the number of children placed in inappropriate detention facilities. Even though the act was largely successful, the practice continues.

Despite such measures, hundreds of thousands of youths, most of whom are already living under difficult circumstances, are placed in pretrial detention each year. Many have suffered long histories of abuse and mental health problems.[31] The detention decision may reflect a child's personal characteristics

**detention**
The temporary care of a child alleged to be a delinquent or status offender who requires secure custody, pending court disposition.

and the quality of his or her home life, rather than any dangerousness or flight risk.[32] Detention is widely misapplied, according to the report by the Justice Policy Institute, a Washington, D.C.–based group, because detention facilities are meant to temporarily house those youths who are likely to reoffend before their trial or who are unlikely to appear for their court date, but many of the youths in this country's more than 750 detention centers do not meet these criteria. Seventy percent of youths in detention are held for nonviolent charges. More than two-thirds are charged with property offenses, public-order offenses, technical probation violations, or status offenses (such as running away or breaking curfew).[33]

The number of delinquency cases involving detention has increased significantly during the past decades. The largest relative increase was for drug offense cases. The data also shows that a disproportionate number of African American youths were detained before trial. Whereas less than 20 percent of delinquency cases involving white juveniles included detention at some point between referral and disposition, about 25 percent of black juveniles involved in delinquency cases and 20 percent of youths of other races are detained. The disproportionate representation of minority youths in detention is a troubling aspect of juvenile justice.

*LEGAL ISSUES*   Most state statutes ordinarily require a hearing on the appropriateness of detention if the initial decision is to keep the child in custody. At this hearing, the child has a right to counsel and may be given other procedural due process safeguards, notably the privilege against self-incrimination and the right to confront and cross-examine witnesses. Most state juvenile court acts provide criteria to support a decision to detain the child. These include (a) the need to protect the child, (b) whether the child presents a serious danger to the public, and (c) the likelihood that the juvenile will return to court for adjudication. Whereas in adult cases most offenders are released if they can afford bail, juveniles may be detained for a variety of reasons, including their own protection. Normally, the finding of the judge that the child should be detained must be supported by factual evidence. In the 1984 case of *Schall v. Martin*, the U.S. Supreme Court upheld the right of the states to detain a child before trial to protect his welfare and the public safety.[34]

*REFORMING DETENTION*   There has been an ongoing effort to reform detention. The most important reform has been the successful effort to remove status offenders from lockups containing delinquents. After decades of effort, nearly all states have passed laws requiring that status offenders be placed in nonsecure shelters, rather than in secure detention facilities, thereby reducing their contact with more dangerous delinquent youths.

Another serious problem is the detention of youths in adult jails. This practice is common in rural areas where there are relatively few separate facilities for young offenders.[35] The OJJDP has given millions of dollars in aid to encourage the removal of juveniles from adult lockups. These grants have helped jurisdictions develop intake screening procedures, specific release or detention criteria, and alternative residential and nonresidential programs for juveniles awaiting trial. By 1980, amendments to the act mandating the absolute removal of juveniles from jails had been adopted. Despite such efforts, many states are not complying with the removal provisions and still detain juveniles in adult jails. Adding to their numbers are youths who commit nonserious acts—such as runaways—but are apprehended in rural areas where there are no juvenile facilities. There are also states that define the age limit for delinquency as 16 or 17 and therefore treat minors of that age as legal adults. At the time of the last available jail census, more than 7,000 persons under age 18 were housed in adult jails. Because jail stays are of short duration, it is likely that hundreds of thousands of minors are held in adult jails each year.

Whatever the actual number jailed today, placing young offenders in adult jails continues to be a significant problem in the juvenile justice system. Juveniles detained in adult jails often live in squalid conditions and are subject to physical and sexual abuse. The practice is widely condemned, but eliminating the confinement of juveniles in adult institutions remains a difficult task.

## Bail

If a child is not detained, the question of bail arises. Federal courts have not found it necessary to rule on the issue of a juvenile's constitutional right to bail because liberal statutory release provisions act as appropriate alternatives. Although only a few state statutes allow release on money bail, many others have juvenile code provisions that emphasize the release of the child to the parents as an acceptable substitute. A constitutional right to bail that on its face seems to benefit a child may have unforeseen results. The imposition of money bail might create a serious economic strain on the child's family, while conflicting with the protective and social concerns of the juvenile court. Considerations of economic liabilities and other procedural inequities have influenced the majority of courts confronting this question to hold that juveniles do not have a right to bail.

## Plea Bargaining

Before trial, prosecutors in the juvenile courts may attempt to negotiate a settlement to the case. For example, if the offender admits to the facts of the petition, she may be offered placement in a special community-based treatment program in lieu of a term in a secure state facility. Or a status offense petition may be substituted for one of delinquency so that the adolescent can avoid being housed in a state training school and, instead, be placed in a more treatment-oriented facility.

If a bargain can be reached, the child will be asked to admit in open court that he did in fact commit the act of which he stands accused. State juvenile courts tend to minimize the stigma associated with the use of adult criminal standards by using other terminology, such as "agree to a finding" or "accept the petition" rather than "admit guilt." When the child makes an admission, juvenile courts require the following procedural safeguards: The child must know of the right to a trial, the plea or admission must be made voluntarily, and the child must understand the charges and the consequences of the plea.

## Waiver of Jurisdiction

Before development of the first modern juvenile court in Illinois in 1899, juveniles were tried for violations of the law in adult criminal courts. The consequences were devastating; many children were treated as criminal offenders and sentenced to adult prisons. Although the subsequent passage of state legislation creating juvenile courts eliminated this problem, the juvenile justice system did recognize that certain forms of conduct require that children be tried as adults. Today, most American jurisdictions provide by statute for **waiver**, or transfer, of juvenile offenders to the criminal courts. Waiver is also widely used in juvenile courts in Europe and Great Britain.[36]

The major forms of waiver administration are

1. *Direct file waiver.* The prosecutor has the discretion of filing charges for certain legislatively designated offenses in either juvenile or criminal court. About 15 states have this provision.

2. *Excluded offense waiver.* State laws exclude from juvenile court jurisdiction certain offenses that are either very minor, such as traffic or fishing violations, or very serious, such as murder. About 29 states now have such laws for certain crimes.

3. *Judicial waiver.* After a formal **transfer hearing** at which both prosecutor and defense attorney present evidence, a juvenile court judge may decide to waive jurisdiction and transfer the case to criminal court. Most commonly

**waiver (juvenile)**
A practice in which the juvenile court waives its jurisdiction over a juvenile and transfers the case to adult criminal court for trial. In some states, a waiver hearing is held to determine jurisdiction; in others, juveniles may be automatically waived if they are accused of committing a serious crime such as murder.

**transfer hearing**
The hearing in which a judge decides whether to waive a juvenile to the criminal court. Waiver decisions are based on such criteria as the child's age, his or her prior offense history, and the nature of the offense.

## EVIDENCE-BASED JUSTICE

# *Is Waiver Effective?*

In all the debate surrounding transfers of juvenile offenders to adult or criminal court, one of the most important issues is whether transfers are effective in reducing crime rates. Are juveniles who are transferred to and convicted in adult court less likely to recidivate than similar youths who are convicted in juvenile court? To answer this question, the Task Force on Community Preventive Services, an independent group that receives support from the U.S. Department of Health and Human Services and the Centers for Disease Control and Prevention, conducted the first comprehensive, methodologically rigorous systematic review of studies measuring the effects of transfer laws and policies on crime rates. The review identified six high-quality evaluation studies that measured the specific deterrent effect of transfers on violent crime rates. Not one of the studies found that transfers produced lower violent crime rates. In fact, four of the studies found a harmful effect; that is, juveniles transferred to adult court had higher violent rearrest rates than their counterparts who were retained in juvenile court. For these four studies, rearrest rates for the transferred juveniles were between 27 percent and 77 percent higher than rates for the nontransferred juveniles. The authors of the review reported that these studies found harmful effects for total crime rates as well. On the matter of a general deterrent effect of transfers, less could be said. The Task Force concluded that there was insufficient evidence at present to make a determination on the effectiveness of transfer laws and policies in reducing juvenile violence generally. Based on the overall findings, the Task Force on Community Preventive Services concluded that transferring juvenile offenders to the adult system is "counterproductive for the purpose of reducing juvenile violence and enhancing public safety." The Task Force did not go so far as to recommend that states repeal their transfer laws and discontinue the practice of transfers altogether, possibly because of the inconsistent results found for general deterrent effects.

Source: Angela McGowan, Robert Hahn, Akiva Liberman, Alex Crosby, Mindy Fullilove, Robert Johnson, Eve Mosciki, LeShawndra Price, Susan Snyder, Farris Tuma, Jessica Lowy, Peter Briss, Stella Cory, Glenda Stone, and Task Force on Community Preventive Services, "Effects on Violence of Laws and Policies Facilitating the Transfer of Juveniles from the Juvenile Justice System to the Adult Justice System: A Systematic Review," *American Journal of Preventive Medicine* 32(4S): 7–28 (2007).

---

considered are the child's age and the nature of the offense alleged in the petition.

4. *Reverse waiver.* State laws mandate that certain offenses be tried in adult court. Once the case is heard in the adult court, the trial judge may decide that the offender would be better served by the juvenile court and order a reverse waiver. About 25 states have this provision for certain circumstances.[37]

Some jurisdictions require that children be over a certain age (typically 14) before they can be waived. Others mandate that the youth be charged with a felony before being tried as an adult, whereas others permit waiver of jurisdiction to the criminal court regardless of the seriousness of the offense when a child is a chronic offender. In 31 states, once a juvenile is tried in adult court, she is no longer eligible for juvenile justice on any subsequent offense (this provision and waiver in general will be discussed again in this chapter).

**LEGAL CONTROLS** Because of the nature of the waiver decision and its effect on the child in terms of status and disposition, the Supreme Court has imposed procedural protections for juveniles in the waiver process. In *Kent v. United States* (1966), the Court held that the waiver proceeding is a critically important stage in the juvenile justice process and that juveniles must be afforded minimum requirements of due process of law at such proceedings, including the right to legal counsel.[38] Then, in *Breed v. Jones* (1975), the Court held that the prosecution of juveniles as adults in the California Superior Court violated the double jeopardy clause of the Fifth Amendment if they had previously been tried on the same charge in juvenile court.[39] The Court concluded that jeopardy attaches when the juvenile court begins to hear evidence at the adjudicatory hearing; thus the waiver hearing must take place before any adjudication.

*THE EFFECT OF WAIVER* Although waiver has its advocates, many experts question its utility, arguing that it does more harm than good. Although some youths transferred to adult court never spend a day in prison, thousands do, and many of them become enmeshed in the daily life of an adult correctional facility. They miss out on being housed in juvenile facilities that are smaller, have much lower inmate-to-staff ratios, and place greater emphasis on treatment, counseling, education, and mentoring of inmates. Some adult facilities do provide easy access to education and treatment, but young inmates still lose out on developing the more supportive, mentoring-focused style of staff–inmate interactions that a juvenile facility provides.[40]

Instead, those forced to serve time in adult prisons are exposed to experienced criminals in what are essentially "schools for crime." In addition, children may be targets of adult predators if they are confined to adult institutions. A recent report of The Campaign for Youth Justice, a group dedicated to ending the placement of youths in adult facilities, found that on an average day, 7,500 young people are held in adult facilities in the United States, and the yearly rate may be several times higher, resulting in the jailing of tens of thousands of young people.[41] The risks they face include

- **Sexual Assault.** When youths are placed with adults in adult jails, they are at risk of physical and sexual assault. More than 20 percent of all substantiated victims of inmate-on-inmate sexual violence were under 18 years old, even though youths make up less than 1 percent of the total jail population.

- **Suicide.** Youths have the highest suicide rates of all inmates in jails. They are 36 times more likely to commit suicide in an adult jail than in a juvenile detention facility, and youths in an adult jail are 19 times more likely to commit suicide than youths in the general population.

- **Damage to Communities and Public Safety.** New evidence shows that placing youths in the adult criminal justice system increases their likelihood of reoffending. Children who are prosecuted in adult court are more likely to be rearrested more often and more quickly for serious offenses.

## Should Youths Be Transferred to Adult Court?

Most juvenile justice experts oppose waiver, because it clashes with the rehabilitative ideal. Basing waiver decisions on type and seriousness of offense rather than on the rehabilitative needs of the child has advanced the *criminalization* of the juvenile court and interfered with its traditional mission of treatment and rehabilitation.[42] And despite this sacrifice, there is little evidence that strict waiver policies can lower crime rates.[43] What is accomplished by treating juveniles like adults? Studies of the impact of the recent waiver statutes have yielded several interesting—and conflicting—results. Research by Benjamin Steiner and Emily Wright on the effect of direct waiver laws found that they have little effect on juvenile violent crime rates in the states that have adopted them into law.[44] Other studies have found that juveniles waived to adult court receive harsher punishment and may be viewed as dangerous and incapable of being rehabilitated.[45] This important issue is explored further in the accompanying Evidence-Based Justice feature.

*PUNISHING JUVENILES: DEATH PENALTY AND LIFE IN PRISON* If juveniles can be waived to adult courts, than it stands to reason that they can be punished as adults . . . or can they? For example, can a minor convicted of murder in an adult court receive the death penalty? You may be surprised to know that the execution of

© AP Images/Joseph Gresser, Pool

*Youngsters who commit serious crimes can be waived to the adult court, but the decision can be a difficult one. Jonas Dixon (left) arrives in Caledonia District Court on January 29, 2007, in St. Johnsbury, Vermont, to face a charge of second-degree murder. The 15-year-old boy pled not guilty in the shooting death of 24-year-old Jacob A. McDowell. Dixon and McDowell, his mother's boyfriend, were involved in a dispute before the shooting. Although Dixon was originally charged as an adult, the waiver decision was appealed, and the Vermont Supreme Court ruled that the lower court did not adequately weigh the events leading up to the shooting, such as the failure of the state Department of Children and Families to protect or remove Dixon and his younger sister from the horrible living conditions they endured in their mother's house. The Supreme Court noted that Dixon and his sister "were living in a remote rural area with a mentally ill and unstable mother with firearms in the house" and that "the combination of acute parental mental illness, desperation, drug and alcohol use, children, and firearms was a recipe for disaster." Dixon eventually plead guilty to manslaughter and received a 15 month sentence and a Youthful Offender Status which allowed him to be treated by the juvenile court.*

minor children has not been uncommon in our nation's history; at least 366 juvenile offenders have been executed since 1642.[46] However, on March 1, 2005, the U.S. Supreme Court, in the case of *Roper v. Simmons*, put an end to infliction of the death penalty on juveniles in the United States. At issue was the minimum age at which juveniles who were under the age of 18 when they committed their crimes could be eligible for the death penalty.[47] At the time, 16- and 17-year-olds were eligible for the death penalty; 21 states permitted the death penalty for juveniles.[48] A total of 72 juvenile offenders were on death row at the time.[49] In a 5 to 4 decision, the Court ruled that the juvenile death penalty was in violation of the Eighth Amendment's ban on cruel and unusual punishment. The Court held that it was cruel and unusual to execute a person who was under the age of 18 at the time of the murder; in reaching its decision, the Court relied on a significant body of sociological and scientific research that showed that juveniles lack the maturity and sense of responsibility found in adults.[50]

What about a life sentence? Experts such as Barry Feld, an opponent of life sentences for kids, have long held that the Supreme Court's reasoning in *Roper v. Simmons* should also apply to cases in which juvenile offenders are receiving life sentences without the possibility of parole.[51] Feld proposes that "states formally recognize youthfulness as a mitigating factor by applying a 'youth discount' to adult sentence lengths."[52] This issue was taken up by the United States Supreme Court when it agreed to take up the matter of juveniles sentenced to life without the possibility of parole in non-homicide cases. The Court accepted appeals from two individuals, both from Florida, who are serving life sentences for non-homicide crimes committed when they were juveniles. In the first case, which goes back to 1989, Joe Sullivan, then 13, was convicted of raping a 72-year-old woman. In the other case, Terrance Graham, who was 17 years old, was convicted of a probation violation for a home invasion robbery in 2004. In their briefs to the Court, both argued that because their crimes did not result in death the sentence of life without the possibility of parole violates the Eighth Amendment's prohibition of cruel and unusual punishment. In oral arguments before the Court, the justices did not revisit the question of whether "juveniles generally are psychologically less mature than adults" but focused, instead, on "whether the mitigating trait of immaturity justified a categorical exclusion of juveniles from the sentence of life without parole."[53] In its final decision, *Graham v. Florida,* the Court ruled that juveniles who commit crimes in which no one is killed may not be sentenced to life in prison without the possibility of parole. Writing for the majority, Justice Kennedy stated: "A state need not guarantee the offender eventual release, but if it imposes the sentence of life, it must provide him or her with some realistic opportunity to obtain release before the end of that term."[54]

## Adjudication

There are usually two judicial hearings in the juvenile court process. The first, typically called an **initial appearance**, is similar to the arraignment in the adult system. The child is informed of the charges against him, attorneys are appointed, bail is reviewed, and in many instances cases are settled with an admission of the facts, followed by a community sentence. If the case cannot be settled at this initial stage, it is bound over for trial.

During the adjudicatory or trial process, which in juvenile proceedings is often called the fact-finding hearing, the court hears evidence on the allegations stated in the delinquency petition. In its early development, the juvenile court did not emphasize judicial rule making similar to that of the criminal trial process. Absent were such basic requirements as the standard of proof, rules of evidence, and similar adjudicatory formalities. Proceedings were to be nonadversarial, informal, and noncriminal. Gradually, however, the juvenile trial process became a target of criticism because judges were handing out punishments to children without affording them legal rights. This changed in 1967 when the Supreme Court's landmark *In re Gault* decision radically altered the juvenile justice system.[55] In *Gault*, the Court ruled that the concept of fundamental fairness is applicable to juvenile delinquency proceedings. The Court granted critical rights to juvenile defendants, the most important being notice of the charges, the right to counsel, the right to confront and cross-examine witnesses, the privilege against self-incrimination, and the right to a transcript of the trial record.

The *Gault* decision completely altered the juvenile trial process. Instead of dealing with children in a benign and paternalistic fashion, the courts were forced to process juvenile offenders within the framework of appropriate constitutional procedures. And though *Gault* was technically limited to the adjudicatory stage, it has spurred further legal reform throughout the juvenile system. Today, the right to counsel, the privilege against self-incrimination, the right to treatment in detention and correctional facilities, and other constitutional protections are applied at all stages of the juvenile process, from investigation through adjudication to parole. *Gault* ushered in an era of legal rights for juveniles.

Once an adjudicatory hearing has been completed, the court is normally required to enter a judgment against the child. This may take the form of declaring the child delinquent or a ward of the court or possibly even suspending judgment to avoid the stigma of a juvenile record. Following the entering of a judgment, the court can begin its determination of possible **dispositions** for the child.

## Disposition and Treatment

At the dispositional hearing, the juvenile court judge imposes on the juvenile offender a sentence based on her offense, prior record, and family background. Normally, the judge has broad discretionary power to issue a range of dispositions

**initial appearance**
A juvenile's first appearance before the juvenile court judge in which the charges are reviewed and an effort is made to settle the case without a trial. If the child does not have legal counsel, an attorney is appointed.

**disposition**
For juvenile offenders, the equivalent of sentencing for adult offenders. The theory is that disposition is more rehabilitative than retributive. Possible dispositions: dismissing the case, releasing the youth to the custody of his or her parents, placing the offender on probation, or sending him or her to an institution or state correctional institution.

Group counseling and other forms of treatment are routine in detention centers and group homes. Residents Miranda Everhart (left), Cheree Williams (second from right), and Brooklin Schaller (right) sit in a group with other residents and discuss the day's events with youth specialist Robert Kofahl (center), at the Rosa Parks Center, a detention home for young girls in Fulton, Missouri.

© AP Images/Jeff Roberson

# CAREERS IN CRIMINAL JUSTICE

## Social Worker

### Duties and Characteristics of the Job

Social workers aid individuals or families who are disadvantaged or facing particular challenges. Social workers pick an area of specialization within one of several larger categories. Public health social workers help individuals and families dealing with the consequences of a serious illness. Child, family, and health social workers will aid families dealing with issues of social functioning, such as child abuse or truancy. Clinical social workers help families deal with issues related to mental health and substance abuse through a rehabilitation program. Other social workers take positions where they aren't dealing with the public; instead, they teach or provide psychotherapy in private practices. There are also policy writers and advocates who attempt to find legislative solutions to social problems and lobby for funding.

Social work is a demanding profession both intellectually and emotionally. Social workers traditionally work a 40-hour office workweek, but working overtime or during evening hours to attend meetings or meet clients is not unusual.

### Job Outlook

The prospects for employment as a social worker are good since jobs are expected to grow faster than average in the near future, and in many places there are more jobs than there are applicants. Because of the impending retirement of the baby boom generation, there are many job opportunities in hospices and nursing homes for social workers specializing in elder care. The employment of school and private social service agencies will also increase.

### Salary

Recent median annual earnings of child, family, and school social workers were $34,820. The lowest 10 percent earned less than $23,130, and the top 10 percent earned more than $57,860. Social

---

**commitment**
Decision of a judge who orders an adjudicated and sentenced juvenile offender to be placed in a correctional facility.

from dismissal to institutional **commitment**. In theory, the dispositional decision is an effort by the court to serve the best interests of the child, the family, and the community. In many respects, this postadjudicative process is the most important stage in the juvenile court system, because it represents the last opportunity for the court to influence the child and control her behavior.

To ensure that only relevant and appropriate evidence is considered by the court during trial, most jurisdictions require a separate hearing to formulate an appropriate disposition. The bifurcated hearing process ensures that the adjudicatory hearing is used solely to determine the merits of the allegations, whereas the dispositional hearing determines whether the child is in need of rehabilitation.

**treatment**
The rehabilitative method used to effect a change of behavior in the juvenile offender; treatment may take the form of therapy or educational or vocational programs.

In theory, the juvenile court seeks to provide a disposition that represents an individualized **treatment** plan for the child. This decision is normally based on the pre-sentence investigation of the probation department, reports from social agencies, and possibly a psychiatric evaluation. The judge generally has broad discretion in dispositional matters but is limited by the provisions of the state's juvenile court act. The following are typical juvenile court dispositions:

- Suspended judgment
- Probation
- Placement in a community treatment program
- Commitment to the state agency responsible for juvenile institutional care

In addition, the court may place the child with parents or relatives, make dispositional arrangements with private youth-serving agencies, or order the child committed to a mental institution.

**DISPOSITION OUTCOMES** In dispositional hearings, juvenile court judges must determine the most appropriate sanction for delinquent youths. Disposition options include commitment to an institution or another residential facility;

workers' salary varies according to their specialization. Social workers who specialize in medical and public health have an average salary of $44,300.

## Opportunities

A majority of social worker positions are in urban and suburban areas; potential social workers will find more competition for a limited number of jobs in urban areas. Because there will be greater competition for these jobs in urban areas, applicants with more education and/or some specialized experience stand a better chance of getting desirable positions and career advancement. It may be considerably easier to find a job in a rural area, and educational requirements will be less stringent. Those who leave social work often successfully pursue careers in related fields, such as counseling.

## Qualifications

The ability to meet the challenging education requirements and certification are the primary qualifications necessary to become a social worker. Personal characteristics such as sensitivity, responsibility, and the ability to work independently are also very important. Potential social workers must have at

least a bachelor's degree in social work to start at entry-level positions, and additional education for higher degrees will prepare them for more advanced duties, such as clinical assessments and supervisory positions. In addition to being well educated, social workers have to meet the particular licensing requirements of the state where they are seeking employment before they can begin to work.

## Education and Training

For entry-level positions, a bachelor's degree in social work (BSW) or in a similar field, such as sociology, is necessary. Those who wish to advance further should earn a master's degree in social work (MSW) or a doctorate (Ph.D. or DSW). Those who wish to ascend to the highest-level positions in an organization employing social workers or design new social work policies or programs should pursue a Ph.D. Social workers' education is never truly complete; they must keep up on recent developments by attending conferences and reading the most recent literature.

Source: Bureau of Labor Statistics, U.S. Department of Labor (2007). Social Worker. *Occupational Outlook Handbook, 2006-07 Edition.* Retrieved June 15, 2008, from www.bls.gov/oco/ocos60.htm.

probation; and a variety of other dispositions, such as referral to an outside agency or treatment program, community service, fines, or restitution. Very often the court imposes some combination of these sanctions. What have been the trends in juvenile disposition? The number of adjudicated delinquency cases resulting in residential placement has increased significantly during the past decade, and today about 10 percent of all cases petitioned to juvenile court get some form of residential treatment. An additional 400,000 kids are put on probation each year.

## Juvenile Sentencing Reform

Over the past decade, juvenile justice experts and the general public have become aroused about the serious juvenile crime rate in general and about violent acts committed by children in particular. As a result, some law enforcement officials and conservative legislators have demanded that the juvenile justice system take a more serious stance with dangerous juvenile offenders. Many state legislatures have responded by toughening their juvenile codes. Some jurisdictions have passed mandatory or determinate incarceration sentences for juveniles convicted of serious felonies. Not all jurisdictions have abandoned rehabilitation as a primary dispositional goal, however, and some still adhere to the philosophy that placements should be based on the least detrimental alternative. This view requires that judges employ the least intrusive measures possible to safeguard a child's growth and development.[56]

A second reform has been the concerted effort to remove status offenders from the juvenile justice system and restrict their entry into institutional programs. Because of the development of numerous diversion programs, many children involved in truancy and incorrigible behavior who ordinarily would have been sent to a closed institution are now being placed in community programs. There are far fewer status offenders in detention or institutions than ever before.

A third reform effort has been to standardize dispositions in juvenile court. As early as 1977, Washington passed one of the first determinate-sentencing laws for juvenile offenders, resulting in other states adopting similar statutes.[57] All children found to be delinquent are evaluated on a point system based on their age, prior juvenile record, and type of crime committed. Minor offenders are handled in the community. Those committing more serious offenses are placed on probation. Children who commit the most serious offenses are subject to standardized institutional penalties. As a result, juvenile offenders who commit such crimes as rape or armed robbery are being sentenced to institutionalization for two, three, and four years. This approach is different from the indeterminate sentencing under which children who have committed a serious crime might be released from institutions in less than a year if correctional authorities believe they have been rehabilitated.

## THE JUVENILE CORRECTIONAL PROCESS

After disposition in juvenile court, delinquent offenders may be placed in some form of correctional treatment. Although many are placed in the community, almost 90,000 are now in secure facilities.

### Probation

The most commonly used formal sentence for juvenile offenders is probation, and many states require that a youth must have failed on probation before being sent to an institution (unless the criminal act is quite serious). Probation involves placing the child under the supervision of the juvenile probation department for the purpose of community treatment. A juvenile may also be required to follow special rules, such as maintaining a curfew or attending substance abuse meetings. Alternative sanctions such as community service or monetary restitution may be ordered. Serious offenders can be placed in intensive supervision or under house arrest. Probation can be revoked if the juvenile violates the probation conditions. Just as in the adult system, probation can be revoked if the rules are not followed, and the court may impose stricter sanctions.

Juvenile probation is an important component of the juvenile justice system. It is the most widely used method of community treatment in juvenile court. Similar in form and function to adult probation, supervising juveniles in the community combines elements of treatment and control. Some probation officers maintain a social work orientation and want to provide needy kids with an effective treatment plan, whereas others maintain a law enforcement orientation, believing that their clients are offenders who need close monitoring.[58]

### Intensive Supervision

**juvenile intensive probation supervision (JIPS)**
A true alternative to incarceration that involves almost daily supervision of the juvenile by the probation officer assigned to the case.

**Juvenile intensive probation supervision (JIPS)** involves treating offenders who would normally have been sent to a secure treatment facility as part of a very small probation caseload that receives almost daily scrutiny.[59] The primary goal of JIPS is decarceration; without intensive supervision, youngsters would normally be sent to secure juvenile facilities that are already overcrowded. The second goal is control; high-risk juvenile offenders can be maintained in the community under much closer security than traditional probation efforts can provide. A third goal is maintaining community ties and reintegration; offenders can remain in the community and complete their education while avoiding the pains of imprisonment.

Intensive probation programs get mixed reviews. Some jurisdictions find that they are more successful than traditional probation supervision and cost much less than incarceration.[60] However, some studies indicate that the failure rate is high and that younger offenders who commit petty crimes are the most likely to fail when placed in intensive supervision programs.[61] It is not surprising that intensive probation clients fail more often, because, after all, they are more serious offenders who might otherwise have been incarcerated and are now being watched and supervised more closely than probationers. In one experimental study of intensive probation supervision plus a coordinated team approach for high-risk juveniles, known as the Los Angeles County Repeat Offender Prevention Program (ROPP), mixed results were found for those who received the program compared to a similar group of youths who received regular probation only. Specifically, recidivism was reduced in the short term, but not over the long-term; school performance was increased; and there was no difference in probation technical violations.[62] In another recent California experiment in juvenile intensive probation supervision, no significant differences were observed in recidivism rates among those youths who received intensive probation compared to a similar group of youths who received regular probation.[63] Further analyses of this program revealed no effects on key family and peer relationship measures.[64]

# Institutionalization

The most severe of the statutory dispositions available to the juvenile court involves commitment of the child to an institution. Juvenile facilities are known by many different names: detention centers, juvenile halls, shelters, reception and diagnostic centers, group homes, wilderness camps, ranches, farms, youth development centers, residential treatment centers, training or reform schools, and juvenile correctional institutions. Some facilities resemble adult prisons or jails, some resemble campuses, and others resemble houses.[65]

State statutes vary when determining the length of the child's commitment. Traditionally, many jurisdictions committed the child up to her or his majority, which usually meant until the individual reached 21 years of age. This normally deprived the child of freedom for an extensive period of time—sometimes longer than an adult sentenced for the same offense would be confined. As a result, some states have passed legislation under which children are committed for periods ranging from one to three years.

As Figure 16.2 indicates, the number of youths being held in some form of incarceration has declined from over 100,000 in 2000 to about 86,000 today, a trend that reflects the on-going decline in juvenile crime. State placement rates vary substantially, from a high of 513 in South Dakota to a low of 69 in

**FIGURE 16.2**
**Number of Juvenile Offenders in Residential Placement**

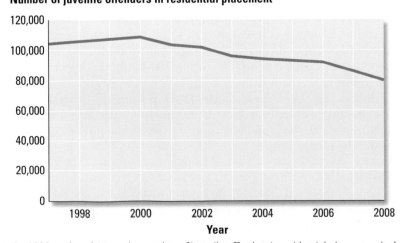

Between the 2000 peak and 2008, the number of juvenile offenders in residential placement, including privately and publicly operated facilities, declined 26 percent.

Source: Melissa Sickmund, *Juveniles in Residential Placement*, 1997–2008 (Washington, D.C.: Office of Juvenile Justice and Delinquency Prevention, 2010).

Vermont. Eleven other states had rates less than 200: Connecticut, Hawaii, Maine, Maryland, Massachusetts, Mississippi, New Hampshire, New Jersey, New Mexico, North Carolina, and Tennessee. Delaware and Wyoming were the only states in addition to South Dakota with rates greater than 400.[66] The efforts made in recent years to keep status offenders out of institutions seem to have paid off.

The typical resident of a juvenile facility is a 15- to 16-year-old white male incarcerated for an average stay of five months in a public facility or six months in a private facility. Private facilities tend to house younger youths, whereas public institutions provide custodial care for older youths, including a small percentage of youths between 18 and 21 years of age.

## Deinstitutionalization

Some experts in delinquency and juvenile law question the policy of institutionalizing juvenile offenders. Many believe that large institutions are too costly to operate and only produce more sophisticated criminals. This dilemma has inspired a number of efforts to remove youths from juvenile facilities and replace large institutions with smaller, community-based facilities. The Commonwealth of Massachusetts closed all its state training schools more than 20 years ago (subsequently, however, public pressure caused a few secure facilities to be reopened). Many other states have established small residential facilities operated by juvenile-care agencies to replace larger units.

Despite the daily rhetoric on crime control, public support for community-based programs for juveniles still exists. Although such programs are not panaceas, many experts still recommend more treatment and less incarceration for juvenile offenders. Utah, Maryland, Vermont, and Pennsylvania, for example, have dramatically reduced their reform school populations, while setting up a wide range of intensive treatment programs for juveniles. Many large, impersonal, and expensive state institutions with unqualified staff and ineffective treatment programs have been eliminated.

*DEINSTITUTIONALIZING STATUS OFFENDERS*  For almost 30 years there has been an ongoing effort to deinstitutionalize status offenders (DSO). This means removing noncriminal youths from institutions housing delinquents in order to prevent them from interacting with violent or chronic offenders.

Since its inception, the DSO approach has been hotly debated. Some have argued that early intervention is society's best hope of forestalling future delinquent behavior and reducing victimization. Other experts maintain that legal control over status offenders is a violation of youths' rights. Still others have viewed status-offending behavior as a symptom of some larger trauma or problem that requires attention. These diverse opinions still exist today.

Since Congress passed the JJDP Act in 1974, all 50 states have complied with some aspect of the deinstitutionalization mandate. Millions of federal, state, and local dollars have been spent on the DSO movement. Programs have been created around the country to reduce the number of juveniles in secure confinement. What remains to be done, however, is to study the effect DSO has had on juveniles and the justice system.

## Aftercare

Aftercare marks the final stage of the formal juvenile justice process. Its purpose is to help youths make the transition from residential or institutional settings back into the community. Effective aftercare programs provide adequate supervision and support services to help juvenile offenders avoid criminal activity. Examples of programs include electronic monitoring, counseling, treatment and community service referrals, education, work training, and intensive parole supervision.

Through the Serious and Violent Offender Reentry Initiative (SVORI), the federal government has invested $150 million in reentry programs for adult and juvenile offenders in all 50 states, the District of Columbia, and the Virgin Islands.[67] Promising results are beginning to emerge from this initiative as well as from other juvenile reentry programs across the country.[68] Take, for instance, the **Intensive Aftercare Program (IAP)** model developed by David Altschuler and Troy Armstrong. This program offers a continuum of intervention for serious juvenile offenders returning to the community following placement.[69] The IAP model begins by drawing attention to five basic principles, which collectively establish a set of fundamental operational goals:

1. Preparing youths for progressively increased responsibility and freedom in the community

2. Facilitating youth–community interaction and involvement

3. Working with both the offender and targeted community support systems (families, peers, schools, employers) on qualities needed for constructive interaction and the youths' successful community adjustment

4. Developing new resources and supports where needed

5. Monitoring and testing the youths and the community on their ability to deal with each other productively

These basic goals are then translated into practice, which incorporates individual case planning with a family and community perspective. The program stresses a mix of intensive surveillance and services and a balance of incentives and graduated consequences, coupled with the imposition of realistic, enforceable conditions. There is also "service brokerage," in which community resources are used and linkage with social networks is established.[70] So far, evaluations of the program indicate that it holds promise.

## Preventing Delinquency

Although the juvenile justice system has been concerned with controlling delinquent behavior, there are now important efforts being made to prevent delinquency before it occurs. "Delinquency prevention" consists of intervening in young people's lives before they engage in delinquency in the first place, thus preventing delinquency from developing at all. In the past, delinquency prevention was the responsibility of treatment-oriented agencies such as day care providers, YMCA and YWCA, Boys and Girls Clubs of America, and other private and public agencies. Today, there are many community-based programs involving a combination of juvenile justice and treatment agencies. Some programs focus on the educational experience and attempt to help kids maintain their bond to society by strengthening their attachments to school. Many of these efforts are conducted by social workers whose specialty is working with troubled youths. The Careers in Criminal Justice feature on page 626 describes this occupation.

Comprehensive community-based delinquency prevention programs take a systematic approach or apply a comprehensive planning model to develop preventive interventions. This includes analyzing the delinquency problems that exist, identifying resources available in the community, prioritizing the delinquency problems, becoming familiar with successful programs in other communities, and tailoring them to local conditions and needs.[71] Not all comprehensive community-based prevention programs follow this model, but evidence suggests that this approach yields the greatest reductions in juvenile delinquency.[72]

An example of a good comprehensive community program is the Children At Risk (CAR) program funded by the federal government. CAR was designed to help improve the lives of young people at high risk for delinquency, gang

**Intensive Aftercare Program (IAP)**
A balanced, highly structured, comprehensive continuum of intervention for serious and violent juvenile offenders returning to the community.

# Significant Cases in the Trial Process

| Case | Issue | Decision |
|---|---|---|
| *Kent v. United States* (1966) | Waiver | Ruled that a child has the right to an attorney at a waiver hearing. |
| *In re Gault* (1967) | Due process | Ruled that a minor has basic due process rights at trial. |
| *In re Winship* (1970) | Level of evidence at trial | Determined that the level of evidence for a finding of "juvenile delinquency" is proof beyond a reasonable doubt. |
| *McKeiver v. Pennsylvania* (1971) | Right to a jury trial | Held that trial by jury in a juvenile court's adjudicative stage is not a constitutional requirement. |
| *Breed v. Jones* (1975) | Double jeopardy | Ruled that a child has the protection of the double jeopardy clause of the Fifth Amendment and cannot be tried twice for the same crime. |
| *Fare v. Michael C.* (1979) | Interrogation | Established that a child has the protection of *Miranda* and may request that a lawyer be provided to protect his or her interests. |
| *Schall v. Martin* (1984) | Preventive detention | Allowed for the placement of children in preventive detention before their adjudication. |
| *New Jersey v. T.L.O.* (1985) | Search | Determined that although the Fourth Amendment protection against unreasonable search and seizure applies to children, school officials can legally search kids who violate school rules (e.g., smoking on campus) even though there is no evidence that the student violated the law. |
| *Vernonia School District v. Acton* (1995) | Drug testing in school | Held that the Fourth Amendment's guarantee against unreasonable searches is not violated by drug testing all students who choose to participate in interscholastic athletics. |
| *Safford Unified School District v. Redding* (2009) | Search in schools | Held that a search cannot be unreasonable and overly intrusive. |
| *Graham v Florida* (2010) | Sentencing of Waived Juveniles | Children waived to adult court cannot receive a life sentence without parole unless they commit murder |

involvement, substance abuse, and other problem behaviors. It was made available to a large number of young people in poor and high-crime neighborhoods in five cities across the country. The program was different in each neighborhood and involved a wide range of preventive measures. The beneficial results for those in the program included less association with delinquent peers, less peer pressure to engage in delinquency, and more positive peer support.[73]

The CAR program is now known as CASASTART, an acronym for the national Center on Addiction and Substance Abuse, Striving Together to Achieve Rewarding Tomorrows. Based at Columbia University in New York, CASASTART is a neighborhood-based, school-centered program aimed at preventing substance abuse and delinquency among high-risk adolescents ages 8 to 13 and reducing drug-related crime in their neighborhoods. The program brings together different organizations, including schools, law enforcement, and social service agencies, to provide clients with eight different services: tutoring, after-school activities, mentoring, counseling, family services, community policing, juvenile justice intervention, and incentives.

Some community delinquency prevention strategies combine the efforts of law enforcement with those of treatment-oriented agencies. An unusual one is located in the city of Lowell, Massachusetts. At a Buddhist temple, the Venerable Khon Sao, a Buddhist monk, teaches young Cambodian youths, many of them gang members, how to meditate. In conjunction with the police department, the temple has begun a program that teaches the fundamentals of Buddhist thought to the teens two evenings a week. In the classes, the youths learn how to pray, meditate, and act peacefully.

© Spencer Platt/Getty Images

Children who may be eligible are referred to CASASTART by school personnel, social service staff, police, or juvenile court personnel. Staff members (called case managers) then determine whether children meet the criteria of being at high risk of substance abuse and crime. Each case manager works on a one-to-one basis with 15 families. In addition to seeking participants and coordinating services, CASASTART case managers engage in a full range of activities:

- Running after-school or recreation programs
- Arranging appointments and sometimes transporting family members to them
- Helping prevent homelessness and utility shutoffs
- Advocating for children and family members in court
- Helping parents resolve problems with schools or social service agencies

The program is now being used in 64 sites around the country, including Denver, Colorado, and San Antonio, Texas.[74]

## The Future of Juvenile Justice

The juvenile justice system is at a crossroads: Can it provide meaningful treatment to youths in an age of budget cutting and reductions in social services? Should it maintain the parens patriae vision of its founders, or should it adopt a law and order approach to dealing with violent kids? Should the system be maintained, or should it be abolished?

Even those experts who want to retain an independent juvenile court have called for its restructuring.[75] Crime control advocates want to reduce the court's jurisdiction over juveniles charged with serious crimes and liberalize the prosecutor's ability to try them in adult courts. In *Bad Kids: Race and the Transformation of the Juvenile Court,* Barry Feld makes the controversial suggestion that the juvenile court system should be discontinued and replaced by an alternative method of justice.[76] During its history, various legal developments have further undermined its purpose—most notably the *In re Gault* ruling, which ultimately led to juveniles being accorded legal protections similar to those accorded to adults and to children being treated like adults in all respects. Then, in the 1980s, the sudden rise in gang membership, gun violence, and homicide committed by juveniles further eroded the juvenile court's mission and resulted in legislation creating mandatory sentences for juvenile offenders and mandatory waiver to the adult court. As a result, the focus of the court has shifted from treating the offender to dealing with the offense. In Feld's words, the juvenile court has become a "deficient second-rate criminal court." The welfare and rehabilitative purposes of the juvenile court have been subordinated to its role as law enforcement agent, so there is little purpose in retaining it in its current state. Robert Dawson suggests that because the legal differences between the juvenile and criminal systems are narrower than they ever have been, it may be time to abolish the juvenile court.[77] The call to abolish juvenile court is substantiated by research showing that at least in some jurisdictions, the spirit of juvenile justice has shifted from a focus on individual needs to the seriousness of the crime, giving the prosecution more power to make decisions and promoting a reliance on the adversarial process at the expense of parens patriae.[78]

Not all experts agree that the juvenile court has become redundant. Some, such as John Kerbs, believe that the "get tough" approach will force the criminal courts to apply harsher sentences and tougher treatment, and that the brunt of these draconian sentences will fall squarely on the shoulders of minority youths. Research efforts routinely show that African American adults are punished with undue severity in adult courts. Sending juvenile offenders to these venues is likely to enmesh them further in an already unfair system.[79] Peter Greenwood contends that, despite these and other limitations, the treatment programs that the "modern" juvenile court currently provides play a central role in society's response to the most serious delinquents.[80] He argues that juvenile courts must take on a number of specific responsibilities to ensure that these programs are indeed effective. Among these responsibilities are awareness of the most up-to-date scientific evidence on the effectiveness of court-based programs, diversion of cases that can be handled informally outside of the system, disposition of cases to appropriate programs, and quality control.[81]

Regardless of which position is correct, there has been an ongoing effort to modify the juvenile justice system in response to the public's fear of predatory juvenile offenders and the reaction to high-profile cases such as the Columbine tragedy. As a result, states began to institute policies that increased the punitive dimensions the juvenile court movement.[82] For example, since 1990, more than 40 states and the District of Columbia have changed their transfer statutes to make it easier to waive juveniles to adult courts.[83] Today, at least 22 states and the District of Columbia specify no minimum age beneath which a juvenile cannot be transferred to adult court.[84] Some states, such as Arizona, have initiated legislation that significantly restricts eligibility for juvenile justice processing and criminalizes acts that heretofore would have fallen under the jurisdiction of the juvenile court. Arizona excludes from the juvenile justice system 15-, 16-, and 17-year-olds charged with any felony if they had two or more prior delinquency adjudications and "dispositions for offenses that would have been felonies if committed by an adult."[85] It also added the provision "once an adult, always an adult," whereby, if a juvenile was previously tried and convicted in criminal court, any future offenses involving that juvenile will be tried in adult court.[86] Thirty-two other states and the District of Columbia have also adopted the "once an adult, always an adult provision."[87]

Those who support the juvenile justice concept believe that it is too soon to write off its rehabilitative principles. Fears of a juvenile crime wave are misplaced, and the actions of a few violent children should not obscure the needs of millions who can benefit from solicitous treatment rather than harsh punishments. Nor have the concepts of rehabilitation and change been lost on the people who actually work in the juvenile justice system. While politicians have passed laws easing the waiver of kids to the adult system, the actual number of juvenile offenders who are waived has been on the decline. The number of delinquency cases judicially waived to criminal court peaked in 1994 at 13,200 cases; since then the number of waivers has declined to about 7,000, which represents less than 0.5 percent of the delinquency caseload.[88] Although a "get tough" approach may seem attractive to some, its costs generally outweigh its benefits.[89]

## Ethical Challenges in Criminal Justice: A Writing Assignment

You are a juvenile court judge. John M. has been arrested for robbery and rape. His victim, a young neighborhood girl, was seriously injured in the attack and needed extensive hospitalization; she is now in counseling. Because the charges are serious, John can be waived to the adult court and tried as an adult even though he is only 14 years old. Under existing state law, a hearing must be held to determine whether there is sufficient evidence that John cannot be successfully treated in the juvenile justice system and therefore warrants transfer to the adult system; the final decision on the matter is yours alone.

At the waiver hearing, you discover that John is the oldest of three siblings living in a single-parent home. He has had no contact with his father for more than ten years. His psychological evaluations show hostility, anger toward females, and deep feelings of frustration. His intelligence is above average, but his behavioral and academic records are poor. John is a loner with few friends. This is his first formal involvement with the juvenile court. Previous contact was limited to an informal complaint for disorderly conduct at age 13, which was dismissed by the court's intake department. During the hearing, John verbalizes what you interpret to be superficial remorse for his offenses.

Write an essay discussing whether you would waive John to the adult court or treat him as a juvenile, and give the reasons for your decision. As you make your decision and prepare to explain your reasoning, refer to the sections on waiver and treatment. Are there treatment alternatives in the juvenile justice system that may work as well as or better than anything in the adult system? What are some of the harmful consequences, such as stigma and labeling, that John may experience if he is waived? What arguments, on the other hand, can be advanced in favor of waiving John to the adult court? What will be your ruling, and why?

## SUMMARY

1. **Describe the nature and purpose of the juvenile justice system.**
   - Conceived at the turn of the twentieth century, the juvenile justice system was originally viewed as a quasi–social welfare agency that was to act as a surrogate parent in the interests of the child.
   - Juvenile justice was originally based on the parens patriae philosophy.

2. **Be familiar with the history and development of juvenile justice.**
   - The modern practice of legally separating adult and juvenile offenders can be traced back to the development of Elizabethan-era poor laws and the creation of the English chancery court.
   - Poor laws and chancery courts were brought from England to colonial America.

- To accommodate dependent youths, local jurisdictions developed almshouses, poorhouses, and workhouses.

### 3. Discuss the child savers and their vision of juvenile justice.

- The child savers were responsible for creating a number of programs for indigent youths, including the New York House of Refuge, which began operations in 1825.

- The child savers also influenced state and local governments to create independent correctional institutions to house minors.

- The first of these reform schools opened in Westboro, Massachusetts, in 1848 and in Rochester, New York, in 1849.

- In 1853, New York philanthropist Charles Loring Brace helped develop the Children's Aid Society, which placed neglected and delinquent youths in private homes in rural communities.

### 4. Describe the efforts of the child savers to create an independent juvenile court.

- The child savers lobbied for an independent, state-supported juvenile court. Their efforts prompted the development of the first comprehensive juvenile court in Illinois in 1899.

- The Illinois Juvenile Court Act set up an independent court to handle criminal law violations by children under 16 years of age, as well as to care for neglected, dependent, and wayward youths.

- The main concern was the "best interests of the child," not strict adherence to legal doctrine, constitutional rights, or due process of law. Youngsters who were found delinquent in juvenile court could spend years in a state training school.

### 5. Cite the changes in juvenile justice that began in the 1960s and continue today.

- In the 1960s and 1970s, the U.S. Supreme Court radically altered the juvenile justice system when it issued a series of decisions that established the right of juveniles to due process of law.

- The trend has been to create family courts, which address a broad range of family- and child-related issues within their jurisdictions.

### 6. Describe the police processing of juvenile offenders.

- Most states do not have specific statutory provisions distinguishing the arrest process for children from that for adults.

- Some jurisdictions give broad arrest powers to the police in juvenile cases by authorizing the officer to make an arrest whenever she or he believes that the child's behavior falls within the jurisdiction of the juvenile court.

- Police may arrest youths for behavior considered legal for adults, such as running away, violating curfew, and being in possession of alcohol.

### 7. Discuss the detention of juveniles.

- After a juvenile is formally taken into custody, either as a delinquent or as a status offender, the prosecutor usually decides whether to release the child to the parent or guardian or to detain the child in a secure shelter pending trial.

- There has been an ongoing effort to reform detention. The most important reform has been the successful effort to remove status offenders from lockups containing delinquents.

- Although only a few state statutes allow release on money bail, many others have juvenile code provisions that emphasize the release of the child to the parents as an acceptable substitute.

### 8. Discuss the problems and legal issues surrounding the waiver decision.

- Before trial, prosecutors in the juvenile courts may attempt to negotiate a settlement to the case.

- Today, most U.S. jurisdictions provide by statute for the waiver, or transfer, of juvenile offenders to the criminal courts.

- Waiver does not seem to influence crime or recidivism rates; one reason may be that juveniles whose cases are waived to criminal court are sentenced more leniently than they would have been in juvenile court.

### 9. Chart the juvenile trial and sentencing process.

- There are usually two judicial hearings in the juvenile court process. The first, typically called an initial appearance, is similar to the arraignment in the adult system.

- During the adjudicatory or trial process, which us often called the fact-finding hearing in juvenile proceedings, the court hears evidence on the allegations stated in the delinquency petition.

- At the dispositional hearing, the juvenile court judge imposes a sentence on the juvenile offender based on his or her offense, prior record, and family background.

- Some jurisdictions have passed mandatory or determinate incarceration sentences for juveniles convicted of serious felonies.

**10. Discuss efforts to treat troubled kids in the juvenile justice system. Next outline the arguments of those who believe that treatment in the juvenile justice system is ineffective and should be abolished. Then cite the arguments of those who believe it should be retained.**

- Although the juvenile justice system has been concerned with controlling delinquent behavior, there are now important efforts being made to prevent delinquency before it occurs.

- Some experts question whether the juvenile justice system should exist in its present form, mainly because it has become so punitive that there is little to distinguish it from the adult criminal court.

- While the "get tough" approach seems to have prevailed, the rehabilitative ideal of juvenile justice still exists. Despite fear of crime, the number of adolescents being waived to the adult court is in sharp decline, signaling a willingness to treat rather than punish young people who violate the law.

## KEY TERMS

parens patriae, 606
poor laws, 606
chancery courts, 606
child savers, 607
Children's Aid Society, 608
juvenile court, 608
status offender, 609

juvenile delinquency, 611
detention, 619
waiver (juvenile), 621
transfer hearing, 621
initial appearance, 625
disposition, 625
commitment, 626

treatment, 626
juvenile intensive probation
supervision (JIPS), 628
intensive aftercare program
(IAP), 631

## CRITICAL THINKING QUESTIONS

1. Should status offenders be treated by the juvenile court? Explain. Should they be placed in confinement for such acts as running away or cutting school? Why or why not?

2. Should a juvenile ever be waived to adult court, with the risk that the child will be incarcerated with adult felons? Why or why not?

3. Do you support the death penalty for children? Explain.

4. Should juveniles be given mandatory incarceration sentences for serious crimes, as adults are? Explain.

5. Is it fair to deny juveniles a jury trial? Why or why not?

6. Do you think the trend toward treating juveniles like adult offenders is desirable? Explain.

## NOTES

1. Patricia Wen, "Odgren Sentenced to Life in Prison, No Parole Option for Teen Killer; Lawyer Brands Ruling 'Barbaric,'" *Boston Globe,* May 1, 2010, www.boston.com/news/local/massachusetts/articles/2010/05/01/odgren_sentenced_to_life_in_prison?mode=PF; Bill Ahearn, "Asperger's Syndrome on Trial? That Behavior Is Determined Has No Bearing on Personal Responsibility," *Psychology Today,* April 14, 2010, www.psychologytoday.com/blog/radical-behaviorist/201004/aspergers-syndrome-trial.

2. Federal Bureau of Investigation, *Crime in the United States, 2009* (Washington, D.C.: U.S. Government Printing Office, 2010). http://www.fbi.gov/ucr/cius2009/data/table_38.html.

3. Material in this section depends heavily on Sanford J. Fox, "Juvenile Justice Reform: A Historical Perspective," *Stanford Law Review* 22 (1970): 1187–1205; Lawrence Stone, *The Family, Sex, and Marriage in England: 1500–1800* (New York: Harper and Row,

1977); Philippe Aries, *Century of Childhood: A Social History of Family Life* (New York: Vintage, 1962); Douglas R. Rendleman, "Parens Patriae: From Chancery to the Juvenile Court," *South Carolina Law Review* 23 (1971): 205–29; Anthony Platt, "The Rise of the Child-Saving Movement: A Study in Social Policy and Correctional Reform," *Annals of the American Academy of Political and Social Science* 381 (1979): 21–38; Anthony M. Platt, *The Child Savers: The Intervention of Delinquency* (Chicago: University of Chicago Press, 1969); Robert S. Pickett, *House of Refuge: Origins of Juvenile Reform in New York State, 1815–1857* (Syracuse, N.Y.: Syracuse University Press, 1969).

4. Douglas Besharov, *Juvenile Justice Advocacy: Practice in a Unique Court* (New York: Practicing Law Institute, 1974), p. 2. See also Jay Albanese, *Dealing with Delinquency—The Future of Juvenile Justice* (Chicago: Nelson-Hall, 1993).

5. 4 Eng.Rep. 1078 (1827).

6. Platt, *The Child Savers*, pp. 11–38.

7. See, generally, Anne Meis Knupfer, *Reform and Resistance: Gender, Delinquency, and America's First Juvenile Court* (London: Routledge, 2001).

8. This section is based on material from the New York State Archives, *The Greatest Reform School in the World: A Guide to the Records of the New York House of Refuge: A Brief History 1824–1857* (Albany, N.Y.: 2001); Sanford J. Fox, "Juvenile Justice Reform: A Historical Perspective," *Stanford Law Review* 22 (1970): 1187.

9. Pickett, *House of Refuge*.

10. Robert Mennel, "Origins of the Juvenile Court: Changing Perspectives on the Legal Rights of Juvenile Delinquents," in *Juvenile Justice Philosophy*, ed. Frederick Faust and Paul Brantingham (St. Paul, Minn.: West, 1974), pp. 69–70.

11. Platt, *The Child Savers*, p. 116.

12. LaMar T. Empey, *American Delinquency: Its Meaning and Construction* (Homewood, Ill.: Dorsey, 1978), p. 515.

13. *Kent v. United States*, 383 U.S. 541, 86 S.Ct. 1045, 16 L.Ed.2d 84 (1966); *In re Gault*, 387 U.S. 1, 87 S.Ct. 1428, 18 L.Ed.2d 527 (1967); *In re Winship*, 397 U.S. 358, 90 S.Ct. 1068, 25 L.Ed.2d 368 (1970); *Breed v. Jones*, 421 U.S. 519, 95 S.Ct. 1779, 44 L.Ed.2d 346 (1975).

14. Public Law 93–415 (1974).

15. *2006 National Report*, pp. 96–97.

16. For a comprehensive view of juvenile law, see, generally, Joseph J. Senna and Larry J. Siegel, *Juvenile Law: Cases and Comments*, 2d ed. (St. Paul, Minn.: West, 1992).

17. Erika Gebo, "Do Family Courts Administer Individualized Justice in Delinquency Cases?" *Criminal Justice Policy Review* 16 (2005): 190–210.

18. Federal Bureau of Investigation, *Crime in the United States, 2009*, http://www.fbi.gov/ucr/cius2009/data/table_38.html.

19. Public Law 93-415, 42 USC 5601 et seq.

20. Emily Cabaniss, James Frabutt, Mary Kendrick, and Margaret Arbuckle, "Reducing Disproportionate Minority Contact in the Juvenile Justice System: Promising Practices," *Aggression & Violent Behavior* 12 (2007): 393–401.

21. Richard J. Lundman, "Routine Police Arrest Practices," *Social Problems* 22 (1974): 127–141; Robert E. Worden and Stephanie M. Myers, *Police Encounters with Juvenile Suspects* (Albany: Hindelang Criminal Justice Research Center and School of Criminal Justice, State University of New York, 2001).

22. Richard Lundman, "Demeanor or Crime? The Midwest City Police–Citizen Encounters Study," *Criminology* 32 (1994): 631–653; Robert Worden and Robin Shepard, "On the Meaning, Measurement, and Estimated Effects of Suspects' Demeanor toward the Police." Paper presented at the American Society of Criminology meeting, Miami, November 1994.

23. Robert A. Brown, Kenneth J. Novak, and James Frank, "Identifying Variation in Police Officer Behavior between Juveniles and Adults," *Journal of Criminal Justice* 37 (2009): 200–208.

24. *Fare v. Michael C.*, 442 U.S. 707 (1979).

25. *Fare v. Michael C.*, 442 U.S. 707 (1979).

26. Barry Feld, "Police Interrogation of Juveniles: An Empirical Study of Policy and Practice," *Journal of Criminal Law & Criminology* 97 (2006): 219–316.

27. *New Jersey v. T.L.O.*, 469 U.S. 325 (1985).

28. *Vernonia School District 47J v. Acton*, 515 U.S. 646 (1995); Bernard James and Jonathan Pyatt, "Supreme Court Extends School's Authority to Search," *National School Safety Center News Journal* 26 (1995): 29.

29. *Board of Education of Independent School District No. 92 of Pottawatomie County et al. v. Earls et al.*, 536 U.S. 822 (2002).

30. *Safford United School District No. 1 v. Redding*, 557 U.S. ___ (2009).

31. Ana Abrantes, Norman Hoffmann, and Ronald Anton, "Prevalence of Co-occurring Disorders among Juveniles Committed to Detention Centers," *International Journal of Offender Therapy & Comparative Criminology* 49 (2005): 179–194.

32. Nancy Rodriquez, "Juvenile Court Context and Detention Decisions: Reconsidering the Role of Race, Ethnicity, and Community Characteristics in Juvenile Court Processes," *Justice Quarterly* 24 (2007): 629–656.

33. Barry Holman and Jason Ziedenberg, *The Dangers of Detention: The Impact of Incarcerating Youth in Detention and Other Secure Facilities* (Washington, D.C.: Justice Policy Institute, 2006), www.cfjj.org/Pdf/116-JPI008-DOD_Report.pdf (accessed March 26, 2009).

34. *Schall v. Martin*, 467 U.S. 253 (1984).

35. See Juvenile Justice and Delinquency Prevention Act of 1974, 42 U.S.C., sec. 5633.

36. Catherine Van Dijk, An Nuytiens, and Christian Eliaerts, "The Referral of Juvenile Offenders to the Adult Court in Belgium: Theory and Practice," *Howard Journal of Criminal Justice* 44 (2005): 151–166.

37. John Burrow, "Reverse Waiver and the Effects of Legal, Statutory, and Secondary Legal Factors on Sentencing Outcomes for Juvenile Offenders," *Crime and Delinquency* 54 (2008): 34–64.

38. *Kent v. United States*, 383 U.S. 541 (1966).

39. *Breed v. Jones*, 421 U.S. 519 (1975).

40. Aaron Kupchik, "The Correctional Experiences of Youth in Adult and Juvenile Prisons," *Justice Quarterly* 24 (2007): 247–270.

41. Campaign for Youth Justice, *"Jailing Juveniles: The Dangers of Incarcerating Youth in Adult Jails in America"* (2008), www.campaignforyouthjustice.org/Downloads/Jailing_Juveniles_Take_Action_Kit.pdf (accessed May 1, 2010).

42. Brandon K. Applegate, Robin King Davis, and Francis T. Cullen, "Reconsidering Child Saving: The Extent and Correlates of Public Support for Excluding Youths from Juvenile Courts," *Crime and Delinquency* 55 (2009): 51–77; Jeffrey Fagan, "Juvenile Crime and Criminal Justice: Resolving Border Disputes," *The Future of Children* 18, no. 2 (2008): 81–118.

43. See Redding, *Juvenile Transfer Laws*; Craig A. Mason, Derek A. Chapman, Chang Shau, and Julie Simons, "Impacting Re-Arrest Rates among Youth Sentenced in Adult Court: An Epidemiology Examination of the Juvenile Sentencing Advocacy Project," *Journal of Clinical Child and Adolescent Psychology* 32 (2003): 205–214; David L. Myers, "The Recidivism of Violent Youths in Juvenile and Adult Court: A Consideration of Selection Bias," *Youth Violence and Juvenile Justice* 1 (2003): 79–101.

44. Benjamin Steiner and Emily Wright, "Assessing the Relative Effects of State Direct File Waiver Laws on Violent Juvenile Crime: Deterrence or Irrelevance?" *Journal of Criminal Law & Criminology* 96 (2006): 1451–1477.

45. Benjamin Steiner, "The Effects of Juvenile Transfer to Criminal Court on Incarceration Decisions," *Justice Quarterly* 26 (2009): 77–106; Megan Kurlychek and Brian Johnson, "The Juvenile Penalty: A Comparison of Juvenile and Young Adult Sentencing Outcomes in Criminal Court," *Criminology* 42 (2004): 485–517.

46. Victor L. Streib, *The Juvenile Death Penalty Today: Death Sentences and Executions for Juvenile Crimes, January 1, 1973–September 30, 2003* (Ada, Ohio: Claude W. Pettit College of Law, Ohio Northern University, October 6, 2003), p. 3.

47. *Roper v. Simmons*, 125 S.Ct. 1183 (2005).

48. Erica Goode, "Young Killer: Bad Seed or Work in Progress?" *New York Times*, November 25, 2003.

49. Adam Liptak, "Court Takes Another Step in Reshaping Capital Punishment," *New York Times*, March 2, 2005.

50. *Roper v. Simmons*, 125 S.Ct. 1183 (2005).

51. Barry C. Feld, "A Slower Form of Death: Implications of *Roper v. Simmons* for Juveniles Sentenced to Life without Parole," *Notre Dame Journal of Law, Ethics and Public Policy* 22 (2008): 9–65.

52. Feld, "A Slower Form of Death," p. 10.

53. Elizabeth S. Scott and Laurence Steinberg, "The Young and the Reckless," *New York Times,* November 13, 2009, http://www.nytimes.com/2009/11/14/opinion/14scott.html.

54. *Graham v. Florida,* 08-7412, May 17, 2010.

55. *In re Gault,* 387 U.S. 1 (1967).

56. See Joseph Goldstein, Anna Freud, and Albert Solnit, *Beyond the Best Interest of the Child* (New York: Free Press, 1973).

57. See Michael Serrill, "Police Write a New Law on Juvenile Crime," *Police Magazine* (September 1979): 47; see also A. Schneider and D. Schram, *Assessment of Juvenile Justice Reform in Washington State,* vols. 1–4 (Washington, D.C.: Department of Justice, Institute of Policy Analysis, 1983); T. Castellano, "Justice Model in the Juvenile Justice System—Washington State's Experience," *Law and Policy* 8 (1986): 479.

58. Emily Gaarder, Nancy Rodriguez, and Marjorie Zatz, "Criers, Liars, and Manipulators: Probation Officers' Views of Girls," *Justice Quarterly* 21 (2004): 547–578.

59. See Richard G. Wiebush, "Juvenile Intensive Supervision: The Impact on Felony Offenders Diverted from Institutional Placement," *Crime and Delinquency* 39 (1993): 68–89.

60. For a review of these programs, see James Austin, Kelly Dedel Johnson, and Ronald Weitzer, *Alternatives to the Secure Detention and Confinement of Juvenile Offenders* (Washington, D.C.: OJJDP Bulletin, 2005), pp. 18–19.

61. James Ryan, "Who Gets Revoked? A Comparison of Intensive Supervision Successes and Failures in Vermont," *Crime and Delinquency* 43 (1997): 104–118.

62. Sheldon X. Zhang and Lening Zhang, "An Experimental Study of the Los Angeles County Repeat Offender Prevention Program: Its Implementation and Evaluation," *Criminology and Public Policy* 4 (2005): 205–236.

63. Jodi Lane, Susan Turner, Terry Fain, and Amber Sehgal, "Evaluating an Experimental Intensive Juvenile Probation Program: Supervision and Official Outcomes," *Crime and Delinquency* 51 (2005): 26–52.

64. Eve Brank, Jodi Lane, Susan Turner, Terry Fain, and Amber Sehgal, "An Experimental Juvenile Probation Program: Effects on Parent and Peer Relationships," *Crime and Delinquency* 54 (2008): 193–224.

65. Melissa Sickmund, *Juveniles in Residential Placement: 1997–2008* (Washington, D.C.: Office of Juvenile Justice and Delinquency Prevention, 2010). www.ncjrs.gov/pdffiles1/ojjdp/229379.pdf.

66. Ibid.

67. Pamela K. Lattimore, "Reentry, Reintegration, Rehabilitation, Recidivism, and Redemption," *The Criminologist* 31 (2006): 1, 3–6; see also Laura Winterfield, Christine Lindquist, and Susan Brumbaugh, *Sustaining Juvenile Reentry Programming after SVORI* (Washington, D.C.: Urban Institute, 2007).

68. Jeffrey A. Bouffard and Kathleen J. Bergseth, "The Impact of Reentry Services on Juvenile Offenders' Recidivism," *Youth Violence and Juvenile Justice* 6 (2008): 295–318; He Len Chung, Carol A. Schubert, and Edward P. Mulvey, "An Empirical Portrait of Community Reentry among Serious Juvenile Offenders in Two Metropolitan Cities," *Criminal Justice and Behavior* 34 (2007): 1402–1426.

69. David M. Altschuler and Troy L. Armstrong, "Juvenile Corrections and Continuity of Care in a Community Context: The Evidence and Promising Directions," *Federal Probation* 66 (2002): 72–77.

70. David M. Altschuler and Troy L. Armstrong, "Intensive Aftercare for High-Risk Juveniles: A Community Care Model" (Washington, D.C.: Office of Juvenile Justice and Delinquency Prevention, 1994).

71. J. David Hawkins, Richard F. Catalano, and associates, *Communities That Care: Action for Drug Abuse Prevention* (San Francisco: Jossey-Bass, 1992).

72. Richard F. Catalano, Michael W. Arthur, J. David Hawkins, Lisa Berglund, and Jeffrey J. Olson, "Comprehensive Community- and School-Based Interventions to Prevent Antisocial Behavior," in *Serious and Violent Juvenile Offenders: Risk Factors and Successful Interventions,* ed. Rolf Loeber and David P. Farrington (Thousand Oaks, Calif.: Sage, 1998).

73. Adele V. Harrell, Shannon E. Cavanagh, and Sanjeev Sridharan, *Evaluation of the Children At Risk Program: Results One Year after the End of the Program* (Washington, D.C.: NIJ Research in Brief, 1999).

74. You can find out more about CASASTART at the following website: www.casacolumbia.org/absolutenm/articlefiles/203-203-casas-tart_field_guide_2003.pdf (accessed March 26, 2009).

75. David Smith, "The Effectiveness of the Juvenile Justice System," *Criminal Justice: International Journal of Policy & Practice* 5 (2005): 181–195.

76. Barry C. Feld, *Bad Kids: Race and the Transformation of the Juvenile Court* (New York: Oxford University Press, 1999).

77. Robert O. Dawson, "The Future of Juvenile Justice: Is It Time to Abolish the System?" *Journal of Criminal Law and Criminology* 81 (1990): 136–155; see also Leonard P. Edwards, "The Future of the Juvenile Court: Promising New Directions in the Center for the Future of Children," in *The Future of Children: The Juvenile Court* (Los Altos, Calif.: David and Lucile Packard Foundation, Center for the Future of Children, 1996).

78. Alexes Harris, "Diverting and Abdicating Judicial Discretion: Cultural, Political, and Procedural Dynamics in California Juvenile Justice," *Law & Society Review* 41 (2007): 387–428.

79. John Johnson Kerbs, "(Un)equal Justice: Juvenile Court Abolition and African Americans," *Annals, AAPSS* 564 (1999): 109–125.

80. Peter W. Greenwood, *Changing Lives: Delinquency Prevention as Crime-Control Policy* (Chicago: University of Chicago Press, 2006); p. 183.

81. Ibid., pp. 193–194.

82. Peter J. Benekos and Alida V. Merlo, "Juvenile Justice: The Legacy of Punitive Policy," *Youth Violence and Juvenile Justice* 6 (2009): 28–46; Hunter Hurst, "Juvenile Court: As We Enter the Millennium," *Juvenile and Family Court Journal* 50 (1999): 21–27.

83. Howard N. Snyder and Melissa Sickmund, *Juvenile Offenders and Victims: 2006 National Report* (Pittsburgh, Pa.: National Center for Juvenile Justice, 2006), p. 113.

84. Patrick Griffin, "National Overviews," in *State Juvenile Justice Profiles* (Pittsburgh, Pa.: National Center for Juvenile Justice, 2008). Available at www.ncjj.org/stateprofiles/ (accessed May 1, 2010).

85. Patrick Griffin, "National Overviews," in *State Juvenile Justice Profiles* (Pittsburgh, Pa.: National Center for Juvenile Justice, 2008). Available at www.ncjj.org/stateprofiles/ (accessed October 29, 2009).

86. Ibid.

87. Ibid.

88. Melissa Sickmund, *Delinquency Cases in Juvenile Court, 2005* (Washington, D.C.: U.S. Department of Justice, Office of Justice Programs, Office of Juvenile Justice and Delinquency Prevention, 2009), p. 3. http://www.ncjrs.gov/pdffiles1/ojjdp/224538.pdf.

89. Simon M. Fass and Chung-Ron Pi, "Getting Tough on Juvenile Crime: An Analysis of Costs and Benefits," *Journal of Research in Crime and Delinquency* 39 (2002): 363–399.

# CHAPTER 17

# Crime and Justice in the New Millennium

## CHAPTER OBJECTIVES

1. Be familiar with the influence of globalization on crime.
2. Discuss the impact of criminal enterprise crime.
3. Describe a Ponzi scheme.
4. Explain what mortgage fraud and subprime mortgages are.
5. Be able to define cyber warfare.
6. Discuss the various forms of cyber crime.
7. Know what is being done to thwart cyber criminals.
8. Understand the concept of transnational crime.
9. Be familiar with some of the most important transnational crime groups.
10. Explain how law enforcement is taking on transnational criminal syndicates.

© Daniel Rosenbaum/New York Times/Redux

**O**n April 16, 2010, the Securities and Exchange Commission (SEC) filed a civil case against investment bank Goldman Sachs, charging "fraudulent misconduct" in the firm's 2007 sale of $1 billion in repackaged subprime mortgage–backed securities. Goldman executives did not deny that they packaged and sold the securities, but the question remains: Did they engage in a criminal act? It seems that Goldman was approached by hedge fund operator John Paulson, who offered the firm $15 million to help put together a package of home loans—known in the trade as a collateralized debt obligation (CDO)—and then market the loans to Goldman's clients, including foreign banks. Paulson believed that the American real estate market was about to collapse, and he sought to make a financial bet against properties soon to be distressed. In order to make his "bet," he, along with Goldman executives, created a fund called ABACUS that comprised home mortgages, personally selected by Paulson, on properties in Arizona, Florida, Nevada, and California, states that were undergoing a collapse in the real estate market.

Goldman Sachs then marketed the ABACUS fund without disclosing that the holdings had been handpicked by Paulson. The government charged that ABACUS fund buyers (including the Royal Bank of Scotland, which lost over $800 million in the deal) had no idea they were buying into such risky obligations. Paulson then made a financial bet that increased in value the more the mortgage-backed securities declined. His foresight was rewarded. By January 2008, nearly all the loans had been downgraded, and Paulson's hedge fund made billions.

After the indictment was filed, Goldman Sachs executives claimed they did nothing wrong in marketing the securities, because purchasers were sophisticated banks and investment companies who knew what they were doing and should have realized that buying mortgage-backed securities was very risky, especially in a down real estate market. The marketing of derivative securities such as CDOs and the short-selling of assets are common practices at virtually all major Wall Street firms. The question is whether Goldman Sachs misled the people who bought the securities and withheld information that would have altered their behavior. While millions of people lost their homes and life savings, Goldman CEO Lloyd Blankfein (who was not named in the indictment) received compensation amounting to $100 million, and John Paulson (also not indicted by the SEC) personally netted $3.7 billion in 2007; the following year his pay plummeted to only $2 billion. ∎

The Goldman Sachs case is but one of many complex financial schemes that have undermined the nation's economy, while presenting new and complex challenges for investigators in the criminal justice system. The techonological revolution has broadened the scope of crime and increased the demands on justice. It is now routine for offenders to use complex and technologically sophisticated methods to secure illegal profits and/or provide criminal services. Sometimes these schemes are so complex that it takes enforcement agencies years to unravel them, even after they are detected. These crimes may not only be national in scope, such as the schemes to defraud some of the nation's largest banking and corporate institutions; they may even be transnational enterprises involving criminal acts that cross nations and continents. However, penalties are often civil and not criminal. On July 15, 2010, Goldman announced they had reached a deal in the case, agreeing to pay the government $550 million in compensation; it was the largest penalty ever paid by a Wall Street Firm. Nonetheless, Goldman's profits exceed more than 13 billion every year.

In some instances, this new brand of crime can involve a single individual who engages in a complex criminal enterprise, such as the multi-billion-dollar fraud perpetrated by financier Bernard Madoff (more on him later). It can also involve people acting in transnational organized crime syndicates that actively traffic in contraband, such as narcotics and weapons—and even in humans for pornography and prostitution.

In this chapter we review three independent, yet interrelated, emerging criminal activities that are presenting challenges for the criminal justice system: *corporate enterprise crime*, *cyber crime*, and *transnational organized crime*. They are linked here because in each category, offenders twist the legal rules of commerce for criminal purposes. Though distinct and independent, these emerging types of crime often overlap: Transnational criminals may use cyberspace to perpetrate fraud and then seek legitimate enterprises to launder money, diversify their sources of income, increase their power and influence, and gain and enhance their surface respectability.[1] Transnational criminals may also borrow from corporate enterprise: They may appropriate marketing concepts from legitimate business enterprise, even though they use threats, extortion, and smuggling to distribute their "products."[2] Otherwise legitimate corporate enterprise executives may turn to international crime cartels to help them with economic problems such as breaking up a strike or dumping hazardous waste products, stifling competition (or threatening competitors), and increasing their influence.[3] Whereas some corporate executives cheat to improve their company's position in the business world, others are motivated purely by personal gain, acting more like organized criminals than indiscreet businesspeople.[4]

## GLOBALIZATION AND JUSTICE

The new global economy is a particularly vexing development for agents of the criminal justice system because it vastly expands the reach of criminal organizations, while at the same time creating new opportunities for criminal conspiracies. The term **globalization** refers to the process of creating transnational markets and political and legal systems; globalization has shifted the focus of crime from a local to a world perspective.

Globalization began when large companies decided to establish themselves in foreign markets by adapting their products or services to the local culture. The process took off with the fall of the Soviet Union, which opened new European markets. The development of China into an industrial superpower encouraged foreign investors to take advantage of China's huge supply of workers. As the Internet and communication revolution unfolded, companies were able to establish instant communications with their far-flung corporate empires, a technological breakthrough that further boosted trade and foreign investments. A series

**globalization**
The process of creating a global economy through transnational markets and political and legal systems.

of transnational corporate mergers and takeovers (such as occurred when Ford bought Swedish car maker Volvo in 1999 and then, in 2010, sold Volvo to the Chinese car company Geely) produced ever-larger transnational corporations.

Some experts believe globalization can improve the standard of living in third world nations by providing jobs and training. Others, however, view it as a means by which larger, more powerful nations exploit the natural resources of third world nations, avoid regulation, and take advantage of desperate workers. When these giant corporations set up a factory in a developing nation, claim critics, it is not to help the local population but to get around environmental laws and exploit needy workers who may be forced to labor in substandard conditions.[5]

It is not surprising, then, that globalization has created a fertile ground for contemporary enterprise crimes. By expanding the reach of both criminal and noncriminal organzations, globalization also increases the vulnerability of indigenous peoples with a traditional way of life.[6] With money and power to spare, criminal enterprise groups can recruit new members, bribe government officials, and even fund private armies. International organized crime has globalized its activities for the same reasons that impel legitimate multinational corporations to expand around the world: New markets bring new sources of profits. As international crime expert Louise Shelley puts it,

> Just as multinational corporations establish branches around the world to take advantage of attractive labor or raw material markets, so do illicit businesses. Furthermore, international businesses, both legitimate and illicit, also establish facilities worldwide for production, marketing, and distribution needs. Illicit enterprises are able to expand geographically to take advantage of these new economic circumstances thanks to the communications and international transportation revolution.[7]

Shelley argues that two elements of globalization encourage criminality, one technological and the other cultural. Technological advances such as efficient and widespread commercial airline traffic, improvements in telecommunications (ranging from global cell phone connectivity to the Internet), and the growth of international trade have all aided the growth in illicit transnational activities. These changes have facilitated the cross-border movement of goods and people—conditions exploited by criminals who now use Internet chat rooms to plan their activities. On a cultural level, globalization brings with it an ideology of free markets and free trade. This cultural shift means less intervention and regulation—conditions exploited by crime groups to cross unpatrolled borders and expand their activities to new regions of the world. Transnational crime groups aggressively exploit this new freedom to travel to regions where they cannot be extradited, base their operations in countries with ineffective or corrupt law enforcement, and launder their money in countries with bank secrecy or few effective controls. Globalization has allowed both individual offenders and criminal gangs to gain tremendous operational benefits and has markedly reduced the risk of apprehension and punishment.

## CORPORATE ENTERPRISE CRIME

In the late 1930s, the distinguished criminologist Edwin Sutherland first used the phrase "white-collar crime" to describe the criminal activities of the rich and powerful: "a crime committed by a person of respectability and high social status in the course of his occupation."[8] As Sutherland saw it, white-collar crime involved conspiracies by members of the wealthy classes to use their positions in commerce and industry for personal gain without regard to the law. These unscrupulous executives crafted elaborate criminal conspiracies designed to improve market share or simply to illegally siphon off corporate profits into their own pockets.[9] Most often these actions were handled by civil courts, because injured parties were more concerned with recovering their losses than with seeing the offenders punished criminally. As a consequence, Sutherland believed, the great majority of white-collar criminals avoided detection, and those who were caught generally avoided punishment.[10] As time has passed, the definition of white-collar crime has been expanded to include almost any type of business-related crime, from simple business fraud to international criminal conspiracies, and today it is widely referred to as **corporate enterprise crime**.

Recent events seem to support Sutherland's original focus on widespread corporate wrongdoing, because it is the crimes of the rich and powerful that seem to be having the most significant impact on society.[11] Experts place its total monetary value in the hundreds of billions of dollars, far outstripping the cost to society of any other type of crime. The FBI is currently pursuing more than 500 corporate fraud cases, several of which involve losses to public investors that individually exceed $1 billion. Bernard Madoff is not the only person to have pulled off a billion-dollar investment scheme: Robert Allen Stanford, owner of Stanford Financial Group and other affiliated companies, has been charged with defrauding investors of approximately $7 billion.[12] In the following sections, some of the most significant illegal corporate enterprise schemes are discussed in some detail.

## Fraud on Wall Street

The creation of global capital markets has created unprecedented opportunities for U.S. businesses to access capital and for investors to diversify their portfolios.[13] Whether through college savings plans or retirement accounts, larger numbers of Americans are choosing to invest in the securities and commodities markets than ever before; the number of people investing in securities and commodities has increased 600 percent since 1980.[14] This large-scale investment growth, however, has also led to significant growth in the amount of fraud and misconduct seen on Wall Street. Investment firms have engaged in deceptive schemes to defraud clients. Investment counselors and insurance agents have used their positions to cheat individual clients by misleading them on the quality of their investments. Financial organizations have cheated their clients by promoting risky investments as being iron-clad safe.

Perhaps the greatest of these crimes was pulled off my financier Bernard Madoff, who operated Bernard L. Madoff Investment Securities LLC. Madoff Investments became one of Wall Street's largest "specialist" trading firms, dedicated to investment management and advice. Managing billions in assets, Madoff was a member of the "jet set" and trusted advisor to many wealthy people, including director Steven Spielberg, as well as to sophisticated financial managers and investors. For a while, Madoff delivered the high returns he had promised, which of course attracted a constant flow of new investors. But things went south when the market crashed and people demanded their money back, only to find there was none available. It turns out that Madoff's asset management firm was a giant Ponzi scheme (see Exhibit 17.1). Madoff had not invested any of the money he had taken in from investors. Instead, he had deposited it in various banks, using the interest and principal to pay off investors when they wanted to take money out of their accounts. Few did so, because they were making fantastic paper profits and kept reinvesting dividends and capital gains. Madoff actively convinced them to keep their profits in the account rather than asking for a distribution. When the market turned and people began asking for their principal, Madoff's house of cards tumbled down: More than $60 billion was missing, and authorities are still trying to figure out where it all went.

When Madoff realized he could never to catch up to the paper profits, he finally told his sons what he had done, and they contacted the FBI. Madoff later claimed that he merely wanted to satisfy his clients' demand for high returns, which simply could not be met by legal means. Instead, he resorted to an illegal scheme that involved false trading activities, illegal foreign transfers, and false SEC filings. He hoped his clients would simply reinvest their gains without

**corporate enterprise crime**
Illegal activities of people and organizations whose acknowledged purpose is to profit through illegitimate business enterprise.

---

**EXHIBIT 17.1**

## *What Is a Ponzi scheme?*

A **Ponzi scheme** is a type of investment fraud that involves the payment of purported returns to existing investors from funds contributed by new investors. Ponzi scheme organizers often solicit new investors by promising to invest funds in opportunities that they claim will generate high returns with little or no risk. In many Ponzi schemes, the perpetrators of the fraud focus on attracting new money to make promised payments to earlier-stage investors and to use for personal expenses, instead of engaging in any legitimate investment activity. With little or no legitimate earnings, the schemes require a consistent flow of money from new investors to continue. Ponzi schemes tend to collapse when it becomes difficult to recruit new investors or when a large number of investors ask to cash out.

Why are they called Ponzi schemes? The term comes from one Charles Ponzi, who duped thousands of New England residents into investing in a postage stamp speculation scheme back in the 1920s. At a time when the annual interest rate for bank accounts was 5 percent, Ponzi promised investors that he could provide a 50 percent return in just 90 days. Ponzi initially bought a small number of international mail coupons in support of his scheme, but he quickly switched to using incoming funds to pay off earlier investors.

Source: Securities and Exchange Commission, "Ponzi Schemes," www.sec.gov/answers/ponzi.htm#PonziCollapse (accessed May 5, 2010).

---

requesting withdrawals until he could figure out a way of investing the money and actually making a profit! When finally caught, Madoff admitted that he knew his day of reckoning was inevitable.

Madoff's Ponzi scheme has been estimated to have cost clients $65 *billion*, and it may have been the largest criminal conspiracy in history. On March 12, 2009, he pled guilty to an 11-count criminal complaint, charging him with violations of the antifraud provisions of the Securities Act of 1933, the Securities Exchange Act of 1934, and the Investment Advisers Act of 1940.[15] On June 29, 2009, Madoff was sentenced to 150 years in prison, a life sentence.

Madoff's attempted Ponzi scheme is not unique. There have been numerous attemts to fraudulently siphon off clients' money, some so great that they have threatened to collapse the financial markets. (See Exhibit 17.2). Among these large-scale securities schemes was the prime bank fraud perpetrated by Robert Allen Stanford, but this one netted only $8 billion.[16] "Sir Robert," as he liked to be called after the Antiguan prime minister knighted him, ran a high-flying investment bank in the Caribbean nation of Antigua that offered investors high-yielding bank certificates of deposit. Sir Robert's financial activities raised eyebrows among American authorities as far back as a decade ago. Like Bernard Madoff, Stanford offered investment opportunities that promised lofty returns on relatively safe certificates of deposit—returns that were often more than twice the going rate offered by mainstream banks. Unfortunately for investors, these assurances were too good to be true. Instead of the safe investments promised, Stanford used the money in very risky long-term real estate and private equity investments, which only he and another associate oversaw; Antiguan auditors neither examined the bank's portfolio nor verified its assets. Stanford withheld this information from investors and told them, instead, that their money was totally safe because it was being monitored by a team of more than 20 analysts and yearly audits by bank regulators in Antigua. Before being seized by the government, Stanford's bank had misappropriated $8.5 billion in assets belonging to 30,000 clients in 131 countries.

## The Subprime Mortgage Scandal

During the period 2008–2009, the nation was rocked by another form of Wall Street fraud that threatened to destroy the financial system, undermine the real estate market, and create a 1929-style depression: the collapse of the subprime

**Ponzi scheme**
An investment fraud that involves the payment of purported returns to existing investors from funds contributed by new investors.

**EXHIBIT 17.2**

## Wall Street Fraud Schemes

- **The Pyramid Scheme:** In much the same way as in Ponzi schemes, the money collected from newer victims of the fraud is paid to earlier victims to provide a veneer of legitimacy. In pyramid schemes, however, the victims themselves are induced to recruit further victims through the payment of recruitment commissions.

- **Prime Bank Scheme:** Victims are induced to invest in financial instruments, alleged to have been issued by well-known institutions, which offer risk-free opportunities for high rates of return. These benefits are alleged to result from the perpetrator's access to a secret worldwide exchange ordinarily open only to the world's largest financial institutions.

- **Advance Fee Fraud:** This type of fraud encompasses a broad variety of schemes that are designed to induce their victims into remitting up-front payments in exchange for the promise of goods, services, and/or prizes. In the securities and commodities fraud context, victims are informed that in order to participate in a promising investment opportunity, they must first pay various taxes and/or fees.

- **Hedge Fund Fraud:** Hedge funds are private investment partnerships that have historically accepted only high-net-worth clients willing to meet significant minimum investment thresholds. The industry as a whole has been largely unregulated but has become increasingly relevant to middle-class investors through their exposure to hedge fund activities via ancillary investments (such as pension funds). The relative lack of regulatory scrutiny has made the industry vulnerable to fraud by fund managers, which may include overstatement/misappropriation of fund assets, overcharging for fund management fees, insider trading, market timing, and late trading.

- **Commodities Fraud:** These schemes typically involve the deceptive or fraudulent sale of commodities investments. False or deceptive sales practices are used to solicit victim funds for commodities transactions that either never occur or are inconsistent with the original sales pitches. Alternatively, commodities market participants may illegally attempt to manipulate the market for a commodity by fraudulently reporting price information or cornering the market to artificially increase the price of the targeted commodity.

- **Foreign Exchange Fraud:** These schemes are characterized by the use of false or deceptive sales practices, such as alleging high rates of return for minimal risk, to induce victims to invest in the foreign currency exchange market. The touted transactions may never occur, or they are inconsistent with the original sales pitches or are executed for the sole purpose of generating excessive trading commissions in breach of fiduciary responsibilities to the victim client

- **Broker Embezzlement:** These schemes involve illicit and unauthorized actions by brokers to steal directly from their clients. Such schemes may be facilitated by the forging of client documents, the doctoring of account statements, unauthorized trading/funds transfer activities, or other conduct in breach of the broker's fiduciary responsibilities to the victim client.

- **Late-Day Trading:** These schemes involve the illicit purchase and sale of securities after regular market hours. Such trading is restricted in order to prevent individuals from profiting on the basis of market-moving information released after the close of regular trading. Unscrupulous traders attempt to illegally exploit such opportunities by buying or selling securities at the market close price, secure in the knowledge that the market-moving information will generate illicit profits at the start of trading on the following day.

Source: FBI, "Financial Crimes Report to the Public, Fiscal Year 2008," www.fbi.gov/publications/financial/fcs_report2008/financial_crime_2008.htm#corporate.

mortgage system. As a result of this financial disaster, several prominent financial institutions, including Bear Stearns and Lehman Brothers, went out of business; banks such as IndyMac Bank and Washington Mutual failed; and the federal government was forced to provide over a trillion dollars in relief to keep other companies, such as American Insurance Group (AIG) and CitiGroup, in business. American taxpayers will be paying for this bailout over the entire course of their lives.

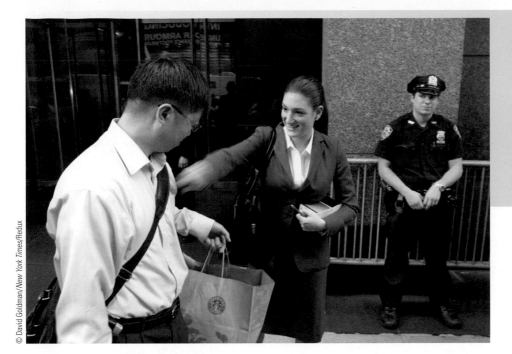

Laura Caputo, a financial job recruiter with Spire Search Partners, puts a business card in the shirt pocket of a man leaving the headquarters of Lehman Brothers, apparently carrying his office belongings, on September 15, 2008, in New York. As Lehman filed for bankruptcy, several of the company's employees emerged from the building throughout the day carrying boxes of belongings. Lehman's collapse resulted in severe financial turmoil that roiled the markets.

© David Goldman/New York Times/Redux

The cornerstone of the crisis was the collapse of the subprime mortgage sector. A subprime mortgage is a home loan given to borrowers who, because of inadequate income, would not ordinarily qualify for bank loans. Once the subprime loans have been issued, the vendors typically bundle them into large pools and sell them as securities, a process known as **securitization.** Because they carry risk, they typically pay a higher interest rate than normal securities, making them attractive to investors. By 2006, subprimes had grown to 20 percent of the mortgage market, up from 2 percent a decade earlier; this means that an estimated $1.3 trillion of the total $4.5 trillion in outstanding mortgage loans is subprime.

Although subprime mortgages can help first-time home buyers of limited means, they also have been the source of fraud by both borrowers and lenders. Borrowers have provided false information to the mortgage broker and/or lender in order to get loans for which they were not qualified. Those involved in mortgage lending, including mortgage brokers, lenders, appraisers, underwriters, accountants, real estate agents, settlement attorneys, land developers, investors, builders, bank account representatives, trust account representatives, investment banks, and credit rating agencies, have gotten involved in criminal fraud to maintain or increase their current standard of living. In addition to traditional industry conspirators, various organized criminal groups and gang members have become involved in mortgage fraud activity.[17]

Subprime lenders made risky loans, assuming that real estate values would always be increasing, enabling borrowers to refinance or sell their properties before going into default. However, when sales slowed down in the housing market, loan defaults increased and the securities lost value. As a result, mortgage companies experienced financial distress and bankruptcy.[18]

Desperate for funds, some subprime lenders, in order to stave off regulators, engaged in false accounting entries and fraudulently inflated their assets and revenues. Some manipulated their reported loan portfolio risks and used various accounting schemes to inflate their financial reports. And in some cases, before these subprime lenders' stocks rapidly declined in value, executives with insider information sold their equity positions and profited illegally. As a result of these practices, some subprime lenders are being investigated by federal agencies for

**securitization**
The process in which vendors take individual subprime loans, bundle them into large pools, and sell them as securities.

corporate fraud and insider trading. In one case, officers of Mercury Finance Company were convicted of intentionally misstating the company's financial records: They falsely reported a profit of more than $120 million instead of a loss of $30 million. Executives provided materially false financial statements to more than 20 financial institutions, enabling Mercury to obtain more than $1.5 billion in loan commitments and lines of credit. When the fraud was discovered, Mercury's stock price dropped significantly, costing shareholders nearly $2 billion in market value. A number of company officers went to prison, including former CEO John Brincat Sr., who pled guilty to wire fraud and making a false statement to a bank and was sentenced to ten years imprisonment.[19]

*FORECLOSURE RESCUE SCAMS* Not only has the availability of subprime mortgages presented opportunities for people to commit fraud, but it also created scams designed to prey upon people who obtained mortagages and now cannot make payments. There have been a variety of foreclosure rescue scams:

- *Phantom help.* Desperate homeowners are offered help by a supposed "expert" in avoiding foreclosures. They are then saddled with charges for things they could have done on their own, such as calling the bank. The phantom helper promises help, collects a fee, and never follows through. Soon it's too late to stop the foreclosure from taking place.

- *Bailout.* In this scam, someone offers to bail out the homeowner by taking the house off their hands with the promise that they can stay on as renters and buy the house back once things have been "fixed." The homeowner soon finds out that he or she cannot buy the house back, and the supposed rescuers get most, if not all, of the equity.

- *Bait and switch.* Scammers tell the victim that they are signing documents for a new loan that will solve their problems. In reality, they are signing forged documents that transfer ownership of the home, which the scammers quickly try to sell to a third party at a reduced rate. The victim still owes whatever remains on the mortgage but no longer has the asset.[20]

*BUILDER-BAILOUT SCHEMES* The housing crisis also induced unscrupulous home builders to engage in fraud in order to unload unsold homes. Buyers have been offered an incentive of a mortgage with no down payment in order to get them to buy a house they could not normally afford. For example, say a builder wishes to sell a property for $300,000, a price that allows him to make a profit. He inflates the value of the property to $360,000 and finds buyers by offering to give them $60,000 to be used as a down payment. The buyers then go to a bank and show that they owe $300,000 on a $360,000 property; the lender funds a mortgage loan of $300,000, believing that $60,000 was paid to the builder and the borrower thus had the required 20 percent home equity. However, the lender is actually funding 100 percent of the home's value. The builder acquires $300,000 from the sale of the home and keeps any profits. If the home goes into foreclosure, the lender who provided the mortgage money finds out that there was actually no equity in the home and loses both the loan and the interest the lender would have collected over the term of the mortgage.[21]

In addition to the subprime mortage scandal, a number of other mortgage schemes have been used by unscrupulous lenders and borrowers (see Exhibit 17.3).

## Billion-Dollar Management Fraud

Sometimes executives in large corporatons take advantage of their position to engage in management frauds, which typically involve falsifying financial information for their own financial benefit. Managers may create false accounting entries and false records of transactions, and they may engage in bogus trades, insider trading, kickbacks, backdating of executive stock options, and misuse or

---

**EXHIBIT 17.3**

## *Common Mortgage Fraud Schemes*

■ *Illegal Property Flipping:* Property is purchased, falsely appraised at an inflated value, and then quickly sold. What makes property flipping illegal is that the appraisal information is fraudulent. The schemes typically involve fraudulent appraisals, doctored loan documentation, and/or inflation of buyer income. Kickbacks to buyers, investors, property/loan brokers, appraisers, and title company employees are common in this scheme.

■ *Silent Second:* The buyer of a property borrows the down payment from the seller through the issuance of an undisclosed second mortgage. The primary lender believes the borrower has invested his own money in the down payment, when in fact, the money has been borrowed. The second mortgage may not be recorded to further conceal its status from the primary lender.

■ *Nominee Loans/Straw Buyers:* The identity of the borrower is concealed through the use of a nominee who allows the borrower to use the nominee's name and credit history to apply for a loan.

■ *Fictitious/Stolen Identity:* A fictitious/stolen identity may be used on the loan application. The applicant may be involved in an identity theft scheme. That is, someone else's name, personal identifying information, and credit history are used without that person's knowledge.

■ *Inflated Appraisals:* An appraiser acts in collusion with a borrower and provides the lender with a misleading appraisal report that deliberately states an inflated property value.

■ *Foreclosure Schemes:* The perpetrator identifies homeowners who are at risk of defaulting on loans, or whose houses are already in foreclosure. Perpetrators mislead the homeowners into believing they can save their homes in exchange for a transfer of the deed and up-front fees. The perpetrator profits from these schemes by remortgaging the property or pocketing fees paid by the homeowner.

■ *Equity Skimming:* An investor may use a straw buyer, false income documents, and false credit reports to obtain a mortgage loan in the straw buyer's name. Subsequent to closing, the straw buyer signs the property over to the investor in a quit claim deed that relinquishes all rights to the property and provides no guaranty to title. The investor does not make any mortgage payments and rents the property until foreclosure takes place several months later.

■ *Air Loans:* Loans are made on property that does not exist, usually without collateral. For example, a broker might invent borrowers and properties, establish accounts for payments, and maintain custodial escrow accounts. Such a fraudulent broker may set up an office with a bank of telephones, one each for the employer, the appraiser, and the credit agency, for verification purposes.

---

misappropriation of company property; solidifying one's position within the company by manipulating accounts and concealing unacceptable performance from stockholders is also a form of management fraud.

Management fraud is not a new phenomenon, but multi-billion-dollar schemes have recently rocked the nation's financial system. And management fraud has involved some of the nation's largest companies and richest people.

■ *Tyco International case.* In 2005, Tyco's chief executive officer L. Dennis Kozlowski and its chief financial officer Marc Swartz were convicted on a variety of fraud and larceny charges, including misappropriating $170 million in company funds by hiding unauthorized bonuses and secretly forgiving loans to themselves. Kozlowski and Swartz were also accused of making more than $430 million by lying about Tyco's financial condition in order to inflate the value of their stock. Kozlowski was convicted of looting the company of $150 million and sentenced to $8\frac{1}{3}$ to 25 years in prison.[22]

■ *Enron case.* Executives of this oil and gas trading firm, once one of the largest companies in the United States, engaged in a massive fraud scheme that caused the company to go bankrupt. Chairman Kenneth L. Lay was charged with conspiracy, securities fraud, wire fraud, bank fraud, and making false statements. Enron CEO Jeffrey K. Skilling and former Enron chief accounting officer Richard Causey were also charged with money laundering and conspiracy. The government claimed that executives oversaw a massive conspiracy to delude investors into believing that Enron was a growing company when, in fact, it was undergoing business setbacks. Why did they do it? Greed. Between 1998 and 2001, Lay received approximately $300 million from the sale of Enron stock options and restricted stock and made over $217 million in profit; he was also paid more than $19 million in salary and bonuses.[23] Lay died suddenly before he could be put on trial.

■ *WorldCom case.* In 2005, WorldCom CEO Bernie Ebbers was found guilty of falsifying the company's financial statements by more than $9 billion. One of the most important elements of the case was the more than $400 million that WorldCom lent or guaranteed to lend Ebbers at an interest rate of 2.15 percent. When the market collapsed, Ebbers was in no position to pay back the loans, and the company collapsed. On May 15, 2005, a federal jury in New York convicted Ebbers on all nine counts with which he was charged and sentenced him to 25 years in prison.[24]

■ *Peregrine Systems case.* Peregrine Systems, Inc., was a business software company headquartered in San Diego, California, and had been one of the region's most celebrated technology companies. Shares of Peregrine were publicly traded on the NASDAQ, and for ten consecutive quarters between 1999 and 2001, executives declared that Peregrine had met or exceeded Wall Street expectations for revenue and earnings. In truth, however, Stephen Parker Gardner, chief executive officer of Peregrine, and others deceptively manipulated Peregrine's financial statements in order to meet those expectations, thereby fraudulently inflating and sustaining the price of Peregrine's stock. Gardner and his co-schemers took steps to conceal from investors the fact that millions of dollars of Peregrine's accounts receivable had not been collected. Gardner gave false and misleading testimony to the SEC about Peregrine's business activity while he himself exercised stock options and sold thousands of shares of Peregrine stock, earning $8.2 million and getting $1 million in annual bonuses. When Peregrine's plight came to light, the company's stock price collapsed, and the company sought federal bankruptcy protection and eventually sold itself to Hewlett-Packard. Shareholders claimed losses in excess of $3 billion resulting from the fraudulent activities of Gardner and others. On December 11, 2007, Gardner was sentenced to serve 97 months in custody and ordered to serve a three-year term of supervised release following his release from prison and to forfeit more than a million dollars in assets. Gardner cooperated by giving evidence against his four co-conspirators, who plead guilty in 2008.

## Strategies to Control Corporate Crime

What efforts have been made to bring violators of the public trust to justice? Controlling corporate criminal activity typically involves two strategies designed to control organizational deviance: civil law (compliance) and criminal law (deterrence).[25]

**CIVIL LAW STRATEGIES** One approach to controlling corporate crime relies on the threat of economic sanctions or civil penalties to control potential violators and gain their compliance with regulations. Compliance strategies use the threat of civil sanctions in an attempt to create a marketplace incentive to obey the law: The more a company pollutes, the more costly and unprofitable that pollution becomes; the less income you report, the greater your civil fine. Compliance strategies also avoid stigmatizing and shaming businesspeople by focusing on the act, rather than the actor.[26]

Compliance is regulated by administrative agencies set up to oversee business activity. For example, the Securities and Exchange Commission regulates Wall Street activities; the Environmental Protection Agency is assigned to oversee pollution, monitor waterways, and prevent illegal dumping of waste products; and the Food and Drug Administration regulates drugs, cosmetics, medical devices, meats, and other foods. The legislation creating these agencies usually spells out the penalties for violating regulatory standards. For example, this approach has been used to control environmental crimes by levying heavy fines based on the quantity and quality of pollution released into the environment.[27] Those who oppose compliance strategies complain that even billion-dollar fines are a drop in the bucket to corporations that routinely earn tens of billions each year. For example, in the five years before the massive Gulf of Mexico oil spill in 2010, British Petroleum (BP) had already paid $485 million in fines in the United States alone. These penalties included an $87.43 million fine paid to the Occupational Safety and Health Administration in October 2009 for a Texas refinery explosion—the largest fine in OSHA's history—and an additional $50 million was paid to the Department of Justice for the same explosion. BP paid $3 million to OSHA for 42 safety violations at an Ohio refinery, and the company was also fined $20 million by the Department of Justice for the Alaska Prudhoe Bay spill, which violated the Clean Water Act. All of these penalties, however, were inconsequential to a company that garners profits of more than $20 billion a year.[28]

**CRIMINAL LAW STRATEGIES** These strategies rely on the threat of punishment of individual offenders to deter other would-be violators. They are deterrence strategies oriented toward apprehending violators and punishing them criminally, rather than creating conditions that induce conformity to the law. Even though law enforcement agencies and the courts have traditionally been reluctant to throw corporate executives in jail, a number of well-publicized cases, such as that of Bernard Madoff, indicate that the gloves are off and the government is willing to punish high-profile corporate criminals with long prison sentences. Because the Madoff, Enron, Worldcom, and other scandals have deprived so many people of their life savings and caused such disruption in the financial markets, both justice system personnel and the general public now consider corporate crimes as more serious offenses than common-law theft offenses and the perpetrators as deserving of severe punishment.[29] Penalties have been increasing, and long prison sentences are being routinely handed out for corporate crimes.[30] In fact, deterrence strategies have become so routine, and punishments so severe, that some commentators now argue that the government may actually be going overboard in its efforts to punish white-collar criminals, especially for crimes that result from negligent business practices rather than from intentional criminal conspiracy.[31]

## Enforcement of Corporate Crime Laws

The detection and enforcement of large-scale corporate crime is primarily in the hands of administrative departments and agencies with investigation arms to police the areas of commerce that are their responsibility. For example, the Securities and Exchange Commission (SEC) has responsibility for overseeing the nation's capital markets; it is assigned the tasks of protecting investors, as well as maintaining fair, orderly, and efficient economic markets.

If SEC investigators detect inappropriate behavior in the financial system, they may decide to bring a case either in federal court or before an administrative law judge, depending on the type of sanction or relief that is being sought. For example, if the commission seeks to bar or remove someone from acting as a corporate officer, it must take the case to a federal district court. During the proceeding, the SEC will ask the judge to issue a court order, called an injunction, prohibiting any further acts or practices that violate the law or SEC rules. An injunction can also require that the offending company open its books for tax

**CourseMate** For more information about the **Securities and Exchange Commission (SEC)**, visit the Criminal Justice CourseMate at CengageBrain.com, then access the "Web Links" for this chapter.

and accounting audits. In addition to barring or suspending the individual from serving as a corporate officer or director, the SEC can seek civil monetary penalties or the return of illegal profits (called disgorgement). A person who violates the court's order may be found in contempt and be subject to additional fines or imprisonment.

The decision to pursue criminal rather than civil violations usually is based both on the seriousness of the case and on the perpetrator's intent, actions to conceal the violation, and prior record. Any evidence of criminal activity is then sent to the Department of Justice or the FBI for investigation. Some other federal agencies, such as the Environmental Protection Agency (EPA) and the U.S. Postal Service, have their own investigative arms. Enforcement generally is reactive (generated by complaints) rather than proactive (involving ongoing investigations or the monitoring of activities). Investigations are carried out by the various federal agencies and the FBI. If criminal prosecution is called for, the case will be handled by attorneys from the criminal, tax, antitrust, and civil rights divisions of the Justice Department. If insufficient evidence is available to warrant a criminal prosecution, the case will be handled civilly or administratively by some other federal agency. For example, the Federal Trade Commission can issue a cease and desist order in antitrust or merchandising fraud cases.

## State-Level Enforcement

Responding to the threat of large-scale corporate fraud, a number of states have created special task forces and prosecution teams to crack down on fraudulent schemes and bring perpetrators to justice. In addition, state legislatures have passed a spate of new laws aimed directly at facilitating prosecution for corporate crimes. For example, in 2007, Florida's Attorney General Bill McCollum created the Mortgage Fraud Task Force to address the issues of mortgage and foreclosure rescue fraud. Since then, the Task Force has reviewed information pertaining to the business practices of more than 200 foreclosure rescue businesses. At the time of this writing, the Task Force had over 50 active investigations, including at least a dozen cases in which lawsuits had been filed, six of which were filed under the Foreclosure Rescue Fraud Prevention Act. The Mortgage Fraud Task Force is made up of representatives from state agencies, law enforcement groups, prosecutorial entities, and the Florida Bar, and its mission is to address the state's mortgage fraud issues and develop a cooperative approach on behalf of Florida's homeowners.

## ▌ CYBER CRIME

On May 15, 2008, a federal grand jury in Los Angeles indicted Lori Drew, a Missouri woman, for her alleged role in a MySpace hoax on a teenage neighbor who later committed suicide. Drew, along with others, created a fake online boy named Josh Evans, who established a cyber romance with 13-year-old Megan Meier. Later, after being spurned by "Josh," Megan took her own life. She had received several messages from "Josh" suggesting that she kill herself and that the "world would be better off without her." Drew was charged with one count of conspiracy and three counts of accessing protected computers without authorization to obtain information to inflict emotional distress. On November 26, 2008, Drew was found guilty on three lesser charges (reduced from felonies to misdemeanors by the jury; her conviction was later overturned on appeal.[32]

This case of cyber bullying, though unusual in its tragic outcome, illustrates one of the newest challenges facing the justice system. **Cyber crime**, a new breed of offenses that can be singular or ongoing, typically involve the theft and/or destruction of information, resources, or funds via computers, computer networks, or the Internet. This new category of crimes presents a compelling challenge for the justice system and the law enforcement community because (a) it is rapidly evolving, with new schemes being created daily, (b) it is difficult

**cyber crime**
The theft and/or destruction of information, resources, or funds via computers, computer networks, or the Internet.

**cyber theft**
The use of computer networks for criminal profits. Copyright infringement, identity theft, and Internet securities fraud are examples of cyber theft.

**cyber vandalism**
Malicious attacks aimed at disrupting, defacing, and destroying technology.

**cyber warfare**
Politically motivated attacks designed to compromise the electronic infrastructure of an enemy nation and disrupt its economy.

to detect through traditional law enforcement channels, and (c) to control it, agents of the justice system must develop technical skills that match those of the perpetrators.[33] It is even possible that the recent decline in crime is actually a result of cyber crime replacing traditional street crime. Instead of robbing a bank at gun point, a new group of contemporary thieves find it easier to hack into accounts and transfer funds to offshore banks. Instead of shoplifting from a bricks-and-mortar store, the contemporary cyber thief devises clever schemes to steal from etailers.

The Internet, coupled with ever more powerful computers, is now the medium of choice for providing a wide range of global services, from entertainment and communication to research and education. The cyber age has also generated an enormous amount of revenue. Spending on IT and telecommunications will grow by more than 6 percent each year and will soon reach about $2 trillion.[34] Today more than a billion people are using email, and 240 million are mobile Internet users. Magnifying the importance of the Internet is the fact that many critical infrastructure functions, ranging from banking to control of shipping on the Mississippi River are now being conducted online.[35] This vast network has now become a target for illegal activities and enterprise.

© AP Images/Tom Gannam

On May 15, 2008, a federal grand jury in Los Angeles indicted Lori Drew for her alleged role in a MySpace hoax on a teen neighbor who later committed suicide. Drew created a fake online boy named Josh Evans, who established a cyber romance with 13-year-old Megan Meier (shown here is Megan's mother Tina, showing pictures of Megan). Later, Megan received several messages from "Josh" suggesting that she kill herself and that the "world would be better off without her." After being spurned by "Josh," Megan took her own life. Drew was charged with one count of conspiracy and three counts of accessing protected computers without authorization to obtain information to inflict emotional distress. On November 26, 2008, Drew was found guilty of three misdemeanors, but her conviction was later overturned on appeal.

There are actually three forms of cyber crime (they are summarized in Concept Summary 17.1). Some cyber criminals use modern technology to accumulate goods and services. **Cyber theft** schemes range from illegally copying material under copyright protection to using technology to commit traditional theft-based offenses such as larceny and fraud. Other cyber criminals are motivated less by profit and more by the urge to commit **cyber vandalism**, or technological destruction. They aim their malicious attacks at disrupting, defacing, and destroying technology they find offensive. A third type of cyber crime is **cyber warfare**, which consists of acts aimed at undermining the social, economic, and political sytem of an enemy nation by destroying its electronic infrastructure and disrupting its economy. This can range from stealing secrets from foreign nations to destroying an enemy's Web-based infrastructure.

Thus some cyber criminals are high-tech thieves and others are high-tech vandals; the property the latter destroy is electronic rather then physical. And some may combine theft and vandalism in cyber terror attacks.

## CONCEPT SUMMARY 17.1
### *Typology of Cyber Crimes*

| Crime | Definition | Examples |
|---|---|---|
| Cyber theft | Use of cyber space either to distribute illegal goods and services or to defraud people for quick profits | Copyright infringement, identity theft, Internet securities fraud, warez |
| Cyber vandalism | Use of cyber space for revenge, for destruction, or to achieve malicious ends | Website defacement, worms, viruses, cyber stalking, cyber bullying |
| Cyber warfare | Politically motivated attacks to disrupt the electronic infrastructure and the economy of an enemy nation | Use of logic bombs to disrupt or destroy "secure" systems or networks, use of the Internet to communicate covertly with agents around the world |

## Cyber Theft: Cyber Crimes for Profit

The new computer-based technology enables criminals to operate in a more efficient and effective manner. Cyber thieves now have the luxury of remaining anonymous, living almost anywhere on the planet, conducting their business during the day or at night, and working alone or in a group, while at the same time reaching a much greater number of potential victims than ever before. No longer are con artists and criminal entrepreneurs limited to fleecing victims in a particular geographic locale; the whole world can be their target. And the technology revolution has opened up novel avenues of attack for cyber theft—ranging from the unlawful distribution of computer software to Internet security fraud—that heretofore were nonexistent.

Cyber thieves conspire to use cyber space either to distribute illegal goods and services or to defraud people for quick profits. Some of the most common methods are described below.

## Computer Fraud

Computer fraud is not a unique offense but, rather, a common-law crime committed using contemporary technology. Consequently, many computer crimes are prosecuted under such traditional criminal statutes as those prohibiting larceny and fraud. However, not all computer crimes fall under common-law statutes because the property stolen may be intangible—that is, it may consist of electronic and/or magnetic impulses. Such crimes include

- *Theft of information.* The unauthorized obtaining of information from a computer (for example, "hacking"), including software that is copied for profit.
- *The "Salami slice" fraud.* The perpetrator carefully "skims" small sums from the balances of a large number of accounts in order to bypass internal controls and escape detection.
- *"One-off kamikaze" fraud.* Similar to a "Salami slice, this manipulation of accounts in the banking system occurs on a much larger and usually more complex scale.
- *Software theft.* The comparative ease of making copies of computer software has led to a huge illegal market, depriving authors of very significant revenues.
- *Corporate espionage.* Trade secrets are stolen by a company's competitors, which can be either domestic or foreign. The goal is to increase the rival company's (or nation's) competitive edge in the global marketplace.[36]

## Pornography and Prostitution

The IT revolution has revitalized the "porn industry." The Internet is an ideal venue for selling and distributing adult material; the computer is an ideal device for storing and viewing it. Because of their vast numbers, it is difficult to estimate how many websites feature sexual content, including nude photos, videos, live sex acts, and Webcam strip sessions, among other forms of "adult entertainment."[37] The number of pornography Web pages has soared during the past six years, and there are now over a million sites containing more than 250 million pages of erotic content, all hoping to cash in on the billions in revenue spent on Internet porn annually.[38]

© Joe Raedle/Getty Images

*Lt. Mike Baute from Florida's Child Predator CyberCrime Unit talks with a man via instant messaging during the unveiling of a new CyberCrime office on March 7, 2008, in Fort Lauderdale, Florida. The person on the other end of the chat told Lt. Baute, who is saying he is a 14-year-old girl, that he is a 31-year-old male and sent Baute a photograph of himself. Florida ranks fourth in the nation in volume of child pornography, and the CyberCrime Unit intends to reduce that ranking through aggressive enforcement.*

Revenue from Internet porn comes from a number of sources: paid subscriptions, advertisements for other porn sites, fees for diverting Web traffic to other sites, sale of sex-related products, and providing auxiliary services such as age verification.

The government has moved to control the broadcast of obscene films via satellite and other technological innovations. However, the First Amendment right to free speech makes legal control of pornography, even kiddie porn, quite difficult. For example, to control the spread of Internet pornography, Congress passed the Communications Decency Act (CDA), which made all Internet service providers, commercial online services, bulletin board systems, and electronic mail providers criminally liable whenever their services were used to transmit material considered "obscene, lewd, lascivious, filthy, or indecent" (§ 314, 1996). However, In *Reno v. ACLU* (1997), the Supreme Court ruled that the CDA unconstitutionally restricted free speech, once again illustrating the difficulty that law enforcement has when trying to balance the need to control obscenity with the First Amendment.[39]

In 1996 Congress again attempted to control the growth of Internet porn when it passed the Child Pornography Prevention Act (CPPA). The CPPA expanded the federal prohibition on child pornography to include not only pornographic images made using actual children but also any visual depiction that is, or appears to be, of a minor engaging in sexually explicit conduct. The careful language of the act was used to ban "virtual child pornography" that appears to depict minors, whether or not minors are actually used.[40] In 2002, however, the U.S. Supreme Court struck down some sections of the CPPA as being unconstitutionally deficient, especially those that ban "virtual porn":

> Finally, the First Amendment is turned upside down by the argument that, because it is difficult to distinguish between images made using real children and those produced by computer imaging, both kinds of images must be prohibited. The overbreadth doctrine prohibits the Government from banning unprotected speech if a substantial amount of protected speech is prohibited or chilled in the process.[41]

Since the Court's ruling, the act has not been enforced. The legal difficulties encountered by the CPPA illustrate the trouble society has controlling the distribution of sexually related materials and why it is today a multi-billion-dollar industry.[42]

## Denial-of-Service Attack

A **denial-of-service** attack is an attempt to extort money from legitimate users of an Internet service by threatening to unterfere with the user's access to that service.[43]

**denial-of-service attack**
Extorting money from an Internet service user by threatening to prevent the user from having access to the service.

Examples include attempts to "flood" a computer network, thereby preventing access by legitimate network traffic; attempts to disrupt connections within a computer network, thereby interrupting access to a service; attempts to prevent a particular individual from accessing a service; and attempts to disrupt service to a specific system or person.

## Copyright Infringement

For the past decade, groups of individuals have been working together to obtain software illegally and then "crack" or "rip" its copyright protections before posting it on the Internet for other members of the group to use. Its criminal purveyors refer to this pirated material as **warez** (pronounced like "wares," as in "software").

Frequently, these new pirated copies reach the Internet days or weeks before the legitimate product is commercially available. The government has actively pursued members of the warez community, and some have been charged and convicted under the Computer Fraud and Abuse Act (CFAA), which criminalizes accessing computer systems without authorization to obtain information,[44] and the Digital Millennium Copyright Act (DMCA), which makes it a crime to circumvent the antipiracy measures built into most commercial software and also outlaws the manufacture, sale, or distribution of code-cracking devices used to illegally copy software.[45] The United States Criminal Code provides penalties for a first-time offender of incarceration for five years and a fine of $250,000.[46] Other provisions provide for the forfeiture and destruction of infringing copies and all equipment used to make those copies.[47]

## Internet Securities Fraud

Internet fraud involves using the Internet to intentionally manipulate the securities marketplace for profit. Three major types of Internet securities fraud are common today.

- *Market manipulation.* Stock market manipulation occurs when an individual tries to control the price of stock by interfering with the natural forces of supply and demand. There are two principal forms of this crime: the "pump and dump" and the "cyber smear." In a pump and dump scheme, erroneous and deceptive information is posted online to get unsuspecting investors interested in a stock, while those spreading the information sell previously purchased stock at an inflated price. The cyber smear is a reverse pump and dump: Negative information is spread online about a stock, driving down its price and enabling people to buy it at an artificially low price before rebuttals by the company's officers reestablish the legitimate price.[48]

- *Fraudulent offerings of securities.* Some cyber criminals create websites specifically designed to sell securities fraudulently. To make the offerings look more attractive than they really are, assets may be inflated, expected returns overstated, and risks understated. In these schemes, investors are promised abnormally high profits on their investments. No investment is actually made. Early investors are paid returns with the investment money received from the later investors. The system usually collapses, and the later investors do not receive dividends and lose their initial investment.

- *Illegal touting.* This crime occurs when individuals make securities recommendations and fail to disclose that they are being paid to disseminate their favorable opinions.

## Identity Theft

**Identity theft** occurs when a person uses the Internet to steal someone's identity and/or impersonate the victim to open a new credit card account or conduct some other financial transaction. It is a type of cyber crime that has grown at startling rates over the past few years.[49]

Identity theft can damage a person's good name and inflict severe losses and inconvenience by manipulating credit records or depleting bank accounts. Some identity thieves create false emails and/or websites that look legitimate but are designed to gain illegal access to a victim's personal information; this is known as **phishing** (and also as *carding* and *spoofing*).

Phishing emails and websites have become even more of a problem now that cyber criminals can easily copy brand names, the names of corporate personnel, and their insignia directly into the email. The look is so authentic that victims believe the email comes from the advertised company. Most phishers send out spam emails to a large number of recipients, knowing that some of those recipients will have accounts with the company they are impersonating. Some phishing schemes involve job offers. Once the unsuspecting victims fill out the "application," answering personal questions and including their Social Security number, the phisher has them in his grasp.[50]

## Etailing Fraud

New fraud schemes are evolving to exploit the fact that billions of dollars of goods are sold on the Internet each year. **Etailing fraud** can involve both buying and selling merchandise illegally on the Internet. Some etailing scams involve failure to deliver promised purchases or services, and others involve the substitution of cheaper or used material for higher-quality purchases.

## Distributing Dangerous Drugs

On May 1, 2009, a jury found employees of Jive Network (which sold controlled substances, mostly stimulants and depressants, using Internet websites) guilty of various drug trafficking crimes; among those convicted were medical doctors. Customers of Jive Network, who had no prescriptions, accessed its websites and purchased controlled substances such as valium, barbiturates, and steroids with a credit card or by money order. Although the customers were required to complete a short "health history,"[51] the doctors employed by Jive, who had no face-to-face contact with the customers, approved orders for the controlled substances without verifying identities or ages, conducting any physical examinations or testing, or reviewing any medical records. For a fee, Jive Network doctors unlawfully approved and issued "prescription" drug orders outside the usual course of their professional practice and for no legitimate medical purpose. During the three-year conspiracy, the organization distributed approximately 5 million dosage units of Schedule III controlled substances (such as codeine, steroids, and Nalline) and approximately 39 million dosage units of Schedule IV controlled substances (such as Rohypnol and valium) to over 500,000 Internet customers who had no valid prescriptions. And in the process it illegally generated revenue in excess of $77 million.

As the Jive Network case illustrates, the Internet has become a prime purveyor of prescription drugs, some of which can be quite dangerous when they are used to excess or fall into the hands of minors. One national survey found 365 websites either advertising or offering controlled prescription drugs for sale online; only two of those sites were registered Internet pharmacy practice sites. More than 80 percent of sites offering drugs for sale required no prescription from a patient's physician. And of the 15 percent of sites that did indicate that a prescription was required, half simply asked that the prescription be faxed, a practice that increases the risk of multiple use of one prescription as well as other fraud.[52]

© AP Images/Suffolk County District Attorney

*Identity theft can be very lucrative. Tax preparer Diana Aliffi (shown here in her mug shot) is accused of taking personal information from former clients and filing phony 2007 state and federal income tax returns in their names, all in a bid to steal as much as $19 million in refunds. Aliffi is suspected of using the personal information from clients' prior tax returns to fill out the fake 2007 returns in their names. She then asked for refunds to be sent to her home office instead of to the victims. Because the bogus returns were filed electronically, Aliffi was able to fake earnings and other information that a client normally would provide through paperwork such as a W-2 form.*

**CourseMate** For more information about the **Federal Trade Commission website on identity theft**, visit the Criminal Justice CourseMate at CengageBrain.com, then access the "Web Links" for this chapter.

**etailing fraud**
Using the Internet to buy or sell merchandise illegally.

## Cyber Vandalism: Cyber Crime with Malicious Intent

Some cyber criminals may be motivated not by greed or profit but by the thirst for revenge, by the desire to inflict wanton destruction, or by other a malicious intent. Cyber vandalism includes sending destructive viruses and worms to attack important computer networks. Cyber vandals are motivated more by malice than by greed:

■ Some cyber vandals target computers and networks, seeking revenge for some perceived wrong.

■ Some desire to exhibit their technical prowess and superiority.

■ Some wish to highlight the vulnerability of computer security systems.

■ Some want to spy on other people's private financial and personal information ("computer voyeurism").

■ Some want to destroy computer security because they believe in open access to all systems and programs.[53]

## What Forms of Cyber Vandalism Currently Exist?

*VIRUSES AND WORMS*  A computer virus is one type of malicious software program (also called malware) that disrupts or destroys existing programs and networks, causing them to perform, instead, the task for which the virus was designed.[54] The virus is then spread from one computer to another when a user sends out an infected file through email, a network, or a disk. Computer worms are similar to viruses, but they use computer networks or the Internet to self-replicate and "send themselves" to other users, generally via email, without the aid of the operator.

*TROJAN HORSES*  Some hackers may introduce a Trojan horse program into a computer system. The Trojan horse looks like a benign application, but it contains illicit codes that can damage the system operations. Sometimes hackers with a cruel sense of irony install a Trojan horse and claim that it is an antivirus program. When it is opened, it spreads viruses in the computer system. Trojan horses do not replicate themselves as viruses do, but they can be just as destructive.

*WEB DEFACEMENT*  Cyber vandals may target the websites of their victims. Web defacement is a type of cyber vandalism that occurs when a computer hacker intrudes on another person's website by inserting or substituting codes that expose visitors to the site to misleading or provocative information.

*CYBER STALKING*  Traditional stalking involves repeated harassing or threatening behavior, such as following a person, appearing at a person's home or place of business, making harassing phone calls, leaving written messages or objects, or vandalizing a person's property. **Cyber stalking** is the use of the Internet, email, or other electronic communications devices to stalk another person.[55] Some cyber stalkers pursue minors through online chatrooms, establish a relationship with a child, and later make contact for the purpose of engaging in criminal sexual activities. Today, Internet predators are more likely to meet, develop relationships with, and beguile at-risk adolescents and underage teenagers, rather than using coercion and violence.[56]

**cyber stalking**
Using the Internet, email, or other electronic communications devices to stalk or harass another person.

## Cyber Bullying

Experts define bullying among children as repeated negative acts committed by one or more children against another.[57] These negative acts may be physical or verbal in nature—for example, hitting or kicking, teasing or taunting—or they may involve indirect actions such as manipulating friendships or purposely excluding other children from activities. Bullying is a problem that remains to be solved, and it has now expanded from the physical environment to the virtual. Because of the availability of cyber space, physical distance is no longer a refuge from the frequency and depth of harm doled out by a bully to his or her victim.[58] **Cyber bullying** is willful and repeated harm inflicted through the medium of electronic text. Like their real-world counterparts, cyber bullies are malicious and cowardly aggressors who seek pleasure or profit through the mistreatment of other individuals. Although power in traditional bullying might derive from physical (stature) or social (competency or popularity) advantage, online power may simply stem from proficiency on the Net. Cyber bullies who are able to navigate the Internet and utilize technology in a way that enables them to harass others are in a position of power relative to their victims. There are four major approaches that cyber bullies employ to harass their victims:

- Bullies can send harassing emails or instant messages.
- They can post obscene, insulting, and slanderous messages to online bulletin boards.
- They can develop websites to promote and disseminate defamatory content.
- They can send harassing text messages to the victim via cellular phones.[59]

> **cyber bullying**
> Willful and repeated harm done through the medium of electronic text.

> **CourseMate** For more information about **cyber bullies**, visit the Criminal Justice CourseMate at CengageBrain.com, then access the "Web Links" for this chapter.

## Cyber Warfare

The justice system must now also be on guard against attacks of cyber warfare that are aimed at the United States by overseas adversaries. Although the term may be difficult to define, cyber warfare can be viewed as an effort by covert forces to disrupt the points where the virtual electronic reality of computers intersects the physical world.[60]

Cyber warfare has been defined as "premeditated, politically motivated attack[s] against information, computer systems, computer programs, and data which result in violence against noncombatant targets by sub-national groups or clandestine agents."[61] Cyber warfare may involve the use of computer network tools to shut down critical national infrastructures or to coerce or intimidate a government or civilian population.[62]

Even though they come from a region where computer databases and the Internet are not widely used, terrorist organizations are beginning to understand the damage that cyber crime can inflict on their targets. Terrorist organizations are now adapting information technology into their arsenal, and agencies of the justice system have to be ready for a sustained attack on the nation's electronic infrastructure.

One form of attack is cyber espionage. This involves hacking into secure computer networks at the target nation's most sensitive military bases, defense contractors, and aerospace companies in order to steal important data or to assess their defenses. Infrastructure attacks can also be aimed at water treatment plants, electric plants, dams, oil refineries, and nuclear power plants. These industries all provide vital services to society by allowing people to go about their daily lives. Terrorist computer hackers could make a dam overflow or cause real property damage to oil refineries or nuclear plants by shutting down safeguards in the system designed to prevent catastrophic meltdowns.

In one well-known cyber espionage case, Chinese agents were able to penetrate computers, enter hidden sections of a hard drive, zip up as many files as possible, and transmit the data to way stations in South Korea, Hong Kong, or Taiwan before sending them to mainland China. The spy ring, known as Titan Rain, is thought to rank among the most pervasive cyber espionage threats ever faced by computer networks in the United States. It is believed that the agents have compromised networks ranging from the Redstone Arsenal military base to NASA to the World Bank; the U.S. Army's flight-planning software has also been electronically stolen. Hundreds of Defense Department computer systems have been penetrated, and similar attacks have been launched against classified systems in Britain, Canada, Australia, and New Zealand.[63] In 2008, the Pentagon issued a report on China's "Cyber Warfare Capabilities," acknowledging that hackers in China had penetrated the Pentagon's computer system and that intrusions, apparently from China, into computer networks used "many of the skills and capabilities that would also be required for computer network attack." It was not clear whether the hackers acted alone or were backed by the Chinese military, but there was ample evidence of Chinese interest in cyber espionage as part of their long-term strategy.[64]

## The Extent and Costs of Cyber Crime

How common are cyber crimes and how costly are they to American businesses and the general public? The Internet has become a major source of illegal profits. Criminal entrepreneurs view this vast pool as a target for cyber crime, and although an accurate accounting of cyber crime will probably never be made because so many offenses go unreported, there is little doubt that its incidence is growing rapidly.

Thousands of of breaches occur each year, but most are not reported to local, state, or federal authorities. Some cyber crimes go unreported because they involve low-visibility acts that are rarely detected, such as copying computer software in violation of copyright laws.[65] Some businesses choose not to report cyber crime because they fear revealing the weaknesses in their network security systems. However, the information that is available indicates that the profit in cyber crime is enormous and continually growing.[66] Losses are now in the billions, and they continue to rise with the continuing growth of e-commerce.

## Controlling Cyber Crime

The proliferation of cyber crimes has created the need for new laws and enforcement processes. Because technology evolves so rapidly, enforcement presents challenges that are particularly vexing. Numerous organizations have been set up to provide training and support for law enforcement agents. In addition, new federal and state laws have been aimed at particular areas of high-tech crimes.[67] What are some of the new legislative initiatives designed to limit or control cyber crime?

*SOFTWARE PIRACY* The government has actively pursued members of the warez community, and some have been charged and convicted under the Computer Fraud and Abuse Act (CFAA), which criminalizes accessing computer systems without authorization to obtain information.[68] The Digital Millennium Copyright Act (DMCA) makes it a crime to circumvent antipiracy measures built into most commercial software and also outlaws the manufacture, sale, or distribution of code-cracking devices used to copy software illegally.[69]

*COPYRIGHT INFRINGEMENT* The United States Criminal Code provides penalties for a first-time illegal copyright offender of five years of incarceration and a fine of $250,000.[70] Infringing copies and all equipment used to make those copies are also subject to forfeiture and destruction.[71]

*IDENTITY THEFT* To meet this increasing threat, Congress passed the Identity Theft and Assumption Deterrence Act of 1998 (the Identity Theft Act) to make it a federal crime knowingly to transfer or use, without lawful authority, a means of identification of another person with the intent to commit, or to aid or abet, any activity that constitutes a violation of federal law, or that constitutes a felony under any applicable state or local law.[72] Violations of the act are investigated by federal investigative agencies such as the U.S. Secret Service, the FBI, and the U.S. Postal Inspection Service. In 2004, the Identity Theft Penalty Enhancement Act was signed into law. The act increases existing penalties for the crime of identity theft, establishes aggravated identity theft as a criminal offense, and establishes mandatory penalties for aggravated identity theft. According to the new law, anyone who knowingly "transfers, possesses, or uses, without lawful authority" someone else's identification will be sentenced to an extra prison term of two years with no possibility of parole. Individuals committing identity fraud while engaged in crimes associated with terrorism—such as aircraft destruction, arson, airport violence, or kidnapping top government officials—will receive a mandatory sentence enhancement of five years.

*INTERNET PORNOGRAPHY* As noted previously, it is difficult to detect and control Internet pornography. Opponents of any controls warn that they may violate the right of free speech. Congress has struggled to create legislation that will restrict objectionable use without violating First Amendment freedoms. For example, the Child Online Protection Act (H.R. 3783) bans web postings of material deemed "harmful to minors."[73] On May 13, 2002, the Supreme Court partly upheld the law when it ruled that the law's use of what it calls "community standards" to define what is harmful to children does not by itself make the law unconstitutional.[74] However, there may be future challenges to COPA on the grounds that it inhibits free speech.

*COMPUTER CRIMES* Congress has treated computer-related crimes as distinct federal offenses since passage of the Counterfeit Access Device and Computer Fraud and Abuse Law in 1984.[75] The 1984 act protected classified United States defense and foreign relations information, financial institution and consumer reporting agency files, and access to computers operated for the government. The act was supplemented in 1996 by the National Information Infrastructure Protection Act (NIIPA), which significantly broadens the scope of the law.

## Enforcing Laws against Cyber Crime

How has the justice system responded to cyber crime? Most of the efforts are being made at the federal level. One approach is to create working groups that coordinate the activities of numerous agencies involved in investigating cyber crime. The Interagency Telemarketing and Internet Fraud Working Group brings together representatives of numerous United States Attorneys' offices, the FBI, the Secret Service, the Postal Inspection Service, the Federal Trade Commission, the Securities and Exchange Commission, and other law enforcement and regulatory agencies to share information about trends and patterns in Internet fraud schemes. One of the most successful federal efforts is the New York Electronic Crimes Task Force (NYECTF), a partnership between the U.S. Secret Service and a host of other public safety agencies and private corporations. Today, the task force consists of over 250 individual members representing federal, state, and local law enforcement; the private sector; and computer science specialists from 18 different universities. Since 1995, the New York task force has charged over 1,000 individuals with causing electronic crime losses exceeding $1.0 billion. It has trained over 60,000 law enforcement personnel, prosecutors, and private industry representatives in cyber crime prevention. Its success has prompted Boston, Miami, Charlotte, Chicago, Las Vegas, San Francisco, Los Angeles, and Washington, D.C., to set up similar task forces.[76]

## RACE, GENDER, AND CULTURE IN CRIMINAL JUSTICE

# *Transnational Sex Trafficking*

Every year, hundreds of thousands of women and children—primarily from Southeast Asia and Eastern Europe—are lured by the promise of good jobs and then end up in the sex trade in industrialized countries. Data is unreliable, but estimates of the number of people trafficked internationally each year range between 600,000 and one million men, women, and children. Japan now has more than 10,000 commercial sex establishments, and 150,000 to 200,000 foreign girls are trafficked into the country each year. It is believed that traffickers import up to 50,000 women and children every year into the United States, despite legal prohibitions and enforcement efforts. According to a 2009 report by the United Nations , the most common form of human trafficking (79%) is sexual exploitation, and the victims are predominantly women and girls; about 20 percent of the victims are children.

The UN report found that the majority of sex traffickers are women. Many were in the sex trade themselves and were encouraged by their recruiter/ trafficker to return home and recruit other women,

often under the scrutiny of people working for the trafficker to make sure they don't try to escape.

Because it is a global enterprise, there is a great deal of cooperation in trafficking; thus in Eastern Europe a single gang may include Russians, Moldavians, Egyptians, and Syrians. Cooperation makes it possible to traffic sex slaves not only to neighboring countries but all around the globe. The UN found that victims from East Asia were detected in more than 20 countries in regions throughout the world, including Europe, the Americas, the Middle East, Central Asia, and Africa.

## Contributing Factors

Human trafficking is facilitated by social problems and disorder, such as disruptions in the global economy, war, and social unrest. Economic crisis hits young girls especially hard. Females victims are often poor and aspire to a better life. They may be forced, coerced, deceived, and psychologically manipulated into industrial or agricultural work, marriage, domestic servitude, organ donation, or sexual exploitation. Some traffickers exploit victims' frustration with low salaries in their home countries,

---

**OTHER SPECIALIZED ENFORCEMENT AGENCIES**  Specialized enforcement agencies are being created to fight cyber crime. The Internet Fraud Complaint Center, based in Fairmont, West Virginia, is run by the FBI and the National White Collar Crime Center. It brings together about 1,000 state and local law enforcement officials and regulators. It then analyzes the fraud-related complaints for patterns, develops additional information on particular cases, and sends investigative packages to law enforcement authorities in the jurisdiction that seem likely to have the greatest investigative interest in the matter. In the first year of its operation, the center received 36,000 complaints, the majority involving auction fraud.

Law enforcement has made remarkable strides in dealing with the crime of identity theft over the last two years. Nonetheless, the problem is serious and may expand despite efforts to control it.

**transnational organized crime**
Use of illegal tactics to gain profit in the global marketplace, typcally involving the cross-border sale and distribution of illegal commodities.

## TRANSNATIONAL ORGANIZED CRIME

The third emerging threat involves **transnational organized crime**—ongoing international criminal enterprise groups whose goal is personal economic gain through illegitimate means. Though sophisticated in the use of technology for communication and recruitment, these criminal groups also use systematic and others take advantage of a crisis in the victim's family that requires her to make money abroad. The traffickers then promise to take the victim abroad and find some traditionally female service sector job, such as waitress, salesperson, domestic worker, or au pair/babysitter.

Victims often come from poorer countries, but the market for labor and sex is found in wealthier countries or in countries that, even though they themselves are economically poor, cater to the demands of citizens from wealthy countries, of corporations, or of tourists.

## Combating Trafficking

Recently, the United States made stopping the trafficking of women a top priority. In 1998, the "Memorandum on Steps to Combat Violence against Women and the Trafficking of Women and Girls" directed the secretary of state, the attorney general, and the president's Interagency Council on Women to expand their work against violence against women to include efforts to stop the trafficking of women.

In the former Soviet Union, prevention education projects are aimed at potential victims of trafficking, and nongovernmental organizations have established hotlines for victims or women seeking information about the risks of accepting job offers abroad.

The UN report found that the number of convictions for human trafficking is increasing, especially in a handful of countries. Nonetheless, most countries' conviction rates rarely exceed 1.5 per 100,000 people, which is even below the level normally recorded for rare crimes such as kidnapping. As of 2008, two out of every five countries covered by the UNODC Report had not recorded a single conviction for sex trafficking. Clearly, the problem remains.

## Critical Thinking

1. If put in charge, what would you do to slow or end the international sex trade? Before you answer, remember the saying that prostitution is the oldest profession, which implies that curbing it may prove quite difficult.

2. Should men who hire prostitutes be punished very severely in order to deter them from getting involved in the exploitation of these vulnerable young women?

Sources: Mark Lusk and Faith Lucas, "The Challenge of Human Trafficking and Contemporary Slavery," *Journal of Comparative Social Welfare* 25 (2009): 49–57; United Nations Office on Drugs and Crime, "Global Reports on Trafficking in Persons," www.unodc .org/documents/Global_Report_on_TIP.pdf (accessed July 7, 2009); Shannon Devine, "Poverty Fuels Trafficking to Japan," *Herizons* 20 (2007): 18–22; Linda Williams and Jennifer Ngo, "Human Trafficking," in Claire Renzetti and Jeffrey Edelson (Eds.), *Encyclopedia of Interpersonal Violence* (Thousand Oaks, Calif.: Sage Publications 2007); Donna Hughes, "The 'Natasha' Trade: Transnational Sex Trafficking," *National Institute of Justice Journal* (January 2001), www.uri .edu/artsci/wms/hughes/natasha_nij.pdf (accessed March 15, 2009).

violence and corruption to achieve their ends. They are involved in money laundering; human smuggling; cyber crime; and the trafficking of humans, drugs, weapons, endangered species, body parts, or nuclear material.[77] There is also a troubling overseas trade in prostitution, in which men from wealthy countries frequent semi-regulated areas in needy nations such as Thailand in order to procure young girls forced or sold into prostitution—a phenomenon known as *sex tourism.* In addition to sex tours, there has also been a soaring demand for pornography, strip clubs, lap dancing, escorts, and telephone sex in developing countries.[78] Transnational sex trafficking, exporting women for the purpose of prostitution, is the subject of the accompanying Race, Gender, and Culture in Criminal Justice feature.

## Transnational Crime Groups

Transnational crime networks may locate themselves in nations whose governments that are too weak to present effective opposition. If they believe that the government may be interfering with their illegal activities, such as drug trafficking, that bring them immense profits, they will carry out a terror campaign, killing police officials and using bribery, violence, or terror to achieve their goals. The political turmoil of the twenty-first century, coupled with advances in telecommunications and computer technology, has had the

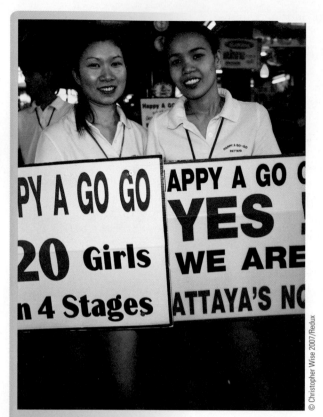

*Young women trying to attract customers to a go-go bar in Pattaya, Thailand. Pattaya is renowned and stigmatized as a tourist destination where the lure of cheap sex is its only "virtue." Pattaya is often referred to as a modern Sodom, where every resident is condemned as sinful or corrupt. The town attracts middle-aged, aging, and young men, from European and Asian countries including China, Taiwan, Korea, and Russian. Sex tourism is one of the world's pressing problems.*

© Christopher Wise 2007/Redux

unintended effect of providing avenues for the rapid expansion of transnational organized crime.[79]

There are a variety of transnational gangs whose membership is spread across the globe. Chinese groups are heavily involved in human trafficking—bringing large numbers of Chinese migrants to North America and essentially enslaving them. Eastern gangs trace their origin to countries spanning the Baltics, the Balkans, Central/Eastern Europe, Russia, the Caucasus, and Central Asia. Though ethnically homogenous, they work with other ethnic groups when perpetrating crimes. Trading in illegal arms, narcotics, pornography, and prostitution, they operate a multibillion-dollar transnational crime cartel. Organized groups prey upon women in the poorest areas of Europe—Romania, the Ukraine, and Bosnia—and sell them into virtual sexual slavery. Many of these women are transported as prostitutes around the world, and some find themselves in the United States. Among the best known of these transnational crime groups are

- *Yakuza.* Japanese criminal group. It is often involved in multinational criminal activities, including human trafficking, gambling, prostitution, and undermining licit businesses.

- *Fuk Ching.* Chinese organized crime group in the United States. It has been involved in smuggling, street violence, and human trafficking.

- *Triads.* Underground criminal societies based in Hong Kong. They control secret markets and bus routes and are often involved in money laundering and drug trafficking.

- *Heijin.* Taiwanese gangsters who are often executives in large corporations. They are often involved in white-collar crimes, such as illegal stock trading and bribery, and they sometimes run for public office.

- *Jao Pho.* Organized crime group in Thailand. It is often involved in illegal political and business activity.

- *Red Wa.* Gangsters from Thailand. They are involved in manufacturing and trafficking methamphetamine.[80]

Two other powerful transnational crime groups, the Russian Mob and Mexican drug trafficking cartels, are discussed in the following sections.

**RUSSIAN TRANSNATIONAL CRIME GROUPS**  Since the collapse of the Soviet Union in 1991, criminal organizations in Russia and other former Soviet republics, such as the Ukraine, have engaged in a variety of crimes: drugs and arms trafficking, stolen automobiles, trafficking in women and children, and money laundering.[81] No area of the world seems immune to this menace, especially not the United States. America is the land of opportunity for unloading criminal goods and laundering dirty money.

Russian organized crime is not based primarily on ethnic or family structures. Instead, Russian organized crime is based on economic necessity that was inflicted by the oppressive Soviet regime. Here, a professional criminal class developed in Soviet prisons during the Stalinist period that began in 1924—the era of the gulag. These criminals adopted behaviors, rules, values, and sanctions that bound them together in what was called the thieves' world, led by the elite *vory v zakone*, criminals who lived according to the "thieves' law." This thieves' world, and particularly the *vory*, created and maintained the bonds and climate of trust necessary for carrying out organized crime.

The following are some specific characteristics of Russian organized crime in the post-Soviet era:

■ Russian criminals make extensive use of the state governmental apparatus to protect and promote their criminal activities. For example, most businesses in Russia—legal, quasi-legal, and illegal—must operate with the protection of a *krysha* (roof). This protection is often provided by police or security officials employed outside their "official" capacities for this purpose. In other cases, officials are "silent partners" in criminal enterprises that they, in turn, protect.

■ The criminalization of the privatization process has resulted in the massive use of state funds for criminal gain. Valuable properties are purchased through insider deals for much less than their true value and then resold for lucrative profits.

■ Criminals have been able to directly influence the state's domestic and foreign policy to promote the interests of organized crime, either by attaining public office themselves or by buying public officials.

Beyond these particular features, organized crime in Russia shares other characteristics that are common to organized crime elsewhere in the world:

■ Systematic use of violence, including both the threat and the use of force.

■ Hierarchical structure.

■ Limited or exclusive membership.

■ Specialization in types of crime and a division of labor.

■ Military-style discipline, with strict rules and regulations for the organization as a whole.

■ Possession of high-tech equipment, including military weapons; threats, blackmail, and violence are used to penetrate business management and assume control of commercial enterprises or, in some instances, to found their own enterprises with money from their criminal activities.

As a result of these activities,

■ Russia has rates of homicide that are now more than 20 times those in western Europe and approximately 3 times the rates recorded in the United States. The rates more closely resemble those of a country embroiled in civil war than those of a country 15 years into the transition to a market economy.

■ Corruption and organized crime are globalized. Russian organized crime is active in Europe, Africa, Asia, and North and South America.

■ Massive money laundering is now common. It allows Russian and foreign organized crime to flourish. In some cases, it is tied to terrorist funding.

The organized crime threat to Russia's national security is becoming a global threat. Russian organized crime operates both on its own and in cooperation with foreign groups. The latter cooperation often comes in the form of joint money-laundering ventures. Russian criminals have become involved in killings for hire in central and western Europe, Israel, Canada, and the United States.

In the United States, with the exception of extortion and money laundering, Russians have had little involvement in some of the more traditional types of organized crime, such as drug trafficking, gambling, and loan sharking. However, thousands of Russian immigrants are believed to be involved in criminal activity, primarily in Russian enclaves in New York City.[82] Russian criminal groups are extensively engaged in a broad array of frauds and scams, including health care fraud, insurance scams, stock frauds, antiquities swindles, forgery, and fuel tax evasion schemes. Russians are believed to be the main purveyors of credit card fraud in the United States. Legitimate businesses, such as the movie business and the textile industry, have become targets of criminals from the former Soviet Union, and they are often used for money laundering and extortion. The first significant conviction against the Russian mob in the United States occurred in 1996 when Vyacheslav Kirillovich Ivankov, who had been dispatched to act as the coordinating authority for all Russian organized crime activity in the United States, was convicted on extortion and conspiracy charges. Ivankov led an international criminal organization that operated mainly in New York, Toronto, London, Vienna, Budapest, and Moscow, but also in numerous other cities in the United States, Canada, and Europe, specializing in extorting money from Russian business interests. Ivankov's conviction was a setback, but Russian groups continue to thrive, engaging in Internet crimes, extortion, and white-collar crimes.

*MEXICAN DRUG CARTELS* Mexican drug cartels have become large-scale suppliers of narcotics, marijuana, and methamphetamines to the United States, and Mexico has become a drug-producing and transit country. In addition, an estimated 90 percent of cocaine entering the United States travels through Mexico. Mexican drug gangs routinely use violence, and the battle for control of the border regions has affected U.S. citizens: More than 60 Americans have been kidnapped, and Mexican drug cartel members have threatened to kill U.S. journalists covering drug violence in the border region. Although Mexican drug cartels, or drug-trafficking organizations, have existed for quite some time, they have grown more powerful since Colombia was able to crack down on the Cali and Medellín cartels in the 1990s. Mexican drug cartels now dominate the wholesale illicit drug market in the United States. As a result, Mexican cartels are the leading wholesale launderers of drug money from the United States. Mexican and Colombian trafficking organizations annually smuggle an estimated $25 billion in drug proceeds into Mexico for laundering.

There are numerous drug cartels operating in Mexico, the main ones being the Gulf, Tijuana, Sinaloa, Juárez, Millennium, Oaxaca, and Colima cartels. Some are dominant in local regions, whereas the major gangs—Gulf, Sinaloa, and Juárez—are present throughout Mexico. In recent years, new cartels have formed and others have become allies, in a constantly shifting landscape of drug activity. The Tijuana cartel formed an alliance with the Gulf cartel, and several cartels (Sinaloa, Juárez, and Valencia) have also formed an alliance known as The Federation. Originated in the 1980s, the cartel known as La Familia Michoacana became an independent drug-trafficking organization and later allied itself with the Gulf cartel. La Familia leadership is philosophically opposed to the sale of methamphetamine to Mexicans and instead supports its export to the United States for consumption by U.S. citizens. La Familia is a heavily armed cartel that has utilized violence (including murders, kidnappings and assaults) to support its narcotics-trafficking business. Associates of La Familia based in the United States have acquired military-grade weapons, assault weapons, and ammunition and have arranged for them to be smuggled back into Mexico for use by La Familia. (See Figure 17.1 for a map of the cartels' approximate areas of influence.)

## Controlling Transnational Crime

Efforts to combat transnational organized crime are typically in the hands of federal agencies. One approach is to form international working groups to collect intelligence, share information, and plot unified strategies among member nations. The FBI belongs to several international working groups aimed at

**FIGURE 17.1**
Mexican Cartels' Areas of Influence

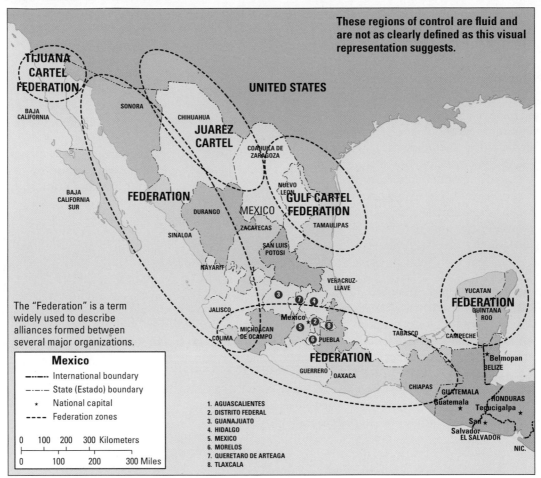

Source: Colleen Cook, *Mexico's Drug Cartels* (Washington, D.C.: Congressional Research Service, 2007), http://ftp.fas.org/sgp/crs/row/RL34215.pdf.

combating transnational gangs in various parts of the world. For example, to combat the influence and reach of Eurasian Organized Crime, the FBI is involved in the following groups and activities:

■ *Eurasian Organized Crime Working Group.* Established in 1994, this group meets to discuss and jointly address the transnational aspects of Eurasian organized crime that affect member countries and the international community in general. The member countries are Canada, Great Britain, Germany, France, Italy, Japan, the United States, and Russia.

■ *Central European Working Group.* This group is part of a project that brings together the FBI and Central European law enforcement agencies to discuss cooperative investigative matters covering the broad spectrum of Eurasian organized crime. A principal concern is the growing presence of Russian and other Eurasian organized criminals in Central Europe and the United States. The initiative works on practical interaction between the participating agencies to establish lines of communication and working relationships, to develop strategies and tactics to address transnational organized crime matters that affect the region, and to identify potential common targets.

## CAREERS IN CRIMINAL JUSTICE

# Drug Enforcement Agent

### Duties and Characteristics of the Job

Drug Enforcement Administration (DEA) agents enforce the controlled substances laws and regulations of the United States of America. They bring to justice organizations—including those with ties to terrorism—and their principal members, who are involved in the growing, manufacture, or distribution of controlled substances. They also work to dismantle drug-trafficking organizations, to prosecute drug traffickers, and to destroy the financial infrastructure of these organizations.

### Job Outlook

Employment of police and detectives is expected to grow 10 percent over the 2008–2018 decade, about as fast as the average for all occupations. Population growth is the main source of increased demand for police services. Competition for jobs in federal law enforcement agencies is significant. Bilingual applicants with a bachelor's degree and several years of law enforcement or military experience, especially investigative experience, have the best opportunities in federal agencies.

### Salary

DEA special agents are generally hired at the GS-7 or GS-9 level, depending on education and experience. The salary includes federal law enforcement officer base pay, plus a locality payment that depends on the duty station. Upon successful graduation from the DEA Training Academy, 25 percent availability pay is added to base and locality pay. After graduation, the starting salaries are approximately $49,746 for a GS-7 and $55,483 for a GS-9. After four years of service special agents are eligible to progress to the GS-13 level and can earn approximately $92,592 or more per year.

### Qualifications

In order to become a DEA special agent, a candidate must successfully complete all phases of a rigorous, in-depth hiring process. This process may take up to 12 months or longer and includes the following phases:

### Qualifications Review

- Written Assessment and Panel Interview
- Urinalysis Drug Test
- Medical Examination
- Physical Task Test
- Polygraph Examination
- Psychological Assessment
- Full-field Background Investigation
- Final Hiring Decision

### Education and Training

The best-qualified candidates possess a bachelor's or master's degree, along with a grade point average (GPA) of 2.95 or higher. Special consideration is given to candidates with degrees in Criminal Justice/Police Science or related disciplines; Finance, Accounting or Economics; foreign languages (with fluency verified) in Spanish, Russian, Hebrew, Arabic, dialects of Nigerian languages, Chinese, and/or Japanese; computer Science/Information Systems; and Telecommunications/Electrical/Mechanical Engineering.

Sources: U.S. Drug Enforcement Administration www.justice.gov/dea/index.htm; Bureau of Labor Statistics, *Occupational Outlook Handbook* (OOH), 2010–2011 Edition.

- *Southeast European Cooperative Initiative.* The Southeast European Cooperative Initiative is an international organization established to coordinate police and customs regional actions for preventing and combating cross-border crime. It is headquartered in Bucharest, Romania, and has 12 fully participating member countries. The United States has been one of 14 countries with observer status since 1998. The initiative's center serves as a clearing house for information and intelligence sharing, allowing the quick exchange of information in a professional and trustworthy environment. The initiative also supports specialized task forces for countering cross-border crime such as the trafficking of people, drugs, and cars; smuggling; financial crimes; terrorism; and other serious cross-border crimes.

In addition, U.S. law enforcement agencies have cooperated in cross-boarder operations to eradicate gang activity. For example, on October 22, 2009, the Drug Enforcement Administration announced the results of "Project Coronado," a four-year multiagency law enforcement investigation that which targeted the *La Familia Michoacana* drug cartel. Coronado, one of the largest operations against the Mexican cartels, resulted in the arrest of more than 300 people in 19 states and involved more than 3,000 agents from a variety of federal, state, and local law enforcement agencies. Before the raids, this cartel was directly responsible for a vast majority of the methamphetamine pouring into our country across our southwestern border. Project Coronado has led to the arrest of 1,186 individuals and the seizure of approximately $33 million in U.S. currency, 1,999 kilograms of cocaine, 2,730 pounds of methamphetamine, 29 pounds of heroin, 16,390 pounds of marijuana, 389 weapons, 269 vehicles, and two clandestine drug labs. To carry off such an elaborate investigation, Project Coronado was coordinated by a multiagency Special Operations Division comprising agents and analysts from the DEA (see the following Careers feature), FBI, U.S. Immigration and Customs Enforcement, Internal Revenue Service, U.S. Customs and Border Protection, U.S. Marshals Service, and ATF (the Bureau of Alcohol, Tobacco, and Firearms and Explosives), as well as attorneys from the Criminal Division's Narcotic and Dangerous Drug Section.[83]

*LAWS TARGETING ORGANIZED CRIME* Congress has passed a number of laws that have made it easier for agencies to bring transnational gangs to justice. One of the first measures aimed directly at organized crime was the Interstate and Foreign Travel or Transportation in Aid of Racketeering Enterprises Act (Travel Act).[84] The Travel Act prohibits travel in interstate commerce, or use of interstate facilities, with the intent to promote, manage, establish, carry on, or facilitate an unlawful activity; it also prohibits the actual or attempted engagement in these activities. In 1970, Congress passed the Organized Crime Control Act. Title IX of the act, probably its most effective measure, is the **Racketeer Influenced and Corrupt Organization Act (RICO)**.[85] RICO did not create new categories of crimes but rather new categories of offenses in racketeering activity, which it defined as involvement in two or more acts prohibited by 24 existing federal and 8 state statutes. The offenses listed in RICO include state-defined crimes, such as murder, kidnapping, gambling, arson, robbery, bribery, extortion, and narcotics violations; and federally defined crimes, such as bribery, counterfeiting, transmission of gambling information, prostitution, and mail fraud. RICO is designed to limit patterns of organized criminal activity by prohibiting involvement in acts intended to

- Derive income from racketeering or the unlawful collection of debts and use or investment of such income
- Acquire through racketeering an interest in or control over any enterprise engaged in interstate or foreign commerce
- Conduct business through a pattern of racketeering
- Conspire to use racketeering as a means of making income, collecting loans, or conducting business

An individual convicted under RICO is subject to 20 years in prison and a $25,000 fine. Additionally, the accused must forfeit to the U.S. government any interest in a business in violation of RICO. These penalties are much more potent than simple conviction and imprisonment.

**Racketeer Influenced and Corrupt Organization Act (RICO)** Federal legislation that enables prosecutors to bring additional criminal or civil charges against people engaged in two or more acts prohibited by 24 existing federal and 8 state laws. RICO features monetary penalties that allow the government to confiscate all profits derived from criminal activities. Originally intended to be used against organized criminals, RICO has also been used against white-collar criminals.

## Why Is It So Difficult to Eradicate Transnational Gangs?

Although international cooperation is now common and law enforcement agencies are willing to work together to fight transnational gangs, these criminal organizations are extremely hard to eradicate. The gangs are ready to use violence and well equipped to carry out threats. One reason why it has proven so difficult for law enforcement to combat the drug cartels is that they employ enforcer gangs to protect them and intimidate enemies. For example, Mexico's Gulf cartel has its own paramilitary force known as the Zetas, whose core members are alleged to be former members of the Mexican military's elite Special Air Mobile Force Group (Grupo Aeromovil de Fuerzas Especiales, GAFES). The military-trained Zetas are able to carry out complex operations and use sophisticated weaponry. The Zetas, who may number up to 200 fighters, are instrumental in maintaining the Gulf cartel's regional domination. Now recruiting from around Latin America, the Zetas act as assassins for the Gulf cartel. They also traffic arms, kidnap, and collect payments for the cartel on its drug routes. In addition to defending the cartel's terrain in northern Mexico, Zetas are believed to control trafficking routes along the eastern half of the U.S.– Mexico border. And when they feel threatened, they are quite willing to fight the law: In July 2006, local police in the southern state of Tabasco unknowingly arrested Mateo Díaz López, a leader of the Zetas. The arrest prompted an assault on the police station that killed four people, including two police officers (Lopez was not freed in the attack). There have even been shocking cross-border attacks by enforcers aimed at intimidating anyone involved in antigang activity or willing to cooperate in antigang investigations. On March 30, 2010, elements of the Mexican military arrested Ricardo Valles de la Rosa, 45 (a leader of the Barrio Azteca gang, which carries out extortion, killings, and drug trafficking) on suspicion of killing three people who worked for the United States consulate in Ciudad Juarez, on the Texas border, perhaps to send a message showing what happens to people who work for or cooperate with "the enemy."[86] Cross-border attacks help quiet witnesses and intimidate local law enforcement agents.

Adding to control problems is the fact that the drug trade is an important source of foreign revenue, and destroying the drug trade undermines the economies of third world nations. Even if the government of one nation were willing to cooperate in vigorous drug suppression efforts, suppliers in other nations, eager to cash in on the sellers' market, would be encouraged to turn more acreage over to coca or poppy production. Today, almost every Caribbean country is involved with narcotics trafficking, and illicit drug shipments in the region are worth more money than the top five legitimate exports combined. Drug gangs are able to corrupt the political structure and destabilize countries. Drug addiction and violent crime are now common in Jamaica, Puerto Rico, and even small islands such as St. Kitts. The corruption of the police and other security forces has reached a crisis point, where an officer can earn the equivalent of half a year's salary by simply looking the other way on a drug deal.[87] There are also indications that the drug syndicates may be planting a higher-yield variety of coca and improving their refining techniques to replace crops lost to government crackdowns.

The United States has little influence in some key drug-producing areas, such as Afghanistan and Myanmar (formerly Burma).[88] War and terrorism also may make gang control strategies problematic. After the United States toppled Afghanistan's Taliban government, the remnants began to grow and sell poppy to support their insurgency; Afghanistan now supplies 90 percent of the world's opium.[89] And although the Colombian guerillas may not be interested in joining or colluding with crime cartels, they finance their war against the government by aiding drug traffickers and "taxing" crops and sales.[90] Considering these problems, it is no surprise that transnational gangs continue to flourish.

## Ethical Challenges in Criminal Justice: A Writing Assignment

A tracking device has been developed that can be implanted in every new computer to constantly monitor every web page visited on the Internet. This device can record every transaction and all activity, and it automatically sends the data to government computers programmed to look for suspicious Web activity This surveillance device will enable the government to keep tabs on what people are doing, what they buy, what they download, and so on. Once a person becomes a suspect in a crime, she or he can be easily monitored from a distance, without the person's knowledge and with no danger to any government agent. Suspects cannot hide or escape detection. Write an essay discussing the pros and cons of employing such a device. You might want to refer to the sections on cybercrime, including etailing fraud and copyright infringement. If you approve of the device, what questions might you want answered before it becomes standard equipment on home computers?

## SUMMARY

### 1. Be familiar with the influence of globalization on crime.

- Globalization has shifted the focus of crime from a local to a world perspective. With money and power to spare, criminal enterprise groups can recruit new members, bribe government officials, and even fund private armies.

- Technological advances ranging from global cell phone connectivity to the Internet, along with the growth of international trade, have contributed to the growth in illicit transnational criminal activities.

- Globalization brings with it an ideology of free markets and free trade that means less intervention and regulation, conditions that crime groups exploit to cross unpatrolled borders and expand their activities to new regions of the world.

### 2. Discuss the impact of criminal enterprise crime.

- The crimes of the rich powerful have the most significant impact on society. Experts place their total monetary value in the hundreds of billions of dollars, far outstripping the expense of any other type of crime.

- Large-scale investment growth has led to significant increases in the amount of fraud and misconduct on Wall Street. Investment firms have engaged in deceptive securities sales that have cost investors billions.

### 3. Describe a Ponzi scheme.

- A Ponzi scheme is an investment fraud that involves the payment of purported returns to existing investors from funds contributed by new investors.

- Ponzi scheme organizers solicit new investors by promising to invest funds in opportunities that they claim will generate high returns with little or no risk.

- Fraudsters focus on attracting new money to make promised payments to earlier-stage investors and use it for personal expenses, instead of engaging in any legitimate investment activity.

### 4. Explain mortgage and subprime mortgages fraud

- Mortgage scandal has rocked the nation.

- Borrowers have provided false information to the mortgage broker and/or lender, enabling them to get loans for which they were not qualified.

- Those involved in mortgage lending have gotten involved in criminal fraud schemes and have falsifued accounting entries and fraudulently inflated assets and revenues.

### 5. Discuss the various forms of cyber crime.

- Cyber crime typically involves the theft and/or destruction of information, resources, or funds via computers, computer networks, and the Internet.

■ Cyber theft is the use of computer networks for criminal profits. Copyright infringement, identity theft, and Internet securities fraud are examples of cyber theft.

■ Cyber vandalism, or technological destruction, involves malicious attacks aimed at disrupting, defacing, and destroying technology.

### 6. Be able to define cyber warfare.

■ Cyberwar consists of politically motivated attacks designed to compromise the electronic infrastructure of the enemy and to disrupt its economy.

■ Cyberwar is an effort by covert forces to disrupt the place where the virtual electronic reality of computers intersects the physical world.

■ Cyber space is a handy battlefield, because attackers can strike at a target that bombs don't directly affect: the economy of their enemy.

### 7. Know what is being done to thwart cyber criminals.

■ Numerous organizations have been set up to provide training and support for law enforcement agents. In addition, new federal and state laws have been enacted to help discourage particular types of high-tech crimes.

■ In the future, technological prowess may make it possible to identify cyber criminals and bring them to justice before they can carry out their attacks.

### 8. Understand the concept of transnational crime.

■ Transnational organized crime involves ongoing international criminal enterprise groups whose purpose is personal economic gain through illegitimate means.

■ Transnational gangs are involved in money laundering; human smuggling; cyber crime; and trafficking of humans, drugs, weapons, endangered species, body parts, or nuclear material.

■ There is also a troubling cross-border trade in prostitution. Transnational gangs export women from third world nations for the purposes of prostitution. Some may be kidnapped or forced into prostitution against their will through violence and threats.

### 9. Be familiar with some of the most important transnational crime groups.

■ Eastern gangs, especially the Russian mob, trace their origin to countries spanning the Baltics, the Balkans, Central/Eastern Europe, Russia, the Caucacus, and Central Asia. Russian organized crime is active in Europe, Africa, Asia, and North and South America.

■ Asian gangs include the Yakuza Japanese criminal group, which is often involved in multinational criminal activities, including human trafficking, gambling, prostitution, and undermining legitimate businesses. Chinese groups are also involved in human trafficking, bringing large numbers of Chinese migrants to North America and essentially enslaving them for profit.

■ A number of powerful Mexican drug cartels that now dominate the cross-border drug trade into the United States.

### 10. Explain how law enforcement is taking on transnational criminal syndicates.

■ Efforts to combat transnational organized crime are typically in the hands of federal agencies. One approach is for them to form international working groups to collect intelligence, share information, and plot unified strategies among member nations.

■ U.S. law enforcement agencies have cooperated in cross-border operations to combat gang activity.

■ Congress has passed a number of laws that have made it easier for agencies to bring transnational gangs to justice. These include the Interstate and Foreign Travel or Transportation in Aid of Racketeering Enterprises Act (the Travel Act) and the Racketeer Influenced and Corrupt Organization Act (RICO).

## KEY TERMS

globalization, 642

corporate enterprise crime, 644

Ponzi scheme, 645

securitization, 647

cyber crime, 652

cyber theft, 652

cyber vandalism, 652

cyber warfare, 652

denial-of-service attack, 655

warez, 656

identity theft, 656

phishing, 656

etailing fraud, 657

cyber stalking, 658

cyber bullying, 659

transnational organized crime, 662

Racketeer Influenced and Corrupt Organization Act (RICO), 669

# CRITICAL THINKING QUESTIONS

1. Should people who illegally download movies or music be prosecuted for theft?

2. How can Internet pornography be controlled, considering that a great deal of adult content is available on foreign websites?

3. Given the threat of transnational drug trafficking, should drugs be legalized and controlled by the government?

4. Should the Internet be more closely monitored and controlled to reduce the threat of cyber warfare?

5. Is there any point in placing economic sanctions on billion-dollar corporations? Should corporate executives be put in prison? What is the purpose of incarcerating someone like 72-year-old Bernard Madoff? Is he a threat to society?

# NOTES

1. Nikos Passas and David Nelken, "The Thin Line between Legitimate and Criminal Enterprises: Subsidy Frauds in the European Community," *Crime, Law, and Social Change* 19 (1993): 223–243.
2. Mark Haller, "Illegal Enterprise: A Theoretical and Historical Interpretation," *Criminology* 28 (1990): 207–235.
3. For a thorough review, see David Friedrichs, *Trusted Criminals* (Belmont, Calif.: Wadsworth, 1996).
4. Kitty Calavita and Henry Pontell, "Savings and Loan Fraud as Organized Crime: Toward a Conceptual Typology of Corporate Illegality," *Criminology* 31 (1993): 519–548.
5. Andrew Nikiforuk, *Pandemonium: How Globalization and Trade Are Putting the World at Risk* (Queensland, NZ: University of Queensland Press, 2007).
6. David Friedrichs and Jessica Friedrichs, "The World Bank and Crimes of Globalization: A Case Study," *Social Justice* 29 (2002): 13–36.
7. Louise Shelley, "The Globalization of Crime and Terrorism," State Department's Bureau of International Information Programs (IIP), 2006, www.america.gov/st/business-english/2008/June/20080608103639xjyrreP4.218692e-02.html.
8. Edwin Sutherland, *White-Collar Crime: The Uncut Version* (New Haven, Conn.: Yale University Press, 1983).
9. Ronald Kramer and Raymond Michalowski, "State-Corporate Crime." Paper presented at the annual meeting of the American Society of Criminology, Baltimore, Maryland, November 1990.
10. Edwin Sutherland, "White-Collar Criminality," *American Sociological Review* 5 (1940): 2–10.
11. Natalie Taylor, "Under-Reporting of Crime against Small Business: Attitudes towards Police and Reporting Practices," *Policing and Society* 13 (2003): 79–90.
12. FBI, "Ponzi Scheme Indictments: Five Charged in $7 Billion Ploy," June 19, 2009, www.fbi.gov/page2/june09/stanford_061909.html (accessed July 2, 2009).
13. FBI, "Financial Crimes," in *Financial Crimes Report to the Public, Fiscal Year 2008*, www.fbi.gov/publications/financial/fcs_report2008/financial_crime_2008.htm#securities (accessed April 28, 2010).
14. Ibid.
15. Securities and Exchange Commission, "SEC Charges Bernard L. Madoff for Multi-Billion Dollar Ponzi Scheme," December 11, 2008, www.sec.gov/news/press/2008/2008-293.htm (accessed April 30, 2009; Joe *Lauria*, "Life Inside the Weird World of Bernard Madoff," Timesonline, *March 22, 2009*, http://business.timesonline.co.uk/tol/business/industry_sectors/banking_and_finance/article5949961.ece (accessed April 28, 2009).
16. Clifford Krauss, Phillip L. Zweig, and Julie Creswell, "Texas Firm Accused of $8 Billion Fraud," *New York Times*, February 18, 2009, www.nytimes.com/2009/02/18/business/18stanford.html.
17. FBI, "2008 Mortgage Fraud Report," in *Year in Review*, www.fbi.gov/publications/fraud/mortgage_fraud08.htm.
18. FBI, "Financial Crimes," www.fbi.gov/publications/financial/fcs_report2007/financial_crime_2007.htm#Mortgage (accessed May 1, 2010).
19. Ibid.
20. Fraudguides, "Mortgage Foreclosure Rescue Scams," www.fraudguides.com/mortgage-foreclosure-rescue-scam.asp (accessed May 5, 2010).
21. FBI, "2008 Mortgage Fraud Report."
22. MSNBC, Ex-Tyco Executives Get Up to 25 Years in Prison, September 20, 2005, www.msnbc.msn.com/id/9399803/ (accessed July 3, 2009).
23. Kurt Eichenwald, "Ex-Andersen Partner Pleads Guilty in Record-Shredding," *New York Times*, April 12, 2002, p. C1; John A. Byrne, "At Enron, the Environment Was Ripe for Abuse," *Business Week* (February 25, 2002): 12; Peter Behr and Carrie Johnson, "Govt. Expands Charges against Enron Execs," *Washington Post*, May 1, 2003, p. 1.
24. Krysten Crawford, CNN, "Ex-WorldCom CEO Ebbers Guilty," March 15, 2006, http://money.cnn.com/2005/03/15/news/newsmakers/ebbers/index.htm; MSNBC, "Ebbers Sentenced to 25 Years in Prison, Ex WorldCom CEO Guilty of Directing Biggest Accounting Fraud," July 13, 2005, www.msnbc.msn.com/id/8474930; Lynne W. Jeter, Disconnected: Deceit and Betrayal at WorldCom (New York: Wiley, 2003);
25. This section relies heavily on Albert Reiss Jr., "Selecting Strategies of Social Control over Organizational Life," in *Enforcing Regulation*, ed. Keith Hawkins and John M. Thomas (Boston: Kluwer Publications, 1984), pp. 25–37.
26. Michael Benson, "Emotions and Adjudication: Status Degradation among White-Collar Criminals," *Justice Quarterly* 7 (1990): 515–528; John Braithwaite, *Crime, Shame, and Reintegration* (Sydney: Cambridge University Press, 1989).
27. John Braithwaite, "The Limits of Economism in Controlling Harmful Corporate Conduct," *Law and Society Review* 16 (1981–1982): 481–504.
28. Tyson Slocum, "BP: The Worst Safety and Environmental Record of All Oil Companies Operating in the United States," *Monthly Review*, http://mrzine.monthlyreview.org/2010/slocum060510.html.
29. Sean Rosenmerkel, "Wrongfulness and Harmfulness as Components of Seriousness of White-Collar Offenses," *Journal of Contemporary Criminal Justice* 17 (2001): 308–328.
30. Jonathan Lechter, Daniel Posner, and George Morris, "Antitrust Violations," *American Criminal Law Review* 39 (2002): 225–273.
31. Mark Cohen, "Environmental Crime and Punishment: Legal/Economic Theory and Empirical Evidence on Enforcement of Federal Environmental Statutes," *Journal of Criminal Law and Criminology* 82 (1992): 1054–1109.
32. Fox News, "Missouri Woman Indicted in MySpace Cyber-Bullying Case That Ended in Teen's Suicide," May 15, 2008, www.foxnews.com/printer_friendly_story/0,3566,356056,00.html.

33. Statement of Michael A. Vatis, director, National Infrastructure Protection Center, Federal Bureau of Investigation, on cyber crime before the Senate Judiciary Committee, Criminal Justice Oversight Subcommittee, and House Judiciary Committee, Crime Subcommittee, February 29, 2000, www.cybercrime.gov/vatis.htm (accessed March 17, 2007).

34. Ed Frauenheim, "IDC: Cyberterror and Other Prophecies," CNET News.com, December 12, 2002 (accessed August 14, 2005).

35. Giles Trendle, "An e-jihad against Government?" *EGOV Monitor*, September 2002.

36. VoGon Interntational, / http://www.vogon-investigation.com/ (accessed April 20, 2010).

37. Andreas Philaretou,"Sexuality and the Internet," Journal of Sex Research 42 (2005): 180–181.

38. N2H2 communication, www.n2h2.com/index.php.

39. *ACLU, Reno v. ACLU*, No. 96–511.

40. ACLU, news release, "*ACLU v. Reno*, Round 2: Broad Coalition Files Challenge to New Federal Net Censorship Law," October 22, 1998.

41. *Ashcroft, Attorney General, et al. v. Free Speech Coalition, et al.* 535 U.S. 234 (2002

42. Flint, "Skin Trade Spreading across U.S." Anthony Flint, Skin Trade Spreading Across U.S., Boston Sunday Globe, Dec. 1, 1996, A1.

43. *This section relies heavily on CERT® Coordination Center Denial of Service Attacks, www.cert.org/tech_tips/denial_of_service.html (accessed September 8, 2010).*

44. The Computer Fraud and Abuse Act (CFAA), 18 U.S.C. §1030 (1998).

45. The Digital Millennium Copyright Act, Public Law 105-304 (1998).

46. Title 18, United States Code, section 2319.

47. Title 17, United States Code, section 506.

48. Jim Wolf, "Internet Scams Targeted in Sweep: A 10-Day Crackdown Leads to 62 Arrests and 88 Indictments," *Boston Globe*, May 22, 2001, A2.

49. These sections rely on "Phishing Activity Trends Report," June 2005, Anti-Phishing Working Group, www.ncjrs.org/spotlight/identity_theft/publications.html#phishing (retrieved August 30, 2005); Special Report on "Phishing" (2004), U.S. Department of Justice Criminal Division, www.ncjrs.org/spotlight/identity_theft/publications.html#phishing (retrieved August 30, 2010).

50. Identity Theft Resource Center (ITRC), "Scams and Consumer Alerts," www.idtheftcenter.org (accessed April 15, 2008).

51. Department of Justice, "Fourteen Convicted on Charges of Internet Trafficking in Controlled Substances as Well as Money Laundering," May 1, 2009, http://tampa.fbi.gov/dojpressrel/2009/ta050109.htm (accessed May 5, 2009).

52. National Center on Addiction and Substance Abuse at Columbia University, "You've Got Drugs!" V: "Prescription Drug Pushers on the Internet," May 2008, www.casacolumbia.org/articlefiles/531-2008%20You've%20Got%20Drugs%20V.pdf.

53. Anne Branscomb, "Rogue Computer Programs and Computer Rogues: Tailoring Punishment to Fit the Crime," *Rutgers Computer and Technology Law Journal* 16 (1990): 24–26.

54. Heather Jacobson and Rebecca Green, "Computer Crimes," *American Criminal Law Review* 39 (2002): 272–326.

55. United States Department of Justice, "Cyberstalking: A New Challenge for Law Enforcement and Industry," A Report from the Attorney General to the Vice President, Washington, D.C., 1999, www.usdoj.gov/criminal/cybercrime/cyberstalking.htm (accessed September 12, 2005).

56. Janis Wolak, David Finkelhor, Kimberly Mitchell, and Michele Ybarra, "Online 'Predators— and Their Victims: Myths, Realities, and Implications for Prevention and Treatment," *American Psychologist* 63 (2008): 111–128.

57. Jane Ireland and Rachel Monaghan, "Behaviours Indicative of Bullying among Young and Juvenile Male Offenders: A Study of Perpetrator and Victim Characteristics," *Aggressive Behavior* 32 (2006): 172–180.

58. This section relies heavily on Justin Patchin and Sameer Hinduja, "Bullies Move beyond the Schoolyard: A Preliminary Look at Cyberbullying," *Youth Violence and Juvenile Justice* 4 (2006): 148–169.

59. Patchin and Hinduja, "Bullies Move beyond the Schoolyard."

60. Barry C. Collin (2004), "The Future of CyberTerrorism: Where the Physical and Virtual Worlds Converge," http://afgen.com/terrorism1.html (accessed August 14, 2005).

61. Mark Pollitt, "Cyberterrorism—Fact or Fancy?" FBI Laboratory, www.cs.georgetown.edu/~denning/infosec/pollitt.html (accessed August 17, 2005).

62. James Lewis, "Assessing the Risks of Cyberterrorism, Cyber War, and Other Cyber Threats," Report submitted to the Center for Strategic and International Studies [CSIS], Washington, D.C., 2002), p. 1.

63. Nathan Thornburgh, Matthew Forney, Brian Bennett, Timothy Burger, and Elaine Shannon, "The Invasion of the Chinese Cyberspies (and the Man Who Tried to Stop Them)," *Time*, September 5, 2005, p. 10.

64. Andrew Gray "Chinese Hackers Worry Pentagon, *PC World*, March 9, 2008. www.pcworld.com/article/id,143242-c,hackers/article.html.

65. Clyde Wilson, "Software Piracy: Uncovering Mutiny on the Cyberseas," *Trial* 32 (1996): 24–31.

66. Deloitte, 2010 Global Security Survey, 2010 TMT Global Security study http://www.deloitte.com/view/en_GX/global/industries/technology-media-telecommunications/c4d38a120c9a8210Vgn VCM200000bb42f00aRCRD.htm (accessed September, 14, 2010).

67. Heather Jacobson and Rebecca Green, "Computer Crime," *American Criminal Law Review* 39 (2002): 273–326; Identity Theft and Assumption Act of 1998 (18 U.S.C. S 1028(a)(7)); Bruce Swartz, Deputy Assistant General, Criminal Division, Justice Department, Internet Fraud Testimony before the House Energy and Commerce Committee, May 23, 2001; Comprehensive Crime Control Act of 1984, PL 98-473, 2101-03, 98 Stat. 1837, 2190 (1984), adding 18 USC 1030 (1984); Counterfeit Active Device and Computer Fraud and Abuse Act Amended by PL 99-474, 100 Stat. 1213 (1986) codified at 18 U.S.C. 1030 (Supp. V 1987); Computer Abuse Amendments Act 18 U.S.C. section 1030 (1994); Copyright Infringement Act 17 U.S.C. section 506(a) 1994; Electronic Communications Privacy Act of 198618 U.S.C. 2510–2520 (1988 and Supp. II 1990).

68. The Computer Fraud and Abuse Act (CFAA) 18 U.S.C. section 1030 (1998).

69. The Digital Millennium Copyright Act, Public Law 105-304 (1998).

70. Title 18, United States Code, section 2319.

71. Title 17, United States Code, section 506.

72. Identity Theft and Assumption Deterrence Act, as amended by Public Law 105-318, 112 Stat. 3007 (October 30, 1998).

73. ACLU, "*ACLU v. Reno*, Round 2: Broad Coalition Files Challenge to New Federal Net Censorship Law," news release, October 22, 1998.

74. *Ashcroft v. ACLU*, 00-1293, 2002.

75. PL 98-473, Title H, Chapter XXI, [sections] 2102(a), 98 Stat. 1837, 2190 (1984).

76. Statement of Mr. Bob Weaver, Deputy Special Agent in Charge, New York Field Office, United States Secret Service, before the House Financial Services Committee, the Subcommittee on Financial Institutions and Consumer Credit, and the Subcommittee on Oversight and Investigations, U.S. House of Representatives, April 3, 2003.

77. National Institute of Justice, "Transnational Organized Crime," www.ojp.usdoj.gov/nij/topics/crime/transnational-organized-crime/welcome.htm (accessed May 5, 2010).

78. Elizabeth Bernstein, "The Meaning of the Purchase: Desire, Demand, and the Commerce of Sex," *Ethnography* 2 (2001): 389–420.

79. Ibid.

80. Ibid.

81. Louise I. Shelley, "Crime and Corruption: Enduring Problems of Post-Soviet Development," *Demokratizatsiya* 11 (2003): 110–114; James O. Finckenauer and Yuri A. Voronin, *The Threat of Russian Organized* Crime (Washington, D.C.: National Institute of Justice, 2001);

82. Omar Bartos, "Growth of Russian Organized Crime Poses Serious Threat," *CJ International* 11 (1995): 8–9.

83. News Release, Drug Enforcement Administration, "DEA Announces Largest Single U.S. Strike against Mexican Drug Cartels," October 22, 2009, www.justice.gov/dea/pubs/pressrel/pr102209ap.html (accessed May 1, 2010).

84. 18 U.S.C. 1952 (1976).

85. Public Law 91-452, Title IX, 84 Stat. 922 (1970) (codified at 18 U.S.C. 1961–68, 1976).

86. William Booth, "Mexican Azteca Gang Leader Arrested in Killings of 3 Tied to U.S." *Washington Post*, March 30, 2010, www.washingtonpost.com/wp-dyn/content/article/2010/03/29/AR2010032903373.html.

87. Orlando Patterson, "The Other Losing War," *New York Times*, January 13, 2007.

88. George Rengert, *The Geography of Illegal Drugs* (Boulder, Colo.: Westview Press, 1996), p. 2.

89. Office of National Drug Control Policy, Drug Facts 2010 http://www.whitehousedrugpolicy.gov/drugfact/index.html. Accessed on September 25, 2010.

90. Francisco Gutierrez, "Institutionalizing Global Wars: State Transformations in Colombia, 1978–2002: Colombian Policy Directed at Its Wars, Paradoxically, Narrows the Government's Margin of Maneuver Even as It Tries to Expand It," *Journal of International Affairs* 57 (2003): 135–152.

# CHAPTER 18

# Terrorism, Homeland Security, and the Future of Criminal Justice

## CHAPTER OUTLINE

- **TERRORISM**
Defining Terrorism
Who Is the Terrorist?
The Contemporary Terrorist

- **HOMELAND SECURITY: THE CRIMINAL JUSTICE RESPONSE TO TERRORISM**
Fighting Terrorism with Law Enforcement
*Criminal Justice and Technology: Using Biometrics to Fight Terrorism: US-VISIT*
Fighting Terrorism in the Courts
*Careers in Criminal Justice: Emergency Management Director*

- **POLITICAL SOLUTIONS TO TERRORISM**
*Images of Justice: al-Hurra versus as-Sahab*

- **CONFRONTING TERRORISM WITH THE LAW**
The USA Patriot Act
Civil Rights and the Struggle against Terrorism
The Supreme Court and Terrorism
*Analyzing Criminal Justice Issues: The Use of Torture*

- **THE FUTURE OF CRIMINAL JUSTICE**
Predicting the Future

## CHAPTER OBJECTIVES

1. Be able to define terrorism.
2. Be familiar with the history of terrorism.
3. Understand the factors that motivate terrorists.
4. Be familiar with the various forms of contemporary terrorism.
5. Explain how the criminal justice system has responded to terrorism.
6. Discuss political solutions to terrorism.
7. Understand the purpose of the Patriot Act.
8. Identify the common theme in Supreme Court terrorism cases since 9/11.
9. Identify trends that are likely to influence criminal justice in the future.

**F**aisal Shahzad, a naturalized U.S. citizen, was born in Pakistan in June 1979. The youngest of four children, he lived a life of privilege by Pakistani standards, attending private secular schools not known for extremist teachings. After moving to the United States, he earned an M.B.A. at the University of Bridgeport in 2005 and took a job as a financial analyst with a cosmetics company. Shortly after his marriage in 2009, Shahzad quit his job, stopped making payments on his house, and then moved to Pakistan with his wife and two children. It is alleged that while he was in Pakistan, he attended a terrorist training camp over the course of his five-month stay. He returned to the United States in February of 2010, bought a Nissan Pathfinder on craigslist for $1,300, and, according to investigators, tried to blow it up with a makeshift bomb on May 1, 2010, in the Times Square section of New York City. He was reported to have loaded the SUV with gas cans and propane bottles, parked it in the city's busy theater district, and used consumer-grade fireworks as igniters. The SUV failed to explode, and Shahzad was captured as he was trying to leave the United States on a Dubai-bound flight from JFK. After his apprehension, Shahzad was promptly charged with multiple terrorism-related offenses. He pled guilty and, on October 5, 2010, was sentenced to life in prison for the botched bombing.

Of course, any attempted bombing is newsworthy, but the most disturbing aspect of this incident is that it is what New York City Police Commissioner Raymond Kelly called "a classic case of homegrown terrorism."[1] Shahzad, like terror suspect Najibullah Zazi, the admitted leader of a New York City subway bomb plot, seems to be part of a growing number of U.S. citizens who have developed extremist religious views and anti-Western values through travels to terrorist hotbeds and visits to websites and chatrooms with connections to terrorist groups. Indeed, of the more than 800 individuals prosecuted for terrorism-related offenses since 9/11, the largest group consisted of U.S. citizens.[2] The government has reacted by passing legislation such as the Prevention of Violent Radicalization and Homegrown Terrorism Act of 2007, but the homegrown threat remains—and continues to grow.[3] ■

As the Shahzad case makes clear, terrorism presents formidable challenges for the justice system and continues to evolve in complexity and seriousness. How is the government supposed to prevent terrorist attacks while respecting citizens' civil rights? At what point do officials go "too far" in their efforts to keep Americans safe? Should the struggle against terrorism be governed by a different set of rules? Should people expect to sacrifice certain rights to protect the security of our homeland? These are difficult questions to answer.

Confronting terrorism is critical because of the lethal tactics now being used—bombings, killing of hostages, chemical warfare, the spreading of toxic biological agents. The tactics of terrorists are alien to most people, who oppose violent solutions to their problems because they enjoy the benefits of living in a society with a secure economic and social system. Even when they wage war, stable governments abide by a standard code of conduct that spells out appropriate and inappropriate behaviors. Because they do not share in its benefits, terrorists not only have no stake in maintaining the economic, social, and political structure but may be actively planning its destruction. They obey few rules of combat and will use any tactic, no matter how violent, to achieve their goals.[4] Agencies of the justice system have little experience in dealing with such ruthlessness.

This chapter looks at terrorism and the homeland security response to it. We begin with some definitions; then we examine the criminal justice system's response to terrorism, particularly since September 11, 2001. We also discuss the legal response to terrorism through a review of the controversial "Patriot Act" and other legislation passed in recent years. This chapter concludes by contemplating the future of criminal justice in these difficult times.

## TERRORISM

Although terrorism is sometimes viewed as a contemporary phenomenon, terrorism and terrorists have been around for quite some time. The first terrorist activities were committed by members of minority religious groups who engaged in violence to (a) gain the right to practice their own form of religion, (b) establish the supremacy of their own religion over others, or (c) meet the requirements of the bloodthirsty gods they worshipped.[5] In some instances, a conquered people used force and violence to maintain their right to worship in their own faith. Zealots—Hebrew warrior groups active during the Roman occupation of Palestine during the first century AD—carried out attacks in broad daylight in order to send the message that the Roman authorities and those Jews who collaborated with them would not be safe.

The term "terrorist" first appeared at the time of the French Revolution, when Edmund Burke, a noted British political philosopher, referred to the violence he observed in Paris as the "reign of terror."[6] Terror was also associated with the unrest in Russia, which led to the 1917 Bolshevik takeover. In May 1881, a terror group killed Czar Alexander II. After the revolution, Bolshevik leaders Vladimir Lenin and Leon Trotsky made terror an instrument of state policy. Terror has also been identified with the civil war in Ireland and the Irish Republican Army, which is considered to be the model for most contemporary terrorist organizations.[7]

Despite its long history, terrorism (from the Latin *terrere*, which means "to frighten") is often difficult to define precisely, and separating terrorist acts from interpersonal crimes of violence is not easy. For example, if a group robs a bank to obtain funds for its revolutionary struggles, should the act be treated as terrorism or as a common bank robbery? In this instance, defining a crime as terrorism depends on the kind of legal response the act evokes from those in power. To be considered terrorism, which is a political crime, an act must carry with it the intent to disrupt and change the government and must not be merely a common-law crime committed for greed or egotism.

# Defining Terrorism

Because of its complexity, an all-encompassing definition of terrorism is difficult to formulate. According to the U.S. State Department, the term **terrorism** means premeditated, politically motivated violence that is perpetrated against noncombatant targets by subnational groups or clandestine agents and is usually intended to influence an audience. The term "international terrorism" means terrorism involving citizens or the territory of more than one country.[8] Terrorism can be distinguished from conventional warfare, because it requires secrecy and clandestine operations to exert social control over large populations.[9]

To be considered terrorism, an act must be aimed at a goal that sets it apart from a common-law crime committed for greed or egotism.[10] It is erroneous to equate terrorism with political goals, because not all terrorist actions are aimed at political change. Some terrorists may try to bring about what they consider to be economic or social reform—for example, by attacking women wearing fur coats or sabotaging property during a labor dispute. "Terrorist" is also often used interchangeably with "guerilla," "insurgent," and "revolutionary," although each is really an independent concept. (See Exhibit 18.1.)

**terrorism**
Premeditated, politically motivated violence perpetrated by subnational groups or clandestine agents against noncombatant targets, usually intended to influence an audience.

# Who Is the Terrorist?

Before terrorism can be effectively fought, controlled, and eradicated, it is important for agents of the justice system to understand something about the kind of people who become terrorists, what motivates their behavior, and how their ideas are formed. Unfortunately, this is not an easy task. Terrorism researchers have generally concluded that there is no single personality trait or behavior pattern that distinguishes the majority of terrorists or sets them apart so they can be easily identified and apprehended. Some seem truly disturbed, but many others have not suffered long-term mental illness or displayed sociopathic traits and/or tendencies; if that were so, bizarre or violent behavior in their early childhood would be a giveaway.[11] Thus there have been a number of competing visions of why terrorists engage in criminal activities such as bombings, shootings, and kidnappings to achieve a political end. Four stand out.

*PSYCHOLOGICAL VIEW* Not all terrorists suffer from psychological deficits, but enough do so that the typical terrorist can be described as an emotionally disturbed individual who acts out his or her psychoses within the confines of violent groups. According to this view, terrorist violence is not so much a political instrument as an end in itself; it is the result of compulsion or psychopathology. Terrorists do what they do because of a wide variety of emotional problems, including but not limited to self-destructive urges and disturbed emotions combined with problems with authority.[12]

*SOCIALIZATION VIEW* Terrorists have been raised to hate their opponents, and they learn at an early age that they have been victimized by some oppressor.[13] Often, this socialization occurred in dysfunctional families from which the father was absent or, if present, was a distant and cold figure.[14] Terrorists report that they were estranged from their fathers, whom they viewed as economically, socially, or politically weak and ineffective. Because of this family estrangement, the budding terrorist may have been swayed to join a group or cult by a charismatic leader who served as an alternative father figure. In this sense, terror groups, like urban street gangs, provide a substitute family that can nurture a heretofore emotionally underprivileged youth.

*IDEOLOGICAL VIEW* Terrorists hold extreme ideological beliefs that prompt their behavior. At first they have heightened perceptions of oppressive conditions, believing that they are being victimized by some group or government. Once these potential terrorists recognize that such conditions can be changed

**EXHIBIT 18.1**

## Terrorist, Guerrilla, Insurgent, Revolutionary

### TERRORIST

A terrorist uses criminal and violent acts to influence an audience beyond the immediate target. "Terrorism is an anxiety-inspiring method of repeated violent action, employed by (semi-)clandestine individual, group or state actors, for idiosyncratic, criminal or political reasons, whereby—in contrast to assassination—the direct targets of violence are not the main targets. The immediate human victims of violence are generally chosen randomly (targets of opportunity) or selectively (representative or symbolic targets) from a target population, and serve as message generators. Threat- and violence-based communication processes between terrorist (organization), (imperiled) victims, and main targets are used to manipulate the main target (audience(s), turning it into a target of terror, a target of demands, or a target of attention, depending on whether intimidation, coercion, or propaganda is primarily sought."

### GUERILLA

Guerillas (from the Spanish term meaning "little war,") are irregular military bands located in rural areas that attack military, police, and government targets. Guerilla warfare employs mobile and surprise tactics, traps, and ambushes to defeat a more powerful foe. Typically, guerillas try to draw their enemy into their terrain so that hit-and-run tactics and ambushes can be used to neutralize the enemy's superior power. Although the objective of some guerillas is to overthrow the existing government or carve out an independent territory, others may fight alongside government troops as they participate in conventional warfare. During World War II, partisan guerilla groups fought the Nazi occupiers in Russia, Poland, and other occupied nations. The goal of such operations is to increase the cost of maintaining an occupation or to exceed the limits of what

the invading army may wish to bear or is capable of enduring.

### INSURGENT

An insurgency is a political movement with a specific aim. Insurgents confront the existing government for control of all or a portion of its territory, or they may force political concessions in sharing political power. Whereas terrorists are inherently violent, insurgents do not necessarily need to use terror or violence to meet their aims; they may employ nonviolent methods or political tactics instead. They may set up food distribution centers and schools in areas where they gain control in order to provide the population with needed services, while contrasting their benevolent rule with the government's incompetence and corruption. Insurgents, unlike terrorists, require the support of a significant portion of the population. They may also seek external support from other nations to bring pressure on the government.

### REVOLUTIONARY

A revolutionary, from the Latin *revolutio* ("a turnaround,"), is generally seen as fighting a civil war between nationalists and a sovereign power that holds control of the land, or between the existing government and local groups over issues of ideology and power. Historically, the American Revolution may be considered an example of a struggle between nationalistic groups and an imperialistic overseas government. Some revolutions rely on armed force, but others can be nonviolent, depending on large urban protests and threats (an example is the Iranian Revolution of 1979).

Sources: United Nations Office on Drugs and Crime, "Definitions of Terrorism," http://web.archive.org/web/20070129121539/ http://www.unodc.org/unodc/terrorism_definitions.html (accessed October 4, 2010); Andrew Silke, "Holy Warriors: Exploring the Psychological Processes of Jihadi Radicalization," *European Journal of Criminology* 5 (2008): 99–123.

by an active reform effort that has not yet been made, they conclude that they must resort to violence to encourage change. The violence need not be aimed at a specific goal. Rather, terror tactics must help set in motion a series of events that enlist others in the cause and lead to long-term change. "Successful" terrorists believe that their "self-sacrifice" outweighs the guilt they incur by harming innocent people. Terrorism, therefore, requires violence without guilt; the cause justifies the violence.

*ALIENATION VIEW* Terrorist operatives are not poor or lacking in education. And yet lack of economic opportunity and recessionary economies are positively correlated with terrorism.[15] Terrorists may be motivated by feelings of alienation

## CONCEPT SUMMARY 18.1
### *The Variety of Terror Groups*

- *Revolutionary terrorism.* Groups that use violence to frighten those in power and their supporters in order to replace the existing government with a regime that holds acceptable political or religious views.

- *Political terrorism.* Political terrorism is directed at people or groups who oppose the terrorists' political ideology or who are defined by the terrorists as "outsiders" who must be destroyed.

- *Eco-terrorism.* Political terror groups today are involved in violent actions to protect the environment.

- *Nationalist terrorism.* Groups whose actions promote the interests of a minority ethnic or religious group that has been persecuted under majority rule and/or wishes to carve out its own independent homeland.

- *Retributive terrorism.* Groups that use violence as a method of influence, persuasion, or intimidation in order to achieve a particular aim or objective.

- *State-sponsored terrorism.* Terrorism carried out by a repressive government regime in order to force its citizen into obedience, oppress minorities, and stifle political dissent.

- *Cult terrorism.* Cults whose leaders demand that followers prove their loyalty through violence or intimidation.

- *Criminal terrorism.* Groups that become involved in common-law crimes such as drug dealing and kidnapping, or even selling nuclear materials.

and by being deprived of the tools to compete in a post-technological society.[16] Some terrorists appear alienated from modern society, and some feel that a suicide mission would cleanse them of the corruption of the modern world.

## The Contemporary Terrorist

On December 27, 2007, Pakistani political leader Benazir Bhutto was assassinated while leaving an election rally in Rawalpindi. Although the exact cause of her death remains a mystery, there is no question that she was shot at by gunmen who then set off a bomb, killing more than 20 people and injuring many others. Bhutto, the daughter of a former prime minister and educated at Harvard and Oxford universities, had been elected prime minister in 1988 and again in 1993. She had just returned to Pakistan after years in exile in order to run once again for public office. Her death was linked to Baitullah Mehsud, a militant leader with links to al Qaeda and other terror groups.

As the death of Benazir Bhutto illustrates, terrorism encompasses many different behaviors and goals. It can be directed toward a foreign occupying power, a local politician, or even a corporation that produces something terrorists find objectionable. Some of the more common forms of terrorism are briefly described here and summarized in Concept Summary 18.1.

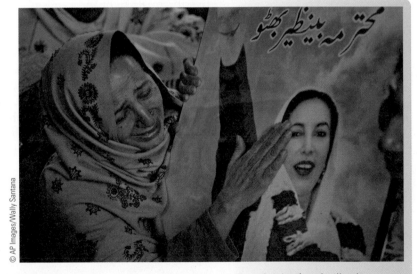

© AP Images/Wally Santana

*Terrorism involves the illegal use of force against innocent people to achieve a political objective. Confronting terrorism is critical because of the lethal tactics being used—bombings, killing hostages, chemical warfare, and spreading toxic biological agents. Another terrorist tactic is assassination. Here, on February 7, 2008, a supporter of the late former Pakistan Prime Minister Benazir Bhutto caresses her portrait at the end of a 40-day Muslim mourning ritual in Islamabad, Pakistan.*

**REVOLUTIONARY TERRORISM** Revolutionary terrorists use violence to frighten those in power and their supporters; their goal is to replace the existing government with a regime that holds political or religious views acceptable to them. Terrorist actions such as kidnapping, assassination, and bombing are designed to elicit repressive responses from governments trying to defend themselves. These responses help revolutionaries to expose, through the skilled use of media coverage, the government's inhumane nature. The terrorists hope that the original reason for the government's harsh response will be forgotten as people who are not philosophically involved witness the effect of its counterterrorist activities.

***POLITICAL TERRORISM***  Political terrorism is directed at people or groups with whom the terrorists live in close connection but who (a) oppose the terrorists' political ideology or (b) are defined as by the terrorists as "outsiders" who must be either exiled or destroyed. Political terrorists want the government to be more sensitive to their views and see things their way. In the United States, right-wing terrorists are organized around such themes as white supremacy, pro-life militancy, militant tax resistance, and religious revisionism. On the left, domestic political terror groups are involved in violent actions to protect the environment and support animal rights (known as eco-terrorism).

***NATIONALIST TERRORISM***  Nationalist terrorism promotes the interests of a minority ethnic or religious group that believes it has been persecuted under majority rule and wishes to carve out its own independent homeland. In Spain, the Basque Fatherland and Liberty (Euzkadi Ta Askatasuna, or ETA) is devoted to establishing a Basque homeland; in the Middle East, Hamas and Hezbollah fight for the destruction of Israel and the establishment of a Palestinian state.

***RETRIBUTIVE TERRORISM***  Rather than fighting for a homeland, retributive terrorists fight for a cause.[17] Their enemies are not local groups whom they oppose or have conflict with but, rather, people anywhere whose ideology and/or religion they find objectionable. Rather than having a unified central command, they are organized in far-flung nets. Not located in any particular nation or area, they have no identifiable address. They are capable of attacking anyone at any time with great destructive force. They may use technology to attack their targets' economic infrastructure—such as through computers and the Internet—and actually profit from the resulting economic chaos by buying or selling securities in advance of their own attack. Because they do not hope to regain a homeland or a political voice, they are willing to engage in suicide missions to achieve their goals.

On February 26, 2010, Palestinians waving the green flag of the fundamentalist group Hamas taunt Israeli soldiers during clashes in Hebron, on the West Bank. Palestinians have been protesting in Hebron since Israel declared that it would add the Cave of the Patriarchs (in Hebron) and Rachel's Tomb (in nearby Bethlehem) to its list of national heritage sites. The move angered Palestinians, who want Israel out of the territory. The United States, the United Nations, and some European countries have expressed concern about Israel's plan.

*STATE-SPONSORED TERRORISM* State-sponsored terrorism occurs when a repressive government regime forces its citizens into obedience, oppresses minorities, and stifles political dissent. Death squads and the use of government troops to destroy political opposition parties are often associated with political terrorism. Countries known for encouraging violent control of dissidents include Brazil, Colombia, Guatemala, Honduras, Peru, Iraq, and the Sudan.

*CULT TERRORISM* Some cults may be classified as terror groups because their leaders demand that followers prove their loyalty through violence or intimidation.[18] These destructive cults are willing to have members commit violence, including murder. Members typically follow a charismatic leader who may be viewed as having god-like powers or even as the reincarnation of an important religious figure. The leader and his or her lieutenants commonly enforce loyalty by severe discipline and by physically preventing members from leaving the group. They may go through doomsday drills and maintain a siege mentality, fearing attacks from the government. It is not uncommon for such destructive groups to begin stockpiling weapons and building defensive barricades.[19]

*CRIMINAL TERRORISM* Sometimes terrorist groups become involved in common-law crimes such as drug dealing and kidnapping, or even selling nuclear materials. Their illegal activities may on occasion become so profitable that they replace the group's original focus. In some cases there has been close cooperation between organized criminal groups and guerillas. In other instances the relationship is more superficial. For example, the Revolutionary Armed Forces of Colombia (FARC) imposes a tax on Colombian drug producers, but evidence indicates that the group cooperates with Colombia's top drug barons in running the trade. In some instances, the line becomes blurred between being a terrorist organization with political support and vast resources and being an organized criminal group engaged in illicit activities for profit. What appears to be a politically motivated action, such as the kidnapping of a government official for ransom, may turn out to be merely a for-profit crime.[20]

Now that this new breed of terrorist has made his mark upon the world, how has the criminal justice system responded to the threat? What has been done in the United States to create homeland security?

## HOMELAND SECURITY: THE CRIMINAL JUSTICE RESPONSE TO TERRORISM

After the 9/11 attacks, agencies of the criminal justice system began to focus their attention on combating the threat of terror. Even local police agencies created antiterror programs designed to protect their communities from the threat of attack. How should the nation best prepare itself to thwart potential attacks? The National Commission on Terrorist Attacks Upon the United States (also known as the 9/11 Commission), an independent, bipartisan commission, was created in late 2002 and given the mission of preparing an in-depth report of the events leading to the 9/11 attacks. In response to the commission report, a **Director of National Intelligence (DNI)** charged with coordinating data from the nation's primary intelligence-gathering agencies was created. The DNI serves as the principal intelligence adviser to the president and as statutory intelligence adviser to the National Security Council.

Among the agencies reporting to the DNI are the newly created National Counterterrorism Center (NCTC), which is staffed by terrorism experts from the CIA, the FBI, and the Pentagon; the Privacy and Civil Liberties Board; and the National Counterproliferation Center. The NCTC serves as the primary organization in the U.S. government for analyzing and integrating all intelligence

**CourseMate** For more information about **state-sponsored terror**, visit the Criminal Justice CourseMate at CengageBrain.com, then access the "Web Links" for this chapter.

**Director of National Intelligence (DNI)** Government official charged with coordinating data from the nation's primary intelligence-gathering agencies.

**CourseMate** For more information about the **Office of the Director of National Intelligence**, visit the Criminal Justice CourseMate at CengageBrain.com, then access the "Web Links" for this chapter.

**CourseMate** For more information about the **National Counterterrorism Center (NCTC)**, visit the Criminal Justice CourseMate at CengageBrain.com, then access the "Web Links" for this chapter.

possessed or acquired by the government pertaining to terrorism and counterterrorism, except purely domestic counterterrorism information.

Thus the 9/11 Commission report outlines what has already been done, what has not been done, and what needs to be done, and agencies of the justice system have begun to respond to the challenge.

## Fighting Terrorism with Law Enforcement

In the aftermath of the attacks on September 11, 2001, even before the 9/11 Commission made its report, it became obvious that the nation was not prepared to deal adequately with the threat of terrorism. One reason is the very nature of American society. Because we live in a free and open nation, it is extremely difficult to seal the borders and prevent the entry of terrorist groups. In his book *Nuclear Terrorism*, Graham Allison, an expert on nuclear weapons and national security, describes the almost superhuman effort it would take to seal the nation's borders from nuclear attack. Every day, 30,000 trucks, 6,500 rail cars, and 140 ships deliver more than 50,000 cargo containers into the United States. Fewer than 5 percent ever get screened, and those that do are inspected using external detectors, which may not detect nuclear weapons or fissile material.

The potential for terrorists to obtain bombs is significant: There are approximately 130 nuclear research reactors in 40 countries. Two dozen of these have enough highly enriched uranium for one or more nuclear bombs.

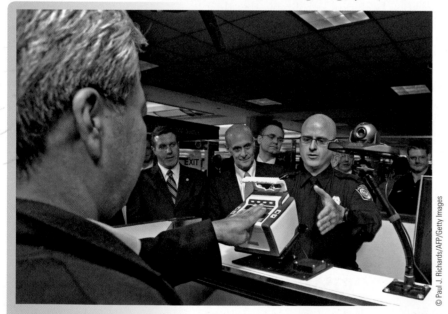

© Paul J. Richards/AFP/Getty Images

If terrorists could get their hands on fissile material from these reactors, they could build a crude but working nuclear bomb within a year. But they may not have to build their own bomb. They may be able to purchase an intact device on the black market. Russia alone has thousands of nuclear warheads and material for many thousands of additional weapons; all of these remain vulnerable to theft. Terrorists may also be able to buy the knowledge to construct bombs. In one well-known incident, Pakistan's leading nuclear scientist, A. Q. Khan, sold comprehensive "nuclear starter kits" that included advanced centrifuge components, blueprints for nuclear warheads, uranium samples in quantities sufficient to make a small bomb, and personal consulting services to assist in nuclear development.[21]

*The Department of Homeland Security has developed a variety of biometric techniques to screen people who want to enter the United States. At Dulles International Airport in Virginia, Officer Brian Pittack (right) stands at his station as Secretary of DHS Michael Chertoff (center) watches a passenger from South Korea get scanned with a new 10-fingerprint scanner for international arriving passengers. Most foreigners between the ages of 14 and 79 who travel to the United States have been required since 2004 to provide U.S. officials with the prints of two fingers and a digital photograph, either when they apply for a visa or when they arrive in the United States.*

Sensing this problem, law enforcement agencies around the country began to realign their resources to combat future terrorist attacks. In response to 9/11, law enforcement agencies increased the number of personnel engaged in emergency response planning; updated response plans for chemical, biological, or radiological attacks; and reallocated internal resources or increased departmental spending to focus on terrorism preparedness.[22] Actions continue to be taken on the federal, state, and local levels.

**FEDERAL LAW ENFORCEMENT** One of the most significant changes has been a realignment of the Federal Bureau of Investigation (FBI), the federal government's main law enforcement agency. The FBI has already announced a reformulation of its priorities, making protecting the United States from terrorist attack its number one commitment. It is now charged with coordinating intelligence collection with the Border Patrol, the Secret Service, and the CIA.

The FBI will also work with and share intelligence with the National Counterterrorism Center (NCTC). At the center of this initiative, the Counterterrorism Division of the FBI collects, analyzes, and shares critical information and intelligence on (a) international terrorism operations both within the United States and in support of extraterritorial investigations, (b) domestic terrorism operations, and (c) counterterrorism related to both international and domestic terrorism. Based in Washington, D.C., the Counterterrorism Division has the following responsibilities:

- Manage a team of analysts who work to put together information gathered by the field offices.

- Operate a national threat-warning system that enables the FBI to instantly distribute important terrorism alert bulletins to law enforcement agencies and public safety departments.

- Send out "flying squads" of specially trained officers to provide counterterrorism knowledge and experience, language capabilities, and analytical support, as needed, to FBI field offices.

- Maintain the Joint Terrorism Task Force (JTTF), which includes representatives from the Department of Defense, Department of Energy, Federal Emergency Management Agency, Central Intelligence Agency, Customs Service, Secret Service, and Immigration and Naturalization Service. Additionally, there are 66 local joint terrorism task forces in which representatives from federal agencies, state and local law enforcement personnel, and first responders work together to track down terrorists and prevent acts of terrorism in the United States.[23]

To carry out its newly formulated mission, the FBI is expanding its force of agents. In addition to recruiting candidates with the traditional background in law enforcement, law, and accounting, the bureau is concentrating on hiring agents with scientific and technological skills as well as foreign-language proficiency in priority areas such as Arabic, Farsi, Pashtun, Urdu, all dialects of Chinese, Japanese, Korean, Russian, Spanish, and Vietnamese, and with other priority backgrounds such as foreign counterintelligence, counterterrorism, and military intelligence. Besides helping in counterterrorism activities, these agents will staff the new Cyber Division, which was created in 2001 to coordinate, oversee, and facilitate FBI investigations in which the Internet, online services, and computer systems and networks are the principal instruments or targets of terrorists.

*DEPARTMENT OF HOMELAND SECURITY* Following the September 11, 2001, attacks, a new cabinet-level agency called the **Department of Homeland Security (DHS)** received congressional approval and was assigned the mission of preventing terrorist attacks within the United States, reducing America's vulnerability to terrorism, and minimizing the damage and aiding the recovery from attacks that do occur. DHS is the third-largest cabinet department in the federal government, after the Department of Defense and the Department of Veterans Affairs. It has approximately 180,000 employees. The various divisions of the DHS are set out in Exhibit 18.2.

The Department of Homeland Security is responsible for securing our nation's borders and transportation systems, which include 350 ports of entry. Its greatest challenge is to prevent the entry of terrorists and the instruments of terrorism, while simultaneously ensuring the speedy flow of legitimate traffic. The DHS is also in charge of securing territorial waters, including ports and waterways. (See the Criminal Justice and Technology feature on page 688 for one method of monitoring entry ports.)

**Department of Homeland Security (DHS)** Federal agency responsible for preventing terrorist attacks within the United States, reducing America's vulnerability to terrorism, and minimizing the damage and facilitating recovery when attacks do occur.

**CourseMate** For more information about the **Department of Homeland Security**, visit the Criminal Justice CourseMate at CengageBrain.com, then access the "Web Links" for this chapter.

**EXHIBIT 18.2**

# Components of the Department of Homeland Security

■ The Directorate for National Protection and Programs works to advance the Department's risk-reduction mission. Reducing risk requires an integrated approach that encompasses both physical and virtual threats and their associated human elements.

■ The Directorate for Science and Technology is the primary research and development arm of the Department. It provides federal, state, and local officials with the technology and capabilities to protect the homeland.

■ The Directorate for Management is responsible for Department budgets and appropriations, expenditure of funds, accounting and finance, procurement, human resources, information technology systems, facilities and equipment, and the identification and tracking of performance measurements.

■ The Office of Policy is the primary policy formulation and coordination component for the Department of Homeland Security. It provides a centralized, coordinated focus to the development of Department-wide, long-range planning to protect the United States.

■ The Office of Health Affairs coordinates all medical activities of the Department of Homeland Security to ensure appropriate preparation for and response to incidents having medical significance.

■ The Office of Intelligence and Analysis is responsible for using information and intelligence from multiple sources to identify and assess current and future threats to the United States.

■ The Office of Operations Coordination is responsible for monitoring the security of the United States on a daily basis and coordinating activities within the Department and with governors, Homeland Security Advisors, law enforcement partners, and critical infrastructure operators in all 50 states and more than 50 major urban areas nationwide.

■ The Federal Law Enforcement Training Center provides career-long training to law enforcement professionals to help them fulfill their responsibilities safely and proficiently.

■ The Domestic Nuclear Detection Office works to enhance the nuclear detection efforts of federal, state, territorial, tribal, and local governments, and the private sector, and to ensure a coordinated response to such threats.

■ The Transportation Security Administration (TSA) protects the nation's transportation systems to ensure freedom of movement for people and commerce.

■ United States Customs and Border Protection (CBP) is responsible for protecting our nation's borders in order to prevent terrorists and terrorist weapons from entering the United States, while facilitating the flow of legitimate trade and travel.

■ United States Citizenship and Immigration Services is responsible for administration of immigration and naturalization adjudication functions and establishing immigration services policies and priorities.

■ United States Immigration and Customs Enforcement (ICE), the largest investigative arm of the Department of Homeland Security, is responsible for identifying and shutting down vulnerabilities in the nation's border, economic, transportation, and infrastructure security.

■ The United States Coast Guard protects the public, the environment, and U.S. economic interests—in the nation's ports and waterways, along the coast, on international waters, or in any maritime region as required to support national security.

■ The Federal Emergency Management Agency (FEMA) prepares the nation for hazards, manages federal response and recovery efforts following any national incident, and administers the National Flood Insurance Program.

■ The United States Secret Service protects the President and other high-level officials and investigates counterfeiting and other financial crimes, including financial institution fraud, identity theft, computer fraud, and computer-based attacks on our nation's financial, banking, and telecommunications infrastructure.

Source: Department of Homeland Security, www.dhs.gov/xabout/structure/ (accessed May 10, 2010).

**STATE LAW ENFORCEMENT EFFORTS TO COMBAT TERRORISM** In the wake of the 9/11 attacks, a number of states have beefed up their intelligence-gathering capabilities and aimed them directly at homeland security. California has introduced the California Anti-Terrorism Information Center (CATIC), a statewide intelligence system designed to combat terrorism. It divides the state into operational zones and links federal, state, and local information services in one system. Trained intelligence analysts operate within civil rights guidelines and use information in a secure communications system; information is analyzed daily.[24] CATIC combines machine intelligence with information coming from a variety of police agencies. The information is correlated and organized by analysts looking for trends. Rather than simply operating as an information-gathering unit, CATIC is a synthesizing process. It combines open-source public information with data on criminal trends and possible terrorist activities. Processed intelligence is designed to produce threat assessments for each area and to project trends outside the jurisdiction. The CATIC system attempts to process multiple sources of information to predict threats. By centralizing the collection and analytical sections of a statewide system, California's Department of Justice may have developed a method for moving offensively against terrorism.

*COUNTY LAW ENFORCEMENT* Some counties are now engaging in antiterror and homeland security activities. For example, the Harris County, Texas, Office of Homeland Security & Emergency Management (OHSEM) is responsible for an emergency management plan that prepares for public recovery in the event of natural disasters or human-caused catastrophes or attacks. It works in conjunction with state, federal, and local authorities, including the city of Houston and other municipalities in the surrounding Harris County area when required. If needed, the Office of Homeland Security & Emergency Management activates an Emergency Operations Center to facilitate coordination of all support agencies to provide continuity of services to the public. OHSEM is responsible for advisement, notification, and assembly of services that are in the best interest of the citizens of Harris County. It prepares and distributes information and procedures governing the same.[25] Similarly, in Montgomery County, Maryland, the Homeland Security Department plans, prevents, prepares, and protects against major threats that may harm, disrupt, or destroy the community, its commerce, and institutions. Its mission is to effectively manage and coordinate the county's unified response, mitigation, and recovery from the consequences of such disasters or events, should they occur. It also serves to educate the public on emergency preparedness for all hazards and conducts outreach to diverse and special populations to protect, secure, and sustain critical infrastructures and ensure the continuity of essential services.[26] See the box on page 690 for career options in the area of emergency management.

*LOCAL LAW ENFORCEMENT* Federal law enforcement agencies are not alone in responding to the threat of terrorism. And, of course, nowhere is the threat of terrorism being taken more seriously than in New York City—one of the main targets of the 9/11 attacks—which has established a new Counterterrorism Bureau.[27] Teams within the bureau have been trained to examine potential targets in the city and are now attempting to insulate those targets from possible attack. Viewed as prime targets are the city's bridges, the Empire State Building, Rockefeller Center, and the United Nations. Bureau detectives are assigned overseas to work with the police in several foreign cities, including cities in Canada and Israel. Detectives have been assigned as liaisons with the FBI and with Interpol in Lyon, France. The city is recruiting detectives with language skills ranging from Pashtun and Urdu to Arabic, Fujianese, and other tongues. The existing New York City Police Intelligence Division has been revamped, and agents are examining foreign newspapers and monitoring Internet sites. The department is also setting up several backup command centers in different parts of the city in case a terror attack puts headquarters out of operation. Several backup senior command teams have been created so that if people at the highest levels of the department are killed, individuals will already have been tapped to step into their jobs.

The Counterterrorism Bureau has assigned more than 100 city police detectives to work with FBI agents as part of a Joint Terrorist Task Force. In addition, the Intelligence Division's 700 investigators now devote 35 to 40 percent of their resources to counterterrorism—up from about 2 percent before January 2002. The department is also drawing on the expertise of other institutions around the

## CRIMINAL JUSTICE AND TECHNOLOGY

# Using Biometrics to Fight Terrorism: US-VISIT

Since the terrorist attacks of September 11, 2001, added security measurements have been installed to help protect the country's citizens. Biometrics, the science of using digital technology to identify individuals, has been implemented in many facets of the country's security system. Biometric technology has been installed in airports, land border points (border crossings), and seaports.

The Department of Homeland Security has implemented the United States Visitor and Immigrant Status Indicator Technology (US-VISIT). US-VISIT was developed to provide more security to the nation's airports while keeping transportation into and out of the country open. This is accomplished by using biometric scans to determine the identity of all travelers from foreign countries who attempt to enter the United States.

### How It Works

Nearly all foreign citizens, regardless of country of origin, who wish to travel into the United States must comply with US-VISIT requirements. The process of registering for travel into the United States sometimes starts far from U.S. soil. Individuals who wish to travel to the United States must first visit the U.S. consular office in their country and apply for a visa. When they apply for the visa, they will have their biometrics collected in two separate ways. First, photographs are taken of every applicant, and those photographs are entered into the US-VISIT database, along with digital finger scans. The digital finger scans are taken of both the right and left index fingers of the applicant. This information is loaded into a database and then checked to see whether the individual matches any criminal or suspected terrorist already in the system.

Once an applicant passes the database check, she can be issued a visa to travel to the United States.

Upon her arrival at a U.S. point of entry, the traveler's left and right index fingers are scanned to determine whether she is the same person who applied for the visa. (This two-finger scanner is gradually being replaced by a more sophisticated ten-finger scanner.)

Entry procedures were started in 115 airports at the beginning of 2004. US-VISIT entry procedures are now in place in 116 airports, 15 seaports, and the secondary inspection areas of 154 land points of entry.

Homeland Security believes that implementing these new security features will result in fewer criminals or terrorists entering the country and will also reduce the incidence of identity theft and fraud that may occur upon entry to or exit from the country. However, there are critics who say that these procedures provide U.S. Customs and Immigration with too much personal information about travelers and U.S. citizens. Despite privacy concerns, the Department of Homeland Security is determined to use the US-VISIT program in conjunction with other government programs to increase the security of the United States.

### Critical Thinking

1. Are you concerned that futuristic security methods such as biometric technology will lead to the loss of personal privacy and the erosion of civil liberties?

2. Would you want your personal medical information to be posted on a computer network where it could potentially be accessed by future employers and others?

Sources: "United States Visitor and Immigrant Status Indicator Technology," (Electronic Privacy Information Center), www.epic.org/privacy/us-visit (accessed May 10, 2010); "US-VISIT" (Travel and Transportation, U.S. Department of Homeland Security), www.dhs.gov/dhspublic/interapp/content_multi_image/content_multi_image_0006.xml (accessed May 10, 2010).

city. For example, medical specialists have been enlisted to monitor daily developments in the city's hospitals to detect any suspicious outbreaks of illness that might reflect a biological attack. And the police are now conducting joint drills with the New York Fire Department to avoid the problems in communication and coordination that marked the emergency response on September 11.

## Fighting Terrorism in the Courts

Terrorism is not just a law enforcement matter. The courts have become increasingly active in this area. Federal trial courts have prosecuted, convicted, and sentenced a number of would-be and successful terrorists. The U.S. Supreme Court, too, has been rather vocal of late with respect to the treatment of terror suspects both here and abroad. We will look later in this chapter at recent Supreme Court cases. Here we consider terrorism prosecutions and convictions, the vast majority of which have occurred in the federal courts. Federal courts are usually the venue of choice because most antiterrorism laws are federal (or because federal statutes provide for harsher penalties).

***TERROR PROSECUTIONS IN FEDERAL COURTS*** In April 2009, the U.S. attorney for the Southern District of New York brought federal charges against Haji Juma Khan, an Afghan who was alleged to have provided the Taliban with funding through his lucrative (and illegal) opium, morphine, and heroin trafficking organization, which has been dubbed the "Khan Organization."[28] In the same month, Wesam al-Delaema pled guilty to conspiring to kill U.S. personnel in Iraq. He is currently serving his sentence in the Netherlands.[29] Other notable terrorism prosecutions in recent years include the following:

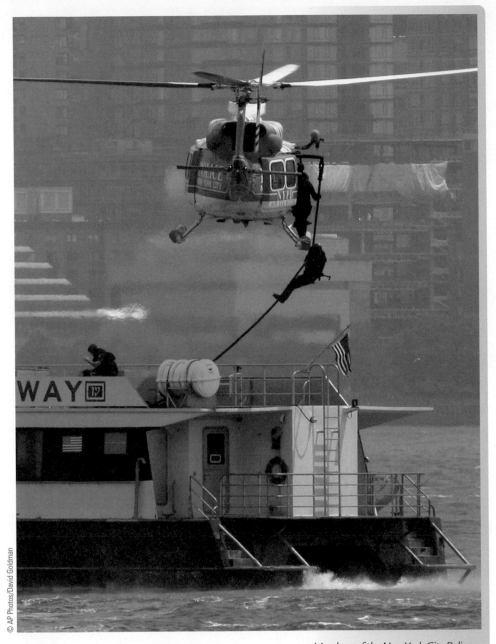

© AP Photos/David Goldman

*Members of the New York City Police Department (NYPD) rappel from a helicopter onto a ferry during a terrorist training exercise in the waters off Ellis Island in New York, on July 2, 2009. Training drills such as this have become commonplace in the wake of the 9/11 attacks.*

- *Toledo Terror Cell (Northern District of Ohio).* In June 2008, Mohammad Amawi, Marwan El-Hindi, and Wassim Mazloum were convicted of conspiracy to commit terrorist acts against Americans overseas, including U.S. armed forces in Iraq, and conspiracy to provide material support to terrorists. Amawi and El-Hindi were also convicted of distributing information regarding suicide bomb vests and Improvised Explosive Devices.

- *Christopher Paul (Southern District of Ohio).* In June 2008, Paul pleaded guilty to conspiring with members of a German terrorist cell to use a weapon of mass destruction (explosive devices) against Americans vacationing at foreign tourist resorts, against Americans in the United States, [and] against U.S. embassies, diplomatic premises, and military bases in Europe.

- *Hassan Abujihaad (District of Connecticut).* In March 2008, Abujihaad, a former member of the U.S. Navy, was convicted of providing material support to terrorists and delivering classified information on the movements of a U.S. Navy battle group to Azzam Publications, a London-based organization alleged to have provided material support to persons engaged in terrorism.

## CAREERS IN CRIMINAL JUSTICE

# Emergency Management Director

### Duties and Characteristics of the Job

Emergency management directors help communities prepare for and respond to natural, technological, and other disasters. Duties may vary, depending on location and on which hazards are typical of the area. In the Northeast, flash flooding from melting river ice is a significant problem, whereas in the midlands, dealing with tornado damage may be the top priority.

Emergency management directors work with and coordinate many different people and groups. Often, directors communicate with everyone from emergency response personnel to high-level officials. Planning and coordination with other agencies is common. This might require combining forces with the departments of social services, public safety, transportation, or health and environmental control; the employment security commission; the state housing authority; or relief organizations, such as the American Red Cross. Emergency management directors work long hours and often have irregular schedules.

The travel and other demands of the work—which include maintaining a constant state of alertness and taking responsibility during a crisis—can take a toll.

### Job Outlook

The number of emergency management specialists of all kinds will grow faster than the average for all occupations until 2014; more than 2,300 jobs will be added. The need for workers in this field is expected to increase more than 28 percent during the next five years. Top employers of emergency management specialists are local governments, state governments, general medical and surgical hospitals, power

generation and supply services, and emergency and other relief services. There is at least one emergency management director for each state, and other directors perform similar functions throughout government and private industry. The job titles for these workers include public safety director and emergency preparedness director.

### Salary and Opportunities

Emergency management specialists earn a median salary of approximately $49,350 per year. First-line supervisors and managers earn $41,690 annually, and they expect to see an 18 percent increase in the number of job opportunities by 2012.

### Qualifications

Management, leadership, and "people skills" are critical for emergency management directors. Experience in local government is valuable, and many directors have a background in firefighting, emergency medical services, or local law enforcement.

People interested in emergency management often volunteer or serve as interns to get field experience and a feel for what the work is really like.

### Education and Training

A college degree in criminal justice, public policy, business administration, public administration, professional management, or a related field is preferred.

Sources: O*Net Online, "Summary Report for 13-1061.00, Emergency Management Specialists," http://online.onetcenter.org/link/summary/13-1061.00 (accessed May 10, 2010); "Guide to Online Schools, More Information about Emergency Management," www.guidetoonlineschools.com/career/emergency-management.html (accessed May 10, 2010).

- *Mohammed Jabarah (Southern District of New York).* In January 2008, Jabarah was sentenced to life in prison after pleading guilty to terrorism charges stemming from his participation in a plot to bomb U.S. embassies in Singapore and the Philippines. Jabarah trained in al Qaeda camps in Afghanistan and spent time with Osama bin Laden, to whom he swore an oath of allegiance.
- *California Prison Plot (Central District of California).* In December 2007, Kevin James, who formed a radical Islamic organization while in California state prison, and two of his recruits, Levar Washington and Gregory Patterson, pleaded guilty to terrorism conspiracy charges, admitting they conspired to attack U.S. military facilities and Jewish facilities in Los Angeles.
- *Jose Padilla and co-defendants (Southern District of Florida).* In August 2007, a federal jury convicted Padilla, Adham Hassoun, and Kifah Jayyousi of conspiracy to murder, kidnap, and maim individuals in a foreign country, conspiracy to provide material support, and providing material support to terrorists. Padilla was sentenced to more than 17 years in prison.

■ *Zacarias Moussaoui (Eastern District of Virginia).* In May 2006, Moussaoui was sentenced to six consecutive life terms after pleading guilty in April 2005 to various terrorism violations [and] admitting that he conspired with al Qaeda to hijack and crash planes into prominent U.S. buildings as part of the 9/11 attacks.

■ *Ahmed Omar Abu Ali (Eastern District of Virginia).* In November 2005, Ali was convicted on all counts of an indictment charging him with, among other violations, providing material support to al Qaeda, conspiracy to assassinate the U.S. president, conspiracy to commit air piracy, and conspiracy to destroy aircraft. Ali was sentenced to 30 years in prison.[30]

These are just a few of the hundreds of terrorism prosecutions that have taken place in the United States since the 1980s. There was a notable spike in prosecutions right after 9/11, but prosecutions continue to this day. In the eight years immediately after 9/11, there were 828 prosecutions of suspected terrorists in the United States.[31] This number continues to grow.

A recent report by the organization Human Rights First concluded that the U.S. criminal justice system is well equipped to handle a broad variety of criminal cases arising from terrorist incidents.[32] The report's authors also claim, however, that "the criminal justice system, by itself, is not 'the answer' to the problem of international terrorism."[33] The criminal justice system, including the courts, is but one piece of a larger puzzle, they argue: "Given the magnitude and complexity of the international terrorism threat, it is plain that the government must employ a multifaceted approach involving the use of military, intelligence, diplomatic, economic, and law enforcement resources in order to address the threat of international terrorism."[34]

*TERRORISM CONVICTIONS* The U.S. Justice Department's National Security Division International Terrorism and Terrorism-Related Statistics Chart tracks all convictions resulting from international terrorism investigations since 9/11. The chart tracks convictions in two categories (a list of offenses appears in Figure 18.1):

■ Category I cases involve violations of federal statutes that are directly related to international terrorism and that are utilized regularly in international terrorism matters. These statutes prohibit, for example, terrorist acts abroad against United States nationals, the use of weapons of mass destruction, conspiracy to murder persons overseas, providing material support to terrorists or foreign terrorist organizations, receiving military-style training from foreign terrorist organizations, and bombings of public places or government facilities.

■ Category II cases include defendants charged with violating a variety of other statutes where the investigation involved an identified link to international terrorism. These Category II cases include offenses such as those involving fraud, immigration, firearms, drugs, false statements, perjury, and obstruction of justice, as well as general conspiracy charges. . . .[35]

Since 9/11, and as of this writing, more than 400 individuals have been convicted under one or more of the aforementioned offenses.[36] In all likelihood, this number will continue to grow. Here are two examples of terrorism convictions resulting from the Category II offenses listed in Figure 18.1:

■ *Fort Dix Plot (conspiracy to murder members of the U.S. military).* In 2008, following a jury trial in the United States District Court for the District of New Jersey, Ibrahim Shnewer, Dritan Duka, Shain Duka, Eljvir Duka, and Serdar Tatar were convicted of violating 18 U.S.C. §1117, in connection with a plot to kill members of the U.S. military in an armed attack on the military base at Fort Dix, New Jersey. The defendants were also convicted of various weapons charges. The government's evidence revealed that one member of the group conducted surveillance at Fort Dix and Fort Monmouth in New Jersey, Dover Air Force Base in Delaware, and the U.S. Coast Guard in Philadelphia. The group obtained a detailed map of Fort Dix, where it hoped to use assault rifles to kill as many soldiers as possible. During the trial, the jury viewed secretly recorded videotapes of the defendants performing small-arms training at a shooting range in the Poconos Mountains in Pennsylvania and of the defendants watching training videos that included depictions of American

**FIGURE 18.1**
Statutes Used to Prosecute and Convict Terrorists

**Category I Offenses**

Aircraft Sabotage (18 U.S.C. § 32)

Animal Enterprise Terrorism (18 U.S.C. § 43)

Crimes Against Internationally Protected Persons (18 U.S.C. §§ 112, 878, 1116, 1201 (a)(4))

Use of Biological, Nuclear, Chemical or Other Weapons of Mass Destruction (18 U.S.C. §§ 175, 175b, 229, 831, 2332a)

Production, Transfer, or Possession of Variola Virus (Smallpox) (18 U.S.C. § 175c)

Participation in Nuclear and WMD Threats to the United States (18 U.S.C. § 832)

Conspiracy Within the United States to Murder, Kidnap, or Maim Persons or to Damage Certain Property Overseas (18 U.S.C. § 956)

Hostage Taking (18 U.S.C. § 1203)

Terrorist Attacks Against Mass Transportation Systems (18 U.S.C. § 1993)

Terrorist Acts Abroad Against United States Nationals (18 U.S.C. § 2332)

Terrorism Transcending National Boundaries (18 U.S.C. § 2332b)

Bombings of place of public use, Government facilities, public transporation systems and infrastructure faciles (18 U.S.C. § 2332f)

Missile Systems designed to Destroy Aircraft (18 U.S.C. § 2332g)

Production, Transfer, or Possession of Radiological Dispersal Devices (18 U.S.C. § 2332h)

Harboring Terrorists (18 U.S.C. § 2339)

Providing Material support to Terrorists (18 U.S.C. § 2339A)

Providing Material Support to Designated Terrorist Organization (18 U.S.C. § 2339B)

Prohibition Against Financing of Terrorism (18 U.S.C. § 2339C)

Receiving Military-Type Training from an FTO (18 U.S.C. § 2339D)

Narco-Terrorism (21 U.S.C. § 1010A)

Sabotage of Nuclear Facilities of Fuel (42 U.S.C. § 2284)

Aircraft Piracy (49 U.S.C. § 46502)

**Category II Offenses**

Crimes Committed Within the special Maritime and Territorial Jurisdiction of the United States (18 U.S.C §§ 7, 113, 114, 115, 1111, 1112, 1201, 2111)

Violence at International Airports (18 U.S.C. § 37)

Arsons and Bombings (18 U.S.C. § 842(m), 842(n), 844(f), 844(I))

Killings in the Course of Attack on a Federal Facility (18 U.S.C. § 930(c))

False Statements (18 U.S.C. § 1001)

Protection of Computers (18 U.S.C. § 1030)

False Information and Hoaxes (18 U.S.C. § 1038)

Genocide (18 U.S.C. § 1091)

Destruction of Communication Lines (18 U.S.C. § 1362)

Sea Piracy (18 U.S.C. § 1651)

Unlicensed Money Remitter Charges (18 U.S.C. § 1960)

Wrecking Trains (18 U.S.C. § 1992)

Destruction of National Defense Materials, Premises, or Utilities (18 U.S.C. § 2155)

Violence against Maritime Navigation and Maritime Fixed Platforms (18 U.S.C. §§ 2280, 2281)

Torture (18 U.S.C. § 2340A)

War Crimes (18 U.S.C. § 2441)

International Traffic in Arms Regulations (22 U.S.C. § 2778, and the rules and regulations promulgated thereunder, 22 C.F.R. § 121–130)

Crimes in the Special Aircraft Jurisdiction other than Aircraft Piracy (49 U.S.C. §§ 46503–46507)

Destruction of Interstate Gas or Hazardous Liquid Pipeline Faciles (49 U.S.C. § 60123(b))

Source: U.S. Justice Department, *Introduction to National Security Division Statistics on Unsealed International Terrorism and Terrorism-Related Convictions*, www .justice.gov/cjs/docs/terrorism-convictions-statistics.pdf (accessed May 11, 2010).

soldiers being killed and of known Islamic radicals urging jihad against the United States.

■ *Fawaz Damrah (citizenship fraud)*. In 2004, following a jury trial in the United States District Court for the Northern District of Ohio, Fawaz Damrah was convicted of violating 18 U.S.C. § 1425 for concealing material facts in his citizenship application. The government's evidence showed that in his

**EXHIBIT 18.3**

## *What Is Jihad?*

According to terror expert Andrew Silke, the term "jihad" derives from the Arabic word for "struggle," and within Islam there are two forms of jihad: the Greater Jihad and the Lesser Jihad. The Greater Jihad is a Muslim's personal struggle to live a good and charitable life and adhere to God's commands. In this sense, jihad is a strictly personal and nonviolent phenomenon. The Lesser Jihad consists of violent struggle on behalf of Islam. Jihadists are "those who struggle," and in this sense, the term refers to individuals who have volunteered to fight in the Lesser Jihad. Members of groups such as al Qaeda use this term to describe themselves and their goals. Jihadists sometimes call themselves Mujahideen, which means "holy warriors," and the term is commonly used to refer to Muslims engaged in the Lesser Jihad.

Source: Andrew Silke, "Holy Warriors: Exploring the Psychological Processes of Jihadi Radicalization," *European Journal of Criminology* 5 (2008): 99–123.

citizenship application, Damrah concealed from the U.S. government his membership in or affiliation with the Palestinian Islamic Jihad (PIJ), a.k.a. the Islamic Jihad Movement in Palestine; the Afghan Refugees Services, Inc., a.k.a. Al-Kifah Refugee Center; and the Islamic Committee for Palestine. Damrah further concealed the fact that he had, prior to his application for U.S. citizenship, "incited, assisted, or otherwise participated in the persecution" of Jews and others by advocating violent terrorist attacks against Jews and others. During the trial, the government's evidence included footage of a 1991 speech in which Damrah called Jews "the sons of monkeys and pigs" and a 1989 speech in which he declared that "terrorism and terrorism alone is the path to liberation."[37]

## POLITICAL SOLUTIONS TO TERRORISM

In the long run, it may simply be impossible to defeat terror groups and end terrorism using military, law enforcement, and legal solutions. Using force may play into terrorists' hands and convince people that the terrorists are freedom fighters valiantly struggling against a better armed and more ruthless foe. No matter how many terrorists are killed or captured, military/deterrence–based solutions may be doomed. Aggressive reprisals will cause terrorist ideology to spread and gain greater acceptance in the underdeveloped world. The resulting anger and alienation will produce more *jihadists* than can be killed off through violent responses (see Exhibit 18.3). In contrast, some believe, if the terrorist ideology is countered and discredited, the appeal of terror groups such as al Qaeda will wither and die.

One approach suggested by policy experts is to undermine support for terrorist groups by being benevolent nation builders giving aid to the nations that house terror groups.[38] This is the approach the United States took after World War II to rebuild Germany and Japan (the Marshall Plan), all the while gaining support for its cold war struggle against the Soviet Union. According to the RAND Corporation, a nonprofit research group, the following steps are required to defeat **jihadist groups** such as al Qaeda:

- Attack the ideological underpinnings of global jihadism.
- Sever ideological and other links between terrorist groups.
- Strengthen the capabilities of frontline states to counter local jihadist threats.

This approach may work, because al Qaeda's goal of toppling "apostate" regimes in Saudi Arabia, Egypt, and Pakistan and creating an ultra-orthodox pan-Islamic government spanning the world does not sit well with large groups of Muslims. That monolithic vision has no room for other Muslim sects, such

**jihadist groups**
Muslim fighters engaged in a holy war or spiritual struggle against infidels.

# IMAGES OF JUSTICE

## al-Hurra versus as-Sahab

Al Qaeda's media network, as-Sahab, is used to distribute the group's views to the world. Traditionally, its videos were posted in Arab chat forums and similar sites, but as-Sahab's Internet presence has grown over time. On YouTube, for example, hundreds of interviews, documentaries, and propaganda clips can be readily accessed. Many of the videos are in English.

This, coupled with al Qaeda's ever-growing capability of getting its message out, has prompted the United States to respond with its own outreach effort, al-Hurra (Arabic for "The Free One"). Funded through the Broadcasting Board of Governors with support from U.S. taxpayers, al-Hurra is a commercial-free Arabic-language television network, broadcast via satellite, to various countries throughout the Middle East. In addition to presenting news and information, the network broadcasts discussion programs, current affairs magazines, and features on a range of subjects.

al-Hurra is a public diplomacy tool, meaning it is used to engage foreign publics, particularly in the American perspective on U.S. foreign policy.

Interestingly, though, the network is barred from broadcasting in the United States because of the 1948 Smith-Mundt Act, which regulates the broadcasting of propaganda domestically. Critics indeed complain that al-Hurra is a United States propaganda tool, but Daniel Nassif, the network's news director, stated in a *Middle East Quarterly* interview that the network does not disseminate U.S. propaganda:

> al-Hurra's role is to report U.S. policy accurately to an audience that has often not received accurate and objective reports, but our role is not to advocate policy. We provide context and analysis so that viewers can make informed decisions. We want to satisfy some of the curiosity about America that many viewers in the Middle East share. The latest political, military, and diplomatic developments tend to drive news coverage, but that does not begin to exhaust the breadth of the engagement between America and the Middle East.

Source: *Middle East Quarterly*, "Daniel Nassif: 'We Do Not Spread Propaganda for the United States,'" Spring 2008: 63–69, available at www.meforum.org/1880/daniel-nassif-we-do-not-spread-propaganda-for (accessed May 11, 2010).

as Shites and Sunni moderates. Therefore, political and social appeals may help fracture local support for al Qaeda. In addition, the United States should seek to deny sanctuaries to terrorist groups and to strengthen the capabilities of foreign governments to deal with terrorist threats, but in an advisory capacity and by providing intelligence. Exhibit 18.4 sets out the RAND Corporation's blueprint for fighting jihadist terrorist groups using political rather than military action.

Another approach is to use the media to win the "hearts and minds" of people in countries that do not hold the United States in high regard. One example of this approach is al-Hurra, the Arabic-language satellite television network for the Middle East funded by the United States. It—and another, anti-U.S. network—are discussed in the accompanying Images of Justice feature.

## CONFRONTING TERRORISM WITH THE LAW

**USA Patriot Act (USAPA)**
The law designed to grant new powers to domestic law enforcement and international intelligence agencies in an effort to fight terrorism.

Soon after the September 11 terrorist attacks, the U.S. government enacted several laws focused on preventing further acts of violence against the United States and creating greater flexibility in the fight to control terror activity. Most important, Congress passed the **USA Patriot Act (USAPA)** on October 26, 2001. The bill is over 342 pages long, creates new laws, and makes changes to over 15 different existing statutes. Its aim is to give sweeping new powers to domestic law enforcement and international intelligence agencies in an effort to fight terrorism, to expand the definition of terrorist activities, and to alter

## *Countering Terror through Political Change*

■ *Attack the ideological underpinnings of global jihadism.* The goal is to deny extremists the high ground of Islamic politico-religious discourse, which has been adroitly exploited by al Qaeda to further the appeal of its own radical rhetoric. Prevailing in the war of ideas requires empowering moderate Muslims to counter the influence of the radicals. Preventing ideologues from continuing to provide justification for terrorism could expedite jihadism's deterioration.

■ *Seek to sever the links—ideological and otherwise— between terrorist clusters and the global jihad.* Contradictions inevitably arise between the global vision promulgated by global jihadist theoreticians and the national agendas that many local movements naturally pursue. Exploiting this friction hinges on decreasing the utility of the relationship with al Qaeda for local groups. To achieve this goal, the United States will need to tailor the specific components of its counterterrorism policy to ensure that they are relevant to extant and emerging patterns of local and regional terrorism.

■ *Strengthen the capabilities of frontline states and moderate civil society groups to counter local jihadist threats.* The object is to deny al Qaeda alternative sanctuaries and, over time, to reduce the clusters that compose the global jihadist movement. These local wars have to be fought and won by local governments and security forces, with the United States in a supporting role. For the U.S. military and the U.S. Air Force, new types of missions may require fusion, not only with other services, but also with the security forces of cooperating countries.

Source: RAND Corporation, "U.S. Counterterrorism Strategy Must Address Ideological and Political Factors at the Global and Local Levels" (2006), www.rand.org/pubs/research_briefs/RB202/index1.html (accessed May 10, 2010).

sanctions for violent terrorism. On March 2, 2006, Congress passed a reauthorization bill that left most of the act intact, and on March 9, President George W. Bush signed it into law.

Although it is impossible to discuss every provision of this sweeping legislation here, a few of its more important elements will be examined.

## The USA Patriot Act

USAPA expands all four traditional tools of surveillance—wiretaps, search warrants, pen/trap orders (installing devices that record phone calls), and subpoenas. The Foreign Intelligence Surveillance Act (FISA) that allows domestic operations by intelligence agencies is also expanded. USAPA gives greater power to the FBI to check and monitor phone, Internet, and computer records without first needing to demonstrate that they were being used by a suspect or the target of a court order.

The government may now serve a single wiretap, or pen/trap order, on any person regardless of whether that person or entity is named in a court order. Prior to this act, telephone companies could be ordered to install, on their networks, pen/trap devices that would monitor calls coming to a surveillance target and to whom the surveillance target made calls; the USAPA extends this monitoring to the Internet. Law enforcement agencies may now also obtain the email addresses and websites visited by a target, as well as the email addresses of the people with whom they communicate. It is possible to require that an Internet service provider install, on its servers, a device that records email and other electronic communications, looking for communications initiated or received by the target of an investigation. Under USAPA, the government does not need to show a court that the information or communication is relevant to a criminal investigation, nor does it have to report where it served the order or what information it received.

The act also allows enforcement agencies to monitor cable operators and obtain access to their records and systems. Before the act, a cable company had to give prior notice to the customer, even if that person was the target of an

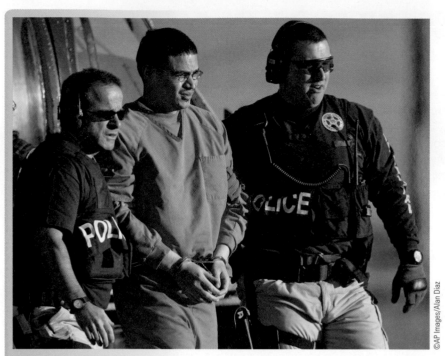

*Jose Padilla is escorted by federal marshals on his arrival in Miami, Florida. On January 22, 2008, Padilla was sentenced by federal judge Marcia Cooke to 17 years and 4 months in prison for conspiring to support Islamic extremists around the world. Padilla, a U.S. citizen, was part of a secret network that supported violent extremists. The government relied largely on wiretapped conversations when it put Mr. Padilla and others on trial as a "North American support cell" that sent money, goods, and recruits abroad to assist "global jihad." The USA Patriot Act makes it easier for U.S. agents to use wiretapping when investigating suspected terrorists in the interests of national security.*

investigation. Information can now be obtained on people with whom the cable subscriber communicates, the content of the person's communications, and the person's subscription records; prior notice is still required if law enforcement agencies want to learn what television programming a subscriber purchases.

The act also expands the definition of *terrorism* and enables the government to monitor more closely those people suspected of "harboring" and giving "material support" to terrorists (Sections 803, 805). It increases the authority of the U.S. attorney general to detain and deport noncitizens with little or no judicial review. The attorney general may certify that there are "reasonable grounds to believe" that a noncitizen endangers national security and is therefore eligible for deportation. The attorney general and secretary of state are also given the authority to designate domestic groups as terrorist organizations and to deport any noncitizen who is a member of such a group.

## Civil Rights and the Struggle against Terrorism

Civil libertarians are troubled by some of the actions taken by the various law enforcement agencies to combat terrorism; they maintain that the harshest measures are eroding civil rights. Some complain that there are provisions that permit the government to share information from grand jury proceedings and from criminal wiretaps with intelligence agencies. First Amendment protections may be violated because the Patriot Act authority is not limited only to true terrorism investigations but covers a much broader range of activity involving reasonable political dissent. But even though many critics have called for its repeal, USAPA was reauthorized in 2006 with a slew of provisions designed to ensure, limiting its surveillance and wiretap authorizations, that the act did not violate citizens' civil rights.[39] More recently, President Obama extended three controversial provisions that were set to expire:

- *Lone wolf.* The government can track individuals who are not connected to a foreign power but who are thought to be affiliated with a terrorist group. This applies only to noncitizens.

- *Business records.* The government can force third parties, such as travel and telephone companies, to provide access to a suspect's records without his or her knowledge.

- *Roving wiretaps.* The government can monitor phone lines and Internet accounts that a terrorist suspect may be using, but it must first get approval from the Foreign Intelligence Surveillance Act court.[40]

Another concern has been the incarceration of terror suspects for extended periods of time without trial or hearing. However, the most sensitive issue has proved to be the use of coercive measures to extract information from terror suspects, an issue explored in the Analyzing Criminal Justice Issues feature on page 698.

## The Supreme Court and Terrorism

During times of national emergency, the government has sometimes taken drastic measures to curtail the rights of its enemies. For example, during the Civil War,

Lamdin Milligan, a civilian and sympathizer with the South, was tried and convicted before a military tribunal (a military court that limits the rights a person would otherwise enjoy in a civilian court) for conspiring to free Confederate prisoners from jail. He challenged his conviction, arguing that since the civilian courts were still functioning, he should have been tried in one of them. In *Ex Parte Milligan*,[42] the Supreme Court agreed. Since then, and especially during times of war, the Court has decided a number of landmark cases. In the wake of 9/11, it has handed down decisions in four important cases. More are sure to follow.

Shortly after the 9/11 attacks, Congress authorized then-President George Bush to use "all necessary and appropriate force" against those responsible for the attacks in New York and Washington, D.C. Yaser Hamdi, an American citizen who had left the United States in his youth, was captured in Afghanistan and detained by military forces at Guantanamo Bay, Cuba, for supposedly aiding the Taliban. He was later moved to a military prison in Norfolk, Virginia, where he filed a writ of habeas corpus, arguing that, as a U.S. citizen, he was entitled to challenge the constitutionality of his confinement in federal court. In *Hamdi v. Rumsfeld* (2004),[43] the Supreme Court agreed with his argument, holding in a 6 to 3 decision that the due process clause of the Fifth Amendment requires that U.S. citizens be given the opportunity to challenge their confinement in this way. The Court also decided, in *Rasul v. Bush* (2004), that the federal courts have jurisdiction to hear habeas corpus petitions from foreign nationals captured outside the United States.[44]

One year later, the Supreme Court heard a case involving Salim Hamdan, a Yemeni and a former driver for Osama bin Laden. He was captured by Afghan warlords and turned over to U.S. forces in 2001. He was transferred to Guantanamo Bay in 2002 and, in 2003, was slated to be tried for various conspiracy offenses before a military tribunal. He filed a habeas corpus petition in the U.S. District Court for the Western District of Washington, basically claiming that he could not legally be tried by a military tribunal. In a 5 to 3 decision, the Supreme Court agreed.[45] It held that the military commission at issue violated the Uniform Code of Military Justice and the four Geneva Conventions signed in 1949. Charges against him were subsequently dropped, but Hamdan was later deemed an "unlawful enemy combatant," tried once again before a military tribunal, and convicted. He was sentenced to five and a half years in prison, given credit for time served, and sent back to Yemen. He was not named a combatant before going into his first trial, which is one reason why the first military tribunal was illegal.

Shortly after Hamdan's case was decided, Congress passed the Military Commissions Act of 2006, which stripped the federal courts of jurisdiction to hear habeas corpus petitions from detainees who have been designated "enemy combatants." But in a 5 to 4 decision, the Supreme Court held that prisoners (even foreign nationals held at Guantanamo Bay) have the right to habeas corpus under the U.S. Constitution and that their arguments can be heard in the federal courts.[46] In effect, the Court held that the Military Commissions Act of 2006 was an unconstitutional suspension of the right to habeas corpus. In October 2009, President Obama signed into law the Military Commissions Act of 2009, which attempted to improve on—and address some of the deficiencies of—the earlier legislation. For example, the new law does not permit a U.S. citizen to be tried by a military commission.[47] As of this writing, the Supreme Court has not decided any cases concerning the new legislation.

It is not particularly easy to understand all the nuances of the Supreme Court's terrorism cases, especially those decided in the wake of 9/11. This is partly because antiterrorism legislation continues to evolve. That said, there is an underlying theme in all of the cases we just considered: Detainees, enemy combatants, terror suspects, and the like enjoy greater protection now than they did in the past. Indeed, all but a few of them enjoy the same rights as anyone else, whether or not they are U.S. citizens.

## ANALYZING CRIMINAL JUSTICE ISSUES

# *The Use of Torture*

On February 23, 2007, Osama Hassan Mustafa Nasr, an Egyptian cleric, made worldwide headlines when he claimed that he had been kidnapped in Italy by American agents and sent to Egypt for interrogation. Nasr claimed, "I was subjected to the worst kind of torture in Egyptian prisons. I have scars of torture all over my body." Italy indicted 26 American and 5 Italian agents accused of seizing him and sending him to Egypt without trial or due process.

Can the torture of a suspected terrorist determined to destroy the government and harm innocent civilians ever be permissible? Most people loathe the thought of torturing anyone, but some experts argue that torture can sometimes be justified in what they call the *ticking bomb* scenario: Suppose the government found out that a captured terrorist knew the whereabouts of a dangerous explosive device that was set to go off and would certainly kill thousands of innocent people. Would it be permissible to inflict torture on this single suspect if it would save the population of a city? Athough the ticking bomb scenario has appeal, opponents of torture believe that it can never be justified, no matter how much destruction its use may prevent. A number of arguments have been constructed:

■ There is a danger that it could become calculated and premeditated; torturers would have to be trained, ready, and in place for the ticking bomb argument to work. We couldn't be running around looking for torturers with a bomb set to go off, could we? Torture then might become routine rather than being reserved for use in extreme cases.

■ What happens if a superior officer tells an enforcement agent to torture someone, but the agent believes the order is unjustified? Should she follow orders or risk punishment for disobeying?

■ There is very little empirical evidence suggesting that torture provides any real benefits, and much more suggests that it can create serious problems. It can damage civil rights and democratic institutions and cause the general public to have sympathy for the victims of torture regardless of their evil intent.

■ The U.S. Constitution limits physical coercion by the government under the Fifth Amendment's due process and self-incrimination clauses and the Eighth Amendment's prohibition of cruel and unusual punishments.

■ Intelligence is rarely, if ever, good enough to provide specific advance warning of a terror attack. If terrorists knew their plan could be foiled by information provided by a prisoner, why would they not change the plan?

Although these arguments are persuasive, noted legal scholar Alan Dershowitz argues that torture can be justified under some circumstances, especially to prevent damaging terror attacks. Moreover,

## THE FUTURE OF CRIMINAL JUSTICE

What will criminal justice be like a decade from now? Two decades from now? A whole generation from now? How will crime itself evolve? What about offenders? The answers are anyone's guess. History tells us as much. In the mid-1990s, for example, several prominent criminologists predicted a surge in serious crime,[48] particularly among juveniles, but the last decade of the twentieth century saw some of the largest crime drops in history, underscoring the difficulty of predicting the future. Even so, inaccurate predictions have not stopped the experts from planning for the future.

Chapter 17 highlighted some of the emerging and cutting-edge problems that the U.S. criminal justice system is coming to grips with. The bulk of this chapter featured the evolving terrorist threat, another problem that will keep criminal justice officials (and the government in general) busy for decades to come. Yet there are other threats and changes that lie in store. Some of them are certainties; others will probably take us by surprise. In this concluding section, we look at some of the possibilities.

he believes that the "vast majority" of Americans would expect law enforcement agents to engage in time-honored methods of "loosening tongues" if the circumstances demanded it. To ensure that torture is not used capriciously, Dershowitz proposes the creation of a "torture warrant" that can be issued by a judge only in cases where (a) there is an absolute need to obtain immediate information in order to save lives and (b) there is probable cause that the suspect has such information and is unwilling to reveal it to law enforcement agents. The suspect would be given immunity from prosecution based on information elicited by the torture; it would be used only to save lives. The warrant would limit the torture to non-lethal means, such as sterile needles being inserted beneath the nails to cause excruciating pain without endangering life.[41]

## The Waterboarding Controversy

Can a bright line be drawn between what is considered torture and what constitutes firm but legal interrogation methods? This issue made headlines when it was revealed that government agents make routine use of the waterboarding technique while interrogating suspected terrorists. Waterboarding involves immobilizing a person on his or her back, with the head inclined downward, and pouring water over the face and into the breathing passages. It produces an immediate gag reflex and an experience akin to drowning; the subject believes his or her death is imminent.

The use of waterboarding is controversial because there seems to be no agreement on whether it is torture or a relatively harmless instrument of interrogation. Official U.S. government policy and government doctrine are vehemently opposed to torture, but authorities have condoned harsh interrogation techniques that combine physical and psychological tactics, including head-slapping, waterboarding, and exposure to extreme cold.

## Critical Thinking

Waterboarding became an issue during the 2008 presidential campaign when Senator John McCain, a former prisoner of war who had experienced torture firsthand in a North Vietnamese prison camp, told the press, "All I can say is that it was used in the Spanish Inquisition, it was used in Pol Pot's genocide in Cambodia, and there are reports that it is being used against Buddhist monks today. . . . They should know what it is. It is not a complicated procedure. It is torture." Do you agree with McCain's assessment, and if not, under what circumstances would you condone the use of waterboarding to interrogate a prisoner?

Sources: Nadia Abou El-Magd, "Accuser in *Case vs. CIA Agents* Tells of Torture: Muslim Cleric Says Egyptians Used Electricity," *Boston Globe*, February 23, 2007, p. A3; Jessica Wolfendale, "Training Torturers: A Critique of the 'Ticking Bomb' Argument," *Social Theory & Practice* 31 (2006): 269–287; Vittorio Bufacchi and Jean Maria Arrigo, "Torture, Terrorism and the State: A Refutation of the Ticking-Bomb Argument," *Journal of Applied Philosophy* 23 (2006): 355–373; Elizabeth Sepper, "The Ties That Bind: How the Constitution Limits the CIA's Actions in the War on Terror," *New York University Law Review* 81 (2006): 1805–1843; Scott Shane, David Johnson, and James Risen, "Secret U.S. Endorsement of Severe Interrogations," *New York Times*, October 4, 2007, www.nytimes.com/2007/10/04/washington/04interrogate .html?_r=1&oref=slogin (accessed May 10, 2010); Michael Cooper and Marc Santora, "McCain Rebukes Giuliani on Waterboarding Remark," *New York Times*, October 26, 2007, www.nytimes.com/2007/10/26/us/politics/26giuliani.html (accessed May 10, 2010); Human Rights Watch, "The Twisted Logic of Torture," January 2005, hrw.org/wr2k5/darfurandabughraib/6.htm (accessed May 10, 2010).

# Predicting the Future

Several organizations are involved in long-range planning and forecasting. One example is the Society of Police Futurists International (PFI). Its Futures Working Group has come up with a number of predictions about crime and the nature of criminal justice over the next decade.[49] The National Institute of Corrections' "Forward Thinking" project works to identify forces that will shape America's correctional landscape going forward.[50] The National Center for State Courts has also focused attention on future trends likely to shape adjudication in America.[51] Even the National Institute of Justice has begun preparing for the future, calling on the experts to speculate about what lies in store.[52] They have come up with a number of shifts, trends, and changes that criminal justice will need to be prepared for. A few of the more notable ones follow.

**CourseMate** For more information about the **Society of Police Futurists International**, visit the Criminal Justice CourseMate at CengageBrain.com, then access the "Web Links" for this chapter.

**DEMOGRAPHIC SHIFTS** The population is aging. Over the next several decades, the proportion of males aged 15 to 19 in the population will shrink. The over-65 population will grow markedly (see Figure 18.2). This will have interesting implications for crime and criminal justice, because young people are typically

**FIGURE 18.2**
Projected Population of the United States, by Age and Sex: 2000 to 2050

Source: U.S. Census Bureau, www.census.gov/population/www/projections/usinterimproj/natprojtab02a.pdf (accessed May 13, 2010).

the most crime-prone group. What will the impact be? According to Bryan Vila, "there will be more people to be either victims or solutions."[53] On the one hand, if there are more elderly people, there is a chance that more of them will become crime victims. On the other hand, the criminal justice system could draw on the volunteer services of retired people to report crime and guide children.

*TECHNOLOGICAL ADVANCES* Technological advances continue at a feverish pace. Surveillance technologies, biometric tools, and DNA analysis, to name just a few, will continue to evolve and improve. Increasingly sophisticated and integrated databases will improve law enforcement's crime fighting capability. The criminal element will improve its technological capabilities, as well, forcing criminal justice to try to keep pace.

*INCREASED DIVERSITY* The number of foreign-born Americans continues to grow. This diversity, though advantageous in many ways, will exert pressures on criminal justice. Chris Stone points to the example of South Africa, noting that its court system now recognizes 11 distinct languages: "Often, the only two people in the courtroom speaking the same language are the victim and defendant—with the judge, prosecutor, and defense lawyer relying on interpreters."[54] Even the racial and ethnic composition of the American population will change markedly. See Figure 18.3 for Census Bureau projections through 2050. According to the Census Bureau, the Hispanic population will nearly triple between 2000 and 2050.

*A FOCUS ON WHAT WORKS* We have introduced a new Evidence-Based Justice feature throughout this book. This focus on *what works and what doesn't* will continue to gain steam as taxpayers increase their efforts to hold the government accountable for spending. The days of throwing money at the crime problem, with little attention to what solutions are best, are surely numbered. The popular Campbell Collaboration reflects this thinking. This organization's goal is to improve decision making in a number of realms, including criminal justice.[55]

*DOING MORE WITH LESS* America's record debt is forcing cutbacks in government services. The same is true of state and local governments. This will pressure criminal justice agencies to do more with less—and again to focus their resources on tried and true successes. Innovative strategies will be necessary, and officials will need to rely increasingly on "civilianization" and related strategies that help to cut costs. Service sharing between municipalities will become more attractive as a means of maintaining a healthy "bottom line." Privatization initiatives will

**CourseMate** For more information about the **Campbell Collaboration**, visit the Criminal Justice CourseMate at CengageBrain.com, then access the "Web Links" for this chapter.

**FIGURE 18.3**
Projected Population of the United States, by Race and Hispanic Origin: 2000 to 2050

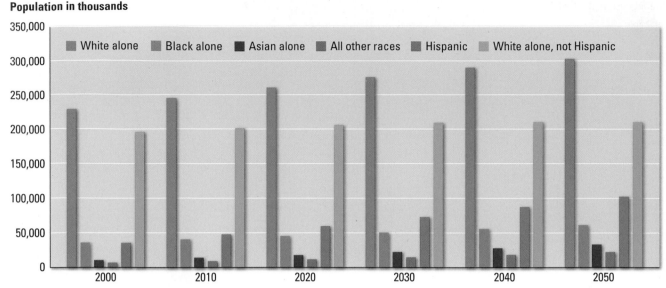

Source: U.S. Census Bureau, www.census.gov/population/www/projections/usinterimproj/natprojtab01a.pdf (accessed May 13, 2010).

continue to gain steam, as well, on the theory that the private sector may be more cost-effective and efficient than the public sector in certain criminal justice operations (such as providing security and running prisons).

*GLOBALIZATION* One of the most significant trends in the future will be globalization. Boundaries will continue to be challenged, and international criminal syndicates will continue to pose threats. Emerging industrial nations will continue to vie for scarce resources. We recently saw gas creep above $4.00 per gallon in certain parts of the country. What if gas prices rise above that? What if they go to, say, $8.00 a gallon? What implications will this hold for police patrols?

*GREEN CRIME* As of this writing, BP's massive oil spill in the Gulf of Mexico has been brought under control, but untold damage to wildlife, ecosystems, and the local economy remain. On June 1, 2010, the Obama administration launched a criminal probe in order to "prosecute to the fullest extent of the law" any persons or companies that broke the law in the time leading up to the spill.[56] It is not yet clear whether criminal charges will be filed, but the government's reaction to the spill is perhaps indicative of a growing concern with crimes against the environment—what some have referred to as green crimes.

Oil spills are just part of the problem. Critical criminologists and environmental activists have long called attention to a variety of environmental threats that they feel should be deemed criminal: ". . . green crimes involve a wide range of actions and outcomes that harm the environment and that stem from corporate behaviors such as decisions about what is produced and how it is produced."[57] Global warming, overdevelopment, population growth, and other changes will continue to bring these issues front and center, but so-called "green-collar" offenders are still not punished as harshly on the whole as their traditional criminal counterparts.[58]

*ILLEGAL IMMIGRATION* Continued immigration is certain to impact crime and criminal justice, though it is less certain what these effects will be. According to some sources, the economic downturn has led to reductions in illegal immigration, but criminal justice officials are still busy.[59] Look no further than Arizona, where lawmakers required police, "when practicable," to detain people they suspected were in the country illegally and to demand proof of citizenship.[60] Shortly after the law was enacted, a federal judge issued an injunction blocking enforcement of the so-called "Papers, please" provision. As of this writing, the law continues to undergo various legal challenges.

## Ethical Challenges in Criminal Justice: A Writing Assignment

A recent federal appeals court decision, *Kiyemba v. Obama*,[61] raised an important question about the treatment of detainees captured in the struggle against terrorism. At issue in the case was whether 17 Chinese citizens who were held at the Guantanamo Bay Naval Base in Cuba should be released into the United States after a finding that they could not be held as enemy combatants. They were by no means "innocents," however. Prior to 9/11, they traveled to the Tora Bora mountains in Afghanistan for firearms training so they could launch an offensive against the Chinese government upon their return to their native land. They were captured by Pakistani forces and turned over to the United States, which made a determination that the 17 were not affiliated with al Qaeda and posed no immediate threat to Americans. Were the United States to return them to China, they would be likely to face execution. Yet they had not been approved for release into the United States, and efforts to find a neutral third nation in which they could be released failed.

Write an essay on the ethical dilemmas posed in this scenario. In doing so, answer these questions: What should the U.S. government do? Would it be ethical for the United States to "wash its hands" of the case and return the men to China? Should the men be released into the United States if they are not enemy combatants? If no option (release into the United States, to China, or to a third nation) is satisfactory, how long should they continue to be detained? Do any of the Supreme Court cases reviewed in this chapter offer guidance in this case? The key question in this case (Can our government be forced to release the men into the United States?) has not yet been answered. As of this writing, the Supreme Court has declined to review the case, leaving the matter up to the federal district court to decide.[62]

## Significant Cases Related to the Struggle Against Terrorism

| Case | Issue | Decision |
|---|---|---|
| *Ex Parte Milligan* (1866) | Military tribunals | It is unconstitutional to try U.S. citizens before military tribunals when civilian courts are available. |
| *Hamdi v. Rumsfeld* (2004) | Detainee rights, U.S. citizens | Detained U.S. citizens enjoy the right to challenge their detentions before an impartial judge. |
| *Rasul v. Bush* (2004) | Detainee rights, foreign nationals | The federal courts have jurisdiction to decide the constitutionality of detaining foreign nationals. |
| *Hamdan v. Rumsfeld* (2006) | Military tribunals, post-9/11 | Bush-era military tribunals violate the Uniform Code of Military Justice and the Geneva Conventions. |
| *Boumediene v. Bush* (2008) | Military tribunals, post-9/11 | Parts of the Military Commissions Act of 2006 that strip federal courts of habeas corpus jurisdiction in cases involving Guantanamo Bay detainees are unconstitutional. |

# SUMMARY

### 1. Be able to define terrorism.

- Terrorism involves the illegal use of force against innocent people to achieve a political objective.
- Confronting terrorism is critical because of the lethal tactics now being used—bombings, killing hostages, chemical warfare, spreading toxic biological agents.

### 2. Be familiar with the history of terrorism.

- The term "terrorist" first appeared at the time of the French Revolution.
- Despite its long history, it is often difficult to precisely define terrorism.
- Terrorism can be distinguished from conventional warfare because it requires secrecy and clandestine operations to exert social control over large populations.
- It is also common to use the term "terrorist" interchangeably with "guerilla," "revolutionary," and "insurgent," although they are independent concepts.

### 3. Understand the factors that motivate terrorists.

- Not all terrorists suffer from psychological deficits, but enough do so that the typical terrorist can be described as an emotionally disturbed individual who acts out his or her psychoses within the confines of violent groups.
- Terrorists have been raised to hate their opponents, and they learn at an early age that they have been victimized by some oppressor.
- Terrorists hold extreme ideological beliefs that prompt their behavior.
- Terrorists may be motivated by feelings of alienation and failure to possess the tools they need to compete in a post-technological society.

### 4. Be familiar with the various forms of contemporary terrorism.

- Revolutionary terrorists use violence to frighten those in power and their supporters in an effort to replace the existing government with a regime that holds acceptable political or religious views.
- Political terrorism is directed at people or groups with whom the terrorists live in close connection but who (a) oppose the terrorists' political ideology or (b) are defined as outsiders by the terrorists.
- Nationalist terrorism promotes the interests of a minority ethnic or religious group that believes it has been persecuted under majority rule and wishes to carve out its own independent homeland.
- Rather than fighting for a homeland, retributive terrorists fight for a cause.
- State-sponsored terrorism occurs when a repressive government regime forces its citizens into obedience, oppresses minorities, and stifles political dissent.
- Some cults may be classified as terror groups because their leaders demand that followers prove their loyalty through violence or intimidation.
- Sometimes terrorist groups become involved in common-law crimes such as drug dealing, kidnapping, or even selling nuclear materials.

### 5. Explain how the criminal justice system has responded to terrorism.

- The justice system has been redirected to fight terror at the federal, state, and local levels.
- The Director of National Intelligence (DNI) is the government official charged with coordinating data from the nation's primary intelligence-gathering agencies.
- One of the most significant changes has been a realignment of the FBI, the federal government's main law enforcement agency.
- The Department of Homeland Security (DHS) is the federal agency responsible for preventing terrorist attacks within the United States, reducing America's vulnerability to terrorism, and minimizing the damage and recovering from attacks that do occur.
- State, county, and local law enforcement agencies have engaged in a number of antiterror initiatives.
- The numbers of terrorism prosecutions and convictions have increased steadily since 9/11.

### 6. Discuss political solutions to terrorism.

- In the long run, it may simply be impossible to defeat terror groups and end terrorism using military, law enforcement, or legal solutions.
- One approach suggested by policy experts is for the United States to undermine support for terrorist groups by being a benevolent nation builder that gives aid to the nations where terror groups operate.

■ Another approach is to use the media to win the "hearts and minds" of people in countries that do not hold the United States in high regard.

### 7. Understand the purpose of the Patriot Act.

■ The Patriot Act gives sweeping new powers to domestic law enforcement and international intelligence agencies in an effort to fight terrorism, to expand the definition of terrorist activities, and to alter sanctions for violent terrorism.

### 8. Identify the common theme in Supreme Court terrorism cases since 9/11.

■ Since 9/11, the U.S. Supreme Court has decided several important cases involving the treatment of terror suspects.

■ The Court's decisions have given terrorism suspects increased opportunities to challenge the legality of their confinement.

### 9. Identify trends that are likely to influence criminal justice in the future.

■ It is difficult to predict what the future holds in store, but experts have identified a number of trends and developments that are likely to affect criminal justice in the future.

■ The criminal justice system will need to be braced for demographic shifts (particularly an older population), technological advances, increased diversity, a focus on what works, continued cutbacks in funding, globalization, green crime, and illegal immigration.

## KEY TERMS

terrorism, 679

Director of National Intelligence (DNI), 683

Department of Homeland Security (DHS), 685

jihadist groups, 693

USA Patriot Act (USAPA), 694

## CRITICAL THINKING QUESTIONS

1. Would you be willing to give up some of your civil rights in order to aid U.S. efforts to defeat terrorism?

2. Should terrorism suspects arrested in a foreign land have all the rights and privileges accorded to an American citizen accused of crime?

3. What groups in America might be the breeding ground of terrorist activity in the United States?

## NOTES

1. Tom Hays, "NYPD Commissioner: NYC Bomb Suspect 'Homegrown,'" *Associated Press*, www.buffalonews .com/2010/05/11/1047342/nypd-commissioner-nyc-bomb-suspect .html (accessed May 12, 2010).

2. Center of Law and Security, New York School of Law, *Terrorist Trial Report Card: September 11, 2001–September 11, 2009* (New York: Center on Law and Security, 2010), www.lawandsecurity.org/ publications/TTRCFinalJan14.pdf (accessed May 12, 2010), p. 20.

3. Violent Radicalization and Homegrown Terrorism Prevention Act of 2007, http://thomas.loc.gov/home/gpoxmlc110/h1955_rfs.xml (accessed May 12, 2010).

4. Thomas P. M. Barnett, *The Pentagon's New Map: War and Peace in the Twenty-first Century* (New York: G. P. Putnam's Sons, 2004), 43–46.

5. Walter Laqueur, *The New Terrorism: Fanaticism and the Arms of Mass Destruction Terrorism and History* (New York: Oxford University Press, 1999).

6. Edmund Burke, *Reflections on the Revolution in France, 1790* (New York: Penguin Classics; reprint edition 1982).

7. Lindsay Clutterbuck, "The Progenitors of Terrorism: Russian Revolutionaries or Extreme Irish Republicans?" *Terrorism and Political Violence* 16 (2004): 154–181.

8. Title 22 of the United States Code section 2656f (d) (1999).

9. Jack Gibbs, "Conceptualization of Terrorism," *American Sociological Review* 54 (1989): 329–340, at 330.

10. Ibid.

11. Stephen J. Morgan, *The Mind of a Terrorist Fundamentalist: The Psychology of Terror Cults* (Awe-Struck E-Books, 2001); Martha Crenshaw, "The Psychology of Terrorism: An Agenda for the 21st Century," *Political Psychology* 21 (2000): 405–420.

12. Andrew Silke, "Courage in Dark Places: Reflections on Terrorist Psychology," *Social Research* 71 (2004): 177–198.

13. Jerrold Post, "When Hatred Is Bred in the Bone: Psycho-Cultural Foundations of Contemporary Terrorism," *Political Psychology* 25 (2005): 615–637.

14. This section leans heavily on Anthony Stahelski, "Terrorists Are Made, Not Born: Creating Terrorists Using Social Psychological Conditioning," *Journal of Homeland Security*, March 2004, www .homelandsecurity.org/journal/Articles/stahelski.html (accessed May 10, 2010).

15. Ethan Bueno de Mesquita, "The Quality of Terror," *American Journal of Political Science* 49 (2005): 515–530.

16. Haruki Murakami, *Underground* (New York: Vintage Books, 2001).

17. Sanjeev Gupta, Benedict Clements, Rina Bhattacharya, and Shamit Chakravarti, "Fiscal Consequences of Armed Conflict and Terrorism in Low- and Middle-Income Countries," *European*

*Journal of Political Economy* 20 (2004): 403–421; Andrew Chen and Thomas Siems, "Effects of Terrorism on Global Capital Markets," *European Journal of Political Economy* 20 (2004): 349–356.

18. Lawrence Miller, "The Terrorist Mind: A Psychological and Political Analysis, Part II," *International Journal of Offender Therapy and Comparative Criminology* 50 (2006): 255–268.

19. Ibid.

20. Chris Dishman, "Terrorism, Crime, and Transformation," *Studies in Conflict & Terrorism* 24 (2001): 43–56.

21. Graham Allison, *Nuclear Terrorism: The Ultimate Preventable Catastrophe* (New York: Times Books, 2004).

22. RAND Corporation, "How Prepared Are State and Local Law Enforcement for Terrorism?" www.rand.org/publications/RB/RB9093/ (accessed May 10, 2010).

23. Federal Bureau of Investigation, *Protecting America against Terrorist Attack: A Closer Look at the FBI's Joint Terrorism Task Forces*, www.fbi.gov/page2/dec04/jttf120114.htm (accessed May 11, 2010).

24. California Anti-Terrorism Information Center (CATIC), www.ag.ca.gov/antiterrorism/ (accessed May 10, 2010).

25. Harris County Homeland Security and Emergency Management, www.hcoem.org/ (accessed May 10, 2010).

26. Montgomery County, Maryland, Homeland Security, www.montgomerycountymd.gov/mcgtmpl.asp?url=/content/homelandsecurity/index.asp (accessed May 10, 2010).

27. William K. Rashbaum, "Terror Makes All the World a Beat for New York Police," *New York Times*, July 15, 2002, p. B1; Al Baker, "Leader Sees New York Police in Vanguard of Terror Fight," *New York Times*, August 6, 2002, p. A2; Stephen Flynn, "America the Vulnerable," *Foreign Affairs* 81 (January–February 2002): 60.

28. U.S. Attorney for the Southern District of New York Press Release No. 09-103, Afghan Drug Kingpin Charged with Terrorist Financing for Funding Taliban Insurgency (April 21, 2009).

29. Del Quentin Wilbur, U.S. Judge Sentences Dutch Man to 25 Years for Crimes in Iraq, *Washington Post*, April 17, 2009, p. A7.

30. U.S. Justice Department, "Fact Sheet: Justice Department Counter-Terrorism Efforts Since 9/11, www.justice.gov/opa/pr/2008/September/08-nsd-807.html (accessed May 11, 2010).

31. Center of Law and Security, New York School of Law, *Terrorist Trial Report Card: September 11, 2001–September 11, 2009.*

32. Richard B. Zabel and James J. Benjamin Jr., *In Pursuit of Justice: Prosecuting Terrorism Cases in the Federal Courts* (Washington, D.C.: Human Rights First, 2008), www.humanrightsfirst.org/pdf/080521-USLS-pursuit-justice.pdf (accessed May 11, 2010).

33. Ibid., p. 2.

34. Ibid.

35. U.S. Justice Department, *Introduction to National Security Division Statistics on Unsealed International Terrorism and Terrorism-Related Convictions*, www.justice.gov/cjs/docs/terrorism-convictions-statistics.pdf (accessed May 11, 2010).

36. Ibid.

37. Ibid.

38. Angel Rabasa, Peter Chalk, Kim Cragin, Sara A. Daly, Heather S. Gregg, Theodore W. Karasik, Kevin A. O'Brien, and William Rosenau, *Beyond al-Qaeda Part 1, The Global Jihadist Movement* and *Part 2, The Outer Rings of the Terrorist Universe* (Santa Monica, Calif.: RAND Corporation, 2006).

39. President Signs USA PATRIOT Improvement and Reauthorization Act, http://georgewbush-whitehouse.archives.gov/infocus/patriot-act/ (accessed May 10, 2010).

40. Obama Signs Reauthorization of Three Patriot Act Provisions, www.mainjustice.com/2010/02/27/obama-signs-patriot-act-reauthorization (accessed May 10, 2010).

41. Alan M. Dershowitz, *Shouting Fire: Civil Liberties in a Turbulent Age* (New York: Little, Brown, 2002); Alan M. Dershowitz, "Want to Torture? Get a Warrant," *San Francisco Chronicle*, January 22, 2002.

42. *Ex Parte Milligan*, 71 U.S. 2 (1866)

43. *Hamdi v. Rumsfeld*, 542 U.S. 507 (2004).

44. *Rasul v. Bush*, 542 U.S. 466 (2004)

45. *Hamdan v. Rumsfeld*, 548 U.S. 557 (2006).

46. *Boumediene v. Bush*, 553 U.S. 723 (2008).

47. See Section 948c of the Military Commissions Act of 2009, www.defense.gov/news/2009%20MCA%20Pub%20%20Law%20111-84.pdf (accessed May 12, 2010).

48. See, for example, James Alan Fox, *Trends in Juvenile Justice: A Report to the United States Attorney General on Current and Future Rates of Juvenile Offending* (Washington, D.C.: Bureau of Justice Statistics, 2006); James Q. Wilson, "Crime and Public Policy," p. 507 in James Q. Wilson and Joan Petersilia (Eds.), *Crime* (San Francisco: ICS Press, 1995).

49. Joseph A. Schafer (Ed.), *Policing 2020: Exploring the Future of Crime, Communities and Policing* (Carbondale, Ill.: Police Futurists International, 2007).

50. National Institute of Corrections, *Forward Thinking*, www.nicic.gov/ForwardThinking (accessed May 13, 2010).

51. T. Peters, N. Kauder, C. Campbell, and C. Flango, *Future Trends in State Courts 2005* (Williamsburg, Va.: National Center for State Courts, 2005).

52. Nancy M. Ritter, "Preparing for the Future: Criminal Justice in 2040," *National Institute of Justice Journal* 255 (2006), www.ojp.usdoj.gov/nij/journals/255/2040.html (accessed May 13, 2010).

53. Ibid.

54. Ibid.

55. The Campbell Collaboration, www.campbellcollaboration.org/ (accessed May 13, 2010).

56. Helene Cooper and Peter Baker, "U.S. Opens Criminal Inquiry into Oil Spill," *New York Times*, www.nytimes.com/2010/06/02/us/02spill.html (accessed June 3, 2010).

57. Michael J. Lynch and Paul Stretesky, "Green Criminology in the United States," pp. 248–269 in Piers Beirne and Nigel South (Eds.), *Issues in Green Criminology* (Portland, Ore.: Willan, 2008), p. 249.

58. Michael M. O'Hear, "Sentencing the Green-Collar Offender: Punishment, Culpability, and Environmental Crime," *Journal of Criminal Law and Criminology* 95 (2004): 133–276.

59. Nathan Thornburgh, "Recession May Be Driving Off Illegals," *Time*, June 4, 2008, www.time.com/time/nation/article/0,8599,1811660,00.html (accessed May 13, 2010).

60. Randal C. Archibold, "Arizona's Effort to Bolster Local Immigration Authority Divides Law Enforcement," *New York Times*, April 21, 2010, www.nytimes.com/2010/04/22/us/22immig.html (accessed May 13, 2010).

61. *Kiyemba v. Obama*, 555 F.3d 1022 (D.C. Cir. 2009).

62. *Kiyemba v. Obama*, No. 08-1234 (2010), cert. denied.

# The Constitution of the United States

## Preamble

We the People of the United States, in Order to form a more perfect Union, establish Justice, insure domestic Tranquility, provide for the common defence, promote the general Welfare, and secure the Blessings of Liberty to ourselves and our Posterity, do ordain and establish this Constitution for the United States of America.

## Article I

**SECTION 1** All legislative Powers herein granted shall be vested in a Congress of the United States, which shall consist of a Senate and House of Representatives.

**SECTION 2** The House of Representatives shall be composed of Members chosen every second Year by the People of the several States, and the Electors in each State shall have the Qualifications requisite for Electors of the most numerous Branch of the State Legislature.

No Person shall be a Representative who shall not have attained to the Age of twenty five Years, and been seven Years a Citizen of the United States, and who shall not, when elected, be an Inhabitant of that State in which he shall be chosen.

Representatives and direct Taxes shall be apportioned among the several States which may be included within this Union, according to their respective Numbers, which shall be determined by adding to the whole Number of free Persons, including those bound to Service for a Term of Years, and excluding Indians not taxed, three fifths of all other Persons. The actual Enumeration shall be made within three Years after the first Meeting of the Congress of the United States, and within every subsequent Term of ten Years, in such Manner as they shall by Law direct. The Number of Representatives shall not exceed one for every thirty Thousand, but each State shall have at Least one Representative; and until such enumeration shall be made, the State of New Hampshire shall be entitled to choose three, Massachusetts eight, Rhode Island and Providence Plantations one, Connecticut five, New York six, New Jersey four, Pennsylvania eight, Delaware one, Maryland six, Virginia ten, North Carolina five, South Carolina five, and Georgia three.

When vacancies happen in the Representation from any State, the Executive Authority thereof shall issue Writs of Election to fill such Vacancies.

The House of Representatives shall choose their Speaker and other Officers; and shall have the sole Power of Impeachment.

**SECTION 3** The Senate of the United States shall be composed of two Senators from each State, chosen by the Legislature thereof, for six Years; and each Senator shall have one Vote.

Immediately after they shall be assembled in Consequence of the first Election, they shall be divided as equally as may be into three Classes. The Seats of the Senators of the first Class shall be vacated at the Expiration of the second Year, of the second Class at the Expiration of the fourth Year, and of the third Class at the Expiration of the sixth Year, so that one third may be chosen every second Year; and if Vacancies happen by Resignation, or otherwise, during the Recess of the Legislature of any State, the Executive thereof may make temporary Appointments until the next Meeting of the Legislature, which shall then fill such Vacancies.

No Person shall be a Senator who shall not have attained to the Age of thirty Years, and been nine Years a Citizen of the United States, and who shall not, when elected, be an Inhabitant of that State for which he shall be chosen.

The Vice-President of the United States shall be President of the Senate, but shall have no Vote, unless they be equally divided.

The Senate shall choose their other Officers, and also a President pro tempore, in the Absence of the Vice-President, or when he shall exercise the Office of President of the United States.

The Senate shall have the sole Power to try all Impeachments. When sitting for that Purpose, they shall be on Oath or Affirmation. When the President of the United States is tried the Chief Justice shall preside: And no Person shall be convicted without the Concurrence of two thirds of the Members present.

Judgment in Cases of Impeachment shall not extend further than to removal from Office, and disqualification to hold and enjoy any Office of honor, Trust or Profit under the United States: but the Party convicted shall nevertheless be liable and subject to Indictment, Trial, Judgment, and Punishment, according to Law.

**SECTION 4** The Times, Places and Manner of holding Elections for Senators and Representatives, shall be prescribed in each State by the Legislature thereof; but the Congress may at any time by Law make or alter such Regulations, except as to the Places of choosing Senators.

The Congress shall assemble at least once in every Year, and such Meeting shall be on the first Monday in December, unless they shall by Law appoint a different Day.

**SECTION 5** Each House shall be the Judge of the Elections, Returns and Qualifications of its own Members, and a Majority of each shall constitute a Quorum to do Business; but a smaller Number may adjourn from day to day, and may be authorized to compel the Attendance of absent Members, in such Manner, and under such Penalties as each House may provide.

Each House may determine the Rules of its Proceedings, punish its Members for disorderly Behaviour, and, with the Concurrence of two thirds, expel a Member.

Each House shall keep a Journal of its Proceedings, and from time to time publish the same, excepting such Parts as may in their Judgment require Secrecy; and the Yeas and Nays of the Members of either House on any question shall, at the Desire of one fifth of those Present, be entered on the Journal.

Neither House, during the Session of Congress, shall, without the Consent of the other, adjourn for more than three days, nor to any other Place than that in which the two Houses shall be sitting.

**SECTION 6** The Senators and Representatives shall receive a Compensation for their Services, to be ascertained by Law, and paid out of the Treasury of the United States. They shall in all Cases, except Treason, Felony and Breach of the Peace, be privileged from Arrest during their Attendance at the Session of their respective Houses, and in going to and returning from the same; and for any Speech or Debate in either House, they shall not be questioned in any other Place.

No Senator or Representative shall, during the Time for which he was elected, be appointed to any civil Office under the Authority of the United States, which shall have been created, or the Emoluments whereof shall have been increased during such time; and no Person holding any Office under the United States, shall be a Member of either House during his Continuance in Office.

**SECTION 7** All Bills for raising Revenue shall originate in the House of Representatives; but the Senate may propose or concur with Amendments as on other Bills.

Every Bill which shall have passed the House of Representatives and the Senate, shall, before it become a Law, be presented to the President of the United States; If he approve he shall sign it, but if not he shall return it, with his Objections to that House in which it shall have originated, who shall enter the Objections at large on their Journal, and proceed to reconsider it. If after such Reconsideration two thirds of that House shall agree to pass the Bill, it shall be sent, together with the Objections, to the other House, by which it shall likewise be reconsidered, and if approved by two thirds of that House, it shall become a Law. But in all such Cases the Votes of both Houses shall be determined by Yeas and Nays, and the Names of the Persons voting for and against the Bill shall be entered on the Journal of each House respectively. If any Bill shall not be returned by the President within ten Days (Sundays excepted) after it shall have been presented to him, the Same shall be a Law, in like Manner as if he had signed it, unless the Congress by their Adjournment prevent its Return, in which Case it shall not be a Law.

Every Order, Resolution, or Vote to which the Concurrence of the Senate and House of Representatives may be necessary (except on a question of Adjournment) shall be presented to the President of the United States; and before the Same shall take Effect, shall be approved by him, or being disapproved by him, shall be repassed by two thirds of the Senate and House of Representatives, according to the Rules and Limitations prescribed in the Case of a Bill.

**SECTION 8** The Congress shall have Power To lay and collect Taxes, Duties, Imposts and Excises, to pay the Debts and provide for the common Defence and general Welfare of the United States; but all Duties, Imposts and Excises shall be uniform throughout the United States;

To borrow Money on the credit of the United States;

To regulate Commerce with foreign Nations, and among the several States, and with the Indian Tribes;

To establish an uniform Rule of Naturalization, and uniform Laws on the subject of Bankruptcies throughout the United States;

To coin Money, regulate the Value thereof, and of foreign Coin, and fix the Standard of Weights and Measures;

To provide for the Punishment of counterfeiting the Securities and current Coin of the United States;

To establish Post Offices and post Roads;

To promote the Progress of Science and useful Arts, by securing for limited Times to Authors and Inventors the exclusive Right to their respective Writings and Discoveries;

To constitute Tribunals inferior to the supreme Court;

To define and punish Piracies and Felonies committed on the high Seas, and Offences against the Law of Nations;

To declare War, grant Letters of Marque and Reprisal, and make Rules concerning Captures on Land and Water;

To raise and support Armies, but no Appropriation of Money to that Use shall be for a longer Term than two Years;

To provide and maintain a Navy;

To make Rules for the Government and Regulation of the land and naval Forces;

To provide for calling forth the Militia to execute the Laws of the Union, suppress Insurrections and repel Invasions;

To provide for organizing, arming, and disciplining, the Militia, and for governing such Part of them as may be employed in the Service of the United States, reserving to the States respectively, the Appointment of the Officers, and the Authority of training the Militia according to the discipline prescribed by Congress;

To exercise exclusive Legislation in all Cases whatsoever, over such District (not exceeding ten Miles square) as may, by Cession of particular States, and the Acceptance of Congress, become the Seat of the Government of the United States, and to exercise like Authority over all Places purchased by the Consent of the Legislature of the State in which the Same shall be, for the Erection of Forts, Magazines, Arsenals, dock-Yards, and other needful Buildings;—And

To make all Laws which shall be necessary and proper for carrying into Execution the foregoing Powers, and all other Powers vested by this Constitution in the Government of the United States, or in any Department or Officer thereof.

**SECTION 9** The Migration or Importation of such Persons as any of the States now existing shall think proper to admit, shall not be prohibited by the Congress prior to the Year one thousand eight hundred and eight, but a Tax or duty may be imposed on such Importation, not exceeding ten dollars for each Person.

The privilege of the Writ of Habeas Corpus shall not be suspended, unless when in Cases of Rebellion or Invasion the public Safety may require it.

No Bill of Attainder or ex post facto Law shall be passed.

No Capitation, or other direct, Tax shall be laid, unless in Proportion to the Census or Enumeration herein before directed to be taken.

No Tax or Duty shall be laid on Articles exported from any State.

No Preference shall be given by any Regulation of Commerce or Revenue to the Ports of one State over those of another: nor shall Vessels bound to, or from, one State be obliged to enter, clear, or pay Duties in another.

No Money shall be drawn from the Treasury, but in Consequence of Appropriations made by Law; and a regular Statement and Account of the Receipts and Expenditures of all public Money shall be published from time to time.

No Title of Nobility shall be granted by the United States: And no Person holding any Office of Profit or Trust under them, shall, without the Consent of the Congress, accept of any present, Emolument, Office, or Title, of any kind whatever, from any King, Prince, or foreign State.

**SECTION 10** No State shall enter into any Treaty, Alliance, or Confederation; grant Letters of Marque and Reprisal; coin Money; emit Bills of Credit; make any Thing but gold and silver Coin a Tender in Payment of Debts; pass any Bill of Attainder, ex post facto Law, or Law impairing the Obligation of Contracts, or grant any Title of Nobility.

No State shall, without the Consent of the Congress, lay any Imposts or Duties on Imports or Exports, except what may be absolutely necessary for executing its inspection Laws: and the net Produce of all Duties and Imposts, laid by any State on Imports or Exports, shall be for the Use of the Treasury of the United States; and all such Laws shall be subject to the Revision and Control of the Congress.

No State shall, without the Consent of Congress, lay any Duty of Tonnage, keep Troops, or Ships of War in time of Peace, enter into any Agreement or Compact with another State, or with a foreign Power, or engage in War, unless actually invaded, or in such imminent Danger as will not admit of delay.

# Article II

**SECTION 1** The executive Power shall be vested in a President of the United States of America. He shall hold his Office during the Term of four Years, and, together with the Vice-President, chosen for the same Term, be elected, as follows:

Each State shall appoint, in such Manner as the Legislature thereof may direct, a Number of Electors, equal to the whole Number of Senators and Representatives to which the State may be entitled in the Congress; but no Senator or Representative, or Person holding an Office of Trust or Profit under the United States, shall be appointed an Elector.

The Electors shall meet in their respective States, and vote by Ballot for two Persons, of whom one at least shall not be an Inhabitant of the same State with themselves. And they shall make a List of all the Persons voted for, and of the Number of Votes for each; which List they shall sign and certify, and transmit sealed to the Seat of Government of the United States, directed to the President of the Senate. The President of the Senate shall, in the Presence of the Senate and House of Representatives, open all the Certificates, and the Votes shall then be counted. The Person having the greatest Number of Votes shall be the President, if such Number be a Majority of the whole Number of Electors appointed; and if there be more than one who have such Majority, and have an equal Number of Votes, then the House of Representatives shall immediately choose by Ballot one of them for President; and if no Person have a Majority, then from the five highest on the List the said House shall in like Manner choose the President. But in choosing the President, the Votes shall be taken by States, the Representation from each State having one Vote; A quorum for this Purpose shall consist of a Member or Members from two thirds of the States, and a Majority of all the States shall be necessary to a Choice. In every Case, after the Choice of the President, the Person having the greatest Number of Votes of the Electors shall be the Vice-President. But if there should remain two or more who have equal Votes, the Senate shall choose from them by Ballot the Vice-President.

The Congress may determine the Time of choosing the Electors, and the Day on which they shall give their Votes; which Day shall be the same throughout the United States.

No Person except a natural born Citizen, or a Citizen of the United States, at the time of the Adoption of this Constitution, shall be eligible to the Office of President; neither shall any Person be eligible to that Office who shall not have attained to the Age of thirty five Years, and been fourteen Years a Resident within the United States.

In Case of the Removal of the President from Office, or of his Death, Resignation, or Inability to discharge the Powers and Duties of the said Office, the same shall devolve on the Vice-President, and the Congress may by Law provide for the Case of Removal, Death, Resignation or Inability, both of the President and Vice-President declaring what Officer shall then act as President, and such Officer shall act accordingly, until the Disability be removed, or a President shall be elected.

The President shall, at stated Times, receive for his Services, a Compensation, which shall neither be increased nor diminished during the Period for which he shall have been elected, and he shall not receive within that Period any other Emolument from the United States, or any of them.

Before he enter on the Execution of his Office, he shall take the following Oath or Affirmation: "I do solemnly swear (or affirm) that I will faithfully execute the Office of President of the United States, and will to the best of my Ability, preserve, protect and defend the Constitution of the United States."

*SECTION 2* The President shall be Commander in Chief of the Army and Navy of the United States, and of the Militia of the several States, when called into the actual Service of the United States; he may require the Opinion, in writing, of the principal Officer in each of the executive Departments, upon any Subject relating to the Duties of their respective Offices, and he shall have Power to grant Reprieves and Pardons for Offenses against the United States, except in Cases of Impeachment.

He shall have Power, by and with the Advice and Consent of the Senate, to make Treaties, provided two thirds of the Senators present concur; and he shall nominate, and by and with the Advice and Consent of the Senate, shall appoint Ambassadors, other public Ministers and Consuls, Judges of the supreme Court, and all other Officers of the United States, whose Appointments are not herein otherwise provided for, and which shall be established by Law; but the Congress may by Law vest the Appointment of such inferior Officers, as they think proper, in the President alone, in the Courts of Law, or in the Heads of Departments.

The President shall have Power to fill up all Vacancies that may happen during the Recess of the Senate, by granting Commissions which shall expire at the End of their next Session.

*SECTION 3* He shall from time to time give to the Congress Information of the State of the Union, and recommend to their Consideration such Measures as he shall judge necessary and expedient; he may, on extraordinary Occasions, convene both Houses, or either of them, and in Case of Disagreement between them, with Respect to the Time of Adjournment, he may adjourn them to such Time as he shall think proper; he shall receive Ambassadors and other public Ministers; he shall take Care that the Laws be faithfully executed, and shall Commission all the Officers of the United States.

*SECTION 4* The President, Vice-President and all civil Officers of the United States, shall be removed from Office on Impeachment for, and Conviction of, Treason, Bribery, or other high Crimes and Misdemeanors.

# Article III

*SECTION 1* The judicial Power of the United States, shall be vested in one supreme Court, and in such inferior Courts as the Congress may from time to time ordain and establish. The Judges, both of the supreme and inferior Courts, shall hold their Offices during good Behaviour, and shall, at stated Times, receive for their Services a Compensation which shall not be diminished during their Continuance in Office.

*SECTION 2* The judicial Power shall extend to all Cases, in Law and Equity, arising under this Constitution, the Laws of the United States, and Treaties made, or which shall be made, under their Authority;—to all Cases affecting Ambassadors, other public Ministers and Consuls;—to all Cases of admiralty and maritime Jurisdiction;—to Controversies to which the United States shall be a Party;—to Controversies between two or more States;—between a State and Citizens of another State;—between Citizens of different States;—between Citizens of the same State claiming Lands under Grants of different States, and between a State, or the Citizens thereof, and foreign States, Citizens or Subjects.

In all Cases affecting Ambassadors, other public Ministers and Consuls, and those in which a State shall be Party, the supreme Court shall have original Jurisdiction. In all the other Cases before mentioned, the supreme Court shall have appellate Jurisdiction, both as to Law and Fact, with such Exceptions, and under such Regulations as the Congress shall make.

The Trial of all Crimes, except in Cases of Impeachment, shall be by Jury; and such Trial shall be held in the State where the said Crimes shall have been committed; but when not committed within any State, the Trial shall be at such Place or Places as the Congress may by Law have directed.

**SECTION 3** Treason against the United States shall consist only in levying War against them, or in adhering to their Enemies, giving them Aid and Comfort. No Person shall be convicted of Treason unless on the Testimony of two Witnesses to the same overt Act, or on Confession in open Court.

The Congress shall have Power to declare the Punishment of Treason, but no Attainder of Treason shall work Corruption of Blood, or Forfeiture except during the Life of the Person attainted.

## Article IV

**SECTION 1** Full Faith and Credit shall be given in each State to the public Acts, Records, and judicial Proceedings of every other State. And the Congress may by general Laws prescribe the Manner in which such Acts, Records and Proceedings shall be proved, and the Effect thereof.

**SECTION 2** The Citizens of each State shall be entitled to all Privileges and Immunities of Citizens in the several States.

A Person charged in any State with Treason, Felony, or other Crime, who shall flee from Justice, and be found in another State, shall on Demand of the executive Authority of the State from which he fled, be delivered up, to be removed to the State having Jurisdiction of the Crime.

No Person held to Service or Labour in one State, under the Laws thereof, escaping into another, shall, in Consequence of any Law or Regulation therein, be discharged from such Service or Labour, but shall be delivered up on Claim of the Party to whom such Service or Labour may be due.

**SECTION 3** New States may be admitted by the Congress into this Union; but no new State shall be formed or erected within the Jurisdiction of any other State; nor any State be formed by the Junction of two or more States, or Parts of States, without the Consent of the Legislatures of the States concerned as well as of the Congress.

The Congress shall have Power to dispose of and make all needful Rules and Regulations respecting the Territory or other Property belonging to the United States; and nothing in this Constitution shall be so construed as to Prejudice any Claims of the United States, or of any particular State.

**SECTION 4** The United States shall guarantee to every State in this Union a Republican Form of Government, and shall protect each of them against Invasion; and on Application of the Legislature, or of the Executive (when the Legislature cannot be convened) against domestic Violence.

## Article V

The Congress, whenever two thirds of both Houses shall deem it necessary, shall propose Amendments to this Constitution, or, on the Application of the Legislatures of two thirds of the several States, shall call a Convention for proposing Amendments, which, in either Case, shall be valid to all Intents and Purposes, as Part of this Constitution, when ratified by the Legislatures of three fourths of the several States, or by Conventions in three fourths thereof, as the one or the other Mode of Ratification may be proposed by the Congress; Provided that no Amendment which may be made prior to the Year One thousand eight hundred and eight shall in any Manner affect the first and fourth Clauses in the Ninth Section of the first Article; and that no State, without its Consent, shall be deprived of its equal Suffrage in the Senate.

## Article VI

All Debts contracted and Engagements entered into, before the Adoption of this Constitution, shall be as valid against the United States under this Constitution, as under the Confederation.

This Constitution, and the Laws of the United States which shall be made in Pursuance thereof; and all Treaties made, or which shall be made, under the Authority of the United States, shall be the supreme Law of the Land; and the Judges in every State shall be bound thereby, any Thing in the Constitution or Laws of any State to the Contrary notwithstanding.

The Senators and Representatives before mentioned, and the Members of the several State Legislatures, and all executive and judicial Officers, both of the United States and of the several States, shall be bound by Oath or Affirmation, to support this Constitution; but no religious Test shall ever be required as a Qualification to any Office or public Trust under the United States.

## Article VII

The Ratification of the Conventions of nine States shall be sufficient for the Establishment of this Constitution between the States so ratifying the Same.

Done in Convention by the Unanimous Consent of the States present the Seventeenth Day of September in the Year of our Lord one thousand seven hundred and Eighty seven and of the Independence of the United States of America the Twelfth IN WITNESS whereof We have hereunto subscribed our Names,

# Amendment 1 [1791]

Congress shall make no law respecting an establishment of religion, or prohibiting the free exercise thereof; or abridging the freedom of speech, or of the press; or the right of the people peaceably to assemble, and to petition the Government for a redress of grievances.

# Amendment 2 [1791]

A well regulated Militia, being necessary to the security of a free State, the right of the people to keep and bear Arms, shall not be infringed.

# Amendment 3 [1791]

No Soldier shall, in time of peace be quartered in any house, without the consent of the Owner, nor in time of war, but in a manner to be prescribed by law.

# Amendment 4 [1791]

The right of the people to be secure in their persons, houses, papers, and effects, against unreasonable searches and seizures, shall not be violated, and no Warrants shall issue, but upon probable cause, supported by Oath or affirmation, and particularly describing the place to be searched, and the persons or things to be seized.

# Amendment 5 [1791]

No person shall be held to answer for a capital, or otherwise infamous crime, unless on a presentment or indictment of a Grand Jury, except in cases arising in the land or naval forces, or in the Militia, when in actual service in time of War or public danger; nor shall any person be subject for the same offence to be twice put in jeopardy of life or limb; nor shall be compelled in any criminal case to be a witness against himself, nor be deprived of life, liberty, or property, without due process of law; nor shall private property be taken for public use, without just compensation.

# Amendment 6 [1791]

In all criminal prosecutions, the accused shall enjoy the right to a speedy and public trial, by an impartial jury of the State and district wherein the crime shall have been committed, which district shall have been previously ascertained by law, and to be informed of the nature and cause of the accusation; to be confronted with the witnesses against him; to have compulsory process for obtaining witnesses in his favor, and to have the Assistance of Counsel for his defence.

# Amendment 7 [1791]

In Suits at common law, where the value in controversy shall exceed twenty dollars, the right of trial by jury shall be preserved, and no fact tried by a jury, shall be otherwise re-examined in any Court of the United States, than according to the rules of the common law.

# Amendment 8 [1791]

Excessive bail shall not be required, nor excessive fines imposed, nor cruel and unusual punishments inflicted.

# Amendment 9 [1791]

The enumeration in the Constitution, of certain rights, shall not be construed to deny or disparage others retained by the people.

# Amendment 10 [1791]

The powers not delegated to the United States by the Constitution, nor prohibited by it to the States, are reserved to the States respectively, or to the people.

# Amendment 11 [Jan. 8, 1798]

The Judicial power of the United States shall not be construed to extend to any suit in law or equity, commenced or prosecuted against one of the United States by Citizens of another State, or by Citizens or Subjects of any Foreign State.

# Amendment 12 [Sept. 25, 1804]

The Electors shall meet in their respective states, and vote by ballot for President and Vice-President, one of whom, at least, shall not be an inhabitant of the same state with themselves; they shall name in their ballots the person voted for as President, and in distinct ballots the person voted for as Vice-President, and they shall make distinct lists of all persons voted for as President, and of all persons voted for as Vice-President, and of the number of votes for each, which list they shall sign and certify, and transmit sealed to the seat of the government of the United States, directed to the President of the Senate;—The President of the Senate shall, in the presence of the Senate and House of Representatives, open all the certificates and the votes shall then be counted;—The person having the greatest number of votes for President, shall be the President, if such number be a majority of the whole number of Electors appointed; and if no person have such majority, then from the persons having the highest numbers not exceeding three on the list of those voted for as President, the House of Representatives shall choose immediately, by ballot, the President. But in choosing the President, the votes shall be taken by states, the representation from each state having one vote; a quorum for this purpose shall consist of a member or members from two-thirds of the states, and a majority of all the states shall be necessary to a choice. And if the House of Representatives shall not choose a President whenever the right of choice shall devolve upon them, before the fourth day of March next following, then the Vice-President shall act as President, as in the case of the death or other constitutional disability of the President.—The person having the greatest number of votes as Vice-President, shall be the Vice-President, if such number be a majority of the whole number of Electors appointed, and if no person have a majority, then from the two highest numbers on the list, the Senate shall choose the Vice-President; a quorum for the purpose shall consist of two-thirds of the whole number of Senators, and a majority of the whole number shall be necessary to a choice. But no person constitutionally ineligible to the office of President shall be eligible to that of Vice-President of the United States.

# Amendment 13 [Dec. 18, 1865]

*SECTION 1* Neither slavery nor involuntary servitude, except as a punishment for crime whereof the party shall have been duly convicted, shall exist within the United States, or any place subject to their jurisdiction.

*SECTION 2* Congress shall have power to enforce this article by appropriate legislation.

# Amendment 14 [July 28, 1868]

*SECTION 1* All persons born or naturalized in the United States, and subject to the jurisdiction thereof, are citizens of the United States and of the State wherein they reside. No State shall make or enforce any law which shall abridge the privileges or immunities of citizens of the United States; nor shall any State deprive any person of life, liberty, or property, without due process of law; nor deny to any person within its jurisdiction the equal protection of the laws.

*SECTION 2* Representatives shall be apportioned among the several States according to their respective numbers, counting the whole number of persons in each State, excluding Indians not taxed. But when the right to vote at any election for the choice of electors for President and Vice-President of the United States, Representatives in Congress, the Executive and Judicial officers of a State, or the members of the Legislature thereof, is denied to any of the male inhabitants of such State, being twenty-one years of age, and citizens of the United States, or in any way abridged, except for participation in rebellion, or other crime, the basis of representation therein shall be reduced in the proportion which the number of such male citizens shall bear

to the whole number of male citizens twenty-one years of age in such State.

*SECTION 3* No person shall be a Senator or Representative in Congress, or elector of President and Vice-President, or hold any office, civil or military, under the United States, or under any State, who, having previously taken an oath, as a member of Congress, or as an officer of the United States, or as a member of any State legislature, or as an executive or judicial officer of any State, to support the Constitution of the United States, shall have engaged in insurrection or rebellion against the same, or given aid or comfort to the enemies thereof. But Congress may by a vote of two-thirds of each House, remove such disability.

*SECTION 4* The validity of the public debt of the United States, authorized by law, including debts incurred for payment of pensions and bounties for services in suppressing insurrection or rebellion, shall not be questioned. But neither the United States nor any State shall assume or pay any debt or obligation incurred in aid of insurrection or rebellion against the United States, or any claim for the loss or emancipation of any slave; but all such debts, obligations and claims shall be held illegal and void.

*SECTION 5* The Congress shall have power to enforce, by appropriate legislation, the provisions of this article.

# Amendment 15 [March 30, 1870]

*SECTION 1* The right of citizens of the United States to vote shall not be denied or abridged by the United States or by any State on account of race, color, or previous condition of servitude.

*SECTION 2* The Congress shall have power to enforce this article by appropriate legislation.

# Amendment 16 [Feb. 25, 1913]

The Congress shall have power to lay and collect taxes on incomes, from whatever source derived, without apportionment among the several States, and without regard to any census or enumeration.

# Amendment 17 [May 31, 1913]

*SECTION 1* The Senate of the United States shall be composed of two Senators from each State, elected by the people thereof, for six years; and each Senator shall have one vote. The electors in each State shall have the qualifications requisite for electors of the most numerous branch of the State legislatures.

*SECTION 2* When vacancies happen in the representation of any State in the Senate, the executive authority of such State shall issue writs of election to fill such vacancies: Provided, That the legislature of any State may empower the executive thereof to make temporary appointments until the people fill the vacancies by election as the legislature may direct.

*SECTION 3* This amendment shall not be so construed as to affect the election or term of any Senator chosen before it becomes valid as part of the Constitution.

# Amendment 18 [Jan. 29, 1919; repealed Dec. 5, 1933]

*SECTION 1* After one year from the ratification of this article the manufacture, sale, or transportation of intoxicating liquors within, the importation thereof into, or the exportation thereof from the United States and all territory subject to the jurisdiction thereof for beverage purposes is hereby prohibited.

*SECTION 2* Congress and the several States shall have concurrent power to enforce this article by appropriate legislation.

*SECTION 3* This article shall be inoperative unless it shall have been ratified as an amendment to the Constitution by the legislatures of the several States, as provided in the Constitution, within seven years from the date of the submission hereof to the States by the Congress.

# Amendment 19 [Aug. 26, 1920]

*SECTION 1* The right of citizens of the United States to vote shall not be denied or abridged by the United States or by any State on account of sex.

*SECTION 2* Congress shall have power to enforce this article by appropriate legislation.

# Amendment 20 [Feb. 6, 1933]

*SECTION 1* The terms of the President and Vice-President shall end at noon on the 20th day of January, and the terms of Senators and Representatives at noon on the third day of January, of the years in which such terms would have ended if this article had not been ratified; and the terms of their successors shall then begin.

*SECTION 2* The Congress shall assemble at least once in every year, and such meeting shall begin at noon on the third day of January, unless they shall by law appoint a different day.

*SECTION 3* If, at the time fixed for the beginning of the term of the President, the President elect shall have died, the Vice-President elect shall become President. If a President shall not have been chosen before the time fixed for the beginning of his term, or if the President elect shall have failed to qualify, then the Vice-President elect shall act as President until a President shall have qualified; and the Congress may by law provide for the case wherein neither a President elect nor a Vice-President elect shall have qualified, declaring who shall then act as President, or the manner in which one who is to act shall be selected, and such person shall act accordingly until a President or Vice-President shall have qualified.

*SECTION 4* The Congress may by law provide for the case of the death of any of the persons from whom the House of Representatives may choose a President whenever the right of choice shall have devolved upon them, and for the case of the death of any of the persons from whom the Senate may choose a Vice-President whenever the right of choice shall have devolved upon them.

*SECTION 5* Sections 1 and 2 shall take effect on the 15th day of October following the ratification of this article.

*SECTION 6* This article shall be inoperative unless it shall have been ratified as an amendment to the Constitution by the legislatures of three-fourths of the several States within seven years from the date of its submission.

# Amendment 21 [Dec. 5, 1933]

*SECTION 1* The eighteenth article of amendment to the Constitution of the United States is hereby repealed.

*SECTION 2* The transportation or importation into any State, Territory, or possession of the United States for delivery or use therein of intoxicating liquors, in violation of the laws thereof, is hereby prohibited.

*SECTION 3* This article shall be inoperative unless it shall have been ratified as an amendment to the Constitution by conventions in the several States, as provided in the Constitution, within seven years from the date of the submission hereof to the States by the Congress.

# Amendment 22 [March 1, 1951]

*SECTION 1* No person shall be elected to the office of the President more than twice, and no person who has held the office of President, or acted as President, for more than two years of a term to which some other person was elected President shall be elected to the office of the President more than once. But this Article shall not apply to any person holding the office of President when this Article was proposed by the Congress, and shall not prevent any person who may be holding the office of President, or acting as President, during the term within which this Article becomes operative from holding the office of President or acting as President during the remainder of such term.

*SECTION 2*  This article shall be inoperative unless it shall have been ratified as an amendment to the Constitution by the legislatures of three-fourths of the several States within seven years from the date of its submission to the States by the Congress.

# Amendment 23 [April 3, 1961]

*SECTION 1*  The District constituting the seat of Government of the United States shall appoint in such manner as the Congress may direct:

A number of electors of President and Vice-President equal to the whole number of Senators and Representatives in Congress to which the District would be entitled if it were a State, but in no event more than the least populous State; they shall be in addition to those appointed by the States, but they shall be considered, for the purposes of the election of President and Vice-President, to be electors appointed by a State; and they shall meet in the District and perform such duties as provided by the twelfth article of amendment.

*SECTION 2*  The Congress shall have power to enforce this article by appropriate legislation.

# Amendment 24 [Feb. 4, 1964]

*SECTION 1*  The right of citizens of the United States to vote in any primary or other election for President or Vice-President, for electors for President or Vice-President, or for Senator or Representative in Congress, shall not be denied or abridged by the United States or any State by reason of failure to pay any poll tax or other tax.

*SECTION 2*  The Congress shall have power to enforce this article by appropriate legislation.

# Amendment 25 [Feb. 10, 1967]

*SECTION 1*  In case of the removal of the President from office or his death or resignation, the Vice-President shall become President.

*SECTION 2*  Whenever there is a vacancy in the office of the Vice-President, the President shall nominate a Vice-President who shall take the office upon confirmation by a majority vote of both houses of Congress.

*SECTION 3*  Whenever the President transmits to the President pro tempore of the Senate and the Speaker of the House of Representatives his written declaration that he is unable to discharge the powers and duties of his office, and until he transmits to them a written declaration to the contrary, such powers and duties shall be discharged by the Vice-President as Acting President.

*SECTION 4*  Whenever the Vice-President and a majority of either the principal officers of the executive departments, or of such other body as Congress may by law provide, transmit to the President pro tempore of the Senate and the Speaker of the House of Representatives their written declaration that the President is unable to discharge the powers and duties of his office, the Vice-President shall immediately assume the powers and duties of the office as Acting President.

Thereafter, when the President transmits to the President pro tempore of the Senate and the Speaker of the House of Representatives his written declaration that no inability exists, he shall resume the powers and duties of his office unless the Vice-President and a majority of either the principal officers of the executive department, or of such other body as Congress may by law provide, transmit within four days to the President pro tempore of the Senate and the Speaker of the House of Representatives their written declaration that the President is unable to discharge the powers and duties of his office. Thereupon Congress shall decide the issue, assembling within forty-eight hours for that purpose if not in session. If the Congress, within twenty-one days after receipt of the latter written declaration, or, if Congress is not in session, within twenty-one days after Congress is required to assemble, determines by two-thirds vote of both Houses that the President is unable to discharge the powers and duties of his office, the Vice-President shall continue to discharge the same as Acting President; otherwise, the President shall resume the powers and duties of his office.

# Amendment 26 [June 30, 1971]

*SECTION 1*  The right of citizens of the United States, who are eighteen years of age or older, to vote shall not be denied or abridged by the United States or any state on account of age.

*SECTION 2*  The Congress shall have power to enforce this article by appropriate legislation.

# Amendment 27 [May 7, 1992]

No law, varying the compensation for the services of Senators and Representatives, shall take effect until an election of Representatives shall have intervened.

**accountability system** A system that makes police supervisors responsible for the behavior of the officers in their command.

**actus reus** An illegal act, or failure to act when legally required.

**adjudication** The determination of guilt or innocence—a judgment concerning criminal charges.

**alternative dispute resolution** A means of settling disputes outside the courtroom.

**anger management** Programs designed to help people who have become dependent on anger as a primary means of expressing themselves and those who inappropriately use anger or the threat of violence to get their way.

**anomie** The absence or weakness of rules, norms, or guidelines on what is socially or morally acceptable.

**antisocial personality** A personality characterized by a lack of warmth and feeling, inappropriate behavioral responses, and an inability to learn from experience (also called sociopath or psychopath).

**appeal** A request for an appellate court to examine a lower court's decision in order to determine whether proper procedures were followed.

**appellate court** A court to which appeals are made on points of law resulting from the judgment of a lower court; the appellate court may be asked to evaluate the impact of new evidence but more typically decides whether the state or federal constitution was improperly interpreted during a case.

**arbitration** A process of dispute resolution in which a neutral third party (arbitrator) renders a decision after a hearing at which both parties agree to be heard.

**arraignment** Initial trial court appearance, at which the accused is read the charges, advised of his or her rights, and asked to enter a plea.

**arrest** Occurs when a police officer takes a person into custody or deprives a person of freedom for having allegedly committed a criminal offense.

**arrest warrant** An order, issued by a judge, directing officers to arrest a particular individual.

**assigned counsel** A private attorney appointed by the court to represent a criminal defendant who cannot afford to pay for a lawyer.

**attorney general** The chief legal officer and prosecutor of each state and of the United States.

**Auburn system** A prison system, developed in New York during the nineteenth century, based on congregate (group) work during the day and separation at night.

**avertable recidivist** A person whose crime would have been prevented if he or she had not been given discretionary release and instead had been kept behind bars.

**bail** The monetary amount required for pretrial release, normally set by a judge at the initial appearance. The purpose of bail is to ensure the return of the accused at subsequent proceedings.

**beats** Designated police patrol areas.

**bench trial** The trial of a criminal matter by a judge only. The accused waives any constitutional right to a jury trial.

**biometrics** Automated methods of recognizing a person on the basis of a physiological or behavioral characteristic.

**blameworthy** Culpable or guilty of participating in a particular criminal offense.

**blue curtain** The secretive, insulated police culture that isolates officers from the rest of society.

**booking** The administrative record of an arrest, listing the offender's name, address, physical description, date of birth, and employer, time of arrest, offense, and name of arresting officer; it also includes photographing and fingerprinting of the offender.

**boot camp** A short-term, militaristic correction facility in which inmates undergo intensive physical conditioning and discipline.

**broken windows model** The role of the police as maintainers of community order and safety.

**brutalization effect** The belief that capital punishment creates an atmosphere of brutality that enhances, rather than reduces, the level of violence in society.

The death penalty reinforces the view that violence is an appropriate response to provocation.

**bus sweep** Police investigation technique in which officers board a bus or train without suspicion of illegal activity and question passengers, asking for identification and seeking permission to search their baggage.

**career criminals** Persistent repeat offenders who organize their lifestyle around criminality.

**center** A mechanism to exchange information and intelligence, maximize resources, streamline operations, and improve the ability to fight crime and terrorism by analyzing data from a variety of sources.

**challenge for cause** Dismissal of a prospective juror by either the prosecution or the defense because he or she is biased, because he or she has prior knowledge about a case, or for other reasons that demonstrate the individual's inability to render a fair and impartial judgment.

**chancery courts** Early English courts established to protect the property rights and welfare of the minor children of affluent families.

**child savers** Civic leaders who focused their attention on the misdeeds of poor children to control their behavior.

**Children's Aid Society** A group created by Charles Loring Brace to place indigent city children with farm families

**chivalry hypothesis** The view that the low rates of crime and delinquency among females reflect the leniency with which female offenders are treated.

**chronic offenders** As defined by Marvin Wolfgang, Robert Figlio, and Thorsten Sellin, delinquents arrested five or more times before the age of 18, who commit a disproportionate amount of all criminal offenses.

**civil law** All law that is not criminal, including tort, contract, personal property, maritime, and commercial law.

**collective efficacy** A condition of mutual trust and cooperation that develops in neighborhoods that have a high level of formal and informal social control.

**commitment** Decision of a judge who orders an adjudicated and sentenced juvenile offender to be placed in a correctional facility.

**community policing** A law enforcement program that seeks to integrate officers into the local community to reduce crime and achieve good community relations. It typically involves personalized service and decentralized policing, citizen empowerment, and an effort to reduce community fear of crime, disorder, and decay.

**community prosecution** A prosecutorial philosophy that emphasizes community support and cooperation with other agencies in preventing crime, as well as a less centralized and more proactive role for local prosecutors.

**community service restitution** An alternative sanction that requires an offender to work in the community at such tasks as cleaning public parks or working with disabled children in lieu of an incarceration sentence.

**community treatment** The attempt by correctional agencies to maintain convicted offenders in the community rather than in a secure facility; it includes probation, parole, and residential programs.

**community-oriented policing** Programs designed to bring police and public closer together and create a more cooperative environment between them.

**complaint** A sworn written statement addressed to a court or judge by the police, prosecutor, or individual alleging that an individual has committed an offense and requesting indictment and prosecution.

**compulsory process** Compelling the production of a witness or evidence via a subpoena

**concurrent sentences** Prison sentences for two or more criminal acts, served simultaneously and run together.

**conflict view of crime** The view that criminal law is created and enforced by those who hold political and economic power and is a tool used by the ruling class to control dissatisfied have-not members of society.

**confrontation clause** The constitutional right of a criminal defendant to see and cross-examine all the witnesses against him or her.

**congregate system** A prison system, originated in New York, in which inmates worked and ate together during the day and then slept in solitary cells at night.

**consecutive sentences** Prison sentences for two or more criminal acts, served one after the other.

**consensus view of crime** The view that the great majority of citizens agree that certain behaviors must be outlawed or controlled, and that criminal law is designed to protect citizens from social harm.

**constable** In early English towns, an appointed peacekeeper who organized citizens for protection and supervised the night watch.

**contract system** A prison industry system, widely employed until after the Civil War, in which officials sold the labor of prison inmates to private businesses, for use either inside or outside the prison.

**contract system** Provision of legal services to indigent defendants by private attorneys under contract to the state or county.

**convict-lease system** A contract system in which a private business leased prisoners from the state for a fixed annual fee and assumed full responsibility for their supervision and control.

**corporate crime** Crime committed by a corporation, or by individuals who control the corporation or other business entity, for such purposes as illegally increasing market share, avoiding taxes, or thwarting competition.

**corporate enterprise crime** Illegal activities of people and organizations whose acknowledged purpose is to profitit through illegitimate business enterprise.

**corruption** Exercising legitimate discretion for improper reasons or using illegal means to achieve approved goals.

**court of general jurisdiction** A state or federal court that has jurisdiction over felony offenses—serious crimes that carry a penalty of incarceration in a state or federal prison for one year or more.

**court of last resort** A court that handles the final appeal on a matter—in the federal system, the U.S. Supreme Court.

**court of limited jurisdiction** A court that has jurisdiction over misdemeanors and conducts preliminary investigations of felony charges.

**courtroom work group** A term used to imply that all parties in the justice process work together in a cooperative effort to settle cases efficiently rather than to engage in a true adversarial procedure.

**crime** A violation of social rules of conduct, interpreted and expressed by a written criminal code, created by people holding social and political power. Its content may be influenced by prevailing public sentiments, historically developed moral beliefs, and the need to protect public safety.

**crime control perspective** A model of criminal justice that emphasizes the control of dangerous offenders and the protection of society through harsh punishment as a deterrent to crime.

**criminal justice system** The system of law enforcement, adjudication, and correction that is directly involved in the apprehension, prosecution, and control of those charged with criminal offenses.

**criminal law** The body of rules that define crimes, set out their punishments, and mandate the procedures for carrying out the criminal justice process.

**criminal negligence** Liability that can occur when a person's careless and inattentive actions cause harm.

**criminology** The scientific study of the nature, extent, cause, and control of criminal behavior.

**critical criminology** The view that crime results because the rich and powerful impose their own moral standards and economic interests on the rest of society.

**cross-examination** The questioning of a prosecution witness by the defense, or of a defense witness by the prosecution.

**cruel and unusual punishment** Physical punishment or punishment that far exceeds that given to people under similar circumstances and is therefore banned by the Eighth Amendment. The death penalty has so far not been considered cruel and unusual if it is administered in a fair and nondiscriminatory fashion.

**culture of poverty** The view that people in the lower class of society form a separate culture with its own values and norms that are in conflict with those of conventional society.

**curtilage** Grounds or fields attached to a house.

**cyber bullying** Willful and repeated harm done through the medium of electronic text.

**cyber crime** The theft and/or destruction of information, resources, or funds via computers, computer networks, or the Internet.

**cyber stalking** Using the Internet, email, or other electronic communications devices to stalk or harass another person.

**cyber theft** The use of computer networks for criminal profits. Copyright infringement, identity theft, and Internet securities fraud are examples of cyber theft.

**cyber vandalism** Malicious attacks aimed at disrupting, defacing, and destroying technology.

**cyber warfare** Politically motivated attacks designed to compromise the electronic infrastructure of an enemy nation and disrupt its economy.

**cynicism** The belief that most people's actions are motivated solely by personal needs and selfishness.

**data mining** The use of sophisticated computer software to conduct analysis of behavior patterns in an effort to identify crime patterns and link them to suspects.

**day fees** A program requiring probationers to pay in part for the costs of their treatment.

**day fine** A fine geared to the average daily income of the convicted offender in an effort to bring equity to the sentencing process.

**day reporting center (DRC)** A nonresidential community-based treatment program.

**deadly force** The intentional use of a firearm or other instrument, resulting in a high probability of death.

**decriminalization** Reducing the penalty for a criminal act without legalizing it.

**defense attorney** Legal counsel for the defendant in a criminal case, representing the accused person from arrest to final appeal.

**deinstitutionalization** The policy of removing from secure confinement as many first offenders of minor, nonviolent crimes as possible and treating them in the community.

**demeanor** The way a person outwardly manifests his or her personality.

**denial-of-service attack** Extorting money from an Internet service user by threatening to prevent the user from having access to the service.

**detention** The temporary care of a child alleged to be a delinquent or status offender who requires secure custody, pending court disposition.

**determinate sentence** A fixed term of incarceration, such as three years' imprisonment. Determinate sentences are felt by many to be too restrictive for rehabilitative purposes; the advantage is that offenders know how much time they have to serve—that is, when they will be released.

**deterrent effect** The assumed ability of the threat of criminal sanctions to discourage crime before it occurs.

**developmental theories** A view of crime holding that as people travel through the life course, their experiences along the way influence their behavior patterns. Behavior changes at each stage of the human experience.

**differential association theory** The view that criminal acts are related to a person's exposure to antisocial attitudes and values.

**direct examination** The initial questioning of one's own (prosecution or defense) witness during a trial.

**directed verdict** A judge's order directing a jury to acquit a defendant because the state has not proved the elements of the crime or otherwise has not established guilt according to law.

**discretion** The use of personal decision making and choice in carrying out operations in the criminal justice system.

**disinhibition** Unconstrained behavior resulting from a loss of inhibition via some external influence, such as drugs or alcohol, or from a brain injury.

**displacement** An effect that occurs when criminals move from an area targeted for increased police presence to another that is less well protected.

**disposition** For juvenile offenders, the equivalent of sentencing for adult offenders. The theory is that disposition is more rehabilitative than retributive. Possible dispositions: dismissing the case, releasing the youth to the custody of his or her parents, placing the offender on probation, or sending him or her to an institution or state correctional institution.

**district attorney** The county prosecutor who is charged with bringing offenders to justice and enforcing the criminal laws of the state.

**diversion** The use of an alternative to trial, such as referral to treatment or employment programs.

**DNA profiling** The identification of criminal suspects by matching DNA samples taken from their person with specimens found at the crime scene.

**double marginality** According to Nicholas Alex, the social burden that African American police officers carry by being both minority group members and law enforcement officers.

**due process perspective** A perspective on criminal justice that emphasizes individual rights and constitutional safeguards against arbitrary or unfair judicial or administrative proceedings.

**e-courtroom** A court that seamlessly integrates technology into its daily operations.

**early onset** The beginning of antisocial behavior during early adolescence, after which criminal behavior is more likely to persist throughout the life span.

**electronic monitoring (EM)** Requiring convicted offenders to wear a monitoring device as part of their community sentence. Typically part of a house arrest order, this enables the probation department to ensure that offenders are complying with court-ordered limitations on their freedom.

**equal justice perspective** A perspective on criminal justice based on the idea that all people should receive the same treatment under the law and should be evaluated on the basis of their current behavior, not on what they have done in the past.

**equity** The action or practice of awarding each person his or her just due. Sanctions based on equity seek to compensate individual victims and the general society for their losses due to crime.

**etailing fraud** Using the Internet to buy or sell merchandise illegally.

**evidence-based justice** Determining whether criminal justice programs actually reduce crime rates and offender recidivism through the use of the scientific method.

**ex post facto law** A law that makes an act criminal after it was committed or retroactively increases the penalty for a crime; such laws are forbidden by the U.S. Constitution.

**excited delirium** An overdose of adrenaline that can occur in heated confrontations with the police.

**exclusionary rule** The principle that illegally obtained evidence cannot be used in a court of law.

**exculpatory evidence** All information that is material and favorable to the accused defendant because it casts doubt on the defendant's guilt or on the evidence the government intends to use at trial.

**excuse defense** A defense in which a person states that his or her mental state was so impaired that he or she lacked the capacity to form sufficient intent to be held criminally responsible.

**exigent circumstances** Emergency or urgent circumstances.

**expressive crimes** Criminal acts that serve to vent rage, anger, or frustration.

**expressive violence** Violent behavior motivated by rage, anger, or frustration.

**Federal Bureau of Investigation (FBI)** The arm of the Justice Department that investigates violations of federal law, gathers crime statistics, runs a comprehensive crime laboratory, and helps train local law enforcement officers.

**fine** Levying a money payment on offenders to compensate society for their misdeeds.

**First Amendment** The amendment to the U.S. Constitution that guarantees freedom of speech, religion, press, and assembly, and the right of the people to petition the government for redress of grievances.

**focal concerns** Central values and goals that, some sociological theorists believe, differ by social class.

**foot patrol** Police patrol that takes officers out of cars and puts them on a walking beat to strengthen ties with the community.

**forfeiture** The seizure of personal property by the state as a civil or criminal penalty.

**fruit of the poisonous tree** Secondary evidence obtained from a search that violates the exclusionary rule.

**furlough** A correctional policy that allows inmates to leave the institution for vocational or educational training, for employment, or to maintain family ties.

**gang tactical detail** A police unit created to combat neighborhood gang problems by targeting known offenders who have shown a propensity toward gang violence or criminal activity.

**general deterrence** A crime control policy that depends on the fear of criminal penalties. General deterrence measures, such as long prison sentences for violent crimes, are aimed at convincing the potential law violator that the pains associated with the crime outweigh the benefits.

**globalization** The process of creating a global economy through transnational markets and political and legal systems.

**good faith exception** The principle that evidence may be used in a criminal trial even though the search warrant used to obtain it was technically faulty, as long as the police acted in good faith when they sought the warrant from a judge.

**grand jury** A group of citizens chosen to hear charges against persons accused of crime and to determine whether there is sufficient evidence to bring those persons to trial.

**grass eater** A term used to describe a police officer who accepts payoffs when everyday duties place him or her in a position to be solicited by the public.

**halfway house** A community-based correctional facility that houses inmates before their outright release so that they can become gradually acclimated to conventional society.

**hands-off doctrine** The legal practice of allowing prison administrators a free hand in running the institution, even if correctional practices violate inmates' constitutional rights; this practice ended with the onset of the prisoners' rights movement in the 1960s.

**hate crimes (bias crimes)** Criminal acts directed toward a particular person or members of a group because they share a discernible racial, ethnic, religious, or gender characteristic.

**hearsay evidence** Testimony that is not firsthand but, rather, relates information told by a second party.

**hot pursuit** A legal doctrine that allows police to perform a warrantless search of premises where they suspect a crime has been committed when delay would endanger their lives or the lives of others and lead to the escape of the alleged perpetrator.

**hot spots of crime** The relatively few locations— bars, malls, the bus depot, hotels, and certain apartment buildings— from which a significant portion of police calls typically originate in metropolitan areas.

**house arrest** A form of intermediate sanction that requires that the convicted offender spend a designated amount of time per week in his or her own home— such as from 6:00 P.M. Friday until 8:00 A.M. Monday.

**hue and cry** In medieval England, a call for mutual aid against trouble or danger.

**hulk** Mothballed ship used to house prisoners in eighteenth-century England.

**hundred** In medieval England, a group of 100 families (ten tythings) responsible for maintaining order and trying minor offenses.

**identity theft** Using the Internet to steal someone's identity and/or impersonate the victim in order to conduct illicit transactions, such as committing fraud using the victim's name and identity.

**impact munitions** Less-lethal weapons that are used to stun or otherwise incapacitate uncooperative suspects so they can be subdued. Examples include rubber bullets and bean bag projectiles.

**in-presence requirement** A police officer cannot arrest someone for a misdemeanor unless the officer sees the crime occur. To make an arrest for a crime the officer did not witness, an arrest warrant must be obtained.

**incapacitation** The policy of keeping dangerous criminals in confinement to eliminate the risk of their repeating their offense in society.

**indeterminate sentence** A term of incarceration with a stated minimum and maximum length, such as a sentence to prison for a period of from 3 to 10 years. The prisoner is eligible for parole after the minimum sentence has been served. Based on the belief that sentences should fit the criminal, indeterminate sentences allow individualized sentences and provide for sentencing flexibility. Judges can set a high minimum to override the purpose of the indeterminate sentence.

**indictment** A written accusation returned by a grand jury, charging an individual with a specified crime after determination of probable cause.

**indigent defendant** A defendant who lacks the funds to hire a private attorney and is therefore entitled to free counsel.

**inevitable discovery rule** The principle that evidence can be used in court even though the information that led to its discovery was obtained in violation of the *Miranda* rule if a judge finds it would have been discovered anyway by other means or sources.

**information** A formal charging document, similar to an indictment, based on probable cause as determined at a preliminary hearing.

**initial appearance** A juvenile's first appearance before the juvenile court judge in which the charges are reviewed and an effort is made to settle the case without a trial. If the child does not have legal counsel, an attorney is appointed.

**inmate social code** An unwritten code of behavior, passed from older inmates to younger ones, that serves as a guideline for appropriate inmate behavior within the correctional institution.

**inmate subculture** The loosely defined culture that pervades prisons and has its own norms, rules, and language.

**instrumental crimes** Criminal acts intended to improve the financial or social position of the criminal.

**instrumental violence** Violent behavior that results from criminal activity designed to improve the financial status of the culprit, such as shooting someone during a bank robbery.

**intake** The process in which a probation officer settles cases at the initial appearance before the onset of formal criminal proceedings. Also, the process in which a juvenile referral is received and a decision is made to file a petition in the juvenile court, release the juvenile, or refer the juvenile elsewhere.

**intelligence-led policing (ILP)** The collection and analysis of information to generate an "intelligence end product" designed to inform police decision making at both the tactical and the strategic level.

**Intensive Aftercare Program (IAP)** A balanced, highly structured, comprehensive continuum of intervention for serious and violent juvenile offenders returning to the community.

**intensive probation supervision (IPS)** A type of intermediate sanction involving small probation caseloads and strict monitoring on a daily or weekly basis.

**intensive supervision parole (ISP)** A form of parole characterized by smaller caseloads and closer surveillance; it may include frequent drug testing and, in some cases, electronic monitoring.

**interactionist view of crime** The view that criminal law reflects the preferences and opinions of people who hold social power in the society and use their influence to impose their own values and moral code on the rest of the population.

**intermediate sanctions** The group of punishments falling between probation and prison ("probation plus"). Community-based sanctions, including house arrest and intensive supervision, serve as alternatives to incarceration.

**internal affairs** The police unit that investigates allegations of police misconduct.

**jail** A correctional facility designed to hold pretrial detainees and misdemeanants serving their criminal sentence.

**jailhouse lawyer** An inmate trained in law, or otherwise educated, who helps other inmates prepare legal briefs and appeals.

**judge** The senior officer in a court of law, who is authorized to hear and decide cases.

**judicial reprieve** The common-law practice that allowed judges to suspend punishment so that convicted offenders could seek a pardon, gather new evidence, or demonstrate that they had reformed their behavior.

**jury nullification** A jury's refusal to render a verdict according to the law and fact regardless of the evidence presented.

**just desert** The philosophy of justice asserting that those who violate the rights of others deserve to be punished. The severity of punishment should be commensurate with the seriousness of the crime.

**justice of the peace** Official appointed to act as the judicial officer in a county.

**justification** A defense for a criminal act claiming that the criminal act was reasonable or necessary under the circumstances.

**juvenile court** A court that has original jurisdiction over persons defined by statute as legal minors and alleged to be involved in juvenile delinquency or status offenses. In some jurisdictions, these are family courts that also deal with custody and neglect issues.

**juvenile delinquency** Participation in illegal behavior by a minor who falls under a statutory age limit.

**juvenile intensive probation supervision (JIPS)** A true alternative to incarceration that involves almost daily supervision of the juvenile by the probation officer assigned to the case.

**Knapp Commission** A public body that conducted an investigation into police corruption in New York City in the early 1970s and uncovered a widespread network of payoffs and bribes.

**latent trait theories** The view that human behavior is controlled by a master trait, present at birth or soon after, that influences and directs behavior.

**Law Enforcement Assistance Administration (LEAA)** Federal agency that provided technical assistance and hundreds of millions of dollars in aid to state and local justice agencies between 1969 and 1982.

**liberal feminist theory** An ideology holding that women suffer oppression, discrimination, and disadvantage as a result of their sex and calling for gender equality in pay, opportunity, child care, and education.

**life course theories** The view that criminality is a dynamic process influenced by people's perceptions and experiences throughout their lives, which may change their behavior for the better or the worse.

**lineup** Placing a suspect in a group for the purpose of being viewed and identified by a witness.

**low-visibility decision making** Decision making by police officers that is not subject to administrative review—for example, a decision not to arrest someone or not to stop a speeding vehicle.

**make-believe families** In female prisons, substitute family groups with a faux father, mother, and siblings.

**mala in se** In common law, offenses that are by their own nature evil, immoral, and wrong; such offenses include murder, theft, and arson.

**mandatory sentence** A statutory requirement that a certain penalty shall be set and carried out in all cases upon conviction for a specified offense or series of offenses.

**mass murderer** Type of multiple killer who kills many victims in a single violent outburst.

**meat eater** A term used to describe a police officer who actively solicits bribes and vigorously engages in corrupt practices.

**mediation** An informal dispute resolution process in which a neutral third party (mediator) helps disputing parties reach an agreement.

**medical model** A view of corrections holding that convicted offenders are victims of their environment who need care and treatment to transform them into valuable members of society.

**medium-security prison** A less secure institution that houses nonviolent offenders and provides more opportunities for contact with the outside world.

**mens rea** A guilty mind: the intent to commit a criminal act.

**Metropolitan Police Act** Sir Robert Peel's legislation that established the first organized police force in London.

**minimum-security prison** The least secure correctional institution, which houses whitecollar and nonviolent offenders, maintains few security measures, and has liberal furlough and visitation policies.

*Miranda* **warning** The requirement that when a person is custodially interrogated, police inform the individual of the right to remain silent, the consequences of failing to remain silent, and the constitutional right to counsel.

**Missouri Plan** A method of judicial selection that combines a judicial nominating commission, executive appointment, and nonpartisan confirmation elections.

**Mollen Commission** An investigative unit set up to inquire into police corruption in New York City in the 1990s.

**monetary restitution** A sanction requiring that convicted offenders compensate crime victims by reimbursing them for out-of-pocket losses caused by the crime. Losses can include property damage, lost wages, and medical costs.

**moral entrepreneurs** People who wage campaigns to control

**National Crime Victimization Survey (NCVS)** The nation's primary source of information on criminal victimization. Each year, data from a national sample measure the frequency, characteristics, and consequences of criminal victimization by such crimes as rape, sexual assault, robbery, assault, theft, household burglary, and motor vehicle theft.

**National Criminal Intelligence Sharing Plan (NCISP)** A formal intelligence-sharing initiative that identifies the security and intelligence-sharing needs recognized in the wake of the 9/11 terrorist attacks.

**National Incident- Based Reporting System (NIBRS)** A form of crime data collection created by the FBI requiring local police agencies to provide at least a brief account of each incident and arrest within 22 crime patterns, including the incident, victim, and offender information.

**National Law Enforcement Officers Memorial** The nation's monument to police officers who have died in the line of duty.

**neurotransmitters** Chemical substances that carry impulses from one nerve cell to another. Neurotransmitters are found in the space (synapse) that separates the transmitting neuron's terminal (axon) from the receiving neuron's terminal (dendrite).

**no bill** The action by a grand jury when it votes not to indict an accused suspect.

**no-frills policy** A correctional policy that stipulates that prisons are intended to punish, not coddle, inmates. This usually means a strict regimen of work and discipline and reduced opportunities for recreation and education.

**nolle prosequi** The decision by a prosecutor to drop a case after a complaint has been made because of, for example, insufficient evidence, witness reluctance to testify, police error, or office policy.

**nolo contendere** A plea of "no contest"—the defendant submits to sentencing without any formal admission of guilt that could be used against him or her in a subsequent civil suit.

**nonintervention perspective** A perspective on criminal justice that favors the least intrusive treatment possible: decarceration, diversion, and decriminalization.

**obitiatry** Helping people take their own lives: assisted suicide.

**open field** Any unoccupied or undeveloped real property outside the curtilage of a home.

**order maintenance (peacekeeping)** Maintaining order and authority without the need for formal arrest ("handling the situation")— keeping things under control by means of threats, persuasion, and understanding.

**overload hypothesis** The theory that police workload influences discretion so that as workload increases, less time and attention can be devoted to new cases, especially petty crimes.

**parens patriae** Latin term meaning "father of his country." According to this legal philosophy, the government is the true guardian of the needy and infirm including dependent children. It refers to the power of the state to act on behalf of a child and provide care and protection equivalent to that of a parent.

**parental efficacy** Parenting that is supportive, effective, and noncoercive.

**parole** The early release of a prisoner from imprisonment subject to conditions set by correctional authorities.

**Part I crimes** Those crimes used by the FBI to gauge fluctuations in the overall volume and rate of crime. The offenses included were the violent crimes of murder and nonnegligent manslaughter, forcible rape, robbery, and aggravated assault and the property crimes of burglary, larceny, motor vehicle theft, and arson.

**Part II crimes** All other crimes reported to the FBI; these are less serious crimes and misdemeanors, excluding traffic violations. cleared An offense is cleared by arrest or solved when at least one person is arrested or charged with the commission

of the offense and is turned over to the court for prosecution.

**particularity** The requirement that a search warrant state precisely where the search is to take place and what items are to be seized.

**penal harm** The belief that during their incarceration inmates should endure pain and suffering, in order to make the punishment deliberately harder so they will not dare recidivate.

**penitentiary** A state or federal correctional institution for incarceration of felony offenders for terms of one year or more.

**Pennsylvania system** A prison system, developed in Pennsylvania during the nineteenth century, based on total isolation and individual penitence.

**penumbral crimes** Criminal acts defined by a high level of noncompliance with the stated legal standard, an absence of stigma associated with violation of the stated standard, and a low level of law enforcement or public sanction.

**peremptory challenge** Dismissal of a prospective juror by either the prosecution or the defense for unexplained, discretionary reasons.

**phishing** Also known as carding and spoofing, phishing consists of illegally acquiring personal information, such as bank passwords and credit card numbers, by masquerading as a trustworthy person or business in what appears to be an official electronic communication, such as an email or an instant message. The term "phishing" comes from the lures used to "fish" for financial information and passwords.

**plain view doctrine** The principle that evidence in plain view of police officers may be seized without a search warrant.

**plea negotiations/plea bargaining** Discussions between defense counsel and prosecution in which the accused agrees to plead guilty in exchange for certain considerations, such as reduced charges or a lenient sentence.

**police brutality** Actions such as using abusive language, making threats, using force or coercion unnecessarily, prodding with nightsticks, and stopping and searching people to harass them.

**police productivity** The amount of order maintenance, crime control, and other law enforcement activities provided by individual police officers and concomitantly by police departments as a whole.

**police styles** The working personalities adopted by police officers that can range from being a social worker in blue to being a hardcharging crime fighter.

**Ponzi scheme** An investment fraud that involves the payment of purported returns to existing investors from funds contributed by new investors.

**poor laws** Sixteenth-century English laws under which vagrants and abandoned and neglected children were bound to masters as indentured servants.

**pre-sentence investigation** An investigation performed by a probation officer attached to a trial court after the conviction of a defendant. The report contains information about the defendant's background, education, previous employment, and family; his or her own statement concerning the offense; prior criminal record; interviews with neighbors or acquaintances; and his or her mental and physical condition (that is, information that would not be made public record in the case of guilty plea or that would be inadmissible as evidence at a trial but could be influential and important at the sentencing stage).

**preliminary hearing** Hearing before a magistrate to determine whether the government has sufficient evidence to show probable cause that the defendant committed the crime.

**preponderance of the evidence** The level of proof in civil cases; more than half the evidence supports the allegations of one side.

**presentment** The report of a grand jury investigation, which usually includes a recommendation of indictment.

**pretrial detainees** People who either are denied bail or cannot afford to post bail before trial and are kept in secure confinement.

**pretrial procedures** Legal and administrative actions that take place after arrest and before trial, including grand jury indictments, preliminary hearings, bail, and plea negotiation.

**preventive detention** The statutory authorization to deny bail to a particular individual who is considered dangerous or a flight risk.

**prison** A correctional facility designed to hold convicted felons while they serve their criminal sentence.

**prisonization** Assimilation into the separate culture of the prison. This loosely defined culture that pervades prisons has its own norms, rules, and language. The traditional prison culture is now being replaced by a violent gang culture.

**private policing** Crime prevention, detection, and the apprehension of criminals carried out by private organizations or individuals for commercial purposes.

**pro bono** The practice by private attorneys of taking the cases of indigent offenders without fee as a service to the profession and the community.

**proactive policing** An aggressive law enforcement style in which patrol officers take the initiative against crime instead of waiting for criminal acts to occur. For example, they stop motor vehicles to issue citations and aggressively arrest and detain suspicious persons.

**probable cause hearing** If a person is subjected to a warrantless arrest, a hearing is held to determine whether probable cause exists that he committed the crime.

**probable cause** The evidentiary criterion necessary to sustain an arrest or the issuance of an arrest or search warrant: a set of facts, information, circumstances, or conditions that would lead a reasonable person to believe that an offense was committed and that the accused committed that offense.

**probation** A sentence entailing the conditional release of a convicted offender into the community under the supervision of the court (in the form of a probation officer), subject to certain conditions for a specified time. The conditions are usually similar to those of parole. (Note: Probation is a sentence, an alternative to incarceration; parole is administrative release from incarceration.) Violation of the conditions of probation may result in revocation of probation.

**probation rules** Conditions or restrictions mandated by the court that must be obeyed by a probationer.

**problem-oriented policing (POP)** A style of police management that stresses proactive problem solving instead of reactive crime fighting.

**procedural criminal laws** The methods that must be followed in obtaining warrants, investigating offenses, effecting lawful arrests, conducting trials, introducing evidence, sentencing convicted offenders, and reviewing cases by appellate courts.

**procedural justice** A concern with making decisions that are arrived at through procedures viewed as fair.

**proof beyond a reasonable doubt** The standard of proof needed to convict in a criminal case. The evidence offered in court does not have to amount to absolute certainty, but it should leave no reasonable doubt that the defendant committed the alleged crime.

**prosecutor** An appointed or elected member of the practicing bar who is responsible for bringing the state's case against the accused.

**prosecutorial discretion** The prosecutor's authority to decide whether to bring a case to trial or to dismiss it outright.

**public account system** A prison industry system, popular after the Civil War, in which employment was directed by the state and the products of the prisoners' labor were sold for the benefit of the state.

**public defender** An attorney employed by the government to represent criminal defendants who cannot afford to pay for a lawyer.

**public law** The branch of law that deals with the state or government agencies and controls their administrative relationships with individuals, corporations, or other branches of government.

**public order crimes** Behaviors that are illegal because they run counter to existing moral standards. Obscenity and prostitution are considered public order crimes

**public safety doctrine** The principle that a suspect can be questioned in the field without a *Miranda* warning if the information the police seek is needed to protect public safety.

**public safety or strict liability crime** A criminal violation—usually one that endangers the public welfare—that is defined by the act itself, irrespective of intent.

**qualified immunity** A legal doctrine that shields government officials from liability if their conduct did not violate clearly established civil rights that a reasonable person would have known about.

**racial threat hypothesis** The view that young minority males are subject to greater police control—for example, formal arrest—when their numbers increase within the population.

**Racketeer Influenced and Corrupt Organization Act (RICO)** Federal legislation that enables prosecutors to bring additional criminal or civil charges against people engaged in two or more acts prohibited by 24 existing federal and 8 state laws. RICO features monetary penalties that allow the government to confiscate all profits derived from criminal activities. Originally intended to be used against organized criminals, RICO has also been used against white-collar criminals.

**recognizance** The medieval practice of allowing convicted offenders to go unpunished if they agreed to refrain from any further criminal behavior.

**recoupment** Process by which the state later recovers some or all of the cost of providing free legal counsel to an indigent defendant.

**rehabilitation perspective** A perspective on criminal justice that sees crime as an expression of frustration and anger created by social inequality that can be controlled by giving people the means to improve their lifestyles through conventional endeavors.

**release on recognizance (ROR)** A pretrial release in which a defendant with ties to the community is not required to post bail but promises to appear at all subsequent proceedings.

**residential community corrections (RCC)** A nonsecure facility, located in the community, that houses probationers who need a more secure environment. Typically, residents are free during the day to go to work, school, or treatment, and return in the evening for counseling sessions and meals.

**restitution** A condition of probation in which the offender repays society or the victim of crime for the trouble the offender caused.

**restorative justice perspective** A perspective on criminal justice that sees the main goal of the criminal justice system as making a systematic response to wrongdoing that emphasizes healing victims, offenders, and communities wounded by crime. It stresses peacemaking, not punishment.

**revocation** An administrative act performed by a parole authority that removes a person from parole, or a judicial order by a court removing a person from parole or probation, in response to a violation on the part of the parolee or probationer.

**risk classification** Classifying probationers so that they may receive an appropriate level of treatment and control.

**routine activities theory** The view that crime is a product of three everyday factors: motivated offenders, suitable targets, and a lack of capable guardians.

**rule of four** The convention that four justices must agree to hear a case before a writ of certiorari is granted.

**search** A government actor's infringement on a person's reasonable expectation of privacy.

**search incident to a lawful arrest** An exception to the search warrant rule, limited to the immediate surrounding area.

**search warrant** An order, issued by a judge, directing officers to conduct a search of specified premises for specified objects.

**securitization** The process in which vendors take individual subprime loans, bundle them into large pools, and sell them as securities.

**self-report survey** A research approach that questions large groups of subjects, such as high school students, about their own participation in delinquent or criminal acts.

**sentencing circles** A type of sentencing in which victims, family members, community members, and the offender participate in an effort to devise fair and reasonable sanctions that are ultimately aimed at reintegrating the offender into the community

**sentencing guidelines** A set of standards that defines parameters for trial judges to follow in their sentencing decisions.

**serial killer** Type of multiple killer who kills over a long period of time but typically assumes a "normal" identity between murders.

**sheriff** The chief law enforcement officer in a county.

**shire reeve** In early England, the chief law enforcement official in a county; forerunner of today's sheriff.

**shock incarceration** A short prison sentence served in boot camp–type facilities.

**shock probation** A sentence in which offenders serve a short prison term before they begin probation, to impress them with the pains of imprisonment.

**social capital** Positive relations with individuals and institutions that foster self-worth and inhibit crime.

**social control** A society's ability to control individual behavior in order to serve the best interests and welfare of the society as a whole.

**social control theory** The view that most people do not violate the law because of their social bonds to family, peer group, school, and other institutions. If these bonds are weakened or absent, individuals are much more likely to commit crime.

**social learning theory** The view that human behavior is learned through observation of human social interactions, either directly from those in close proximity or indirectly from the media.

**social reaction (labeling) theory** The view that society produces criminals by stigmatizing certain individuals as deviants, a label that they come to accept as a personal identity.

**social structure** The stratifications, classes, institutions, and groups that characterize a society.

**specialized court** A court that has primary jurisdiction over specific types of offenses and that operates differently than a traditional criminal court, such as with a concern over outcomes and extensive judicial monitoring.

**specific deterrence** A crime control policy suggesting that punishment should be severe enough to convince convicted offenders never to repeat their criminal activity.

**split sentence** A practice that requires convicted criminals to spend a portion of their sentence behind bars and the remainder in the community.

**spree killer** Type of multiple killer who spreads the murderous outburst over a few days or weeks.

**stalking** The willful, malicious, and repeated following, harassing, or contacting of another person. Such behavior becomes a criminal act when it causes the victim to feel fear for his or her safety or the safety of others.

**stare decisis** To stand by decided cases: the legal principle by which the decision or holding in an earlier case becomes the standard by which subsequent similar cases are judged.

**state (organized) crime** Criminal acts committed by state officials in pursuit of their jobs as government representatives.

**status offender** A noncriminal youth who falls under the jurisdiction of the juvenile court by reason of having engaged in behavior prohibited to minors, such as being truant from school, running away from home, or being habitually disobedient and ungovernable.

**sting operation** Organized groups of detectives who deceive criminals into openly committing illegal acts or conspiring to engage in criminal activity.

**stop and frisk** The situation in which police officers who are suspicious of an individual run their hands lightly over the suspect's outer garments to determine whether the person is carrying a concealed weapon; also called a threshold inquiry or pat-down.

**strain** The emotional turmoil and conflict caused when people believe that they cannot achieve their desires and goals through legitimate means.

**strategic intelligence** Information about the changing nature of certain problems and threats for the purpose of developing response strategies and reallocating resources.

**subpoena** A court order requiring a witness to appear in court at a specified time and place.

**substantive criminal law** A body of specific rules that declare what conduct is criminal and prescribe the punishment to be imposed for such conduct.

**substantive rights** Civil rights that include the right of inmates to receive mail and medical benefits and to practice their religion.

**super-maximum-security prison** The newest form of a maximum-security prison, which uses high-level security measures to incapacitate the nation's most dangerous criminals. Most inmates are in lockdown 23 hours per day.

**suspended sentence** A prison term that is delayed while the defendant undergoes a period of community treatment. If the treatment is successful, the prison sentence is terminated.

**tactical intelligence** Gaining or developing information related to threats of terrorism or crime and using this information to apprehend offenders, harden targets, and use strategies that will eliminate or mitigate the threat.

**Taser** A nonlethal conducted energy device that administers a shock to an uncooperative suspect by way of an electrified dart.

**thermal imager** A device that detects radiation in the infrared range of the electromagnetic spectrum and is used in law enforcement to detect variations in temperature (warm images stand out against cool backgrounds).

**three-strikes laws** Sentencing codes that require that an offender receive a life sentence after conviction for a third felony. Some states allow parole after a lengthy prison stay—for example, 25 years.

**tier system** A type of prison in which cells are located along corridors in multiple layers or levels.

**time-in-rank system** The promotion system in which a police officer can advance in rank only after spending a prescribed amount of time in the preceding rank.

**torts** The law of personal injuries.

**total institution** A regimented, dehumanizing institution, such as a prison, in which like-situated people are kept in social isolation, cut off from the world at large.

**transfer hearing** The hearing in which a judge decides whether to waive a juvenile to the criminal court. Waiver decisions are based on such criteria as the child's age, his or her prior offense history, and the nature of the offense.

**transnational organized crime** Use of illegal tactics to gain profit in the global marketplace, typcally involving the cross-border sale and distribution of illegal commodities.

**treatment** The rehabilitative method used to effect a change of behavior in the juvenile offender; treatment may take the form of therapy or educational or vocational programs.

**true bill of indictment** A written statement charging a defendant with the commission of a crime, drawn up by a prosecuting attorney and considered by a grand jury. If the grand jury finds sufficient evidence to support the indictment, it will issue a true bill of indictment.

**true bill** The action by a grand jury when it votes to indict an accused suspect.

**truth in sentencing** A sentencing scheme requiring that offenders serve at least 85 percent of their original sentence before being eligible for parole or other forms of early release.

**truth-in-sentencing laws** Laws requiring convicted felons to spend a significant portion of their sentence behind bars.

**tything (tithing)** In medieval England, a collective group of ten families that pledged to help one another and provide mutual aid.

**U.S. court of appeals** An appellate court in the federal court system

**U.S. district court** A trial court in the federal court system.

**U.S. Supreme Court** The highest appellate court in the United States

**Uniform Crime Report (UCR)** The official crime data collected by the FBI from local police departments.

**United States attorneys** The nation's principal (federal) litigators, appointed by the president. Assistant United States attorneys are tasked with, among other duties, prosecuting criminal defendants in federal court.

**venire** The group called for jury duty from which jury panels are selected.

**verdict** The finding of a jury or a judge on questions of fact at a trial.

**vice squads** Police units assigned to enforce morality-based laws, such as those addressing prostitution, gambling, and pornography.

**victim impact statement** A postconviction statement by the victim of crime or the victim's family that may be used to guide sentencing decisions.

**victim precipitation** The role of the victim in provoking or encouraging criminal behavior.

**vigilantes** In the Old West, members of a vigilance committee or posse called upon to capture cattle thieves or other felons.

**voir dire** The process in which a potential jury panel is questioned by the prosecution and the defense in order to select jurors who are unbiased and objective.

**waiver (juvenile)** A practice in which the juvenile court waives its jurisdiction over a juvenile and transfers the case to adult criminal court for trial. In some states, a waiver hearing is held to determine jurisdiction; in others, juveniles may be automatically waived if they are accused of committing a serious crime such as murder.

**Walnut Street Jail** The birthplace of the modern prison system and of the Pennsylvania system of solitary confinement.

**warez** Copyrighted software illegally downloaded and sold by organized groups without license to do so.

**watch system** In medieval England, groups of men who organized in church parishes to guard at night against disturbances and breaches of the peace under the direction of the local constable.

**white-collar crime** White-collar crimes involve the violation of rules that control business enterprise. They include employee pilferage, bribery, commodities law violations, mail fraud, computer fraud, environmental law violations, embezzlement, Internet scams, extortion, forgery, insurance fraud, price fixing, and environmental pollution.

**Wickersham Commission** Formally known as the National Commission on

Law Observance and Enforcement, a commission created in 1929 by President Herbert Hoover to study the U.S. criminal justice system, including the police.

**work release** A prison treatment program that allows inmates to be released during the day to work in the community, returning to prison at night.

**writ of certiorari** An order of a superior court requesting that a record of an inferior court (or administrative body) be brought forward for review or inspection.

**writ of habeas corpus** A judicial order requesting that a person who detains another person produce the body of the prisoner and give reasons for his or her capture and detention. Habeas corpus is a legal device used to request that a judicial body review the reasons for a person's confinement and the conditions of confinement. Habeas corpus is known as "the great writ."

**zero tolerance** The practice of seizing all instrumentalities of a crime, including homes, boats, and cars. It is an extreme example of the law of forfeiture.

*Note: "nn" following a page reference indicates multiple note numbers on a single page.*

# PHOTO CREDITS

**Chapter 1. 3:** © *Sacramento Bee*/MCT / Landov **10:** © AP Photo/Elaine Thompson **16:** © AP Photo/Marcio Jose Sanchez **23:** © Luke Sharrett/*New York Times*/Redux **28:** © AP Photo/Michael Wilson, Pool **30:** © AP Photo/*Summit Daily*, Mark Fox **31:** © AP Photo/Jeff Roberson **35:** © AP Photo/*Hutchinson News*, Jon Ruhlen

**Chapter 2. 43:** © AP Photo/Huntsville Police Dept. **45:** © Michael Appleton/*New York Times*/Redux **50:** © Andrew Lichtenstein/The Image Works **51:** © AP Photo/Moises Castillo, File **65:** © Douglas Engle/Austral Foto/archi/Redux **71:** © AP Photo/*Dayton Daily News*, Jim Noelker **75:** © Associated Press/AP Photo/*Antelope Valley Press*, Kelly Lacefield **78:** © Luke Sharrett/*New York Times*/Redux **80:** © AP Photo/Kiichiro Sato

**Chapter 3. 89:** © Timothy A. Clary/AFP/Getty Images **92:** © NY *Daily News* Archive via Getty Images **93:** © AP Photo/Louis Lanzano **94:** © AP Photo/Shizuo Kambayasi **100:** Dr. Alan Zametkin/Clinical Brain Imaging, courtesy of Office of Scientific Information, NIMH **106:** © AP Photo/*Daily Press*, Sangjib Min **112:** © AP Photo/Garfield County Sheriff **117:** © AP Photo/Fernando Sturla, Telam/File

**Chapter 4. 135:** © Darcy Padilla/Redux **144:** © AP Photo/Justin L. Fowler/*State Journal-Register* **150:** © Chip Litherland/*New York Times*/Redux **158:** © AP Photo/Dave Martin **161:** © AP Photo/Gloria Ferniz

**Chapter 5. 169:** © AP Photo/Jeff Chiu **172:** © Popperfoto/Getty Images **175:** © AP Photo/Boston Public Library **177:** © Associated Press/AP Photo **180:** © AP Photo/Steve Helber **181:** © Paul J. Richards/AFP/Getty Images **188:** © AP Photo/Jae C. Hong

**Chapter 6. 203:** © Justin Sullivan/Getty Images **206:** © AP Photo/*West Bend Daily News*, Nathan Pier **208:** © AP Photo/*Winchester Star*, Scott Mason **213:** © AP Photo/Denis Poroy **217:** © Kirk Condyles/*New York Times*/Redux **219:** © AP Photo/John Storey **221:** © Michel Du Cille/*Washington Post*/Getty Images

**Chapter 7. 241:** © AP Photo/Guillermo Arias **247:** © AP Photo/Stephanie Sinclair/VII **252:** © Robert Stolarik/*New York Times*/Redux **254:** © AP Photo/Tracy Gitnick **256:** © AP Photo/Ross D. Franklin **262:** © AP Photo/*Independent Florida Alligator*, Andrew Stanfill **276:** © AP Photo/*Free Lance–Star*, Robert A. Martin

**Chapter 8. 285:** © Yellow Dog Productions/Getty Images **287:** © AP Photo/Mary Altaffer **288:** © Wade Payne/*Knoxville News Sentinel* **289:** © AP Photo/Tony Dejak **298:** © AP Photo/Ross D. Franklin, File **300:** © AP Photo/Branimir Kvatuc **314:** © AP Photo/Gerry Broome

**Chapter 9. 327:** © AP Photo/*Anchorage Daily News*, Bill Roth **330:** © AP Photo/Steve Pope **339:** © AP Photo/Dave Einsel **342:** top, © AP Photo/*Miami Herald*, Cammy Clark **342:** bottom, © AP Photo/Elaine Thompson **349:** © *Syracuse Newspapers*/Al Campanie /The Image Works **351:** © The Center for Legal and Court Technology's McGlothlin Courtroom at William & Mary Law School

**Chapter 10. 359:** © AP Photo/Gail Burton **363:** top, © AP Photo/Kathy Willens **363:** bottom, © AP Photo/Sara D. Davis **364:** bottom, © AP Photo/Louis Lanzano **365:** © Monica Almeida/*New York Times*/Redux **375:** © AP Photo/*Tyler Morning Telegraph*, Herb Nygren Jr. **378:** © AP Photo/Mario Anzuoni **383:** © Nikki Kahn/*Washington Post*/Getty Images

**Chapter 11. 391:** Chuck Cook @ 2009 *Times-Picayune*. All rights reserved. Reprinted with permission. **393:** © AP Photo/Matthew West **396:** © AP Photo/*Indianapolis Star*/Mike Fender **407:** © Elaine Thompson/Reuters/Pool/Landov **411:** © Bob Daemmrich/The Image Works **415:** © Scott Dalton/*New York Times*/Redux **419:** © AP Photo/Sue Ogrocki

**Chapter 12. 435:** © AP Photo/Florida Department of Corrections **436:** © The Granger Collection, New York **439:** © AP Photo/Jim Cole **442:** © AP Photo/*Texarkana Gazette*, Eric J. Shelton **453:** © AP Photo/John Lovretta, Pool **456:** © AP Photo/Michael Goulding, Pool **459:** © Nicholas Kamm/AFP/Getty Images

**Chapter 13. 477:** © Rahav Segev/*New York Times*/Redux **480:** © David Jacobs, left, Brian Harkin/*New York Times*/Redux **488:** © AP Photo/Chris O'Meara **493:** © Mark Ralston/AFP/Getty Images **495:** © AP Photo/Ric Feld **498:** © AP Photo/John Bazemore **500:** © AP Photo/Jeffrey M. Boan **507:** © AP Photo/*Daily Star*, Kari Wheeler

**Chapter 14. 519:** © Joshua Lott/*New York Times*/Redux **521:** © van Gogh, Vincent: Prisoner's Round, (detail), 1890. Pushkin Museum of Fine Arts, Moscow. Scala/Art Resource, New York. **525:** © Courtesy of the Library Company of Philadelphia **527:** © The Granger Collection, New York **528:** © American Correctional Association **534:** © Q. Sakamaki/Redux **539:** © AP Photo/*Idaho Statesman*, Chris Butler **540:** © AP Photo/*Maryland Gazette*, Andy Carruthers

**Chapter 15. 549:** © Joyce Dopkeen/*New York Times*/Redux **552:** © AP Photo/Charlie Riedel **557:** © AP Photo/James MacPherson **560:** © Shaul Schwarz/Getty Images **569:** © AP Photo/Oscar Sosa **581:** © AP Photo/Rich Pedroncell **595:** © AP Photo/Oscar Sosa

**Chapter 16. 605:** © AP Photo/Elise Amendola **607:** © The Granger Collection, New York **617:** © Thomas Barwick/The Image Bank/Getty Images **618:** © Jim Wilson/*New York Times*/Redux **624:** © AP Photo/Joseph Gresser, Pool **625:** © AP Photo/Jeff Roberson **633:** © Spencer Platt/Getty Images

**Chapter 17. 641:** © Daniel Rosenbaum/*New York Times*/Redux **647:** © David Goldman/*New York Times*/Redux **653:** © AP Photo/Tom Gannam **655:** © Joe Raedle/Getty Images **657:** © AP Photo/Suffolk County District Attorney **664:** © Christopher Wise 2007/Redux

**Chapter 18. 677:** © AP Photo/U.S. Marshals Service **681:** © AP Photo/Wally Santana **682:** © Rina Castelnuovo/*New York Times*/Redux **684:** © Paul J. Richards/AFP/Getty Images **689:** © AP Photo/David Goldman **696:** © AP Photo/Alan Diaz